THE OXFORD HANDBOOK OF

STATE AND LOCAL GOVERNMENT FINANCE

THE OXFORD HANDBOOK OF

STATE AND LOCAL GOVERNMENT FINANCE

Edited by

ROBERT D. EBEL AND JOHN E. PETERSEN

Foreword by

ALICE M. RIVLIN

OXFORD

UNIVERSITY PRESS

OXFORD
UNIVERSITY PRESS

Oxford University Press, Inc., publishes works that further
Oxford University's objective of excellence
in research, scholarship, and education.

Oxford   New York
Auckland   Cape Town   Dar es Salaam   Hong Kong   Karachi
Kuala Lumpur   Madrid   Melbourne   Mexico City   Nairobi
New Delhi   Shanghai   Taipei   Toronto

With offices in
Argentina   Austria   Brazil   Chile   Czech Republic   France   Greece
Guatemala   Hungary   Italy   Japan   Poland   Portugal   Singapore
South Korea   Switzerland   Thailand   Turkey   Ukraine   Vietnam

Copyright © 2012 by Oxford University Press

Published by Oxford University Press, Inc.
198 Madison Avenue, New York, New York 10016
www.oup.com

Oxford is a registered trademark of Oxford University Press.

Library of Congress Cataloging-in-Publication Data
The Oxford handbook of state and local government finance / edited
By Robert D. Ebel and John E. Petersen.
p. cm.
Includes bibliographical references and index.
ISBN 978-0-19-976536-2 (cloth : alk. paper)
1. Finance, Public—United States—States—Handbooks, manuals, etc.
2. Local finance—United States—Handbooks, manuals, etc. 3. Intergovernmental fiscal
relations—United States—Handbooks, manuals, etc.
I. Ebel, Robert D. II. Petersen, John E. III. Title: Handbook of state
and local government finance.
HJ275.O94 2012
336'.01373—dc23
2011034089

3 5 7 9 8 6 4 2
Printed in the United States of America
on acid-free paper

CONTENTS

....

PART I   THE ECONOMIC, DEMOGRAPHIC, AND INSTITUTIONAL FRAMEWORK

PART II   REVENUE STRUCTURES AND SYSTEMS

PART III   SPENDING, BORROWING, AND FINANCIAL MANAGEMENT

PART IV   LOOKING AHEAD: REFORMING AND RESTRUCTURING

FOREWORD

....

WHILE many citizens care deeply about the tax and spending policies in their own
state or city, the general subject of state and local finance does not attract widespread public interest except in a crisis. Scholars of fiscal federalism rarely become
media stars. Now, however, two such crises have converged to put state and local
finance in the cross hairs and virtually guarantee that long-accepted policies will
be reexamined by the federal government and state and local jurisdictions all over
the country. The first is the Great Recession, which has undermined state and local
revenues while at the same time increasing state and local expenditure responsibilities to a far greater extent than recent recessions. The other crisis is the unsustainable trajectory of federal debt. Absent substantial policy change, federal debt
will grow faster than the economy in the years ahead even as the economy recovers.
Some combination of reductions in projected federal spending and increases in revenues will be necessary for achieving federal financial stability, and both will put
pressure on state and local finances for the foreseeable future. Will these two crises
result in a weakening of state and local fiscal viability—fewer federal grants, more
mandates, increasing federal preemption revenue sources, and a declining quality
of services? Or will the stresses lead to a serious rethinking of federal, state, and
local roles and finances that could strengthen the effectiveness of government? The
chapters in this volume address these questions with short- as well as medium- and
long-term perspective.

The Great Recession dramatized the vulnerability of states and localities to
economic downturns as both the dependence on the income tax and other cyclically sensitive revenue sources increased along with their spending obligations.
At the same time it showed how difficult it is for federal fiscal policy to stabilize
the economy in the face of procyclical state and local spending cuts, as substantial
amounts of federal stimulus were negated by fiscal drag from the state and local
sector. The Great Recession further revealed the worrisome structural weakness
in state and local finance as consumer spending shifted from goods to less easily
taxed services, internet sales increased, and anti-tax sentiment capped revenues at
unrealistic levels. These stresses might be forgotten—as they have been after past
recessions—if the economy were soon to start growing robustly; but rapid recovery is highly unlikely in the face of the collapsed housing market and the federal
debt crisis. Furthermore, the oncoming tsunami of retirees combined with relent-
less health care cost increases will continue to drive up spending for Medicare,
Medicaid, and Social Security even if significant reforms reduce some of the currently projected growth in these programs. Federal revenues will have to rise to

offset part of the increasing federal debt, and interest rates are very likely to rise. All of these factors can be expected to lead to higher state and local borrowing costs, greater resistance to revenue increases, and a congressional proclivity to push the federal deficit "down," through actions such as reducing federal grants to states and localities and adopting a policy of enacting costly unfunded expenditure mandates.

Efforts to deal with the looming federal debt have also revealed public ambivalence about federal spending and great confusion about the appropriate federal role. Politicians are often applauded when they deplore federal spending or Washington "overreach" in the abstract, but meet resistance if they propose specific cuts in spending large enough to make a dent in the total. Part of the problem is that federal spending programs have proliferated over the years in response to changing needs and pressure from particular interest groups. The public often does not have a clear idea what the federal government actually does, what specific activities accomplish, and what they cost. This is true not only in the domestic arena, but also with regard to national security, where changing threats have led to a costly legacy of outdated but well-entrenched programs and a public with little idea of how they contribute to security and at what cost. Federal budget numbers are all very large and confusing, so it is possible for wishful thinkers to harbor the hope that cutting our "waste and fraud" or "welfare" or "foreign aid" would reduce federal spending significantly and balance the budget without the necessity of touching well-beloved programs such as Social Security and Medicare or raising more revenues.

Over several decades many have argued for a sharper division between federal responsibilities and those of state and local government for clearer accountability (see, for example, Alice M. Rivlin, *Reviving the American Dream; The Economy, the States, and the Federal Government*, 1992). The federal government could retain clear responsibility for national security, foreign affairs, air traffic control, problems that move across state boundaries (air and water pollution), Social Security and health care financing, while devolving to the states and their localities functions that require adaptation to local conditions, citizen input, and community support. These include education, housing, most law enforcement and transportation, economic development, and social services. This sharper intergovernmental allocation of expenditure responsibilities and revenue authority would take some of the spending pressure off the federal taxpayer, as well as help citizens understand which type of government is required to do what and, thus, whom to hold accountable. It would also force politicians to explain their tax and spending proposals instead of talking vaguely about federal overreach and avoiding hard choices.

Recognizing the need to reinforce a cooperative federalism, new federal revenue structures could not only reduce federal debt and stabilize state and local revenues, but also reduce competitive state and local tax reductions ostensibly designed to attract business (the "race to the bottom"). For example, a national consumption tax, such as a value added tax, could be coordinated in a manner that would preserve state revenue autonomy as well as provide funds for reducing the inherent fiscal disparities among the states. A carbon tax shared with the states could create incentives to reduce greenhouse gases and raise revenue at the same time. A uniform shared corporate income tax base could generate new revenues, reduce tax gaming by multistate corporations, and lower the costs of taxpayer compliance and revenue administration.

As documented in this handbook , the Great Recession and its aftermath have been a shock to the public finances of federal and state and local governments alike. But, as history attests, the US system of fiscal federalism is one of proven resiliency that time and time again has been key to adjusting to such shocks and, thus, to the accomplishment of the nation's broader goals of financial soundness, growth, and stability and a return to fairness in the distribution of income and wealth. Despite all its very real and deep negative impacts, the Great Recession also brings with it an opportunity to act wisely. Many innovations in fiscal federalism are possible. However, retaining many of the current practices of how we tax and spend and the division of responsibilities and tax structures in the face of recurring crises is a bad option. Refusing to act will guarantee continuing confusion over governmental roles and deteriorating government services.

Written for practitioners and scholars alike, this handbook provides a comprehensive and timely knowledge base of the trends in and current status of the nation's intergovernmental and financial arrangements and the policy and practice of US state and local finance. It also identifies options for policy and administrative changes that range from adjustments to specific programs and tax structures to a broad rethinking of how the public finance systems can help fulfill the American dream of an economy that is both just and productive. The messages here are of optimism as well as of urgency to act. The optimism stems from the proposition that a well-informed democratic political system can produce fair and efficent fiscal systems that people can understand and will support. The second message is that now is the time to institute fiscal policies that will require making the difficult but necessary choices that will revitalize and rationalize how the United States' public sector is financed.

Alice M. Rivlin
The Brookings Institution and Georgetown University
Co-Chair, Debt Reduction Task Force, Bipartisan Policy Center
November 2011

PREFACE

....

THIS handbook came into being not on a "dark and stormy night," but rather on a crystal clear day in January 2010, following a wintry storm that left a bright deep mantle of fresh snow. Such days encourage taking a new look at things. In the case of state and local government finance, a reappraisal was very much in order, as several decades of relatively sunny fiscal times were rapidly coming to an end in the midst of great economic uncertainty and a faltering, deeply divided political system. The two editors met to outline what this book should contain and to round up as contributors their colleagues who worked in the various disciplines of state and local public finance. The very large and disparate state and local sector had seen its speed-ups and slow-downs in growth—with occasional bad patches for particular cities and states—over the nearly six decades since World War II. But this time it was clear that things were different. This was not just another occasional bad patch.

What states and localities had to offer in the way of more schools, more roads, and improved public services and facilities had evidently been what the voters wanted and were willing to pay for. Yet the economic and political tides were turning to alter that pattern of slow but steady expansion. Fiscal systems of states and localities, a legacy of earlier times, had become increasingly vulnerable to changes in the US economic, demographic, and institutional framework. But the need for spending and revenue decisions more responsive to changing conditions had been deflected or deferred. In the view of many experts, the financial framework of the state and local government sector was becoming "obsolete." Indeed, the massive financial and economic downturn of 2008–09 (the Great Recession) coupled with a shifting political environment would prove to be "game-changer" as the full impact finally hit state and local governments. So we assigned topics to contributors that matched their expertise, and asked them to update state of the art in their discipline and to prognosticate about how changes they perceived would affect policies and practices in the future.

The Great Recession of 2008–09 devastated, in succession, state as well as local government revenues, which over the years had become increasingly reliant on the low-hanging fruits of growth. This was best exemplified by the boom in real estate values and the tide of income and transactions associated with building, furnishing, and financing new structures. Added to this was the legislative narrowing of tax bases and the increases in rates applied to those contracting bases that had made them increasingly sensitive to changing economic conditions. The Great Recession ushered in five consecutive quarters of decline in state revenues and

drove an unprecedented forty-eight of the nation's fifty state budgets into unexpected deficits in fiscal year 2009. As this erosion in state revenues accumulated, it
soon exhausted many states "rainy day" funds and other reserves.

At the outset the states were not left totally bereft of help. In the spring of 2009,
the federal government, which had earlier stepped in to assist the financial sector,
launched a $787 billion stimulus program that included $180 billion in financial aid
for the states, with most of that aid flowing in 2010 and 2011. Amid the numerous
initiatives were programs to bolster state spending on Medicaid, education, and
capital spending. The stimulus provided a burst of support and helped fill in state
budget gaps, dampening the decline in output and employment. Nonetheless, the
stimulus program became politically controversial as the increased federal spending in the face of diminished revenues added to the deficit. Thus, the stimulus
spending turned out to be only a transitory buffer for the states.

The year 2010 ended with two important events: the elections of November
2010 and the release of two reports on the deficit problems of the federal government, each of which underscored the overarching fiscal and political ties that exist
between the state and local sector and the federal government. First, the November
elections ended Democratic control of the House of Representatives and increased
the number of Republicans in the US Senate. The "wave" election results brought
many new Republican governors into office and resulted in Republicans gaining
increased control over state legislatures. The newly elected officials reflected the
rise of an electorate that was avowed to constrain tax revenues as part of a long-
term political strategy to downsize the public sector in American life. Furthermore,
some newly elected Governors and legislative majorities became engaged in controversial state budgetary battles, often with unionized state government workers who resisted losing their right to organize and collectively bargain for various
retirement and health benefits. But while not every state was subject to pyrotech-
nics, legislatures on both sides of the aisle and governors of both parties have since
had to deal the new normal of prolonged austerity.

Locally, revenues raised have historically been tied to property values and
activities associated with real estate transactions. Yet the continuing national
depression in housing markets, best illustrated by the sustained decline in housing
prices and the high level of mortgage foreclosures, has deeply eroded the revenue
base. Meanwhile, the fiscal problems of the states compounded those of the local
governments as the amount of state aid provided to them declined. By the end
of 2011 the state and local sector had become a pro-cyclical damper on economic
recovery having reduced employment by 600,000, which is a 3.2 percent cut since
the high water mark of early 2009.

Two reports on the federal fiscal outlook focused the growing discontent
with the federal budget deficits and the consequences of rapidly growing federal
debt. First, in November 2010, the Debt Reduction Task Force of the Bipartisan
Policy Center released its recommendations for *Restoring America's Future*. That
report was followed in December by one authored by the presidentially appointed
National Commission on Fiscal Responsibility and Reform. These documents,

which varied in particulars but not in the fundamental substance and immediacy of their findings, detailed the steps that would have to be taken to address present and future federal imbalances. Moreover, the various schemes for balancing the budget made clear that addressing the federal deficit and debt issue would likely mean future austerity for state and local government, which would see not only a decline of federal assistance but also increased competition with the federal tax collectors in generating revenues.

The federal budgetary battles, which consumed the US Congress in early 2011, reached a crescendo that summer in the dispute over raising the federal government's debt limit amid threats of closing the government down and, perhaps, defaulting. A temporary solution was devised that avoided those outcomes; but the substance of the problem—restructuring the federal entitlement programs, the costs of which may outweigh what the public's willingness to pay—remained unresolved. Meanwhile, the economy has continued to languish with high unemployment, depressed consumer and investment demand, and a volatile securities market. One casualty of the congressional deadlock was the US government's bond rating, which was lowered by rating firm Standard and Poor's from the highest level (AAA) for the first time ever. Meanwhile, many AAA-rated obligations of states and localities were put on "negative watch" by Moody's. "Political risk" has now become an increasingly important factor in government credit ratings in the United States, a novel and unsettling development.

As this preface is written in late 2011, the future of the nation's public finances remains cloudy at best, and, at worst, dismal. The Great Recession and its aftermath exceeded our expectations in becoming the Great Contraction, where unemployment remains high and with a projected rate of economic growth that is insufficient to soon close the gap between the actual and full employment level of national income and output. Moreover, the fiscal fortunes of state and local governments are tied not only to the domestic economy, but have increasingly become global as well. At present, the fate of the European economy, beset with public finance crises of its own, is hanging in the balance, with the United States very much affected, but seemingly diminished in power to influence the outcome.

The times ahead will be difficult. Choices will have to be made. It is our hope that this collection of chapters will contribute to understanding the options for finding a sustainable balance between the public's demands for services and its willingness to provide resources to deliver them. No one has all the answers, but each author contributes her or his perspective, experience, and analysis to the issues at hand. To the extent that experience and reason have a place in today's noisy and excitable public forum, then these contributions can help in deciding what can be done to restore economic vigor and public confidence. This book is dedicated to that end.

Acknowledgments

FIRST, we wish to thank all the contributing authors to this volume. They were valiant in their efforts to abide with our editorial demands on their chapters, which were written under the press of time and in the face of rapidly changing conditions. Moreover, we were assisted at every step by Ha T.T. Vu, who brought structure to an otherwise chaotic process of editing thirty-five chapters involving nearly sixty different contributors. In the process of helping us with this book, she completed her dissertation at George Mason University and co-authored the introductory chapter with us.

We would also like to express our thanks to our the team of editors at Oxford University Press, who were professional as well as collegial throughout the entire process and diligent in keeping this book's deadlines. We wish to especially acknowledge Terry Vaughn, Catherine Rae, and Amy Whitmer at Oxford University Press; copyeditor Christine Dahlin; and Molly Morrison and her team at Newgen North America.

Last, we would like to thank our spouses, Leslie Steen and Mary Petersen, for their unstinting support over the years. We look forward to their continued encouragement and forbearance in times to come.

December 2011

Contributors

Michael E. Bell is a Research Professor in the Institute for Public Policy at The George Washington University.

Carolyn Bourdeaux is an Associate Professor at Andrew Young School of Policy Studies and Associate Director of the Georgia State University Fiscal Research Center.

Donald Boyd is a Senior Fellow in the Nelson A. Rockefeller Institute of Government at the University at Albany, State University of New York.

Andrew Bristle is a Research Assistant in the Department of Economics at Michigan State University.

David Brunori is a Research Professor at The George Washington University and is a Contributing Editor of *State Tax Notes*.

Robert M. Buckley is a Senior Fellow in the Milano School of International Affairs, Management and Urban Policy at The New School.

Richard Ciccarone is Chief Research Officer and Managing Director at McDonnell Investment Management LLC, Chicago, Illinois.

Lee Cokorinos is a Principal at Democracy Strategies LLC, Silver Spring, Maryland.

Timothy J. Conlan is a Professor of Government at George Mason University.

Joseph J. Cordes is a Professor of Economics at The George Washington University.

Lucy Dadayan is a Senior Policy Analyst in the Nelson A. Rockefeller Institute of Government at the University at Albany, State University of New York.

Bernard Dafflon is a Professor of Public Finance and Policies in the Department of Political Economy at the University of Fribourg in Switzerland.

Ellen Dannin is a Fannie Weiss Distinguished Faculty Scholar and Professor of Law in the Dickinson School of Law at Pennsylvania State University.

Harley Duncan is Tax Managing Director at KPMG LLP.

James R. Eads, Jr., is Director of Public Affairs at Ryan LLC, Austin, Texas.

Robert D. Ebel is a Professor of Economics and Public Administration at the University of the District of Columbia.

Ronald C. Fisher is a Professor of Economics at Michigan State University and a Visiting Professor at Zhongnan University of Economics and Law.

William F. Fox is Director of the Center for Business and Economic Research and William B. Stokely Distinguished Professor of Economics at the University of Tennessee.

Norton Francis is Director of Revenue Estimation and Research in the Office of the Chief Financial Officer, District of Columbia.

Robert J. Freeman is a Professor of Accounting Emeritus in the Rawls College of Business at Texas Tech University.

Thomas Gais is Director of the Nelson A. Rockefeller Institute of Government at the University at Albany, State University of New York.

Jonathan Gifford is a Professor in the School of Public Policy at George Mason University.

Tracy M. Gordon is a Fellow in Economic Studies at The Brookings Institution.

Adam Greenwade is a Research Assistant, School of Public Affairs, University of Colorado, Denver

Billy C. Hamilton of Hamilton Consulting is a Former Texas Deputy Comptroller of Public Accounts in Austin.

W. Bartley Hildreth is a Professor in the Andrew Young School of Policy Studies at Georgia State University.

Jason N. Juffras is a Research Associate in the Trachtenberg School of Public Policy and Public Administration at The George Washington University.

Daphne A. Kenyon is a Visiting Fellow at the Lincoln Institute of Land Policy.

John Kincaid is a Robert B. and Helen S. Meyner Professor of Government and Public Service and Director of the Meyner Center for the Study of State and Local Government at Lafayette College.

Iris J. Lav is a Teaching Fellow in the Center for Advanced Governmental Studies at Johns Hopkins University.

Siona Listokin-Smith is an Assistant Professor in the School of Public Policy at George Mason University.

LeAnn Luna is an Associate Professor of Accounting in the Department of Accounting and Information Management in the Center for Business and Economic Research at the University of Tennessee.

Justin Marlowe is an Assistant Professor in the Daniel J. Evans School of Public Affairs at the University of Washington.

Christine R. Martell is an Associate Professor in the School of Public Affairs at the University of Colorado–Denver.

Richard H. Mattoon is a Senior Economist and Economic Advisor at the Federal Reserve Bank of Chicago.

Leslie McGranahan is a Senior Economist at the Federal Reserve Bank of Chicago.

Matthew N. Murray is a Professor of Economics at the University of Tennessee.

Robert H. Nelson is a Professor in the School of Public Policy at the University of Maryland.

Rudolph G. Penner is an Institute Fellow at The Urban Institute.

John E. Petersen is a Professor of Finance and Public Policy in the School of Public Policy at George Mason University.

Paul L. Posner is a Professor in the School of Public and International Affairs at George Mason University.

Alice M. Rivlin is a Professor of Public Policy at Georgetown University and Senior Fellow, Economic Studies, at The Brookings Institution.

Raymond Scheppach is a Professor of Practice in the Frank Batten School of Leadership and Public Policy and a Fellow in the Miller Center of Public Affairs at the University of Virginia.

Alex F. Schwartz is an Associate Professor and Chair of the Graduate Program in Urban Policy Analysis and Management in the Milano School for International Affairs, Management, and Urban Policy at The New School.

Craig D. Shoulders is a Professor and Chairman in the Department of Accounting and Information Technology at the University of North Carolina–Pembroke.

David L. Sjoquist is a Professor of Economics and the Dan E. Sweat Distinguished Chair in Educational and Community Policy in the Andrew Young School of Policy Studies at Georgia State University.

James E. Spiotto is a Partner at Chapman and Cutler LLP, Chicago, Illinois.

Rayna Stoycheva in a Lecturer in the Department of Economics at the University of Miami.

François Vaillancourt is a Fellow at CIRANO and Professeur Honoraire at the Université de Montréal.

Ha T. T. Vu is an Economist at The World Bank.

Sally Wallace is a Director of the Fiscal Research Center and Professor and Chair of the Department of Economics in the Andrew Young School of Policy Studies at Georgia State University.

Robert B. Ward is a Deputy Director of Fiscal Studies in the Nelson A. Rockefeller Institute of Government at the University at Albany, State University of New York.

Zhou Yang is an Assistant Professor of Economics at Robert Morris University.

Serdar Yilmaz is a Senior Economist at The World Bank.

THE OXFORD HANDBOOK OF

STATE AND LOCAL GOVERNMENT FINANCE

CHAPTER 1

INTRODUCTION: STATE AND LOCAL GOVERNMENT FINANCE IN THE UNITED STATES

ROBERT D. EBEL, JOHN E. PETERSEN, AND HA T. T. VU

FOUR significant developments of US state and local finance are converging in a manner that will newly frame the practices of state and local governance in the next decade and beyond. First, the dominant role of these governments in providing day-to-day essential services makes it a national interest to maintain a fiscally healthy state and local sector. Second, there is a growing vulnerability of state and local fiscal systems to economic recessions and to slow growth in the national economy. Third, the "fiscal obsolescence" of the state and local fiscal structure represents the continuing failure of state and local policymakers to adapt to changes in the nation's economic structure, demographic trends, and institutional and technical arrangements in an increasingly globalized economy. Fourth, there is a trend away from a "cooperative" to a "coercive" system of federalism that leads one to reflect on the continuing validity of Alexander Hamilton's confidence that the people "would always take care to preserve the Constitutional equilibrium" among the general government and the states.[1]

These trends can move from low-priority "problems to be addressed" to becoming urgent, high-priority concerns when the governments face economic and political shocks that are beyond their direct control. Just such a shock occurred with the financial crisis of the late 2000s and the onset of a pervasive and prolonged economic downturn that has become labeled as the Great Recession (2007–2009). An examination of six key economic indicators reveals that the contraction that began in 2007 has been the deepest in the last sixty years and has lasted longer than any since the Great Depression of 1929–1933. The six key indicators—employment, wages, personal income, gross domestic product (GDP), the consumer price index, and the Standard & Poor's 500 Index—all contracted in 2009. The last time that happened was in 1948–1949, and even then the eleven-month duration was shorter than that of the eighteen months of the Great Recession, and buoyant growth soon ensued.[2]

Of course, similar external shocks have occurred throughout US history. But, nearly always the resiliency and built-in-flexibility of the system of fiscal federalism and state and local financial steadfastness and continuity have allowed the nation to regain its momentum and move on. Whether this legacy of state and local resilience, flexibility, and steadfast continuity remains in place today is conjectural. Clearly the deteriorating conditions of the federal and state and local government finances call for an understanding of what went wrong with the fiscal system of state and local governments, and what can be done to make it go right in the post–Great Recession era.

Given this setting, this handbook brings together the existing knowledge on the principles and practices of state and local finance. It takes an explicit look at how the issues addressed in this volume fit into the broader framework of the practice of US intergovernmental relations (fiscal decentralization) as well as the historical trends of, and outlook for, the US federal system. It is also a book that lays out options for bringing a twentieth-century system of state and local finance into the twenty-first century.

Following this introductory chapter, the handbook is organized in four sections. The chapters in part I examine the institutional, economic, and political framework that explains the financial structure and performance of the state and local sector. The chapters in part II provide an overview of how state and local revenue systems performed during (and are performing) as a result of the Great Recession, and they detail analytical and prescriptive consideration of several forms of taxes and charges and their implications for future revenue performance. The chapters in part III discuss spending, borrowing, and financial management. For spending, the focus is on the "big six" service delivery sectors: education, health care, human services, transportation, public pension, and housing. The chapters in this section also address the capital spending and financial-market activities of the state and local governments. Part IV contains chapters that are dedicated to looking ahead and that speculate about how the state and local sector could adjust to their new circumstances.

Accordingly, this book combines technical treatments of state and local finance with considerations of the "political economy" of the post–Great Recession era that is evolving. State and local governments will face historic challenges in matching spending needs and revenue sources given the present set of institutional, legal, and organizational arrangements that characterize the US governmental system.

BACKGROUND

The State and Local Government Sector at a Glance

There is a dominant national interest in what happens to the state and local sector, which Justice Louis Brandeis labeled a "laboratory" federalism.[3] Moreover, the theoretical and empirical record is clear that a well-designed decentralized fiscal system of shared fiscal autonomy among the federal, state, and local sectors is key to enhancing the nation's broader goals of economic efficiency in the allocation of its scarce resources and in the delivery of local public goods, economic growth, macroeconomic stability, and social cohesion.

The fifty states and their ninety thousand local governments (as measured by their final expenditures) represent just over 12 percent of the GDP. This is one and a half times the size of the federal sector with national defense spending included, and it is four and a half times federal government spending when one considers only federal nondefense spending.[4] And, unlike the federal sector, the states and localities typically (but not always) make these contributions to GDP while having balanced budgets. Furthermore, when taken together, the states and localities employ about one out of every eight workers; provide all basic governmental services consumed by individuals and firms such as education, public safety, and public works; and deliver much of the federal government services that are domestically consumed, including passing on many federal transfer payments to people and organizations.

Over the last decade the federal government has pursued a policy of tax cuts and spending increases, which has resulted in large debt. The United States now has its lowest ratio of taxes as a percentage of GDP since 1950, and it has one of the lowest tax-to-GDP ratios among the industrialized nations of the world. The nation has spent heavily on the expenses of waging war and has enacted new domestic programs, including a prescription drug benefit program for Medicare recipients and two recession "stimulus" packages, all largely paid for by issuing debt. The Congressional Budget Office (CBO) projects that under current law the US federal government will accumulate $7 trillion of additional debt during 2013–2021.[5]

Consequently, as warned by many experts, a federal government on an unsustainable financial path may try to address its financial mess in part by "pushing the deficit down" to state and local budgets in the form of a more "coercive federalism" of regulations, unfunded mandates, and preemptions of state revenues. But yet another outcome might be a federal government that is bereft of resources and shorn of powers to govern effectively and that may fade away in importance, leaving the scope and content of the nation's governance increasingly up to the individual states to decide and finance.

Emerging Fiscal Vulnerability

Concerns about the viability and growth of state and local taxes had long been well documented but largely ignored before the Great Recession. Postwar resurgence of the state and local sector was characterized by the divergence of shifts in the nation's economic, demographic, and institutional arrangements. The 1980s ended with robust fiscal performance by the states, many of which experienced increased revenue flows following the recessions of the early 1980s. The relatively brief recession of 1991–1992 caused a relatively minor downswing in the revenues, but it left the major spending trends unaffected and was viewed as a cyclical event, largely not affecting the long-term trend in state spending. Localities had to adjust to the diminished growth in property values in view of the slowdown in real estate values, but the effect was short-lived. Housing construction, as usual, quickly resumed and picked up the tempo of the economy. By 1993, state and local governments (along with the federal government) entered into a phase of prolonged economic prosperity and sustained growth, as the national economy ticked along. What problems there were seemed most associated with the secular decline in manufacturing employment. As a result, in the aggregate, states began to experience surpluses, as personal income and corporate profits grew, especially in the last half of the 1990s. A reflection of the period was the continuing state policy actions that led to permanent tax-rate reductions. With full employment and low inflation, the evident need for revenues appeared to be diminishing. But, as the 1990s ended, there awaited the recession in 2001, which stuck state finances with unanticipated fury. Observers noted the severity of the impacts and, aware of changing demographics and the increasing importance of health-care costs, began to worry about the longer-term fiscal future.[6]

The Recession of 2001

The strong economy and soaring stock market of the late 1990s significantly boosted the growth of government revenues, which enabled states and localities to cut taxes, begin new programs, and hike spending for existing activities at the same time they were building their reserves to high levels.[7] But the deep stock-market slump of 2000 and the relatively mild recession that began in 2001 severely reduced the growth of government revenues and raised the prospect of substantial state budget deficits, requiring remedial actions to be taken. While most states have sundry constitutional or statutory requirements for balancing their general fund operating budgets, these requirements may be fairly loose and allow for the use of temporary sources of financing. Faced with impending budget shortfalls, states had various alternative actions. Initially, states responded to slowing revenues by using accumulated reserves and tapping other sources of temporary funding.

The budgetary actions by state and local governments, because they reduced the growth of aggregate demand, likely acted as a minor offset to the federal government's stimulus actions. The 2003 federal tax cut included about $20 billion of aid to states that was spread over fiscal years 2003 and 2004, which helped bolster their finances. Overall, up to the early 2000s, fluctuations in state and local budgetary balances were much less than those of the federal government.

The fiscal difficulties of states and localities were due to a combination of a slow-down in the growth of their revenues that exceeded the slowdown in the growth of their spending. Throughout most of the 1990s, total state and local spending rose relative to GDP, but revenues grew even faster, which produced growing surpluses. In the late 1990s, spending grew faster than revenues, but the years of state and local surpluses did not end until the recession began in 2001. With the recession, the growth of revenues slowed dramatically, but the growth of spending did not slow quickly enough to avoid the onset of deficits.

The recession of 2001 brought some consideration as to what the outcome of the structural changes of the 1990s meant for state and local government finances. Experts laid out the longer-term worries about the impact of the changes in the underlying economy on the viability of the state and local revenue systems.[8] Among other things, the states had persistently narrowed their sales tax bases or failed to keep up with economic changes, which narrowed those bases. In many cases, states had made permanent reductions in their income taxes and had foregone changes in major taxes, while favoring various fees and charges that are sensitive to economic conditions.

The political mood of the country was consistently one of lowering taxes in order to promote economic growth, a formula that appeared to be magically working because tax cuts were followed by even more surpluses. Moreover, the fastest growth in the economy was coming in sectors that were legally or practically exempted from sales taxes, namely most professional services and mail-order or Internet sales. Furthermore, the increasingly footloose nature of industries brought recurring rounds of interstate competition for jobs, which eroded state corporate and local property-tax bases through the use of various tax-reducing incentives. In addition, the role of real property in commercial and industrial use was decreasing as a component of value, effectively shifting more of the burden to residential properties.

At about the same time, the financial-market meltdown brought into bold relief another long-term problem that was gathering steam: the condition of the state and local public pension plans. The plans over the years had largely moved from a pay-as-you-go basis to achieving advanced funding for their liabilities. They had also invested heavily in the stock market, which had been rewarded with strong returns as the markets grew. As a result, the systems were in unusually good shape by the end of the 1990s and had begun to skip employer contributions and enrich benefits with their surpluses. However, the stock-market crash (the "dot-com bust") of the early 2000s led to widespread losses in portfolio values and meant that the funds had to increase their contributions in order to remain sound actuarially. That episode perhaps should have led to reconsideration of the rates of return assumptions that the funds used to calculate their liabilities. Most funds continued to assume that their investments would earn at elevated historic rates of return, which effectively amounted to a bet that the spectacular growth in the nation's economy and financial markets in the twentieth century would continue into the twenty-first century.

The states recovered slowly after the early 2000s, and the local governments were relatively unaffected because real estate taxes and residential building activity held up. But, as the nation was soon to find out, the bases of recovery were to prove insubstantial and fleeting. State surpluses and rainy-day reserves grew in the mid-2000s, but state balances in reserves peaked at $69 billion by fiscal year 2006.[9] Given the size of the deficits that emerged starting in 2008, these reserves were to provide little protection.

The Great Recession of 2007–2009

The Great Recession began in late 2007 with a weakening of demand for housing and consumption spending, as the first inklings of the financial meltdown began to surface. It gathered considerable steam in 2008 and reached its trough in early 2009 as unemployment quickly rose and consumption spending plummeted. The woes of the housing sector quickly spread throughout the financial system, which had built up tremendous leverage based on the low interest rates. The huge inflation in the capital values in the markets and, accordingly, in the balance sheets of households and commercial firms evaporated, as a huge deleveraging took place.

The details of the financial meltdown and the accompanying contraction in the real economy are detailed elsewhere and are dealt with in individual chapters in this book. All aspects of the state and local finance and intergovernmental relations were affected, given the severity of both the capital market crash and the ensuing economic decline, which was felt nationwide. The increased sensitivity of the state and local revenue systems was brought into full relief, as was the existence in many states of persistent structural deficits.

An illustration of the severity of the Great Recession in contrast with the two earlier national recessions of 1991–1992 and 2001 can be seen in table 1.1. As is often cited, the impacts of recessions tend to lag behind in their effects when it comes to the state and local sector, with both government revenues and expenditures absorbing major impacts after the recession has formally started and ended. The impact of the earlier 2001–2002 recession was about four times as great as that of 1991–1992, when viewing state budget shortfalls as a percentage of GDP. These in turn were further magnified in the case of the recession that began in the fourth quarter of 2007 and ended by the second quarter of 2009, which showed shortfalls as being relatively twice as great as those of 2001–2002. State shortfalls in fiscal year 2010, at $191 billion, were estimated to equal 1.3 percent of GDP. It was not that

Table 1.1 Impact of Recession on State Budget Deficit Gaps

Fiscal Year	States Deficit Gaps (billions)	National GDP (billions)	State Deficit Gap as % GDP	State Deficit as % of State-Local Spending
Recession of 1990–91				
1991	–8	5,896	–0.14%	–1.16%
1992	–13	6,167	–0.21%	–1.79%
Recession of 2001–02				
2002	–40	10,464	–0.38%	–3.15%
2003	–75	10,892	–0.69%	–5.64%
2004	–80	11,506	–0.70%	–5.79%
2005	–45	12,254	–0.37%	–3.10%
Great Recession of 2007–09				
2008		14,215		
2009	–110	14,244	–0.77%	–6.16%
2010	–191	14,390	–1.33%	–10.73%
2011e	–130	14,930	–0.87%	–7.25%
2012e	–112	15,500	–0.725	–6.20%

Sources: Estimated deficits: 1991–1992 (NASBO surveys), 2002–2005 and 2009–2012 (est) (CBPP) GDP (Bureau of Econoic Analysis, National income Accounts, Table 1.15): Estimated for Fiscal Years by using average of adjacent calendar years.

state and local spending had become relatively more important, but rather that their revenues had become increasingly sensitive to changes in the economy.

The difficult fiscal situation for states has attracted considerable attention and a spate of special studies and analyses. The seemingly intractable problems of the state of California have been a centerpiece of attention. Even during the recovery of the late 2000s, the state suffered continuing deficits, having balanced its budget only once during that decade.

States in Disarray: Beyond California

The Pew Center for the States in late 2009 examined ten states that shared attributes that were similar to those that had led to California's continuing fiscal crisis.[10] The analysis illustrated the point that fiscal performance was determined by the interaction of the underlying economy and the state's fiscal system, which itself is a product of the political structure, "public culture," and the types of fiscal institutions and constraints that the state adopts.

For example, California, Nevada, Arizona, and Florida are all states that have oriented their tax systems to a model of continuing economic growth and, in particular, the sustained housing boom. These states were heavily hit by the subprime housing crisis, increased foreclosures, and the collapse in housing prices. Then there are the older industrial states (e.g., New Jersey, Rhode Island, Illinois, Michigan, Ohio, and Wisconsin) that are undergoing long-term adjustments due to the deep losses within their manufacturing bases. These are also states that have a unionized public sector. And there are the unbalanced revenue systems. Thus, Oregon, almost solely dependent on the income tax, paid the price for that tax's great sensitivity to income fluctuations. The fiscal institutional setting is also important. Several states require a "super majority" to pass a tax or to approve a budget or both, with California being the classic example of a state that could not pass credible, let alone timely, budgets even in good years.[11] The final factor is the "money management score," which is a summary score of an inability of states to plan for or to implement their fiscal affairs in a logical, systematic fashion (which is usually tied to the underlying political culture and governmental structure).

State and Local Financial Challenges

While the Great Recession pointed out these problems, the persistent budgetary difficulties of the states are not an unexpected result of dysfunctional systems. The past decade or two have provided a poor environment for tax reform because antigovernment and antitax sentiments are very strong. A decade of continuing tax cutting in the 1990s, even when program expansions occurred, made support for even *fiscally neutral* reforms (that means no change in total revenues) difficult to muster. There are deep ideological divisions as to what governments should do. The slow economic recovery from 2003 through early 2007 glossed over many fiscal weaknesses. The sharp slowdown in 2007 was followed by the deep recession dive of 2008 and 2009, which exposed the problems. There are now huge arguments over the wages and benefits for government employees. State and local employment has been contracting. As of April 2011, state and local governments had cut 700,000 jobs since 2008, a figure that was growing steadily.[12]

Tax systems are not compatible with changing economic and political circumstances and becoming obsolete. Primary causes are the following: (1) there is a high level of dependency on intergovernmental aid that is slow to grow and unreliable, and such aid is largely passed through to persons (e.g., Medicaid); (2) state and local own-source tax bases have declined in comparison to the economy; and (3) there is increased interjurisdictional competition, especially in retaining and attracting jobs by giving tax concessions, and this has restricted growth in tax bases. The pressure on revenue systems is primarily due to rapid increases in health-care costs, both in terms of Medicaid and employee benefits.

The concentration of some states on only one dominant revenue source is a major problem. Five states levy no sales tax and eleven levy no income tax. This makes trade-offs among revenue sources difficult and places great competitive pressure on tax rates. The local property tax is the mainstay local tax (representing almost 40 percent of own-source revenues); and, although once a stable source, the real estate base has become subject to erratic behavior. While there are delays and loose linkages, the base of assessed values is ultimately market-driven and has now gone into a prolonged decline as the tax has become a favorite vehicle for tax-base erosion for often ostensible gains in equity and economic development, and economic change has lessened the role of industry in the property-tax base and has added more weight on residential properties. More corporate value is now found in intangibles (patents, databases, and intellectual property).

Consumption spending is shifting to various services and away from goods. Many of the latter are exempted and preferred items. The sales tax has pro-cyclical behavior, but generally its base has been on a downtrend as a fraction of GDP. A continued narrowing of the sales tax base has occurred whenever taxes are cut. Sales taxes became disproportionately influenced by home building and relocation activity, as well as the purchase of large appliances and building materials. Lower prices on taxed consumer items are due to low inflation rates, and this has hurt growth in tax revenues. On the other hand, exemptions of taxes on food and medical "necessities" like drugs shrink the sales tax base.

Due to the US Supreme Court intervention (and congressional failure to correct the problem) regarding of collection of sales tax on Internet purchases, sales-tax revenue losses are growing as well as creating a disadvantage for physical (versus virtual) businesses (i.e., whatever happened to those small bookstores?).

Tax competition has increased and this can enforce efficiency. But how much is too much? Pressure on a state that is losing jobs forces large concessions, cutting back its tax base, and ultimately reducing public goods. The corporate income tax has been a major loser. These taxes were affected by federal tax cuts. In the 1990s and early 2000s, personal income taxes climbed as a percentage of revenue, but they are increasingly cyclical. Corporations now pay states about the same percentage tax on their profits as persons pay on their personal incomes (3.5%). Corporate taxation has also been eroded by tax concessions that are given to attract businesses and jobs.

There are no easy alternatives and competing goals need to be recognized and policy trade-offs addressed. New taxes on the sales of services may increase the regressive nature of taxes. More business-to-business sales taxes favor integration of businesses and hurt small firms. The federal government may get into the state-local taxing act by efforts such as competing for the retail sales base and disallowing the deductibility of state and local taxes in the computation of one's federal tax liability. deductions. Other options for states: make corporate tax breaks be based on "performance" or abandon the corporate profits tax altogether and replace it with a gross receipts or value-added tax.

The remainder of this introduction provides a short summary of the key messages—the "headline story"—of each of the chapters. As was noted, the chapters are grouped in major sections that deal respectively with the institutional framework; the sources of revenues; spending, borrowing, and financial management; and future prospects for state and local government finances. Unless otherwise cited, the quotations in each section are directly from the chapter that is being discussed.

The Demographic, Economic, and Institutional Framework

Chapter 2: Constitutional Frameworks of State and Local Government Finance

In having the oldest federal constitutional government in the world, the United States is organized as a system of divided and concurrent powers. The national ("federal") government has sovereign authority with respect to the powers delegated to it by the federal Constitution, while the fifty states remain sovereign over all nondelegated powers, including constitutional authority for the country's 89,526 (in 2007) local governments. In chapter 2, John Kincaid provides a primer of the fiscal frameworks set forth in the US Constitution and the fifty state constitutions. Recognizing that "neither the United States nor any constituent state has a free-standing fiscal constitution," Kincaid works through the labyrinth of fiscal provisions that are embedded in the constitutions and constitutional law. Because what the US Constitution "says" about the practice of fiscal federalism is largely about what the federal courts (past and present) have decided it should be (ostensibly based on what the framers meant by federalism), Kincaid's chapter begins with a review of *The Federalist* on federal and state fiscal powers ("Despite the comparatively sparse references to public finance in the U.S. Constitution, the tax power was one of the principal issues underlying the country's transition from confederation to federation..."). He then lays out the core public finance provisions in the federal Constitution: direct taxes and apportionment; federal tax, spending, and borrowing powers and limits (albeit not always respected by the courts); and the nature of state and local powers ("Each state possesses inherent authority to do whatever it pleases, as long as the U.S. Constitution or the state constitution does not prohibit it from doing so" whereas "local governments possess...only powers granted to them by their state"). Kincaid next turns his analysis to reinforcing the message that what is notable about the US Constitution compared to other federal constitutions is the absence of detail and, thereby, the lack of significant constraints on the federal and state governments.

The chapter concludes with a section on state constitutional frameworks of public finance (when the US Constitution was ratified, eighteen state constitutions were already in place). Some state constitutions say little about state fiscal powers, while others contain detailed provisions. At the same time, Kincaid makes clear that while there is no federal-state fiscal hierarchy (that is, the states are not a lower constitutional "level" of government), there is a state and local fiscal hierarchy set out in state constitutions.

Chapter 3: Federalism Trends, Tensions, and Outlook

The chapter by Timothy Conlan and Paul Posner (chapter 3) details the development of the US federal system over the past two and a half centuries. Their effort not only establishes the proposition that if one is to understand the history of this country then one must understand its federalism platform, but also that that platform sets the initial conditions for determining the future options for US public finance policy and administration. To develop this theme, Conlan and Posner take us through a series of stages—from that of a "dual federalism" that lasted until the 1860s whereby the federal and state governments had little overlap in functions and responsibilities to a post-Civil War era centralizing impulse that strengthened what had been a very weak antebellum national government. The early twentieth century saw the establishment of many of the institutions that are now part of today's intergovernmental system (e.g., the Federal Reserve System and the income tax amendment, "which laid the fiscal foundation for subsequent expansion" of the federal sector). What ensued was "cooperative federalism," a model of governance whereby the federal government and the states shared responsibilities in a collaborative manner.

Then came the Great Depression. State and local finances collapsed and, consequently, "the states turned toward the federal government for assistance" in the era of the New Deal. Even with the "centralizing trend" of the New Deal (1933–1936), there was still a "cooperative" federalism. Beginning with the Great Society of Lyndon B. Johnson (despite widely heralded moves toward devolution during the Richard Nixon and Ronald Reagan administrations), cooperative federalism gave way to a continued expansion of "more coercive regulatory tools." This included major new federal-to-state spending mandates and the passage of new intergovernmental regulations and the preemption of state regulatory authority. This transition from "cooperation to coercion in contemporary federalism" is where, according to them, we are today.

What about the future? Conlan and Posner have two things to say. First, the maintenance of a robust decentralized federal system is essential to accomplishing many of the nation's broader societal goals such as economic growth, macroeconomic stability, and public-sector innovation. Second, they pose a question as to "whether the federal system retains its historic capacity for adaptation and flexibility" in order to provide the needed robustness. On the "yes" side, the authors argue that if the tradition of resilience of the states and their longstanding roles as policy laboratories collide with "national political and policy gridlock," citizens may again turn to states and localities for new policy ideas and reforms. However, on the "no" side, the authors cite several forces that are eroding the state and local position, such as a political culture whereby a new generation of national officials have converted from "being ambassadors" of state and local parties to being "independent political entrepreneurs" for national programs and legislation. Also, an increasingly globalized business sector has shifted from a "traditional position supporting decentralization of policy" to that of seeking "national legislation to standardize, restrict, or actually prohibit states' initiatives."

Thus, Conlan and Posner have provided a conditional answer. There is a history of state and local resilience that the United States needs to turn to if it is to continue to address unique needs and priorities across its diverse communities.

Chapter 4: State and Local Government Finance: Why It Matters

Serdar Yilmaz, François Vaillancourt, and Bernard Dafflon lay out the economists' view of why state and local government matters. To establish the economic framework, the authors systematically work through the seminal contributions of Paul Samuelson's theoretical arguments of the importance of a public-sector role for efficiency in resource allocation; Charles Tiebout's thinking on the difference between national and local public goods; Richard Musgrave's classification of the fiscal "branches" of a decentralized federalist system; and Wallace Oates's Decentralization Theorem, which posits that a uniform, centrally determined level of local public goods and services will result in a lower level of social welfare than will decentralized service provision.[13]

It is from this platform that Yilmaz, Vaillancourt, and Dafflon proceed to address three fundamental fiscal policy issues for a multigovernmental society (e.g., US fiscal federalism): (1) the sorting out of expenditure responsibilities among different types of governments ("expenditure assignment"); (2) the question of which type of government should use which type of revenue ("revenue assignment"), and (3) what happens when, for many state and local governments, the costs of the allocation of expenditure responsibilities are greater than that which can be financed from their "own" state/local revenues (the role of "intergovernmental transfers"). The result is a straightforward theoretical analysis that demonstrates the two opportunities for welfare gains from fiscal decentralization: when across jurisdictions there are divergences in demand for, or costs of, local public goods and services. Having established the case for fiscal decentralization, the authors then lay out the conceptual framework in a decentralized system of "own" revenues, expenditure need, and the variants of intergovernmental grant arrangements.

Chapter 5: State and Local Governments and the National Economy

Rick Mattoon and Leslie McGranahan in chapter 5 take a longer-term look at the roles of the state and local government sector in the nation's economy. Over the last four decades, the sector has played a fairly constant, but substantial, role in the national economy as contributors to GDP when measured by their purchases. But there have been important changes in the composition of the sector's spending and revenues. An increasing share of expenditures has gone to social benefits (in particular, for Medicaid) and there has been growing reliance on the federal government as a source of funds. There has also been increasing dependence by states on the personal income tax and a heightened sensitivity of state tax revenues to economic conditions. For the states, revenues thus have become more unreliable, while spending has been relatively unaffected by changing economic conditions. Localities and their sources of funds have presented a more stable picture. But changes by the states increasingly affect local governments, which now get approximately one-third of their revenues as transfers from states.

The authors see the roles of the states and local governments continuing to evolve, but there will be growing pressures to better balance revenues and spending. The aging population and increasing medical costs mean that Medicaid and other health-care programs will grow as a share of state budgets. On the revenue side, the income tax is likely to continue to be a major, but cyclically sensitive, source of funds for states. The property tax, the pillar of most local government revenue systems, may see long-term erosion as taxable property values decline and increases in tax rates are widely resisted.

The authors conclude by assessing ways that states in particular can mitigate the increased cyclical nature of their revenues. States can smooth revenues by either returning to the historic practice of raising tax rates for major tax bases (sales and income) during bad times or restructuring and broadening tax bases to mitigate their volatility. Other self-help alternatives amount to states saving more and building reserves (rainy-day funds) or reducing expenditures aggressively to close budget gaps. A final option is relying on the federal government for help, which occurred most vividly and recently with the American Recovery and Reinvestment Act (ARRA) during the Great Recession. The problem with that strategy is that such relief is "no sure thing" because the federal government has its own long-term fiscal problems to confront. In fact, fiscal misery runs downhill: Efforts to solve the federal deficit problem by cutting its expenditures and increasing its revenues will intensify the pressure on state and local government finances.

Chapter 6: The Evolving Financial Architecture of State and Local Governments

Sally Wallace addresses the impact on state and local budgets of the "underlying trends and tensions facing state and local governments" as the United States pulls out of the Great Recession. Noting that recessions are cyclical and there will be a recovery, she draws attention to the "more fundamental challenge for the US state and local fiscal system—indeed for the sustainability of our system of fiscal federalism." She focuses on the demographic, economic, and institutional trends that determine expenditure needs and shape revenue sources but that are largely beyond the control of state and local policymakers.

Demographic characteristics include the changing rate of growth of the population and its age and ethnic composition as well as shifts in migration flows and household composition across regions. Economic trends of importance are primarily those of economic structure and output (e.g., the rapid growth of employment in the health and social services sectors versus that of the manufacturing sector). Institutional changes refer to not only what is happening to tax and administration and budget preparation and execution, but also to the many legal constraints that the federal government imposes on the state revenue autonomy and that the states impose on local governments. Thus, for example, on the expenditure side, there is the link between the aging of the population and the composition of the demand for local public goods (health-based spending) as well as for state and local labor costs. On the revenue side, there is the relative increase in the number of the elderly (for purposes of their income taxes, most states exempt all or part of pension income despite the option of means testing); the feasibility of sales taxation of some rapidly growing sectors in a mobile economy (e.g., professional services), and whether the property-tax and general-business taxes can be structured to capture changes in the production of wealth and income.

Recognizing how the fiscal architecture is shaping up for the next decade is fundamental to understanding what makes "fiscal sense" for state and local taxation and spending policies. As Wallace notes, even though the trends themselves are largely beyond the control of state and local policymakers and administrators, "forward-thinking governments can capture the implications of these changes in their expenditure forecasts" as well as tailor their revenue systems so as to both minimize the negative impacts on budgets and to capture the potential fiscal benefits of changes in the fiscal architecture. The trends may be beyond policymakers' control, but that state and local revenue systems must therefore become obsolete in the twenty-first century "is not a fait accompli."

Chapter 7: Profiles of Local Government Finance

Christine R. Martell and Adam Greenwade provide a profile of the structure and diversity of local government finance. Nearly ninety thousand local governments in the United States provide most public services. It is such a diverse subsector that no one set of political or fiscal arrangements can be said to be standard. This scale and complexity make the local governments in the United States unique among the world's nation-states.

The main revenue sources for local governments are own-source revenues that they raise within their jurisdictions (including revenue from property taxes, sales taxes, personal income taxes, and user fees and charges) and from transfers they receive from the state and federal governments. Local government own-source revenue options are determined by each respective state, although local jurisdictions typically have some power to set rates and exemptions. Martell and Greenwade find that, on average, per capita local government revenue has grown 70 percent from 1980 to 2008, most of which can be attributed to growth in own-source revenue. Notably, property-tax and sales-tax revenue has decreased in the percentage of total own-source revenue, while revenue from charges and fees increased its relative contribution. Nonetheless, property-tax revenue generally remains the largest source of local government own-source revenue. Despite rising property values, the property-tax base has been declining due to development incentives and tax limitations that cap assessments. From 1980 to 2008, the share of federal revenue transfers to local governments decreased in relationship to the share of state revenue transfers.

Martell and Greenwade find that expenditure assignments vary among local governments whose services may include general government, public safety, K-12 public education, community colleges, public works, planning, parks and recreation, economic development, and public health and welfare. However, local government spending by function has remained remarkably consistent over the last thirty years. The largest single spending of local governments is education (39 percent), followed by public welfare spending (11 percent), the environment (10 percent), and public safety (9 percent). On a per capita basis, local government expenditure has grown slowly but steadily and all major categories of local government spending have grown at similar rates over the past three decades.

Local governments have been stressed by the Great Recession, which reduced the property-tax base, slowed consumer spending, increased unemployment, and restricted access to credit. That recession also led to a decline in state aid. At the same time, employee pension and health-care costs have increased. Local governments responded to the harsh economic climate by employing a number of revenue-raising and expenditure-reducing strategies. They increased fee levels and property or sales tax rates, added new fees and taxes, and broadened tax bases. Local governments have laid off personnel, cancelled or delayed infrastructure investments, abandoned specific city services, modified health-care benefits, and cut spending on public safety and human services.

Chapter 8: Federal Preemption of Revenue Autonomy

Starting with *Federalist* No. 30 on "Concerning Taxation," Alexander Hamilton devotes seven essays to the topic of national and state taxing powers.[14] As an advocate of a strong national government, Hamilton argued that the federal government ought to possess the power to tax for not only "providing for the support of the national forces" but also to "embrace provision for the support of the national civil list." Hamilton then turned (in No. 32) to the "justice of reasoning, which requires that the individual states should possess an independent and uncontrollable authority to raise their own revenues for the supply of their own wants" with the "sole exception of duties on imports and exports" and that the states should "retain that authority in the most absolute and unqualified sense; and that an attempt on the part of the national government to abridge them in the exercise of it, would be a violent assumption of power, unwarranted by any article or clause of its constitution."

This Hamiltonian view fit well with what Kincaid refers to in chapter 2 as "the contemplation of a dual federalism whereby the state and federal governments would tax, spend, and borrow independently." And, indeed, throughout much of the first two US centuries, the federal government pretty well held to a policy of nonencroachment on state and local taxing powers. One notable exception was in *McCulloch v. Maryland* whereby the US Supreme Court held that, under the Supremacy Clause, the state of Maryland did not have the authority to tax the Second Bank of the United States. However, even that decision was about state taxation of the federal government and not, as one now increasingly observes, an argument for the federal preemption of state and local taxation of private activity.[15]

However as James R. Eads writes in his chapter on state revenue autonomy (chapter 8), "in the past quarter century there has been an increasing—and troubling—trend of an abandonment the historical notion of US federalism as a federal-state-local partnership whereby the Congress would show a great deal of deference to state and local governments in formulating national policy, toward one of coercive federalism" characterized by, inter alia, "preemptions of state and local revenue authority." Citing the evolving limits on the power of state and local government to tax, Eads then catalogues the major federal preemptions (more than half of which have been enacted since 1969) of state and local taxing powers, starting with those that relate to federal government instrumentalities and the treatment of federal employees (including service members) to that of interstate telecommunications and employment matters.

He concludes by arguing that though a "case can be made for selective federal preemptions of the state tax base" there is "an equally important concern that the federal government will overreach." By drawing on the work of the US Advisory Commission on Intergovernmental Relations, Eads then offers a set of guidelines for avoiding what Alexander Hamilton would have likely regarded as a "usurpation of power not granted by the constitution."[16]

Chapter 9: State Intergovernmental Grant Programs

Although much of the state and local literature regarding grants is focused on federal aid to state and local governments, much of the action in grants policy and practice is that of state-to-local transfers, which are larger in absolute as well as relative magnitude than federal aid. Moreover, for those who want to know what lessons, if any, the United States has to offer to developing and transitional countries, the practice of "state aid" as examined by Ronald C. Fisher and Andrew Bristle (chapter 9) will be relevant.

Fisher and Bristle identify the reasons that, for efficiency, a well-designed system of fiscal decentralization will utilize intergovernmental transfers. Their discussion begins with details about the vertical imbalance within the aggregate numbers for state-to-local aid.

The authors then turn their attention to a topic that is perennially at or near the top of nearly every state and local legislative body. This topic is the level and structure of financial support for general-purpose local governments (counties, municipalities, and townships). Among the authors' findings is that only about half of the states provide true general revenue sharing aid to localities (i.e., the aid unrestricted as to use) and for those that do provide unrestricted support, the amount is relatively small ("only ten states grant more than 10 percent of local revenue").

The authors then discuss the diverse ways in which states allocate assistance. For example, regarding transportation, most states collect revenue mainly from fuel taxes and vehicle taxes and fees, even though the division of transportation responsibilities between state and local governments varies substantially. Such tax earmarking generally meets the conventional wisdom of matching the user and the user fee. Or does it? When Fisher and Bristle look in further detail at factors such as state versus local road ownership and the advances in increasing fuel efficiency, it turns out that per capita distributions are becoming an increasingly used factor to allocate grants for transportation as well as for general-purpose grants. The authors conclude that population is, however, often not an appropriate guide and it is time for state aid formula allocations that better reflect the diverse economic and institutional circumstances of the states.

Chapter 10: State and Local Fiscal Institutions in Recession and Recovery

Tracy M. Gordon analyzes the recent budget challenges that have prompted examination of the role of state and fiscal institutions such as balanced budget rules, tax and expenditure limits, debt restriction, and "rainy-day," or budget stabilization, funds. Some commentators argue that stronger fiscal rules could have helped avert the 2008–2011 (and, still continuing) state and local budget crises. Others contend that rules already in force have exacerbated budgetary effects of the Great Recession and that continuing with them as currently structured will not only make more difficult fiscal recovery but will also undermine the traditional role of the states in the federal system. California's demonstration of how such institutions can take a state from fiscal health and stability to near bankruptcy is a dramatic case, especially for those critics who are currently making the argument that institutions can lead to particularly severe unintended consequences, including enhanced sensitivity to business cycles. In contrast, as Gordon notes, legislatively imposed institutions, if well designed, can lead to increased public and social accountability.

In her chapter, Gordon looks first at the broad question of "why legislatures may adopt enact restrictive fiscal institutions that bind themselves." The reasons range from the relevance of median voter models and state concerns regarding policies of "their" local governments, to a response to judicial rulings and political responses "to constrain opposition...elements." Recognizing the diversity of state practices, Gordon finds that states with strict balanced budget rules tend to run larger surpluses and to be quicker to adjust to deficit shocks by making spending cuts more often than using tax increases. States with both tax and expenditure limits were less likely to raise taxes, but they were no more likely to cut spending than other states because they turned to other nontax sources of funds, including fees and charges. Some states with restrictions on general obligation debt found that the rules may have precipitated the proliferation of special-purpose entities, which can typically issue debt without voter approval. Regarding budget stabilization funds, the degree of stringency depends on rules governing deposits, withdrawals, and the sizes of the fund. In some cases (e.g., New York, the District of Columbia), rules on replenishment and repayment of the funds can inhibit their use.

Gordon concludes that proponents and critics of stricter rules have probably overstated their roles in protecting states and localities in the recent fiscal crisis. One solution she suggests is to borrow from international experience with cyclically adjusted, or "over the cycle," multiyear budget targets that allow for a more activist fiscal policy during recessions while maintaining longer-term budget discipline.

Revenue Structures and Systems

Chapter 11: Real Property Tax

A good place to start a discussion of the United States' state and local revenue systems is with the single largest source of state and local own-source revenues—the property tax. Beginning with a comparative review of traditional measures used to examine tax trends, Michael E. Bell then proceeds to an analysis and evaluation as to that tax's performance in recent years and through the Great Recession, concluding with a look to the fiscal future.

The property tax today still remains as the local government revenue "mainstay"—97 percent of property tax revenue accrues to local governments. Over the past four decades, however, the property tax has declined in its relative importance as a share of local government revenues (43 percent of local general revenues in 1968 to 28 percent in 2008), and as a percentage of local own-source revenues (56 percent in 1968 to 45 percent in 2008).

As with any overall trend data, the numbers mask a wide diversity among the state and local systems. The data presented in Bell's chapter show a clear regional character. In 2008 the six states that topped the list of property taxes as a percentage of own-source revenues were all in the Northeast: Connecticut, Maine, Massachusetts, New Hampshire, New Jersey, and Rhode Island. The three states with the lowest property-tax dependence are clustered in the Southeast: Alabama, Arkansas, and Louisiana. Diversity is also the case for the property-tax rates, because effective rates among localities varied from a high of 3.26 percent in Detroit, Michigan, to just 0.28 percent in Honolulu, Hawaii.

There are several "stories" about the tax on real property. Bell focuses on three of particular importance as they set the stage for the future of the real property tax. First, based on traditional criteria for evaluating a revenue system (revenue adequacy, neutrality/efficiency, simplicity, and equity), the local property tax emerges as a very defensible source of local revenues. The property tax is especially attractive when compared with other potential sources of local tax revenues.

Second, there is a long-term trend for the increasing relative importance of residential properties in the real property-tax base compared to the commercial and industrial base of the "old" economy. States have responded with a variety of tax relief measures in an effort to reduce the burden on residential property owners. Bell argues that, as a result of such state policies, the property tax is moving further and further from its ideals because of its increasingly narrow focus, policies that create distortions to private decision making by favoring some land use types, and the administration of the tax. The tax is becoming less uniform and less fair as a result of special provisions that accumulate as the broad base of the property tax is decimated and destroyed.

Finally, in spite of its base having been eroded over the past three decades by special interests, the property tax helped local governments avoid some of the more severe difficulties experienced by state governments during the Great Recession. That's good news in terms of revenue stability. That said, this may amount to only a buying of time. As Bell notes, local governments are experiencing significant post–Great Recession declines in property tax collection for the same reasons that the slowly reacting tax bought them time during the recession.

Chapter 12: State Personal Income Taxes

In chapter 12, Joseph J. Cordes and Jason N. Juffras examine the economics of the personal income tax (PIT), which is the second largest source of state and local government own-source revenues, after the property tax. When viewed from the state perspective (91 percent of PIT collections are made by states), the PIT is the largest source of own-source revenue, surpassing the general sales tax (26 percent for PIT versus 23 percent for general sales tax). Because policymakers make tax choices given their own economic, demographic, and institutional circumstances, there is wide diversity in its use: forty-one states and the District of Columbia tax a broad base of wage and capital income, while two other states tax only interest and dividend income. The seven states that do not levy a state personal income tax typically have an especially large capacity to tax alternative bases, such as consumption or the extractive industries.

Following a state-by-state description of key statutory provisions, Cordes and Juffras evaluate how the PIT performs when judged against the criteria of revenue elasticity, equity, efficiency, and administration. The record on how the PIT performed during the Great Recession is ambiguous. Despite a dramatic drop in personal income during the recession, states with a strong reliance on the PIT were not "at jeopardy of larger revenue losses during the recession." Nor did conformity with the federal income tax lead to sharper revenue losses (indeed, states that conformed to the federal treatment of Social Security showed a gain in stability).

With respect to the legislative response, a number of Northeastern and Western states reacted to the Great Recession by creating new upper-income tax brackets with higher rates, enough so that the authors suggest that "the pendulum" may be moving away from two decades of flattening tax rates before the Great Recession toward greater progressivity. States have also made their income-tax systems more progressive by adopting earned income tax credits, which are now offered by a majority of states with a broad-based PIT. But states have not made concerted efforts to broaden their personal income-tax bases or curtail tax expenditures. This pattern may leave some states with no choice but to maintain higher rates.

Cordes and Juffras analyze short-run versus long-run revenue elasticity that supports earlier findings and find that there is no necessary linkage between long-run elasticity (which is relatively high for the PIT) and short-run swings in revenue when the economy and tax base have contracted during a recession. They similarly confirm the warnings by Wallace (in chapter 6) that unless states respond to the erosion of the PIT base due to the aging of the US population, the state personal income-tax base will be in jeopardy.

Chapter 13: State Corporate Income Taxes

Addressing the state corporate income tax (CIT), David Brunori goes immediately to the question of whether the states can "rescue the state corporate income tax from near irrelevancy." Even though the tax is used in forty-five states and the District of Columbia (only Nevada, Ohio, South Dakota, Washington, and Wyoming do not impose any taxes on corporate net income), it has diminished—dropping from a high of 9.5 percent of state revenues in 1997 to less than 5 percent today. In addition to simply broadening the tax base, the CIT is primarily justified on two grounds: as a complement to the tax on real property (which ignores the returns to the input of intangible property) and a need for a mechanism that integrates with the state personal income tax (to ensure some degree of neutrality by type of business organization). At the same time, he largely dismisses the frequently cited justification that a state CIT adds to the progressivity of state public finance systems, noting that depending on the nature of the market, the tax is just as likely to be shifted forward to consumers in the form of higher prices or backward to factor suppliers such as labor as it is to be shifted to landholders in the form of lower rents and by reducing the shareholder return to equity.

Key to his theme that the "corporate income tax requires much-needed reform if it is to once again become a viable part of the state revenue system," Brunori examines four reasons for the erosion of the CIT tax base that explain the decline of its importance: (1) the proliferation in the last three decades of "economic development" incentives; (2) abandonment of uniformity in formula apportionment of multistate business receipts; (3) adeptness of corporate tax planners to convert what would normally be considered business income to nonbusiness income allocated to a low- or no-income-tax state; and (4) changes in the federal law in 1995 that have ushered in the use of pass-through entities such as limited liability companies (LLCs) and limited liability partnerships (LLPs). These latter entities allow taxpayers to switch from a traditional "C" corporation status to a pass-through structure as states have conformed to the federal law, which treats LLCs and LLPs as partnerships for tax purposes.

To have some chance to "save" the CIT, Brunori discusses several policy initiatives: (1) require combined reporting (a trend that is catching on as nearly half the states now have such a statute in place); (2) return to the traditional three-factor formula ("uniformity is essential" and the formula is a "fair and efficient solution among a set of imperfect options"); (3) use more aggressive forms of "throwback" (untaxed sales to the state of origin) and "throw-out" (exclude from the sales denominator any sales not assigned to any states) rules; and (4) cut back on the granting of corporate tax incentives. With these initiatives in a postrecession era of fiscal stress, policymakers can consider the "overall ineffectiveness" of this form of tax-base erosion.

Chapter 14: Entity Taxation of Business Enterprises

Picking up on Brunori's discussion of the pending "irrelevancy" of the state tax on business net income, LeAnn Luna, Matthew N. Murray, and Zhou Yang in chapter 14 report that some states have responded by complementing the CIT with "business activity" or "entity" taxation—that is, a general business tax based on gross receipts (GRT) or on state value-added taxes (VAT). At present, ten states have some form of broad-based tax on gross receipts or a "hybrid" value-added base, with three of the ten relying on an entity approach such as an alternative minimum tax.

The chapter begins with an introduction to the variants of state general business taxes, noting that the range of choices can be thought of as a continuum, with the options distinguished primarily by the deductions allowed at arriving at the taxable base. On one end of the continuum of equal-revenue yield taxation is the narrowly based CIT. On the other end is the pure GRT, or "turnover," tax that disallows any deductions from gross receipts. This technique leads to tax pyramiding. Falling in between the CIT and GRT is the value-added tax, which can be computed either by the "subtraction method" of business gross receipts minus interfirm purchases or by the "addition method" of the sum of payments to the factors of production—land (rents), labor (payroll), the use of capital (interest), and entrepreneurship (profits). Although in practice the taxes along the continuum are not "pure," the business activity taxes have the merit of including in the tax base business firms regardless of their levels of profitability.

Following a description of how each of the alternative entity taxes operates and the performance of current examples of business activity taxes, the authors proceed to evaluate the two forms of entity taxes versus existing taxes (the CIT and the retail sales tax). The comparisons are done vis-à-vis the conventional normative criteria of (1) justification for business taxation and taxpayer fairness; (2) efficiency (organizational form, neutrality over imports and exports, and neutrality across and within state borders); (3) revenue performance (i.e., yield, elasticity, buoyancy, stability, and cyclicality); and (4) costs of taxpayer compliance and the ease of tax administration.

Chapter 15: Implications of a Federal Value-Added Tax for State and Local Governments

Harley T. Duncan addresses the question as to whether the United States may join many other central governments in enacting a national VAT—a question that he argues is in urgent need of discussion in chapter 15. The idea of a federal VAT, which in its final incidence operates like a national retail sales tax, is not new. Duncan reviews the performance of the current system of state and local retail sales taxes (RSTs) and compares this to what a "well-designed" consumption tax should look like (tax-base comprehensiveness, minimization of the taxation of intermediate products and services, destination-based taxation, and compliance and administrative costs). He concludes that state RSTs not only "fall well short" of meeting these policy goals, but also that their defects are not likely to be corrected.

There are two powerful arguments for a federal VAT: the national government needs the money, and it has the better potential of growing with the economy. The state RST, while it will not disappear from the intergovernmental revenue system, cannot be counted on as the state revenue mainstay that it once was. But can federal and state consumption taxes (the VAT and RST) be coordinated without a loss in state revenue autonomy and without leading to an overly complex and cumbersome intergovernmental revenue system? Duncan's answer is that a federal VAT can work with and for state and local governments. However, to get it "right" will require a thorough sorting out of the alternative forms a federal VAT might take. With that observation, Duncan takes us through a step-by-step description and evaluation of national VAT alternatives and what each may mean for a federal system. He concludes that although the federal adoption of a VAT will be certain to "create significant issues and challenges for states and localities," a national VAT could be structured to preserve a high degree of state and local revenue autonomy while at the same time providing a basis for addressing the "long-overdue modernization" of the state and local revenue systems.

Chapter 16: Retail Sales and Use Taxation

When discussions turn to the growing "obsolescence" of state and local taxation in the economy of the twenty-first century, two state taxes are at the top of the list: the tax on corporate net income and the retail sales tax. William F. Fox takes on the general retail sales tax. Whereas during the 1990s and into the 2000s that tax was the most important own-source revenue for state governments, it is now second to the state personal income tax. Fox begins with a brief history of the tax and then examines a convergence of factors explaining its declining importance.

Fox identifies three factors that have contributed to the sales tax-base shrinkage. The first factor is a range of state-legislated exemptions from specific exemptions that were ostensibly designed to reduce the tax impact on low-income families to that of "sales tax holidays" to encourage commerce. The second factor is the failure of policymakers to keep pace with the changing economy and, thus, the composition of a potential tax base that has shifted from a largely tangible goods orientation to one that is increasingly that of services, particularly professional services. The third factor is the operational weakness of the compensating use tax, a matter that has become particularly problematic with the growth of mail-order and Internet-based sales. The e-commerce sales tax losses for the forty-six sales-tax states and the District of Columbia have amounted to more than $12 billion a year (as of 2012).

Fox next evaluates all key facets of the RST against the test of economic efficiency (that is, the principle that a tax ideally should minimally interfere with, or "distort," private consumer, labor, and producer decisions). Noting the important discussion of the fundamentals of destination versus origin taxation, Fox examines the merits and demerits of the exemptions for the retail destination base, tax treatment of inputs that are intermediate in the production process, arguments to expand the sales tax to a wide range of services, and expanded taxation of remote transactions.

The general conclusion is that much of the obsolescence of the sales tax is institutional in nature rather than economic or demographic; thus, the sales tax can remain a key component of state tax systems. However, as to whether the required actions will be taken by the states or the US Congress, Fox concludes that "the past decade offers little confidence" for improvement of sales tax policy.

Chapter 17: Local Revenue Diversification: User Charges, Sales Taxes, and Income Taxes

From broad-based taxes on sales and income and employer payrolls, to fees and charges on school lunches, medical equipment, parking, harbor maintenance, lab testing, camping sites, sewer connections, ambulance services, plastic bags at supermarkets, driveways, and false fire alarms, and more, few topics take one into more aspects of public economics than the study of local revenue diversification. In chapter 17, David L. Sjoquist and Rayna Stoycheva provide a thorough review of this topic, bringing to their discussion new data as well as some new evidence on the measurement of the degree of revenue diversity among the states.

Sjoquist and Stoycheva begin with a set of measures as to the growth of the level and degree of revenue diversification by type of government, and, from there, they address the questions of "why diversify," where diversification works well, and where, in contrast, it has led to unintended negative outcomes. They present several reasons that justify local revenue diversification, beginning with the fundamental proposition that, just as is true for nations and states, different localities have different revenue-raising capacities. But arguments "against" are also considered, such as "diversification" is not only about different revenue tools but also about different services and type of governments, so one cannot make sweeping generalizations about efficiency. The useful guideline that a "charge should reflect the marginal cost of an additional user of the publicly provided good or service" often "needs to be adopted with caution" as it may result with "too little of the public service" or "higher administrative costs than the revenues" collected.

From this foundation, Sjoquist and Stoycheva take a close look at the US practice of state and local user fees and charges versus the use of local sales and income taxation. They further report on the use of fees and charges in response to the fiscal crisis of 2008, noting that while "local governments have overwhelmingly turned to fees and charges to shore up their revenues," for many local governments the untapped revenue potential of user charges is likely to still be large. Given all the institutional (including administrative) economic tax-base variables at play, getting revenue diversification policy "right" is a very complex task.

Chapter 18: State Tax Administration: Seven Problems in Search of a Solution

Steady periods of budget surpluses can hide, and effectively defer attention being given to, systemic problems that only a fiscal squeeze can reveal. This is the situation that Billy Hamilton addresses in his chapter on state tax administration. For the past quarter century, state tax administration has largely operated smoothly.

But a problem with largely uninterrupted growth is that those processes that worked from year to year in the "good times" are not necessarily reliable for the "bad times." Thus, the Great Recession "did not as much create new problems for state tax administration as it exposed the challenges that already confronted the profession and now need attention." Taking a cue from the "tax gap" literature that administrators and academics often talk about, Hamilton identifies seven major "gaps that pose significant challenges to tax administration" as the states address (or at least ought to address) in the postrecession years ahead. The seven gaps, each of which has several dimensions, include *data* (for "own" state data mining and multistate efforts alike); *resources* (legislators seeing what they considered adequate revenues tended to underresource tax agency enforcement efforts); *tax* (the typical three "u" problems: unfiled returns, unreported income, and underpaid taxes on filed returns); *knowledge* (e.g., salaries that cannot keep pace with private-sector practice, including the practice of tax avoidance); *technology* (many advances have been state pioneered but some agencies are still stuck with outdated computers); *policy* (tax-collection systems often reflect "tax structures that were created to tax an economy that no longer exists"); and *politics* ("the toxic mix of…antitax rage and distrust for government" has abetted the practice of some successful lobby policymakers to prevent administrators from doing their jobs).

Although the gaps are "interrelated to varying degrees, finding a solution to them requires addressing them separately as well as a group." If there is a post-Great Recession structuring of intergovernmental fiscal relations, that may happen (or it may not).

Chapter 19: Revenue Estimation

In chapter 19, Norton Francis poses three questions: "Where did the forecasting models go wrong? Who's to blame for the forecast errors? and How can [state and local] revenue estimation improve?" To answer all three, he starts out with a look at just how severe the 2007–2009 recession was, and he then empirically examines how five common features of revenue-estimating models were affected by the second longest business-cycle contraction of the past eighty years.

The Great Recession (eighteen months, peak to trough) was the most severe decline of any recession since the Great Depression of 1929–1933 (which lasted forty-three months). Norton carefully works through each of the key indicators that a state revenue estimator watches, and he demonstrates that not only was the Great Recession dramatically deep ("the last time all six major indicators contracted was 1948–1949, and even that was of shorter duration") but also that it has been "very different than prior recessions."

Several outcomes—and lessons—are revealed from the analysis. The most fundamental is that, for a series of very explainable and understandable technical reasons, even the most sophisticated of revenue-estimation models were not structured to handle the dramatic turning points in the business cycle. The Great Recession was, literally as well as metaphorically, uncharted territory. The time-series data that revenue estimators had been using with much prerecession accuracy "did not contain the information that would show the kind of downturn that was to occur." This chapter is not an apology for the poor performance of the models of the community of revenue estimators. Rather, it is a clear set of statements about why the models got it wrong and, thus, why nearly all the states have had to grapple with unexpected revenue shortfalls. It is also a chapter that takes what has been learned and suggests what might be done to improve the next generation of revenue-estimating models so as to be better prepared for when the next great contraction comes along.

In addition to drawing lessons about the method and technique of state and local revenue estimating, Norton also alerts us to the dangers of how, during a prolonged era of economic growth, policymakers can forget about the dangers of assuming that the business cycle has been tamed and can thereby engage in easy-to-make short-term policies without regard to difficult-to-reverse long-term consequences.

Spending, Borrowing, and Financial Management

Chapter 20: Providing and Financing K-12 Education

Spending for public elementary and secondary education, K-12, accounts for the single largest piece (about 25 percent) of the pie chart of total state and local spending. If one considers education as a whole (to include community colleges and state universities), the share is 36 percent. And even though private alternatives exist, the United States largely educates its youth within state and local public government schools. Of today's approximately sixty million K-12 students, 86 percent are in public schools, 11 percent are in private schools, and 3 percent are home schooled.

The public education sector is complex and manifests a variety of intertwining institutional and financial aspects that reflect its intergovernmental nature, where the state governments set standards and provide a share of funding, but the day-to-day delivery of services, much of the financing, is done at the local government level. Daphne Kenyon lays out the multidimensional aspects of how the US public school system works and points out that there are several variants of how the "system" is structured from state to state and across the country's nearly fourteen thousand school districts.

In terms of the history of the US federal system, the intervention of the courts in K-12 education is relatively recent ("since the 1960s...forty-five states have dealt with such lawsuits"). As Kenyon explains, the basis for going to court, which in nearly all cases is based on state and not US constitutional grounds, has changed from lawsuits based on equity and equal protection to that of the now more-frequent set of "adequacy lawsuits that put a greater emphasis on education outcomes."

The chapter then turns to the topic of how public education is financed. Recognizing the differences among the states, Kenyon examines the split among governments in how they provide school revenues. In the process she provides a primer on the development of and status of the property tax and the level and structure of state aid formulas.

Kenyon next turns to a discussion of current and future challenges for the delivery of education services and finance: "demographic challenges" of age as well as the ethnic composition of the population "are likely to generate the greatest pressures." She concludes that even "with elementary and secondary education becoming more essential" for national growth and competitiveness, fiscal pressures make it "difficult to be optimistic about the future of education."

Chapter 21: The Social Safety Net, Health Care, and the Great Recession

Safety net programs, as defined by Thomas Gais, Donald Boyd, and Lucy Dadayan (chapter 21), are those that assist people who have great difficulty in meeting basic needs such as food, clothing, shelter, and medical care, and those who have been unable to find work. These difficulties can result from age, illness, or disability, or they can be caused by events such as economic recession or natural disasters. The scope is huge as are the dollars involved. Overall, in 2008, federal, state, and local government spending on safety net programs (other than Social Security and Medicare) amounted to almost $700 billion, which equaled nearly 5 percent of the nation's GDP. Two out of three dollars of this total were financed by the federal government, while the remaining one-third ($235 billion) was supported by state and local government revenues.

These amounts were pushed rapidly higher by the federal government's response to the Great Recession. The size of its stimulus was "breathtaking," as federal assistance to state and local governments jumped from 3.3 percent of GDP to an unprecedented 4.6 percent between fiscal years 2008 and 2010. Federal assistance for social programs (including health care, income security, education, employment, and social services) increased from 2.6 percent to 3.7 percent of GDP. This effort was not just a matter of fiscal pump priming. The federal government used the ARRA not just to stimulate the economy and sustain state and local programs, but also as a lever to influence state policies and promote institutional reforms.

The Great Recession's countercyclical spending jolt was impressive. But the authors worry whether the nation can continue the regime of shared responsibilities for safety net programs between the national and state governments. They fear that many of the states will not be able to sustain their financial part of the bargain.

In any event, if the federal government is to provide financial support to states, it will need to fashion some sort of accountability. Accountability in the past has relied on matching formulas, data reporting, regulations, and performance measures and requirements. However, many states, aside from being politically recalcitrant, may not be able to meet the matching requirements. The authors worry that requiring too much "accountability" will restrict federal programs to those states that have greater financial resources and stronger bureaucracies. They conclude that creating "effective partnerships between the national and state governments in social welfare policy...is surely one of the more difficult and important tasks for US social policies."

Chapter 22: Transportation Finance

No area of state and local government finance has a longer lineage of public spending and intergovernmental relationships (or is more visible to citizens on a daily basis) than the sprawling, physically intertwined, absolutely essential transportation sector. Jonathan L. Gifford (in chapter 22) provides a tour through the labyrinth of financing arrangements that are now used to meet the nation's surface, air, and water transportation needs. Once the major claimant on state and local spending, transportation's role has eroded in the face of the demands of education and the spiraling needs of health-related programs. Likewise, the shifting public mood and the new age of austerity have brought transportation funding to a crossroads.

Federal Highway Trust Fund revenues are no longer are sufficient to meet program spending levels. No longer self-sufficient, the program has received "bailouts" from the federal government's general fund. Despite widespread agreement that the federal surface transportation program needs to be restructured, there is no consensus about what restructuring should look like. With stagnant revenues and little prospect for raising more funds, federal highway programs seem destined to shrink and to focus on maintaining existing roads and facilities. Visions of achieving broader goals such as smart growth, more urban "livability," and the bolstering of metropolitan prosperity are, at best, only aspirational for the foreseeable future. Similarly, federal plans for initiatives in aviation and water transportation are largely stalled. Stringent times may cause the government to move away from the traditional formula-based allocation of aid funds toward other allocating devices, such as project cost-benefit analysis or evaluations based on criteria such as environmental impact and energy-efficiency policies.

With prospects for added federal transportation funding bleak because of the long-term pressures on the federal budget, any future initiatives will be seen in the state and local sector. The challenge for them is replacing declining federal funding in an economic and political climate that opposes any new taxes. By necessity, states and localities will make difficult choices in allocating limited resources and in finding new ways to provide transportation infrastructure and services. Gifford concludes the chapter by reviewing an assortment of structures for public-private partnerships (PPPs) that might be enlisted to provide transportation facilities and services and for possible innovations for achieving greater use of user fees.

Chapter 23: Housing Policy: The Evolving Subnational Role

Providing for housing for moderate and low-income families ("affordable housing") as well as for the homeless has been geared to three policy parameters. First, there is a measurable need when the housing cost burdens equal or exceed 30 percent of a resident's income. Forty-five percent of all renters have an affordability problem; plus when housing is less available, homelessness increases. Second, inadequate housing increases a wide range of troubles for society as a whole. Third, this type of market failure has in the past elicited financing partnership between state and local and federal entities that is in the nation's tradition of a "cooperative federalism."

In chapter 23, Robert M. Buckley and Alex F. Schwartz provide both a policy primer and an analytical guide to the evolving subnational role in US housing. They trace developments that began in the 1970s "when the federal government began to relinquish its role as the preeminent player in US housing policy... through a convergence of strategies including the curtailment of highly centralized programs" to the growth of grant and tax "policies that provide state and localities much more latitude to devise their own programs," including that of "providing new subsidies to people rather than to places."

The chapter begins with an overview of housing's role in the economy ("what was seen as an unbroken success came apart with the mortgage crisis that began in 2007"). It then moves along to trends in housing tenure and an analysis of why concern for the affordability problem is increasing due largely to the interplay between the functioning of the housing market and the nation's widening wealth and income inequality.

From there, the authors delve into, and demystify, the large array of federal housing programs and then turn to the growth of state and local activism that took off in the 1980s, where most of the action was within local governments rather than the states.

Despite the evolving state and local roles, the provision of affordable housing remains heavily dependent upon a federal commitment. Examples examined range from project-based programs such as the HOME Investment Partnership Program, which is the largest federal block grant focused exclusively on low- and moderate-income households, and the Low Income Housing Tax Credit, which "has evolved from an esoteric financial instrument to the most important source of equity for low-income rental housing in the country," to rental housing vouchers (rent subsidies) that directly help low-income households to "obtain housing that already exists in the private market." Throughout their chapter, the authors also make the case that due to diversity of needs across the country there is a need for a variety of intergovernmental strategies, as well as of requirements that a certain percentage of federal funds be directed to community-based nonprofit organizations.

The chapter concludes with a strong endorsement of the importance of a continued federal-state-local partnership, recognizing that "state and local governments often have greater flexibility than federal agencies in designing programs more closely attuned to the needs of specific places and populations." But localities rarely offer the deep subsidies provided by the federal programs, which make it possible to house very low-income families. Thus, if federal, state, and local governments do not continue to collaborate and work in concert with nonprofits, the United States will never be able to serve all the neediest households.

Chapter 24: Capital Budgeting and Spending

Justin Marlowe first lays out the broad contours of state and local government capital spending and the precepts of the capital budgeting process. He then considers how capital spending levels and budgeting processes were affected by the Great Recession. State and local capital spending, which had grown rapidly before the downturn, was slowed considerably by the Great Recession's onset. Federal aid helped to cushion the blow, but capital spending began to decline as many jurisdictions exhausted their influx of federal funds. The Great Recession's effect on capital spending was found by Marlowe to be consistent with the impacts of past recessions, but he warns that its depressing effects will coninue for several years. Thus, the Great Recession, when its aftershocks are played out, will likely result in unprecedented declines in state and local capital spending and an erosion of the public capital stock.

However, austerity may bring improvements to state and local capital budgeting practices. Jurisdictions, faced with doing more with less money, will redesign capital budgeting processes in order to achieve tighter linkages between capital spending and community goals. Marlowe reports, based on survey information, that communities also have shifted resources away from new construction toward more efficient maintenance of existing infrastructure. Pressed for diminishing resources, jurisdictions are considering comprehensive approaches to capital budgeting, with thorough analyses that are driven by transparent criteria and quantifiable benefits.

The Great Recession has strained intergovernmental relations regarding capital budgeting and spending. Intergovernmental transfers designed to bolster local capital spending did sustain spending. But they also restructured capital budgeting in ways that may inhibit, rather than promote, intergovernmental cooperation in the future. With prospects of growth dimmed, the competition for limited resources may create both more prudence in capital spending decsions and rougher competition when trying to get access to more resources.

Chapter 25: Financial Markets and State and Local Governments

As John E. Petersen and Richard Ciccarone describe, subnational governments are important players in the financial markets, both as issuers of debt securities that pay for infrastructure and as investors that invest funds in the private markets to meet their cash management and employee retirement system needs.

The financial markets changed dramatically in the late 2000s and these changes affected the state and local sector. After a discussion of the aggregate balance sheet of state and local governments, the authors give a brief reprise of the financial-market developments in the early 2000s and the subsequent meltdowns of 2007 and 2008, which affected state and local governments. As was true with the entire economy, the financial system debacle was followed by a widespread downturn in activity and this had a disproportionate impact on state and local government revenues. The financial stresses growing from the Great Recession led to major changes in the municipal bond market. These largely centered on the demise of the bond insurers and the related disruptions in the credit-rating system. A key question relates to the continuing creditworthiness of individual governments. Their ability to contend with the increasingly sophisticated demands of the financial markets is a continuing concern.

Credit ratings have been of special importance to state and local securities, and the shortcomings and disruptions in that business had special consequences for state and local borrowers. In addition, the onslaught of exotic financing structures, poorly understood by unsophisticated issuers, led to a number of losses for governments. A short-lived, federally subsidized program, which was part of the federal stimulus, had a large impact on the municipal bond market, lowering interest rates and promoting an increase in volume. By the same token, the widespread fear of defaults by state and local securities led to volatility in the market as the condition of governments gained unaccustomed attention during 2010 and early 2011.

Petersen and Ciccarone detail the impacts of the federal financial reform act that was passed in 2010, which has led to more federal regulatory activity. As this chapter was written, the reforms remain controversial and the content of the new regulatory scheme is uncertain. Furthermore, federal-level spending cutbacks and tax reforms will likely have adverse implications for state and local finances. There are many problems that are arising from the long-term structural imbalances and weakening financial condition of state and local governments and, these, in turn, will affect their continuing access to the private financial markets.

Chapter 26: Infrastructure Privatization in the New Millenium

Traditionally, state and local public infrastructure has been funded through the use of state and local taxes and user fees, intergovernmental transfers, and through borrowing from the tax-exempt municipal bond market. In the last half of the twentieth century, the federal government became a major participant in providing and financing for infrastructure. But, with competing needs and a lack of appetite for paying taxes, the nation is faced with deteriorating infrastructure. In chapter 26, Elizabeth Dannin and Lee Cokorinos examine an alternative means of obtaining infrastructure funding, which consists of various techniques that involve private ownership and the operation of public-use facilities. Their focus is on highway projects, which constitute a major area for privatization proposals and can involve large-scale projects.

After recounting many of the technical and contractual issues that are entailed in the private provision of infrastructure and reviewing the results of large deals done thus far, the authors note that privatization has been around in the United States for a short time, but long enough to raise some important policy issues. Infrastructure privatization has been seen as a novel innovation in financing, building, operating, and maintaining infrastructure. However, the revenue-guarantee measures used to protect investors—the various adverse action or stabilization clauses—can be contrary to the public interest.

The United States can benefit from domestic and international experience. It may want to emulate the United Kingdom's decision to provide infrastructure through a network of agencies that provide oversight and guidance. Also, the United States needs national legislation that addresses comprehensive transportation needs and provides strong protection of the broader public interest. The highway funding mechanisms that have been used for the last fifty years and are falling out of date must be improved and updated. The least expensive way to provide high-quality infrastructure may be through well-designed taxes, rather than relying on private investors and complex decades-long contracts.

Finally, privatization schemes are leaving an unexpected legacy of lawsuits as the validity of various concessions and their associated contracts are being tested. Such lawsuits will clog courts for years and, because they often involve foreign corporations, they present a mixture of complex law and politics. As the authors conclude, financial innovation, such as that embodied in infrastructure privatization, while often attractive, can lose its appeal as time goes by and more knowledge is gained.

Chapter 27: Financial Emergencies: Default and Bankruptcy

The Great Recession and its aftermath resurrected concerns that state and local governments would begin to default on their obligations. Many feared that the long and successful history of state and local borrowing in the capital markets was destined to end. As spending needs swamped resources, finding easier ways out of public debt than repaying it as promised might become politically fashionable. James Spiotto in this chapter explains and evaluates the various mechanisms that might deal with municipal and state defaults and insolvencies in the United States.

He first explores the historical underpinnings of restructuring municipal debt, providing examples of successes and failures of such efforts in the United States. The era of the Great Depression of the 1930s and its precursors is examined, as is the existing statutory framework for municipal bankruptcy ("Chapter 9") in the United States. Sovereign debt by states and its resolution is also discussed. His overall conclusion is that these devices are painful, expensive to apply, and leave a wake of uncertainty that in the long run ends up costing taxpayers more than they save.

Spiotto believes that the present fiscal crises should stimulate designing new, creative ways for states and municipalities to meet their obligations. One approach would be the increased use of Chapter 9 by municipalities and the creation of a bankruptcy court for the states. But, he notes, bankruptcy courts do not provide bridge financing or interim provision of essential services: "bankruptcy affects virtually all constituents, taxpayers, government workers, suppliers, and essential services; it is an expensive, time-consuming, disruptive process that should only be used when there is no feasible alternative." Better options need to be considered and put in place before disaster strikes.

Ideally, a new generation of debt-resolution mechanisms should be tied to increased use of oversight; assistance and refinancing vehicles that transfer certain services to other entities provide bridge financing and, if needed, engage new tax sources. These mechanisms should work surgically, focusing precisely on what is broken. According to Spiotto, experiences with New York City, Cleveland, Philadelphia, and other distressed situations where state authorities have taken the lead provide useful frameworks for future mechanisms to relieve fiscally distressed local governments.

Chapter 28: Government Financial Reporting Standards: Past, Present, and Anticipating the Future

Financial reporting is an arcane area and one that is complicated by the difficulties of achieving a balance between accountability and control (how every cent is spent) versus efficiency and efficacy (what spending on inputs will achieve in outcomes). These difficulties are heightened by the fact that government activities, and hence its associated bookkeeping, are strewn over a landscape where thousands of governments are engaged in countless programs that range from picking up the trash to running high-tech medical facilities. The job of setting standards is up to the Government Accounting Standards Board (GASB). As Craig D. Shoulders and Robert J. Freemen discuss, winnowing out and compiling the critical financial information and reporting it on a timely and accurate basis are arduous and often controversial tasks.

Starting off with a brief description of the basis of governmental accounting principles (and how they are set), the authors recount the ongoing efforts to address long-standing problems and newly emerging issues. A major difficulty has been trying to tailor presentations to satisfy the various user groups—such as government managers, the general public, and bond market investors—while preserving the overall integrity of financial statements. One complexity is reporting on the separate self-balancing funds, of which there can be a multitude for an individual government. The scope and number of audits, which cost money and take time, are constraints and affect how quickly financial reports can be published. Potential regulations in the securities area may force rapid changes. Another major pressure, evolving from the profession itself, is to move governments closer to the accrual-based accounting concepts (and associated principles) used by the private sector and to achieve greater conformity with international standards.

Shoulders and Freeman conclude that the most influential determinant on where the GASB decides in the future to steer government financial reporting likely will be the bond market participants. These users, with money on the line, rely on fund-based financial information and demand that it be audited. Their need for detail on the individual funds and assurance that the numbers are in conformance with the standards will likely keep the fund-based structure in place for financial reports.

Chapter 29: Pullback Management: State Budgeting under Fiscal Stress

Carolyn Boudreaux and W. Bartley Hildreth analyze the challenge of state budgeting during periods of dramatic and unplanned declines in state revenue collections. Most public finance textbooks describe the budget process as an orderly cycle of preparation, approval, execution, and evaluation. When governments are "experiencing a steady growth or only marginal declines" in revenues such as during the past two decades (1989–2009), it's easy to see how state budget officials can become accustomed to a predictable, "regular rhythm." Thus, when the Great Recession hit, a series of month-after-month and quarter-after-quarter revenue shortfalls affected nearly all state budgets. The result was that with little warning and preparation, policymakers faced midyear budget deficits.

Boudreaux and Hildreth take on the topic of managing midyear budget adjustments. Beginning with a review of the institutional tools available to governors and legislatures (e.g., allotments, apportionment, budgeting, impoundments, special fund transfers, fund withholdings, furloughs), the authors carry out a study of how five states went about balancing their budgets in 2009–2010 and how the lessons from these state responses can inform those dealing with the next fiscal crisis.

The five cases provide a continuum, from a state where the governor had "almost unlimited authority" to make midterm adjustments to one in which the executive had "almost no authority to withhold or move funds." Between these two extremes is a representative middle range of three states that had a more mixed executive/legislative system of budgetary power sharing.

For each of the case studies, the authors lay out the initial fiscal conditions and the nature of the external shock to the state's economy and its finances. Next, they examine the range of midyear budget options available to state officials and the actions finally taken—actions that in each case "worked" as a means of solving the short-term goal of balancing the budget. Boudreaux and Hildreth conclude with a review of what has been learned and how the outcome serves to inform scholars and policy practitioners alike about how to think about the next such external shock to state budgets (which, of course, will be different from previous shocks).

Chapter 30: Public Employee Pensions and Investments

Nineteen million public employees are covered by state and local retirement systems. These funds in 2010 had a total of $3.2 trillion in assets. But those weren't near enough, because the systems also had up to $3 trillion in unfunded liabilities. The public retirement systems depend heavily on investment earnings to pay future benefits and, as Siona Listokin-Smith reports, the returns on investments have been terrible over the last decade. Consequently, state and local governments need to rapidly increase their annual contributions to the pension funds if they are to pay promised benefits. The underlying forces affecting public pension funds— changing demographics and a declining number of public employees relative to retirees—have been long visible. Moreover, changes in accounting rules have also underscored the liabilities tied to retirement health-care benefits.

Listokin-Smith surveys the landscape of state and local retirement systems and assembles a long list of policy ideas and concerns. On average, public pension funds are in trouble, and the unfunded liabilities promise to strain tight public budgets. But not all systems are having difficulties: "Any description of public pension fund reform must distinguish between those state and local government funds facing severe funding problems and those that have been responsibly managing their retirement systems." Overall, there are many dark clouds on the horizon. What are needed are more realistic actuarial assumptions, setting contribution floors, reducing the generosity of benefit structures, and sharing more costs with employees. States facing severe underfunding of pensions need dramatic reforms. Pensions are only part of the problem: other postretirement benefits (particularly those involving health care) exacerbate the financial trauma that lies ahead. The author notes that the states with severe funding problems face unsavory choices. They should assume a lower rate of return on investments. They also need mechanisms that force the payment of the required pension contributions. Both employee and employer contribution rates must increase and governments should restrict future benefit increases, tying them to higher employee contributions or requiring explicit taxpayer approval. Finally, governments need to shift toward defined contribution plans for new employees, and, if employees are not already participants, they should join Social Security. These are difficult but necessary prescriptions to avoid a fiscal Armageddon for many public employee funds and the associated misery that would be visited on retirees and taxpayers alike.

Looking Ahead

Chapter 31: Accomplishing Budget Policy and Reforms

Iris Lav in this chapter tackles an issue that is often talked about, but where little has been done lately: comprehensive state budget reform. With structural deficits rampant, reform is needed to maintain the current level of programs that states and localities now provide, but cannot support over time with current revenue policies. Recent "reforms" have mainly focused on cutting both spending and taxes. Nonetheless, the author believes, rhetoric to the contrary, that people want their services and will vote to pay for them, if given that option.

The author notes that there have been very few successful state tax reforms in recent years. But she says that modernization of tax systems is needed to alleviate structural deficits. Part of the problem is institutional myopia: improved multiyear budgeting can warn policymakers when proposed actions are likely to create budget problems over the long term. An area that needs reform is the proliferating use of tax expenditures (credits, exemptions, and deductions) that erode tax bases and engender inequitable and inefficient tax systems. Changes in a spending program, or in the tax code, are sometimes designed to have a modest budget impact in the initial year, but they end up having a much larger one in subsequent years. Such backloading of costs so as to squeeze programs into a current year's budget leaves a legacy of future unbalanced budgets. Cyclical downturns can intensify longer-term problems when hastily adopted tax cuts stifle future revenues and accumulate over time, curbing future levels of public services.

Limiting overall spending or revenues through rigid formulas and severe caps will distort budgets and reduce flexibility. Multiperiod budgeting techniques that carefully cost out programs and register the effects of changes in taxes as those of direct spending totals can help avoid long-term mismatches of revenues and expenditures. To drive the message home, states need to use "pay-as-they-go" approaches to match proposed changes in current expenditures with changes in revenues. More visibility and discipline will help states to do more with less, both in the good times and bad.

Chapter 32: Fiscal Austerity and the Future of Federalism

Fiscal relationships among the federal and state and local governments will change significantly in the future. As Rudolph G. Penner documents, the federal government is saddled with unsustainable tax and spending policies, and the changes that are necessary to restore fiscal stability are far larger than anything that has been experienced since World War II. State and local governments, beset with their own structural issues, will have to adjust to and share in a new world of fiscal austerity.

The deepest domestic federal spending problems lie with Social Security, Medicare, and Medicaid. All three entitlement programs are growing faster than the economy and tax revenues can provide. The overall federal tax burden has remained remarkably constant, varying between 17 and 19 percent of the GDP for all but eleven of the past fifty years. However, the Great Recession drove the federal tax burden below 15 percent of GDP in fiscal year 2010, the lowest level since 1950.

Federal budget policies have to change, and Penner walks through a list of candidates for cost cutting as well as revenue-raising cures, and he discusses their impacts on the state and local sector. If much of the federal deficit problem is solved by tax increases, it will be much harder for the states and localities to raise their own taxes. For example, depending on its design, a federal consumption tax (VAT) could compete with state taxes. Elimination of the federal income-tax deduction for state and local taxes will give these taxes higher after-federal tax costs. The elimination of tax exemption of interest income on state and local bonds would make that form of borrowing more expensive.

Federal tax increases might take some pressure off the spending side of the budget, but in any case it is likely that intergovernmental grants will be curtailed. But there are some dim rays of hope. Federal budget pressures may lead to vigorous health-cost control measures and more efficiency in health-care programs, lessening the burden on states. Although the federal government will be tempted to pass the responsibility for some activities "down" to the states, that will be muted by the fact that federal politicians enjoy the power to control those activities and prohibitions on unfunded mandates.

The impact on subnational governments will depend on the process surrounding federal budget reform. A comprehensive deal that is struck after a careful deliberative process might allow more time to design and to phase in long-run reforms. But if a financial crisis (or political hysteria) drives reforms, acting quickly probably means that spending cuts and tax increases will likely be both dramatic and haphazard.

Penner concludes that state and local governments should be strong advocates for federal budget reform. It will be easier for them to protect their interests if reform comes about from a thought-through, deliberative process rather than from an economic or political crisis.

Chapter 33: Achieving Fiscal Sustainability for State and Local Governments

Over the last decade, observers of state and local finances have been alarmed over an emerging picture of long-term, structural imbalances. Robert B. Ward in this chapter examines the concept of fiscal sustainability in several formulations and explains that it essentially means limiting expenditure commitments to those that can be met by available revenue streams. He investigates why fiscal sustainability in actual practice, however it might be measured in theory, has fallen into disrepair. The usual lineup of budget-busting culprits is next examined, with the proliferation of entitlement programs standing at the head of the line. Over the past four decades, state and local budget increases reflected the strength of the economy during an unprecedented run of prosperity. Meanwhile, the array of entitlement programs that drove spending was increasingly shaped by political, demographic, and institutional forces, each with its own clientele of beneficiaries. That has made adjustments more difficult when revenues do not keep pace with spending patterns. In addition, public employee compensation was allowed to spiral in costs, even as those costs were not fully accounted for, as in the case of retirement and employee health benefits. Meanwhile, revenue systems were allowed to be squeezed and pruned, making them politically acceptable but ever more sensitive to changing economic conditions.

Ward sees the decay of a state and local "budgetary culture" as a major issue in achieving sustainability. When that culture no longer undergirds the budgetary process, the spending and taxing sides of budgets lose their connection. This is a separate issue from how large or small a government might be: "[we] may debate the appropriate size and nature of governmental budgets. Such issues are separate from the question of whether a given set of revenue and expenditure policies is sustainable. Often, the most popular spending and tax policies will not be sustainable. Indeed, the problem of fiscal sustainability arises precisely because elected leaders have increasingly responded affirmatively to voters' desires for more spending without more taxes."

According to Ward, the deepest problems facing US state and local governments may ironically stem from the nation's success. The notion of fiscal sustainability is itself a public good. It thus represents a commonly shared, but one with low visibility, benefit to the individual citizen. Citing Mancur Olson, Ward worries that the nation's long run of political stability and prosperity has engendered powerful special-interest constituencies that benefit from state and local programs and tax policies. Thus, operating in their self-interest (highly visible to the few), they will retard efficiency in the overall economy and in the national government (less visible to the many).

Chapter 34: The Intergovernmental Grant System

As Raymond B. Scheppach indicates, history will write the two-year period of 2009 to 2010 as a watershed in the federal-state-local fiscal relationship. The outpouring of aid (about $150 billion in ARRA money and another $100 billion in other grants) helped states to avoid cutting spending and increasing taxes in the depths of the Great Recession. Federal grants dramatically increased as a percentage of total state revenues, from 26 percent to 35 percent. The fiscal relief packages were harbingers for the future, because 70 percent of the federal grants were devoted to health and education. But the relief supplied by the federal stimulus was short-lived. The expected "new normal" revenue path means that states will continue to downsize and streamline along all fronts.

Health-care spending holds the key. Existing health programs and the new Affordable Care Act, if is fully implemented, will mean that 130 million individuals will look to the states to help meet or, at least, control health-care costs. That is the difficult and expensive mission confronting the states in the future. Because of the growth in the Medicaid program and the expansion of coverage in the new national health-reform law, federal grants will become a significantly larger part of the total revenues for state and local governments. As health care consumes a growing share of state budgets, education, training, social services, and transportation are destined to receive smaller shares of the budget. The consequent reductions in spending on education and training and public infrastructure will reduce the nation's long-run competitiveness, productivity, and economic growth as well as the real wages and real incomes of citizens.

Scheppach unhappily concludes that none of these trends is positive for the nation. The growth of federal health-care entitlements promises to erode public investment in human and infrastructure capital. Health-care cost containment is the top national priority. But it may take another financial crisis for the nation to face this growing problem.

Chapter 35: Community Associations at Middle Age: Considering the Options

Robert H. Nelson in chapter 35 surveys what has been a leading development for American housing and local governance of the past half century: the meteoric rise of community associations. These quasi-government organizations usually are created by land developers and, as the new communities are developed, they evolve into self-governing entities owned by the homeowners and provide an extensive array of local services. In 2010 there were more than three hundred thousand community associations, which housed more than 60 million Americans, or 20 percent of the US population. (This is in contrast to the approximately ninety thousand local governments in the United States.) The growth of these associations has been rapid: between 1980 and 2000, half of the new housing in the United States was built and organized under the private governance of a community association. Most of that growth occurred in the sunny and sandy regions of the West and the South.

In many ways, the associations serve as substitutes for traditional local governments or can augment their services. Important issues are their financial viability, stability and longevity, and the nature of their governance they provide. Nelson's chapter focuses on the maturation of community associations, where the communities' age and homeownership changes and, perhaps, communities are abandoned. The recent plunges in housing prices and then subsequent foreclosures, particularly in those states where community associations have flourished, have exacerbated the problems of how to restructure or terminate them through bankruptcy. Nelson examines these options, which range from financial renewal of the associations to their legal interment, and the required state laws to facilitate those actions.

While community associations face midlife challenges, the pressures on traditional local governments may evince greater use of the "neighborhood-government" concept and similar special-purpose, self-governing, service-providing organizations. This model might be extended to older areas of the country. Nelson says new legal authority might allow for the "retrofitting" of community associations to be used in existing neighborhoods. Thus, an older neighborhood now governed within a larger political jurisdiction could elect to have its own "private government," with its own agenda of tailored services. A community association may become an increasingly enticing option if the capacity of local governments to provide adequate services at affordable tax prices diminishes.

Notes

The views of John Petersen are his alone and do not represent those of the Municipal Securities Rulemaking Board of which he is currently a member.

1 For reference, see Kincaid (this volume).
2 National Bureau of Economic Research (2011).
3 Brandeis (1932): "It is one of the happy incidents of the federal system that a single courageous State may, if its citizens choose, serve as a laboratory; and try novel social and economic experiments without risk to the rest of the country."
4 Economic Report of the President (2011).
5 CBO (2011).
6 See Wallace (this volume).
7 Snell et al. (2003).
8 Tannenwald (2001); Snell (2004).
9 National Conference of State Budget Officers (2010).
10 PEW (2009).
11 *Economist* (2011).
12 Petersen (2011).
13 Oates (1998) and Bird (2005) address many of the other classics and contributions to the fiscal federalism literature.
14 Carey and McClellan (2001). The eighty-five essays of the *Federalist* were all signed by "Publius," a reference to a Roman statesman (during the sixth century B.C.) who was a strong proponent of republican government. The essays were written during 1787-1788 by Alexander Hamilton, James Madison, and John Jay.
15 *McCulloch v. Maryland* (1819).
16 Carey and McClellan (2001), *Federalist* No. 33.

REFERENCES

Bird, Richard (2005). "Fiscal Federalism." In Joseph J. Cordes, Robert D. Ebel, and Jane G. Gravelle (Eds.), *The Encyclopedia of Taxation and Tax Policy*. Washington, DC: Urban Institute Press. 146–149.

Brandeis, Louis (1932). *Dissent: New Ice Co. v. Liebmann*, 285 U.S. 262, 52 S.CT. 371, 76 L.ED 747.

Carey, George W., and James McClellan (Eds.) (2001). *The Federalist: Gideon Edition by Alexander Hamilton, John Jay, and James Madison* (2nd ed.). Indianapolis: The Liberty Fund.

CBO, United States Congress (2011). "The Budget and Economic Outlook: Fiscal Years 2010 to 2020." Washington, DC. January 2011. www.cbo.gov.

Economic Report of the President (2011). Washington, DC: US Government Printing Office. Table B-1.

Economist (2011, April 23). "The People's Will: A Special Report on Democracy in California."

National Bureau of Economic Research (NBER) (2011). www.nber.org.

National Conference of State Budget Officers (2010). *Fiscal Survey of the States*. Washington, DC: National Conference of State Budget Officers.

McCulloch v. Maryland, 17 U.S. 316 (1819).

Oates, Wallace E. (Ed.) (1998). *The Economics of Fiscal Federalism and Local Finance*, Cheltenham, UK: Edward Elgar.

Petersen, John E. (2011) "Who's the First to Go?" *Governing* (July).

Pew Center for the Study of the States (2009). "Beyond California." Washington, DC: Pew Foundation.

Snell, Ronald (2004). "New Realities in State Finance." Presentation. Denver: National Conference of State Legislatures.

Snell, Ronald K, Corina Eckl, and Graham Williams (2003). "State Spending in the 1990s." Presentation. Denver: National Conference of State Legislatures.

Tannenwald, Robert (2001). "Are State and Local Revenue Systems Becoming Obsolete?" *New England Economic Review*, 27–43.

PART I

THE ECONOMIC, DEMOGRAPHIC, AND INSTITUTIONAL FRAMEWORK

CHAPTER 2

....

THE CONSTITUTIONAL FRAMEWORKS OF STATE AND LOCAL GOVERNMENT FINANCE

....

JOHN KINCAID

NEITHER the United States nor any constituent state has a free-standing fiscal constitution; provisions for government finance (principally taxing, spending, and borrowing) are embedded in various articles of the United States Constitution and in the fifty state constitutions. The US Constitution has no single section devoted to public finance, and it does not say much about finance. By contrast, the constitutions of most other federal countries have detailed finance articles—for example, Germany (Article X), India (Part XII), and Switzerland (Articles 126–135). Given that modern written constitutions were invented by the US states, and that the Massachusetts Constitution of 1780 is the world's oldest written constitution still in force while the US Constitution is the oldest national constitution, the American constitutions are organized somewhat differently than later federal documents, although some post-World War II state constitutions have features more in tune with contemporary ideas.

Unlike other federal constitutions, the US Constitution contains no detailed tax assignments to the federal and state governments. It merely vests the federal government with exclusive authority to tax foreign imports and with concurrent authority (i.e., with the states) to levy other unspecified taxes. No taxes are assigned to the states because the states already possessed inherent, plenary tax powers. The Constitution's framers also contemplated a dual fiscal structure whereby the federal and state governments would tax, spend, and borrow independently of each other. Hence, there was no need to specify the detailed fiscal arrangements found in most other federal constitutions. Even with the passage of more than two hundred years, the finance provisions have experienced only one major amendment (i.e., the Sixteenth Amendment in 1913, which authorized federal income taxes). Despite the absence of tax assignments, however, there is some informal specialization. The federal government relies heavily on personal income and payroll taxes; the states depend mainly on income and sales taxes; and local governments rely greatly on property taxes and fees.

POWER DELEGATION IN THE US CONSTITUTION AND POWER LIMITATION IN THE STATE CONSTITUTIONS

There is a fundamental difference between the federal and state constitutions. The US Constitution is one of delegated powers; through it, the peoples of the states delegate specific powers to the federal government and reserve all nondelegated powers to the states or to the people, as reaffirmed in the Constitution's Tenth Amendment. Strictly speaking, the federal government has no inherent powers. It possesses only limited, enumerated powers, although the US Supreme Court has opined that Congress does, in effect, possess some inherent powers, including the authority to declare its paper currency as legal tender for paying debts.[1] Basically, the federal government can do only what it is permitted to do by the US Constitution; however, the "necessary and proper" clause (Art. I, Sec. 8, Cl. 18) allows Congress to interpret its enumerated powers very broadly. This implied powers clause soon became known as the sweeping, or elastic, clause.

In their state constitutions, the people limit rather than delegate powers because the sovereign people of each state possess inherent powers, which, prior to the Articles of Confederation (1781) and the US Constitution (1789), were plenary. Each state possesses inherent authority to do whatever it pleases, as long as the US Constitution or the state constitution does not prohibit it from doing so. Thus, while the federal government can do only what it is constitutionally permitted to do, a state government can do anything it is not constitutionally prohibited from doing. (Local governments possess no inherent powers; their powers are only granted to them by their respective states. In many states, the courts construe local powers strictly and narrowly by using Dillon's Rule.[2])

Consequently, a state government can levy any conceivable tax, spend money for any purpose, and borrow money without limit unless it is prohibited from doing so by the federal Constitution or its own state constitution. As a result, the peoples of the states have placed various limits on taxing, spending, and borrowing in their state constitutions.

The US Constitution is not laden with such limits because many of its framers expected the federal government to be limited to the prescribed scope of powers delegated to it. Believing that the federal government lacked inherent powers, the only explicit fiscal limits placed in the US Constitution are equity limits on the federal government's tax power (see below). The spending power was merely implicitly limited by the expectation that the federal government would spend only to execute its enumerated powers. There are no legal limits on borrowing in the federal Constitution.

However, debates since ratification of the Constitution in 1788 have generated disagreements about the founders' intentions. Some observers argue that the Constitution grants the US Congress very broad,[3] even "complete,"[4] powers of taxation and, thereby, extensive spending and borrowing powers, too. Others argue that the founders and subsequent generations construed the Constitution and, therefore, the federal government's fiscal powers narrowly, such that by the late 1920s, federal expenditures still accounted for only 2.6 percent of US GNP. The New Deal of the 1930s then dismantled this fiscal constitution and thereby liberated each Congress to "write its own fiscal constitution, subject only to the restraint that the appropriations must serve some vague concept of public purpose."[5]

Whatever the intentions of the founders were, the latter view has prevailed since the New Deal. Politically, the federal government possesses virtually plenary power to tax, spend, and borrow. At the same time, the federal government has circumscribed state tax powers, especially by using the federal Constitution's commerce clause (Art. I, Sec. 8, Cl. 3) to sequester certain matters from state taxation. The constitutional tables were turned during American history, making the federal government the dominant fiscal power while the states have become the subordinate, even substantially dependent, fiscal power.

THE FEDERALIST ON FEDERAL AND STATE FISCAL POWERS

Despite the comparatively sparse references to public finance in the US Constitution, the tax power was one of the principal issues underlying the country's transition from confederation to federation in 1787–1788. The importance of taxation is amply illustrated in *The Federalist*, to which Alexander Hamilton, who became the first secretary of the US Treasury (1789–1795), contributed seven papers about taxation

(Nos. 30–36). This was the most attention given by the authors[6] of *The Federalist* to any policy element of the Constitution. Hamilton termed taxation "the most important of the authorities proposed to be conferred upon the Union."[7]

In framing the US Constitution, the founders invented modern federalism by extending "the authority of the Union to the persons of the citizens,"[8] thereby empowering the new "general" government created by the Constitution to legislate for individuals (e.g., to levy taxes, regulate commerce, conscript men into military service, imprison individuals, and enforce treaties). This fundamental feature of the Constitution transformed the ancient notion of federalism as confederation into the modern notion of federalism as a mode of governance whereby at least two governments rule the same territory and independently legislate for citizens within their respective spheres of authority. The Articles of Confederation (1781–1789) reflected the ancient idea of federalism because the union government lacked authority to legislate for individuals. This, argued Hamilton, was "the great and radical vice...of the...Confederation."[9]

The founders' transformation of ancient federalism required them to authorize the new general government to acquire its own revenues independently of the states. They did not want the new union government to depend, like the confederal government, on financial contributions from the states, contributions that fell far short of the amounts requested by the confederal government. This fiscal arrangement placed the confederal government at the mercy of the states and left the confederal government with only one independent source of revenue—borrowing. The willingness of creditors to lend it money, however, was limited by the government's lack of taxation authority.

The Continental, and then confederal, Congress issued some $241,552,780 of paper money,[10] called "Continental dollars," during the Revolutionary War. The Continental dollar's value depreciated so steeply that in 1779 George Washington complained "that a wagon load of money will scarcely purchase a wagon load of provisions."[11] Massive counterfeiting by the British accelerated the money's devaluation. After the new Constitution came into force, Continentals could be traded at 1 percent of their value for US bonds. Benjamin Franklin observed that the currency's depreciation was a de facto tax to help finance the Revolutionary War.[12]

Authorizing the new union government to levy taxes was, therefore, a momentous change that sparked considerable fear among opponents of the Constitution and triggered Hamilton's extensive treatment of taxation in *The Federalist*. "Money is," he wrote, "the vital principle of the body politic.... A complete power, therefore, to procure a regular and adequate supply of revenue, as far as the resources of the community will permit, may be regarded as an indispensable ingredient in every constitution."[13] While at pains to defend the federal government's "unqualified" and "indefinite constitutional power of taxation," Hamilton assured readers "that the individual States would...retain an independent and uncontrollable authority to raise revenue to any extent of which they may stand in need, by every kind of taxation, except duties on imports and exports."[14]

It is in the context of taxation that *The Federalist* defends some of the most transformative provisions of the Constitution: the necessary and proper clause and the supremacy clause (Art. VI, Cl. 2). Absent the supremacy clause, the federal tax power would be meaningless. At the same time, Hamilton assured readers that "the composition and structure" of the federal government would prevent it from employing the necessary and proper clause to usurp state taxes and that, in any event, the people would "always take care to preserve the constitutional equilibrium between the General and the State governments."[15]

Hamilton emphasized that the power to tax all articles other than exports and imports is "a concurrent and coequal authority" of the federal and state governments.[16] This concurrency, he averred, is essential for ensuring that the federal and state governments can secure sufficient revenue to meet their respective needs and that one order of government does not dominate the other fiscally. He acknowledged that "the particular policy of the national and of the State systems of finance might now and then not exactly coincide"[17] and that there might be a certain "inconvenience" for citizens when both governments tax the same article, but, he argued, the "effectual expedient" will be for both governments "mutually to abstain from those objects, which either side may have first had recourse to. As neither can *controul* the other, each will have an obvious and sensible interest in this reciprocal forbearance."[18] As such, Hamilton advocated cooperation and coordination on taxation between the federal and state governments.

Hamilton also contended that the primary rationale for an indefinite federal tax power was to enable it to secure "the public peace against foreign or domestic violence."[19] Because wars and rebellions know no predetermined fiscal limits and "future contingencies...are illimitable,"[20] the federal tax power should know no limits. Hamilton argued that wars and rebellions would primarily account for "an immense disproportion between the objects of federal and state expenditure" and thereby justify an indefinite federal tax power. By contrast, even taking into account "all the contingencies" that face state governments, the total amount of revenue needed by each state "ought not to exceed" 200,000 pounds per year.[21] Hence, the states need not fear that the federal government would gobble up so much revenue as to cripple the states' more modest domestic-governance tax needs. Furthermore, suggested Hamilton, "when the states know that the Union can supply itself without their agency, it will be a powerful motive for exertion on their part,"[22] thereby implying intergovernmental competition for tax bases.[23]

Unlike most contemporary fiscal theorists,[24] Hamilton opposed the assignment of particular taxes to the federal government, arguing that such an assignment "would naturally occasion an undue proportion of the public burdens to fall upon"[25] those taxes and, thereby, also produce inequitable tax burdens. The "most productive system of finance will always be the least burdensome."[26] Hamilton also defended the US House of Representatives as being sufficiently representative of the people's interests to restrain burdensome taxation. He famously contended that no legislature can simply mirror the makeup of the population. The electoral process itself frequently elevates "landholders, merchants, and men of the learned professions" to legislatures where they develop "strong chords of sympathy" with their constituents. These elected representatives are most likely to understand the principles of taxation, and "the man who understands those principles will be least likely to resort to oppressive expedients, or to sacrifice any particular class of citizens to the procurement of revenue."[27]

Hamilton contended that in the case of certain taxes, such as those on "houses and land," the federal government would not fashion its own system because local conditions vary so widely. Instead, it would make "use of the *system of each State within that State*."[28] The "probability is that the United States would either wholly abstain from" tax bases already occupied by the states or, if it must intrude upon such bases, "make use of the State officers and State regulations for collecting" such taxes.[29] Hamilton also sought to allay fears of "double sets of revenue officers, a duplication of [citizen] burdens by double taxation, and...frightful forms of odious and oppressive poll taxes."[30] Overall, he suggested, federal taxes would fall mainly on commerce, which would expand tremendously under the new Constitution and, thereby, prevent federal taxes from becoming burdensome. One key objective of the Constitution was to establish relatively free trade domestically, whereby reduced state barriers would foster economic growth.

Public Finance Provisions in the US Constitution

Constitutionally, Congress's power to tax is subject only to one exception and two equity qualifications. Congress cannot tax articles exported from any state. Direct taxes must be apportioned among the states according to their respective populations, and indirect taxes must be uniform nationwide. Otherwise, the tax power "reaches every subject, and may be exercised at discretion."[31] The Constitution also places Congress in the fiscal driver's seat. Only Congress can levy taxes, and only Congress has the "power of the purse" because "No Money shall be drawn from the Treasury, but in Consequence of Appropriations made by Law" (Art. I, Sec. 9, Cl. 7). This "clause is the most important single curb in the Constitution on Presidential power."[32]

Taxation with Representation

In accordance with the Revolutionary War slogan "no taxation without representation," the Constitution requires all bills for levying taxes to originate from the House of Representatives (Art. I, Sec. 7, Cl. 1), which is the people's chamber, not the Senate, which is the states' chamber. Furthermore, more populous states have more weight in the House, whereas less populous states have more weight in the Senate. The House once contended that this clause also applies to appropriations and repeals of tax laws.

This provision is consistent with the transformation of federalism wrought by the Constitution, which allows the federal government to legislate for individuals. The provision also copied state constitutional rules requiring House origination, which, in turn, were derived from Britain's practice of having revenue bills start in the House of Commons. As a practical matter, though, this procedural limit on the tax power is insignificant because the Senate can amend any House revenue bill.

This section also includes the presidential veto process. Although no mention is made of finance here, it is worth noting that the president, unlike most governors, has no line-item veto.

DIRECT TAXES AND APPORTIONMENT

The first mention of taxes in the federal Constitution occurs in conjunction with representation, slavery, and Indians.

> Representatives and direct Taxes shall be apportioned among the several States which may be included within this Union, according to their respective Numbers which shall be determined by adding the whole Number of free Persons, including those bound to Service for a term of Years [i.e., indentured servants], and excluding Indians not taxed, three fifths of all other Persons. [Art. I, Sec. 2, Cl. 3]
>
> [This clause should be read together with the following clause:] No Capitation, or other direct, Tax shall be laid, unless in Proportion to the Census or Enumeration herein before directed to be taken. (Art. I, Sec. 9, Cl. 4)

The former clause limits direct (e.g., per capita) federal taxes by requiring them to be apportioned among the states according to population. The clause contains the infamous compromise whereby each slave was counted as three-fifths of a person for direct taxation and for representation in the US House. This compromise was extinguished by the Thirteenth Amendment (1865), which abolished slavery. The clause also acknowledged that members of Indian nations lived outside of the federal government's tax jurisdiction. This provision was mooted by the Indian Citizenship Act of 1924, which gave US citizenship to all Indians, whether they wanted it or not.

The meaning of "direct Taxes" is ambiguous, although it was believed that the federal government would levy such taxes only under exigent circumstances. In his notes on the Constitutional Convention, James Madison wrote, "Mr. King asked what was the precise meaning of *direct* taxation? No one answered."[33] Even so, the term was widely understood to include a capitation or poll tax (deemed odious by Hamilton) and taxes based on the value of land and real property—hence, the fierce debate over how to assess the property value of slaves. Apportioning property taxes among the states according to population is challenging, but the federal government did levy one-time property taxes to address a war possibility in 1798 and to meet war exigencies in 1813, 1815, and 1861.[34] After 2012, the Patient Protection and Affordable Care Act of 2010 imposes a 3.8 percent Medicare tax on high-income home sellers whose home-sale profits exceed a certain threshold, but this is apparently not being construed as a direct tax. Otherwise, the US Supreme Court held in 1796 that a $16 carriage tax, which was, in effect, a luxury tax, was an excise tax, not a direct tax.[35] The historical effect of the apportionment requirement was to leave property taxes to state and local governments.

THE CORE FEDERAL TAX, SPENDING, AND BORROWING POWERS

The core federal fiscal powers are found at the start of Article I, Section 8:

> The Congress shall have Power to lay and collect Taxes, Duties, Imposts and Excises, to pay the Debts and provide for the common Defense and general Welfare of the United States; but all Duties, Imposts and Excises shall be uniform throughout the United States... To borrow Money on the credit of the United States.

Duties are customs duties or tariffs. Excises are taxes on the production, sale, or use of goods and services as well as on certain privileges and procedures of doing business. Imposts encompass both duties and excises. The uniformity rule refers to geography; for example, an article or service taxed at 7 percent in Maine must be taxed at 7 percent in every other state as well. The uniformity rule is not violated, however, if a federal tax has a different incidence across states due to state laws. The US Supreme Court ruled, for instance, that the federal estate-tax law permitting deductions for state estate-tax payments does not violate the uniformity rule merely because some states levy no estate tax.[36]

The power to tax set forth here has been held to be so broad that it "embraces every conceivable power of taxation."[37] Nevertheless, the US Supreme Court has, over the centuries, imposed and removed limits on the federal tax power. For example, the Court in the 1920s held that imposing a federal income tax on federal judges violated the Constitution's prohibition on lowering the salaries of judges during their tenure. The Court reversed itself in 1939. The Court also has held that Congress cannot use its tax powers to violate the US Bill of Rights (e.g., it cannot tax speech or the free exercise of religion) or the due process and equal protection clauses of the Fourteenth Amendment (1868).

Another issue involves intergovernmental tax immunities articulated in *McCulloch v. Maryland* (1819) wherein Chief Justice John Marshall opined: "The power to tax involves the power to destroy." This case established the precedent, derived from the very nature of the federal system being a compound of two sovereigns, that the states cannot tax instrumentalities of the federal government and the federal government cannot tax instrumentalities of the state governments.[38] However, since 1928, the Court has circumscribed state immunity from federal taxation. In 1939, for example, the Court reversed an 1871 ruling that the salary of a state judge is immune from federal income taxation, although the Court did seek to maintain the principle that the federal tax power cannot be wielded to impair the states' sovereignty.[39] In 1939, the Court tried to establish two guidelines for immunity: (1) activities "essential to the preservation of State governments" and (2) activities where the federal tax is not "substantially or entirely absorbed by private persons."[40]

However, the Court sometimes splits over such matters, as in 1946 when two justices dissented from a ruling upholding a federal tax on the sale of mineral waters from properties owned and operated by New York. The dissenters contended that the Court placed "the sovereign States on the same plane as private citizens" and compelled them to "pay the Federal Government for the privilege of exercising powers of sovereignty guaranteed them by the Constitution."[41] The chief justice opined that what might remain immune from federal taxation is the "State's capitol, its State-house, its public school houses, public parks, [and] its revenues from taxes or school lands."[42] The principal fiscal residue of the doctrine is the federal income-tax exemption for interest earned on most state and local bonds, although this was circumscribed, too, in 1988 when the Court held that federal taxation of certain types of bonds does not violate the intergovernmental immunity doctrine or the Tenth Amendment.[43]

Beyond intergovernmental concerns, the Court has held that Congress can regulate or suppress activities via taxation, tax an activity whether or not it is authorized by federal or state laws (e.g., illegal gambling and drug selling so long as the tax does not violate the constitutional protection against self-incrimination), and employ taxation, such as a protective tariff, to promote desired economic objectives. A protective tariff was the second law adopted by the new Congress in 1789, in part because it was to be a major source of federal revenue.

A current controversy involves the "individual mandate" contained in the Patient Protection and Affordable Care Act of 2010. This provision requires uninsured US citizens and legal residents to purchase federally approved health insurance by 2014 if they are not exempt from the mandate (e.g., for religious reasons). A person who fails to buy such insurance will have to pay to the US Treasury a penalty of $695 per year or 2.5 percent of his or her annual income, whichever is higher. When Congress debated this legislation, the president said that this penalty was "absolutely not" a tax or tax increase, but when some twenty-eight states challenged the mandate in federal courts in 2010–2011, the US Department of Justice defended the mandate as a proper exercise of Congress's "power to lay and collect taxes."[44]

The spending power was initially seen by some of the founders as a qualification of the tax power. Thomas Jefferson argued that Congress could tax only to pay debts and promote the general welfare; Congress could not do anything it pleased to provide for the general welfare. Since the outset of the federal union, however, the spending power has been construed to be broadly in line with Hamilton's view as opposed to the views of Jefferson and Madison, who also believed that the federal government's fiscal powers could be deployed only to execute its enumerated powers. In 1936, the US Supreme Court sided with Hamilton, opining "that the power of Congress to authorize expenditure of public moneys for public purposes is not limited by the direct grants of legislative power found in the Constitution."[45] The Court also has held that neither a citizen nor a state is entitled to a judicial remedy against an allegedly unconstitutional appropriation of federal funds. Only the Fourteenth Amendment and the Bill of Rights impose implicit limits on the spending power (e.g., Congress cannot spend to establish a religion).

Politically, the broad view of the spending power resulted partly from state tolerance of federal spending, which has often benefited the states. At the outset of the republic in 1790, Hamilton convinced Congress to take over payment of the remaining debts that some states still owed from the Revolutionary War. This measure was controversial. Many opponents recognized it as a substantial enhancement of federal power over the states, but the measure prevailed, and ever since 1790, states have rarely complained about federal spending on their behalf. By contrast, the Canadian provinces, especially Quebec, have contested Ottawa's spending power in order to shield themselves from federal intrusions.

In a challenge to provisions of the unemployment section of the Social Security Act of 1935, the Supreme Court held that the provisions were not "weapons of coercion, destroying or impairing the autonomy of the States" and that unemployment relief is a legitimate expenditure for the general welfare.[46] The Court also has upheld federal spending on, for example, old-age assistance and loans and grants to state and local governments.[47] Congress also can earmark the proceeds of a tax for a specific use.

In a 1969 challenge to funding the Vietnam War, the plaintiff argued that the funding did not meet the constitutional criteria of paying the nation's debts or providing for the country's common defense and general welfare. An appellate court held, however, that "congressional appropriations for the war are made under authority of the powers 'to raise and support Armies' and 'to provide and maintain a Navy,'" not the "general welfare" clause.[48]

Nevertheless, challenges to the spending power continue, with conservatives especially asserting a narrower Madisonian view of the spending clause. In 2010, for example, US Senator-elect Mike Lee (R-UT) declared that "the Constitution doesn't give Congress the power to redistribute our wealth."[49] Although calls to abolish the major federal welfare programs may not succeed, the projected fiscal problems of the federal government will likely incite political and legal efforts to constrain the federal spending power. In 2010, the US Government Accountability Office projected that under current policies, demographic changes (mainly a growing senior-citizen population), rising health-care costs, and deficit spending will require the federal government's major entitlement programs, plus net interest payments, to consume "93 cents of every dollar of federal revenue" by 2030.[50]

Such challenges could substantially affect state and local governments because the states especially have become dependent on federal grants-in-aid, which, on average, account for more than one-quarter of state general spending. The Supreme Court has repeatedly held that the federal government can attach conditions (i.e., regulations) to grants-in-aid, such as conditions requiring states to enforce the Hatch Act, lower the blood alcohol level for drunk driving to 0.08, and reduce to twenty-one the legal age for purchasing alcoholic beverages or else suffer reductions in their highway grant monies. South Dakota challenged the 1984 drinking age condition, arguing, in part, that Congress has no authority to mandate a drinking age because the Twenty-First Amendment (1933) to the Constitution reserves alcoholic beverage regulation to the states. The Supreme Court rejected the challenge, holding that such conditions pass constitutional muster so long as they are unambiguous, promote "the general welfare," pertain "to the federal interest in particular national projects or programs," and are not independently prohibited by another provision of the Constitution.[51] By ruling that the Twenty-First Amendment's limit on the spending power did not prohibit Congress from achieving federal objectives indirectly, the Court allowed Congress to use grants-in-aid to do what it lacks constitutional authority to do directly itself.

The power to pay debts also has been construed broadly, including authority for the federal government to give itself priority in the distribution of the estates of its debtors.[52] It should be noted, as well, that Article VI of the Constitution provides that "all Debts contracted and Engagements entered into, before the Adoption of this Constitution, shall be valid against the United States under this Constitution, as under the Confederation." This seemingly innocuous clause was crucial for two reasons. It was vital reassurance to creditors that the new union government would not abrogate past debt obligations. It also reaffirmed that the United States had come into existence in 1781 and that the new constitution created "a more perfect Union" (Preamble), not a new union. During the Civil War (1861–1865), President Abraham Lincoln made much of the idea that the union preceded the Constitution.

The borrowing power has been interpreted along broad Hamiltonian lines as being limited by nothing in the Constitution. The only limit stated there is that of "the credit of the United States." Congress may not, though, revise the terms of outstanding US obligations without compensating the holders of such obligations for an "actual loss" produced by the change.[53] However, the Supreme Court has held that the Fifth Amendment's takings clause does not protect holders of US obligations from reductions in value due to inflationary fiscal policies.

In the original draft of the Constitution, the borrowing clause stated the following: "To borrow money and emit bills on the credit of the United States." By a vote of 9–2, the Constitutional Convention deleted the words "and emit bills." Nevertheless, in 1871, the Supreme Court ruled that Congress can issue Treasury notes and make them legal tender for paying debts.

In summary, the above clauses constitute the core of the fiscal constitution of the federal government. The broad interpretation of this fiscal constitution has allowed the federal government, for example, to establish national banks and shield them from state taxation, issue paper money as legal tender for debts, alter the metal content and value of US coins, tax state banknotes out of existence in 1865, create the Federal Reserve System, and create such entities as the Farm Loan Bank, the Federal National Mortgage Association (Fannie Mae), and the Federal Home Loan Mortgage Corporation (Freddie Mac).

Coinage and Counterfeiting

The Constitution also authorizes Congress "to coin Money, regulate the value thereof, and of foreign Coin, and...To provide for the Punishment of counterfeiting the securities and Coin of the United States" (Art. I, Sec. 8, Cl. 5 and 6). These provisions have been interpreted broadly to give Congress authority over virtually all aspects of currency. The framers of the Constitution apparently anticipated gold and silver coinage, but during the Civil War, Congress authorized paper money, which in the twentieth century was expanded to include paper currency not redeemable for gold or silver, namely, fiat money.

It has been argued that the counterfeiting clause "is superfluous. Congress would have had this power without it, under the" necessary and proper clause.[54] Even the Supreme Court has ruled this clause to be unnecessary and not exclusive. States, too, can punish coin counterfeiters.

LIMITS ON FEDERAL FISCAL POWERS

An often-overlooked fiscal limit on the federal government is that "no Appropriation of Money" to raise and support armies "shall be for a longer Term than two Years" (Art. I, Sec. 8, Cl. 12). This clause reflects the founders' considerable fear of a standing army that could become oppressive of the people and the states or topple the federal government or state governments. The clause served as a potential restraint on the president's ability to prosecute an unpopular war or maintain a large force after an insurrection beyond the two-year appropriations limit—although, historically, it never fulfilled this role. The clause does not apply to the Navy or, by later interpretation, to the Air Force, both of which require building programs longer than two years. The clause is basically a dead letter.

Section 9 of Article I begins with authorization of a temporary, now moot, federal tax, namely, a tax of not more than $10 on each imported slave. The clause was one of several compromises made on slavery. It somewhat satisfied opponents of slavery by allowing Congress to tax slave trading. It also satisfied supporters of slavery by preventing Congress from using its broad tariff power to tax the slave trade out of existence until 1808 when Congress could, under the first part of this clause, ban the slave trade. Hence, from a political perspective, the clause was both a preservation of and limit on the federal power to tax imports.

Section 9 prohibits Congress from enacting ex post facto laws, but the Supreme Court has deemed this to apply only to criminal laws. Hence, Congress can enact a tax law in the midyear and make its provisions retroactive to the start of the tax year.

This section also provides that "No Tax or Duty shall be laid on Articles exported from any State. No Preference shall be given by any Regulation of Commerce or Revenue to the Ports of one State over those of another; nor shall Vessels bound to, or from, one State, be obliged to enter, clear, or pay Duties in another."

The word "export" refers to goods exported to a foreign country, and the prohibition is by reason of export. The clause does not prohibit a tax levied on all goods, including those destined for export. The Supreme Court also held that the clause does not prohibit a fraud-prevention stamp tax on tobacco intended for export.

The ports clause prohibits discrimination among the ports of different states but not between individual ports. Under cover of the commerce clause (Art. I, Sec. 8, Cl. 3), Congress can establish ports of entry, construct and operate lighthouses, improve harbors and rivers, and provide structures to handle port traffic. Indeed, port appropriations have been a classic case of pork-barrel spending in American history.

In addition to requiring expenditures to be made by law (as cited above), clause 7 of this section stipulates that "a regular Statement and Account of the Receipts and Expenditures of all public Money shall be published from time to time." Although this is seemingly a minor provision, such transparency is extremely important for democratic accountability and had already existed in some of the eighteen state constitutions that preceded the US Constitution. In many countries, fiscal transparency is nonexistent.

The last clause of Section 9 prohibits the granting of titles of nobility and forbids federal officeholders from accepting any gifts, emoluments, offices, or titles "from any King, Prince, or foreign State." By implication, the clause also precludes favorable financial treatment of a particular class of citizens and guards against federal officers receiving or giving favorable fiscal treatment to foreign rulers and states. Provisions of this nature exist in most state constitutions, including some of those that predated the US document.

LIMITS ON STATE FISCAL POWERS

Section 10 of Article I begins by stating, among other things: "No State shall...coin Money; emit Bills of Credit; make anything but gold and silver Coin a Tender in Payment of Debts; pass any...Law impairing the Obligation of Contracts, or grant any Title of Nobility." Except for the contracts provision, the limits in this clause have not been contested significantly in US history and have been largely moot because state banknotes were taxed out of existence by Congress in 1865. The contracts provision is not, strictly speaking, a fiscal provision, although it has fiscal implications insofar as the honoring of contracts is fundamental to the operation of the nation's economy. As such, the clause has experienced extensive litigation throughout US history. The clause was inserted in the Constitution mainly to prevent states from altering financial contracts so as to relieve debtors of their obligations. This clause also was needed for consistency with the bankruptcy clause (Art. I., Sec. 8, Cl. 4).

The second clause of Section 10 provides:

> No State shall, without the Consent of the Congress, lay any Imposts or Duties on Imports or Exports, except what may be absolutely necessary for executing its inspection Laws; and the net Produce of all Duties and Imposts, laid by any State on Imports or Exports, shall be for the Use of the Treasury of the United States, and all such Laws shall be subject to the Revision and Controul of the Congress.

This clause prevents states with large ports from disadvantaging other states by exacting levies from goods passing through them. It also reinforces the federal government's sole authority to levy customs duties, which was expected to be a major source of federal revenue.

The clause, according to the US Supreme Court, applies only to goods imported from or exported to foreign countries and mainly to the acts of importing and exporting. Once an imported good is unpackaged and enters the stream of domestic commerce, it is subject to nondiscriminatory state taxation. The Supreme Court has held that the clause does prevent states from, for example, requiring importers to purchase a license to sell imported goods, imposing a franchise tax on foreign corporations engaged in importing, and taxing sales by brokers and auctioneers of imported merchandise in their original packages. States can, however, levy piloting fees and tax the gross sales of a purchaser from an importer, among other things. Regarding inspections, the Court defined the acceptable elements of state inspection laws to be the "quality of the article, form, capacity, dimensions, and weight of package, mode of putting up, and marking and branding of various kinds."[55]

The last clause of Section 10 prohibits states from levying "any Duty of Tonnage" without congressional consent. This prohibition includes all levies, whether or not they are measured by vessel tonnage, that impose charges to enter, trade in, or lie in a port. However, it does not ban charges for vessel services, even if calibrated by tonnage, such as piloting, towing, and mooring; loading and unloading cargo; and storing goods.

PRESIDENTIAL AND JUDICIAL PROVISIONS

Interestingly, Article II says nothing about the president's now prominent role in the budget process, his responsibilities in expending appropriated funds, or establishment of the US Department of the Treasury. Instead, the Constitution specifies general presidential duties, which were modeled after gubernatorial provisions in some state constitutions, namely, that he serve as commander in chief of the US military and state militias when called into federal service, "take Care that the Laws be faithfully executed," and inform Congress about the state of the union. The document is silent about specific presidential fiscal roles. The president's veto power can be deployed as a fiscal weapon, but it is weakened by the lack of a line-item veto.

The budget process is dominated finally by Congress. The president plays a major role in proposing a budget every year because the landmark Budget and Accounting Act of 1921 authorized him to do so and provided for the White House agency now known as the Office of Management and Budget (OMB). In 1974, Congress enacted the Budget and Impoundment Control Act to rein in certain presidential abuses, such as refusals to spend appropriated funds because of policy disagreements with Congress. This act also reorganized the congressional budgeting process and created the semi-independent Congressional Budget Office, which acts, in part, as an informational check on the OMB.

Article III on the Supreme Court says nothing about public finance. Yet, in line with the expansion of federal power since 1789, the Court has played a large role in public finance, especially in legitimizing broad interpretations of the federal government's constitutional fiscal powers and constraining state fiscal powers.

FISCAL GUARANTEES OF INSTITUTIONAL INTEGRITY AND SEPARATION OF POWERS

The Constitution also contains fiscally relevant restraints that help to protect the institutional integrity of the federal government and the separation of powers. These include a requirement that members of Congress be paid by the federal government (Art. I, Sec. 6, Cl. 1), not by their states, as was the practice under the Articles of Confederation, and a prohibition on members of Congress voting to increase the salary for a civil office and then being appointed to that office during their congressional term (Art. I, Sec. 6, Cl. 2). Article II, clause 7, provides for compensation of the president (now $400,000 per year) and prohibits Congress from decreasing or increasing a president's salary during his term of office. Similar provisions regarding the governor and other independently elected executive officials, such as the attorney general, exist in some state constitutions. Such provisions reinforce the separation of powers by preventing the legislative body from bribing or punishing the executive in order to secure his or her compliance with the legislature's will. The president also is prohibited from receiving additional pay from the United States or from any state of the union. A number of state constitutions also prohibit state executive officials from receiving additional pay from other sources.

Article III on the Supreme Court mandates that justices "receive for their Services, a Compensation, which shall not be diminished during their Continuance in Office" (Sec. 1). Given that justices serve, in effect, for life (unless they resign or are impeached and removed from office), it is necessary to allow salary increases for them, but congressional authority to decrease their salaries would jeopardize judicial independence. This constitutional protection has been extended legislatively to judges on the twelve federal circuit courts of appeals and ninety-four district courts. Given that most state judges serve fixed terms subject to direct or retention elections, some state constitutions prohibit increases or decreases of a judge's salary during any given fixed term.

CONSTITUTIONAL AMENDMENTS

Only three of the US Constitution's amendments deal explicitly with a fiscal matter. Most momentous is the Sixteenth Amendment (1913), which authorizes the federal government "to lay and collect taxes on incomes, from whatever source derived, without apportionment among the several States." This is a broad grant of power. In the view of many observers, this amendment, more than any other change in the Constitution, fueled the rise of federal dominance in the twentieth century. (The first state to enact an income tax was Wisconsin in 1911.)

The amendment was necessitated by an 1895 Supreme Court decision (*Pollock*) that struck down a flat income tax of 2 percent on incomes over $4,000 enacted by Congress in 1894. A federal income tax was strongly supported by Democrats, Progressives, Populists, and Socialists. At that time, the federal government relied on excises and tariffs, the burden of which fell heavily on the less affluent. Advocates also saw in an income tax the potential for requiring the wealthy to bear more of the costs of government, redistributing income from the rich to the poor, and preventing enactment of a land tax that would hit farmers hard. All four 1912 presidential candidates[56] supported an income tax. Ratification of the amendment was strongest in the more agricultural West and South and weakest in the urban-industrial Northeast.

Today, the federal government derives about 45 percent of its revenue from a personal income tax, 36 percent from a payroll tax (i.e., Social Security and Medicare), 12 percent from a corporate income tax, and only 3 percent from excises.

The Twenty-Fourth Amendment (1964) abolished poll taxes for federal elections. These were taxes levied by states, mostly southern states, on voters. One had to pay the tax in order to vote (although Alabama's constitution dedicated the revenue to education). The states that levied these taxes employed them mostly to suppress voting by black citizens and low-income whites. The amendment was championed by the Civil Rights Movement that had emerged by the late 1950s.

The Twenty-Seventh Amendment (1992) states, "No law varying the compensation for the services of Senators and Representatives shall take effect until an election of Representatives shall have intervened." This amendment was proposed in 1789 as part of the Bill of Rights, but it was not ratified then. An undergraduate student in Texas revived it in 1982, and enough additional states ratified it to place it in the Constitution. The amendment mimicked provisions in some state constitutions that required an election after legislators proposed a pay raise for themselves and before the legislature could enact the raise in the next session. It is intended to give voters an opportunity to unseat legislators who support a pay raise. The amendment is moot, however, because in 1989, Congress had established automatic annual cost-of-living increases that require no vote. Federal courts later ruled that such increases do not violate the amendment.

The Third Amendment, contained in the Bill of Rights and also modeled after comparable state constitutional protections, prohibits an implicit tax, namely, the quartering of soldiers in private homes without the owners' consent. This was, in part, a reaction against the British practice of requiring colonial residents to house and feed its soldiers.

The Fifth Amendment provides that private property cannot "be taken for public use, without just compensation." This clause, also found in state constitutions, restrains the government's ability to tax indirectly by exercising its power of eminent domain. It also places the burden on the government to show why it should not pay equitable compensation. The Supreme Court has expanded this protection to include certain regulatory takings (e.g., when a government regulation reduces the value of property so deeply as to constitute a de facto taking). This clause has become controversial, however, especially since a 2005 Supreme Court decision upheld the authority of local governments to take property from one owner and sell it to another private party for economic development purposes.[57]

The Eighth Amendment, which prohibits excessive bail and fines, protects individuals from excessive government financial burdens and restrains such penalties as a revenue source. State constitutions also provide this protection. Bail is ordinarily calibrated in relation to the severity of the criminal charge and flight risk. Fines are ordinarily set at flat rates in relation to levels of infraction (e.g., miles per hour over a highway speed limit), unlike some other federal countries, such as Switzerland, where a driver was fined $290,000 in 2010 for speeding because the fine is calibrated in terms of both speed and the driver's wealth.[58]

Section 4 of the Fourteenth Amendment (1868) upholds the validity of public debt incurred by the federal government for prosecuting the Civil War but invalidates debt "incurred in aid of insurrection or rebellion against the United States." Some contemporary observers argue that this clause allows the president to increase the federal debt ceiling without congressional consent, but no president has done so.

SUMMARY

The US Constitution, as interpreted over 223 years, delegates nearly plenary taxing, spending, and borrowing authority to the federal government. At the same time, the document contemplates a dual system of public finance, with each order of government (i.e., federal and state) acting independently. What is notable about the US Constitution compared to other federal constitutions is the absence of detail and, thereby, of significant constraints on the federal and state governments. There is no authorization for federal grants to state and local governments; there are no requirements for the federal government to engage in tax sharing or fiscal equalization; there are no provisions on state and local government borrowing and no mention of hard or soft budget constraints on those governments; and there are no provisions requiring a balanced federal budget or establishing federal operating and capital budgets.

STATE CONSTITUTIONAL FRAMEWORKS
OF PUBLIC FINANCE

Nevertheless, the federal government used its powers sparingly during the first 145 years of US history. The United States became a world power while public functions were financed mainly by local property taxes. From 1789 to about 1842, states were the major fiscal actors. They financed infrastructure, development, and government operations from asset income derived from canal tolls, bank-stock dividends, and land sales, as well as some indirect business taxes. By 1841, state debt stood at $193 million compared to $25 million for local governments and $5 million for the federal government.[59] From 1842 to the mid-1930s, local governments were the major fiscal actors, relying heavily on property taxes. By 1902, property taxes accounted for 42 percent of all federal, state, and local revenues.[60] Even by 1932, local governments accounted for more than half of all government revenue. Of federal spending in 1932, 22 percent went to veterans' benefits, 19 percent to the post office, 17 percent to defense, and 5 percent to state and local aid. Only after the mid-1930s did the federal government ascend to fiscal dominance, relying heavily on income taxes.

States and localities were fiscally prominent for so long, in part because the states possess inherent fiscal powers, and the federal Constitution did not significantly constrain those powers. Instead, constraints have come from the people. Especially since the 1840s when some states teetered on bankruptcy from excessive debt, the people have imposed some constitutional limits on various aspects of state taxing, spending, and borrowing. Consequently, the fifty constitutions are diverse. They also range from 8,565 words (Vermont) to 367,000 words (Alabama) because some states handle many matters through their constitution while others rely mostly on statutes. Hence, all states might have the same particular fiscal rule, but it may not be found in every state constitution. Many of the early constitutions (e.g., for Connecticut, New Hampshire, and Vermont) said little or nothing about public finance, and some still say little about it. Making general statements about the state constitutional frameworks of public finance is, therefore, difficult.

HISTORICAL ORIGINS

The states invented modern written constitutions, starting with the eight states that adopted their first constitutions in 1776. Eighteen state constitutions were ratified before ratification of the US Constitution in 1788. Since 1776, the states collectively have had 144 constitutions. These documents originally derived largely from an evolving line of colonial charters and self-governing covenants dating back to the Mayflower Compact of 1620. Arguably, the first "constitution" was the "the laws and liberties of Massachusetts" promulgated in 1647. This was the first published code of laws in Anglo-American history. The eighth article of the code is entitled "Charges Publick." It provided for regular assessments of "persons & estates" pursuant to lawful procedures. Taxation was important because Britain gave the colonies substantial self-governing authority. Colonial governments taxed for self-governing purposes and also collected taxes for the Crown. Upon independence, states mostly incorporated historical tax practices—minus Crown taxes—into their new constitutions, all of which provided for taxation with representation.

More than half of the state constitutions have an article regarding taxation and revenue. A few have one on debt, too, but fiscal issues also inhabit the legislative article, amendments, and some other articles, such as local government and education. However, except for somewhat detailed provisions on property taxation and debt, most taxing, spending, and borrowing matters are left to legislative action because taxation is an inherent power. The Arkansas Constitution states this rather explicitly: "The State's ancient right of eminent domain and of taxation is herein fully and expressly conceded" (Art. 2, Sec 23). Hence, the myriad taxes levied by most states are not mentioned in their constitutions. Thus, those documents are poor guides to the states' finance systems. What is notable instead is the emphasis on institutional structures, such as the separation of powers, institutional procedures, such as legislative voting rules, and public referendums as key means to restrain state governments' exercises of their inherent fiscal and nonfiscal powers. The people's hope that these mechanisms will work is expressed in the Vermont

Declaration of Rights' admonition that before any law is "made to raise a tax, the purpose for which it is to be raised ought to appear evident to the Legislature to be of more service to community than the money would be if not collected" (Chap. I, Art. 9). North Carolina's charter mandates: "The power of taxation shall be exercised in a just and equitable manner for public purposes only" (Art. 5, Sec. 2).

State constitutions address some issues of fiscal equity, but they do not wax philosophic about efficiency, economies of scale, externalities, or ability-to-pay versus benefit taxes. Instead, the fiscal provisions usually reflect the state's political culture as well as historical political conflicts and compromises. Indeed, a peculiar feature of US state constitutions compared to most constitutions in the world (except Switzerland) is the roles the people reserve for themselves to exercise some of the fiscal powers of their states directly (e.g., the initiative process) and to check their state's exercise of fiscal powers (e.g., referenda).

GENERAL STATE CONSTITUTIONAL PROVISIONS AND LIMITS ON STATE FISCAL POWERS

As noted above, powers are not delegated to the states; instead, the people limit their state's inherent powers through their constitution, although a few constitutions seek to ensure that the legislature will do its duty by stipulating the following: "The legislature shall provide by law for an annual tax sufficient to defray the estimated expenses of the state for each fiscal year" (Nevada Art. 9, Sec. 2). Oklahoma's constitution spells out such powers:

> The Legislature shall have power to provide for the levy and collection of license, franchise, gross revenue, excise, income, collateral and direct inheritance, legacy, and succession taxes; also graduated income taxes, graduated collateral and direct inheritance taxes, graduated legacy and succession taxes; also stamp, registration, production or other specific taxes. (Art. X, Sec. 12)

Declarations of Rights

The inherent nature of state powers is why the first section of forty-nine state constitutions is a declaration of rights. These declarations impose the same constraints on state fiscal powers as those imposed by the US Bill of Rights on the federal government, but they also impose some different and more rigid limits. For example, many state documents have detailed prohibitions on taxing, spending, or borrowing on behalf of religious schools. About eleven declarations state that the people cannot be taxed without the consent of themselves or their elected legislature.

Maryland's declaration says "that paupers ought not to be assessed for the support of the government" (Art. 15). The North Carolina Constitution forbids the state and its local governments to levy any "poll or capitation tax." Most state declarations of rights prohibit irrevocable grants of any privilege, franchise, or immunity; perpetuities, primogeniture, entailments, or monopolies; exclusive public emoluments or privileges; or hereditary emoluments, privileges, or powers. Nearly all rights declarations prohibit imprisonment for debt, and some constitutions extend the takings principle to prohibit private property from being "taken or sold for the payment of the corporate debt of municipal corporations."[61]

Taxpayer Bill of Rights

In 1992, Coloradans added a Taxpayer Bill of Rights (TABOR) to their constitution (Art. 10. Sec. 20). Other states have not followed suit, and voters in some states have rejected a TABOR.[62]

TABOR originally prohibited the state and its local governments from increasing tax rates without voter approval and required governments to obtain voter approval in order to spend funds collected through currently approved tax rates if the revenues exceeded the rates of inflation and population growth. Revenues above TABOR's limit had to be returned to taxpayers unless voters approved a revenue offset. However, TABOR did not accommodate productivity increases and recessions. This prevented the state and its localities from taxing additional income from year to year due to a "ratchet-down effect" whereby revenue falling below TABOR's limit in one year pushed the next year's limit below the level it would have been if the prior-year revenues had met or surpassed the limit.

TABOR was weakened when voters approved Amendment 23 in 2000, which responded to decreased K–12 education funding due to TABOR. This amendment required general and per-pupil education funding to be increased at least at the rate of inflation plus 1 percent for ten years and at the inflation rate thereafter. As a result, the state and its local governments cut funding for many other services in order to fund education, thereby eroding TABOR's popularity. In 2005, voters allowed the state to spend all revenue subject to TABOR limits for five years through FY 2009–2010. Thereafter, the state could spend above TABOR up to a cap that increases from the prior year's cap so as to eliminate the ratchet-down effect. Revenues above the TABOR limit but below the new cap must be spent on education, health care, police and firefighter pensions, and transportation priorities.

Other Tax and Expenditure Limits

More than thirty states operate under some type of tax-and-expenditure limits (TELs), although only a few are embedded in the constitution. For instance, the North Carolina Constitution stipulates the following: "No poll or capitation tax shall be levied by the General Assembly or by any county, city or town, or other taxing unit" (Art. 5, Sec. 1). The Delaware document states that "shares of the capital stock of corporations created under the laws of this State, when owned by persons or corporations without this State, shall not be subject to taxation by any law now existing or hereafter to be made" (Art. IX, Sec. 6).

Arizona's constitution provides that "the legislature shall not appropriate for any fiscal year state revenues in excess of seven per cent of the total personal income of the state for that fiscal year as determined by the economic estimates commission" (Art. 9, Sec. 17[3]). The Arkansas legislature cannot levy taxes in any year that would exceed, in the aggregate, 1 percent of the assessed valuation of the property of the state (Art. 16, Sec. 8). In Michigan, "property taxes and other local taxes and state taxation and spending may not be increased above the limitations specified herein without direct voter approval" (Art. IX, Sec. 25).

Although not a limit per se, Hawaii's constitution mandates a tax review commission to be appointed every five years to evaluate "the State's tax structure [and] recommend revenue and tax policy" (Art. VII, Sec. 3).

Public Purpose Rule

Many constitutions (often the declaration of rights) require taxes to be levied and monies spent or borrowed only for public purposes. The meaning of "public purpose" is, of course, debatable. The final arbiter is usually a state's high court, although judges frequently defer to the legislature's definition of "public purpose." In deciding whether a tax meets a public purpose, courts also consider judicial precedents, whether voters approved the tax, general public benefits derived from the tax, whether a large number or broad class of people benefits from the tax, the need for the tax, and the extent to which the tax competes with private-sector provisions of public goods. One historically controversial area has been borrowing to assist private enterprises for purposes of economic development. This has sometimes produced constitutional amendments to permit or limit such borrowing.

Related rights guarantees prohibit any tax power from being delegated to a private corporation or association and any suspension of taxes on corporations and corporate property via a grant or contract. A number of constitutions (e.g., Minnesota) have a provision similar to that of North Carolina: "The power of taxation shall be exercised in a just and equitable manner, for public purposes only, and shall never be surrendered, suspended, or contracted away" (Art. 5, Sec. 2).

Uniformity and Equality Rules

Most state constitutions—usually the declaration of rights—require some or all taxes to be uniform. Equal protection clauses impose additional equality requirements. One scholar identified twelve types of uniformity clauses.[63] Delaware's constitution, for example, has a broad rule: "All taxes shall be uniform upon the same class of subjects within the territorial limits of the authority levying the tax" (Art. VIII, Sec. 1). However, this rule applies most frequently to property taxes. Basically, equals must be taxed equally, and similarly situated people taxed similarly. The Nebraska Constitution created a Tax Equalization and Review Commission that has the "power to review and equalize assessments of property for taxation" (Art. IV, Sec. 28). A few constitutions also specify that in-state property belonging to out-of-state residents cannot be taxed more highly than in-state property owned by state residents (although the US Constitution implicitly prohibits such discriminatory taxation in any event).

One controversy surrounding uniformity is whether some people or activities can be exempted from a tax, such as exemptions of prescription drugs and certain foods from a sales tax, exemptions of pension income from an income tax, and special assessments that benefit certain property owners. Obviously, numerous exemptions exist; satisfying this rule is a matter of legislative and judicial interpretation. Another controversy is whether or how a state can tax at different rates, such as progressive income taxes, different rates for license and gross-receipts taxes, and property-tax abatements and circuit breakers. There are numerous examples of such differential tax rates. Legislatures ordinarily manage these differences by placing persons, objects, and activities into classifications. So long as every member of a class is taxed uniformly and so long as the classification is rational and not discriminatory, it passes constitutional muster.

Initiative and Referendum Rules

Some unusual features of many state constitutions are their initiative and referendum rules. Most important is that eighteen state constitutions (e.g., California, Colorado, and Ohio) allow citizens to bypass the legislature and place constitutional amendments concerning fiscal and nonfiscal matters directly on the ballot for voter action. As with TABOR in Colorado, initiatives can have huge impacts on state finances. Over time, voter initiatives also can produce clashing outcomes, sharply limit the fiscal discretion of the legislature, and earmark substantial amounts of tax dollars to specific purposes. Some observers argue, for example, that initiatives in California have contributed greatly to the state's fiscal crisis.

In an effort to deal with this problem, Arizona's constitution demands the following:

> An initiative or referendum...that proposes a mandatory expenditure of state revenues for any purpose, establishes a fund for any specific purpose or allocates funding for any specific purpose must also provide for an increased source of revenues sufficient to cover the entire immediate and future costs of the proposal. The increased revenues may not be derived from the state general fund or reduce or cause a reduction in general fund revenues. (Art. 9, Sec. 23)

In all states except Delaware, voters must approve amendments to their constitution; hence, they can reject unwanted fiscal amendments proposed by an initiative or by the legislature. Many constitutions also require certain state and especially local fiscal policy proposals (most often general-obligation borrowing) to be put to a referendum. In 2010, for example, voters in twenty-eight states approved twenty-five of forty-one ballot measures on taxes, nineteen of twenty-one bond and debt measures, and fifteen of twenty-two budget measures.

Voting and Procedural Rules

Many states (e.g., Delaware and New Hampshire) require revenue bills to originate from the House of Representatives. This rule is partly due to the formerly quasi-federal character of many states whereby representation in the Senate was based on towns and counties.

A constraining rule on almost all state legislatures as compared to Congress is that votes are based on the entire membership of each house, not quorums. In addition, super-majorities are needed to raise some or all taxes in about fifteen states. "No tax or license fee may be imposed or levied except pursuant to an act of the General Assembly adopted with the concurrence of three-fifths of all members of each House" (Delaware Art. VIII, Sec. 11[a]). The same rule applies in Oregon (Art. IV, Sec. 25[2]). In Arizona, a net increase in state revenues requires approval of two-thirds of the members of each house of the legislature. If the governor vetoes the measure, three-fourths of the members of each house must approve the measure (Art. 9 Sec 22[A]). In 2010, California voters repealed a requirement that the state budget be passed by a two-thirds vote of the legislature but mandated that state and local fees be enacted by a two-thirds legislative vote so as to prevent legislators from disguising taxes as fees. That same year, Washington voters approved a rule requiring a two-thirds vote of the legislature or a majority vote of the people to approve state tax increases.

Alaska's constitution is complex:

> Except for appropriations for Alaska permanent fund dividends, appropriations of revenue bond proceeds, appropriations required to pay the principal and interest on general obligation bonds, and appropriations of money received from a non-State source in trust for a specific purpose...appropriations...made for a fiscal year shall not exceed $2,500,000,000 by more than the cumulative change, derived from federal indices as prescribed by law, in population and inflation since July 1, 1981. Within this limit, at least one-third shall be reserved for capital projects and loan appropriations. The legislature may exceed this limit in bills for appropriations to the Alaska permanent fund and in bills for appropriations for capital projects...if each bill is approved by the governor, or passed by affirmative vote of three-fourths of the membership of the legislature over a veto or item veto, or becomes law without signature, and is also approved by the voters....Each bill for appropriations for capital projects in excess of the limit shall be confined

to capital projects of the same type, and the voters shall, as provided by law, be informed of the cost of operations and maintenance of the capital projects. No other appropriation in excess of this limit may be made except to meet a state of disaster declared by the governor.... (Art. 9. Sec. 15)

Alabama's constitution prohibits any revenue bill from being passed during the last five days of the legislative session. Arizona's charter stipulates: "Every law which imposes, continues, or revives a tax shall distinctly state the tax and the objects for which it shall be applied; and it shall not be sufficient to refer to any other law to fix such tax or object" (Art. 9, Sec. 9).

Some states (e.g., Alabama and Pennsylvania) have a rule such as:

The general appropriation bill shall embrace nothing but appropriations for the ordinary expenses of the executive, legislative, and judicial departments of the state, for interest on the public debt, and for the public schools. The salary of no officer or employee shall be increased in such bill, nor shall any appropriation be made therein for any officer or employee unless his employment and the amount of his salary have already been provided for by law. All other appropriations shall be made by separate bills, each embracing but one subject. (Alabama, Art. 4, Sec. 71)

Constitutional Provisions and Limits on Specific Aspects of State-Local Finance

Most state constitutions contain provisions about specific taxes and other finance matters.

Property Taxes

Property, or *ad valorem* (Latin for according to value), taxes have long been a staple of state and local revenue systems.[64] These taxes are levied in all states on real property such as land, improvements on land (e.g., a home), and business property and on personal property (e.g., an automobile) by a few states. The property-tax levy typically consists of the property's assessed value multiplied by an assessment ratio (i.e., percentage of property value subject to taxation) multiplied by the tax rate. Although states levy some property taxes, especially on public utilities such as railroad tracks and power lines, the lion's share of property taxation was devolved during the nineteenth century to local governments (e.g., counties, municipalities, townships, independent school districts, and levee districts). A few constitutions (e.g., Nebraska, North Dakota, and Texas) prohibit the state from taxing property for state purposes.

Given the historic importance of property taxes to local governments and the tax's ubiquitous incidence on landowners, it frequently arouses taxpayer ire. The element of the tax attacked most often is the rate. Limits on property-tax rates began to appear in constitutions during the late nineteenth century (e.g., Alabama) when local governments used it to finance roads, streets, sewers, and other infrastructure and to retire debt. During the Great Depression (1929–1938), voters revolted against property-tax rates that precipitated foreclosures. Perhaps the most famous (or infamous) property-tax revolt was Proposition 13 (the Jarvis-Gann citizen initiative) that amended California's constitution in 1978. This initiative shifted property-tax valuation away from current market values toward acquisition values. It limited tax increases to 2 percent per year (unless a property is sold) and required two-thirds majorities to approve state statutes and local referendums increasing other types of taxes. Many observers argued that Proposition 13 triggered a nationwide tax revolt and helped usher Ronald Reagan (California's governor in 1967–1975) into the White House in 1981, although empirical evidence for these claims is weak.

In 2010, Indiana voters approved a constitutional amendment capping property taxes. A few states limit the amount of revenue or revenue increase derived from the property tax, thereby requiring a rate reduction if, for example, inflation increases assessed values, which then produce revenues above the cap. Many limits exempt tax increases dedicated to debt service, but some, such as Proposition 13, permit no exceptions.

Many constitutions have special provisions for agricultural property, usually requiring it to be valued in terms of current agricultural uses, not alternate uses of higher value (e.g., a shopping center). The Washington Constitution allows the legislature to extend this principle to "standing timber and timberlands, and…other open space lands which are used for recreation or for enjoyment of their scenic or natural beauty" (Art. VII, Sec 11).

Constitutions may require property to be taxed at "fair market value," "fair cash value," "true and full valuation in money," or "just valuation." A few constitutions prohibit local governments from assessing property owners for the costs of sidewalks, street paving, sewers, and the like at levels exceeding the increased value enjoyed by the property owner from such improvements.

Most states require uniformity of assessment, and some require reassessment at regular intervals. Given the importance and subjectivity of property assessment, twenty-two states mandate elected local assessors, fourteen allow localities to elect or appoint assessors, and ten require appointment.[65]

All state constitutions permit property-tax exemptions. These may include religious, charitable, educational, cemetery, cultural, historical, and water facilities plus federal, state, and local government properties. Exemptions also exist for widows, senior citizens, veterans, and disabled persons, though these are usually enacted via statutes. Circuit breakers, too, are usually provided by statute. Almost half of the state constitutions provide for a homestead exemption whereby a certain portion (e.g., $3,000) of the value of one's home is exempt from the tax. A few constitutions (e.g., Amendment 27 to the Arkansas Constitution) authorize property-tax exemptions or abatements to attract or expand business firms. At least two states, New Mexico and Oklahoma, exempt property (including commercial goods) that is "moving in interstate commerce" through the state, even if it is placed in a warehouse where "the property is assembled, bound, joined, processed, disassembled, divided, cut, broken in bulk, relabeled or repackaged." Utah has a broad provision going beyond the property tax: "Nothing in this Constitution may be construed to prevent the Legislature from providing by statute for taxes other than the property tax and for deductions, exemptions, and offsets from those other taxes" (Art. XIII, Sec. 4).

Sales and Excise Taxes

Forty-five states levy a sales tax and all levy excises (e.g., on cigarettes and alcoholic beverages), although most of these levies are not rooted constitutionally.[66] State constitutions say little about these taxes. Montana's constitution simply limits the sales tax rate to 4 percent. Michigan's charter limits the rate to 4 percent but allows a later 2 percent add-on to help fund education. Michigan further mandates that 15 percent of the revenue from the 4 percent tax "be used exclusively" to assist "townships, cities and villages, on a population basis" (Art. IX, Sec. 10). California limits sales taxation on food. Nevada's constitution exempts "all household goods and furniture used by a single household and owned by a member of that household" and "food for human consumption" but does not exempt "prepared food intended for immediate consumption" or alcoholic beverages (Art. 10, Sec. 3). The Ohio Constitution (Art. 12, Sec. 13) has a complex provision prohibiting taxation of food, ingredients, and packaging from wholesale to retail purchases. Colorado's Constitution (Art. 10, Sec. 20) authorizes cigarette taxes specifically to reduce smoking.

All states levy motor-fuel taxes, nearly all of which are statutory. However, a number of constitutions require such taxes to be dedicated to highway programs. Arizona's rule is indicative: "No moneys derived from fees, excises, or license taxes relating to registration, operation, or use of vehicles on the public highways or streets or to fuels or any other energy source used for the propulsion of vehicles on the public highways or streets, shall be expended for other than highway and street purposes including the cost of administering the state highway system" (Art. 9, Sec. 14). Massachusetts amended its constitution to permit such revenues to support mass transportation (Art. CIV).

Income Taxes

Income taxes, which are levied on all or some personal income by forty-three states, also are based mostly on statutes. Only a few constitutions (e.g., Indiana and Kansas) authorize the legislature to enact a personal or corporate income tax.

Ohio has the most extensive provision: "The taxation of incomes, and the rates of such taxation may be either uniform or graduated, and may be applied to such incomes and with such exemptions as may be provided by law" (Art. 12, Sec. 3). A few constitutions (e.g., Kansas) authorize the legislature to couple the state income tax to the federal income-tax code.

Otherwise, a few constitutions contain restrictions. Delaware prohibits income-tax increases from being made retroactive from their date of enactment (Art. VIII). The Illinois Constitution says, "A tax on or measured by income shall be at a non-graduated rate. At any one time there may be no more than one such tax imposed by the State for State purposes on individuals and one such tax so imposed on corporations. In any such tax imposed upon corporations the rate shall not exceed the rate imposed on individuals by more than a ratio of 8 to 5" (Art. IX, Sec. 3[a]). Michigan's document holds that "no income tax graduated as to rate or base shall be imposed by the state or any of its subdivisions" (Art. IX, Sec. 7). Utah dedicates income-tax revenues to public schools. A 1975 amendment (Art. VIII, Sec. I, Para. 6) to New Jersey's constitution requires all personal income-tax revenues to be placed in a perpetual Property Tax Relief Fund and appropriated annually to reduce or offset property taxes.

No constitution specifically prohibits an income tax, but Florida's charter effectively blocks enactment of a personal income tax, as does the Texas constitutional rule requiring any income tax enacted by the legislature to be approved by a majority of the state's voters before taking effect (Art. 8, Sec. 24).

Estate Taxes

The Alabama and Ohio constitutions authorize estate taxes, and a few constitutions authorize the "pick-up tax" whereby the state tax equals the allowable federal estate-tax credit. South Dakota's constitution, however, prohibits any inheritance tax (Art. 11, Sec. 15). Other constitutions are silent on estate taxes.

Severance Taxes

Forty states levy severance taxes on natural resources; only Ohio's constitution specifically authorizes them. Nevada limits the tax to a rate not to exceed 5 percent of the net proceeds (Art.10, Sec. 5). A few states earmark some severance-tax revenues. In North Dakota, "Not less than fifteen percent of the tax imposed for severing coal shall be placed into a permanent trust fund…administered by the board of university and school lands, which shall have full authority to invest said trust funds…and may loan moneys from the fund to political subdivisions" (Art. X, Sec. 21).

Corporation Taxes

Although many state constitutions have provisions on the chartering and governance of corporations, corporate taxation is handled mostly by statute. There are only some miscellaneous provisions such as New York's charter: "Where the state has power to tax corporations incorporated under the laws of the United States there shall be no discrimination in the rates and method of taxation between such corporations and other corporations exercising substantially similar functions and engaged in substantially similar business within the state" (Art. XVL, Sec. 4).

Earmarking

In 2010, Iowa voters approved a constitutional amendment providing that when the legislature next increases the sales tax, three-eighths of each cent of the new revenue shall be deposited in a new, permanent Natural Resources and Outdoor Recreation Trust Fund. As noted above, all states earmark motor-fuel tax revenues to highways, but various other earmarks of specific tax revenues (e.g., from tobacco and alcoholic beverages), as well as lottery proceeds, can be found in some constitutions.

Public Education

All state constitutions provide for public education, usually instructing the legislature to provide for free public schools (K-12). In some cases, the constitution may provide for the structure of schools, specify tax authority for education, and dedicate certain state revenues to education. Trends in recent decades have included state assumption of more responsibility for financing education and litigation arguing that state constitutional education and equal protection provisions mandate state equalization of school funding across local districts or pupils.

Campaign Financing

Public financing for statewide office campaigns was approved by voters in Maine in 1996 and in Arizona in 1998.[67] There are partial programs in some other states, but nearly all are statutory. Hawaii's document, though, instructs the legislature to "establish a campaign fund to be used for partial public financing of campaigns for public offices of the State and its political subdivisions" (Art. II, Sec. 5). However, most constitutions say little about campaign financing, except for occasional provisions such as "No fee shall ever be required in order to have the name of any candidate placed on the official ballot for any election or primary" (Arizona, Art. 7, Sec. 14).[68]

Rainy-Day Funds

Forty-seven states have one or more budget stabilization funds. Such funds are constitutionally authorized in twelve states (i.e., Alabama, Alaska, California, Delaware, Louisiana, Missouri, Oklahoma, Oregon, South Carolina, Texas, Virginia, and Washington). The constitutional authorization ordinarily specifies the level of revenues to be deposited in the fund at regular intervals and the procedures for spending and replenishing the fund.

Trust Funds and Other Funds

A number of constitutions establish permanent trust funds and other funds for specific purposes, such as a Veterans Land Fund and a Water Development Fund in Texas. This is another form of revenue earmarking insisted upon by the people. Revenue for the funds usually comes from specific sources (e.g., specific taxes, land proceeds, or levies on minerals or oil). Some funds can borrow money.

In 2010, North Dakotans approved a constitutional amendment establishing a state legacy fund to be stocked with certain oil and gas tax revenues. New Mexico has a "severance tax permanent fund" from which the legislature can make appropriations "for the benefit of the people" (Art. VIII, Sec. A). The recently established Idaho Millennium Permanent Endowment Fund gets the revenues received by the state from the 1998 master settlement agreement with tobacco companies. Perhaps most well known is the Alaska Permanent Fund, created in 1976. It is funded by oil and gas tax revenues, and it distributes money to all residents each year. Each resident gets the same amount because the US Supreme Court ruled that payments calibrated to years of Alaska residency violated the US Constitution's right to interstate travel.[69]

Borrowing and Debt Limits

State constitutions originally said little about borrowing and debt. States were assumed to possess inherent borrowing authority, and they made little peacetime use of borrowing until New York made money from financing construction of the Erie Canal in 1817. Other states also borrowed to finance infrastructure, but the Panic of 1837 drove many states toward bankruptcy, and about ten states defaulted on bonds. The federal government declined to bail out such states. This fiscal crisis triggered reforms, which, since the 1840s, have produced extensive provisions in most constitutions.

A few constitutions (e.g., Connecticut, New Hampshire, and Vermont) have no specific debt provisions. The most frequent restriction is a referendum requirement to approve state general-obligation debt except in cases of war, insurrection, natural disasters, and debt refinancing, although a few states (e.g., Florida) limit refinancing to reducing interest payments.

Another common restriction is a super-majority legislative vote to incur debt. Delaware requires a three-fourths majority of each legislative chamber to approve general-obligation debt except in cases of war, insurrection, and debt refinancing (Art. 8, Sec. 3). Many constitutions (e.g., Arizona) establish debt limits for general-obligation borrowing. A typical example is Mississippi: "Neither the State nor any of its direct agencies, excluding the political subdivisions and other local districts, shall incur a bonded indebtedness in excess of one and one half (1½) times the sum of all the revenue collected by it for all purposes during any one of the preceding four fiscal years, whichever year might be higher" (Art. 4, Sec. 115). Hawaii also establishes a limit, but if the governor declares an emergency, debt can exceed the limit if approved by a two-thirds vote of each legislative house.

Most documents permit borrowing only for public purposes. Some constitutions (e.g., Alaska and Delaware) additionally require specification of reasons for debt and require borrowed money to be spent for those reasons only. Most constitutions also prohibit the state from giving or lending its credit to aid any individual, association, or corporation, although the Massachusetts Constitution, while having this prohibition, allows the state to "give, loan or pledge its credit" if approved by a two-thirds vote of a quorum in each house of the legislature (Art. LXXXIV).

However, public purpose rules and other debt restrictions do not usually apply to revenue bonds, although a few state constitutions (e.g., Florida and Nebraska) explicitly exclude all or certain revenue bonds from debt restrictions.

Many constitutions also stipulate rules such as this: "Neither the state nor any county, school district, municipality, special district, or agency of any of them, shall become a joint owner with, or stockholder of...any corporation, association, partnership or person" (Florida Art. VII, Sec. 10).

Some constitutions place a dollar ceiling on debt (e.g., $100,000, Nebraska, Art. XIII, Sec. 1) but then permit debt for specific purposes (e.g., infrastructure) spelled out in the constitution if approved by a majority or usually super-majority vote of the legislature.

State Budgeting

One of the most prominent budget features is that forty-four constitutions require some type of annually balanced operating budget. Most constitutions also require all appropriations and expenditures of public funds to be made by law; a few specify annual or biennial state budgeting and designate the fiscal year (usually July 1 to June 30); most allow the governor to propose the state budget; all allow the governor to veto appropriations bills (and forty-four states allow a line-item veto); and some provide for appointed or elected finance officials, such as state treasurer, auditor, and comptroller. Some constitutions (e.g., Pennsylvania) specifically prohibit appropriations for charitable, educational, or benevolent institutions not under absolute state control and for any denomination or sectarian institution, corporation, or association. Missouri's constitution requires all revenues to be placed in the state treasury and then appropriated by the legislature in the following order of priority (1) payment of sinking fund and interest on state debt, (2) public education, (3) costs of assessing and collecting state revenue, (4) payment of the civil lists, (5) support of eleemosynary and other state institutions, (6) public health and welfare, (7) all other state purposes, and (8) expenses of the general assembly (Art. 3, Sec. 36).

State and Local Relations

Given that local governments are legal creatures of the states, most constitutions have provisions pertinent to local government finance, although a few, such as New Hampshire and Vermont, say nothing about regulating local governments. By contrast, Oklahoma's document has lengthy provisions, including delineation of the boundaries of the state's seventy-seven counties. Many of the provisions affecting local governments, such as property-tax rules, were discussed above.

A number of constitutions (e.g., California and Colorado) prohibit the state legislature from levying taxes for local purposes but allow it to grant specific tax powers to local governments. New Mexico's constitution specifies, though, that "no tax or assessment of any kind shall be levied by any political subdivision whose enabling legislation does not provide for an elected governing authority" (Art. VIII, Sec. 9). Generally, in Dillon's Rule states, local governments cannot levy taxes or fees not explicitly authorized by their charters; in home-rule states, municipalities and sometimes counties have some revenue flexibility so long as they do not contradict state law. The Illinois Constitution (Art. VII, Sec 6[g]) allows the legislature, by a three-fifths vote, to deny or limit tax powers and also limit debt for home-rule units. Many amendments to the Alabama Constitution authorize specific local taxes for specific units so long as the locality's voters approve the taxes. Most constitutions prohibit the legislature from enacting laws that apply to specific counties or municipalities, requiring instead general laws applicable to classes of local governments (e.g., by population size). Some also prohibit the legislature from enacting special laws on certain local subjects, such as laws amending charters, regulating local affairs, creating local offices, or prescribing local officials' duties.

Usually, all of the general constitutional rules that apply to state public finance also apply to local governments. However, many state constitutions place additional tax-rate and tax-level restrictions on local governments, as well as debt limits. Michigan's constitution states, "Property taxes and other local taxes and state taxation and spending may not be increased above the limitations specified herein without direct voter approval" (Art. IX, Sec. 25). A few constitutions contain specific restrictions. An Arizona amendment states that any local jurisdiction having "authority to impose any tax, fee, stamp requirement or other assessment, shall not impose any new tax, fee, stamp requirement or other assessment, direct or indirect, on the act or privilege of selling, purchasing, granting, assigning, transferring, receiving, or otherwise conveying any interest in real property" after 2007 (Art. 9, Sec. 24). Debt limits may be framed in terms of a fixed percentage (e.g., 6 percent in Arizona) of the assessed value of the locality's property subject to property taxes, a fixed limit such as the locality's current-year revenues, or a local referendum requirement. Many constitutions prohibit the state from assuming responsibility for local debts. Some constitutions also spell out accounting, auditing, and other rules intended to minimize local financial corruption.

In a few states, the constitution can provide for some revenue sharing with local governments. Ohio's charter states that "Not less than fifty per cent of the income, estate, and inheritance taxes that may be collected by the state shall be returned to the county, school district, city, village, or township in which said income, estate, or inheritance tax originates, or to any of the same, as may be provided by law" (Art. 12, Sec. 9). In the realm of the idiosyncratic, Kentucky's constitution requires each county to have a fiscal court, which is the county legislative body.

A big issue for local officials, however, is unfunded state mandates. Some constitutions (e.g., Maine and Michigan) prohibit various forms of unfunded mandates. Michigan's Headlee Amendment (1978) provides the following rule: "The state is prohibited from requiring any new or expanded activities by local governments without full state financing, from reducing the proportion of state spending in the form of aid to local governments, or from shifting the tax burden to local government" (Art. IX, Sec. 25). A common complaint of local officials is that legislatures find many ways to circumvent such mandate restrictions, as has happened in Michigan.

Summary

Although, on average, state constitutions, compared to the US Constitution, contain more details about and specific restrictions on taxing, spending, and borrowing, most state constitutions are not, on balance, excessively restrictive of state fiscal powers. This chapter, however, has not attempted to assess the actual impacts of these provisions. Those impacts have been examined elsewhere.[70]

FEDERAL STATUTORY AND JUDICIAL RESTRAINTS ON STATE FISCAL POWERS

Today, some of the most significant restraints on state tax powers, though less so for state spending and borrowing, stem from federal statutes and court rulings. Even though the federal Constitution imposes no significant restraints on state tax powers, Congress and the courts have employed the Constitution's commerce clause, export-import clause, and privileges and immunities clause, as well as the Fourteenth Amendment's due process and equal protection clauses, to restrict state taxation. Some of the growth of these federal restrictions has been associated with the general expansion of federal power, especially since the 1960s.[71] Rising federal restrictions have been due also to the rise of a national, now global, economy in which so many taxable activities involve interstate and foreign commerce. A leading state concern today is the federal prohibition on state collections of sales taxes on most out-of-state purchases made by their residents via the Internet, telephone, and mail order. The unwillingness of Congress to authorize such taxation costs states about $18 billion per year in sales-tax revenue. A related concern is the 1998 Internet Tax Freedom Act, which was extended to 2014 in 2007. This act prohibits federal, state, and local taxes on Internet access as well as such Internet levies as bandwidth, bit, and e-mail taxes.

Although the federal government does not regulate state and local spending in a general way, numerous policies affect, co-opt, and mandate state and local spending. Federal court orders, for example, can require expenditures of billions of state and local revenues for institutional reform, such as school desegregation and prison improvements; matching requirements attached to federal grants co-opt state and local funds for federally desired policies; and unfunded mandates require state and local spending on specific federal objectives (e.g., environmental protection). The National Conference of State Legislatures estimates that Congress shifted about $130 billion in unfunded costs to the states in fiscal years 2004–2008.[72]

By contrast, the federal government has subsidized state and local borrowing by allowing taxpayers to exclude from their federal income-tax liability interest earned on many state and local bonds. This allows state and local governments to borrow at comparatively low interest rates. The 2009 federal stimulus act provided for taxable Build America Bonds (BABs) by which the federal government subsidizes the interest payments that local governments make to investors, increasing the bonds' yield by 35 percent. About $174 billion in BABs were issued by states by late 2010. Critics, however, contend that BABs merely encouraged state and local governments to accumulate more debt. The program was allowed to expire at the end of 2010.

Conclusion

The federal-state tax coordination envisioned by Hamilton never came to pass. Political restraints kept the federal government out of state and local tax lairs for some 145 years, but during the 1930s, the federal government began to circumscribe and intrude upon state and local taxation in unilateral ways. Changes in federal tax laws occur with little consultation with state and local officials, and enactment of a federal sales or value-added tax, as proposed by some, could squeeze state consumption taxes, such as the sales tax. Full discussion of federal-state issues, however, is beyond the scope of this chapter.

Acknowledgment

I wish to thank Richard L. Cole, University of Texas at Arlington, Troy E. Smith, Brigham Young University-Hawaii, and Conrad Weiler, Temple University, for their helpful comments.

Notes

1 *Juillard v. Greenman* (1884) 110 US 421.
2 This rule, articulated in 1868 by Iowa Supreme Court Justice John Dillon, holds that municipal governments possess only the powers that are expressly granted to them by their state legislature, although they may also exercise powers necessarily implied from those grants of power and powers indispensable to the municipality's existence and operation. However, ambiguities in legislative grants of power should be interpreted as denials of municipal power.
3 Dam (1977).
4 Chase and Ducat (1973), 33.
5 Niskanen (1992), 14.
6 The other two authors were James Madison and John Jay.
7 Cooke (1961), 205.
8 Ibid., 95.
9 Ibid., 93.
10 Newman (1976), 13.

11 Stahr (2005), 105.

12 Newman (1976), 17.

13 Cooke (1961), 188.

14 Ibid., 208.

15 Ibid., 198.

16 Ibid., 201.

17 Ibid., 202.

18 Ibid., 227 (emphasis in original).

19 Ibid., 195.

20 Ibid., 211.

21 Ibid., 213.

22 Ibid., 227.

23 Kincaid (1991).

24 Shah (2007), 19-21.

25 Cooke (1961), 216.

26 Ibid., 222.

27 Ibid., 221-222.

28 Ibid., 226 (emphasis in original).

29 Ibid., 227.

30 Ibid.

31 *License Tax Cases* (1866), 462.

32 Chase and Ducat (1973), 101.

33 Farrand (1966), II:350.

34 *Pollock v. Farmers' Loan & Trust Co.* (1895) 572-573.

35 *Hylton v. United States* (1796) 171.

36 *Florida v. Mellon* (1927) 12.

37 *Brushaber v. Union Pacific R. Co.* (1916) 12.

38 However, Congress may legislate permission for state and local taxation of federal
    property. US ACIR (1981-1982).

39 *Collector v. Day* (1871) 113.

40 *Helvering v. Gerhardt* (1938) 419-420.

41 *New York v. United States* (1946) 596.

42 Ibid., 587-588.

43 *South Carolina v. Baker* (1988) 505.

44 Cited in Blackwell and Klukowski (2010), A19.

45 *United States v. Butler* (1936) 66.

46 *Steward Machine Co. v. Davis* (1937) 591.

47 *Massachusetts v. Mellon* (1923).

48 Quoted in Chase and Ducat (1973), 38.

49 Quoted in Rosen (2010), 34.

50 US Government Accountability Office (2010), 6.

51 *South Dakota v. Dole* (1987).

52 *United States v. Fisher* (1805).

53 *Perry v. United States* (1935).

54 Chase and Ducat (1973), 74.

55 *Turner v. Maryland* (1883) 55.

56 Eugene V. Debs (Socialist), Theodore Roosevelt (Progressive Republican), William
    Howard Taft (Republican), and Woodrow Wilson (Democrat and winner).

57 *Kelo v. City of New London* (2005) 469.

58 BBC News Europe (2010).

59 Wallis (2000), 67.

60 Ibid., 70.

61 Colorado Constitution, Art. X, Sec. 14.

62 See Gordon (this volume).

63 Newhouse (1984), 16-18.

64 See Bell (this volume).

65 Bell (2005), 307.

66 Alaska, Delaware, Montana, New Hampshire, and Oregon levy no sales tax.

67 The US Supreme Court struck down a key provision of Arizona's law. See *Arizona Free Enterprise Club's Freedom PAC v. Bennett* (2011).

68 For state campaign finance laws, see the Campaign Finance Institute at http://www.cfinst.org.

69 *Zobel v. Williams* (1982) 55.

70 See, e.g., Rose (2010).

71 Kincaid (1993).

72 National Conference of State Legislatures (2010), 1.

References

BBC News Europe (2010, August 12). "Swede Faces World-Record $1 Million Speeding Penalty," http://www.bbc.co.uk/news/world-europe-10960230, accessed December 2, 2010.

Bell, Michael (2005). "Property Tax Assessment." In *The Encyclopedia of Taxation & Tax Policy*, edited by Joseph J. Cordes, Robert D. Ebel, and Jane G. Gravelle. Washington, DC: Urban Institute Press. 307–310.

Blackwell, J. Kenneth, and Kenneth A. Klukowski (2010, July 22). "Why the Obama-Care Tax Penalty Is Unconstitutional." *Wall Street Journal*, A19.

Brushaber v. Union Pacific R. Co. (1916) 240 US 1.

Chase, Harold W., and Craig R. Ducat (1973) *Edward S. Corwin's The Constitution and What It Means Today.* Princeton: Princeton University Press.

Collector v. Day (1871) 11 Wall. (78 US) 113.

Cooke, Jacob E. (Ed.) (1961). *The Federalist.* Middletown, CT: Wesleyan University Press.

Dam, Kenneth W. (1977). "The American Fiscal Constitution." *University of Chicago Law Review* 44:2 (Winter 1977): 271–320.

Farrand, Max (Ed.) (1966). *The Records of the Federal Convention of 1787.* Vol. 2. New Haven: Yale University Press.

Florida v. Mellon (1927) 273 US 12.

Helvering v. Gerhardt (1938) 304 US 405.

Hylton v. United States (1796) 3 US 171.

Juillard v. Greenman (1884) 110 US 421.

Kelo v. City of New London (2005) 545 US 469.

Kincaid, John (1991). "The Competitive Challenge to Cooperative Federalism." In *Competition among States and Local Governments: Efficiency and Equity in American Federalism*, edited by Daphne A. Kenyon and John Kincaid. Washington, DC: Urban Institute Press. 87–114.

Kincaid, John (1993). "From Cooperation to Coercion in American Federalism: Housing, Fragmentation, and Preemption, 1780–1992," *Journal of Law and Politics* 9 (Winter): 333–433.

License Tax Cases (1866) 72 US (5 Wall.) 462.

Massachusetts v. Mellon (1923) 262 US 447.

National Conference of State Legislatures (2010) *Mandate Monitor* 7:1 (January 4, 2010) 1–2.

New York v. United States (1946) 326 US 572.

Newhouse, Wade J. (1984). *Constitutional Uniformity and Equality in State Taxation*. 2nd ed. Buffalo, NY: W. S. Hein.

Newman, Eric P. (1976). *The Early Paper Money of America*. Racine, WI: Western Publishing.

Niskanen, William A. (1992). "The Case for a New Fiscal Constitution." *Journal of Economic Perspectives* 6:2 (Spring): 13–24.

Perry v. United States (1935) 294 US 330.

Pollock v. Farmers' Loan & Trust Co. (1895) 157 US 429.

Rose, Shanna (2010). "Institutions and Fiscal Sustainability." *National Tax Journal* 63:4 (December): 807–837.

Rosen, Jeffrey (2010, November 28). "Radical Constitutionalism." *New York Times Magazine*, 34, 36.

Shah, Anwar (2007). "Introduction: Principles of Fiscal Federalism." In *The Practice of Fiscal Federalism: Comparative Perspectives*, edited by Anwar Shah. Montreal: McGill-Queen's University Press. 3–42.

South Carolina v. Baker (1988) 485 US 505.

South Dakota v. Dole (1987) 483 US 203.

Stahr, Walter (2005). *John Jay: Founding Father*. New York: Hambledon Continuum.

Steward Machine Co. v. Davis (1937) 301 US 548.

Turner v. Maryland (1883) 107 US 38.

United States v. Butler (1936) 297 US 1.

United States v. Fisher (1805) 6 US (2 Cr.) 358.

US Advisory Commission on Intergovernmental Relations (ACIR) (1982). *Payments in Lieu of Taxes on Federal Real Property*. Report A-90. Washington, DC: ACIR.

US Government Accountability Office (2010). *The Federal Government's Long-Term Fiscal Outlook: January 2010 Update*. GAO-10-468SP. Washington, DC: GAO.

Wallis, John Joseph (2000). "American Government Finance in the Long Run: 1790 to 1990." *Journal of Economic Perspectives* 14:1 (Winter): 61–82.

Zobel v. Williams (1982) 457 US 55.

CHAPTER 3

FEDERALISM TRENDS, TENSIONS, AND OUTLOOK

TIMOTHY J. CONLAN AND
PAUL L. POSNER

FOUNDATIONS OF US FEDERALISM

FEDERALISM is a system of government in which power and authority are divided among two or more tiers of government, each of which is directly accountable to the people and enjoys some degree of extraordinary legal protection.[1] Modern federalism first appeared in the United States Constitution. The framers of that document sought to design a governmental system that overcame the weaknesses of confederation while still ensuring a substantial degree of decentralization and protection of individual liberties. The Articles of Confederation (1781–1788) were essentially a treaty among separate and sovereign states, in which the national government was almost wholly dependent on the states for revenue and for the implementation of policies within the very limited sphere of federal responsibilities. In contrast, the federal Constitution (1789) was based on the principle of popular sovereignty, in which the people of the United States, rather than the states themselves, were the ultimate source of authority. The people, through their Constitution, established both the state and federal governments in order to carry out their distinctive public responsibilities.[2]

The new national government was given much more extensive powers than under the Articles, including, among others, the power to tax and spend for the general welfare, responsibility for national defense and foreign affairs, and the power to regulate commerce among the states and with foreign nations. To provide a check on this stronger national government, its powers were limited to those listed or enumerated in Article 1, Section 8 of the Constitution. However, ambiguities in wording and differences of interpretation left considerable uncertainty as to the actual scope of those powers. States retained all governmental powers not granted to the national government, which ensured considerable decentralization and state autonomy in the system, and their interests were thought to be further protected by equal state representation in the Senate, a state role in the selection of presidents (through the electoral college) and, prior to the Seventeenth Amendment, state legislative selection of US senators.

History and Development

Until the 1860s, American federalism in practice resembled what has come to be known as "dual federalism." In dual federalism, there is little overlap in the functions and responsibilities of the federal government and the states. Each government has its own, largely separate, sphere of responsibilities.[3] In this system, the national government concentrated on defense, foreign affairs, developing the western territories, and the promotion of American industry and commerce through the use of tariffs and "internal improvements." The states were almost wholly responsible for the administration of justice, public education, welfare, and most public infrastructure.

Within this accepted division of responsibilities, there remained considerable political debate about the size and scope of government, especially regarding the national government. Those favoring a more expansive and energetic national government interpreted the constitutional grants of power to Congress broadly. Expressing themselves at different times through the Federalist, Whig, and Republican parties, they favored policies such as a national bank to service public debt, the promotion of economic development through national road and waterway projects, grants to assist states in caring for the blind and needy, and high protective tariffs to promote domestic industries. Followers of the Democratic Party believed, on the other hand, in reading Article I, Section 8 narrowly, thus keeping the federal government small and limited in its responsibilities. These divergent political views were reinforced by the social and economic effects of slavery, as well as by the divergent patterns of economic modernization in the North and South. The latter sought to protect slavery and lagged behind in industrial development. The North, in contrast, experienced rapid population growth and dramatic expansion of industrial and agricultural productivity.

These underlying economic and social factors fed political conflict over the nature of American federalism and led eventually to southern secession and the Civil War. The North's victory strengthened both the legal and political authority of the national government. The Fourteenth Amendment to the Constitution strengthened Congress's authority vis-à-vis the states, by guaranteeing all citizens due process and equal protection of the law, by prohibiting states from infringing on those rights, and by granting Congress the power to enforce equal protection and due process through federal legislation. Moreover, the policy agenda of the Civil War–era Republican Party expanded the scope of federal policy activism and laid the foundation for future policy expansions, through such varied initiatives as the Morrill land grant college act, promotion of an intercontinental railroad, creation of the Departments of Agriculture and (briefly) Education, establishment of the first federal income tax, and initiatives to assist the newly freed slaves and to care for disabled veterans and their dependents and survivors.

Following the Civil War, a long period of gradual government expansion ensued, along with the first tentative ventures into "cooperative" federalism. As the nation's economy expanded, the limits of state economic regulation were exposed. States attempted but ultimately were unable to effectively regulate the developing national systems of rail transportation, food processing, mining, and heavy industries.[4] Their jurisdictional reach was inadequate to the geographic scope of the economic externalities that were created by national markets and industries. Consequently, the latter nineteenth and early twentieth centuries saw the gradual creation of federal railroad regulation, antitrust legislation, food and drug safety legislation, and the creation of the Federal Reserve Bank system.[5] This same period also witnessed the development of the first significant federal cash grants to states; these grants were for agricultural research, forestry, vocational education, and highway construction. All of these grants laid the foundations for greater federal-state cooperation in the years to come.[6]

The Supreme Court slowed and moderated this centralizing trend but did not block it entirely. The Court's restrictive reading of the Constitution overturned the federal income tax in the 1890s, and federal child labor and minimum wage laws in the early twentieth century (holding that these exceeded Congress's authority to regulate interstate commerce, interfered with private contracts, and invaded the sphere of state policy).[7] On the other hand, the Court upheld federal laws regulating or prohibiting harmful goods and practices in interstate commerce, including impure food and drugs, lottery tickets, and prostitution, and it upheld Congress's power to affix conditions to federal grants-in-aid.[8]

The federal income tax was subsequently restored upon passage of the Sixteenth Amendment in 1913, which laid the fiscal foundation for subsequent expansion of federal spending. The enactment of the Seventeenth Amendment, also in 1913, further enhanced federal power by replacing state legislative selection of US senators with popular elections. This action simultaneously shrank state influence over national policy making and strengthened the Senate by enhancing its democratic legitimacy.

The federal government's growing role during the late nineteenth and early twentieth centuries was more than matched by the growth and sophistication of municipal governments. At the turn of the twentieth century, major cities were in many ways the central actors in domestic governance, spending by far the largest share of government expenditures and providing the bulk of domestic services. They were also the focal point for government reform initiatives, often leading the way with innovations in public-sector management. Many, though by no means all, states were also innovative policymakers during the Progressive era. But virtually all states were handicapped by inadequate revenue systems and by small and often highly unprofessional workforces.[9]

This latter problem was gradually improved by the rise of cooperative federal grant programs. Federal grants often required improvements in state bureaucracies, and they stimulated the development of state services and new state revenues by requiring states to match federal contributions, typically on a dollar-for-dollar basis. The first major program of federal highway grants, adopted in 1916, stands as a notable example. It required states to establish a "single state agency" to implement highway programs, administered by a civil engineering professional, and it required states to provide matching funds. In the process, it helped to launch the development nationwide of professionalized state highway agencies.

By necessity, this model of cooperative federalism, in which the federal government and the states shared responsibilities in a collaborative manner, came of age during and after the 1930s. The New Deal readjusted the balance of power and the operational practices of the federal system as profoundly as the Civil War had done. State and local finances collapsed under the pressure of the Great Depression, as tax revenues contracted sharply and demands for services increased. Consequently, states and localities turned increasingly to the federal government for assistance.[10]

The federal government responded initially with massive employment and relief programs, limits on agricultural and industrial production to boost prices and halt deflation, new regulations of securities and banking industries, and large-scale deficit spending. The initial agricultural and industrial policies were overturned by the Supreme Court, which held that they exceeded the bounds of Congress's authority under the Constitution. But the Court eventually accepted the expansion of federal responsibilities, adopting broader interpretations of the interstate commerce power and allowing broad federal involvement in state responsibilities through federal grants-in-aid.[11] Congress responded with the passage of assistance for the elderly, unemployment insurance, cash welfare assistance, federal wage and hours laws, public housing, and more.

By 1936, government spending had doubled as a share of the economy, and the federal share of public expenditures equaled combined state and local spending for the first time during peacetime.[12] Because the federal government relied on states and cities to implement many of these new programs, it also worked to modernize and professionalize state governments and to promote broader sharing and cooperation across many domestic functions. Most states also engaged in fiscal and institutional modernization, including the adoption of state income and sales taxes by many more states.

This system of cooperative federalism, marked by shared involvement by all types of general-purpose government across most domestic functions, became the norm in American governance in the 1950s. It was greatly expanded during the 1960s with the "Great Society" program of President Lyndon B. Johnson. Hundreds of new federal grant programs were adopted; the total number of federal grants tripled from 132 in 1960 to 397 in 1969.[13] Many of these new programs, such as the Model Cities program for urban renewal, bypassed state governments and went directly to local governments. In other cases, federal involvement expanded deeply into traditional state and local fields such as K-12 education and local law enforcement, as well as newer functions such as health care for the needy. Some of the largest and most important federal aid programs in existence today, such as education grants for disadvantaged children and Medicaid, were established during this period. A new programmatic focus on fighting poverty was also adopted by the federal government, as were new forms of federal mandates and other forms of regulations affecting state and local governments.

This explosion of new federal spending programs, and the conflicts caused by the federal government's new focus on civil rights, poverty, and governmental reform, created a political backlash and intergovernmental policy changes in the Nixon and Reagan administrations.[14] President Richard M. Nixon launched a "new federalism" initiative, which sought to reduce the strings on federal grant programs and decentralize decision making. Although he failed to enact all of his proposed reforms, President Nixon succeeded in winning congressional approval for General Revenue Sharing—a multibillion-dollar program of largely no-strings aid to state and local governments—as well as broad flexible block grants for community development and employment and training programs. But Nixon also oversaw the continued expansion of more coercive, regulatory tools with the adoption of major new federal mandates in areas such as air and water pollution, occupational safety, and protection of endangered species.

President Ronald Reagan, too, sought to reduce federal power and influence by cutting federal spending (and taxes) and by consolidating smaller, more tightly controlled federal grant programs into more flexible block grants. Despite this widely heralded move toward devolution, he, too, accommodated the continued rise of regulatory federalism, supporting or acquiescing in the passage of costly new intergovernmental regulations and the preemption of state regulatory authority by Congress.

THE CHALLENGES OF CONTEMPORARY FEDERALISM

As we enter the second decade of the twenty-first century, our federal system remains a central vehicle used by national, state, and local officials to satisfy an ever-expanding range of needs and goals. Whether it is homeland security, health care, education, or environmental policy, national policymakers have increasingly turned to state and local governments as the critical workhorses. State and local governments have stepped up as well to mount new initiatives to address health, safety, education, and infrastructure needs, much as they have done for decades. Federal initiatives have changed the agendas of state and local governments, just as the policy innovations from below have influenced the priorities and choices of federal decision makers.

The fiscal and policy fortunes of each type of government in our system have become increasingly intertwined over the past several decades. While citizens increasingly have demanded federal action and many policy areas have been nationalized, this has been accompanied by a growing reliance on state and local governments to implement national goals. These arrangements confer benefits— the federal government gains valuable political and fiscal partners, and state and local governments gain the opportunity to negotiate a balance between national goals and differing state and local needs and interests.

However, the increasing connections among governments in our system have raised vexing governance challenges as well. State and local governments have been confronted with the challenge of addressing their own unique needs while at the same time assuming stewardship for a growing plate of national needs. The federal government struggles with the gap between its accountability for compelling national concerns and its relative lack of control over achieving national outcomes. The public is presented with the dilemma of sorting out responsibilities for outcomes when so many hands are in the public policy soup.

The intergovernmental system is now being tested by a complex array of short-term and long-term challenges. For example, in areas ranging from homeland security to education, federal, state, and local governments face daunting problems in managing programs that involve numerous actors inside and outside of government. Moreover, the unique advantages of a federal system—the flexibility and capacity to respond to the unique local needs of a diverse nation—are threatened by long-term trends such as advances in technology and communications that span state and even national boundaries and inspire demands for consistent national and even international regulatory and tax policies.

The system's challenges are most sharply defined by increasingly acute expenditure and revenue pressures occurring at among all governments. In the short term, the recent economic downturn and stock-market declines have caused revenues to slide, while other developments, such as health-care cost increases, have greatly increased spending demands for all governments. Longer-term trends, such as the aging of the population, will continue to put spending demands on all governments, while other trends, such as globalization and advancing technology, will affect traditional sources of government revenues by eroding tax bases.[15] The financial challenges facing all governments threaten to erode the fiscal foundations that have underwritten cooperative federalism in the past and enabled partners to join together in expanding public services to meet rising public expectations. In its place, the fiscal future of our federal system could feature heightened intergovernmental conflict where US governments vie to preempt revenues, shift costs, and shift blame for the difficult choices that will be necessary to resolve fiscal deficits.

Nationalization of the Policy Agenda

The extension of the federal policy regime to an ever broader range of issues is premised on the emergence of a broad consensus supporting the nationalization of both problems and solutions. Questions about the legitimacy of the federal role—once among the most contentious issues dividing our party system—have largely been settled. Conservative Republican, moderate Democratic, and liberal Democratic regimes have all affirmed a secular preference for a strong national and intergovernmental response to emerging issues through our federal system. The public, too, has shown little patience for observing the structural constraints of the federal design, supporting national interventions from community policing to educational accountability.

The institutional erosion of state and local governments' political influence on our system helped set the stage for this nationalization of policy agendas and solutions. Fundamental political forces have eroded the traditional bastions of state and local influence that undergirded our federal system for decades. State and local party organizations declined while national parties gained influence. Individualization of congressional politics further diminished state and local influences on the political system, as did the proliferation of interest groups in Washington after 1960.[16]

Other shifts in our political system have contributed to the nationalization of policy agendas and politics. The growth of national media institutions focused on Washington created a powerful resource for those groups wishing to nationalize problems and issues, as reporters increasingly sought to find national dimensions or applications for state and local problems or solutions. The advent of lobbies representing broad, diffuse interests, the so-called public interest groups, has fueled national policy advocacy because many of these groups have settled in Washington, DC, rather than in other states. Perhaps the most important development in the interest-group sector was the pronounced, but little noticed, shift of business groups from allies of the states to advocates of national regulation by federal agencies. This trend underscores the impact of the nationalization and globalization of the economy on our federal system. As corporations increasingly operate in a global environment, coping with fifty separate state regulatory regimes is seen by some as a hindrance to economic efficiency and competitiveness.

This secular tendency was put to the test in the administration of George W. Bush. Some anticipated that a conservative Republican administration, led by a former governor and matched with a Republican-controlled Congress for the first time in nearly fifty years, would halt or reverse the historical trajectory of an expanded federal role and increasing intergovernmentalization of domestic governance. Yet the Bush administration consolidated the national policy regime by using the familiar pattern of tapping the state and local sectors to advance national goals. Indeed, far from slowing down the nationalization of the policy agenda, the Bush administration, working with a Republican-controlled Congress, accelerated it in several policy domains and further seeded it with new ideas that warranted a federal response. Whether it was No Child Left Behind or the Real ID Act, President Bush and the Congress followed a muscular domestic policy agenda, relying on federal mandates and preemptions on states and localities to carry out national policy priorities.[17]

Upon his election in 2008, President Barack Obama pursued a bold and ambitious set of national policy goals. While never articulating a federalism vision during the campaign, the new administration, like those before it, found that it would have to stand on the shoulders of state and local governments to achieve economic recovery, to reform financial markets, and to implement its ambitious new health-reform program. The Obama administration had all of the tools that previous administrations had at their disposal such as preemptions, mandates, grants, and tax expenditures. Indeed, it used mandates and preemptions of states to extend health insurance to the uninsured and to establish new regulatory frameworks to govern health insurance previously regulated by the states. However, the depth of the recession also legitimized significant expansion of federal grants to state and local governments to mitigate the effects of recession. Consequently, the Obama administration had access to the federal aid toolbox at a level not seen since the days of Lyndon Johnson and the Great Society. The 2009 American Recovery and Reinvestment Act (ARRA) included $285 billion in expanded, temporary funding for more than ninety federal grant programs, including increased matching funds for Medicaid, highly flexible funding for education, and support for stimulative grant programs in education, high-speed rail, and energy conservation. Consequently, federal aid increased from $461 billion in FY2008 to $654 billion in FY 2010 and rose to 17.6 percent of total federal spending, one of the highest levels in history.[18]

From Cooperation to Coercion in Contemporary Federalism

In many respects, the expanding federal role in setting the agenda for the intergovernmental system has been a feature of American government for the past fifty years. However, such policies were often spawned and implemented through the institutions of cooperative federalism. The older cooperative model expanded the federal role while at the same time strengthening the state and local foundations for that role. Recognizing the growing federal fiduciary and functional interest in a strong state and local sector, the federal government in the cooperative era provided fiscal assistance and capacity building to enhance the vitality and capacity of their state and local partners. State and local governments retained vital bargaining power with national leaders because they could at least threaten to withhold their cooperation that was so vital for national programs to succeed.[19]

Most studies of the etiology of federal policy initiatives during this period show that grants were usually the initial tool used to stimulate interest and adoption throughout the intergovernmental system, only to be followed by more coercive mandates as the federal role became more legitimate and gaps in implementation became less acceptable.[20] Notwithstanding the perennial efforts to devolve many federal grant programs to the states, federal aid continues to be significant, as grants totaled $654 billion in federal outlays in FY 2010, making up more than 25 percent of state and local expenditures (figure 3.1).[21] Most federal dollars are still highly categorical in nature. There are more than 950 federal grant programs according to the Congressional Research Service.[22] Only twenty-five of these programs are block grants, reflecting the continuing propensity of Congress to claim credit for highly specific programs, as well as practical difficulties in the design and implementation of such programs.[23]

The politics of grant design suggested above lead to a grant system that is often at odds with the theoretical insights offered by economists. In public finance theory, grants are justified to correct problems involved with external benefits and costs not fully captured by "lower-level" jurisdictions. Accordingly, the provision of public services is suboptimal because of a mismatch between benefits and costs, and a federal grant is warranted to correct for these externalities. Grants are also justified to rectify the distributional implications of state and local reliance on regressive taxation and to level the fiscal playing field between low- and high-income communities.[24]

An open-ended categorical matching grant is the most appropriate way to overcome externalities by changing the prices faced by recipient jurisdictions for each additional marginal increment of the service. A matching requirement should be imposed to reflect the ratio of external to internal benefits. As Edward Gramlich and others have noted, however, this dictum is rarely followed in the design of grants. Nearly all grants are close-ended in nature. The predominantly close-ended nature of most grants suggests that Congress intends to underwrite a minimum level of services for each state, as operationalized by the fixed funding

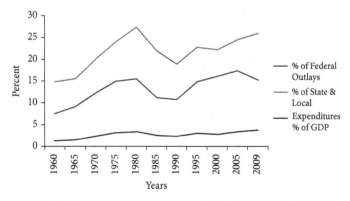

Figure 3.1 Federal Grants as a Percentage of Outlays, Expenditures, and GDP
Source: US Office of Management and Budget.

ceiling, rather than a less controllable and more potentially troublesome marginal cost-matching formula.[25]

Congress has also resisted economists' prescriptions on redistributive grants. Disparities clearly exist in public services due to the mismatch between needs and fiscal capacity.[26] General-purpose equalizing grants are the recommended solution to this problem, but the short, troubled life of General Revenue Sharing shows that general-purpose aid has little political attraction to a Congress needing to claim credit for program accomplishments. Although redistributive goals may also be sought by allocating federal categorical grants in proportion to needs and capacity, studies have generally found that aid is not well targeted based on these criteria. The Government Accountability Office (GAO) found, for example, that fiscal capacity was included in formulas in only twenty-three of the ninety-seven largest grant programs in 1996.[27] Reflecting the role that formulas play in cementing political coalitions behind grant programs, the most significant variable explaining grant allocations in the GAO's analysis was the minimum grant levels provided to small states, due to obvious political factors.

The numerous federal categorical grants meet not only the credit-claiming needs of federal officials, but also a broader coalition of clientele and state and local bureaucrats who stand to gain additional resources and leverage from specific grant programs. The design and management of grants typically reflect the need to strengthen and broaden the coalition behind the program.[28] Formula design provisions, reporting requirements, beneficiary protections, and fiscal maintenance of effort and matching provisions are often bargaining chips that gain the support of both beneficiary interest groups and state and local implementers.

Cooperative federalism thus tended to generate a "picket-fence" structure of program specialists among types of governments. Intergovernmental relationships flowed up and down through "vertical functional autocracies," which cut across the horizontal governance structures of our multitiered federal system.[29] Specific techniques to build the picket fences of the federal system include personnel qualification standards, single state agency requirements, and advisory board requirements that enhance the role played by like-minded professionals within state governments. These functional "stovepipes" became the channels for federal grants and other forms of cooperative intergovernmental relationships, and they defined the space for intergovernmental bargaining and negotiation. In many respects these intergovernmental networks of specialists proved capable of negotiating cooperative intergovernmental relationships if granted sufficient time.[30] Bargaining characterized these relationships, as neither the states nor the federal government had sufficient leverage to act unilaterally.

Because neither the federal government nor the states enjoyed sufficient leverage to act unilaterally, each had to settle for a level of influence and results that were suboptimal to their own interests. From the federal perspective, gaining participation is more critical politically to program survival than promoting compliance with goals. Holding grantees to overly rigid and demanding requirements risk losing their participation and support, which are so critical to the survival of the program. For instance, there has been a secular trend over the years to reduce or drop matching from federal grants. Before 1935, for instance, most grants required matching and nearly all had a 50 percent nonfederal match. The GAO's research found that only 9 percent of all grant programs in 1978 required a match of 50 percent or greater and that 37 percent of grants had no required match.[31] By 1995, 50 percent of all grants had no matching requirement.[32]

From the state and local perspective, federal grants have cumulative effects on the priority setting and capacity of state and local officials to respond to the unique needs of their citizens. Joseph Zimmerman catalogued an inventory of sixteen criticisms of federal grant provisions including reduction in discretionary authority of states and localities, distortion of state and local priorities to meet national mandates and matching requirements, and the greater independence won by state bureaucrats at the expense of their nominal politically accountable superiors.[33] Although each federal program requirement may make sense on its own terms, this literature pays more attention to the global impacts of grants in the aggregate on state and local governance and accountability.[34]

The collective consequences of grants for state and local decisions are illustrated by examining the budgetary implications of federal grants for the state and local fiscal commons. On the one hand, federal grants provide potential opportunities for state and local cost savings if grants can be used to supplant existing state and local funds for aided programs. Studies suggest that fiscal substitution can be considerable for broad-based programs where state and local governments already have significant investments. Moreover, the absence of a federal maintenance of effort provision also facilitates substitution.

By contrast, federal matching provisions in open-ended programs generate a stimulative state and local spending response, which distorts state and local budgetary priorities. Studies of fiscal retrenchment have found that state and local governments protect federal grants by sustaining their matching and maintenance of effort at the expense of purely state- or local-funded programs. The most pronounced effect of federal grants on state spending in particular arises from the matching requirements of the federal Medicaid program. With a median nonfederal match of 40.57 percent, the states' share of Medicaid has now grown to rival education as the top state spending priority.[35]

Coercive Federalism

In recent years, we have witnessed a transition away from cooperative federalism featuring grants to a more coercive, opportunistic model. In contrast with the earlier cooperative model, federal officials are increasingly enticed and pressured to respond to a prodigious agenda of national problems through more centralized and nationalizing policy actions and tools, whether it be mandates or preemptions in various forms. Regardless of how small or localized it may be, seemingly no issue of domestic governance is off the table for a national policy response.

Intergovernmental regulations can range from direct orders imposed on state and local governments by federal statute to more indirect actions that force state and local policy change as a consequence of other independent federal policies, such as the implications of federal immigration policies for local health clinics. The United States Advisory Commission on Intergovernmental Relations (ACIR) usefully defined a taxonomy of "federally induced costs," which suggested discrete policy actions that the federal government could take to increase state and local costs.[36]

Such policy actions could consist of either affirmative obligations for state and local governments to take action on a policy issue—what might be generically termed a "mandate"—or a constraint preventing or preempting certain actions. While conceptually distinct, the intergovernmental impacts can be quite similar. For instance, the fiscal impacts of mandates ordering cleaner water can be every bit as costly as preemptions of state or local revenue sources. Many other distinctions can be drawn—some federal regulatory actions affect public and private sectors equally, such as fair labor standards, while others specifically focus on state and local governments such as voting or educational requirements.

Thus, the instruments of coercive federalism go well beyond the popular concept of "unfunded mandates." This conceptualization was formalized when Congress passed the Unfunded Mandates Reform Act (UMRA) in 1995. While the passage of this act did indeed mark an attempt to reverse or at the very least arrest the growth of intergovernmental regulation or coercive federalism, in fact, the UMRA primarily addressed only one of these instruments: statutory direct orders. The relatively narrow definition embraced in the UMRA has served to limit the potential effectiveness of this reform in influencing these policy decisions.

The secular trends toward a more coercive and centralized federalism have survived the passage of both Republican and Democratic administrations, as well as Democratic and Republican Congresses. The Nixon administration, while following a principled federalism approach in creating both block grants and revenue sharing, nonetheless presided over a major expansion of federal regulation with important federalism implications.[37] The Reagan administration, notwithstanding major policy proposals to rebalance the federal role in the federal system, nonetheless found itself endorsing new federal mandates in areas including environmental protection, highway safety, health care, and social welfare policy.[38] These trends continued through the 1990s and 2000s.

Recent centralizing actions succeeded in overturning cooperative federalism frameworks that had evolved over many years. Recent examples in the Bush and Obama administrations encompass many areas of traditional state and local responsibility—education reform, electoral administration, local emergency communications, and the issuance of state driver's licenses[39] are among the new areas that were covered by new federal mandates and preemptions in the Bush era. The Obama administration has added health reform to the list—states have become the primary instrument used to extend health insurance to the uninsured through both expansive new Medicaid coverage mandates and the new health exchanges, which states will administer under close federal supervision and standards. Ironically, the familiarity and political support spawned by these more cooperative forerunners may very well have paved the way for their more coercive successors.

Intergovernmental tensions and consequences have been accentuated by simultaneous federal actions that both increase intergovernmental fiscal burdens through spending mandates while at the same time limiting revenues available to state and local governments to finance these far-flung federal policy initiatives. Recent federal tax policy actions broke new ground in constraining state revenues. In the estate-tax area, a shared federal-state regime begun in 1924, which encouraged states to continue their own estate taxes through a federal credit, was overturned in 2001. Prior to the passage of the federal estate-tax cut in 2001, every state levied an estate tax that allowed them to "pick up" a share of federal estate-tax revenues. The state "pick-up" estate taxes did not increase total estate-tax liability for estates, because taxpayers received a dollar-for-dollar credit against their federal estate-tax liability. The 2001 tax cuts phased out both federal estate taxes as well as the state credit, which expired four years before the federal tax. Notwithstanding this change, twenty-one states decoupled from the federal tax code to continue to collect their own estate taxes in 2010.[40]

Moreover, the pace of federal preemptions of state and local tax law has accelerated in recent years. As early as 1985, the Congress acted to prohibit states from imposing business taxes on out-of-state companies with limited nexus in 1985. This was reinforced by Supreme Court decisions that prevented states from collecting sales taxes on the sales of goods produced by remote sellers, although the Court left the door open for Congress to overturn this preemption by statute.[41] Congress has not acted on this invitation to enable states to extend their sales tax to mobile sales, notwithstanding the efforts by a majority of states to adopt a more uniform sales tax base through the Streamlined Sales Tax Project. Congressional preemptions of state taxation proceeded further than the Court's ruling. In 2007, Congress extended the preemption of state authority to tax Internet access, an action that will reduce state and local revenues by at least $80 million per year according to the Congressional Budget Office.[42]

The intergovernmental capacity to manage change is being put to the test by coercive, opportunistic federalism. The changes in political parties, the media, and interest groups discussed earlier have opened up the intergovernmental system to more and more rapid, exogenous policy changes. Assertive national policies in welfare, education, homeland security, and electoral reform have their roots in crises, events, or political agendas outside of the professional subsystems that have shaped policy and managed implementation under the cooperative federalism model of the past.

THE STATE AND LOCAL SECTOR IN AMERICAN FEDERALISM: RESILIENT BUT BATTERED

The federal system, thus, has become more complex, volatile, and conflictual. Against the backdrop of growing interdependence, the question remains whether the federal system retains its historic capacity for adaptation and flexibility. In a culture that is historically ambivalent about the power and size of the federal government, states' participation helps legitimize new programs and adapts them to the differing conditions and priorities throughout the nation. Moreover, states provide vital laboratories for the nation itself to learn about the efficacy of differing approaches to emerging problems and challenges.

The Tradition of State Resilience

In this regard, states have sustained, and enhanced, their longstanding roles as policy laboratories of innovation in our system. Whether it is global warming or health-care coverage for the uninsured, states have retained their traditional role in our system to serve as policy laboratories. Frustrated by national political and policy gridlock, many groups are finding states to be hospitable and eager champions of new policy ideas and reforms.[43] There are reasons to believe that the reliance on states to generate national policy ideas has accelerated in recent years.

The capacity of our intergovernmental system to pilot and champion policy innovation is found not only in states but also in other intergovernmental settings as well. The Regional Greenhouse Gas Initiative pursued by northeastern states is an example of how states are organizing themselves into regional groups to take the lead on an international policy problem in the face of federal political gridlock.

While state and local governments have traditionally assumed the role of central recipients of grants, even under more coercive instruments such as preemptions, federal officials often have been forced to rely on state and local regulatory regimes to supplement paltry staff levels and to promote greater political support. Partial preemption strategies, for instance, provide states with vital opportunities to exceed federal regulatory standards when participating in federal regulatory enforcement regimes. While perhaps falling short of the cooperative partnerships observed for federal grants, nonetheless the substantial state roles promote a degree of decentralization thanks to the critical role played by states in implementing federal standards, and in some cases in promulgating the standards themselves.

Even under direct order mandates, states have collectively shown a resilience that has prompted greater resistance to centralized programs hatched in the nation's capital. Mandates have a political life cycle that is centralizing in passage and decentralizing in implementation. During the initial passage, state and local government officials are prone to being divided, ambivalent, and actually supportive of the purposes. However, these political dynamics are reversed during the implementation cycle. State and local cohesion grows as the costs and program design challenges become more salient to officials throughout the country; conflict between the goals and priorities of state and local and federal officials heightens at this stage as well, not surprisingly. Thus, for instance, while state and local officials offered little opposition to initial passage of No Child Left Behind, many have joined forces with teachers' unions to mount vigorous protests of the program's standards and constraints, including attempting to gain court injunctions against the program's most onerous mandates. Most states refused to pass broad sweeping changes to their driver's license procedures to comply with the federal Real ID Act of 2005, forcing the federal government to back off and search for a compromise with state leaders.[44] And an emerging coalition of conservative state attorneys general are teaming up to challenge the Obama health-care reform, epitomized by the lawsuits filed by nearly half of the states' attorneys general.

The Eroding Positions of State and Local Governments in the Federal System

While states retain considerable leverage in our federal system, their resilience and capacity to achieve their own unique public policy goals have eroded in recent years. Two forces at work—the growing centralization of the political and economic systems of the nation and the eroding fiscal foundations of state and local budgets—have undermined the voice and capacity of state and local governments to articulate and defend their unique priorities and prerogatives.

Ironically, in the presence of powerful centralizing forces, greater state policy activism has sparked greater federal policy ambition in its wake. Far from earning them forbearance, federal officials have increasingly seized on state-based reforms to institute more centralized federal programs. While many of these programs provide federal funds to hard-pressed states, they also often come laden with centralizing and coercive federal policies as well.

The national adoption of state initiatives results from both state push and national pull. In one recent study of the nationalization of state policies, the advocacy of state officials proved to be the most important factor promoting the national adoption of state policy reforms.[45] Where state policies have external benefits or costs, the initiatives of leading states can often be undermined by the inaction of or opposition by other states. Thus, for instance, states with strong gun-control laws cannot effectively police their borders, because their regulatory regimes are undermined by the importation of guns purchased in states with weaker regulation. Similarly, states with strong climate-change programs could suffer as businesses relocate to states with weaker regulatory profiles. Accordingly, state policy leaders often seek federal policy action to place a floor under the competition from other states.

While states have become more fertile sources of policy innovation, shifts in national political institutions have ensured that national officials will seize on states' initiatives to advance their own policy and political interests. Fundamental changes in our party system have converted national political officials from being ambassadors of state and local party officials to becoming independent political entrepreneurs who seek to gain favor with their constituents by sponsoring national programs and legislation. In a nation with a "24-7" news cycle and thousands of interest groups located in Washington, DC, state issues are often quickly placed on the policy agendas of national leaders. State initiatives are frequently used to illustrate that the new policies are (1) feasible, (2) effective, and (3) popular. At some point, the states' policy initiatives reach a "tipping point" where the policy benefits constitute a national minimum standard or even entitlement.[46] The role of business as a force promoting nationalization of state policies is particularly noteworthy. As business becomes more global, they have shifted from their traditional position of supporting decentralization of policy to the states to seeking national legislation to standardize, restrict, or actually prohibit states' initiatives.[47] Financially, a globalized, technological economy is working to gradually undermine the fiscal underpinnings of state and local finance. A key example is that the retail sales tax, a mainstay of most states' revenue systems, is threatened by the shift to a service-based economy and the rise of purchases made on the Internet.[48] What is more, the growing mobility of investment, employment, and population constricts other revenue sources as well, lest high marginal tax rates prompt a race, slide, or shuffle to the bottom. On the spending side, an aging society will place yet additional demands on the state and local sector to finance health care and pensions for their own employees, as well as serving as fiscal partners in providing national long-term care for an aging population.[49] Already the states' share of Medicaid has become the largest spending item in their budgets, increasingly crowding out other spending priorities for state and local needs. The GAO concludes that, over the next forty years, state and local governments' fiscal outlooks will deteriorate, driven in great part by the exponential growth of health-care costs (figure 3.2).[50]

The aging population, rising health-care costs, and the shifting nature of the economy are secular long-term forces that are difficult for any government to reverse in the short term. These forces are exacerbating vertical fiscal imbalances in our system. Traditional prescriptions in public finance argue that the national government is best positioned to aid the state and local sector due to the superior revenue-raising base enjoyed by national officials. However, the federal government is beset with long-term fiscal deficits due to the very same forces afflicting state and local fiscal capacity. While the federal government has recently provided antirecession assistance to states and localities in the short term, escalating deficits in the short and long term will sap the flexibility and capacity of the federal government to play its time-honored role as the equalizer in public finance.

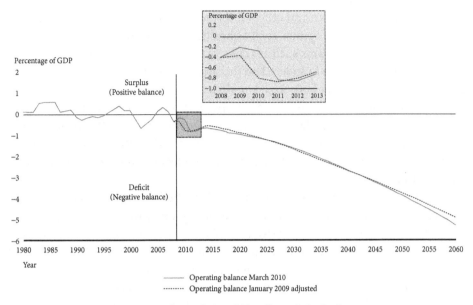

Figure 3.2 State and Local Fiscal Trends and Outlook, 1980–2060
Note: Historical data are from the Bureau of Economic Analysis's National Income and
Product Accounts from 1980 to 2008. Data in 2009 are GAO estimates aligned with
published data where available. GAO simulations are from 2010 to 2060, using many
Congressional Budget Office projections and assumptions, particularly for the next
10 years. Simulations are based on current policy. The term "January 2009 Adjusted"
refers to the results of GAO 09 320R, which we adjusted to reflect the effect of reduced
oil prices on the sector's expenditures. "March 2010" refers to the results of
our most recent simulation in GAO-10-358.
Source: CBO (2007).

CONCLUSION: THE FISCAL FUTURE

The US federal system is at a crossroads. The system has become the central vehicle
for implementing all manner of complex national policy initiatives, whether it is
ready or not. The intergovernmental system has become more contentious, difficult to manage, and less satisfying to all partners in the process. Each type of
government must persevere to pursue conflicting objectives in a complex environment that at best consists of an uneasy and fragile compromise between numerous
competing actors and interests. The public itself has difficulty assigning responsibility for outcomes achieved through this system—a problem that could erode
confidence in government over the longer term.

It is no wonder that serious efforts were made in the 1980s to sort out and
"decongest" the system, with the hope that roles and responsibilities could be clarified and simplified. A common approach was to rethink the fundamental assignment of responsibilities among the national government and the states. Work by

Alice Rivlin, Paul Peterson, and others informed proposals to centralize responsibility for redistributive programs such as health care while devolving responsibilities for distributive programs such as transportation and education.[51]

However, such efforts foundered on the shoals of political opposition, as political actors disagreed about both what should be done and who should do it in such programs as welfare, Medicaid, food stamps, and others. Beyond this, it became apparent that there was little appetite among federal or state officials to surrender control over programs that economists such as Alice Rivlin asserted should be delivered locally while centralizing welfare and health programs that called for national financing and control.[52]

It is difficult to envision a future scenario where the federal government responds to fiscal constraints by sorting out roles or avoiding intergovernmental approaches. Instead, it is more likely to need partners to share costs and responsibilities during such times. Ultimately, as long as vexing and emerging problems continue to be laid at the federal doorstep, intergovernmental systems remain the most optimal way to address complex problems in a compound republic. Intergovernmental systems are best suited for policy areas where there is (1) conflict over the goals and objectives that inhibit the development of purely national programs and (2) wide distribution of resources and capacities necessary to address particular problems or goals. Ultimately, our intergovernmental system is well suited for many of the "wicked" problems we face today—problems with contestable definitions and dimensions and no fixed boundaries.

As federal officials continue to rely on the federal system, it will be increasingly important to understand the capacity of that system to reach national goals. What is the collective capacity of states and localities to achieve national objectives and at what cost to other priorities and objectives that are important? What models of authority allocation and distribution work well for intergovernmental programs and how do they vary across policy areas? What reforms piloted by states can best inform federal initiatives as problems become nationalized? In searching for the answers to these national questions, it is equally important to understand the implications of national programs for the resilience and capacity of state and local governments to address unique needs and priorities across the diverse communities in our nation.

Ironically, as policy agendas and finances became more intertwined and intergovernmentalized, our national capacity to answer these questions and monitor our federal system has withered away. The Advisory Commission on Intergovernmental Relations disappeared more than fifteen years ago. While the GAO and CBO have retained an intergovernmental analytic capacity, the Congress itself has not sustained vital subcommittees with a focus on intergovernmental management. The Office of Management and Budget and the Treasury Department no longer harbor divisions and offices dedicated to focusing on intergovernmental grants and fiscal federalism. Restoring the institutional capacity to analyze our federal system is critical to sustaining a healthy federal system for the trying times ahead.

Notes

1 Bird (2005); Kincaid (this volume).

2 *Federalist* No. 46.

3 See Corwin (1950) and Scheiber (1975). For a contrasting view emphasizing a greater degree of intergovernmental cooperation and sharing, see Elazar (1962).

4 Beer (1975).

5 Walker (1998).

6 Johnson (2006).

7 *Pollock v. Farmers' Loan & Trust Company* (1895), *Adkins v. Children's Hospital* (1923), and *Hammer v. Dagenhart* (1918).

8 *Hipolite Egg Co. v. United States* (1911), *Hoke v. United States* (1913), and *Massachusetts v. Mellon* (1923).

9 Derthick (2001).

10 Leuchtenburg (1963); Patterson (1981).

11 *United States v. Darby* (1941); *United States v. Butler* (1936); *Wickard v. Filburn* (1942).

12 Wallis (2006).

13 Walker (1998), 17.

14 Conlan (1998).

15 Scheppach and Shafroth (2008).

16 US Advisory Commission on Intergovernmental Relations (1986).

17 Eads (this volume).

18 Conlan and Posner (forthcoming).

19 Derthick (1970).

20 See US Advisory Commission on Intergovernmental Relations (1984); Kincaid (1990); Posner (1998).

21 US Office of Management and Budget (2010), 246.

22 Dilger (2009), 6.

23 Reischauer (1977).

24 Yilmaz, Vaillancourt, and Dafflon (this volume); Break (1980), chapter 3.

25 Beam (1980).

26 Yilmaz and Zahradnik (2008).

27 US Government Accountability Office (1997), 27.

28 Ingram (1977), 509.

29 Seidman (1997).

30 Peterson, Rabe, and Wong (1986).

31 US Government Accountability Office (1981), 17.

32 US Advisory Commission on Intergovernmental Relations (1995), 18.

33 Zimmerman (1992) 119.

34 Walker (1998).

35 Kaiser Family Foundation (2011). For fiscal years 2009 and 2010, the federal Medicaid matching rate was temporarily increased by 6.2 percentage points, which decreased the median state matching rate in those years to just over 30 percent.

36 US Advisory Commission on Intergovernmental Relations (1994).

37 US Advisory Commission on Intergovernmental Relations (1984).

38 Posner (1998).

39 The implementation of Real ID—a federal law requiring additional security provisions in the issuing of state driver's licenses—has been postponed by the federal Department

of Homeland Security following actions by nearly two-thirds of the states registering opposition or prohibiting their participation. "Real ID Postponed by the Department of Homeland Security," *Government Technology News,* December 18, 2009.

40 McNichol (2010).

41 Fox (this volume); *National Bellas Hess Inc. v. Illinois Department of Revenue,* 386 US 753 (1967); *Quill Corporation, Petitioner v. North Dakota, by and through its Tax Commissioner, Heidi Heitkamp,* 504 US 298 (1992).

42 CBO report on HR 3778, Internet Tax Freedom Act Amendments of 2007.

43 Nathan (2008).

44 "Real ID Postponed by the Department of Homeland Security," *Government Technology News,* December 18, 2009.

45 Aulisi, Larsen, Pershing, and Posner (2007).

46 Posner (1998).

47 Posner (2008).

48 Scheppach and Shafroth (2008); Fox (this volume).

49 Wallace (this volume).

50 US Government Accountability Office (2007).

51 Peterson, Rabe, and Wong (1986); Rivlin (1992).

52 Rivlin (1992).

References

Adkins v. Children's Hospital, 261 US 525 (1923).

Aulisi, Andrew, John Larsen, Jonathan Pershing, and Paul Posner (2007). *Climate Policy in the State Laboratory: How States Influence Federal Regulation and the Implications for Climate Change Policy in the United States.* Washington, DC: World Resources Institute.

Beam, David R. (1980). Economic Theory as Policy Prescription: Pessimistic Findings on "Optimizing" Grants. In Helen Ingram and Dean Mann (Eds.), *Why Policies Succeed or Fail.* Beverly Hills, CA: Sage Publications.

Beer, Samuel. H. (1973). The Modernization of American Federalism. *Publius: The Journal of Federalism, 3* 49–96.

Bird, Richard. M. (2005). Fiscal Federalism. In Joseph J. Cordes, Robert D. Ebel, and Jane G. Gravelle (Eds.), *The Encyclopedia of Taxation and Tax Policy, Second Edition.* Washington, DC: Urban Institute Press. 146–149.

Break, George. (1980). *Financing Government in a Federal System.* Washington, DC: Brookings Institution.

Conlan, Timothy J. (1998). *From New Federalism to Devolution: Twenty-five Years of Intergovernmental Reform.* Washington, DC: Brookings Institution.

Conlan, Timothy J., and Paul L. Posner (2011). Inflection Point? Federalism and the Obama Administration. *Publius: The Journal of Federalism, 41,* 421–446.

Corwin, Edwin S. (1950). The Passing of Dual Federalism. *Virginia Law Review, 36,* 1–22.

Derthick, Martha (2001). *Keeping the Compound Republic: Essays on American Federalism.* Washington, DC: Brookings Institution.

Derthick, Martha (1970). *The Influence of Federal Grants,* Cambridge, MA: Harvard University Press.

Dilger, Robert J. (2009). *Federal Grants in Aid: An Historical Perspective on Contemporary Issues.* Washington, DC: Congressional Research Service.

Elazar, Daniel J. (1962). *The American Partnership: Intergovernmental Cooperation in the United States.* Chicago: University of Chicago Press.

Hammer v. Dagenhart, 247 US 251 (1918).

Hipolite Egg Co. v. United States, 220 US 45 (1911).

Hoke v. United States, 227 US 308 (1913).

Ingram, Helen (1977). Policy Implementation through Bargaining: The Case of Federal Grants-in-Aid. *Public Policy,* 25, 499–526.

Johnson, Kimberly (2006). *Governing the American State: Congress and the New Federalism.* Princeton, NJ: Princeton University Press.

Kaiser Family Foundation. (2011). *Federal Medical Assistance Percentage [FMAP] for Medicaid and Multiplier.* Retrieved January 28, 2011, from www.statehealthfacts.org/comparetable.jsp?ind=184&cat=4

Kincaid, John (1990, May). From Cooperative to Coercive Federalism. *Annals of the American Academy of Political and Social Science,* 509, 139–152.

Leuchtenburg, William E. (1963). *Franklin D. Roosevelt and the New Deal, 1932–1940.* New York: Harper & Row.

Massachusetts v. Mellon, 262 US 447 (1923).

McNichol, Elizabeth (2010). State Taxes on Inherited Wealth Remain Common. Washington, DC: Center for Budget and Policy Priorities.

Nathan, Richard. P. (2008). Updating Theories of American Federalism. In Timothy J. Conlan and Paul L. Posner (Eds.), *Intergovernmental Management in the 21st Century.* Washington, DC: Brookings Institution. 13–25.

National Bellas Hess Inc. v. Illinois Department of Revenue, 386 US 753 (1967).

Patterson, James T. (1981). *The New Deal and the States; Federalism in Transition.* San Francisco: Greenwood Press.

Peterson, Paul E., Rabe, Barry, & Wong, Kenneth (1986). *Making Federalism Work.* Washington, DC: Brookings Institution.

Pollock v. Farmers' Loan & Trust Company, 157 US 429 (1895).

Posner, Paul L. (1998). *The Politics of Federal Mandates: Whither Federalism?* Washington, DC: Georgetown University Press.

Posner, Paul L. (2008). Mandates: The Politics of Coercive Federalism. In T. Conlan and P. L. Posner, *Intergovernmental Management for the 21st Century.* Washington, DC: Brookings Institution. 286–309.

Quill Corporation, Petitioner v. North Dakota, by and through its Tax Commissioner, Heidi Heitkamp, 504 US 298 (1992).

Reischauer, Robert. D. (1977). Government Diversity: Bame of the Grants Strategy in the United States. In Wallace E. Oates (Ed.), *The Political Economy of Fiscal Federalism.* Lexington, MA: D. C. Heath. 115–128.

Rivlin, Alice (1992). *Reviving the American Dream: The Economy, the States and the Federal Government.* Washington, DC: Brookings Institution.

Scheiber, Harry N. (1975). Federalism and the American Economic Order, 1789–1910. *Law and Society Review,* 57–118.

Scheppach, Raymond C., and Shafroth, Frank (2008). Intergovernmental Finance in the New Global Economy: An Integrated Approach. In Timothy J. Conlan and Paul Posner (Eds.), *Intergovernmental Management for the 21st Century.* Washington, DC: Brookings Institution. 42–76.

Seidman, Harold (1997). *Politics, Position and Power* (5th ed.). New York: Oxford University Press.

United States v. Butler, 297 US1 (1936).

United States v. Darby Lumber Co., 312 US 100 (1941).

US Advisory Commission on Intergovernmental Relations. (1995). *Characteristics of Federal Grant-in-Aid Programs to State and Local Governments, M-195*. Washington, DC: US ACIR.

US Advisory Commission on Intergovernmental Relations,. (1994). *Federally Induced Costs Affecting State and Local Governments, M-193*. Washington, DC: US ACIR.

US Advisory Commission on Intergovernental Relations. (1986). *The Transformation in American Politics: Implications for Federalism, A-106*. Washington, DC: US ACIR.

US Advisory Commission on Intergovernmental Relations. (1984). *Regulatory Federalism: Policy, Process, Impact and Reform, A-95*. Washington, DC: US ACIR.

US Government Accountability Office. (1997). *Federal Grants: Design Improvements Could Help Federal Resources Go Further, GAO/AIMD-97-7*. Washington, DC: GAO.

US Government Accountability Office. (1981). *Proposed Changes in Federal Matching and Maintenance of Effort Requirements for State and Local Governments, GGD-81-7*. Washington, DC: GAO.

US Government Accountability Office. (2007). *State and Local Governments: Persistent Fiscal Challenges Will Likely Emerge Within the Next Decade, GAO-07-1080SP*. Washington, DC: GAO.

US Office of Management and Budget (2010). *Analytical Perspectives, Budget of the United States Government, Fiscal Year 2009*. Washington, DC: OMB.

Walker, David B. (1998). *The Rebirth of Federalism: Slouching toward Washington*. Chatham, NJ: Chatham House.

Wallis, John J. (2006). Government Finance and Employment. In Susan B. Carter (Ed.), *Historical Statistics of the United States, Earliest Times to the Present*. New York: Cambridge University Press. 5–11.

Wickard v. Filburn, 317 US 111 (1942).

Yilmaz, Yesim, and Robert Zahradnik (2008). Measuring the Fiscal Capacity of the District of Columbia: A Comparison of Revenue Capacity and Expenditure Need, FY 2005. Washington, DC: National Tax Association.

Zimmerman, Joseph F. (1992). *Contemporary American Federalism: The Growth of National Power*. Westport, CT: Praeger.

CHAPTER 4

···

STATE AND LOCAL GOVERNMENT FINANCE: WHY IT MATTERS

···

SERDAR YILMAZ, FRANÇOIS VAILLANCOURT, AND BERNARD DAFFLON

Intergovernmental reforms have been at the center of public-sector change in countries across the globe. Indeed, the World Development Report on *Entering the 21st Century* asserts that two forces will influence development policy in the first part of this century: *globalization* (the continuing integration of countries) and *localization* (self-determination and the devolution of power).[1] This force of "localization," which in the international literature is also referred to as "decentralization," is that of the division of public-sector functions among multiple types of government, both central and subnational. Such "decentralization" is occurring in unitary and federal states alike.

Established theories in economics and political science have articulated the efficiency and accountability gains that could accrue from decentralization reforms. The efficiency and accountability gains promised by a well-designed intergovernmental system range from the internalization of spillover effects,[2] alleviation of information asymmetry and better accountability due to the proximity of principals and agents,[3] and the improvements in service delivery and revenue policy that may result from the fiscal competition among local governments.[4]

This chapter, which is designed to inform fiscal federalism policy in the United States by laying out a set of "fiscal decentralization" principles that apply to not only the United States but also to countries around the world, begins with a generalized discussion of the "assignment" or functional roles among different types of governments and then proceeds to develop the theoretical case for decentralized governance. Recognizing that a well-designed assignment of functions among different types of governments will likely result in both vertical and horizontal fiscal imbalances, the paper concludes with a conceptual examination of the critical role of intergovernmental transfers in making intergovernmental finance "work."

DISTRIBUTION OF FUNCTIONS AMONG TYPES OF GOVERNMENTS

A seminal contribution to the theory of the intergovernmental assignment of functions was provided by Richard Musgrave in his *Theory of Public Finance*[5] in which he identifies three functions of the public sector: (1) macroeconomic stabilization; (2) income redistribution; and (3) efficient allocation of resources. At a very general level, the central (in the United States, federal) government should have basic responsibility for macroeconomic stabilization and income redistribution functions. There are two tools in carrying out stabilization policy: fiscal policy tools and monetary policy tools. The three usual pro-centralization arguments for stabilization policy tools are the following:[6] (1) local economies are open economies and, as such, there is little chance that stabilization efforts initiated locally will bear fruit in this same local arena; (2) given that fact, local government units could adopt a do-little-or-nothing strategy, letting the other local governments implement stabilization policies whose effects would spill over in their favor; and (3) limiting local deficits and debt may be appropriate if financial markets do not function properly to ensure budget discipline.[7] With respect to this last point, there are two perspectives among public finance experts, known respectively under the terms of budget "discipline" versus "accountability."[8]

The second tool, monetary policy, is obviously one that can be used by only the central government bank (in the United States, this is the Federal Reserve Bank). Thus, stabilization is assigned to the center.

Under Musgrave's model, policies to adjust the inter-individual/household distribution of a nation's income and wealth—thus the distribution function—also accrue to the center. This is because the full (assumed) mobility of both the rich and the poor between subnational entities makes it impossible for one such government to have more generous policies toward the poor than others if it has to finance these policies itself, be it only at the margin. Either the poor will move in (overloading the expenditure side and thus requiring higher taxes), or the rich will move out (starving the revenue side), or both will happen simultaneously. A subnational government (SNG) could have pro-rich policies to encourage outmigration of the poor but this would be undesirable from an overall allocative perspective. This would lead to segregation and thus to a reduction in the externalities that emerge from mixing in a given territory various groups.[9] However, there are costs associated with mobility. In small countries (Belgium, for example), differences in ethno-linguistic-religious characteristics between subnational entities could reduce mobility from one jurisdiction to another. In large countries, distance and its associated costs may be a barrier to mobility even if there are no differences in these characteristics. Thus it is conceivable to have some subnational income distribution policies.

This leaves the efficiency argument—i.e., *allocation* policy—as the traditional *raison d'être* for the subnational role. This is not to say that an efficient provision of public goods requires only subnational activity. Indeed, that is not the case. Some social goods are such that the incidence of their benefits is nationwide (i.e., national defense, certain aspects of public health, some court systems), while others are geographically limited (i.e., street lighting, water distribution, public safety, fire protection).

The recognition that the allocation function is an intergovernmental responsibility applies not only to broad functions of services, but also within functions. Elementary education provides a good example. A nation as a whole has a strong interest in a well-educated population, as does the locality where the service is provided. This fact, when combined with the spatial limitations of benefit incidence, suggests that the responsibility for education can be broken into several subfunctions (e.g., financing, which is primarily a local function, especially with respect to capital expenditures; setting the curricula, such as a national "core" curriculum supplemented by local options; teacher certification, to which the central goverment may wish to set minimum standards; staff hiring, firing, and salary determination; and textbook selection).

The Allocation Function

In the "next seminal" contribution to the theory of intergovernmental finance, Wallace Oates presented four criteria for assigning functional responsibilities across types of governments:[10]

  i. *Economies of scale* will vary across goods and services. Economies of scale are significant in broadcasting, for example, where the unit cost per viewer drops by half (absent the need for additional broadcasting equipment) when the number of viewers of a given program doubles, but negligible in the provision of individualized health services such as surgical treatment. The existence of significant economies of scale constitutes an argument for a national or regional (e.g., special purpose) government to provide a particular good or service.

ii. *Heterogeneity of preferences and of circumstances* also matters. Groups living in different parts of a country may display strong heterogeneity of preferences or may be faced with different environments in terms of climate or topography. They may therefore prefer or may need different amounts (more or fewer) of services, a different quality of service (for a given amount), or a different language for delivering public services. Decentralization is an appropriate vehicle to address these needs.[11]

iii. *The presence of externalities*, negative or positive, has an impact. If some of the activities of one government have important external effects on the individuals or businesses located in other jurisdictions or on other government types, then these activities should be well coordinated among the affected governments.

iv. *Emulation*, also referred to as competition, which helps increase or introduce best practices in government, requires at least two, and probably more, units involved in a given activity. This is an argument for decentralizing government activities.

In general, governments have three mechanisms to carry out their assigned functions: "functional" spending made through the budgetary process, regulation of private activities, and tax expenditures. The most common one is the *functional budget*—that is, the cost and accounting financial plan of the government's spending.[12] *Regulations* are both complements and substitutes to budgetary spending. This typically involves mandating private agents to spend on tasks that the government would otherwise carry out or requiring them to modify their behaviors, with or without a cost to them. For example, business firms are often required to dispose of their "own" solid waste, with such regulations accompanied by fines for noncompliance. The use of such regulation to impose costs on households or firms cannot be justified on the basis that it reduces budgetary government spending. Regulation can, however, be appropriate if they are designed to "internalize" what are appropriately private-sector costs of production and/or privately generated external costs to society as a whole.[13] They are also appropriate if private provision is less expensive than public provision due to low density, for example; hence, requiring residents to have septic tanks can be a substitute for installing a sewer system in a given jurisdiction with both high- and low-density parts. The distinction between national and local regulations is relevant. Noise regulations are by nature mostly local while the regulation of greenhouse gases is national in scope.

A third, and often much less transparent, way of spending is by the use of "tax expenditures"—revenue losses resulting from tax provisions that grant special tax relief designed to encourage certain kinds of taxpayer behavior or to aid taxpayers in special circumstances. Tax expenditures may take one of several forms, can be hard to measure, and are typically not given the periodic budget review required for good public financial management.[14]

Governments, by using these three mechanisms, provide goods and services that are not produced by the private sector in efficient amounts for various reasons.

The Case for the Provision of Local Public Goods

Different goods and services provided by the government have beneficiary areas with different sizes. Certain publicly provided goods and services including public goods, such as national defense and environmental protection, have a beneficiary area defined by both national boundaries and treaties obligations and explicit and implicit agreements. These kinds of goods and services are national and sometimes international in terms of their beneficiary areas; other publicly provided goods and services, such as street lighting and garbage collection, have beneficiary areas limited to local jurisdictions. Some of these publicly provided goods are called local public goods, being understood that local is non-national and thus can yet also be regional.[15]

While the theoretical argument for public goods comes from Paul Samuelson, he did not make a distinction between public goods with large catchment (benefit) areas such as defense and other public goods that are similar in outcomes (protection from unwarranted use of force) but more local in nature, such as policing.[16] Charles Tiebout subsequently makes the distinction and examines the difference between national and local public goods.[17] He argues that when citizens have differing personal valuations on local public services and varying ability to pay the attendant taxes, they will move from one jurisdiction to another until they find the one that maximizes their personal utility.[18]

Although conceptually the distinction between national and local public goods is very intuitive, practically it is not always clear. The question is, what kinds of services are local public goods and what kinds of services are national public goods? A classic example is the difference between street lighting and national defense. Street lighting is a local public good with a defined catchment area whereas national defense is a national public good that covers the entire territory of a country and perhaps that of its allies. However, one should note that broad headings of public activities can be misleading. For example in health, vaccination or food inspection activities have national impacts while the provision of ambulance services has a local impact.

The difference in the sizes of beneficiary areas for national and local publicly provided goods and services and regulations lends itself to decentralized delivery of these goods and services. The economic case for decentralized service delivery is based on the welfare gains from an improved allocation of resources. Decentralization allows local governments to tailor the levels of public services to the particular tastes and circumstances of their communities. Local governments are closer to the people and they possess knowledge of local preferences. Decentralized governments have their *raison d'être* in the provision of goods and services whose consumption is limited to their own jurisdictions. Since the efficient level of output (quantity and associated characteristics) of a local public good is likely to vary across jurisdictions, decentralized provision of services increases overall economic welfare. By tailoring local service delivery to the particular preferences and circumstances of their population, local government provision of local publicly provided goods and services increases economic welfare above that which results from the more uniform levels of national government service delivery. Furthermore, differential level of unit cost of service delivery across jurisdictions provides overall welfare gains to an economy.

Therefore, divergence in demand across jurisdiction and interjurisdictional cost differentials are two important sources of welfare gains from decentralization: divergences in demand for local public goods and services, and divergences in the cost of local public goods and services.

1. Divergences in Demand for Local Public Goods and Services

Figure 4.1 depicts the demand curves for local services of jurisdictions one (D_1) and two (D_2) per household. If we assume that local publicly provided goods and services can be provided at a constant cost per unit of MC, the optimal output levels are Q_1 in jurisdiction one and Q_2 in jurisdiction two—assuming that there are no interjurisdictional spillover effects. If the central government decides on the level of output and is unwilling to or is unable, due to legal/regulatory constraints, to provide anything but a uniform output, a uniform level of output of Q_C could be provided in all jurisdictions.[19] If the central provision of Q_C replaces the independent local provision Q_1 and Q_2, then the loss of social welfare from centralized provision would be the sum of triangles ABC for residents of jurisdiction one and DCE for residents of jurisdiction two.[20] A uniform, centrally determined level of local public goods and services will result in a lower level of social welfare than decentralized service provision, where each local government provides an optimal level of local service in its jurisdiction. This is the Decentralization Theorem.[21] The greater the divergence between D_1 and D_2—the population is more heterogeneous— the larger will be the triangles ABC and DCE—the greater the potential gains from decentralization. And if either Q_1 or Q_2 were provided, then one triangle would shrink to zero but the other would increase.

In a Tiebout equilibrium, individuals locate in jurisdictions that satisfy their demands for local public services; thus, localities are perfectly homogeneous in terms of demand for local public goods and services. In Tiebout's model, mobile households "vote with their feet": they choose their jurisdictions in which to reside according to the fiscal package (revenue and expenditure) that is best suited for their preferences. Decentralization is thus more important where the demand and

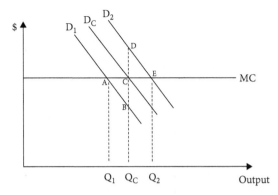

Figure 4.1 Decentralization theorem: divergent demands for local public goods
Source: Adapted from Oates (1997).

ensuing supply for local public goods has greater variation across local governments. In places where the population is homogeneous and has similar tastes and preferences for local publicly provided goods and services, the potential welfare gains from decentralization are smaller.

Table 4.1, which is adapted from Oates (1997), shows an example of the impact of the mobility implicit in the Tiebout model. There are three areas in one country that can become three local jurisdictions (I, II and III) that are susceptible of producing two local public services, either S_1 or S_2. There are seventy-one residents in the country who are also beneficiaries and voters. With central provision, a majority vote gives thirty-six voices to S_2; the unsatisfied minority is thirty-five. With devolution, residents (or voters) in jurisdictions I and III choose to produce for local public provision S_1 while S_2 is chosen for jurisdiction II. Without an alternative, there would be altogether twenty-five unsatisfied residents. The "central" versus "devolved provision" solutions correspond to that of figure 4.1 (that is, D_c and D_1/D_2). In the Tiebout model, unsatisfied minorities could move to a preferred jurisdiction; in the example, minorities in I and III could choose to move to jurisdiction II. In this solution, no one is forced to accept the provision of an unwanted local service. Of course, the cost of moving remains to be taken into consideration; also, jurisdictions I and III, which provide the same service, should consider the possible economies of scale in producing S1.[22]

2. Divergences in Cost of Local Public Goods and Services

Cost differentials of service delivery across jurisdictions can also be a source of welfare gains from fiscal decentralization. Figure 4.2 (as with Figure 4.1, also adapted from Oates, 1997) depicts a case where the demand curve, D_c, is the same for local publicly provided services but the marginal cost of local services differs between the two jurisdictions. MC_1 is the marginal cost of local service delivery in jurisdiction one and MC_2 is the marginal cost of local service delivery in jurisdiction two. In figure 4.2 the Pareto efficient outcomes are Q_1 and Q_2. In this case, centralized provision of a uniform level of output at the average marginal cost,

Table 4.1. Example of a Tiebout model.

Jurisdiction	Central provision		Devolved provision No mobility		Tiebout model	
(wards with central provision, independent entities when devolved or Tiebout)	S_1	S_2	Majority choice	# in minority	Choice	Mobility *Vote by moving (with their feet)* Mobile population Final population
I	10	8	$10-S_1$	8	S_1	8 go to II	$10 + 5 = 15$
II	5	16	$16-S_2$	5	S_2	5 go to I	$16 + 8 + 12 = 36$
III	20	12	$20-S_1$	12	S_1	12 go to II	20
Majority		36	46				36 and 35
Unsatisfied	35			25			0
Characteristics of outcome	Central command		Specialization respect of minorities creativity, proximity		Specialization, respect of minorities, proximity, fiscal competition	

Source: Authors.

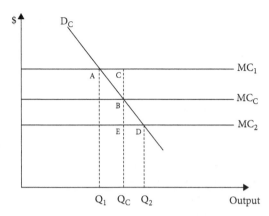

Figure 4.2 Decentralization theorem: divergent costs for local public goods
Source: Adapted from Oates (1997).

Q_C, results in the welfare loss of triangle ABC in jurisdiction one and triangle BED in jurisdiction two. The size of the welfare loss depends on the distance between MC_1 and MC_2. The welfare gains from decentralization will be greater if the demand for local services is more price-responsive.

REVENUES

Once the assignment of service delivery responsibilities is decided, the next question is to assign financing sources to local governments to carry out those responsibilities. In an effective local government system, local governments must have control over some of their revenues. Local governments that lack independent sources of revenue can never truly enjoy fiscal autonomy, because they may be—and probably are—under the financial thumb of the central government. A rational assignment of revenue-raising powers helps each type of government control its fiscal destiny.

The important question is which revenue sources can and should be assigned to which type of government. This is commonly referred to as the tax assignment problem.[23] It is closely related to the assignment of expenditures, both because of the importance, at least in principle, of benefit taxation and because of the need for adequacy of revenues to finance local expenditures. An adequate assignment of revenue-raising powers permits choice in the level of public spending by each type of government.

Each type of government should be assigned taxes that finance the costs of the benefits derived from the services delivered by that governmental unit (this is the "matching principle" of public finance). Thus, the proper assignment of taxes that are related to benefits depends on the assignment of service delivery responsibilities. In other words, to the fullest extent possible, local services should be financed by user charges and fees. This is both fair and efficient in the sense of encouraging the responsible use of economic resources.[24] However, user charges, fees, and taxes related to the benefits of public spending are likely to be regressive. Therefore they are unlikely to reduce income inequality.[25] For both equity and efficiency purposes, tax rates should reflect the costs and benefits of public services. For example, taxes levied on motor vehicles and motor fuels are benefit-related and receipts from these taxes can be used to construct and maintain roads. Furthermore, such taxes can also be levied for the purpose of reducing congestion and pollution—or both when the direct value of the service provided to the user as well as social costs are factored in.

The notion of subsidiarity in taxation means a given tax should be "exercised by those authorities which are closest to the citizens" (and "where practicable").[26] Compliance with subsidiarity principle is important to minimize the tendency toward vertical imbalance.[27]

Another guiding principle in designing an intergovernmental fiscal system is that subnational governments must have enough "own" revenues to finance the services they provide.[28] Even if such subnational governments rely on grants from a central government, if the grants are determined in an objective way and are guaranteed by the constitution or by long-standing legislation, they may be considered to be own revenues at least in the short term, such as the agreed period of a transfer formula. But these revenues are revenues that cannot be increased or decreased by these subnational governments because they do not have access to the base or rate so it is incomplete ownership as in the private ownership of a protected wetland. On the other hand, if grants are made at the sole discretion of the donor government, perhaps on an ad hoc, arbitrary, or unpredictable basis, and even well into the fiscal year and subject to renegotiation, subnational governments may be considered to have an inadequate level of revenues. In between these extremes, other arrangements include tax surcharges levied by one type of government (e.g., a local general-purpose government) but collected by another government (e.g., the state unit) as in the case of revenue base sharing and tax piggybacking. All of these arrangements may be seen as own revenues if there is no substantial risk for revenues accruing to the subnational governments.

If subnational governments are to be truly autonomous, they must be assigned marginal sources of own revenues—that is, they have some level of control over their revenues.[29] If they can legislate[30] and implement their own taxes and if they are allowed to impose surcharges on the taxes levied by the central government at rates they choose, they can influence the amount of revenues they receive at the margin—thus, they control their revenues. Marginal revenue-raising powers allow residents of subnational jurisdictions to choose the level of public services they want.

In assigning revenue-raising powers to subnational governments, it is important to distinguish four aspects of revenue assignment: which government (1) determines tax policy choices, in other words, who makes policy decision on taxes from which subnational governments receive revenues, (2) defines the tax bases, (3) sets the tax rates, and (4) administers the taxes.

- *Tax policy*: For the public finance economist, the goal of taxation is to pay for collectively demanded goods and services (as discussed above) that are required in order to achieve an efficiency in the allocation of resources. For the jurist, to cite US Justice Oliver Wendell Holmes, "taxes are what we pay for civilized society."[31] The *efficiency* aspects have been addressed above. *Equity* in taxation has both horizontal and vertical components. Horizontal equity is present when there is equal tax treatment of taxpayers who are in the same circumstances to pay taxes. Vertical equity concerns the proper relationship between the relative tax burdens paid by individuals with different capacities to pay taxes. There is no agreed-upon formula for setting the proper degree of progressivity of taxation. "Progressivity" depends on factors such as the degree of inter-individual solidarity in a society and the degree of shirking by potential recipients of transfers. But it is likely that, given the issues raised with respect to income distribution above, subnational taxes will be less progressive than national ones. In this context, which type of government decides which taxes are to be levied by which type of government is an important aspect of the revenue assignment issue. However, subnational governments clearly cannot be allowed total discretion in the choice of the taxes they can levy. For example, given administrative and efficiency considerations, they should not be allowed to levy import duties on international trade or trade between subnational jurisdictions.[32]
- *Tax base*: For efficiency purposes, it is important for subnational governments to have some control over tax bases. But for shared taxes, it is preferable for administrative and compliance reasons to have the same base used by all tax-levying jurisdictions.[33]
- *Tax rate*: For subnational governments, setting the tax rates is clearly the most important aspect of their fiscal sovereignty. If subnational governments have the authority on the local tax rate (or fee, or charge), one then has an "own" tax. If the subnational does has not have control over the tax rate (e.g., if the rate is set by a state or central government), the tax is not a "local" own revenue.[34]
- *Tax revenue administration*: Choosing which type of government collects local own revenues often entails weighing the trade-offs among collection efforts, collection rates and administrative (including enforcement) and taxpayer-incurred compliance costs vis-à-vis revenue generated. While central governments may have low marginal collection costs, they may also have low marginal collections because collecting local taxes may not be a priority for their tax collectors. The answer will thus depend on a thorough examination of institutional arrangements. While some argue that, in allocating revenue administration functions, overall administrative and

compliance costs for the entire national and subnational system should be taken into consideration,[35] this is not the sole consideration. Local autonomy may come with higher administrative or collection costs; central collection may come with lower local revenues than would otherwise be generated. One workable intergovernmental arrangement that is typical in many US states is for the local government to maintain its tax autonomy by "piggybacking" the local rate on a state-determined and state-administered tax base.[36]

These dimensions of revenue-raising powers have important implications for how revenues are linked to services that are provided. Some of the services that subnational governments provide can be described as producing generalized benefits, or benefits that cannot be closely related to taxes on the beneficiaries.[37] The general benefits of subnational government spending may be loosely related to income or to private consumption. In these cases, unless there is some reason to believe that benefits rise more or less rapidly than income or consumption, relying on flat-rate taxes on income or consumption to finance such services may be reasonable. If people do not work where they live (or if they do not invest their savings where they live), an important tax policy choice is whether production or consumption (income earned or income spent) is the better measure of generalized benefits. If the benefits of public spending are more closely related to production or the earning of income than to consumption or the spending of income, origin-based taxes on value-added taxes (VATs) and payroll taxes levied where employment occurs would be superior to destination-based VATs, retail sales taxes, and residence-based income taxes as measures of benefits received.

Consumption (the spending of income) is more closely related to the benefits of public spending than is production (the earning of income). For example, public education is usually provided where people live, not where they work, and the same tends to be true for health care and social aid. Therefore, for the purpose of taxing generalized benefits of public services, residence-based income taxes are probably superior to employment-based payroll taxes, and destination (consumption)-based sales taxes are better than origin (production)-based ones. This may be difficult if personal income taxation is not available to subnational governments. In that case, payroll taxation levied in the region of employment but allocated (e.g., by compact) on the basis of the place of residence of workers (share of wage bill) may be a solution.

Various approaches to assigning revenues to subnational governments differ in the degree of fiscal autonomy they provide to subnational governments. In certain countries, like Canada (provincial), Switzerland (cantonal), and the United States (state), the national constitution (as in the case of the United States), or independent subnational legislation and administration, provides subnational governments with very high fiscal autonomy.[38] In these countries, subnational governments choose the taxes they levy, define the tax bases, set the tax rates, and administer the taxes.[39] In some cases, subnational jurisdictions enter into competition to attract businesses and wealthy individuals to their localities.[40]

Although tax competition can protect citizens from the rapaciousness of politicians and bureaucrats, excessive subnational latitude in the choice of tax bases and in tax administration can create unacceptable complexity and administrative burdens, as well as inequities and distortions in the allocation of resources. In extreme cases, tax competition exposes the public finance system to inconsistency, duplication of effort, and excessive complexity of compliance and administration. These problems can occur if different jurisdictions choose radically different taxes (for example, if some levy retail sales taxes, but others levy VATs as is the case in Canada), define their tax bases in different ways (as in the case of state corporate income taxes and retail sales taxes in the United States), or administer the same taxes in different ways.[41]

In other countries (but also, as noted above for the United States), local governments may (but only with the approval of the state) employ surcharges or piggyback taxes on a state tax. For a surcharge, the surcharge rate is set locally but both the main tax and the surcharge are collected by the government responsible for the main tax. For a piggyback tax, the rate is set locally and the tax is also collected locally; it is piggybacking on an existing tax base. It is, thus, using information already available to the taxpayer to compute a different tax.[42] Ideally, in these countries, the intergovernmental finance system is less prone to the problems that occur when different subnational jurisdictions define the tax base in conflicting ways, use different apportionment formulas, and administer the tax in different ways. In a surcharge regime, although subnational governments don't have the ability to define the tax base and administer taxes, they have the power to set surcharge rates—the most important attribute of fiscal sovereignty.

Subnational surcharges provide appropriate means with their own marginal revenues in cases where revenue bases are scarce. However, an incentive problem in subnational surcharge regimes is that the tax-collecting government may not collect a tax for itself but only for others. In those cases where the tax rate of the collecting government is low or zero, the case for uniformity and efficiency advantages from centralized collection must be high.

The last approach is that of tax sharing. Under tax-sharing arrangements, subnational governments receive fixed fractions of revenues from particular national taxes originating within their boundaries. In general the sharing rates are uniform across jurisdictions, but there is always variation across taxes. This approach restricts subnational governments' fiscal autonomy. Although individual subnational governments have autonomy over how to spend a given amount of the shared revenue, they do not have the power to alter the amount of revenue they receive. Therefore, they have limited control over the level of public spending.[43] In general, there is a formula to determine the deemed origin of tax revenues. Thus, the degree of the loss of autonomy will depend on whether the formula is written in the constitution (as in Switzerland), in the financial law, or is annually decided by a legislative body as part of the budget process.

TRANSFERS

Intergovernmental transfers may compose a significant portion of subnational governments' revenues in all countries and are therefore an essential component of intergovernmental fiscal arrangements. [44] Their design has important efficiency and equity implications on the provision of local public service. In general, intergovernmental transfers have three principal objectives: (1) to equalize vertically (improve revenue adequacy); (2) to equalize horizontally (interjurisdictional redistribution); and (3) to minimize interjurisdictional spillovers (externalities). They may also be used to allow the federal government a presence in policy areas where it has no direct role in the provision of publicly provided goods and services. This is the case for education in the United States (No Child Left Behind) or health in Canada (Canada Health Transfers).[45]

Vertical fiscal imbalance is the disparity between revenue sources and expenditure needs of subnational governments. A vertical imbalance occurs when the expenditure responsibilities of subnational governments do not match with their revenue-raising powers. A horizontal imbalance occurs when own fiscal capacities to carry out the same functions differ across subnational governments resulting from the following factors:

- Unequal distribution of revenue bases, natural resources, and wealth across subnational governments
- Variations in the socioeconomic characteristics of population
- Differences in the geography and climate across jurisdictions that lead to disparities in subnational economic opportunities or costs in the provision of goods and services

A third objective of intergovernmental transfers is to correct for interjurisdictional spillovers. Some subnational government services' benefits (or costs) extend beyond the borders of the jurisdiction. For example, an outbreak of a disease in one jurisdiction may have an impact on the overall health situation in neighboring communities. However, the subnational units may be unwilling to provide an efficient level of certain services if they believe that people who reside outside the jurisdiction will benefit from many of the resulting benefits. To ensure that local governments provide a greater amount of those services, the central (e.g., federal) government may transfer resources to them.

There are two general kinds of transfers: conditional and unconditional. In conditional transfers, the transferring authority specifies the purpose of use for these funds. The use of conditional transfer funds is limited to a specific sector that is highly important to the transferring government, such as education, health, housing, and environmental. These types of transfers are sometimes called specific purpose grants or categorical grants. There are different types of conditional transfers:

A. *Open-Ended, Matching:* For a unit of money given by the donor, the recipient should spend some amount and there is no cap on the amount of funds transferred to the recipient. Open-ended means as long as the recipient provides cofinancing; the donor government will contribute its share as well.

B. *Close-Ended, Matching:* Very similar arrangements but the transferring authority puts a ceiling on the total amount to be transferred.

C. *Nonmatching:* The recipient is not required to provide cofinancing. The transferring authority sends a fixed sum of money with the stipulation that it be spent on a specific publicly provided good or service.

In unconditional transfers the transferring authority places no restrictions on the use of funds. In both conditional and unconditional transfer systems, one can explicitly factor equalization into the transfer formula. The reasons for introducing equalization are multiple because intra-country and inter-region solidarity is often not explained only by economic arguments. No federal or decentralized country is perfectly homogeneous; therefore, the different levels of taxation by the subnational governments do not necessarily mirror differences in preferred local public services. Local financial capacities depend on both the tax bases accessible to subnational governments and the territorial distribution of those bases. Local needs vary according to the particular preferences of the local residents, but they also depend on geographic, demographic, and socioeconomic factors. They are further determined by constitutional or legal requirements as to the type and nature (quantity, quality) mandatory public goods and services that SNGs must provide.

Box 4.1 reviews the possible origins of fiscal disparities in the relevant literature.[46] The logic behind this classification in five categories is twofold:

1. "External" items that are outside the scope of local decision making should be compensated, at least partly, if they result in a significant spread in the relative fiscal position of governmental units. We call them "disparities."

2. Those items that are within the scope of decision making and the fiscal management of SNGs should not be taken into consideration for equalization. They belong to the sphere of local autonomy and responsibility. We call them "differences."

Category A concerns resource equalization: revenue sources depend in part on the geographic locations of subnational governments in the national territory (proximity of urban areas or economic centers or located at the periphery), on the kind of economic activities, and on communication networks. Within an open market economy, subnational governments cannot influence these characteristics; thus, they must be treated as exogenous variables.

Categories B and C cover the two determinants of expenditure equalization. Both items require more attention than differences in taxable capacity. Needs disparities when measured using simple indicators should not be influenced by subnational governments' decisions. But one must be careful as to the interrelation between specific policies and outcomes; the possible origin of needs disparities deserves careful consideration.

Box 4.1 Five sources of fiscal differences across subnational governments and their appropriateness for equalization

Appropriate for equalization: Disparities

A Differences in the territorial distribution of revenue bases (taxes, natural-resource royalties) or access to them usually measured per head. This can result from differences in endowments (land, minerals), location (access to sea or trade routes), or constitutional/legal constraints (some tax bases are off-limits).

B Need differences in the number of units of standardized service required per capita owing to demographic reasons (age structure, migrant/nonmigrant structure) and territorial (length of shoreline or border to be patrolled).

C Cost differences per unit of standardized public service that arise from factors such as differences in the quantity and composition of inputs that are necessary for producing the public service, differences in factor or input prices, differences in physical characteristics (environmental factors) and presence or absence of economies of scale in the service provision.

Not appropriate for equalization: Differences

D Differences in local preferences either for optional services, for quantities or quality above the minimum standard level in the provision of services, or for autonomy that hinders the achievement of optimal size.

E Differentials that are attributable to strategic behavior on the part of the SNGs with respect to federal transfer payments; local preferences between (nonbenefit) taxes and user charges (benefit taxes), including the choice—if any—among different forms of taxes.

Source: Adapted from Dafflon and Mischler (2008), 215.

Well-measured cost disparities in input factors most often also fall outside the SNGs' decision-making competence. But this requires using input prices from the private sector for measurement purposes. Having examined what are reasonable grounds for equalization, we turn in the next section to revenue equalization, which is equalization justified under Category A of box 4.1.

Revenue Equalization

In this section and in the following one, we put forward both a graphical depiction of revenue (expenditure) equalization and a discussion of issues that cannot be included in such a graph. Figure 4.3 is taken from a work by Dafflon and Vaillancourt that addresses a first set of four issues.[47]

The first issue is the level of the public revenues available to subnational governments to both satisfy the needs of their populations and to be shared in a horizontal equalization scheme. The vertical axis records subnational revenue divided by population (per capita). At point A on the vertical Y-axis, the subnational government receives the average amount of public revenue per resident for that type of jurisdiction in a given country, represented by the standardized value 1.0. In this figure, assume that all revenues available to satisfy the needs of the population are also available for financing an equalization scheme. But this may not be the case; for example, natural-resource revenues may be treated differently for each purpose.

The second issue is that equalization requires jurisdictions to be ranked according to some indicator of contribution/entitlement to equalization; this is addressed by the positioning of the various jurisdictions along the horizontal X-axis. In Figure 4.3, this is revenue capacity because we are presenting revenue equalization; in figure 4.4 it will be cost-adjusted needs. The basic revenue equalization rule is as follows: jurisdictions with higher-than-average revenue capacity should receive less (pay more); jurisdictions with lower-than-average capacity should receive more (pay less). In figure 4.3, average capacity is given a value of 100. For ease of exposition, the lower value for the "poorest" jurisdiction is given a value of 30 and the highest a value of 150. In practice, ranking SNGs is not easy. There are numerous indicators that can be used for ranking purpose and good ad hoc reasons for each being deemed "best" by one actor or another such as a public finance economist,[48] a macroeconomist, a politician, the winning jurisdiction(s) or the losing jurisdiction(s).

Let us assume that these two issues have received an appropriate answer. The third issue is the equalization formula. To understand this, let us compare

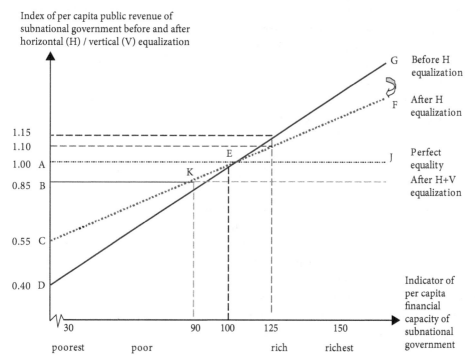

Figure 4.3 A stylized representation of a revenue equalization scheme
Source: Dafflon and Vaillancourt (2003), 401.

the "before" and "after" situations. With no equalization, and the possibility of identifying exactly the origin of the tax revenues, "poor" jurisdictions would certainly receive less than average per capita endowments, and "rich" ones would receive higher than average amounts, something like the line DEG (labeled "before H equalization") in figure 4.3. Any equalization formula would have to give more to "poor" jurisdictions than they would receive following the origin principle and "rich" jurisdictions would receive less, something along the CEF line. The equalizing performance is represented by the distance between lines DE and CE for beneficiary jurisdictions, and between EG and EF for the jurisdictions supporting the financial cost of equalization. Thus, for example, for the poorest jurisdiction with a revenue capacity of 30, equalization increases public revenue per capita from 0.40 (at point D) to 0.55 (at point C), but for a rich region with capacity of 125, equalization reduces public revenues available to it from 1.15 to 1.10. Of course, a balanced solution with horizontal (H) equalization requires that benefits (amounts received, represented by the surface of triangle CDE) and payments (amounts contributed, represented by the surface of triangle EFG) coincide. The importance of equalization depends on the equalization formula, which gives the position of the slope CF around the central point E.

The fourth issue is whether an equalization policy would introduce further limits to the redistribution formula. In figure 4.3, E represents an exactly neutral position with regard to equalization: with an average financial capacity and average per capita tax revenues, a jurisdiction at this point would neither pay nor receive any equalizing amount. But the central point need not be at E. Other equalization targets are possible and often controversial. Two specific points must be noted.

First, it can be debated whether jurisdictions with just below average financial capacity should also benefit from equalization. One could argue on financial, political, and equity grounds that only jurisdictions below a certain level (e.g., an indicator of capacity = 90) should qualify. Financial considerations could be one argument: at 90, the triangle equivalent to CDE would be smaller, which means smaller contributions by richer SNGs. But more crucial are political considerations; at what value does fragmentation of the nation into poor and rich jurisdictions endanger national coherence? Or, how much poorer is too poor?

A second related question is illustrated by the triangle BCK. The resources available after applying the horizontal equalization formula are those corresponding to line CE (above DE): the poorer a jurisdiction, the more it receives. But the horizontal equalizing payments in the example can be argued to be far from giving poor jurisdictions sufficient resources, increasing the resources for the poorest SNG from (in our example) 40 percent to 55 percent of the national average. Should they be increased? In the affirmative, what would be the appropriate limit? The example in figure 4.3 ensures that poor jurisdictions receive equalizing payments so that their revenue endowment reaches at least 85 percent of the national average, along line BK. Because "rich" jurisdictions already pay EFG to cover CDE (equal by construction), financial resources for paying BCK come from a contribution from the center through a vertical equalization scheme.[49] But is 85 percent a proper level? Fragmentation, equity, and incentives must be considered. But note that in figure 4.3, beneficiary jurisdictions have no incentive to take initiative for their development if they are satisfied with public spending compatible with 85 percent of the national average per capita public revenues, and if they have no preference for autonomous revenues rather than transfers.

Not all the key issues of revenue equalization are captured in figure 4.3. For example, we do not discuss how equalization is financed. The questions are which revenue (tax) source is to be shared and according to which decision procedure? Several answers are possible, each with pros and cons; two are discussed below with reference to vertical equalization but the questions are also relevant to horizontal equalization.

- The amount is financed out of the general resources of the central government and established in its annual budget. This is a very flexible solution. But it has two main defects: (1) recipient governments are not sure that they will receive a comparable amount (in real value) from one year to another, which render medium-term planning and multiannual policies very difficult; (2) annual budgetary debates are subject to ad hoc political arrangements.
- The exact calculation of the amount is explicitly stated in the constitution or in a law, in the form of revenue sharing from at least one, but preferably several or all, specific tax source used by the central government (the use of only one tax source for sharing purposes may result in the central government either not collecting it as vigorously as it could since its efforts in part would reward subnational governments or selecting the less buoyant tax source). In this case, the political debate on equalization takes place once when the constitution is amended or the law is passed and not on an annual basis at the time the budget is discussed. And if the tax sources are sufficiently diversified, such that they partly alleviate macroeconomic cycles, it avoids important variations in the amounts available. If they are not, it is possible to solve this potential cyclical problem with the introduction of an equalization fund that can smooth equalization payments over time.

Expenditure Equalization

The focus of this section is on expenditure equalization, a combination of items B and C in box 4.1. Figure 4.4 presents a stylized expenditure equalization scheme. The reader should note that contrary to figure 4.3, the recipients of equalization are to the right of the pivot point and not to the left. As with figure 4.1, one must answer four questions.

First, what are the equalizable expenditures carried out by SNGs? In this figure, we assume that all expenditures are eligible for equalization. If we did not do this, then the vertical Y-axis would be drawn only for eligible expenditures, which means that the total SNG expenditures could be higher for some or all SNGs. As in figure 4.3, we present it in per capita terms. Second, how should we rank SNGs for expenditure equalization?

To answer this question, recall that as noted by Bird and Vaillancourt, average per capita expenditure differences in providing a public service reflect two factors: need differences (box 4.1, B above) and cost differences (box 4.1, C).[50]

- Need differences—differences in the number of units of standardized service required per capita—usually arise owing to demographic reasons such as the age structure of the population and different participation rates in social programs by persons of different ages.[51]
- Cost differences are differences in the cost per unit of a "standardized" public service. They may arise from climatic or geographic features, density or distance factors, or differences in labor costs across regions. Costs should be calculated using real (not nominal) private-sector wages for equivalent inputs and not on the basis of public-sector wages, which may reflect such political factors as the government's political philosophy or the relative strength of workers' unions.[52]

Plausible factors related to needs differences are the share in the total population of various age groups such as infants (postnatal care), elders (health care), and school-aged children, and the share of population with special needs (either temporary, such as new immigrants who need language skills acquisition, integration into society, or ongoing, such as an aboriginal population). The relevance of many of these indicators depends on the role that SNGs play in delivering public services. For instance, if it is the central government or the private sector that provides health care, the share of infants or elders in the population of an SNG may not be relevant in determining transfers.

Various factors determining cost differences have been proposed. Some are natural ones that vary with geography such as climate (snowfall, heavy rain), frequency of natural disasters (floods, earthquakes), topography (mountainous or desert regions), and distance (remoteness from providers of inputs into public services). Others are demographically based, such as population density and urbanization. The difficulty is to estimate in monetary units the impact of such factors on costs. In some cases, it may be not too difficult, such as using private transportation costs per kilometer or mile to estimate the impact of remoteness on the cost of schoolbooks being delivered to a school. But if snow removal is done only by public maintenance crews, then how does one distinguish between true differences in costs and the relative strength of public-sector unions in various SNGs, assuming that each sets its own wages (not set centrally)?

We thus use a cost-adjusted needs index on the X-axis of figure 4.4. What does this mean? Let us assume that we have two regions with identical revenue capacity (the same ranking on the vertical Y-axis of figure 4.3): one (A) has a proportion of 10 percent of older individuals in need of specific health services in its population and the other (B) has 30 percent. In terms of needs, B has higher needs. If the cost

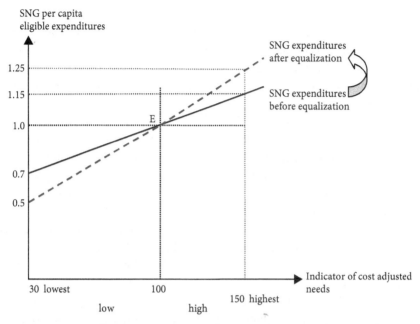

Figure 4.4 A stylized representation of an expenditure equalization scheme
Source: Adapted from Dafflon and Vaillancourt (2003).

per percentage point of the older population is one monetary unit, then B should receive twenty more units of resources than A to be able to provide the required services without having to levy more taxes than A. But if A is more mountainous than B and the cost of getting the services to the older residents is higher because of this, say 1.5 unit per percentage point in A and still one in B, then the difference in cost-adjusted needs is only fifteen: $(30 \times 1) - (10 \times 1.5) = 15$. Hence, adjusting for cost changes, the relative position of these SNGs on the X-axis of figure 4.4. Depending on original positions and the importance of cost differentials, it could invert the rankings.

The third issue is the equalization formula. To understand how it works, let us compare the "before" and "after" situations. With no equalization, "needier" jurisdictions to the right of E spend less per capita than with equalization, and "un-needy" ones to the left of E spend more. Note that per capita expenditures in figure 4.4 are for the populations as a whole and not for the specific populations (e.g., older, immigrants, school-aged children) that may be deemed to have specific needs. Horizontal equalization in this context means than un-needy SNGs spend less overall on their residents after equalization is implemented and implicitly spend for residents of other jurisdictions. Needier jurisdictions can now spend to better satisfy the needs of their residents without, given the assumption of equal revenue capacity, having to levy higher taxes while before equalization they spent less because we assumed no additional tax effort. Thus, for example, for the neediest jurisdiction with a cost-adjusted needs indicator of 150, equalization increases expenditures per capita from 1.15 to 1.25, but for an un-needy region with a needs indicator of 30, equalization with its diversion of revenues reduces the public expenditures it can finance from 0.7 to 0.5. As in figure 4.3, a balanced solution with horizontal (H) equalization requires that benefits and costs coincide. The importance of equalization depends on the equalization formula, which gives the positions of the lines around the central point E. It is conceivable that the slopes of these two lines are not the same.

The fourth issue is whether an equalization policy would introduce further limits to the redistribution formula. In figure 4.4, E represents an exactly neutral position; a jurisdiction at this point would neither pay nor receive any equalizing amount. But the central point need not be at E. Other equalization targets are possible. It can be debated whether jurisdictions with just-above-average needs should benefit from equalization; one could argue that this would be a disincentive to become more productive or that measurement errors of needs are upwardly biased and thus that a cushion of say 5 percent should be used. One could also argue on financial, political, and equity grounds that only jurisdictions above a certain level (e.g., 110) should qualify.

As noted earlier for box 4.1 and its discussion, while disparities are eligible for equalization, differences (items D and E) should not be. One now comes back to this because it is relevant to expenditure equalization. Figure 4.5 illustrates the difficulty of drawing the border between genuine disparities and local preferences or management abilities that result in expenditure or cost differences. The first scenario relates to the optimal size of SNGs and their capacity to realize scale economies. The second scenario illustrates the difficulty of distinguishing between higher production costs that arise from justifiable factors and those that result from X-inefficiencies.

Scenario 1: Impossible Economies of Scale or Reluctance to Cooperate

The jurisdictions face the usual simplified U-shaped production function for a local public good S. Start with the production function PF I for SNG1. Resident beneficiaries pay for the service on a quid pro quo basis (for simplification: one resident, one unit of local service S, one tax unit—that is, there is no spillover). The efficient solution is at E for a total of $N_{optimal}$ residents served. The E solution shows two key results: the minimal average cost at AC_1 and the total local public expenditure at the optimal level for PF I.

Consider SNG2: assume it has an identical production function PF I, but only N_2 residents. Average cost is AC_2. Why is this so? There are three plausible answers: (1) the number of beneficiaries is low because of sociodemographic characteristics of the resident population in SNG2 (less school-aged children if S is a primary school); (2) SNG2 is not in a position (for topographic reasons or distance) to cooperate with neighboring SNGs in order to increase the number of beneficiaries towards $N_{optimal}$; or (3) SNG2 (for reasons of differences in preferences or the desire to remain autonomous) is not willing to cooperate with neighboring SNGs. In this last case, SNG2 should also bear the fiscal consequences of the decision and not receive equalization to make up for the *difference*, which is not due to equalizable disparities in cost.

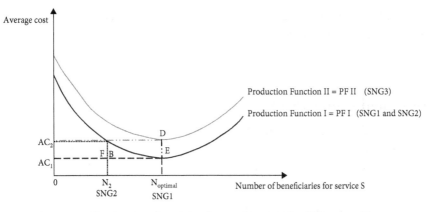

Figure 4.5 Production functions for a subnational public expenditure
Source: Dafflon and Mischler (2008), 218.

Scenario 2: Genuine Cost Disparities versus X-Inefficiencies

Now let's look at a third local unit, SNG3 in figure 4.5 with production function PF II, characterized by higher costs for the whole range of production. Even with the optimal number of beneficiaries served, SNG3 cannot provide an equal level of service S at the same tax price $[N_{optimal} D > N_{optimal} E]$. If the cost difference AC_1EDAC_2 is a genuine disparity, then the situation suggests some kind of equalization so as to restore the fiscal balance. This would not only reduce the average cost (tax price AC_2) of service S that residents in SNG3 face, but it should also reduce fiscally induced migration, thereby enhancing efficiency.[53]

But does PF II represent the real costs or does it hide any X-inefficiencies? How can one interpret the difference *ED* in average costs if SNG1 and SNG3 serve the same number of beneficiaries?[54] Can SNG3 do anything about the high costs?

Figure 4.5 thus identifies three situations that need to be examined if expenditure needs equalization is on the political agenda to be able to rank SNGs on the X-axis. Cost-adjusted needs can be determined in relative terms only if sources of cost differentials are clearly traced and identified. This is not simple; it requires information about the number of beneficiaries and the production function of each public service selected for equalization for several SNGs in order to set the standard cost function within a reasonable range. Such information is not always available.[55] And are costs set by beneficiary or by a production-determined grouping of beneficiaries? For example, for primary school, is it the average cost per pupil that matters or is it the average cost per class with different results if regulations require a minimum and set a maximum number of pupils per class? And who determines when mergers or at least cooperation between SNGs should be required to lower average production costs? Are mixed-language or mixed-religion classes to be mandated either centrally or by SNGs that pay horizontal equalization?

From this perspective, one can see that any policy of expenditure-based equalization is a tremendous challenge. Because expenditure needs equalization is complex, should one conclude that one should renounce the approach, as the Canadian Expert Panel on Equalization recently proposed?[56] Or should there be an attempt to try to design expenditure needs equalization as best as possible with imperfect knowledge, information, and data?[57]

Combined Equalization

Can one combine the two types of equalization in one formula? Yes, but one must be clear on the sequence in which to do this. Equalization is about providing similar levels of public services at similar levels of taxation. Hence, to combine both types of equalization, the following steps are appropriate:

- First, establish the needs index and compute the expenditure equalization entitlement, positive or negative, of each SNG according to it.
- Second, correct the needs-based index for cost differences and compute anew the expenditure equalization entitlement, positive or negative of each SNG according to it.
- Third, compute the revenue capacity index and compute the revenue equalization entitlement, positive or negative of each SNG according to it.
- Fourth, combine the expenditure and revenue equalization entitlements together to get total equalization.

Horizontal versus Vertical Equalization

A last issue deserves attention, which is whether equalization is horizontal or vertical. In figure 4.3, surface CDE = EFG implies that equalization is horizontal, between contributing and beneficiary SNG units; CBK, if it exists in total or partially, is vertical. In figure 4.4, a balanced solution (around E) with horizontal equalization requires that benefits coincide: but the solution could be also to grant equalization to the jurisdictions with cost-adjusted needs higher than average (100 points on the horizontal axis) without asking the jurisdictions with cost-adjusted needs lower than average to contribute; needs equalization would then be vertical and centrally funded.

Horizontal equalization is typically a "Robin Hood"-type of equalization: high-capacity SNGs directly transfer public revenues to a fund that serves low-capacity SNGs. This is less conceivable for expenditure needs equalization.[58] This would imply that SNGs with relatively low needs and costs of service provision accept higher tax prices, which allow subsidizing other SNGs with relatively high expenditure needs. This would distort the relative local tax prices of public services and result in allocative inefficiencies.

Two further arguments against horizontal expenditure equalization are that (1) for those public services that are financed through user charges, if the "price" does not reflect benefit, consumers will face false price signals; and (2) when the difference between SNG choices, X-inefficiencies, and genuine disparities is not clear, SNGs might indulge in strategic behavior with the aim of placing themselves in a more favorable equalizing position (in this case, higher costs and more needs). Vertical needs equalization can be set on expenditure standards that eliminate functions based on the benefit principle for their financing and that ignore SNGs' potential strategies but this adds to complexity.[59]

Conclusion

This chapter has demonstrated that if a society is to achieve an efficient allocation of its scarce resources, then not only is there a clear case for collective (public-sector) provision of good and services, but also, to achieve efficiency, the system of government should be decentralized—that is, economic efficiency requires state and local fiscal autonomy.

Thus, we make the case for a well-designed and implemented intergovernmental fiscal system that addresses three fundamental questions of (1) which type of government (federal, state, or local) should provide which set of public goods and services; (2) how those services shall be financed; and (3) the role for fiscal transfers among types of governments when there is an efficient "assignment" of expenditure responsibilities and revenue authority. What's "right" for one intergovernmental system may not be "right" for another. [60] But even though the answers to these questions may differ across systems (e.g., among the thousands of different governments in the United States), there are fundamental principles that are common not only across the United States but also apply to other countries—and that is that addressing these intergovernmental answers "correctly" is not only critical to the achievement of a nation's broader goals of stabilization and economic growth, the efficient provision of public goods and services and fairness in the distribution of income and wealth, but that there are conceptual guidelines for making those decisions. Throughout its history, the United States has done a remarkably good job of recognizing the importance of maintaining a robust decentralized government; indeed, the US structure of federalism is a model often of interest in other countries, although it needs to be implemented by taking into account the unique situation of each country. However, whether the United States can maintain this record of "achieving federalism" is yet to be seen.

Notes

1 World Bank (2000).
2 Oates (1972); Mueller (1996).
3 Cremer et al. (1996); Raff and Wilson (1997); Bucovetsky et al. (1998).

4 Tiebout (1956).

5 Musgrave (1959).

6 Rossi and Dafflon (2002), 20–25.

7 As in the case of a federal or state "financial control board" that is temporarily established to restructure fiscally fragile local governments. For a US case, see Gandhi, Yilmaz, Zahradnik, and Edwards (2009). For a global and international review, see Ter-Minassian and Craig (1997); Dafflon and Beer-Tóth (2009), 337.

8 Yilmaz, Beris, and Serrano-Berthet (2010).

9 These can occur in the schooling environment, for example.

10 Oates (1972).

11 Bird and Ebel (2007).

12 The related technical issues of "off" versus "on" budgeting and extra-budgetary accounts are not discussed here. For a discussion, see Wong, Martinez-Vazquez, and Gooptu (2002).

13 Whenever one economic actor (a firm or individual) undertakes an action that has a (net) added value or cost to another economic actor, there is an externality. If these values (positive externalities) are not paid for by the recipient or net costs (negative externalities) are not paid for by the first actor, the result is inefficient resource allocation.

14 Gravelle (2005) identifies four variants: (1) exclusions, exemptions, and deductions, which reduce taxable income; (2) preferential rates, which apply lower rates to part or all of a taxpayer's income; (3) credits subtracted from taxes and ordinarily computed, and (4) deferrals of tax, resulting from delayed recognition of income, which allow within the current year deductions of what are properly attributable to a future year. Levitis, Johnson, and Koulish (2009) note that although forty-one states and the District of Columbia publish tax expenditure reports, many of these forty-two have significant shortcomings. There are, however, some very comprehensive tax expenditure reports (e.g., District of Columbia, Michigan, Minnesota, Oregon, and Washington).

15 Governments also provide private goods. Indeed, in many countries, the provision of private goods dwarfs that of public goods in the budget. Education services, most of health services, and some income insurance/support schemes are joint "private-public" goods: private because the service is delivered to individuals and, as such, the consumption is rival and price exclusion is possible; public because the service provides externalities, which are of collective nature (education is a key factor in social and cultural homogeneity, labor capacity and mobility, health, and the exercise of democracy) The distinction between national and local applies to such private goods. The provision of education is more a local good while the provision of a pension scheme is more national.

16 Samuelson defined public goods (or "collective consumption goods" as he calls them) as goods that "all enjoy in common in the sense that each individual's consumption of such a good leads to no subtractions from any other individual's consumption of that good" (Samuelson [1954], 387).

17 Tiebout (1956).

18 For a succinct explanation, see Oates and Schwab (2005).

19 We assume that the output will be a compromise between the two desired levels, a reasonable outcome in a democratic system.

20 For Qc, group D1 would be ready to pay B, but has to pay much more in C; and for a price equal to C, group D2 would rather obtain quantity Q2 but has to satisfy itself

with Qc only. Note that the two jurisdictions could enter into a cooperative agreement, producing more in total than in the independent solution at a lower cost for each of them (Buchanan, 1968).

21 Oates (1972).

22 If they are neighbors, amalgamation could be on the agenda because the residents' preferences are now identical at least for this public service.

23 Musgrave (1953). The tax assignment problem may be seen as part of a larger set of questions that can be referred to as the revenue assignment problem. The latter includes the design of intergovernmental grants and the framework for borrowing by subnational governments.

24 Where strict compliance with benefit finance is infeasible because of the difficulty or undesirability of exclusion from the benefits of public spending, the principle is, nonetheless, instructive.

25 This statement is incomplete if the benefits of public spending, as well as tax burdens, are considered. Taxes related closely to marginal benefits may finance expenditures that involve substantial inframarginal benefits. These inframarginal benefits may be of special value to low-income families. Obvious examples include the provision of safe drinking water. Many consumers would probably consider themselves better off if they had access to safe water, even if they had to pay for it. The problem is often access, not cost.

26 Drawing on the Council of Europe's European Charter of Local Self Government (1985), subsidiarity in taxation was introduced to the European Union with the *Maastricht Treaty* amendments to the *Treaty of Rome* (Article 3B). The Commission of the European Communities (1991, p. 7) explained that subsidiarity requires that "Member States should remain free to determine their tax arrangements, except where these would lead to major distortions." See Marcou (2007).

27 A vertical imbalance may exist because subnational governments have difficulty implementing many taxes, but "higher" governments—that is, governments with a larger tax catchment area—can implement almost any tax that a "lower" level of government can implement.

28 If a subnational government legislates and collects its own taxes, protected by meaningful constitutional safeguards of its right to do so, it clearly has a source of own revenues.

29 Even if subnational governments have own revenues, they may be unable to influence the amount of revenue they receive. This is true, for example, if the central government shares revenues from certain taxes with subnational governments. In such a case, these are own revenues but are not marginal revenues of subnational governments.

30 An important prerequisite for the exercise of subnational fiscal autonomy is the ability to choose statutory tax rates. An issue here is why statutory and not effective tax rates. Effective tax rates would vary if subnational governments could alter deductions, exemptions, and so on, but this would mean changing the base and not the rates. This would increase the complexity of the system and the compliance costs of firms operating in multiple jurisdictions.

31 Holmes (1927).

32 McLure Jr. (1983).

33 In the case of Canada, for example, provinces that use the harmonized sales tax (HST), a VAT collected by the federal government for both it and the province at a jointly agreed rate (5 percent federal and a provincial rate) are allowed a maximum 5 percent variation in their base from the federal government base.

34 Jensen (2002). Furthermore, if the state or center "caps" a tax rate and the local government has reached that cap but cannot then exceed it, some argue that it is no longer an "own" local tax (Ebel and Taliercio [2005]).

35 Mikesell (2003).

36 See Cordes and Juffras (this volume).

37 Ebel and Taliercio (2005).

38 For the US case, see Kincaid (this volume)

39 Subnational constitutions or laws may limit any of these, but self-imposed restrictions in the constitutions of subnational governments differ from restrictions imposed from above by law or as part of a national constitution. In the case of Switzerland, for example, the definition of the income-tax base and tax deductions is federal and applies to the twenty-six cantons. The cantons can choose their own tax rate schedule and the amount of deduction (but cannot add one to the federal list). The communes (local government units) can only decide the tax coefficient for balancing their budgets in a true piggyback tax system.

40 Note first that "tax competition" is distinct from the Tiebout model: in Tiebout, it is the best alternative "basket of local public services, or taxes," that determines the localization of economic agents. "Fiscal competition" is achieved through benchmarking and mobility. In tax competition, it is assumed that the basket of local public services is almost identical so that only taxes may be considered. Brennan and Buchanan (1983) provide an argument for tax competition (see also McLure 1986). This is only part of the story, although an important part. Because those who have access to public goods cannot be excluded from enjoying their benefits, they have little incentive to reveal their preferences for such goods. There is thus a tendency to underprovide public goods that tax competition might aggravate. See Gordon (1983) for a theoretical analysis of the inefficiencies that can result from decentralization, including tax competition. Benefit taxation helps to combat this source of market failure (Wildasin 1986). Tax competition makes it difficult for subnational governments to tax mobile factors—capital and highly educated or skilled labor—and therefore to engage in progressive taxation.

41 Inequities and economic distortions can also occur if the tax systems of various subnational governments do not mesh, resulting in gaps or overlaps in taxation. Within limits, these problems—which differ in importance from tax to tax—can and should be tolerated in the interest of gaining the benefits of fiscal decentralization. Serious complexities, inequities, and distortions can be achieved without greatly compromising (indeed, by enhancing) the fiscal autonomy of subnational governments through intergovernmental compacts such as the Multistate Tax Commission arrangement (www.mtc.gov).

42 See the Cordes and Juffras discussion (in this volume) of state-to-federal tax conformity.

43 Although all subnational governments, acting as a group, can attempt to influence their share of revenues from these taxes, no subnational government, acting unilaterally, can hope to do so.

44 See Fisher and Bristle (this volume) and Sheppach (this volume).

45 See Kenyon (this volume).

46 For a review of the literature on this, see Dafflon (2007), 363–366.

47 Dafflon and Vaillancourt (2003).

48 Public finance economists have proposed that SNGs' revenue capacity would be better measured with RTS methods (for Representative Tax or Representative

Revenue System, RTS and RRS). The RTS/RRS measures the per capita tax potential of SNGs and not the actual tax yield. The RTS methodology was developed in 1962 by Selma Mushkin and Alice Rivlin for the United States Advisory Commission on Intergovernmental Relations. In 1990 Robert Rafuse extended the analysis of "representative expenditures." See Rafuse (1990); Kenyon (2005); Yilmaz and Zahradnik (2008).

49 Which may well be paid for by residents of SNGs already contributing to horizontal equalization, if central and SNG tax capacity are correlated.

50 Bird and Vaillancourt (2007).

51 Wallace (this volume).

52 Courchene (1998); Rechovsky (2007), 400-409.

53 Bird and Vaillancourt (2007), 262.

54 Take the example of primary education. Suppose SNG1 and SNG3 buy the same number of books for the same number of pupils. Does SNG3 overspend on fancier books, try harder to keep up with new pedagogical trends, or teach a different language group and thus face higher unit costs for otherwise identical books? Yet if one refers to the logic behind box 4.1, further questions arise. Is SNG3's choice to follow a new pedagogical path an item of laboratory federalism, a decision taken in coordination with other SNGs (in this case, equalization is acceptable), or is it an own decision following the specific tastes of the constituency (no equalization)? If language is different, is the higher government concerned with the protection of minorities (equalization is acceptable) or are language differences not an issue (no equalization)? Not only is it difficult to isolate variables that affect costs from variables that indicate differences in public-good preferences, but the answers (to laboratory federalism and preoccupation with minorities protection in the example)—and therefore the justification of expenditure needs equalization—belong to the realm of politics.

55 Dafflon and Mischler (2007), 183-185.

56 Boothe and Vaillancourt (2007), 48.

57 Boex and Martinez-Vazquez (2007), 291.

58 Dafflon (2007), 370-371.

59 Dafflon and Mischler (2008), 235.

60 Wallace (this volume).

REFERENCES

Bird, Richard M., and Robert D. Ebel (2007). *Fiscal Fragmentation in Decentralized Countries: Subsidiarity, Solidarity, and Asymmetry.* Northampton, MA: Edward Elgar.

Bird, Richard M., and François Vaillancourt (2007). "Expenditure-Based Equalization Transfers." In Jorge Martinez-Vazquez and Bob Searle (Eds.), *Fiscal Equalization: Challenges in the Design of Intergovernmental Transfers.* New York: Springer. 259-284.

Boex, Jameson, and Jorge Martinez-Vazquez (2007). "Designing Intergovernmental Equalization Transfers with Imperfect Data: Concepts, Practices and Lessons." In Jorge Martinez-Vazquez and Bob Searle (Eds.), *Fiscal Equalization: Challenges in the Design of Intergovernmental Transfers.* New York: Springer. 291-344.

Boothe, Paul, and Francois Vaillancourt (2007). "A Fine Canadian Compromise: Perspectives on Equalisation and Territorial Funding Financing." Edmonton and Montréal: Institute for Public Economics and CIRANO, http://www.cirano.qc.ca/pdf/Perequation_07.pdf.

Brennan, Geoffrey, and James Buchanan (1983). "Normative Tax Theory for a Federal Polity: Some Public Choice Preliminaries." In Charles E. McLure Jr. (Ed.), *Tax Assignment in Federal Countries*. Canberra: Centre for Research on Federal Financial Relations. 52–65.

Buchanan, James (1968). *The Supply of Public Goods*. Chicago: Rand McNally.

Bucovetsky, Sam, Maurice Marchand, and Pierre Pestieau (1998). "'Tax Competition and Revelation of Preferences for Public Expenditure.'" *Journal of Urban Economics* 44, 367–390.

Commission of the European Communities (1991). "Removal of Tax Obstacles to the Cross-Frontier Activities of Companies," Supplement 4/91 to the Bulletin of the European Communities, available at http://aei.pitt.edu/5420/1/003921_1.pdf.

Courchene, Thomas (1998). "Renegotiating Equalization: National Polity, Federal State, International Economy." C. D. Howe Institute Commentary 113. Toronto: C. D. Howe Institute.

Cremer, Jacques, Antonio Estache, and Paul Seabright (1996). "'Decentralizing Public Services: What Can We Learn from the Theory of the Firm?" *Revue d'Economie Politique* 106, 37–60.

Dafflon, Bernard (2007). "Fiscal Capacity Equalization in Horizontal Fiscal Equalization Programs." In Robin Boadway and Anwar Shah (Eds.), *Intergovernmental Fiscal Transfers: Principles and Practice*. Washington, DC: World Bank. 361–390.

Dafflon, Bernard, and Krisztina Beer-Tóth (2009). "Managing Local Public Debt in Transition Countries: An Issue of Self-Control." *Financial Accountability and Management* 25(3), 337–365.

Dafflon, Bernard, and Peter Mischler (2007). "Réforme de la péréquation intercommunale dans le canton de Fribourg." Centre d'études en Economie du Secteur Public, série Etudes et Rapports, Fribourg: Université de Fribourg.

Dafflon, Bernard, and Peter Mischler (2008). "Expenditure Needs Equalisation at the Local Level: Methods and Practice." In Junghun Kim and Jorgen Lotz (Eds.), *Measuring Local Government Expenditure Needs*. Seoul and Copenhagen: The Korea Institute of Public Finance and the Danish Ministry of Social Welfare. 213–240.

Dafflon, Bernard, and François Vaillancourt (2003). "Problems of Equalization in Federal Countries." In Raoul Blindenbacher and Arnold Koller (Eds.), *Federalism in a Changing World—Learning from Each Other*. Montreal: McGill-Queen's University Press. 395–411.

Ebel, Robert D., and Robert Taliercio (2005). "Subnational Tax Policy and Administration in Developing Economies." *Tax Notes International*, March 2005.

Gandhi, Natwar, Yesim Yilmaz, Robert Zahradnik, and Marcy Edwards (2009). "Washington, District of Columbia." In Enid Slack and Rupak Chattopadhyay (Eds.), *Finance and Governance of Capital Cities in Federal Systems*. Montreal: McGill-Queens's University Press. 263–291.

Gordon, Roger H. (1983). "An Optimal Taxation Approach to Fiscal Federalism." In Charles E. McLure Jr. (Ed.), *Tax Assignment in Federal Countries*. Canberra: Centre for Research on Federal Financial Relations. 26–42.

Gravelle, Jane G. (2005). "Tax Expenditures." In Joseph C. Cordes, Robert D. Ebel, and Jane G. Gravelle (Eds.), *Encyclopedia of Taxation and Tax Policy*. Washington, DC: Urban Institute Press. 406–408.

Holmes, Oliver Wendell, Jr. (1927). *Compania General de Tobacos de Filipinas v. Collector of Internal Revenue* 275 US 87, 100 (1927).

Jensen, Leif (2002). *Fiscal Design Surveys across Levels of Governments: Tax Policy Studies No 7.* Paris: Organisation for Economic Cooperation and Development.

Kenyon, Daphne (2005). "Tax and Revenue Capacity." In Joseph C. Cordes, Robert D. Ebel, and Jane G. Gravelle (Eds.), *Encyclopedia of Taxation and Tax Policy.* Washington, DC: Urban Institute Press. 389–391.

Levitis, Jason, Nicholas Johnson, and Jeremy Koulish (2009). *Promoting State Budget Accountability through Tax Expenditure Reporting.* Washington, DC: Center on Budget and Policy Priorities.

Marcou, Gerard (2007). "Legal Framework and the European Charter of Local Self Government." In Robert D. Ebel and Gabor Peteri (Eds.), *The Kosovo Decentralization Briefing Book.* Prishtine: Kosovo Foundation for Open Society. 49–59.

McLure, Charles E., Jr. (Ed.) (1983). *Tax Assignment in Federal Countries.* Canberra: Centre for Research on Federal Financial Relations.

McLure, Charles E., Jr. (1986). "Tax Competition: Is What's Good for the Private Goose Also Good for the Public Gander?" *National Tax Journal* 39(3), 341–348.

Mikesell, John (2003, March). "International Experiences with Administration of Local Taxes: A Review of Practices and Issues." Paper prepared for the World Bank Thematic Group on Taxation and Tax Policy. Washington, DC: World Bank.

Mueller, Dennis C. (1996). *Constitutional Democracy.* Oxford: Oxford University Press.

Musgrave, Richard A. (1959). *The Theory of Public Finance.* New York: McGraw-Hill.

Oates, Wallace E. (1972). *Fiscal Federalism.* New York: Harcourt, Brace and Jovanovic.

Oates, Wallace E. (1997). "On the Welfare Gains from Fiscal Decentralization." *Journal of Public Finance and Public Choice* Vol. 2–3. 83–92.

Oates, Wallace E., and Robert M. Schwab (2005). "Tiebout Model." In Joseph Cordes, Robert D. Ebel, and Jane G. Gravelle (Eds.), *Encyclopedia of Taxation and Tax Policy.* Washington, DC: Urban Institute Press. 437–439.

Raff, Horst, and John D. Wilson (1997). "Income Redistribution with Well-Informed Local Governments." *International Tax and Public Finance* 4, 407–427.

Rafuse, Robert (1990). *Representative Expenditures: Addressing the Neglected Dimension of Fiscal Capacity.* Washington, DC: US Advisory Commission on Intergovernmental Relations.

Rechovsky, Andrew (2007). "Compensating Local Governments for Differences in Expenditure Needs in a Horizontal Fiscal Equalization Program." In Robin Boadway and Anwar Shah (Eds.), *Intergovernmental Fiscal Transfers: Principles and Practice.* Washington, DC: World Bank. 397–429.

Rossi, Sergio, and Bernard Dafflon (2002). "The Theory of Subnational Balanced Budget and Debt Control." In Bernard Dafflon (Ed.), *Local Public Finance in Europe: Balancing the Budget and Controlling Debt.* Cheltenham UK: Edward Elgar. 15–44.

Samuelson, Paul A. (1954). "The Pure Theory of Public Expenditure." *Review of Economics and Statistics* 36(4), 387–389.

Ter-Minassian, Teresa, and Jon Craig (1997)."Control of Subnational Government Borrowing." In Teresa Ter-Minassian (Ed.), *Fiscal Federalism in Theory and Practice.* Washington, DC: International Monetary Fund.

Tiebout, Charles (1956). "A Pure Theory of Local Expenditures." *Journal of Political Economy* 64, 416–424.

Wildasin, David E. (1986). "Interstate Tax Competition: A Comment." *National Tax Journal* 39(3), 353–356.

Wong, Christine, Jorge Martinez-Vazquez, and Sudarshan Gooptu (2002). China National Development and Subnational Finance, Report No. 22951-CHA. Washington, DC: World Bank.

World Bank (2000). *Entering the 21st Century: World Development Report, 1999–2000.*
     Oxford: World Bank and Oxford University Press.
Yilmaz, Serdar, Yakup Beris, and Rodrigo Serrano-Berthet (2010). "Linking Local
     Government Discretion and Accountability in Decentralisation." *Development Policy
     Review* 28, 259–293.
Yilmaz, Yesim, and Robert Zahradnik (2008). "Measuring the Fiscal Capacity of the
     District of Columbia: A Comparison of Revenue Capacity and Expenditure Need, FY
     2005." Washington, DC: National Tax Association.

CHAPTER 5

STATE AND LOCAL GOVERNMENTS AND THE NATIONAL ECONOMY

RICK MATTOON AND LESLIE MCGRANAHAN

THE Great Recession, beginning in 2007 and officially ending in mid-2009, placed both state and local governments under extreme fiscal pressure. While downturns in the business cycle have always caused stress for state and local governments, the two recessions of the first decade of the 2000s, the Great Recession and that of 2001, have been particularly challenging.[1] This chapter examines expenditure and revenue patterns for state and local governments both over time and relative to the performance of the national economy.[2] In particular, the focus will be on the performance of these governments in the periods surrounding national recessions. The authors will illustrate that state and local expenditure patterns have followed their traditional pattern in the two most recent recessions. But, in contrast, revenue patterns have become very different from past experience. There has been increased cyclicality of state revenues, particularly in the income tax, and an enhanced role of federal grants. The broad impact of the state and local sector over the past four decades has been to maintain its major significance in the national economy and to generally behave in a countercyclical fashion, with lagging adjustments to changes in the overall economy. This behavior has not been a conscious choice by policy-makers but is instead an outcome of the goods and services these governments provide and the revenue sources they depend on, including the influx of federal assistance in times of fiscal stress. However, the increased volatility of state and local own-source revenues may cause that behavior to change.

The State and Local Sector in Relation to GDP and Employment

We begin by measuring the state and local sector's contribution to two broad aggregate measures of the US economy—gross domestic product (GDP) and total employment.[3] The first figure shows total state and local consumption expenditures and gross investment relative to GDP (figure 5.1).

In the most recent quarter for which data were available (the third quarter of 2010), state and local consumption and gross investment spending represented 12.1 percent of GDP. Figure 5.2 expands this definition to include social benefits and other transfer expenditures (most of which are interest payments). While the first figure includes the data that underlie the contribution to GDP in the National Income and Product Accounts (NIPA), the second figure shows the amount of funds that is being injected by the sectors into the economy.

A number of patterns emerge from these two figures. First, the share of national economic output derived from the direct spending of state and local governments has been basically flat with a modest upward trend since the mid-1980s. This upward trend becomes more pronounced and longer in duration when the payments of social

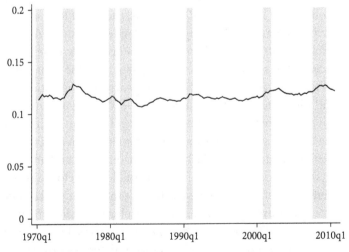

Figure 5.1 State and local government consumption and gross investment: Share of GDP
Source: US Bureau of the Census, US Bureau of Economic Analysis, authors calculations.

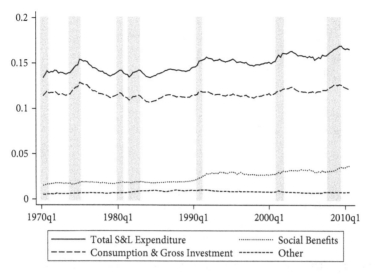

Figure 5.2 State and local current expenditure plus gross investment: Share of GDP
Source: US Bureau of the Census, US Bureau of Economic Analysis, authors calculations.

benefits are incorporated into the definition of state and local spending, as seen in figure 5.2. Social benefits are transfers to individuals and firms. These transfer payments are primarily Medicaid expenditures, but scholarships and family assistance from Aid to Families with Dependent Children (AFDC) and Temporary Assistance to Needy Families (TANF) also fall into this category. While state and local social benefit payments represented 1.6 percent of GDP in 1970, this percentage rose to 3 percent in prerecession 2006 and then increased to 3.5 percent in 2009. So while the sector's direct spending has been close to flat in general, there have been pronounced upward movements in social benefits, in particular in Medicaid payments. While the sector has maintained its traditional role as a direct provider of services, it has increased its influence in the national economy as a payer for services, in particular medical services that are provided by other sectors of the economy.

Figure 5.3 illustrates state, local, and combined state-and-local employment as a share of total nonfarm employment for a forty-year period. The pattern here is consistent with that shown in figure 5.1. In particular, state and local employment as a share of total employment has been basically flat. This is not surprising given that employee compensation is the single largest component of state and local consumption expenditures. In November 2010, state and local government employment represented 15 percent of total nonfarm employment. The sector's share of nonfarm employment is larger than its share of GDP.[4] This outcome arises because provision of education and other government services is labor-intensive relative to most other national output.[5] Studies have found that total hourly wages are higher for both state and local employees relative to the private sector (for 2008, hourly wages were $22.15 for local government workers, $22.17 for state government workers, and $20.57 for private-sector workers). When adjusting for the greater educational intensity and comparable earnings determinants of state and local government jobs, state and government workers typically earn less than private-sector

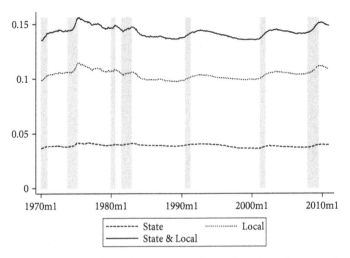

Figure 5.3 State and local employment as a share of total nonfarm employment
Source: US Bureau of Labor Statistics, authors' calculations.

counterparts. However, this differential tends to decline or even reverse itself when benefits (particularly pensions and health care) are added to wage compensation.[6]

Local government employment is more than two times the size of state government employment throughout this period. In terms of shares of total nonfarm US employment, local government represents between 10 and 11 percent of total employment while state government employment ranges from 3.5 to slightly above 4 percent. Just under half of state and local employees work in public schools or state higher education institutions.

From figures 5.1, 5.2, and 5.3, one can see that state and local governments have basically been growing in line with the overall economy with the exception of social benefits, which have been growing more rapidly. Moderate average economic growth in the overall economy throughout this period means that the level of state and local government economic activity has increased even though the fraction it represents has been stable at 12 percent. While the sector has been close to flat in terms of its contribution to national GDP in the last forty years, one would see a strikingly different pattern if the horizon were extended back an additional three decades, as there was a rapid expansion in the economic role of states and localities in the national economy throughout the 1940s, 1950s, and 1960s.[7]

Cyclical Factors

Over the past forty years, there were six recessions that occurred beginning in 1973, 1980, 1981, 1990, 2001, and 2007. Overall, state and local government expenditure patterns are countercyclical as the demand for government services increases in

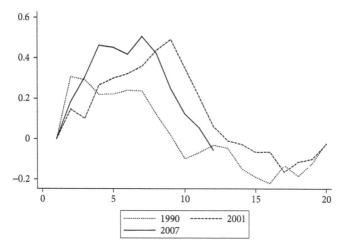

Figure 5.4 Spider graph of consumption and gross investment (detrended)
Source: US Bureau of the Census, US Bureau of Economic Analysis, authors' calculations.

the face of economic stress while tax revenues are procyclical because revenues are related to economic activity such as income and consumption. Figures 5.1, 5.2, and 5.3 seem to show a rise in state and local expenditures relative to overall GDP during recessions (shaded in gray in the figures) and no discernible trend in economic activity in the quarters leading up to a recession. To better examine state and local spending during recessionary periods, we detrend the data and use spider graphs in Figures 5.4, 5.5, and 5.6. For the purpose of visual clarity, these figures will show only state behavior for the 1990, 2001, and 2007 recessions. (The prior recessions of 1973, 1980, and 1981 exhibit a similar pattern to that of 1990.) We detrend the data in order to adjust for long-term trends in expenditures so as to better isolate cyclical patterns. Each leg of the spider represents one post-1970 recession. We start

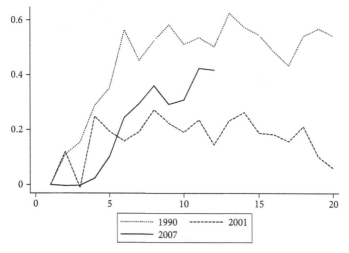

Figure 5.5 Spider graph of social benefits (detrended)
Source: US Bureau of the Census, US Bureau of Economic Analysis, authors' calculations.

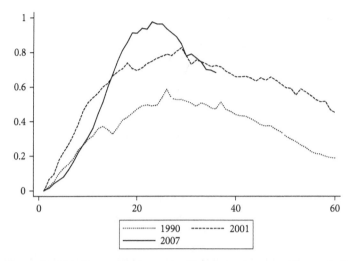

Figure 5.6 Spider graph of state and local employment (detrended)
Source: US Bureau of the Census, US Bureau of Economic Analysis, authors' calculations.

the line at t = 0, which represents the time period when the recession started and then trace out the pattern of the variable relative to its level during that inaugural quarter. Each line ends twenty quarters (or five years) after the recession started. The line for the 2007 recession is shorter because as of this writing we are waiting to see the evolution of economic variables and what the postrecession experience will be.

Figure 5.4 displays a recession spider graph for (detrended) state and local government consumption and investment as a percent of GDP. The values on the horizontal axis indicate the quarters since the beginning of the recession and the values on the vertical axis indicate the percentage of GDP represented by the sector's spending relative to its level at the beginning quarter of the recession. During all recessions, state and local expenditures as a percent of GDP moved upward in the period following the beginning of the recession. For all six recessions, the state and local sector experienced growth (relative to trend) during the first quarters following the start of each recession. The patterns for the recessions are broadly similar, with steady increases in the share of the state and local sector in the economy during the first couple of years following the start of the recession.

Figure 5.5 uses the same methodology to display patterns of social benefit payments.[8] The patterns here are more varied. In 1990 and 2001, social benefits trended generally upward. In 2007, a flat initial period was followed by an upward trend beginning in early 2008, about four quarters into the recession (which was at about the time of the passage of the American Recovery and Reinvestment Act [ARRA]).[9] For these social benefit payments, detrending the data is crucial because, otherwise, the long-term upward trend in spending as a portion of GDP would dominate these figures. Figure 5.6 illustrates the pattern for state and local employment. For employment, the numbers on the horizontal axis represent the months since the beginning of the recession because employment data are released on a monthly frequency. Again, the figure ends sixty months (or five years) after the start of each recession.

All three figures display the same general pattern. In particular, the state and local sector becomes an increasing share of national output at the start of the recessions. These patterns persist even if we detrend the underlying data. When the economy begins to shrink, the state and local sector either continues to grow or shrink more slowly than the overall economy. In other words in the early phases of recessions the state and local sector acts in a countercyclical fashion as it reacts more slowly to the changing economy than the private sector does.

These patterns are not surprising. Demand for many state and local government services, such as education, are not cyclically sensitive. We may even anticipate that demand increases when the economy is bad because people substitute public options for private ones as the economy sours. Another thing to note is that the expenditure responses during the two most recent recessions (2001 and 2007) have been broadly similar to those experienced during the earlier recessions as represented by the 1990 recession.

Expenditure Detail: Changes in Government Functions over the Period

In this section, we investigate the evolving composition of state and local spending. We are interested in the services provided by sub-national governments and how these roles have changed over the past forty years. In tables 5.1 and 5.2, we display direct expenditure shares for three separate years for the different levels of governments. These figures suggest that the role of state governments has evolved during this forty-year period while the role of local governments has been more stable.

State Expenditures

The composition of direct state government spending is shown for 1972, 1990, and 2008 in table 5.1. We note four patterns in the data. First, transportation spending, primarily in the form of highway spending, has declined in percentage terms. Much of this decline from 21 to 10 percent occurred between 1972 and 1990, although it continued to fall between 1990 and 2008. Second, state education spending increased from 10 to 19 percent of direct state expenditures between 1972 and 1990. Education's share of state level spending remained at 19 percent in 2008. This rise in education spending is almost exclusively due to increased

Table 5.1 Shares of state government expenditures by function

	1972	1990	2008
Transport (Including Highways)	21%	10%	7%
Public Safety and Corrections	4%	6%	5%
Education and Libraries	10%	19%	19%
Public Welfare (Excluding Medicaid)	23%	17%	14%
Medicaid Vendor Payments	9%	14%	23%
Employee Retirement	5%	7%	12%
Unemployment Insurance/Workers' Comp	9%	6%	4%
Other	19%	21%	16%

Source: US Census Bureau, authors' calculations.

costs for higher education institutions such as state universities. Third, Medicaid vendor payments grew dramatically during this period, from 9 percent in 1972 to 23 percent of direct expenditures. Fourth, other public welfare payments fell. This fall was primarily due to the development of the Supplemental Security Income[10] program (in the early 1970s), which federalized state programs serving the aged, blind, and disabled, and due to the 1990s welfare reform.

On balance, between 1972 and 2008, direct spending by state governments shifted from being dominated by public welfare (primarily in the form of cash payments) and transportation to eventually being dominated by higher education and Medicaid expenditures. The implications of this shift in terms of the ability of state governments to adapt to recessions on the spending side is unclear because while public welfare and Medicaid are both sensitive to economic conditions, transportation and higher education are less so. In fact, states may have some leeway to cut back on capital spending in these latter areas to adapt to budget stress.

Table 5.2 Shares of local government expenditures by function

	1972	1990	2008
Transport (Including Highways)	7%	6%	6%
Public Safety and Corrections	7%	9%	9%
Education and Libraries	42%	38%	39%
Public Welfare (Excluding Medicaid)	15%	13%	13%
Medicaid Vendor Payments	1%	0%	0%
Employee Retirement	1%	2%	2%
Other	27%	33%	31%

Source: US Census Bureau, authors' calculations.

Local Expenditures

The composition of local government expenditures by function is shown for 1972, 1990, and 2008 in table 5.2. Local government expenditure shares have been relatively stable during this period. In addition, within the broad categories displayed in this table, spending shares have been fairly constant. Throughout, provision of education, almost exclusively at the elementary and secondary levels, has dominated local government direct expenditures. Demand for this major local government service is likely fairly independent of business-cycle conditions.

Turning to Revenues

Figure 5.7 displays state and local current receipts as a percentage of GDP for the four-decade period. State and local governments raised about $2.15 trillion at an annual rate in the third quarter of 2010. This makes the sector's revenue base slightly smaller than that of the federal government. These revenues come from three primary sources; tax receipts (62 percent of total current receipts in this time period for 2010), federal transfers (25 percent) and other revenues (13 percent). While states and localities raise money from taxation and other own-source revenues, they also rely heavily on the federal government for funds. In turn, states and localities implement many federally funded grants, sponsored programs, or mandated programs, including Medicaid, unemployment insurance, and public education. These subnational levels of government also spend on federal highways and various other categorical grant funds.

In figure 5.7 is a general upward trend in state and local government revenues as a fraction of GDP starting in the early 1980s and accelerating during the 2007 recession. When we break these revenues into their component parts, in figure 5.8, we find that tax receipts have been fairly flat while federal government assistance payments have been increasing.

We next investigate the business-cycle behavior of state and local government revenues. We use the same methodology used above for plotting the sector's expenditures. Namely, we detrend the data, which measure the variables as a percentage of GDP, and then we use spider graphs to display behavior over the three most recent recessions. Once again for visual clarity, we do not include the 1973, 1980, and 1981 recessions, but the patterns for these recessions were similar to the pattern for 1990. The graph for total receipts is figure 5.9, the graph for tax receipts is figure 5.10, and the graph for federal grants is figure 5.11.

There was an upward movement in receipts as a share of GDP in response to the 1990 and 2007 recessions, and there was a dramatic decline in revenues in 2001. When we look at the behavior of tax receipts in figure 5.12, we see that taxes have behaved differently in the two most recent recessions than in the earlier downturn.

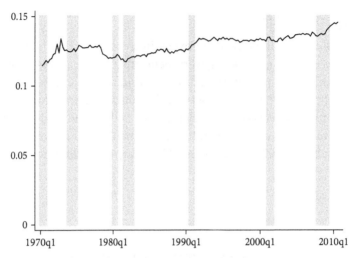

Figure 5.7 State and local current receipts: Share of GDP
Source: US Bureau of the Census, authors' calculations.

In particular, while tax revenues either increased or stayed steady as a share of GDP in previous episodes, in the more recent 2001 and 2007 recessions, revenues fell off dramatically in response to declining economic conditions.

In earlier work, we investigated the increasing sensitivity of state tax revenues to economic conditions.[11] This phenomenon of greater income elasticity has occurred both during recessions (as shown in figure 5.10) as well as during better economic times. In particular, changes in state and local revenues have also become more synchronized with the economy when times are good as well as bad. Most of this change in cyclical responsiveness can be attributed to changes in revenues from the individual income tax. Much of this change in the income tax arises from two factors. First, income-tax revenues have grown far more sensitive

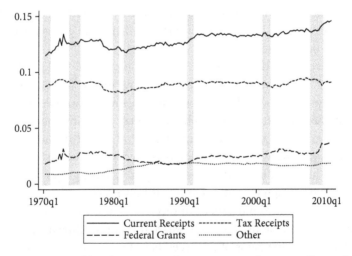

Figure 5.8 State and local receipts and components of receipts: Share of GDP
Source: US Bureau of the Census, authors' calculations.

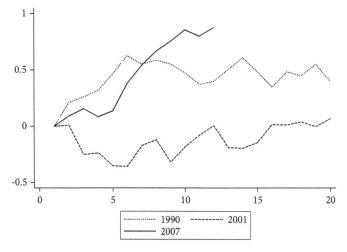

Figure 5.9 Spider graph of state and local receipts (detrended)
Source: US Bureau of the Census, US Bureau of Economic Analysis, authors' calculations.

to economic conditions due to increasing reliance on the volatile capital gains portion of income. Second, state and local policymakers have changed their behavior
in response to recessions. While prior to the 2001 recession, tax rates in many states
would be increased in response to economic downturns to preserve revenues, in
more recent years, tax rates have been more independent of economic conditions.
However, we did not find that the shift from sales to income taxes (discussed in
more detail below) has been a major source of increasing revenue responsiveness.

Figure 5.11 displays a detrended spider graph of grants received by state and local
governments from the federal government, again expressed as percentages of GDP.
Here we see evidence of the major countercyclical aid packages that were enacted
during recent recessionary periods. One can see clear signs of the commencement

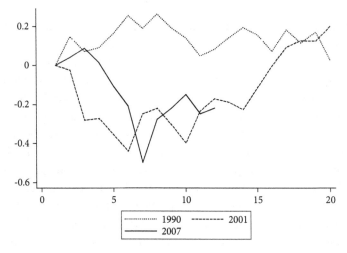

Figure 5.10 Spider graphs of state and local tax receipts (detrended)
Source: US Bureau of the Census, US Bureau of Economic Analysis, authors' calculations.

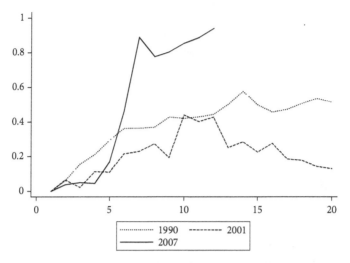

Figure 5.11 Spider graphs of federal grants (detrended)
Source: US Bureau of the Census, US Bureau of Economic Analysis, authors' calculations.

of the federal stimulus package, the ARRA. Comparing figure 5.11 with figures 5.9 and 5.10, one can see that the increase in total receipts during the most recent recession was due to a decline in tax receipts, which was more than offset by an increase in federal aid. In the next section, we discuss the role of federal aid in more detail.

The Wild Card: Countercyclical Federal Aid

When states hit recessions, a common response has been to turn to Washington for relief. In general, countercyclical aid from the federal government has been a frequent component of revenues available to the states during or following recessions, although the level and terms of the aid change from recession to recession.[12] Table 5.3 describes the types and levels of federal aid provided during the last five recessions. Only once, in the 1990–1991 recession, did the federal government fail to provide a specific countercyclical aid package to state and local governments. But, given the passage of a massive roads and infrastructure program (ISTEA) in 1991, that initiative likely took the place of any recession-targeted aid package.[13]

A couple of things are notable about federal aid packages and their impact. First, federal aid almost always comes with a lag. Most of the packages were authorized after the official end dates of recessions, which typically have lasted for only a quarter or two. Only the ARRA, enacted in early 2008, was actually created amid the downturn. This may well reflect the lag in fiscal stress that states experience in their finances during the onset of a recession, as well as the legislative lag that Congress

Table 5.3 Federal state and local government countercyclical aid

Recession Date	Recession Duration	Federal Program Response
1973–1975	16 months	Three programs were launched in 1976 and focused on job training/public employment, public works, and general assistance. Total aid was $14.5 billion.
1980, 1981–1983	1980: 6 months 1981–1983: 16 months	The Emergency Job Act (1983) provided $9 billion through 77 different federal programs designed to stimulate economic and job growth.
1990–1991	8 months	No specific federal program was passed; however, the $151 billion Intermodal Surface Transportation Efficiency Act was passed in 1991.
2001	8 months	The Job and Growth Relief and Reconciliation Act of 2003 paid out $10 billion in fiscal years 2003 and 2004.
2007—2009 (estimated)	Estimated at 20 months	The American Recovery and Reinvestment Act (2009) had two components for state and local governments. The first was $224 billion in fiscal stabilization targeted for education, health care, and unemployment insurance. The second was $275 billion for infrastructure. An additional $10 billion was paid out in 2010.

Source: Mattoon, Haleco-Meyer, and Foster (2010).

faces in designing and approving the aid package. Initially, state tax revenues hold up and social welfare program expenditures are only beginning to expand in the early phases of a recession. States and localities have resources (such as fund balances, rainy-day reserves, or access to other one-time money-raising measures) to balance their budgets. Thus, it is not until the recession wears on that it becomes clear that federal aid is needed. Second, with the exception of the ARRA, most of the federal aid is modest in scope relative to the size of the sector. For example the $14.5 billion in federal aid provided in 1976 only represented roughly 5.5 percent of the direct expenditures made by state and local governments in 1975.[14]

REVENUES

We next display breakdowns in the sources of state and local government own-source revenues, that is, revenues excluding federal transfers. Subsequently, we will display breakdowns in tax dollars, which is the single largest revenue source.

Table 5.4 State government own-source revenue composition

	1972	1990	2008
Taxes	83%	76%	72%
Charges	11%	11%	14%
Utility and Liquor Stores	3%	2%	2%
Miscellaneous	4%	12%	12%

Source: US Census Bureau, authors' calculations.

Table 5.4 shows the share of state own-source revenues from taxes, charges, government utilities (including liquor stores), and miscellaneous sources in 1972, 1990, and 2008. While tax revenues have consistently been the largest source of state government funds, there has been a shift toward charges and miscellaneous sources. Increases in interest earnings, lottery revenues, and one-time funds such as those from the tobacco settlement have contributed to the rise in miscellaneous revenues.

Table 5.5 shows the breakdown of local government revenues. Localities also show a shift from taxes toward charges and miscellaneous sources. The growth in revenue from charges has been fairly broad-based and has occurred in a diverse set of areas including air transport, public hospitals, and water-sewer systems. Also, in keeping with the pattern for states, interest earnings have been an important source of revenue growth.[15]

We now turn to the sources of state and local government tax dollars. Table 5.6 displays the share of tax revenues that come from the major state tax sources in 1972, 1990, and 2008. There has been a major shift from selective sales taxes into personal income taxes over this period. Within selective sales, motor fuel taxes fell from 13 percent of state tax revenues in 1972 to less than 5 percent in 2008. At the same time, the individual income tax grew from 22 percent of state tax revenues in 1972 to 36 percent of state tax revenues in 2008. This increase has little to do with new states adopting personal income taxation because only one state has added an income tax

Table 5.5 Local government own-source revenue composition

	1972	1990	2008
Taxes	68%	54%	55%
Charges	15%	20%	22%
Utility and Liquor Stores	11%	14%	12%
Miscellaneous	6%	13%	10%

Source: US Census Bureau, authors' calculations.

Table 5.6 State government tax composition

	1972	1990	2008
Property	2%	2%	2%
General Sales	29%	33%	31%
Selective Sales	26%	16%	15%
Licenses	9%	6%	6%
Personal Income	22%	32%	36%
Corporate Income	7%	7%	6%
Other	4%	4%	4%

Source: US Census Bureau, authors' calculations.

since 1972 (New Jersey in 1976). Instead, this growth is the result of increasing reliance on the income tax in those states that already had adopted income taxes. Due to the shift to the income tax, states and the federal government both now increasingly rely on the same base for their principal source of funds. While the individual income tax has been the largest revenue source for the federal government since 1950, it first became the largest source for state governments in 1998.

In table 5.7, we display local government tax revenue shares by tax base. In all three years, property taxes have represented the lion's share of local tax revenues.[16] At the same time the share of revenues in total revenues from the property tax has been steadily falling. In its place, local tax revenues from the general sales tax have been increasing. This increase has been due to the commencement of local sales taxes in a number of states, as well as expansions in the role of the sales tax in numerous states. It also reflects the growing economic importance of those regions that have emphasized the use of the sales tax.

Table 5.7 Local government tax composition

	1972	1990	2008
Property	84%	75%	73%
General Sales	5%	11%	12%
Selective Sales	3%	5%	5%
Licenses	1%	0%	3%
Personal and Corporate Income	4%	5%	6%
Other	2%	4%	2%

Source: US Census Bureau, authors' calculations.

CONCLUSION: POLICY OPTIONS FOR DEALING
WITH THE BUSINESS CYCLE

We have examined trends in the state and local government sector in the aggregate economy over the last four decades. Subnational governments have maintained a fairly constant and substantial role in the national economy throughout this period. The forty-year period is marked by the increasing share of expenditures made for social benefits (in particular, for Medicaid) and a growing reliance on the federal government as a source of funds. There has also been an increasing dependence on the personal income tax by the states and a heightened responsiveness of state tax revenues to economic conditions. However, there has been no similar change in the responsiveness of expenditures. Unlike the federal government, virtually all states and municipalities are required to produce budgets that are at least balanced on paper. As a result, there is a question as to how states are going to adjust to this change, where revenues are more volatile but spending is relatively unaffected by changing economic conditions. While the role of localities and their sources of funds have been more stable, changes at the state level are also relevant for localities because approximately one-third of local government revenues are transfers from states.

The role of the states and local governments will likely continue to evolve, and while many of the patterns in place will probably continue, there are growing pressures of change. In particular, the aging population and increases in medical expenses are likely to cause Medicaid to continue to grow as a share of state budgets. On the revenue side, the income tax is likely to continue to be a major and cyclically sensitive source of funds. The property tax, which has been the pillar of most local government revenue systems, may see long-term erosion in its tax base as residential and commercial property values decline and as increases in tax rates are widely opposed.

States may want to consider ways to adapt to the increased cyclical nature of their revenue base.[17] States could attempt to smooth their own-source revenues by either returning to the historic practice of raising tax rates for major tax bases (sales and income) during bad times or by restructuring state taxes to mitigate their volatility. That latter action could be achieved by broadening the base to include less cyclically sensitive forms of income and sales. For example, states could remove exemptions for items such as food and clothing or expand their base to include some basic services. They could also decrease their reliance on the capital gains portion of the income tax, which is now treated as ordinary income in many state tax codes. States could also generate revenues during bad times by using asset sales to smooth out revenue fluctuations, although these one-shots are controversial, especially if the assets are revenue-producing. States could also garner extra funds during downturns by increasing their reliance on rainy-day funds. Given the role of investment-related receipts in generating fluctuations, states could have dedicated rainy-day funds that are explicitly connected to capital gains income-tax revenues. A second strategy would be to adjust expenditures more aggressively. This approach would assume that revenues will always be volatile and thus would force budget gaps to be closed by more rapid changes on the spending side. Another option is to simply permit states to run operating deficits. The idea that a state has to have a balanced budget each year regardless of economic conditions may be an anachronism. A final option is to look to the Federal government for help. This occurred most recently through the ARRA in 2009, and countercyclical aid was provided in response to recessions to states and localities in 2003 and in 1975. But the problem with such a strategy is that such aid is not a sure thing because the federal government also its own long-term fiscal problems to confront as well. In fact, movement toward solving the federal deficit problem will likely cause even more pressure on state and local government finances.

NOTES

The opinions expressed in this chapter are those of the authors and do not represent the opinions of the Federal Reserve Bank of Chicago or of the Federal Reserve System.

1 Maag and Merriman (2003).
2 Another approach to measuring the fiscal response of states and localities to the national business cycle uses the high employment budget structure that decomposes state responses into cyclical and structural components. For more on this, see Follette, Kuska, and Lutz (2008).
3 There are two primary sources of information on state and local government economic activity—data from the Census Bureau and data from the Bureau of Economic Analysis (BEA). The Census Bureau releases data on annual government financial activity in the quinquennial Census of Governments (which is based on a full census) and the related Government Finance annual survey (which is based on statistical sampling). This source provides detailed data on state, local and combined state and local revenues, expenditures and debt. Data are also available separately for each state. The Census Bureau also provides quarterly data on state, local and combined state and local tax collections by revenue source and by state. The BEA, on the other hand, releases quarterly data on state and local government economic activity as part of the quarterly release of the National Income and Product Accounts (NIPAs). These data treat the state and local government sector as a whole. We use both sources of data for this chapter. When we are interested in differences between states and localities we use the Census Bureau data. When we are concerned about business-cycle behavior, we use data from the NIPAs because we prefer the quarterly frequency. There are important differences between the treatment of state and local government receipts and expenditures in the NIPAs and the Census Bureau's Government Finances (GF) series. The NIPAs are based on the GF series, but the data are then adjusted to conform to the standards of national income accounting. In particular, the NIPAs recognize activity in the sectors where the final demand takes place. As a result, services considered to be sold by the government are recorded in the sector that purchases them. For example, the consumption of government enterprises (such as utilities) is treated as personal or business consumption. The GF series, on the other hand, includes the revenues and expenditures of these enterprises. In addition

most transactions of employee pension funds are included in the NIPA personal sector. Also, the NIPAs treat Unemployment Insurance as part of the federal sector while it is part of the state sector in the GF data. Table 3.19 in the NIPAs details the relationship between measures derived directly from the GF data and the NIPAs.

4 This is also higher due to the exclusion of farm employment. However, farm employment is less than 2 percent of total employment so it cannot explain much of this gap.

5 US Bureau of Economic Analysis (2010).

6 For a recent discussion on trends in state, local, and private-sector compensation and benefits using comparability measures, see Bender and Heywood (2010).

7 The expansion in state and local governments from the 1940s to the 1970s was due in part to the creation of the Medicaid program in 1965 and to the expansion in education funding as the baby boomers entered the public education system. Penner (1998) provides a concise description of these forces.

8 The unemployment insurance program is not included here because the NIPAs place it in the federal sector. Were it included, we would observe more dramatic social benefits growth in response to recessions.

9 ARRA http://www.recovery.gov/About/Pages/The_Act.aspx. The ARRA program affected state and local government social insurance payments primarily through increasing the portion of Medicaid paid for by the Federal government. The ARRA also included emergency TANF funds and increased grants for employment and training programs. The ARRA, in addition, increased unemployment insurance spending, but this spending is treated as part of the federal sector in the NIPAs.

10 See http://www.ssa.gov/ssi/text-understanding-ssi.htm

11 Mattoon and McGranahan (2008).

12 Mattoon, Haleco-Meyer, and Foster (2010).

13 See http://ntl.bts.gov/DOCS/istea.html.

14 Mattoon, Haleco-Meyer, and Foster (2010).

15 Much of the rise in interest revenue can probably be attributed to changes in the treatment of interest from public debt for private purposes. If we exclude interest revenues, the share of state own-source revenues from miscellaneous sources increases from 2 percent in 1972 to 8 percent in 2008. The share of local own-source revenues from miscellaneous sources increases from 4 percent in 1972 to 6 percent in 2008.

16 For an excellent discussion of property tax revenue performance over the business cycle, see Lutz (2008).

17 Mattoon and McGranahan (2008).

References

....

American Recovery and Reinvestment Act (ARRA) of 2009. http://frwebgate.access.gpo.gov/cgi-bin/getdoc.cgi?dbname=111_cong_bills&docid=f:h1enr.pdf

Bender, Keith A., and John S. Heywood (2010)."Out of Balance? Comparing Public and Private Sector Compensation over 20 Years," National Institute on Retirement Security and Center for State Local Government Excellence, April 2010. http://www.slge.org/vertical/Sites/%7BA260E1DF-5AEE-459D-84C4-876EFE1E4032%7D/uploads/%7B03E820E8-F0F9-472F-98E2-F0AE1166D116%7D.PDF.

Boyd, Donald J., (2009, February 19). "What Will Happen to State Budgets When the Money Runs Out," Nelson A. Rockefeller Institute of Government, *Fiscal Features*.

Follette, Glenn, Andrea Kuska, and Byron F. Lutz (2008). "State and Local Finances and the Macroeconomy: The High-Employment Budget and Fiscal Impetus," *National Tax Journal* LXI(3), 531–545.

Fox, William F. (2003). "Three Characteristics of Tax Structures Have Contributed to the Current State Fiscal Crises," *State Tax Notes,* 30(5), 369–378.

Lutz, Byron F. (2008). "The Connection between House Price Appreciation and Property Tax Revenues," *National Tax Journal,* LXI(3), 555–572.

Maag, Elaine, and David Merriman (2003). "Tax Policy Responses to Revenue Shortfalls," *State Tax Notes,* 30(5), 393–404.

Mattoon, Richard, Vanessa Haleco-Meyer, and Taft Foster (2010). "Improving the Impact of Federal Aid to the States," *Economic Perspectives* (Third and Fourth Quarter 2010) Federal Reserve Bank of Chicago, 66–92.

Mattoon, Richard, and Leslie McGranahan (2008). "Structural Deficits and Revenue Bubbles: What's a State to Do?" Federal Reserve Bank of Chicago, Working Paper WP2008-15.

McGranahan, Leslie, and Richard Mattoon (2010). "Revenue Cyclicality and State Policy Options," unpublished manuscript.

Penner, Rudolph G. (1998, October). "A Brief History of State and Local Fiscal Policy," The Urban Institute, No A-27.

Ross, Casey (2009, June 17). "Lawmakers Look to Capital Gains Tax to Bolster Savings," *Boston Globe.*

Sjoquist, David, and Sally Wallace (2003). "Capital Gains: Its Recent, Varied and Growing (?) Impact on State Revenues," *State Tax Notes,* 30(5), 423–432.

US Bureau of Economic Analysis, National Income and Product Accounts, Gross Domestic Product, various years, http://www.bea.gov/national/nipaweb/index.asp, http://www.bea.gov/national/index.htm#gdp.

US Census Bureau, state government finances, various years, http://www.census.gov/govs/www/state.html.

....

CHAPTER 6

THE EVOLVING FINANCIAL ARCHITECTURE OF STATE AND LOCAL GOVERNMENTS

....

SALLY WALLACE

DEMOGRAPHIC, economic, and institutional trends define the "fiscal architecture" of state and local governments. Changes in these trends are largely beyond the control of governments, but they put pressure on expenditures and revenue sources of state and local governments and may constrain options for reforming public finances. The trends include demographic changes (e.g., growth and age composition of the population, sizes of households, life expectancy) and economic changes that affect the structural mix of the state's economy (e.g., employment level, distribution of income, the mix of sectors). How institutions and organizations change also constrains and frames the nature of revenue and expenditure pressures and options (e.g., the way citizens communicate among themselves about their government and how governments communicate and become accountable to their citizens); federal government interventions in the form of expenditure mandates and preemptions of the revenue base; or the intergovernmental implications of federal (and, in this era of rapid globalization, other nations') fiscal policy.[1]

Thus, what state and local governments can and cannot do is based on the fiscal architecture of those individual governmental units as well as on the fact that all governments are a part of a vibrant federal union and a global economy. For example, some states might want to impose import duties as globalization opens world markets, but they are constitutionally prohibited from doing so because taxation of imports falls under the purview of the federal government. Or states, and/or their governments, might want to alter minimum funding for schools but federal (and for the locality, state) regulations and rules may preclude them from doing so. If not that, at least, states must determine the conditions under which such an intergovernmental transfer is designed. Taxing capital might look like a good idea for a state, but the global mobility of capital makes taxation administratively difficult. And then there are the rules and regulations of entitlement programs such as Medicaid that constrain the abilities of federal and state governments to adjust expenditures in the face of a burgeoning elderly population.

PURPOSE AND SCOPE

This chapter provides an analysis of the current state of the fiscal architecture of state and local governments in the United States in the late 2000s and of the potential pressures and options for state and local governments to deal more effectively with the economic and demographic changes that face them. The analysis is not meant to be revisionist, but rather to lay out a framework for looking forward by suggesting changes to the fiscal architecture that might increase the sustainability of state and local finances over the next quarter century—that is, given the changing nature of demographic, economic, and institutional trends, we need to look at what choices make "fiscal sense" for a sustainable state and local sector, and, therefore, a vibrant and sustainable system of fiscal federalism. The backdrop of the 2007–2009 recession is difficult to ignore, but in this chapter, the focus is not on that particular fiscal crisis but on the underlying trends and tensions facing state and local governments over the past two decades and the next to come.

Accordingly, the chapter is organized as follows. The next section lays out the analytical links among economic and demographic change and the fiscal architecture of state and local governments in the United States. The third section presents data to analyze the trends in revenues and expenditures from 1980 to the present, with a focus on the current decade. The fourth section provides an overview of major economic and demographic changes that have impacted and will continue to impact state and local fiscal options over the next decade. In the fifth section, quantitative analysis of these impacts is developed, and the final section concludes with options for state and local governments to deal with the changes they face.

Linking Fiscal Architecture with Economic, Demographic, and Institutional Factors

Efficiency requires that the structure of public finances reflect citizen demands for public goods and services. More often than not, however, it takes time for governments to adjust to new demands and to alter the way they do their "revenue business." The relationships among economic, demographic, and institutional changes and the fiscal structure are quite straightforward. A couple of simple examples make the case.

Expenditure Impacts

Public goods and services provided by state and local governments are driven by the needs of the client population.[2] A very basic relationship between public expenditures and demographic factors is as follows:

$$\text{Exp}_i = Q_g \times C_g \tag{1}$$

$$Q_g = f \text{ (client population)} \tag{2}$$

$$d\text{Exp}_i = dQ_g \times C_g + Q_g \times dC_g \tag{3}$$

where Q_g is the output of the public good and C_g is the cost per unit.[3]

Expenditures are a function of demand "Q" and the price of production "C." Changes in demand (equation (3)) are brought about by changes in the client population and changes in the cost of production. Changes in the client population might include demographics (e.g. elderly population, school-aged population), changes in economic base (bringing forth different demands for infrastructure), and other factors. Changes in the cost of production are associated with the cost of inputs (e.g., wages, materials, rents). Demographic changes can influence the cost and demand components of the expenditure calculation. For example, consider a change in the age distribution of the population. If a population is becoming increasingly elderly, this will increase the need for expenditures for retirement and health based expenditures.[4] However, such a trend will also influence the direct cost of providing those services as labor shortages may also ensue, thus driving up the cost of labor inputs.

Revenues

A relationship for revenues can be similarly expressed as a function of the tax-paying population ("pop"), tax rate, and tax base as follows:

$$\text{Rev}_i = (\text{tax base}_i \times \text{tax rate}_i) \times \text{pop}_i \tag{4}$$

$$dRev_i = dtax\ base_i \times tax\ rate_i \times pop_i + tax\ base_i \times dtax\ rate_i \times$$
$$pop_i + tax\ base_i \times tax\ rate_i \times dpop_i \qquad (5)$$

On the revenue side, the "tax base" is determined by the tax code of the appropriate jurisdiction and economic activity of a particular revenue source, and the "tax rate" is determined by the relevant legislature and executive bodies.[5] Pop_i is the tax-paying population for a given revenue source. For personal or individual income taxes, the tax base would be some measure of taxable income per unit, and the population would be the number of individuals who have that taxable income. Tax compliance and administration might also be captured in this relationship, but those important considerations are excluded from this discussion.

Economic and demographic changes will directly influence these tax bases as well as the relevant population. In the case of a consumption-based revenue source, for example, the level of population will affect the total potentially taxable consumption, and the age distribution of the population will affect the type of consumption that is made. The breadth of the tax base of each state and local government will determine how much revenue will fluctuate as a result of these demographic changes. For example, if a state or local government taxes individual income broadly, it will be less subject to changes in the composition of income. The tax rate, while exogenous to these demographic and economic changes, is a policy variable that can be used to compensate for changes in the tax base.

These simple relationships among expenditures and revenues and their component parts demonstrate that economic and demographic trends will affect state and local public finances through various means if the overall structure is not adjusted. There is a third important component of this analysis. The fiscal structure is built on numerous institutional components. For example, the US Constitution provides only the most basic assignment of revenues between the federal and state governments, whereas state constitutions typically are quite explicit on the nature (and limits) of local revenue authority.[6] State governments in turn provide different regulations regarding local revenue sources. Intergovernmental relations in the form of revenue sharing and nondiscretionary expenditure programs determine a large share of the public finances in the United States. Changes in these and many other institutions will affect the fiscal structure of the entire federal-state-local system potentially as much as changes in demographic and economic characteristics will directly affect fiscal choices of governments.

CURRENT FISCAL ARCHITECTURE

Over the past thirty years, the financial structures of state and local governments have undergone some changes.[7] It is important to highlight these past trends to better understand the current and future financial architecture of state and local governments (tables 6.1 and 6.2; figure 6.1).

As a share of personal income, state and local government revenue has increased from 19.7 percent of personal income in 1980 to 25.9 percent in 2007 before falling with the recession to 21.8 percent in 2008. On a per capita basis, revenues have grown steadily, with downturns in 2002 and 2008. State revenue and local revenue separately show similar patterns of growth. Over this period, there was some movement in the level of intergovernmental revenues. As a share of personal income, intergovernmental revenues hit a high of 4.3 percent in 2004 and a low of 2.8 percent in 1988–1989. Federal transfers directly to local governments continue to play a relatively small role (making up $244 per capita in real terms in 1980 and $191 in 2008). Federal transfers to state governments increased from $716 in 1980 (real per capita) to $1,363 in 2008. States in turn increased their intergovernmental transfers to the local governments from $958 in 1980 to $1,533 in 2008 (all in real, per capita terms).

The data in figure 6.1 demonstrate that the upward trend in per capita total revenue was substantially impacted during the most recent recessions (2001 and 2007+). These general trends suggest that revenues have indeed been affected by economic downturns in the last thirty years, but they tell us less about how the underlying structure of the economy and socioeconomic and demographic changes have influenced the structure and level of revenue.

A general look at expenditures also suggests an overall pattern of growth in real per capita state and local expenditures between 1980 and 2008. Expenditure reactions to the economic downturns of this period are a bit more lagged than revenues and less dramatically affected.

A more detailed look at state and local revenues and expenditures is necessary to help understand the implications of changes in demographics and other factors on the fiscal structures of state and local governments in the United States. The data in table 6.1 summarize the trends in the level of revenues and expenditures for major classifications by using the US Census Bureau classification as follows:

Total Revenue = general revenue + utility revenue + liquor store revenues + social insurance trust revenue.

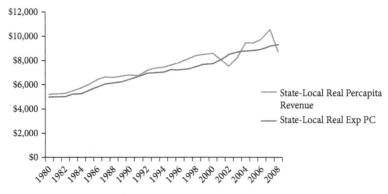

Figure 6.1 State and local real per capita expenditures and revenues
Source: State & Local Government Finance Data Query System.
http://www.taxpolicycenter.org/slf-dqs/pages.cfm.

General revenue is further classified to include taxes, intergovernmental revenue, charges, and miscellaneous general revenue. *Total expenditures* are comprised
of intergovernmental expenditures and direct expenditures. *Direct expenditures*
are further classified into four sectors: direct general, utilities, liquor stores, and
social insurance trust. Finally *direct general expenditures* are comprised of various
functions including education, health, and transportation.

As seen in table 6.1, state governments obtain the largest share of revenue
from own-source taxes, while local governments receive similar shares from
own-source taxes and intergovernmental revenues. The variation in tax revenue
is cyclical (as expected) but the overall trend demonstrates a decreasing concentration of tax revenue at the state but locally. Both state and local governments
have seen an increase in the importance of user fees and charges, while the share
of intergovernmental revenue to general revenue has declined for local governments and increased for states. In general, insurance trust revenue (which is
largely earmarked for pension payments) has increased for both state and local
governments—one hint of the impact of an aging population. On the expenditure
side, the high-level aggregation reveals few provocative trends. For state and local
governments, direct general expenditures tend to dominate the public finance
systems.

The data in table 6.2 provide more detail on the composition of tax revenues
and general expenditures, in order to shed more light on general trends. The taxes
listed in that table represent almost 90 percent of state tax revenues and 95 percent of local tax revenues.[8] The noteworthy state revenue trends are the decline in
the importance of the corporate income tax and general sales tax and an increase
in individual income tax. For local governments, a decrease in the concentration
of the property tax and an increase in general sales tax revenues are noteworthy
trends.

On the expenditure side of the budget, there has been some movement in the
concentration of expenditures in certain sectors. State governments have witnessed
an increased share of general expenditures to public welfare (payments to vendors including payments for Medicaid-provided services are the largest share of
the public welfare category). For local governments, expenditures on education
account for nearly 44 percent of general expenditures, and this concentration has
not changed over the period. These expenditure choices are a function of federal
mandates related to nondiscretionary expenditures as well as demand from the
constituent population.

These trends suggest rather sluggish movements in the fiscal structures of state
and local governments over this period. The questions that remain are whether the
sluggishness is in line with the underlying demographic and economic changes
and whether it serves to increase the fiscal vulnerability of state and local governments in the future. To analyze these questions, one must turn next to an analysis
of the underlying demographic and economic changes that will influence finances
and should be accounted for by adjusting the fiscal structure of state and local
governments.

Table 6.1 Distribution of revenue and expenditure

Percentage of General Revenue	Revenues Average 1980–2008 (min/max)		Percentage of General Expenditures	Expenditures Average 1980–2008 (min/max)	
	State	Local		State	Local
Taxes	55.2 (49.4/59.5)	38.3 (36.7/39.8)	Intergovernmental	29.8 (27.5/32.8)	1.0 (0.6/1.2)
Intergovernmental	27.8 (24.0/33.0)	38.9 (37.0/44.1)	Direct General	57.9 (55.0/59.3)	85.7 (83.8/86.8)
Fees and Charges	17.0 (13.8/18.9)	22.7 (18.8/23.7)	Utilities-Liquor	1.7 (1.2/2.0)	11.5 (10.1/13.7)
Utility and Liquor	1.3 (0.9/1.8)	9.7 (8.6/11.0)	Insurance	9.4 (7.6/11.5)	1.8 (1.5/2.1)
Insurance Trust	20.9 (1.7/35.7)	3.1 (0/5.6)			

Source: State and Local Government Finance Data Query System, http://www.taxpolicycenter.org/slf-dqs/pages.cfm.

Table 6.2 Detailed distribution of revenue and expenditure

Tax Revenues 1980–2008			Expenditures 1980–2008		
Percentage of Total Tax Revenue	State	Local	Percentage of General Expenditures	State	Local
Individual Income	27.1	5.8	Education	24.5	43.8
	35.6	4.8		22.7	43.2
Corporate Income	9.7	0.0	Health and Hospitals	10.9	7.4
	6.5	1.3		9.0	8.5
General Sales	49.5	14.0	Public Welfare	23.1	5.5
	45.9	16.4		34.6	3.7
Property	2.1	76.0	Corrections	2.9	1.0
	1.6	72.3		4.6	1.9
			Highways	14.4	5.7
				8.8	4.6

Source: State and Local Government Finance Data Query System, http://www.taxpolicycenter.org/slf-dqs/pages.cfm.

ECONOMIC AND DEMOGRAPHIC TRENDS

The US population is growing older, but unlike a country such as Japan, there is still a healthy growth in the number of children to help bolster the labor force.[9] The country has witnessed long-term migration from the Northeast and Midwest to the South and West regions of the country. There is considerable growth in the number of Hispanics. *The Economist* magazine points out, correctly, that to make matters more complicated, the demographic changes are not evenly spread over the country.[10] One specific example mentioned is that the percentage of the elderly in Maine now surpasses that of Florida.

In this section, a handful of the major economic and demographic trends and projections are highlighted. The analysis is not exhaustive, but the factors analyzed here are illustrative of the types of factors that are affecting state and local finances and should be considered in reform options aimed to increase the fiscal health of state and local governments.

One of the most talked-about demographic changes is the aging of the population. Countrywide, there is an increased concentration of individuals age sixty-five and older (table 6.3) and the US Census projects a continued increase in this age group over the next two decades.[11] At the same time, the absolute level of population in each major age category is expected to grow. These trends portend some important conflicts for state and local finances. From the perspective of expenditure demand, the elderly will increase the demand for health services, while the constituents of an expanding school-aged population will need increasing education expenditures.

Table 6.3 Distribution of population (US)

Age Group	1980	1990	2000	2010	2025
	Percentage of Total Population				
5 to 19	24.6	21.3	21.7	20.3	19.8
20 to 64	56.8	58.7	59	59.9	55.8
65 and older	11.3	12.5	12.4	13	17.9
80 and older	2.3	2.8	3.3	3.7	4.2

Source: US Census International Database, http://www. census.gov/ipc/www/idb/informationGateway.php.

The growing trend of exempting the elderly from a portion of the property tax could signal increased fiscal pressures related to school financing. There is no compendium of the value of these property-tax exemptions for the United States, but there are tax expenditure estimates for some states. In the state of Georgia, the tax expenditure estimate associated with elderly exemptions (homestead) was $207 million in 2007 relative to property-tax revenues of greater than $7.5 billion.[12]

From the data in table 6.4, it is clear that the Northeast is aging relatively quickly. Census projections show that the youngest age groups, those under eighteen, will make up 22 percent of the population in the Northeast in 2020 (based on Census projections)—down from 24.3 percent in 2000. The percent of the population who are sixty-five and older in the Northeast will grow to more than 17 percent by 2020, which is a substantial increase from 13.8 percent in 2000. A convenient way to capture the fiscal complications associated with the aging demographic is to track the "old-age dependency ratio" (DR), a ratio of the population aged sixty-five and older to the population aged between twenty and sixty-four. As this ratio increases, all else equal, there are fewer working-aged individuals to support those close to or in retirement. For state and local budgets, increasing ratios suggest less wage income and tax revenue to support public pension systems. In all regions of the country, the ratios are expected to increase by 6.4 to 8.4 percentage points between 2000 and 2020. The Northeast is projected to have the largest ratio in 2020 (29.7), but states in the West will see the largest percentage point growth (18.5 to 26.9 between 2000 and 2020).

A specific example of the implications of the aging population on state and local fiscal structures can be seen by way of an example of public pension funding. Many public pensions are funded through general tax revenue (or, in the case of the federal government, payroll taxes) as well as other forms of contributions and capital earnings. Many state income taxes (which comprise a large portion of general fund revenues) exempt various portions of retirement income, thereby increasing the burden of pension systems on working individuals. If the portion of financing coming from taxes on working individuals is "α" and the remainder funded by other means is $1 - \alpha$, a simple expression for pay-as-you-go pension financing may be expressed as follows:[13]

$$P_b{*}B = \alpha{*}t{*}P_w{*}w + (1 - \alpha){*}Rev_j$$

Table 6.4 Regional distribution of population by age
(percentage of total population)

	Under 18 years	
Region	2000	2020
Northeast	24.3	22.0
Midwest	25.9	23.8
South	25.5	24.3
West	26.9	24.7
	18 to 64 years	
Region	2000	2020
Northeast	61.9	60.7
Midwest	61.3	59.9
South	62.1	59.3
West	62.1	59.9
	65 years and over	
Region	2000	2020
Northeast	13.8	17.3
Midwest	12.8	16.3
South	12.4	16.3
West	11.0	15.4

Source: US Census International Database, http://www.census.gov/
population/www/projections/regdivpyramid.html.

P_b is the number of pensioners, B is an average of the benefit per pensioner, t is the income-tax rate on wages, P_w is the number of workers, w is the average covered wage per worker, and Rev_i is the revenue from nonincome-tax sources. Rearranging this expression slightly yields the following expression:

$$t = (P_b/P_w) * (B/\alpha w) (1 - \alpha)*Rev_j$$

The first term on the right-hand side of the equation is the age-dependency ratio—the ratio of the working population to pensioners. The second term is the replacement ratio—the ratio of average benefits paid to wages that supply the financing for the pension system (weighted by the amount of financing from the income tax as our example) and the second part of the expression is the share of pension financing from other means.[14] As the number of beneficiaries grows relative to the number of workers who are paying income tax, the aged-dependency ratio grows and if a system does not have adequate reserves, there will not be enough of the various revenue sources to support the increased benefits liability. A standard of best practice in funding state and local pensions is that systems have an active member-to-annuitant ratio of three or better, but recent research of more than one hundred public pension systems demonstrates that only six have ratios greater than three.[15]

In addition to impacts on pensions and income-tax revenue, the aging demographic will change the demands for various goods and services, coupled with increased voting participation by the elderly. This will continue to increase the need for services preferred by the elderly, including health, hospital, and medical services; social security; transportation services; and some types of recreational services. Elderly populations consume different types of goods, including substantial health- and medical-related goods and services—most of which are largely untaxed.[16]

Changes in the economic base (income composition and sectoral distribution of production and employment) will also have important impacts on state and local government budgets. Employment data serve as the best measure of sectoral changes in the economy. A thirty-plus-year trend in the US economy is a move from manufacturing to service production and employment. According to the Bureau of Economic Analysis (BEA), this general trend has continued through 2009.[17] Interestingly, the BEA data show an increase in state and local government employment between 1990 and 2009 with a slight decline in federal government employment over the same period. This trend is found in all regions except the Rocky Mountain region. However, the big "news" on the composition of the economy is increased concentration of employment (and in output) in the health care and social assistance sector. In the New England and Mideast regions, this sector now makes up over 15 percent of private employment—up from less than 12 percent in 1990. In all regions, this sector is now more than 10 percent of private employment and it competes with retail trade as the single largest sector in each region of the country. Manufacturing employment and output has continued its slide. In the Great Lakes region, manufacturing employment made up 20.9 percent of private employment in 1990; by 2009 it was 11.9 percent. In the Southeast, the decrease is from 17.3 percent in 1990 to 8.4 percent in 2009.

These trends in employment (and output) of the service sector relative to the manufacturing sector may have a significant impact on property taxes. The service sector is less heavily invested in tangible property and capital than the manufacturing sector, and this will cause a potential reduction in the amount of equipment and machinery subject to the property tax.[18] Regarding personal income, there has been a large increase in the share of income from transfer payments. While this is certainly expected in economic downturns, the trend has existed for the past two decades. Table 6.5 summarizes the distribution of personal income for the United States as a whole, and these data show quite clearly the substantial rise in transfer payments from 12.3 percent of personal income in 1990 to 17.5 percent in 2009. Capital income (interest, dividends, rent, and proprietors' income) are more "noisy" in that their concentration fluctuates over the years. Intervening years show the same general pattern, the most consistent of which is the increase in transfer payments as a share of personal income. Transfer payments are largely made up

Table 6.5 Composition of personal income (US, 1990–2009)

Year	1990	2000	2009
Wages	56.50%	56.39%	51.50%
Dividends, interest, and rent	20.07%	18.41%	18.03%
Transfer payment	12.32%	12.66%	17.52%
Proprietors' income	7.60%	9.59%	8.39%

Source: Bureau of Economic Analysis, http://www.bea.gov/regional/spi/default.cfm?selTable=summary.

of social security and other payments to individuals; many of these payments are nontaxable income by state and local governments.

A relatively simple example helps to demonstrate the potential impact of the income composition dynamic on the state individual income tax, which is an important source of revenue. Consider a base year, where the composition of income is 60 percent wages (taxable), 30 percent capital income and proprietors' income (largely taxable), and 10 percent pensions, transfer payments, and other forms of nontaxable income. If the average tax rate were 5 percent and the composition of income remained constant but grew with the general trends in the economy, the taxing state would expect state income-tax revenues to maintain a growth rate approximately equal to the growth in the overall economy. If instead the state witnessed a change in the composition of income such that, over a ten-year period, wages fell to 57.3 percent, capital plus proprietors' income fell to 25.5 percent and pensions and transfer payments increased to 17.2 percent, the growth in income-tax revenues would fail to keep up with the growth in the economy. With a starting income base of $100 billion, the difference in revenue between the two scenarios at the end of the ten-year period would be 4.3 percent of income-tax revenues. Given the importance of income-tax revenues in most state fiscal structures, this is not an insignificant revenue loss. At the same time, state and local governments would be faced with more pressure to provide services such as education and health due to the increasing elderly and school-aged populations.

In summary, these demographic and economic sector changes portend reduced elasticities for several important state and local revenue sources (including the income and sales tax) and increased demand for public goods (including health care). Most of these trends have been documented for the past twenty to thirty years, and forecasts suggest that they will continue to intensify over the next decade. The aging of the population and the number of retirees put increased pressure on public health expenditures at a time when increasing components of income (pensions and social security) are untaxed. The elderly also consume a larger share of health- and medical-related goods than the nonelderly—and many of those goods are not taxed. The growth of service-based consumption (including Internet sales) increases the complexity and cost of taxing sales. The loss of manufacturing employment and output and the increase in the service-based economy increase the complexity of administering taxes. An increase in the concentration of minorities in the population and changes in demand for public services (including in the medium-term demands for language services in schools) and changes in consumption patterns also will affect the level of taxable sales.

In the next section, an empirical analysis of the potential impact of economic and demographic changes on the current fiscal health of state governments is conducted and discussed to provide additional quantitative evidence of those changes.

A Closer Look at Impacts

The early 2000 and the 2007+ recessions have made more evident the fiscal stresses on state and local finances, but the underlying changes in demographic and economic characteristics have signaled this pressure on the state and local fiscal systems for the past three decades. The deterioration of state and local governments' fiscal situations during the Great Recession is almost legendary. The National Association of Budget Officers (NASBO) and the Center on Budget and Policy Priorities (CBPP) reported near-record reductions in per capita tax revenue, cutbacks in spending, and shrinking end-of-the-year funds ("rainy-day funds").[19] These fiscal outcomes are quite expected given the depth and length of the recession.

But recessions are cyclical; there will be a recovery. Thus the more fundamental challenge for the US state and local fiscal systems—indeed for the sustainability of our system of fiscal federalism—is whether there is evidence of a longer-term decline in the growth of per capita revenue or signs of fiscal stress associated with the economic and demographic trends presented in the earlier sections.[20] There is no attempt here to define a theoretical or complete structural model of these relationships. Instead, we are looking for correlations among fiscal balances and per capita revenue and the underlying economic and demographic variables that are expected to affect revenue productivity—in particular, the aging demographic and income composition trends.

Simple correlations between state individual income-tax revenues per capita and the percentages of the elderly and of wages in personal income provide some interesting results. From 1988 to 2000, there is a positive and statistically significant correlation between the wage share of personal income and income-tax revenue, and the coefficient remains relatively constant at about 0.27. There is no significant correlation with the percentage of the elderly. From 2002 on, the wage share correlation is stronger, with a magnitude of between 0.31 and 0.38 from 2002 to 2008. Again, the elderly coefficient is insignificant. Correlations between a per capita measure of fiscal stress (calculated as expenditures minus revenue minus stabilization funds), the percentage of the elderly, and the percentage of wages also demonstrate an important pattern. Before 1999, the correlations between the stress measure (state government) and the percentages of elderly and of wages are erratic in sign and size. After 1998, the sign of the correlation between stress per capita and the elderly is positive—meaning that there is a simple correlation between the percentage of the elderly and a higher level of stress. The correlation between stress and the wage share variable is positive (which is not expected) but typically not significant.[21]

In addition to these simple correlations, an OLS regression was run as follows:

$$\text{Stress\_pc} = \alpha_0 + \alpha_1{}^*\text{GDPPC} + \alpha_2{}^*\text{PctELD} + \alpha_3{}^*\text{PctWAGE} + \alpha_4{}^*\text{GrantPC} + \mu$$

GDPPC is gross domestic product per capita, PctELD is the percentage of the elderly, PctWAGE is the ratio of wages to personal income, GrantPC is total grants per capita, and μ is the error term. This regression was run for the state with and without year dummy variables. For various combinations of years, the coefficient on PctELD is positive and significant, while that for wages is often positive but less significant. The coefficient on GrantPC is negative and significant in all cases, but doubles in size between the early years (1988–2000) and the later years (2000–2007). These results suggest that the impact of demographic change (aging of the population) may be reflected in the fiscal status of state (and, by extension, local) governments. Per capita grants mitigate the impact, as might be expected.

These results are far from conclusive but they merit attention because they reveal a measurable impact of some demographic and economic variables on the fiscal health of state and local governments. In addition, there is some limited evidence that the impact of demographic change may be stronger after the early 2000 recession. More work needs to be done to fully quantify these relationships. However, at the very least, these results reinforce the need for policymakers and practitioners to understand the systematic long-term links between the fiscal architecture of the state and local sectors and their long-term financial position within the federal system.

OUTLOOK AND OPTIONS

While the constitutional framework of the fiscal structure of state and local governments can remain constant in the face of these challenges, the concentration of revenues and demand for particular services will change. What is important is that, from a public finance perspective, the implications of the economic and demographic pressures touched on in this chapter are not *fait accompli*. Forward-thinking governments can capture the implications of these changes in their expenditure forecasts and tailor their revenue systems in such a way as to reduce the impact on their revenue stream of changes in their constituents' economic base, income, or demographics. Governments can ignore the underlying pressures in which case we would expect to see decreases in the growth in revenue from most sources and a misaligned system of expenditures, resulting in a sort of cognitive dissonance for governments that will be hard to reconcile. By taking a proactive approach, state and local governments can adjust their fiscal structures to maintain fiscal balances while producing the public goods demanded by their changing populations. Instituting tax changes and veering from the status quo of expenditures are difficult policy changes to implement. However, medium- to long-term budget analysis and forecasting that incorporate the economic and demographic changes presented in this chapter may provide time to "politic" the necessary adjustments.[22]

What options are out there for state and local governments? In table 6.6, a series of pressures and options are presented. This table is illustrative, but it does highlight the likely pressures and the potential impact on major components of the public finance systems of state and local governments. The general expectation is that the economic and demographic changes that state and local governments face will reduce the elasticity of most major sources of revenue, including individual income, sales, and property tax. State and local governments can increase awareness of these impacts if they regularly analyze their tax expenditures in the form of an official tax expenditure budget as is done in many states; and then make the political decision to act on those items that undermine—indeed, may threaten—the fiscal sustainability of the state and local sector. Exemptions and deductions may have had merit at the time they are made law but their merit may diminish over time while their costs rise. Income-tax exemptions for retirement income are one example of a tax expenditure whose cost will continue to increase in all regions of the country. As this erosion on the tax base converges with the expenditure implications of increased demand for health-care expenditures for the elderly, the long-term result is more, not less, budget stress, unless such currently exempt income is, for tax purposes, brought into the state and local revenue base. Another overarching policy prescription for state and local governments in light of the challenges put forth by the economic and demographic changes is for continued collaboration to rationalize sales tax bases and collections across jurisdictional boundaries. Consider, for example, the interplay of the institutional fact of the congressional preemption from state and local sales taxes on consumer purchases made via the Internet (estimatedly $45.9 billion in 2012)[23] and the demographic that 90 percent of Generation Y (the "Millennials" born between 1981 and 1999) over the age of eighteen use the Internet regularly when compared with three-quarters of the population as a whole.[24] How can a sales tax be modern—that is, capturing the fiscal architecture—if federal policymakers ignore such developments?

Expanding tax bases is old advice, but in the face of these types of challenges, it could be effective in mitigating the decrease in elasticities of various revenue sources. In general, as outlined in table 6.6, there are important implications for

Table 6.6 Matrix of economic and demographic impacts on state and local budgets and options

Economic/ Demographic Variables	Recent and Future Trends	Anticipated Impact on State and Local Government Budgets	Options
Personal income	Growth in overall personal income. The composition has changed and shows an increase in nonwage and salary components including transfer payments. Higher income families hold an increasing share of total US income. Fast-growth regions of the 1980s (West and parts of the South) have slowed considerably.	**REVENUE:** Reduced taxable income base, most directly affecting state and local individual income taxes. Relative increases in income for high-income families could increase income-tax revenues for states with progressive marginal tax-rate structures.	Broad-based income taxes may mitigate some of the issues related to growing retirement income. In general, an annual review of tax expenditures could help to highlight the impact of exemptions over time.
Population	Increased proportion of the elderly in the population and increased growth in school-aged children over the next ten to fifteen years. Increased dependency ratio in all US regions, with the largest growth coming in the West.	**REVENUE:** Property-tax exemptions for the elderly could expand. Changes in consumption patterns may reduce the growth of taxable sales by the elderly and changes in ethnicity may also affect the sales tax base. **EXPENDITURE:** Increased demand for services, especially health care and transportation. Increased demand for improved educational outcomes (and a likely call for increased expenditures for education to support diverse population).	Broad-based sales and income taxes will reduce the impact of changes in consumption patterns and income generation. Diversification of school financing to include support from the federal and state governments should be further investigated

(Continued)

Table 6.6 Continued

Economic/ Demographic Variables	Recent and Future Trends	Anticipated Impact on State and Local Government Budgets	Options
Employment/Output	Continued shift from manufacturing employment and output to service employment and output. E-commerce as an increasing way to do business.	**REVENUE:** Increased cost of tax administration to locate service-based and Internet sales. Potential reduction of property tax on inventories and other capital. **EXPENDITURE:** Increased demand for expansion of technology and telecommunications infrastructure.	Continued development of cooperation in sales taxation across jurisdictions is important to reduce the impacts of Internet sales. Expanding the sales-tax base and training to improve the efficiency of tax administration for a service-based economy may bolster the sales tax.
Consumption	Increase in consumption of services throughout the last decade. Diversification in consumption due to demographic changes (ethnicity, elderly).	**REVENUE:** Increased consumption of largely nontaxed goods will lower the growth in sales tax revenue over time.	Broad-based sales taxation will help to mitigate changes in consumption.

what makes "fiscal sense" for state and local governments given the economic and demographic changes that the nation is experiencing. Recognizing that in tax policy there is no "one-size-fits-all" solution for structural problems, the table lists some further options as a starting point for policy action.

Thus, for example, with respect to the aging of the population, state governments should consider a reduction of the retirement income exclusion, subjecting such income to the same rules as, say, wage income. Property-tax exemptions should be analyzed and possibly redesigned to consider income as an index of equity versus providing blanket exemptions based on age. The changing structure of the economy calls for a review of the differential property-tax treatment of manufacturing inventories and equipment (to the extent they exist) and a renewed focus on taxing the service sector, including purchases over the Internet. Expanding the sales tax bases to include more services and the expanded use of user fees and charges might be considered as ways to capitalize the growth in demand for specific items as consumption becomes more diverse.

The reform options considered here and in table 6.6 are starting points for state and local governments that cannot afford to be left behind with the changes in the state and local fiscal architecture. For some states, reform may be politically difficult and require a renewed effort at federal and state as well as multistate institutional cooperation. However, if the state and local roles in our system of fiscal federalism are to remain robust, there is very little choice but to act. In this regard, the increased pressure of sluggish revenues and heavy demands on the public sector that have been dramatically highlighted by the cyclical impact of the Great Recession may provide the political room for federal, state and local policymakers to look back as to why and how our system of a flexible fiscal federalism served the nation as a whole. At the same time, the fiscal crisis from 2007 on is forcing us to look ahead and adapt to a state and local fiscal architecture that has changed dramatically.

NOTES

1 Eads (this volume).
2 This simplification does not ignore externalities but assumes that they are a component of client population demand.
3 The "i" subscript refers to a particular public good.
4 The concept and measurement of expenditure "need" is discussed in Yilmaz and Zahradnik (2008).
5 The "i" subscript refers to a specific revenue source.
6 Kincaid (this volume).
7 The data presented in this section are from the Urban-Brookings Tax Policy Center State and Local Finance Data Query System (http://slfdqs.taxpolicycenter.org/pages.cfm).
8 The remaining percentage is made up of myriad taxes, including death and gift taxes, severance taxes, and transfer taxes. Some of these specific taxes may be important to

a few states (such as severance taxes in Alaska), but on average, they represent a small share of total tax revenue.

9 *Economist* (2010).

10 Ibid.

11 US Census (2010).

12 Sjoquist, Winters, and Wallace (2007), 24.

13 This is a very simplistic view of pension financing but the point here is to focus on the impact of aging on the financing of a portion of public pensions. Novy-Marx and Rauh (2010a, 2010b) provide more detailed discussions of state and local pension financing and point out that for a variety of reasons, these pensions are unfunded by billions of dollars in the case of state pensions.

14 To keep this example simple, "Rev" is not a function of the aging demographic. In practice, it may also be affected by economic and demographic changes.

15 These are the Arkansas Teachers Retirement System, Nebraska Retirement Systems, Texas County and District Retirement System, North Carolina Retirement Systems, Georgia Employees Retirement System, and Teacher Retirement System of Texas (Willoughby [2008], 18-21).

16 Mullins and Wallace (1996, 247-254) find that the elasticity of consumption with respect to age (head of household over the age of sixty-five) is positive for medical and health, personal, and household services. Most state and local governments do not tax these items or tax few of the specific service items.

17 BEA (2010).

18 Fox (1996).

19 NASBO (2010), i-iii; CBPP (2010), 1-3.

20 For further perspectives on the context of US fiscal federalism, see Conlan and Posner (this volume), Lav (this volume), and Penner (this volume).

21 The hypothesis here is that a higher wage share would increase the elasticity of the income tax and thus reduce stress. A counterargument, however, is that a higher wage share allows state governments to provide a higher level of expenditures, thus increasing stress according to this measure.

22 Fox (this volume).

23 Ibid.

24 *Kiplinger* (2010); Eads (this volume).

REFERENCES

Bureau of Economic Analysis [BEA]. (2010). "Regional Information System." http://www.bea.gov/regional/docs/footnotes.cfm?tablename=SA25N. Accessed October-November 2010.

Center on Budget and Policy Priorities [CBPP]. (2010, December 9). "States Continue to Feel Recession's Impact." Report, Washington, D.C.

Economist. (2010, November 20–26). "One Nation, Divisible." 33–34.

Fox, William. (1996). "Sales Tax: Current Condition and Policy Options." In *Taxation and Economic Development: A Blueprint for Tax Reform in Ohio*, edited by Roy W. Bahl. Columbus, OH: Battelle Press.

Kiplinger (2010, December 17). "Make Way for Generation Y." 1–4.

Mullins, Daniel, and Sally Wallace. (1996). "Changing Demographics and State Fiscal Outlook: The Case of Sales Taxes." *Public Finance Quarterly* 24: 237–262.

National Association of Budget Officers [NASBO]. (2010, June). "The Fiscal Survey of the States." Washington, DC.

Novy-Marx, Robert, and Joshua D. Rauh (2010a). "Policy Options for State Pension Systems and Their Impact on Plan Liabilities." Northwestern University Working Paper.

Novy-Marx, Robert, and Joshua D. Rauh (2010b). "The Crisis in Local Government Pensions in the US." Working Paper: http://www.kellogg.northwestern.edu/faculty/rauh/research/NMRLocal20101011.pdf. Accessed December 5, 2010.

Sjoquist, David, Jonathan Winters, and Sally Wallace. (2007, September 26). "Selected Fiscal and Economic Implications of Aging." Paper presented at the conference "Georgia's Aging Population: What to Expect and How to Cope," Andrew Young School of Policy Studies, Atlanta, GA.

Urban Institute-Brookings Institution Tax Policy Center. (2010, October-November). Data from US Census Bureau, Annual Survey of State and Local Government Finances, Government Finances, Volume 4, and Census of Governments (1980–2009). State & Local Government Finance Data Query System, http://www.taxpolicycenter.org/slf-dqs/pages.cfm.

US Census International Data Base. (2010), http://www.census.gov/ipc/www/idb/informationGateway.php.

Wallace, Sally (2003). "Changing Times: Demographic and Economic Changes and State and Local Finances." In *State and Local Finance at the Beginning of the 21st Century*, edited by David L. Sjoquist. Northampton, MA: Edward Elgar. 30–59.

Willoughby, Katherine. (2008, April 21). "Financial Management Capacity in US State Governments: Assessing GPP Grades." Presentation at the 40th annual Georgia Fiscal Management Council Conference, Center for Continuing Education, University of Georgia, Athens, Georgia.

Yilmaz, Yesim, and Robert Zahradnik (2008). "Measuring the Fiscal Capacity of the District of Columbia: A Comparison of Revenue Raising Capacity and Expenditure Need." *Proceedings of the Annual Conference of the National Tax Association*. Washington, DC: National Tax Association.

CHAPTER 7

....

PROFILES OF LOCAL
GOVERNMENT
FINANCE

....

CHRISTINE R. MARTELL
AND ADAM GREENWADE

ONE of the most important features of fiscal federalism in the United States is the local government sector and its diversity and robustness. It is not only a key component of the federal-state-local system of governance, but, arguably, it is the very foundation of day-to-day citizen interactions with the delivery of public services. It is certainly the largest part of the system. In the United States there is one central, federal government, then there are the state governments for the fifty states plus the city-state of District of Columbia and several other "middle-tier" governments (commonwealths, territories, possessions, and sovereign Indian nations). To attest to the importance of localization, as of 2007, there are 89,526 local governments, general plus special purpose, including public school systems.[1] Reflecting the diversity of the country's demographic, economic, and institutional characteristics, it is a sector for which no one set of political or fiscal arrangements can be said to be the "standard case."[2]

The purpose of this chapter is to profile the structure and diversity of local government finance. It begins with a section on the legal structure and organization of local government. The second section, the bulk of this chapter, focuses on the composition of, and trends in, local government finance, with emphases on expenditure assignments, revenue sources, and intergovernmental transfers. The third section addresses current issues in local government finance, including the fiscal conditions that have been brought on by recession, the changing role of municipal debt finance, growing fiscal pressure from unfunded employee pensions, and variation in local government autonomy. The last section considers the direction and future of local government finance as it reacts to what promises to be an era of continuing stringency.

LEGAL STRUCTURE AND ORGANIZATION OF LOCAL GOVERNMENTS

Forms of Local Government

The collective "local government" sector in the United States is a system of highly diverse entities working in and across thousands of jurisdictions. Its scale and complexity make it unique among the world's nation-states (table 7.1).[3] It is common for citizens to be simultaneously served by multiple forms of local government. In the most basic formulation, local governments fall into two classes: general-purpose and special-purpose governments. General-purpose governments have general taxing powers and provide a broad collection of services. Special-purpose governments, on the other hand, are limited in the scope of services and revenue sources, and typically serve a single function.

The number and composition of local governments have changed over time. In particular, there have been steady increases in special districts and in the consolidation of school districts (table 7.1).

General-purpose governments fall into two main classes: county governments and municipal governments.[4] County governments are administrative subdivisions of the state, and their role as local governments varies regionally. In the regions of the early colonies, primarily the Northeast, counties serve a very limited role in local governance. Conversely, the county government is considered the primary unit of local government in some regions, such as the South and West, where historically the county served as an economic engine.

Municipal governments, which are composed of cities, towns, and townships, are generally considered corporate entities brought into existence by the state and its progeny. They are created through incorporation, subject to state legislature as solidified in 1868 by Dillon's Rule.[5] Yet, despite being subjects of the state, practically speaking, municipal governments are self-governing. Given authorization by the state, the local governments' activities are based on voter approval by the affected citizens. This is based on the concept of *home rule*, "the power of a local government to conduct its own affairs—including specifically the power to determine its own organization, the functions it performs, its taxing and borrowing authority, and the numbers, types, and employment conditions of its personnel."[6] The metes and bounds of local government autonomy vary among the states, depending on the legal traditions of the various states.

Typically, townships are governed by elected commissioners, towns by the voters, themselves and cities by an elected council. In some areas of the country, like the Northeast and the Midwest, all land in a state is incorporated into municipalities so that one municipality borders others in a contiguous fashion. In other parts of the country, such as the South and West, some areas remain unincorporated. These latter areas are not served by local general-purpose municipal governments, but rather by county services. The county may contain a number of contiguous municipalities, be an area composed of municipalities and unincorporated areas, or be geographically coincident with a municipality as in some urban cities.

Although municipal government structures are subject to the broad provisions of the state, there is significant variation among municipalities. In the mayor-council form, mayors are elected officials who serve as the head of the local government. A weak mayor-council system limits the veto and appointment powers of the mayor, whereas a strong mayor-council system empowers the mayor in an executive branch position. The alternative is the council-manager system, which strives to accord with Woodrow Wilson's idea that policy making and administration are separate and are to be conducted by legislative and administrative bodies, respectively.[7] In the city manager form, the council is in charge of setting the policy mandates, and the manager oversees a professional staff that implements policy. In practice, there are a myriad of adaptations to both of these governance structures.[8] Less common forms of municipal governance structures are the *commission*, whereby commissioners serve a combination of legislative, executive, and administrative functions, and the *town meeting*, in which the citizenry at town meetings passes laws and a board of selectmen attends to administrative functions.

One form of local government, the special district, is common in the United States, particularly in the western states. Special districts are defined by the US Census Bureau as "independent limited-purpose local governmental units that exist as separate legal entities with substantial administrative and fiscal independence from general purpose governments."[9] Authorized by the state, special-purpose governments levy taxes or charges on the residents of a particular area to provide services that are not typically provided by other general-purpose governments.[10] Common special district functions include water, sanitation, fire protection, library services, and business improvement.[11] Enabled by state laws, special district functions vary by state and, as multistate instrumentalities, across states.

Special districts are the most common form of government in the United States (table 7.1).[12] The number of special districts in the United States grew an average of 9 percent per decade between 1972 and 2007.[13] Special district growth was actually faster in the 1950s and 1960s, averaging nearly 40 percent growth per decade. Overall growth between 1952 and 2007 is 203 percent, representing the creation of about 25,000 new special districts. The number of special districts (37,381) in the United States in 2007 exceeded the number of municipalities, which numbered 36,011 (including towns and townships). Special districts accounted for the

Table 7.1 Local governments by type, US totals

	Counties	Municipalities	Towns/ Townships	Special Districts	School Districts	Total Local Governments
1952	3,052	16,807	17,202	12,340	67,355	*116,756*
1962	3,043	17,997	17,144	18,323	34,678	*91,185*
1972	3,044	18,517	16,991	23,885	15,781	*78,218*
1982	3,041	19,076	16,734	28,078	14,851	*81,780*
1992	3,043	19,279	16,656	31,555	14,422	*84,955*
1997	3,043	19,372	16,629	34,683	13,726	*87,453*
2002	3,034	19,429	16,504	35,052	13,506	*87,525*
2007	3,033	19,492	16,519	37,381	13,051	*89,476*

Source: US Census Bureau (2007).

majority of new local-government growth over the end of the twentieth century. Illinois leads the country with 3,145 special districts, followed by California (2,830), and Texas (2,245). Four states account for nearly 30 percent of overall growth in special districts over the last fifty years—Texas (8 percent), Pennsylvania (8 percent), Illinois (7 percent), and California (6 percent).

Special districts are designed to provide urban services such as water, sanitation and fire protection by aligning them with the needs of citizens in a particular geography. They are commonly justified as being efficient, flexible, professional, and responsive in providing public goods.[14] Yet they have been criticized as leading to fragmented and inefficient governments, being discriminatory, motivated by self-interest, and designed to support private rather than public interests.[15] A specific critique of the proliferation of special districts is the claim that they lack direct accountability to voters because they are less politically visible than general-purpose governments, which can bear negatively upon accountability and popular participation.[16]

With the exception of most school districts in New England where school finance is an instrumentality of a general-purpose (municipal) government and thus a "dependent" school district, most school districts are designated as "independent" bodies, which are typically governed by an elected school board and an appointed superintendent.[17]

Fiscal Autonomy

As the form of government varies, so do revenue sources and expenditure assignments. Local government own-source revenue options are enabled by the state, although local jurisdictions typically have some power to set rates and exemptions.

Local governments raise own-source revenues via property taxes, sales taxes, income taxes, and user fees and charges. In addition, local governments receive intergovernmental monies, from both the states and the federal government, usually for the provision of explicit functions. Most states empower local governments to raise one or two of the three tax bases; thirty-six allow local sales tax; and fourteen allow local income taxes.[18]

By and large, the property tax has been the most important single source of revenue for local governments, and it continues to generate nearly 75 percent of own-source tax revenue.[19] The property tax has been the main financing tool of public schools, although states are funding an increasing share of education due to school funding equalization measures.

Local governments also often offer tax incentives to attract businesses with the goal of stimulating economic development. A common form is tax increment financing, whereby a portion of the growth in government revenues (usually the property tax or, less frequently, the sales tax) is used to repay the financing that enabled redevelopment.[20] Other incentives include payments in lieu of taxes and multiyear waivers on tax obligations. Some states regulate local use of tax incentives to encourage economic development that does not induce "race to the bottom" type zero-sum local level competition.[21]

Expenditure assignments vary among local governments, as well as by state and region. Services may include general government, public safety, K-12 public education, community colleges, public works, planning, parks and recreation, economic development, and public health and welfare (usually subsidized by state and federal monies).[22]

Composition of and Trends in Spending and Revenues

Local Government Expenditures

Data on subnational government spending are often lumped into "state and local" expenditures. Yet expenditure assignments are considerably different across the states.

While state spending largely consists of public welfare, including health-care costs like Medicaid, the single largest spending priority of local governments is education. More than one-third (39 percent) of all local government expenditures goes toward education. Another 11 percent of local government spending is for public welfare services, including medical assistance and public hospitals, aid for needy families, and various social safety-net programs. Other major categories of local government spending include that for environment purposes (10 percent), which consists of natural-resource management, parks and recreation, sewers, and solid-waste management; public safety services such as police and fire protection and corrections (9 percent); and transportation (6 percent), which consists mostly of road maintenance and local transit.

In the United States as a whole, the proportion of local government spending devoted to each major expenditure category has remained remarkably consistent over the last thirty years. As figure 7.1 illustrates, no category of spending at the local level has varied as a portion of overall spending by more than a few percentage points.

Growth in Local Government Expenditures

On a per capita basis, local government expenditures are growing slowly but steadily.[23] Between 1980 and 2008, inflation-adjusted spending per capita by local governments increased 72 percent, from about $3,000 to about $5,000, at an average annual rate of around 2 percent, or 75 dollars per person, per year (2008 dollars). In 2008, local governments in the United States spent nearly $1.6 trillion collectively, amounting to about $5,000 for every resident.

Over the same period, local government spending has grown only slightly faster than personal income, increasing from around 11 percent of income to slightly more than 13 percent. Local government spending as a percentage of personal income ranges from 5 percent in Hawaii to 17 percent in Nebraska.

Sources of Expenditure Growth

Consistent with figure 7.1 and overall local expenditure growth, all major categories of local government spending have grown at similar rates over the past three decades

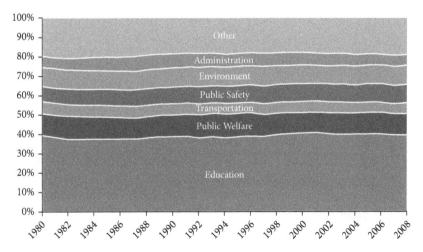

Figure 7.1 Local government expenditures by function, 1980–2008
Source: U.S. Census Bureau, State and Local Government Finances, 2008.

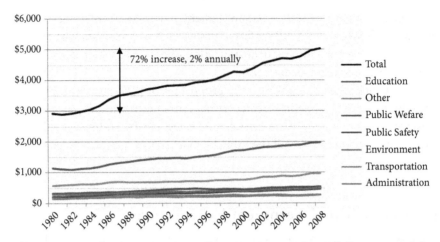

Figure 7.2 Local government expenditures, 1980–2008 (2008 dollars per capita)
Source: U.S. Census Bureau, State and Local Government Finances (2008).

(figure 7.2). Education is responsible for the largest share (39 percent) of growth in local government spending since 1980, increasing by more than $800 per person, or $30 per year. The fastest growing component of public welfare spending is health care (5 percent annual growth). Growth in other categories ranges from 1.6 percent annually (transportation) to 2.0 percent (administration). The fastest growing component of administration is interest on general debt (3.7 percent annually).

Expenditure Consistency across Regions

Local government spending varies by state and region and among the types of local governments. Yet in the aggregate, local government expenditures by function are fairly consistent across regions of the United States. No major spending category varies regionally by more than a few percentage points.

Local Government Revenues

Local governments pay for the services and facilities they provide through a number of revenue sources. The two major data categories are that of local "own-source" revenues and intergovernmental revenues.[24] Own-source revenues are generated by the jurisdiction through the use of its power to tax and set fees and charges.[25] Intergovernmental revenues consist of aid from the federal government and the states (figure 7.3).

Revenue Sources

As figure 7.3 illustrates, most local revenue is own-source, generated through taxes, charges, and fees. Local government taxes make up 13 percent of US taxes.[26] Local government taxes are largely directed at wealth and consumption (e.g., property and

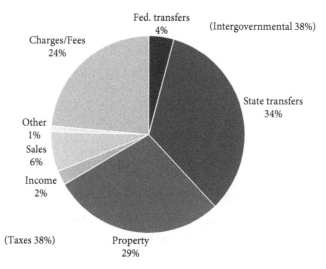

Figure 7.3 Local government revenue by source, US averages (2008)
Source: U.S. Census Bureau, State and Local Government Finances, 2008.

retail sales), unlike federal taxes, which are primarily directed at income. Property taxes constitute the largest component of local government own-source revenue, accounting for 29 percent of local revenue collections, on average. Sales and income taxes contribute 6 percent and 2 percent, respectively. Charges—which include utility charges, licenses, fees for sewer and garbage collection, parking tickets, and other miscellaneous charges and fees—account for 24 percent of local revenue.

Growth in Local Government Revenue

Adjusted for inflation, per capita local government general revenue has grown 70 percent from 1980 to 2008, increasing from about $2,600 to $4,600 per person. Most of this growth (70 percent) can be attributed to growth in own-source revenues, associated with a relative decline in intergovernmental transfers over the same period. Taxes account for slightly more than half of the growth in own-source revenue (58 percent), while charges and fees make up the other 42 percent. Nationally, local own-source revenues have remained steady as a percentage of personal income, growing from under 6 percent in 1980 to just over 7 percent in 2008.

Sources of Revenue Growth

Two notable trends in local government finance are decreasing share of taxes represented by property-tax revenues and the associated increase in the share of revenue collected from charges and fees.[27] Figure 7.4 illustrates the near symmetry of these opposing trends. Whereas the share of local revenue accounted for by property-tax revenues decreased from about 50 percent in 1980 to about 45 percent in 2008, the share accounted for by charges and fees increased from 34 percent to 37 percent over the same period. The downward trend of property-tax revenue is explained

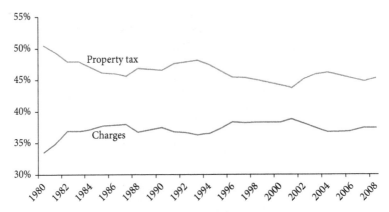

Figure 7.4 Charges and property taxes as a percentage of local own-source revenue
Source: U.S. Census Bureau, State and Local Government Finances, 2008.

by the rising popularity of tax and expenditure limitations, led by California's property-tax revolt, Proposition 13, in 1978; by Massachusetts' Proposition 2 1/2 in 1980; and by struggles to finance education.[28]

Variation in Local Government Revenues

Reliance on particular revenue sources varies by type of local government and across regions of the country. Figure 7.5 shows how cities, counties, and special districts vary in their revenue collections, especially with respect to property, income, and sales taxes. Property-tax collections vary by type of local government due to differing legal and political structures, differing state laws, and different tax characteristics of small and large cities.[29] Note that special districts do not generate any income tax. Special districts generate the majority of their own-source revenue from charges for services such as water and fire protection, followed by property-tax collections. The high level of intergovernmental revenue to counties reflects county-level implementation of state programs directed at health and human services.

There is also a fair degree of regional variation in the composition of revenue sources, partially illustrated by figures 7.6 and 7.7. Most pronounced is the reliance on the property tax. Over time, the property-tax base of local governments has been declining due to the use of development incentives and tax limitations that have limited the growth in assessments.[30]

Three trends have eroded the sales tax base over time: exemptions (i.e., food and clothing), growth in nontaxable services, and the advent and expansion of electronic commerce.[31] Although in the aggregate sales tax as a percentage of total local tax revenue has only decreased 1 percent since 1980, there is considerable regional variation in reliance on sales tax revenue (see figure 7.7).

Special-Purpose Districts

Special-purpose (or special-district) government revenue and spending has grown at twice the rate of city revenue and spending over the last several decades.

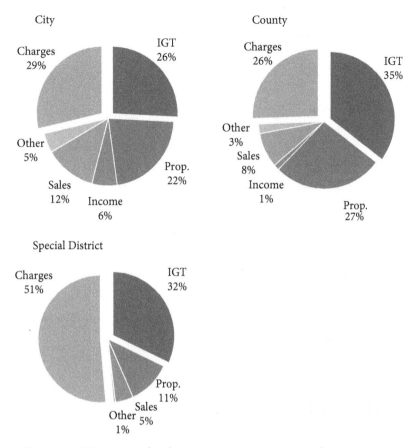

Figure 7.5 Variation in local government revenue source by type (2008)
Source: U.S. Census Bureau, State and Local Government Finances, 2008.

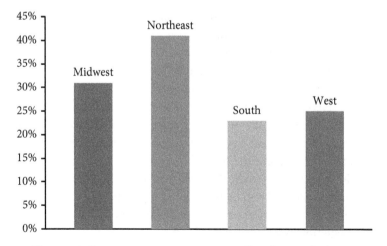

Figure 7.6 Property tax as a percentage of local general revenue
Source: U.S. Census Bureau, State and Local Government Finances, 2008.

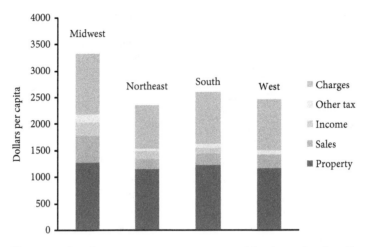

Figure 7.7 Local own-source revenue composition by region (2008)
Source: U.S. Census Bureau, State and Local Government Finances, 2008.

Between 1980 and 2007, city revenue and spending grew around 105 percent, while special-district revenue and spending grew by 217 percent.

Intergovernmental Revenues

In addition to own-source revenue, local governments rely on intergovernmental grants and transfers.[32] Intergovernmental revenues are sent to local governments directly from the federal government, indirectly from the federal government through states, and directly from state governments. These revenues are used largely to subsidize health expenditures, welfare and safety programs, transportation capital, and education.

Intergovernmental revenue accounts for 38 percent of total local government revenue, on average. Although it accounts for nearly 30 percent of the growth in per capita general revenue, this share has decreased as a percentage of general revenue from about 44 percent in 1980 to 37 percent in 2008.

The relative share of intergovernmental revenue coming directly from the federal government has decreased over the years from 9 percent of total local government revenue in 1980 to 4 percent in 2008. The share of intergovernmental revenue coming directly from the state governments also has decreased over the years, from 35 percent in 1980 to 33 percent in 2008.

Federal transfers directly to local governments grew by more than 300 percent nominally between 1980 and 2002, but declined more than 50 percent as a proportion of local general expenditures over the same period.[33] Change in state-to-local transfers was negligible over the same period.

As of September 2010, just over $111 billion in American Recovery and Reinvestment Act (ARRA) funding had been paid out to state and local governments

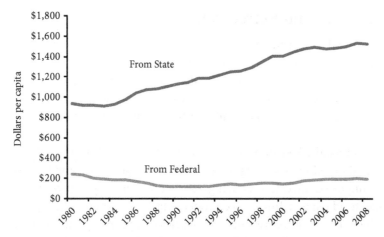

Figure 7.8 Local intergovernmental revenue by source
Source: U.S. Census Bureau, State and Local Government Finances, 2008.

by the federal government since February 2009.[34] Another $139 billion had been awarded but not paid out. Nearly 70 percent ($536 billion) of the total $787 billion package was allocated but not yet made available. Most of the money was to be spent by 2011. The ARRA specified that $144 billion be directed toward stabilizing state and local government budgets, in order to minimize service reductions and tax increases.[35] Thus, the share of local government revenues attributed directly or indirectly to federal assistance was expected to increase from 2009 to 2011.

State transfers have been responsible for the dollar volume growth in local intergovernmental revenue since 1980.[36] As figure 7.8 shows, between 1980 and 2008, the amount of state transfers to local governments increased by more than 60 percent. During the same period, federal transfers decreased by just over 20 percent. However, with states' budget gaps growing, states were cutting aid to local governments. For fiscal year 2011, fourteen states had explicitly introduced the idea or enacted legislation to reduce aid to local governments.[37]

EMERGING ISSUES IN LOCAL GOVERNMENT FINANCE

Local governments face a number of financial challenges. In the current fiscal environment, local governments are stressed by the economic recession and reduced state revenue; they borrow in a disrupted municipal credit market; they must finance underfunded pensions and health-care liabilities; and they are subject to unstable structural arrangements that affect local financial autonomy and performance.

The Recession and Retrenchment

The housing and subprime mortgage crisis of 2008 resulted in a subsequent recession, which slowed consumer spending, increased unemployment, and restricted
credit markets. This chain of events affected local governments in three distinct ways: it reduced the property-tax base and associated revenues; it reduced
nonproperty-tax revenues; and it altered the means by which local governments
borrow.

State and local governments were susceptible to the housing crisis, which hit
even before the credit markets tightened.[38] As mortgage default and foreclosure rates
soared to unprecedented levels during 2007–2009, municipal governments in particular had to adjust to a diminished property-tax base. Among the repercussions of
the housing crisis are lower revenues from sales and property transfer (recordation)
taxes; decreased fees associated with construction activity; and reduced property
taxes. In addition, there were increased expenditures due to the cost associated with
monitoring vacant lots and the limited ability to insure debt.[39]

The current environment of local governments is characterized by further
revenue declines, high unemployment, and poor fiscal conditions. Poor fiscal
management choices, such as an inability to address unfunded pension liabilities
and offering tax abatements for economic development, magnify the adverse fiscal impact of the crisis.[40] Moreover, although the national economy gave signs of
slowly improving, the rebound in local finances was expected to exhibit a lag.[41]
Specifically, the fiscal condition of cities weakened from 2008 to 2010, and it is
expected to remain weak through at least 2012.

That local fiscal systems have become increasingly stressed has been documented elsewhere.[42] Among local governments surveyed, 87 percent of cities
reported being less able to meet fiscal needs in 2010 than in 2009. In 2010 general-
fund revenues experienced a second year of decline of 2.5 percent from 2008 to
2009, and of 3.2 percent from 2009 to 2010.[43] Local governments that rely on revenue from property and sales taxes have been affected more than those that depend
mainly on income-tax revenue. While sales tax revenues decreased in both 2009
and 2010, property-tax revenues experienced their first decrease in 2010. Local
income-tax revenues, driven primarily by income and wages, held steady or experienced slight declines in 2010, in part because some major states increased their
income-tax rates. Moreover, the economic crisis has led to a decline in investment
income and decreases in state aid.[44] Expenditures remained nearly stable from
2008 to 2009, but declined from 2009 to 2010 by 2.3 percent. Increases in the costs
of employee health benefits, pensions, infrastructure, and public safety contributed
to increased expenditure demand. In addition, the health of the local economy and
the level of state aid contributed to local government financial stress.[45]

The declining fiscal conditions are likely to persist into 2012, with expected
shortfalls totaling between $56 billion and $83 billion from 2010 to 2012.[46] The third
year of real revenue decline was 2010.[47] These conditions at the local government
level have national implications, primarily because of local governments' important

positions as employers, accounting for 10 percent of nonfarm metropolitan employment.[48] In early 2011, it was reported by the Bureau of Labor Statistics that local government employment had declined by 416,000 from its high point in the fall of 2008.[49]

Local governments responded to the economic climate by employing a number of revenue-raising and expenditure-reducing strategies.[50] Strategies on the revenue-raising side have included increasing fee levels, adding new fees and new taxes, increasing property or sales tax rates and broadening the tax bases. To reduce local government expenditures, local governments instituted hiring freezes and laid off personnel, canceled or delayed infrastructure investments, abandoned specific city services, modified health-care benefits, and cut spending on public safety and human services.[51] Other personnel-related cuts included salary freezes, the elimination of travel and development budgets, furloughs, and reduced pension benefits.

The federal government provided some relief to local educational needs through $48 billion in State Fiscal Stabilization Funds, authorized by the ARRA of 2009. In an effort to stimulate the economy, ARRA required a rapid spend-down of funds, which will quickly lead to a drastic drop-off in federal aid in 2011 as well as a noticeable hole in subnational budgets.

While the average share of ending balances to expenditures still exceeds the share over the last twenty-five years, the share was expected to fall again in 2010 to 19.9 percent, from a high of 25.2 percent in 2007. "Bond underwriters...look at reserves as an indicator of fiscal responsibility, which can increase credit ratings and decrease the costs of city debt, thereby saving the city money."[52] Thus, to bond raters and investors alike, municipalities appeared more vulnerable.

Municipal Debt Finance

Local governments typically finance capital investments by selling bonds to investors, who expect full and timely payments of principal and interest. Bonds can broadly be classified as either secured with the full faith and credit of the issuing jurisdiction (general obligation bonds) or with a specific revenue source (revenue bonds).[53] As general obligation bonds obligate the local government's entire revenue system to make payments, they are considered the most secure and therefore bear the lowest interest costs. Revenue bonds are used more often when an identified revenue stream can be connected with the project, such as charges associated with water utilities or toll roads. The "municipal" bond market, as a matter of convention, includes borrowing done by both states and their subdivisions (including local governments). A keystone of the US municipal credit market has been that the interest on most bonds is exempt from federal and (often) state income taxes. The exemption allows state and local governments to borrow at lower rates of interest. While most jurisdictions sell debt that is not enhanced, other jurisdictions buy insurance or liquidity support to make their issues more attractive in the market and to reduce interest costs.

A number of significant changes affected the structure of municipal credit markets as a consequence of the housing crisis.[54] The most notable changes were the collapse of the market for variable-rated securities, a withdrawal from the market of traditional bond insurers, and the diminished availability of credit enhancement instruments from banks, such as standby bond-purchase agreements. Collectively, these changes meant a restricted credit environment and an increase in the borrowing costs for local governments.

As an initial reaction, many local governments deferred capital investment needs to finance, waiting for more market stability and lower interest costs before borrowing.[55] Municipal debt issuance levels fell about 14 percent from September 2008 to September 2009. During 2009, approximately $330 billion in new tax-exempt municipal debt was issued, the lowest volume since 2002. But the drop-off in tax-exempt bond sales was only part of the picture. A new federally subsidized instrument, Build America Bonds (BABs), accounted for another $70 billion in municipal issuance activity, bringing the total to around $400 billion.

The implications of the recession, unemployment, and low wage growth on credit quality became clear: municipal credit quality was seen as stressed.[56] In addition to the weakness in revenues, there was a concern that municipalities were taking on too much debt, in part due to the stimulus funds provided through the BABs program.[57] A further risk was that the stimulus funds, which kept spending levels from dramatic drops, would dry up before economies recovered enough to generate own-source revenues to replace them.[58]

The introduction of the BABs program, which was terminated in December 2010, when Congress failed to re-enact the program, temporarily altered how the federal government treated the subsidization of local government investment costs.[59] Bonds that are tax exempt from federal, and some state, income taxes have been the mainstay of local government finance. But, the BABs funds were not tax exempt. Rather, a direct subsidy, set at 35 percent, was given to the issuing state or local government that agreed to sell their bonds on a taxable basis. BABs bonds were attractive to nontax-paying investors and broadened the investor pool. Yet some felt they introduced the potential for the federal government to override local investment interests with federal priorities and provided too much relief to deficit-running states.

Pensions and Liabilities

Unfunded pension benefits have strained local government budgets.[60] These long-term liabilities have been hit from both sides of the balance sheet. On the obligation side, the demographics of an aging and retiring workforce increases the demand for the payout of pension benefits. This phenomenon is exacerbated for pension packages that include health-care benefits, because the cost of health care has increased at rates faster than those of other goods. On the investment side, pension funds experienced severe losses in the financial crisis, in some cases upward of 35 percent.[61] Moreover, local governments, long accustomed to rising economies and increasing revenues, have not had the management foresight or political will to bring their unfunded liabilities under financial control. Their ability to make changes themselves has also been limited by state mandates or membership in state-managed employee pension systems. As a result, local governments are left with shortfalls in their pension assets. Faced with higher contribution requirements, localities will be inclined to reduce those contributions, pass them on to employees, or seek to limit pension benefits.

Fiscal Autonomy

Local government fiscal autonomy refers to the jurisdiction's ability to decide how to fund its residents' needs. On the revenue side, this can be measured across a number of dimensions including its control over revenue sources and rates versus constraining tax and expenditure limitations and unfunded mandated spending requirements.[62] Municipal autonomy is enhanced when jurisdictions control the local tax rate and the revenues are non-earmarked; when a mix of both inelastic and elastic revenues contribute to fiscal stability and growth; when jurisdictions can use locally raised revenues for general purposes defined by the discretion of the local government; when well-structured state aid allows for equalization; and when local government revenue is not bound by property or general-revenue limitations.[63]

There has been interest in whether local government autonomy affects the structure of local government finance or the relationship between local and state governments. Early research suggests that local fiscal autonomy does influence fiscal outcomes.[64] Tax and expenditure limitations that restrict local property-tax revenues have shifted expenditure burdens to the states.[65] Conventional wisdom increasingly supports the view that state limitations on local government autonomy—especially tax, expenditure, or debt limitations—yield unintended consequences such as the proliferation of non-general-purpose governments and authorities. But empirical support for such claims is mixed.[66]

FUTURE CONSIDERATIONS

Local governments assume a myriad of shapes and forms, and the finance arrangements vary accordingly. There are variations across and within types of local governments, as well as among the regions of the country. Collectively, local governments have been stressed by the Great Recession. They have seen deteriorations in their tax bases due to internal development policies and external limitations. They have experienced a decrease in intergovernmental revenues from states. They face increasing employee pension and health-care costs and uncertain prospects in the bond markets.

A number of directions have been suggested for how local governments should approach their diminishing fiscal fortunes. One standard recommendation is to improve fiscal management. This recommendation addresses a number of trends in local public finance, such as the erosion of tax bases and the expansion of unfunded liabilities. With a constrained budget, local jurisdictions need to be very transparent about, and carefully weigh the costs and benefits of, granting tax abatements and exemptions. Moreover, pension benefits need to be sustainably financed and likely will be renegotiated and diminished. These are tough, contentious political decisions about allocating limited resources that have become increasingly unavoidable.

A second recommendation is to create a stronger federal-state-local partnership.[67] Muro and Hoene recommend a stronger federal role in (1) providing direct fiscal assistance to cities, (2) assisting cities with a public service employment program, (3) stabilizing the housing market, (4) investing in local transportation projects, and (5) providing municipal credit enhancement.[68] Honadle has recommended that the federal government use improved fiscal management as a precondition for federal assistance.[69] In view of the large-scale spending cutbacks that appear certain at the federal level, the outlook of initiatives from that quarter must be seen as bleak. More likely, federal (and state) aid will be reduced and further pressure on municipal spending lies ahead.

Finally, while improving fiscal management is important, recent popular dissatisfaction with government at all levels suggests that there is an underlying paramount issue: the "social compact" between the citizenry and government. Recently, Hoene presented a number of recommendations to engage the citizenry and focus the role of local government on redefining its role in the social compact.[70] First, instead of focusing on jobs per se, as in traditional economic development strategies, focus should be on innovations in local government, especially those related to education, research and development, and the incubation of new ventures.[71] Second, public-sector compensation must be restructured in order to attract talent, thereby encouraging employment in local government to be a first, not a default, choice. Third, the focus on taxation and spending should be lessened in favor of focusing on public conversations with citizens about the social compact. These conversations will challenge the assumptions of local government finance, especially regarding how jurisdictions should prioritize core services. Finally, the value of leadership must be emphasized, in order to encourage difficult choices about the direction of local governance in a period of slow growth and austerity.

Whether or not these recommendations are followed, local governments will be forced to change their taxation and spending priorities, their fiscal management strategies, and their relationships with state and federal governments. Moreover, adjusting to slower growth, they may begin distinguishing between increased *economic activity* and enhanced *development*, where the latter term encompasses a broader, perhaps less materialistic, concept of livability and quality of life. In any event, it appears certain that the "new normal" will embrace the notion of local governments doing just enough (if no longer more) with less.

NOTES

1 US Census Bureau (2007).
2 Wallace (this volume).
3 Hoene and Pagano (2008).
4 Miller (2002).
5 *City of Clinton v. Cedar Rapids and Missouri River Railroad* (24 Iowa 455: 1868).
6 Advisory Commission on Intergovernmental Relations (ACIR) (1987), 1.
7 Wilson (1887).
8 Frederickson, Wood, and Logan (2001).
9 Axelrod (1992), 13.
10 US Census Bureau (2009).
11 Scott and Bollens (1950); Bollens (1961).
12 Berry (2009).
13 US Census Bureau (2002).
14 Bish and Ostrom (1973); Cape et al. (1969); Blair (1986); ACIR (1987).
15 ACIR (1964); Bollens (1961); Burns (1994); Foster (1997).
16 Savitch and Vogel (2004); Miller (2002); Foster (1997).
17 Kenyon (this volume).
18 Mikesell (2009); Fox and Slack (2009).
19 Bell (this volume).
20 Michael (2005), 411-413.
21 Hoene and Pagano (2008).
22 Yilmaz, Vaillancourt, and Dafflon (this volume).
23 Brunori et al (2005).
24 Fisher (this volume).
25 The technical definition of what makes a tax or fee local "own-source" is examined in de Kam (1999) and Jensen (2002).
26 NCSL (2009).
27 Sjoquist (this volume).
28 Brunori et al (2006).
29 Brunori et al (2006).
30 Gordon (this volume).
31 Tannenwald (2004); Fox and Slack (2009).
32 Sheppach (this volume).
33 Mullins and Pagano (2005).
34 ARRA (2009); www.recovery.gov.
35 ARRA (2009), section 3.
36 Fisher (this volume).
37 NCSL (2009); Greenblatt (2010).
38 Honadle (2009).
39 Urban Institute (2008).

40 Honadle (2009); Bullock (2010); Pew Center on the States (2010).

41 Hoene and Pagano (2010); Temple-West (2010).

42 Dadayan (2010); Pew Center on the States (2010); Hoene and Pagano (2010).

43 Hoene and Pagano (2010).

44 Leech (2009); NCSL (2009); Honadle (2009).

45 Hoene and Pagano (2010).

46 Hoene (2009).

47 Hoene (2010).

48 Muro and Hoene (2009).

49 US Department of Labor (2011)

50 Hoene and Pagano (2010).

51 Ibid.

52 Ibid., 6.

53 See Mikesell (2009), 639.

54 Martell and Kravchuk (2010).

55 Honadle (2009); Stone & Youngberg (2009).

56 Temple-West (2010).

57 Ibid.

58 McGee (2010).

59 Martell and Kravchuk (2010).

60 Honadle (2009).

61 Ibid.

62 Hoene and Pagano (2008); Wolman et al. (2009).

63 Hoene and Pagano (2008).

64 Wolman et al. (2009).

65 Skidmore (1999).

66 Carr (2006); Bollens (1986); Feiock and Carr (2001); Foster (1997); McCabe (2000); Lewis (2000); Bowler and Donovan (2004).

67 Muro and Hoene (2009).

68 Ibid.

69 Honadle (2009).

70 Ibid.

71 Muro and Hoene (2009).

References

Advisory Commission on Intergovernmental Relations (ACIR) (1964). *The Problem of Special Districts in American Government*. Washington, DC: US Government Printing Office.

Advisory Commission on Intergovernmental Relations (ACIR) (1987). *The Organization of Local Public Economies*. Washington, DC: US Government Printing Office.

American Recovery and Reinvestment Act (ARRA) (2009). Public Law 111–5.

Axelrod, Donald (1992). *Shadow Government: The Hidden World of Public Authorities— And How They Control over $1 Trillion of Your Money*. New York: John Wiley and Sons.

Barbour, Elisa (2007). *State-Local Fiscal Conflicts in California: From Proposition 13 to Proposition 1A*. San Francisco: Public Policy Institute of California.

Berry, C. (2009). *Imperfect Union: Representation and Taxation in Multilevel Governments*. Cambridge, MA: Cambridge University Press.

Bish, Robert L., and Vincent Ostrom (1973). *Understanding Urban Government: Metropolitan Reform Revisited*. Washington, DC: American Enterprise Institute for Public Policy Research.

Blair, G. S. (1986). *Government at the Grassroots*. Pacific Palisades, CA: Palisades Publishers.

Bollens, John (1961). *Special District Governments in the United States*. Westport, CT: Greenwood.

Bollens, Scott A. (1986). "Examining the Link between State Policy and the Creation of Local Special Districts." *State and Local Government Review* 18(3): 117–124.

Bowler, Shaun, and Todd Donovan (2004). "Evolution in State Governance Structures: Unintended Consequences of State Tax and Expenditure Limitations." *Political Research Quarterly* 57(2): 189–196.

Boyd, Donald J. (2010). "Recession, Recovery, and State-Local Finances" (presentation). New York: Rockefeller Institute of Government.

Brunori, David, Michael E. Bell, Harold Wolman, Patricia Atkins, Joseph J. Cordes, and Bing Yuan (2005). *State and Local Fiscal Trends and Future Threats*. Prepared for the National Center for Real Estate Research. Washington, DC: George Washington Institute of Public Policy.

Brunori, David, Richard Green, Michael Bell, Chanyung Choi, and Bing Yuan. (2006). *The Property Tax: Its Role and Significance in Funding State and Local Government Services*. Washington, DC: George Washington Institute of Public Policy.

Buettner, Thiess, and David E. Wildasin (2006). "The Dynamics of Municipal Fiscal Adjustment." *Journal of Public Economics* 90(6–7): 1115–1132.

Bullock, Nicole (2010, February 26). "US States Struggle in the Shadow of Greece." *Financial Times*.

Burns, Nancy (1994). *The Formation of American Local Governments: Private Values in Public Institutions*. New York: Oxford University Press.

Cape, William, Leon Graves, and Burton Michaels (1969). *Government by Special District*. Government Research Series 37. Lawrence: University of Kansas.

Carr, Jered B. (2006). "Local Government Autonomy and State Reliance on Special District Governments: A Reassessment." *Political Research Quarterly* 59(3): 481–492.

City of Clinton v. Cedar Rapids and Missouri River Railroad (24 Iowa 455: 1868). Dadayan, L. (2010). *State Revenue Flash Report: Final Quarter of 2009 Brought Still More Declines in State Tax Revenue*. Albany, NY: Nelson A. Rockefeller Institute of Government, State University of New York at Albany.

de Kam, Flip (1999). *Taxing Powers of State and Local Governments*. Paris: Organisation of Economic Cooperation and Development.

Feiock, Richard C., and Jered B. Carr (2001). "Incentives, Entrepreneurs, and Boundary Change: A Collective Action Framework." *Urban Affairs Review* 36(3): 382–405.

Foster, Kathryn A. (1997). *The Political Economy of Special-Purpose Government*. Washington, DC: Georgetown University Press.

Fox, William F., and Enid Slack (2009). "Local Public Finance in North America." Unpublished working paper.

Frederickson, H. George, Curtis Wood, and Brett Logan (2001). "How American City Governments Have Changed: The Evolution of the Model City Charter." *National Civic Review* 90(1): 3–18.

Greenblatt, Alan (2010). *Local Squeeze.* Washington, DC: National Conference of State Legislatures.

Hildreth, W. Bartley, and C. Kurt Zorn (2005). "The Evolution of the State and Local Government Municipal Debt Market over the Past Quarter Century." *Public Budgeting and Finance* 25(4): 127–153.

Hoene, Christopher (2009). *City Budget Shortfalls and Responses: Projections for 2010–2012.* Washington, DC: National League of Cities.

Hoene, Christopher. (2010, December 3). "Local Governance in Times of Fiscal Crisis." Buechner Institute of Governance, University of Colorado, Denver.

Hoene, Christopher, and Michael A. Pagano (2008). *Cities and State Fiscal Structure.* Washington, DC: National League of Cities.

Hoene, Christopher, and Michael A. Pagano (2009). *City Fiscal Conditions in 2009.* Washington, DC: National League of Cities.

Hoene, Christopher, and Michael A. Pagano (2010). *City Fiscal Conditions in 2010.* Washington, DC: National League of Cities.

Honadle, Beth Walker (2009). "The Other 'S&L Crisis': A Policy Window for Reform?" *Municipal Finance Journal* 29(4): 65–76.

Jensen, Leif (2002). *Fiscal Design Surveys across Levels of Government.* Paris: Organisation of Economic Development and Cooperation.

Leech, B. S. (2009). "Holding a Hot Potato? The Credit Crisis and Its Impact on State Cash and Short-Term Investment Portfolios." *Municipal Finance Journal* 29(4): 125–137.

Lewis, Paul G. (2000). "The Durability of Local Government Structure: Evidence from California." *State and Local Government Review* 32(1): 34–48.

Martell, Christine R., and Robert S. Kravchuk (2010, November 4–6). "Implications of Current Policy Reverberations of the Municipal Bond Markets." *Association for Public Policy Analysis and Management* annual conference, Boston, MA.

McCabe, Barbara C. (2000). "Special-District Formation among the States." *State and Local Government Review* 32(2): 121–131.

McFarland, Christina (2010). *State of America's Cities Survey on Jobs and the Economy.* Washington, DC: National League of Cities.

McGee, P. (2010). "Municipalities Are Set to Handle Upcoming Turmoil, Raters Say." *The Bond Buyer.* Retrieved from http://www.bondbuyer.com/issues/119_276/rating-agencies-municipalities-1007316-1.html.

Michael, Joseph (2005). "Tax Increment Financing." In *The Encyclopedia of Taxation and Tax Policy*, edited by Joseph J. Cordes, Robert D. Ebel, and Jane G. Gravelle. Washington, DC: Urban Institute Press. 411–413.

Mikesell, John L. (2009). *Fiscal Administration.* 8th ed. Boston, MA: Wadsworth.

Miller, David Y. (2002). *The Regional Governing of Metropolitan America.* Boulder, CO: Westview.

Mullins, Daniel R. (2004). "Tax and Expenditure Limitations and the Fiscal Response of Local Government: Asymmetric Intra-Local Fiscal Effects." *Public Budgeting & Finance*, Winter, 11–147.

Mullins, Daniel R., and Michael A. Pagano (2005). "Local Budgeting and Finance: 25 Years of Developments." *Public Budgeting and Finance* 25(4): 3–45.

Muro, Mark, and Christopher W. Hoene (2009). *Fiscal Challenges Facing Cities: Implications for Recovery.* Washington, DC: Metropolitan Policy Program at Brookings.

National Conference of State Legislatures [NCSL] (2009). *State, Federal and Local Taxes.* Retrieved from http://www.ncsl.org/documents/fiscal/StateFederalandLocalTaxes.pdf.

Neiman, Max, and Daniel Krimm (2009). *Perceptions of Local Fiscal Stress during a State Budget Crisis.* San Francisco: Public Policy Institute of California.

Pew Center on the States (2010). *State of the States 2010: How the Recession Might Change States.* Washington DC

Savitch, H. V., and Ronald K. Vogel. (2004). "The United States: Executive-Centered Politics." In *Comparing Local Governance*, edited by B. Denters and L. E. Rose. New York: Palgrave Macmillan.

Scott, Stanley, and John C. Bollens (1950). "Special Districts in California's Local Government." *Western Political Quarterly* 3(2): 233–243.

Skidmore, Mark (1999). "Tax and Expenditure Limitations and the Fiscal Relationships between State and Local Governments." *Public Choice* 99(1/2): 77–102.

Stone & Youngberg (2009). *The Municipal Bond Market: One Year Later.* Retrieved from www.syllc.com/userfiles/file/sy_FinMarketsOneYearLater_r8.pdf.

Tannenwald, Robert (2004). "Are State and Local Revenue Systems Becoming Obsolete?" Washington, DC: National League of Cities.

Temple-West, Patrick. (2010). "Governments Facing Slower Recovery and Lower Ratings." *The Bond Buyer.* Retrieved from http://www.bondbuyer.com/issues/119_250/state-local-governments-1005598-1.html.

Urban Institute (2008, February 26). "The housing crisis and what it means for state and local governments." *Policy Nutshells* No.7. http://www.urban.org/decisionpoints08/archive/07housingcrisis.cfm

US Census Bureau (2002). *Census of Governments*, Volume 1, Number 1, Government Organization. GCO 2(1)-1. Washington, DC: US Government Printing Office. http://www.census.gov/prod/2003pubs/gco21x1.pdf.

US Census Bureau (2007). *County and City Databook: 2007. A Statistical Abstract Supplement*, 14th ed. Washington, DC: US Census Bureau. http://www.census.gov/prod/2008pubs/07ccdb/ccdb-07.pdf.

US Census Bureau (2009). *Population of interest- special districts.* Retrieved from http://www.census.gov/govs/go/special_district_governments.html.

US Census Bureau (2008). State and Local Government Finances. Retrieved from http://www.census.gov/govs/estimate/.

US Census Bureau, Census of Governments, Volume 1,Number 1, Government Organization, Series CG07, www.census/gov/govs/cog/.

US Department Of Labor (2011, April). Bureau of Labor Statistics. Current Employment Statistics, Table 7: Most-Recent Industry Specific Peaks. ftp://ftp.bls.gov/pub/suppl/empsit.tab7.txt

Ward, Robert B. (2010, April 15). "State Fiscal Trends and the Federal Role." Testimony to the Congressional Subcommittee on Commercial and Administrative Law, Committee on the Judiciary, US House of Representatives.

Wildasin, David E. (2009). *State and Local Government Finance in the Current Crisis: Time for Emergency Federal Relief?* IFIR Working Paper No. 2009-2007. Lexington, KY: Institute for Federalism and Intergovernmental Relations.

Wilson, Woodrow (1887). "The Study of Administration." *Political Science Quarterly* 56(4): 481–506.

Wolman, Hal, Robert McManmon, Michael Bell, and David Brunori (2008). *Comparing Local Government Autonomy across States.* Washington, DC: George Washington Institute of Public Policy.

CHAPTER 8

FEDERAL PREEMPTION OF REVENUE AUTONOMY

JAMES R. EADS JR.

In the past quarter century there has been an increasing—and troubling—trend of an abandonment of the historical notion of US federalism as a federal-state-local partnership, whereby Congress shows deference to state and local governments in formulating national policy, toward one of coercive federalism characterized by federally imposed expenditures and federally imposed mandates and preemptions of state and local revenue authority.[1] Indeed, it is not unreasonable to say that the lines separating national and state powers are disappearing.

The question of mandates (expenditures, direct orders, regulations) has been adequately discussed elsewhere.[2] This chapter focuses on the relatively neglected dimension of the growing trend of the federal preemption of the states' power of taxation.[3] The underlying theme of the chapter is that one of the most fundamental rights of a unit of government, whether federal, state, or local, is the right to determine its own fiscal destiny; with this right comes an obligation that a government that has the power to tax its citizens should do so in such a way that the revenue produced is then used to provide the goods and services to benefit those citizens. It is a theme that is well established in the Federalist Papers, wherein James Madison, in *Federalist No. 46* asserted that the states and national government "are in fact but different agents and trustees of the people, constituted with different powers."[4] And, in *Federalist No. 28*, Alexander Hamilton wrote that the government should exercise authority to the citizens' benefit: "If their [the peoples'] rights are invaded by either, they can make use of the other as the instrument of redress."

Similarly James Madison in *Federalist No. 39* stated that "each state in ratifying the Constitution is considered a sovereign body independent of all others" and that "in this relation then the new Constitution will, if established, will be federal and not a national constitution."[5]

The original thirteen states were preexisting political entities at the time the US Constitution was adopted in 1789. The adoption of the new Constitution changed in a meaningful way the prior construct of government, the Articles of Confederation (1781–1789). Under the Constitution, the federal government has certain express powers, enumerated powers, which are powers specifically set forth in the Constitution, including the right to levy taxes, declare war, and regulate interstate and foreign commerce. In addition, the Necessary and Proper Clause gives the federal government the implied power to pass any law "'necessary and proper' for the execution of its express powers." But powers that the Constitution does not delegate to the federal government or forbid to the states, the "reserved" powers, are specifically stated as belonging to the people or the states.[6]

Thus, the authority of the federal government of the United States proceeds ultimately from the Constitution. The Constitution also contains limits on the powers of states. The principal sources of constitutional limits on the power of the states and local governments to tax are the Commerce and Import-Export Clauses of Article I, the Privileges and Immunities Clause of Article IV, the Due Process and Equal Protection Clauses incorporated in the Fourteenth Amendment, and the Supremacy Clause of Article VI.[7] A complete explication of the intricacies and case law of each of these provisions is beyond the scope of this chapter, but they are noted because they are the foundation for preemption of state tax authority by the federal government. In addition to these constitutional provisions, only some of which are self-implementing, there have been many federal statutory enactments that limit the power of the states. The basic authority for these enactments superseding state and local government power is the Supremacy Clause.

Indeed, the landmark opinion from the US Supreme Court regarding the principle that the states could not act to frustrate the power of the federal government involved a state tax. Chief Justice John Marshall's landmark opinion held that Congress had the constitutional authority to create the Bank of the United States and that Maryland did not have the authority to tax the bank under the Supremacy Clause.[8]

Although it deals with all forms of preemption and not just tax authority, one of the most, if not *the* most, comprehensive reports on federal preemption of state authority was published in 1992 by the US Advisory Commission on Intergovernmental Relations (ACIR). The commission reported that the pace and breadth of federal preemptions of state and local authority have increased significantly since the late 1960s. As the ACIR noted at the time, of the approximately 439 significant preemption statutes enacted by Congress since 1789, more than 53 percent (233) had been enacted since 1969.[9] Noting this explosion in preemption, one commentator stated, "It strains credulity to suppose that the world became, all of a sudden, as utterly different after 1970 as to warrant a doubling of the amount of centralization in American government."[10]

Cataloging Federal Preemption Statutes

Broadly purported reasons for federal preemptions are defined in five categories: (1) protecting the government of the United States, its instrumentalities, and its employees, including members of the military and its property; (2) protecting interstate transportation and telecommunication; (3) protecting sovereign states and nations, territories, possessions, and the Alaska Native Fund; (4) nondiscriminatory treatment of federal employees, and those relating to; and (5) salary, retirement, and miscellaneous matters.

1. Federal Preemption for the United States and Its Instrumentalities

This category of preemption relates to specific federal government instrumentalities that are protected by federal law from state taxation.

Stocks and bonds issued by the US government are exempt from all taxes imposed by state or local governments except for nondiscriminatory franchise taxes, other nonproperty taxes, or estate taxes (Stocks and obligations of the US government: 31 USC.A. § 3124(a)).[11]

Federal Reserve banks are exempt from all state and local taxes except real estate taxes (*Federal Reserve Banks 12 USCA § 531*). *Federal Reserve Bank of St. Louis v. Metrocentre Improvement District* (657 F.2d 183 [8th Cir. 1981]) held that the statutory exemption for Federal Reserve banks extended to special assessments for city improvements in the city in which a bank was located. This assessment was deemed not to be a tax upon real estate.[12]

The following federal financial institutions along with their attendant real property, income holdings, and corporate assets are exempt from all state and local taxes except uniformly based real property taxes: Government National Mortgage Association and Federal National Mortgage Association, 12 USCA § 1723a; Federal Home Loan Mortgage Corporation, 12 USCA § 1452(e); Federal Home Loan Banks, 12 USCA § 1433; Federal Deposit Insurance Corporation, 12 USCA § 1825; Thrift Depositor Protection Oversight Board and Resolution Trust, 12 USCA § 1441a; Federal Crop Insurance Program, 7 USCA § 1511; and Federal Credit Unions, 12 USCA § 1768.

2. Federal Preemption for Interstate Transportation, Telecommunication, and Other Commerce

Special preemptive rules apply to state taxation of various interstate authorities and businesses. Below are significant examples.

Authorities and Business Providers

- Amtrak and commuter authorities that were eligible to contract with Amtrak as of October 1, 1981, are exempt from state and local tax on their rail services (Amtrak, 49 USCA § 24301).
- Northeast rail service-transfer taxes, 45 USCA § 1106(a) (1). For states located in the Northeast Rail Service District, special rules apply to state and local taxes on certain northeastern railroad property. In these states, transfers of interests in northeastern rail property, whether real or personal, are exempt from any state or local taxes.
- Northeast (Rail) Corridor Improvement Program, 49 USCA § 24908. Transfers of interests in railroad property that are part of the Northeast Corridor Improvement Program are exempt from state and local taxes.
- Retirement of railroad employees, 45 USCA 231. The National Rail Retirement Investment Trust is exempt from all state and local taxes, including income, sales, use, property, or any other taxes.
- Railroad Revitalization and Regulatory Reform Act (4-R Act), 49 USCA § 11501. Under this act, state and local taxes cannot be assessed at a higher rate on rail property than other surrounding commercial property. In the case of *Dept. of Revenue v. ACF Indus.*, 510 US 332 (1994), the Supreme Court held that states could exempt other nonrailroad commercial and industrial property from generally applicable property taxes without running afoul of the 4-R Act. They held that, in this case, it was proper to compare the differential tax bases between taxed commercial property and taxed railroad property rather than the exempt commercial property and taxed railroad property.
- Head taxes on airlines, 49 USCA § 40116. State and local governments are not permitted to levy taxes on individuals traveling in air commerce, the sale of air transportation, the carrying by air of people or things, or the gross receipts from any air commerce. However, state and local governments may tax a commercial air carrier and related services if the aircraft takes off or lands in the state. Thus, in order to properly tax an air carrier, the flight must take off or land within the state or local government's taxing jurisdiction.
- Head taxes on motor carriers, 49 USCA § 14505. This is similar to the previous entry but applies to motor carriers.

Compensation of Transportation Employees

- Airline employees, 49 USCA § 40116. The income of air carrier employees who work in more than one state is only taxable in the employees' state/municipality of residence and the state/municipality in which the employees earn more than 50 percent of their salaries. In cases of authorized leave, the same rules apply such that income is only taxable in the state/municipality of residence in which more than 50 percent of pay would have been earned had the employees performed their regularly assigned duties.
- Merchant seamen, 46 USCA § 11108(b). Merchant seamen are only subject to taxes on their income from merchant seamen activities in the state or other political subdivision in which they reside. The withholding provision under this statute only applies to withholding of state and local taxes, not federal taxes.[13]
- Rail carrier employees, 49 USCA § 11502. Rail carrier employees are only taxed on their rail carrier income in their states of residence, regardless of the states in which they work. With regards to these cross-jurisdictional workers, employers should only withhold taxes within the appropriate jurisdictions.
- Motor/water carriers, 49 USCA § 14503. Employers may only withhold taxes in the states of the employees' residence.

Federal Preemption for Interstate Telecommunications

- Internet access, 47 USCA § 151. Internet tax freedom has undergone a number of changes and an extension was first enacted in 1998 and renewed in 2001 and 2007, with an expiration set for November 1, 2007. Among its initial provisions was a moratorium on the ability of state and local governments to impose new taxes on Internet access (a limited "grandfather clause" permits states that are already taking steps to tax access to continue to do so). That moratorium has now been extended to November 1, 2014.[14]
- Sourcing mobile telecommunications services, 4 USCA § 117. All charges for mobile telecommunications services that are deemed to be provided by a customer's home service provider are authorized to be subjected to tax, charge, or fee by the taxing jurisdictions whose territorial limits encompass the customer's place of primary use, regardless of where the mobile telecommunication services originate, terminate, or pass through, and no other taxing jurisdiction may impose taxes, charges, or fees on charges for such mobile telecommunications services.
- State and local taxation of direct-to-home satellite services, 47 USCA § 152. A provider of direct-to-home satellite service shall be exempt from the collection or remittance, or both, of any tax or fee imposed by any local taxing jurisdiction on direct-to-home satellite service.
- Right-of-way charges, 47 USCA § 253.

(a) In general: No state or local statute or regulation, or other state or local legal requirement, may prohibit or have the effect of prohibiting the ability of any entity to provide any interstate or intrastate telecommunications service.

(b) State regulatory authority: Nothing in this section shall affect the ability of a state to impose, on a competitively neutral basis, requirements necessary to preserve and advance universal service, protect the public safety and welfare, ensure the continued quality of telecommunications services, and safeguard the rights of consumers.

(c) State and local government authority: Nothing in this section affects the authority of a state or local government to manage the public rights-of-way or to require fair and reasonable compensation from telecommunications providers, on a competitively neutral and nondiscriminatory basis, for use of public rights-of-way on a nondiscriminatory basis, if the compensation required is publicly disclosed by such government.

(d) Preemption: If, after notice and an opportunity for public comment, the FCC determines that a state or local government has permitted or imposed any statute, regulation, or legal requirement that violates subsection (a) or (b) of this section, the FCC shall preempt the enforcement of such statute, regulation, or legal requirement to the extent necessary to correct such violation or inconsistency.

- States are permitted to tax telecommunication service providers for the use of public rights-of-way, provided that such taxes are not discriminatory and are competitively neutral between foreign and domestic service providers.

- Universal service fees, 47 USCA 254(f). A state may adopt regulations not inconsistent with the FCC's rules to preserve and advance universal service. Every telecommunications carrier that provides intrastate telecommunications services shall contribute, on an equitable and non-discriminatory basis, in a manner determined by the state to the preservation and advancement of universal service in that state. A state may adopt regulations to provide for additional definitions and standards to preserve and advance universal service within that state only to the extent that such regulations adopt additional specific, predictable, and sufficient mechanisms to support such definitions or standards that do not rely on or burden federal universal service support mechanisms.

- Cable communications, 47 USCA 542(b). For any twelve-month period, the franchise fees paid by a cable operator with respect to any cable system shall not exceed 5 percent of such cable operator's gross revenues derived in such period from the operation of the cable system to provide cable services. For purposes of this section, the twelve-month period shall be the twelve-month period applicable under the franchise for accounting purposes. Nothing in this subsection shall prohibit a franchising authority and a cable operator from agreeing that franchise fees that lawfully could be collected for any such twelve-month period shall be paid on a prepaid or deferred basis; except that the sum of the fees paid during the term of the franchise may not exceed the amount, including the time value of money, which would have lawfully been collected if such fees had been paid per annum.

- Sales of tangible personal property, P.L. 86–272; 15 USCA § 381. No state, or political subdivision thereof, shall have power to impose, for any taxable year ending after September 14, 1959, a net income tax on the income derived within such state by any person from interstate commerce if the only business activities within such state by or on behalf of such person during such taxable year are either, or both, of the following:
  (a) the solicitation of orders by such person, or his representative, in such state for sales of tangible personal property, which orders are sent outside the state for approval or rejection, and, if approved, are filled by shipment or delivery from a point outside the state; and
  (b) the solicitation of orders by such person, or his representative, in such state in the name of or for the benefit of a prospective customer of such person, if orders by such customer to such person to enable such customer to fill orders resulting from such solicitation are orders described in paragraph (a).

3. Federal Preemption for Sovereign States and Nations, Territories, Possessions, and the Alaska Native Fund

The US government also operates preemptively in the area of sovereign states, territories, and nations.

- Bonds and other financial operations. Bonds issued by sovereign states, nations, and territories are exempt from US state and local taxes. Sovereign state or territory local taxes may be imposed on these bonds, however, if so allowed. This differs in each jurisdiction, so each law must be examined.
- Puerto Rico, 48 USCA § 745. All bonds issued by the government of Puerto Rico, or by its authority, shall be exempt from taxation by the government of the United States, or by the government of Puerto Rico or of any political or municipal subdivision thereof, or by any state, territory, or possession, or by any county, municipality, or other municipal subdivision of any state, territory, or possession of the United States, or by the District of Columbia.
- Virgin Islands, 48 USCA § 1403. All bonds issued by the government of the Virgin Islands or any municipality thereof, including specifically interest thereon, shall be exempt from taxation by the government of the United States, or by the government of the Virgin Islands or any political subdivision thereof, or by any state, territory, or possession or by any political

subdivision of any state, territory, or possession, or by the District of Columbia: Provided further, the government of the Virgin Islands and any municipality thereof shall be obliged to levy and collect sufficient taxes for servicing any of the outstanding bonds, even if such taxation is required at a rate in excess of or in addition to the tax or tax rate of 1.25 percent of the assessed value.

- Foreign trade zones, 19 USCA § 81o(e). Tangible personal property imported from outside the United States and held in a zone for the purpose of storage, sale, exhibition, repackaging, assembly, distribution, sorting, grading, cleaning, mixing, display, manufacturing, or processing, and tangible personal property produced in the United States and held in a zone for exportation, either in its original form or as altered by any of the above processes, shall be exempt from state and local *ad valorem* taxation. A foreign trade zone is an area designated by the federal government, outside of US customs jurisdictions, where duty-free trade is permitted. Activity occurring in these zones is considered international and is protected from various domestic laws governing the jurisdiction in which the foreign trade zone sits.

- Continental shelf, 43 USCA 1333(a)(2)(A). To the extent that they are applicable and not inconsistent with this subchapter or with other federal laws and regulations of the Secretary now in effect or hereafter adopted, the civil and criminal laws of each adjacent state, now in effect or hereafter adopted, amended, or repealed are declared to be the law of the United States for that portion of the subsoil and seabed of the outer Continental Shelf, and artificial islands and fixed structures erected thereon, which would be within the area of the state if its boundaries were extended seaward to the outer margin of the outer Continental Shelf, and the president shall determine and publish in the *Federal Register* such projected lines extending seaward and defining each such area.[15] All of such applicable laws shall be administered and enforced by the appropriate officers and courts of the United States. State taxation laws shall not apply to the outer Continental Shelf.

- Note that the prohibition on state taxation of the Continental Shelf does not prohibit states from including extraction activity income from the Continental Shelf in income-tax apportionment formulas. The act only prohibits direct taxes on the Continental Shelf, such as severance and production taxes.[16]

- Navigable waters, 33 USCA § 5 (originally enacted 1884). No taxes, tolls, operating charges, fees, or any other impositions whatever shall be levied upon or collected from any vessel or other watercraft, or from its passengers or crew, by any nonfederal interest, if the vessel or watercraft is operating on any navigable waters subject to the authority of the United States, or under the right to freedom of navigation on those waters, except for (i) fees charged under section 2236 of the title; (ii) reasonable fees charged on a fair and equitable basis that are used solely to pay the cost of a service to the vessel or watercraft; enhance the safety and efficiency of interstate and foreign commerce; and do not impose more than a small burden on interstate or foreign commerce; and (iii) property taxes on vessels or watercraft, other than vessels or watercraft that are primarily engaged in foreign commerce if those taxes are permissible under the United States Constitution.

- *Alaska Native Claims Settlement*, 43 USCA § 1620(a). Revenues originating from the Alaska Native Fund shall not be subject to any form of federal, state, or local taxation at the time of receipt by a regional corporation, village corporation, or individual native through dividend distributions (even if the regional corporation or village corporation distributing the dividend has not segregated revenue received from the Alaska Native Fund from revenue received from other sources) or in any other manner. This exemption shall not apply to income from the investment of such revenues.

4. Federal Preemption for Tax Treatment of Federal Employees

Civilians Including Members of Congress

- Treatment of federal employees, 4 USCA § 111.
    - (a) General rule.—The United States consents to the taxation of pay or compensation for personal service as an officer or employee of the United States, a territory or possession or political subdivision thereof, the government of the District of Columbia, or an agency or instrumentality of one or more of the foregoing, by a duly constituted taxing authority having jurisdiction, if the taxation does not discriminate against the officer or employee because of the source of the pay or compensation.
    - (b) Treatment of certain federal employees employed at federal hydroelectric facilities located on the Columbia River: pay or compensation paid by the United States for personal services as an employee of the United States at a hydroelectric facility that is owned by the United States and located on the Columbia River, portions of which are within the states of Oregon and Washington, shall be subject to taxation by the state or any political subdivision thereof of which such employee is a resident.
    - (c) Treatment of certain federal employees employed at federal hydroelectric facilities located on the Missouri River: pay or compensation paid by the United States for personal services as an employee of the United States at a hydroelectric facility that is owned by the United States and located on the Missouri River, portions of which are within the states of South Dakota and Nebraska, shall be subject to

taxation by the state or any political subdivision thereof of which such employee is a resident.

- Residence of members of Congress, 4 USCA § 113. No state, or political subdivision thereof, in which a member of Congress maintains a place of abode for purposes of attending sessions of Congress may, for purposes of any income tax (as defined in section 110(c) of this title) levied by such state or political subdivision thereof treat such member as a resident or domiciliary of such state or political subdivision thereof; or treat any compensation paid by the United States to such member as income for services performed within, or from sources within, such state or political subdivision thereof, unless such member represents such state or a district in such state.

- Federal Employee Health Benefits Act (FEHBA), 5 USCA § 8909. No tax, fee, or other monetary payment may be imposed, directly or indirectly, on a carrier or an underwriting or plan administration subcontractor of an approved health benefits plan by any state, the District of Columbia, or the Commonwealth of Puerto Rico, or by any political subdivision or other governmental authority thereof, with respect to any payment made from the fund. [This preemption] shall not be construed to exempt any carrier or underwriting or plan administration subcontractor of an approved health benefits plan from the imposition, payment, or collection of a tax, fee, or other monetary payment on the net income or profit accruing to or realized by such carrier or underwriting or plan administration subcontractor from business conducted under this chapter, if that tax, fee, or payment is applicable to a broad range of business activity.

- Members of the armed forces. As another area of express statutory preemption, Congress has enacted several provisions relating to the jurisdiction and timing for taxation of members of the armed forces.
  - Servicemembers Civil Relief Act, 50 app. USCA 570 and 571. 570(a) Deferral of tax—Upon notice to the Internal Revenue Service or the tax authority of a state or a political subdivision of a state, the collection of income tax on the income of a service member falling due before or during military service shall be deferred for a period not more than 180 days after termination of or release from military service, if a service member's ability to pay such income tax is materially affected by military service.
  - 571(a) Residence or domicile: A service member shall neither lose nor acquire a residence or domicile for purposes of taxation with respect to the person, personal property, or income of the service member by reason of being absent or present in any tax jurisdiction of the United States solely in compliance with military orders.
  - Military service compensation and personal property. Compensation of a service member for military service shall not be deemed to be income for services performed or from sources within a tax jurisdiction of the United States if the service member is not a resident or domiciliary of the jurisdiction in which the service member is serving in compliance with

military orders. Similarly, the personal property of a service member shall not be deemed to be located or present in, or to have a situs for taxation in, the tax jurisdiction in which the service member is serving in compliance with military orders. This preemption does not prevent taxation by a tax jurisdiction with respect to personal property used in or arising from a trade or business, if it has jurisdiction. Eligibility for relief from personal property taxes under this subsection is not contingent on whether or not such taxes are paid to the state of domicile.

○ Spouses. In November 2009, the president signed the Military Spouses Residency Relief Act (P.L. 111–197 [2009]) into law, which gives military spouses the same domiciliary rules as soldiers but with respect to nonmilitary compensation, provided the military spouse is only present in a jurisdiction to be with the military member on military orders.

5. Federal Preemptions of Salary, Retirement, and Other Matters

- Pension income, 4 USCA § 114. No state may impose an income tax on any retirement income of an individual who is not a resident or domiciliary of such state (as determined under the laws of such state).
- ERISA, 29 USCA § 1144. No state may impose an income tax on any retirement income of an individual who is not a resident of such state.
- Unemployment taxes, 26 USCA § 3304. The Secretary must approve all state laws regarding taxes on unemployment income. There are various requirements for these state laws under the Federal Unemployment Tax Act. If the law satisfies these enumerated requirements, then the state law will be approved.
- Food stamp program, 7 USCA § 2013. Subject to the availability of funds, the Secretary is authorized to formulate and administer a supplemental nutrition assistance program under which, at the request of the state agency, eligible households within the state shall be provided an opportunity to obtain a more nutritious diet through the issuance to them of an allotment and, through an approved state plan, nutrition education, except that a state may not participate in the supplemental nutrition assistance program if the Secretary determines that state or local sales taxes are collected within that state on purchases of food made with benefits issued under this chapter. The benefits so received by such households shall be used only to purchase food from retail food stores that have been approved for participation in the supplemental nutrition assistance program. Stated simply, if a state or other locality wishes to participate in the federal food stamp program, then it must not tax purchases of food made with food stamps.

- Agricultural credit, 7 USCA § 1984. All property subject to a lien held by the United States or the title to which is acquired or held by the Secretary under this chapter other than property used for administrative purposes shall be subject to taxation by state, territory, district, and local political subdivisions in the same manner and to the same extent as other property is taxed: Provided, however, that no tax shall be imposed or collected on or with respect to any instrument if the tax is based on
    (1) the value of any notes or mortgages or other lien instruments held by or transferred to the Secretary;
    (2) any notes or lien instruments administered which are made, assigned, or held by a person otherwise liable for such tax; or
    (3) the value of any property conveyed or transferred to the Secretary,
- whether as a tax on the instrument, the privilege of conveying or transferring or the recordation thereof; nor shall the failure to pay or collect any such tax be a ground for refusal to record or file such instruments, or for failure to impart notice, or prevent the enforcement of its provisions in any state or federal court.
- Any property subject to a lien held by the United States or whose title has been acquired by the Secretary, if used for any nonadministrative purpose, is subject to normal state and local taxes on property; however, no state and local tax may be assessed on any instrument if the tax is based on the value of any notes or mortgages held by the Secretary or the value of any property conveyed or transferred to the Secretary.
- Discrimination in the taxation of the generation or transmission of electricity, 15 USCA 391. No State, or political subdivision thereof, may impose or assess a tax on or with respect to the generation or transmission of electricity which discriminates against out-of-state manufacturers, producers, wholesalers, retailers, or consumers of that electricity. A tax is discriminatory if it results, either directly or indirectly, in a greater tax burden on electricity that is generated and transmitted in interstate commerce than on electricity that is generated and transmitted in intrastate commerce.

CONCLUDING COMMENT

Based on the foregoing, it is obvious that the federal government has little hesitancy when it comes to circumscribing the power of the states to impose and administer their own schemes of taxation. And, to be balanced, of the preemptions, such as those that make clear the objective is nondiscriminatory taxation, have merit. Moreover, the increasing complexity of the US economy over the past half century is surely one of the reasons—and, again, in some cases, the justification for Congress to step in—to add to the clarity and transparency of how a federation ought to treat its taxpayers, individuals, and businesses alike. A case can be made for selective federal preemptions of the state tax base.

At the same time there is an equally important concern that, in order to maintain the proven benefits of a robust system of federal federalism, the federal government will overreach. This concern is heightened by what some might well argue is the political pressure on Congress to "do something" to demonstrate its political role in an era of growing federal fiscal austerity.

And herein lies the question of how to cope with the preemption issue in the next decade: if Congress continues to justify its interventions into these limitations on the basis of arguments that it must either protect itself or protect the "national market" from state interference, when does it cross the line between providing for transparency and nondiscriminatory intervention and creating coercive federalism? That is, when is it appropriate for the government to limit the power of subnational governments to raise and spend the funds necessary to provide services? The answer is, as for many answers to complicated issues, is "it depends."

But that the answer is complex is not a reason to shy away from framing the decision of whether or not to intervene through tax base preemption in terms of a set of criteria as to how to judge a "good" (or "bad") preemptive activity. Establishing such a list of criteria is the very method that public finance economists have conventionally—and successfully—pursued in order to judge what makes a good efficient and fair revenue system for different types of governments.[17]

Drawing on the ACIR criteria [18] as well as on subsequent contributions[19] and beginning with the important and broad guideline that the presumption against any federal fiscal preemption of the sovereign states is high and to take such action requires the exercise of consideration, a respect by the federal government for subnational government decisions and their prerogatives and legitimacy in solving their own problems, and respect by the federal government for the roles of state and local governments in the system of fiscal federalism—a system that, as Richard Nathan reminds us, was "born in America."[20] Thus, preemptions must be invoked only for the following reasons:

1. Protecting the basic political and civil rights guaranteed to all citizens by the Constitution.
2. Ensuring national defense and the proper conduct of foreign relations.
3. Establishing certain uniform and minimum standards in areas clearly affecting the flow of interstate commerce.
4. Assuring essential fiscal and programmatic integrity in the use of federal grants and contracts into which state and local governments may freely enter.
5. Ensuring that there is no fiscal harm: Legislation dealing with state taxing authorities should not disproportionately reduce existing state revenues. This principle is especially important at a time when states are cutting core services to meet balanced budget requirements. Federal unfunded

mandates or restrictions on state taxation will only exacerbate the fiscal problems that states currently face.

6. Preserving flexibility: The fiscal crisis is forcing all policymakers to revisit fundamental principles about the role of government. These questions will lead to changes that could have long-term, positive effects on the delivery of services, modernizing revenue systems, and holding government accountable. States should not be hindered in their pursuit of these reforms by federal legislation that restricts a state's authority to act.

7. Ensuring transparency: Federal legislation, especially in the context of state taxation, should be clear to limit ambiguity or the need for expensive and time-consuming litigation.

Notes

1 Kincaid (this volume); Conlan and Posner (this volume).

2 The National Conference of State Legislatures (NCSL) has identified at least $130 billion in cost shifts from the federal government to states from fiscal year 2004 to fiscal year 2008. NCSL (2011).

3 The focus is on the federal-state relationship, which includes the recognition that preemptions may also have important implicit actions for the autonomy of local governments. For an empirical analysis of the trends in and status of local government autonomy see Wolman, McManmon, Bell, and Brunori (2010), and MTC (2003).

4 Carey and McClellan (2001), 242–248.

5 Ibid., 136–139.

6 Kincaid (this volume).

7 Hellerstein et al. (2009).

8 *McCulloch v. Maryland* 17 US (4 Wheat) 316 (1819).

9 ACIR (1992).

10 Nivola (2000).

11 See also *McCulloch v. Maryland*, 17 US 316 (1819) (holding that, in order to preserve the tenets of the federal system, federal obligations are exempt from state taxation).

12 See also *United States v. Hartford Co.*, 572 F. Supp 238 (D. Md. 1983).

13 See *Henderson v. Sea-Land Service, Inc.*, 468 A.2d 1064 (N.J. 1983).

14 This topic is further discussed by Fox (this volume).

15 Throughout this chapter the authority of the "Secretary" is kept general so as to recognize that overtime Congress may change the name of the federal agency headed by a secretary. Thus before 1979 when the Department of Education, and, thus, the Secretary of Education, was created, there had been a Secretary of Health Education and Welfare.

16 See *Shell Oil Co. v. Iowa Dept. of Revenue*, 488 US 19 (1988); *Kelly-Springfield Tire Co. v. Iowa State Bd. of Tax Review*, 414 N.W.2d 113 (Iowa 1987).

17 Watson (2005); Musgrave (2005); Hildreth (2005).

18 ACIR (1992).

19 Eads (2010).

20 Nathan (2005).

REFERENCES

ACIR (1992, September). *Federal Statutory Preemption of State and Local Authority: History, Inventory, and Issues.* Report A-121. Washington, DC: US Advisory Commission on Intergovernmental Relations.

Budget and Revenue Standing Committee (2012). *Mandate Monitor.* Denver: National Conference of State Legislatures.

Carey, George W., and James McClellan (Eds.) (2001). *The Federalist: Gideon Edition* by Alexander Hamilton, John Jay, and James Madison (2nd ed.). Indianapolis: The Liberty Fund. 242–248.

Eads, James R., Jr. (2010, April 23). "Federal State Tax Relations in the 21st Century." American Tax Policy Institute Roundtable.

Hellerstein, Walter, Kirk Stark, John Swain, and Joan Youngman (2009). *State and Local Taxation, Cases and Materials* (3rd ed.). St. Paul, MN: West Publishing Co.

Henderson v. Sea-Land Service, Inc., 468 A.2d 1064 (N.J. 1983).

Hildreth, Bartley (2005). In *The Encyclopedia of Taxation and Tax Policy*, edited by Joseph J. Cordes, Robert D. Ebel, and Jane G. Gravelle. Washington DC: Urban Institute Press. 429–430.

Kelly-Springfield Tire Co. v. Iowa State Bd. of Tax Review, 414 N.W.2d 113 (Iowa 1987).

Law and Criminal Justice Standing Committee (2012). *Preemption Monitor.* Denver: National Conference of State Legislatures.

McCulloch v. Maryland, 17 US (4 Wheat) 316 (1819).

Multistate Tax Commission. (2003). "Federalism at Risk." Washington, DC: Multistate Tax Commission.

Musgrave, Richard (2005). "Fairness in Taxation." In *The Encyclopedia of Taxation and Tax Policy*, edited by Joseph J. Cordes, Robert D. Ebel, and Jane G. Gravelle. Washington DC: Urban Institute Press. 135–138.

Nathan, Richard (2005). "Updating Theories of American Federalism." In *Intergovernmental Management for the Twenty-First Century*, edited by Timothy J. Conlan and Paul L. Posner. Washington, DC: Brookings Institution Press. 13–25.

Nivola, Pietro (2000, June). "Last Rites for States Rights?" *Brookings Reform Watch* No. 1.

Posner, Paul (1998). "The Politics of Unfunded Mandates." In *American Intergovernmental Relations*, 4th ed., edited by Laurence O'Toole Jr. Washington, DC: CQ Press. 280–292.

Shell Oil Co. v. Iowa Dept. of Revenue, 488 US 19 (1988).

United States v. Hartford Co., 572 F. Supp. 238 (D. Md. 1983).

Watson, Harry (2005). "Excess Burden." In *The Encyclopedia of Taxation and Tax Policy*, edited by Joseph J. Cordes, Robert D. Ebel, and Jane G. Gravelle. Washington DC: Urban Institute Press. 121–122.

Wolman, Harold, Robert McManmon, Michael E. Bell and David Brunori. In *The Property Tax and Local Autonomy*, edited by Michael E. Bell, David Brunori, and Joan Youngman. Cambridge, MA: Lincoln Institute of Land Policy. 69–114.

CHAPTER 9

STATE INTERGOVERNMENTAL GRANT PROGRAMS

RONALD C. FISHER AND ANDREW BRISTLE

INTERGOVERNMENTAL fiscal flows, or resource transfers between governments, are an inherent characteristic of federal systems.[1] State governments receive 28 percent of their revenue from the federal government, and local governments receive 4 percent of revenue from the federal government in addition to 34 percent from state governments. Part of that revenue transferred from state governments to localities effectively can be considered federal grants in that the state governments have "passed on" funds to local governments. The interdependence flows in both directions, however, because although the federal and state governments provide substantial financial support to state and local governments, respectively, those governments also rely on the states and localities, respectively, to provide services with the transfers that were received. This second aspect of the interdependence raises issues about the public service goals of intergovernmental transfers and the appropriate structure of grant programs, given the goals.

Federal government transfers to states and localities are dominated by grants for medical assistance, principally for Medicaid, which make up 44 percent of all federal aid. Other substantial categories of federal aid include grants for education (8 percent), for highways (7 percent), for food assistance (5 percent), and for income support (4 percent). The structure and effects of many of these federal transfer programs have been examined in detail elsewhere.[2]

In contrast, state government transfers to support local governments, which are larger in absolute and relative magnitude than the federal transfers to states, have not been studied as extensively. State intergovernmental transfers are especially interesting also because the magnitude, structure, and effects often vary among the states. There is no standard model for state financial support of localities. State transfers are similar to federal transfers in one respect: one category is dominant. School districts are the recipients of the largest component of state government aid, which is 55 percent of total state grants to local governments. State education grants also have been studied extensively.[3]

The objective in this chapter, therefore, is to focus on state financial support for general-purpose local governments in the United States. We attempt to address this issue by (1) reviewing carefully the magnitude of state financial support for general-purpose local governments, (2) tabulating an up-to-date summary and comparison of such programs nationwide, (3) exploring common characteristics of these programs, (4) considering the various objectives of these grant programs, and (5) beginning an analysis of how and why state aid programs and magnitudes differ among the states.

REASONS FOR STATE INTERGOVERNMENTAL GRANTS

Intergovernmental grants traditionally have one of four objectives (or rationales): (1) provide regional resource redistribution, (2) allow for scale economies in revenue generation, (3) correct for externalities and spillovers, and (4) promote macroeconomic stabilization and economic growth. Each of these potential reasons for intergovernmental transfers may not apply equally across various types of governments in a federal system. Some may be relatively more appropriate for federal-to-state interaction, whereas others may apply more in the case of state-to-local intervention. In addition, the importance of each rationale varies from state to state and for different state and local public services. Each rationale is considered in turn in relation to potential state support of local governments.

Regional Redistribution

First, grants can be used for explicit redistribution of resources among regions or localities within states, most commonly for equity reasons.[4] If taxes that are collected by a state government are then allocated or distributed to local governments in that state using any factor other than "origin" or "derivation," then some redistribution among localities is likely to occur.[5] If state funds are distributed inversely proportional to local area income or property value, this results in an explicit transfer from taxpayers in higher-income jurisdictions to governments in lower-income jurisdictions.

Regional or local redistribution of resources traditionally has been a central factor in state grants to local governments for education purposes.[6] State grants are intended, at least somewhat, to alter large differences in educational spending driven in part by substantial differences in local property-tax bases. However, resource redistribution also can be an explicit or implicit objective of state grants for general-purpose local governments. This often is particularly true for unrestricted or revenue-sharing grants to counties and municipalities, as discussed later in this chapter.

The effects of this type of income redistribution are not always clear, however, because jurisdictions seldom are completely homogeneous in income or wealth and because the local government determines how the grant funds are to be spent. Even jurisdictions that have low-income residents on average may have high-income residents (in some cases a substantial number of the latter). If the objective is to assist low-income individuals and families, it may be preferable to give grants directly to those individuals, rather than to the local government where they reside. On the other hand, if the objective is to address local government spending or service differences, then grants to the local governments are appropriate, although the structure of those grants also will be crucial.

Efficiency of Revenue Collection

Grants also may be used to substitute one tax structure for another or one tax collection administration for another (e.g., to take advantage of scale economies in tax collection). This is commonly the case for many state transfers to local governments. Intergovernmental grants effectively substitute the granting government's tax revenue or tax collection for that of the recipient government.[7] If the taxes used by the granting government are more efficient than the ones they replace, this tax substitution is one way that grants may improve the efficiency of the federal system.

Because economic mobility is so much greater among local jurisdictions than among states, a tax levied statewide may generate less inefficiency than a set of similar local taxes. Centralized revenue collection may also provide economies of scale in tax collection and compliance. The revenue can be generated through the state government but spent locally, with a system of intergovernmental grants. This is at least part of the rationale for revenue-sharing programs. For instance, rather than instituting a set of county or municipal income taxes, a state might increase the state income-tax rate (or adopt a state income tax) and distribute the revenue to local governments. If the revenue is distributed to localities based on the origin of the funds, then there is no local redistribution, and the sole objective or benefit of this structure is the efficiency in centralized revenue generation. However, if the revenue is allocated by some factor other than origin, then the grant program may serve both to improve the efficiency of tax collection and to redistribute resources for equity or public service reasons.

In the United States, centralized revenue collection is in some states an important factor underlying state government transfers, because state governments are responsible for generating a substantially larger fraction of state and local revenue than they are for providing state and local public services directly. The degree of "vertical fiscal imbalance" in the United States is reflected in table 9.1. For the state and local sector in 2008, state governments received about 61 percent of total revenue (also 62 percent of general revenue and 59 percent of taxes), but state governments were responsible for only about 44 percent of direct state and local spending (that is, spending for directly providing public services). Therefore, because local governments have more responsibility for direct spending than for generating revenue, the difference is made up through financial transfers from the state governments.

Indeed, the degree of fiscal imbalance in the United States in 2008 understates the long-run situation, because state government revenue was affected more by the recession that began in 2007 than was local government revenue. In 2005 and 2006, for example, before the effects of the recent recession, state governments generated about 65 percent of revenue and were responsible for only about 45 percent of direct spending. This suggests that the vertical fiscal imbalance between state governments and their respective local governments in the United States averages about twenty percentage points.

Of course, due to the economic, demographic, and institutional diversity among the states, the difference between revenue and spending responsibility also differs

Table 9.1 Relative fiscal magnitude of state governments compared to the state and local sector

	State Government Share of State and Local Revenue	State Government Share of State and Local General Revenue	State Government Share of State and Local Taxes	State Government Share of State-Local Direct Expenditure*
2008	60.9%	62.4%	58.8%	44.3%
2007	65.1%	62.4%	59.0%	44.2%
2006	64.9%	63.5%	59.7%	45.0%
2005	65.0%	63.5%	59.2%	45.1%
2004	65.2%	63.2%	58.4%	44.9%
2003	63.3%	63.1%	58.5%	45.2%
2002	60.7%	63.1%	59.1%	44.8%
2001	62.4%	63.7%	61.2%	44.1%
2000	64.9%	63.9%	61.9%	43.4%

* Direct expenditures are made up of payments by governments for providing goods and services; they are considered a measure of spending after intergovernmental transfers.
Source: US Census Bureau, State and Local Government Finances, various years

widely among the states, as shown in table 9.2. Spending responsibility is relatively more centralized in some states, with the state governments being responsible for at least 60 percent of direct spending in eight states (Alaska, Delaware, Hawaii, Kentucky, Maine, Rhode Island, Vermont, and West Virginia). In contrast, the fiscal imbalance (difference between revenue and spending responsibility) is largest (at least twenty percentage points) in Arkansas, New York, North Carolina, Texas, Vermont, and Wyoming.[8] Vermont is an interesting case; although the state government is responsible for nearly 62 percent of direct spending, it generates almost 85 percent of revenue. Thus, in Vermont both revenue raising and spending are relatively centralized, but a large vertical imbalance remains. Because of the variations in the vertical fiscal imbalance among the states, one also expects the importance of state aid to local governments to differ substantially among the states.

Transportation funding provides a specific example of centralized revenue generation. States clearly have opted for a centralized (state) collection of revenue: principally, this is composed of state motor fuel taxes and vehicle registration fees that are often referred to as "user-related" taxes. Most states earmark these revenues solely for transportation purposes, with a substantial component distributed to counties and municipalities that have substantial responsibility for providing transportation services.

Spillovers

Grants may be intended to stimulate additional public spending by recipient governments, perhaps to correct for externalities or spillovers that arise from the structure of subnational governments. This is another way that grants may improve the efficiency of fiscal decisions. The existence of interjurisdictional externalities, or spillovers, can cause service decisions by individual local governments to be inefficient from the society's viewpoint. If nonresidents benefit from a locally provided service, but those nonresident benefits are not considered in the decision about the amount of the service to provide, social marginal benefits will be underestimated and too little of the service provided. In such a case, an intergovernmental grant can be used to induce the local government to provide more of that specific service, as efficiency requires.[9] Moreover, because the grant funds are generated from taxes collected by the state government, those nonresidents who benefit from the service end up paying for part of the service through their state taxes.

Individual migration among local communities also may involve a type of externality, if that migration imposes costs on the other residents.[10] Individuals may move to avoid subnational taxes or to gain services. If the new residents pay less than the average cost of services they consume, however, existing residents face either service reductions with constant taxes or higher taxes to maintain services. The potential migrants have no incentive to include those costs imposed on other residents in their decision about whether to relocate, so the distribution of population among localities may become inefficient. Again, intergovernmental grants

Table 9.2 Relative fiscal magnitude of state governments compared to the state and local sector, by state in 2008

	State Government Share of State and Local Revenue	State Government Share of State and Local General Revenue	State Government Share of State and Local Taxes	State Government Share of State and Local Direct Expenditure*
Alabama	57.7%	67.7%	64.6%	47.6%
Alaska	85.3%	86.5%	86.5%	66.9%
Arizona	58.1%	63.1%	59.6%	39.1%
Arkansas	76.9%	80.2%	80.1%	55.8%
California	56.8%	59.3%	63.1%	37.2%
Colorado	56.3%	52.7%	49.0%	39.0%
Connecticut	66.6%	68.0%	63.2%	55.0%
Delaware	79.2%	83.2%	78.9%	65.9%
Florida	46.4%	49.8%	48.9%	36.3%
Georgia	56.3%	57.4%	53.7%	39.6%
Hawaii	77.9%	79.8%	76.4%	78.7%
Idaho	67.4%	67.7%	73.9%	52.3%
Illinois	56.2%	57.9%	55.1%	42.0%
Indiana	63.1%	66.1%	65.9%	46.3%
Iowa	63.8%	64.9%	59.7%	48.0%
Kansas	59.7%	63.3%	60.3%	45.8%
Kentucky	69.8%	73.8%	71.0%	60.3%

Louisiana	68.6%	70.5%	61.3%	58.7%
Maine	71.2%	72.0%	63.8%	61.1%
Maryland	62.5%	63.8%	56.8%	49.8%
Massachusetts	70.4%	70.6%	64.4%	53.7%
Michigan	61.6%	67.2%	65.8%	44.5%
Minnesota	65.1%	68.4%	74.1%	45.4%
Mississippi	68.9%	71.6%	73.5%	53.8%
Missouri	59.8%	62.0%	55.2%	46.9%
Montana	75.1%	73.3%	71.3%	59.4%
Nebraska	47.2%	59.2%	56.3%	35.3%
Nevada	52.3%	52.2%	57.8%	32.5%
New Hampshire	65.2%	63.9%	45.4%	51.7%
New Jersey	64.1%	63.2%	56.9%	51.9%
New Mexico	76.2%	79.6%	72.9%	59.4%
New York	60.4%	58.1%	47.3%	39.8%
North Carolina	66.6%	66.8%	68.6%	46.0%
North Dakota	75.2%	75.4%	72.8%	59.1%
Ohio	65.0%	62.4%	56.0%	48.3%
Oklahoma	69.7%	71.5%	67.6%	55.2%

(Continued)

Table 9.2 Continued

	State Government Share of State and Local Revenue	State Government Share of State and Local General Revenue	State Government Share of State and Local Taxes	State Government Share of State and Local Direct Expenditure*
Oregon	59.1%	61.2%	58.1%	48.5%
Pennsylvania	64.8%	63.3%	59.4%	48.2%
Rhode Island	70.9%	71.2%	56.7%	61.1%
South Carolina	65.3%	65.6%	60.6%	55.0%
South Dakota	56.1%	63.6%	52.9%	51.7%
Tennessee	53.5%	64.2%	60.7%	40.2%
Texas	60.6%	60.3%	51.7%	39.2%
Utah	67.1%	69.6%	65.2%	50.6%
Vermont	84.6%	87.3%	86.7%	61.8%
Virginia	62.2%	63.9%	56.3%	45.4%
Washington	58.0%	61.3%	62.8%	45.8%
West Virginia	78.2%	79.5%	75.9%	61.9%
Wisconsin	61.5%	66.6%	61.9%	45.7%
Wyoming	71.6%	69.2%	65.1%	44.0%

* Direct expenditures are made up of payments by governments for providing goods and services; they are considered a measure of spending after intergovernmental transfers.

Source: US Census Bureau, State and Local Government Finances, 2008.

may be used to resolve this difficulty. Grants to high-tax or low-service localities may forestall some of the migration in search of lower taxes or more services and contribute to a more efficient structure of local government. Such grants may appear to be for resource redistribution purposes, but in fact may be thought of as more accurately advancing efficiency objectives.

Stabilization

Grants have also been considered as a macroeconomic stabilizing mechanism for the subnational government sector, but this argument applies more appropriately to federal grant possibilities than to state grant programs. It is common during national macroeconomic downturns—including the recession that began in 2007—for the federal government to provide additional financial support to state and local governments through the intergovernmental grant system. Here the federal government is following traditional fiscal policy objectives of attempting to maintain or increase demand (spending) by using state and local governments as the spending vehicle.

However, similar behavior by a state government toward the local governments in the state is not common; indeed, the opposite is often the case. In some cases, state governments target particular grants or components of specific grants to local governments that are exhibiting characteristics of "fiscal distress." But rather than being part of an effort to stimulate overall economic growth or stability in a state, such targeted aid is often a short-run measure to forestall a fiscal crisis in that locality. It is more common for states to react to state government fiscal problems by reducing state government aid to local governments, especially for local revenue sharing or for primary and secondary education. In contrast to common federal-to-state interaction, a state government's fiscal difficulties often are transferred on to local governments within that state.

GRANT STRUCTURE

Intergovernmental grants may either be *lump-sum*, in which case the grant amount is fixed and does not change as a recipient government changes its taxes or expenditures, or may be *matching*, which requires that recipient government taxes or spending "match," at some rate, the amount of the grant. In that case, the size of the grant depends on the amount of the recipient government taxes or spending that is allocated for that purpose. Both lump-sum and matching grants may be allocated either by a formula or on a project-by-project basis and may be either open-ended (no limit on the grant amount) or closed-ended (the grant amount is somewhat limited because the funds appropriated for the grant program are fixed). If the formula used to distribute grant funds uses factors outside of the recipient government's direct control, such as population or per capita income, the grant is a pure lump sum to the government. If the formula used to distribute grant funds uses factors selected by the recipient government, such as tax revenue or public spending, then the grant is a matching grant and creates an incentive for the recipient government to increase taxes or spending. Finally, grants may be targeted to specific spending categories, called categorical grants, or they may be unrestricted (or general) grants, allowing the recipient government to allocate the grant funds to any expenditure or public service area.

If the objective is to increase recipient government expenditures on a specific function or public service, for instance to offset externalities, economic theory implies that open-ended, categorical matching grants are most effective. A matching grant with a matching rate equal to the nonresident share of benefits offsets the effects of interjurisdictional externalities by reducing the local tax price. The lower price induces the increase in expenditures necessary for economic efficiency. For instance, if the external (nonresident) benefit of additional highway spending is half of the total, a matching grant to the government that is responsible for the road that pays $1 for each $1 of local funds reduces that government's cost by half and restores efficiency. Although other grants also could be used to increase expenditures, an open-ended matching grant induces the desired expenditure response with the smallest possible grant; matching grants provide the largest expenditure effect per dollar of the grant.

As shown in the next section, the great majority of state government grants to local governments (excluding those for education to school districts) are lump-sum grants distributed by formula. In some instances the formula creates a geographic redistribution of resources, whereas in other cases the formula simply returns grant funds to the location where the state tax revenue was generated. Matching grants by state governments outside of the education arena are rare. State government grants to general-purpose local governments are most often intended for specific functions, although unrestricted state grants are used in roughly half of the states.

Magnitude and Composition of State Intergovernmental Grants

Amount and Growth of State Aid

In 2008, state governments provided about $467 billion of intergovernmental revenue to local governments, representing almost 27 percent of state expenditure and accounting for about 33 percent of local government general revenue, as shown in figure 9.1. Although state aid grew by about 31 percent from 2002 to 2008, the real value of state aid payments to localities declined over this period, as did the importance of state aid to local budgets and the share of state government expenditures for this purpose. Among the states, the relative importance of state intergovernmental grants compared to local general revenue varied from 66.7 percent (in Vermont) to 23 percent (in Colorado).[11] Of course, this includes the substantial

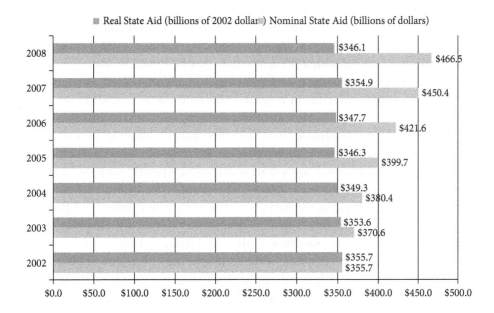

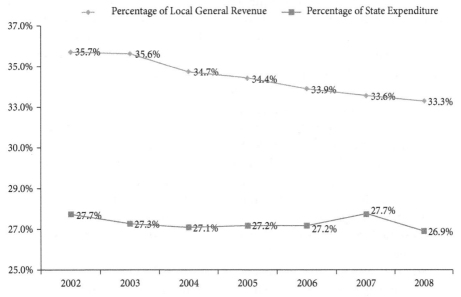

Figure 9.1 Local government intergovernmental revenue from states, 2002–2008
Source: U.S. Census Bureau, Governments Division, State and Local Finances.

support provided by state governments to finance public K–12 education, which accounts for the high ratio in Vermont.

The possible relationship between federal aid and state and local governments and of state government aid to local governments is an intriguing issue that has received less attention in the academic literature than may be warranted. The magnitude of these potentially connected intergovernmental flows is shown in table 9.3. In 2008, state governments received about $423 billion from the federal government, which represents about 26 percent of state government revenue. In turn, state governments transferred about $467 billion to local governments, accounting for about 31 percent of aggregate local government revenue.[12] At least in aggregate, there is some rough sense that these amounts may be linked because the fraction of state government revenue from federal aid is highly correlated over time with the fraction of local government revenue from state aid (a correlation coefficient of 0.73).

However, the mechanism for how federal-to-state and state-to-local aid might be linked is not clear. Federal intergovernmental grants to state governments all are categorical grants, which are grants restricted for specific purposes. The largest category of federal aid by a substantial margin is for health-care provision, essentially Medicaid and associated programs. Only a few federal aid programs require a "pass through" of aid to local governments explicitly. However, federal aid clearly increases the economic resources in a state, and perhaps more important, the resources at the disposal of the state government. If a state government would, in any case, have spent state-generated funds on a public service program supported by federal aid, then the federal aid may just substitute for state funds, freeing resources to be spent by the state government on other functions. This is the familiar issue of "fungibility of money," implying that a substantial portion of categorical grants (whether matching or lump-sum) may be diverted to uses other than those nominally intended.[13] Those other functions might include providing intergovernmental aid to local governments for specific service provisions. This option may be reinforced by the "flypaper effect," which suggests that diverting funds to other public service areas is more likely than reducing state taxes. The relationship between federal-to-state grants and state-to-local aid would seem to be a fruitful topic for additional research.

State intergovernmental transfers in the United States are especially important for the largest subnational government service area, which is education. As shown in figure 9.2, school districts are the recipients of the largest component of state aid by far: about 55 percent of the total in 2007. As a result, local K–12 public education institutions receive 56 percent of their revenue from state and federal governments. In contrast, county governments are the recipients of about 23 percent of state aid (about $105 billion in 2007), whereas municipal and township governments receive about 20 percent of state aid ($84 billion).

Although state intergovernmental grants provide about 20 percent of revenue to municipalities and 30 percent to counties, the structure of the grant programs that states use to provide financial support to general-purpose local

Table 9.3 Federal-to-state government and state-to-local government aid, 2000–2008[*]

Year	Intergovernmental Aid from the Federal Government to the State Governments (Billions of Dollars)	Intergovernmental Aid from the State Governments to Local Governments (Billions of Dollars)	Intergovernmental Aid from the Federal Government to State Governments as a Percentage of State Government Revenue	Intergovernmental Aid from State Governments to Local Governments as a Percentage of Local Government Revenue
2000	$259.11	$317.06	20.6%	31.3%
2001	$288.31	$340.25	24.4%	31.9%
2002	$317.58	$355.68	28.9%	32.8%
2003	$343.30	$370.65	26.5%	32.5%
2004	$373.51	$380.36	23.5%	30.5%
2005	$386.31	$399.86	23.5%	30.6%
2006	$398.20	$418.42	22.4%	29.7%
2007	$410.18	$446.64	20.5%	29.0%
2008	$423.15	$466.51	26.1%	30.5%

*The federal government also provides direct grants to local governments.
Source: US Census Bureau, State and Local Government Finances, various years.

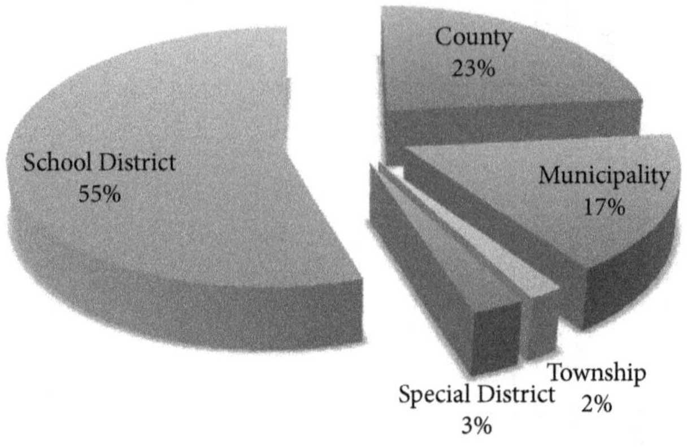

Total Aid = $446.7 billion

Figure 9.2 State aid by type of local government, 2007 (billions of dollars)
Source: U.S. Census Bureau, Census of Governments, 2007.

governments and the public service responsibilities targeted by these grants have not received substantial attention in the academic and policy literature. In contrast, the magnitude and structure of state government grants for local public education has been studied extensively and is well documented. Daphne Kenyon examines the topic of education grants in chapter 20 of this volume. Accordingly, state government grants to general-purpose local governments is the focus of this chapter.

One seemingly rough but straightforward method to exclude state support for K-12 education is to subtract both state aid for public education and the general revenue for public education in the calculation. The resulting ratio is state intergovernmental aid, excluding that for public education as a fraction of local general revenue and excluding the revenue for elementary and secondary education. This estimation is possible because the US Census Bureau reports data for both state aid and revenue for elementary and secondary education that includes both public independent and dependent school systems.[14]

For 2006, such a calculation reveals that state intergovernmental aid represents about 24.7 percent of local general revenue, *excluding* primary and secondary public education. State government financial support for local governments, excluding public primary and secondary education, varied from 35.6 percent (in California) to 6 percent (in Alaska). These estimates still fall short of an ideal measurement of state support for general-purpose localities because (1) they include fiscal magnitudes for special districts other than schools, (2) no information is provided about the relative magnitude of different local public service functions supported by this intergovernmental revenue, (3) the interstate comparisons are greatly influenced by how responsibility for provision of specific public services is divided between state and local governments in each case, and (4), as the US Census Bureau notes, it is not possible to make a complete fiscal separation in the case of dependent school systems.

Magnitude and Composition of State Aid to General-Purpose Localities

The most accurate and detailed perspective about state support for general-purpose local governments (that is, excluding school districts and other special districts) arises from examining the finances of counties, municipalities, and townships separately, which is possible with data from the Census of Governments. As shown in table 9.4, in aggregate in 2007, county governments received 31.1 percent of their general revenue from state governments, whereas state aid provided 19.5 percent of general revenue for municipalities (cities and townships). The relative importance of state aid to both counties and municipalities declined between 2002 and

Table 9.4 State aid to counties and municipalities-townships, 2002 and 2007

State Aid to Counties and Municipalities		
Total and Selected Categories	2002	2007
TO COUNTIES		
Total Aid (Billions of Dollars)	$86.80	$104.90
As a Percentage of State Expenditure	6.7%	6.6%
As a Percentage of County Revenue	33.8%	31.1%
For County General Government Support	$9.0	$10.8
As a Percentage of County Revenue	3.5%	3.2%
For County Highway Support	$6.87	$8.18
As a Percentage of County Revenue	2.6%	2.4%
For County Mass Transit Support	$0.39	$0.35
As a Percentage of County Revenue	0.1%	0.1%
TO MUNICIPALITIES AND TOWNSHIPS		
Total Aid (Billions of Dollars)	$69.20	$84.20
As a Percentage of State Expenditure	5.4%	5.2%
As a Percentage of Municipality and Township Revenue	21.6%	19.5%
For Municipality and Township General Government Support	$16.8	$20.6
As a Percentage of Municipality and Township Revenue	5.3%	4.8%
For Municipality and Township Highway Support	$5.50	$6.75
As a Percentage of Municipality and Township Revenue	1.7%	1.6%
For Municipality and Township Revenue Mass Transit Support	NA	$3.65
As a Percentage of Municipality and Township Revenue	NA	0.8%

Source: US Census Bureau, Census of Governments, 2002 and 2007.

2007, when compared to local revenue and state government expenditure. Detailed examination of the composition of this aid is necessary both to clarify the role that state governments play in financing general-purpose local governments and to focus on specific categories of support.

The distribution of state aid to counties, on the one hand, and to cities and townships on the other, by functional category is shown in figure 9.3. For counties, the largest amounts of state aid are for welfare (29 percent), education (24.6 percent), and health and hospitals (13.1 percent). The magnitudes for welfare and health, in many cases, likely reflect payments as part of the TANF and Medicaid programs,

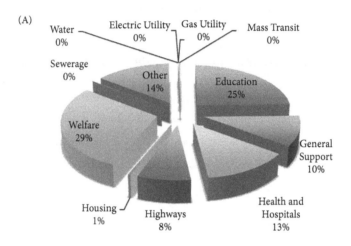

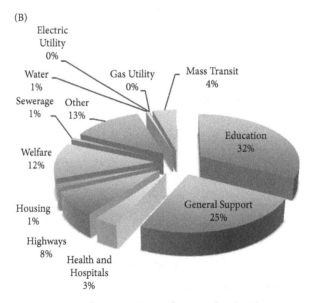

Figure 9.3 Functional composition of state aid to local governments, 2007. (A) counties, (B) municipalities and townships
Source: U.S. Census Bureau, Governments Division, 2007 Census of Governments.

whereas the state support to counties for education likely represents support for elementary and secondary schools operated by counties (so-called dependent school systems) and for community colleges. In contrast, the share of state aid to counties that is targeted for transportation (highways and mass transit) is about 8 percent of the total.

The situation for cities and townships is similar (see figure 9.3). Education accounts for 32.4 percent of state aid to municipalities and townships, which largely represents state aid to dependent elementary and secondary school systems, with grants for general support the second largest at 25 percent. Grants to cities and townships for transportation purposes represent about 12 percent of total state aid to municipalities (8 percent for highways and 4 percent for mass transit).

Returning to table 9.4, the relative levels of importance of state grants for general local government support and for transportation purposes, for both counties and municipalities, are shown separately. State grants for general support, on average, provide slightly more than 3 percent of revenue for county governments and nearly 5 percent of municipal government revenue. State grants for transportation purposes represent about 2.5 percent of revenue for both county and municipal governments. So, taken together, these two categories of state aid account on average for roughly 5 to 8 percent of the revenue of general-purpose local governments. Of course, as we shall see, these magnitudes vary widely among the states.

In the remainder of this chapter, the structures of state unrestricted grants for general support (revenue sharing) and of state grants for transportation purposes are examined in greater detail. These two categories of state intergovernmental grants were selected for additional examination because these two programs have received little analytical attention in recent years in the academic or policy literature, because the categories are relatively well defined and have easily identified related grants, because survey information about grant characteristics has become available, and because they are relatively important in magnitude and policy impact.[15]

State Grants for General or Unrestricted Government Support

Using the Census of Governments data as the measure, there is wide variation in the existence and structure of general revenue sharing by state governments for their respective local governments. State general revenue sharing to county governments provides at least 5 percent of general revenue in only thirteen states, whereas state general support to counties is not substantial at all (providing less than 2 percent of revenue) in nearly half (twenty-four) of the states. Similarly, state grants for general government support of municipalities and townships (as measured by the Census of Governments) provide at least 10 percent of municipal and township general revenue in only ten states, and at least 5 percent of revenue in twenty states. State revenue sharing for cities and townships is very minor or nonexistent in more than half (twenty-six) of the states.

For a number of states, the Census of Governments data show exceedingly small amounts of state support both to counties and to municipalities and townships for general government support. Many of these small amounts likely reflect state-collected taxes that are distributed to local governments based on their origin. An example might be an excise tax levied on the sale of alcoholic beverages or hotel rooms and collected by the state government, with the revenue distributed to the localities where the sales took place. In addition, some large state grants for general government support may arise effectively from the state collection of local taxes. One example could be a local option sales tax that is collected by the state (along with the state sales tax) and distributed to the localities that adopted the local option.

Obviously, there is an important semantic or categorization issue with such taxes and state distributions. Do they provide state revenue that is then used for grants to localities, or are they local taxes collected administratively by states? Traditionally, revenue sharing has been thought of as requiring some redistribution of resources among recipient governments, whether based on differential resource or cost factors. It is useful to note that whether grants are allocated on a redistributive basis and whether the funds are restricted to specific uses are independent issues. Some of the funds distributed based on origin are earmarked for specific public service functions, whereas others are for general use. Similarly, some state aid that is redistributive is earmarked for specific purposes and some is unrestricted. Our definition of state government unrestricted distributions for general local government support ("general revenue sharing") includes *only* state aid allocated by a formula that redistributes resources among localities.[16]

To determine the structure of state aid programs that are used to fund counties and municipalities, including both the sources of revenue and the distribution of the funds, Fisher and Prasad reviewed and collected the details of such programs from state sources.[17] The review relied on publicly available information from state agencies (budget, finance, or treasury departments and legislative analysis offices, depending on the state organizational structure), from local government associations (municipal league or associations of counties), and from state governmental research associations (NGOs and expenditure or tax foundations). In some cases, direct discussions with staff members of those organizations and recommendations and information provided by other academic researchers were used to clarify understanding.

The list of states operating state grant programs to counties or municipalities in order to provide general (unrestricted) financial support by the Fisher-Prasad definition (redistributing formula) is shown in table 9.5. Beside each state's name in

Table 9.5 State grant programs for general local government support

State with Intergovernmental Grants for General Government Support (Unrestricted Revenue Sharing)[a]

Counties and Municipalities	Counties Only	Municipalities Only
Arkansas (1.5%, 2.5%)	Hawaii (5.2%)	Arizona (13.8%)
California (3.3%, 7.1%)	Iowa (3.5%)	Maine (5.2%)
Florida (6.3%, 6.2%)	Louisiana (1.7%)	Massachusetts (6.2%)
Idaho (5.9%, 6.5%)		New Jersey (12.8%)
Indiana (7.2%, 8.9%)		New York (0.6%)
Illinois (8.9%, 19.2%)		Rhode Island (5.4%)
Kansas (0.8%, 0.8%)		
Michigan (0.9%, 10.7%)		
Minnesota (5.3%, 8.6%)		
Montana (4.6%, 10.4%)		
Nevada (17.7%, 22.3%)		
North Carolina (0.2%, 4.2%)		
North Dakota (6.7%, 5.5%)		
Ohio (4.0%, 5.7%)		
South Carolina (6.1%, 3.3%)		
Tennessee (0.8%, 3.2%)		
Wisconsin (5.7%, 16.4%)		
Wyoming (9.5%, 30.3%)		

[a] Number in parentheses is grant percentage of local general revenue, according to the 2007 Census of Government data.
Source: Fisher and Prasad (2009).

parentheses is a number showing the percentage of local general revenue provided by state intergovernmental revenue for general government purposes, as reported by the Census of Governments. Thus, there are two independent measures of state general revenue sharing combined in this table.

Structure of State Revenue Sharing

This review of state sources uncovered twenty-seven states operating state programs that provided general (unrestricted) financial assistance to counties and municipalities (cities and townships), as shown in the tables. Of these twenty-seven states, eighteen provide support to both counties and municipalities through these programs. Only municipalities receive funds in six states (including some without functioning counties), whereas county governments are the sole recipients in three states. There is no substantial regional pattern to which states operate local revenue-sharing programs, with a number of states in every region included (although state revenue-sharing programs seem most common relatively in the Midwest).

Examination of the structures of these state revenue-sharing (unrestricted aid) programs reveals five features that stand out. The first of these is that population (per capita distribution) is by far and away the most common allocation factor used in distributing state unrestricted aid funds; at least nineteen of the twenty-seven identified states use population as at least part of the allocation formula. But population is used exclusively as the allocation factor in only two of these states.[18]

The second key feature is that, in a number of cases, states establish ad hoc limits or constraints on whatever allocation formula is used. Minimum grant amounts by the type of local government are set in two states (Arizona and Florida), and special allocations for identified localities are used in another seven states (Hawaii, Michigan, Minnesota, Montana, New Jersey, New York, and Rhode Island). In the cases of Michigan and New York, there are special allocations for the City of Detroit and New York City. In Minnesota, specific amounts are identified for a large set of cities. In New Jersey and Rhode Island, there are separate allocations for cities that are in "fiscal distress." In Hawaii and Montana, the shares to each county are measured as specific, fixed percentages.

A third important feature is that none of these state revenue-sharing programs use cost measures in the distribution formula. Although a number of states use traditional "need" or resource measures, such as per capita income and per capita property value, to target aid to "poorer" communities, none of them attempt directly to distribute more resources to local areas where public service costs are higher. Even such a simple cost measure as population density never appears. This stands in contrast to an extensive academic literature, suggesting the importance of considering cost differences, not just for education, but for general-purpose governments, as well.[19]

A fourth observation is that when fiscal difficulties of state governments result in reductions to local revenue-sharing distributions, states often suspend the statutory allocation formula in favor of some ad hoc adjustment. Importantly, states seldom seem to make major structural changes to or redesigns of their revenue-sharing programs during periods of fiscal stress, electing instead for temporary limits of some type.

Fifth, and finally, an analysis of the relationship between the use of state revenue-sharing programs and state economic and fiscal characteristics shows no clear pattern, either for all states with state revenue sharing or only among the states using "equalizing or needs" allocation factors (income or property value). For all states with revenue-sharing programs, possible relationships to state household income, to per capita state and local expenditures, and to the fiscal role of state governments are shown in table 9.6. For each characteristic, about half of the revenue-sharing states are above the national measure and about half are below.

Table 9.6 Relationship of state characteristics to state revenue sharing

States with Unrestricted Revenue Sharing	2008 Median Household Income	2007 Per Capita State and Local General Expenditures	State Government Share of State and Local Direct General Expenditures
AZ	−	−	−
AR	−	−	+
CA	+	+	−
FL	−	Med	−
HI	+	+	+
ID	−	−	+
IL	+	+	−
IN	−	+	+
IA	−	+	+
KS	−	−	+
LA	−	+	+
ME	−	+	+
MA	+	+	+
MI	−	−	−
MN	+	+	−
MT	−	−	+
NV	+	−	−
NJ	+	+	+
NY	+	+	−
NC	−	−	+
ND	−	+	+
OH	−	+	−
RI	+	+	+
SC	−	+	+
TN	−	−	+
WI	+	+	−
WY	+	+	−
US	$52,029 Median	$7,311 Median	42.70% Mean

Source: Fisher and Prasad (2009).

In addition, twelve states with revenue-sharing programs (Florida, Idaho, Kansas, Maine, Massachusetts, Michigan, Minnesota, New Jersey, New York, Rhode Island, Wisconsin, and Wyoming) allocate funds to local governments by using the needs-based factors of local incomes or property values. A similar analysis again shows no obvious relationship for these states with income, state-local spending, or the state government role. Therefore, both the reasons why some states have adopted or continued state revenue sharing to provide general financial support for local governments and the reasons why a particular structure for such programs is adopted are unresolved and provide interesting topics for future research.

STATE GRANTS FOR TRANSPORTATION SUPPORT

The magnitude and structure of state grants to general-purpose local governments for transportation purposes are related to two important institutional factors. First, states differ substantially in the division of ownership and maintenance responsibility for roads between the state government and local governments, counties, or cities. Thus, as one would expect, in states where relatively more responsibility for roads is allocated to local governments than the state government, a greater share of state transportation revenue will be transferred to local governments. Second, unlike many intergovernmental grants for other purposes, grants for transportation purposes are derived from specific revenue sources related to and earmarked for transportation. The distribution of those earmarked revenues is expected to create regional redistribution because those sources of revenue to be shared with local governments may not have been generated in the same jurisdictions where they are ultimately distributed.

Road Ownership

The ultimate fiscal responsibility (i.e., ownership) for various types of roads is divided among various governments in the US federal system, and this division is not at all uniform across the nation. In total, local governments (counties and municipalities principally) are responsible for 76 percent of public road mileage in the United States and state government highway departments about 19 percent.[20] The division of road ownership between the state and local governments in different states results from differences in the relative importance of federal aid and nonfederal aid highways and from the geographic mix of urban and rural areas in a state. In addition, however, a number of states have explicit policy arrangements that alter the division of road ownership compared to the national averages.[21]

Accordingly, the division of road ownership (by mileage) between the state government and local governments varies dramatically among the states. In 2008, local government ownership of public roads varied from 91.8 percent in Kansas to 8.2 percent in West Virginia. With a coefficient of variation equal to 0.29, these interstate differences are indeed quite substantial. Even a quick review of the data suggests that these differences arise as much, if not more, from explicit state policy decisions as from the degree of interstate traffic or the rural and urban nature in these states. The states where local government ownership of roads is very high include some that are quite rural (Kansas and Iowa) and some that are relatively urban (New Jersey and Massachusetts). Similarly, some of those states are expected to have substantially more interstate traffic (New Jersey) than others (Wisconsin). Therefore, an important issue is whether the formula used to distribute highway funds to local governments is different in states that have elected to emphasize local ownership of roads.

State Transportation Revenues

The two major state revenues that are shared with local governments to fund transportation are motor fuel taxes and motor vehicle license taxes and fees. In 2008, state and local governments collected about $37.9 billion from motor fuel taxes and $21.3 billion in vehicle license taxes. Together, then, these two sources generated nearly $60 billion in 2008, which represents about 2.5 percent of state and local general revenue. These predominantly are state rather than local government revenues; 95 percent of revenue from these two sources went to state governments. Since 2002, vehicle license taxes have grown at a faster rate (about 26 percent) than motor fuel taxes (about 15 percent). This likely reflects the fact that most motor fuel taxes are per-gallon excise taxes. As fuel efficiency of vehicles has risen or miles driven per vehicle have declined, fuel consumption and fuel taxes increase relatively less than the number of vehicles. It is the sharing of these two revenue sources by state governments with local governments that largely makes up state grants for transportation.

State Transportation Grants

The US Department of Transportation collects and reports information about the methods used by states to distribute state motor fuel taxes and state motor vehicle taxes and fees to local governments. The DOT information is exceptionally detailed, essentially reporting the key aspects of the various state statutes through which these distributions are legislated. Therefore, based on the DOT information, Fisher and Bristle summarize four types of grants: motor fuel tax distributions to county and municipal governments, separately, and motor vehicle taxes and fees to county and municipal governments, separately, all of which are lump-sum, formula grants.[22] They report, for each category of grant, whether one of six primary allocation factors are used: (1) origin (funds returned to the local jurisdiction from which they were collected), (2) equal share (total amount to be distributed divided by the number of recipient jurisdictions), (3) population (per capita), (4) area, (5) vehicle registrations, and (6) road miles. Although these allocation factors easily represent the bulk of distribution formulas, a few states utilize different specialized factors that are grouped into an "other" category.

A summary of the frequency of use of the various distribution factors is shown in figure 9.4 (for motor fuel taxes) and figure 9.5 (for motor vehicle taxes and fees). For fuel taxes, the most prevalent factors used to allocate fuel tax revenue both to counties and municipalities are population and road mileage. In contrast, allocation by the origin (the jurisdiction where the tax was collected) of fuel tax revenue is the least-used allocation method. This suggests that distribution of state motor fuel taxes generally does create geographic resource redistribution in those counties and municipalities from which the most fuel tax revenue is generated may not necessarily be the biggest beneficiaries of fuel tax distribution.

Importantly, only three states—Iowa, Kansas, and Nevada—allocate fuel tax revenue to localities on the basis of explicit road use.[23] In Iowa, "daily vehicle miles traveled" is one of five factors in the distribution formula for counties. Kansas uses "average daily road miles traveled, exclusive of the interstate system" for counties, and Nevada uses "vehicle miles of travel" for cities.[24] In no case does a state include an explicit cost index in any allocation formula to account for regional

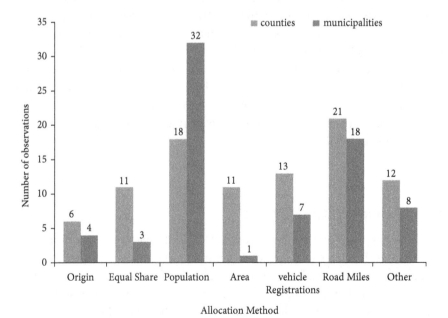

Figure 9.4 Frequency of allocation methods for motor fuel taxes
Source: U.S. Department of Transportation, Federal Highway Administration, 2008.

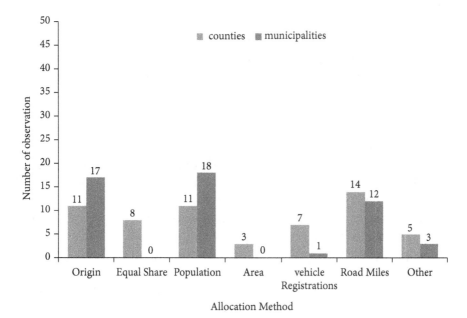

Figure 9.5 Frequency of allocation methods for vehicle registration taxes
Source: U.S. Department of Transportation, Federal Highway Administration, 2008.

road production or maintenance cost differences (input prices, such as labor cost differences). Of course, states often take account of one obvious explicit quantity measure in miles of roads, but due to factors such as road use, weather, and land prices, the cost to construct or maintain one mile of road will vary geographically. These components of road cost differences generally are not recognized.[25]

For distributing vehicle taxes and fees (shown in figure 9.5), origin (the jurisdiction where the vehicle tax originated) is used far more frequently as an allocation method, equal in relative frequency of use to population or per capita allocation. In some cases, origin distribution may have arisen because local government offices are responsible for collecting the vehicle taxes or fees, and simply retain them. The quantity of road miles also is used often as an allocation factor for vehicle taxes and fees.

Population and road mileage are among the most frequently used allocation methods for both transportation revenue sources (fuel taxes and vehicle fees) because, in many states, motor vehicle fee revenues and motor fuel tax revenues are deposited into the same budgetary fund, and they are thus distributed in the same fashion. In those instances where motor vehicle tax revenue was allocated separately from motor fuel tax revenue, the most common allocation methods are origin and road mileage.

Thus, no single distribution mechanism is apparent or dominant for how state governments share motor fuel and motor vehicle registration taxes with local governments. Even states that use the same allocation factors (e.g., population or road miles) do not necessarily define them in the same way, give them the same weights, or apply them to the same shares of revenue. To examine any patterns in the states' choices about how to share these taxes, Fisher and Bristle elected to identify the sets of states that use (to some degree) three different allocation factors: (1) road miles, (2) population, and (3) vehicle registrations or road-use data.[26] These are interesting not only because they are among the most commonly used factors, but also because population or measures vehicle registrations or road use might be interpreted as serving as proxies for transportation service demand. In contrast, allocation by road miles is more related to traditional measures of "cost." Of course, this characterization is rather imprecise because the measure used is a simple dichotomous (0, 1) distinction of whether that factor is used by that state at all. And it is common for states to use more than one allocation factor, even for the same tax or the same type of local government.

The use of each allocation factor was then related both to general characteristics of the state (per capita income, population, land area, and density) and to characteristics of the state's transportation financing structure (local government ownership of public roads, the importance or magnitude of state transportation grants to counties and municipalities). The simple correlation coefficients for these various combinations are shown in table 9.7. This analysis provided only limited information to help understand state choices about grant allocation systems.

The main observations from this research are as follows:

- First, states that allocate relatively larger amounts of state government funds to local governments for transportation are slightly more likely to use demand or road-use proxies as an allocation factor. The correlation coefficient between the set of states that use vehicle registrations or road use to allocate transportation funds and the percentage of public roads "owned" by local governments is 0.30, and the correlation coefficient between the set of states that use vehicle registrations or road use to allocate transportation funds and the percentage of municipal government revenue provided by state transportation grants is 0.39.
- Second, relatively more densely populated states and higher income states are, to some degree, the less likely states to allocate state transportation funds on the basis of population. The correlation coefficients between the set of states using population as an allocation factor and both state density and state per capita income is -0.26. Other correlations among state characteristics and state transportation financing arrangements and state transportation grant allocation factors were quite small.
- There is little substantial correlation between the set of states allocating grants based on road miles, on the one hand, and state characteristics, local road ownership, or the local revenue share from state transportation grants, on the other.

Therefore, just as with state governments' general (unrestricted support) for local governments, there also does not appear to be a consistent or cogent policy or structure underlying state government grants to localities for transportation. The existing research has not identified a clear relationship between a state government objective for the grant program and a resulting grant distribution structure.

Table 9.7 Correlation coefficients, state characteristics vs. state with specific allocation factors

		State transportation Grants	Allocation Factors	
		Road Miles (29 States)	Population (35 States)	Vehicle Registrations and/or Road Use (18 States)
State Economic Characteristics	Per Capita Income	−0.04	−0.26	0.06
	Population	0.15	0.09	0.20
	Land Area	−0.02	0.02	−0.01
	Density	−0.16	−0.26	−0.11
State Fiscal Characteristics	Local Road Ownership	0.08	0.07	0.30
	State Grant Percentage of County Revenue	0.02	0.39	0.23
	State Grant Percentage of Municipality Revenue	0.02	0.13	0.38

Source: Fisher and Bristle (2010).

CONCLUDING COMMENTS

The case of state government intergovernmental fiscal transfers to local governments in the United States is a classic example of the diversity that both arises from and defines the notion of fiscal federalism. There is no "standard" model for these programs. The magnitude, structure, and even existence, of state grant programs varies widely among the states, with current research providing little understanding of why these different fiscal choices have been made.

The $467 billion of intergovernmental revenue provided by state governments to local governments in 2008 accounted for almost 27 percent of state government expenditures and provided about 33 percent of local government general revenue. School districts are the recipients of the largest component of state aid by far—about 55 percent of the total in 2007—whereas county governments receive about 23 percent of state aid and municipal and township governments about 20 percent. Intergovernmental grants from state governments provided about 31 percent of general revenue to counties and about 20 percent of revenue to municipalities and townships, most of which was targeted to specific functions, including education and welfare.

A review of state aid program structures suggests that only about half of the states provide true general revenue-sharing aid to localities (aid that redistributes resources among localities and is unrestricted as to use). Where state revenue-sharing grant programs do exist, they commonly provide only a relatively small share of local government revenue. State revenue-sharing grants provide at least 10 percent of local revenue in only ten states. Allocation formulas differ widely even for states offering unrestricted revenue-sharing grants, suggesting that the objectives of the aid programs also may differ by state.

State intergovernmental grants are nearly ubiquitous in the case of state and local transportation provision and funding in the United States. States typically have opted for state government collection of revenue, principally motor fuel taxes and vehicle registration fees, which are related to transportation use or benefit, and in most cases earmarked solely for transportation purposes. However, the states differ substantially in how responsibility for highway and road transportation is divided between state and local governments, so the magnitude of state government financial support for transportation that is transferred or provided to local governments also varies substantially. When state governments do transfer state tax revenue to local governments for transportation services, the mechanisms and formulas used to allocate those resources also are not standard, and instead they differ greatly in the parameters and weights used.

A striking finding is that population or per capita distribution is the most commonly used factor to allocate grants both for general local government support and for state transportation aid to localities. In contrast, there is little evidence that different and specific allocation factors that are appropriate for specific objectives of the grants are utilized often. This use of population to allocate state grants also reinforces the importance of the Census of Population data, which are also used in allocating federal grants to subnational governments. In addition, allowance for geographic differences in costs is not common in any state aid programs, so that the distribution of real aid amounts may differ dramatically from the nominal allocations. Finally, special allocations for individual localities or special adjustments by states to the aid distribution often occur.

The variation in the structure of state governments' grants for general-purpose local governments raises the issue of whether there is a preferable method for allocating state funds among local governments. Are some allocation factors or formulas "better" than others? One way to think of this issue is to consider the traditional purposes for intergovernmental grants, often identified as regional redistribution, scale economies in revenue generation, correcting for externalities, or macroeconomic stabilization and growth. Clearly, the allocation method should also depend on the targeted public service, if any, as well as the intended outcome.

For state revenue-sharing programs used to support general-purpose local governments, presumably the goal is either direct substitution of state government tax systems for local ones or regional resource redistribution. If the intent is merely to substitute tax structures to take advantage of economics of scale, then distribution of the state taxes based on origin is appropriate. Indeed, there are many such examples among the US states, although this method tends to be relatively more common for taxes with relatively narrow bases (such as on natural resources, tourism, or consumption of specific commodities). If regional resource distribution is the goal, then presumably distribution based on needs-based parameters (e.g., per capita income or wealth) is most appropriate. Such distribution measures are used in a few US states, but most state revenue-sharing programs, if they exist, distribute funds based on other measures, especially population.

Of the twenty-seven US states identified by Fisher and Prasad as having redistributive state revenue-sharing programs, twenty distributed funds based on population, which is especially used for distributing broadly based state taxes.[27] The geographic distribution of population is likely to be different than the distribution of state tax collections, so population involves some degree of regional redistribution. But that redistribution is not expected to target to local governments with concentrations of low-income residents or localities with unusually high costs specifically. Only twelve of the twenty-seven states with state revenue-sharing programs distribute funds at least partly based on incomes or wealth.

In addition, the fact that only about half of US states have state revenue-sharing programs, some of which are relatively small in magnitude, has a number of possible policy implications. The low level of state revenue sharing may be one factor contributing to continuing high reliance on property taxes by many local governments.[28] And if a state desired to pursue more substitution of increased state taxes for local government taxes, an extensive and appropriate state aid distribution system to allocate those state government taxes may not exist currently.

In the case of grants for transportation, one option is to think of allocating transportation grants on the basis of either cost or demand for transportation infrastructure and services. "Cost" might include only construction, maintenance, and depreciation (private cost) or be expanded to include congestion and effects on vehicle damage from poor-quality roads (social cost). Allocation based on measures of road mileage, road use, or direct measures of road quality would seem to correlate best with cost. Transportation "demand," on the other hand, would seem to be best measured by direct road-use data, or to a lesser extent by vehicle registrations or the jurisdictional origin of motor fuel and vehicle registration taxes. Indeed, if state motor fuel taxes and vehicle registration fees are intended to be user charges, then one might argue that allocation based on transportation "use" makes most sense.[29]

In comparison, Fisher and Bristle's analysis shows that allocation of state funds to localities for transportation is rarely based on direct road-use data, is based on vehicle registrations or tax origin in relatively few instances, and never includes cost differences based on geographic cost factors.[30] The most commonly used factor to allocate state transportation aid to localities—population, or per capita distribution—does not serve as a relatively good measure of either cost or demand. Areas with relatively low populations may have a relatively large number of miles of roads, whereas urban local governments with relatively large populations may have substantially more relative road use because of commuters (the case for many central cities or cities that have large retail centers, for instance).

The dominance of population as an allocation factor for state government grants to local governments raises the obvious questions of why population is so commonly used and what are the implications for distribution and efficiency.[31] If the production of local government services exhibits constant returns to scale, that is, if the average cost of providing a unit of local public service to one person is constant, then total cost will be proportionate to population. In that case, one can think of per capita allocation as reimbursement based on average cost.[32] But constant returns with respect to population are not expected in the case of many local government services. For instance, because of the use of a fixed grade structure for elementary and secondary education, a 10 percent reduction in the number of students does not easily translate into a 10 percent reduction in spending.[33] Other local government services are thought to be "congestible public goods" for which the marginal and average costs rise with population increases. Thus, per capita distribution will correspond to average cost only in some limited circumstances. Per capita distribution also does not account for costs that arise from providing local public services to nonresidents.

Another policy issue is the degree to which per capita distribution of grants results in resource redistribution and, if so, of what type. Regional resource distribution will occur with per capita distribution of grant funds if the generation of state tax revenue to be shared is not based solely on population. For instance, one might imagine an increase in a state income, with the additional revenue distributed to local governments on a per capita basis. Clearly, per person state income tax is expected to be greater in higher income localities than lower income ones, so equal per capita distribution will generate regional resource redistribution. The amount of redistribution, however, will be less than if the grant funds were distributed based on a needs-based factor, although the degree of difference will depend on the specific distribution of income and wealth in that state. In addition, the nature of the regional redistribution is expected to vary based on the source of state government revenue to be shared.

Perhaps, then, per capita allocation is used commonly more because of its simplicity and familiarity in state and local finances than for its allocation characteristics being related to grant program objectives.

The review in this chapter suggests several areas for further academic and policy study. In many cases state governments in the United States have not identified clearly the objectives of state transfer programs. With unclear or unspecified objectives, it then follows that the structure of those grant programs—especially whether they should be matching or lump-sum and what parameters should be used to distribute lump-sum grants—may be inappropriate. Therefore, policy analysts might want to examine further the specific public service areas where state transfers make most sense and to help state and local officials identify specific objectives for each program. With objectives identified, economists can then assist in analyzing the most appropriate or effective structure for each grant program in order to achieve those objectives. In any case, the topic of state government transfers to support general-purpose local governments deserves substantially more attention from public finance specialists than it has received in the past.

Notes

1 Bird (2005).
2 Sheppach (this volume).
3 Fisher and Papke (2000).
4 Ladd (2005).
5 The exception would be if the geographic distribution of tax payments and grants happened to be identical, which would only happen in very special cases or by accident.
6 Kenyon (2007).
7 Hamilton (this volume).
8 Hawaii is a special case. Its state revenue responsibility (77.9 percent) and state spending share (78.7 percent) are essentially equal. In large part, this occurs because of state government responsibility for K-12 education in Hawaii.
9 It is also possible that tax exporting will cause a locality to underestimate the cost of public services and thus provide more than is efficient.
10 Flatters et al. (1974).
11 This excludes Hawaii, because the data for Hawaii are not easily comparable to other states because of the state government provision of public education in Hawaii.
12 Local governments also received about $58.2 billion in direct aid from the federal government.
13 For discussion of this issue, see Fisher (2007), 210–212.
14 Thus, state grants and aggregate elementary and secondary revenue for schools operated by municipalities or counties are added to grants and revenue of independent public school districts. See US Census Bureau (2008).
15 In contrast, it would be more difficult to examine grants to counties for welfare or in the health and hospitals categories (both of which are relatively large, because each category includes numerous grants, some of which are quite small).
16 Although controversial and sometimes difficult to separate, we believe state revenue sharing must be more than simply the state collection of local taxes.
17 Fisher and Prasad (2009).
18 This is quite similar to the situation in 1973, as reported by the ACIR, in which eleven of the thirteen large state unrestricted revenue-sharing programs allocated funds at least partly by population.
19 For example, see Ladd and Yinger (1994) and Duncombe and Yinger (1998). For a discussion on the measurement of fiscal capacity and need by state, see Yilmaz and Zahradnik (2008).
20 The small remainder is either the direct responsibility of the federal government (federal parks, federal forest land, and so on) or other state government agencies (including state toll roads operated by agencies that are independent of the state highway department).
21 We are not familiar with the history of how road ownership and responsibility between the state government and local governments evolved. An obvious issue is how this policy decision was influenced by state characteristics and whether road ownership and the state transportation grant allocation method were influenced by the same characteristics. These are issues that we have begun to explore.
22 Fisher and Bristle (2010).

23 In New York, the shares of revenue to be distributed among counties, cities, and towns are determined by vehicle miles of travel in the past, but allocations to specific jurisdictions are then based on lane miles.

24 States are required to report estimates of vehicle miles traveled on various categories of roads annually to the Federal Highway Administration, a process that provides data that can be used as a grant allocation factor.

25 Michigan is an exception, because snowfall over a specific threshold is an allocation factor.

26 Fisher and Bristle (2010).

27 Fisher and Prasad (2009).

28 Bell (this volume).

29 How allocation factors are measured can be important. "Road miles" has a very different implication than "lane miles," and even "vehicle miles of travel per day" does not account for vehicle differences.

30 Fisher and Bristle (2010).

31 An equivalent of per capita distribution—specifically per student distribution—has also become more common in recent years for allocating state government funds to school districts. In foundation aid programs, per student distribution is common.

32 Even in this instance it makes sense to adjust for price differences based on geographic input.

33 If there are twenty students per grade and class in an elementary school, a 10 percent reduction in enrollment across all ages leaves eighteen students per grade. It is not clear in such a case how spending could be reduced by 10 percent.

References

Bird, Richard M. (2005). "Fiscal Federalism." In *The Encyclopedia of Taxation and Tax Policy*, edited by Joseph J. Cordes, Robert D. Ebel, and Jane G. Gravelle. Washington, DC: Urban Institute Press. 146–149.

Boyer, Kenneth D. (2003). "Michigan's Transportation System and Transportation Policy." In *Michigan at the Millennium*, edited by Charles Ballard, Paul Courant, Douglas Drake, Ronald Fisher, and Elisabeth Gerber. East Lansing: Michigan State University Press, 2003. 323–349.

Boyer, Kenneth D., and Ronald C. Fisher (2005, February 8). "Vital Options Could Drive Up Quality of Michigan's Roads." *Detroit Free Press*.

Bradbury, Katherine L., Helen Ladd, Mark Perrault, Andrew Reschovsky, and John Yinger (1984, June). "State Aid to Offset Fiscal Disparities across Communities." *National Tax Journal*, 37: 151–170.

Citizens Research Council of Michigan (2008, February). "Improving the Efficiency of Michigan's Highway Revenue Sharing Formula." CRC Memorandum, http://www.crcmich.org.

Connolly, Katrina D., David Brunori, and Michael E. Bell (2010). "Are State and Local Finances Becoming More or Less Centralized, and Should We Care?" In *The Property Tax and Local Autonomy*, edited by Michael Bell, David Brunori, and Joan Youngman. Cambridge, MA: Lincoln Institute of Land Policy. 121–160.

Duncombe, William, and John Yinger (1998, June). "School Finance Reform: Aid Formulas and Equity Objectives." *National Tax Journal*, 51: 239–262.

Fisher, Ronald C. (2007). *State and Local Public Finance*. Mason, OH: Thomson South-Western.

Fisher, Ronald C., and Leslie E. Papke (2000, March). "Local Government Responses to Education Grants." *National Tax Journal*, 53: 153–168.

Fisher, Ronald C. and Jeffrey P. Guilfoyle (2003). "Fiscal Relations among the Federal Government, State Government, and Local Governments in Michigan." In *Michigan at the Millennium*, edited by Charles Ballard, Paul Courant, Douglas Drake, Ronald Fisher, and Elisabeth Gerber. East Lansing: Michigan State University Press. 645–665.

Fisher, Ronald C., and Anupama Prasad (2009, November). "An Overview and Analysis of State Intergovernmental Aid Programs." Working paper presented at the Annual Research Conference, Association for Public Policy and Analysis.

Fisher, Ronald C., and Andrew Bristle (2010, November). "An Overview and Analysis of State Transportation Grant Programs." Working paper presented at the Annual Research Conference, Association for Public Policy and Analysis.

Flatters, Frank, J. Vernon Henderson, and Peter Mieszkowski (1974). "Public Goods, Efficiency, and Regional Fiscal Equalization." *Journal of Public Economics*, 3: 99–112.

Kenyon, Daphne A. (2007). *The Property Tax—School Funding Dilemma*. Cambridge, MA: Lincoln Institute of Land Policy.

Ladd, Helen F (2005). "Fiscal Equalization." In *The Encyclopedia of Taxation and Tax Policy*, edited by Joseph J. Cordes, Robert D. Ebel, and Jane G. Gravelle. Washington, DC: Urban Institute Press. 145–146.

Ladd, Helen F., and John Yinger (1994, March). "The Case for Equalizing Aid." *National Tax Journal*, 47: 211–224.

Pelissero, John P (1985, September). "Targeting State Highway Aid to Needy Cities." *Journal of Urban Affairs*, 7(4): 29–36.

Reschovsky, Andrew (2004, Spring). "The Impact of State Government Fiscal Crises on Local Governments and Schools." *State and Local Government Review* 36(2): 86–102.

US Advisory Commission on Intergovernmental Relations (1974). *Significant Features of Fiscal Federalism: 1974*. Washington, DC.

US Census Bureau. *Census of Governments*, 2002 and 2007. Washington, DC.

US Census Bureau (2005). *Finances of County Governments: 2002*. Washington, DC: US Government Printing Office.

US Census Bureau (2005). *Finances of Municipal and Township Governments: 2002*. Washington, DC: US Government Printing Office.

US Census Bureau. *State and Local Government Finances*, various years. Washington, DC.

US Census Bureau (2008). *Public Education Finances: 2006*. Washington, DC.

US Department of Transportation (2008). *Highway Statistics*. Washington, DC.

US Department of Transportation, Federal Highway Administration (2008). "Policy Information, Motor Fuel and Highway Trust Fund 2008." http://www.fhwa.dot.gov/ohim/hwytaxes/2008/index.cfm.

US Department of Transportation, Federal Highway Administration (n.d.). "Policy Information, State Practices Used to Report Local Area Travel." http://www.fhwa.dot.gov/ohim/statepractices.cfm.

Yilmaz, Yesim, and Robert Zahradnik (2008). "Measuring the Fiscal Capacity of the District of Columbia: Comparison of Revenue Capacity and Expenditure Need with the States, FY 2005." In *Proceedings of the National Tax Association*. Washington, DC: The Association.

Yinger, John (1986). "On Fiscal Disparities across Cities." *Journal of Urban Economics* 19 (1986): 316–337.

CHAPTER 10

....

STATE AND LOCAL FISCAL INSTITUTIONS IN RECESSION AND RECOVERY

....

TRACY M. GORDON

In 1991, the late public finance expert Edward R. Gramlich remarked that "every decade or so the state and local government sector begins to behave strangely."[1] Although he was referring to the 1970s and 1980s, this observation could just as easily capture state and local finances today. In the past decade, states and localities have twice accumulated large budget surpluses only to return to record deficits in the years that followed.

The recession that began in December 2007 was particularly hard on state and local governments. States suffered historic revenue declines as enrollments swelled for Medicaid, postsecondary education, and other public programs. At the local level, revenues held steadier but are expected to dip as state aid evaporates and property-tax assessments catch up with market values.

Federal policymakers extended significant aid to states and localities through the American Recovery and Reinvestment Act of 2009 (ARRA). However, ARRA covered at best 40 percent of state budget shortfalls and most of its payments expired in 2011. Revenues, on the other hand, are not expected to recover for at least another two to three years due to standard lags in rehiring and reinvestment. As a result, states and localities, which normally contribute to US employment and output, may be a drag on economic growth for the next few years.

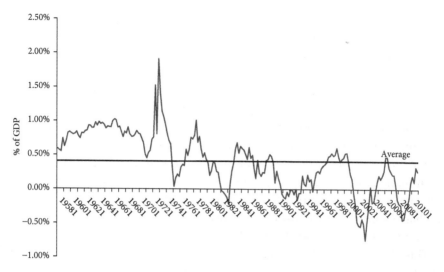

Figure 10.1 State and local government net saving
Source: U.S. Bureau of Economic Analysis, Table 3.3. State and Local Government
Current Receipts and Expenditures, downloaded April 28, 2011.

Looking ahead, state and local governments will also have to contend with unfunded pension and retiree health-care obligations estimated at $1 trillion and possibly up to $4 trillion.[2] Before the Great Recession, the US Government Accountability Office (GAO) projected that states and localities would face major long-term funding challenges due to rising health-care costs and aging populations.[3] In its most recent projection, the GAO suggests that state and local operating shortfalls will reach 2 to 4 percent of GDP by 2060.[4]

In light of these difficulties, some commentators have called on the federal government to provide additional state and local aid.[5] Others have warned that doing so will only create moral hazard problems or diminished incentives for state and local fiscal prudence. They point to cases of excessive lower level government borrowing, which have generated macroeconomic instability in federations such as from Brazil and Argentina.[6]

A traditional solution to moral hazard is to require aid recipients to undertake actions that are costly and especially so for imposters or those that are not truly needy.[7] The International Monetary Fund (IMF), for example, frequently requires countries to enact structural reforms as a condition of participating in stabilization agreements. Similarly, members of the US Congress have proposed that states be forced to adopt stricter pension accounting and disclosure standards to retain their federal tax-exempt bond authority.[8] Others have suggested that states themselves should enact tougher tax-and-spending caps, debt restrictions, and budget stabilization funds (BSFs).[9]

However, critics charge that these rules already exist at the state and local levels, where they have also exerted real costs. Even under favorable economic circumstances, overly restrictive institutions can compel severe spending reductions.[10] In a downturn, these rules can prevent smoothing tax and spending adjustments over several years, actions that can compound a recession.[11] Hansen and Perloff referred to this phenomenon as "fiscal perversity."[12] Others have suggested that similar failures to coordinate national and subnational fiscal policies extended the Great Depression and Japan's Lost Decade of the 1990s.[13]

Although it may be premature to assess these institutions' roles in the recent economic downturn, it is an opportune time to review their effectiveness. This chapter considers four fiscal institutions: balanced budget rules, tax and expenditure limitations, debt restrictions, and BSFs. It focuses on the states, including state limits on local governments, although it incorporates local rules where possible.[14] The chapter omits political institutions, such as the voter initiative or gubernatorial term limits, which may also affect budget outcomes.[15]

This chapter argues that evaluating fiscal rules is not always straightforward. Institutions vary widely in their design and structure. Some rules apply to only specific revenues or expenditure categories. Others are easily evaded through gimmicks such as rosy scenarios, borrowing, fund shifts, and deferrals. More fundamentally, institutions may be adopted for various reasons, including changing political preferences and previous state or local fiscal performances. These factors may exert their own consequences, thereby obscuring independent contributions of fiscal institutions.

Nevertheless, the bulk of research in this area suggests that "institutions matter." States with strict balanced budget rules tend to run larger surpluses and they are quicker to adjust to deficit shocks, usually by cutting spending. States with binding tax and expenditure limits raise less revenue, and rainy-day funds are associated with higher saving rates.

However, institutions also produce unintended consequences. States with restrictions on general obligation debt borrow more from other sources, including revenue-backed bonds and special-purpose entities. States with TELs spend more at the local level. Perhaps most worrying, states with restrictive fiscal institutions appear to be more exposed to the volatility of business cycles.

This outcome arises because of a classic tradeoff between rules and discretion. As in monetary policy, lawmakers may want to commit to lower spending targets but they will face incentives to deviate from this position once it is announced. Fiscal rules may help overcome this commitment problem but at a cost of reduced discretion. A better resolution of this tradeoff may be more flexible rules or cyclically adjusted targets.

The remainder of this chapter proceeds as follows. After a brief review of state and local fiscal institutions and their prevalence, it surveys the empirical literature on their effectiveness. The chapter then examines reasons for fiscal institutions based on models of political economy as well as a dynamic perspective rooted in macroeconomics and behavioral public finance. The chapter concludes by offering directions for reform.

Overview of State and Local Fiscal Institutions

Balanced Budget Rules

Among the oldest and best-known fiscal institutions are balanced budget rules (BBRs). Commentators frequently invoke these rules in debates about federal aid to states, noting that all states except Vermont are constitutionally or statutorily required to balance their budgets. The argument is that states, unlike the federal government, therefore cannot borrow to cover a deficit.

In fact, the picture is more nuanced. Many state BBRs are prospective in nature. As of 2008, 44 states required governors to submit and 41 states required legislatures to enact a balanced budget.[16] More restrictive rules prohibit states from carrying over a deficit into the next fiscal year. At least thirty-eight states had such retrospective limits in 2008.[17] Although most BBRs were enacted at the close of the nineteenth century, stronger rules emerged in recent years.

The strength of BBRs also depends on their constitutional or legislative status. Constitutional rules are generally viewed as more binding because they require a legislative supermajority and/or popular vote to override. For example, a stringency index developed by the Advisory Commission on Intergovernmental Relations (ACIR) assigned the highest score to constitutional rules with no-carry-over provisions.[18]

Yet even the most stringent BBRs may be evaded. Rules usually apply to operating budgets and not capital or pension funds. Within current expenditures, they cover general funds and not federal funds or special funds dedicated to specific purposes such as local governments or transportation. As a result, BBRs typically apply to less than 75 percent of state budgets.[19]

It is also worth noting that BBRs rarely specify an enforcement mechanism such as automatic, across-the board spending cuts.[20] They often stipulate penalties—including removal from office, fines, and jail terms—for elected officials who fail to enforce the rules but there are no reported instances of these sanctions. Lawsuits are also rare and typically involve parties concerned about effects of spending cuts rather than a lack of enforcement.[21]

On the other hand, there is evidence that bond markets and voters penalize politicians' failures to meet BBRs.[22] Similarly, adhering to BBRs may be a political tradition.[23] Researchers have thus drawn varying conclusions about which rules are truly binding. For example, Hou and Smith suggest that technical versus political distinctions (e.g., deficit prohibitions versus procedural requirements to submit a balanced budget) are more important than constitutional versus statutory ones.[24]

Tax and Expenditure Limits

Tax and expenditure limits (TELs) restrict revenue or expenditure growth to a fixed numerical target or index such as population, inflation, or personal income. They emerged in the late nineteenth century but at that time applied only to local property taxes. More general revenue and expenditure limitations were a product of the "tax revolt" movement initiated by California's Proposition 13 in 1978.

Proposition 13, a constitutional citizen initiative, limited both state and local revenues. It capped property-tax rates at 1 percent, rolled back assessed values to 1975–1976 levels, limited future increases to 2 percent per year unless a property was sold, and required a two-thirds legislative majority for all new state taxes and a two-thirds popular vote for new local special taxes. A companion measure, Proposition 4, passed in 1979, and it restricted state spending but was later modified and substantially weakened when voters passed Proposition 111, which altered the spending target from population growth plus inflation to faster-growing personal income.

Soon after the passage of Proposition 13, similar measures followed in other states. By one estimate, Proposition 13 increased a state's probability of enacting a tax limitation measure from once every decade to twice per year.[25] In Massachusetts, citizens enacted Proposition 2½ in 1980, reducing effective property-tax rates to 2.5 percent and limiting future growth in levies to 2.5 percent per year unless local voters passed an override by referendum.

Another round of more stringent TELs began in the 1990s with Oregon's Measure 5 and Colorado's Taxpayer Bill of Rights (TABOR). TABOR was the most restrictive limit yet, applying to all taxing districts in the state and requiring voter approval for any changes to rates or assessment practices as well as the adoption of any new taxes. The law explicitly prohibited certain taxes, including new or increased real estate transfer taxes, local income taxes, state property taxes, and state income-tax surcharges.

Perhaps most important, TABOR restricted general revenues to the prior year's level adjusted for population growth and inflation, a more stringent limit than personal income. It further required any revenues beyond the limit to be returned to taxpayers. TABOR spawned a wave of similar proposals in other states. For example, in 2005, legislatures in twenty-three states considered TABOR-style amendments. However, in that year Colorado citizens also voted to suspend TABOR for five years and to permanently reset the revenue limit at a higher level.[26]

As of 2007, most states (thirty) had at least one TEL. The bulk of states (twenty-three) had spending limits, four had revenue limits, and three had both types of limits.[27] In addition, thirty-six states restricted revenues or spending of local governments. Although many prominent TELs were enacted by citizen initiative, most originated in state legislatures. Legislatures passed fourteen TELs in place as of 2007 and proposed another ten that were ultimately enacted by popular vote. Voters passed eight TELs through the initiative process, and the remaining two emerged from constitutional conventions.[28]

Like balanced budget rules, TELs vary in their stringency. As with BBRs, constitutional rules are generally viewed as more binding. However, statutory TELs can also require a legislative supermajority or popular vote to override or amend, as eighteen TELs did in 2007. Beyond TABOR, only five other measures rely on population plus inflation, compared to nineteen based on personal income. Other strict TELs include mandatory tax rebates or BSF deposits if revenues exceed the limit and prohibitions on transferring programs to local governments to evade the limit.[29]

Closely related to TELs are legislative supermajority and voter-approval requirements for new taxes. Sixteen states had such requirements in place as of 2007, with voting thresholds ranging from three-fifths to three-fourths. These requirements can pertain to all taxes or only specific taxes, such as corporate or sales taxes.[30]

As noted earlier, local property-tax limits were among the first TELs. Property-tax limits can apply to tax rates, assessments, levies (yields), or some combination of all three. Limits on rates or assessments alone are generally viewed as nonbinding because changes to one parameter can offset the other. More recently, local TELs have focused on general revenues or expenditures. Today, forty-seven states impose some restriction on local revenues, expenditures, or both.[31] Many localities also operate under their own limits. Although data on local institutions are rare, through their own survey Brooks and Phillips identified locally imposed TELs in one out of eight large and mid-sized American cities.[32]

Debt Restrictions

Debt restrictions were the first state and local fiscal institutions. They grew out of the financial panic of 1837 and the defaults that followed.[33] Prior to the crisis, states had provided infrastructure such as railroads, turnpikes, and canals through "taxless finance," in which private firms built projects in exchange for exclusive operating rights. States helped secure access to capital funds or issued bonds themselves, using tolls or dividends for debt service. This arrangement proved extremely popular, leading to the construction of landmarks, including New York's Erie Canal. By 1841, states had borrowed over $200 million, or 86 percent of all federal, state, and local debt.[34]

The whole system unraveled, however, when projects failed to generate anticipated returns. Failures peaked during the recession of the 1840s, when deflation also grew real debt burdens. As a result, eight states and the Territory of Florida defaulted, five states repudiated all or part of their debts, two states renegotiated with creditors, and two states delayed but ultimately repaid their obligations.[35] In the ensuing political crisis, eleven states drafted new constitutions explicitly curtailing state and local borrowing, while Indiana banned state debt altogether.[36]

Today, most states (forty-six) have constitutional or statutory limits on total debt outstanding as a percentage of the state budget or at a specific dollar amount.

Apart from these limits, many states impose procedural requirements on debt issuance (e.g., requiring state legislatures to identify the purpose of public debt and specify annual debt service costs). Debt issuances beyond a certain amount may also require legislative supermajority or voter approval.[37]

In response to state restrictions, localities issued more debt. This prompted another debt crisis in the 1870s. States then took steps to limit local debt as an absolute dollar amount or share of property values and to impose procedure hurdles on its issuance. By 1890, thirty-six states either implemented or asserted the right to implement such restrictions. As Wallis and Weingast note, these rules may have precipitated the proliferation of special-purpose entities, such as water and sewer districts, which can typically issue debt without voter approval.[38]

Budget Stabilization Funds

Budget stabilization funds (BSFs) are among the most recent and fastest-growing fiscal institutions. Although a few date to the 1940s, most BSFs were enacted in the early 1980s in response to what was then the worst economic crisis since the Great Depression. BSFs are intended to help states save for a "rainy day" and thereby ease economic downturns.

As of 2008, only two states, Kansas and Montana, lacked BSFs, and several had multiple funds.[39] Although most BSFs are constitutional, eleven are statutory and five states have both kinds of funds. Some BSFs are linked to specific revenue sources, such as lotteries, motor fuel taxes, or tobacco settlements. Beyond BSFs, many states also have contingency or emergency funds for natural disasters and other nonrecurring expenditures.

The stringency of a BSF depends on the rules governing its deposits, withdrawals, and size. At one extreme, BSFs may allow for deposits by legislative appropriation, or discretion. More stringent funds specify that a fixed proportion of year-end balances must be set aside, if they in fact materialize. The strictest savings vehicles dedicate a portion of revenues to the BSF each year, regardless of economic or fiscal conditions. Some states rely on a combination of triggers—including revenue, expenditure, and economic growth—as specified by formula.

Analogously, withdrawals may be accomplished by legislative appropriation or by satisfying a previously specified definition of a budget shortfall or fiscal emergency. Sixteen states further require legislative supermajority approval for BSF withdrawals.[40] Withdrawals often must be repaid with interest and within a specified period, sometimes before the fiscal year end.[41] Observers note that these rules can inhibit the use of BSFs. For example, New York lawmakers did not access the state's Tax Stabilization Reserve Fund in twenty years of state budget woes.[42]

Finally, most states cap BSFs at less than 10 percent of general revenues or expenditures. A common "rule of thumb" is 5 percent of spending, although some analysts suggest targets as high as 15 percent.[43] In fact, state fund balances (including

BSFs and end-of-year surpluses) often exceed 10 percent of total spending, as during economic expansions in 2000 and 2006.[44] Excessive balances can also provoke a political backlash, however. For example, large state surpluses in the early 1970s may have contributed to California's popular tax revolt.[45]

EFFECTS OF FISCAL INSTITUTIONS

Academics have long been drawn to the study of state and local fiscal institutions. Political scientists and public administration scholars were at the forefront of efforts to bring the concept of an executive prepared budget from municipal governments to the federal government at the turn of the twentieth century.[46] More recently, economists have drawn lessons from the US states for the design of a federal balanced budget amendment and for the European Monetary Union.[47]

Focusing on states and localities enables researchers to take advantage of rich institutional variation while avoiding large unobserved differences that can confound international comparisons.[48] However, it does not avoid the problem of unobserved differences entirely. State and local fiscal institutions may be proxies for the "congealed preferences" of voters and legislators who enacted them or summary statistics for previous fiscal performance.[49] This endogeneity may bias measured effects in either direction if, for example, fiscally conservative voters are more likely to enact TELs or states that default are more likely to adopt debt restrictions. In both cases, observed relationships between institutions and outcomes will be spurious.

Although the exogeneity assumption may be intuitively appealing for long-standing institutions like debt restrictions and BBRs, it is worth noting that political preferences can also persist over time. States with lower deficits at the turn of the century may have been more likely to enact strict fiscal institutions and they may yet run lower deficits today. Maintaining existing rules without modification or amendment is itself a policy choice.

Endogeneity plagued many early studies of state and local fiscal institutions. For example, an early ACIR report found lower deficits in states with strict BBRs.[50] Another study by Abrams and Dougan did not detect any differences between states with and without BBRs or debt restrictions although they did find weakly higher spending in TEL states. However, both investigations were based on a single snapshot or cross-section of data. Abrams and Dougan noted that "it is quite possible the endogenous nature of such limits may obscure their true effects."[51]

A second generation of research has sought to address endogeneity by incorporating additional controls and years of data. These studies typically employ panel regressions with state fixed effects to absorb persistent political or cultural differences and year effects for transitory economic or other shocks. However, state fixed effects are infeasible when institutions do not change over time. To counter this difficulty, researchers have pursued how institutions mediate time-varying relationships, such as between income and public spending. Alternatively, they have used instrumental variables that theory or institutional knowledge suggest are correlated with the institution of interest but are unrelated to fiscal outcomes.

Taken together, this literature tends to confirm that "institutions matter."[52] Starting with balanced budget requirements, von Hagen found no relationship between deficits and strict rules as measured from 1975 to 1985.[53] Alt and Lowry expanded on this analysis by considering the role of politics. They modeled revenues and expenditures based on income and federal intergovernmental grants as well as lagged values of the dependent variable and fund balances. They then estimated separate models based on legislative and executive party control, strict anti-deficit rules, and regional fixed effects. Results suggested that states with stronger BBRs were quicker to close budget deficits, but only under unified party control.[54]

Poterba focused on a more precise measure of unexpected deficits from 1988 to 1992.[55] Using data from the National Association of State Business Officers (NASBO), he constructed actual versus forecasted revenues and expenditures and then took the difference between these two measures, also subtracting midyear tax and spending changes. Like Alt and Lowry, Poterba detected faster adjustments to deficit shocks in states with strong BBRs and unified party control. Adjustments occurred mainly through spending cuts rather than tax increases.

Unfortunately, the Poterba data series only covered a limited range of fiscal years. Bohn and Inman addressed the longer-run consequences of BBRs by using Census of Governments data from 1970 to 1999.[56] Similar to Alt and Lowry, they modeled general-fund surpluses as a function of income, unemployment, and intergovernmental aid as well as accumulated assets, political controls, and state fixed effects. They then regressed state fixed effects on BBR provisions. Bohn and Inman detected higher surpluses in states with constitutional anti-deficit-carry-over provisions, particularly when rules were enforced by an elected rather than appointed Supreme Court. Political variables were individually and jointly insignificant, suggesting that Alt and Lowry's results may have stemmed from omitted variables.

Bohn and Inman further studied effects of strict BBRs on budget volatility. As noted above, a frequent concern about BBRs and other fiscal institutions is that they prevent states and localities from responding to changing economic conditions or running countercyclical fiscal policy. For example, Bayoumi and Eichengreen found that strict BBRs limited state responsiveness to business cycles by 40 percent.[57] However, Bohn and Inman observed that budgets in BBR states were less sensitive to changes in income but not unemployment. They also noted higher accumulated savings that could function as a cushion or buffer stock in these states.

Other studies have investigated links between BBRs and economic volatility. For instance, Alesina and Bayoumi found a negative, but statistically insignificant relationship between strict BBRs and standard deviations of Gross State Product from 1965 to 1992.[58] However, they did not consider potential reverse causality or omitted variables. Levinson addressed these shortcomings by examining interactions between BBRs and the relationship between personal income and population. A maintained assumption of this model was that larger states experienced milder income swings, perhaps because of activist fiscal policy or economic diversity. Levinson hypothesized that BBRs would attenuate this relationship and found support for this view in higher income volatility among large states with strict BBRs.[59]

Similar to BBRs, much of the early work on TELs detected little to no effects on the size or growth of government.[60] Exceptions include Crain and Miller and Elder, who found that TEL states had lower taxes. However, neither study explicitly addressed endogeneity.[61] Moreover, because Elder's sample was restricted to states with limits, the only identifying variation came from differences in TEL adoption dates. Kousser et al. repaired this omission by considering differences between states with and without TELs before and after adoption.[62] Nevertheless, their quasi-experimental approach still did not eliminate the possibility of time-varying unobservable factors, such as shifts in preferences, leading to both TELs and fiscal outcomes.[63]

By contrast, instrumental variable (IV) approaches have detected significant TEL consequences. Using the availability of citizen initiative and recall procedures as instruments, Rueben found that states with strict limits (i.e., requiring a supermajority to override) raised and spent less as a share of personal income.[64] However, local spending was also higher in these states. Similarly, Knight used the availability of direct legislation and the ease of amending state constitutions as instruments for supermajority tax-vote requirements. He found that states with these requirements had lower tax rates and collections as a share of income from 1963 to 1995.[65] In his study of fiscal adjustment, Poterba also found that states with TELs were less likely to raise taxes but no more likely to cut spending in response to a deficit shock.[66]

A related literature has examined effects of state limits on local taxes and spending. In general, strict property-tax limitations (e.g., assessment limits coupled with rate limits) are associated with lower property taxes but higher revenues from nontax sources including user fees and charges, borrowing, and state funds.[67] Local TELs may also alter local government structure by encouraging more special district formation.[68] They may depress education spending and performance as well as government wages and employment.[69]

In general, studies of local TELs lack the attention to endogeneity found in state studies. One reason may be limited data. This constraint has also hindered research into locally adopted fiscal institutions, such as municipal TELs. An exception is a recent study by Brooks and Phillips, who conducted their own survey of large and mid-sized American cities as noted above. Using a difference-in-difference approach, they found lower spending in TEL cities, although they noted that they could not reject other explanations such as shifting preferences.[70]

Many of the studies noted above also examined effects of debt restrictions. For example, von Hagen detected lower general obligation debt in states with borrowing restrictions. However, this response was offset by higher revenue-backed bonds not subject to voter approval. Bunch obtained similar results on the expanded use of public authorities in states with debt limits, although she looked only at a single cross-section of data.[71] In their panel regressions, Bohn and Inman found that debt restrictions were associated with less long-term borrowing but also lower capital investments.

Thus far, this section has considered balanced budget rules, tax and expenditure limits, and debt restrictions. As noted earlier, a frequent criticism of these institutions is that they prevent activist countercyclical fiscal policies. By contrast, BSFs can help states and localities "save for a rainy day," thereby avoiding procyclical tax increases or spending cuts. In fact, states with BSFs appear to save more than other states. Using a difference-in-difference approach, Levinson and Knight determined that states adopting a BSF increased their savings on a dollar-for-dollar basis, although the authors noted that they could not rule out shifting preferences or other time-varying omitted variables.[72] Other researchers have detected similarly positive but smaller responses that suggest some "crowd out" of general fund balances.[73]

If BSFs increase overall savings, do they also reduce budget and economic volatility? Sobel and Holcombe found that states with BSFs exhibited less "fiscal stress," or deviations of taxes and expenditures from long-run averages, especially when fund contributions were mandatory instead of discretionary.[74] As Knight and Levinson point out, states with BSFs often also have strict BBRs.[75] Levinson found that the combined effect of these institutions was to smooth business-cycle fluctuations, and that BSFs offset volatility enhancements from BBRs.

Fatás and Mihov offered an intriguing explanation for these mixed findings.[76] They suggested that BBRs together with rainy-day or budget stabilization funds could exert two countervailing effects: (1) limiting government responsiveness to changing conditions, which would enhance economic volatility, and (2) diminishing the variability of fiscal policy, which would mitigate economic volatility. Consistent with this explanation, the authors found that state spending was less elastic with respect to income in the presence of strict BBRs, but these differences did not translate into greater economic volatility. They attributed this result to fiscal rules curbing unhelpful aspects of discretionary fiscal policy. The sources of such policies are explored below.

REASONS FOR FISCAL INSTITUTIONS

Fiscal institutions are puzzling from the perspective of the median-voter model that undergirds most political economy research. The model holds that as long as certain conditions hold, the voter at the midpoint of the preference distribution will be decisive.[77] Although the model performs well in empirical tests, at the local level, the presence of restrictive fiscal institutions raises an important question.[78] If the median voter prefers a smaller public sector and his or her preferences are decisive, why are institutions needed?

One explanation is that majority-voting outcomes will be inefficient because they do not take into account the intensity of individual preferences. If voters who prefer less government have more inelastic demand yet all voters face the same tax price, fiscal rules will yield welfare gains. However, it is not immediately clear how such a rule would actually pass into law without a mechanism for winners under the rule to compensate those who have lost.

Another possibility is that fiscal limits arise because the median voter's preferences have changed, perhaps in response to an exogenous shock.[79] For example, Fischel attributes passage of California's Proposition 13 to a state Supreme Court school finance equalization decision that effectively severed the relationship between local property taxes and public schools.[80] Implementing a new fiscal institution may be a quicker and more effective signal than waiting for the next electoral cycle. In addition, legislators may enact fiscal limits to signal that they recognize a shock has occurred despite inevitable lags in budget adjustment.

In practice, the median voter model's assumptions may also be violated. For example, preferences may be multipeaked in the presence of private alternatives to public services, such as elementary and secondary education. Under these circumstances, a coalition of low- and high-income voters who both prefer lower public spending can form a winning coalition against the median voter. Similarly, policy choices often involve multiple dimensions beyond public spending, including regulation, ideology, and even candidate personality.

On the other hand, some scholars reject the median voter model altogether on the grounds that it ignores the supply side of politics, including the role of interest groups and motivations of elected and appointed officials. According to the public choice school, governments may seek to maximize their budgets rather than the general welfare, they may exploit their agenda power to achieve spending beyond the level preferred by the median voter, and they may pursue campaign contributions rather than informed votes to increase their overall odds of electoral success.[81] In addition, voters may suffer from "fiscal illusion," or they may systematically overestimate benefits and underestimate costs of government.[82] In this environment, constitutional rules will be the only way to restrain a government Leviathan.[83]

However, legislatures are themselves often the source of fiscal institutions. For example, as noted above, nearly half of all TELs emanated from state legislatures. In many of these states, voters do not have access to the initiatives, meaning there is no threat of an alternative, more restrictive citizen-backed measure.

Why would legislatures willingly cede their own power? The new institutional economics literature suggests that one reason is to obtain costly information or actions.[84] In particular, legislatures may wish to solve a common resource problem or the tendency toward overspending whenever benefits are geographically concentrated and costs are diffuse or borne by all taxpayers.[85] Alternatively, legislatures may adopt restrictive institutions to bind their successors, especially when they anticipate a change in party control.[86]

Finally, legislatures may adopt restrictive fiscal institutions to bind themselves. The problem of dynamic inconsistency is well known in macroeconomic policy. In the classic formulation, a government will have incentives to renege on a previously announced inflation target once firms have set their own wage contracts because inflation will appear as output gains. Knowing this, forward-looking rational agents will not believe announcements unless they are credible or self-enforcing. One way to achieve credibility is through building a reputation in repeated interactions. Another is through rules followed by an independent central bank.[87]

Similarly, individuals often face self-control issues in domains ranging from health to savings behavior.[88] Knowing this, sophisticated consumers will adopt strategies to curb their own future behaviors. Potential commitment strategies include establishing separate mental accounts for savings and consumption or accumulating illiquid assets as a constraint.[89] The cost is reduced flexibility. The next section explores alternative resolutions to this trade-off between rules and discretion.

Alternatives to Traditional Fiscal Institutions

Although more frequently contemplated in monetary policy, dynamic inconsistency problems can also arise in fiscal policy. Spending and revenue decisions affect expectations, which in turn can affect future states of the world and future policies. This effect serves as a constraint on current policy. For example, announcing a lower spending target may itself induce vigorous interest-group lobbying, which will tempt legislators to deviate from their announcement. Knowing this, rational forward-looking agents will discredit the announcement. States and localities may thus be forced to pay higher borrowing costs than they otherwise would. Fiscal institutions can alleviate this problem by anchoring expectations in the present and raising the costs of deviating in the future. Indeed, Alt and Lowry and Poterba and Rueben have shown that states with binding BBRs pay lower borrowing costs.[90]

However, as noted above, binding fiscal rules can also prevent governments from responding to changing conditions and especially engaging in countercyclical fiscal policy. To counter this problem, many countries have implemented more flexible fiscal rules. For example, "structural balance rules" adjust targets for projected output gaps, whereas "growth-based balance rules" consider deviations from long-term average growth trends. A recent IMF report notes that such rules allowed for more flexible fiscal policy responses to the recent economic crisis.[91]

Should states adopt similar rules? The danger is that they can weaken fiscal discipline, particularly when there is strategic manipulation or simply random error in revenue and spending forecasts. For example, in the boom years that preceded the recent recession, several European countries routinely evaded deficit targets outlined in the EMU Stability and Growth Pact because they perceived ongoing growth.[92] Another issue is whether states can and should be running activist fiscal policy. Musgrave's taxonomy put macroeconomic stabilization squarely under central government responsibility on the grounds that benefits from local stimulus would leak into neighboring states.[93] However, Gramlich countered that recessions are often regionally focused and states are well situated to respond to these shocks.[94] Evidence from the recent recession may prove useful in responding to this debate. In particular, the American Recovery and Reinvestment Act of 2009 (ARRA) directed significantly more resources ($282 billion) to states and localities than in previous recessions with the goals of stimulating the economy, stabilizing budgets, and protecting the disadvantaged.[95]

CONCLUSIONS

State and local government finances are again in the national spotlight. As the economy emerges from the worst recession since the Great Depression, state and local governments continue to face severe budget challenges. In the longer term, they will contend with rising health-care costs and aging populations: these are the same spending pressures busting the federal budget.

This focus has also brought renewed attention to state and local fiscal institutions. Proponents suggest that stricter rules could have helped protect states and localities from boom-and-bust economic cycles. Critics argue that existing rules may have compounded the crisis by preventing states and localities from borrowing or otherwise smoothing tax increases and spending cuts over the several years.

In fact, both views are probably overstated. Researchers have generally concluded that "institutions matter." However, the magnitudes are often limited and sensitive to modeling choices. In addition, institutions may have unintended consequences, such as enhanced exposure to business-cycle fluctuations. One solution to this dilemma borrowed from international contexts is cyclically adjusted or "over the cycle" multiyear budget targets. These targets allow for more activist fiscal policy during recessions while maintaining longer-term budget discipline. A key question going forward is whether this kind of flexibility is possible, or desirable, for the state/local government area.

NOTES

1 Gramlich (1991), 249.
2 Pew Center on the States (2010a); Novy-Marx and Rauh (2010a); Novy-Marx and Rauh (2010b).

3 US Government Accountability Office (2007).

4 US Government Accountability Office (2011).

5 E.g., Shiller (2010).

6 E.g., Inman (2010).

7 Nichols and Zeckhauser (1982).

8 Nunes et al. (2011).

9 E.g., Mitchell (2010); Malaga (2011).

10 E.g., Lav and Williams (2010).

11 Barro (1979).

12 Hansen and Perloff (1944).

13 Brown (1956); Kuttner and Posen (2001).

14 See the chapter by John Kincaid on state and local fiscal constitutions in this volume.

15 See Rose (2010) and Besley and Case (2003) for reviews of fiscal and political institutions.

16 National Association of State Budget Officers (2008).

17 National Conference of State Legislatures (2010). The National Association of State Budget Officers (2008) reports the number at 43.

18 Advisory Commission on Intergovernmental Relations (1987).

19 Poterba (1995).

20 NCSL (2010).

21 US General Accounting Office (1993).

22 Lowry and Alt (2001); Poterba and Rueben (2001).

23 US GAO (1993).

24 Hou and Smith (2010).

25 Martin (2009).

26 McGuire and Rueben (2006).

27 National Conference of State Legislatures (2007).

28 Ibid.

29 Ibid.

30 Ibid.

31 Mullins (2010); Downes and Figlio (2008).

32 Brooks and Phillips (2010).

33 Rodriguez-Tejedo and Wallis (2010).

34 Wallis and Weingast (2006).

35 McGranahan (2010).

36 Wallis and Weingast (2006), 20.

37 Rodriguez-Tejedo and Wallis (2010).

38 Wallis and Weingast (2006), 34.

39 NASBO (2008).

40 Pew Center on the States (2010b).

41 Ibid.

42 Goodman (2010).

43 McNichol and Filipowich (2007).

44 NASBO (2010).

45 Doerr (2008).

46 Previously, federal budgets were piecemeal appropriations summarized in the US Congress's *Book of Estimates*: "rather a more or less well-digested mass of information submitted by agents of the Legislature to the Legislature" according to the final report of President Taft's 1910 Commission on Economy and Efficiency. See Rabin and Hildreth (2007).

47 See, e.g., Poterba (1995) and von Hagen (1991).

48 See, e.g., Besley and Case (2003).

49 Riker (1980).

50 ACIR (1987).

51 Abrams and Dougan (1986).

52 Poterba (1995).

53 von Hagen (1991).

54 Alt and Lowry (1994).

55 Poterba (1994).

56 Bohn and Inman (1996).

57 Bayoumi and Eichengreen (1995).

58 Alesina and Bayoumi (1996).

59 Levinson (1998).

60 Kenyon and Benker (1984); Abrams and Dougan (1986); Dougan (1988); Bails (1990); Joyce and Mullins (1991); Shadbegian (1996).

61 Elder (1992); Crain and Miller (1990).

62 Kousser at al. (2008).

63 Besley and Case (2000).

64 Rueben (1996).

65 Knight (2000). Knight notes that Crain and Miller (1990) obtained consistent results. By contrast, Temple and Nannenhorn (1998) found no effect of supermajority requirements. However, they controlled for potential endogeneity with state-specific linear time trends, which like state fixed effects may not capture shifts in voter attitudes over time. Bails and Tieslau found that expenditure limits and supermajority requirements interacted with BBRs were associated with lower combined state and local spending in a random effects model from 1964 to 1999.

66 Poterba (1994).

67 Shadbegian (1999); Joyce and Mullins (1991); Mullins and Joyce (1996); Sokolow (2000); Preston and Ichniowski (1991).

68 Mullins (2004).

69 Downes and Figlio (2007); Poterba and Rueben (1995).

70 Brooks and Phillips (2010).

71 Bunch (1991).

72 Knight and Levinson (1999).

73 Wagner (2003); Hou and Duncombe (2008).

74 Sobel and Holcombe (1996). See also Douglas and Gaddie (2002), Hou (2004), Knight and Levinson (1999)

75 Knight and Levinson (1999).

76 Fatás and Mihov (2006).

77 Conditions include restrictions on individual preferences, in particular single-peakedness or symmetry, as well as a single-dimensional policy space.

78 Fischel (2001).

79 Dougan (1988).

80 Fischel (1989).

81 Niskanen (1971); Romer and Rosenthal (1979); Stigler (1971).

82 Buchanan and Wagner (1977).

83 Brennan and Buchanan (1980).

84 E.g., Weingast and Marshall (1988); Cox and McCubbins (1993).

85 Weingast et al. (1981); see also Primo and Snyder (2008).

86 Persson and Svensson (1987); Alesina and Tabellini (1990); de Figueiredo, 2003.

87 Kydland and Prescott (1977); Barro and Gordon (1983).
88 Thaler and Shefrin (1981).
89 E.g., Angletos et al. (2001).
90 E.g., Lowry and Alt (2001); Poterba and Rueben (1995).
91 Kumar et al. (2009).
92 E.g., Anderson and Minarik (2006).
93 Musgrave (1959).
94 Gramlich (1991).
95 US Office of Management and Budget (2011).

References

Anderson, Barrett, and Joe Minarik (2006). "Design Choices for Fiscal Policy Rules."
    OECD Journal on Budgeting 5(4): 159–208.
Angletos, George-Marios, David Laibson, Andrea Repetto, Jeremy Tobacman, and
    Stephen Weinberg (2001). "The Hyperbolic Consumption Model: Calibration,
    Simulation, and Empirical Evaluation." *Journal of Economic Perspectives*
    15(3): 47–68.
Abrams, Burton A., and William R. Dougan (1986). "The Effects of Constitutional
    Restraints on Governmental Spending." *Public Choice* 49(2), 101–116, 111.
Advisory Commission on Intergovernmental Relations (1987, July). *Fiscal Discipline in
    the Federal System: National Reform and the Experience of the States.* Washington,
    DC: ACIR.
Alesina, Alberto, and Tamim Bayoumi (1996). "The Costs and Benefits of Fiscal Rules:
    Evidence from US States," *NBER Working Paper No. 5614.* National Bureau of
    Economic Research, Cambridge, MA.
Alesina, Alberto, and Guido Tabellini (1990). "A Positive Theory of Fiscal Deficits and
    Government Debt." *Review of Economic Studies* 57(3): 403–414.
Alt, James E., and Robert C. Lowry (1994). "Divided Government, Fiscal Institutions, and
    Budget Deficits: Evidence from the States." *American Political Science Review* 88(4):
    811–828.
Bails, Dale G. (1990). "The Effectiveness of Tax-Expenditure Limitations: A
    Re-Evaluation: In 19 States They Resulted in Virtually No Success in Limiting
    Growth in Their Budgets." *American Journal of Economics and Sociology* 49(2):
    223–238.
Bails, Dale G., and Margie A. Tieslau (2000). "The Impact of Fiscal Constitutions on State
    and Local Expenditures." *Cato Journal* 20(2): 255–277.
Barro, Robert J. (1979). "On the Determination of the Public Debt." *Journal of Political
    Economy* 87: 940–971.
Barro, Robert J., and David B. Gordon (1983). "A Positive Theory of Monetary Policy in a
    Natural Rate Model." *Journal of Political Economy* 91: 589.
Bayoumi, Tamim, and Barry Eichengreen (1995). "Restraining Yourself: The Implications
    of Fiscal Rules for Economic Stabilization." *International Monetary Fund Staff
    Papers* 42(1): 32–48.
Besley, Timothy, and Anne Case (2000). "Unnatural Experiments? Estimating the
    Incidence of Endogenous Policies." *Economic Journal* 110(467): F672–F694.
Besley, Timothy, and Anne Case (2003). "Political Institutions and Policy Choices:
    Evidence from the United States." *Journal of Economic Literature* 41(1): 7–73.

Bohn, Henning, and Robert P. Inman (1996). "Balanced Budget Rules and Public Deficits: Evidence from the US States." *NBER Working Paper No. 5533*. National Bureau of Economic Research, Cambridge, MA.

Brennan Geoffrey F., and James M. Buchanan (1980). *The Power to Tax: Analytical Foundations of a Fiscal Constitution*. Cambridge University Press.

Brooks, Leah, and Justin Phillips (2010, July). "Constraining the Local Leviathan? The Existence and Effectiveness of Municipally-Imposed Tax and Expenditure Limits." University of Toronto Working Paper.

Brown, E. Cary (1956, December). "Fiscal Policy in the 1930s: A Reappraisal." *American Economic Review* 46: 857–879.

Buchanan, James M., and Wagner, Richard E. (1977). *Democracy in Deficit: The Political Legacy of Lord Keynes*. New York: Academic Press.

Bunch, Beverly S. (1991). "The Effect of Constitutional Debt Limits on State Governments' Use of Public Authorities." *Public Choice* 68(1–3): 57–69.

Cox, Gary W., and Mathew D. McCubbins (1993). *Legislative Leviathan*. Berkeley: University of California Press.

Crain, W. Mark, and James C. Miller III (1990). "Budget Process and Spending Growth." *William and Mary Law Review* 31(4): 1021–1046.

de Figueiredo, Rui J. P., Jr. (2003). "Endogenous Budget Institutions and Political Insulation: Why States Adopt the Item Veto." *Journal of Public Economics* 87: 2677.

Doerr, David R. (2008). *California's Tax Machine: A History of Taxing and Spending in the Golden State*. Sacramento: California Taxpayer's Association.

Dougan, William R. (1988). "The Effects of Tax and Expenditure Limits on State Governments." *George G. Stigler Center for Study of Economy and State Paper No. 54*.

Douglas, James W., and Ronald Keith Gaddie (2002). "State Rainy Day Funds and Fiscal Crises: Rainy Day Funds and the 1990–1991 Recession Revisited." *Public Budgeting and Finance* 22(1): 19–30.

Downes, Thomas, and David Figlio (2008). "Tax and Expenditure Limits: School Finance and School Quality." In *Handbook on Research and Education Finance Policy*, edited by Helen F. Ladd and Edward B. Fiske. New York: Routledge.

Elder, Harold W. (1992). "Exploring the Tax Revolt: An Analysis of the Effects of State Tax and Expenditure Limitation Laws." *Public Finance Quarterly* 20: 47–63.

Fatás, Antonio, and Ilian Mihov (2006). "The Macroeconomic Effects of Fiscal Rules in the US States." *Journal of Public Economics* 90(1–2): 101–117.

Fischel, William A. (1989) "Did Serrano Cause Proposition 13?" *National Tax Journal* 42(4): 465–473.

Fischel, William A. (2001). *The Homevoter Hypothesis: How Home Values Influence Local Government Taxation, School Finance, and Land-Use Policies*. Cambridge, MA: Harvard University Press.

Goodman, Josh (2010, November 16). "Why Rainy Day Funds Can't Always Be Used on Rainy Days." *Stateline*. Washington, DC: Pew Center on the States.

Gramlich, Edward M (1991). "The 1991 State and Local Fiscal Crisis." *Brookings Papers on Economic Activity*. Washington, DC: The Brookings Institution, 22: 249–288.

Hansen, Alvin H., and Harvey S. Perloff (1944). *State and Local Finance in the National Economy*. New York: W. W. Norton.

Hou, Yilin (2004). "Budget Stabilization Fund: Structural Features of Enabling Legislation and Balance Levels." *Public Budgeting and Finance* 24(3): 38–64.

Hou, Yilin, and Daniel Smith (2010). "Do State Balanced Budget Requirements Matter? Testing Two Explanatory Frameworks." *Public Choice* 145: 57–79.

Hou, Yilin, and William Duncombe (2008, Fall). "State Saving Behavior: Effects of Two Fiscal and Budgetary Institutions." *Public Budgeting and Finance* 28(3): 48–67.

Inman, Robert (2010). "States in Fiscal Distress." Federal Reserve Bank of St. Louis, *Regional Economic Development* 6(1): 70–80.

Joyce, Philip G., and Daniel R. Mullins (1991). "The Changing Fiscal Structure of the State and Local Public Sector: The Impact of Tax and Expenditure Limitations." *Public Administration Review* 51(3): 240–253.

Kenyon, Daphne A., and Karen M. Benker (1984). "Fiscal Discipline: Lessons from the State Experience." *National Tax Journal* 37(3): 433–446.

Knight, Brian G. (2000). "Supermajority Voting Requirements for Tax Increases: Evidence from the States." *Journal of Public Economics* 78(1): 41–67.

Knight, Brian, and Arik Levinson (1999). "Rainy Days Funds and State Government Savings." *National Tax Journal* 52(3): 459–472.

Kousser, Thad, Matthew D. McCubbins, and Ellen Moule (2008). "For Whom the TEL Tolls: Testing the Effects of State Tax and Expenditure Limitations on Revenues and Expenditures." *State Politics and Policy Quarterly* 8(4): 331–362.

Kumar, Manmohan, Emanuele Baldacci, Andrea Schaechter, Carlos Caceres, Daehaeng Kim, Xavier Debrun, Julio Escolano, Jiri Jonas, Philippe Karam, Irina Yakadina, and Robert Zymek (2009, December 16). "Fiscal Rules—Anchoring Expectations for Sustainable Public Finances." *IMF Staff Paper*. Washington, DC: International Monetary Fund.

Kuttner, Kenneth N., and Adam S. Posen (2001). "The Great Recession: Lessons for Macroeconomic Policy from Japan." *Brookings Papers on Economic Activity*, Economic Studies Program, The Brookings Institution 32: 93–186.

Kydland, Finn E., and Edward C. Prescott (1977). "Rules Rather Than Discretion: The Inconsistency of Optimal Plans." *Journal of Political Economy* 85: 473.

Lav, Iris J., and Erica Williams (2010, March 15). *A Formula for Decline: Lessons from Colorado for States Considering TABOR*. Washington, DC: Center for Budget and Policy Priorities.

Levinson, Arik (1998). "Balanced Budgets and Business Cycles: Evidence from the States," *National Tax Journal* 51(4): 715–732.

Lowry, Robert, and James Alt (2001). "A Visible Hand? Bond Markets, Political Parties, Balanced Budget Laws, and State Government Debt." *Economics and Politics* 13(1): 49–72.

Malaga, Steven (2011, Winter). "State Budget Bunk." *City Journal* 21(1).

Martin, Isaac William (2009). "Proposition 13 Fever: How California's Tax Limitation Spread." *California Journal of Politics and Policy* 1(1): 1–28.

McGranahan, Leslie (2010, June). "Measuring State and Local Indebtedness: How Much Is Too Much?" Presentation to the Chicago Federal Reserve Bank.

McGuire, Therese J., and Kim S. Rueben (2006, March). "The Colorado Revenue Limit: The Economic Effects of TABOR." *Economic Policy Institute Briefing Paper*.

McNichol, Elizabeth, and Brian Filipowich (2007, April 16). "Rainy Day Funds: Opportunities for Reform." Washington, DC: Center for Budget and Policy Priorities.

McNichol, Elizabeth, Phil Oliff, and Nicholas Johnson (2010, December 9). *States Continue to Feel Recession's Impact*. Washington, DC: Center for Budget and Policy Priorities.

Mitchell, Matthew (2010, December 10). "How to Control State Spending." *Wall Street Journal*.

Mullins, Daniel R. (2004). "Tax and Expenditure Limitations and the Fiscal Response of Local Government: Asymmetric Intra-local Fiscal Effects." *Public Budgeting & Finance* 24(4): 111–147.

Mullins, Daniel R. (2010) "Fiscal Limitations on Local Choice." In *State and Local Fiscal Policy*, edited by Sally Wallace. Northampton, MA: Edward Elgar.

Mullins, Daniel R., and Philip G. Joyce (1996). "Tax and Expenditure Limitations and State and Local Fiscal Structure: An Empirical Analysis." *Public Budgeting and Finance* 16(1): 75–101.

Musgrave, Richard A. (1959). *The Theory of Public Finance*. New York: McGraw-Hill.

National Association of State Budget Officers [NASBO] (2008, Summer). *Budget Processes in the States*. Washington, DC: National Association of State Budget Officers.

National Conference of State Legislatures [NCSL] (2007). *State Tax and Expenditure Limits*. Denver: National Conference of State Legislatures.

National Conference of State Legislatures (2010, November 12). *NCSL Fiscal Brief: State Balanced Budget Provisions*. Washington, DC: National Conference of State Legislatures.

Nichols, Albert L., and Richard J. Zeckhauser (1982). "Targeting Transfers through Restrictions on Recipients." *American Economic Review* 72: 372–377.

Niskanen, W. A. (1971). *Bureaucracy and Representative Government*. Chicago: Aldine-Atherton.

Novy-Marx, Robert, and Joshua Rauh (2010a). "Policy Options for State Pension Systems and Their Impact on Plan Liabilities." *NBER Working Paper* #16453. Cambridge, MA: National Bureau of Economic Research

Novy-Marx, Robert, and Joshua Rauh (2010b). "The Crisis in Local Government Pensions in the United States." Working paper.

Nunes, the Honorable Representative and Reps. Ryan and Issa (2011). *To amend the Internal Revenue Code of 1986 to provide for reporting and disclosure by State and local public employee retirement pension plans.* 112th Congress 1st Session H. R. ll (January 5)

Persson, Torsten, and Lars O. Svensson (1989, May). "Why a Stubborn Conservative Would Run a Deficit: Policy with Time-Inconsistent Preferences." *Quarterly Journal of Economics* 104: 325.

Pew Center on the States (2010a). *The Trillion Dollar Gap: Underfunded State Retirement Systems and the Road to Reform*. Washington, DC: Pew Charitable Trusts.

Pew Center on the States (2010b). *Budget Stabilization Funds*. Washington, DC: Pew Charitable Trusts.

Poterba, James M. (1994). "State Responses to Fiscal Crises: The Effects of Budgetary Institutions and Politics." *Journal of Political Economy* 102(4): 799–821.

Poterba, James M. (1995, September). "Balanced Budget Rules and Fiscal Policy: Evidence from the States." *National Tax Journal* 48(3): 329–336.

Poterba, James M., and Kim Rueben (1995, May). "The Effect of Property-Tax Limits on Wages and Employment in the Local Public Sector." *American Economic Review Papers and Proceedings* 85(2): 384–389.

Poterba, James M., and Kim Rueben (2001). "Fiscal News, State Budget Rules, and Tax-Exempt Bond Yields." *Journal of Urban Economics* 50: 537–562.

Preston, A. E., and Ichniowski, C. (1991). "A National Perspective on the Nature and Effects of the Local Property Tax Revolt." 1976–1986. *National Tax Journal* 44(2): 123.

Primo, David M., and James M. Snyder, Jr. (2008, April). "Distributive Politics and the Law of 1/n*." *The Journal of Politics* 70(2): 477–486.

Rabin, Jack, and W. Bartley Hildreth (2007). *Handbook of Public Administration*. CRC Press. 163.

Riker, William (1980). "Implications for the Disequilibrium of Majority Rule for the Study of Institutions." *American Political Science Review* 74: 432.

Rodriguez-Tejedo, Isabel, and John Wallis (2010). "Lessons for California from the History of Fiscal Constitutions." *California Journal of Politics and Policy* 2(3): 1–19.

Romer, T. and Rosenthal, H. (1979). "The Elusive Median Voter." *Journal of Public Economics* 12: 143–170.

Rose, Shanna (2010). "Institutions and Fiscal Sustainability." *National Tax Journal* 63(4, Part 1): 807–838.

Rueben, Kim S. (1996) "Tax Limitations and Government Growth: The Effect of State Tax and Expenditure Limits on State and Local Government." *PPIC Working Paper.*

Shadbegian, Ronald J. (1996). "Do Tax and Expenditure Limitations Affect the Size and Growth of State Government?" *Contemporary Economic Policy* 14(1): 22–35.

Shadbegian, Ronald J. (1999). "The Effect of Tax and Expenditure Limitations on the Revenue Structure of Local Government, 1962–1987." *National Tax Journal* 52(2): 221–237.

Shiller, Robert J. (2010, August 28). "The Case for Reviving Revenue Sharing." *New York Times.*

Sobel, Russell S., and Randall G. Holcombe (1996). "The Impact of State Rainy Day Funds in Easing State Fiscal Crises during the 1990–1991 Recession." *Public Budgeting and Finance* 16(3): 28–48.

Sokolow, Alvin D. (2000, Spring). "The Changing Property Tax in the West: State Centralization of Local Finances." *Public Budgeting and Finance* 20: 85–104.

Stigler, George J. (1971) "The Theory of Economic Regulation." *Bell Journal of Economics and Management Science* 2(1): 3–21.

Temple, Judy A., and Edward J. Nannenhorn (1998). "State Supermajority Requirements for Tax or Revenue Increases: An Overview." *Proceedings of the 90th Annual Conference of the National Tax Association.*

Thaler, Richard H., and H. M. Shefrin (1981). "An Economic Theory of Self Control." *Journal of Political Economy* 89: 392.

US General Accounting Office (1993). *Balanced Budget Requirements: State Experiences and Implications for the Federal Government.* GAO AFMD-93.58BR. Washington, DC: US Government Printing Office.

US Government Accountability Office (2007, July 18). *State and Local Governments: Persistent Fiscal Challenges Will Likely Emerge within the Next Decade.* Washington DC: US Government Printing Office.

US Government Accountability Office (2010, March). *State and Local Governments' Fiscal Outlook: April 2011 Update GAO-11–495SP.* Washington DC: US Government Printing Office. April 6, 2011

US Office of Management and Budget (2011). "Aid to State and Local Governments." *Analytical Perspectives, Budget of the United States Government, Fiscal Year 2012.* Washington, DC.

von Hagen, Jürgen (1991). "A Note on the Empirical Effectiveness of Formal Fiscal Restraints." *Journal of Public Economics* 44: 199.

Wagner, Gary A. (2003). "Are State Budget Stabilization Funds Only the Illusion of Savings? Evidence from Stationary Panel Data." *Quarterly Review of Economics and Finance* 43(2): 213–238.

Wallis, John Joseph, and Barry R. Weingast (2006, February). "Dysfunctional or Optimal Institutions? State Debt Limitations, the Structure of State and Local Governments, and the Finance of American Infrastructure." Working paper: 9.

Weingast, Barry R., and William J. Marshall (1988). "The Industrial Organization of Congress; or, Why Legislatures, Like Firms, Are Not Organized as Markets." *Journal of Political Economy* 96: 132.

Weingast, Barry R., Kevin A. Shepsle, and C. Johnsen (1981). "The Political Economy of Benefits and Costs: A Neoclassical Approach to Distributive Politics." *Journal of Political Economy* 89: 642–664.

PART II

REVENUE STRUCTURES AND SYSTEMS

CHAPTER 11

....

REAL PROPERTY TAX

....

MICHAEL E. BELL

INTRODUCTION

....

THE tax on real plus personal property serves as the largest source of state or local own-source revenues. In FY 2008, the property tax generated $409.7 billion for state and local governments—96.9 percent of which was received by local governments.[1] In contrast, general sales taxes generated $304.4 billion for state and local governments (20.8 percent being received by local governments) and the personal income tax generated $304.6 billion of which just 8.6 percent was received by local governments.[2]

Although the relative importance of the property tax has declined over time, it is nevertheless still the local government revenue "mainstay." Forty years ago, in 1968, the property tax accounted for 42.9 percent of local general revenues, 56.1 percent of local own-source revenues, and 86.1 percent of local taxes. In 2008 the comparable property-tax shares were 28.3 percent, 45.3 percent, and 72.3 percent, respectively.

According to the US Census Bureau, in 1968 the property tax generated $26.8 billion in local revenues. By 2008 it generated $397 billion in revenues for local governments—an increase in nominal property-tax collections of 1,381 percent over this forty-year period. Adjusting for inflation, the increase in real property-tax revenues over this period was 101 percent.[3]

A number of metrics are commonly used to describe the role of total property-tax revenues in local finances. For example, in 1972 total local property taxes per capita were $198.87, increasing to $1,305.65 per capita in 2008—an increase of 557 percent. Figure 11.1 presents a number of other common metrics documenting the changing role of property taxes during this period—property tax collects relative to local general revenues, own-source revenues, tax revenues, and personal income.[4] From 1972 to 1982 local property taxes declined significantly as a share of local general,

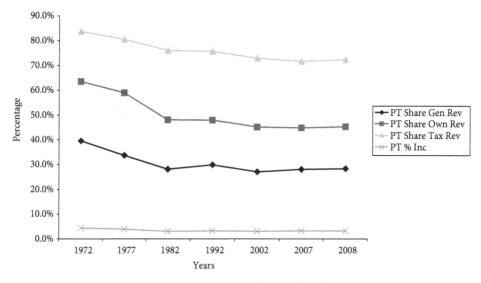

Figure 11.1 Property taxes as share of local revenues
Source: Data for 1972, 1977 and 1982 come from 1982 Census of Governments, Volume
6: Topical Studies, Number 4: Historical Statistics on Government Finances and
Employment, selected tables, GC82(6)-4. Government finance data for 1992, 2002 and
2007 come from Census of Governments for each year accessed at http://www.census.
gov/govs/. Government finance data for 2008 come from the state and local government
finance annual series which can be accessed through the same web site. Data for population and personal income come from the 2010 Statistical Abstract of the United States
accessed at http://www.census.gov/compendia/statab/

own-source, and tax revenues, while its share of own-source and tax revenues continued to decline modestly from 1982 to 2007.[5] Local property taxes increased as a
share of local general, own-source, and tax revenues from 2007 to 2008, in part as a
result of the impact of the Great Recession on local income and sales tax revenues.

The relative importance of total property taxes as a source of local revenue varies
across states. Such variations reflect differences across states in state income, assessment levels, property-tax rates, and the relative importance of personal property
in the property-tax base. Appendix 11.1 reports data on the variation in reliance on
total property taxes across the fifty state systems of local government. In 2008, four
states have local governments that generate more than three-fourths of their own-
source revenues from property taxes—Connecticut (83.4 percent), New Hampshire
(80.7 percent), Rhode Island (79.3 percent), and New Jersey (76.6 percent). At the
other extreme, seven states had local governments that depended on property taxes
for less than one-third of their own-source revenues.[6] Their variation is not as great
when looking at the role of the property tax in local tax revenues. In 2008, thirteen states had local governments that generated more than 90 percent of local tax
revenues from the property tax, but only three states with local governments that
generated less than 50 percent of tax revenues from the property tax.

In 2008 total property taxes generated an average of $1,306 per capita. The prop-
erty tax generated more than $2,000 per capita in four states—New Jersey ($2,615),

Connecticut ($2,378), New Hampshire ($2,029), and New York ($2,005). At the other extreme, the property tax generated less than $600 per capita in six states.[7]

The property tax is a tax on wealth, but the liability must be paid out of annual income. One common measure of the "burden" of the property tax is the share of personal income required to pay annual property-tax liabilities. In terms of the claim on personal income, property taxes declined somewhat between 1972 and 1982, and they have been relatively constant at about 3 percent of personal income since 1982 (see figure 11.1).

The claim of the property tax on state income also varies across states. In 2008, on average the property tax claimed $32.85 for each $1,000 of personal income. The local property tax accounted for more than $45 of personal income in four states—New Jersey ($51.35), Rhode Island ($47.87), New Hampshire ($47.37), and Maine ($45.51). Alternatively, the local property tax accounted for less than $20 per $1,000 personal income in eight states.[8]

Another measure of "burden" that economists typically consider is the tax liability relative to the tax base (market value), or the effective property-tax rate. Bell and Kirschner review a number of alternative measures of effective property-tax rates as described in box 11.1.

They conclude that the most comprehensive measure of effective property-tax rates is the one calculated annually for the largest city in each state by the Minnesota Taxpayers Association (MTA).[9] Appendix 11.2 presents data from the MTA's annual survey of effective property-tax rates for largest cities that have the highest and lowest effective property-tax rates on the median priced urban residential property in 2006 and 2009.[10] Four of the five cities with the highest effective property-tax rates in 2009 were among the five cities with the highest effective tax rates in 2006. The median residential property value fell in three of these four cities (Buffalo, New York, was the exception) during the Great Recession. Of the four with the highest property-tax rates in both years the effective property-tax rate increased in two cases (Aurora and Philadelphia) and declined in two others (Detroit and Buffalo).

Three of the five states with the lowest effective tax rates in 2009 were also among the lowest in 2006—Honolulu, Denver, and Boston. For these three cities, the effective property-tax rate fell in two (Honolulu and Boston) and was unchanged in Denver. In other words, effective property-tax rates vary significantly across the largest cities in the fifty states and there has been no systematic pattern of change in effective tax rates as a consequence of the Great Recession.[11]

While Census data include revenues from both real and personal property, the focus of the rest of this chapter is on the real property tax. When judged with respect to the conventional standards for what makes a "good" local tax, the real property tax gets high marks: in principle it meets the tests of revenue productivity and stability, and, because it generally satisfies the "matching principle" between the benefits of local services received and the payment for such services, it satisfies the efficiency and equity criteria. In practice, however, the property tax is moving further and further from these ideals because of its increasingly narrow focus, policies that create distortions to private decision making by favoring some land-use types more than others and the administration of the tax is becoming less uniform

---

Box 11.1 Summary of Characteristics of Various Measures of Effective Property-Tax Rates

| | Source of Data | | Base of Comparison | Jurisdiction for which Effective Tax Rate is Computed |
	Property Taxes	Property Value/Income		
American Association of Retired Persons	American Community Survey	American Community Survey	Income	Average for state*
National Association of Home Builders	American Community Survey	American Community Survey	Property value	Average for state
Minnesota Taxpayers Association	Calculated for each state	Calculated for each state	Property value	Largest city and one rural jurisdiction in each state
District of Columbia Government	Calculated for each state	American Community Survey	Property value	Largest city in each state
Fiscal Policy Institute	Calculated for individual properties	Actual sales data	Property value	Individual jurisdictions in the D.C. metro area

*Property-tax burdens are computed for three groups in each state: all homeowners, homeowners under sixty-five years of age, and homeowners over sixty-five years of age.

---

and less fair and the tax is becoming less accountable because of "the confusing and opaque jumble of special provisions that accumulate as the broad base of the property tax is destroyed."[12]

The purpose of this chapter is to discuss the trends considered to be undermining the broad base of the real property tax and the implications these trends have for the credibility and legitimacy of the local real property tax.

THE PROPERTY TAX AS A REVENUE SOURCE

Revenue Stability

As noted above, the property tax is the foundation of local government revenue. Moreover, it tends to be a stable revenue source because it is based on asset value, not on an annual stream of income or sales.

A stable tax generates revenues that change relatively more slowly than income—that is, the tax revenue is income-inelastic. And, because real estate markets reflect long-term asset values, which tend to respond more slowly to annual changes in the level of economic activity than economic flows like sales, personal income, and profits, the property tax tends to be more stable than the general sales tax or the personal income tax. Also, fluctuations in the property-tax base are moderated because few jurisdictions have annual assessment practices that completely capture changes in real estate values. Therefore, the property tax is regarded as a relatively stable revenue source—especially compared with other potential local tax sources (local personal income and local general sales taxes).

The relative stability of the property tax protects local budgets in periods of economic downturns. For example, figure 11.2 documents the continued growth of property-tax revenues from the first quarter of 2008 through the second quarter of 2009 while income and sales tax revenues declined significantly during the Great Recession.

The property tax represents a critical anchor for funding local governments. In a recent study of the impact of the Great Recession on local revenues generally, and property taxes specifically, Alm, Buschman, and Sjoquist concluded that

> local government reliance on the property tax rather than more elastic revenues sources like income, sales, and excise taxes has—so far, in any event—helped local governments avoid some of the more severe difficulties experienced by many other governments in the current economic situation.[13]

Giertz documented a similar stabilizing impact of the growth in property-tax revenues as income and sales tax revenues declined, albeit more modestly, as a result of the stock market decline in 2000 and the recession of 2001.[14]

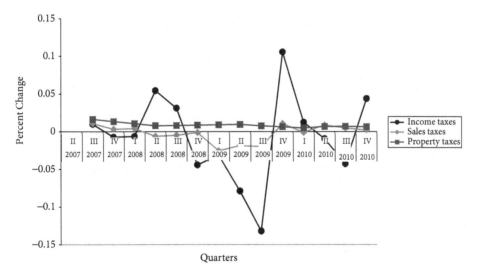

Figure 11.2 Quarterly percentage change in tax collections by type of tax
Source: Author's calculations based on Bureau of Economic Analysis, National Income and Product Account Tables, Table 3.3 State and Local Current Government Receipts and Expenditures, found at http://www.bea.gov/national/nipaweb/TableView.asp?SelectedTab le=88&ViewSeries=NO&Java=no&Request3Place=N&3Place=N&FromView=YES&Fre q=Qtr&FirstYear=2007&LastYear=2010&3Place=N&Update=Update&JavaBox=no

Neutrality/Efficiency

Neutrality, or efficiency, in taxation requires that taxes minimize unintended influence on private economic decisions. What is to be avoided, or minimized, to the extent possible, is a tax that causes taxpayers to adjust their behaviors in ways that shift the ultimate burden of the tax to others or avoid the tax entirely. To the extent that economic actors adjust their behaviors to shift or avoid the tax, the tax has distorted private economic decisions and the economy is moved to a less efficient, or lower, welfare position because of the tax.[15] As a general rule, such inefficiencies are best avoided by a system with a broad tax base (e.g., allow few, if any, tax exemptions, deductions, and credits) combined with low rates.[16]

In this context, an ideal real property tax would be broad based and include all forms of real property (i.e., land and structures for both residential and commercial properties, as well as agricultural land and property owned by governments and non-profit organizations alike). In addition, because the property tax is assessed against real property, which, in the short run, is immobile, there is little that owners can do to avoid the tax. Thus, the tax has little impact on their economic decisions in the short run. In this respect, the property tax tends to distort private economic decisions less than other local taxes—especially when the base of the tax is defined as broadly as possible.

Simplicity

Taxes may cause distortions in the allocation of economic resources if they are complex and difficult to administer. In such a situation, the taxpayer may have to spend substantial resources to comply with the tax law, and the local jurisdiction may expend substantial resources administering it.

The property tax is generally considered to be taxpayer-passive because taxpayers face minimal compliance costs. Alternatively, the property tax is considered to have higher administrative costs for the local government associated with preparing and maintaining the tax roll, annually estimating the property-tax base,[17] generating and delivering tax bills, collecting tax revenues, and enforcing the payment of the property tax when it is not paid in a timely fashion. Relative to other potential local tax sources with tax bases that are annual flows that must be monitored and verified (high compliance costs for both taxpayers and the government), the property tax is relatively easy to administer and involves low taxpayer compliance costs, except in the case of commercial and industrial property that may have higher compliance costs for both the taxpayers and the government.[18]

Another virtue of the property tax, from the government's perspective, is that taxpayers cannot easily hide or move real property. Thus, unlike income and sales taxes, the real property tax is difficult to evade. Moreover, the property provides collateral for the tax liability. If the property owner fails to pay the taxes, a lien is placed on the property. That lien prevents the property from being sold or mortgaged until the tax liability is satisfied. If collection efforts are unsuccessful, the local government can seize and sell the property. The local government retains the taxes owed, penalties, interests, and administrative costs, and it then remits the remainder to the owner. While property-tax sales are often the last resort for local governments, such sales provide powerful incentives to comply with the law.

Finally, the property tax presents equally attractive compliance benefits for the taxpayer. Most residential property owners face minimal compliance costs. Unlike the much more onerous (from a compliance standpoint) federal and state income taxes, there are no forms to file when complying with property taxes. There are generally no calculations to be made. Indeed, the government calculates the property tax and the taxpayer's role begins and ends when the tax is paid. And it is rare for an individual property owner to incur fees for professional tax assistance (i.e., accountants, attorneys) when complying with the property tax, even if the assessed value is appealed (unless it ends up in court, which is generally rare).

Equity

The property tax funds the delivery of community services. How the cost of these services is distributed across properties determines the fairness of the property tax. In this context, the property tax is consistent with both the ability-to-pay and the benefits-received principles of taxation.

The case for ability-to-pay principle of taxation of real property is based on two arguments. First, there is general agreement that the annual stream of housing benefits (or the annual stream of similar benefits accruing to commercial and industrial properties) escape taxation under the current income tax.[19] In other words, there is agreement that the taxation of income is generally imperfect because it does not capture all consumption (or unrealized capital gains to stocks, bonds, and other intangible property). As discussed above, in order to minimize the distortions of individual decision making as a result of a tax, the income tax should be comprehensive. This requires that all additions to income—whether in the form of money income, imputed income, changes in net wealth, or, as in the case of real property like housing, the annual flow of housing services—should be included in the taxable base.

To the extent that the annual flow of benefits escapes taxation, equity and efficiency concerns mandate that the asset be taxed. For example, in the case of housing, the value of the asset is the capitalized value of the annual stream of housing benefits received. Thus, a property tax, especially on residential and agricultural property, is a necessary complement to an imperfect tax on income.

The second argument that the property tax is consistent with the ability to pay rests on how the ultimate economic impact, or incidence, of the property tax is shifted from the taxpayer to others. It is generally agreed by most economists that the ultimate incidence of the property tax rests on all capital. According to Aaron, the "new" view of the incidence of the property tax holds "that *all* owners of capital bear the property tax" in large part because a uniform tax on the value of all land

and capital goods would reduce the rate of return to owners of capital.[20] Because property, and most other forms of capital, is concentrated in the top income groups, it is generally argued that the property tax is a progressive tax.

In addition, the property tax is generally considered to be consistent with the benefits-received principle of taxation. Because the property tax funds community services—e.g., police officers, fire stations, street maintenance—the level and quality of these site-oriented services benefit property owners and increase the values of their properties. This argument assumes implicitly that the benefits of public services are distributed across properties in proportion to market value. In turn, this implies that expenditure benefits are capitalized in the values of the properties.

The property tax, then, is consistent, to some extent, with both the benefits-received and ability-to-pay rationale. As implemented, however, it is fundamentally a tax on wealth with property-tax liabilities defined in terms of the value of real estate. Therefore, to promote fairness, property values must be estimated uniformly across all properties within a property-use class and across property-use classes.

Again, the base of the property tax is not observed annually, it is estimated. To achieve a fair allocation of the responsibility for financing local public services, properties need to be assessed for tax purposes uniformly. Eckert argues that uniformity, both within and across different classes of property, relates to the fair and equitable treatment of individual properties. Appraisal uniformity requires the equitable treatment of individual properties within groups (use classes, neighborhoods, etc.) and between groups. When individual property valuations are at the same percentage of market value, they are most likely to be accepted as fair. The ultimate policy objective, therefore, should be to implement the property tax uniformly across all property-use classes at 100 percent of market value, which promotes transparency.[21]

This notion of uniformity means that the property tax treats similarly situated taxpayers the same, that similar real property values should be taxed alike. Dissimilar treatment—real differences in the taxation of equals—undermines confidence in the property-tax system. Consider the homeowner who discovers that because of assessment limits, and valuation for tax purposes based on acquisition value, his neighbor, with essentially the same house, pays substantially less in property taxes simply because he has lived in the house longer. Such situations can only breed cynicism and distrust not only of the tax system, but also of government in general.

Because the property tax is, to some extent at least, an imperfect proxy for ability to pay, uniformity requires that higher valued properties pay more property taxes than lower valued properties. In other words, taxpayers with properties of different value have tax differences proportionate to their underlying market-value differences.

In conclusion, based on traditional criteria for evaluating a revenue system, the local property tax emerges as a very defensible source of local revenues. The property tax is especially attractive when compared with other potential sources of local tax revenues.

While most economists would embrace this conventional wisdom, this conventional wisdom is being re-evaluated in light of the consequences of legislative efforts to limit the ability of local governments to raise revenues from the property tax. The manner in which the property tax is administered greatly influences its productivity, neutrality, simplicity, and equity. Bahl et al. conclude that "bad practice has overtaken many of the potential advantages of taxing property....In the United States, voter preferences in recent years appear to be to trade an equitable property tax for one whose revenue growth is restrained."[22]

Giertz is more direct:

> Rather than a broad-based, low-rate tax that treats all types of real property uniformly, the tax in most states is characterized by a bewildering array of constraints and preferences including classified bases, rate limits, revenue limits and caps, assessment exemptions, freezes and caps, circuit breakers, and special incentives for business.[23]

Anderson concludes that such efforts by state legislatures to limit the volatility of individual property-tax liabilities through assessment limits, nonannual assessment, revenue limits, or tax rate limits undermine the horizontal and vertical equity of the property tax.[24]

These issues, as they relate to the erosion of the real property-tax base over time, are explored in more detail in the next section.

TRENDS IN THE REAL PROPERTY-TAX BASE

The real property tax is a mechanism for sharing the cost of providing general local goods and services to the community. It shares those costs across the community in relationship to the composition of the property-tax base. Therefore, trends impacting the composition of the property-tax base are critical in obtaining a fair distribution of the responsibility of funding locally provided goods and services across members of the community.

The property tax can be either general or selective in nature. A general property tax applies broadly to all types of property and treats individual types of property uniformly. Alternatively, a selective property tax is characterized by nonuniformity of tax treatment across property types. Nonuniformity can be introduced in a number of ways, including total exclusion of some property types from the base, by differential tax treatment of various property types, or by a combination of these two.

A general property tax, therefore, would be imposed on all classes of property—e.g., land, improvements, machinery, household goods, automobiles, and business inventories—in a uniform manner regardless of the nature of the property, its use, or ownership. Typically, the base of a general ad valorem property tax is the estimated market value of each property type. The property-tax liability is then determined by applying a single statutory rate uniformly to the estimated market value of the base.

In contrast, a selective property tax is imposed on a well-defined subset of all classes of property, usually based on the type of asset, its use, or its ownership. Given these characteristics, some property may be totally or partially excluded from the property-tax base (e.g., business machinery, inventories, and homestead properties).

The property tax in the United States was initially a selective property tax imposed on certain classes of wealth easily identifiable in an agrarian economy (e.g., land, improvements, and cattle).[25] Tax rates were generally *in rem* (i.e., levied at so many cents per unit rather than as a percentage of value like the current ad valorem property tax). Starting in the early nineteenth century, the various forms of tangible wealth increased and intangible property became more prominent. As a result, the nature of the property tax evolved through the mid-nineteenth century to a more general ad valorem property tax that was uniformly applied to the value of this broader set of assets regardless of their form.[26]

There are two main categories of property—*real property* and *personal property*. Real property consists of two component parts—land plus any improvements permanently attached to the land. Personal property is every kind of property other than real property and consists of two component parts: tangible and intangible personal property. Tangible personal property includes things such as inventories that can be seen, touched, or moved about. It also includes things like cars, boats, office equipment, and machinery. Alternatively, intangible personal property has no physical existence other than certificates or accounts that represent the property value. Fixtures may be either tangible personal or real property, depending on whether or not they can be removed without damaging the real property to which they are attached.

For the last several decades, however, the property tax in the United States has reverted back into a selective property tax focused on real property generally, and residential property more specifically. The personal property tax has been, and is continuing, to decline in relative importance. In terms of locally assessed property values, the personal property tax declined from 17.2 percent of local gross assessed value in 1956 to just 9.8 percent in 1986.[27] According to a recent study by the International Association of Assessing Officers, the importance of personal property has continued to decline with twelve states taxing inventories in 2009 (compared with fifteen in 1999), thirty-eight states taxing machinery and equipment (down from forty-three in 1999), thirty-eight taxing tangible business personal property (up slightly from thirty-five in 1999), and seven states taxing intangible personal property (down from ten in 1999).[28]

Increasing Importance of Residential Property

One of the most important trends in the composition of the property-tax base is the increasing importance of residential property and the declining relative importance of commercial and industrial property. According to Census data, in 1956 residential properties accounted for 54.1 percent of gross assessed values and increased to 61.2 percent in 1986. Over the same period, the commercial share of gross assessed values increased modestly, from 16.6 percent in 1956 to 17.3 percent in 1986, while the industrial share fell from 10.8 percent in 1956 to 7.0 percent in 1986. Over this same period, the relative importance of personal property fell from 17.2 percent of gross assessed values in 1956 to 9.8 percent in 1986.[29] These Census data, however, must be viewed with some caution. For example, the data presented are gross assessed values and do not reflect partial exemptions. As a result, these figures may overstate the relative importance of residential property.[30]

The Census Bureau stopped collecting such data in 1987, but anecdotal evidence from individual states suggests that the trend has continued unabated. For example, Giertz documents the increasing importance of residential property to the property-tax base in Illinois from 1982 (less than 50 percent of the base) to 2002 (more than 60 percent of the base). This trend is a result of a steady increase in residential property values and a reduction in the importance of real-property-intensive manufacturing in the state.[31]

Bowman provides other anecdotal evidence of the increasing importance of residential property in the property-tax base for selected states:

- in 1987 the Census of Governments estimated that single-family nonfarm residential property in Virginia accounted for 60.6 percent of the real property-tax base, while an estimate from the University of Virginia estimated this share was 71 percent in 2005; and[32]
- in 1987 the Census of Governments estimated that all residential property in Ohio accounted for 67.7 percent of the real property-tax base, while state data estimated this share at 72.9 percent in 2004.[33]

Gravelle and Wallace reached a similar conclusion about the increasing importance of residential property values as a share of the local property-tax base. Using estimates of the shares of assessed value attributable to residential and commercial/industrial properties between 1981 and 2004 for states that provide data broken down in these categories, they conclude that the share of assessed value in the sample states attributable to residential property increased over the period from about 52 percent to about 64 percent for the sample as a whole.[34]

Factors Contributing to the Increasing Residential Share of Real Property-Tax Base

The Knowledge-Based Economy

The high-technology, service, and knowledge-based economy adversely affects the local property-tax base. When heavy manufacturing dominated the American economy, a large portion of the property-tax base consisted of business land, plants, and equipment. Factories and heavy equipment, as well as extensive business ownership of land, filled the coffers of local governments with property-tax revenues for much of the twentieth century.

Modern businesses, which tend to rely more on computers and technology, however, have fewer plants and less equipment relative to large manufacturing firms.[35] These businesses do not own significant amounts of real property; this lack of ownership leads to a decrease in business property-tax revenue.[36] In fact, there has been a significant drop in the capital-to-labor ratio economywide, which may have reduced the growth in some types of taxable property.[37] This results in a shift in property-tax burdens from businesses to residential properties.[38]

In addition, the new economy has created another problem for the property tax. Capital-intensive firms (that is, those with relatively large amounts of plants and equipment) now incur a larger share of commercial and industrial property tax liabilities than high technology or service-centered businesses.[39] That inequity undermines support for the tax, particularly within the business community. Such inequities may lead to calls for lower tax burdens on capital-intensive firms in an effort for the local government to compete for jobs.

Competition for Jobs

The decade between 2000 and 2009 saw no net new job growth in the United States. As a result, some state and local governments reacted by adding to a plethora of property-tax incentives ostensibly intended to stimulate economic growth and job development.

Wassmer catalogued the growth in property-tax incentives for businesses across states.[40] Wassmer adopted the classification of such programs as "stand-alone property tax abatement programs" (or SAPTAPs), which (1) allow for a full or partial reduction in property-tax liability for selected manufacturing, commercial, or retail parcels; (2) impose a time limit on the reductions; (3) have a stated purpose beyond relief from high property taxes; and (4) need not be used with other state or local economic development programs. Wassmer identified fourteen states with such programs in 1963[41] and thirty-five states in 2007 with such programs. In 2007, six other states had property-tax abatement programs that did not fit the definition of SAPTAP. He concluded that for a state or region that theory and empirical evidence show that abatement does little but deplete the entire base of property taxation.[42]

Preferential Treatment

Most states provide multiple programs that extend preferential treatment to a variety of properties based on land-use type. Appendix 11.3 indicates that all fifty states provide preferential treatment for farmland, thirty provide preferential treatment for timber land, twenty-three have programs providing preferential treatment to open spaces, and eleven have programs providing preferential treatment for historic preservation. Such preferential treatment might include the total exemption of the taxable value of certain property based on ownership or use. Alternatively, the taxable values of such properties might be reduced through preferential assessment practices. In addition, most states provide property-tax relief to nonprofit organizations by exempting their real property from property taxes.

Property owned by nonprofit organizations is generally, although not always, exempt from the property tax. Utilizing the flow of funds accounts of the Federal Reserve Board, Bowman and others estimated that the value of real estate owned by nonprofit organizations increased from $1,233.5 billion in 2000 to $1,792.8 billion in 2005—a 45 percent increase in just five years.[43]

In addition, all fifty states have programs that provide preferential assessments for farmlands. Typically, farmland, and in many states forest land and open space land, are valued at use value, not market value. Most states do not estimate the impact these programs have on the property-tax base, but some that produce tax expenditure budgets that include property taxes estimate the revenues lost because of such preferential treatment. For example, Minnesota estimated that in 2006 their Green Acres program reduced property taxes by $42.8 million and their open space program reduced property taxes by $5.1 million; in 2006 preferential treatment of farmland cost Nebraska $145.9 million in foregone property-tax revenues; in 2005 to 2007 local governments in Oregon lost $181 million in property-tax revenues; and local governments in Texas experienced foregone property-tax revenues of $1.6 billion.[44]

Green and Weiss estimated that the preferential treatment of farmland in Wisconsin reduced the taxable value of agricultural land by 44 percent. The impact of preferential treatment of farmland in Kansas is even more significant as it is estimated that the market value of agricultural land is nearly five times its taxable value.[45]

RESPONSES TO THE INCREASING
IMPORTANCE OF RESIDENTIAL PROPERTY

Given the increasing share of property-tax liabilities falling on residential property owners, it is no surprise that legislators and local elected officials pursue policies to ameliorate those pressures. This trend toward limiting the property tax on residential property is exacerbated by the fact that the property tax tends to be consistently unpopular.

For two decades the Advisory Commission on Intergovernmental Relations conducted a survey of public attitudes toward taxes and government. From 1972, the first year of the survey, until 1979, the property tax was considered the worst, or least-fair, tax, followed by the federal income tax. From 1979 to 1993, the last year of the survey, the property tax was considered the second worst, or least-fair, tax after the federal income tax.

Nearly a decade later the property tax was still considered the worst tax by 22 percent of survey respondents compared with 30 percent who thought the federal income tax was least fair.[46] Most recently, a Gallup/CNN/*USA Today* poll in April

)3 found that 38 percent of Americans thought the local property tax was the worst ιαx compared to 21 percent who chose the federal income tax. This environment makes it easier for some to argue for the complete elimination of the property tax.[47]

In part, the property tax is unpopular with taxpayers because it is a tax on wealth that must be paid out of current income. When the market value of residential property is increasing more rapidly than income, people feel the pressure from increasing property-tax liabilities. In fact, a common theme that emerges in states considering eliminating the property tax is the growth rate of tax liabilities, especially for homeowners (i.e., voters), which creates what has been called the "monthly payment problem."[48]

Over the last several decades there have been a number of efforts to provide both *direct* and *indirect* property-tax relief to residential property owners. Direct property-tax relief reduces the tax liabilities for individual property owners. Indirect property-tax relief reduces reliance on property taxes by providing local governments access to alternative own-source revenues, or greater reliance on state grants. Sjoquist, Sweat, and Stoycheva explore in their chapter for this volume the issue of revenue diversification through increased reliance on user fees and local sales and income taxes. The focus here is on tools used to provide direct property-tax relief.

Property-Tax Rates and Levy Limits

According to data in Appendix 11.4, thirty-six states impose limits on the property-tax rate that can be levied by local governments. Most rate limits are set by legislation, but some are included in the state's constitution. Some rate limits do not allow for any increases, while some can be overridden in particular circumstances. Alabama, Ohio, and Michigan, for example, allow their rate limits to be increased by a simple majority of the electorate, while Oregon and Nebraska require a supermajority vote of the electorate.[49]

Data in Appendix 11.4 indicate that thirty-four states impose a limit on the total property-tax levy that can be raised by a local government. In some states the growth in property-tax revenues is limited to a flat percentage increase from year to year. In other cases, the limit allows for growth to reflect a combination of population growth and inflation. In most states, the levy limit can be overridden by the electorate or the legislative body in the taxing jurisdiction.[50]

According to data in Appendix 11.4, twenty-five states have both a property-tax rate and levy limit, while seven states have neither.

Such property-tax rate and levy limits constrain the ability of local governments to raise revenues from the property tax. Such relief, however, benefits all property owners equally. Thus, the property-tax rate and levy limits are intended to hold the line on the growth in property-tax liabilities in a manner that maintains the uniformity of the administration of the property tax and does not impose distortions on the system.

Classification

Other initiatives by state legislators and local decision makers are intended to impact different land-use classes differently. For example, the explicit policy objective of classification is to introduce different effective property-tax rates—taxes that are different percentages of market value—for different land uses.[51] A general classified property tax can be accomplished in two ways. Most states imposing a classified property-tax system achieve the desired goal by having different assessed values for different land-use classes. Alternatively, many states achieve the goal of differential effective tax rates by applying differential rates to uniform valuations of all classes of property.

Sexton identified twenty-five states that have some form of classified property-tax system. The list identified nineteen states that vary the effective tax rate across land-use types by varying assessment ratios, while six states provide differential effective tax rates across land-use types by varying the tax rate.[52] Bowman argued that the number is closer to thirty if you include states with local options for classification and states that hold constant some historic relationship between the tax shares of residential property and other property—what Gold called dynamic classification.[53]

Assessment Limits

While classified property-tax systems have the objective of shifting tax liabilities from residential to commercial and industrial properties by creating different effective tax rates for each land-use class, assessment limits go an extra step by creating different effective tax rates across properties within the same land-use class, as well as across land-use classes. Such limits destroy the notion of uniformity in property-tax administration, thereby undermining the efficiency and equity of the property tax.

Terri A. Sexton identified nineteen states and the District of Columbia as having some form of limitation on the growth in assessed values.[54] According to Sexton, fifteen of the nineteen states have statewide, uniform assessment limits, three states (Connecticut, Georgia, and Illinois) offer assessment limits as a local option, and New York mandates assessment limits in New York City and Nassau County. Ten states—Arkansas, California, Colorado, Florida, Georgia, Michigan, Oklahoma, Oregon, South Carolina, and Texas—enacted assessment limits as constitutional amendments.

Assessment limits vary by state ranging from 2 percent in California to 15 percent in Minnesota. The assessment limits in other states include 3 percent in Florida, Oregon, and New Mexico; 15 percent over five years in South Carolina; 5 percent in Arkansas, Michigan, and Oklahoma; a range of 6 to 8 percent in New York City; 7 percent in Cook County, Illinois; and 10 percent in Arizona, District of Columbia, Maryland, and Texas. Georgia provides a local option of an assessment freeze, and 19 of 159 counties have frozen residential values. Unlike the other states, Iowa applies its 4 percent assessment limit to classes of properties (residential, agricultural, and commercial) rather than to individual parcels. Colorado also applies an aggregate cap by limiting the residential part of the tax base to 45 percent of the total.[55]

Most limits on assessed values include a provision called the acquisition value feature, which recalibrates the assessed value to reflect market value when the property changes ownership. Only three states—Arizona, Minnesota, and Oregon—do not have the acquisition value feature of the eighteen states that limit assessment value increases of individual parcels.[56]

Resetting values to reflect market values when a property is sold undermines horizontal equity. Property-tax systems with horizontal equity apply similar tax burdens to similar properties. Under a system with the acquisition value feature, long-time owners are taxed less than new owners of properties similarly valued.[57] O'Sullivan, Sexton, and Sheffrin calculated that a new owner of a Los Angeles property sold in 1991 would pay five times more in property taxes than an owner of an identical property who has lived there since 1975, the base assessment value that increases 2 percent each year.[58] In a study of four counties (Alameda, Los Angeles, San Bernardino, and San Mateo) O'Sullivan, Sexton, and Sheffrin found that California's acquisition value system benefited lower-income homeowners and the elderly on average relative to other homeowners because they tended to move less often.[59]

The acquisition value feature creates a disincentive for people to move because property owners lose their tax break when they sell and buy a new place. The longer an owner stays, the larger his or her tax benefits are. Property-tax liability can increase drastically even if the resident moves to a home of equal or lesser value. Faced with a large increase in property taxes, growing families may not move to a larger house, putting pressure on the entry-level housing market. Seniors may not downsize to a smaller house. Homeowners may not relocate with a job and deal with a longer commute. The disincentive to move is called the lock-in effect.[60]

California passed Proposition 60 in 1986 and this allowed homeowners fifty-five years and older to transfer the assessed values of their former homes to new homes of equal or lesser value within the same county. This portability feature is allowed only once in a lifetime. Proposition 90 in 1988 allowed senior homeowners to transfer the assessed value to a new home in a different county if the receiving county agrees.[61]

Sexton argued that the acquisition value property taxes add another transaction cost to moving.[62] It creates a loss in economic well-being from "suboptimal housing consumption, inefficient labor market outcomes, longer commutes with associated environmental and congestion costs, a reduction in the supply of smaller homes for young and old home buyers, and reduced incentives for households to vote with their feet, thereby impeding the efficient provision of local public goods."[63]

Assessment limits are generally considered to be the least effective, least equitable, and least efficient approaches for providing property-tax relief. Assessment limits give the greatest property-tax relief to those properties growing most rapidly. Such limits result in substantial shifts in property-tax burdens and differences in effective property-tax rates within and across property classes. In short, they are the most destructive property-tax relief tool because they undermine the adequacy, efficiency, and equity of the local property tax.

THE FUTURE OF THE PROPERTY

The property tax is the mainstay of local finances. As such, it provided relative stability for local governments, especially those most reliant on property taxes, during the Great Recession of 2007 to 2009. The real property tax, however, is performing less well against generally accepted criteria for evaluating local revenues because of what Witte has called "the confusing and opaque jumble of special provisions that accumulate as the broad base of the property tax is destroyed."[64]

The challenge then becomes how to preserve and strengthen the role of the property tax in funding the delivery of critical local government services by moving it back toward a broad-based tax with low rates.

Dye considered the issues of what the future property tax will look like and what might replace the property tax as a source of local revenues. He concluded that given the current budget pressures on state and local governments and the important role of the property tax in local finance that it is hard to imagine drastic reductions in property-tax revenues going forward.[65]

Dye proposed four recommendations for improving the property tax in the future:

- pay attention to the features of property-tax limitations and make sure there is a reasonable provision for override by local voters to maintain local control;
- consider alternatives to broad limitations on the property tax;
- provide better education on the vertical distribution of the burden of the property tax to refine the message and figure out how to get it to a broader audience; and
- provide better information on the fiscal challenges faced by state and local governments as a result of an aging population so there is greater appreciation for the important role of the property tax in state and local finance.[66]

These concerns are echoed by Brunori who argued that the most important first step in restoring the property tax is educating the public about the many virtues of this specific revenue source vis-à-vis other potential local revenue sources. This should include making the public aware that government reforms, many instituted in response to popular discontent with the tax, have largely addressed the causes of public concern.[67]

Part of the issue may be the terminology used to describe the frustration of taxpayers with tax bills that increase faster than income does. Youngman made the point "that in many cases 'regressive' is simply a dramatic way of calling the tax unfair." Thus, a set of initiatives is necessary to strengthen the role of the property tax by educating the taxpayer and policymakers. Policymakers and analysts need to do more in addressing the myth of regressivity. In popular discussion the property tax is generally thought to be regressive, with a disproportionate burden falling on those who earn low incomes. In theory, and practice, however, the tax is not regressive.

What can be done to promote the argument that the property tax is fair? A number of things seem in order. First, policymakers should move back toward the goal of uniformity of assessment, which has been abandoned over the years, resulting in significant and visible inequities in the tax. Second, once uniformity is restored, there needs to be a serious review of various types of exemptions, as well as what they cost and who they benefit. This should be part of a tax expenditure budget for the property tax.

Fisher expressed the view that the main concern with the property tax is what he termed the "monthly payment problem."[68] In this context, policymakers should avoid providing property-tax relief to all taxpayers and concentrate such tax relief on those with high property-tax burdens relative to current income. The appropriate policy tool for addressing such a need is the circuit breaker.[69]

Pomp provided an array of recommendations, which might be reasonable but will be difficult to implement. Specifically, he suggested that property can only be purchased by tax-exempt organizations with the approval of the local government, limiting the number of acres qualifying for exemption, setting dollar limits on the amount of property that can be exempt, imposing user charges (or payments in lieu of taxes) on tax-exempt organizations, and requiring that the state reimburse local governments for revenues foregone because of state action.[70]

In search of a solution for reducing the gap between ideal and actual property-tax systems, Witte suggested that strengthening transparency of the property-tax system may help by informing citizens of the costs and benefits of various property-tax relief programs. He mentioned two tools that improve overall transparency: first, there are truth-in-taxation laws that give voters more information about property taxes and rates. Taxpayers need more information regarding the factors that contribute to increasing property-tax liabilities for individual homeowners. Are property taxes going up because property values are increasing, or are local decision makers increasing property-tax rates? Transparency, and therefore accountability, is improved when taxpayers are better informed about changes in property-tax revenues and related changes in property-tax rates.[71]

Second, there is the idea of a tax expenditure budget that identifies public policies that deprive local governments of property-tax revenues and result in distortions that could ultimately undermine the legitimacy of the tax. Tax expenditures, however, should not be viewed simply as a government accounting and reporting system. Surrey argued that these special provisions in the tax code were equivalent to taxing everyone at the full tax rate and then giving some taxpayers preferred treatment by subsidizing taxpayer activities. Thus, tax expenditures should properly be viewed not as revenue policies, but as spending programs.

By converting what appear to be problems with tax reform to problems of spending reform, the tax expenditure mind-set involves asking a different set of questions associated with spending programs: what is the goal of the program, how cost-effective is the approach, what are the distributional consequences of the program, and should the program be replaced with a direct expenditure program?[72]

A tax expenditure budget for local property taxes should including the following type of information:

- A description of each property-tax relief mechanism;
- The cost of each property-tax relief mechanism in terms of foregone revenues for the current fiscal year;
- The estimated cost of each property-tax relief mechanism for future years to allow comparison with other proposed expenditures;
- The relevant legal citation for each property-tax relief mechanism and the year of enactment; and
- Details on the taxpayers who benefit from each property-tax relief mechanism.

Developing such a tax expenditure budget for local property taxes will achieve the following benefits:

- Improve transparency by making the consideration of the costs and benefits of each property-tax relief mechanism an explicit part of each year's budget process;
- Encourage accountability by requiring state and local policymakers to annually consider and approve the costs and distribution of benefits associated with each property-tax relief mechanism;
- Save money as property-tax relief is treated in a more informed way so that relief can be concentrated on those most in need at a lower overall cost of foregone revenues to state and local governments; and
- Promote efficiency in taxation by broadening the base of the property tax and reducing the tax rate needed to raise a given amount of tax revenue.

Developing such a tax expenditure budget for the property tax will create an environment where property-tax relief can be targeted to those most in need and relief going to those not in need can be reduced or eliminated, thereby broadening the base of the tax.

Appendix 11.1 Reliance of total property-tax revenues (real and personal), 2008

	% Gen Rev	% Own Rev	% Tax Rev	PT Per Capita	PT Per $1000 PI
United States	28.3%	45.3%	72.3%	$ 1,306	$ 32.85
Alabama	11.6%	19.8%	40.3%	$ 430	$ 12.78
Alaska	26.2%	44.4%	75.3%	$ 1,438	$ 33.19
Arizona	22.7%	38.7%	62.5%	$ 893	$ 27.09
Arkansas	9.9%	22.9%	41.6%	$ 273	$ 8.74
California	22.3%	39.5%	73.5%	$ 1,373	$ 32.17
Colorado	26.7%	36.2%	61.2%	$ 1,241	$ 29.29
Connecticut	56.7%	83.4%	97.7%	$ 2,378	$ 42.27
Delaware	23.2%	45.8%	77.4%	$ 693	$ 16.96
District of Columbia	17.2%	24.6%	32.0%	$ 2,920	$ 44.93
Florida	33.5%	46.6%	80.7%	$ 1,651	$ 42.26
Georgia	26.4%	38.6%	65.1%	$ 1,047	$ 30.81
Hawaii	47.9%	57.9%	78.9%	$ 973	$ 24.03
Idaho	22.3%	37.9%	91.7%	$ 775	$ 24.11
Illinois	37.2%	56.4%	81.9%	$ 1,646	$ 38.82
Indiana	29.9%	46.9%	88.4%	$ 1,086	$ 31.86
Iowa	29.8%	46.8%	80.0%	$ 1,239	$ 33.77
Kansas	30.8%	47.3%	76.5%	$ 1,288	$ 33.91
Kentucky	19.1%	32.5%	55.5%	$ 533	$ 16.75
Louisiana	15.2%	24.2%	40.2%	$ 633	$ 17.45
Maine	48.5%	74.5%	98.7%	$ 1,610	$ 45.51
Maryland	25.1%	38.2%	50.1%	$ 1,062	$ 22.07
Massachusetts	43.0%	72.2%	96.5%	$ 1,795	$ 35.37
Michigan	28.1%	52.8%	92.2%	$ 1,186	$ 33.59
Minnesota	24.5%	45.1%	92.5%	$ 1,134	$ 26.52
Mississippi	20.3%	37.0%	92.1%	$ 765	$ 25.88
Missouri	26.5%	38.4%	61.2%	$ 922	$ 26.18
Montana	30.1%	52.4%	96.4%	$ 987	$ 28.81
Nebraska	32.1%	44.8%	75.7%	$ 1,392	$ 36.90
Nevada	22.5%	36.8%	67.6%	$ 1,163	$ 28.82
New Hampshire	55.0%	80.7%	98.4%	$ 2,029	$ 47.37
New Jersey	53.7%	76.6%	98.0%	$ 2,615	$ 51.35
New Mexico	14.1%	32.2%	50.8%	$ 537	$ 16.75
New York	26.0%	40.0%	53.6%	$ 2,005	$ 41.70
North Carolina	23.0%	39.5%	75.5%	$ 853	$ 24.78
North Dakota	32.6%	52.9%	85.6%	$ 1,151	$ 29.26
Ohio	26.1%	43.5%	66.1%	$ 1,182	$ 33.28
Oklahoma	18.6%	30.7%	53.0%	$ 580	$ 15.72
Oregon	26.6%	44.5%	80.6 %	$ 1,118	$ 31.08
Pennsylvania	28.1%	47.9%	70.4%	$ 1,243	$ 30.88
Rhode Island	52.5%	79.3%	97.6%	$ 1,963	$ 47.87
South Carolina	26.4%	39.8%	82.8%	$ 958	$ 30.03
South Dakota	32.7%	48.0%	72.9%	$ 1,068	$ 28.57
Tennessee	23.2%	34.6%	62.6%	$ 751	$ 21.89
Texas	34.9%	51.0%	80.4%	$ 1,379	$ 35.74
Utah	25.0%	41.2%	68.0%	$ 811	$ 26.76
Vermont	17.3%	56.4%	93.8%	$ 591	$ 15.19
Virginia	33.8%	53.1%	73.8%	$ 1,358	$ 31.66
Washington	20.0%	31.3%	57.1%	$ 926	$ 21.87
West Virginia	25.6%	46.4%	79.7%	$ 680	$ 22.04
Wisconsin	36.1%	63.7%	93.8%	$ 1,547	$ 41.45
Wyoming	22.7%	38.0%	76.1%	$ 1,842	$ 37.05

Source: US Bureau of Census, Statistical Abstract of the US (2010), selected tables; US Bureau of Census, Government Finances (2008).

Appendix 11.2 Effective property-tax rates, 2006 and 2009

Median Priced Urban Residential

	2006				2009		
State	City	Median Value	Effective PropTax Rate	State	City	Median Value	Effective PropTax Rate
Highest Five Effective Tax Rates							
Michigan	Detroit	$ 156,200	3.33%	Michigan	Detroit	$ 10,735	3.26%
New York	Buffalo	$ 99,800	2.46%	Connecticut	Bridgeport	$ 380,200	2.71%
Pennsylvania	Philadelphia	$ 215,100	2.43%	Illinois	Aurora	$ 204,300	2.69%
Illinois	Aurora	$ 265,600	2.40%	Pennsylvania	Philadelphia	$ 211,000	2.62%
Wisconsin	Milwaukee	$ 214,900	2.32%	New York	Buffalo	$ 115,400	2.39%
Lowest Five Effective Tax Rates							
Hawaii	Honolulu	$ 620,000	0.34%	Hawaii	Honolulu	$ 569,500	0.28%
Colorado	Denver	$ 247,500	0.53%	Colorado	Denver	$ 223,700	0.53%
New York	New York City	$ 454,100	0.59%	South Carolina	Columbia	$ 137,900	0.54%
Wyoming	Cheyenne	$ 165,000	0.65%	Massachusetts	Boston	$ 336,100	0.55%
Massachusetts	Boston	$ 397,500	0.65%	Arizona	Phoenix	$ 131,000	0.59%

Source: Minnesota Taxpayers Association (2010).

Appendix 11.3 Significant features of the property tax: Preferential treatment of properties, 2008

State	Farmland	Timber	Historic*	Open Space
Alabama	X		X	
Alaska	X			
Arizona	X			X
Arkansas	X	X		
California	X	X	X	X
Colorado	X	X		X
Connecticut	X	X		X
Delaware	X	X		
District of Columbia			X	
Florida	X		X	X
Georgia	X	X	X	X
Hawaii	X		X	
Idaho	X	X		
Illinois	X	X	X	X
Indiana	X	X		
Iowa	X		X	
Kansas	X			
Kentucky	X			
Louisiana	X			
Maine	X	X		X
Maryland	X			
Massachusetts	X	X		X
Michigan	X	X		X
Minnesota	X	X		X
Mississippi	X			
Missouri	X	X		
Montana	X	X		
Nebraska	X			
Nevada	X			X
New Hampshire	X	X		X
New Jersey	X			
New Mexico	X			
New York	X	X		
North Carolina	X	X	X	
North Dakota	X	X		X
Ohio	X	X		X
Oklahoma	X			
Oregon	X	X	X	X
Pennsylvania	X	X		X
Rhode Island	X	X		X
South Carolina	X			
South Dakota	X			
Tennessee	X	X		X
Texas	X	X		X
Utah	X			
Vermont	X	X		X
Virginia	X	X		X
Washington	X	X		X
West Virginia	X	X		
Wisconsin	X	X	X	
Wyoming	X			

* Does not include any property tax relief based on the increased value due to improvements made to historic properties.

Source: Lincoln Institute of Land Policy and George Washington Institute of Public Policy, "Significant Features of the Property Tax," https://www.lincolninst.edu/subcenters/significantfeatures-property-tax

Appendix 11.4 Significant features of the property tax: State limits on property-tax levies

State	Levy Limit	Rate Limit
Alabama		X
Alaska	X	X
Arizona	X	X
Arkansas	X	X
California		X
Colorado	X	X
Connecticut		
Delaware	X	
District of Columbia	X	X
Florida		X
Georgia		X
Hawaii		
Idaho	X	X
Illinois	X	X
Indiana	X	X
Iowa		X
Kansas		
Kentucky	X	X
Louisiana	X	X
Maine	X	
Maryland		
Massachusetts	X	X
Michigan	X	X
Minnesota	X	X
Mississippi	X	
Missouri		X
Montana	X	X
Nebraska	X	X
Nevada	X	X
New Hampshire		
New Jersey	X	
New Mexico	X	X
New York	X	X
North Carolina		X
North Dakota	X	X
Ohio	X	X
Oklahoma		X
Oregon		X
Pennsylvania	X	X
Rhode Island	X	
South Carolina	X	
South Dakota	X	X
Tennessee		
Texas	X	X
Utah		X
Vermont		
Virginia	X	
Washington	X	X
West Virginia	X	X
Wisconsin	X	X
Wyoming	X	

Source: Lincoln Institute of Land Policy and George Washington Institute of Public Policy, "Significant Features of the Property Tax," https://www.lincolninst.edu/subcenters/significantfeatures-property-tax.

Notes

1 The US Census Bureau collects and publishes information on property-tax revenues for state and local governments. The reported revenue figures include revenues from taxes on both real and personal property.

2 The Census Bureau defines property-tax revenues to include revenues from general property taxes including real property (e.g., land and structures) as well as personal property, which may be either tangible (e.g., automobiles and boats) or intangible (e.g., bank accounts and stocks and bonds). General sales-tax revenues include taxes applicable to sales of all types of taxable goods and services or to all gross receipts, whether at a single rate or at classified rates; and sales use taxes. Personal income taxes are taxes on individuals measured by net income and taxes on special types of income (e.g., interest, dividends, income from intangible property, etc.). For local governments, the personal income tax includes wages, salaries, and other compensation earned by both residents and nonresidents that are subject to tax collections by the reporting government. See US Census Bureau (2006).

3 The state and local government implicit price deflator is used to adjust for inflation. It is heavily weighted by wages and salaries in state and local government but also includes estimates for the entire range of government purchases. The deflator equals 100 for 2005 and can be found at http://www.bea.gov/national/nipaweb/TableView.asp ?SelectedTable=13&ViewSeries=NO&Java=no&Request3Place=N&3Place=N&From View=YES&Freq=Year&FirstYear=1972&LastYear=2008&3Place=N&Update=Upda te&JavaBox=no.

4 General revenue comprises all revenue except that classified as liquor store, utility, or insurance trust revenue. There are four types of revenue within general revenue sector: taxes, intergovernmental revenue, current charges, and miscellaneous general revenue. Taxes are compulsory contributions exacted by a government for public purposes, other than for employee and employer assessments and contributions to finance retirement and social insurance trust systems. Tax revenue comprises gross amounts collected (including interest and penalties) minus amounts paid under protest and amounts refunded during the same period. It consists of all taxes imposed by a government whether the government collects the taxes itself or relies on another government to act as its collection agent. Own-source revenues are all general revenues minus intergovernmental revenues including taxes, current charges, and miscellaneous revenues. See US Census Bureau (2006).

5 Data for 1972, 1977, and 1982 come from 1982 Census of Governments, Volume 6: Topical Studies, Number 4: Historical Statistics on Government Finances and Employment, selected tables, GC82(6)-4. Government finance data for 1992, 2002, and 2007 come from Census of Governments for each year accessed at http://www. census.gov/govs/. Government finance data for 2008 come from the state and local government finance annual series, which can be accessed through the same website. Data for population and personal income come from the 2010 Statistical Abstract of the United States accessed at http://www.census.gov/compendia/statab/.

6 Kentucky (32.5 percent), New Mexico (32.2 percent), Washington (31.3 percent), Oklahoma (30.7 percent), Louisiana (24.2 percent), Arkansas (22.9 percent), and Alabama (19.8 percent).

7 Vermont ($591), Oklahoma ($580), New Mexico ($537), Kentucky ($533), Alabama ($430), and Arkansas ($273).

8 Louisiana ($17.45), Delaware ($16.96), Kentucky ($16.75), New Mexico ($16.75), Oklahoma ($15.72), Vermont ($15.19), Alabama ($12.78), and Arkansas ($8.74).

9 Bell and Kirschner (2009).

10 The MTA approach to calculating effective property-tax rates assumes that the property-tax calculation has five distinct components:
- a "true" market value (TMV)
- a local assessment/sales ratio (SR)
- a statutory classification rate to determine the proportion of the assessor's estimated market value that is taxable (CR)
- the total local property-tax rate (TR)
- applicable property-tax credits (C)

Thus the net local property-tax liability for each parcel of property can be written:

$$\text{Net Property Tax} = \text{TMV} \times \text{SR} \times \text{CR} \times \text{TR} - \text{C}$$

These net tax liabilities are then compared with the true market value for each individual property to determine effective property-tax rates.

11 Minnesota Taxpayers Association (2010).

12 Witte (2009), 314.

13 Alm et al. (2010), 23.

14 Giertz (2006).

15 Fisher (1996), 303.

16 NCSL (1992).

17 The property tax is different from other state and local taxes because the tax base, estimated market value, must be determined by the government. The property tax is a tax on wealth, a stock variable, which does not change hands annually. In contrast, the base of the personal income tax or general sales tax is based on annual economic flows.

18 For example, see Bowman (1998), 132; Brunori (2007), 48–50.

19 Stiglitz (1988), 545–546.

20 Aaron (1975), 38–55.

21 Eckert (1990), 516.

22 Bahl et al. (2010), 14.

23 Giertz (2006), 695. For a discussion of tax limitations, see Gordon (this volume).

24 Anderson (2006), 692–693.

25 Lynn (1969).

26 Wallis (2001) describes how the property tax evolved from a fixed amount per acre of agricultural land in the early nineteenth century to an ad valorem tax because the ad valorem tax was thought to place a larger (and fairer) share of the tax burdens on properties where land values were rising most quickly as a result of large public investments like canals.

27 Bowman (1995), 8, table 1.3.

28 Dornfest et al. (2010), 12, table 8.

29 Bowman (1995), 8, table 1.3.

30 Cornia (1995), 26–27.

31 Giertz (2006), 697–698.

32 Bowman (2007), 32.

33 Ibid.

34 Gravelle and Wallace (2009), 37.

35 Bonnet (1998).

36 Strauss (2001).

37 Gravelle and Wallace (2009), 26.
38 Strauss (2001).
39 Green, Chevrin, and Lippard (2002).
40 Wassmer (2009).
41 Wassmer derives these estimates from Johnson (1962), table 1, and Bridges (1965), table 1.
42 Wassmer (2009), 249.
43 Bowman, Cordes, and Metcalf (2009), 274, table 9.1.
44 Ibid., table 9.3.
45 Green and Weiss (2009), 64–65.
46 Kincaid and Cole (2001), 207.
47 Fisher et al. (2010).
48 Ibid., 197.
49 Yuan et al. (2009), 155.
50 Ibid., 155–156.
51 For a fuller discussion of classified property taxes, see Bowman (2009, 1998).
52 Sexton (2003).
53 Bowman (2009), 93–94.
54 Sexton (2009), table 5.1.
55 Haveman and Sexton (2008), 8, 12–15; Sexton (2009), table 5.1.
56 Haveman and Sexton (2008), 14.
57 Ibid., 26.
58 O'Sullivan, Sexton, and Sheffrin (1995).
59 O'Sullivan et al. (1994).
60 Sexton (2008).
61 Ibid.
62 Ibid.
63 Ibid.; O'Sullivan et al. (1995).
64 Witte (2009), 314.
65 Dye (2010), 231.
66 Ibid., 232–235.
67 Brunori (2007), 124–125.
68 Fisher (2009).
69 See Bowman (2009) and Bowman, Kenyon, Langley and Paquin (2009) for a discussion of the various types of circuit-breaker programs, a survey of current practices across states and design issues to consider as such programs are expanded.
70 Pomp (2002), 389, as cited in Brunori (2007), 130.
71 Witte (2009), 332–333.
72 Gravelle (2005), 406–408; Ladd (1994), 50–51.

References

Aaron, Henry J. (1975). *Who Pays the Property Tax: A New View.* Washington DC: The Brookings Institution.

Alm, James, Robert Buschman, and David L. Sjoquist (2011). "Rethinking Local Government Reliance on the Property Tax." *Regional Science and Urban Economics* 41(4): 320–331.

Anderson, Nathan B. (2006, September). "Property Tax Limitations: An Interpretive Review." *National Tax Journal* 59(3): 685–694.

Augustine, Nancy, Michael E. Bell, David Brunori, and Joan M. Youngman (Eds.) (2009). *Erosion of the Property Tax Base: Trends, Causes and Consequences.* Cambridge, MA: Lincoln Institute of Land Policy.

Bahl, Roy, Jorge Martinez-Vazquez, and Joan Youngman (2010). "Whither the Property Tax: New Perspectives on a Fiscal Mainstay." In *Challenging the Conventional Wisdom on the Property Tax*, edited by Roy Bahl, Jorge Martinez-Vazquez, and Joan Youngman. Cambridge: Lincoln Institute of Land Policy. 3–14.

Bell, Michael E., David Brunori, and Joan M. Youngman (Eds.) (2010). *The Property Tax and Local Autonomy.* Cambridge, MA: Lincoln Institute of Land Policy.

Bell, Michael E., and Charlotte Kirschner (2009). "A Reconnaissance of Alternative Measures of Effective Tax Rates." *Public Budgeting and Finance* 29(2): 111–136.

Bonnet, Thomas W. (1998). *Is the New Global Economy Leaving State and Local Tax Structures Behind?* Washington, DC: National League of Cities.

Bowman, John H. (1995). "Taxation of Business Property: Overview." In *Taxation of Business Property: Is Uniformity Still a Valid Norm?* edited by John H. Bowman. Westport, CT: Praeger. 1–23.

Bowman, John H. (1998). "Real Property Taxation." In *Taxing Simply, Taxing Fairly: District of Columbia Tax Revision Commission.* Washington DC: Greater Washington Research Center. 119–201.

Bowman, John H. (2007). *Issues in State and Local Finance: Questions and Answers on Selected Topics with an Emphasis on Property Taxes*, unpublished manuscript prepared for the Lincoln Institute of Land Policy, Cambridge, MA.

Bowman, John H. (2009). "Residential Property Tax Relief Measures: A Review and Assessment." In *Erosion of the Property Tax Base: Trends, Causes and Consequences*, edited by Augustine et al. Cambridge, MA: Lincoln Institute of Land Policy. 73–110.

Bowman, John H., Daphne A. Kenyon, Adam Langley, and Bethany P. Paquin (2009). *Property Tax Circuit Breakers: Fair and Cost-Effective Relief for Taxpayers.* Policy Focus Report, Cambridge, MA: Lincoln Institute of Land Policy.

Bowman, Woods, Joseph Cordes, and Lori Metcalf (2009). "Preferential Tax Treatment of Property Used for Social Purposes: Fiscal Impacts and Public Policy Implications." In *Erosion of the Property Tax Base: Trends, Causes and Consequences*, edited by Augustine et al. Cambridge, MA: Lincoln Institute of Land Policy. 269–294.

Bridges, Benjamin (1965). "State and Local Inducements for Industry." *National Tax Journal* 18: 1–14.

Brunori, David (2007). *Local Tax Policy: A Federalist Perspective.* 2nd ed. Washington DC: Urban Institute Press.

Cornia, Gary C. (1995). "Perspectives on the Business Property Tax Base." In *Taxation of Business Property: Is Uniformity Still a Valid Norm?* edited by John H. Bowman. Westport, CT: Praeger. 25–44.

Dornfest, Alan S., Steve Van Sant, Rick Anderson, and Ronald Brown (2010). *State and Provincial Property Tax Policies and Administrative Practices (PTAPP): Compilation and Report*, Kansas City, MO: International Association of Assessing Officers, at http://www.iaao.org/sitePages.cfm?Page=442.

Dye, Richard F. (2010). "What Will the Future Property Tax Look Like, and What Will Take Its Place?" In *The Property Tax and Local Autonomy*, edited by Bell et al. Cambridge, MA: Lincoln Institute of Land Policy. 211–238.

Eckert, Joseph K., with Robert J. Gloudemans and Richard R. Almy (1990). *Property Appraisal and Assessment Administration.* Chicago: International Association of Assessing Officers.

Fisher, Ronald C. (1996). *State and Local Public Finance.* 2nd ed. Chicago: Irwin.

Fisher, Ronald C. (2009). *Property Taxes for Local Finance: Research Results and Policy Perspectives (Reconsidering Property Taxes: Perhaps Not So Bad after All).* Working Paper WP09RF1, Lincoln Institute of Land Policy, Department of Valuation and Taxation.

Fisher, Ronald C., Andrew Bristle, and Anupama Prasad (2010). "An Overview of the Implications of Eliminating the Property Tax: What Do Recent State Debates and Priori State Experience Tell Us?" In *The Property Tax and Local Autonomy,* edited by Bell et al. Cambridge, MA: Lincoln Institute of Land Policy. 165–202.

Giertz, J. Fred (2006, September). "The Property Tax Bound." *National Tax Journal* 59(3): 695–705.

Gravelle, Jane (2005). "Tax Expenditures." In *The Encyclopedia of Taxation and Tax Policy,* edited by Joseph J. Cordes, Robert D. Ebel, and Jane J. Gravelle. Washington, DC: Urban Institute Press.

Gravelle, Jennifer, and Sally Wallace (2009). "Overview of the Trends in Property Tax Base Erosion." In *Erosion of the Property Tax Base: Trends, Causes and Consequences,* edited by Augustine et al. Cambridge, MA: Lincoln Institute of Land Policy. 17–46.

Green, Harry A., Stan Chevrin, and Cliff Lippard (2002, May 27). "The Local Property Tax in Tennessee." *State Tax Notes:* 851–877.

Green, Richard K., and Elaine Weiss (2009). "Property Tax Expenditures, Revenues, and Equity: Some Lessons from Wisconsin." In *Erosion of the Property Tax Base: Trends, Causes and Consequences,* edited by Augustine et al. Cambridge, MA: Lincoln Institute of Land Policy. 51–68.

Haveman, Mark, and Terri A. Sexton (2008). "Property Tax Assessment Limits: Lessons from Thirty Years of Experience." Policy Focus Report, Cambridge, MA: Lincoln Institute of Land Policy.

Johnson, William A. (1962). "Industrial Tax Exemptions: Sound Investment of Foolish Giveaway?" *Proceedings of the 55th Annual Conference on Taxation.* Washington, DC: National Tax Association. 421–437.

Kincaid, John, and Richard L. Cole (2001). "Changing Public Attitudes on Power and Taxation in the American Federal System." *Publius: The Journal of Federalism* 31(3): 205–214.

Ladd, Helen (1994). "The Tax Expenditure Concept after 25 Years." Presidential address to the National Tax Association 86th Annual Conference on Taxation, Charleston, SC. Washington, DC: National Tax Association. 50–57.

Lynn, Arthur D. Jr. (1969). "Property-Tax Development: Selected Historical Perspectives." In *Property Taxation USA,* edited by Richard W. Lindholm. Madison: University of Wisconsin Press. 7–19.

McGuire, Therese J. (2001). "Alternatives to Property Taxation for Local Governments." In *Property Taxation and Local Government Finance,* edited by Wallace Oates. Cambridge, MA: Lincoln Institute of Land Policy. 301–314.

Minnesota Taxpayers Association (2010). *50-State Property Tax Comparison Study: Payable Year 2009.*

National Conference of State Legislatures (1992). *Principles of a High-Quality State Revenue System.* 2nd ed. Washington, DC: NCSL.

Oates, Wallace (2001). "Property Taxation and Local Government Finance." In *Property Taxation and Local Government Finance,* edited by Wallace Oates. Cambridge, MA: Lincoln Institute of Land Policy. 21–31.

O'Sullivan, Arthur, Terri A. Sexton, and Steven M. Sheffrin. 1994. "Differential Burdens from the Assessment Provisions of Proposition 13." *National Tax Journal* XLVII(4): 721–729.

———. 1995. *Property Taxes and Tax Revolts: The Legacy of Proposition 13.* New York: Cambridge University Press.

Pomp, Richard (2002). "The Collision between Nonprofits and Cities over the Property Tax: Possible Solutions." In *Property Tax Exemption for Charities*, edited by Evelyn Brody. Washington, DC: Urban Institute Press. 383–391.

Sexton, Terri (2003). *Property Tax Systems in the United States: The Tax Base, Exemptions, Incentives, and Relief.* Center for State and Local Taxation, Institute for Governmental Affairs, University of California-Davis, unpublished report, http://iga.ucdavis.edu/Research/CSLT/Publications/PropTaxUS.pdf.

Sexton, Terri A. (2008, October 6). "Proposition 13 and Residential Mobility." *State Tax Notes*: 29.

Sexton, Terri A. (2009). "Assessment Limits as a Means of Limiting Homeowner Property Taxes." In *Erosion of the Property Tax Base: Trends, Causes and Consequences*, edited by Augustine et al. Cambridge, MA: Lincoln Institute of Land Policy. 117–142.

Sexton, Terri, and Steven M. Sheffrin (1995, December 18). "Five Lessons from the Tax Revolts." *State Tax Notes*: 1763–1768.

Sheffrin, Steven (1999, December 14). "Interview: Steven M. Sheffrin on the Worst Tax, Local Options and Proposition 13." *State Tax Notes*: 1721–1723.

Sokolow, Alvin D. (1998). "The Changing Property Tax and State and Local Relations." *Publius: The Journal of Federalism* 28 (Winter): 165–187.

Stiglitz, Joseph E. (1988). *Economics of the Public Sector.* 2nd ed. New York: W. W. Norton.

Strauss, Robert (2001, June 4). "Pennsylvania's Local Property Tax." *State Tax Notes*: 1963–1983.

Tannenwald, Robert (2002, September). "Are State and Local Revenue Systems Becoming Obsolete?" *National Tax Journal* 55(3): 467–489.

US Census Bureau (2006). *Federal, State, and Local Governments, 2006 Government Finance and Employment Classification Manual: Part 2. Government Finance Statistics.*

Wallis, John Joseph (2001). "A History of the Property Tax in America." In *Property Taxation and Local Government Finance*, edited by Wallace Oates. Cambridge, MA: Lincoln Institute of Land Policy. 123–147.

Wassmer, Robert W. (2009). "Property Tax Abatement as a Means of Promoting State and Local Economic Activity." In *Property Taxation and Local Government Finance*, edited by Augustine et al. Cambridge, MA: Lincoln Institute of Land Policy. 221–259.

Witte, John F. (2009). "The Politics of the Property Tax Base." In *Property Taxation and Local Government Finance*, edited by Augustine et al. Cambridge, MA: Lincoln Institute of Land Policy. 307–334.

Wolman, Harold, Robert McManmon, Michael E. Bell, and David Brunori (2010). "Comparing Local Government Autonomy across States." In *The Property Tax and Local Autonomy*, edited by Bell et al. Cambridge, MA: Lincoln Institute of Land Policy. 69–119.

Yuan, Bing, Joseph Cordes, David Brunori, and Michael E. Bell (2009). "Tax and Expenditure Limitations and Local Public Finances." In *Property Taxation and Local Government Finance*, edited by Augustine et al. Cambridge, MA: Lincoln Institute of Land Policy. 149–191.

CHAPTER 12

STATE PERSONAL INCOME TAXES

JOSEPH J. CORDES
AND JASON N. JUFFRAS

THE personal income tax is now 101 years old. Wisconsin was the first jurisdiction to adopt the tax (also known as the "individual income tax") in 1911. Levied on a broad base of wages and salaries, dividends, interest, and other income, the personal income tax added $304.6 billion to state and local coffers in 2008, or 15.7 percent of own-source revenue. Property taxes represent the most important source of state and local government revenue ($409.7 billion, or 23.1 percent of state and local own-source revenue in 2008).[1] The personal income tax barely eked out second place over the general sales tax, which generated $304.4 billion (15.7 percent) of own-source revenue for state and local governments in 2008. The corporate income tax is much smaller, with receipts totaling only $57.8 billion (3 percent) of state and local own-source revenue that same year.[2]

A MAINSTAY OF STATE
GOVERNMENT FINANCE

As a component of the US state and local revenue systems, the personal income tax is primarily a revenue source for states, which collected 91 percent ($278.4 billion) of state and local personal income tax revenue in 2008, the last year for which comparable data are available. The personal income tax generated the largest share of own-source revenue (26.1 percent) for states in 2008, surpassing the general sales tax, which raised $241 million (22.6 percent).[3]

A broad-based personal income tax is in effect in forty-one states. New Hampshire and Tennessee impose the personal income tax only on interest and dividend income, while seven states (Alaska, Florida, Nevada, South Dakota, Texas, Washington, and Wyoming) do not levy a personal income tax. The District

Table 12.1 State personal income-tax revenue as a percentage of total own-source revenue, 2008

State	Personal Income Tax (%)	State	Personal Income Tax (%)
Alabama	21.6%	Montana	24.4%
Alaska	0.0	Nebraska	29.8
Arizona	18.7	Nevada	0.0
Arkansas	22.9	New Hampshire	3.0
California	39.2	New Jersey	31.4
Colorado	34.6	New Mexico	12.9
Connecticut	42.3	New York	42.3
Delaware	19.3	North Carolina	37.3
Florida	0.0	North Dakota	9.3
Georgia	37.5	Ohio	26.4
Hawaii	21.4	Oklahoma	23.0
Idaho	30.2	Oregon	42.1
Illinois	25.5	Pennsylvania	23.3
Indiana	23.2	Rhode Island	25.4
Iowa	27.4	South Carolina	21.2
Kansas	29.4	South Dakota	0.0
Kentucky	24.5	Tennessee	1.7
Louisiana	20.2	Texas	0.0
Maine	29.9	Utah	26.6
Maryland	32.6	Vermont	18.1
Massachusetts	39.6	Virginia	35.2
Michigan	20.1	Washington	0.0
Minnesota	34.7	West Virginia	20.3
Mississippi	17.6	Wisconsin	31.7
Missouri	32.6	Wyoming	0.0

Source: US Bureau of the Census (2010).

of Columbia, which performs both state and local functions, also imposes a broad-based personal income tax but is classified as a local government by the US Census Bureau in its studies of government finances.[4]

Among the states with a broad-based personal income tax, the percentage of own-source revenue raised by the tax in 2008 varied from a low of 9.3 percent in North Dakota to a high of 42.3 percent in Connecticut and New York (see table 12.1).

A Minor Role in Local Government Finance

Local governments collected only $26.3 billion in personal income tax revenue in 2008, less than one-tenth the amount of state personal income tax revenue and a mere 3 percent of total own-source revenue for local governments.[5] For local governments, property taxes are the most important revenue source ($397 billion in 2008), followed by charges and user fees ($222.7 billion), sales and gross receipts taxes ($90.2 billion), and other taxes ($26.7 billion).[6] In fact, local governments in only twelve states recorded personal income tax revenue in 2008.[7]

Table 12.2 Percentage of local own-source revenue raised by the personal income tax in twelve states and the District of Columbia, 2008

State	Percentage (%) of Local Own-Source Revenue Raised by Personal Income Tax
Alabama	1.1
Delaware	4.3
District of Columbia	19.3
Indiana	3.7
Iowa	1.0
Kentucky	15.0
Maryland	27.1
Michigan	2.1
Missouri	2.5
New York	10.1
Ohio	13.4
Oregon	0.1
Pennsylvania	12.1

Source: US Bureau of the Census (2010).

Personal income tax rates imposed by local governments are usually low, often in the 1 to 2 percent range.[8] In 2008, the percentage of local own-source revenue generated by the personal income tax in the twelve states and the District of Columbia ranged from a minuscule 0.1 percent in Oregon to 27.1 percent in Maryland (see table 12.2). Although more than 4,000 local governments collect the income tax, approximately two-thirds are located in Pennsylvania.[9]

Most of the general-purpose local jurisdictions imposing personal income taxes are cities (such as Cleveland and Philadelphia) and townships, but school districts and counties in several states also levy personal income taxes.[10] In some cases, the taxes are structured as surcharges to the state income tax (as in the case of counties in Maryland), or as local earnings taxes (as in the case of Fayette and Jefferson counties in Kentucky). Several cities, such as Los Angeles, San Francisco, and Newark, New Jersey, impose gross earnings or wage taxes that are not classified as personal income taxes by the Census Bureau because they are paid by employers as a percentage of their total payroll, instead of being paid by employees.[11]

LONG-TERM STABILITY AS A REVENUE SOURCE

The personal income tax grew substantially as a source of state revenues during the 1960s and 1970s, largely due to the adoption of the tax by Michigan and Nebraska (1967), Illinois and Maine (1969), Ohio, Pennsylvania, and Rhode Island (1971), and New Jersey (1976). Since the 1980s, the personal income tax has been marked by long-term stability as a revenue source for state governments. Connecticut (1991) has been the only state to introduce a broad-based personal income tax since 1976. Looking at the three most recent recessions to isolate similar points in the economic cycle, one finds that the personal income tax inched up from 23.9 percent of state own-source revenue in 1992 to 25.5 percent in 2002 and 26.1 percent in 2008.[12] At the same time, the personal income tax remained almost unchanged as a minor source of local own-source revenue (2.9 percent in 1992 and 3 percent in 2008).[13]

MECHANICS OF THE STATE PERSONAL INCOME TAX

Most state personal income taxes are based on the federal personal income tax, largely for administrative simplicity. Twenty-eight of the states with a broad-based income tax, plus the District of Columbia, use the federal definition of adjusted gross income (AGI) as the starting point for determining tax liability.[14] AGI excludes most types of nonmonetary resources (such as employer-provided fringe benefits, unrealized capital gains, and the imputed rent on owner-occupied housing) as well as some types of money income such as welfare payments and interest on state and local government bonds. Another eight states use federal taxable income (AGI minus personal exemptions and deductions that are intended to reflect individual circumstances) as the starting point for computing personal income tax liability. States that base their tax liabilities on federal AGI or taxable income typically allow or require their own adjustments to income but the federal rules shape the tax structure. The other five states with a broad-based personal income tax use their own definitions of income and allowable adjustments.[15]

After calculating taxable income, tax filers must apply the relevant marginal tax rates and then subtract tax credits to determine their personal income tax liability. States face a tradeoff in conforming tax codes to federal definitions of adjusted gross income or taxable income. Both tax administrators and taxpayers benefit from the increased simplicity, which can also promote voluntary compliance and enforcement, but states also lose some control over policy choices and revenue levels if federal changes are automatically mirrored in state tax codes. Accordingly, during the past ten years, many states have decided to "decouple" from certain federal tax rules to avoid the revenue loss that would result from federal conformity.[16]

In 2010, thirty-four states and the District of Columbia had progressive personal income tax structures, in which the tax rate rises along with income; only seven states had flat rates that apply to all income.[17] Nevertheless, there is much variation in progressive rate structures. In some states, the top rate begins at a very low income level, meaning that almost all income is subject to a single rate. Alabama, where the top tax rate of 5 percent starts at an annual income level of $3,000 for a single filer, is one such example. By contrast, in California the top rate of 10.3 percent applies to annual income greater than $1,000,000. As will be discussed later, a number of states have moved in recent years to make their personal income tax systems more progressive, adding new top tax rates for high-income households.

PRINCIPLES OF TAXATION

From the standpoint of the traditional criteria used to judge revenue sources, individual income taxes generally get good, although somewhat mixed, marks. The important criteria include revenue elasticity, equity, efficiency, and administration.

Revenue Elasticity. Total personal income in the United States is now 13 trillion annually,[18] creating a strong revenue base for the personal income tax prior to exclusions, deductions, and credits. In addition, the tax provides an elastic revenue source if the rate structure is progressive, pushing taxpayers into higher tax brackets as the economy grows and income rises. The US Government Accountability Office found that state personal income taxes grew faster than income in all but four states between 1977 and 2007.[19]

Nevertheless, the elasticity of the personal income tax can be a double-edged sword during economic slowdowns because revenue yields tend to fall faster than economic activity, particularly if capital income represents a significant part of the state tax base. David Sjoquist, Andrew Stephenson, and Sally Wallace attributed increased volatility in the annual growth of state personal income tax revenue since 1996 to the increase in capital gains income. Capital gains almost tripled from 5.3 percent of personal income to 15 percent in 2000 before falling sharply at the end of the dot-com boom and then rising again during the subsequent economic recovery.[20]

Equity. Compared with sales and excise taxes, income taxes are not inherently regressive. Because income is considered a good measure of an individual's resources, the personal income tax directly incorporates the concept of ability to pay, facilitating both horizontal equity (treating taxpayers with similar levels of resources similarly) and vertical equity (treating taxpayers with different levels of resources differently). Not only does a broad-based personal income tax build in elements of tax progressivity (for example, by including capital income, which is concentrated among wealthy households), but the rate structure can also be designed to offset the regressivity of other state taxes such as those on consumer expenditures.

Efficiency. Because the income tax is a personal tax, it can be more readily adapted to varying individual or household circumstances.[21] Nevertheless, high marginal taxes may discourage work, savings, and investment, although most evidence suggests that the effect of taxes on labor supply is modest.[22]

Administration. Administration and compliance costs of the personal income tax, if not low, are modest because collection of the tax relies heavily on employer withholding and voluntary self-reporting by taxpayers. Nevertheless, individuals incur significant costs to maintain the necessary records and compute the amount of tax owed (or to hire a professional tax preparer). Administrative and compliance costs can be lowered by conforming the state income tax to the federal tax, although conformity also has the advantages and disadvantages discussed earlier. Enforcement costs also rise along with the complexity of the tax system and the associated exclusions, deductions, and credits.

Due to its importance as a revenue source and the way it can be tailored to meet the normative criteria of a "good" state revenue source, the personal income tax will clearly continue to play an important role in state and local public finance. Accordingly, the remainder of this chapter focuses on (1) how states that rely on the personal income tax have fared in the economic and fiscal crisis triggered by the Great Recession of 2007–2009, (2) changes that states have made in their personal income taxes in response to the crisis, and (3) possible challenges facing the state personal income tax in the coming decades.

STATE REVENUE PERFORMANCE DURING THE GREAT RECESSION

Has greater reliance on the state personal income tax placed states in greater jeopardy of a significant decline in state revenues during the Great Recession that began in December 2007 and officially ended in June 2009? The answer to this question is ambiguous. Donald Bruce, William F. Fox, and M. H. Tuttle found that state personal income taxes have an average long-run elasticity of 1.832, more than double that of state sales taxes (the other major source of state-tax revenue).[23] This suggests that the state personal income tax puts states at greater risk of significant revenue loss during periods of economic contraction. Nevertheless, Bruce, Fox, and Tuttle also point out that short-term patterns may differ from the long-term trend; they find that the short-run elasticities of both taxes are very similar when the tax base falls below its long-run "trend level."[24] As a result, their estimates "do not provide a firm conclusion as to whether the sales or the income tax is more volatile, with the conclusion depending upon the definition of volatility. The income tax has a higher long-run elasticity, but that...tells little about whether the growth path is volatile."[25]

An empirical analysis of the percentage decline in total state revenue between 2008 and 2009 and the percentage of state revenue that is raised from the personal income tax reveals no systematic relationship between reliance on the personal income tax, and the severity of overall declines in state revenue. The implication is that greater reliance on the personal income tax did not put states at greater jeopardy of a large drop in overall tax revenue during the recession.[26]

STATE POLICY CHANGES IN RESPONSE TO THE RECESSION

How did states with personal income taxes adapt to the fiscal pressures created by abruptly declining revenue during the Great Recession? To what extent did more reliance on the personal income tax facilitate or hinder the ability of states to make such adjustments? As the longest and deepest downturn since the Great Depression, the Great Recession provides an interesting case study of the personal income tax in a time of severe economic duress. The nationwide decline in employment during the recession was approximately three times the drop in the previous four recessions,[27] and at one point (the second quarter of 2009) state personal income tax revenue had fallen by 28 percent from the level of the prior year.[28]

When the Great Recession began in December 2007, states began cutting spending, increasing taxes, and drawing down reserves—a retrenchment that continued as of this writing in early 2011. Nevertheless, during 2008 several states such as New Mexico and Ohio continued to phase in multiyear reductions in the personal income tax that had been enacted in prior years, and several other states approved new reductions.[29] Maryland, which approved higher tax rates for upper-income households as well as a temporary top rate for millionaires, was the only state to implement personal income tax rate increases in 2008. Among all states, the net change in personal income taxes in 2008 due to legislative action was a reduction of $254.3 million—the only such reduction among all tax types.[30]

State policy regarding the personal income tax shifted sharply toward austerity in 2009, as budget gaps widened and fund balances fell. By the second quarter of 2009, total state tax collections had fallen almost 17 percent from the prior year.[31] States responded by raising personal income taxes by an estimated $11.4 billion, representing 40 percent of the total increase in state taxes in 2009.[32] The legislative changes included higher taxes on upper-income groups in eight states (Connecticut, Delaware, Hawaii, New Jersey, New York, North Carolina, Oregon, and Wisconsin), while California enacted an across-the-board increase and Ohio suspended the last phase of a tax reduction approved in 2005. The rate increases imposed by these states (along with the Maryland increases that took effect in 2008) are described in table 12.3.

The sharp change in policy between 2008 and 2009 suggests that governors and state legislators prefer to raise other taxes before increasing the personal income tax—perhaps due to the visibility of the tax—but will raise the tax when budget crises persist or worsen. The National Conference of State Legislatures (NCSL) finds that legislators often delay tax increases during a recession because they believe that upward tax adjustments may (1) harm consumers and businesses that are already seeing their real incomes decline due to the recession, (2) make policymakers seem insensitive to the economic distress of their constituents, and (3) be premature if a recession turns out to be short-lived or recovery seems imminent.[33]

As shown in table 12.4, state tax increases in 2008 were concentrated on the corporate income tax, which accounted for more than $2.3 billion (62 percent) of the net $3.8 billion in tax increases imposed by states that year.[34] Nevertheless, the corporate income tax base is too small to generate the revenue increases that many states decided were necessary in 2009; as a result, state policymakers turned to the two

Table 12.3 Increases in state personal income-tax rates since 2007

State	Statutory Change
California	0.25 percentage point increase in each tax bracket—tax years 2009 and 2010 only.
Connecticut	New top tax rate of 6.5% for income of $500,001 or more for single filers and $1,000,001 or more for joint filers. Previous top tax rate was 5%, applied to income of $10,001 or more for single filers and $20,001 or more for joint filers.
Delaware	Top tax rate, which applies to income greater than $60,000, rose from 5.95% to 6.95%.
Hawaii	Three new top tax brackets will apply through tax year 2015. For joint filers, the top rates will be 9% for income between $300,001 and $350,000; 10% for income between $350,001 and $400,000; and 11% for $400,001+. Previous top tax rate was 8.25% for joint filers with income over $48,000.
Maryland	New top rate was 6.25% on income greater than $1 million for tax years 2008 through 2010. Maryland also added three new permanent brackets. For joint filers, the new rates are 5% on income from $200,001 to $350,000; 5.25% on income from $350,001 to $500,000; and 5.5% on income from $500,001 to $1 million. The previous top rate was 4.75 percent on income over $3,000.
New Jersey	For tax year 2009, two new top brackets were 10.25% on income from $500,001 to $1 million and 10.75% on income over $1 million. The tax rate was also raised from 6.37% to 8% for taxpayers with income from $400,001 to $500,000. New Jersey repealed the higher rates for tax year 2010, reverting to a top tax rate of 8.97% on income greater than $500,000. The second-highest bracket of 6.37% applies to income from $75,001 to $500,000.
New York	Two new top brackets will apply through tax year 2011. The tax rate will be 7.85% for single filers with income above $200,000 and joint filers with incomes above $300,000, and the top rate will be 8.97% for all filers with income above $500,000. Previous top tax rate was 6.85% for single filers with income over $20,000 and joint filers with income over $40,000.
North Carolina	Temporary surcharge on upper-income taxpayers for tax years 2009 and 2010. The surcharge is 2% of tax liability for single filers with income from $60,001 to $150,000 and joint filers with income from $100,001 to $250,000. The surcharge is 3% for single filers with income above $150,000 and joint filers with income above $250,000. The top marginal tax rate would be 7.98 percent as a result of the surcharge.
Oregon	Two new top brackets will apply for tax years 2010 and 2011. Joint filers will pay 10.8% on income from $250,001 to $500,000, and 11% on income over $500,000. After 2011, the top rate will drop to 9.9% for income above $250,000. The previous top tax rate was 9% on all income over $15,200.
Wisconsin	The new top tax bracket applies 7.75% tax to single filers with incomes above $225,000 and joint filers with income over $300,000.

Sources: National Conference of State Legislatures (2009); National Conference of State Legislatures (2010); National Conference of State Legislatures (2011a); Wisconsin Legislative Fiscal Bureau (2011).

Table 12.4 Net revenue change from legislative action, 2008–2010 (millions of dollars and percentage of total changes)

Tax	2008		2009		2010	
Personal Income	−$254.3	−6.6%	$11.406.1	39.9%	−$656.4	−16.6%
Corporate Income	2,347.0	61.7	2,014.5	7.0	494.3	12.5
Sales and Use	688.9	18.1	7,236.5	25.3	1,736.5	43.9
Health Care	237.2	6.2	2,535.4	8.9	1,298.1	32.8
Tobacco	464.0	12.2	1,898.2	6.6	602.7	15.2
Alcoholic Beverage	141.1	3.7	192.6	0.7	34.2	0.9
Motor Fuel/Excise	35.4	0.9	1,871.2	6.5	48.2	1.2
Miscellaneous	144.1	3.8	1,434.1	5.0	401.8	10.1
Total	3,803.4	100.0	28,588.2	100.0	3,959.4	100.0

Sources: National Conference of State Legislatures (2009), 3; National Conference of State Legislatures (2010), 3; and National Conference of State Legislatures (2011a), 3.

taxes with the largest bases—the personal income tax and the general sales tax—to help close budget gaps. During 2010, when the net tax increase imposed by states dropped sharply once again, states provided a net reduction of personal income taxes of $656.4 million at the same time that all other taxes were being raised. This pattern is consistent with a longer-term trend identified by NCSL—namely that "increases in the personal income tax spike more decisively in response to recessions than increases in the sales tax, which tend to be more spread out over more years."[35]

A Shift Toward more Progressive Taxation

Although the income tax increases implemented during 2008 and 2009 are clustered among northeastern (Connecticut, Delaware, Maryland, New Jersey, and New York) and western states (California, Hawaii, and Oregon), they may reflect a shift among an important subgroup of states toward a more progressive income tax structure. Between 1988 and 2008, state personal income tax structures became flatter: fourteen states and the District of Columbia reduced their top rates, and Utah replaced its graduated income tax with a flat tax. In some cases, the reductions were sharp: Connecticut reduced its top rate from 12 percent to 5 percent;

Montana dropped its top rate from 11 percent to 6.9 percent, and North Dakota slashed its top rate from 12 percent to 5.54 percent.[36] Now the pendulum appears to be moving back. One reason why is that the federal government in effect subsidizes state personal income taxes by allowing an itemized deduction for state and local taxes paid; for some taxpayers this federal deductibility reduces the effective cost of a state tax increase by the amount of the tax paid multiplied by the taxpayer's federal marginal tax bracket rate.[37]

In 2007, no state exceeded the 10 percent threshold for its top income tax rate; by 2011, three states had breached that level: California (10.55 percent), Hawaii (11 percent), and Oregon (11 percent). Oregon's top rate is scheduled to drop back to 9.9 percent after tax year 2011 and Hawaii's top rate is scheduled to revert to 8.25 percent after tax year 2015, but states may find it difficult to roll back higher income tax rates. As discussed later, state personal income tax systems will be under increased pressure in coming years if significant percentages of retirement income are excluded from the tax base and policymakers continue to use exclusions, exemptions, credits, and other tax preferences as a favorite tool of economic and social policy. Without expanding the base, states may need to maintain graduated tax rates with higher top rates. (New Jersey, however, provides a counterexample. In 2010, New Jersey policymakers allowed a temporary top tax rate of 10.75 percent

Table 12.5 State thresholds for the top income-tax bracket, 2007 and 2011 (single filers in states with a top threshold > $100,000)

State	2007 Threshold	2011 Threshold
Arizona	$150,000	$150,000
California	$1,000,000	$1,000,000
Connecticut	$10,000	$500,000
Hawaii	$48,000	$200,000
Maryland	$3,000	$500,000
New Jersey	$500,000	$500,000
New York	$20,000	$500,000
North Carolina	$120,000	$150,000
North Dakota	$336,550	$379,150
Ohio	$200,000	$201,800
Oregon	$6,850	$250,000
Rhode Island	$336,550	$125,000
Vermont	$336,550	$379,150
Wisconsin	$137,410	$224,210

Sources: Urban-Brookings Tax Policy Center (2011b); Tax Foundation (2011).

to expire, despite efforts to extend the tax. Therefore, the top rate dropped back to the previous level of 8.97 percent.)

Also striking is the extent to which states have created new top tax brackets at much higher income levels. In 2000, only two states (Arizona and Ohio) started their top marginal tax rate for single filers at incomes over $100,000; in 2011, by 2011 twelve other states joined Arizona and Ohio (California, Connecticut, Hawaii, Maryland, New Jersey, New York, North Carolina, North Dakota, Oregon, Rhode Island, Vermont, and Wisconsin).[38] Nor have the increases in the top rate threshold been modest, predictable amounts that would arise from inflation and economic growth; most of the changes have been almost exponential. For the states with a top tax bracket that begins over $100,000, table 12.5 shows the changes in the top tax threshold between 2007 and 2011.

Expansion of the Earned Income Tax Credit

Another source of progressivity in state personal income tax systems is the earned income tax credit (EITC), which is usually provided to low- and moderate-income families with earned income as a percentage of the federal EITC. The amount of the EITC rises with income until it reaches a maximum, and it then is phased out at income levels that are adjusted for family size.[39] State EITCs have grown steadily since Rhode Island enacted the first one in 1986, and they are now offered by twenty-three states and the District of Columbia,[40] up from fifteen states and DC in 2005.[41] Thus, the EITC is now offered in a majority of states with a broad-based personal income tax.

State EITCs generally maintained strong political support during the recent recession. In fact, elected officials sometimes used an EITC expansion to soften the impact of tax increases on low-income households and make their tax plans more palatable politically.[42] Indiana, Kansas, New Mexico, and North Carolina increased existing credits. Although Michigan and Wisconsin scaled back their EITCs in 2011, Connecticut authorized a state EITC equal to 25 percent of the federal credit. Several localities, including Denver, New York City, San Francisco, and Montgomery County, Maryland, also offer local supplements to the EITC.

Table 12.6 shows the amount of each state EITC and whether it is refundable. Almost all of the EITCs (nineteen states and the District of Columbia) are fully refundable (as is the federal EITC). Credit levels vary widely, from 3.5 percent in Louisiana to 40 percent in the District of Columbia.

Despite the EITC's steady growth, state adoption patterns remain uneven. Most midwestern states (Iowa, Illinois, Indiana, Kansas, Michigan, Minnesota, Nebraska,

Table 12.6 State EITCs, 2011

State	Percentage of Federal Credit	Refundability
Connecticut	25	Refundable
Delaware	20	Nonrefundable
District of Columbia	40	Refundable
Illinois	5	Refundable
Indiana	9	Refundable
Iowa	7	Refundable
Kansas	18	Refundable
Louisiana	3.5	Refundable
Maine	5	Nonrefundable
Maryland	25	Refundable (option)
Massachusetts	15	Refundable
Michigan	6 (as of January 1, 2012)	Refundable
Minnesota	33 (average)	Refundable
Nebraska	10	Refundable
New Jersey	20	Refundable
New Mexico	10	Refundable
New York	30	Refundable
North Carolina	5	Refundable
Oklahoma	5	Refundable
Oregon	6	Refundable
Rhode Island	25	Partially Refundable
Vermont	32	Refundable
Virginia	20	Nonrefundable
Wisconsin	4—one child 11—two children 34—three children	Refundable

Notes: Iowa has decoupled from federal EITC policy changes included by the American Recovery and Reinvestment Act of 2009. Those provisions added a third schedule of benefits for families with three or more children and increased the benefits for married couples with children. Thus, Iowa uses the "pre-2009" federal EITC structure to calculate the benefits provided by the state EITC.
Maryland allows taxpayers to choose between a 25 percent refundable credit and a 50 percent nonrefundable credit. Minnesota bases its credit on a percentage of earned income, rather than as a percentage of the federal credit. Rhode Island refunds 15 percent of the amount by which the EITC exceeds taxable income.
Sources: Tax Credits for Working Families (2011); Williams, Johnson, and Shure (2010); Internet sites of state departments of revenue.

and Wisconsin) and northeastern states (Connecticut, Maine, Massachusetts, New Jersey, New York, Rhode Island, and Vermont) offer an EITC, whereas adoption has been limited to New Mexico in the Mountain states and to Louisiana, North Carolina, and Virginia in the South. EITCs in the Southern states are either small (3.5 percent in Louisiana and 5 percent in North Carolina) or nonrefundable (Virginia).

Continued Pressure on the Tax Base: The Case of Tax Expenditures

The other option for increasing tax revenue in response to a shrinking base is to broaden the base of what is taxed. While some states increased their personal income tax rates during the Great Recession, particularly on high-income taxpayers, they did not make significant efforts to broaden their definitions of income or to curtail tax expenditures, which are defined as special exclusions, exemptions, deductions, credits, or deferrals that depart from the general tax structure. Jane Gravelle observed that "tax expenditures may, in effect, be viewed as spending programs channeled through the tax system."[43]

Tax expenditure reports, which are periodically issued by most states to estimate the revenue loss resulting from tax preferences, indicate that policymakers continue to rely on these preferences as a tool of economic and social policy.[44] Oregon, which prepares a particularly detailed tax expenditure report, has identified 184 personal income tax expenditures resulting from federal income tax conformity or state law, resulting in a revenue loss that could exceed $10 billion for the FY 2011–2013 period.[45] Similarly, the District of Columbia has itemized 102 personal income tax expenditures resulting from federal tax conformity and 26 personal income tax expenditures authorized by local law.[46] The District of Columbia absorbed a revenue loss of approximately $700 million from the federal conformity provisions and $90 million from local personal income tax expenditures during FY 2010.[47] (Estimates of the total cost of tax expenditures are inevitably rough because there are interaction effects among the different provisions.) California's Commission on the 21st Century Economy estimated that total personal income tax expenditures equaled approximately 60 percent of personal income tax collections.[48]

Rhode Island can be singled out for undertaking significant reform of its personal income tax since 2007. Effective in tax year 2011, the new structure reduces the number of tax brackets from five to three and drops the top income tax rate (which applies to taxable income of more than $125,000) from 9.9 percent to 5.99 percent. Rhode Island was able to lower its personal income tax by broadening the base. Policymakers eliminated itemized deductions and repealed several credits. In addition, Rhode Island also opted to tax capital gains as ordinary income, regardless of how long an asset has been held.[49] Although Rhode Island increased its standard deduction, it is now phased out for incomes over $175,000.

Nationwide, measures to broaden the personal income tax base appear to have been roughly offset by the expansion of exclusions, deductions, and credits, as described below. Several states broadened their definitions of taxable income and curbed tax expenditures by decoupling from federal tax breaks, reducing capital gains exclusions, capping various deductions, and taxing income from legalized gambling, but these efforts were fairly sporadic. Table 12.7 describes selected state policies enacted since 2007 to broaden the tax base.

Despite large drops in state tax revenues, a number of states continued to create and expand tax subsidies, particularly for health insurance, military pay, retirement income, and energy conservation. Table 12.8 summarizes selected state policies enacted since 2007 to expand tax exclusions, deductions, and credits.

Table 12.7 Selected state policies to broaden the personal income-tax base, 2008–2010

Policy	State Action
Federal Decoupling	Alabama—decoupled from bonus depreciation and section 179 expensing provisions of the federal Economic Stimulus Act of 2008 Oklahoma—decoupled from bonus depreciation and section 179 expensing provisions in the federal Economic Stimulus Act of 2008, and from net operating loss, motor vehicle excise tax deduction, and increased unemployment benefits exemption in the American Recovery and Reinvestment Act of 2009 Oregon—decoupled from section 179 business expensing provision of the American Recovery and Reinvestment Act of 2009 Vermont—decoupled from bonus depreciation provisions of the federal Economic Stimulus Act of 2008
Exemption Limits	Hawaii—limited itemized deductions for high-income taxpayers, using federal phase-out rules New York—limited itemized deductions for high-income taxpayers Oregon—phased out deduction for state and local taxes Vermont—capped deductions for state and local taxes at $5,000
Capital Gains	Rhode Island—taxed capital gains as ordinary income Vermont—limited capital gains deduction to 40% of federal taxable income Wisconsin—reduced capital gains exclusion from 60% of net long-term gain to 30%
Taxation of Legalized Gambling	Delaware—imposed tax on lottery winnings New Hampshire—imposed tax on gambling winnings New Jersey—applied income tax to lottery winnings over $10,000

Sources: National Conference of State Legislatures (2009); National Conference of State Legislatures (2010); National Conference of State Legislatures (2011a); Internet sites of state revenue departments.

Table 12.8 Selected state policies to expand tax preferences, 2008–2010

Policy	State Action
Health Insurance	Alabama—allowed small businesses to deduct 50% of health insurance premiums paid for employees who earn less than $50,000 per year, and allowed employees who earn less than $50,000 per year to deduct 50% of their health insurance premiums. Georgia—authorized deduction for high-deductible health savings account premiums Utah—provided a nonrefundable credit for contributions to medical savings accounts and certain amounts paid for insurance by those who lack employer-provided coverage for themselves or their families.
Military Pay	Minnesota—created a nonrefundable credit for veterans with twenty years of service or a service-related total and permanent disability; increased a refundable credit for active military service in a combat zone from $59 to $120 per month; and authorized a military pay subtraction for military pay that is not already exempt. Ohio—exempted military pay to surviving spouses. Oklahoma—provided a 100% deduction for salary of active military Wisconsin—expanded eligibility for the veterans' and surviving spouse property-tax credit (which is provided through the income tax)
Retirement Income	Kansas—established an income tax credit to offset property taxes for certain low-income senior citizens Ohio—exempted military retirement pay from the income tax Wisconsin—exempted Social Security benefits from taxation and authorized a deduction of up to $5,000 of income from a qualified retirement plan or an individual retirement account for taxpayers with federal AGI less than $15,000 (single) or $30,000 (joint)
Energy and Environment	Arizona—created a renewable energy companies credit Georgia—authorized credits for installation of clean energy equipment and systems Iowa—provided wind energy production tax credits South Carolina—introduced a 25% nonrefundable credit for the production and distribution of alternative fuels
Earned Income Tax Credit	Indiana—repealed EITC sunset date and increased credit from 6% to 9% Kansas—increased the EITC from 17% to 18% for 2010–2012 New Jersey—increased EITC from 20% in 2007 to 22.5% in 2008, and to 25% in 2009. The EITC returned to the 20% level in 2010 New Mexico—increased EITC from 8% to 10% North Carolina—increased EITC from 3.5% to 5%

Sources: National Conference of State Legislatures (2009); National Conference of State Legislatures (2010); National Conference of State Legislatures (2011a); Internet sites of state revenue departments.

IMPLICATIONS OF AN AGING
POPULATION FOR THE TAX BASE

States have not adjusted their personal income tax systems to reflect the aging of the population; in fact, considerable evidence suggests that state policy changes will make their tax systems *more* vulnerable to revenue losses as the population ages.[50] The growing elderly population will present states with increased service demands, particularly for health care, while much of the income flowing to the elderly—not only Social Security, but also civil service and private pension income—is more likely to be exempt from state personal income taxes.

The Census Bureau has projected that the percentage of the US population aged sixty-five or older will grow by half between 2010 and 2030, from 13 percent to 19.3 percent.[51] The aging of the baby boomers will also result in a near-doubling in the percentage of the very old—those aged eighty-five and over—from 2.3 percent to 4 percent of the population between 2030 and 2050.[52]

In a 2006 study, the Iowa Department of Revenue examined the implications of the aging population for the state tax system. The department concluded that "the amount of individual income tax revenue the State will collect may be expected to decline as the State's population ages.... If future taxpayers have similar individual income tax liabilities as taxpayers of the same age as for 2003 the total amount of tax revenue generated from this source will top out in about 2015."[53]

Two factors explain this outcome. First, average income falls with age, resulting in a lower revenue yield as the population ages. In Iowa, average gross income in 2003 fell steadily from a peak of $77,019 among fifty-five- to sixty-four-year-olds to $50,379 for sixty-five- to seventy-four-year-olds, $41,940 for seventy-five- to eighty-four-year-olds, and $32,002 for those over eighty-five.[54] Second, for older Iowans the sources of income shifted sharply away from wages and toward interest, dividends, capital gains, private pensions, and Social Security income. The latter forms of income are more likely to be tax exempt. The Iowa Department of Revenue found that 37.2 percent of income reported by sixty-five- to seventy-four-year-olds is subject to exclusion thresholds, compared to only 10 percent of the income reported by the fifty-five- to sixty-four-year-olds.[55]

Similar challenges likely await most states as the population ages, because preferential treatment of Social Security and other retirement income is common among the states. Ronald Snell identified two primary approaches to the taxation of pension income among states: some states provide specific exclusions for particular types of pension income (such as civil service and military pensions), while others provide a blanket exclusion that applies both to civil service and private pensions, as well as Social Security in some cases. Among states with broad-based personal income taxes, ten exclude all federal, state, and local government pension income from taxation, while eleven states and the District of Columbia provide partial exclusions. In addition, twenty states provide a fixed exemption that applies to most sources of retirement income.[56] Some states also offer tiered exemptions for different age groups, such as fifty-five- to sixty-four-year-olds, and those sixty-five and over. Although sixteen states provide no exemption for private pension income, Mississippi and Pennsylvania allow a complete exemption.

States largely exempt Social Security benefits from taxation, departing from federal policy in which as much as 85 percent of benefits are taxable based on a measure known as "provisional income."[57] Among the forty-one states with a broad-based personal income tax, twenty-seven provide a total exemption for Social Security benefits (as does the District of Columbia), while only seven states conform to the federal rules. The other seven states have created their own rules for taxing Social Security benefits, shielding more income from taxation than the federal government does in at least six of those states.[58] The exemptions for Social Security income mean that states are leaving most of the $168.1 billion in federally taxable Social Security benefits (2008 data) out of their personal income tax bases.[59]

Even as the population ages and poverty among the elderly remains the lowest of all age groups, states continue to expand tax preferences for the elderly. The most recent example is Wisconsin, which exempted all Social Security benefits from the personal income tax beginning in tax year 2008; prior to that time, Wisconsin taxed as much as 50 percent of Social Security benefits. Beginning in tax year 2009, Wisconsin also authorized deductions of private pension income for low-income residents. Both Missouri and Iowa are also phasing out the taxation of Social Security benefits, which will be fully exempt from state personal income tax in tax year 2012 for Missouri and tax year 2014 for Iowa.

Georgia provides an example of how growing tax preferences for the elderly (or any other group) can slowly but steadily erode state personal income tax bases. Researchers at Georgia State University estimated that the foregone revenue from tax exemptions for the elderly would rise tenfold, from $15.8 million in 2000 to $165.4 million in 2010, due largely to an increase in the retirement income exemption from $13,000 to $35,000 during that period.[60] For the 2005 to 2015 period, Barbara Edwards and Sally Wallace projected that tax preferences for the elderly would lead to annual reductions in state personal income tax between 0.11 percent (New York) and 4.81 percent (Georgia) in the ten largest states.[61] Although the lost revenue appears relatively small, the reduction in revenue capacity makes it more difficult for states to weather difficult economic times and the drop in revenue could grow over time.

STATE TREATMENT OF CAPITAL GAINS INCOME

Approximately two-thirds of the states with broad-based personal income taxes (twenty-seven states plus the District of Columbia) conform to the federal definition of capital gains as ordinary income, with minor exceptions in some states

for in-state investments or industries. Nevertheless, several states provide preferences for capital gains, most notably Arkansas and North Dakota (which exclude
30 percent of long-term capital gains) and South Carolina (which excludes
44 percent of long-term gains). Changes in state treatment of capital gains income
can be expected to have significant effects on the size of state personal income tax
bases because capital gains have become a larger share of total income over the long
term despite their considerable short-term volatility. Between 1981 and 2005, wages
and salaries (which account for approximately two-thirds of federal adjusted gross
income) grew at an annual rate of 2.4 percent while capital gains grew at an annual
rate of 6.3 percent.[62]

Capital gains taxation also has major implications for the distribution of taxes.
As a percentage of federal AGI (which serves as a proxy for the total state personal
income tax base in the absence of comprehensive state-by-state data on the components of the tax base), capital gains and dividend income rises from 1.7 percent
of income for taxpayers with AGI of $50,000 to $99,999, to 12.9 percent for taxpayers with AGI of $500,000 to $999,999, and 47.5 percent for taxpayers with AGI of
$10,000,000 or more.[63] The data attest that the capital gains preference reduces the
overall progressivity state personal income tax systems.

IMPLICATIONS OF FEDERAL AND STATE
PERSONAL INCOME TAX CONFORMITY

As noted earlier, states have virtually complete flexibility in defining the personal
income tax base. Over time, many states have decided to conform all or a part
of their tax base to the base of the federal income tax. "Automatic conformity"
(also known as "rolling" conformity) means that a state automatically adopts
provisions of the US Internal Revenue Code (IRC) as they are enacted; no legislative or administrative action is necessary. "Fixed conformity" means that the
state adopts the provisions of the IRC as of a specific date. Fixed-conformity states
must periodically take legislative action to align the state tax code with the IRC.
Finally, "selective conformity" means that a state adopts only specified provisions
of the IRC. The state rules on federal personal income tax conformity are shown
in table 12.9.

Some analysts have viewed decisions by states to conform their income-tax
bases to federal rules as a form of tax-base erosion, presumably because conformity incorporates federal departures from a comprehensive tax base into the state
tax system. Nevertheless, there is no statistical evidence that states with personal
income taxes that were in "full conformity" with the federal tax base experienced
larger drops in income-tax revenues than states that were not. Among states that

Table 12.9 Conformity of state personal income-tax bases to federal-income-tax base

	Social Security Income	Private Pension Income Exemption	Capital Gains
Federal Rule	Two-tier system in which 50% of provisional income above $25,000/single and $32,000/married is taxed, and 85% of income above $34,000/single and $44,000/married is taxed.	States cannot tax railroad retirement benefits, but other private pension income is taxable.	For gains held more than one year, capital gains tax is 15% for those whose marginal tax rate is 25% or more. Capital gains tax is 0% for those in 10% and 15% tax brackets. Net capital losses are deductible up to $3,000/yr., and unused capital losses can be carried forward.

State	Federal Conformity	Social Security Income	Private Pension Income Exemption	Capital Gains
Alabama	Automatic	Exempt	Defined Benefit Payments Exempt	Modified[8]
Arizona	Fixed	Exempt	None	Federal
Arkansas	Selective	Exempt	$6,000	Modified[9]
California	Selective	Exempt	None	Federal
Colorado	Automatic	Modified[1]	$20,000 (55–64)/ $24,000 (65+)	Federal[10]
Connecticut	Automatic	Modified[2]	None	Federal[10]
Delaware	Automatic	Exempt	$2,000 (under 60)/$12,500 (60+)	Federal
District of Columbia	Automatic	Exempt	None	Federal

(Continued)

Table 12.9 Continued

		Social Security Income	Private Pension Income Exemption	Capital Gains
Georgia	Fixed	Exempt	$35,000	Federal
Hawaii	Fixed	Exempt	Exempt if Employer-Funded	Own System[11]
Idaho	Fixed	Exempt	None	Federal[10]
Illinois	Automatic	Exempt	Exempt for Employer-Funded or Self-Employed Plans	Federal
Indiana	Fixed	Exempt	None	Federal
Iowa	Fixed	Modified[3]	$6,000 (single)/$12,000 (joint)	Modified[12]
Kansas	Automatic	Modified[4]	None	Federal[10]
Kentucky	Fixed	Exempt	$41,110	Federal[10]
Louisiana	Automatic	Exempt	$6,000	Federal
Maine	Fixed	Exempt	$6,000 minus Social Security and Railroad Retirement Benefits	Federal[10]
Maryland	Automatic	Exempt	$24,500	Federal
Massachusetts	Automatic	Exempt	None	Own System[13]
Michigan	Fixed	Exempt	$45,120 (single)/$90,240 (joint)	Modified[14]
Minnesota	Fixed	Federal	None	Federal[10]
Mississippi	Selective	Exempt	Exempt	Federal

Missouri	Automatic	Modified[5]	$6,000	Modified[15]
Montana	Automatic	Modified[6]	$3,600 for Income < $30,000	Modified[16]
Nebraska	Automatic	Federal	None	Federal[10]
New Jersey	Selective	Exempt	$15,000 (single)/$25,000 (joint)	Federal[10]
New Mexico	Automatic	Federal	None	Modified[17]
New York	Automatic	Exempt	$20,000	Federal
North Carolina	Fixed	Exempt	$2,000	Federal[10]
North Dakota	Automatic	Federal	None	Modified[18]
Ohio	Fixed	Exempt	$200 credit	Federal[10]
Oklahoma	Automatic	Exempt	$10,000	Federal[10]
Oregon	Fixed	Exempt	9% Credit for Low-Income	Federal[10]
Pennsylvania	Selective	Exempt	Exempt	Modified[19]
Rhode Island	Automatic	Federal	None	Federal
South Carolina	Fixed	Exempt	$3,000 (under 65)/$10,000 (65+)	Modified[20]
Utah	Automatic	Modified[7]	Retirement Credit of $450 (Income-Tested)	Federal[10]
Vermont	Fixed	Federal	None	Modified[21]
Virginia	Fixed	Exempt	None	Federal[10]

(Continued)

Table 12.9 Continued

		Social Security Income	Private Pension Income Exemption	Capital Gains
West Virginia	Fixed	Federal	None	Federal
Wisconsin	Fixed	Exempt	$5,000 for 65+ (Income-Tested)	Modified[22]

Sources: Federation of Tax Administrators (2011a); Internet sites of state revenue departments; Wisconsin Legislative Fiscal Bureau (2011).

[1] Colorado exempts up to $20,000 of federally taxable Social Security benefits and pension income for individuals aged fifty-five to sixty-four, and up to $24,000 for those who are sixty-five and older.

[2] Connecticut exempts Social Security benefits from taxation for those with income below $50,000 (single filers) or $60,000 (joint filers or heads or household); federal rules apply above those thresholds.

[3] Iowa is phasing out the taxation of Social Security benefits, which will be exempt from state personal income taxation in tax year 2014. In tax year 2010, Iowa taxed only 22.5 percent of Social Security benefits.

[4] Kansas does not tax Social Security benefits for taxpayers with adjusted gross income less than or equal to $75,000. Federal rules apply above that threshold.

[5] Missouri exempts 65 percent of federally taxable Social Security benefits, subject to income limits.

[6] Montana taxes Social Security benefits for taxpayers with income above $25,000 (single filers) or $32,000 (joint filers), but uses a different measure of income than is used for federal taxation of Social Security benefits.

[7] Utah provides a retirement income tax credit for private pension and Social Security benefits. The credit is phased out at income limits beginning at $25,000 (single filers) and $32,000 (joint filers).

[8] In Alabama, all capital gains are taxable and all capital losses are deductible in the year incurred.

[9] Arkansas excludes up to 30 percent of long-term capital gains.

[10] State conforms to the federal rules with a very minor exception or exceptions, such as excluding gains from in-state investments or industries.

[11] Hawaii imposes an alternative tax on capital gains.

[12] Iowa provides a 100 percent exclusion for qualifying capital gains on business assets.

[13] Massachusetts imposes separate personal income tax rates on capital gains, ranging from 5.3 percent to 12 percent.

[14] Michigan allows persons age sixty-five and over to exempt up to $10,058 in interest, dividends, and capital gains.

[15] Missouri allows a 25 percent exclusion for certain sales of low-income housing.

[16] Montana allows a 40 percent exclusion for installment sales entered into before 1987, and gains from certain small business investment companies are exempt.

[17] New Mexico allows taxpayers to deduct the greater of 50 percent or $1,000 of federally taxable capital gains.

[18] North Dakota excludes 30 percent of net long-term gains.

[19] In Pennsylvania, all capital gains are taxable and all capital losses are deductible in the year incurred, with certain limitations for taxpayers who are married and filing jointly.

[20] South Carolina offers a 44 percent exclusion for long-term capital gains (held more than one year).

[21] Vermont allows an exemption for the first $2,500 of eligible capital gains.

[22] Wisconsin permits an exclusion of 60 percent for farm assets and 30 percent of other assets held for more than one year. The deduction for net capital losses is limited to $500. Gains from qualified small business stock and family business sales are also excluded.

experienced declines in income-tax revenue between 2008 and 2009,
percentage decline among states listed as conforming automatically in
equaled twelve percentage points, while the mean percentage decline ar
without automatic conformity equaled fifteen percentage points. The d.....
means was not statistically significant.

STATE PERSONAL INCOME TAX FEATURES
AND THE GREAT RECESSION

The following tables present the results of simple regressions that explore the roles
of several factors discussed above on the performance of state personal income
taxes during the Great Recession. The dependent variable in each regression is the
percentage change in state personal income-tax revenue. Table 12.10 includes all
states with a broad-based personal income tax, while table 12.11 is limited to states
that experienced a decline in personal income tax revenue. The main results of the
analysis are summarized below.

Personal Income Tax Declines Strongly Correlated with Personal Income.
As one would expect, the percentage decline in state personal income-tax revenue between 2008 and 2009 was positively associated with the percentage
decline in state personal income. The magnitude of the coefficient suggests
that state personal income-tax revenue declined between 2.5 and 4.8 percentage
points for each percentage point decline in state personal income, for all states
with personal income-tax revenue. When the analysis is limited to states experiencing declines in revenue, the effect size is a decline of approximately three
percentage points.

*States That Automatically Conformed to the Federal Tax Base Did Not
Experience Sharper Drops in Personal Income Tax Revenue.* Despite concerns that
have been expressed about the effect of federal and state tax-base conformity, the
coefficient of the interaction term between automatic conformity to the federal
tax code and a state's percentage change in the potential tax base firmly rejects a
hypothesis that conformity increased the vulnerability of a state to the downturn.
Indeed, although the coefficient is estimated imprecisely in the full regression, the
results suggest that states with automatic conformity experienced smaller percentage declines in personal income-tax revenue.

*Personal Income Tax Is Less Volatile When the Tax Base Is Below Its Long-
Run Equilibrium Path.* When one includes the long-run tax-base elasticity estimated by Bruce, Fox, and Tuttle as a proxy for "structural features of the personal
income tax" that contribute to long-run volatility, the variable is not significant
in any of the regressions. This result is broadly consistent with the work of Bruce,

Table 12.10 State personal income tax features and changes in revenue, 2008–2009 (all states with broad-based personal income tax)

	(1)	(2)	(3)	(4)
	% Decline PIT Revenues	% Decline PIT Revenues	% Decline PIT Revenues	% Decline PIT Revenues
% Change in Personal Income	2.529[*] (2.09)	3.867[**] (2.95)	3.726[**] (2.77)	4.162[**] (2.95)
% Change in Personal Income Interacted with Federal Tax Base Conformity		−3.405[*] (−2.16)	−3.919[*] (−2.22)	−3.462 (−1.71)
Long-Run Elasticity			1.485 (0.70)	1.997 (0.98)
Share of AGI from Capital Gains				1.543 (1.18)
Share of AGI from Pensions				4.424[**] (2.90)
Share of AGI from Pensions × Pension Exemption				−0.964[*] (−2.06)
Share of AGI from IRAs				4.728 (1.38)
Share of AGI from Social Security				−8.850 (−1.71)
Share of Social Security × Social Security Exemption				0.909 (0.63)
Constant	7.136[**] (3.55)	7.558[***] (3.91)	5.283 (1.20)	−18.88 (−1.19)
Observations	41	41	39	39
R^2	0.101	0.199	0.223	0.497
Adjusted R^2	0.078	0.157	0.156	0.341

Note: For ease of interpretation of the coefficients, the actual percentage change in personal income tax revenue, which was negative in all but four states, was multiplied by -1. Thus a positive coefficient means that a unit change in the respective variable increased the percentage decline in PIT revenues, holding other factors constant.
Source: Authors' calculations.

Fox, and Tuttle, who found that the state personal income tax may be more volatile to swings in income over the long run but that there is no necessary linkage between long-run volatility (as measured by the long-run elasticity) and short-run swings in revenue when the tax base (income) is not on its long-run equilibrium path.

Table 12.11 State personal income tax features and decline in revenue, 2008–2009 (all states with broad-based personal income tax that experienced revenue loss)

	(1)	(2)	(3)	(4)
	% Decline PIT Revenues	% Decline PIT Revenues	% Decline PIT Revenues	% Decline PIT Revenues
% Change in Personal Income 2009/2008	2.398* (2.21)	3.243** (2.80)	3.043* (2.53)	3.285** (3.00)
% Change in Personal Income Interacted with Federal Tax Base Conformity		−2.299* (−1.75)	−2.796* (−1.84)	−2.511 (−1.68)
Long-Run Elasticity			1.306 (−0.75)	0.00118 (0.00)
Share of AGI from Capital Gains				2.208* (2.37)
Share of AGI from Pensions				3.354** (3.15)
Share of AGI from Pensions × Pension Exemption				−1.158* (−3.55)
Share of AGI from IRAs				3.871 (1.62)
Share of AGI from Social Security				−2.759 (−0.75)
Share of Social Security × Social Security Exemption				1.629 (1.62)
Constant	9.058*** (5.14)	9.263*** (5.39)	12.31** (3.17)	−20.75 (−1.87)
Observations	37	37	35	35
R^2	0.123	0.195	0.217	0.630
Adjusted R^2	0.098	0.148	0.141	0.497

Note: For ease of interpretation of the coefficients, the actual percentage change in personal income-tax revenue, which was negative in all but four states, was multiplied by −1. Thus a positive coefficient means that a unit change in the respective variable increased the percentage decline in PIT revenues, holding other factors constant.
Source: Authors' calculations.

Capital Income Adds to the Short-Run Volatility of Personal Income Tax Revenue. As expected, income from capital gains contributes to the short-run volatility of personal income-tax revenue. Among states that experienced a decline in personal income-tax revenue from 2008 to 2009, a one-percentage point increase in the share of federal AGI from capital gains is correlated with a decrease of approximately two percentage points in state personal income tax revenue.

Retirement Income Has an Unclear Impact on Changes in State Personal Income Tax Revenue. The pattern of results for the various sources of retirement income, like the findings reported by Bruce, Fox, and Tuttle, is complex. The coefficient on the variable "pension share in AGI" implies that states in which pension income was a larger share of AGI experienced larger proportional declines in state personal income-tax revenue (on the order of three to four percentage points). On the other hand, exempting all or part of private pensions from state personal income taxation, at least in the short run, had a countervailing effect. The results indicate that income from individual retirement accounts had an effect similar to that of pensions. Although not precisely estimated, the signs of the coefficients of the Social Security variables are opposite of those of the pension variables.

The results for pensions and Social Security are a bit puzzling. The positive correlation between pensions as a share of AGI and the size of the percentage drop in PIT revenues seems counterintuitive. One would think that pension income would not be that cyclical. The negative sign of the pension/pension exemption interaction term may reflect the fact that excluding a portion of income from the tax base to begin with reduces short-run volatility. With regard to the results for Social Security income, it may be that the share of Social Security as a percentage of AGI is a proxy for the presence of relatively better-off senior citizens in a state because, under the federal tax code, for high income earners up to 85 percent of an individual's social security benefits may be included in the computation of gross income (table 12.9).

Much of the Variation in State Personal Income Tax Revenue Remains Unexplained. Overall, a considerable proportion of the variation in the decline in state personal income-tax revenue during the Great Recession remains unexplained by the variables included in the model. For example, one might have expected that variations in the decline in state personal income would have had a larger effect on the decline in state personal income-tax revenue. The failure of the data to support this claim suggests that the volatility of the state personal income tax is complex and that a variety of factors are at play.[64]

SUMMARY AND CONCLUSIONS

The personal income tax has been a source of long-term stability and strength in state government finances, generating approximately 25 percent of state own-source revenue for the last two decades. Drawing on a broad base of wages and salaries, interest, dividends, capital gains, and other income, the personal income tax is likely to remain a mainstay of state fiscal policy because of its revenue-generating capacity, its adaptability to individual circumstances, and its relative ease of administration based on considerable conformity with the federal tax code.

Although for most states personal income tax is more elastic than other major taxes, statistical analysis suggests that greater reliance on the personal income tax did not place states at jeopardy of larger revenue losses during the recession that began in December 2007. When the economy is below its long-run growth path (as during a time of recession), the personal income tax appears to be less volatile. State conformity with federal income tax rules did not appear to place states at greater risk of revenue losses; states that automatically conform to changes in federal tax law did not experience sharper drops in revenue. In some cases, federal conformity can increase the capacity and stability of state income tax systems: for example, the federal government taxes 40 percent of all Social Security benefits[65] while twenty-seven of forty-one states with a broad-based personal income tax exempt all Social Security income from taxation.

As part of an effort to close large budget gaps during the recession, a number of states concentrated in the Northeast and the West raised personal income tax rates, and eight states made their tax systems more progressive by adding top rates for high-income households. In particular, there has been an almost exponential increase in the income thresholds for top tax brackets in those states. At the same time, state EITCs, which reduce the tax burden for low- and moderate-income working families (and in some cases create a negative tax burden because the credits are usually refundable), are now offered in a majority of states with a broad-based personal income tax. Although this movement toward a more progressive personal income-tax structure could merely reflect the latest swing of a pendulum rather than a lasting change, it may also be that voters who prefer a more progressive tax system are registering these preferences through state policy. Federal income-tax policy has emphasized lower marginal tax rates since the enactment of major tax cuts in 2001 and 2003.[66]

The overall strength and stability of state personal income-tax systems may also mask growing pressure and a slow erosion of the tax base. States continue to offer dozens of tax exclusions, deductions, exemptions, abatements, and credits at the same time that federal conformity introduces many other tax preferences into state personal income-tax systems. In particular, states exempt large proportions of retirement income—a growing share of total personal income as the society continues to age—from their personal income taxes. States also exempt some capital gains income, another fast-growing component of the tax base. If states allow continued erosion of the tax base, they may have no choice but to maintain higher rates. Few states have followed (or carefully considered) an alternate approach, reflected most prominently in the federal Tax Reform Act of 1986, of broadening the definition of income, curbing tax preferences, and lowering marginal tax rates even though such a policy could enhance the equity, efficiency, and simplicity of the personal income tax.

Notes

....

1 Own-source revenue includes taxes, current charges, and miscellaneous revenue, such as amounts received from the public for fees, rents, and sales, as well as income from commercial enterprises and interest earnings.

2 US Bureau of the Census (2010), table 1: State and Local Government Finances, 2007–2008.

3 Ibid.

4 Ibid.

5 Ibid.

6 Ibid.

7 These states were Alabama, Delaware, Indiana, Iowa, Kentucky, Maryland, Michigan, Missouri, New York, Ohio, Oregon, and Pennsylvania. See US Bureau of the Census, *2008 Annual Surveys of State and Local Government Finances*, tabulated July 7, 2010, available at www.census.gov.

8 Urban-Brookings Tax Policy Center (2011a).

9 Henchman (2008).

10 Ibid.

11 US Bureau of the Census (2006).

12 US Bureau of the Census (2001, 2005, 2010).

13 Ibid.

14 Federation of Tax Administrators (2011a).

15 Ibid.

16 For example, many states have decoupled from "bonus depreciation" provisions that have been authorized periodically by the federal government. Bonus depreciation allows individuals and businesses to claim larger up-front deductions (or total up-front deductions) for machinery and equipment expenses. Singham and Johnson report that thirty-three states decoupled from a federal bonus depreciation provision enacted in 2008 to avoid the revenue loss that would result from federal conformity. See Singham and Johnson (2011), 2.

17 Federation of Tax Administrators (2011b).

18 US Department of Commerce, Bureau of Economic Analysis. *Relation of Gross Domestic Product, Gross National Product, Net National Product, National Income, and Personal Income*, Data is updated quarterly at www.bea.gov.

19 US Government Accountability Office (2010), 26–27.

20 Sjoquist, Stephenson, and Wallace (2010), 1–3, 22. Norton Francis (in this volume) discusses this volatility in the context of the state revenue estimation problem during the 2007–2009 Great Recession.

21 State individual income taxes mimic (though at a smaller scale due to their lower rates) the efficiency effects of the federal income tax.

22 Slemrod and Bakija (2008), 124–127.

23 Bruce, Fox, and Tuttle (2006), 323.

24 Ibid., 330.

25 Ibid., 331.

26 Controlling for the severity of the state downturn, as measured by the change in the state unemployment rate from 2008 to 2009, does not change the result.

27 Francis (this volume); Dadayan and Boyd (2011), 18.

28 Dadayan and Boyd (2011), 4.

29 Louisiana rolled back its personal income tax rates to the levels that prevailed in 2002. Rhode Island continued phasing in reductions in its optional personal income flat tax, as required by legislation enacted in 2006. Rhode Island's flat tax dropped from 7.5 percent in tax year 2007 to 7 percent in tax year 2008 and 6.5 percent in 2009 (the flat tax was repealed in 2010).

30 National Conference of State Legislatures (2009), 3.

31 Dadayan and Boyd (2011), 4.

32 National Conference of State Legislatures (2010), 3.

33 National Conference of State Legislatures (2011a), 4.

34 National Conference of State Legislatures (2009), 10.

35 National Conference of State Legislatures (2011a), 6.

36 National Conference of State Legislatures (2011b), 9–10.

37 Maguire (2005) and Rueben and Burman (2005) examine the implications of the interplay of the federal and local income tax, including that of a federal tax base broadening that would eliminate the deductibility of state and local taxes.

38 Urban-Brookings Tax Policy Center (2010b); Tax Foundation (2011).

39 In tax year 2011, the EITC is available to single-parent families with annual income less than $36,372 (one child), $41,341 (two children), or $44,404 (three or more children). The EITC is also available to married-couple families with annual income less than $41,502 (one child), $46,471 (two children), or $49,534 (three or more children). In addition, households without children qualify if their income is lower than $16,840 (single individuals) or $21,970 (married couples). See Williams, Johnson, and Shure (2010), 4–5.

40 Washington State, which does not have an income tax, also offers a state EITC that is administered by the state's Department of Revenue as a rebate program.

41 Holt (2006), 3.

42 Williams, Johnson, and Shure (2010), 3.

43 Gravelle (2005), 406.

44 Levitis, Johnson, and Koulish (2009) provide a detailed discussion of the strengths, weaknesses, and uses of state tax expenditure reports (also known as "tax expenditure budgets").

45 State of Oregon (2011), 5–6.

46 Government of the District of Columbia (2010), ix–xiii, 107–152.

47 Ibid., ix–xiii.

48 Commission on the 21st Century Economy (2009), 16.

49 This change took effect in tax year 2010.

50 Wallace (this volume).

51 US Bureau of the Census (2008).

52 Ibid.

53 Iowa Department of Revenue (2006), 4.

54 Ibid., 3.

55 Ibid., 4.

56 Snell (2011), 2–3.

57 Provisional income equals adjusted gross income plus one-half of Social Security benefits and otherwise tax-exempt interest income, such as interest from tax-exempt bonds.

58 Wisconsin Legislative Fiscal Bureau (2011), 14–57.

59 Bryan (2010), 39.

60 Landers, Richie, Sjoquist, Wallace, and Viceisza (2005), 17–19.

61 Edwards and Wallace (2004), 17–19.

62 Institute on Taxation and Economic Policy (2009), 9.

63 Bryan (2010), 11.

64 This is a conclusion also reached by Bruce, Fox, and Tuttle (2006), 337–338.

65 The statistic on federal taxation of Social Security benefits is calculated from data provided by Bryan (2009), 39.

66 US Congress, Economic Growth and Tax Relief Reconciliation Act (2001); US Congress, Jobs and Growth Tax Relief Reconciliation Act (2003)

References

Bruce, Donald, William F. Fox, and M.H. Tuttle (2006). "Tax Base Elasticities: A Multi-State Analysis of Long-Run and Short-Run Dynamics." *Southern Economic Journal* 73(2): 315–341.

Bryan, Justin (2010). "Individual Income Tax Returns, 2008." *SOI Bulletin* 30(1): 5–78.

Commission on the 21st Century Economy (2009). *Commission on the 21st Century Economy.* http://www.cotce.ca.gov.

Dadayan, Lucy, and Donald J. Boyd (2011). "State Tax Revenues Gained New Strength in Fourth Quarter: Every Quarter of 2010 Showed Growth, But Recession's Harsh Impact Will Linger." State Revenue Report, February 2011, No. 82. Albany, NY: The Nelson A. Rockefeller Institute of Government, State University of New York, University at Albany.

Edwards, Barbara, and Sally Wallace (2004). "State Income Tax Treatment of the Elderly." *Public Budgeting and Finance* 24(2): 1–20.

Federation of Tax Administrators (2011a). "State Personal Income Taxes: Federal Starting Points (as of January 1, 2011)." Washington, DC: Federation of Tax Administrators.

Federation of Tax Administrators (2011b). "State Individual Income Taxes (Tax Rates for Tax Year 2011—as of January 1, 2011)." Washington, DC: Federation of Tax Administrators.

Government of the District of Columbia (2010). *District of Columbia Tax Expenditure Report.* Washington, DC: District of Columbia Office of the Chief Financial Officer.

Gravelle, Jane G. (2005). "Tax Expenditures." In *The Encyclopedia of Taxation and Tax Policy*, edited by Joseph J. Cordes, Robert D. Ebel, and Jane G. Gravelle. Washington, DC: Urban Institute Press. 406–408.

Henchman, Joseph (2008). "County and City Income Taxes Clustered in States with Poor Tax Climates: Fiscal Fact No. 133." Washington, DC: Tax Foundation.

Holt, Steve (2006). "The Earned Income Tax Credit at Age 30: What We Know." Metropolitan Policy Program Research Brief. Washington, DC: The Brookings Institution. 1–39.

Institute on Taxation and Economic Policy (2009). "A Capital Idea: Repealing Tax Breaks for Capital Gains Would Ease Budget Woes and Improve Tax Fairness." Washington, DC: Institute on Taxation and Economic Policy.

Iowa Department of Revenue (2006). "Issue Paper: State Tax Policy Implications of an Aging Population." Issue paper of the Iowa Department of Revenue.

Landers, Glenn, Clare S. Richie, David Sjoquist, Sally Wallace, and Angelino Viceisza (2005). "Georgia's Aging Population: What to Expect and How to Cope." Atlanta, GA: Healthcare Georgia Foundation.

Levitis, Jason, Nicholas Johnson, and Jeremy Koulish (2009). *Promoting State Budget Accountability through Tax Expenditure Reporting.* Washington, DC: Center on Budget and Policy Priorities. 1–43.

Maguire, Steven (2005). "State and Local Tax Deductibility." In *The Encyclopedia of Taxation and Tax Policy*, edited by Joseph J. Cordes, Robert D. Ebel, and Jane G. Gravelle. Washington, DC: Urban Institute Press. 367–370.

National Conference of State Legislatures (2009). *State Tax Actions, 2008.* Denver: National Conference of State Legislatures.

National Conference of State Legislatures (2010). *State Tax Actions, 2009.* Denver: National Conference of State Legislatures.

National Conference of State Legislatures (2011a). *State Tax Actions, 2010.* Denver: National Conference of State Legislatures.

National Conference of State Legislatures (2011b). "NSCL Fiscal Brief: How State Tax Policy Responds to Economic Recessions." Denver: National Conference of State Legislatures.

Rueben, Kim, and Len Burman (2005). "Deductibility of State and Local Taxes." *Tax Analysts Tax Facts.* http://www.taxpolicycenter.org/taxfacts/index.cfm.

Singham, Ashali, and Nicholas Johnson (2011). "States Can Avert New Revenue Loss by Decoupling from Federal Expensing Provision." Washington, DC: Center on Budget and Policy Priorities.

Sjoquist, David L., Andrew Stephenson, and Sally Wallace (2010, May 14). "The Impact of Tax Revenue from Capital Gains Realizations on State Income Tax Revenue and Budget Conditions." Working paper of the Department of Economics, Andrew Young School of Policy Studies, Georgia State University.

Slemrod, Joel, and Jon Bakija (2008). *Taxing Ourselves: A Citizen's Guide to the Debate over Taxes.* 4th ed. Cambridge, MA: The MIT Press.

Snell, Ronald (2011). "State Personal Income Taxes on Pensions and Retirement Income: Tax Year 2010." Denver, CO: National Conference of State Legislatures.

State of Oregon (2011). *Tax Expenditure Report, 2011–2013.* Salem: Oregon Department of Administrative Services and Oregon Department of Revenue.

Tax Credits for Working Families (2011). "Tax Credits for Working Families." http://www.taxcreditsforworkingfamilies.org./earned_income_tax_credit.

Tax Foundation (2011). "State Individual Income Tax Rates, as of January 1, 2011." http://www.taxfoundation.org/taxdata.

Urban-Brookings Tax Policy Center (2011a). "Individual Local Income Tax Rates 2006." http://www.taxpolicycenter.org/taxfacts/index.cfm.

Urban-Brookings Tax Policy Center (2011b). "Individual State Income Tax Rates, 2000–2010." http://www.taxpolicycenter.org/taxfacts/index.cfm.

US Bureau of the Census (2001). "State and Local Government Finances by Level of Government and State: 1991–1992." Document created March 30, 2001, and last revised on September 9, 2009. http://www.census.gov.

US Bureau of the Census (2005). "State and Local Government Finances by Level of Government and by State: 2001–2002." Document created December 9, 2005. http://www.census.gov.

US Bureau of the Census (2006). *Government Finance and Employment Classification Manual.* Suitland, MD: US Bureau of the Census.

US Bureau of the Census (2008). "Table 3: Percent Distribution of the Projected Population by Selected Age Groups and Sex for the United States: 2010 to 2050," August 14, 2008. http://www.census.gov.

US Bureau of the Census (2010). *2008 Annual Surveys of State and Local Governments.* Suitland, MD: US Bureau of the Census.

US Congress, Economic Growth and Tax Relief Reconciliation Act of 2001 (Pub. L. 107–116, 115 Stat. 38), June 7, 2001.

US Congress, Jobs and Growth Tax Relief Reconciliation Act of 2003 (Pub. L. 108–127, 117 Stat. 752), May 28, 2003.

US Government Accountability Office (2010). *State and Local Governments: Fiscal Pressures Could Have Implications for Future Delivery of Intergovernmental Programs* (GAO-10–899). Washington, DC: US Government Accountability Office.

Williams, Erica, Nicholas Johnson, and Jon Shure (2010). *State Earned Income Tax Credits: 2010 Legislative Update.* Washington, DC: Center on Budget and Policy Priorities.

Wisconsin Legislative Fiscal Bureau (2011). *Individual Income Tax Provisions in the States.* Madison: Wisconsin Legislative Fiscal Bureau.

CHAPTER 13

....

STATE CORPORATE INCOME TAXES

....

DAVID BRUNORI

STATE corporate income taxes (CIT) on business profits are among the most controversial and complicated components of the state revenue system. Such a tax is difficult to administer, capricious in its "tax cost" impact across types of businesses, and is characterized by a narrow tax base and high statutory rate when compared to a general value-added tax and gross receipts tax alternatives. These characteristics of the taxes lead to numerous political and economic challenges.[1] Formulary apportionment, distinctions between business and nonbusiness income, and a myriad of tax-planning opportunities constantly test tax practitioners and administrators. Attorneys and accountants struggle with laws designed to raise revenue, spur economic development, and comply with constitutional and federal statutory limitations on state taxing authority.

Forty-five states tax corporate net income, including traditionally anti-income-tax jurisdictions such as Tennessee, New Hampshire, and Florida. In 2009, the tax accounted for about $40 billion in tax revenue for the states.[2] Only Nevada, Ohio, Washington, South Dakota and Wyoming do not impose any taxes on corporate net income.[3]

Corporate income taxes make up a surprisingly small portion of state revenues. And the relative importance of the state corporate income tax has steadily declined for decades. From its high of about 9.5 percent in 1977, the state CIT dropped to about 5 percent of total state tax revenue in 2009. And, to provide further perspective, the tax accounts for less than 2 percent of total state revenue (tax and nontax revenue), its quantitative importance being dwarfed by the much larger amount of revenue collected from personal income, consumption, and excise taxes.[4] Nonetheless, inordinate amounts of resources and intellectual capital are used in administering and complying with state corporate income and franchise taxes. Tax commentators and scholars have noted the difference in administrative and compliance costs for the CIT relative to other levies.[5] The reason for this cost/benefit imbalance is that corporations generally have the resources to plan and dispute tax matters. The private sector's highly trained, well-paid attorneys and accountants also significantly raise the costs of administering the corporate income tax for the states. To meet the companies' intellectual firepower, the states must hire, train, and retain equally qualified tax professionals. Although the state CIT raises very little revenue compared with other levies, it devours a disproportionate amount of tax-planning and litigation resources.

The amount of time and resources devoted to the tax outweighs its financial contribution to the states. Even in states with long traditions of progressive taxation, which would seem most likely to rely on the tax, the revenue gained from corporate taxes is minimal. For example, Oregon, historically one of the most progressive states in terms of taxation, has no sales tax and a history of relatively high personal income taxes. Despite this progressive tradition, the state raised only 3.4 percent of its tax revenue from corporate levies in 2009. Oregon raised more than twice the amount from excise taxes ($744 million) than it did from its corporate income tax ($224 million). Montana, another state with a progressive tax history, raised only $164 million from corporate income taxes in 2009 compared to over $529 million from excise taxes.

The three states that depend the most on the CIT are Alaska, New Hampshire, and Delaware; in these states, the tax accounts for 12.7 percent, 23 percent, and 7.4 percent of total state tax revenue, respectively. It should be noted, however, that these three states do not impose statewide sales tax. Alaska and New Hampshire also do not tax personal income.

HISTORY OF THE CIT

Although states have imposed taxes on various business activities since the nation's start, today's corporate net income tax can be traced to Wisconsin's Income Tax Law of 1911. The tax proved successful in progressive Wisconsin, and its success quickly led to adoption of the CIT by five other states. By 1930, seventeen more states had adopted the tax; by 1940, an additional seventeen states had begun taxing corporate income.

The relatively rapid spread of state corporate taxation is attributable to a number of political and economic factors. Progressive and populist political leaders with a skeptical view of corporations controlled many states in the early part of the twentieth century. The opportunity to raise revenue from corporations fit naturally with their political philosophies. These same leaders also fought successfully to implement progressive federal and personal income taxes.

The growth of the corporate tax in the mid-1900s also reflected a developing movement in most states to diversify their tax systems. Throughout the nineteenth century, state governments financed their operations mainly through excise taxes and some form of property tax. These financing systems, however, did not raise enough revenue to meet growing public service demands. The early and mid-twentieth century saw the adoption of personal income taxes as well as sales and use taxes throughout the country. The tax on corporate income was part of the expansion to diversify the overall tax base. These fundamental changes to how states collect revenue persisted into the start of the twenty-first century.

Like other levies, the state corporate income tax was developed for a far different economy than at present. The tax was designed at a time when most corporations manufactured tangible personal property. It was also designed to function in an environment in which interstate tax competition was not nearly as intense as it is today. Although that economy no longer dominates, the structure of the tax has largely remained the same.

RATIONALE FOR THE CORPORATE INCOME TAX

The state CIT has been justified on a number of grounds. One widely noted rationale is that it compensates for deficiencies in the property tax.[6] The property tax does not take into account that businesses require varying degrees of property inputs to produce the same level of profit. Consequently, some capital-intensive operations (e.g., manufacturing companies) are taxed more heavily by the property tax than are labor-intensive companies, including knowledge-based enterprises such as high-technology companies. This inequity is compounded by the difficulties in assessing property taxes for intangible property. Instead of relying entirely on taxing business inputs, states, in the interest of greater equity, have included the CIT in their mix of revenue sources.

A more common rationale for the CIT is that it protects the much more significant (in terms of revenue) personal income tax. Without a levy on corporate income, taxpayers might have an incentive to shelter personal income in corporate holdings. For example, business owners seeking to avoid personal income tax would incorporate their operations; the corporation itself would then accumulate the dividends or salary that normally would be paid out to the individual. The shareholders could thus escape personal income taxation on these monies until they were paid out as dividends or the company was sold. The federal government has adopted rules to prevent the accumulation of corporate profits as a means of avoiding personal income tax liability.

This rationale—that the CIT helps protect the personal income tax—makes sense intuitively. However, the decline of the corporate tax over the past several decades undermines its validity. Personal income tax revenue has grown dramatically in the last decade, a period when corporations increasingly avoided state taxation of income. It is difficult to see how the personal income tax could receive protection from a tax that has proved quite ineffectual in the past quarter-century. Indeed the CIT is badly in need of reform if it is to become a viable source of income for the states.

An effective corporate income tax system may add to the tremendous success of the personal income tax. But the deficiencies in the state corporate tax system do not generally stem from individuals trying to shelter profits from personal income taxes but rather from corporations' attempts to escape entity-level taxation. Thus, based on the historical record, it is unclear whether the CIT can be justified based on the need to protect the personal income tax.

The most compelling rationale for imposing tax on corporate profits is that such levies reimburse the states for the significant services provided to the business community.[7] Requiring corporations to pay for services provided by the community satisfies the benefits theory of taxation—that is, that tax liabilities are imposed to compensate for the benefits that had been received.[8]

Corporations use public services provided by the state as much as individuals and unincorporated businesses. They benefit from a state's transportation infrastructure—the roads, railways, airports, and harbors—in order to receive materials and to move products to market. Corporations also benefit from public safety operations, including police, fire, and medical emergency services. In addition, the state judicial system protects the contractual, intellectual property, and other legal rights of businesses. Corporations also depend on the state's school system to produce an educated workforce—an especially important role in this highly specialized age of electronic commerce. High-quality school systems also help attract qualified employees.

A corporation's success depends on the adequate provision of these services. In numerous cases, businesses have opposed state tax cuts (or, less frequently, advocated tax increases) to protect public services deemed vital to companies' operations.[9] Many studies have shown that corporations make decisions on where to expand (or relocate) largely based on the availability of adequate public services.[10]

Opponents of corporate taxes often argue that the economic development and the wealth created by corporations are greater than the benefits that they receive from the state. It is true that corporate enterprises usually result in additional tax revenue for the state in which they operate. The corporation itself, as well as employees of the corporation, pay property and consumption taxes. Employees also pay personal income taxes. But corporate activities can have an even larger impact on state revenue. When the corporation and its employees spend money, other businesses in the state (e.g., vendors to the corporation and their employees) end up paying income, consumption, and property taxes.

Finally, a frequently cited justification for the corporate tax is that it eases—to some extent—the regressivity of state public finance systems, which rely heavily on consumption taxes. The corporate tax is often viewed as an effective means of lessening the burden on poorer citizens.

But the effect on the overall regressivity of the tax system is dependent on the incidence of the tax. There has been much debate over who bears the corporate tax burden.[11] Studies have found that shareholders bear the cost in the form of lower returns. But other studies have found that consumers bear the cost in the form of higher prices for goods. And still other studies have found that labor bears the costs in the form of lower wages.[12] The progressive effect on the system would be minimized if consumers or labor were bearing the cost of corporate taxation. Still, there is widespread belief that along with the personal income tax, the corporate income tax offsets the regressive effects of the sales and use taxes as well as the excise taxes imposed by many states.

THE CRISIS OF THE STATE CIT

The state corporate income tax presents numerous issues for policymakers. Although many of these issues have existed since the inception of the tax, others are the result of modern economic, technological, and political developments.

The state corporate income tax has not been a particularly reliable or stable source of income for state governments. The percentage of total state tax revenue collected from levies on corporate income has declined steadily for more than two decades.[13] Many commentators expect that decline to continue.[14]

In all states imposing the tax, the share of CIT relative to total state tax revenue fell between 1995 and 2009. As noted above, only New Hampshire collects more than 20 percent of its total tax revenue from corporate taxes. But even its unusually heavy reliance on the tax reflects its policy of not taxing personal income and sales.

More important, in every year since 1959 the corporate tax base has failed to keep pace with company profits (either worldwide or domestic).[15] In other words, in relative terms, state governments are collecting less in corporate income taxes while corporations are earning more profits. Some of the major reasons for the decline in the state CIT are discussed below.

Tax Incentives

One important factor in the steady erosion of the state corporate tax base is the pervasive use of targeted tax incentives. Each year, hundreds of tax breaks are granted to corporations to encourage economic development. In addition to sales and property-tax incentives, states provide significant corporate income-tax incentives as part of their efforts to retain or attract businesses. Corporate income-tax incentives generally include tax credits for investment, job creation, and worker training as well as expanded deductions for accelerated depreciation. These tax expenditures cost state governments (and state taxpayers) billions of dollars in forgone revenue. They are offered every year by states that tax corporate income. Despite their ineffectiveness, tax incentives have proliferated in the past three decades.[16]

The most noteworthy example is the "Mercedes-Benz" law. Enacted in Alabama, the law was meant to entice the German automaker to remain in the state. Under the law, companies that invested at least $5 million and employed at least fifty people in the state were allowed to issue tax-exempt bonds to finance their operations. The companies could then claim corporate income tax credits for the amount that was spent servicing the debt on the bonds. The law provided Mercedes-Benz with more than $250 million in tax breaks, the majority of which reduced the company's CIT liability. Alabama raises less than 4 percent of its total tax revenue from corporate taxes, a below-average percentage that is almost certainly related to the Mercedes-Benz law. While the Alabama example is the most cited example, there are hundreds of other similar instances.

Tax incentives limit a state's ability to tax corporations on net profits. But the problem is that such incentives are rarely limited to a small number of companies. The willingness of states to offer tax incentives creates an atmosphere that encourages companies to seek the same type of tax preferences offered to other companies. Corporations count on the states' propensity to offer tax incentives, and many corporate investment decisions are coupled with a request for incentives. Often these requests are made after the company has already made its investment and location decisions. Once states begin offering tax incentives to a few corporations, it can become politically difficult to not offer similar incentives to many companies. The result is a declining corporate tax base.

Abandonment of Uniformity

States have also attempted to use their corporate tax laws to foster economic development with another, less publicly known, method. To promote interstate commerce, many states have modified the formulas they use to calculate the CIT of multistate firms with a location within the taxing state. The use of different apportionment formulas among the states essentially disregards the notion that an effective corporate income-tax system requires uniformity across state lines.[17] When the CIT was first implemented, many corporations manufactured, sold, and had headquarters in one or a few states. There were few problems in determining which states had jurisdiction to tax corporate profits. In the modern economy, however, it is difficult to find many corporations that do not conduct multistate business.

For the state CIT to work effectively for interstate business, uniformity is essential.[18] The principle of uniformity requires that all states imposing corporate income taxes use the same (or very similar) rules for determining how corporations are taxed and which states have authority to tax corporate income. The use of uniform laws facilitates the accurate determination of tax liability among multistate taxpayers, including the equitable apportionment of tax bases. Uniformity also reduces the compliance costs (return preparation and filing) for taxpayers. Perhaps most important, if every state used the three-factor formula, corporations would neither be taxed twice on the same income nor be able to avoid taxation on 100 percent of their income. Moreover, corporations would not have the incentive or the ability to base business decisions on corporate tax consequences.

For state governments, uniformity decreases the costs of administration. Uniformity also ensures that corporations conducting business in states that impose CITs will pay their fair share of taxes. If all states adopted the same or very similar rules, corporations would be unable to create "nowhere income" that is not subject to tax.

To achieve a measure of uniformity, in the past most states relied on the evenly weighted three-factor apportionment formula adopted by the 1957 Uniform Division of Income for Tax Purposes Act (UDITPA). This three-factor formula apportions taxable income according to the relative amount of sales, property, and payroll that a corporation has in a particular state. These three factors approximate the value added to the corporation's business in the various states. But as interstate tax competition increased, states began to adopt different apportionment formulas as a way to foster economic development. In 2010, only thirteen states imposing the tax still used the traditional three-factor formula. Twenty-two states imposing the CIT used a double-weighted sales factor. Five states (Pennsylvania, Oregon, Ohio, Minnesota, and Michigan) allowed for greater than double-weighted sales factor formulas. And, Iowa, Nebraska, Texas, and Illinois[7] use a single-sales factor to determine corporate tax liability.

Using a double-weighted or single-sales factor usually results in lower tax costs for corporations that have substantial operations within a state (as measured by payroll and property) but that sell most of their goods and services out of state. Indeed, scholars have found that moving to a single-sales factor apportionment formula results in a 10 percent decrease in CIT revenue.[19] In effect, double-weighting the sales factor benefits corporations with significant property and payroll in the state. Accordingly, many corporations have lobbied for a formula that double-weights sales.[20]

Not all corporations benefit from using an apportionment formula with a double- or single-sales factor, because this method increases the tax burdens on corporations that sell a significant share of their products in a particular state but do not maintain sizable physical operations in that state. State policymakers often accept this imbalance, however, to meet the larger goal of attracting investment. They reason that corporations are unlikely to stop selling their products and making profits in a state merely because their tax burdens are somewhat higher than those of businesses located within the state.

Although lawmakers believe that a double- or single-sales factor will encourage companies to expand their presences in a state, there is no real evidence that deviating from the traditional three-factor formula promotes economic development.[21] The ultimate effect is to shrink the in-state corporate tax base.[22]

Tax-Planning Opportunities

Another important shortcoming of the modern CIT system is that most states fail to combine the apportionment factors of related entities when calculating tax liabilities. In these "separate-entity states," the property, sales, and payroll of related corporations engaged in the same business are not taken into account. Thus, each corporation calculates its corporate tax liability without regard to related-party transactions.

As an alternative to the separate-entity policy, states could require related corporations engaged in the same "unitary business" to calculate their apportionment formula as if they were operating one business. This requirement would eliminate intercompany transactions and combine the sales, property, and payroll of the related parties.

Failure to require combined reporting results in a direct link between corporate income-tax liability and the legal structure of the corporate group. The choice to operate as a subsidiary or division will often create dramatically different tax consequences even though there is no real economic difference between the two arrangements. Corporate tax planners routinely take advantage of the opportunity to avoid or lessen corporate tax liability by simply incorporating a division or liquidating a subsidiary. Often, this action has no other business or economic reason; it is taken solely to avoid the tax.

The states' failure to require combined reporting also allows related corporations to shift profits from states with relatively high tax costs to states with lower or no corporate tax burdens. When related corporations conduct a single unitary business, they have the opportunity to manipulate prices, a practice known as transfer pricing. For example, a corporation in state A (with a high effective tax rate) might sell products to a related corporation in state B (with a low effective tax rate) at prices well below market. If the related corporation's operations are not combined with the original seller's operations for tax purposes, the companies will have shifted the profits from state A to state B and reduced the overall tax burden. Policing such transfer pricing is an expensive and difficult endeavor for the states.

The failure to require combined reporting also gives companies incentive to establish holding companies in states that do not impose CIT, such as Delaware and Nevada. The holding company is established to do little more than collect royalties and interest from its related companies. The royalties and interest are usually deducted from the related party's taxable income, but the holding company typically is not taxed on the receipts.

Pomp proposes another reason for states' inability to collect the amount of corporate tax revenue that the potential tax base suggests is possible.[23] He theorizes that aggressiveness on the part of corporate tax planners has allowed corporations to escape taxation.

Like federal tax practices, state corporate tax firms attract the top accountants and lawyers in the field. The corporate tax-planning and litigation resources in this area continually challenge state revenue departments. Corporations and their representatives in large law and accounting firms have the resources (and the incentive) to develop sophisticated planning devices to legally minimize state tax liability. Developments in the past decade illustrate that they have successfully used those resources to reduce corporate tax burdens.

For example, only "business income" (income from the same business operations) is subject to apportionment among the states in which the corporation has sales, payroll, and property. Nonbusiness income (interest, dividends, and income unrelated to the operations of the taxable business) is not subject to apportionment but is allocated to the state that is considered the source of the income. Corporate planners have been particularly adept at converting what would normally be considered business income to nonbusiness income allocated to a low- or no-income tax state.[24]

Pass-Through Entities: The Rise of "Limited Liability" Entities

Part of the decline of the amount of the state CIT has been caused by the dramatic growth in the use of pass-through entities to carry out multistate business. A limited liability company (LLC) or limited liability partnership (LLP) has increasingly become an entity of choice for many businesses that traditionally would have opted for traditional "C" corporate status. Changes in federal law in 1995 made electing an LLC and LLP entity status much easier for the purposes of federal taxation. Under most states' laws, LLCs and LLPs that are treated as partnerships for federal tax purposes are treated the same way for state tax purposes.

Businesses operating as LLCs and LLPs are not taxed at the entity (i.e., at the corporate or partnership) level. Rather, the taxable income passes through to the shareholders and partners. This arrangement avoids one of the oldest complaints about the corporate tax (within both federal and state systems): double taxation of dividends and profits.[25] Partnerships and federal S corporations have always avoided this pitfall. But the advantage of LLCs and LLPs is that the shareholders and partners enjoy virtually the same protections against personal liability as do traditional C corporations.

The potential problem for state revenue departments is that more and more businesses will choose to operate as LLCs and LLPs, further shrinking the corporate tax base. While a serious concern, the growth of the use of pass-through entities may not continue at the same pace.[26] LLCs and LLPs do not offer easy access to capital, and they offer no opportunity to trade stock publicly. In an economy driven by the need for capital at a moment's notice, many businesses will continue to choose to operate as traditional C corporations.

Still, studies of the advent of limited liability companies and other pass-through entities have found that states have lost up to a third of their corporate tax revenue due to these practices.[27]

Relationship with the Federal Corporate Income Tax

In virtually every state the CIT is calculated by reference to the federal CIT. In most states, the starting point for computing corporation income tax is income as reported on the federal CIT return. Twenty-five states begin with federal taxable income before special deductions (line 28 of Form 1120). Twenty states begin with federal taxable income (line 30 of Form 1120). Only Arkansas, Kentucky, and the District of Columbia do not start with any reference to federal taxable income. For filing purposes, every state except Texas and Tennessee requires some portion of the federal Form 1120 to be attached to the state return.

Then additions and subtractions are made to arrive at each state's corporate tax base. Typical additions to federal income are state and local bond interest, deductions for state and local taxes paid, federal special deductions like dividends received, and deductions for cost recovery if assets are not depreciable for state purposes. Typical subtractions are interest on federal bonds, refunds of state and local taxes paid, and dividends received from out-of-state corporations.

Nonbusiness income is also subtracted from any income that must be apportioned. The net amount of adjusted federal taxable income must then be apportioned to the state according to the state's apportionment formula—which, as noted above, is often some weighted average of in-state sales to total sales, in-state employee compensation to total compensation, and in-state property to total property. Taxable income apportioned to the state is then adjusted again for gains and losses allocable to the state.

Because the state and federal corporate income-tax regimes are so interrelated, any change in the federal law can and often does have significant effects on state revenue for those states that substantially conform to the federal tax base.[28] For example, the states lost approximately $16 billion of income tax revenue as a result of federal tax changes made in 2001 and 2002.[29] The states lost another $1.3 billion in revenue as a result of federal corporate tax changes in 2004.[30] Those federal tax changes involved increasing depreciation and other business deductions that narrow the federal CIT base. As the federal base is narrowed, there is a direct reduction in the amount of income that is subject to tax by the states.

The only way to avoid substantial revenue losses is for the states to "decouple" from the federal corporate tax laws. That is, states would no longer peg their corporate tax base to the federal tax base. In the early 2000s, thirty-one states decoupled their tax laws from some or all of the federal tax-reduction provisions.[31] Those actions saved the states an estimated $13 billion. In 2011, the failure to decouple from the federal domestic production deduction will cost twenty-one states $500 million.[32]

While it is certainly possible to decouple from federal tax changes, there are several problems associated with departing from a close linkage between federal and state tax systems. The conformity between state and federal tax laws is intended to reduce compliance and administrative burdens on both taxpayers and governments. The more nonconformity that arises as a result, the more complicated and expensive the corporate tax laws become. Moreover, decoupling, while possible, can be a difficult political choice. A reduction in federal taxes will mean in a reduction in state taxes if state laws are not changed.

SHOULD STATES TAX CORPORATE INCOME?

Given the relatively small amount of revenue generated by the corporate income tax, as well as the high costs of compliance and administration, a relevant question is whether the states should impose the tax at all. The tax fails to achieve many of the rationales thought to justify its imposition. It has not played a role in protecting the personal income tax. Given the small revenue, it is doubtful the tax has a meaningful impact on the overall incidence of state fiscal systems. Most observers have also concluded that it has much to be desired as a benefits tax. Indeed, with respect to paying for services, the business community pays far more in other types of taxes than it does in CITs.[33] In 2009, business entities paid over $590 billion in state and local taxes. Only 8 percent of that amount consisted of CITs.

Thus, one can argue that the CIT is neither an efficient nor an effective method for raising state revenue. There are several reasons for ending the corporate income tax. The problems with the tax discussed above have decimated the tax; most of the problems are difficult if not impossible to fix. There is little chance of ending the use of corporate tax incentives. There is little political support for addressing the problems associated with separate accounting or business and nonbusiness income. The amount of money raised by the CIT does not justify the administrative and compliance costs.

James Peters, a nationally known practitioner who has served with the California Franchise Tax Board, has concluded that "there is little theoretical support for the tax."[34] The economist Peggy Musgrave noted that the "corporate income tax at the state level has run counter to the recommendations of most economists who have traditionally seen the tax as a particularly inefficient and inequitable instrument, singularly unsuited for use at the state level."[35] As far back as 1981, former Deputy Assistant Secretary of the Treasury for Tax Analysis Charles McLure asserted that state corporate income taxes have manifest disadvantages that disqualify them for use by states.[36] McLure noted, "The primary reasons for a state corporate income tax are cosmetic and political; it is simply not politically acceptable for individuals to pay income taxes if corporations do not."[37] And more recently, McLure asserted:

> There is little good to be said for state corporate income taxes. Corporate profits are a poor measure of the benefits of public services the state provides to business. Thus corporate income taxes interfere with economic neutrality and undermine the state's competitive position. They are neither fair nor transparent. The best that can be said for them is that they act as a backstop for the individual income tax, which might otherwise be avoided through incorporation.[38]

In 2005, Ohio was the first state to take steps to formally abandon its CIT. The legislatures passed and the governor signed a law that would phase out the CIT over a five-year period. The new law replaced the lost revenue with a broad-based, low-rate commercial activity tax, which is essentially a gross receipts tax.[39] The new law was supported by the corporate business community but was opposed by retailers and antitax groups. One prominent commentator, who supports repeal of corporate income taxes, opposed the imposition of a gross receipts tax as a replacement on the grounds that such taxes are regressive, nontransparent, and detrimental to economic growth.[40]

Despite these notable detractors, and the new legislation in Ohio, there has been no widespread public or political support for eliminating the tax. Support may be lacking because the revenue and burdens generated by the tax are too inconsequential to give rise to serious dissatisfaction. But the reason may be that, despite the problems discussed above, political leaders and the public sincerely agree with the rationale for imposing a tax on corporate profits. Without the tax, even the pretense that corporations (or rather their shareholders) pay for the government services they receive would disappear.

With no serious opposition to the tax on the horizon, the state CIT will no doubt continue to exist. Unless states strengthen the tax considerably, however, it will remain a minor source of revenue.

SAVING THE CORPORATE INCOME TAX

How can states rescue the state CIT from near irrelevancy and make it a more significant source of income? Several policy changes could strengthen the tax.

Require Combined Reporting

The most effective way of increasing corporate tax revenue is the adoption of combined reporting as a tool for countering the tax-avoidance strategies of corporations. Combined reporting treats the parent company and most or all of its subsidiaries as a single corporation for state income tax purposes. States should require unitary-based combined reporting for all related corporations. Under this requirement, all related corporations would apportion their respective state tax returns as a single business. Combined reporting would severely limit corporations' ability to avoid state corporate tax liability through a variety of tax-avoidance strategies that are based on artificially shifting profits to subsidiaries located in no-tax or low-tax states. It would also add billions of dollars to state tax revenue.[41]

There is a growing recognition that states that do not mandate combined reporting are vulnerable to a variety of corporate tax-avoidance strategies. Sixteen states have mandated combined reporting for at least two decades. Vermont enacted the policy in 2004, and it went into effect there in 2006.[42] New York enacted a combined reporting law in April 2007, retroactive to the beginning of the year. Texas and West Virginia have implemented combined reporting in 2008 and 2009, respectively. Combined reporting is also included in a "Michigan Business Tax" that went into effect in 2008. As of 2009, a total of twenty-three states now require combined reporting.

There are, however, critics who question the basic arguments that proponents have made in advocating for combined reporting. Cline has identified several ways in which combined reporting leads to a less favorable outcome than separate filing. He found that combined reporting does not necessarily raise additional revenue, reduces investment, and increases administrative and compliance costs.[43]

A Return to the Three-Factor Formula?

States could return to the UDIPTA three-factor formula, which is considered by many experts to be an efficient and fair rule among the set of imperfect options.[44] More important, most public finance experts agree that using the three-factor formula will raise additional corporate tax revenue in states with significant plant space, equipment, and employees.

The rationale for using these three factors to determine taxable income is that companies benefit from a state's public services in a variety of ways, including owning property in a state, making sales within a state, and having an in-state employee base. The three-factor formula ensures that corporate tax liability reflects the benefits received by each type of corporation.

Using the apportionment rule that UDITPA recommends would be an important step toward ensuring that all corporate profits are subject to taxation. However, over the past twenty years many states have chosen to reduce the importance of the property and payroll factors and to increase the importance of the sales factor.

The majority of states now use apportionment formulas that give "double-weight" or greater to the sales factor: in such formulae, a corporation's in-state sales are at least twice as important as each of the other factors. At the extreme, more than a dozen states now rely entirely on the sales factor in determining at least some corporations' tax liabilities. This is the "single-sales factor." Returning to a more uniform set of apportionment rules is an important first step in preventing widespread tax avoidance and ensuring that state corporate income taxes are applied fairly.

Use "Throwback" or "Throw-Out" Rules to Deal with "Nowhere Income"

States should consider implementing "throwback" or "throw-out" rules to deal with "nowhere income."[45] Ideally, all of a company's sales would be attributed to the states in which it operates, but, due to differences among states' CIT rules, this is not always the case. In some instances, a portion of a company's sales are not attributed to any state, either because that state does not levy such a tax or because the company doesn't have sufficient level of activity in the state to be subject to the tax. This means that a corresponding portion of its profits go untaxed, a phenomenon often referred to as "nowhere income." Corporations are aware that they can significantly reduce their corporate tax burdens by carefully planning their tax liabilities. Such tax planning often entails little more than creating subsidiaries with little or no assets or business activity within low-tax and no-tax states.

One remedy for the problem of nowhere income is enacting a "throwback rule," which mandates that sales into other states that are not taxable will be "thrown back" into the state of origin for tax purposes. Twenty-seven states use the throwback rule. But the following eighteen states that tax corporate income do not: Arizona, Connecticut, Delaware, Florida, Georgia, Iowa, Kentucky, Louisiana, Maryland, Massachusetts, Minnesota, Nebraska, New York, North Carolina, Pennsylvania, South Carolina, Tennessee, and Virginia.

One alternative to the throwback rule is the "throw-out" rule. Rather than seeking to assign all sales to the states in which the company operates, the throw-out rule simply excludes from the denominator of the sales factor any sales that are not assigned to any states. By reducing the denominator while leaving the numerator unchanged, the sales factor is increased and the portion of the taxpayer's income that is subject to tax is increased. West Virginia and New Jersey are the only states with a throw-out rule, although New Jersey's throw-out rule is scheduled to be repealed in 2011.

Companies aggressively pursuing this "nowhere income" tax-avoidance strategy can reduce their state tax bills far below what they ought to pay—and far below the taxes paid by competing companies. Allowing companies to minimize their tax liability through these strategies distorts the economic incentives they face,

puts other businesses at a disadvantage, and drains tax revenue that could be us
to finance vitally important long-term public investments. Throwback and throv
out rules can help to level the economic playing field among all businesses and t
reduce state fiscal stress, by simply ensuring that all of the profits that companies
earn are subject to taxation in the states in which they do business.

Use of Tax Incentives

The granting of tax incentives to corporations has proliferated in the past quarter-
century. Every state offers some form of tax benefit to corporations that relocate to
or remain within their jurisdiction. And most states offer tax incentives for particular types of investment. States should minimize the granting of tax incentives to
corporations. In addition to forgoing significant amounts of revenue, such actions
violate every principle of sound tax policy by shrinking the tax base, undermining
equity, and subverting efficiency.

There is an abundance of research that has found corporate tax incentives are
largely unnecessary (the corporation would have taken the desired action even
without the tax break). Thus, tax incentives cost states tremendous amounts of
revenue.

States have given out far more corporate tax incentives than can be listed herein.
But some examples illustrate the size of the foregone revenue. Under the threat of
moving facilities and jobs elsewhere, Citigroup received a total of at least $285.9
million from 1989 to 2007 in subsidies just in New York, New Jersey, Kentucky,
and Texas combined.[46] It is no surprise for one commentator to conclude that "all
the evidence points to a single conclusion: state tax incentives are a thoroughly
unproven tool for promoting economic development."[47]

CONCLUSION

The state CIT has a long and controversial history. It raises relatively little revenue, yet it consumes a disproportionate amount of administrative and compliance
resources. The tax has the potential to raise significantly more revenue. But the
arguments that the tax deters economic growth and renders states less competitive
have been seen as compelling by political leaders. To save the CIT from irrelevancy,
policymakers must find ways to strengthen and enforce the tax.

This book goes to print during the greatest economic crisis for state governments since the Great Depression. From 2008 to the present, state governments
have faced historically high budget deficits. The states have raised taxes and

substantially reduced service levels. In this environment, the debate over state CITs has become more intense. That debate has centered on whether the tax deters economic development and job creation. It has also hinged on the states' dire need for additional revenue. The economic crisis is sure to keep the debate over whether and how to tax corporate profits at the state level alive and well for many years.

NOTES

1 Luna, Murray, and Yang (this volume).
2 All data on corporate income tax revenue are for 2009 and are from the US Census Bureau (2010).
3 Washington's business and occupation tax is viewed as a business activity tax on gross income. Ohio repealed its corporate net income tax in 2005 and replaced it with a gross receipts tax. Each of these noncorporate net income tax states subjects the business enterprise to specific business levies (e.g., Ohio imposes a corporate franchise tax on either taxable income or net worth; Wyoming on the sum capital, property, and other in state assets and property; and all four levy some form of corporate organization fee). CCH (2009).
4 US Census Bureau (2010).
5 Pomp (1998); Brunori (2002); Brunori (2005).
6 Brunori (2011).
7 Brunori (1999a); McLure (2005a).
8 Luna, Murray, and Yang (this volume).
9 Brunori (2004); Brunori (1999b).
10 Bartik (1991); Lynch (1996).
11 Gravelle (2010).
12 Harberger (2006); Carroll (2009).
13 Cornia et al. (2005); Fox (2003).
14 Brunori (1999c); Brunori (1999d); Fox (2003).
15 Sullivan (2008); Dubin (1999).
16 Brunori (2011).
17 Strauss (2005), 14–16; Edmiston (2005); Gordon (1986).
18 Brunori (2011); Brunori (2000); Pomp (1998).
19 Edmiston (2002).
20 Pomp (1998).
21 Pomp (1987).
22 Fox (2003).
23 Pomp (1998).
24 Ibid.
25 Cordes (2005).
26 Lee (2000).
27 Fox and Luna (2002).
28 Brunori (2011); Fox and Luna (2002).
29 Johnson (2003).
30 Johnson and McNichol (2005).
31 Ibid.

32 Johnson and Singham (2010).

33 Cline et al. (2010).

34 Peters (1995), 1404.

35 Musgrave (1984), 51.

36 McLure (1981), 51.

37 Brunori (1999c), 1227.

38 McLure (2005a), 30.

39 Luna, Murray, and Yang (this volume).

40 McLure (2005b).

41 Mazerov (2007).

42 Ibid.

43 Cline (2008).

44 Bucks (2005); Miller and Gravelle (2005); Edmiston (2005).

45 Luna (2005) provides a review of empirical research on "throwbacks."

46 Stecker and Steinberg (2007).

47 Enrich (1996), 424.

References

Bartik, Timothy (1991). *Who Benefits from State and Local Economic Development Policies?* Kalamazoo, MI: W.E. Upjohn Institute for Employment Research.

Brunori, David (1997, Winter). "Principles of Tax Policy and Targeted Tax Incentives." *State and Local Government Review* 29(1): 50–61.

Brunori, David (1999a, October 25). "Interview: CBPP's Iris Lav on Fairness, Progressivity, and the Net." *State Tax Notes*: 1103–1108.

Brunori, David (1999b, September 13). "Business Makes Its Case—for Higher Taxes." *State Tax Notes*: 683–686.

Brunori, David (1999c, November 8). "Interview: Charles McLure on Sales Tax, E-Commerce, and the Pros and Cons of a VAT." *State Tax Notes*: 1225–1230.

Brunori, David (1999d, October 18). "Interview: FTA's Harley Duncan on the MTC, Cooperation, E-Commerce." *State Tax Notes*: 1037–1041.

Brunori, David (2000, July 31). "Interview with Dan Bucks of the Multistate Tax Commission." *State Tax Notes*: 303–309.

Brunori, David (2002, July 1). "The Politics of State Taxation: Stop Taxing Corporate Income." *State Tax Notes*: 47–50.

Brunori, David (2004, March 8). "The Politics of State Taxation: Corporate Taxes Are All the Rage." *State Tax Notes*: 811–813.

Brunori, David (2011). *State Tax Policy: A Political Perspective.* 3nd ed. Washington, DC: Urban Institute Press.

Bucks, Dan (2005). "Multistate Tax Commission." In *The Encyclopedia of Taxation and Tax Policy*, edited by Joseph J. Cordes, Robert D. Ebel, and Jane G. Gravelle. Washington, DC: Urban Institute Press. 14–16.

Carroll, Robert (2009). "The Corporate Income Tax and Workers' Wages: New Evidence from the 50 States." Washington, DC: The Tax Foundation.

Cline, Robert (2008, June 23). "Understanding the Competitive and Revenue Effects of Combined Reporting." *State Tax Notes*: 959–980.

Cline, Robert, Thomas Neubig, Andrew Phillips, and Julia Thayne (2010, April 26). "50-State Total State and Local Business Taxes for 2009." *State Tax Notes*: 275–295.

Commerce Clearing House, CCH (2009). *State Tax Handbook*. Chicago: CCH/Wolters Kluwer.

Cordes, Joseph J. (2005). "Dividends, Double Taxation." In *The Encyclopedia of Taxation and Tax Policy*, edited by Joseph J. Cordes, Robert D. Ebel, and Jane G. Gravelle. Washington, DC: Urban Institute Press. 83–84.

Cornia, Gary, Kelly Edmiston, David Sjoquist, and Sally Wallace (2005). "The Disappearing State Corporate Income Tax." *National Tax Journal* LVIII(1): 115–138.

Dubin, Elliot (1999, July 29). Paper presented to the Multistate Tax Commission Annual Conference, Traverse City, Michigan.

Edmiston, Kelly (2002). "Strategic Apportionment of State Corporate Income Tax." *National Tax Journal* LV(2): 239–260.

Edmiston, Kelly (2005). "State Formula Apportionment." In *The Encyclopedia of Taxation and Tax Policy*, edited by Joseph J. Cordes, Robert D. Ebel, and Jane G. Gravelle. Washington, DC: Urban Institute Press. 370–371.

Ely, Bruce, and Christopher Grissom (2000, July 24). "LLC and LLP Scorecard: An Update." *State Tax Notes*: 235–243.

Enrich, Peter D. (1996, December). "Saving the States from Themselves: Commerce Clause Constraints on State Tax Incentives for Business." *Harvard Law Review* 110: 377.

Fox, William (2003, August 4). "Three Characteristics of Tax Structures Have Contributed to the Current State Fiscal Crisis." *State Tax Notes*: 369–376.

Fox, William F., and LeAnn Luna (2002). "State Corporate Tax Revenue Trends: Causes and Possible Solutions." *National Tax Journal* 55: 491–508.

Gordon, Roger (1986). "A Critical Look at Formula Apportionment." In *Final Report of the Minnesota Tax Study Commission*, Vol. 2, edited by Robert D. Ebel and Therese J. McGuire. Boston: Butterworth. 209–222.

Gordon, Roger (2003, January 16). "Does the Advent of LLCs Explain Declining State Corporate Tax Revenue?" Working Paper. Knoxville: University of Tennessee.

Gravelle, Jennifer (2010). "Corporate Tax Incidence: Review of the General Equilibrium Estimates and Analysis." Congressional Budget Office Working Paper 2010–2003.

Harberger, Arnold (2006). "Corporate Tax Incidence: Reflections on What Is Known, Unknown, and Unknowable." In *Fundamental Tax Reform: Issues, Choices, and Implications*, edited by John Diamond and George Zodrow. Cambridge, MA: MIT Press. 283–308.

Johnson, Nicholas (2003, June 9). "Federal Tax Changes Likely to Cost States Billions in Coming Years." *State Tax Notes*: 909–912.

Johnson, Nicholas, and Elizabeth McNichol (2005, February 22). "States Can Decouple from the Qualified Production Activities Deduction." *State Tax Notes*: 545–550.

Johnson, Nicholas, and Ashali Singham (2010, January 14). "States Can Opt Out of the Costly and Ineffective Domestic Production Deduction Corporate Tax Break." Center on Budget and Policy Priorities.

Lee, John William, III. (2000, May 8). "Choice of Small Business Tax Entity: Fact and Fiction." *State Tax Notes*: 1605–1620.

Luna, LeAnn (2005). "Throwback Rules, Multistate Corporations." In *The Encyclopedia of Taxation and Tax Policy*, edited by Joseph J. Cordes, Robert D. Ebel, and Jane G. Gravelle. Washington, DC: Urban Institute Press. 436–439.

Lynch, Robert (1996). "Do State and Local Tax Incentives Work?" Washington, DC: Economic Policy Institute.

Mazerov, Michael (2007, April 30). "Growing Number of States Consider Combined Reporting." *State Tax Notes*: 335–340.

McLure, Charles (1981, July 13). "Toward Uniformity in Interstate Taxation." *Tax Notes*: 51.

McLure, Charles (2005a, April 4). "How—and How Not to—Tax Business." *State Tax Notes*: 29–34.

McLure, Charles (2005b, April 18). "Why Ohio Should Not Impose a Gross Receipts Tax." *State Tax Notes*: 213–215.

Miller, Ben, and Jane G. Gravelle (2005). "Foreign Corporations, State Taxation of." In *The Encyclopedia of Taxation and Tax Policy*, edited by Joseph Cordes, Robert D. Ebel, and Jane G. Gravelle. Washington, DC: Urban Institute Press. 155–158.

Multistate Tax Commission (2003). "Corporate Tax Sheltering and the Impact on State Corporate Income Tax Revenue Collection." *State Tax Notes*: 237–244.

Musgrave, Peggy (1984). "Principles for Dividing the State Corporate Tax Base." In *The State Corporation Income Tax*, edited by Charles McLure. Palo Alto, CA: Hoover Institution Press. 51.

Peters, James H. (1995, April 3). "The State Corporation Income Tax in the 21st Century." *State Tax Notes*: 1400–1404.

Pomp, Richard (1987). "Reforming a Corporate Income Tax." *Albany Law Review* 51: 393–409.

Pomp, Richard (1998). "The Future of the State Corporate Income Tax: Reflections (and Confessions) of a State Tax Lawyer." In *The Future of State Taxation*, edited by David Brunori. Washington, DC: Urban Institute Press. 49–72.

Stecker, Sarah, and Dan Steinberg (2007, June 10). "Pay, or We (Might) Go: How Citigroup Games the States and Cities." *New Jersey Policy Perspective*, www.goodjobsfirst.org/pdf/citigroupplays.pdf.

Strauss, Robert (2005). "Apportionment." In *The Encyclopedia of Taxation and Tax Policy*, edited by Joseph J. Cordes, Robert D. Ebel, and Jane G. Gravelle. Washington, DC: Urban Institute Press. 14–16.

Sullivan, Martin (2008, May 20). "Corporate Reports Show Taxes on Profits Falling." *State Tax Notes*: 527–532.

Swenson, Charles W. (1997, November 3). "Does Your State Overtax Business Income?" *State Tax Notes*: 1129–1135.

US Census Bureau (2010). "Federal, State, and Local Governments: 2009 State Government Finance Data." www.census.gov/govs/www/state09.html.

CHAPTER 14

....

ENTITY TAXATION
OF BUSINESS
ENTERPRISES

....

LEANN LUNA, MATTHEW N. MURRAY,
AND ZHOU YANG

STATE governments rely on three major sources of tax revenue: corporate income taxes (CITs), individual income taxes, and sales taxes. In recent years, all three sources have been under tremendous pressure. The recent collapse in state and local revenues can be largely attributed to the economic recession, but the long-term threats to these traditional revenue sources are structural and will only partially reverse themselves when the economy recovers. Corporate income-tax collections have been in decline for a number of years partially due to effective tax-planning efforts by businesses as well as the growing popularity of limited liability corporations (LLCs) and other pass-through entities that effectively shift business income to individual tax returns.[1] At the same time, the sales tax base is threatened by the shift of the US economy toward generally untaxed services and the rise of electronic commerce as a means to market and deliver goods and services.[2] States impose a use tax on the e-commerce of goods, but the use tax is easily and frequently evaded by consumers; services delivered electronically are typically excluded from the sales and use tax base by statute. Further, both corporate income taxes and sales taxes are cyclically sensitive and naturally rise and fall with the economy. Attempts to reverse the revenue trends with loophole-closing provisions and higher tax rates have only been partially successful, leaving states with few options under their existing tax regimes to generate needed tax revenue.

The combination of budgetary pressures and structural problems has led states to consider new options to supplement or replace existing taxes. One option considered by a growing number of states, and recently adopted by a few, are taxes such as gross receipts taxes (GRTs) and variants of subtraction value-added taxes that are imposed on business activities rather than on profits. Lawmakers hope these alternative revenue sources, which can include elements of both income and sales taxes, will prove more stable and elastic and politically easier to implement than raising rates or expanding corporate income or sales-tax bases.

The policy challenge confronting the states is not new. Pressures on the state CIT emerged as early as 1959 when Congress enacted P.L. 86–272, intended as a temporary measure, which limits the ability of states to tax business whose only activity within their borders is the solicitation of sales. Additional pressures on the CIT have surfaced in recent decades because of tax planning, tax competition, and policy choices, which have narrowed the base and diminished revenue productivity. The erosion of the sales-tax base can be dated back to at least 1960 when largely untaxed services began their noticeable ascent as a share of consumption. Further, the US Supreme Court limited the ability of states to require remote sellers (e.g., mail order and online vendors) to collect sales tax with two decisions: *National Bellas Hess, Inc. v. Department of Revenue* in 1967 and *Quill Corp. v. North Dakota* in 1992. Despite these pressures and other trends that have conspired to weaken state revenue performance, there have been few if any fundamental shifts in state tax policy toward business.[3]

The focus of this chapter is on the nature, structure, and policy implications of nontraditional taxes on business activity. The chapter begins with an introduction to the various alternatives and the important differences between the viable options. The discussion then turns to an evaluation and comparison of the alternative tax instruments, primarily the gross receipts tax and the value-added tax. We also compare these alternatives to the CIT and retail sales tax applying four criteria: (1) justification for business taxation and taxpayer fairness; (2) economic efficiency (neutrality); (3) revenue performance; and (4) ease of administration and compliance.[4] Framing the analysis of entity taxation within the context of other taxes currently used by the states is important because the various tax instruments are often viewed as policy substitutes.

DESCRIPTION OF GROSS RECEIPT TAXES AND VALUE-ADDED TAXES

The options for broadly taxing business activity can be thought of as a continuum, with the options distinguished primarily by the deductions (if any) allowed in arriving at the tax base. On one end is the CIT, which taxes apportioned corporate

Table 14.1 Taxonomy of Business Taxes*

	Tax Base	Example	Description of Tax Base
Taxes with Broad Bases	General gross receipts tax (GRT)	Ohio CAT, Washinton B&O, Delaware	Gross receipts (GR) with few, if any, deductions
	Modified GRT	Texas tax base option Michigan	GR minus labor costs or 70 percent of GR GR minus purchases of *tangible* propcrty
	Gross margin tax	Texas base option; Kentucky and New Jersey AMTs	GR minus cost of goods sold
	Net receipts tax/ Subtraction method VAt	California (proposed)	GR minus purchases from other firms, resulting in incomplete border adjustments
	Credit invoice VAt	EU credit-invoice VAt	GR minus purchases from other firms with border adjustments
	Corporate income tax	Traditional business entity tax imposed in 45 states; applies to C corps only	GR minus labor costs, depreciation, interest, purchases from other firms, other operating expenses
Taxes with Narrow Bases			

*We draw this from Cline and Neubig (2008) 187 and have updated it for recent reforms.

profits and, for a given total tax yield, has the smallest base and the highest tax rate. On the other end is the pure GRT, which taxes gross sales (i.e., turnover), allows for no deductions, and imposes much smaller rates on the vastly larger tax base. The subtraction method value-added tax (VAT)—like the proposed business nets receipts tax (BNRT) in California[5]—falls between the CIT and the GRT. Each of these taxes can be destination-based or origin-based, depending on the factor or factors used to apportion interstate activity. Table 14.1 lists these alternatives, along with some of the variants of the GRT and the VAT, and reflects the differences in the tax bases.

Gross Receipts Tax

A broad GRT begins with the gross proceeds from business activity. Typically, taxable gross receipts include all in-state sales of tangible goods and services but often exclude income from financial transactions (interest, dividends, proceeds from the sales of stock). The most recent GRTs are intended to be destination taxes on domestic business activity, which is accomplished by using the location of the final customer to situs (i.e., source) interstate sales and efforts to exempt out-of-state sales from the tax base.[6] In its simplest form, the GRT base is simply the numerator of the sales-factor apportionment formula, commonly used to apportion income of multistate businesses for income-tax purposes. The amount includes items shipped to a state for final consumption as well as sitused services and nonbusiness sales allocated to the state.

Washington and Delaware have maintained GRTs for many years;[7] more recently (2005–2010), Michigan, Ohio, Oklahoma, and Texas added variants of GRTs.[8] New Mexico has a sales tax that is named a GRT, but the tax effectively operates as a sales tax.[9] The GRT is an attractive alternative to the traditional CIT for various reasons. Because the GRT is levied on the gross proceeds from business activities conducted within the state, the base is very large and allows states to levy the tax at a very low rate. Furthermore, the GRT generally applies to broadly defined business activity, rather than corporations per se; therefore, individuals, partnerships, and limited liability companies are also subject to the GRT.[10]

As a broad tax on sales, GRTs are often compared to the retail sales tax (RST), but the two taxes have different intended tax bases. While the sales tax intends (but in practice fails) to fully tax consumption, the GRT taxes the value of all transactions.[11] Unlike the sales tax, which exempts purchases intended for resale or integral to the manufacturing process, the GRT does not allow deductions for purchases of previously taxed materials or labor, causing the tax to pyramid each time a product changes hands during the production and distribution process. Some GRT systems attempt to mitigate pyramiding by allowing deductions for some input costs, imposing differential tax rates on different categories of sales, or imposing lower tax rates on business sectors such as manufacturing with multiple steps in the production chain.[12] Net receipt taxes (NRTs) more broadly allow deductions for certain business–to-business purchases, which moves them closer to a pure sales tax or a subtraction VAT.

GRTs also broadly tax services (largely excluded from the RST among the states) and sales to organizations that are typically exempt from the sales tax (e.g., some government and nonprofit organizations). A GRT can also potentially expand the reach of state business taxes by expanding the scope of taxpayers subject to the tax. Businesses whose activities within a state are protected by nexus concerns and federal law are often subject to the GRT because states assert that a lower nexus threshold applies to privilege taxes than to sales and corporate income taxes (see discussion below).[13]

Because of the much larger tax base, gross receipts tax rates are much lower than CIT tax rates. Most GRT rates are less than 1 percent; thus, the median corporate tax rate is at least seven times larger than the typical gross receipts tax rate for US states. The GRT rates vary considerably by state; the rates depend on the size of the tax base, revenue need, and whether the GRT is in addition to or a substitute for other taxes. In addition, the rate may vary by firm-specific factors such as whether the firm is a wholesaler or retailer, and sometimes the specific industry, as with the Washington Business & Occupation (B&O) tax. The legal incidence of the GRT falls on the business entity (the seller of the good or service) rather than on the consumer as is the case with most state RSTs.

Value-Added Taxes

Value-added taxes have a long history, with early proposals being introduced in France in the 1920s. By the late 1960s VAT adoptions accelerated; some version of the VAT is now in use in at least 137 countries, primarily as a national tax.[14] Because US states lack an enforceable border, a state-level VAT has fundamentally more conceptual and operational issues than a national tax. However, economists and policymakers adapted VAT concepts to the state and local levels almost immediately after their introduction abroad. The Brookings Institution advanced the earliest recommendations for a state VAT for Iowa (1930) and Alabama (1932). In 1932, Hawaii became the first governmental unit in the United States to employ the value-added concept with its business excise tax.

In 1953, with strong support from the automotive sector, Michigan became the first state to adopt a VAT—the business activities tax (BAT)—as a replacement for the corporate net income tax. While it was adopted as a reasonably pure origin tax, over time the BAT became eroded with numerous special provisions, and in 1968 Michigan returned to conventional corporate profits taxation.[15] However, by 1975, legislators determined that the Michigan business tax system had again become unstable and overly complex, and they replaced the corporate profits tax (plus several "nuisance" taxes) with the single business tax (SBT). In 2008, the SBT was replaced with the Michigan Business Tax (the MBT), which includes a modified gross receipts tax that allows for deductions for purchases from other firms. In 1993, New Hampshire became the second state to enact a VAT, the business enterprise tax (BET), which is still in place today.[16]

As the name suggests, a VAT attempts to tax only the value added by each business in the life cycle of a product or service from the extractive and fabrication processes to product distribution (wholesale and retail trade) and service delivery. Conceptually, the value added at each stage of production is the selling price of a good or service minus the cost of purchases of tangible goods and services from other firms. Purchases include the typical components of costs of goods sold (excluding in-house labor costs) as well as indirect costs such as expenditures on office supplies, computers, and telecommunications equipment. A consumption VAT levies a tax each time a good passes between vendors and at the final sale; a deduction or credit is allowed for any previously taxed activity. The sum of the VAT paid at each stage of production and distribution is equivalent to a tax on final household consumption. An income-type VAT, sometimes referred to as a business value tax (BVT),[17] is a tax on production and is levied on business activity during a taxable period, such as a year, rather than on a transaction basis. The state VATs in the United States most closely resemble a BVT.

Because deductions often cannot be sited to particular locations, multistate businesses must apportion the "value added" as they must apportion taxable income for CIT purposes. The VAT can be destination-based or origin-based, depending on the apportionment factors used. For example, the original Michigan business activity tax (the BAT) used an equally weighted three-factor formula of property, payroll, and sales, which resulted in a largely origin-based tax. Using the location of final sales to apportion the value added converts the tax to a destination basis.

Governments use one of three types of VATs to calculate the value added: credit invoice, subtraction, and addition VATs.[18] Many national governments (including the nation-state members of the European Union) use the credit-invoice method to determine the tax base. The credit-invoice VAT is in principle similar to the retail sales tax[19] in that both impose the tax on final sales to consumers. Although there has been some academic consideration regarding the application of a credit/invoice approach for US state taxation, the approach has not received any serious legislative attention.[20] Because no US state has seriously considered the credit-invoice VAT, we limit the remainder of the VAT discussion to the addition and subtraction method types of VATs.

The addition and subtraction methods VATs are typically imposed on all businesses regardless of organizational form. The two methods arrive at an equivalent tax base but from different directions. For the addition method, the tax base equals the sum of the costs that generate added value, primarily labor (payroll), rent, interest, and the firm's profits. For the subtraction method VAT,[21] the tax base is equal to gross receipts minus qualified purchases from other firms. Taxable gross receipts typically include all sales of tangible goods and services but exclude income from financial transactions (e.g., interest, dividends, proceeds from the sales of financial assets). Allowable deductions include purchases of raw materials and intermediate goods (but not in-house labor) that would make up the cost of goods sold under the income tax, the full cost of capital purchases, and expenditures for office supplies, computers, and indirect materials necessary but not integral to the production process.

Under either method, lawmakers must also decide between income or consumption variants of the VAT, depending on how capital purchases are treated.[22] For the income variant (IVAT), capital purchases are treated similar to the income tax, with taxpayers taking depreciation deductions over time and maintaining inventory accounts. Most states have decided to use the consumption variant (CVAT), where deductions for capital and inventory are taken at the time of purchase rather than when an item is sold. This approach eliminates the need for tracking depreciation or inventory levels for tax purposes.

The subtraction method VAT, which, like the addition method, is imposed at the entity level on an aggregated taxable base, resembles an income tax but is distinguishable from the CIT both by the types of income included in the base and allowable deductions. For example, the CIT base includes receipts of interest and dividends, frequently excluded from the VAT base.[23] Wages are deductible for purposes of the CIT but are disallowed for the subtraction method VAT. The subtraction method VAT typically allows immediate expensing of capital purchases (a CVAT) while the CIT requires most capital purchases to be depreciated over time. There is no reason, however, why a VAT could not be structured as an IVAT and could treat capital goods the same as the CIT.

Current Examples of US Business Activity Taxes

In this section, we discuss examples of business activity taxes that states currently employ, while noting some of the differences and similarities between these taxes. Precise classification of these taxes into particular categories, such as GRTs,[24] NRTs, or subtraction VATs is not practical because some of the taxes have elements of more than one type of tax.

At present three states employ a GRT in the United States: these taxes are the Ohio Commercial Activity Tax (CAT), the Washington Business and Occupation tax (B&O), and the Delaware gross receipts tax.[25] Both the Ohio CAT and the Washington B&O are levied on businesses or persons with taxable gross receipts and an economic presence in the respective states. However, Ohio and Delaware GRTs do not tax returns to capital (e.g., interest, dividends, and capital gains), although the states' personal and corporate income taxes will capture this income. Washington does not have an income tax but does include returns to capital in its B&O tax base. Further, while Washington's B&O tax applies to almost all business income, the B&O tax does provide for limited exemptions, deductions, and credits. Delaware allows for no deductions, but it imposes the tax only on receipts above a threshold amount. Most businesses receive a monthly exemption of $80,000; manufacturers receive a monthly exemption of $1 million. Recent business activity taxes enacted by Michigan and Texas are hybrid systems that fall between a general GRT and a subtraction method VAT and resemble NRTs. For example, the Michigan Business Tax allows a deduction for tangible personal property purchased from other firms. The Texas Gross Margin Tax permits firms to choose to deduct either the cost of goods sold or wages and compensation, and it applies lower rates to retailers, wholesalers, and restaurants.[26]

Similarly, the new Oklahoma business activity tax (BAT), which began in 2010 as a replacement for the Oklahoma franchise tax, combines elements of a GRT and a subtraction method VAT.[27] Although described as a tax on business activity, the tax is imposed on "net revenue" and allows for many deductions. To begin with, the tax base excludes several types of revenue such as interest, dividends, real estate rentals, royalties, and net capital gains. Receipts also exclude compensation received by an employee for services performed for the employer. Taxpayers reduce adjusted revenue by ordinary trade or business deductions, with some important exceptions. For example, deductions are not allowed for interest, depreciation, and amortization. The excluded items of income and deduction are still taken into account for Oklahoma income-tax purposes.

New Hampshire imposes the business enterprise tax (BET), the only subnational VAT currently operating in the United States.[28] The BET is an addition VAT; the tax base consists of wages and other compensation plus interest and dividends paid. An addition VAT normally includes profits in the tax base, but because New Hampshire retained a separate tax on business income, the BET does not include profits in the base.

Several states do not impose a stand-alone GRT or NRT, but they rely on the concept as part of an alternative minimum tax (AMT). In these jurisdictions, taxpayers pay the greater of the traditional income tax or the alternative tax based on some measure of gross profits or gross receipts. For example, New Jersey imposes an Alternative Minimum Assessment (AMA) based on gross receipts at rates ranging from 0.1389 percent for taxpayers with receipts from $2 million to $20 million to 0.4 percent for taxpayers with gross receipts of more than $75 million. Tax rates on gross profits range from 0.2778 percent to 0.8 percent. Kentucky assesses a Limited Liability Entity Tax, creditable against corporate or individual income tax of members and shareholders, based on gross receipts or gross profits, whichever calculation results in the lowest tax liability. Because all AMTs are characterized by a broader base with a lower rate than the income tax they complement, these AMTs can best be thought of as being on the same continuum as the GRT and VAT, with their location determined by how broadly the state determines the AMT base.

EVALUATION OF ALTERNATIVE BUSINESS TAXES

The Rationale for Business Taxation

The taxation of business entities is generally premised on the benefit principle where a firm receives public services or regulatory and legal benefits from the state. A classic example is a privilege (or franchise) tax where the state charters a corporation and then taxes the corporation for the receipt of this privilege.[29] This perspective is formalized under the benefit principle where the alignment of taxes paid with services provided by the state establishes a quid pro quo that could be viewed as both fair and nondistortionary. In practice, however, the base of traditional business taxes does not correspond precisely to the privileges bestowed upon the firm by the state or the services that firms receive from government. A more general view holds that the taxation of business is appropriate not only because of benefits directly bestowed on the firm, but also because of benefits that accrue to nonresident owners of the firm, to visitors, and to local residents and workers.[30] The benefit principle offers the strongest and most general rationale for the taxation of business activity.

Application of the benefit principle to the state CIT would imply that apportioned profits serve as the government service benefit proxy. But unique state policies like apportionment rules and throwback provisions are not intended to align profits with benefits received, while tax-planning behavior allows firms with otherwise similar profits to pay unique liabilities depending on the nature and scope of their reported activities across states. In addition, non-corporate entities and corporations with an economic presence but without nexus pay no CIT.

In contrast, a destination-based VAT is generally understood as a tax on domestic consumption. As such, the benefit principle must apply to public services provided to consumers, whether they are residents or nonresidents. In this instance the firm is simply serving as a tax handle and collection instrument for the public sector.

A gross receipts levy like the Ohio CAT is defined as a privilege tax with statutory incidence falling on the business entity. Application of the benefit principle would imply that in-state receipts (including any embedded tax pyramiding) from delineated taxable activities constitute the benefit tax proxy. Like apportioned profits, there is no reason to believe that gross receipts align closely with the services that a firm receives from the state. In addition, the GRT will lead to varying degrees of forward and backward shifting of tax depending on market conditions in factor and product markets, with differential effects for factors and consumers in different local markets. Accordingly, one must appeal to a general benefit argument rather than a specific quid pro quo to rationalize the use of the GRT.

An entity-level GRT has considerable appeal from this broader perspective of the benefit principle by virtue of including a broader array of firms and economic activity in the tax net. Importantly, the GRT overcomes the sales-tax nexus constraint created by the Supreme Court's *National Bellas Hess v. Department of Revenue* and *Quill Corp. v. North Dakota* decisions. These two court decisions require some form of physical presence to trigger the sales-tax nexus and tax-collection obligations. Equally important is that the GRT overcomes the hurdle created by P.L. 86–272 under the state CIT; P.L. 86–272 is a congressional preemption that protects firms from an income-tax nexus if the firm's only contact with the state is the solicitation of sales of tangible goods. A GRT is neither a sales nor a net income tax but is instead a form of privilege tax that can be applied to a broader set of firms consistent with the notion of economic nexus. Tax-planning opportunities are muted under a GRT relative to a CIT because of a common structure for all firms (as opposed to separate personal and corporate income taxes), a broader nexus standard, and uniform treatment of in-state intercompany transactions. A GRT can be viewed as being fairer because it taxes all firm transactions with a common tax instrument.

The use of a policy criterion like fairness in the context of the taxation of business is problematic. Ultimately, people pay taxes, not the firm, as a legal entity. Fundamental measures of fairness like horizontal equity (the equal treatment of those with similar ability to pay) and vertical equity (the differential treatment of taxpayers with differential ability to pay) are rooted in utilitarianism and do not lend themselves to the analysis of business equity. Discussions regarding the fairness of business tax policy are nonetheless commonplace and typically centered on statutory tax liabilities rather than on economic incidence and who bears the true burden of the tax.

The issue of business tax "fairness" in the debate over GRTs has largely been disconnected from the benefit tax view and is often placed in the context of horizontal and vertical equity and thus the ability to pay. This is inappropriate. While there are legitimate concerns regarding how alternative forms of general-business taxes are distributed across firms with different legal structures, of different size and in different sectors, in the end firms do not have ability to pay in the same sense as a household does.

There are, indeed, concerns over how changes in business-tax policy might redistribute tax burdens across firms. For example, there are specific concerns regarding the "high volume, low margin firm" that might be compelled to remit significant liabilities under a GRT but face little or no tax under a CIT or a VAT.[31] The presumption is that the high volume, low margin firm has little profit or possibly short-run losses and thus a lower ability to pay taxes. Moreover, this view considers the GRT, as well as a CIT or VAT, in a vacuum, rather than in the context of other taxes that must be remitted by firms. For example, businesses must pay property, sales, franchise/privilege, and other taxes regardless of their cash flow or profitability. In addition, the ability to pay and liquidity arguments ignore the possibility of the shifting of tax liabilities forward to consumers.

Adoption of a GRT would fundamentally alter both the statutory and economic burdens of state tax systems. If coupled with reduced reliance on or elimination of the CIT, statutory burdens on regular corporations would fall while burdens on pass-through entities, manufacturers, and service enterprises would rise. A subtraction method VAT or NRT would have similar effects but would also shift statutory burdens from low value-added to high value-added firms.[32] Economic incidence is more complicated because it depends on the complexities of product and factor markets.

Efficiency or Neutrality

An efficient or neutral tax does not alter relative prices and thus does not distort business decision making, including investment, input, and location choices. A well-defined benefit tax would be nondistortionary, but as noted above, aligning taxes with services is problematic, especially if "benefits" are narrowly defined. In practice, any business or entity tax is likely to create distortions.

This section considers the relative efficiency of the GRT, VAT, and CIT from three perspectives. First is neutrality across and within industries, which accounts for influences on the vertical structure of the industry and input choices through the stages of extraction, production, and distribution. Second is neutrality across state borders, including location choices and the treatment of imports and exports. Third is neutrality with respect to business organizational form. The first and third perspectives potentially involve in-state and multistate transactions, while the second area focuses primarily on interstate business activity. Ideally the analysis would be guided by the classical equal-yield approach to evaluating alternative tax instruments. However, in practice the alternative taxes are not always considered as equal-yield substitutes.[33] Moreover, the numerous practical distortions associated with each tax instrument would necessitate rigorous second-best considerations. The analysis below generally operates from the premise that broad bases and low rates are preferred to narrow bases and high rates.

Neutrality Across and Within Industries: Extraction, Production, and Distribution

As shown in table 14.1, the base varies across different business taxes, with a general GRT having the broadest base and the CIT having the narrowest base. The differences in the base and overall structure determine how businesses would be taxed through various stages of extraction, production, and distribution. A significant disadvantage of the GRT relative to a VAT or CIT is that the tax is levied at every link in the interfirm supply chain. For example, wood is taxed as raw timber, as processed lumber, as furniture sold at wholesale, and at the final retail sale. These multiple layers of taxation create tax "pyramiding"—the repeated taxation of the same input or product—that yields a tax base that is larger than the total value of output for the taxing jurisdiction. Depending on the vertical structure of the supply chain (and nuances of the tax structure including differential rates), the degree of tax pyramiding will vary across industries.[34] The issue is greatest for industries with many stages of production and is of lesser importance for an industry with few stages of production. The service sector, for example, will often have fewer stages of production than the manufacturing sector. Pyramiding under a GRT can distort the firm's optimal input choice, the degree of vertical integration, and ultimately consumption choice via differing effective tax rates across industries and products.

The degree of tax pyramiding depends on the degree of vertical integration within an industry. A recent study shows that the technology intensity of both suppliers (upstream firms) and producers (downstream firms) in the same industry significantly influences the likelihood of vertical integration.[35] In general, the total impact of the tax on an industry will vary with the number of firms involved in the production process. Firms that combine multiple steps of the process within a single entity will reduce the overall tax on the final product versus production that is accomplished by different firms at each stage. Thus GRTs can create an incentive for vertical integration. Consequently, the product of the integrated company becomes relatively more competitive than the output of nonintegrated firms within the same industry. In practice, the low tax rates of most GRTs, typically less than 1 percent of sales, will mitigate the incentive to vertically integrate so that factors other than taxes will generally drive the decision to bring production in-house.

Unfortunately, there is no empirical evidence on the extent to which a GRT affects vertical integration. A recent theoretical analysis identified situations where a GRT may create incentives or disincentives for vertical integration.[36] The model considered firm behavior under various market structures where a downstream firm could choose to purchase an input from an upstream input supplier or alternatively to self-supply the same input. The downstream firm used the input to produce a final product that was then sold to consumers. The results showed that a GRT pushes down the input price that an upstream supplier charges, though the extent of this price effect depended on the relative competitiveness of upstream and downstream markets.

As an example, if the downstream market is highly competitive compared to that of the upstream market, a GRT will lead to a greater reduction in the input price than from what an upstream supplier charges. This induces downstream firms to consider buying from the upstream supplier. Intuitively, suppliers in this case have less ability to pass on the additional tax through higher prices. The incentive of the GRT to vertically integrate is reduced by the extent to which the tax is absorbed by suppliers. Thus, the downstream firm will prefer buying inputs over self-supplying as long as the marginal cost of self-producing the inputs is higher than the price that the upstream firm charges for the inputs. In general, market structure influences a GRT's ability to reduce input prices, thus affecting firms' make-or-buy decisions and the degree of pyramiding.

In practice, states with GRTs have taken various steps to modify the tax structure to reduce tax pyramiding. Washington estimates that its GRT pyramids an average of 2.5 times, ranging from only 1.5 times for many services to 6.7 times for some manufacturing processes. To mitigate the pyramiding problem, Washington has made a number of changes to the B&O tax that was implemented in the 1930s, including lower tax rates on industries that are known to pyramid more frequently. For example, the B&O rate for the service sector is 1.8 percent, but the manufacturing sector has a rate of less than 0.5 percent because the industry involves many stages of production. California's proposed BNRT addressed pyramiding in a different fashion by broadly allowing deductions for business-to-business purchases, yielding a system very close to a VAT without border adjustments.

While pyramiding may be extensive with a GRT, effective tax rates will depend on the tax rate and the number of links in the taxable production chain. Washington State, for example, calculated the mean effective B&O tax rate for each industry and found that it varied from a low of 0.32 percent of gross income for the agricultural, forestry, and mining sectors to a high of 0.93 percent for the transportation, communication, and utilities sectors. The mean effective tax rates of the GRT on durable and nondurable goods manufacturing were 0.42 percent and 0.41 percent of gross income, respectively. However, most of the within- and across-sector differences in the total tax burden were caused by the property tax, not the B&O tax. States differ in GRT structure and industry characteristics so that the degree of tax pyramiding and industry-effective tax rates will vary.

The distortions introduced by GRTs due to tax pyramiding need to be compared to alternative business taxes and their potential degree of pyramiding. A VAT is neutral across industries and the supply chain, except in the situation that firms sell (provide) exempt goods or services. Because firms cannot enjoy relief from a VAT paid on any purchases related to exempt sales, tax pyramiding might still occur, though this is not likely to be pervasive because the scope of exempt sales to business will be limited. (Exempt transactions are different from zero-rated sales under a VAT in that the latter allows for a reclamation of tax paid.) A CIT could conceivably lead to pyramiding to the extent that prices rise as a result of formulary apportionment, especially with respect to the sales factor, assuming that tax burdens are shifted forward.[37]

Other taxes on business may also lead to distortions associated with tax pyramiding. Most prominent is the state sales and use tax, which falls on a significant share of business input purchases and pyramids across the production chain, yielding distortions for products and sectors.[38] For example, one estimate indicates that nearly 40 percent of the state sales tax falls on business input purchases.[39] The degree of tax pyramiding will vary depending on the nature of the production process and the types of sales-tax exemptions that states provide to business. Given that sales tax rates are much higher than GRT rates, sales-tax pyramiding will be more pronounced than GRT pyramiding for a given market structure and set of taxable production stages.

Neutrality over Imports and Exports: Interstate Activity

The way that a tax treats imports and exports can influence a state's domestic market for goods and services, a firm's decision to import and export, and the decision on where to locate production facilities. In theory, a sound tax system designed to realize destination-based taxation should tax imports and domestically produced goods in an equal manner; exports should be exempt from taxation and then taxed as imports in other states. The combination of origin-based and destination-based taxation will lead to multiple taxation on exports and can distort the location of production activities.

A general GRT does not allow deductions for inputs or rebates for taxes paid at previous stages of production. A GRT tends to favor imported goods over domestically produced goods because imports from states without GRTs pass through fewer, if any, taxable stages of production.[40] If transactions are sitused at their destination, there is no distortion in location choice, but distortions arise if sales are situed at the origin. The incentive to locate in non-GRT states must be balanced against any source-based taxation arising from the sales taxation of business inputs.

A GRT is similarly nonneutral with respect to exports. Tax pyramiding embeds the tax paid during intermediate stages of production into the product price. Exclusion of the tax at the final stage of production reduces the distortion but fails to account for taxes paid at previous points of production. Therefore, exporters that locate in states with GRTs may be at a competitive tax disadvantage relative to firms located in non-GRT states. However, the presence of any tax pyramiding from the sales tax in market states will mitigate this disadvantage.

National credit-invoice VATs employ border adjustments in order to subject imports to tax and relieve exports of tax. However, no US state uses a credit-invoice VAT. The proposed California BNRT was designed to approximate a subtraction method VAT with a sales-based formula apportionment used to realize destination taxation. In practice, this type of tax operates similarly to an income tax in that the tax is levied on the firm rather than on the transaction, making it difficult to attribute taxes to in-state versus out-of-state sales. Taxes like the BNRT do not fully eliminate taxes on exports because they do not fully relieve tax paid at previous links in the production chain.[41] The effects on prices will depend on market structure, which influences the price elasticity of demand. For example, businesses selling a homogeneous product in many different states may find it difficult to shift the tax forward.

State CITs with a single sales-factor apportionment formula achieve destination-based taxation and can reduce distortions on the location of production that would otherwise arise from origin-based taxation. However, the same apportionment rule can discourage corporate location and the creation of nexus to create untaxed "nowhere" income.[42] Many state CITs still use the three-factor apportionment formula to distribute profits among the states where economic activity has taken place. The three-factor apportionment formula transforms the CIT into an excise tax on the three factors in the formula: sales, property, and payroll.[43] While the sales factor promotes destination-based taxation, the property and payroll factors reflect origin-based taxation. The three-factor formula means that the CIT applies to both imports and exports (assuming nexus is established), though the specific tax impacts would depend on the market structure and the extent of forward and backward shifting of the tax.

Neutrality and Business Organizational Form

A neutral business tax should not distort the choice over organizational form. A CIT distorts the choice of business organizational form by taxing corporate entities with a different structure than noncorporate entities.[44] For instance, a firm may choose to be a pass-through entity such as a sole-proprietorship or limited liability company to avoid potentially higher tax rates and the double taxation of dividends under the CIT. Corporate income taxation can lead to large amounts of shifting of businesses across organizational forms in a setting in which both corporate and noncorporate production coexist, and the deadweight loss from the CIT can be significant.[45] A study using cross-sectional state data on organizational form choices of retailers suggested that there was a significant impact of the relative taxation of corporate versus personal income on corporations' share of real economic activity.[46] Evidence from a more general study that encompasses firms across all sectors found that state tax rates and other tax policy parameters affect the entity choice between corporations and pass-through firms.[47] In contrast to the CIT, which taxes only profitable businesses organized as corporations, both GRTs and VATs include most firms, regardless of their form, and thus have less impact on the choice of organizational form.

The more neutral treatment of different business structures under a GRT and VAT reduces incentives and opportunities to strategically choose business forms based only on tax considerations, potentially increasing efficiency by saving resources spent on tax planning and combating perceived abuses. For example, corporations often have the easiest access to national capital markets, which in turn may lower costs, but income-tax regimes can create incentives to organize as noncorporate entities. Firms may then choose to forgo the nontax benefits of incorporation and become pass-through entities for tax considerations, depending on the relative importance of these two factors. With GRTs or VATs, firms can largely ignore these tax considerations when making the entity choice decision. Efficiency gains occur to the extent that businesses are able to make decisions based on market rather than tax considerations.

Although GRTs are less likely to affect entity choice decisions such as the option of a C corporation versus an LLC, distortions involving organizational structure can still arise. Examples have been developed around Washington's B&O tax.[48] In one case, a manufacturer in Washington created an out-of-state subsidiary as the legal primary manufacturer. This subsidiary then shipped the goods into Washington and contracted with the Washington entity to process the intermediate goods into final products. The manufacturer paid tax on the contract payments received as the processor, rather than on the value of the goods produced. Similarly, a Washington wholesaler could establish itself as the purchasing agent that acquires goods from manufacturers and transfers them to retailers in exchange for a commission. The wholesaler owed tax on the commission, rather than on the value of the goods the retailer receives. These remaining organizational issues are a product of businesses taking advantage of different state tax structures and cannot be eliminated unless states harmonize their systems.

Overall Assessment

This section considered the relative neutrality of major state-level business taxes by considering possible effects on different industries and the chain of extraction, production, and distribution; on imports, exports, and firm location; and on organizational form choices. Among the three taxes, a pure VAT would be the

most efficient, though there are practical problems of making appropriate border adjustments across states. Both GRTs and CITs distort input choices while the
VAT is neutral (aside from border issues). None of the taxes would distort location
choice if designed as destination taxes, but distortions would arise if there were
origin-based elements to the taxes. Both GRTs and VATs are neutral with respect
to business organizational form, though GRTs can create incentives for vertical
integration; there is ample conceptual and empirical evidence to show that state
CITs distort the choice of organizational form. Finally, there has been little explicit
discussion above about how business taxes may distort relative prices and the consumption choices of final consumers. A pure VAT would be neutral by not altering
relative product prices (though prices relative to leisure would be distorted), while
both a CIT and GRT would be distortionary. The problem with the GRT arises
from the differential degree of pyramiding for different producers and products,
while distortions from the CIT are rooted in potentially different degrees of the
forward shifting of tax.

Revenue Performance

Revenue need and near- and long-term concerns over how to tax the business sector have been primary motivations for considering broad-based levies like a GRT.
Ultimately revenue performance—including revenue yield, revenue elasticity and
buoyancy, and revenue stability and cyclicality—will be determined by policy
choices that define the tax base and tax rate.

Because GRTs are turnover taxes with few if any business-to-business exemptions, the base will generally be some multiple of state gross domestic product,
greatly enhancing revenue potential vis-à-vis other tax instruments. For example,
Mikesell noted that Washington's B&O tax base was 177 percent of state gross
domestic product in 2005.[49] The effects of pyramiding on revenue yield can be
pronounced, with evidence from New Mexico suggesting that this is the source of
about one-third of collections from the state's GRT.[50] The potential size of the gross
receipts base, along with the tax's invisibility in the eyes of households, has raised
some concerns that revenue yield may become excessive.

The potential revenue yield of a GRT is enhanced further by the capacity to
include all businesses and all market transactions in the tax net. A transactions
tax like the retail sales tax is limited in its ability to collect revenue from remote
vendors while the state corporation income tax cannot capture firms protected
by P.L. 86–272. These constraints do not apply to a GRT because it is deemed a
privilege tax rather than a transaction or net income tax (though it may still be
administratively problematic to capture all firms in the tax net using the concept
of economic nexus). As such, a GRT can include a larger number of firms and
thus more economic activity in the state tax base. In principle, this encompasses
all business forms rather than only corporations, including nonprofit firms, and
all business activity regardless of whether the firm shows a profit. In addition, the

state sales tax typically exempts sales to and from nonprofit entities, along with a wide range of services, and it often subjects other consumption items (like food or clothing) to reduced rates of taxation. A gross receipts tax could conceivably tax all components of consumption.

The revenue potential of a GRT gives policymakers wide latitude in how to define business tax policy and overall state tax structure. For example, Washington relies on its long-standing B&O tax as the only broad-based levy imposed by the state on business. Reforms that introduced GRTs in Texas and Ohio yielded a similar outcome because they were coupled with the elimination of corporate franchise and excise taxes. Because of their capacity to generate significant amounts of revenue, however, GRTs could conceivably be used to support reductions in any of a number of state taxes. This was the intent with the proposed BNRT in California in 2009, which was to be coupled with elimination of the state CIT and reduced reliance on sales and personal income taxes.

In practice, behavioral effects will temper revenue yield over time. Vertical integration will reduce the scope of business-to-business transactions that are subject to gross receipts taxation. Under Ohio's CAT, firms may choose to report as a consolidated group to avoid taxation of intercompany transactions. The presence of pyramiding under a GRT may induce firms to purchase inputs from out-of-state suppliers, reducing in-state economic activity and revenues.[51] *De minimis* provisions such as in Delaware may lead to a proliferation of small firms below tax thresholds. While there is no empirical evidence on the scope of any of these or other behavioral responses that might narrow the effective tax base, it is unlikely that behavior would seriously compromise the revenue yield and elasticity of a GRT as long as rates remained low.

Policy choices also can be expected to erode revenue performance as has been the case with VATs outside the United States and state sales and corporate income taxes inside the United States. One might anticipate special rates or base exemptions to emerge for sectors of the economy to protect specific industries and promote economic development. The likelihood of this policy response will grow as more states adopt a GRT and horizontal competitive pressures mount. Consumer products may also be granted preferential tax status to achieve equity objectives. Revenue buoyancy will be compromised to some extent by these policy choices. However, revenue elasticity should be enhanced under GRTs and VATs relative to the sales tax by virtue of the broad and diversified base and the inclusion of services, which are a rising share of household consumption.

There is little empirical evidence on the year-to-year stability and peak-to-trough/trough-to-peak performance of broad gross receipts, consumption, and corporate income taxes for the American states.[52] A broader tax-base portfolio should enhance the stability of consumption and gross receipts bases while diminishing cyclicality relative to the narrower base of state sales taxes that disproportionately include durable goods. Building materials and consumer durables are volatile components of the state sales-tax base and the addition of services to the base will offer a stabilizing influence. There is evidence showing that the standard deviation of aggregate personal consumption expenditures is smaller than the standard deviation of any of the broad individual components of personal consumption. This evidence indicates that base broadening can enhance stability.[53] One evaluation of the New Hampshire BET compares its stability against the state's business profit tax and shows that the BET is the more stable of the two taxes.[54] A comparison of proxies for the GRT and a hypothetical CIT in Washington produced higher coefficients of variation for the CIT for all firms and for manufacturing firms from 1995 to 2003.[55]

Compliance and Administration

This section provides an overview of the compliance and administration issues inherent in each type of tax and some of the efforts required to address them. Where appropriate, we use examples from the state taxes currently in effect in the United States to highlight issues. Note that the financial services industry—banking, insurance, investment, and related activities—is inherently difficult to tax under the GRT or VAT systems. In almost every case, states exempt the financial sector from activity-based taxes and instead levy an alternative tax (frequently some measure of gross receipts). In Michigan, for example, in lieu of the modified GRT, insurance companies pay a tax on gross direct premiums written, and financial institutions pay a tax on net capital. For industries outside the financial sector, states typically exclude interest, dividends, and proceeds from the sale of financial assets from the base, but tax that income with an income tax or other alternative. A detailed discussion of how states tax the financial services industry is beyond the scope of this chapter.

Simple and unambiguous taxes with broad bases and few exemptions are less costly to administer and should increase compliance by reducing opportunities for errors and abuse. Comparison of the compliance and administration costs for the GRT, VAT, and CIT will depend on the specific structure of each tax that is implemented.[56] In the United States the GRT and the closely related subtraction method VAT are administratively similar and differ primarily in the number and type of allowable deductions.

The GRT and, to a lesser extent, the NRT and subtraction method VAT reduce both the means and the incentives to avoid tax. US states typically begin the calculation with in-state sales, an amount that is more difficult to shift among jurisdictions than profits but that is still subject to potential underreporting. Furthermore, business activity taxes sharply limit the type of allowable deductions, and those deductions that are allowed (materials purchased in the case of the Michigan MBT, for example) are relatively simple to audit compared to the types of expenses that businesses can use to shift profits under the CIT. For example, common CIT planning techniques utilize intercompany transactions to shift expenses into high tax jurisdictions, often using charges for management support, interest, and charges for the use of intangibles. These expenses are disallowed in the business activity taxes currently in use by states and eliminate some of the tax-planning techniques. Finally, because the GRT and VAT often have nominal rates of 1 percent or less, the marginal payoff per dollar of income shifted is much lower with the GRT and VAT than with the CIT or the RST.

In addition to reducing the incentive for existing taxpayers to shift income, the GRT and the VAT typically expand the pool of taxpayers subject to tax. First, the taxes apply to business activity rather than to specific categories of taxpayer. Therefore, taxpayers who are not subject to the CIT, such as individuals and pass-through entities, are subject to VATs and GRTs. Service providers are often excluded from the RST but are subject to business activity taxes. The expanded pool of taxpayers will increase compliance costs for those taxpayers brought into the system for the first time and administrative costs for governments that must deal with more returns, but the overall compliance costs for taxpayers within a state will depend in large part on whether the activity-based taxes replace or supplement existing taxes, such as the CIT and the RST. If a VAT or GRT replaces existing taxes, existing taxpayers would likely see a decrease in compliance costs, though this would depend on the complexity of the new regime.

Compliance with a subtraction method VAT or GRT is in principle relatively simple. The tax base is gross receipts, excluding specifically identified items such as interest or dividends, less a limited number of allowable deductions. As with any tax, the conceptual simplicity often hides a tremendous amount of operational complexity, especially for large taxpayers involved in multiple lines of business, and it ignores the likelihood of increased tax complexity with the passage of time as policymakers respond to the inevitable political pressure to favor certain activities with targeted tax incentives and deductions. Because taxes on business activity are relatively new, the regulations that accompany them are incomplete because legislators are unable to anticipate all issues that will arise, and businesses, tax professionals, and revenue officials are less familiar with the issues presented and workable solutions. These transitional compliance and administrative issues will diminish with experience as taxpayers become familiar with the new laws and administrators become more skilled in recognizing and addressing gray areas with expanded regulations and communications that address frequently asked questions. More contentious issues will be resolved over time through the legislative, judicial, and administrative law processes.

The tax base for addition method VATs, such as the New Hampshire BET, is the sum of a limited number of items and is deceptively simple on its face. In the case of the BET, the tax base equals wages, dividends, and interest paid, less any special deductions or credits allowed for business development and incentive purposes. However, an addition VAT in theory includes a measure of income, such as retained earnings or earned income during the period, which requires companies to perform a calculation similar to that required for the traditional CIT. New Hampshire excludes net income or retained earnings from the base, but it maintains a parallel business profits tax (a CIT) that captures business taxable income. Including a measure of taxable income in the addition VAT base or maintaining a separate income tax undermines any argument that an addition VAT simplifies compliance for taxpayers.

While a business activity tax without exemptions and a single rate is possible, this is not likely in the United States.[57] For example, policymakers generally attempt to reduce the distortions caused by the cascading of activity-based taxes by applying lower tax rates to the business activities of industries most likely to be adversely affected (e.g., manufacturing). The Washington B&O tax illustrates some of the potential difficulties. This tax has twenty-eight different classifications of income that are taxed at several different rates. Taxpayers with diversified transactions must segregate their receipts into the proper categories, classify each category of receipts into the appropriate B&O classification, and apply the correct tax rate to each applicable category. This task will often be simple, but for many transactions that bundle both goods and services, such as the purchase and installation of an item of equipment, the problems become immediately apparent. Some purchases come with a limited period of "free" customer support. In other cases, retailers will, at no charge, extend the manufacturer's warranty on products they sell. For each of these transactions, taxpayers must first determine if the sales price must be allocated among various categories, and if so, they must choose the allocation method.

The Texas Margin Tax deduction for cost of goods sold provides an additional example of administration and compliance issues that arise when states diverge from common federal tax concepts when implementing a new law. Cost of goods sold is a familiar term for federal income-tax purposes, but the Texas law defined the term more broadly ("costs required to produce or acquire a good") and included write-offs for research and development and certain costs incurred by the oil and gas industry. The expanded definition introduced uncertainty, which taxpayers apparently exploited to take aggressive tax positions and deductions not contemplated by lawmakers. Many service firms claimed deductions for cost of goods sold, for example. As a result, actual collections from the tax fell far below projections, and taxpayers, while enjoying the tax savings allowed under the expanded definition, are left wondering how the state will finally interpret the rules.[58]

Because the VAT is collected at each stage of the production process, proponents argue that there is less evasion than with a tax like the RST, which is levied only once on the final sale.[59] However, this conclusion is based largely on the presumed self-enforcing credit-invoice element of European-style VATs. For the subtraction method VATs used in the United States, the enforcement mechanisms of the credit-invoice method are absent, and the multiple stages of taxation through the production chain produce many opportunities for evasion, even if the incentive and the taxes evaded at each stage are small.

A common criticism of the CIT is its complexity because it both increases compliance costs and provides for tax-planning opportunities, particularly in a multistate setting.[60] Firms doing business across state lines face similar complexity issues with the VAT and GRT. Identifying out-of-state taxpayers who are subject to the tax is the first hurdle. For example, P.L. 86–272 prohibits states from levying income-based taxes unless the taxpayer has nexus in the taxing state. Because the law applies only to income taxes, states ignore P.L. 86–272 for purposes of the GRT and instead assert the right to subject firms to activity-based taxes by using a different standard. Recently enacted GRTs assert nexus under the broadest definition to require firms to have only economic presence, a standard that can be met with a threshold level of sales.[61] Accordingly, many firms that are not subject to income tax because of P.L. 86–272 will be subject to the GRT and subtraction method VATs. The unanswered question is the point at which a subtraction method VAT, differing from an income tax primarily by the type of allowable deductions, is treated as a type of income tax for the purposes of P.L. 86–272. Courts have not yet resolved constitutional challenges to the economic nexus standards, such as to Ohio's CAT.

Multistate operations must also apportion and allocate both income and expenses to the taxing jurisdiction. For the CIT, many states have adopted combined reporting requirements that treat related businesses as a single entity for apportionment purposes. States adopting the VAT or GRT will also have to consider combined reporting for the purposes of these taxes. National VATs achieve destination taxation by using border adjustments. However, for US states, such border adjustments are impracticable.[62] States attempt to achieve a destination basis by using a single sales-factor apportionment formula, but problems frequently arise in determining the destination state, particularly for services and intangibles. Furthermore, additional distortions of the destination principle arise when exempting exports that include previously taxed inputs (i.e., the rebate will be too low) and when levying the tax on the entire value of imports that were taxed by other jurisdictions at previous stages of production (i.e., the tax will be too high).

Enforcement of business activity taxes would be done through mechanisms including taxpayer audits and possibly interstate tax audits like those undertaken by the Multistate Tax Commission for sales and corporate income taxes. Academic literature has examined compliance with credit-invoice VATs; however, there are no academic studies that have examined these issues for the US state GRT and its variants.[63]

Significant transition issues come with implementing new taxes such as a GRT or VAT if that tax replaces the CIT. Carryovers of tax credits, losses, and various tax attributes must be planned for and accounted for by taxpayers.

Conclusion

The state business tax structure in the United States has long been strained by behavioral choices, policy decisions, and a shifting economic and business structure that have narrowed tax bases and weakened revenue performance. As the states have sought to meet their revenue needs they have considered—and in several instances adopted—variants of gross receipts taxes and aggregate subtraction method VATs. This chapter has provided an overview of the key issues that need to be considered in an evaluation of gross receipts and other business taxes.

The policy options for taxing business entities follow a continuum where a GRT offers the broadest possible base and the state corporate income tax yields the narrowest base. While there is considerably complexity associated with each alternative tax instrument, the differences are best understood in terms of the definition of income and any deductions from income that produce the taxable base. A pure GRT is a turnover tax with no deductions, while the CIT falls on apportioned profits.

GRTs and the application of economic nexus can be broadly justified by the benefit principle. While taxes will not align perfectly with public service benefits, the linkage may be closer with a GRT tax that falls on virtually all firms and transactions than other forms of business taxation. Fairness will depend on the eyes of the taxpayer. A common objection is that firms will incur a GRT liability regardless of whether they earn a profit. But businesses currently pay an array of taxes regardless of profitability, including property taxes and sales tax on business inputs.

Business taxes are nonneutral and a GRT is no exception. A GRT introduces pyramiding, which can distort economic activity across industries, input markets, and final product markets. The inability to fully suspend tax along the production chain may also place in-state suppliers at a competitive disadvantage against imports. A retail sales tax that does not fully exempt input purchases may have similar effects. GRTs and VATS have less impact on the choice of organizational form for businesses than the CIT.

Revenue yield and elasticity would be enhanced under a GRT relative to sales and corporate income taxes. Yield would expand by increasing the scope of firms and transactions subject to tax while elasticity would benefit from the inclusion of services in the tax base. A GRT should improve stability by diversifying the tax base.

Finally, a GRT would likely lead to reduced costs of compliance and administration, at least after dealing with issues of transition in moving to the new tax regime. Compliance should improve by including all firms in the tax net, reducing the number of ambiguities associated with line items of income and expense, and tempering the marginal incentive to evade via the low rate of taxation.

NOTES

1 Brunori (this volume); Fox and Luna (2005); Luna (2004).
2 Fox (this volume); Fox and Luna (2002).
3 Wallace (2005) framed trends such as these more generally in the context of "fiscal architecture," which accounts for the way that demographic, economic, and institutional forces can affect revenue performance.

4 For a detailed discussion of the corporate income, value-added, and sales taxes, see chapters 13, 15, and 16, respectively (this volume).

5 The proposed California BNRT would tax gross receipts less deductions for purchases of goods and services from other firms with net receipts apportioned using a single-factor sales formula. The BNRT was negatively received and is not currently being considered.

6 Washington's Business and Occupation Tax is an exception, and it levies the tax based on the seller's location resulting in an origin-based tax.

7 Washington enacted the tax in 1933 and Delaware's GRT has been in existence prior to 1930.

8 Refer to the following publications for more detail. Michigan: McIntyre and Pomp (2009); Ohio: Church and Hall (2007); Oklahoma: Jones, Sutton, and Yenowitz (2010); Texas: Hamilton (2010).

9 Fox (this volume).

10 States with the traditional CIT tax the noncorporate sector with the individual income tax.

11 Fox (this volume).

12 For the purposes of this chapter, "production chain" refers to the entire range of stages of production, including extraction, fabrication, and distribution.

13 Firms selling into a state are often protected from income taxes or having to collect the sales or use tax because the selling firm lacks nexus in the destination state.

14 Martinez-Vasquez and Bird (2010), 2.

15 Ebel (1972); Hines (2003).

16 For more detail on the New Hampshire BET, see Kenyon (1996).

17 Bird (2007).

18 See Cnossen (2009); Duncan and Sedon (2009); and Duncan (this volume) for more detailed discussions of how these three VATs work.

19 See Zodrow (1999) for an excellent comparison of the VAT and the RST.

20 See Duncan (this volume), and Tait, Ebel, and Le (2005) for a discussion of a national VAT.

21 The subtraction method VAT and a net receipts tax are conceptually equivalent (see table 14.1). Because of political opposition to taxes labeled as a VAT, current state tax reforms and proposals label the tax as a business transfer tax or a business cash-flow tax.

22 Ebel and Kalambokidis (2005).

23 Typically, interest and dividends excluded from the VAT base do not escape taxation but are instead captured by other business taxes.

24 For a discussion of features of state GRTs in the United States, see Mikesell (2007) and Testa and Mattoon (2007).

25 States and localities frequently impose GRTs on narrow forms of economic activity. For example, states typically tax financial institutions by using receipts as the tax base; localities frequently apply gross receipts taxes to public utilities. Due to the limited reach of these taxes, we limit the discussion here to broad state-level taxes on business.

26 Texas also allows firms to elect a deduction equal to 70 percent of gross receipts.

27 For more detail on the Oklahoma BAT, see Jones, Sutton, and Yenowitz (2010). The tax is currently intended to be temporary and to be in effect for tax years 2010 through 2012.

28 Kenyon (1996).

29 Murray (1999).

30 General arguments for the taxation of the business enterprise are provided by Oakland and Testa (1996) and Ebel and Taliercio (2005). There may be specific arguments in support of the use of specific tax instruments. For example, the CIT has been viewed as a backstop to the personal income tax (Brunori, this volume); the VAT has been advocated as a nondistortionary tax (Ebel and Kalambokidis, 1999), and the gross receipts tax can overcome nexus hurdles under both the sales tax and the state corporate income tax as discussed in this chapter.

31 Church and Hall (2007).

32 Cline and Neubig (2010).

33 Cline and Neubig (2008), 187, showed the relative size of the tax base for six types of business taxes by using the overall US economy to show the tax rate that would be necessary to raise the same amount of revenue, $50 billion. Specifically, they showed that a GRT required a tax rate of 0.28 percent compared to a 1.1 percent tax rate for a "pure" VAT and a 5.8 percent tax rate for a CIT.

34 Other taxes have differential impacts on different industries aside from the issue of pyramiding. For example, the property tax places a larger burden on capital-intensive industries, such as utilities and manufacturing, than it does on more labor-intensive industries (e.g., retail and professional services).

35 Acemoglu, Aghion, Griffith, and Zilibotti (2007).

36 Yang (2010).

37 Mieszkowski and Zodrow (1985).

38 See Fox (this volume).

39 Ring (1999).

40 Chamberlain and Fleenor (2006).

41 For example, McLure (2010).

42 See Brunori (this volume).

43 McLure (1980).

44 This is true of the federal and state corporate income taxes. For example, see Ayers, Cloyd, and Robinson (1996); Goolsbee (2004).

45 Gravelle and Kotlikoff (1993); Goolsbee (1998).

46 Goolsbee (2004).

47 Luna and Murray (2010).

48 See Mikesell (2007).

49 Ibid.

50 del Valle (2005).

51 Purchases from out-of-state vendors would be subject to gross receipts taxation. However, the importing state would lose any gross receipts tax revenue that would have been associated with earlier links in the production chain for the imported product.

52 There is a small empirical literature that looks at actual and hypothetical state tax bases and short-run and long-run revenue performance. For example, Bruce, Fox, and Tuttle (2006) examined short-run and long-run sales tax elasticities by using state-level data on sales-tax bases. But actual state sales-tax bases tend to be far narrower than true consumption or value-added taxes, as well as GRTs. Sobel and Holcombe (1996) considered hypothetical state tax bases by using national aggregates. They relied on corporate taxable income as a proxy for the state corporate income and showed that it is much more stable in the short run than national retail sales. However, the retail sales measure relied on national data and did not include the range of services that might be taxed under a broad consumption levy.

53 Dye and McGuire (1991).

54 Kenyon (1996).

55 Wheeler and Senoga (2007).

56 Very little is known about the administration and compliance costs of these taxes. European-style VATs differ markedly from the aggregate subtraction VATs introduced in the United States and thus offer little guidance on costs. Gupta and Mills (2003) used a small sample of only 295 firms and concluded that compliance costs of the state CIT are 0.02 percent of sales.

57 Thuronyi (2010), 858, discussed this at a national level and noted that the US political process is fundamentally different from that in other countries with a VAT.

58 Hamilton (2010).

59 Bloomfield and McLure (1987).

60 Tax planning is one of the primary reasons that corporate tax revenues as a share of corporate profits have fallen dramatically over the last two decades. See Fox and Luna (2002) and Fox, Luna, and Murray (2005).

61 For example, in both Ohio and Oklahoma, nexus for purposes of the GRT is established if the business has at least $500,000 of in-state sales.

62 McLure (2000) has suggested an alternative to border adjustments: the compensating VAT (CVAT), a uniform rate levied on all interstate sales.

63 See Agha and Houghton (1996) and Keen and Smith (2006) for a discussion of evasion in the context of credit-invoice VATs. We are not aware of any empirical evidence on the scope of the noncompliance problem for the state CIT. The Washington Department of Revenue (2010) reported that the ratio of noncompliance to total tax liability for the 2006 tax year was 1 percent for the sales tax, 23 percent for the use tax and 2.4 percent for the business and occupation tax.

References

Acemoglu, Daron, Philippe Aghion, Rachel Griffith, and Fabrizio Zilibotti (2007). "Vertical Integration and Technology: Theory and Evidence." Institute for Empirical Research in Economics, University of Zurich, Working Paper Series ISSN 1424–0459.

Agha, Ali, and Jonathan Houghton (1996, May). "Designing VAT Systems: Some Efficiency Considerations." *Review of Economics and Statistics* 78: 303–308.

Ayers, Benjamin C., C. Bryan Cloyd, and John R. Robinson (1996). "Organizational Form and Taxes: An Empirical Analysis of Small Businesses." *Journal of the American Taxation Association* 18 (Supplement): 49–67.

Bird, Richard (2007, August). "Is a State VAT the Answer? What's the Question?" Fiscal Research Center Report No. 162, Georgia State University.

Bloomfield, Mark A., and Charles E. McLure Jr. (1987). *The Value-Added Tax: Key to Deficit Reduction?* Washington DC: American Enterprise Institute.

Bruce, Donald, William F. Fox, and Markland H. Tuttle (2006, October). "Tax Base Elasticities: An Analysis of Long-Run and Short-Run Dynamics." *Southern Economic Journal* 73: 315–341.

Chamberlain, Andrew, and Patrick Fleenor (2006). "Tax Pyramiding: The Economic Consequences of Gross Receipts Taxes." Tax Foundation Special Report No. 147.

Church, Frederick, and Christopher Hall. (2007, January 8). "Ohio Tax Reform: Cuts and Repeals and That Darn CAT." *State Tax Notes* 43: 23–37.

Cline, Robert. and Tom Neubig (2008, January 21). "Future State Business Tax Reforms: Defend or Replace the Tax Base." *State Tax Notes* 47: 179–192.

Cline, Robert. and Tom Neubig (2010, June 7). "Five Federal Lessons from California's Near-VAT Experience." *State Tax Notes*: 821–825.

Cnossen, Sijbren (2009, August 17). "A VAT Primer for Lawyers, Economists, and Accountants." *Tax Notes* 124: 687–698.

del Valle, Manuel (2005, September). "Pyramiding Transaction Taxes in New Mexico: A Report on the Gross Receipts Tax." New Mexico Tax Research Institute.

Duncan, Harley, and Jon Sedon (2009, December 21). "How Different VATs Work." *Tax Notes: Views on VATs*: 1367–1374.

Dye, Richard F., and Therese J. McGuire (1991, March). "Growth and Variability of State Individual Income and General Sales Taxes." *National Tax Journal* 44: 55–66.

Ebel, Robert (1972). *Michigan Business Activities Tax*. East Lansing: Michigan State University Press.

Ebel, Robert, and Laura Kalambokidis (2005). "Value-added Tax, State." In *The Encyclopedia of Taxation and Tax Policy*, edited by Joseph Cordes, Robert Ebel, and Jane Gravelle. Washington, DC: Urban Institute Press: 464–467.

Ebel, Robert, and Robert Taliercio (2005, March 7). "Subnational Tax Policy and Administration in Developing Economies." *Tax Notes International*: 919–936.

Fox, William F., and LeAnn Luna (2002, September). "State Corporate Tax Revenue Trends: Causes and Possible Solutions." *National Tax Journal* 55: 949–956.

Fox, William F., and LeAnn Luna (2005, November). "Do Limited Liability Companies Explain Declining State Tax Revenues?" *Public Finance Review* 33: 690–720.

Fox, William F., LeAnn Luna, and Matthew N. Murray (2005, March). "How Should a Subnational Corporate Income Tax on Multistate Businesses Be Structured?" *National Tax Journal* 53: 139–159.

Goolsbee, Austan (1998, July). "Taxes, Organizational Form and the Deadweight Loss of the Corporate Income Tax." *Journal of Public Economics* 69: 143–152.

Goolsbee, Austan (2004, September). "The Impact of the Corporate Income Tax: Evidence from State Organizational Form Data." *Journal of Public Economics* 88: 2283–2299.

Gravelle, Jane, and Lawrence Kotlikoff (1993, October). "Corporate Tax Incidence and Inefficiency When Corporate and Noncorporate Goods Are Close Substitutes." *Economic Inquiry* 31: 501–516.

Gupta, Sanjay, and Lillian F. Mills (2003, June). "Does Disconformity in State Corporate Tax Systems Affect Compliance Cost Burdens?" *National Tax Journal* 56: 355–372.

Hamilton, Billy (2010, May 24). "This Is Not an Income Tax: Problems with Texas's Margin Tax." *State Tax Notes* 56: 629–633.

Hines, James R., Jr. (2003). "Michigan's Flirtation with the Single Business Tax." In *Michigan at the Millennium*, edited by Charles L. Ballard, Douglas C. Drake, Paul N. Courant, Ronald Fisher, and Elisabeth R. Gerber. East Lansing: Michigan State University Press. 603–628.

Jones, Chuck, Giles Sutton, and Jamie C. Yenowitz (2010, August 23). "Oklahoma's New Business Activity Tax: A Sign of Things to Come?" *State Tax Notes* 57: 495–499.

Keen, Michael, and Stephen Smith (2006, December). "VAT Fraud and Evasion: What Do We Know, and What Can be Done?" *National Tax Journal* 49: 861–887.

Kenyon, Daphne (1996, September). "A New State VAT? Lessons from New Hampshire." *National Tax Journal* 49: 381–399.

Luna, LeAnn (2004, May). "Corporate Tax Avoidance Strategies and States' Efforts to Prevent Abuses." *Journal of MultiState Taxation and Incentives*: 6–17, 46–48.

Luna, LeAnn, and Matthew N. Murray (2010, December). "The Effects of State Tax Structure on Business Organizational Form." *National Tax Journal* 63: 995–1022.

Martinez-Vasquez, Jorge, and Richard Bird (2010, August). "Value Added Tax: Onward and Upward?" International Studies Program Working Paper 10–26, Georgia State University.

McIntyre, Michael J., and Richard D. Pomp (2009, March 2). "Michigan's New Apportioned Value Added Tax." *State Tax Notes*: 673–687.

McLure, Charles E., Jr. (1980). "The State Corporate Income Tax: Lambs in Wolves' Clothing." In *The Economics of Taxation*, edited by H. Aaron and M. Boskin. Washington DC: Brookings Institution: 247–268.

McLure, Charles E., Jr. (2000, December). "Implementing Subnational Value Added Taxes on Internal Trade: The Compensating VAT (CVAT)." *International Tax & Public Finance* 7: 723–740.

McLure, Charles E., Jr. (2010). "The Business Net Receipts Tax: A Dog That Will Not Hunt." http://taxprof.typepad.com/files/mclure.pdf.

Mieszkowski, Peter M., and George R. Zodrow (1985, December). "The Incidence of a Partial State Corporate Income Tax." *National Tax Journal* 38: 489–496.

Mikesell, John L. (2007). "Gross Receipts Taxes in State Government Finances: A Review of Their History and Performance." Background Paper Number 53. Tax Foundation and Council on State Taxation.

Murray, Matthew N. (1999). "The Franchise Tax." In *The Encyclopedia of Taxation and Tax Policy*, edited by Joseph Cordes, Robert Ebel, and Jane Gravelle. Washington, DC: Urban Institute Press. 139–140.

Oakland, William H., and William A. Testa (1996, January/February). "State and Local Business Taxation and the Benefits Principle." *Economic Perspectives* 20: 2–19.

Ring, Raymond J. (1999, March). "Consumers' Share and Producers' Share of the General Sales Tax." *National Tax Journal* 52: 79–90.

Sobel, Russell S., and Randall G. Holcombe (1996, December). "Measuring the Growth and Variability of Tax Bases Over the Business Cycle." *National Tax Journal* 49: 535–552.

Tait, Alan, Robert Ebel, and Tuan Minh Le (2005). "Value-added Tax, National." In *The Encyclopedia of Taxation and Tax Policy*, edited by Joseph Cordes, Robert Ebel, and Jane Gravelle. Washington, DC: Urban Institute Press: 461–464.

Testa, William A., and Richard Mattoon (2007, December). "Is There a Role for Gross Receipts Taxation?" *National Tax Journal* 55: 821–840.

Thuronyi, Victor (2010, August 23). "A VAT for the United States?" *Tax Notes* 128: 856–863.

Wallace, Sally (2005). "Fiscal Architecture." In *The Encyclopedia of Taxation and Tax Policy*, edited by Joseph Cordes, Robert Ebel, and Jane Gravelle. Washington, DC: Urban Institute Press. 141–143

Washington Department of Revenue (2010, August 20). "Department of Revenue Compliance Study." Research Report 2010–2014, Olympia, Washington.

Wheeler, Laura, and Edward Senoga (2007, August 20). "Alternative State Business Tax Systems: A Comparison of State Income and Gross Receipts Taxes." *State Tax Notes* 45: 487–501.

Yang, Zhou (2010). "Essays on Gross Receipts Taxes." PhD diss., University of Tennessee.

Zodrow, George R. (1999, September). "The Sales Tax, the VAT and Taxes in Between—or, Is the Only Good NRST a 'VAT in Drag'?" *National Tax Journal* 52: 429–442.

··

CHAPTER 15

IMPLICATIONS OF A FEDERAL VALUE-ADDED TAX FOR STATE AND LOCAL GOVERNMENTS

··

HARLEY T. DUNCAN

THE impacts of the financial crisis of 2008–2009 and the resulting "Great Recession" on the federal government's fiscal posture have generated increased discussion in the popular press about the United States adopting a value-added tax (VAT).[1] There has also been a noticeable uptick in the volume of academic and tax-policy literature concerning the merits and demerits of a VAT for the United States as well as the issues involved in implementing a VAT in this country.[2] And, in November 2010, the Debt Reduction Task Force of the Bipartisan Policy Center recommended that the United States adopt a VAT—the "Debt Reduction Sales Tax"—as part of a "pro-growth tax system" to divert the "federal budget from its present dangerous, unsustainable path."[3] Proposals for the adoption of a VAT in the United States are not new. In the 1970s, President Nixon asked the Advisory Commission on Intergovernmental Relations to examine the use of a federal VAT to reduce the role of property taxes in financing elementary and secondary education.[4] There was also extensive discussion of broad-based consumption taxes in the mid-1980s.[5]

The urgency associated with the current discussion is driven primarily by the fiscal outlook for the federal government. While a VAT would increase federal revenues, implementing a federal VAT in this country would raise issues of fiscal federalism, tax coordination, and state autonomy that are several orders of magnitude more complex than in most of the other 150-plus nations that have adopted a VAT because of the extent to which US states and localities utilize retail sales taxes (RSTs) and the autonomy they enjoy in the design of their tax systems. This chapter examines the fiscal environment driving the current discussion of a federal VAT and the political, policy, and practical issues that are involved in adopting a federal VAT and coordinating it with state and local consumption taxes, given the US system of federalism and the current utilization of state and local (RSTs).

TIME FOR ACTION? A LOOK AT BUDGET DEFICITS

Both the near-term and the longer-range outlooks for the federal budget are largely responsible for the current VAT discussion. As discussed below, the federal budget deficit is projected to average nearly $1 trillion annually over the next decade under what many consider to be reasonable policy assumptions. In addition, as baby boomers (those born from 1946 to 1964) retire in increasing numbers, spending for Social Security, Medicare, and other government-financed health care could require significant tax increases, spending cuts in other areas, or an additional revenue stream.[6] Put another way, most observers believe the federal government must make substantial changes in its current tax and spending policies if it is to avoid an unprecedented accumulation of debt in the coming years.

The Congressional Budget Office (CBO) released its most recent examination of the outlook for the federal budget in January 2011.[7] The CBO used a "baseline" forecast, which is premised on current law with respect to both revenues and expenditures, as the benchmark for evaluating the federal government's fiscal future. The current baseline forecast reflected the December 2010 enactment of the Tax Relief, Unemployment Insurance Reauthorization and Job Creation Act,[8] which reduced the payroll tax and indexed the alternative minimum tax (AMT) index for inflation for tax year 2011 and extended for 2011 and 2012 the tax-rate reductions and other cuts that had been scheduled to expire in 2010.[9] Under the baseline scenario, the CBO projected federal budget deficits of more than $1 trillion in each of FY 2011 and 2012; the deficits would then average about $650 billion annually for FY 2013–2021 (about 3 percent of GDP) as revenues increase because of the expiring rate reductions and other tax cuts. The federal government would accumulate about $7 trillion in additional debt over the next decade, and the amount of debt held by the public would reach about 75 percent of GDP under the baseline scenario.[10]

Because most observers do not expect the "baseline" scenario to actually occur, the CBO also calculated expected deficits under other possible scenarios. According to CBO estimates, if the tax provisions that are scheduled to expire in 2011 and 2012 are extended through 2021 and certain expenditure assumptions are made, the volume of accumulated debt over the next decade would soar by an additional $5 trillion, and annual deficits would exceed 6 percent of GDP. Under this scenario, the debt held by the general public would approach 100 percent of GDP and be at its highest level since 1947.[11]

If this isn't enough to give one pause, the long-term projections over the next thirty to fifty years almost certainly will. The long-term outlook for the budget is driven almost exclusively by two factors: (1) the aging of the US population and what that means for Social Security and related Medicare and Medicaid expenditures along with (2) the rate of growth in health-care costs generally.[12] As summarized in the CBO's 2009 report on the long-term outlook for the federal fiscal posture:

> Under current law, the federal budget is on an unsustainable path, meaning the federal debt will continue to grow much faster than the economy over the long run. Although great uncertainty surrounds long-term fiscal projections, rising costs for health care and the aging of the US population will cause federal spending to increase rapidly under any plausible scenario for current law. Unless revenues increase just as rapidly, the rise in spending will produce growing budget deficits and accumulating debt. Keeping deficits and debt from reaching levels that would cause substantial harm to the economy would require increasing revenue significantly as a percentage of [GDP], decreasing projected spending sharply, or some combination of the two.[13]

The Debt Reduction Task Force of the Bipartisan Policy Center used more graphic terms to describe the long-term fiscal fortunes of the country. Using CBO data, the Task Force found that without changes in our current policies, the combination of spending on Social Security, Medicare, Medicaid, and interest on the debt will consume all available federal revenues by 2025, leaving all other services, including defense and homeland security, to be eliminated or financed through additional borrowing.[14] It also noted that CBO data indicated that without substantial changes in our financial policies, the total level of debt held by the public would be roughly four times its historic average by 2040 and reach 200 percent of our GDP, a situation that it said could lead to a "death spiral" of "rising debt and interest costs...feeding off one another in an ever-more vicious cycle."[15]

Another way to look at the issue is what is termed as the "fiscal gap," which is a calculation of the amount (relative to GDP) by which the government needs to "immediately and permanently" increase revenues, decrease spending, or some mix of both in order to keep the debt-to-GDP ratio at the level it is at the beginning of the measurement period.[16] Recent estimates put the US government fiscal gap at about 7 percent to 9 percent of GDP.[17] A gap of this magnitude is essentially equal to the total of federal individual income taxes at the current time and is described as being "difficult to close...entirely via modifications to existing taxes and spending programs."[18] In other words, the long-term costs of health care and retirement for the aging US population could require an immediate and permanent doubling of federal income taxes or a new revenue source to potentially avoid deterioration of the government's fiscal position.

There are, of course, a wide range of choices available to policymakers for dealing with the fiscal issues facing the country. A VAT may or may not be in the nation's future. One thing is clear, however. As the CBO wrote in 2009, "The difficulty of the choices notwithstanding, CBO's long-term budget projections make clear that doing nothing is not an option: Legislation must ultimately be adopted that raises revenue or reduces spending or both. Moreover, delaying action simply exacerbates the challenge."[19]

ADOPTING A VAT IN THE UNITED STATES

Adopting and implementing a federal US VAT would create a wide range of issues. Many of these are largely the province of the federal government, such as the macroeconomic effects of a VAT, treatment of various economic sectors, and the distribution of the tax burden across income groups. Such issues are beyond the scope of this chapter. Instead, the focus here is on a set of intergovernmental issues involving how best to coordinate a federal VAT with state and local consumption taxes, given the extent to which states and localities rely on RSTs and the degree of autonomy they have in designing them. More fully stated, the issue is how overlapping national and subnational consumption taxes should be structured to achieve a sound consumption tax system and recognize the legitimate authority of both the federal government and the states, while at the same time minimizing complexity for sellers and avoiding opportunities for noncompliance and fraud.

Achieving a coordinated federal-state consumption tax system involves political, policy, and practical challenges. To a considerable extent, the political challenges derive largely from the extent to which state and local governments utilize a broad-based consumption tax in the form of an RST and the degree of autonomy they exercise currently in the design of their RSTs. The policy challenges arise from attempting to deploy a federal VAT in a manner that can be leveraged to improve state and local RSTs and move them closer to accepted policy norms for consumption taxes. The practical challenges largely revolve around implementing a coordinated federal-state VAT in a fashion that guards against substantial compliance issues for both states and the federal government, minimizes seller burdens, and encourages states to coordinate their RSTs with the federal VAT. While coordinated national and subnational VATs have been more or less successfully implemented in some countries with a federal system,[20] notably Canada,[21] the number of states and localities that employ sales taxes as well as the autonomy of states to design their tax systems will increase the difficulty of implementing a coordinated federal-state consumption tax in the United States.

The federal government adoption of a VAT would present states with a bit of a dilemma. On the one hand, it would constitute a significant move by the federal government into the consumption tax arena, an area that to this point has largely been the province of states and localities. This could constrain state and local government utilization of such taxes in the future. On the other hand, if state and local RSTs could be modified to emulate and be coordinated with a well-designed federal VAT,[22] the VAT could improve their operation as a comprehensive tax on individual consumption of goods and services that is more broadly based than current RSTs and does not tax business inputs. It might also serve to reduce the compliance burden faced by sellers and improve compliance; experience in other countries, however, indicates this is likely to be achieved only with the loss of a substantial portion of the autonomy that states currently exercise over the design and operation of their taxes.

State Angst Over a Federal Vat

For a considerable period of time, some state officials have expressed opposition toward—or at least apprehension about—a federal VAT.[23] One concern among states is that a federal VAT, or at least coordinating with a federal VAT, explicitly or as a practical matter, could force the states to structure their consumption taxes to piggyback on the federal VAT. Such a requirement could decrease a state's autonomy if the tax rate, the tax base, the administration of the tax, or the allocation of revenue among states is "*de facto* dictated by the national government."[24] As even casual observers of state RSTs are quick to realize, state legislators and policy officials guard quite jealously their ability to establish the RST base and other features of the RST.[25] A related concern is that the policy decisions of the national government may not be in a particular state's best interest. For example, a federal government decision to exempt or zero-rate certain items, industries, or activities could cause a state to lose a source of revenue by virtue of its conformity to the federal base. This situation would resemble situations in which the federal government amends the federal income tax to stimulate the overall economy (e.g., through bonus depreciation, increased expensing) at the same time states are struggling to balance their budgets. This practice often causes states to decouple from the particular federal change, resulting in increased complexity for taxpayers.[26]

States, it seems, are justifiably concerned about such constraints on their current autonomy (regardless of how exercised), considering the types of coordinated

VATs that have been adopted in other countries with a federal system and the degree to which they require uniformity among the federal and state tax bases.[27] As other commentators have pointed out, a system under which a state VAT or RST is not coordinated with a federal VAT is not necessarily unworkable, but it could significantly diminish any administrative advantages that would arise from a coordinated federal-state VAT.[28]

State officials also fear that implementation of a federal VAT may diminish consumer spending and cause state revenues to decrease. Most economists consider this concern to be misplaced, but it nonetheless motivates state resistance.[29] A more likely consequence of a federal VAT that also concerns states is that a federal VAT may begin to restrain states' use of the consumption tax base. Federal movement into consumption taxes—traditionally the exclusive territory of states— could result in an aggregate tax rate that "cannot be enforced satisfactorily" (i.e., evasion will balloon).[30] From the states' point of view, "the concern is that if federal reform causes the national government to dominate a base that has traditionally been used primarily by states, it could reduce the fiscal flexibility of states and disrupt the current balance in the intergovernmental system."[31]

OPPORTUNITIES TO IMPROVE STATE AND LOCAL RETAIL SALES TAXES

The policy challenges involved in implementing a coordinated federal-state VAT in the United States are complex. From one perspective, coordinating state RSTs with a well-designed federal VAT could significantly improve the policy underpinnings of state RSTs. From another, such coordination in other countries has come at the expense of a significant degree of subnational autonomy over the design of the tax base. Implementing a coordinated federal-state VAT in a system as complex as the United States is not necessarily easy, and models developed elsewhere in the world may not work without significant modification.

From a tax-policy perspective, a "well-designed" consumption tax generally has four features: (1) the tax should apply to virtually all consumption of goods and services by individuals and households, (2) intermediate purchases of inputs by businesses should not be subject to tax, (3) goods and services should be taxed on a destination basis (i.e., where consumption occurs), and (4) compliance and administrative costs should be minimized.[32] Current RSTs fall well short of these policy norms.

Taxation of Goods and Services. Present-day RSTs are generally applied primarily to sales of tangible personal property and are not applied generally to service transactions.[33] This is largely an artifact of the genesis of state RSTs during the Great Depression of the 1930s. Even today, however, over one-half of the states refrain from taxing installation and labor services, and most states do not tax personal services, computer services, or professional services.[34] While there is no reason, as a matter of principle, why a state RST cannot be applied to services, recent efforts to do so have failed.[35] A federal VAT could provide a vehicle for states to modify their tax bases to include a broad range of services.

Business Inputs. State RSTs also fall short of the norm of not taxing business purchases of goods and services used in the production process, thus allowing the entire consumption tax burden to fall on individual or household consumption. Taxing business inputs is to be avoided because the tax "cascades" or "pyramids," when it becomes embedded in the costs of goods and services moving through the production process, which ultimately can distort consumer and producer choices. States use such techniques as "sale for resale" or "exempting manufacturing machinery and equipment" to ease the burden on business inputs, but no state exempts all business purchases.[36] In fact, some studies suggest that more than 40 percent of RST revenues result from tax paid on purchases by businesses.[37] Conforming state RSTs to a federal VAT that uses the credit-invoice mechanism to eliminate tax on purchases for business purposes could enable states to improve their consumption taxes. Relieving the tax burden on business inputs has resulted in a marked increase in business investments in other countries, which may suggest that conforming to a federal VAT could have desirable impact on state economies.[38]

Destination-Based Taxation. Current RSTs generally impose ultimate taxation on a destination basis.[39] Nonetheless, so many business inputs are taxed under current RSTs that export to other states and nations often bear an embedded RST from the state of production that would not occur in a VAT with appropriate border adjustments. Again, conforming RSTs to a well-designed VAT could improve the functioning of RSTs as a consumption tax.

Reducing Compliance Burden. Complying with current state and local RSTs is complex. A retailer operating in multiple jurisdictions must be aware of the tax base and tax rate in each jurisdiction, retain proper documentation of exempt sales, and properly and timely file returns and payments.[40] Evidence suggests that the average cost of collection of RSTs is more than 3 percent of the total tax collected, but it ranges significantly higher for small-volume sellers.[41] The compliance burden under a VAT is also estimated to fall within the 3–5 percent of revenue collected range.[42] Continuing RSTs without coordinating with a federal VAT would add the burden of a federal VAT without diminishing RST compliance costs. Coordinating state RSTs with a federal VAT and disposing of the original state RSTs would eliminate the need to comply with two separate systems. Moreover, to the extent that states conform to the federal VAT base, the retailers' need to monitor and comply with different RST bases in each state would be obviated.

Two other features of the current environment that will likely affect the manner in which state consumption taxes can be coordinated with a federal VAT are state diversity and local government concerns.

State Diversity. At present, not all states currently impose an RST.[43] Likewise, even if some states opted to convert their RSTs to VATs, it is highly unlikely that all would do so, especially at the outset.[44] The resulting patchwork would likely make it impractical to implement certain coordination mechanisms that would involve a uniform approach across the country.

Local Government Concerns. More than eight thousand local governments also impose an RST.[45] While the vast majority of these are administered along with state RSTs, the existence of such a large number of local RSTs would compound exponentially some of the complexities involved in ensuring final taxation on a destination basis. Put another way, the large number of local government RSTs effectively precludes the adoption of certain mechanisms that are commonly used to produce destination-based taxation and would require alternative arrangements.

COORDINATING FEDERAL AND STATE CONSUMPTION TAXES

The central issue to be addressed in designing a coordinated national-subnational VAT structure for a country with a federal system is dealing with sales that involve two jurisdictions (termed "interstate sales" here), or more specifically, ensuring that interstate sales are taxed on a destination basis.[46] If the sales were between two countries, one would rely on the normal border-tax adjustment process[47] wherein the sale would be zero-rated[48] in the country from which the good is exported (and the seller would claim a refund for taxes it had paid on in its inputs) and a VAT would be imposed at the rate of the importing country either through border controls or by having the importing entity (presuming it is a registered trader) use a "reverse-charging" mechanism to impose a VAT on the imported good.[49]

The traditional border-tax adjustment process, however, is considered impractical and unworkable at the subnational level for at least two reasons. First, there are no physical interstate borders or "fiscal frontiers" at which a tax may be collected on imports,[50] meaning the tax on imports under the traditional approach must be collected via reverse charging. This leads, in turn, to concerns about potential fraud and noncompliance, particularly given the volume of interstate trade that is to be expected in the United States.[51] The noncompliance concerns emanate from two sources. First, a considerable amount of VAT revenue would be collected and then subject to refund as supplies are exported from one jurisdiction to another, thus creating an opportunity for fraudulent refund claims.[52] Second, the reverse-charging mechanism that would be used for interstate sales[53] also presents opportunities for evasion, because it means that goods would essentially enter the flow of commerce and be free of tax. That is, with reverse charging, there is a "break in the VAT chain" in that tax is not paid on the imported good, and the importer is required to self-impose the tax and then immediately claim the corresponding input tax credit.[54] There is growing concern about the development of sophisticated fraud schemes in the EU, in particular, that exploit the reverse-charging approach.[55] The volume of interstate sales of services and the growth of electronic commerce, particularly involving digital products and services, add significantly to the compliance issues that face a destination-based, subnational VAT if it is implemented with traditional border-adjustment processes.[56]

Approaches to Interstate Trade. As the interest in deploying subnational VATs has increased, various academics and practitioners have suggested several approaches to dealing with the interstate trade issues that would plague a destination-based subnational VAT.

Revenue Sharing or Tax Sharing. One approach used in some countries (e.g., Australia, Austria, and Germany)[57] does not involve a separate subnational VAT. Instead, these countries essentially share a single national tax between the national and subnational governments. In these systems, subnational governments receive either a specified proportion of the tax collected from consumption within the subnational area (tax sharing) or an allocation of overall VAT revenue based on a formula (revenue sharing). The formula may reflect consumption patterns in the country, or it may be based on other factors aimed at achieving some degree of fiscal equalization among subnational units.[58] A revenue-sharing or tax-sharing system would be a substantial departure from the US system of federalism where states and localities can structure their own taxes and establish their own tax rates. Given the vast number of local governments, there are also questions of whether equalization efforts are effective or practical.[59]

Clearinghouse Operations. The EU, for one, has considered establishing a clearinghouse operation to deal with the interstate trade issues. Under the EU proposal, a VAT would be collected on exports at the rate in the exporting state (or the country in the case of the EU), and the purchaser would receive an input credit on the return that it filed in the importing state. All exports and imports would be reported to the clearinghouse, which would be responsible for arriving at the net balances owed from one state to another. Concerns about the volume of transactions that would be involved and potential compliance issues have prevented implementation of the EU clearinghouse.[60] The EU instead uses a "reverse-charge" system for transactions involving member-states. A clearinghouse-type system has been used between Israel and the West Bank and the Gaza Strip, but the experience there indicates some of the pitfalls that can befall such an arrangement.[61]

Compensating VAT. Charles McLure, senior fellow (emeritus) at the Hoover Institution at Stanford University and a former US Treasury official, has written widely on subnational VATs, in particular on the potential coordination of a US federal VAT with state and local RSTs.[62] Building on a proposal originally made for Brazil,[63] McLure has suggested a coordinated national and subnational VAT that consists of three separate levies: a national VAT levied at a single rate throughout the country, a subnational VAT levied on *intrastate* sales within the jurisdiction, and a compensating VAT (CVAT) levied at a uniform rate on all *interstate* sales.[64] The CVAT would be fully creditable, so it would generate no net revenue except for that associated with interstate sales to individual consumers and unregistered traders.[65] Sales to final consumers would reflect a combination of the national VAT and the subnational VAT in the destination jurisdiction.[66] The intent of the CVAT is to avoid a "break in the VAT chain" and to avoid an excessive amount of refund claims. In addition, the CVAT would be collected by and accounted for by the national government, thus eliminating any need for a clearinghouse to net export tax and import credits. [67]

Viable Integrated VAT. The International Monetary Fund economists Michael Keen and Stephen Smith have developed an approach similar to the CVAT to deal with "interstate trade" between member-states of the EU, where there is no over-arching central government VAT.[68] A uniform viable integrated VAT (VIVAT) rate would be applied to all sales to *registered traders* regardless of whether the sale occurred wholly within a member-state of the EU or between traders in multiple member-states. The VIVAT would be fully creditable. Individual member-states would establish their own tax rates to be applied to sales to final consumers and unregistered traders.[69] Like the CVAT, the VIVAT would use a uniform levy on cross-border sales to registered traders to avoid compliance issues with zero-rating, refunds, and reverse charging. Some clearing mechanism would be necessary to reconcile the credits on imports and exports among countries, as credits for VIVAT paid on intermediate purchases would be taken against the returns filed with individual member-states, rather than against a central EU-wide tax (as with a CVAT).[70]

Dual VAT. Richard Bird and Pierre-Pascal Gendron, noted public finance economists, have written widely on VATs around the world; much of their writing has focused on Canada. Based on their experience, they believe that it is eminently possible for both a national VAT and a subnational VAT to coexist and operate effectively without a uniform levy such as the CVAT or VIVAT to handle cross-border trade.[71] Bird and Gendron posit that a dual VAT system (a federal VAT and separate provincial VAT) where interprovincial sales are subject to traditional border-adjustment mechanisms is preferable to a more complicated CVAT or VIVAT. They believe that strong working relationships between the national and subnational tax authorities can serve as an effective enforcement mechanism and can obviate the need for an additional levy such as the CVAT or VIVAT.[72]

Two Important Caveats. In virtually all discussions about achieving an optimal coordination of national and subnational VATs, the underlying assumption is that the national and subnational tax bases will be substantially identical.[73] Some countries have developed mechanisms for allowing the federal and subnational governments to share in decision making about their tax bases or have minor variances between the bases. In general, however, there is little concern with the ability of subnational governments to establish their own tax bases. Instead, the focus is on preserving the ability of the subnational units to establish their own tax rates on sales to consumers within their jurisdiction.[74] In addition, it is generally considered most efficient to have one tax authority administer both the national and subnational VATs. However, insistence on a single-entity administration as a prerequisite to a well-coordinated VAT is decreasing, provided that there are effective information exchanges and other coordination and working relationships between the national government and the states.[75]

Options for the States. Not all of the approaches designed to deal with interstate trade and subnational VATs seem well-suited to the United States. The revenue-sharing or tax-sharing approach, for example, runs against the grain of some states that desire not to have an RST and others that desire to design and administer the RST themselves. Similarly, the CVAT and VIVAT, besides being untested models, would seem to rely on all states (or a substantial number) using the same approach. Given these considerations, the predilection of states to retain a separate state consumption tax of some sort, and the experience in other federal systems,[76] an individual state would seem to have four options available to it for retaining or modifying its RST if the US government adopts a VAT: it could (1) maintain the status quo and retain its sales tax as it currently exists, (2) "harmonize" its RST with the VAT and have it treated essentially as an "add-on" to the federal VAT, (3) adopt a state-level VAT that is coordinated with and emulates the federal VAT but is administered separately by the state, or (4) adopt an "Integrated Sales Tax" (IST), a type of RST that relies on certain VAT techniques and could benefit from implementation with a federal VAT to achieve the aims of an ideal RST in terms of taxing individual consumption. (The IST is discussed more fully below.) Given the traditions of US states and the experience in Canada, we should not expect that all states will make the same choice, and we should expect that the preferences of states may change over time in terms of the manner in which they modify (or do not modify) their RSTs in response to the federal adoption of a VAT.

Status Quo. A state could, if it so desires, maintain its RST and make no changes in its operation, structure, or administration in response to the adoption of a federal VAT. This is, in fact, the predominant approach adopted by Canadian provinces immediately following adoption of the federal Goods and Services Tax (GST) in 1991. Each province with a sales tax maintained its separate tax with the exception of Quebec, which implemented its provincial VAT. In 1997, three provinces—Nova Scotia, New Brunswick, and Newfoundland and Labrador—moved to harmonize their sales taxes with the GST;[77] they were followed into the harmonized system over a decade later by British Columbia and Ontario in 2010. Manitoba, Prince Edward Island, and Saskatchewan maintain separate provincial sales taxes.[78]

Maintaining the status quo seems likely to be the initial response of many states given that it requires no modification of a state's tax structure. The primary impact of such a decision will be borne by US businesses that will be required to comply not only with the federal VAT, but also with what is acknowledged to be an exceedingly complex RST system. If states maintain their RSTs, there will be few policy dislocations. Then again, there will be no tax-policy improvements at the subnational level, and the combined federal and state compliance burden faced by multistate sellers may increase significantly.

"Harmonized" Sales Tax. At the opposite end of the policy spectrum, a state could opt to "harmonize" its sales tax with the federal VAT, or adopt a system that is similar in key aspects to the Harmonized Sales Tax (HST) system that is currently in place for the Canadian provinces of Nova Scotia, New Brunswick, Newfoundland and Labrador, British Columbia, and Ontario.[79] In that arrangement, the provincial tax is essentially a surcharge applied to the provincial portion of the federal GST base. From the state perspective, the most relevant HST features are that the tax base is identical (or nearly so) to the federal tax,[80] the tax is administered by the federal government on behalf of the states, and each state is responsible for establishing the rate at which sales of goods and services sourced to the state are taxed.[81] International exports would be zero-rated as to both the federal and state taxes, imports by registered traders would be reverse charged, and the federal Bureau of Customs and Border Protection, a part of the Department of Homeland Security, could collect the federal and state taxes (for an HST state) on international imports by others.[82]

Presuming a well-designed federal VAT, the HST approach, if adopted by a significant number of states, would yield the greatest policy and administrative benefits to the overall consumption tax system. It would adjust the state tax base away from taxing business inputs and toward taxing all final personal consumption of goods and services. It could also reduce the administrative and compliance burdens facing multistate sellers by reducing the number of different tax bases with which they are expected to comply.[83] Finally, if the federal government administers the HST on behalf of participating states, the HST would relieve participating states of the cost of administering their RSTs, a feature used as a "selling point" for harmonization in Ontario.[84]

Achieving these improvements would also require states to surrender substantial autonomy to define the tax base as well as administration of the tax to the federal government. Compliance with the HST would be made significantly more complicated, or impossible, if each state defined its own tax base, and it would become nigh impossible to have a single level of government administer the tax.[85] The requirement for base uniformity, along with concerns about forgoing state administration, effectiveness of federal enforcement, and the manner and timeliness for distributing revenues to the states, makes it seem unlikely that a significant number of states would opt for the HST approach, at least at the outset. As any observer of state RSTs knows, states have wielded their near-plenary authority[86] over the RST to create countless differences from state to state.[87] The fervor with which state officials guard their authority over the tax base is demonstrated by the fact that an underlying principle of the Streamlined Sales and Use Tax Agreement (SSUTA), the most far-reaching effort to promote uniformity in sales-tax practices across states, is that states should be free to determine their own tax bases.[88] While the SSUTA contains uniform definitions for certain products that states are required to use, the determination of whether an item is taxed or not in a state is reserved for the state legislature.[89] Adopting an HST would also expose states to potential revenue swings if the federal government were to enact laws that affected the shared HST and VAT tax base.[90]

State VAT. If the HST approach is considered problematic for states, the question becomes whether states could implement a state-level VAT that addresses some of the fiscal autonomy concerns but at the same time improves the policy underpinnings of subnational consumption taxes. Internationally, successful administration of a destination-based subnational VAT is limited primarily to Quebec, which administers both the Quebec Sales Tax (QST)—a destination-based subnational VAT—and the Canadian federal GST.[91]

As noted above, there are several options for dealing with the central issue of taxing interstate trade on a destination basis without risking substantial exposure to fraud and noncompliance. Those that involve actual administration of a separate state VAT include the CVAT, VIVAT, and dual VAT approaches. McLure, who has devoted the most attention to the design of subnational VATs, has concluded that these approaches are not optimal for implementing a destination-based state-local VAT in the United States for several reasons.[92] First, the volume of interstate trade in the United States and the resulting VAT refunds on zero-rated business-to-business sales would create a substantial risk of fraud and noncompliance, making the zero-rating/reverse charge regime of a dual VAT unworkable, in his estimation.[93] Second, either the VIVAT or CVAT approach would work best if all states adopted it—an unlikely occurrence. Third, a VIVAT would require a revenue clearinghouse and an agreed-upon VIVAT rate, each of which McLure also considers a long shot.[94] Finally, he finds that the CVAT also comes up short in the US setting because it would rely on administration by the federal government or a consortium of states and could not be transported to the local level.[95]

Integrated Sales Tax. To address these shortcomings, McLure developed the IST, which he believes can be used to implement a destination-based sales tax that comports with a well-designed consumption tax.[96] The IST is essentially an ideal form of RST that uses certain VAT techniques to exclude business inputs from taxes and to tax individual consumption on a destination basis. Under the IST, all sales between registered traders (both intrastate and interstate sales) would be zero-rated, and only sales to individual consumers and unregistered traders would be subject to a positive tax rate that would be established by the states.[97] Under McLure's proposal, states would administer the IST, but its administration would be closely coordinated with the federal VAT, particularly in the registration of taxpayers and monitoring of sales between registered traders (i.e., business-to-business sales).[98] As formulated by McLure, the base of the state tax on sales to consumers would conform to the federal VAT base, in part to facilitate coordination in administering the state and federal taxes.[99]

McLure believes the IST approach is the best choice for those states desiring to modify their sales taxes in a fashion that would be coordinated with a federal VAT for several reasons. First, it is consistent with the state tradition of imposing RSTs, while eliminating the shortcomings that currently characterize the RSTs, such as taxing business inputs and not taxing all sales to individuals. Second, not all states would be required to adopt the IST for it to be useable by those that did. Third, it does not require federal administration of a state tax or a clearinghouse to distribute funds among states. Fourth, it would avoid the refunds that would be necessary under the standard border-tax adjustment process as well as avoid possible fraudulent practices. Finally, like existing sales taxes, it could be used by local governments.[100]

Issues for States. As proposed, the IST represents a radical departure from current RSTs that would appear to bring state RSTs into closer alignment with the accepted policy norms for consumption taxes. At the same time, it raises several significant issues that states would have to evaluate carefully in assessing whether to adopt the IST as a vehicle for coordinating with a federal VAT.

Tax Rate. Probably, the first consideration for states would be the tax rate that would need to be applied to the new tax base of intrastate sales to final consumers to compensate for the revenue currently collected on sales to businesses that would not be taxed under an IST. Some recent analyses have suggested that a well-designed federal VAT could have a base equal to roughly 60 percent of GDP.[101] This translates to a federal VAT base of roughly $8 trillion based on 2009 GDP, meaning that an average state IST rate of about 3 percent would generate revenues roughly equal to the $240 billion in general sales taxes collected by states in 2008.[102] Among Organisation for Economic Co-operation and Development (OECD) countries, the average VAT base is equal to roughly 60 percent of final household consumption. A US federal VAT base commensurate with the OECD average would translate to a VAT base of about $6 trillion,[103] meaning an average state-tax rate of about 4 percent would be necessary to be revenue neutral with current state RST collections.[104]

Tax Base. As noted, McLure proposed for both administrative and policy reasons that the base of the state-level IST conform to that of the federal VAT. The same is true in other countries that attempt to coordinate national and subnational VATs, whether it is the HST or the QST in Canada or the proposals for an integrated GST now being considered in India.[105]

In Canada, some differences in tax base are accommodated through "on-the-spot" rebates (a refund paid to a customer at the point of sale) or varying rebates to certain types of taxpayers without unduly complicating compliance for sellers. As a state IST would apply only to in-state sales to final consumers and would be administered by the states, it might be possible to allow states to vary to some degree from the federal base without making compliance or administration overly complicated. If experience is a guide, it would seem necessary to minimize such deviations, or the differences from state to state and the complexity could soon become overwhelming. Differences in federal and state tax bases would also complicate coordinated enforcement and administration with the federal government as discussed below. Given the need to have a single federal and state taxpayer registration, it would not seem possible for a state-tax base to deviate from the federal base in a manner that would require a seller to register and collect a state VAT when it was not required to do so for federal purposes. Likewise, imposition of tax on business inputs would complicate such coordinated administration.

Compliance. The state IST would be collected entirely on the final sale to an individual consumer. As a result, there will be a substantial volume of trade moving among registered traders without payment of tax, thus creating opportunities for evasion and noncompliance for states. Some of these compliance risks might be overcome by coordinating the administration of an IST with a federal VAT.

Taxpayer Registration. The cornerstone of a cooperative approach to administration would be a common taxpayer registration system in which the federal government and the states would rely on a single registration process and registration number for each taxpayer. The possession of a valid VAT registration number would identify the holder as being eligible to engage in zero-rated purchases from another registered trader for the IST and as being eligible for the input credits associated with the federal VAT.[106] Common registration and identification numbers would also be integral to meaningful information exchanges between the federal government and the states to promote compliance.[107]

Establishing a common registration system would create issues. Most countries with a VAT use a "registration threshold," wherein businesses with an annual sales volume below some specified level are not required to charge and collect a VAT on their sales.[108] The registration threshold, while reducing revenues somewhat, simplifies administration of the VAT for both the government and sellers by eliminating the requirement that a large number of sellers collect and remit tax. Given the difference in the way the two taxes operate (single-stage ISTs versus multistage VATs) as well as differences in scale, it should be expected that the states would support a lower threshold than might be optimal for the federal government.[109] Likewise, states are likely to be interested in more aggressive sanctions against a broader range of noncompliant taxpayers than the federal government.[110] Some accommodation of the different interests would be necessary for a coordinated VAT system.

Information Sharing. An active program of exchanging information between the IRS and state tax administration agencies is a centerpiece of state income-tax enforcement, particularly for individual income taxes.[111] Similar information exchanges could benefit the states in dealing with compliance issues. In particular, sharing information about taxpayer registration applications; data on purchases, sales, and tax collections by taxpayer; and the results of federal audits and compliance activities would be beneficial to states.[112]

Under the IST, there would likely be a greater volume of cross-border sales between registered traders on which no tax is collected than under current RSTs. Moreover, no record of the sale would be necessary at the state level to claim any input tax credit. Information on these transactions, however, would be available to the federal government as part of the process of verifying input credits and output tax liability. As a result, it has been suggested that either the states or the federal government should establish a database on these cross-border sales between registered traders as a compliance aid to states.[113] This database would enable each state to monitor the flow of goods and services into and out of the state and to ascertain whether the appropriate tax has been paid and remitted when sold to an individual consumer. This proposal is similar to the VAT Information Exchange System (VIES) in place in the European Union and is being considered as part of the VAT reform in India.[114] To be most helpful to the states, such a database would have to include information that is not necessary to federal VAT administration, such as the state of origin and the state of destination. It would also require a likely significant level of financial resources.

Distance Selling. Under current constitutional interpretation, a seller without a physical presence or the requisite "substantial nexus" in a state with an RST cannot be required to collect the RST on sales into that state.[115] While states have been focused on this issue for several decades, it arguably may be more important to states with an IST because tax will only be collected on final sales to individuals and not on any intermediate business transactions. To aid compliance with ISTs and to provide an incentive for states to move from an RST to the IST, the federal government could adopt a "distance-selling rule," which would mean that sellers above a certain sales threshold would be required to collect the IST on all sales to final consumers, even in states where they would not be considered to have a collection obligation under current law.[116] The EU has similar rules for the intra-European Community supply of goods to final consumers.[117]

Tax on International Imports. The federal government could also aid compliance with ISTs and encourage their adoption by agreeing to collect tax on imports into the United States when the importer is not a registered trader.[118] Given the presumed similarity between the federal VAT base and IST base, the US Customs and Border Protection Bureau would need confirmation that the importer is not a registered trader and the appropriate tax rate in the destination state to make such a system work.

Local Government Sales Taxes. Local government sales taxes present a unique set of challenges to the coordination of national and subnational consumption taxes that is not encountered in Canada or other federal countries. About 8,000 local governmental units in over 30 US states employ RSTs. In all states except Alabama, Arizona, Colorado, and Louisiana, the state administers the local tax, which is generally, but not always, imposed on a base that is substantially the same as the state RST base. In 2007, local governments collected about $61 billion in general sales taxes, or just under one-fifth of their total tax revenues,[119] meaning the issue of local taxes is not inconsequential. Local RSTs are often considered to add complexity to the administration of RSTs because they are generally not levied uniformly across the state and are levied at different rates among localities. In some cases, special-purpose districts (e.g., transit districts), whose boundaries do not coincide with general-purpose local governments, are authorized to levy a sales tax.

McLure has examined the issues involved in implementing a VAT at the local government level. He drew three conclusions:[120]

1. Imposition of a traditional VAT with standard border adjustments is impractical at the local level because of the fraud potential as well as general complexity given the number of jurisdictions involved and the volume of trade expected.
2. If a state administered a VAT, local VATs could be handled through a VIVAT, but this would be complicated by the patchwork pattern and varying rates of local taxes.

3. If a state adopts an IST, local governments could add a surcharge on the state IST. Even if states and localities were both to adopt a coordinated IST, it would add complexity for traders making taxable sales to final consumers; the traders would be required to determine the appropriate tax rate of the local jurisdiction into which they are selling. In addition, states and localities would need to determine whether to distribute local VAT revenue on the basis of actual sales (which require significant reporting and accounting) or on the basis of a formula that is intended to replicate where consumption occurs.

In short, replacing local RSTs with a local IST is feasible; it is not, however, without some complexities.

CONCLUSION

The severity of the Great Recession and its impact on the finances of governments at all levels, coupled with the long-term structural issues they all face, may occasion a thorough evaluation of the services that the federal government provides and the manner in which they are financed. These pressures may lead to a close examination of a federal VAT. Such a move would create significant issues and challenges for states and localities. At the same time, it could also provide a platform for substantially improving state consumption tax systems and aid in a long-overdue modernization of a major component of the state and local revenue structure. Using a well-designed federal VAT could pay substantial rewards by improving the policy underpinnings of state consumption taxes and reducing the compliance burden imposed on US businesses. The complexity of the current RST structure and history of political autonomy enjoyed by states in designing their RSTs would present substantial obstacles to achieving such a coordinated system. Regardless of the approach that states individually or collectively may choose, successful implementation of a coordinated federal-state consumption tax system is likely to depend on the degree of uniformity that can be achieved between the federal VAT base and the state consumption tax base. Achieving that uniformity is a step that is not likely to come easily to many state policymakers.

NOTES

The information contained in this chapter is general in nature and based on authorities that are subject to change. Applicability to specific situations is to be determined through consultation with your tax advisor. This chapter represents the views of the author only.

1 See, for example, Altman (2009); Bartlett (2009); and Montgomery (2009).

2 See, for example, Graetz (2008) (arguing that revenues from a VAT should be used to reform the federal income-tax system, lower rates, and eliminate the tax for many low- and middle-income taxpayers) and Burman (2009) (arguing that the revenues from a VAT should be used to finance expanded health-care coverage in the United States). The American Tax Policy Institute (www.americantaxpolicyinstitute.org) held a conference in February 2009 that addressed various issues in designing and implementing a VAT in the United States. Papers presented at that conference, several of which are referenced here, were published by the *Tax Law Review* in the Winter and Spring 2010 editions.

3 Debt Reduction Task Force (2010), 40–43.

4 US Advisory Commission on Intergovernmental Relations (1973).

5 See, for example, Bradford (1986); Aaron, Galper, and Pechman (1988).

6 Wallace (this volume).

7 US Congressional Budget Office (2011).

8 111th Congress, P.L. 111–312.

9 US Congressional Budget Office (2011), 1. On the expenditure side, the baseline reflects a continuation of all entitlement and discretionary programs as they currently exist, and implementation of the health-care reform act passed in 2010.

10 Ibid., 2. The Budget Control Act of 2011 was adopted in August 2011. The act imposed caps on certain discretionary spending for the period 2011–2021. The caps would reduce spending by about $945 billion over ten years. The act also charged a select committee of the Congress with formulating recommendations for an additional $1.2 trillion in deficit reduction over a ten-year period. Congress would need to adopt the additional deficit reductions and could alter the spending caps at any time. If the deficit reductions of the Budget Control Act are achieved, it would substantially alter the long-term budget projections discussed below.

11 Ibid., 24.

12 Wallace (this volume).

13 US Congressional Budget Office (2009), xi.

14 Debt Reduction Task Force (2010), 25.

15 Ibid., 12.

16 Ibid., 15.

17 Auerbach and Gale (2009), 3.

18 Ibid.

19 US Congressional Budget Office (2009), 8.

20 Duncan (2010b), 1643.

21 For a complete discussion of the Canadian system, see Bird and Gendron (2010).

22 Throughout this chapter, the assumption is that the federal government would adopt a well-designed credit-invoice VAT that taxes final individual consumption broadly on a destination basis and relieves any burden on business inputs. The merits of coordinating with a federal VAT that did not meet these criteria are open to question.

23 US General Accounting Office (1989), 44–45.

24 Fox and Luna (2003), 875, 878.

25 For a rather stinging critique of the manner in which states have exercised this autonomy, see McLure (2002a, 2005b).

26 Hellerstein (2000), Sec. 7.02; Brunori (this volume).

27 Duncan (2010b), 1643, 1647–53.

28 Bird and Gendron (2010), 517, 579–580.

29 Under a well-designed VAT, a reduction in consumption (i.e., an increase in savings) merely defers taxation until savings are spent. However, even a temporary reduction

in state revenues can be problematic, given state balanced-budget requirements. The impact of a VAT on state revenues also needs to be contrasted with raising a similar amount of federal revenue via another federal revenue source. Interestingly, the same concern motivates some retailer opposition to a potential federal VAT as expressed by the National Retail Federation (NRF). See Carroll, Cline, Neubig, Diamond and Zodrow (2010) who estimate that a 10.3 percent add-on VAT would reduce retail spending by $2.5 trillion over 10 years.

30 McLure (1988), 1517, 1530.

31 Duncan (2005), 8.

32 See, for example, McLure (2000c; 2002b; 2005a, 35–36).

33 Fox (this volume).

34 Federation of Tax Administrators (2008).

35 Duncan (2010a), 717. Duncan noted that the state legislatures in Florida, Massachusetts, and Michigan have passed legislation to impose sales tax on a broad array of services, but in each case, the tax was repealed shortly before or shortly after it was implemented. These failures were, in part, attributable to the inappropriate imposition of the tax on the purchase of services by a business, which leads to inordinately complicated sourcing issues.

36 Durner and Bui (2010), 983.

37 Phillips, Cline, and Neubig (2008), 1; Fox (this volume).

38 Bird and Smart (2009), 591.

39 Carlson (2005).

40 Duncan (2010a), 720–724.

41 Ibid.

42 Holcombe (2010), 26.

43 Alaska, Delaware, Montana, New Hampshire, and Oregon do not levy a broad-based retail sales tax.

44 The Canadian experience is instructive here in that most provinces chose to retain their RSTs when the federal government adopted the GST. In 1997, Nova Scotia, New Brunswick, and Newfoundland and Labrador replaced their RSTs with a single federal-provincial harmonized sales tax collected by the federal government. In 2009, Ontario and British Columbia announced that they would replace their RSTs with a harmonized sales tax beginning July 1, 2010. See Sullivan (2010); Duncan (2010b), 1649–1650.

45 Fox (this volume).

46 Duncan (2010b), 1644. The remainder of the discussion presumes that an interstate sale is between two registered traders. With a VAT (as with the retail sales tax in the United States), sales from a seller in one jurisdiction to a final consumer in another raise compliance issues unless there is an enforceable requirement that the seller collect the tax imposed in the destination jurisdiction. In *Quill Corp. v. North Dakota*, 504 US 298 (1992), the Supreme Court held that a state could not require a seller that did not have a physical presence in the taxing jurisdiction to collect tax on sales of goods and services into that jurisdiction. The Quill, or distance-selling, issue is discussed further below.

47 Duncan and Sedon (2009), 1370–1371. In theory, the same principles apply to cross-border sales of services and intangibles, although the rules in this context have not always conformed to them and it is only in recent years that many governments have sought to extend them to services. For a discussion of the European Union practices, see Hellerstein and Gillis (2010), 467–470.

48 A zero-rated sale is within the scope of the tax (i.e., subject to tax), but the rate applied is zero. While no VAT is collected on the sale, the seller or supplier is eligible to claim an input credit for tax paid on its purchases. This contrasts with an exempt sale in which no tax is collected, but the seller is not eligible for an input credit on taxes paid on inputs. For more explanation, see Hellerstein and Duncan (2010), 989–991; Duncan and Sedon (2009), 1369–1370.

49 In a reverse charge transaction, the exporter zero-rates the sale and takes any input credit available in the jurisdiction from which the export was made. The importer, on the other hand, makes a self-assessment of the VAT and records an accounting entry to accrue the VAT due on the import at the rate imposed in the destination jurisdiction; at the same time, the importer makes another entry to claim the input tax credit on its next VAT return. In this manner, the tax on the imported item is equivalent to what it would have been if it had been produced and purchased domestically, but the input credit ensures no tax is attached to the business inputs of the importer. See Duncan and Sedon (2009), 1370–1371.

50 Hellerstein (2003), 61 (noting that actual fiscal frontiers, though inimical to the concept of a common market, may serve the interests of effective consumption tax enforcement).

51 See Bird and Gendron (2001), 5; Ebrill et al. (2001), 184–88; McLure (2010), 650–652.

52 See Ebrill et al. (2001), 188; Keen and Smith (2006), 867–870.

53 It is fair to assume that physical border controls would not exist in a federal system. To contemplate, one simply has to imagine a long line of trucks heading west on the George Washington Bridge waiting for a New Jersey tax compliance officer to administer the New Jersey VAT on cargo destined for New Jersey purchasers. Similar lines once existed in the European Union, before they abolished fiscal frontiers in 1993.

54 Keen and Smith (2006), 870–872; see also Cnossen (2010), 599–604. Unlike Keen and Smith, Cnossen does not believe the basic VAT structure needs to be altered to deal with VAT evasion, but rather that evasion can be dealt with through various other enforcement approaches.

55 McLure (2010), 663–672 (discussing carousel or missing trader fraud); Keen and Smith (2006), 870–872 (the same).

56 Ebrill et al. (2001), 184–188; Keen and Hellerstein (2010), 400–406.

57 Perry (2010), 624–625. See also Bird and Gendron (2001), 6–7. The German VAT is administered at the subnational level, and revenues are allocated on a formula basis.

58 McLure (2000a), 628.

59 Yilmaz, Vaillancourt, and Dafflon (this volume).

60 Ebrill et al. (2001), 189–190. Some clearing mechanism is necessary in any destination-based system in which a tax is charged on an export and remitted to the exporting state and a credit is taken for the tax paid in the importing state. Without the clearing mechanism, the exporting state will receive revenues from a supply that took place outside its jurisdiction, and the tax will have been paid by the importing jurisdiction through the credit granted.

61 Ibid., 190. Operation of a clearinghouse would in some ways be similar to the distribution by state governments of local government sales taxes collected on their behalf. Distributions by such an entity must be current, must be transparent and verifiable, and must not be used to achieve political aims.

62 His writings on coordinating a US VAT with state and local sales taxes include McLure (2005a, 2010).

63 Varsano (1995).

64 The CVAT proposal was first explored in McLure (2000b), 725–726.

65 Ibid., 726. Registered traders would be eligible for a credit of all national VAT and subnational VAT on their inputs so that only final consumers and unregistered traders would bear the burden of any form of VAT. The state VAT on interstate sales would be collected through a reverse charge in the state of import.

66 Ibid. International exports would be zero-rated. No national or subnational VAT or CVAT would apply to an international export. Imports would be subject to the national VAT and CVAT at the border.

67 McLure (2000b), 732–733.

68 The VIVAT was first explained in Keen and Smith (1996). It was further developed in Keen and Smith (2000).

69 Keen and Smith (2000), 741.

70 McLure (2000b), 734.

71 Bird and Gendron (1998, 2000, 2001).

72 Ibid. The issue of whether the CVAT, VIVAT, or dual VAT is the most effective method of dealing with cross-border trade in a subnational VAT has been the subject of a rather vigorous academic debate. See McLure (2000b); Bird and Gendron (2000); Keen and Smith (2000).

73 McLure (2010), 645–646; McLure (2000b), 724–725. Substantial symmetry between the federal and provincial base is seen by Bird and Gendron as being important to effective coordination and utilization of federal GST enforcement to aid in the enforcement of the Quebec provincial VAT. Bird and Gendron (1998) 434, 438. McLure considers symmetry in the base to be essential to effective coordination.

74 McLure (2010), 645–646.

75 Bird and Gendron (1998), 434; Bird and Gendron (2001), 13.

76 While it is beyond the scope of this chapter, the experience of other federal systems (Brazil, India, and Canada) and the European Union can be instructive. See Perry (2010) (Brazil and India); Cnossen (2010) (European Union); Bird and Gendron (2010) (Canada); and Duncan (2010b).

77 Bird, Mintz, and Wilson (2006), 894.

78 Duncan (2010b), 1647. In August 2011, the voters of British Columbia rejected the law adopting the Harmonized Sales Tax. As a result, the provincial sales tax that existed prior to July 2010 will be reinstated by 2013.

79 Professors Bird and Gendron, the leading authorities on the Canadian consumption taxes, have written extensively on the topic. For a thoughtful and comprehensive article on the Canadian GST and RST experience, see Bird and Gendron (2010).

80 Some variations are accomplished in Canada through point-of-sales rebates and other rebates. See Bird and Gendron (2010), 549–553.

81 The Atlantic provinces in Canada each adopted the same HST rate by mutual agreement, rather than being required to do so by law. By agreement they also place limits on the ability of the provinces to increase or decrease their HST rates. Ontario and British Columbia have each determined its own rate for HST, and Nova Scotia has set its own rate, effective July 1, 2010. See Duncan (2010b), 1649.

82 These provisions would achieve a destination-based tax. They are similar to those in place in Canadian HST provinces, except that the Canada Border Security Agency collects the provincial HST only on sales to nonregistered traders and final consumers. See Duncan (2010b), 1649. An additional issue that would need to be addressed is distribution of HST revenues to the participating states. In Canada, HST revenues are distributed on the basis of a formula that is intended to estimate

taxable consumption by province instead of tracking and reporting sales and tax collections by province. Using this approach in the United States would seem to be problematic given that there may be a large number of local governments with varying tax rates that would also be included in the HST and given that not all local governments within a state will necessarily levy the HST. This would seem to necessitate the tracking and reporting of sales by state and local jurisdiction, a feature that would make the HST in the United States more complex than in Canada.

83 The reduction in compliance burden is due largely to the assumed condition that the HST base is identical to the federal VAT base. Sellers would still be required to determine the appropriate state and local tax rates to apply. Determining the appropriate local tax rate to apply could still be problematic. Reductions in complexity would also be frustrated to the extent that a state was allowed to use multiple HST rates for different types of goods and services.

84 Duncan (2010b), 1649-1650, and accompanying text. Central administration is not required for an effective HST regime.

85 The essential uniformity of tax bases is required of a HST province in Canada. It is also being set as a condition for state-level VATs being proposed in India. See Duncan (2010b), 1652.

86 State actions in establishing and implementing an RST must comport with the requirements of the US Constitution. The primary constraint in terms of defining the tax base is that a state tax must not discriminate against interstate commerce and may not be imposed on the US government or its instrumentalities. Federal statutory law also limits state sales-tax bases in some areas, as in prohibiting the imposition of sales taxes on purchases made under certain federal nutrition programs. See 7 USC 2011-2025 (Food Stamp Act); 42 USC § 1786 (Special supplemental nutrition program for women, infants, and children).

87 For a taste of the different treatments accorded to different products from state to state, see CCH (2009), 531-599. In addition to product exemptions, states also provide exemptions to various types of entities on either their purchases or their sales or both. Moreover, in many cases, the taxability of a product is based on the use to which it is put. See McLure (2002a, 2005b); Duncan (2010a), 721-722.

88 For a complete discussion and description of the SSUTA, see Hellerstein and Swain (2006-2007). The principle of state determination of the tax base is contained in section 103 of the SSUTA, available at www.streamlinedsalestax.org.

89 Some observers argue that a state's ability to establish the tax base should not be an overriding concern and the focus should instead be on preserving to states the authority to establish tax rates, because that is the key element of state autonomy: the ability to choose the level of spending and how to finance it. McLure, for example, argued, "The case for state autonomy over tax rates is taken as axiomatic" (2010, 645). He argued further that states have not used their authority to establish the tax base wisely and that the taxation of business inputs and the innumerable exemptions that cause the tax to be less than comprehensive in the taxation of individual consumption contribute needlessly to complexity, inefficiency, and distortions. See McLure (2002a, 2005b).

90 McLure (2010), 694-695, argued that this would not be likely—certainly not as likely as under the income tax.

91 For further discussion of the QST and provincial administration of the GST, see Bird and Gendron (2010). Possible state-level administration of the federal VAT is

not considered further here since such an approach seems unlikely to be transported to the United States, given that many states are unlikely to adopt a VAT and some states do not have an RST—not to mention concerns about allowing subnational administration and enforcement of a national tax.

92 McLure (2010), 665–672.

93 Ibid., 662–663.

94 Ibid., 668.

95 Ibid., 669–670.

96 The Integrated Sales Tax is most fully explained in McLure (2010), 643, note 20.

97 By zero-rating all sales to registered traders, the IST uses some of the mechanics of a VAT to achieve the results of an "ideal" sales tax (i.e., a tax collected at a single stage on sales to final consumers and no tax on business inputs).

98 McLure (2010), 680–681.

99 Ibid., 685–687.

100 Ibid., 680–681. States could achieve the same results as an IST under their current RSTs by allowing an unlimited exemption for all business-to-business transactions and taxing all business-to-consumer transactions. The presence of a federal VAT, however, is believed to strengthen the ability of states to ensure compliance with the tax.

101 Duncan and Sedon (2009), 1372–1373.

102 Based on data from the US Bureau of the Census, State Government Tax Collections in 2008.

103 Based on data on final household consumption as reported by the OECD, which can be accessed at http://stats.oecd.org/Index.aspx?DatasetCode=SNA_TABLE1.

104 The calculations of the required state tax rate do not make adjustments to GDP our household consumption for the four states (Alaska, Montana, New Hampshire, and Oregon). Given the sizes of these states, such an adjustment would not be expected to alter the conclusions significantly.

105 See Duncan (2010b), 1647–1652, for a review of these systems and proposals.

106 McLure (2010), 680–684; Duncan (2010a), 759–763.

107 See Duncan (2010a), 755–759, for a discussion of the types of exchanges that could be fruitful. Pages 730–734 discuss various information exchanges under the individual income tax.

108 McLure (2010), 682. Businesses below the threshold would pay a VAT on their inputs, and they would not receive input credits on those purchases.

109 Duncan (2010a), 759–763; McLure (2010), 680–681. State retail sales taxes generally do not have such thresholds. The revenue loss from such a threshold will be less under a VAT than under an RST because tax will be collected on inputs purchased by sellers under the threshold.

110 Duncan (2010a), 762–763.

111 See Duncan (2010a), 730–734; Duncan and McLure (1997) for a review of these programs.

112 Duncan (2010a), 755–756.

113 Ibid., 756–757.

114 Madhavan, Renavikar, and Arawattigi (2010) 132.

115 *Quill Corp. v. North Dakota*, 504 US 298 (1992).

116 McLure (2010), 702–703; Duncan (2010a), 764. States, through the Streamlined Sales Tax Project, have been working to simplify sales tax administration and to encourage Congress to adopt a similar rule for the RST in certain states. A distance-selling rule

for ISTs might be considered more palatable to some given that the presumption is that the IST base would, for all practical purposes, be identical to the federal VAT with which the seller would be required to comply.

117 Hellerstein and Gillis (2010), 466.

118 Duncan (2010a), 764. The Canada Border Security Agency performs this function for Quebec and the HST provinces.

119 US Bureau of the Census, State and Local Government Finances, 2007.

120 McLure (2010), 673–678.

References

Altman, Roger C. (2009, June 30). "We'll Need to Raise Taxes Soon." *Wall Street Journal*: A15.

Auerbach, Alan J., and William G. Gale (2009, September). "The Economic Crisis and the Fiscal Crisis: 2009 and Beyond, An Update," http://www.brookings.edu/papers/2009/06_fiscal_crisis_gale.aspx.

Bartlett, Bruce (2009, June 5). "VAT Time?" http://www.forbes.com/2009/06/04/value-added-tax-opinions-columnists-bartlett.html.

Bird, Richard M., and Pierre-Pascal Gendron (1998). "Dual VATs and Cross-Border Trade: Two Problems, One Solution?" *International Tax and Public Finance* 5: 429–442.

Bird, Richard M., and Pierre-Pascal Gendron (2000, December). "CVAT, VIVAT, and Dual VAT: Vertical 'Sharing' and Interstate Trade." *International Tax and Public Finance* 7: 753–761.

Bird, Richard M., and Pierre-Pascal Gendron (2001). "VATs in Federal States: International Experience and Emerging Possibilities." Working Paper #01–4. Atlanta: Georgia State University, Andrew Young School of Public Policy Studies.

Bird, Richard M., and Pierre-Pascal Gendron (2010, Spring). "Sales Taxes in Canada: The GST-HST-QST-RST 'System.'" *Tax Law Review* 63: 517–582.

Bird, Richard M., Jack M. Mintz, and Thomas A. Wilson (2006, December). "Coordinating Federal and Provincial Sales Taxes: Lessons from the Canadian Experience." *National Tax Journal* 59: 889–903.

Bird, Richard M., and Michael Smart (2009, December). "The Impact on Investment of Replacing a Retails Sales Tax with a Value-Added Tax: Evidence from Canadian Experience." *National Tax Journal* 62: 591–609.

Bradford, David F. (1986). *Untangling the Income Tax*. Cambridge, MA: Harvard University Press.

Burman, Leonard E. (2009, Spring). "A Blueprint for Tax Reform and Health Reform." *Virginia Tax Review* 28: 288–323.

Carlson, George (2005). "Destination Principle." In *The Encyclopedia of Taxation and Tax Policy*, edited by Joseph J. Cordes, Robert D. Ebel, and Jane G. Gravelle. Washington, DC. Urban Institute Press. 82–83.

Carroll, Robert, Robert Cline, Tom Neubig, John Diamond, and George Zodrow (2010). *The Macroeconomic Effects of an Add-On Value Added Tax*. Prepared for the National Retail Federation. Washington: Ernst and Young.

CCH (2009). *State Tax Handbook—2009*. Chicago: CCH.

Cnossen, Sjbren (2010, Spring). "VAT Coordination in Common Markets and Federations: Lessons from European Experience." *Tax Law Review* 63: 583–622.

Debt Reduction Task Force (2010). *Restoring America's Future: Reviving the Economy, Cutting Spending and Debt, and Creating a Simple, Pro-Growth Tax System.* Washington: Bipartisan Policy Center.

Duncan, Harley (2005, October 3). "Federal Tax Reform and State Taxes: A Framework for Analysis." In *Federal Tax Reform and the States, Special Supplement*, edited by Harley T. Duncan. *State Tax Notes*: 5–15.

Duncan, Harley (2010a, Spring). "Administrative Mechanisms to Aid in the Coordination of State and Local Retail Sales Taxes with a Federal Value-Added Tax." *Tax Law Review* 63: 713–770.

Duncan, Harley (2010b, March 29). "VATs in a Federal System." *Tax Notes*: 1643–1653.

Duncan, Harley T., and Charles E. McLure, Jr. (1997, February). "Tax Administration in the United States of America: A Decentralized System." *Bulletin for International Fiscal Documentation* 51: 74–85.

Duncan, Harley, and Jon Sedon (2009, December 21). "How Different VATs Work." *Tax Notes*: 1367–1374.

Durner, Leah, and Bobby Bui (2010, February 22). "Comparing Value Added and Retail Sales Taxes." *Tax Notes*: 983–987.

Ebrill, Liam, Michael Keen, Jean-Paul Bodin, and Victoria Summers (2001). *The Modern VAT.* Washington: International Monetary Fund.

Federation of Tax Administrators (2008). "Taxation of Services—Update, July 2008." *By the Numbers.* http://www.taxadmin.org/fta/pub/services/btn/0708.html.

Fox, William F., and LeAnn Luna (2003, March 10). "Subnational Taxing Options: Which Is Preferred, a Retails Sales Tax or a VAT?" *State Tax Notes*: 875–884.

Graetz, Michael J. (2008). *100 Million Unnecessary Returns: A Simple, Fair and Competitive Tax Plan for the United States.* New Haven, CT: Yale University Press.

Hellerstein, Walter (2000). *State Taxation.* 3rd ed. New York: Warren, Gorham & Lamont.

Hellerstein, Walter (2003, Fall). "Jurisdiction to Tax Income and Consumption in the New Economy: A Theoretical and Comparative Perspective." *Georgia Law Review* 38: 3–70.

Hellerstein, Walter, and Harley Duncan (2010, August 30). "VAT Exemptions: Principles and Practice." *Tax Notes*: 989–999.

Hellerstein, Walter, and Timothy H. Gillis (2010, April 26). "The VAT in the European Union." *Tax Notes*: 461–471.

Hellerstein, Walter, and John A. Swain (2006–2007). *Streamlined Sales and Use Tax.* New York: Warren, Gorham and Lamont of RIA.

Holcombe, Randall G. (2010, June). "The Value Added Tax: Too Costly for the U.S." Working Paper No. 10–32. Mercatus Center George Mason University. Available at http://mercatus.org/sites/default/files/publication/VAT.Holcombe.pdf.

Keen, Michael, and Walter Hellerstein (2010, Winter). "Interjurisdictional Issues in the Design of a VAT." *Tax Law Review* 63: 359–408.

Keen, Michael, and Stephen Smith (1996, October). "The Future of the Value Added Tax in the European Union." *Economic Policy* 23: 375–411.

Keen, Michael, and Stephen Smith (2000, December). "Viva VIVAT!" *International Tax and Public Finance* 6: 741–751.

Keen, Michael, and Stephen Smith (2006, December). "VAT Fraud and Evasion: What Do We Know and What Can Be Done?" *National Tax Journal* 59: 861–887.

Madhavan S., Rahul Renavikar, and Praveen William Arawatigi (2010, March-April). "Taxation of Interstate Transactions under the Proposed Indian GST." *International VAT Monitor*: 128–132.

McLure, Charles E., Jr. (1988, March 28). "State and Local Implications of a Federal Value-Added Tax." *Tax Notes*: 1517–1535.

McLure, Charles E., Jr. (2000a, December). "Tax Assignment and Subnational Fiscal Autonomy." *Bulletin for International Fiscal Documentation* 630: 626–635.

McLure, Charles E., Jr. (2000b, December). "Implementing Subnational Value Added Taxes on Internal Trade: The Compensating VAT (CVAT)." *International Tax and Public Finance* 7: 723–740.

McLure, Charles E., Jr. (2000c). "The Taxation of Electronic Commerce: Background and Proposal." In *Public Policy and the Internet: Privacy, Taxes, and Contracts*, edited by Nicholas Imparato. Stanford, CA: Hoover Institution Press. 49–113.

McLure, Charles E., Jr. (2002a, September 16). "The Nuttiness of State and Local Taxes—and the Nuttiness of Responses Thereto." *State Tax Notes*: 841–856.

McLure, Charles E., Jr. (2002b). "Thinking Straight about the Taxation of Electronic Commerce: Tax Principles, Compliance Problems, and Nexus." *Tax Policy and the Economy* 16: 115–140.

McLure, Charles E., Jr. (2005a, October 3). "Coordinating State Sales Taxes with a Federal VAT: Opportunities, Risks, and Challenges." In *Federal Tax Reform and the States, Special Supplement*, edited by Harley T. Duncan. *State Tax Notes*: 35–48.

McLure, Charles E., Jr. (2005b, September). "Understanding the Nuttiness of State Tax Policy: When States Have Both Too Much Sovereignty and Not Enough." *National Tax Journal* 58: 565–573.

McLure, Charles E., Jr. (2010, Spring). "How to Coordinate State and Local Sales Taxes with a Federal Value-Added Tax." *Tax Law Review* 63: 639–704.

Montgomery, Lori (2009, May 27). "Once Considered Unthinkable, U.S. Sales Tax Gets Fresh Look." *Washington Post*: A15.

Perry, Victoria J. (2010, Spring). "International Experience in Implementing VATs in Federal Jurisdictions: A Summary." *Tax Law Review* 63: 623–638.

Phillips, Andrew, Robert Cline, and Tom Neubig (2008). *Total State and Local Business Taxes: 50-State Estimates for Fiscal Year 2007*. Washington: Ernst and Young and Council on State Taxation.

Sullivan, Martin A. (2010, May 3). "Economic Analysis: VAT Lessons from Canada." *Tax Notes*: 493–496.

US Advisory Commission on Intergovernmental Relations (1973). *The Value-Added Tax and Alternative Sources of Federal Revenue*. Washington, DC: US Government Printing Office. http://digital.library.unt.edu/ark:/67531/metadc1129/?q=value%20added%20tax.

US Congressional Budget Office (2009). *Long-Term Budget Outlook, June 2009*. Washington, DC: Congressional Budget Office. http://www.cbo.gov/doc.cfm?index=10297&zzz=39116.

US Congressional Budget Office (2011). *The Budget and Economic Outlook: Fiscal Years 2011 to 2021*. Washington, DC: Congressional Budget Office. http://www.cbo.gov/doc.cfm?index=12039.

US General Accounting Office (1989). *Value-Added Tax Issues for U.S. Policymakers*. Briefing Report to the Joint Committee on Taxation. GAO/GGD-89-125BR. Washington, DC: US General Accounting Office. http://archive.gao.gov/d26t7/139626.pdf.

Varsano, Ricardo (1995). "A Tributação do Comércio Interestadual: ICMS versus ICMS Partilhado" ["Taxation of Interstate Commerce: ICMS versus Shared ICMS"]. Instituo de Pesquisa Econômica Aplicada, Brasilia, Texto para Discussão No. 382.

....

CHAPTER 16

RETAIL SALES AND
USE TAXATION

....

WILLIAM F. FOX

A sales tax is intended as a tax on the disposition of income (consumption) rather than as a tax on the sources of income (such as an income, estate, or gift tax). General sales taxes are intended to apply to a broadly inclusive base of goods and services sold at retail; a selective sales tax, in contrast, is levied on a specific commodity, such as motor fuel, tobacco, or alcohol. General and selective sales taxes can be, and often are, used simultaneously.

All states that levy a general retail sales tax (RST) also levy some form of compensating use tax. The use tax applies at the same rate as the sales tax and is imposed on purchases of taxable items made outside the state for use within the state or when items purchased for a tax-exempt purpose are transferred to a taxable purpose. The use tax is complementary to the sales tax and does not apply if the taxable sale already has been, or will be, subject to the sales tax. Unless otherwise specified, the references to sales taxes below generally mean both the sales and use tax.

The discussion in this chapter focuses on the states' use of the sales tax, and this use is based on the presumption that the tax is intended as a tax on consumption, though it is difficult to make a case that states chose sales taxes with the clear understanding that they were meant to be broad-based consumption taxes.[1] The chapter begins with a brief summary of sales tax history and proceeds to (1) overview the statutory features of the tax as it is currently structured in the United States; (2) examine performance of the tax as reflected by three reasons the sales tax base has declined relative to economic activity; (3) place the sales tax in the context of alternative consumption taxes and other related taxes, such as gross receipts and value-added taxes; (4) provide a normative evaluation of the tax; and

(5) lay out directions for reform of the tax base. A concluding section brings this together in the context of the need to maintain the integrity and importance of the sales tax as a pillar of state and local finance. Key aspects of the empirical literature are presented throughout.

Sales Tax History

Sales taxes have a long and storied history because taxes on transactions can be found through much of modern civilization.[2] Tomb paintings illustrate Egyptian tax collectors at least as early as 2000 B.C. and sales taxes on individual commodities, such as cooking oil, can be tracked to that time. Egypt, Rome, and Athens were all reported to have general sales taxes. Indeed, the Romans are credited with taking sales taxes to the rest of Europe. Later, Spain had a national sales tax in place from 1342 until the eighteenth century, with rates reaching 10 to 15 percent. Specific commodity taxes were so broadly imposed during the US Civil War, that when combined, they nearly formed a general sales tax.

US sales taxes date back at least to the Pennsylvania mercantile license tax that was introduced in 1821, though this and other early taxes were not broad-based. Buehler attributed the development of modern state sales taxes to the Depression era, wherein twenty-three states first enacted their sales taxes during the 1930s.[3] Commerce Clearing House credits Mississippi with the first sales tax, also in 1930 (see table 16.1). In 1969 Vermont was the last state to impose a sales tax.

Table 16.1 State adoption of general sales tax

State	Year	State	Year
Mississippi	1930	Louisiana	1938
Arizona	1933	Connecticut	1947
California	1933	Maryland	1947
Illinois	1933	Rhode Island	1947
Indiana	1933	Tennessee	1947
Iowa	1933	District of Columbia	1949
Michigan	1933	Florida	1949
New Mexico	1933	Georgia	1951
North Carolina	1933	Maine	1951
Oklahoma	1933	South Carolina	1951

(Continued)

Table 16.1 Continued

State	Year	State	Year
South Dakota	1933	Pennsylvania	1953
Utah	1933	Nevada	1955
Washington	1933	Kentucky	1960
West Virginia	1933	Texas	1961
Missouri	1934	Wisconsin	1961
Ohio	1934	Idaho	1965
Arkansas	1935	New York	1965
Colorado	1935	Massachusetts	1966
Hawaii	1935	New Jersey	1966
North Dakota	1935	Virginia	1966
Wyoming	1935	Minnesota	1967
Alabama	1936	Nebraska	1967
Kansas	1937	Vermont	1969

*States without general sales tax: Alaska, Delaware, Montana, New Hampshire, and Oregon.
Source: Authors.

CURRENT SALES-TAX STRUCTURE

Forty-five states and the District of Columbia levy a general sales tax.[4] Alaska, Delaware, New Hampshire, Montana, and Oregon do not impose a general state sales tax, though some cities in Alaska use a local sales tax. In addition, around eight thousand cities and counties impose a local sales tax. Sales taxes raised $285.7 billion in 2010 with state sales taxes generating $223.8 billion and local taxes collecting another $61.9 billion.[5] During the recession, combined state and local 2010 sales-tax revenues declined 6.9 percent from their 2008 peak of $306.9 billion. There is no single sales-tax structure in the United States, but instead there are forty-six often widely differing systems. For example, states may have a "general tax rate" accompanied by higher rates on selected goods and services (see the District of Columbia, for example), such as surtaxes on the retail rate for tangible personal property sold in vending machines, liquor sold for off-premises consumption, restaurant meals, and parking and transient accommodations.[6]

Moreover, states differ dramatically in their reliance on sales taxes. The average state raised 31.9 percent of its tax revenues from a sales tax in 2009,[7] but the tax raised at least 60 percent of revenues in three states (Washington, Tennessee, and Florida). Vermont, at the other extreme, generated only 12.8 percent with sales taxes. At least thirty-four states levy a local sales tax, but the tax is generally a smaller share of tax revenues. The average local government collected 11.6 percent of its 2008 tax revenues with the sales tax, but local governments in Arkansas and Louisiana generate about one-half from sales taxes.

Among the states that impose the tax, the basic state tax rates (not including the varying surtaxes noted above) range from a low of 2.9 percent in Colorado to a high of 8.25 percent in California. Tennessee has the highest combined state and local tax rate at 9.4 percent.[8] Sales tax rates have been rising continuously for decades, though rate increases tend to be bunched during the fiscal crises surrounding recessions. More than thirty states increased their rates around the early 1980s recessions and more than twenty did so around the 1990s recession. Rate increases were somewhat less common around the 2000 recession but at least ten states have increased their rates since 2009. The median state rate was 3.25 percent in 1970 and has now reached 6 percent.

Revenues are declining as a share of economic activity despite the rising pattern of rates. State revenues peaked at 1.83 percent of the US gross domestic product (GDP) in 1996 and fell to 1.60 percent of GDP in 2009. A cyclical decrease has caused some of the decline, but revenues were down significantly as a share of GDP even before the downturn. As discussed below, whether this policy of narrowing the tax base can be sustained in the coming decade is not only problematic if the US state and local sector is to continue as the foundation for US fiscal federalism, but also whether it is incompatible with the nature of the nation's changing economic structure.[9]

A shrinking tax base relative to economic activity explains the fall in revenues relative to state GDP. The average states' tax base had fallen from 53 percent of personal income in 1979 to 39 percent by 2008. Again, this masks dramatic variation. Hawaii's General Excise Tax (GET) base is 116 percent of personal income, larger than the state's economy; whereas Illinois is only 24 percent of personal income. The composition of tax bases can also differ within a state. Colorado, for example, allows counties to define their own tax bases. The variation across states depends in part on the extent to which states tax consumer expenditures. For example, thirty-two states fully exempt food for home consumption from taxation (though the local rate is applied in five of these states) and another seven states tax food at a reduced rate of the usual sales tax.[10] Furthermore, the Federation of Tax Administrators identifies 168 services, of which the median state taxes 57.[11] Hawaii's GET taxes 160 and New Mexico taxes 158 while Colorado taxes 11 and Illinois taxes 17. Variation also exists to the extent that states tax intermediate goods used in business production. Differences in input taxation are harder to quantify because the exemptions are often firm- or industry-specific, but the wide range in the estimated breadth of state tax bases suggests that states have very different practices.

Legislative Narrowing of the Tax Base

Base shrinkage can be attributed to three main causes. First, states legislate new exemptions on a seemingly continuous basis. Exemptions are granted for many reasons, including concerns about fairness, administrative difficulties in collection, and concerns that other states fail to tax the same good or service and that the loss of a sales tax base and other economic activity could result if the tax were imposed. The justifications for exemptions have differing degrees of validity depending on the vendor and item, but the bottom line is that many fail the tests of a well-designed sales tax in an era of the nation's changing economic structure. Commonly legislated exemptions include the growing number of states providing tax-favorable treatment for food for home consumption and clothing as well as "tax holidays" that usually entail exemptions of specified products for a weekend or two per year. At present, eighteen states allow tax holidays that exempt items such as clothing, school supplies, and computers.[12] There have been comprehensive analyses of the history and policy implications of sales-tax holidays.[13]

Growth in Service Consumption

Second, consumption is shifting away from goods and to services. Service expenditures as a percentage of consumption in the US GDP accounts has risen from 47.4 percent in 1979 to 59.7 percent in 2007. As noted above, taxation of services varies widely across states, but the median state taxes only about 55 of the 168 services. As a result, changing consumption behavior shrinks the relative size of the taxable base because services are less likely to be taxable than are goods.

Remote Commerce

Third, cross-border shopping is growing and states are less able to collect tax on many remote transactions. Remote sales happen in many ways, including through e-commerce, mail order catalogs, and consumers physically making purchases while traveling within another state or country. Among these, at least, remote commerce is growing. For example, Bruce, Fox, and Luna have estimated that 2012 e-commerce transactions will total $4 trillion, nearly double the 2005 level, and their forecast represents a slowing in the e-commerce growth rate.[14]

The distinction between remote and local commerce can be very important for revenues because of the greater potential to apply administrative jurisdiction over vendors operating in the state. The taxability of transactions very seldom depends on the mode of purchase or delivery so in most cases purchases made remotely belong in the base if they are taxable when purchased within the state. All sales-taxing states levy a corresponding use tax that is imposed on the use or enjoyment of taxable purchases in a state when the sales tax has not been paid. Thus, the distinction is whether the tax is collected on remote sales, not whether it is due. The administrative mechanism normally differs between the sales and the use tax. Efficient and reliable sales-tax collection normally relies on the tax being collected and remitted by the selling vendor. There are far fewer vendors to audit and financial accounts of companies can be used to identify sales. Counterpart records on purchases are generally not available for individuals. Unfortunately, vendors can only be required to remit the sales-tax information if they have nexus in the state, which is based on a physical presence standard.[15] Use-tax compliance generally requires remittance by the purchaser, which has proven to be much less reliable.

Noncompliance with use taxes, which is much higher than vendor noncompliance with the sales tax, occurs in two ways. First, firms purchase items for an exempt use (like resale) and later convert the purchase to a taxable use, such as operating the business. Use-tax noncompliance results in cases where firms fail to report the change to a taxable use and do not remit the tax. Second, businesses and households make purchases in one jurisdiction for consumption in another and then fail to remit their use-tax liability. Sales-tax noncompliance comes largely when firms fail to remit tax that is due. Sometimes the vendor has collected the tax from purchasers and sometimes it has not. A State of Washington study found that noncompliance with the sales tax by registered vendors was only 1.7 percent compared with 25.5 percent with the use tax.[16] Thus, firms generally remit almost all of the sales tax that is due, but they fail to remit about one-fourth of the use tax. The Washington study focused on nonpayment of use tax by registered vendors, not on all forms of noncompliance. Noncompliance with the use tax by nonregistered firms is likely much greater, at least in relative terms, than with registered firms. Further, individual consumer compliance with the use tax is expected to be particularly poor for all purchases except for those that must be registered in a state, such as automobiles. Twenty-three states[17] provide a space on the individual income-tax return to remit use tax, but collections based on this option are very low.

States have aggressively sought to expand vendor collections by expanding the nexus requirement. As discussed below, one avenue has been to encourage Congress to enact a sales-tax nexus standard that allows states to require remote vendors to collect the tax. The Supreme Court ruling in *Quill Corp. v. North Dakota* was based on the Commerce Clause of the US Constitution, which is in Congress's control.[18] The Streamlined Sales Tax Project (SSTP) has been an important avenue for the states to raise the issue to Congress.[19] Also, states have sought to apply attributional nexus standards. For example, a number of states have enacted legislation requiring a firm to collect the sales tax if firms with a presence in the state direct sales to the selling firm's website. These laws are often referred to as "Amazon Laws" because they are partly aimed at requiring the very large business-to-consumer remote retailer, Amazon.com, to collect the tax. Further, several states, including Colorado and Oklahoma, have passed provisions requiring remote vendors to report on sales made to in-state residents even if these firms are not required to collect the tax. Colorado's law is being challenged in court by the Direct Marketers' Association on a number of grounds, including a violation of interstate commerce.

The inability to collect tax that is due results in further shrinkage of the base. Most e-commerce purchases are exempt sales of intermediate goods or are nontaxable services. Still, Bruce, Fox, and Luna have estimated that 18.2 percent of e-commerce transactions are taxable, and if the tax were fully collected, states would reap $45.9 billion in 2012. Many large e-commerce vendors also have a physical presence in states, so they estimated that between 46.1 percent and 89.3 percent of the tax due on sales made by large vendors is remitted through the sales tax.[20] But these large firms are only responsible for about 37 percent of e-commerce sales.[21] Smaller remote vendors are expected to be much less likely to have physical presence in most states where they make sales, so use-tax compliance becomes necessary. Bruce, Fox, and Luna estimated that state and local governments will fail to collect about $12 billion in 2012 because of noncompliance on use-tax collections, which represents about one-fourth of the taxes that are due. They estimated that losses from business-to-consumer mail-order sales are nearly an additional $7 billion. The total loss is expected to be much greater when these losses are combined with business-to-business mail order sales and shopping while traveling. Further, companies located on one side of a state border may fail to register for tax purposes on the other side of the border even though they have substantial sales and may send salesmen, service representatives, and others into the other state.

SALES TAXES IN THE CONTEXT OF OTHER TAXES

Sales taxes, value-added taxes, and consumable income taxes are three different mechanisms that have their conceptual basis in taxing consumption. Conceptually, all three approaches can be designed to have the identical aggregate tax base. In practice, differences arise in the ability to administer the tax, the costs of compliance, the ability to target incentives and provide relief to certain individuals, and so forth.

A comprehensive sales-tax base equals the total consumption if all sales to final consumers are taxable. Consumable income taxes are collected from individual taxpayers by defining the tax base as income less a deduction for savings, the difference of which by definition equals consumption. If income and savings are properly measured, then the resulting consumption must equal the final sales to individuals.[22]

The value-added tax equals consumption if the value added of all businesses is taxed.[23] A major difference between the VAT and the sales tax is how intermediate goods are treated. The credit-invoice VAT that is generally used around the world allows credit for taxes paid earlier in the chain by registered traders and the sales tax allows deduction or exemption of intermediate sales (though in principal it could also be structured on a credit basis). By definition, the sum of all value-added tax equals total final sales if investment is immediately expensed in the VAT and the VAT and sales taxes are both levied on a destination basis.[24]

Sales taxes also have some similarities with gross receipts taxes.[25] In fact, a number of states, such as New Mexico, describe their sales tax as a gross receipts tax even though these taxes are better categorized as sales taxes. The differences between gross receipts and sales taxes are in degree and in the intended base. The sales tax is intended to tax consumption[26] and the gross receipts tax is levied on the value of all transactions. In practice, gross receipts taxes generally have broad coverage across nearly all industries while sales taxes in the United States are targeted to many goods and a relatively small set of services (which, of course, is one of the tax's greatest weaknesses). Further, sales taxes allow deductions and exemptions for some intermediate purchases and true gross receipts taxes do not. Net receipts taxes, such as Michigan and Texas have imposed, allow deductions for certain business-to-business purchases, moving them closer to a sales tax. The recently enacted gross receipts taxes have all been levied on a destination basis, like the sales tax. The net receipts tax recently recommended in California would have allowed deductions for all intermediate purchases and would have been levied on a destination basis. It would have worked much like a consumption tax, but with incomplete border adjustments.[27]

Efficiency (Tax Neutrality)

Two broad rules define the economist's guidance for structuring sales taxes. Both go to the goal of increasing the neutrality (efficiency) of a tax—that is, the principle that taxes should be designed to minimize interference ("distortions" with private [consumer, laborer, producer] economic decisions). The first is that in order to minimize nonneutrality, consumption taxes should be levied at flat rates on the broadest possible base of consumption.[28] Second, intermediate transactions should be exempt from sales taxation. An exception may be that intermediate transactions belong in the tax base in cases where the final sale is not taxable.[29]

The sales tax must be levied on a destination basis if the tax is to work as a consumption tax. Destination taxation, if fully enforced, also eliminates the potential for revenue competition between governments and gives governments greater control over their revenues because consumers can only avoid taxes by not purchasing taxable items, not by purchasing out-of-state.[30]

Destination taxation and origination taxation treat neutrality differently for different markets. Destination taxation creates neutrality in each consumption market, so governments do not have an incentive to lower their rates to attract sales. But neutrality may not exist in each production market because goods produced at a particular location may be subject to different tax rates when sold. Origin taxation creates neutrality within each production market, but not in the consumption markets. Tax rates that differ across production markets create incentives to compete for tax revenue and production by lowering the rate.[31]

Destination taxation can increase the costs of taxpayer compliance and administrative costs alike. Compliance concerns are that firms must abide with the tax structure in every state (and potentially local government) where sales are made. This may require firms to situs sales based on the location of buyers and understand the tax bases, rates, schedules, and rulings in multiple states. This is almost surely more costly than abiding by the statutes of a single state without the need to situs the destination of sales.[32] Destination taxation also creates larger administrative difficulties because it is generally easier to enforce payment on firms that are physically present (at least, given current nexus restrictions).[33] An origin-based structure would likely lower compliance costs relative to destination taxation because firms only need to accommodate the tax structures of a home state. Of course, both origin and destination taxes require knowing certain characteristics of the buyer so that business purchases can be exempted (usually with an exemption certificate).

In practice, the sales tax deviates widely from good tax policy as espoused in these rules, and the resulting deviations can have important implications for economic efficiency and incidence. Wide differences exist in practice between consumption and the sales-tax base. As noted above, the base is generally much too narrow with many services and increasingly consumer goods (food for consumption at home, some clothing) are exempt. Similarly, many intermediate transactions are taxable. Ernst and Young estimated that state and local governments collected $133 billion in taxes on intermediate goods purchases in 2008.[34] This is consistent with 43.8 percent of sales taxes being collected on intermediate transactions.

Distortions from the Narrow Sales-Tax Base

A key issue is the extent to which narrow bases and different rates both within and across states distort the types and locations of consumption decisions. Estimates of the sales-tax incidence and specifically whether the tax is ultimately paid by consumers through higher tax-inclusive prices or by business owners, workers, or landowners through lower earnings is one dimension of these issues. Two empirical articles provide some insight into incidence. Both of these studies provide support for the conclusion that the sales tax is paid by the consumer, as is typically assumed. Besley and Rosen used data from 155 cities to examine whether the tax results in higher gross of tax consumer prices for twelve specific commodities.[35] The research suggested that the tax is forward-shifted to consumers, and in a number of cases the price paid by consumers would rise by more than the amount of the tax (that is, the tax is overshifted). In another key study, Poterba found that sales taxes are fully shifted to consumers.[36]

The conclusion that consumers pay the sales tax, however, is based on research for a series of standard consumer items that are likely to be purchased locally and does not necessarily apply to goods or services commonly sold across state lines or for the tax imposed on business inputs. The research does not indicate that the tax on business inputs is borne by final consumers, only that the final levy on a taxed sale is paid by consumers.[37] Thus, a tax on intermediate goods may raise the cost of doing business in the taxing locale versus others.

Sales taxes affect consumers' decisions to buy exempt versus taxable items and the effects on behavior and tax revenues depend on how responsive consumers are to the tax-induced price differentials. Such tax avoidance can arise in various ways, including from self-supply, altering where goods are purchased and shifting to nontaxed purchases. Granting exemptions (or not) can potentially affect decisions on what to purchase (e.g., taxed goods or untaxed services), where to make the purchases (e.g., a low or high tax jurisdiction), and when to make purchases (e.g., during a sales-tax holiday). The higher gross of tax price paid by consumers can raise the excess burdens of taxes and harm state economies as they distort consumer decisions. Merriman and Skidmore indirectly investigated the effects of differential prices as they examined the allocation of expenditures between the retail and service sectors between 1982 and 1992.[38] Their research indirectly tested the effects that sales taxes have on the consumption of exempt versus nonexempt purchases since services are generally exempt and goods are generally taxable. Merriman and Skidmore found evidence that the share of the economy in the retail sector fell, and the share in the service sector rose in high sales-tax-rate states. Their findings indicated that differential taxation can explain as much as one-third of the relative decline in the retail sector and as much as one-eighth of the relative gain in the service sector. These results suggest that sales taxes alter consumption behavior by increasing the quantity demanded for exempt items compared with taxable items. A broader sales-tax base should lessen the extent of such behavioral distortions.

Hawkins examined the responsiveness to price differentials (including sales-tax rates) of several items that are often exempt from the sales tax.[39] He finds that gasoline, tobacco, and food for consumption at home have the greatest responsiveness to tax-induced price changes and utilities and services have lower responsiveness. The excess burden of taxes rises with the price elasticity, suggesting that exemption of gasoline and food is more costly than exemption of services and utilities.[40] Overall, Hawkins found that the sales tax's excess burden rises with the narrowness of the tax base. Thus, a narrow base that exempts food for consumption at home, most services, gasoline, and utilities has a 38.5 percent higher excess burden than one that taxes consumption broadly. Baum also found that broadening the sales-tax base to include food lowers the excess burden of the tax.[41]

Russo used a simulation model to study how a broad-based versus narrow-based sales tax affects overall economic activity.[42] He found no evidence that the breadth of a state's sales-tax base affects the size of the state's economy, but it seemed that a broader base results in a small reduction in the tax's excess burden. A broader base increases well-being by permitting a lower tax rate that lessens incentives to buy those remaining exempt items and by reducing the set of choices between exempt and taxable items. States with broad bases may have less to gain at the margin from additional base broadening (and, there are relatively few opportunities because the base is so broad), but the reverse effect still arises—additional exemptions raise the excess burden of taxes. It should be noted that Russo observed an even larger gain in well-being for states when they combine taxing all consumption with eliminating taxation of business inputs.

Sales taxes can also influence where consumers choose to make purchases. The tax should have no effect on where people shop to the extent that the use tax can be enforced (effectively meaning that destination taxation can be enforced), but both households and businesses have a tax incentive to buy from vendors that do not collect tax for their state given the relatively weak ability to enforce use taxes. A number of studies, most of which were undertaken some years ago, have been conducted on how tax differentials influence on which side of the border people prefer to shop.[43] The research generally found that people are very responsive to tax differentials by doing relatively more shopping on the low-tax side of the border and the price elasticity of cross-border shopping is inversely related to the distance to the border.

Corlett and Hague concluded that in a second-best world, taxation of goods that are complementary with leisure increases efficiency.[44] This suggests that the current structure that results in local goods being taxed more effectively than remote goods is preferred if local goods are more complementary with leisure. A Ramsey-type argument may also be applied if items purchased remotely are viewed differently from the otherwise same goods purchased locally. Differential taxation is preferred if the own price elasticities differ, with the current structure preferred if the own price elasticity for local goods is lower than for remotely purchased goods.[45] Zodrow simulated the optimal tax rates for local versus remote goods by using various parameter values and concluded that the uniform taxation of remote and local sales is "much more likely to be desirable."[46]

Two recent studies investigated the empirical effect that sales taxes have on the propensity to shop online. Goolsbee examined the effects of sales taxes on Internet shoppers and found that higher sales-tax rates increased the incentive and propensity to shop online.[47] His analysis relied on 1997 data, which were early in the e-commerce buying age, at least raising the question of what more current data would evidence. Ellison and Ellison examined the effects of sales taxes on the online purchasing of memory modules.[48] They concluded that sales at online retailers would fall by about 30 percent in the average state if the sales tax were eliminated at the offline stores.

Russo also examined the effects of extending the sales tax to Internet sales.[49] He found that state economies would be slightly larger and the excess burden of taxes would be smaller if all Internet sales could be taxed.[50] Presumably this is because the incentives to avoid the tax by purchasing out of state via the Internet are eliminated. The result is also consistent with the conclusion that a lower sales-tax rate is better for a state's economy because it reduces the incentive to buy outside the state.

Distortions from Taxing Intermediate Inputs

All intermediate purchases should be exempt from the sales tax, recognizing that sales taxes are intended as taxes on final consumption. Every state allows some exemptions for intermediate purchase but every state also taxes many intermediate purchases. This requires providing exemptions based on characteristics of the buyer and how the purchased items will be used. Essentially all states exempt goods that become component parts of manufactured goods and exempt goods purchased for resale. A number of other specified purchases are also exempt in every state. But this leaves many taxable inputs. It may be efficient to tax inputs in cases where there are constraints on the ability to tax the final output.[51] Effectively this means it may be justifiable to tax inputs when final sales of the service outputs are outside the tax base. Bruce, Fox, and Murray have argued that sales taxation of business inputs as it occurs under most state statutes is roughly consistent with greater taxation of industries where many services are taxed. Accordingly, computers, vehicles, office equipment, cash registers, shelving, and packaging are often taxable when purchased for business purposes.

Taxation of some business inputs is also justified on administrative grounds. Exemption of business purchases puts the vendor in the position of needing to know who the buyer is and how the purchases will be used. Exemption of all business purchases would likely lead to widespread evasion as companies are formed to take advantage of the special tax treatment and businesses make purchases for personal use.

Nonetheless, the efficiency argument holds that in principle all inputs—transactions that are intermediate in production and distribution—should be exempt. Indeed, the propensity to impose the sales tax on inputs is often seen as the greatest weakness of the sales tax. An obvious reason for exemption of input purchases is that the intended sales-tax base is consumption, and intermediate purchases are not consumption. However, the bigger concern is that taxes on business inputs have the potential to alter firm behavior and cascade into higher product prices that further distort consumption decisions. Three main distortions are identified here. First, taxing intermediate inputs can alter business practices as firms seek to limit their tax liability. Firms can substitute nontaxable inputs for taxable ones (for example, use untaxed labor rather than taxable purchased inputs), to the extent that input substitution is possible. Also, firms can vertically integrate and bring more production within a single company. For example, printing services purchased by businesses are often sales-taxed. Firms could develop in-house capacities to produce the service and avoid the sales tax on printing services purchased from outside vendors. Presumably vertical integration entails some efficiency loss because firms would vertically integrate without the tax if it were the best business structure.[52] No evidence exists on the extent to which taxes distort decisions to vertically integrate, but big firms are presumably in the best position to vertically integrate creating some relative price advantages. Not only are smaller businesses less able to vertically integrate, perhaps because of the lumpiness of many integrated services, but small businesses as a group also are likely made less profitable as larger companies decrease their outsourcing in response to taxation of transactions between firms.

Recent theoretical research has examined some aspects of vertical integration.[53] Luna, Murray, and Yang found that taxing inputs may provide an incentive for firms to vertically integrate, but this would depend on the extent to which intermediate good pricing in the upstream market is affected by the fall in demand that occurs with imposition of the tax in the downstream market.[54] The sales tax may discourage vertical integration if upstream prices are sufficiently flexible downward in response to the tax. On the other hand, Hortacsu and Syverson suggested that the extent of vertical integration is less than has often been thought.[55]

Second, input taxes raise the cost of producing in a state, which can cause some firms to locate their production in states that impose lower tax burdens on business transactions. There is no empirical research that directly examines the extent to which taxes on business inputs harm a state's economy, though some research has considered whether higher sales-tax rates generally harm a state's economy. Here the empirical results are somewhat conflicting. Bruce, Deskins, and Fox found that the gross state product falls as states increase their sales-tax rates.[56] Further, they argued that the effects of taxes on location are growing because technology makes it increasingly easy for firms to geographically separate their production from their markets. Carroll and Wasylenko studied how a number of fiscal variables, including the sales tax, affect total employment and manufacturing employment in a state.[57] They observed no relationship between sales taxes and *total* employment but found that states with higher sales-tax rates had lower *manufacturing* employment in the years between 1967 and 1983. The sales-tax effects on manufacturing employment were no longer present when they studied 1984 to 1988. This suggested that the impacts of taxes on business location were diminishing (the opposite conclusion of Bruce, Deskins, and Fox). The Carroll and Wasylenko study entirely predated recent technology and the Internet and may be less applicable to today's more mobile economy.

Third, taxation of business purchases cascades into higher taxes on final products. The extent of cascading depends on the complexity of the production process (how many levels of production a good or service goes through), the tax treatment of the various business inputs, and the propensity to vertically integrate in the industry. As a result, the amount of cascading can vary significantly across economic sectors. Assuming that business purchases of capital equipment, communications equipment, utilities, and office supplies are taxable, Hawkins found that the sales tax is imposed on inputs equal to 14.7 percent of the revenues of electric producers, 11.2 percent for firms taking fees and admissions, 46.7 percent for producers of shelter, 2.6 percent for gasoline stations, and 11.5 percent for firms providing nonshelter lodging.[58] Derrick and Scott used input-output analysis to investigate the extent to which sales taxes fall indirectly on consumers in Maryland through taxation of business inputs (with their ultimate goal to examine equity issues).[59] They found the weighted average indirect tax rate through inputs is somewhat higher than the direct tax on final goods (suggesting greater cascading than Hawkins). The highest tax on business inputs (as a share of spending on the transaction) occurs in industries where the output is generally exempt, such as utilities and housing. Also, input taxation is below average in all industries where the output is broadly taxed. But the relationships are not simple because some industries with low direct taxes on outputs, such as education and household operations, also have low input taxes.

Cascading can have important nonneutrality effects because it raises the relative price of certain goods and causes people to purchase fewer of them. Interestingly, Hawkins found that the excess burden associated with narrow tax bases is lower with the cascading from taxation of business inputs, because the taxes cascade most in areas that are likely to be exempt, such as many services.[60] This suggests that exempting all business transactions may not be the best policy for states that choose relatively narrow tax bases, because taxing the business transactions may be an indirect means of taxing the final consumption.

Moreover, as noted above, taxing intermediate goods broadens the sales-tax base and allows a lower tax rate to raise a specific amount of revenue, given the resulting larger tax base. The lower tax rate reduces the distortions described above, such as for purchasing untaxed items relative to taxed items, particularly to the extent that the inputs are taxed more in cases where the final product is exempt. Thus, the net effect on a state's economy from taxing business inputs depends on the relative size of benefits from the lower tax rate versus costs from altering business behavior. In addressing the broader efficiency gains, for an "equal yield" of revenues to the state fiscal budget, Russo found that eliminating the tax on business inputs resulted in a small increase in the size of the state's economy and a small reduction in excess burden, even though the tax rate must be higher.[61] The conclusion on excess burden differs from Hawkins, but it may suggest that the effects on excess burden depend on the specific set of exemptions.

SALES-TAX REFORM

In the context of the foregoing discussion, the policy prescriptions are not difficult to identify, given the current environment of state sales taxes. Recent experience with the sales tax points to increasing inefficiency as rates have risen consistently for decades and the base has narrowed.[62] There is also no convincing evidence that taxation of business inputs has shrunk. Areas can be identified where business-input taxation has been reduced, such as manufacturing equipment, but there are others where greater taxation is occurring, such as with software. Further, many of the exemptions are firm-specific, such as part of an economic development policy, and do not provide broad relief from taxation of intermediate inputs. Administrative and legal reforms are necessary to allow states to collect the sales tax more effectively on a destination basis[63] and policy changes are appropriate to broaden the base more to consumption and narrow the taxation of business inputs.

On net, this could expand the tax base, which would allow states to lower the tax rate for a given amount of revenue.

Limit New State Exemptions of Consumer Goods

State actions that further narrow sales taxation of consumer goods should be avoided and, where possible, states should seek to bring some exempt items back into the tax fold. Food and clothing are obvious examples. Base expansion has proven to be politically difficult, but states must certainly avoid any further narrowing of the consumer base. Economic efficiency and vertical equity are often used to defend exempting these items. In the efficiency context, economic development is a common justification for tax-base narrowing with the argument that a neighboring state does not tax the item or it is available without tax remotely so the state's economy is harmed if tax treatment for in-state purchases is not similar to competitive out-of-state purchases. For example, clothing is generally exempt in New Jersey, yet generally taxable in New York, which provides consumers with an incentive to purchase clothing in New Jersey and/or wait for prices to fall in New York to offset all or part of the tax difference. However, research on cross-border shopping indicates that while some buyers will travel across state lines to take advantage of state-tax differences, at least along the border, the effects are likely too small to justify narrowing the base. More important, taking stronger steps to administer sales taxes on a destination basis is a better route to limiting the economic distortions from differential taxation across states.[64]

With respect to vertical equity (distribution of the tax payment by income class), exemption of food for home consumption is often sought on the grounds that food purchases are regressive against current income. Analysis of the Consumer Expenditure Survey[65] confirms that the tax on food purchases is regressive but also evidences that most items are regressive in consumption, so it is very difficult to design a sales tax that is not regressive.[66] Also, the sales tax and specifically the tax on food, is much less regressive against lifetime income than against current income, so the equity concerns may not be as great as is often asserted. Further, most states could provide tax relief to low-income consumers with credits against the personal income tax or some other mechanism at much lower cost to fiscal budgets than poorly targeted broad exemptions.

Expand the Taxation of Services

Greater taxation of services is frequently considered by states across the United States. Generally, states with broad taxation of services effectively included many services in the base when the sales tax was created. Other states have found expansion of the base politically very difficult despite the frequent recommendations, and the propensity has been to bring a set of relatively small services into the base. Florida broadened the base to many services in the mid-1980s but quickly repealed the legislation. Texas also undertook a relatively significant base expansion in the 1990s, but other examples are hard to find. Expansion of the base to services is particularly difficult because most sales-tax structures are written so that tangible personal property is broadly in the base. Exemptions of goods must normally be articulated by item. Services were often not anticipated in the tax legislation and must be individually itemized. The need to itemize each service and to vote specifically on its taxation has created much of the political problem.

The case for taxing services is not straightforward. Ultimately the question is not whether services should be taxed, but which services belong in the base. Each service must be considered after weighing the advantages and disadvantages as they apply to the specific service. Health care, construction services, and some other professional services offer the greatest potential for additional revenue and are seldom considered. Consumer services should be in the base to enhance horizontal equity and limit the extent of behavioral distortions, both by reducing untaxed alternatives and permitting a lower sales tax rate for a given amount of revenue. Greater revenue elasticity is probably another advantage of expanding taxation of services. Bruce, Fox, and Tuttle found that revenue elasticities are larger for broader-based sales taxes but the effect on elasticity depends on the specific services that are included in the base.[67] Health care services would likely be very revenue elastic but many personal services may not be.

Some services should not be included in the base, such as those that are intermediate inputs. Many services, such as legal and accounting services, are primarily purchased by businesses and expansion of the base to these services could increase taxation of intermediate inputs unless business purchases can be exempted. Administrative and compliance costs will likely rise as more services are taxed because service vendors tend to be smaller on average than goods vendors. Also, states may choose not to tax services that are easily sold across wide distances. Enforcement of tax on remotely produced services could prove difficult, increasing the chance that the services will be produced outside the state to avoid collection of the tax.

States should not only tax more services but also align the way they tax services that are sold across state lines with the way that they tax goods. Effectively, the reform means that sales-tax structures must move to a destination basis for services. Currently, services are more likely to be taxed on an origination basis, using legislation with wording such as "the tax is due where the greatest performance of the service takes place." As a result, states often do not impose use tax on services produced outside the state for consumption within the state. Hawaii is an exception, having amended its sales-tax law in the late 1990s to tax services on a destination basis and impose use tax on services produced outside the state. The origin approach is fine if services are produced and sold in the same state (though even within states there can be problems across local governments). But technology likely expands the opportunities for producing services at remote locations, and taxation on an origin basis provides a cost incentive to produce in the lowest tax jurisdiction.

Reduce the Taxation of Inputs

The taxation of inputs should be reduced as the consumption base is expanded. Broader exemption of inputs in the sale of services to businesses will be particularly important because relatively few services are currently exempted when sold to businesses. Of course, statutory tax rates would need to be much higher to raise the same revenue if input taxation is reduced without sufficient other base expansion, such as to services. Enacting significantly higher rates to maintain revenues as input taxation is reduced is likely to be politically difficult for elected officials, but the tax structure would be more efficient.

States must balance the exemption of more inputs with the ability to administer the tax. Significant evasion could result because of the difficulty of determining what constitutes a business within current administrative practices. Plus, fully ensuring that buyer's exemption certificates are used solely for purchases for exempt business purposes further increase administrative costs. Households have an incentive to create businesses or use existing businesses to make exempt purchases. The requirement with the sales tax to exempt business purchases is often criticized relative to a VAT. Exemption is often granted based on vendors' good-faith acceptance of a buyer's exemption certificate and of businesses using the certificates appropriately; the VAT relies on the self-enforcing credit/invoice system that requires misrepresentation to revenue authorities for evasion to take place.

Tax Remote Transactions

Expanded taxation of remote transactions is a key to enhanced sales-tax efficiency. The shrinking tax base and incentives to buy out of state cannot be eliminated until the tax is enforced on a destination basis, which can only happen with vendor collection of the tax. Two means are possible for creating a collection responsibility for all vendors. Ultimately, both approaches will rely on interstate, and likely international, cooperation if the world's governments are to effectively collect sales and value-added taxes on a destination basis. The Supreme Court could be approached about reversing its decision in *Quill Corp. v. North Dakota*. The decision turned heavily on the higher compliance costs faced by remote vendors versus local vendors and the Court's view that interstate commerce would be harmed if remote vendors were required to collect the tax. The states working together with the business community formed the SSTP in 2000 to provide a mechanism for lessening compliance burdens. Twenty states are currently full participants in the resulting agreement and nearly every sales-taxing state is involved in the discussions. Uniformity and simplification measures implemented by the project include (1) requiring that both state and local taxes are administered by state governments, (2) requiring identical state and local tax bases, and (3) allowing only one state rate plus one for food, electricity, and prescription drugs and one local rate in each jurisdiction. The agreement also includes a mechanism for voluntary multistate compliance. Each of these provides significant compliance advantages and provides significant collection benefits even in the absence of authority to require remote vendors to collect the tax.

Alternatively, Congress controls interstate commerce and has the capacity to require remote vendors to collect sales tax, but it has so far proven unwilling to do so. Congress bears the political costs of passing the legislation but gains none of the revenues, making passage a political challenge. Several technical challenges also remain. A small seller exception has been proposed, whereby only vendors with sales above a certain threshold would be required to comply. No agreement has been reached on the appropriate threshold. The lost revenues to states and potential means to abuse the threshold rise rapidly with the threshold's size because the distribution of remote vendors includes many relatively small firms. Also, there is general agreement that vendor compensation for collecting the tax must be part of the agreement. Twenty-five states currently allow some form of compensation,[68] but the agreement could require all states to provide compensation and could increase the payments for many states that are already providing some form of compensation. Again, the level of compensation could dramatically lower the net new revenues available to states because the compensation would apply to all sales and not only to remote sales.

Not-for-Profit Entities

Many states allow exemptions for either the sale of taxable goods and services or the purchase of taxable goods and services or both for not-for-profit entities. Sales by not-for-profits should generally be taxable.[69] Their purchases often should be exempt because they represent inputs purchased for use in production or for resale. Most states do not explicitly require that the entities or the transactions are in the public interest and still permit the exemption. Further, there seems to be little audit of these transactions, raising the chance that these provisions are abused to make purchases for personal use. No strong justification exists for exempting sales by not-for-profits because the intention is to tax the consumption, and the not-for-profit is only collecting the tax on behalf of the state. The exemption is sometimes seen as a subsidy for the not-for-profit. But, the subsidy is poorly targeted, likely very expensive in foregone tax revenue relative to a direct subsidy that offered the same benefit to the firm (since the purchaser may reap much of the benefit from the exemption), and the amount provided as a subsidy is not transparent because it depends on the magnitude of sales by the firm. Subsidies provided directly on the expenditure side of state budgets would receive much greater scrutiny, be better targeted to the not-for profit, and be less expensive.

CONCLUSION

The past decade offers little confidence that sales-tax policy is improving. The base was narrowed further as more states exempted food for home consumption, as well as clothing and selected other consumer purchases (for sales-tax holidays). Some base expansion to services occurred, but it was primarily to smaller services, leaving those services with greater economic and revenue effects untaxed in most states. Tax rates continued their upward plod as thirty-four rate increases were enacted during the past decade and the median state rate reached 6 percent. Nonetheless, tax revenues continue to fall as a share of GDP as the rate increases were insufficient to offset the base narrowing. The diminishing revenue benefits make the sales tax increasingly unreliable as a mainstay of state revenues and have slowly diminished the sales-tax share of total tax revenues. Not surprisingly, research has showed that higher rates on a narrower share of consumption distort what people buy and where they make their purchases, thereby creating what are surely growing economic distortions. States need to move strongly to maintain the sales tax and the policy strategies to achieve this goal are clear: (1) maintain taxation of consumer goods purchases, (2) expand the taxation of appropriate services, (3) reduce the taxation of intermediate inputs, (4) tax remote purchases evenly with their local counterparts, and (5) rely on natural tax-base growth rather than rate increases to maintain revenues.

NOTES

1 Local sales taxes are addressed by Sjoquist and Stoycheva (this volume).
2 Buehler (1940); Fox (2004).
3 Gold and Ebel (2005); Snell (2009).
4 The District of Columbia is treated as a state for the remainder of this chapter.
5 Tax collections are calculated based on quarterly data taken from the US Bureau of the Census. See http://www.census.gov/govs/qtax/.
6 Due and Mikesell (1994).
7 See http://www.taxadmin.org/fta/rate/09taxdis.html.
8 As of December 20, 2010. See http://www.taxch.com/STRates.stm.
9 Fox (1998a) also raised the question of the long-term sustainability in an earlier article.
10 See http://www.taxadmin.org/fta/rate/sales.pdf.
11 See http://www.taxadmin.org/fta/pub/services/btn/0708.html#table.
12 See http://www.taxadmin.org/fta/rate/sales_holiday.html.
13 Cole (2008); Hawkins and Mikesell (2001); Robyn et al. (2009).
14 Bruce, Fox, and Luna (2009).
15 Based on the US Supreme Court ruling in *Quill Corp. v. North Dakota*, firms can only be required to collect the tax in states where they have a physical presence. Firms can choose to voluntarily collect and remit the tax for states.
16 See http://dor.wa.gov/Docs/Reports/Compliance_Study/compliance_study_2010.pdf.
17 See Wisconsin Legislative Fiscal Bureau (2009).
18 *Quill Corp. v. North Dakota*, 504 US 298 (1992).

19 Congress passed several versions of the Internet Tax Freedom Act, which precludes specific axes on the Internet, but it does not prevent the application of sales and use taxes to transactions over the Internet. See Eads (this volume).

20 The differences among states arise because firms are more prone to have a physical presence in some states than others and states vary in their aggressiveness in seeking collection of the tax.

21 See Bailey (2008).

22 Technical issues could lead to differences in the bases, such as how consumer durables are treated in defining savings.

23 Detailed differences could arise, such as how sales to the public sector are treated.

24 See Carlson (2005a), 82–83; Duncan (this volume).

25 See Luna, Murray, and Yang (this volume).

26 State legislation differs as to who is legally liable for the tax. About one-third of the states impose the tax on buyers (even though the tax is often collected by the seller), about one-third impose the tax on sellers, and about one-third use a mixture of these policies.

27 Fox (2010), 88–101.

28 In this regard, it is important to remember that this conclusion can only be derived theoretically in the specialized case where all goods are equally complementary with leisure (Auerbach and Hines, 2002). Slemrod (2003) provided an interesting discussion of the distinction between the folk (or policy) theorems and rigorous theoretical results.

29 Bruce, Fox, and Murray (2003), 25–40.

30 Kanbur and Keen (1993), 877–892.

31 Carlson (2005b), 283–384.

32 The Streamlined Sales Tax Project requires states to post certain information about their tax rates and bases on a website to help lessen the costs of complying with destination taxation across multiple states.

33 Hellerstein (2003), 38.

34 Ernst and Young (2010).

35 Besley and Rosen (1999).

36 Poterba (1996).

37 Besley and Rosen's finding of overshifting may be the result of forward shifting of the tax on inputs.

38 Merriman and Skidmore (2000).

39 Hawkins (2002).

40 Excess burden, also called efficiency cost or dead-weight loss, occurs when a tax interferes with a taxpayer's decisions and efficient choices but generates no additional benefit to the tax collection agent (Watson 2005).

41 Baum (1998).

42 Russo (2005).

43 See Fox (1986), 387–401; and Walsh and Jones (1988), 261–265, for examples.

44 Corlett and Hague (1954).

45 Goolsbee and Zittrain (1999), 413–428.

46 Zodrow (2006).

47 Goolsbee (2000).

48 Ellison and Ellison (2006).

49 Russo (2005).

50 For example, the gross state product would rise by about 0.5 percent if the tax was extended to Internet sales of tangible goods and if tax relief was provided for business inputs.

51 Input taxation may also be efficiency enhancing when imposed on industries subject to decreasing returns to scale. See Bruce, Fox, and Murray (2003), 25–40.

52 Of course, vertical integration is the best business model for some activities in some firms even without the encouragement from taxes.

53 The research is focused on gross receipts taxes on intermediate inputs.

54 Luna, Murray and Yang (this volume).

55 Hortacsu and Syverson (2009).

56 Bruce, Deskins, and Fox (2007).

57 Carroll and Wasylenko (1994).

58 Hawkins (2002).

59 Derrick and Scott (1993).

60 Hawkins (2002).

61 Russo (2005).

62 Snell (2004).

63 The public-choice view is that the loss of horizontal competition with destination taxation encourages Leviathan tendencies, and it can result in inefficiencies from excessive government.

64 Kanbur and Keen (1993), 877–892, also argue for minimum tax rates to lessen incentives for tax competition, but there is no mechanism to enforce minimum rates across states.

65 http://www.bls.gov/cex/.

66 Fox (2006).

67 Bruce, Fox, and Tuttle (2006).

68 http://www.taxadmin.org/fta/rate/vendors.pdf.

69 Fox (1998b).

References

Auerbach, Alan J., and James R Hines, Jr. (2002). "Taxation and Economic Efficiency." In *Handbook of Public Economics: Volume 3*, edited by Alan J. Auerbach and Martin Feldstein. Amsterdam: Elsevier Press. 1347–1421.

Bailey, Joe (2008). "The Long Tail Is Longer Than You Think: The Surprisingly Large Extent of Online Sales by Small Volume Sellers." Unpublished paper, University of Maryland.

Baum, Donald N. (1998). "Economic Effects of Eliminating the Sales Tax Exemption for Food: An Applied General Equilibrium Analysis." *Journal of Economics* 24(1): 125–148.

Besley, Timothy J., and Harvey S. Rosen (1999, June). "Sales Taxes and Prices: An Empirical Analysis." *National Tax Journal* 52: 157–178.

Bruce, Donald, John Deskins, and William F. Fox (2007). "On the Extent, Growth and Efficiency Consequences of State Business Tax Planning." In *Corporate Income Taxation in the 21st Century*, edited by Alan Auerbach, James Hines, and Joel Slemrod. Cambridge University Press. 226–257.

Bruce, Donald, William F. Fox, and LeAnn Luna (2009, August 16). "State and Local Sales Tax Revenue Losses from E-Commerce." *State Tax Notes* 33: 511–518.

Bruce, Donald, William F. Fox, and Matthew Murray (2003). "To Tax or Not to Tax: The Case of Electronic Commerce." *Contemporary Economic Policy* 21(1): 25–40.

Bruce, Donald, William F. Fox, and Markland Tuttle (2006, October). "Tax Base Elasticities: A Multistate Analysis of Long Run and Short Run Dynamics." *Southern Economic Journal*: 315–341.

Buehler, Alfred G. (1940). *Public Finance*. New York: McGraw-Hill.

Carlson, George (2005a). "Destination Principle." In *The Encyclopedia of Taxation and Tax Policy*, edited by Joseph J. Cordes, Robert D. Ebel, and Jane G. Gravelle. Washington: Urban Institute Press. 82–83.

Carlson, George (2005b). "Origin Principle." In *The Encyclopedia of Taxation and Tax Policy*, edited by Joseph J. Cordes, Robert D. Ebel, and Jane G. Gravelle. Washington: Urban Institute Press. 283–384.

Carroll, Robert, and Michael Wasylenko (1994, March). "Do State Business Climates Still Matter—Evidence of a Structural Change." *National Tax Journal* 47: 19–37.

Cole, Adam J. (2008, March 31). "Sales Tax Holidays, 1997–2007: A History." *State Tax Notes*: 1001–1025.

Corlett, W. J., and D. C. Hague (1954). "Complementarity and the Excess Burden of Taxation." *Review of Economic Studies* 21(1): 21–30.

Derrick, Frederick W., and Charles E. Scott (1993, April). "Businesses and the Incidence of Sales and Use Taxes." *Public Finance Quarterly* 21: 210–226.

Due, John, and John Mikesell (1994). *Sales Taxation: State and Local Structure and Administration*. 2nd ed. Washington DC: Urban Institute Press.

Ellison, Glen, and Sara Fisher Ellison (2006, May). "Internet Retail Demand: Taxes, Geography, and Online-Offline Competition." NBER Working Paper No.12242.

Ernst and Young (2010, March). "Total State and Local Business Taxes: State by State Estimates for 2009." Report prepared for the Council of State Taxation.

Fox, William F. (1986, December). "Tax Structure and the Location of Economic Activity along State Borders." *National Tax Journal* 39: 387–401.

Fox, William F. (1998a). "Can the Sales Tax Survive a Future Like Its Past?" In *The Future of State Tax Policy*, edited by David Brunori. Washington, DC: Urban Institute Press. 33–48.

Fox, William F. (1998b). "Sales Taxes in the District of Columbia: Current Conditions and Policy Options." In *Taxing Fairly, Taxing Simply: The Final Report of the District of Columbia Tax Revision Commission*, edited by Philip M. Dearborn. Washington, DC: District of Columbia Government.

Fox, William F. (2004). "History and Economic Impact of the Sales Tax." In *Sales Taxation*, edited by Jerry Janata. Institute for Professionals in Taxation.

Fox, William F. (2006). "Hawaii's General Excise Tax: Should the Base Be Changed?" Report Prepared for the 2005–2007 Hawaii Tax Review Commission.

Fox, William F. (2010). "Can State and Local Governments Rely on Alternative Tax Sources?" Federal Reserve Bank of St. Louis. *Regional Economic Development* 6(1): 88–101.

Gold, Steven D., and Robert D. Ebel (2005). "Tax Reform, State." In *The Encyclopedia and Taxation and Tax Policy*, edited by Joseph J. Cordes, Robert D. Ebel and Jane G. Gravelle. Washington, DC: Urban Institute Press. 424–427.

Goolsbee, Austan (2000, May). "In a World without Borders: The Impact of Taxes on Internet Commerce." *Quarterly Journal of Economics* 115: 561–576.

Goolsbee, Austan, and Jonathan Zittrain (1999). "Evaluating the Costs and Benefits of Taxing Internet Commerce." *National Tax Journal* 52: 413–428.

Hawkins, Richard (2002, December). "Popular Substitution Effects: Excess Burden Estimates for General Sales Taxes." *National Tax Journal* 55: 755–770.

Hawkins, Richard, and John Mikesell (2001, March 5). "Six Reasons to Hate Your Sales Tax Holiday." *State Tax Notes*: 801–805.

Hellerstein, Walter (2003). "Jurisdiction to Tax Income and Consumption in the New Economy: A Theoretical and Comparative Perspective." In *Symposium on Jurisdiction to Tax in the New Economy: International, National, and Subnational Perspectives* 38. *Georgia Law Review*.

Hortacsu, Ali, and Chad Syverson (2009). "Why Do Firms Own Production Chains?" Unpublished paper, University of Chicago.

Kanbur, Ravi, and M. Keen (1993). "Jeux Sons Frontieres: Tax Competition and Tax Coordination When Countries Differ in Size." *The American Economic Review* 83: 877–892.

Merriman, David, and Mark Skidmore (2000, March). "Did Distortionary Sales Taxation Contribute to the Growth of the Service Sector?" *National Tax Journal* 53: 125–142.

Poterba, James (1996, June). "Retail Price Reactions to Changes in State and Local Sales Taxes." *National Tax Journal* 44: 165–176.

Quill Corp. v. North Dakota, 504 US 298 (1992).

Robyn, Mark, Micah Cohen, and Joseph Henchman (2009, August). "Sales Tax Holidays: Politically Expedient but Poor Tax Policy." *Tax Foundation Special Report*: 171.

Russo, Benjamin (2005). "An Efficiency Analysis of Proposed State and Local Sales Tax Reforms." *Southern Economic Journal* 72: 443–462.

Slemrod, Joel. (2003). "Michigan's Sales and Use Taxes: Portrait and Analysis." In *Michigan at the Millennium*, edited by Charles Ballard, Paul Courant, D. Drake, Ronald Fisher, and E. Gerber. East Lansing: Michigan State University Press: 559–576.

Snell, Ronald K. (2004), *New Realities in State and Local Finance*. Denver: National Conference of State Legislatures.

Snell, Ronald K. (2009). *State Finance in the Great Depression*. Denver: National Conference of State Legislatures.

Walsh, Michael J., and Jonathan D. Jones (1988, June). "More Evidence on the Border Effect—The Case of West Virginia, 1979–1984." *National Tax Journal* 41: 261–265.

Watson, Harry (2005). "Excess Burden." In *The Encyclopedia of Taxation and Tax Policy*, edited by Joseph J. Cordes, Robert D. Ebel, and Jane G. Gravelle. Washington: Urban Institute Press. 107–108.

Wisconsin Legislative Fiscal Bureau (2009, January). "Individual Income Tax Provisions in the States." Informational Paper No. 4.

Zodrow, George R. (2006, March). "Optimal Commodity Taxation of Traditional and Electronic Commerce." *National Tax Journal* 59: 7–31.

CHAPTER 17

LOCAL REVENUE DIVERSIFICATION: USER CHARGES, SALES TAXES, AND INCOME TAXES

DAVID L. SJOQUIST AND RAYNA STOYCHEVA

A common and well-documented concern regarding the state and local revenue systems is that the US economic structure and demographics have dramatically changed, but state and local revenue systems have yet to adjust to these changes.[1] While this chapter does not necessarily challenge this general proposition, it is also true that the structure and composition of the local revenue system looks much different than it did seventy years ago. While the property tax remains the mainstay of local government revenue, the importance of other revenue sources has increased. For example, in 1942, property taxes accounted for 92.2 percent of local government taxes and 88.3 percent of own-source revenue.[2] By 2008, property taxes had fallen to 72.3 percent of local tax revenue and 45.3 percent of own-source revenue.[3]

This decrease in the relative importance of property taxes is the result of at least two developments. First, there has been a growth in the use of local sales taxes and local income taxes. In 1942, local sales and income taxes accounted for less than 3.4 percent of tax revenue, but by 2008, these revenue sources had increased to 17.6 percent of tax revenue. Second, the use of charges and miscellaneous revenue increased from 10.5 percent of own-source revenue in 1942 to 37.4 percent in 2008.

As a result of these changes, local revenue systems have become more diverse. By this, it is meant that local governments now raise revenue from a larger number of tax sources, and the composition of revenue across revenue sources is more balanced, that is, less dependent on just one revenue source. Because state governments have substantial control over the taxing authority of local governments, the ability of local governments to diversify their revenue systems has required state governments to provide local governments with the ability to adopt alternative revenue sources and to adjust the rates for these revenue sources. Even if a local government is granted the authority to use a particular revenue source, the state government can still impose restrictions or limitations on the use of the revenue source. But if given the authority to use other revenue sources, revenue diversity still requires that local governments use that authority.

This chapter explores this diversity in local government revenue, focusing on user charges and fees, local sales taxes, and local income taxes. The chapter begins with a discussion of the degree of revenue diversity among local governments and the arguments for and against revenue diversity. The chapter then presents a discussion of the use of the three revenue sources: user charges, local sales taxes, and local income taxes. The concluding section provides a summary and concluding thoughts.

REVENUE DIVERSITY

Level of Diversification

While the relative reliance on the property tax has decreased among local governments, there is large variability in the degree of revenue diversification among local governments in the United States. Consider, for example, the variation across states in the share of own-source revenue derived from nonproperty-tax revenue in 2008. At one end was Connecticut, where local governments generated only 17.6 percent of own-source revenue from sources other than property taxes; while at the other end was Alabama, where local governments collected 80.2 percent of its own-source revenue from nonproperty-tax sources.

A more rigorous way of measuring revenue diversification is to construct a Herfindahl index, which allows one to measure the diversity of local revenue composition. The index is calculated as the sum of the square of the share of each source of own-source revenue. The greater the number of revenue sources available and the more equal the share of revenue from the available revenue sources, the greater is the diversity of revenue sources. Thus, the greater the diversity of revenue, the lower is the value of the Herfindahl index. If a local government had only

---

Box 17.1   Calculating the Herfindahl index

With nine revenue sources and with each source yielding the same amount of revenue, each revenue source accounts for one-ninth of total revenue. To calculate the index, one would square one-ninth and then sum over the nine revenue sources, that is, $\Sigma(1/9)^2 = 0.11$. On the other hand, if one revenue source accounted for 60 percent of the revenue and another eight accounted for 5 percent each, the index would equal 0.38, or $\Sigma(0.6^2 + 0.05^2 + 0.05^2 + 0.05^2 + 0.05^2 + 0.05^2 + 0.05^2 + 0.05^2 + 0.05^2) = 0.38$.

---

one source of revenue, the Herfindahl index would equal one, while if there were nine revenue sources and each source yielded the same amount of revenue, the Herfindahl index would equal 0.11. Box 17.1 illustrates how the Herfindahl index is calculated.

Herfindahl indices were calculated for each state by using the nine local government revenue sources identified in the government finance data of the Bureau of the Census.[4] Figure 17.1 shows the distribution of these state-level Herfindahl indices. The value of the index for the aggregate of local governments in the United States is 0.292, while the unweighted average of the state indices is 0.350. This suggests a substantial diversity of revenue sources. Twenty-three states have index values between 0.300 and 0.400 and 35 have values between 0.250 and 0.450, suggesting similarity across many states in the level of local government diversity. The five states with the highest index values, and thus the smallest degree of local government revenue diversity, are Connecticut (0.708), New Hampshire (0.670), Rhode Island (0.648), Maine (0.593), and New Jersey (0.614). Given that these states do not have very diverse local government revenue structures, it is not surprising that they rely heavily on property taxes. For example, in Connecticut 83.4 percent of local own-source revenue comes from the property tax. On the other hand, states with

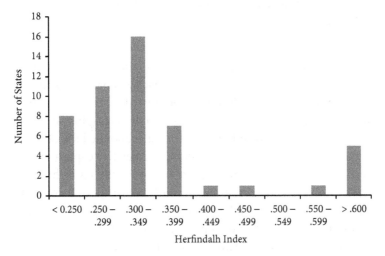

Figure 17.1   State Herfindahl index, 2008
Source: Authors' Calculations.

low values of the index do not rely heavily on property taxes and are states that rely more heavily on local sales or local income taxes. For example, New York has the lowest Herfindahl index at 0.225 and its reliance on property taxes is 40 percent of local own-source revenue. The Herfindahl index is 0.236 for New Mexico and 0.245 for Washington State, while property taxes are 32.2 percent and 31.3 percent of own-source revenue, respectively. Property taxes as a share of own-source revenue is lowest in Alabama (19.8 percent), but that state's Herfindahl index is 0.292.

There are differences in the degree of revenue diversity by the type of local government. Herfindahl indices by type of local government for the United States for 2007 were calculated. School districts have the least diverse own-source revenue systems; this is not surprising because school districts generally rely nearly completely on property taxes for local revenue. Municipalities have the most diverse revenue structure, with an index value of 0.191, in general because local sales and local income taxes are more common among municipalities than for other types of local governments. The index values for counties, special districts, and townships are 0.278, 0.396, and 0.540, respectively. Given the diverse nature of special districts, in the aggregate they generate revenue from many sources. Some are transit districts that rely on sales taxes, some are hospital and sewer districts that rely heavily on charges, and others are urban improvement districts that rely on property taxes. Thus, while most individual special districts rely on one revenue source, as a category they have a diverse revenue stream.

Why Diversify?

Local governments are responsible for funding a set of public services that benefit local constituents. Obviously, to accomplish this, local governments need to raise the appropriate level of revenue, and they do so by matching expenditure responsibilities with community revenues. Five arguments emerge to justify local revenue diversification:[5]

- Capture Local Revenue Capacity. Just as is true for state (and national) revenue systems, the revenue-raising capacity of particular revenue sources can differ across local jurisdictions, because the capacities of revenue sources depend on the local economic and demographic circumstances.[6] Thus, for example, a locality with a robust economic base of manufacturing and/or office building will rank high in relative capacity to tax income, whereas a locality with a large visitor industry will have a high revenue capacity in taxing consumption. Similarly, a jurisdiction dominated by elderly residents may rank low in terms of income-tax revenue capacity but high on the taxation of consumption and assets (e.g., property taxation). For this reason, local governments should have a diverse set of potential revenue sources available to them to finance public services.
- Reduced Reliance on the Property Tax. A second often-cited reason for revenue diversification is that by allowing local governments to use

nonproperty-tax revenue, local governments can reduce their reliance on the traditional "mainstay" property tax. Advocates of increased diversity cite public opinion polls[7] that find that citizens do not like the property tax; one way to reduce the anti-property-tax view is to simply use it less intensively. As noted above, greater revenue diversity is associated with a smaller relative reliance on property taxes, but that is not the same as an absolute reduction in property taxes. The simple correlation coefficient across states between property taxes per capita in 2008 and the Herfindahl index is 0.60. Thus, states with a more diverse local revenue structure do rely less on property taxes. However, it is possible that states with more diverse revenue structures simply have lower revenue per capita overall. That is in fact the case, although the correlations coefficient between the Herfindahl index and own-source revenue per capita is only −0.04.

- Horizontal Equity. Another argument for revenue diversity is premised on the notion that some beneficiaries of local public services may avoid paying a fair share of the cost of public services if the local government relies on just one type of tax. This is a violation of the principle of horizontal equity, which, as broadly applied here, calls for a local tax contribution by all beneficiaries of like local services. For example, the property-tax base for some households, or businesses, may be very small, yet they may obtain significant benefits from public services. Tourists and commuters impose costs on local governments but do not pay any property taxes to the local government. By employing other revenue sources, these individuals or businesses are less likely to avoid paying their fair share of the cost of the public services provided.

- Revenue Stability. A fourth argument for a diversified revenue structure concerns the stability of total revenue over the business cycle. Just as a diversified individual or business investment portfolio can reduce the overall risk of a loss, a diversified revenue structure can reduce the risk of revenue loss to the local government. The argument for a diversified investment portfolio is based on the assumption that the likelihood that one asset, for example the stock of one company, will decrease in value is not highly correlated with the likelihood that other assets will incur a loss. But to the extent that all assets are driven by economic conditions, the losses and gains will be correlated. In a similar manner, the year-to-year revenue growth in each revenue source is largely driven by the national and state economies. Thus, if the revenue from one revenue source declines, it is very likely that the revenue from other sources will also fall. But the extent of the decline may differ and thus a diversified revenue system may suffer a smaller decline than a nondiversified revenue system.

    In more general terms, the argument for a diversified revenue structure is analogous to the argument for a diversified financial portfolio. Just as an investor will create a portfolio of different investments, a local government, given the options made available to it, would choose among available revenue options to create a portfolio of revenue sources.

Investments differ in terms of their characteristics, in particular different risks and returns, and thus investors choose different portfolios so as to achieve their individually desired mix of risk and returns. Similarly, revenue sources have different characteristics. Revenue sources differ in terms of their growth rates over time, stability over the business cycle, equity, ease of administration, economic effects, acceptability by citizens, etc. Thus, alternative revenue portfolios could be constructed, each of which would yield a different mix of characteristics. Several authors have explored this idea and estimated the trade-offs among some of these characteristics.[8]

Just as investors have different preferences for risk and return, local governments may differ in their preferences over the various revenue characteristics. The citizens of one jurisdiction may have a preference for taxes that are tied to the benefits received from public services, while another jurisdiction may be more concerned with keeping taxes low for low-income families. Thus, if a local government can use alternative revenue instruments, the local government can choose the revenue portfolio that achieves its desired mix of characteristics.

- Economic Efficiency. A final reason for revenue diversification is that financing local public services through user charges and fees promotes an efficient level of public services.[9] Charges and fees, when designed appropriately, serve as signals of the cost of the public service, similar to prices for private goods. Because user charges vary with the amount of service consumed, individuals can adjust their consumption in response to the charge. Taxes, on the other hand, are paid regardless of the level of consumption, and therefore the effective marginal cost that the citizen pays to consume one more unit of the public service is zero.
  As a result, the quantity demanded of public services financed with taxes will be higher than what is socially optimal because each individual taxpayer ignores the extra cost that results from his consumption.

There are two principal counterarguments against a diversified revenue structure. First, some writers suggest that a benefit tax should be used by local governments, since, given the mobility of labor and capital, attempts to tax on the basis of income or consumption is likely to result in the migration of businesses and households. Furthermore, a theory has been advanced that the property tax is a benefit tax and an ideal tax for local governments.

As formally presented by Bruce Hamilton and by William Fischel, the premise is that local jurisdictions offer alternative tax-public service packages and that households choose among the jurisdiction based on the household's most preferred package.[10] Thus, the property-tax liability is equal to the benefits a household receives from the public services that the local government provides. In this world, the property tax is essentially the price that a resident pays for the public services that are provided. However, others argue that the theory that the property tax is a benefits tax is not supported by empirical evidence.[11] A more ad hoc argument is that the benefits of public services such as police protection, fire service, and street maintenance are positively associated with the value of one's property.

The second argument against local revenue diversification is that if a local government gains access to additional revenue options, it will increase revenue, and thus expenditures, beyond what the citizens truly desire. There are several reasons why this might happen, but the main argument is based on the Leviathan view of government, as espoused by James Buchanan and by Buchanan and Richard Wagner.[12] Under this view, government decision makers rather than voters are assumed to determine expenditure levels. Furthermore, it is assumed that the government bureaucrats prefer greater public spending than the citizens. Government bureaucrats, the argument goes, are able to increase expenditures because more revenue instruments lead to a more complex tax structure, which allows greater manipulation of voters by government officials. The empirical evidence of the effect of the revenue structure on the level of expenditures is mixed; see, for example, Wagner, who found support for the Leviathan view of government, and Helen Ladd and Dana Weist, who obtained contrary results.[13]

We now consider three specific nonproperty-tax revenue sources: user fees, local sales taxes, and local income taxes. The discussion focuses first on the reliance on each source and then turns to issues associated with using each of these sources to diversify local government revenue structures.

State and Local User Charges and Fees

User charges can be separated into those that apply to general public services, referred to as current charges, and those associated with utilities such as water. While the primary focus below is on current charges, some discussion of utility revenue is also included.

Reliance on User Charges and Fees

User charges and fees have become an increasingly important source of state and local revenues. In the last two decades, current charges and fees grew steadily in real terms, as indicated in figure 17.2.[14] Total state and local revenues in real terms from current charges almost doubled between 1992 and 2008, increasing from about

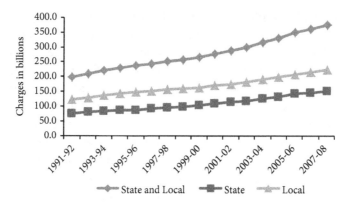

Figure 17.2 Current charges, FY 1992–FY 2008 (in 2008 dollars)
Source: Bureau of the Census, *Government Finances: FY 1992–2008.*

$200 billion to $374 billion. The growth of state revenues from charges was some-what faster than total local revenues over that period. In 2008, current charges by local government made up 59.6 percent of total state and local current charges; local government made up 45.1 percent of state plus local government own-source revenue. The increase in charges per capita, on the other hand, while substantial, has not been as large as the growth in total revenues (figure 17.3). The per capita current charges by state and local governments increased from $784 to $1,240, or by 58.2 percent.

However, the relative share of current charges of own-source revenues did not increase significantly between 1992 and 2008 (figure 17.4). The average share of current charges of own-source revenue increased from 17.3 percent in 1992 to only 19.2 percent in 2008 for state and local governments combined. The state revenue share of charges increased from 12.1 percent to 14.1 percent and from 23.6 percent to 25.4 percent for local governments. These data reflect the situation noted above: local governments rely relatively more heavily on current charges than do state governments.

Utility revenue, including water, electricity, gas, and transit, increased at a slower pace than current charges, with an overall increase of about 60 percent.

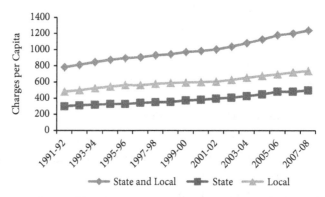

Figure 17.3 Current charges per capita, FY 1992–FY 2008 (in 2008 dollars)
Source: Bureau of the Census, *Government Finances: FY 2008.*

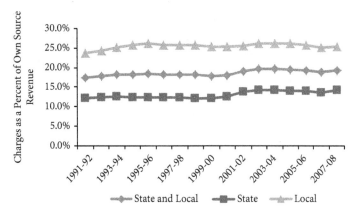

Figure 17.4 Current charges as a percentage of own-source revenue, FY 1992–FY 2008
Source: Bureau of the Census, *Government Finances: FY 2008*.

In FY 1992, utility revenue was 30.1 percent of total current and utility charges, but this fell to 27.1 percent in FY 2008.

While there have not been significant changes in the overall share of charges, the use of current charges differs across states and between state and local governments, as illustrated for FY 2008 in table 17.1. The minimum share of current charges revenue is 7 percent (Alaska), while the maximum is almost 34 percent (South Carolina). Alaska, the District of Columbia (DC) and Connecticut have the

Table 17.1 Current and utility charges as a percentage of own-source revenue by type of government, 2008

	State and Local	State	Local
Alabama	30.5%	24.4%	39.0%
Alaska	7.2%	4.1%	26.6%
Arizona	16.0%	9.6%	23.8%
Arkansas	21.2%	18.9%	28.0%
California	20.4%	10.5%	31.4%
Colorado	23.8%	19.7%	27.3%
Connecticut	9.6%	9.5%	9.8%
Delaware	20.7%	19.6%	25.0%
District of Columbia	6.9%		6.9%
Florida	21.3%	12.6%	27.7%
Georgia	22.5%	13.8%	30.3%
Hawaii	18.0%	17.2%	20.6%
Idaho	26.1%	12.4%	46.9%

(Continued)

Table 17.1 Continued

	State and Local	State	Local
Illinois	14.7%	10.5%	19.2%
Indiana	22.4%	15.9%	31.6%
Iowa	26.0%	21.0%	32.6%
Kansas	22.1%	19.9%	25.0%
Kentucky	22.2%	19.5%	27.6%
Louisiana	18.4%	12.2%	26.8%
Maine	14.5%	12.1%	18.8%
Maryland	15.1%	13.9%	16.8%
Massachusetts	14.3%	11.8%	19.2%
Michigan	22.4%	17.6%	30.2%
Minnesota	18.6%	10.0%	33.3%
Mississippi	29.2%	15.8%	48.6%
Missouri	20.3%	15.4%	25.7%
Montana	19.5%	14.7%	28.8%
Nebraska	23.0%	15.5%	30.8%
Nevada	20.4%	9.1%	30.8%
New Hampshire	17.0%	20.9%	12.3%
New Jersey	14.0%	13.0%	15.4%
New Mexico	15.0%	12.5%	22.0%
New York	13.0%	9.5%	16.2%
North Carolina	23.0%	13.1%	37.6%
North Dakota	20.2%	20.6%	19.3%
Ohio	20.0%	18.8%	21.4%
Oklahoma	22.3%	17.4%	30.9%
Oregon	23.4%	19.3%	28.5%
Pennsylvania	17.5%	15.8%	19.8%
Rhode Island	13.7%	14.4%	12.6%
South Carolina	33.7%	29.0%	39.6%
South Dakota	18.5%	14.2%	23.9%
Tennessee	21.9%	12.1%	34.1%
Texas	19.5%	15.5%	23.6%

(Continued)

Table 17.1 Continued

	State and Local	State	Local
Utah	24.8%	24.6%	25.0%
Vermont	16.6%	14.8%	26.1%
Virginia	20.9%	22.2%	19.0%
Washington	23.5%	15.4%	33.5%
West Virginia	20.2%	17.1%	29.0%
Wisconsin	19.3%	16.8%	23.1%
Wyoming	20.3%	5.0%	40.7%

Source: US Bureau of the Census (2008).
Note: Own-source revenues are general revenues from taxes, charges, and miscellaneous general revenue. Own-source revenue does not include intergovernmental revenue or revenue from utilities, liquor stores, and trust funds. Charges are amounts received from the public for performance of specific services that benefit the person charged and from the sale of commodities or services other than utilities and liquor stores. Charges includes fees, maintenance assessments, and other reimbursements for current services; rents and sales derived from commodities or services furnished incident to the performance of particular functions; gross income of commercial enterprises; and the like.

lowest share of charges overall, while Mississippi, Alabama, and South Carolina collect almost one-third of their revenues from user charges and fees. At the state level, revenue from user charges ranges from 4 percent (Alaska) to 29 percent (South Carolina) of own-source revenue. Alabama, Utah, and South Carolina generate more than 24 percent of their state revenues from user charges. The variation among local governments is much greater, with DC and Connecticut collecting less than 10 percent of their local revenues from user charges, while Alabama, South Carolina, Idaho, Mississippi, and Wyoming get 40 percent or more of their revenues from charges.

What Services Are Financed by User Charges and to What Extent?

Table 17.2 presents the share of user-charge revenue by service category, separately for current charges and utility revenue. Education and hospitals account for more than 50 percent of total state plus local current charges and slightly more that 80 percent of current state charges. The heavy reliance by the state on charges for education is largely explained by tuition at colleges and technical schools. Among local governments, hospital fees, sewerage charges, and other charges are the major source of current-charge revenue. Among utilities, a charge for electric power is the largest source of revenue at both the state and local levels. State governments generate very little in water-user charges. Box 17.2 illustrates the types of charges associated with various public service categories.

Table 17.2. Distribution of current charges by type, 2008

	State and Local	State	Local
Current Charges			
Education	29.57%	56.66%	11.21%
Hospitals	26.03%	24.02%	27.40%
Highways	2.99%	4.25%	2.13%
Air Transportation (Airports)	4.76%	0.88%	7.39%
Parking Facilities	0.52%	0.01%	0.87%
Sea and Inland Port Facilities	1.11%	0.81%	1.31%
Natural Resources	1.07%	1.68%	0.66%
Parks and Recreation	2.57%	1.05%	3.60%
Housing and Community Development	1.51%	0.45%	2.23%
Sewerage	10.19%	0.03%	17.07%
Solid Waste Management	4.09%	0.30%	6.65%
Other Charges	15.59%	9.86%	19.47%
Total	100.0%	100.0%	100.0%
Utility			
Water Supply	32.64%	1.45%	36.84%
Electric Power	52.23%	83.90%	47.96%
Gas Supply	6.42%	0.10%	7.27%
Transit	8.71%	14.55%	7.93%
Total	100.0%	100.0%	100.0%

Source: US Bureau of the Census (2008).

The extent to which user fees and charges are used to cover the expenditures for government services varies significantly. Generally, utility charges for electricity, gas, and water recover most of the expenses for these services. Other services with a large ratio of revenue to expenditures are air and water transportation facilities, sewerage and waste management, and hospitals. Parking revenues generally significantly exceed the costs of the service. On the other hand, education, highways and public transportation, parks and recreation, and housing and community development have low charge-to-expenditure ratios. Charges for education cover a much larger share of expenditures for the states than for local governments because states charge tuition for postsecondary education while tuition is not generally imposed in K-12 education (table 17.3).

To provide some additional detail regarding how the use of charges differs across cities, three small cities are compared for 2010–2011: Smyrna, Georgia;

Box 17.2 Examples of fees and charges	
Public Function	Fees and Charges
Education—K-12	School lunches; activity fees
Higher Education	Tuition; student activity fees; transportation fees
Hospitals	Room charges; supplies; medical equipment
Highways and Roads	Motor vehicle license and registration fees; trucks (55,000 + pounds) user charge; tolls
Air Transportation (airports)	Landing fees; passenger facility charges; parking and concession charges
Parking Facilities	Parking fees
Sea and Inland Port Facilities	Harbor maintenance user fees
Natural Resources	Charges for agricultural fairs; lab testing fees
Parks and Recreation	Vehicle entrance fees; camping site fees; recreation facility rental fees
Housing and Community Development	Impact fees; stormwater fees; permits for building, plumbing, air and heating, etc.
Sewerage	Capital and distribution charges; per-gallon charges
Solid Waste Management	Fixed annual collection fees; pay-as-you-throw bags (Decatur, GA)
Water Supply	Sanitary commission fees; connection charges; capital and distribution charges; per-gallon charges
Electric Power	Connection charges metered charges
Gas Supply	Connection charges; metered charges
Transit	Fares
Other Charges	Ambulance services fees; alarm permits; fire response charges; library fees

Garner, North Carolina; and Ramsey, Minnesota.[15] Smyrna and Ramsey charge variable water rates based on usage, although the increase at each step is higher in Smyrna. The water rate in Garner, on the other hand, is a fixed fee, which is based on zoning and acreage, but not usage. The sewer rate is a fixed fee in Ramsey, but in Smyrna the fee is based on gallons of water used, but the rate does not increase with water consumption.

There is substantial variation in the type of recreation services and fees used in each location. Smyrna provides extensive recreational services and facilities for rent. The schedule for recreation services for Garner specifies that most of the services should cover 100 percent of direct cost and includes a surcharge of 30 percent for nonresidents. Garner also explicitly specifies the rules for low-income subsidies

Table 17.3 Distribution of utility and current charges as a percentage of expenditures by government sector, 2008

	State & Local	State	Local
Current charges			
Education	13.4%	36.8%	4.2%
Hospitals	75.5%	69.8%	79.3%
Highways	7.3%	7.1%	7.6%
Air Transportation (Airports)	83.6%	75.4%	84.4%
Parking Facilities	122.1%	241.5%	121.5%
Sea and Inland Port Facilities	83.8%	81.9%	84.6%
Natural Resources	13.4%	12.8%	14.7%
Parks and Recreation	23.7%	28.9%	22.8%
Housing and Community Development	11.1%	6.2%	12.4%
Sewerage	81.5%	3.5%	83.7%
Solid Waste Management	64.3%	18.7%	69.5%
Other Charges	48.1%	37.3%	53.5%
Utility			
Water Supply	82.3%	67.8%	82.4%
Electric Power	94.8%	89.8%	96.0%
Gas Supply	84.8%	134.5%	84.8%
Transit	23.8%	23.4%	23.9%

Source: US Bureau of the Census (2008).

for recreational access and sets a limit for the total value of the subsidy for each individual. Smyrna does not have extra police and fire fees, such as for false alarms. Garner charges for each false alarm after the third false alarm, with an increasing rate for each instance. Ramsey implemented several new user charges in 2010 in addition to the false alarm charge. These include a charge for a gas line hit by contractors of $300, an illegal burning fee of $200, and a personal injury and extrication charge for nonresidents of $500.

Setting the Levels of Charges

As noted in the arguments presented above for revenue diversification, charges and fees, when designed appropriately, serve as signals of the cost of the service, similar to prices for private goods.[16] Because user charges vary with the amount of service consumed, individuals can adjust their consumption in response.

In addition to covering the marginal cost of providing a public service, user charges can be used to reduce congestion when the demand for a public service exceeds capacity. The use of congestion tolls on highways has been widely discussed.[17] But fees can be imposed to limit the use of facilities such as swimming pools and golf courses on weekends, electricity during heat waves, and water during droughts.

User charges are also expected to resolve an efficiency problem on the supply side, which leads to overproduction of public services. According to William Niskanen's bureaucracy theory, the goal of public bureaucracies is to maximize their budgets, which may lead to higher than optimal levels of public services.[18] When financing of services is not clearly linked to the costs, as it is in the case of general taxes, it is more difficult to observe the efficient level of output.

Finally, user charges may be attractive as a means to promote fairness in the financing of public goods.[19] For services that do not involve distributional concerns, user charges ensure that those who benefit from a service pay for it. This is particularly relevant for services that may be consumed by nonresidents, since they would not be taxed for the provision of those services. On the other hand, it is necessary to consider the potential vertical equity issues that may arise as a result of user charge financing. Because user charges would be based on marginal cost and usage, for many public services the user charge would constitute a larger percentage of income for lower-income individuals and therefore may be regressive. The extent to which this is the case would vary with different public services. For example, higher-income individuals may consume more recreational services such as golfing courses, so public provision financed through general taxes subsidizes the consumption of higher-income individuals. One way to remedy regressive user charges would be to provide a subsidy to lower-income residents through discounts or waivers.

In order for user charges to achieve the goal of efficient provision of public services, user fees need to meet several criteria. First, the user charge should reflect the marginal cost of an additional user of the publicly provided good or service.[20] Consider first the case of a public service that requires one more unit of the public service in order for one more citizen to consume the public service. The marginal cost can be divided in two main components: the capital cost and the operating cost, where the capital cost is relatively fixed over a certain range of output, and the operating cost varies with the level of output. The operating cost is the one that is most easily identified as a user charge because it represents the extra cost of one more user. The distribution of the capital cost depends on whether the beneficiaries are only the users or are all of the residents in a location. For example, the existence of a bridge may benefit the community overall through improved transportation, although not every resident uses the bridge. Therefore, the capital cost in that case should be allocated to all residents through general taxes, and only the variable costs for maintaining the bridge should be collected through user charges.

At the other extreme is a public service that can be enjoyed by many people without an increase in the cost of the public service for another person. For example, consider a 4th of July fireworks display. For this type of service, there are no additional costs for allowing one more family to watch the fireworks. In this case, no user charge should be imposed.

The case for user charges is built on the assumption that consumers can and will adjust their consumption in response to different prices. The price elasticity of the demand for the public service is a measure of the responsiveness of the use of public services to user charges. The more elastic the demand, that is, the greater the response of individuals to the price incentives, the more important it is to reduce consumption because with no user charge, the consumption of the public service will be well beyond an efficient level. A more elastic demand also indicates that people have other alternatives, which may alleviate vertical equity concerns about user charges.

The literature on user charges has extensively examined the price elasticity of demand for various services. In general, these studies find that citizens are relatively responsive to user charges. For example, the price elasticity for tolls on bridges, roads, and tunnels in the United States has been found to range from −0.10 to −0.50.[21] In a meta-analysis of public transportation studies, Johan Holmgren reported that the short-run price elasticity of public transportation in the United States is −0.59 and the long-run price elasticity is −0.75.[22]

Generally, the fee for solid waste collection is a flat amount, independent of the amount of solid waste generated. Such a fee is not associated with the cost of providing the service, which depends on front footage and the amount of solid waste that the family generates. A number of cities have adopted a fee structure that depends on the volume of solid waste generated. Typically, in these cities households have to purchase special trash bags, the price of which includes the user charge. Does such a fee actually reduce the volume of solid waste? Thomas Kinnaman reviewed the literature on solid waste fees for households, and he reported that the studies, on average, found that a fee of $1.00 per bag would reduce the number of twenty-pound bags per week by about 0.60, after controlling for the presence of a curbside recycling program.[23]

The second criterion is that an efficient user charge needs to take into account external benefits generated by the publicly provided good or service. For example, education and health care provide external benefits beyond the individual who sits in the classroom or who receives an inoculation. The social marginal benefit of such services is higher than the individual's marginal benefit. This additional social benefit is not taken into account by the individual when she decides how much to consume. Thus a user charge set at the marginal cost would result in too little of the public service. Therefore, the user charge should be reduced by the amount of the external marginal benefit in order to obtain a socially efficient level of the public service. Of course, measuring the external benefit is a challenge.

Third, the user charge must be administratively feasible. For that purpose, it should be relatively easy to identify the beneficiaries of the good or service and to exclude them from consuming it without paying the charge. In some cases it may be very costly to exclude direct users, even though it may be easy to identify them. For example, to collect entrance fees to parks it is necessary to have limited entry points and someone to collect fees. For some parks with a low number of visitors, the revenue may not offset the administrative costs. It may also be relatively costly to implement a variable charge based on use if the use does not vary significantly.

Current Trends in User Charges and Fees

In response to the financial crisis of 2008, local governments have overwhelmingly turned to user charges and fees to shore up their revenues. According to the 2009 International City and County International City/County Management Association (ICMA) State of the Profession Survey, 46 percent of the responding local governments indicated that they had increased existing fees and 23 percent had added new fees.[24] Fee increases were across all types of services, including utilities, recreation, sanitation, development, and administrative services. Some governments implemented automatic increases based on the consumer price index, while others implemented more steep one-time increases, ranging from 5 percent to 20 percent. Georgia recently passed legislation increasing nearly all state fees. Colorado state parks are expected to increase user fees for daily passes, camping, and lodging by about 15 percent.[25]

The new fees for services also range across all categories of services, with the most common ones being recycling, pay-to-throw (trash collection), parks and recreation, facility, and development fees. In addition, local governments have expanded recreation programs and added community space for lease. A library in Sausalito, California, offers new services, including exam proctoring and notary services for which it charges a fee.[26] Other cities have turned to less traditional areas for user charges. Mission City, Kansas, has approved a "driveway" fee based on the amount of traffic generated by businesses and homeowners.[27] Other non-traditional approaches to fees include a proposal in Pontiac, Illinois, to charge each accident victim $300 for being rescued from their cars.[28] More examples from the ICMA survey include fees for ambulance response for nonresidents and false alarm fees. The controversy surrounding less traditional user charges is illustrated by California public schools, which are facing lawsuits for increasingly charging fees for required school activities.[29]

The Potential for Expanding the Use of User Charges

In 1992, Downing estimated a significant revenue potential of user charges based on municipal information about user-charge rates and differences among cities.[30] He found that cities differ significantly in the extent to which they finance services with user charges and that these differences are masked by the kind of average percentages presented here for state and local governments. Taking into account the higher reliance on user charges in some cities and applying it to all cities provides one way to project the revenue potential of user charges. This approach yields an estimate of significant potential revenue increases, ranging from 100 percent to 400 percent for different services. The other option for expanding the revenue potential of user charges is by changing the pricing from average cost to marginal cost. This would result in higher user charges because it takes into account the implicit costs of capital and land, among others.

Although municipal data necessary to develop an estimate using this precise approach are not available, there are reasons to suggest that the revenue potential of user charges is likely to still be large. It appears from the ICMA survey that many cities have been moving in the direction suggested by Downing as a result of the current fiscal crisis. The fact that 23 percent of respondents introduced new fees, although most of the new fees were very similar to fees already being used in other cities, indicates that many cities have not tapped into this revenue source. The total share of user charges as a percentage of own-source revenue for local governments has remained constant since the early 1990s, so there does not appear to be evidence of a systematic increase in the reliance on user charges, and thus the potential discussed by Downing has continued.

Furthermore, it does not appear from the anecdotal evidence that cities are in effect using marginal cost pricing. While marginal cost pricing needs to be adopted with caution because a variable rate may have higher administrative costs than the revenues it will collect, this need not be the case for all services. The most significant challenges of marginal cost pricing are associated with the costs of measuring and billing for variable rates of use. For example, while it may be efficient to have a peak charge for electricity use at different times during the day, at this point it is not technologically feasible to have such meters for all users. Similarly, the volume charge for refuse is approximated by some fixed amount (a bag or can), not the actual volume of the trash because it is very costly to measure the actual volume with current technology.

One final note concerns the political feasibility of user charges, as discussed extensively by David Duff.[31] Although user charges may be economically efficient and feasible to implement, there might be significant opposition to user charges. Some of this opposition may be based on the view that these services are already financed through taxes, so it is necessary to clarify the difference between what portion of the public good is financed with general taxes and what portion is more appropriate to be financed with a user charge. User charges may be opposed by politicians and bureaucrats, as well, on the basis that revenues collected from user charges are essentially earmarked for the specific public service and therefore restrict the flexibility of government budgets.

LOCAL SALES TAXES

Reliance on Local Sales Taxes

In 1934, New York City became the first local government to adopt a local sales tax. Use of local sales taxes spread, and as of 2008, local sales taxes were used in thirty-three states (see table 17.4). The growth in local sales-tax revenue (and local income-tax revenue) as a share of local government taxes is illustrated in figure 17.5.

Table 17.4 Local sales tax revenue as a percentage of local tax revenue, 2008

State	Percentage	State	Percentage
Louisiana	52.5%	Alaska	16.4%
Arkansas	48.2%	California	13.3%
New Mexico	38.8%	Texas	13.0%
Oklahoma	38.0%	Iowa	12.7%
Alabama	37.4%	North Dakota	10.7%
Colorado	29.4%	Nebraska	10.4%
Arizona	28.8%	Ohio	8.1%
Tennessee	26.3%	Virginia	7.6%
Georgia	25.5%	Illinois	5.3%
South Dakota	23.0%	Nevada	4.4%
Washington	22.5%	Florida	3.6%
Missouri	20.5%	Wisconsin	3.2%
Utah	19.9%	South Carolina	2.4%
North Carolina	18.8%	Minnesota	1.8%
Wyoming	18.2%	Vermont	1.4%
Kansas	16.8%	Pennsylvania	1.4%
New York	16.1%		

Source: US Bureau of the Census (2008).

Sales taxes grew from 5 percent of total local taxes in 1970 to a high of 12.4 percent in 2001, before falling to 11.6 percent in 2008. There is wide variation across states in the reliance on local sales taxes; local sales-tax revenue as a share of local tax revenue varies from 0 to over 50 percent (table 17.4).

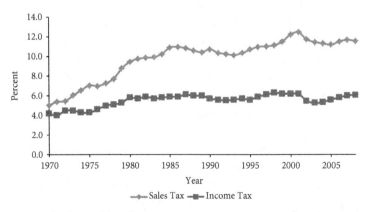

Figure 17.5 Local sales and local income taxes as a percentage of total taxes (1970–2008)
Source: Tax Foundation; U.S. Bureau of the Census.

How local sales taxes are imposed and how the revenues are used vary across states. For example, in Georgia there are six alternative local option sales taxes. The first was adopted to fund rapid transit (Metropolitan Atlanta Rapid Transit Authority, MARTA) in the two central counties in the Atlanta region. There is now a local option sales tax (LOST) that was designed for property-tax relief, with the revenue shared between the county and municipal governments within the county based on a negotiated sharing agreement; a special-purpose LOST (SPLOST) that is used to fund capital improvements by the county and municipal governments; an education SPLOST (ESPLOST) that is used for capital improvements for schools; a homestead option sales tax (HOST) that is used to fund homestead exemptions of up to 100 percent of value; and a municipal option sales tax (MOST) in the city of Atlanta that is used to fund a massive upgrade of Atlanta's water-sewer system. Finally, in 2010, the state legislature approved the potential use of another local sales tax that would be imposed within designated regions of the state with the revenue used to fund transportation within the region.

All of the local sales taxes in Georgia are levied at 1 percent, are countywide (with the exception of the MOST and the new regional transportation sales tax), and must be approved through a referendum. Some taxes are permanent while others have term limits, but they can be reauthorized through referenda. The statewide average local sales-tax rate in Georgia is about 2.8 percent compared to the 4 percent state sales-tax rate.

California allowed locally administrated sales taxes as early as 1944, with local governments adopting their own sales tax ordinances, tax rates, and exemptions. In an effort to bring order to the complexity of having many locally administered sales taxes, the state established the Bradley-Burns uniform sales tax in 1955. The Bradley-Burns sales tax is imposed at 1 percent and is then split as 25 percent from the county government and 75 percent from the city or county (depending on the location of the sale), with the revenue going to the general fund. All counties in California have adopted a Bradley-Burns sales tax. In addition to the Bradley-Burns tax, a local option sales tax of up to 1.5 percent can be imposed by referendum by either a city or a county. The revenue of the majority of these sales taxes is earmarked, especially for transportation.

In Utah, cities were given the authority in 1960 to impose a local sales tax; the rate, which is uniform across the state, is set by the state legislature and has been changed from time to time. Revenue is shared, with 50 percent allocated on the basis of the point of sale and 50 percent on a per capita basis within the county. In 1975, cities in urban counties were given authority, subject to approval in a referendum, to levy a local sales tax to fund mass transit. More recently, authority was granted to impose, subject to a referendum, sales taxes that are earmarked for rural hospitals, rural highways, and cultural support. In addition, counties can adopt, without a referendum, a local sales tax for property-tax relief.

In Tennessee, counties can impose a local sales tax, and all have done so, up to a rate of 2.75 percent. Municipalities within that county can impose a tax at a rate equal to the difference between 2.75 percent and the county sales-tax rate, although not many cities have imposed a local sales tax. Half of the revenue is allocated to education; tax revenue from the sale of certain goods and services is earmarked for tourism promotion.

It is clear that the use of local sales taxes is widespread, but it is not close to universal. Generally, the administration of the sales tax follows that of the state sales tax, and while there are some administrative issues, they are not overwhelming.[32] As discussed above, there is substantial variation across states in what local sales-tax revenue can be used for.

Characteristics of Local Sales Taxes

The decision of whether to use local sales taxes to diversify the local revenue structure depends on the characteristics the tax brings to the revenue portfolio. This section discusses the relevant features of the local sales tax.

In most states, the allowable sales-tax rate and the sales-tax base are set by the state. In this situation, local governments have no control, at the margin, over the revenue structure of their sales taxes. Allowing local governments to determine their own definition of the sales-tax base independent of the state's sales-tax base, would, however, be bad tax policy. The compliance cost of having to determine whether a product or service is taxed in any given jurisdiction would likely be very high. Firms already struggle to determine what sales-tax rate applies for a specific address. That would be compounded if businesses also had to determine what products the tax applied to, including determining the definition of products that were exempt.

Limiting the sales-tax rate means that a local government has to choose between a zero percent (i.e., not having a sales tax), and, say, a 1 percent sales-tax rate. But it might be that the optional degree of revenue structure diversity for a given local government might imply a sales-tax rate of 0.5 percent or 1.5 percent. Thus, this limitation on the sales-tax rate means that the local government may not be able to achieve its desired level of revenue structure diversity. However, to the extent that the sales-tax revenue is used to reduce property taxes, the local sales tax does provide the local government with additional fiscal freedom. Thus, for example, if in the future the local government needs to raise additional revenue, there may be less resistance to increasing property-tax rates given that the local government reduced property taxes in an earlier period.

Typically sales-tax revenue is earmarked for expenditures on specific services or categories of services. This further limits the fiscal freedom of local governments to diversify its revenue structure. This restriction, combined with a specified sales-tax rate, has two possible effects. If the revenue from the sales tax exceeds the desired expenditure on the allowable services, expenditures on the allowable services will increase, leading to an inefficiently high level of expenditures. On the other hand, if the sales-tax revenue is less than the current existing expenditures on the designated activity, the other revenues that were used to fund the designated service can be used for other purposes.

The local sales tax is not a benefit tax, that is, there is no link between sales taxes paid and the benefits an individual receives from the public services. Residents typically shop in many jurisdictions, not just in the jurisdiction of their residence. This is especially true if a household's residential jurisdiction does not have a large retail center. Thus, a substantial percentage of local sales taxes that an individual pays is likely paid to a jurisdiction other than the jurisdiction of residence, and this percentage is likely to vary widely across jurisdictions. Therefore, the sales tax paid to the jurisdiction of residence will not be closely tied to the benefits of public services provided.

The sales tax will generate revenue from tourists, shoppers, and commuters. To the extent that these individuals require local governments to provide additional public services, the sales-tax revenue can be used to pay for these additional expenditures. It is unlikely, however, that the additional revenue will exactly match the additional expenditures required. In addition, commuters are likely to impose higher additional public service costs but are likely to generate relatively less sales-tax revenue than tourists and shoppers would.

The property-tax base is thought to be immobile in the short run, which is considered one of its desirable features. But that is not a feature of the sales tax. There is a substantial literature on the mobility of the sales-tax base, although much of the focus on the mobility has been on the effect of differential sales-tax rates on cross-border shopping.[33] These studies generally find that a one percentage point higher sales tax rate is associated with per capita sales along a state's border that are between 1 and 7 percent lower. For example, Michael Walsh and Jonathan Jones studied West Virginia's phased-in reduction of the sales-tax rate on grocery purchases.[34] For each percentage point reduction in the sales-tax rate they found that grocery sales along the West Virginia border increased by about 5.9 percent. It is expected that differential sales-tax rates across jurisdictions within a state would have similar, if not greater, effects on the location of purchases.

There is also related research on tax-base mobility that uses an interstate tax-rate differential to estimate the effect on economic activity. Stephen Mark, Therese McGuire, and Leslie Papke examined economic activity over nine jurisdictions in the DC metropolitan area, which includes two states and DC, and found a negative relationship between sales taxes and economic activity.[35] In addition, there is some evidence that increased reliance on sales taxes increases the competition for retail development among local governments.[36]

Regarding vertical equity, compared to the property tax, sales taxes are more regressive, when measured as a percentage of current income. The Institute on Taxation & Economic Policy has estimated the tax burden for the property tax and sales tax for all fifty states.[37] As can be seen in figure 17.6, which uses Georgia as an example, the sales tax is very regressive and is much more regressive than the property tax. While the distribution of tax burdens would differ across states, the pattern would be similar. However, if one measures the sales-tax burden by using lifetime income, the sales tax is much less regressive, and perhaps proportional.[38]

An important characteristic of a particular tax base is its cyclical stability. Most studies of tax-base stability find that the sales-tax base is more volatile than the

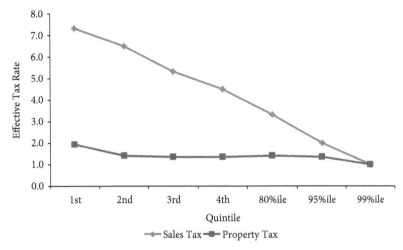

Figure 17.6 Effective tax rates, Georgia
Source: Institute on Taxation & Economic Policy.

property-tax base.[39] Property-tax revenue is even more stable than the property-tax base because the rate is set after the jurisdiction determines the property-tax base.[40]

A final feature of the sales tax is the purported benefit that it is nearly invisible (i.e., one hardly notices the few pennies paid on each purchase). While this may be a benefit from the elected official's point of view, it weakens the link between the decision regarding the level of public expenditures and the tax price. Given the visibility of the property tax and voter resistance to property-tax increases, elected officials are thought to be more conservative in their budget decisions when they rely on the property tax.

LOCAL INCOME TAX

Reliance on Local Income Taxes

The late 1940s and the 1960s were two periods of substantial increases in the adoption of local income taxes. In 2008, local income taxes were imposed in thirteen states (excluding DC) (table 17.5). New Jersey (Newark) and California (San Francisco) have local payroll taxes, but the Census Bureau does not classify them as income taxes and therefore does not report revenue as income tax; thus, these two states are not included in table 17.5.[41] In most of the states with local income taxes, very few local governments actually have local income or payroll taxes; for example, one city in Delaware, two cities in Missouri and in New York (including New York City),

Table 17.5 Local income-tax revenue as a percentage of local tax revenue, 2008

State	Percentage	State	Percentage
Maryland	35.6%	Missouri	4.0%
Kentucky	25.6%	Michigan	3.6%
New York	22.2%	Alabama	2.2%
Ohio	21.0%	Iowa	1.8%
Pennsylvania	17.9%	Oregon	1.4%
Delaware	7.3%	Kansas	0.1%
Indiana	7.0%		

Source: US Bureau of the Census (2008).

and two transit districts in Oregon have local income taxes. Box 17.3 provides a description of the local income or payroll tax in each state.

In 2008, local income taxes accounted for more than 10 percent of local tax revenue in only five states (table 17.5): Pennsylvania at 17.9 percent; Ohio at 21 percent; New York at 22.2 percent; Kentucky at 25.6 percent; and Maryland at 35.6 percent. Figure 17.5 shows the growth in local income taxes as a share of total local-tax revenue; there has been little growth in local income taxes as a percentage of taxes since 1980. In 2008, local income taxes were 6.1 percent of local tax revenue. Most large cities that currently use the income tax adopted it by 1970.

Characteristics of Local Income Taxes

Sally Wallace and Barbara Edwards have provided an overview of the structure of local income taxes. In most cases, the local income tax is a relatively simple tax.[42] Rates vary from less than 1 percent to almost 5 percent (with 1 percent being a common tax rate); in Iowa the tax is a percentage of the state income tax. Typically the tax applies to wages and salaries, but not income from capital. The income tax in Kansas, however, applies only to the return on intangible assets. Some local income taxes are levied by place of work, while others are based on place of residence. An exception is in the Detroit area where essentially the tax is split evenly between the jurisdiction of residence and the jurisdiction of employment. While there is some uniformity across states in local income taxes, the differences are larger than for the local sales tax. Like with the local sales tax, the types of jurisdiction that are eligible to use an income tax vary across states.

Local governments in Ohio are significant users of local income taxes. Nearly all municipal governments impose an income tax at rates that generally range from 1 percent to 3 percent, with an average rate of 1.3 percent. The municipal income tax is a worksite-based tax. There is also a school district income tax in Ohio that is used by about 35 percent of the school districts. The rate for a school district

Box 17.3 Descriptions of local income taxes, 2011

State	Jurisdictions	Tax Rates	Tax Base
Alabama	Cities of Bessemer, Birmingham, and Gadsen; Jefferson and Macon Counties	Tax rates range from 0.45% to 2%	Gross receipts of people engaged in trade, occupation, or business; worksite based
California	Los Angeles and San Francisco have a payroll tax on employers	Tax rate is 1.5%	Payroll by place of work
Delaware	Wilmington	Tax rate is 1.25%	Earnings, including net profits, of residents and for work within Wilmington by nonresidents
Indiana	Indiana County AGI Tax (CAGIT) is used in all fifty-six counties	Allowable tax rates are 0.5%, 0.75%, or 1.0%, although ten counties can impose a rate in excess of 1%; actual tax rates range from 0.5% to 1.3%; tax rate for nonresidents is 0.25%	Indiana taxable income of county residents and income attributed to the county for nonresidents who do not reside in a county with a CAGIT, COIT, or CEDIT
	Indiana County Economic Development Tax (CEDIT) is used in seventy-five counties	Allowable tax rates range from 0.1% to 0.5% (with some exceptions); actual tax rates vary from 0.1% to 0.56%; the combined CAGIT and CEDIT tax rates cannot exceed 1%	Indiana taxable income of county residents and income attributed to the county for nonresidents who do not reside in a county with a CAGIT, COIT, or CEDIT
	Indiana County Option Income Tax (COIT) is used in twenty-eight counties	Tax rates cannot exceed 0.6%, but can go to 1% with voter approval	Indiana taxable income of county residents and income attributed to the county for nonresidents who do not reside in a county with a CAGIT, COIT, or CEDIT
	Indiana Local Option Income Tax (LOIT) is used in 24 counties. Revenue is used to freeze property tax levy, for property tax relief, or for public safety	Maximum tax rate is 1%, but restrictions apply to the tax rates depending on the purpose	Indiana Taxable Income of county residents and income attributed to the county for nonresidents who do not reside in a county with a county tax

(Continued)

Box 17.3 Continued

State	Jurisdictions	Tax Rates	Tax Base
Iowa	The tax is used by 554 school districts and Appanoose County	Tax rates range from 1% to 20%	A surtax on state income tax
Kansas	The Intangible Income Tax is imposed in most municipalities and counties	Most tax rates are set at 2.25%	Imposed as tax on income from intangibles
Kentucky	First class cities, and large counties and school districts may levy an occupational license tax on the net profits of businesses and/or on the salaries and wages of employees earned in the jurisdiction. The tax is used in many jurisdictions	Maximum tax rate for cities and counties over 300,000 population is 1.25%. Counties with a population over 30,000 can levy a tax up to 1%. Maximum tax rate for school districts is 0.5%. Actual tax rates range from 0.25% to 2.5%	Earned income by worksite. The school district tax does not apply to non-residents. Where both the city and county levy an occupational license tax, a credit may be given, at the option of the local governments, for the amount paid to the city against the occupational license tax of the county
Maryland	All 23 counties plus the City of Baltimore	Tax rates range from 1.25% to 3.20%	Maryland taxable income. Applies to residents and to nonresidents deriving compensation in the taxing county
Michigan	Twenty-two cities	Maximum tax rates are 1% for residents and corporations; the rate for nonresidents is half of the applicable rate for residents. Maximum rates are higher in Detroit (2.5%) Highland Park (2%), Saginaw (1.5%) and Grand Rapids (1.5%)	Applies to all income for residents and income arising from sources within the city for nonresidents. Residents receive a credit for tax imposed on income from outside the city of residence
Missouri	Kansas City and St. Louis	Tax rate is 1%	Applies to earnings of residents and net profits of unincorporated business in the city and earnings within the city for nonresidents

(Continued)

Box 17.3 Continued			
State	Jurisdictions	Tax Rates	Tax Base
New Jersey	Newark has a payroll tax on employers	Tax rate is 1%	Payroll by place of work
New York	New York City has a progressive income tax. Yonkers has an income tax surtax	The top New York City tax rate is 3.648%. Yonkers tax rate is 5%	For NYC: New York state taxable income. For Yonkers earnings (of individuals, trusts and estates) for residents and earning (of individuals, trusts, and estates) within Yonkers for nonresidents
Ohio	Municipal Income Tax is imposed in 710 municipalities	The maximum tax rate without voter approval is 1%. Actual rates range from 0.4% to 3%	Wages, salary, and other compensation plus net profits attributable to the municipality
	The School District Income tax is imposed in 278 school districts	There is no limit on the tax rate, but it is subject to voter approval. Actual tax rates vary from 0.25% to 2%	There are two possible tax bases. Most districts use the state taxable income. 29 districts used earned income
Oregon	The Tri-Met Transit District (Portland) and Lane County Transit District (Eugene and Springfield)	Rate is 0.6319% in Portland and 0.6% in Eugene	Gross earnings by place of work
Pennsylvania	The Earned Income Tax is imposed in most of the 2621 townships and cities as well as by local school districts	Combined tax rates are 2.00% or less, except for Philadelphia (3.98%), Pittsburgh (3%), Reading (2.7%), Scranton (3.4%), Wilkes-Barre (2.85%)	Earned income. Both residents and nonresidents are subject to taxes. In most cities, nonresidents get a credit if the resident's city imposes an income tax

Sources: Henchman (2008); Lohman (2005); Advisory Commission on Intergovernmental Relations (1988); various state departments of revenue websites.

income tax is generally 1 percent, and the school districts have a choice between an income tax that is residence based and an earnings tax that is worksite based. In Iowa, the local income tax is used only by school districts; about 82 percent of the districts have adopted the local income tax, which is a surtax on the state income-tax liability. Rates generally range between 6 percent and 10 percent.

As with local sales taxes, in most states, the allowable local income-tax rate is generally set by the state. And thus as was the case with the local sales tax, local governments have no control at the margin over its revenue structure.

To the extent that a household's demand (and thus marginal benefit) for local public services is positively related to household income, then the income tax is related to benefits. However, because preferences can vary across households with the same income levels, the association between benefits and income tax will be closer for some households than others. Furthermore, there is no formal theory similar to that for the property tax that concludes that the income tax is a benefits tax. Thus, as with the local sales tax, the argument that the local income tax is a benefits tax has not been demonstrated.

One possible exception is K-12 education. Robert Strauss has argued that the benefits of K-12 education are more closely associated with income than with property wealth.[43] He argued that education generates social benefits and is a form of social insurance; he concluded that education should be financed by a broad-based, ability-to-pay tax. Thus, a broad income or consumption tax would be an appropriate revenue instrument for financing education. In some states (Arkansas, Iowa, Kentucky, and Ohio), local income taxes are used to fund school districts.

Like the local sales tax, a local income tax, if it is imposed on workers, will impose a tax burden on nonresident workers and thus generate revenue to pay for local public services provided to nonresident workers. However, in many states the local income tax is mainly taxed on residents. Furthermore, a local income tax will generate revenue only from workers and not from other visitors (e.g., tourists) to the jurisdiction.

Much of the research on the effect of local income taxes on tax-base mobility has focused on Philadelphia, for which differential income-tax rates have been shown to result in the migration of workers across the region. Ronald Grieson estimated that Philadelphia lost 14 percent of its employment between 1965 and 1975 as a result of its high income-tax rate, which was three to four times the tax rate in surrounding jurisdictions.[44] Robert Inman and others obtained an estimated elasticity of employment with respect to the wage tax rate of between −0.11 and −0.14 for Philadelphia. That is, for every 10 percent increase in the tax rate, employment fell by 1.1 to 1.4 percent.[45] Thomas Luce obtained an elasticity of −0.6 for the wage tax-rate differential by using data from the Philadelphia area, that is, an increase of 10 percent in the tax differential results in an estimated decrease in employment of 6 percent.[46]

Because local income taxes are generally flat-rate taxes with few if any exemptions, they score well in terms of economic efficiency, although they provide an incentive to increase the capital-to-labor ratio. Local income taxes can also affect the size of the city. David Wildasin constructed a monocentric urban model and demonstrated that under certain conditions an income tax results in a larger, more dispersed urban area and in a reduction in welfare.[47]

Local income taxes are probably slightly regressive because not all income sources are taxed and the excluded income (largely returns to capital) is largely associated with higher-income households. However, no study of the equity of local income taxes was identified. States that tie the local income tax to the state income tax (for example, Maryland) have a progressive local income tax, and the local income tax has less horizontal inequities because a larger percentage of total income is taxed. New York City's income is more like a state income tax, in that most sources of income are taxed and there is a progressive tax-rate structure.

CONCLUSIONS

Reliance on the property tax has declined among local governments, particularly for counties and municipalities, as these governments have increased user fees, local sales taxes, and local income taxes. The result has been an increase in the level of diversity of local government revenue structures over the past sixty years, although there was little increase in diversity over the past twenty years. But there is wide variation across the country in the level of local government revenue diversity. One indicator is that local governments in Connecticut generated only 17.6 percent of own-source revenue from sources other than property taxes, while in Alabama it was 80.2 percent.

There are many advantages to having a diversified local government revenue structure. First, the revenue-raising capacity of particular revenue sources differs across local jurisdictions. Thus, a diverse set of potential revenue sources is more likely to allow local governments to generate needed revenue in the most effective way for a jurisdiction. More broadly, if a local government can use alternative revenue instruments, it can choose the revenue portfolio that achieves the desired mix of characteristics such as growth, stability, equity, and so on. Second, having access to nonproperty-revenue sources means that local governments can reduce their reliance on property taxes. Third, a diverse revenue system reduces the likelihood that beneficiaries can avoid paying a fair share of the cost of public services. Fourth, a diversified revenue structure is likely to add to the stability of total revenue over the business cycle. Fifth, a final advantage for revenue diversification is that financing local public services through user charges and fees promotes a more efficient level of public services.

The principal sources of nonproperty-tax revenue are user fees, local sales taxes, and local income taxes, which composed 25.4 percent, 7.2 percent, and 3.8 percent of own-source revenues, respectively, in 2008. But there has been little increase in their shares of own-source revenues over the past twenty years, despite voter opposition to property taxes.

User charges are very desirable because they lead to a more economically efficient level of public services. But user fees can be difficult to implement and inappropriate for many public services, and thus their importance varies across public services. In response to the financial crisis of 2008, local governments overwhelmingly turned to user charges and fees to shore up their revenues. The 2009 ICMA State of the Profession Survey found that 46 percent of the responding local governments indicated that they had increased existing fees and 23 percent had added new fees.[48]

Nonetheless, given the wide variation in the reliance on fees and charges, there is room for an increase in their usage. The fact that 23 percent of respondents introduced new fees, although most of the new fees were very similar to fees already being used in other cities, indicates that many cities have not tapped into this revenue source.

Sales and income taxes are thought to be tax options that are preferred to the property tax, and thus it is surprising that there has not been an increase in the reliance on these two taxes. In 2008, local sales taxes were used in thirty-three states and accounted for 11.6 percent of total local taxes while local income or payroll taxes were imposed in fifteen states and made up 6.1 percent of total local-tax revenue. There is wide variation across states in the reliance on local sales and income taxes.

There are several potential drawbacks with local sales or local income taxes. First, unlike the property tax, they are not related to the benefit of local public services. Second, there is concern that they will result in increases in expenditures. Third, these taxes are less stable and are more geographically mobile than the property tax.

One of the main reasons for the lack of adoption of these two taxes seems to be that states have not granted all local governments permission to adopt these taxes. Furthermore, in most states the allowable tax rate is set by the state, and revenue is frequently earmarked for expenditures on specific services. This reduces the control that local governments have over the use of these taxes. However, it is also the case that many local governments have not adopted local sales and income taxes even when allowed to do so, and they have not relied on user fees to the greatest extent. So, increased local revenue diversity will occur only if state governments grant permission to more local governments to use these two taxes and allow more discretion in the use of the revenues, and if local governments exercise their existing authority to impose sales and income taxes and increase their reliance on user fees.

Notes

1 Snell (1993); Tannenwald (2001); Wallace (2010).
2 US Bureau of the Census (1951).
3 US Bureau of the Census, State and Local Government Finance (2008). Property tax revenues include the taxes imposed on the value of real property and personal property, whether tangible or intangible, as well as penalties and interest on delinquent property taxes and the proceeds of tax sales and tax redemptions. Payments-in-lieu-of-taxes are not included.
4 The revenue sources used are the property tax, general sales tax, specific selective sales taxes, personal income taxes, corporate income taxes (which are zero in nearly all states), motor vehicle licenses, other taxes, current charges, and miscellaneous revenue.
5 See, for example, Advisory Commission on Intergovernmental Relations (1988).
6 Yilmaz and Zahradnik (2008); Wallace (2010).
7 Cole and Kincaid (2000).
8 White (1983); Misiolek and Perdue (1987); Dye and McGuire (1991); Harmon and Mallick (1994).
9 Bierhanzl and Downing (1998); Downing (1999); Duff (2004).

10 Hamilton (1975); Fischel (2001).

11 See Zodrow (2001).

12 Buchanan (1967); Buchanan and Wagner (1977).

13 Wagner (1976); Ladd and Weist (1987). For a review of the literature, see Sjoquist, Walker, and Wallace (2005); Sjoquist, Wallace, and Edwards (2004).

14 Further detail is available at US Bureau of the Census, *State and Local Government Finances,* various years.

15 Boyd and Jones (2010); Garner, North Carolina (2010); Ramsey, Minnesota (2010).

16 Bierhanzl and Downing (1998); Downing (1999); Duff (2004).

17 Gómez-Ibáñez and Small (1994); Small and Gómez-Ibáñez (1998).

18 Niskanen (1971).

19 Duff (2004); Fisher (2007).

20 Fisher (2007); Downing (1999).

21 Odeck and Brathen (2008).

22 Holmgren (2007).

23 Kinnaman (2006).

24 ICMA (2010).

25 Finley (2010).

26 National League of Cities (2009).

27 Watts (2010).

28 Leinwand (2010).

29 Dillon (2010).

30 Downing (1992).

31 Duff (2004).

32 Due and Mikesell (1994).

33 See, for example, Mikesell (1971); Mikesell and Zorn (1986); Fisher (1980); Fox (1986); Walsh and Jones (1988); Tosun and Skidmore (2007).

34 Walsh and Jones (1988).

35 Mark, McGuire, and Papke (2000).

36 Lewis (2001).

37 Institute on Taxation & Economic Policy (2009).

38 Fullerton and Rogers (1993).

39 Dye and Merriman (2005).

40 Matthews (2005); Winters (2007).

41 The Census Bureau considers payroll taxes imposed on businesses a business tax, not an income tax.

42 Wallace and Edwards (1999).

43 Strauss (1995).

44 Grieson (1980).

45 Inman, Hines, Preston, and Weiss (1987).

46 Luce (1994).

47 Wildasin (1985).

48 ICMA (2010).

References

Advisory Commission on Intergovernmental Relations (ACIR) (1988). *Local Revenue Diversification: Local Sales Taxes.* SR-12. http://www.library.unt.edu/gpo/acir/Reports/staff/SR-12.pdf.

Bierhanzl, Edward J., and Paul B. Downing (1998). "User Charges and Bureaucratic Inefficiency." *Atlantic Economic Journal* 26(2):175–189.

Boyd, David A., and Monica J. Jones (2010). *City of Smyrna, Georgia, Schedule of Fees and Charges, 2010.* http://www.smyrnacity.com/Modules/ShowDocument. aspx?documentid=1012. Accessed September 15, 2010.

Buchanan, James M. (1967). *Public Finance in a Democratic Process.* Chapel Hill: University of North Carolina Press.

Buchanan, James M., and Richard Wagner (1977). *Democracy in Deficit: The Political Legacy of Lord Keynes.* New York: Academic Press.

Cole, Richard L., and John Kincaid (2000). "Public Opinion and American Federalism: Perspectives on Taxes, Spending, and Trust—An ACIR Update." *Publius* 30(1):189–201.

Dillon, Sam (2010, September 10). "Public Schools Face Lawsuit over Fees." *New York Times.* http://www.nytimes.com/2010/09/10/education/10education.html?_r=1.

Downing, Paul B. (1992). "The Revenue Potential of User Charges in Municipal Finance." *Public Finance Quarterly* 20(4): 512–527.

Downing, Paul B. (1999). "User Charges, Impact Fees, and Service Charges." In *Handbook on Taxation*, edited by W. Bartley Hildreth. New York: Marcel Dekker. 239–262.

Due, John F., and John L. Mikesell (1994). *Sales Taxation: State and Local Structure and Administration.* 2nd ed. Washington, DC: Urban Institute Press.

Duff, David G. (2004). "Benefit Taxes and User Fees in Theory and Practice." *University of Toronto Law Journal* 54: 391–447.

Dye, Richard F., and Therese J. McGuire (1991). "Growth and Variability of State Individual Income and General Sales Taxes." *National Tax Journal* 44(1):55–60.

Dye, Richard F., and David F. Merriman (2005). "State Revenue Stability: Alternative Conceptualizations." *Proceedings of the Ninety-Seventh Annual Conference on Taxation.* Washington, DC: National Tax Association. 258–268.

Finley, Bruce (2010, September 12). "Budget Cuts Leave State Parks Struggling to Handle More Visitors." *Denver Post.* http://www.denverpost.com/news/ci_16053952.

Fischel, William A. (2001). "Municipal Corporations, Homeowners, and the Benefit View of the Property Tax." In *Property Taxation and Local Government Finance*, edited by Wallace E. Oates. Cambridge, MA: Lincoln Institute of Land Policy. 33–77.

Fisher, Ronald C. (1980). "Local Sales Taxes: Tax Rate Differentials, Sales Loss, and Revenue Estimation." *Public Finance Quarterly* 8:171–188.

Fisher, Ronald C. (2007). "Pricing of Government Goods—User Charges." In *State and Local Public Finance.* Mason, OH: Thomson South-Western. 170–196.

Fox, William F. (1986). "Tax Structure and the Location of Economic Activity along State Borders." *National Tax Journal* 39:387–401.

Fullerton, Don, and Diane Lim Rogers (1993). *Who Bears The Lifetime Tax Burden?* Washington, DC: The Brookings Institute.

Gómez-Ibáñez, José A. and Kenneth A. Small (1994). *Road Pricing for Congestion Management: A Survey of International Practice.* Washington, DC: Transport Research Board, National Academy Press.

Garner, North Carolina (2010). *2010–2011 Town of Garner Fees and Charges.* http://www. ci.garner.nc.us/Publications/Administration/FeeSchedule_2010_2011.pdf. Accessed October 24, 2010.

Grieson, Ronald E. (1980). "Theoretical Analysis and Empirical Measurements of the Effects of the Philadelphia Income Tax." *Journal of Urban Economics* 8(1):123–137.

Hamilton, Bruce W. (1975). "Zoning and Property Taxation in a System of Local Governments." *Urban Studies* 12:205–211.

Harmon, Oskar Ragnar, and Rajiv Mallick (1994). "The Optimal State Tax Portfolio Model: An Extension." *National Tax Journal* 47(2):395–402.

Holmgren, Johan (2007). "Meta-Analysis of Public Transport Demand." *Transportation Research Part A* 41: 1021–1035.

ICMA (2010). *ICMA State of the Profession Survey Report 2009.* http://icma.org/en/icma/knowledge_network/documents/kn/Document/100267/ICMA_2009_State_of_the_Profession_Survey. Accessed June 2010.

Inman, Robert P., Sally Hines, Jeffrey Preston, and Richard Weiss (1987). "Philadelphia's Fiscal Management of Economic Transition." In *Local Fiscal Issues in the Philadelphia Metropolitan Area*, edited by Thomas F. Luce and Anita A. Summers. Philadelphia: University of Pennsylvania Press. 98–115.

Institute on Taxation & Economic Policy (2009). *Who Pays? A Distributional Analysis of the Tax Systems in All 50 States.* Washington, DC: Institute on Taxation & Economic Policy.

Kinnaman, Thomas C. (2006). "Examining the Justification for Residential Recycling." *Journal of Economic Perspectives* 20(4): 219–232.

Ladd, Helen F., and Dana R. Weist (1987). "State and Local Tax Systems: Balance among Taxes Versus Balance among Policy Goals." In *The Quest for Balance in State-Local Revenue Structures*, edited by Frederick D. Stocker. Tax Policy Roundtable/Property Tax Papers Series #TRP-16. Cambridge, MA: Lincoln Institute of Land Policy. 39–69.

Leinwand, Donna (2010, March 18). "Cities, States Tack on More User Fees." *USA Today.* http://www.usatoday.com/news/nation/2009–03–17-user-fees_N.htm.

Lewis, Paul G. (2001). "Retail Politics: Local Sales Taxes and the Fiscalization of Land Use." *Economic Development Quarterly* 15(1):21–35.

Lohman, Judith (2005). "Local Income Taxes." OLR Research Report 2005-R-08760. http://www.cga.ct.gov/2005/rpt/2005-r-0860.htm.

Luce Jr., Thomas F. (1994). "Local Taxes, Public Services, and the Intrametropolitan Location of Firms and Households." *Public Finance Quarterly* 22(2):139–167.

Mark, Stephen T., Therese J. McGuire, and Leslie E. Papke (2000). "The Influence of Taxes on Employment and Population Growth: Evidence from the Washington, DC Metropolitan Area." *National Tax Journal* 53(1):105–123.

Matthews, John (2005). *Tax Revenue Volatility and a State-Wide Education Sales Tax.* FRC Policy Brief No.109. Atlanta: Fiscal Research Center, Andrew Young School of Policy Studies, Georgia State University.

Mikesell, John L. (1971). "Sales Taxation and the Border County Problem." *Quarterly Review of Economics and Business* 11:23–29.

Mikesell, John L., and C. Kurt Zorn (1986). "Impact of the Sales Tax Rate on Its Base: Evidence from a Small Town." *Public Finance Quarterly* 14(3):329–338.

Misiolek, Walter, and D. Grady Perdue (1987). "The Portfolio Approach to State and Local Tax Structure." *National Tax Journal* 40(1):111–114.

National League of Cities (2009). *Alternative Revenue Sources for Cities.* http://www.nlc.org/ASSETS/ABE8C4B51BE744C0BDECB5B81A985F89/CPB%20-%20Alternative%20Revenue%20Sources%20for%20Cities%20Mar09.pdf.

Niskanen, Jr., William A. (1971). *Bureaucracy and Representative Government.* Chicago: Aldine.

Odeck, James, and Svein Brathen (2008). "Travel Demand Elasticities and Users Attitudes: A Case Study of Norwegian Toll Projects." *Transportation Research Part A* 42: 77–94.

Ramsey, Minnesota (2010). *City of Ramsey 2010 Adopted Schedule of Rates, Fees, and Charges.* http://www.ci.ramsey.mn.us/Documents/CMS/finance/rates/2010_Rates,_Fees,_and_Charges%5B1%5D.pdf. Accessed October 24, 2010.

Small, Kenneth A., and José A. Gómez-Ibáñez (1998). "Road Pricing for Congestion Management: The Transition from Theory to Policy." In *Road Pricing, Traffic Congestion and the Environment: Issues of Efficiency and Social Feasibility*, edited by Kenneth J. Button and Erik T. Verhoef. Northampton, MA: Edward Elgar. 213–246.

Sjoquist, David L., Mary Beth Walker, and Sally Wallace (2005). "Estimating Differential Responses to Local Fiscal Conditions: A Mixture Model Analysis." *Public Finance Review* 33(1):36–61.

Sjoquist, David L., Sally Wallace, and Barbara Edwards (2004). "What a Tangled Web: Local Property, Income and Sales Taxes." In *City Taxes, City Spending: Essays in Honor of Dick Netzer*, edited by Amy Ellen Schwartz. Northampton, MA: Edward Elgar. 42–70.

Snell, Ronald (1993). *Financing State Government in the 1990s*. Denver: National Conference of State Legislatures.

Strauss, Robert P. (1995). "Reducing New York's Reliance on the School Property Tax." *Journal of Education Finance* 21(1):123–164.

Tannenwald, Robert (2001). "Are State and Local Tax Systems Becoming Obsolete?" *New England Economic Review* 4:27–43.

Tosun, Mehmet S., and Mark L. Skidmore (2007). "Cross-Border Shopping and the Sales Tax: An Examination of Food Purchases in West Virginia." *B.E. Journal of Economic Analysis & Policy* 7(1):Art 63. http://www.bepress.com/bejeap/vol7/iss1/art63.

US Bureau of the Census (1951). *US Statistical Abstract*. 72nd ed. Washington, DC: US Printing Office.

US Bureau of the Census (2008). *State and Local Government Finances*. http://www.census.gov/govs/estimateWagner, Richard E. (1976). "Revenue Structure, Fiscal Illusion, and Budgetary Choice." *Public Choice* 25(Spring):45–61.

Wallace, Sally (2010). *State and Local Fiscal Policy: Thinking Outside the Box*. Northampton, MA: Edward Elgar.

Wallace, Sally, and Barbara M. Edwards (1999). "Personal Income Tax." In *Handbook on Taxation*, edited by W. Bartley Hildreth and James A. Richardson. New York: Marcel Dekker. 149–190.

Walsh, Michael J., and Jonathan D. Jones (1988). "More Evidence on the 'Burden Tax' Effect: The Case of West Virginia, 1979–1984." *National Tax Journal* 61(2):261–265.

Watts, Jim (2010, August 31). "Kansas 'Driveway Tax' Derided." *Bond Buyer*. http://www.bondbuyer.com/issues/119_416/driveway-tax-derided-1016651-1.html.

White, Fred C. (1983). "Trade-Off in Growth and Stability in State Taxes." *National Tax Journal* 36(1):103–114.

Wildasin, David E. (1985). "Income Taxes and Urban Spatial Structure." *Journal of Urban Economics* 18(3):313–333.

Winters, John V. (2007). *Tax Revenue Stability of Replacing the Property Tax with a Sales Tax*. FRC Policy Brief. http://aysps.gsu.edu/frc/1415.html164. Atlanta: Fiscal Research Center, Andrew Young School of Policy Studies, Georgia State University.

Yilmaz, Yesim, and Robert Zahradnik (2008). "Measuring the Fiscal Capacity of the District of Columbia—A Comparison of Revenue Raising Capacity and Expenditure Need, Fiscal 2005." Washington, DC: National Tax Association.

Zodrow, George R. (2001). "Reflections on the New View and the Benefit View of the Property Tax." In *Property Taxation and Local Government Finance*, edited by Wallace E. Oates. Cambridge, MA: Lincoln Institute of Land Policy. 79–111.

CHAPTER 18

STATE TAX ADMINISTRATION: SEVEN PROBLEMS IN SEARCH OF A SOLUTION

BILLY HAMILTON

THE current era of state-tax administration, like the current era of state-tax policy, began as the 1970s ended. The basic form of today's state-tax agencies essentially was in place by 1980. By that time, the states had adopted a number of structural reforms that were intended to centralize tax-collection activities and improve their efficiency and effectiveness. Most states had begun appointing rather than electing heads of tax agencies, and the administration of major taxes had been consolidated in most states into a single agency. In addition, departments had been reorganized along functional rather than tax-type lines.[1]

The first computerized tax systems had made their appearance, although these were the early days of information processing. The Internet would not gain its public face, the World Wide Web, for another decade, but the basic elements that would enable the Internet revolution were falling rapidly into place. Still unknown to most people, the Internet already existed in its early form, and the first successful commercial personal computers had been introduced in 1977. The IBM PC made its appearance in 1981.

At the same time, the elements also were falling into place for what would become a seismic transformation of the environment in which revenue agencies operate. The tax revolt flared in California with the passage of Proposition 13 in 1978, and the movement eventually spread nationally. Tax policy became a political pinball, and in the difficult years surrounding the 1981–1982 recession, an increasing focus of corporate tax interest. Beginning in 1978 and extending well into the new century, states cycled through periods of lowering, raising, and then lowering taxes once again in reaction to a mixture of tax protests, economic recession, and economic recovery. Business-tax incentives began to proliferate, and states began to offer tax amnesties in the early 1980s. Between the end of 1981 and early 1990, at least thirty states had run amnesty programs.[2]

Beyond their potential to produce a quick shot of revenue, the proliferation of tax amnesties also showed that states were becoming more conscious of the challenges posed by noncompliance with their tax laws. While the Internal Revenue Service (IRS) had undertaken detailed studies of tax compliance as early as 1962, states were only just beginning to worry about the "tax gap," an issue brought to prominence in the late 1970s by news reports of billions of dollars of unreported transactions in the "underground economy." Tax administration was also lagging. Clara Penniman observed in 1980, for example, that while income-tax administration had improved since the late 1950s, it had not "kept pace with the growing volume of taxpayers or the increasing complexities of enforcement."[3]

Penniman's observations might apply equally well today. Tax administrators must deal with a world that has changed fundamentally in the past three decades relying on an administrative structure that is still fundamentally the same as one that could be found in 1980. Certainly, there have been many innovations in the profession in the past thirty years. It has become faster and more automated. Data collection and analysis have become more sophisticated, and audit techniques have been refined. More attention has been directed at "customer service." Still, the structure itself isn't so very different than it was when the tax revolt first burst into the national consciousness.

Although configurations vary from agency to agency, the core functions of tax administration—collection and processing, policy and compliance—are the same. And it remains a challenge for agencies to keep pace with the growing volume of taxpayers and the increasing complexities posed by the tax system. If anything, the problems have become even more acute. In effect, states are dealing with a twenty-first-century economy with a twentieth-century administrative structure, just as it equally can be said that they are trying—and often failing—to deal with a twenty-first-century economy with a twentieth-century tax structure.

These problems were magnified beginning in late 2007 by the financial system meltdown and the resulting "Great Recession," which put enormous stress on state budgets.[4] State-tax collections plummeted nationwide with few exceptions during the period from late 2007 through 2010, and states were forced to take drastic measures to bring budgets into balance. Tax agencies were not always immune from these cuts as they often had been in past budget crises.

With revenues declining at unprecedented rates, revenue agencies also found themselves under increased pressure to collect every dollar owed to the state to help close budget shortfalls, often while dealing with the problem of a workforce that was shrinking in relation to the taxpayer population. Agencies were called on to implement, often without adequate resources, the often lurching attempts of lawmakers to find ways, through taxes and other policies, to fill revenue gaps, to bolster economic development, or to constrain the tax system in various ways (often conflicting goals), and these goals were often pursued simultaneously and generally were higher in political than policy content.

The recession did not just create new problems for state-tax administration; it also exposed the challenges that already confronted the profession. Taking a cue from the "tax gap" that administrators and academics often talked about, there are at least seven "gaps," including the tax gap, that pose significant challenges to state-tax administration today.

THE DATA GAP: HOW LITTLE WE KNOW
ABOUT WHAT WE KNOW

States are diverse political entities. Still carrying vestiges of the preindustrial society that created them, they have been, for much of their existence, relatively free to develop their own institutional arrangements. Certainly they share many common features, but each state has developed its own vision of how its state and local governments should function and relate to one another. The list of differences is practically inexhaustible. Some states have strong governors and a cabinet-style administrative structure, while others rely on a series of more or less autonomous boards and commissions. Some have legislative-centric budgeting and a weak governor. Some elect a number of top administrative heads; most do not. Some put a greater burden on local governments, while others provide extensive aid to local governments. This list goes on.

This diversity is one of the strengths of a federal system. It is one explanation for why states have been, in the words of Justice Louis Brandeis, "laboratories of democracy." They have been free to innovate according to their own needs and political constraints. It is not an entirely closed loop though. Over time, states also have learned from one another, although as an active and extensive process, this is largely the product of the late twentieth century. While the National Governors Association dates from 1908, the National Conference of State Legislatures was not created until 1975. The National Association of State Budget Officers was created in 1945. The two chief associations of state tax agencies—the Federation of Tax Administrators (FTA) and the Multistate Tax Commission (MTC)—were created in 1937 and 1967, respectively.

The MTC, which has never included all of the states in its membership, was created to avoid federal preemption in the state treatment of multistate taxpayers and has always had a more limited focus than the FTA, which is an association of tax administrators from all of the states plus the District of Columbia and New York City. The FTA was organized during the Depression by representatives of the North American Gasoline Tax Conference (NAGTC), the National Association of Tax Administrators (NATA), and the National Tobacco Tax Association (NTTA), all separate organizations at that time and for a long period thereafter. In 1984, the three associations consolidated into a single organization: the NATA. The NAGTC became the NATA Motor Fuel Tax Section, and the NTTA became the NATA Tobacco Tax Section. In June 1988, the NATA merged with the FTA, taking the Federation of Tax Administrators as its name.

The two associations' multistate structures provide numerous opportunities for information sharing through meetings, training, and, more recently, through electronic information sharing. Agencies can learn from one another and join together to act collectively on issues of common interest, often involving federal government involvement in state-tax issues. The Streamlined Sales Tax Project (SSTP) is a recent example of this cooperation.[5] The FTA also provides a forum for state interaction with the IRS, which has paid dividends to tax administrators in terms of improved filing methodologies and information sharing.

These associations have, however, proved of only limited value in providing a collective set of information on state-tax administration. With limited staffs, the associations of necessity focus on policy matters—how services are taxed under the sales tax, for example, or what Congress is doing on a given matter—and not on the comparative structure of tax administration. There are exceptions. The FTA has sections that deal specifically with issues with motor fuel tax and tobacco tax collection, and technology and revenue estimating. States also share successful programs in a sort of "how-to" format at annual conferences where the best of these ideas are recognized and presented awards. However, a clear understanding of the actual inner workings of the agencies themselves has proven more elusive, a result of the diverse nature of the agencies themselves.

Efforts to provide greater detail on the nitty-gritty of tax administration have proven difficult to sustain. During the 1990s and early 2000s, the FTA, under the initial leadership of William Remington, then director of the Revenue Division of the Delaware Department of Finance, made a concerted effort to develop a common set of core performance measures for comparison among the states. The task proved difficult (and ultimately unsuccessful) partly because of differences in the definition of various measures and partly because the task often required reprogramming or reordering state systems to produce the information—and most state staff had other priorities.

This lack of a common database makes it difficult to effectively analyze the issues facing tax administrators today, except anecdotally. In effect, we have a sense of what the problems are and we understand their common features, but there is no common system for collecting and presenting that information. There is some research literature on the topic, but even that is limited by the passage of time and the changes that occur from one state administration to the next. Very few people spend years and years heading revenue agencies. Such jobs tend to be short-term assignments, although many of the people who actually work in the agencies are around for extended periods.

As a result, we know more about the range of state-tax policy choices than we do about the specifics of how individual states administer those choices. This is another gap that should be filled if the goal is improved tax administration. But this particular gap poses a major limitation on researchers. Agencies can, through the FTA, share information when they wish. It is surprising, though, how limited the information sharing is except on a few specific issues of common interest—federal preemption being a primary example.[6] Tax agencies are, to some degree, islands in a chain, each isolated yet part of a whole, each more focused on its own issues than on those of its neighbors. And yet, for all that, the problems are pretty much the same no matter which island you visit. In the current economic climate, they begin with the limits on resources for administering the tax laws.

THE RESOURCE GAP

It is axiomatic in public administration that administrators seldom have all of the resources they believe they need to do their jobs properly. State-tax agencies face this issue like any other public agency. They must subdivide their legislative appropriations among a large number of tasks and make decisions on the right balance between, for example, technology investments and additional compliance staff. These decisions have a certain inertial logic from year to year—the tax compliance staff is in place, the computers are available—but the decisions are never simple. What is the right mix of auditors to phone collection staff? How important is tax enforcement in the mix? Which goal has the highest priority: making tax information available as quickly as possible, extending audit coverage, or making sure that current collections are deposited rapidly? There is no set formula. Each can lay claim to being important, and they all depend on resources—mainly in the form of budget dollars—to succeed.

Staffing, though, is a particular concern. Tax administration still depends on people, for processing, customer service, auditing, and enforcement. Although revenue departments have used privatization to some degree (mainly to collect out-of-state taxes), more than half of the operating budget in any tax agency is committed to staff salaries and benefits. Tax administrators complain that they are unable to pay skilled staff—and particularly tax auditors—enough to slow an ongoing exodus to the private sector. The growing importance of state-tax and local-tax practices among accounting firms and the increased emphasis on state and local taxes by multistate corporations since the early 1980s has guaranteed that there will be a steady demand for knowledgeable staff from state tax agencies, which often, to their chagrin, wind up serving as training schools for the private sector.

In addition, technology is expensive and frequently risky to implement. Scan any state's capital news stories, and you'll find cases of large-scale computer system project failures in state government. Seizing on this, lawmakers, facing resource limitations in many budget areas, are hesitant to plow additional millions of dollars into computer systems that may be of a dubious pedigree or yield results only after years of expensive investment.

These work-a-day problems in state government budgeting were, however, seriously complicated by the 2007–2009 recession. The national recession that began in December 2007 created unprecedented budget challenges in virtually all states. The phrase "worst conditions since the Great Depression," whether true or not, was frequently heard in state after state. Some states experienced revenue declines as early as late 2007 as a result of the collapse of the housing market. Others did not experience severe fiscal challenges until after the financial sector crisis occurred in the fall of 2008. Some states, particularly those with prominent energy sectors, did not begin to feel the effects of the recession until much later, if at all. In addition, the large increase in federal funding for states under the American Recovery and Reinvestment Act of 2009 (ARRA) produced a major benefit in helping to limit the recession's immediate budget impact in many states but also created a situation where states faced a steep budget "cliff" in fiscal year 2011 as federal funding began to run out.

According to an analysis by the Washington-based Center on Budget and Policy Priorities, budget cuts were enacted in at least forty-six states plus the District of Columbia between 2008 and 2010 and occurred in all major areas of state services, including health care and services to the elderly and disabled, K-12 education, and higher education.[7] No budget area was entirely safe, including tax administration. States generally have invested more in tax agencies during past budget difficulties in an effort to increase revenues to help close the budget gap. In the 2007–2009 recession and its aftermath, though, the results were more mixed. While some agencies maintained their budgets, particularly in the tax compliance area, most experienced one or more of the following: across-the-board reductions, targeted budget cuts, hiring freezes, staff furloughs, early retirement programs, or layoffs as lawmakers searched for ways to balance state budgets.

Unfortunately, there is no good single source of information on the size and extent of these cuts or their effects on the revenue system, and much of the data that are available are anecdotal. However, by combining these data with what is known about the budget strategies followed in the states, it is possible to get a sense of the scope of the budget situation that confronted many tax administrators as the first decade of the new century came to a faltering end.

Table 18.1 shows the extent to which the states made use of various budget strategies in fiscal years 2009 and 2010 based on information from the National Association of State Budget Officers, the Center on Budget and Policy Priorities, and individual state budgets. These strategies cover a wide range of budget approaches from cuts in services to tax increases. From the standpoint of tax agencies, the key budget effects primarily have been felt in the changes that reduce staffing or make

Table 18.1 Strategies used to reduce or eliminate state budget shortfalls, fiscal years 2009–2010

Budget Option	Number of States		Notes
	2009	2010*	
Layoffs	19	26	Includes eliminating unfilled positions and actual reductions in the workforce.
Furloughs	15	22	Essentially, giving employees unpaid days off.
Early Retirement	6	6	
Salary Reductions	9	12	Pay cuts, often in lieu of layoffs.
Cuts in Benefits	6	9	Reductions in current or future retirement benefits or health-care commitments.
Across-the-Board Cuts	29	28	Five to ten percent is common.
Targeted Cuts	33	36	Many options: Closure of state facilities, cuts in K-12 eduction and higher education (often large budget items), reductions in budgeted travel, cancelation of scheduled pay increases, deferral of payments (e.g., deferral of payments to local school districts), and so on.
Reductions in Local Aid	17	22	Some states have (or had) large aid programs for local governments other than schools.
Reorganization of Agencies	7	14	Normally done to consolidate and reduce administrative costs.
Privatization	3	3	Examples include privatizing mail service, state-managed ports, state-run liquor stores and lotteries.
Rainy-Day Fund, Reserves	26	19	May include sweeping balances from other state funds.
Lottery Expansion	1	2	Typically adding Power Ball or Mega Millions multistate games.
Gaming Expansion	0	3	Not many, because most states already have broadest politically acceptable level of gaming and because gaming revenues are in a steep decline at present.

(Continued)

Table 18.1 Continued

Budget Option	Number of States 2009	Number of States 2010*	Notes
General Tax Increases	29	–	Total is number with net increases. May include some tax reductions along with increases. The figures for 2010 are not available because tax bills tend to be passed late in legislative sessions. Nine states had net tax cuts in 2009. The largest increases were in the sales and personal income taxes, mainly because of increases in California, Massachusetts, and New York.
User Fees	8	15	
Higher Education Fees	6	10	Often tuition or student fees that are exchanged for regular general fund appropriations.
Court-Related Fees	5	14	For example, states are considering new Super Speeder fines that add $200 to a speeding fine above 85 mph.
Transportation-Motor Vehicle Fees	8	11	Often higher vehicle registration fees.
Business-Related Fees and Taxes	3	9	Often higher license fees.
Other	16	23	Includes, among other things, sale and lease back of state assets, borrowing, debt restructuring, hiring freezes, and use of federal stimulus funds to fund current operations.

* Totals for 2010 reflect actions up to June 2010. Some legislatures are still in session.
Source: National Association of State Budget Officers, Federation of Tax Administrators, Center on Budget and Policy Priorities.

across-the-board or targeted cuts in agency budgets. The available data suggest that much of the impact was, in fact, a result of agency furloughs, which covered most agencies in the states where they were employed.

The range of results for individual tax agencies can be seen more clearly in table 18.2, which compiles data collected by the Federation of Tax Administrators through a survey of tax agencies (to which not all responded), with information about state budget documents and new accounts. It presents a limited (but the best available) picture of the effects of the recession on tax agencies.

Table 18.2 Budget reduction measures, selected state tax agencies, fiscal years 2009–2011

Arizona	Layoffs in fiscal 2009. Furloughs in fiscal years 2010, 2011, and 2012.
California	Furloughs. The state tax agencies, the Board of Equalization and Franchise Tax Board, were exempted from furloughs beginning in late 2010.
Colorado	Furlough days in fiscal 2010.
Connecticut	Hiring freeze and furloughs.
Florida	Authorization to continue hiring auditors.
Georgia	Added tax auditors to increase state revenues.
Hawaii	Need governor's approval to hire. Furloughs twice a month; reduction in force (layoffs) prior to furlough.
Illinois	Hiring freeze but agency was allowed to continue hiring auditors. Management has twenty-four mandatory furlough days in the fiscal year, while union supervisors and auditors have voluntary furlough days.
Kentucky	Furlough and hiring freeze.
Louisiana	State had a state hiring freeze but the agency was exempted. The agency was also given funding to hire twenty additional auditors. No furloughs or layoffs were made in the audit program, but the agency did undertake a layoff-avoidance measure whereby employees that were eligible to retire were given an incentive of approximately six months of the payroll savings realized by their retiring no later than August 13, 2010. The agency was required to keep these positions vacant for a year. Fifty-three employees took advantage of this measure agencywide, which included a number of field audit employees.
Maine	Hiring freeze and ten furlough days in fiscal 2010 and another ten furlough days in fiscal 2011.
Massachusetts	State imposed a hiring freeze and furloughs. It also offered voluntary incentives to reduce the state workforce. Layoffs were considered but not adopted in the fall of 2009.
Montana	None
Nebraska	Two furlough days in July 2010 after end of year revenue shortfall.
Oregon	Ten furlough days in 2010–2011
Texas	Agency given additional funding in 2009 for added auditors. All agencies required to make a 5% reduction in fiscal 2010–2011 budget and submit budgets for fiscal 2012–2013 that is 10% below current funding. Approximately 300 jobs reduced through attrition.
Washington	State furlough program. Revenue agents exempted.
Wisconsin	Sixteen furlough days for each full-time equivalent position from July 1, 2009, through June 30, 2011. On a case-by-case basis, the agency is allowed to fill vacant positions such as office auditors, field auditors, audit supervisors, etc.
Wyoming	Hiring freeze; reduction of four positions

Source: Federation of Tax Administrators Survey, summer 2010; survey of individual agency budgets and websites.

Based on the survey findings, revenue departments were most heavily affected by state furlough policies. As states struggled with the need to cut state budgets, they often found it necessary to reduce labor costs, because, as is the case with tax agencies, salaries and benefits are a major component of the total operating budget in many state agencies. Reviewing the news articles surrounding some of these furlough programs, it is obvious that the goal was to cut labor costs without the necessity of staff layoffs. Layoffs are often discussed, often in chilling terms, but a furlough plan is eventually adopted. Under such plans, employees take unpaid leave for a scheduled number of days in a fiscal year or in two or more fiscal years. Typically, the furlough days are distributed over the course of the year to avoid excessive disruption of services. This strategy gave rise, for example, to the common term "Furlough Fridays" in California where the furlough program, imposed on two different occasions, proved especially controversial, winding up, in the case of the fiscal 2011 program, in the state courts that ruled in the governor's favor. However, the revenue agencies had already been exempted from the second round of furloughs.

Only a handful of state-tax agencies were found to have experienced actual staff layoffs, and they were often limited in size. Perhaps the most significant tax agency staff reductions occurred in Arizona, one of the states hardest hit by the recession. In February 2009, the Arizona Department of Revenue laid off about two hundred staff members in an effort to reduce its budget by $9.5 million. Earlier, the agency had released fifty-three probationary employees. The department had an authorized work force of 1,164 but had a "soft" hiring freeze in place since the spring of 2008, which had reduced the workforce down to roughly 950 at the time of the layoffs. It had also used furloughs prior to the staff reduction. The loss was later reported as representing 44 percent of tax collection workers and auditors in the agency.

Of course, most people would recognize that tough budget times often place strains on government agencies like any other business, and they need to cut staff costs, if reasonable, particularly in a time when many private-sector firms faced similar difficulties and made similar decisions. The issue that arises in the case of staffing cuts at revenue agencies is whether they should be exempted because of their role in collecting money for the state. In Arizona's case, the department projected that the state would lose about $174 million through fiscal year 2010 in reduced collections of delinquent sales, income, and corporate taxes as a result of the reductions. However, prospective losses of even this magnitude are difficult to prove in a concrete way to lawmakers: at times, they are skeptical. In this case, the Arizona governor's office said tax collections would have dropped anyway as more companies wrestled with the recession, implying that the loss of collection workers had little effect.

A similar debate surrounded the proposed furlough of tax agency staff in California. After Governor Arnold Schwarzenegger ordered most of the state workforce to take two unpaid days off work starting in February 2009, he rejected a plea from the state Franchise Tax Board to be excluded. The 5,300 workers at the agency took an overall 14 percent cut in pay when a third furlough day was added by the governor on July 1. The unpaid days saved an estimated $65 million in Franchise Tax Board salaries by the time the furloughs ended in July 2010.

Under California's bifurcated administrative structure, the state's other major tax collector, the Board of Equalization, is an independent agency outside the governor's direct control. As such, it avoided furloughs. Eventually, in 2010 and extending into state fiscal year 2011, the courts were asked to measure the extent of the governor's authority to furlough employees, although by that time the revenue agencies were excluded from the governor's directive. The courts sided with the governor on his ability to furlough employees without legislative approval, and he subsequently vetoed legislation that specifically protected both the Franchise Tax Board and Board of Equalization.

However, escaping furloughs didn't mean either tax agency escaped the budget ax. Take, for example, the Board of Equalization. Like other constitutional offices that refused to impose furloughs on all workers, the tax agency had its budget cut by the administration by about as much as a 14 percent salary reduction. The Board of Equalization was directed to cut $41.5 million from its $465 million budget in 2009–2010. To meet the budget requirements, the board stopped hiring and promoting. It also dipped into its operating budget, with more than one thousand employees taking voluntary leave. In all, the agency cut about the $41.5 million demanded by the budget agencies.

The furloughs were not renewed for the two tax agencies when the governor sought to impose a new furlough plan in 2010 The new order exempts departments that collect revenue, such as the Franchise Tax Board. However, the extent of the damage to state-tax collections from the earlier furlough program was measured and laid out in a report by the California Senate Office of Oversight and Outcomes in a February 2010 report.[8] According to the report, the Franchise Tax Board estimated that $465 million in taxes would be lost because furloughed workers would not be on the job to pursue the money through audits and collection efforts.

The report found that, spared from furloughs, the Board of Equalization "did a better job of minimizing harm to tax revenue collection than the Franchise Tax Board could with furloughs. The Board of Equalization cut $41.5 million and will be unable to collect an estimated $264 million in tax money as a result." Taken together, the revenue lost at the two agencies offset almost half of the $1.66 billion in general fund saving that the state expected to save by furloughing *all* state workers two to three days a month. In total, the report concluded that California lost $6.36 tax dollars for every dollar saved through budget cuts at the Board of Equalization and lost $7.15 for every dollar saved through furloughs at the Franchise Tax Board.

This is not to argue that state-tax agencies should be exempt from reviews of their operations or that they should be immune to the ongoing search for budget savings. However, policymakers need to recognize that the decision to cut revenue department budgets can carry significant consequences—an experienced tax auditor on a business account can often produce a $600-per-hour return—and the effects of well-intended budget policies that are imposed across the board can be a major impediment to actually accomplishing budget goals.

This problem has been magnified by the recession and the difficulty of the budget decisions required, but it applies in the normal course of state business. With the resistance to tax increases that has grown up in many states in the last thirty years in the wake of the tax revolt and the increasing demands on state budgets in areas like public education, social services, and health care, budget issues and the resource gap they create are a persistent problem for most tax agencies. This is an unfortunate development for the fair and efficient administration of the tax laws, and it adds to the next important gap in current state-tax administration—the tax gap—how much of the existing tax due to a state is finally collected and how much escapes collection.

THE TAX GAP

The tax gap is the difference between taxes theoretically owed and taxes paid. The size of the difference between these two numbers is not an inconsiderable issue, even for the federal government. The IRS estimates that over the past thirty years the federal tax gap has ranged from 16 to 20 percent of total federal-tax liability—that is, up to one dollar in five that is owed to the government can only be collected through tax enforcement efforts—and maybe not then. Despite vigorous enforcement by the IRS, a significant amount of revenue remains unreported and unpaid. In 2005, the IRS estimated what it characterizes as the "gross tax gap" to be approximately $345 billion, or slightly more than 16 percent of tax liability.[9] About $55 billion of this total eventually is collected through enforcement actions and other late payments, leaving a net tax gap of approximately $290 billion. These estimates, which are the most recent estimates available, were conducted using data collected in tax year 2001 and before. The size of the tax gap, obviously, could have grown significantly in the succeeding years simply because of economic growth and increases in the taxpayer population.

The IRS describes the tax gap as having three primary components—unfiled tax returns, taxes associated with underreported income on filed returns, and underpaid taxes on filed returns.[10] Within the underreported income component, the IRS has further delineated specific categories of taxes, such as individual, corporate, employment, estate, and excise taxes. The IRS's problem—and one as great or greater for state-tax agencies—is finding all of this unreported income. Nonfiling and underpayment of reported taxes account for less than 20 percent of the gross tax gap; underreporting on timely filed tax returns makes up the bulk of the gap. Underreporting on individual income-tax returns alone accounted for about 68 percent of the gross tax gap in 2001. More than 60 percent of underreported individual tax is estimated to be from business and self-employment income, which the IRS has no easy way to locate without extensive audits. Only 10.5 percent of the underreporting gap is attributable to corporate income tax, and only 1.4 percent to the estate tax and excise taxes. Individual-income taxpayers fail to report about 54 percent of income from sources for which there is no information reporting, such as sole proprietorships. In contrast, less than 5 percent of income from easily verified sources such as interest, dividends, and pensions goes unreported. When income is subject to both information returns and tax withholding, as is the case with wages, just over 1 percent goes unreported.

Once again, the states' analyses of their own tax gaps vary widely. Table 18.3 shows the major tax-gap studies that have been completed by states or outside sources in the past decade.[11] Only a handful of states have prepared these studies, and because of the enormous amount of analysis associated with them, they appear only at irregular intervals. They also differ in which taxes they examine, the personal and corporate income taxes being the most common because of the IRS tax-gap model, but the sales tax is also examined in some of the states. One state, Wisconsin, also included the cigarette tax in its estimates because high tax rates in some states, along with the product's portability, makes tobacco products, along with motor fuel, particularly susceptible to tax evasion through smuggling and other illegal schemes.[12]

Table 18.3 Estimates of tax gaps in selected states

State	Year of Tax Gap Study	Taxes Included	Tax Gap Estimate	Estimated Compliance Rate
California	2005–2006	Personal and corporate income tax	$6.5 billion	85%
	2007	Sales and use tax	$1.5 billion	
Georgia			$2.28–2.88 billion	80.15–84.55%
Idaho	2009	Personal and corporate income tax; sales tax	$255 million	82.90%
Minnesota	1999	Sales and use tax	$451.1	89.5%
Montana	2006	Personal income tax	N/A	78–82%
New York	2002	Personal income tax	$2.338 billion	86.10%
Oregon	2006	Personal income tax	$1.248 billion	81.5%
Wisconsin	2009	Personal and corporate income tax; sales tax; cigarette tax	$1.2 billion	90.0%

Source: The table is made of data from California Legislative Analyst's Office (2005); Borders (2009); Idaho Tax Commission (2009); American Economics Group (2002); Montana Legislative Audit Division, (2008); Oregon Department of Revenue (2009); Washington Department of Revenue (2006); Collier and Norman (2010).

As the table shows, most states found that their level of noncompliance falls into the range found by the IRS in its own studies, ranging from a low of 80 percent compliance to 90 percent. Still, the numbers represent a considerable amount of lost tax revenue, and the states that have focused their attention on the issue typically have invested in efforts to close the gap. Other states proceed, presumably, with the recognition that a tax gap exists but with no understanding, even a theoretical one, of its size or cost. The issue was neatly framed by Henry Aaron and Joel Slemrod in *The Crisis in Tax Administration*:

> Most people pay their taxes. They do so for two reasons, despite the cost and complexity of complying with the tax law. On the positive side, many recognize, even if grudgingly, that paying taxes is a duty of citizenship rather than the outcome of a cost-benefit calculation. On the negative side, taxpayers know that the law requires payment, that evasion is a crime, and that willful failure to pay taxes is punishable by fines or imprisonment, even if the chances of being caught are remote. The practical questions for tax administration how much to spend on enforcement to maintain the second of these motives for payment and how to organize administration to get the best results for each dollar spent?[13]

All states maintain some combination of tax enforcement and account auditing, coupled with efforts to maintain or increase voluntary compliance through various methods. The preferred compliance strategy, of course, is to avoid the tax audit and enforcement processes altogether, focusing instead on "soft" collection techniques based on educating and assisting taxpayers to comply. These techniques are often useful in dealing with unintentional noncompliance, which accounts for a sizable portion of the tax gap.

A significant amount of this unintentional noncompliance results from the lack of knowledge—or outright confusion—about the tax laws. Filing relies on taxpayers to voluntarily gather their information and fill out the tax forms, so education and assistance are essential to facilitating compliance. Many taxpayers have difficulty filing a correct return without education and information. This includes a variety of activities from the design of forms to providing one-on-one tax assistance, often, but not always, in field offices maintained by the tax agency. States also have moved in recent years to greater use of telephone assistance and collection techniques as a way of increasing the coverage and reducing unintended noncompliance. Agencies may also conduct regular workshops for new taxpayers or in cases where the tax laws have changed to reach as many taxpayers as possible.

A second major component of the compliance effort is auditing. This, too, is a multilayered process. After a return is filed, it goes through a process of checks to ensure accuracy, a process greatly enhanced by the application of computer technology. Simple things like addresses, names, and social security numbers are checked to match existing records. Returns also are checked for math errors and adjustments are made for obvious errors. In many states, a second check determines if values are reasonable in terms of statutory or other logical limits. For example, if a credit is limited to $500 and a return is claiming $5,000 for the credit, the return would then be manually reviewed in more detail. After this initial screening, a further review may be made based on audit results or by comparing the return to external information such as IRS form 1099 information. Taxpayers may be asked to verify the information on the return by providing more information.

In some cases, these quick, highly automated reviews are a prelude to more detailed field audits. States select accounts for detailed review if there are significant questions about the information on the return or in the case of some taxpayers selected by size or because of past or suspected compliance issues because experience has shown that closer review will often yield additional tax due—though not always. Beginning in the 1990s, some states began to apply sophisticated data warehousing technology to combine information from a variety of sources—state unemployment information, state incorporation data, federal tax and customs data, and even information from telephone directories—to look for patterns of noncompliance in the overall taxpayer population by comparing individual taxpayers to patterns found among all taxpayers in a given industry. These efforts generally yield additional leads for tax auditors.

Once identified, some of the selected audit reviews may be conducted through the mail simply by asking taxpayers to provide more detailed information. In other cases, a more detailed review of a taxpayer's records may appear warranted, particularly in the case of business taxpayers where the transactions are more complex. Auditors in field offices or at the home office conduct most of these complex audits. They typically require face-to-face contact with taxpayers or their representatives. When the State of Oregon surveyed other states about their approach in this area, they found that "a majority of other states surveyed about audit methods told us that both face-to-face and correspondence audits are effective, depending on the extent of the issue under audit."[14]

A final component of the compliance cycle is tax enforcement. This can be as simple as contacting a taxpayer about a return that has not been filed. Telephone contacts with taxpayers (sometimes called "dialing for dollars," though not within earshot of taxpayers or legislators) can resolve many of these delinquency problems. For those taxpayers who did not file a return, states may assess an estimated tax amount once the return becomes delinquent based on the best information available and issue a delinquency notice to the taxpayer's address on record with the state. At any time after the taxpayer has been issued a delinquency notice, he or she can file an accurate return, although interest and administrative penalties may apply depending on how late the return proves to be. Failure to file once these actions are taken may result in an escalation of enforcement efforts that vary from state to state but may include seizure of property, the imposition of bank liens, forfeiture of the right to do business (if applicable), and court action designed to compel compliance. States may also maintain criminal enforcement groups that work with law enforcement in cases of overt and criminal tax evasion, such as cigarette or motor fuel smuggling.

Despite the innovations in technology and the greater use of "phone power" and other techniques to improve compliance, the tax gap has remained stubbornly persistent. In part, this is related to the fact that tax systems have become more, not less, complex over time, and taxpayers may continue to have problems complying correctly. Education and assistance help, but they do not reach the entire taxpaying population. In addition, some taxpayers are simply going to avoid taxes wherever possible and depend on the sheer size of the taxpayer population to shield their evasion. This problem becomes even more acute during economic recessions when taxpayers are stretched to the limit, and paying taxes is only one more unpaid bill. Too often the avoidance strategy can work altogether too well. While all returns may be "examined" by computerized collection systems, actual detailed audits of taxpayer accounts cover only a fraction of the taxpayer population in any given year. In fact, in many states detailed audit coverage amounts to 1 percent or less of the potential accounts. Agencies simply do not have the resources and staff to cover a larger segment of taxpayers.

There are, of course, other ideas about how to make further inroads into the tax gap. For example, several potential solutions derived from academic research have been posed by James Alm. He suggested many of the more "standard suggestions," such as increasing the number of audits, improving the quality of audits and of the auditors and increasing penalties for tax cheating. He also proposed more unique approaches such as allowing third-party audits, increasing source withholding and implementing expanded information sharing between states as effective means of reducing the tax gap. In his analysis, he argues that out that there is now theoretical, empirical, and experimental evidence that individuals respond predictably, if not always significantly, to such administrative policies as: increased audit rates, more 'productive' audits, repeated audits, strategic audit selection, public disclosure of audit, public dissemination of audit information, increased administrative penalties, greater use of source-withholding, more targeted audit programs, more use of information-sharing between government audit agencies, greater rewards for compliance, closer taxes-services linkage, increased taxpayer participation in group decisions, tax amnesties, as well as increased complexity and uncertainty.[15]

Alm also suggests that treating the taxpayer more as a client rather than as a potential criminal can yield greater taxpayer compliance. Methods to improve the service of tax agencies include simplification of tax payments, forms, and the tax laws themselves, as well as improvements in agency efforts to aid taxpayers in the filing process. Finally, he proposes reinforcing the norm regarding payment of taxes through the use of the media and other organizations to portray payment of taxes as a civic duty, a strategy some states have begun to adopt. He concluded that "an administrative strategy based only on enforcement may well be a reasonable starting point but not a good ending point for closing the tax gap."

How successful these or other approaches might be is a matter of speculation. The tax gap has been a controversial subject and the nature of this controversy illustrates how little is really understood about the extent and nature of the problem of underreporting in federal and state tax systems alike. Some view the tax gap as a major potential revenue source that can be used to close the federal budget deficit or other reforms without raising taxes. Others believe that the potential revenue gains from proposals to improve enforcement are quite limited.[16]

In general, state-tax administrators probably would agree that more could—and should—be done to close the tax gap, but the issue remains fundamentally one of resources, particularly during the recession and its aftermath. For most agencies, the answer is straightforward: investments in tax auditors, enforcement staff, and collection-related technology yield more tax dollars recovered for the state. As the Idaho Tax Commission reported in a 2009 study of its tax gap, "The best demonstration of actual returns from investment in tax compliance comes from our own experience. In 2003 (another year characterized by declining revenues and budget holdbacks), the Governor signed legislation which boosted the compliance budget of the Tax Commission by $926,000. This allowed us to create new tax compliance positions which brought in more than $10 million in additional revenue within a year, and over the first four years produced an average return on investment (ROI) of 13 to 1."[17] The agency found this conclusion to be very consistent with results in other states, which are summarized in table 18.4, which shows the comparative ROI from compliance investment in various states as reported in the Idaho study.

On the other hand, the Idaho report pointed out the same lesson associated with the argument against tax agency layoffs and furloughs in Arizona and California—that cuts to revenue-producing agencies cost far more budget dollars than they save. The first two gaps in state tax administration—the resource gap and the tax gap—then can be seen to be inversely related. As the investment in tax compliance rises, the tax gap should shrink, and as the investment falls, the gap will expand. There is, however, one other factor that must be added to this formulation—not only is the level of staffing important, but the knowledge and experience of the staff is as well.

Table 18.4 Selected state compliance initiatives

State	Year	Cost to the State	Added Revenue	Return on Investment (ROI)
Idaho	2003	$926,000	$12,000,000+	13 to 1
Kansas	2002	$6,000,000	$54,000,000	9 to 1
Minnesota	2003	$10,300,000	$97,200,000	9.4 to 1
Kansas	2005	$1,440,000	$15,000,000	10.4 to 1
Washington	2009	$10,700,000	$67,800,000*	6.3 to 1
New Mexico	2009	$5,000,000	$29,000,000*	6 to 1
New Mexico	2010	$5,000,000	$45,000,000*	9 to 1
Average Return on Investment				**9 to 1**

Source: Idaho Tax Commission, Idaho's Tax Gap, November 2009.

THE KNOWLEDGE GAP

One of the long-standing problems of state-tax administration is attracting and retaining skilled staff, particularly in specialty areas like tax policy, tax auditing, and information technology. People do not emerge from college with a good working knowledge of state taxation, much less the intricacies of the specific tax laws of individual states. While they may have the skills to gain such information, acquiring a thorough understanding of tax policy or the tax law usually takes place over a period of years and is best taught through on-the-job experience. State agencies invest in training to varying degrees, but there is still no substitute for actual experience with the tax administration process itself. New auditors, for example, return far fewer dollars per hour of effort than do auditors who over time have gained the ability to audit tax accounts efficiently and are able to handle larger and more complex assignments, such as reviewing the tax returns for multinational corporations. The same can be said for tax enforcement staff and for those who work in tax policy. It is one thing to have read the tax laws and quite another to actually understand what they mean and how they are applied in a given situation.

At some point, too, states run into a second problem: salaries that do not keep pace with what skilled professionals can make in the private sector. With the rise of state and local practices at major accounting and law firms, state-tax agencies have become, to a certain extent, training grounds for private companies. In addition, information technology workers may also be attracted by the larger salaries offered by private-sector employers, a particular problem in the technology boom of the 1990s when states often lost skilled staff and then faced the almost impossible task of finding replacements in a tight and competitive job market.

Despite these challenges, many tax agencies have been able to hold on to a core of experienced staff. For various reasons, many of the individuals who entered the public service in the 1970s and 1980s—prior to the economic boom of the 1990s—remained in state employment, and most tax agencies, along with many government agencies generally, have a fairly large cohort of workers with twenty or more years of experience. This has been important to maintaining the continuity of state-tax administration, but it may also pose a problem in the future. That problem is the aging of the public-sector workforce, a problem most widely identified and publicized in conjunction with the federal government but which also applies to most state government agencies, including revenue departments.

The federal problem has been widely documented and is indicative of the problem at all levels of government. The aging of the Baby Boom generation and the downsizing of the federal government workforce over the past fifteen years has produced an aging workforce and the potential for what has been called a federal retirement "tsunami". According to a report compiled by the Congressional Research Service, the federal workforce increased in age significantly in the past decade. The percentage of federal employees aged fifty-five or older rose from 15 percent in 1998 to almost one-quarter of the total in 2008.[18] The *Washington*

Post reported that the federal Office of Personnel Management projects that 20 percent of all permanent, full-time federal employees will retire by the end of 2014.[19]

The IRS faces this issue along with the rest of the government. In an August 2009 report, the Treasury Inspector General for Tax Administration noted that the IRS "faces a loss of leadership and technical employees that could threaten its ability to provide American taxpayers the service they have come to expect."[20] The IRS employs about 106,000 workers, including 9,100 managers. Half of all employees are over age fifty, and 39 percent of IRS executives are already eligible for retirement. The agency has said it would have to hire a manager a day for the next decade to keep up with attrition.

Although it has received less scrutiny, this same challenge faces state and local governments. The difficulty in understanding the full extent of the problem facing the states is that, once again, there is no single source of data on workforce trends in the fifty states, a fact that applies equally to state-tax agencies. Nonetheless, the studies that are available show that the situation is similar to the federal problem or perhaps worse.

In a study of public-sector employment, the economist Stuart Greenfield reported that, based on Census data, "45.3 percent of the civilian labor force is between 40 and 61 years of age. However, the proportion of the workers the same age in the public sector is substantially greater. Among federal workers, 64.1 percent of the workforce is within this age group, while 54.3 percent of those in the state government workforce and 57.2 percent of the local government workforce are within this group."[21] A 2009 study by Gregory Lewis and Yoon Jik Cho found that the state government problem may be even more acute: "State workers are even older than federal workers, so the retirement tsunami may hit states sooner and harder than the federal service. State employees have the highest share of old workers and the lowest share of young workers, making them likely to experience the biggest increases in turnover."[22]

According to the data presented in the analysis by Lewis and Cho, state government workers in 1980 were only 1.7 years older than the labor force as a whole and were 0.4 years younger than the local government workforce. By 2006, the state sector had the oldest workforce across the federal-state-local sectors, the lowest percentage of workers under the age of thirty (10.3 percent) and the highest percentage of workers who were fifty years or older (40.4 percent).

The distribution of older workers is not uniform. The prevalence of older workers is higher in occupations that require specialized education, training, or skills. This includes health-care workers, legal professionals, natural scientists, engineers, educators, managers, and presumably tax specialists. A 2002 analysis by the Rockefeller Institute of Government found that more than half of government workers have occupations that can be classified as within the knowledge worker category, compared to about 29 percent in the private sector.[23] Older workers constituted 49.3 percent of knowledge workers in government, they found, but only 34.8 percent of private-sector knowledge workers.

Similarly, there is little reliable data available specifically on the age demographics of state-tax agencies other than anecdotal examples. For example, data provided at a Federation of Tax Administrators conference in 2002 highlighted the New Jersey Division of Taxation's workforce-planning efforts in recognition of the graying agency workforce at that time.[24] The division, in its research on the issue, found that 57 percent of its employees were eligible for retirement within ten years, and that the percentages were far higher in some areas than others. The examples given included:

- Property Administration
  - Local Assessment Compliance at 92 percent
  - Local Property Tax Field Assistance at 81 percent
  - Local Property Tax Policy and Planning at 77 percent
- Field Audit at 57 percent
- Field Investigations at 57 percent
- Special Procedures at 71 percent
- Inheritance Tax at 77 percent

It is reasonable to assume that these trends confront most state-tax agencies in varying degrees and with certain exceptions. One likely exception is the audit workforce. Audit staff members, because of their technical knowledge of the state tax system, often are hired away by the private sector because of their skills. If anything, that segment of the agencies' workforce seems likely to be younger on average than the overall agency because of this attrition, although that fact likely provides cold comfort for administrators trying to retain experienced staff of whatever age.

Both the federal and state governments have gotten some reprieve from the workforce problem because of the economic downturn. A great number of retirement-eligible personnel are delaying their departure from the workforce because of economic uncertainties. Federal retirements, for which there are good data, are instructive. They dropped to a seven-year low in 2009. Only about 43,600 full-time, permanent federal employees retired in fiscal 2009, about 27 percent fewer than expected by the Office of Personnel Management and the lowest total since fiscal 2002, another period of economic problems. Eventually, though, time will push the Baby Boomer generation out of the workforce and into retirement despite economic circumstances. The workforce "tsunami" may be delayed but the fundamental demographics of the workforce have not vanished.

This particular gap could have both good and bad aspects for state government. On the one hand, the size of the older segment of the workforce means that as these workers leave the government, a considerable body of institutional knowledge could be lost. The need to transfer and retain institutional knowledge, build leadership skills, improve the efficiency of agency processes, and acquire and retain new talent has never been more important. In this regard, states have only recently begun implementing serious worker succession planning, and tax policy and related skills are difficult to teach in any case. It could be a bumpy transition within many states.

On the other hand, the aging of the workforce, handled correctly, provides opportunities to tax administrators. According to Charles Fay, some industries, of which government is one, could actually benefit from mass retirements.[25] Fay argued that the government sector, higher education, and highly unionized industries that still operate on seniority could see some benefits from large-scale retirements because their older workers are more costly. In general, they use more health care and earn more, and in labor-intensive jobs, they are less productive. However, those benefits may only be realized over a long period of time and have the most benefit for state budgets and not the effective administration of the tax laws.

The question, then, is how well states will respond actively to the demographic changes ahead.[26] This implies taking a far more systematic approach to the issue of succession planning than has typically been the case in the past. For example, agencies will need to develop comprehensive, agencywide information on the skills of its employees in mission-critical occupations. This information is needed to effectively assess current and future workforce needs. Administrators will need to develop an agencywide recruitment strategy that included a long-term plan for all functions involved in recruiting, and this will require an agencywide process to consistently and accurately project future human resource needs for more than the following fiscal year. It also means having a methodology in place for systematic knowledge transfer and training to maintain skill levels as older employees leave state service.

Even if economic conditions improve and the retirement process begins to speed up again, state government workforces will not change overnight—but they will change relentlessly. This also is true of the general labor force. As it moves through the workforce demographic, the Baby Boom generation has inaugurated a protracted graying of the workforce that will increase the average age in most industries for some years before it starts to drop again. The youngest baby boomers are unlikely to retire until 2026. The knowledge gap will be an ongoing issue that tax administrators will have to address.

THE TECHNOLOGY GAP

Revenue agencies have tried to make up for budget-related hiring problems—and more recently their graying workforce—by investing in technology. Technology can speed operations that were, three decades ago, brutally time-consuming and paper-intensive processes. The application of technology is a reasonable strategy, and it has become an imperative in modern business operations, both in the private and public sectors, and there has been widespread hope that the emergence of digital or e-government marks a new era of greater convenience for citizens and the ability of government agencies to work smarter, not harder as the familiar catchphrase goes. Tax agencies' commitment to technology development, in fact, is nothing new. States have been investing in tax administration technology at least since the 1950s and 1960s when the first mainframe computers were deployed by state governments. Since then, and particularly since the early 1980s, states have added a number of technology innovations as summarized in table 18.5.

There are, however, barriers to the full realization of this goal, which means that a technology gap continues to plague state-tax administration. These include cost, risk, time, and simple inertia. Large-scale information technology projects are expensive, and while some states have pursued some innovations, like integrated tax systems and large data warehousing projects, many have been held back

Table 18.5 Timeline of state tax agency technology innovations

1950s–1970s	States deploy first mainframe computer systems
1980s	Early document management systems appear
	Electronic funds transfer and electronic data interchange
	Development of first integrated tax systems
	Desktop computers become available
	Federal income tax e-filing begins
1990s	Internet begins to be available and World Wide Web makes first widespread appearance
	First state tax agency websites appear
	States begin tele-filing option for taxes
	Second-generation integrated systems with client-server interfaces
	E-correspondence eventually to become e-mail
	Federal-state e-filing begins
	First use of Internet for tax filing
	First data warehouse projects
	States begin to accept credit card payments
	States begin to offer direct deposit refunds
	First self-funded revenue system contracts
	e-Pay used for tax payments for the first time
	Barcode-based paper tax-return digital capture
2000s	Video/webinar conferencing
	True secure e-mail with taxpayers and practitioners
	E-filing expanded to the forms of tax, including partnership and corporate returns
	Sophisticated data mining/matching compliance databases
	Third-generation integrated systems with web-based interfaces and/or use of enterprise resource planning systems for backbones
	States begin to offer e-services such as secure electronic communications, account maintenance, online offers in compromise
	First uses of social media (Second Life, YouTube, Twitter)

by a lack of funds, a problem exacerbated in the past decade by the budget upheavals that most states confronted as a result of the 2002–2003 recession and during the recession of 2007–2009.

Tax-system modernization is rarely an ongoing budget item because of the price tag, and it typically requires incremental legislative funding that competes with other state needs and, indeed, may compete with other needs within the agency. Where tax agencies are concerned, lawmakers often want to see a clear ROI for the dollars they appropriate, and that is often difficult to show when the result is more efficient handling of tax records or better customer service rather than improved audit performance—or where the results will not be realized for several years and well outside the current budget period. What's more, in the eyes of lawmakers and agency administrators as well, legacy applications may be seen as "paid for" with ongoing maintenance, which is a standard IT budget line item, as their only cost. They also are "safe" in the sense that they are a known quantity, and there also may be a perception that modernization projects primarily maintain the status quo, only adding a few bells and whistles to an already working system.

Nonetheless, some of the state systems are as aged as the staff that use them. For example, the Pennsylvania Department of Revenue was recently reported to be relying on a computer system that originally was installed in 1975 and had, in fact, been at the agency longer than most of the current staff. The department had different computer systems processing different tax types. One handled only corporate taxes, another the income tax, and another the sales tax and employer withholding. Another system handled smaller tax types such as the inheritance tax. The newest tax systems were reported to be twenty years old, although they had been updated through the years for tax law changes and to add improvements. Nonetheless, the systems were information silos that could not communicate with one another. Revenue Secretary C. Daniel Hassell told a reporter in July 2010 that he worried that the systems were living on borrowed time and could crash, bringing the department to its knees.[27] In this case, there was little argument from lawmakers about the need for updating the systems, although the price tag for this was estimated to be $100 million.

Even if an agency can secure the commitment of funds necessary for major system modernizations, the risk of failure remains. This is not unique to tax agencies. In fact, there is little evidence to suggest that it is a particular problem for state governments generally, although many states have seen major system failures of one sort or another in the past decade. Installing a complex new system is difficult, and there have been many prominent (and not so prominent) large-scale systems failures in both the private and public sectors in recent years. An information technology research firm, the Standish Group, prepares a periodic survey of the success of information technology projects in a range of industries. Its 2009 report concluded that only 32 percent of all projects were successful, which meant, in the study's terms, that they were delivered on time and on budget with required features and functions.[28] Another 44 percent were deemed to be "challenged," which meant that they were late, over budget, and/or had less than the required features and functions. The remaining 24 percent of projects were found to have failed, which meant that they were canceled prior to completion or delivered and never used.

The experience in the federal government may be even worse. As part of an analysis of the federal IT Dashboard, the Office of Management and Budget (OMB) compiled statistics regarding risky information technology projects. The OMB found a 42 percent decline in the number of major federal IT projects executed during the period 2004–2009. However, the average budget per project more than doubled during this period, from $42 million in 2004 to $87 million in 2009. Most important, though, in 2009, 72 percent of major federal IT projects were on the Management Watch list, which highlights projects "containing one or more planning weaknesses." These projects have been deemed vulnerable to failure.

The pressure for more technology investment will only increase in the future, assuming that agencies can secure the funding for needed changes. The pace of technological change in the broader economy is rapid and unrelenting, and there will be new demands on tax agencies in the years ahead. Tax agencies will increasingly move toward expanded electronic filing options and providing taxpayers with greater direct access to manage their tax records. These improvements will, in turn, raise new security and privacy concerns.

One of the newest challenges is likely to be how to integrate new social media, such as Twitter, Facebook and YouTube, into tax administration. To date, tax agencies have made limited use of social media, mainly Twitter and YouTube, although state governments generally are beginning to use them. A recent survey by the National Association of State Chief Information Officers (NASCIO) found that "social media tools are being actively adopted and used throughout state governments across the country. Much as was the case with the explosive growth of the Web itself over a decade ago, the early adopters of social media are most frequently the public relations, messaging-focused segments within state governments. As was also the case in that earlier time, the survey in the aggregate documents a parallel lag between use and policy or governance mechanisms, even while a number of states have moved aggressively to adopt the technologies strategically and to govern their use through enterprise policies, guidelines, or standards."[29]

According to the NASCIO, the survey revealed continued concerns of state CIOs in the areas of security, legal terms of service, privacy, records management, and acceptable use, and this has led to wide variation in patterns of adoption. Less than one-quarter of the respondents indicated they are moving full-speed-ahead in use of social media. Relatively few have developed policies or guidelines to provide an enterprise context for managing social-media tool use. Some states have completely balked at legal use of the tool. It can be concluded that overall, state tax agencies are being (appropriately) cautious to adopt social media until there is a legal and institutional sorting out of the implications to adopt.

THE POLICY GAP

Tax laws are the framework on which actual administrative practice is hung in bits and pieces by tax administrators and taxpayers as they go about implementing, enforcing, and complying with the tax laws. Some policy is borne out of administrative rulings that interpret the law, while some policy stems directly from challenges to the law and administrative rulings by taxpayers that may be settled through an agency review process or in the courts. Thus, tax administrators do not shape the overall state tax policy, but they play a central role in giving it substance. And right now, that substance is shaky at best. Katherine Barrett and Richard Green summed up the problem in a January 2008 report on state taxes for the Pew Charitable Trusts' Center on the States that appeared in *Governing* magazine. "It's been known for a long time that obsolete state tax systems are not producing the revenue states need," they wrote. "But what's becoming clear today is that those tax systems are not only failing to keep up with the dramatic shifts in the US economy. They are a drag on economic growth."[30]

The problem, which has been well documented, is the gap between what tax systems are and what they need to be in the twenty-first century. More than a decade ago, David Brunori wrote, "State and local taxation has generally not changed much in the last half-century. To be sure there have been innovations with respect to collection, periodic Supreme Court pronouncements on state tax power, and the trauma of the property tax revolt movement. But the structure of state and local tax systems has remained the same."[31] A decade has passed. State-tax systems have been rocked by two major recessions; the second recession was perhaps the most extreme to batter state governments since the Great Depression, and what, in reality, has changed?

States still rely on a combination of sales, income, and business taxes, much as they did thirty years ago—or seventy years ago in many cases. The sales and use taxes began in many states as a temporary revenue measure during the Great Depression. The personal income tax was first enacted a generation before that. States have talked about tax system reform on and off at least since the recession of the 1980s, but taken as a whole, the changes have been marginal and have proceeded incrementally. Organizations like the MTC and the FTA have helped to provide forums for coordinated action by states on issues of common interest, but even those efforts have had limited success, mainly in the realm of information sharing and multistate auditing of large taxpayer accounts. The one clear effort at state collective action to deal with a major policy problem in state taxation, the SSTP, which began in 2000, has made some progress, but, judged against the size of the problem it was designed to confront, again, not much has changed.

The problem for tax policy today—the gap that administrators confront—is that the tax systems in use today were created to tax an economy that no longer exists. The US economy has changed dramatically in the past three decades, largely due to new technology and telecommunications that enable instantaneous transactions in the global market. The economy in many states has shifted from manufacturing jobs to services. These changes have made taxation extremely challenging by using old tax policies. In 2000, Tom Neubig and Satya Poddar pointed out the developing problem with old tax systems confronting the new economy, which they called "blurred boundaries." They wrote about national tax policies, but their conclusions apply equally well to the states. "The tax systems of the world rely on many definitions that are increasingly blurred as a result of the rapid changes in technology and financial innovations. A major question for tax policy and tax administration at the beginning of the 21st century is whether governments can adapt their tax systems to the new economy with the speed necessary to minimize adverse economic distortions from the blurring of the many tax boundaries."[32]

The problems created by the collision of twentieth-century policy and the twenty-first-century economy are familiar to anyone who follows state taxation. The problems can be cast in different ways but with much the same general conclusion. For example, in an article in *State Tax Notes*, Bruce Johnson, a commissioner on the Utah Tax Commission, wrote that the two greatest challenges for state tax policy were interstate and international commerce and intangible property.[33] His point on interstate and international commerce echoes Neubig and Poddar's idea of "blurred boundaries." In short, Johnson wrote, "Geographical boundaries have been the primary basis of state and local jurisdiction to tax. Such boundaries, however, are increasingly irrelevant to commerce. Accordingly, there is a growing mismatch between the tax collector and the tax base."[34] The problem with intangibles shares some of the same elements—the difficulty of state-tax systems to compensate for the changing economy. He wrote, "The problem with intangibles is similar to the problem with interstate commerce. State and local tax systems were simply not designed to deal with it. As more wealth is represented by intangibles, proportionately less wealth is subject to property tax. As more sales involve intangibles, proportionately fewer sales are taxable. The economy is changing and our tax system has been left behind."

Charles McLure, in testimony to the California Commission on the 21st Century Economy in 2009, provides one list of the problems with the states' two major taxes—many of which, he says, are tied to the "nuttiness" of state-tax systems.[35]

These are among the many nutty characteristics of state sales and use taxes:[36]

- Many services are exempt.
- Internet access is exempt.[37]
- Many business purchases are taxed.
- The sales tax "system" is incredibly complex, in large part because of interstate differences in tax bases, product definitions, and administrative practices, but also because of the existence of local taxes.
- A state cannot require a vendor to collect its use tax unless the vendor has a physical presence in the state.

Nuttiness also permeates the state corporate income tax:[38]

- Not all states provide for combination of unitary businesses.

- States that do provide for combination do not necessarily define a unitary business the same way.
- Even when states use the same apportionment factors to divide the business income of multistate corporations, they do not all assign the same weights to the various factors.
- States do not use identical definitions of the apportionment factors, especially sales.
- The existence of substantial sales in a state does not imply a taxable nexus, even if the state employs only sales to apportion income.[39]

An individual may agree or disagree with McLure's list, and certainly it would be possible to add to it, but it illustrates the scope of the problem confronting state-tax systems. This policy gap has serious consequences not just for the concept of fair and efficient tax administration but for the successful management of state government in general. Tax-system problems make it more difficult to fund government services, a problem exacerbated by the recession but one that lingers after the recession is passed.

It is possible to argue that state taxes have never been as important as they are today because of the demands on the states to provide a wider and more expensive range of services. Brunori wrote, "In addition to providing traditional services (e.g., state police, prisons, higher education, and highway maintenance), states are providing many services once supplied and paid for almost exclusively by the federal and local governments."[40] These include two critical areas of state budgets: public education and public assistance. The problem, then, is not simply that the tax system is mismatched to the economy. That mismatch also leads to a mismatch between the services states are expected to provide and the revenue available to provide them. Without significant changes in policy, states face long years of struggling to meet obligations—or, in all likelihood they will be forced to shed obligations they already have undertaken. It is at this point that the final gap in state tax administration comes to the forefront—the political gap.

THE POLITICAL GAP

Tax policy is the product of politics, so a complete understanding of the challenges facing tax administrators today requires an explicit recognition of the political environment within which tax policy is made. The political environment is important for several reasons. Most obviously, because a state's tax structure is a product of a political process, one must understand that process to completely understand the tax system. In addition, the politics of taxation in any state have a direct effect on the other challenges facing tax administrators that have already been discussed. Lawmakers create the basic policies that govern state taxation. They provide the funding for operating the state tax agency and the oversight that determines how successful the tax administrator is in securing funding for staff and new technology: two issues very often high on a tax agency's wish list.

Tax politics also play a role in shaping the daily work of tax administration. Each legislative session brings new tax legislation, which must be implemented. Tax systems must be changed, tax forms revised, rules written, staff trained, websites revised, and taxpayers notified. Eventually auditors must evaluate how well taxpayers have complied, and tax compliance officers must deal with the taxpayers who did not comply. Lawmakers may add new tax incentives, extend old ones, enact tax amnesties, raise or lower rates, expand or contract tax bases, or provide tax holidays. The list is long, and all of these issues impact a tax agency. It also is the case that because the tax system can become a political lightning rod, and tax agencies may find they are on the political hot seat when things go wrong. State-tax agencies have recently received unfavorable political attention because of delays in providing income-tax refunds, computer glitches that prevented some taxpayers from filing their income taxes on time, and charges of favoritism and sweetheart deals in tax cases for large taxpayers.

Aside from these specific problems, the political environment in which tax agencies operate today is a toxic mix of partisan politics that simmers around antitax rage and distrust for government in general, with taxes as a focal point. Raising taxes has become an extremely difficult proposition politically in most states, and while there is nothing wrong with major tax changes being difficult to enact, the political problems associated with such changes have made a rational examination of the tax system and its problems increasingly difficult to undertake.

Many of these environmental problems can be traced to the tax revolt that sprung up in the wake of the passage of Proposition 13 in California in 1978.[41] Antitax politics fueled the passage of Proposition 13 and lead to similar tax revolts in other states. Candidates for public office began to use taxes as a central issue in their campaigns. Tax cuts became a regular theme for gubernatorial and legislative candidates seeking election in virtually every state. These developments also increased the prominence of initiative and referendum movements, which have been dominated in recent years by antitax proponents.[42]

What Brunori has called the "politics of antitaxation" have limited state governments' ability to raise revenue precisely at the moment when the demand for services, particularly in education and human services, has increased. As an echo of this political movement, some lawmakers talk about slashing state budgets, and during the current recession, they have made some sizable budget cuts. For many state agencies, the situation has become a new version of what John Shannon of the US Advisory Commission on Intergovernmental Relations once labeled "fend-for-yourself federalism," only in this case, it is "fend-for-yourself budgeting" where agencies must raise the fines and fees at their disposal to prevent the loss of services, where higher education institutions must raise tuitions, and where transportation systems are awash in debt or must build miles of toll roads or sell portions of the road system to private operators while leaving much of the remainder of the system to deteriorate because of inadequate funding.

Revenue agencies occupy a central and uncomfortable position in this roiling process because they are expected to squeeze more dollars out of the existing tax system, often leading them to take more aggressive action to collect taxes and creating an inevitable and undesirable rift with taxpayers. The response from taxpayers is greater unhappiness with the tax system, resistance to changes in even the most dire budget circumstances, and, in the case of business taxpayers, a marked increase in their investments in tax representatives—the lawyers and accountants who help them deal with audit issues and plan around the tax system.

In this regard, it is important not to underestimate the role of business taxpayers in the politics of modern state-tax policy. In the legislative arena, many lawmakers focus on job creation and economic development. Although much of the rhetoric associated with these policies involves creating a strong education system and a skilled workforce, much of the actual policy involves tax incentives and other concessions to attract and retain businesses. Thus, while the recession raged, states continued to pursue tax incentives to attract filmmakers and "green" jobs and to attract individual businesses to a state.

The efforts of the business community do not stop at the state-house doors. They extend into the administrative process as well. As businesses have whittled down other costs, state and local taxes have become a more prominent focus of their cost-reduction efforts. According to Richard Pomp, this trend began in 1981, when for the first time many corporations paid greater state corporate income tax than federal corporate income taxes.[43] It continued throughout the 1980s and 1990s and into this century. As a result, business taxpayers spend enormous amounts on lobbying, audit defense, tax planning, and litigation of state-tax issues. They also have become more actively involved in the national debate over state-tax policy. Business interests have had a prominent (and appropriate) role in the SSTP, and some multinational businesses and their associations also have been active in Congress on various federal policies designed to preempt state-tax policies that they do not like. This trend is unlikely to abate in the immediate future, governed as it is by the dueling desires of states to chart their own courses and businesses to carve out some sort of consistency in the state-tax policies that affect their operations.

This, then, is the dilemma—the gap—in state taxation produced by the current nature of state-tax politics. It seems clear that the recession and the rapidly changing nature of the economy have magnified the need for elected officials to make essential long-term changes in tax systems so states can live within their means yet still educate children, keep people safe, and create jobs, but there is no political will for making such changes. Most tax agencies do not plan adequately for long-term change in the tax system, but administrators are familiar with the issues. The problem is that tax politics, as much as any of the gaps, stands in the way of real progress—and is likely to do so for the foreseeable future. The double irony is that it is uncertain whether, if the clouds suddenly parted and states had free rein to rewrite their tax systems to be fairer and more reflective of the new economy, that they would have any real idea about how to go about doing so.

Conclusion

The title of this chapter implies that that there are seven major gaps in state tax administration that need a single solution. That might be taken as an indication that there is some grand unified field theory of tax administration that could unite and solve all of the problems in one stroke (rather than just an attempt at a clever title). Perhaps in the right circumstances, that would be possible, but it is highly unlikely, not in an individual state and certainly not in all of the states collectively. The seven problems described in this chapter are discrete. Some have been around throughout the history of state-tax administration; some are newer and all have been shaped by events like the recent recession. They all are interrelated to varying degrees, but finding a solution to them requires addressing them individually as well as a group.

That is a daunting challenge. It is tempting to write, as Henry Aaron and Joel Slemrod did of the federal tax system, that we face a "crisis in tax administration." The observation very likely is true. State-tax systems today work but face mounting problems. The tax administrator's job is essential to this process, and yet their motives and means are suspect, not just in the antitax community but also in the business community that suspects the tax agency's interests lie in collecting more tax dollars than in administering the system fairly. The administrator watches the taxpayer population growing year by year, but that growth is not matched by growth in the agency's budget. The solutions to any one of the six problems must seem vanishingly remote.

By the same token, it is important to remember that tax administrators, like most public managers, always face administrative obstacles in varying degrees, particularly those of limited resources and lagging technology. The problems only seem more obvious and pressing today because of the severity of the recent recession and because of the enormous pressures on state governments to meet new service demands in a period when people want services but, in effect, do not want to pay more in taxes to get them.

Nevertheless, the political and economic pressures on state revenue systems have not changed the fundamental purpose of state taxation or the fundamental responsibility of the tax administrator. State governments need revenue to fund the services they provide to their citizens. Political rhetoric criticizing taxes and government spending is thick in the air these days, but the simple fact is that many of the services that state governments provide are essential for the state's economic progress and well-being. Those services cannot continue without proper funding. The problems of state-tax administration, then, should be addressed and, if not solved, at least ameliorated, for that reason alone—to have a functioning government, states need a functioning revenue system. The viability of state governments as entities in the next fifty years rests heavily on how the states choose to address the gaps in administration that exist today.

When he was asked about the solutions to the current problems facing tax policy, Bruce Johnson wrote that the answer was cooperation: "At the risk of sounding naïve, there is a solution to these problems. That solution is—cooperation. Cooperation between taxpayers and tax administrators. Cooperation between states. Cooperation between state and local governments. If tax administrators are to propose new tax systems that are both effective and efficient in a highly dynamic economy, they need the knowledge and assistance of the taxpayers that live in that economy. Together, taxpayers and tax administrators can design reasonable solutions to problems that would otherwise be intractable." Add cooperation between tax administrators and lawmakers, and it sounds like a good place to start.

Notes

1 Snavely (1988), 903.
2 Dubin, Graetz, and Wilde (1992).
3 Penniman (1980), 266.
4 Francis (this volume).
5 Fox (this volume).
6 Eads and Hecht (this volume).
7 Johnson, Oliff, and Williams (2010).
8 Adkisson, Hill, Korber, and Vogel (2010).
9 US Internal Revenue Service (2006).
10 George (2007), 1.
11 California Legislative Analyst's Office (2005); Borders (2009); Idaho Tax Commission (2009); American Economics Group (2002); Montana Legislative Audit Division (2008); Oregon Department of Revenue (2009); Washington Department of Revenue (2006); Collier and Norman (2010).
12 Collier and Norman (2010).
13 Aaron and Slemrod (2004), 1.
14 Oregon Department of Revenue (2009), 10.
15 Alm (2007), 1–2.
16 See, for example, Toder (2007).
17 Idaho Tax Commission (2009), 11.
18 Congressional Research Service (2008), 17.
19 Vogel (2009).
20 US Department of Treasury, Inspector General—Tax Administration (2009), 2.
21 Greenfield (n.d.), 1.
22 Lewis and Yoon (2009), 17.
23 Abbey and Boyd (2002), 7.

24 Thompson (2002).

25 Hennessey (2006).

26 Wallace (this volume).

27 Murphy (2010).

28 Standish Group (2009).

29 National Association of State Chief Information Officers (2010), 5.

30 Barrett and Green (2008), 20.

31 Brunori (1998), 1.

32 Neubig and Poddar (2000), 1153.

33 Johnson (2002), 949–951.

34 Johnson (2002), 950.

35 McLure (2009).

36 For further discussion, see Fox (this volume).

37 Due to congressional preemption. See Eads (this volume).

38 For further discussion, see Brunori (this volume).

39 Ibid.

40 Brunori (2005), 5.

41 See, for example, Schrag (1999).

42 Brunori (1999), 1635.

43 Pomp (1998), 47–92.

References

Aaron, Henry J., and Joel Slemrod (Eds.) (2004). *The Crisis in Tax Administration*. Washington DC: The Brookings Institution.

Abbey, Craig W., and Donald J. Boyd (2002, July). "The Aging Government Workforce." Nelson A. Rockefeller Institute of Government. http://www.rockinst.org/pdf/ workforce_welfare_and_social_services/2002–07-the_aging_government_ workforce.pdf.

Adkisson, John, John Hill, Dorothy Korber, and Nancy Vogel (2010, February 12). "Furloughs at the Franchise Tax Board: Loss Is Seven Times Greater Than the Savings." Senate Office of Oversight and Outcomes, Report to the Senate Rules Committee.

Alm, James (2007, July). *Administrative Options to Close the Tax Gap: Insights from Research*. Atlanta: Georgia State University Andrew Young School for Policy Studies.

American Economics Group (2002, November). *Minnesota Sales and Use Tax Gap Project: Final Report*. Prepared for the Minnesota Department of Revenue.

Barrett, Katherine, and Richard Green (2008, January). "Taxes and Growth." *Governing*. The Pew Charitable Trusts, Center on the States.

Borders, Kyle (2009). "Estimates and Implications of the Georgia Personal Income Tax Gap," Georgia State University, Andrew Young School of Policy Studies.

Brunori, David (Ed.) (1998). *The Future of State Taxation*. Washington, DC: Urban Institute Press.

Brunori, David (1999, May 17). "Initiatives and Referendums Are Here to Stay." *State Tax Notes*: 1635–1637.

Brunori, David (2011). *State Tax Policy: A Political Perspective*, Washington, DC: Urban Institute Press.

California Legislative Analyst's Office (2005, February). *California's Tax Gap.* Sacramento.

Collier, Dennis, and Jack Norman (2010). *Wisconsin's Billion-Dollar Tax Gap How Uncollected Taxes Can Help Fill the State's Budget Hole.* Glendale, WI: Institute for Wisconsin's Future.

Congressional Research Service (2008). "The Federal Workforce: Characteristics and Trends." http://www.policyarchive.org/handle/10207/bitstreams/19381.pdf.

Dubin, Jeffery, Michael J. Graetz, and Louis L. Wilde (1992). "State Income Tax Amnesties: Causes." *Quarterly Journal of Economics* 107(3): 1057.

George, J. Russell (2007, February 16). Treasury Inspector General for Tax Administration, Hearing before the US House of Representatives, Committee on Budget, "IRS and the Tax Gap."

Greenfield, Stuart (n.d.). *Public Sector Employment: The Current Situation.* Center for State and Local Government Excellence.

Hennessey, Melissa (2006, February 22). "The Retirement Age." *CFO Magazine.* Available at: http://www.cfo.com/article.cfm/5491083/c_10671787.

Idaho Tax Commission (2009, November). *Idaho's Tax Gap: Estimating Idaho's Tax Gap and Developing Strategies to Reduce It.* Boise.

Johnson, Bruce (2002, June 3). "The Greatest Challenge Facing Our State and Local Tax Systems." *State Tax Notes:* 949–951.

Johnson, Nicholas, Phil Oliff, and Erica Williams (2010, August 4). "An Update on State Budget Cuts." Center on Budget and Policy Priorities. http://www.cbpp.org/files/3-13-08sfp.pdf.

Lewis, Gregory B., and Yoon Jik Cho (2009, September). "The Aging of the State Government Workforce: Trends and Implications." Paper prepared for presentation at the American Political Science Association Annual Meeting. http://papers.ssrn.com/sol3/papers.cfm?abstract_id=1450764

McLure, Charles (2009, February 12). "How to Improve California's Tax System: The Good (But Infeasible), the Bad, and the Ugly." Testimony to the California Commission on the 21st Century Economy. http://www.cotce.ca.gov/meetings/testimony/documents/1-CHARLES%20McLURE%20-%20COTCE%20paper.pdf.

Montana Legislative Audit Division (2008, December). "Financial-Compliance Audit: Department of Revenue, For the Two Fiscal Years Ended June 30, 2008."

Murphy, Jan (2010, July 31). "Pennsylvania Department of Revenue's $100 Million Computer Upgrade Questioned." Pennlive.com. http://www.pennlive.com/midstate/index.ssf/2010/07/pennsylvania_department_of_rev_.

National Association of State Chief Information Officers (2010). *Friends, Followers and Feeds: A National Survey of Social Media Use in State Government.*

Neubig, Tom, and Satya Poddar (2000, August 28). "Blurred Boundaries: The New Economy's Implications for Tax Policy." *Tax Notes:* 1153–1161.

Oregon Department of Revenue (2009, January 30). *2009 Report on Personal Income Tax Compliance in Oregon.* Salem, Oregon.

Penniman, Clara. (1980). *State Income Taxation.* Baltimore: Johns Hopkins University Press. 266.

Pomp, Richard (1998). "The Future of the State Corporate Income Tax: Reflections (and Confessions) of a Tax Lawyer." In *The Future of State Taxation,* edited by David Brunori. Washington, DC: Urban Institute Press. 47–92.

Schrag, Peter (1999). *Paradise Lost: California's Experience, America's Future.* Berkeley: University of California Press.

Snavely, Keith (1988). "Innovations in State Tax Administration." *Public Administration Review* 48(5): 903–910.

Standish Group (2009, April 23). "New Standish Group Report Shows More Project Failing and Less Successful Projects." http://www.standishgroup.com/newsroom/chaos_2009.php.

Thompson, Robert (2002, June 5). New Jersey Division of Taxation, "Taxation's Retirement Planning." Presentation at the Federation of Tax Administrators Annual Conference, Nashville, Tennessee. http://www.taxadmin.org/fta/meet/am02_sum/thompson.pdf.

Toder, Eric (2007, July 3). "Reducing the Tax Gap: The Illusion of Pain-Free Deficit Reduction." Urban Institute and the Brookings Institution. http://www.taxpolicycenter.org/publications/url.cfm?ID=411496.

US Department of Treasury, Inspector General—Tax Administration (2009, August 19). "To Address Its Human Capital Challenge, the Internal Revenue Service Needs to Focus on Four Key Areas." Report 2009-10-118: 2. http://www.treas.gov/tigta/auditreports/2009reports/200910118fr.pdf.

US Internal Revenue Service (2006, February 14). "IRS Updates Tax Gap Estimates." IR-2006-2028. http://www.irs.gov/newsroom/article/0,,id=154496,00.html.

Vogel, Steve (2009, January 12). "Federal Workers Delaying Retirement Because of Economic Crisis." *Washington Post*. http://www.washingtonpost.com/wp-dyn/content/article/2009/01/12/AR2009011202572.html.

Washington Department of Revenue (2006, June 30). "Department of Revenue Compliance Study." Research Report #2006-2.

CHAPTER 19

....

REVENUE ESTIMATION

....

NORTON FRANCIS

THE Great Recession that began in December 2007 has exposed limitations in state and local revenue-estimating models that state and local policymakers rely on to make budget decisions. Even though the unemployment rates have not risen to the level or duration of the Great Depression, and today's social and financial safety net is much stronger than in the 1930s, an examination of several indicators reveals that in several ways the depth of the recession has been unprecedented. As the dust settles and the crises abate, each individual state—that is, state and local system—will go through a period of soul-searching because, as was true in many states, as each time the revenue estimators thought they had been conservative enough to have made what in their judgment was a "worst-case" forecast, the next forecast led to yet another report of a deteriorating revenue outlook.

Where did the models go wrong? Who's to blame for the forecast errors? How can the estimates improve in the future? These questions have been asked in the past but there are many features of the latest business cycle that make them harder to answer this time. This chapter looks at the recent history in the revenue-estimating context and attempts to draw some conclusions about the state of the science of revenue estimations.

A look at key indicators reveals that the Great Recession has been very different than prior recessions.[1] Of six key indicators—employment, wages, personal income, gross domestic product (GDP), consumer price index (CPI), and the Standard & Poor's 500 index (S&P500)—all six were contracting in 2009. In the previous two recessions, a maximum of two indicators contracted: employment and S&P500.

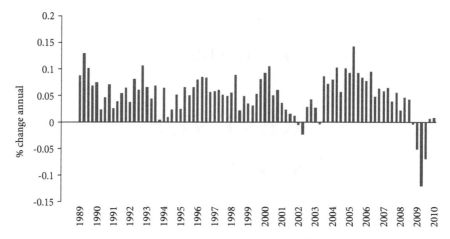

Figure 19.1 State and local tax revenue
Source: US Census Bureau.

The last time all six contracted was in 1949. This had important implications for revenue estimating, particularly at the beginning of the recession:

- The largest annual contraction in real GDP since 1946 had been less than 2 percent and there had not been more than one year of contraction in a row since the 1946 recession.
- During the 2009 recession, real GDP contracted 0.3 percent in 2008 and 3.5 percent in 2009.[2]
- Personal consumption expenditures (PCE) had never contracted two years in a row since the Great Depression and had not contracted for a single year since 1980.
- During the 2009 recession, PCE declined two years in a row and the contraction in 2009 was the largest since 1942.[3]
- Personal income (PI) had not contracted since 1949 and the wage component not since 1954.
- During the 2009 recession, PI contracted $197 billion from the fourth quarter 2007 to the second quarter 2009, or 1.6 percent, and wages contracted $245 billion, or 3.8 percent.[4]
- Total nonfarm employment only contracted two years in a row twice since data collection started in 1939 and never more than the 3.6 percent, the contraction in 1945 after World War II ended.
- During the 2009 recession, employment contracted 4.3 percent in 2009 and from 2007 to 2010 lost almost eight million private sector jobs and taking the employment level back to 2003. Employment fell three years in a row by 2010.[5]
- Even the S&P 500, a notoriously volatile time series, had two consecutive years of decline worse than the dot.com bust that started in 2001.
- From 2007 to 2009, the S&P500 dropped 36 percent compared to the 2000 to 2003 period when it dropped 32 percent.[6]

As revenue estimators built models and analyzed data to compile revenue estimates for FY 2009 and FY 2010, the time-series data they relied on did not contain the information that would show the kind of downturn that was to occur.

In addition to the exogenous variables that drive the revenue estimates, history of collections is also used. Here again, collections provided no help in predicting the contraction in state and local revenues.

- Since 1951, total state-level revenues have only contracted twice. In 2002, total state revenues contracted $24.4 billion, or 4.4 percent. The contraction in 2009 was $66 billion, or 8.5 percent.[7] Forty-five states contracted in 2009.
- Most revenue forecasts from the late summer and fall of 2007 for FY 2009 and FY 2010 were "pessimistic" at the time when compared to the high levels of growth that had just occurred. A slowdown was projected but not a big downturn.
- In New Mexico, there were words of caution regarding the state of the economy and the estimate for personal income tax was for growth of 3 to 4 percent, "low by historic standards."[8]
- In Vermont, the economic outlook was revised down significantly but did not include a recession though the report did warn policymakers that "most recent estimates put Vermont's chances of two consecutive declines in real GSP at better than 50%."[9]

The summer of 2008 was the end of the good times for revenue estimators across the states. Most states were just beginning fiscal year 2009 and were closing their books on one of the highest revenue years ever.[10] All states had fully recovered from the 2001 recession, which had had a bigger impact on state budget experts than the taxpayers and workers. States had also built up what was thought to be adequate reserves.[11] In fact, there was discussion in many states about the right level of reserves and whether the states were keeping too much revenue. By the end of FY06, states had built up reserves to 11.5 percent, up from 3.2 percent in FY 2003.[12]

When the revenues started turning and an official recession was declared, experience was still acting against accurate forecasts. Before December 2007, a handful of states had never been through a long recession. Since 1991, there were six states that had fewer than ten months (nonconsecutive) of contraction in employment prior to December 2007. Many of those states have now been in recession for one to two years. For example, New Mexico had only one month (June 1991) when employment declined from the prior year from January 1991 to November 2008, a period of 215 months; from December 2008 to August 2011, a period of 33 months, year-over-year employment declined for 31 of those months. When the first few months of contraction were reported at the end of 2008, it was simply implausible to consider a continued two-year string of declines that occurred.[13]

Personal income, likely found in more models than employment because of its stronger correlation with tax revenue, is even more complicated. From 1970 to the start of the recession at the end of 2007, a span of 152 quarters, only eighteen

Table 19.1 States with fewer than 15 months of annual employment contraction before December 2007

	January 1991 to November 2007 (203 Months)	% of Months	December 2007 to August 2011 (45 Months)	% of Months
New Mexico	1	0.5%	31	68.9%
Alaska	2	1.0%	9	20.0%
Wyoming	3	1.5%	18	40.0%
Montana	6	3.0%	24	53.3%
Idaho	9	4.4%	32	71.1%
North Dakota	9	4.4%	9	20.0%
Arizona	12	5.9%	36	80.0%
Nevada	13	6.4%	40	88.9%
South Dakota	13	6.4%	18	40.0%
Nebraska	14	6.9%	23	51.1%
Average	37	18.2%	26	57.8%

Note: The data are the number of months, consecutive or not, of year-over-year declines in seasonally adjusted nonagricultural payroll employment.
Source: BLS, author's calculations.

states had ever experienced a downturn.[14] From the fourth quarter of 2007 to the third quarter of 2010, a span of eleven quarters, all fifty states and the District of Columbia experienced negative growth rates in personal income and the average number of quarters was 4.2 (table 19.2).

Unprecedented declines in all of the major variables made it a challenging environment in which to look to the future. In a report published by the Pew Center

Table 19.2 States and District of Columbia with at least one quarter of personal income contraction

Recession End	# of States
1975	3
1980	2
1982	3
1991	0
2001	1
2009	51

Source: US Bureau of Economic Analysis, author's calculations.

on the States in 2011, the median forecast error grew to over 10 percent in 2009, up from a median of 3.5 percent in prior years. The conclusion of the report is that the volatility of revenue estimates has increased in recent years and that "errors in revenue estimates have worsened progressively during the fiscal crises that have followed the past economic downturns. During the 1990–1992 revenue crisis, 25 percent of all state forecasts fell short by 5 percent or more. During the 2001–2003 revenue downturn, 45 percent of all state forecasts were off by 5 percent or more. And in 2009, fully 70 percent off all forecasts overestimated revenues by 5 percent or more."[15]

The Pew Center report concentrated on the revenue estimate at the time in the fall of 2007 for fiscal year 2009 and compared that with earlier data in order to frame the issue as an ominous trend in the accuracy of revenue estimates. However, a few missing elements added to the complexity. The variables noted above and many others—housing indicators, oil and natural gas prices, and interest rates—deviated from a fairly long history that formed the basis for revenue estimates.

Revenue Estimating Methods

There are as many methods of forecasting revenues as there are states but there are common features and a common sequence:

1. Adopt a forecast of the national economy.
2. Forecast the state economy.
3. Model and forecast revenues by using historical collections and exogenous forecasts of appropriate variables.
4. Compile recent changes in legislation.
5. Test and evaluate the completed forecast.

1. Adopt a forecast of the national economy

The starting point of a revenue estimate process is to evaluate the US economy. The interconnectedness of the states requires that attention be paid to the national economy and, in the case of states that have a higher concentration of exporting industries, the global economy. Typically, state governments rely on external contractors for this service.[16] The largest and most widely used are IHS Global Insight (GI) and Moody's Analytics (also known as Economy.com). These vendors provide forecast data that are used in econometric models and narratives outlining the outlooks and the risks. In addition to a baseline forecast, they may provide scenarios and assign probabilities of their occurrence.[17] These vendors also made presentations at conferences where state economists assemble, providing context to the forecasts being compiled.[18]

There were some warning signals in these forecasts but the baseline, or most plausible, forecasts from both Moody's and GI in late 2007 did not include a recession (figure 19.2).[19] In the fall of 2008, the recession was predicted to be narrow because it was restricted to housing markets. The sentiment at the time was that

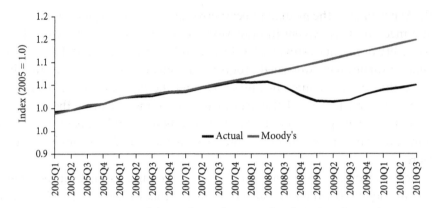

Figure 19.2 Moody's Analytics forecast of real GDP and actual
Source: Moody's Analytics, August 2007; US Bureau of Economic Analysis (BEA).

housing market crises were localized and had a more limited impact on the national economy. At this point, only a few economists were waving the red flag that would be the financial crisis and reveal the web that lay beneath the mortgages.[20]

Another source of information, more as a benchmark, are the federal agencies charged with economic forecasts for federal budgeting purposes. The Office of Management and Budget (OMB) and the Congressional Budget Office both produce economic forecasts. Their track record was similar to the private forecasters (figure 19.3). When preparing the budget for FY 2009, the OMB and CBP were forecasting 4.7 to 5.1 percent growth in nominal GDP in FY 2009. One year later, the forecast was reduced to essentially zero growth, still missing the actual decline of 1.7 percent.

2. Forecast the state economy

The national forecast is subsequently used to generate a forecast of the local economy. States have a variety of approaches for determining the best forecast for the

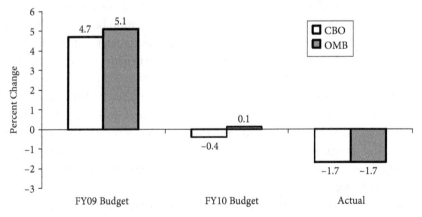

Figure 19.3 OMB and CBO forecasts of 2009 GDP
Source: US Office of Management and Budget (OMB); US Congressional
Budget Office (CBO).

local economy. States with a consensus process for revenues will generally start by agreeing on a forecast for important economic variables. There are also states that have advisory groups that discuss and may agree on a forecast.[21] In some states, a higher education institution has been charged with developing a forecast for the state's economy. These institutions have an appreciation developed by experience and research of the nuances of a particular geographic locale that help customize the forecast to the locale. Additionally, many of these institutions are integrated with government institutions by providing new graduates to work in the revenue and budget offices, by having experienced government staff as adjunct professors or by taking on special academic research that pertains to public policy. The universities also have connections in the private sector—for many of the same reasons—and may have a more direct connection to what is going on in the local economy that models built on national data would not be able to project

Some states also use national macroeconomic forecast vendors to compile forecasts of the local economy. This can either be an alternate forecast to compare to the locally developed one or used as the official forecast. Using a respected private vendor gives the *imprimatur* of independence that is sometimes helpful. Regionally, there are several private economic consulting firms that specialize in the geographic area. Forecasts can also be purchased for specific industries if that industry is sufficiently important that a general economic forecast will not capture the specialization. This is the case for states whose industrial makeup is far different than the national economy, such as Michigan (motor vehicles) or Kansas (agriculture) or Wyoming (energy). In these cases, specialty forecasts are included in the official forecast.[22]

Variable Selection. Regardless of the source, most revenue estimators rely on a handful of economic variables that, when combined, capture most taxable activity. Each revenue stream has a particularly meaningful or useful driver. The first criterion of variable selection is the availability of good data. There are some variables that are ideal for inclusion in a model but are difficult to collect, have too long a lag time in publication, do not occur frequently, or are difficult to forecast. It would be very useful to include GDP by state in revenue models, but the data are provided annually and are two years old by the time they are released.[23]

Table 19.3 Examples of variables used to forecast revenues

Revenue	Variables
PIT—Withholding	Wages and Salaries
PIT—Nonwithholding	S&P500, Personal Income
CIT	S&P500, Corporate Profits
Sales Tax	Wages and Salaries, National Retail Sales
Motor Vehicle Excise	Car Registrations, Employment
Motor Fuel	Oil Price, Wages, and Salaries
Severance	Price at wellhead, Production volume

The withholding of personal income tax, for example, is correlated to wages and salaries or employment—these are direct measures of paychecks that are the source of withholding. Withholding makes up the lion's share of personal income-tax revenue. Nonwithholding is made up of final tax payments that are included with tax returns, estimated quarterly payments, and refunds of taxes. Because final payments and quarterly payments are often related to investment activity, the S&P500 is often used for the model. A reliable forecast of stock-market prices is a difficult proposition and is the cause of significant error in forecasting income-tax revenue. Also, the reliability of the S&P500 as an explanatory variable was brought into question in 2010 when it rebounded more than expected but nonwithholding continued to decline.[24]

The sales tax has historically been a stable revenue stream because it was thought to have a fairly straightforward relationship to employment.[25] As long as the base was broad enough, regardless of economic conditions, people still had to buy things and that would keep up sales-tax revenues. In the two recessions prior to the 2007–2009 recession, sales growth rates slowed considerably but never contracted and then rebounded in the recovery.[26] Beginning in 2009, the narrative changed and now there is a full year of contraction in the data. Further complicating conventional forecast tools, the environment of taxable sales is changing. Three trends have emerged that require attention: housing market exposure, a move away from goods toward services in the states' output, and the rise in Internet purchases.[27]

- *Housing market exposure.* One of the most significant effects of the 2007–2009 recession was the magnitude of damage caused by the housing collapse. The complete shutdown of new housing construction caused an immediate loss of relatively high-paying construction jobs and an immediate loss of spending on construction materials. The former reduced both sales and income taxes and increased demand for public services, particularly unemployment compensation. The latter was felt mostly in lower sales-tax revenue. At the peak of the housing bubble, sales of building materials and furniture as a share of total retail sales (excluding food service) also peaked at 11.7 percent.[28] It had been steadily growing since 2000 and was contributing more and more to the growth of retail sales. In 2007, building and furniture declined for the first time since the data began in 1992 and declined for three consecutive years. In 2010, these sales represented less than 10 percent of retail trade. This is exacerbated by mortgage equity withdrawal that was financing other consumption outside of the housing markets like automobiles and travel. In a discussion about risks to the forecast, the Minnesota Department of Finance in its November 2007 forecast directly confronts the challenges facing estimators: "Historically, increases in wealth, other things equal, have been found to produce small additions to consumer spending. But forecasters attempting to project the impact of the current decline in housing values on consumption find themselves in uncharted territory because there has not been a yearlong decline in housing values since the Great Depression."[29]

- *Services replacing goods.* In the 1930s, goods made up 55 percent of personal consumption expenditures.[30] By the 1970s, there was a shift to services as the major share of consumption and by 2009 the share of goods had dropped to 22 percent. This change in emphasis has decreased the efficiency of the sales tax for many states that exempt most or all services.[31] Increasingly, states are attempting to add services to the base, starting with services that are less likely to be part of business-to-business transactions (thus to avoid pyramiding) but it has proved as difficult as any other type of tax increase.[32] The FTA maintains a listing of the services that states include in their tax bases and over time there have not been significant moves toward broader bases.[33] There has, however, been an increase in the rates, which drives up the costs of those items remaining in the base. This narrowing of the base makes the sales tax less efficient as a revenue generator.
- *Internet sales.* The other trend is increased purchases over the Internet. This is not a new issue. For a state to collect tax revenue from a company, that company must have some nexus in the state.[34] Sales over the Internet are comparable to sales made through catalogs—and like catalog sales they are generally exempt from sales tax unless the company has a physical presence. The increasing share of commerce that occurs over the Internet, however, is creating significant problems for sales-tax revenues. In 2003, the Census Bureau began keeping statistics about online commerce and its survey showed about 1.8 percent of retail sales were through e-commerce. By 2008, the share had doubled to 3.6 percent. A significant amount of these sales are taxable due to the company's "brick and mortar" presence but there is a considerable amount that is not.[35] A study from the University of Tennessee Center for Business and Economic Research projects that the total revenue loss to state and local governments is $12 billion in 2012.[36]

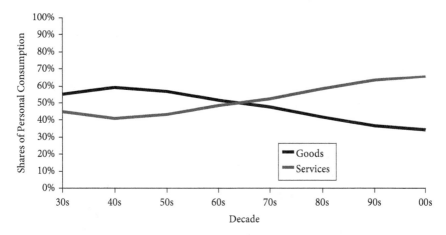

Figure 19.4 Goods versus services
Source: US Bureau of Economic Analysis.

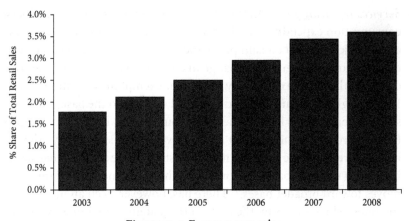

Figure 19.5 E-commerce sales
Source: US Census Bureau.

Income taxes and sales taxes are the revenues that get the most attention from revenue estimators due to their relative importance to total revenue. The taxes and nontax revenue—fees, permits, fines, charges for service—that make up the remaining third of revenues also must be forecast.[37] In many cases, such as fees and many permits, the models do not require external variables because the models are simple models. There are cases where it is helpful to aggregate different revenues and model as a group with an economic variable. Building permits and other construction-related revenues can be compiled into an aggregate, modeled using a construction-related variable that has a good forecast and then disaggregated for reporting purposes.

3. Model the data

To model revenue data appropriately, the historic collections have to be prepared for modeling. Collections data are often very "lumpy," in that it is not as smooth as it should be because of problems associated with the collection process and the accounting processes. For example, in 2010, there was a tremendous snowstorm in the mid-Atlantic region that closed District of Columbia operations for several days. This closure resulted in delays in processing tax collections and so made January activity (which is reported in February) seem artificially low and February activity (reported in March) seem high due to the catch-up. These two months are called "paired opposite outliers" and should be averaged if the model is based on monthly data. Most forecast data are quarterly so this particular example would be corrected by transforming the monthly data into quarterly data.[38]

The estimator must also know the timing of collections and the accrual process used so that the collections data can be as closely matched to the selected explanatory variable as possible and also to select the appropriate frequency for modeling. Lags are used for this purpose to shift the data backward. In most jurisdictions, sales tax collected in the current month are required to be sent in by a certain date next month so the collections data are always one month off the activity month. Income-tax withholding follows the same pattern but nonwithholding does not. Estimated payments are quarterly but are generally equal distributions of prior year tax liability though they are adjusted as changes in a particular taxpayer's circumstances warrant. Because the actual data are more closely related to an annual series—last year's total tax liability—an annual model may be more desirable over a quarterly model.

Once the data are prepared for analysis, the next step is model selection. Selecting the model depends on the revenue stream. There are several types of models that are useful and they range from simple moving averages and trend models to more sophisticated linear regression and time-series models. It can be informative to model the same revenue using a simple and complex model as a way to validate the results. The model selection is also matched to the importance of the revenue. As with any activity, resources must be prioritized and the most attention paid to the largest revenues. In other words, the model sophistication increases with the importance of the revenue. Alternatively, as mentioned above, revenues may be aggregated and modeled using more sophisticated techniques than would be the case if they were modeled individually.

There are some revenues—fees and licenses, for example—that are required to be renewed or applied for. Simple models that calculate a multiyear average are often sufficient and can be adjusted for any increase in rates. There are other revenues that are so volatile and unpredictable that a simple average is often the best or even the only appropriate method. Examples are unclaimed property or estate taxes.[39] A history of collections will indicate whether a simple model is appropriate.

A trend model is used when revenue follows a consistent trend. This is more sophisticated than a simple average because it allows for growth in the forecast. Revenues that increase with population or inflation can be modeled with a simple trend model, and trend models are useful as benchmarks to validate other more complicated models. Trend models are not useful in identifying turning points, unfortunately.

Some revenues, theoretically, can be modeled using an explicit ratio to another variable. For example, the sales-tax base is usually highly correlated to wages and salaries. A ratio model would apply the historic ratio to the forecast of wages and then apply the appropriate tax rate. This model uses an exogenous forecast as the primary driver.

Most estimators rely on econometric models for the most important revenues.[40] The standard form is the original least squares (OLS) model modified for time-series analysis. Modification may be the inclusion of an autoregressive term to address serial correlation or using lags of the dependent variable (the tax revenue being modeled). There is an abundance of academic research on this level of model selection and there are infinite variations on the way to treat both the dependent variable and the independent or exogenous variables.[41] Most estimators have software that will perform the most common tests and provide forecasts that are based on "best practices" in the field.

While model form is important, variable selection is critical. The model has to be easily understood and based on a theory about the movement of the revenue. Data mining for good "fits" may make a model's coefficients look robust but, when the model is used to forecast, the interactions have to be well understood. The estimator has to be able to explain *why* a particular variable is used and often to a public audience that is not composed of economists. An example is the use of dummy variables, which is a technique used to account for seasonality or regime shifting (such as when a new tax rate is applied). Dummy variables serve an important role in identifying shifts in the data (e.g., before and after a tax-rate increase, or summer sales of ice cream) but they should not be used as a substitute for variability. In cases where there is an observable outlier or spike in the data and there is a rationale for it, a dummy can be used to mitigate its effect on the model. An example of a case where there is justification for using a single period dummy is Microsoft: in the fourth quarter of 2004, Microsoft paid out a dividend that was large enough that it was noticeable in the quarterly data at the national level.[42] In this case, because it was a one-time event, the model should reflect an adjustment for this quarter. There are other large dividend payouts by other companies but they occur with regularity so are already included in the base data.

As noted above, however, the forecast of explanatory variables upon which the data are being modeled is crucial. A simple model of total state-level revenue using wages and salaries as the primary driver has excellent model attributes and, as figure 19.6 shows, the modeled values closely track the actual values.[43] This is the way the world looked in the fall of 2007. Figure 19.7 compares the forecast would have been using a fall 2007 forecast of wages and salaries with the actual outcome: a significant deviation. In this case, the forecast of the explanatory variable did not capture the downturn.

4. Change legislation, policy, and behavior

Once the variables are selected and forecast, the revenue estimators evaluate whether the base needs to be adjusted to reflect changes in tax law, tax policy, or taxpayer/tax-administrator behavior. There are not only recent changes in tax law

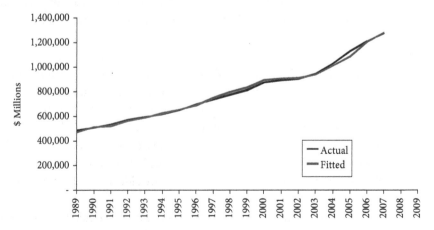

Figure 19.6 Fitted versus actual of total revenue model using wages
Source: US Bureau of Economic Analysis; author's calculations.

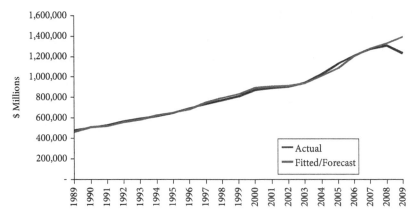

Figure 19.7 Forecast of total revenue model using wages
Source: US Bureau of Economic Analysis; author's calculations.

but also changes that are phased-in or triggered by events that estimators have to be conscious of. At times, policymakers will not want to absorb the impact, positive or negative, of a particular policy in a single year and will instead phase it in over several years. A fiscal estimate that is generally calculated and reported at the time of passage must be reviewed as each phase is entered. Major reforms are often phased in to give taxpayers ample time to adjust; alternatively, they are phased out through sunsets.[44] The danger is that these changes are reflected very slowly in the tax base that is used to forecast revenues and also are not usually reflected in the economic variables. The revenue estimator has to review all policies to determine if the impact is in the base or has to be added or removed. For example, a change in the sales-tax rate begins to show up in the base immediately but is not in the history that is used to calculate the estimation coefficients so it has to be added after the fact until the revenue estimator is comfortable that the model is capturing the rate change. One way to accommodate this is to model tax bases rather than tax collections and then any rate can be applied at any time.

According to an annual survey conducted by the National Association of State Budget Officers (NASBO), states other than Michigan enacted $1.6 billion of budget cuts in FY 2008.[45] Forty-two states (including Michigan) enacted tax changes: more than half decreased either sales or personal income taxes, taxes that make up two-thirds of state revenue.

There are also other policy changes that are not legislated but that affect revenue collections. A concerted effort by the compliance division of the tax department increases revenues but may require an appropriation. Innovations in compliance such as bank-account attachments or reciprocal agreements with the Internal Revenue Service can also lead to more revenue. To the extent that a collection rate is either implicit or explicit in the revenue model, an increase in the rate has a direct impact on the revenue forecast. Similarly, an environment that discourages extensive and comprehensive auditing of taxpayer returns could lower the collection rate. These types of variables, however, are extremely difficult to

Table 19.4 Tax legislation in 2008

	NASBO Reported Changes	FY 2008 State Tax Revenue		Number of States Enacting Tax Changes	
			Share	Increases	Decreases
Sales	(716)	241,008	−0.30%	2	22
Personal Income	(1,778)	278,373	−0.64%	4	24
Corporate Income	275	50,759	0.54%	9	8
Cigarette	762	16,068	4.74%	8	0
Other	(235)	195,436	−0.12%	18	24
Total	(1,692)	781,644	−0.22%		

Source: US National Association of State Budget Officers (NASBO); US Census Bureau.

quantify and so are not typically incorporated explicitly in the revenue forecast. It is important to be aware of collections activity because recent history of collections is often the strongest driver of the forecast.

A corollary of compliance is taxpayer behavior. The success of the US economy and the ability to fund federal, state, and local government services is the high compliance rate for the payment of major taxes, particularly income taxes. Most of the income tax is collected through the withholding from paychecks and employees have little control over that process. Without this established method of collecting taxes, the compliance rate could be more volatile as individuals weigh alternatives to paying a tax bill like businesses do. Particularly in times of economic contraction, taxpayers who control the amount of estimated taxes may decrease or delay the payment of taxes to improve cash flow despite penalties and interest. If the choice is not paying employees or shutting down and making an estimated tax payment, the taxpayer may choose the latter and risk the penalty with the goal of paying the tax and penalties when the environment improves.

In addition to taxpayer behavior around the payment of taxes, there is also avoidance behavior either through tax planning, illegal evasion, or substitution. Changes in tax law that affect high-income taxpayers, individual or business, may result in additional emphasis on tax planning to lower the taxpayers' taxable income. For example, including a service such as legal services in the sales-tax base may induce companies to hire lawyers as staff rather than hiring law firms, thus reducing the amount they spend on a taxable activity. Changes that increase the audit requirements of the tax administrators may increase opportunities to illegally evade the tax. Credits and deductions may be claimed with no supporting evidence if there is no mechanism for tracking the credits. Finally, taxpayers may simply stop the taxable activity to avoid the tax. An example is increasing Internet purchases in response to an increase of the sales tax.

5. Test the results

Once the models have been identified and run, the results have to go through another series of tests, outside of the econometric tests in the model output, that the revenue estimators must conduct: reasonableness, validation, and range of result. The irony of the past few years is that an accurate forecast of revenues in the fall of 2007 would likely have been rejected or modified because it would not have made sense given the history for the reasons outlined above.

Reasonableness. A test for reasonableness is simply asking the question: given the economic outlook and the policy environment, does this result make sense? In the last few years, the reasonableness test may have caused estimators to throw out results because the models wanted to return to a norm when the outlook was for continued contraction. A test for reasonableness may also be related to the particular characteristics of the revenue that would not be captured by a model. One place this occurred probably more than others was capital gains income. In the history of capital gains, a period of decline has been followed by a fairly sharp increase. This was the case with the stock market in the Great Recession. Following a decline of 30 percent in 2008, the S&P500 ended 20 percent higher in 2010. A model using the S&P500 would have shown a similar bounce-back. This is where the estimator might use expert judgment and reject the model output, knowing that there will be extraordinary losses or that at a certain point, the relationship between the stock market and capital gains no longer holds.[46]

Validation. Another test is a validation test. As mentioned, often a trend model or ratio model can be used to validate the results of a more complicated model. The validation is not to confirm the exact results but is more another test of reasonableness. A simple test may not point to the magnitude of a particular trend but it should point to the direction. If a simple test shows a negative direction and the model shows a positive direction, there must be something in the model data that is changing the course of the revenue and has to be explained or revised. Billy Hamilton, a frequent contributor to *State Tax Notes*, uses a simple benchmark to validate his analysis of sales-tax revenue: sales-tax growth should be about two to three times employment growth and so any model estimate can be compared to this rule of thumb.[47]

Range of result. Finally, econometric models will provide a confidence interval or band of probability results along with a point estimate. If there is concern that the forecast of the economic variable may be too optimistic, the estimator can pick the lower band and intentionally build in more pessimism to the model without disregarding the model output. The inability to provide a range estimate for revenues rather than a point estimate means that the band of uncertainty, the confidence interval, is not usually explicit in presentations and reports. Unfortunately, policymakers cannot appropriate in ranges but rather to a particular level so a point estimate is required.

The final step in the revenue-estimate process is to write the narrative and answer a set of questions about each revenue stream:

1. What are the primary drivers of the forecast and are they included in the economic outlook discussion?

2. How has the forecast changed since the last forecast?
3. Was the model reviewed? Did the model capture the latest data reasonably well?
4. What are the risks to this forecast?

Because the nature of estimating is uncertain by definition, it is important to include clues about the direction of uncertainty. The answers to these questions will help write the narrative and prepare for any questions regarding the forecast from policymakers or the public. As forecast accuracy is examined, looking back on these questions at the time that a revenue estimate is made provides additional depth. In the fall of 2007, there were many risks outlined that had to do with housing markets and energy prices but the financial crisis had not emerged yet and employment did not start falling until December 2007.

Revenue estimators are applied economists rather than theoretical economists and must balance the requirement of theoretical robustness with the ability to generate consistent and meaningful forecasts. In the final report, the revenue estimator must be able to explain how a forecast was arrived at and the more sophisticated the techniques, the more difficult the explanation. The unfortunate nature of revenue estimating is that, while it can be sheltered from political influence, the estimate is placed squarely in a political environment and the revenue estimator is often called upon to describe and explain the estimate in a public forum of noneconomists.

The recent years have provided a new set of information that in many ways conflict with historic data and add new extremes to the time series used for revenue estimating. The future of revenue estimating will have to take the new information and incorporate it into the existing models or develop new models. Not only are there new lows and new contractions to understand but also new data that were not fully appreciated before. Over the next few years, housing measures will be looked at much more closely as they relate to revenues and whether the collapse set up a new trend or reverted to a pre-bubble trend. For revenue estimators, the task of variable selection and forecast selection is harder because the traditional methods failed to capture the magnitude of the decline. In this environment, estimators will adapt by adding new models and new methods of evaluating models.

NOTES

1 Mier (2009), slide 2. In a presentation to the National Association of State Treasurers, a strategist from Loop Capital Markets compared the conditions in the financial markets to the ten plagues of Egypt in the Bible.
2 US Bureau of Economic Analysis (BEA).
3 Ibid.
4 Ibid.
5 US Bureau of Labor Statistics.
6 Yahoo! Finance (finance.yahoo.com).

7 US Census Bureau, Annual Summary of State Taxes (last revised January 18, 2011). Note that this does not include the District of Columbia, which shows up in the local tax data: DC also contracted in 2009.

8 New Mexico Department of Finance and Administration (2007) 10.

9 Kavet (2008), 7.

10 BEA and author calculations. In 2008 thirty-eight states and the District of Columbia had the highest revenues.

11 Eckl and Klee (2005, 327–328) note that while there is no "ideal" amount that should be accumulated in a budget reserve ("rainy-day fund"), a combination of general fund surpluses and budget reserves should be at least 5 percent of total state expenditures.

12 NASBO (2010).

13 The author was the chief economist of the NM Legislative Finance Committee and participated in the consensus revenue forecast.

14 BEA; the data are quarterly changes in four quarters of the moving average of personal income.

15 Urahn and Gais (2011), 4.

16 The larger states—California, New York, and Florida—may have resources to compile in-house forecasts of the national economy and use outside forecasts.

17 In the fall of 2007, IHS Global Insight began increasing the probability of their pessimistic forecast.

18 Every fall, the Federation of Tax Administrators convenes a revenue-estimating conference that includes tax-policy experts from many states as well as private and federal experts. The 2007 conference included presentations by both IHS Global Insight and Economy.com that played down the probability of a broad recession.

19 At the FTA conference, Economy.com predicted that although a recession would be avoided, the probability increased from the low 20s to almost 40 percent, the highest probability since the 2001 recession.

20 WSJ (2007). A *Wall Street Journal* forecast survey reported only three economists of fifty-four at the time projected a contraction in US GDP and only four thought that the probability of a recession was greater than 50 percent.

21 NASBO (2008). Twenty-nine states have economic advisory groups, and twenty-eight use a consensus revenue process.

22 Alaska, Colorado, New Mexico, Utah, and Wyoming all include forecasts of the price of oil and/or natural gas in the official forecasting reports; West Virginia includes the coal outlook; Kansas includes agricultural statistics in its forecast documents.

23 The BEA released advanced estimates of 2009 GDP by state in November 2010 and then the final 2009 numbers plus revisions in July 2011.

24 It's likely that losses from prior years are now offsetting gains and depressing nonwithholding.

25 Hamilton (this volume).

26 In the 2001 recession, sales-tax growth reported in the Census *Annual Survey of State Tax Collections* was 0.2 percent and grew 2.7 percent the following year. In 1991, the growth rate was 3.5 percent. Up-to-date quarterly state-by-state estimates are provided by the Nelson A. Rockefeller Institute of Government (quarterly at www.rockinst.org).

27 Fox (this volume).

28 US Census Bureau Monthly Retail Trade (downloaded January 23, 2011).

29 Minnesota Department of Finance (November 2007), forecast, http://www.mmb.state. mn.us/doc/fu/07/forecast-nov07.pdf.

30 US Bureau of Economic Analysis (BEA).

31 Efficiency of a tax is defined as the ability to generate adequate revenue with minimal administration. A very efficient tax has the broadest base possible. See Watson (2005), 121–122.

32 Pyramiding is when there are taxes applied throughout the production process rather than on the final sale.

33 www.taxadmin.org.

34 Nexus is usually defined as a physical presence through facilities or agents but the Internet has created new questions about what nexus is and is not. States have recently been trying to address this, because online sales become a much larger share of commerce. The Streamlined Sales Tax Initiative that has been joined at some level by every state that has a sales tax is an example. States are also challenging online retailers like eBay and Amazon or rewriting statutes to capture these sales.

35 For example, a purchase made online at BestBuy is likely subject to sales tax because BestBuy has locations in every state but the identical purchase from Amazon.com would be exempt in most states.

36 Bruce, Fox, and Luna (2009). To put it into context, the total decline in state sales-tax collections in 2009 was $12.9 billion, according to the Census Survey of Governments.

37 Sjoquist and Stoycheva (this volume).

38 Williams (2008), 351.

39 It may be possible, using mortality models, to model the number of deaths but it is almost impossible to combine that with the wealth of the deceased!

40 Some states also have microsimulation models for income taxes but these models are more useful for estimating the fiscal impacts of changes in parameters and not useful for forecasting. Similarly, input-output models (such as REMI) are generally not used for forecasting variables but for fiscal impact estimating.

41 Willoughby and Guo (2008), 31.

42 BEA Frequently Asked Questions. Answers can be found at http://www.bea.gov/faq/index.cfm?cat_id=0&searchQuery=&start=0.

43 The data are from a simple Cochrane-Orcutt model using GRETL econometric software where total state revenue is regressed against US wages and salaries and is for illustration only.

44 The Joint Committee on Taxation issues a report every year of tax provisions that are expiring because of sunset provisions in the statutes.

45 NASBO (2007). Michigan enacted $1.6 billion in tax increases because of the prolonged budget and economic problems there. Including Michigan would offset almost all of the other states' tax decreases.

46 Losses are extremely difficult to model because (a) details about the magnitude are not well known, (b) they can be claimed on amended returns or have been carried forward from prior years and taken out of current year collections, and (c) modifying the way losses are treated is a popular form of tax relief, particularly for the federal government.

47 Hamilton (this volume).

References

Bruce, Donald, William F. Fox, and LeAnn Luna (2009, August). "State and Local Government Sales Tax Revenue Losses from E-Commerce." http://cber.utk.edu/ecomm.htm. 511–518.

Congressional Budget Office (2008, January). "The Budget and Economic Outlook: Fiscal Years 2008 to 2018."

Congressional Budget Office (2009, January). "The Budget and Economic Outlook: Fiscal Years 2009 to 2018."

Eckl, Cornia, and Jed Klee (2005). "Rainy day funds (budget stabilization, budget reserve funds).", "In *The Encyclopedia of Taxation and Tax Policy*, edited by Joseph J. Cordes, Robert D. Ebel, and Jane G. Gravelle. Washington, DC: Urban Institute Press. 327–328.

Geweke, John (2007, October 3). "Revenue Predictions," memo from University of Iowa Institute for Economic Research to Revenue Estimating Conference, http://tippie. uiowa.edu/economics/institute/.

Hamilton, Billy (2011, January 24). "Worried Man: Trying to Predict the Turnaround in Tax Revenue." *State Tax Notes* 59: 295–299.

Kavet, Rockler and Associates (2008, January 16). "January 2008 Economic Review and Revenue Forecast Update." Prepared for the State of Vermont Emergency Board and Legislative Joint Fiscal Committee.

Lutz, Byron, Raven Molloy, and Hui Shan (2010). "The Housing Crisis and State and Local Tax Revenue: Five Channels." Federal Reserve Board Finance and Economic Discussion Series, 2010–2049.

Maki, Wilbur R., Carlo del Ninno, and Peter L Stenburg (1980). "Forecasting State Economic Growth in Recession and Recovery." *Journal of Regional Analysis and Policy* 13(2): 39–50.

Massachusetts Department of Revenue (2007, December 13). "Briefing Book: FY2009 Consensus Revenue Estimate Hearing." Boston: Massachusetts Department of Revenue.

McCullen, Mark (2007, September 17–19). "Regional Economic Fallout." Presentation to annual Federation of Tax Administrators' revenue-estimating conference, Raleigh, North Carolina.

McNichol, Elizabeth, and Kwame Boadi (2011, February 3). "Why and How States Should Strengthen Their Rainy Day Funds." Center on Budget and Policy Priorities.

Mier, Chris (2009, May 12–15). "The Current Environment in Financial Markets." Presentation to the National Association of State Treasurers' 2009 Treasury Management Conference, Atlanta, Georgia.

Minutes of the Delaware Economic and Financial Advisory Council (2008, September 15). Buena Vista.

National Association of State Budget Officers (NASBO) (2008). "Budget Process in the States, Summer 2008." www.nasbo.org.

National Association of State Budget Officers (NASBO) (2010). *Annual Report on Fiscal Survey of the States*. www.nasbo.org.

Nelson A. Rockefeller Institute of Government (current quarterly). State Revenue Report. Albany: State University of New York at Albany. www.rockinst.org.

New Mexico Department of Finance and Administration (2007, October 23). "General Fund Consensus Revenue." Presentation to the New Mexico Legislature.

Office of Management and Budget (OMB) (2008, February 4). "Budget of the United States Government: Fiscal Year 2009."

Urahn, Susan, and Thomas Gais (2011, March). "States' Revenue Estimating: Cracks in the Crystal Ball." Joint Project of Pew Charitable Trusts and Rockefeller Institute.

US Bureau of Economic Analysis (BEA) (monthly and annual) National Income and Products Table. www.bea.gov

US Bureau of Labor Statistics (BLS) (monthly and annual) Employment Situation.

US Census Bureau (2011). Annual Survey of State Tax Collections. http://www.census.gov/govs/statetax/.

Watson, Harry (2005), "Excess Burden." In *The Encyclopedia of Taxation and Tax Policy*, edited by Joseph J. Cordes, Robert D. Ebel, and Jane G. Gravelle. Washington, DC: Urban Institute Press. 121–122.

Williams, Daniel W (2008). "Preparing Data For Forecasting." In *Government Budget Forecasting*, edited by Jinping Sun and Thomas D. Lynch. Boca Raton, FL: CRC Press. Chapter 14.

Willoughby, Katherine, and Hai Guo (2008, March). "The State of the Art." *Government Budget Forecasting*: 27–42.

WSJ.com (2007). "WSJ Forecasting Survey—December 2007." http://online.wsj.com/public/resources/documents/info-flash08.html?project=EFORECAST07, accessed January 30, 2011.

PART III

SPENDING, BORROWING, AND FINANCIAL MANAGEMENT

CHAPTER 20

··

PROVIDING AND FINANCING K-12 EDUCATION

··

DAPHNE A. KENYON

ELEMENTARY and secondary education spending is the single largest category of United States state and local government spending, representing about one-quarter of the total. In 2006 state and local spending on public kindergarten through grade 12 (K-12) education totaled $500.5 billion, nearly 4 percent of GDP.[1] Although private alternatives exist, in 2007 50.6 million children or nearly 86 percent of schoolchildren in the United States attended public schools. Eleven percent of children attended private schools and three percent were homeschooled.[2]

The financing and quality of elementary and secondary education is critically important for many reasons. The future of America's youth depends on their educational opportunities, and educational opportunity is a stepping stone to economic success for many. Education is critical to the vitality of our democratic political system. A quality education makes individuals more productive in the workplace, thereby contributing to economic growth and increasing our country's international competitiveness.

The United States has one of the most decentralized education finance systems in the world. Although the US Constitution makes the direct provision of education a state function, all states but Hawaii delegate important educational responsibilities to local governments. At the core of the system is a long-standing commitment to local control and finance. But local financing of education has fallen since the 1920s and the role of state governments has increased (figure 20.1).

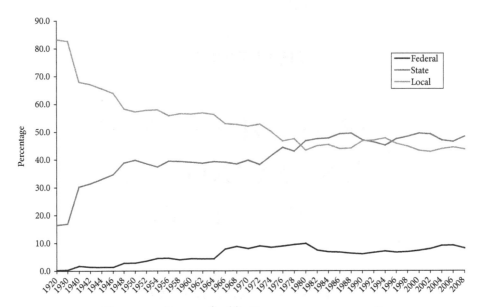

Figure 20.1 Source of public K-12 revenues, 1920–2008
Source: National Center for Education Statistics, 2007; U.S. Census, 2010.

Beginning in the 1980s, the state contribution to public K-12 revenues first exceeded the local contribution; since then both state and local contributions have been nearly equal. In recent years the federal role in K-12 education has increased, but the federal government still provides less than 10 percent of total funding.

Today, technological changes and other forces appear poised to force major changes in the provision of education. This chapter will focus on education finance in the context of the changing provision of education. Unless otherwise noted, references to education should be interpreted as referring to K-12 education.

EDUCATION AS A LOCAL GOVERNMENT RESPONSIBILITY

The provision and financing of K-12 education in the United States has traditionally been a responsibility of local government, but the nature of local government involvement varies as does the degree of local control.

Education can be provided by independent school districts or dependent school districts. In the case of independent school districts, voters consider budgets for general-purpose local governments and school districts independently. In the case of dependent school districts, the school district is a department of a larger general-purpose government such as a municipality or county. In 2007 there were 14,561 public school districts in the United States—13,051 independent and 1,510 dependent. Thirty states had independent school districts only; four states had dependent school districts only;[3] and fifteen states had a mix of independent and dependent school districts.[4]

The degree of local control varies dramatically by state, depending on the number of school districts. For example, Nevada, where school districts are organized by county, has seventeen school districts, whereas New Hampshire, which has a mix of dependent and independent school districts, has 178 school districts. New Hampshire has approximately half the population of Nevada but ten times as many school districts, making the degree of local control much greater in New Hampshire than in Nevada.

The size and character of local school districts also vary enormously. Vermont has the most fragmented system of local school districts in the United States, with 292 regular school districts serving just over 90,000 students.[5] Contrast this with Fairfax County, Virginia, which constitutes a single school district with 169,000 students. An even greater contrast is the New York City Department of Education, the largest public school system in the country, with 1.1 million children in 1,700 schools.[6]

In 2007–2008, the federal government contributed 8 percent of public K-12 revenue, state governments contributed 48 percent, and local governments contributed 44 percent (figure 20.2). The local contribution is made up of local property taxes (29 percent), parent government contributions (approximately 8 percent) and other local sources (7 percent). However, most parent government contributions likely derive from the property tax[7] and certainly the property tax is the predominant local source of revenue for K-12 education.

At the same time, reliance on local property taxation for school funding has declined over time due to school reform efforts (discussed in the next section) and taxpayer antipathy toward the property tax. According to McGuire and Papke, the percentage of total school funding from the local property tax was 47 percent in

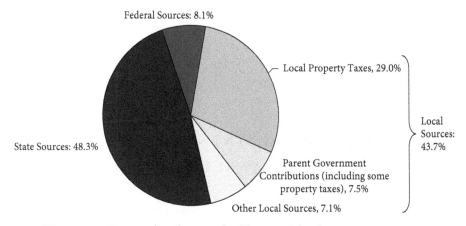

Figure 20.2 Percent distribution of public K-12 School revenue, 2007–2008
Source: U.S. Census (2010) Public Education Finances 2008.

1956, continued to exceed 40 percent until 1972, but fell to 34 percent in 1982, and has since declined to 29 percent.[8] The following discussion will focus on the pros and cons of relying on local property taxes to fund schools.

One of the strongest criticisms of funding schools through property taxation is that it creates fiscal disparities. That is, because property values per pupil vary among school districts, reliance on the property tax for K-12 financing allows some communities to fund high per-pupil expenditures with low tax rates while other communities need to impose high tax rates to fund even modest school expenditures. The example drawn from the 1971 California lawsuit *Serrano v. Priest* compares Beverly Hills, which had assessed value per pupil of $50,885, to Baldwin Park, which had an assessed value per pupil of $3,706. Beverly Hills was able to fund more than twice the level of spending per pupil with a tax rate half as high.[9] The fiscal disparities created by relying on local property taxes to fund education have long been a sore point with some. For example, in commenting on their study of the New England region, which relies more heavily on the property tax than any other region, Neal Pierce and Curtis Johnson emphatically criticized this reliance: "High property taxes—the burdens and perverse incentives they create, the rage they generate, the town-to-town school funding inequities they proliferate—...represent an endless New England nightmare."[10]

In a less dramatic fashion, other analysts have asked whether local governments, including school districts, need a local source of revenue, and if they do, whether better alternatives than the property tax exist. McGuire and Papke argued that fiscal empowerment of local governments is important, both to cater to differences in tastes for public goods and to promote fiscal responsibility.[11] Next they compared the property tax to the two main alternatives: a local sales tax and a local income tax. For several reasons, including the revenue productivity and stability of the property tax, McGuire and Papke have appeared to favor the property tax. Many other analysts agree. To the degree that voters prefer local autonomy and local involvement in education, a local revenue source is necessary because control is linked to financing. Furthermore, many support the property tax as the best revenue source to fund independent local governments. For example, the National Research Council concluded that "the local property tax remains the best way to raise *local* revenue for education."[12]

The Growing State Role, State School-Funding Lawsuits, and State Aid

But the role of state governments in funding education changed dramatically over the twentieth century. In 1920, state governments provided less than 20 percent and local governments provided more than 80 percent of the revenues for public K-12 education. The percentage of revenues provided by state governments increased dramatically so that since the 1970s, state governments and local governments in the United States have each provided just under 50 percent of total education revenues, although state-local funding ratios vary dramatically by state.

School-Funding Lawsuits. Since the 1960s and continuing until today, various lawsuits across the country have challenged states' school-funding systems. Forty-five states have dealt with such lawsuits; the only states without school-funding lawsuits are Delaware, Hawaii, Mississippi, Nevada, and Utah.[13] In one of the first such cases, *McInnis v. Shapiro* (1968), an Illinois case, the plaintiffs charged that the state was failing to distribute education based on the needs of the districts; a similar suit, *Burrus v. Wilkerson* (1969), was filed in Virginia.[14] Federal courts rejected the claims for each case. For example, the Virginia Supreme Court argued that the "courts have neither the knowledge, nor the means, nor the power to tailor the public monies to fit the varying needs of the students throughout the state."[15] For these early "need-based" lawsuits, appeals to the United States Supreme Court were unsuccessful, and this led lawyers who were concerned with school finance equity to seek a new approach to litigation.

From the late 1960s to 1973, so-called equity lawsuits were brought in both federal and state courts. These lawsuits were based on the theory that school spending per pupil should not depend on the school district's property wealth. *Serrano v. Priest* (1971), in which the California Supreme Court found that the state's school system violated the equal protection clauses of both the federal and California constitutions, was one of the most significant decisions of this era.[16] But the US Supreme Court's decision in *San Antonio Independent School District v. Rodriguez* (1973) shut the door on efforts to pursue equitable school funding through federal courts.[17] In that 5–4 decision, the US Supreme Court ruled that education was not a fundamental right and property wealth per pupil was not a suspect class so that school-funding disparities in Texas did not violate the Equal Protection Clause of the US Constitution.

From 1973 to 1989 a number of equity school-funding lawsuits were filed in state courts also resting on equal protection claims and on claims that the state constitution imposed a duty to educate. This included California's *Serrano II* (1976), in which California's highest court reaffirmed its finding on the basis of the state constitution and New Jersey's *Robinson v. Cahill*.[18] But the ratio of plaintiff victories to lawsuits filed was low (plaintiffs prevailed in only seven of twenty-two final decisions),[19] which led to another type of school-funding lawsuit, based on adequacy claims.

The first adequacy lawsuit was the 1989 *Rose v. Council for Better Education, Inc.*, decision in Kentucky.[20] Adequacy lawsuits are typically based on education clauses in state constitutions, in which the state might be required to "cherish" education, as in New Hampshire and Massachusetts, with the usual focus being to ensure that all children in the state have the opportunity to receive an adequate education. Two broad differences between adequacy and equity lawsuits are that adequacy lawsuits put greater emphasis on education outcomes than equity lawsuits, and adequacy lawsuits tend to emphasize whether children are able to meet some absolute standard of education quality rather than a relative equity standard.

Although this thumbnail sketch of the history of school-funding lawsuits is by now standard, it is important to emphasize the limits of this simple taxonomy. Individual states have often had both equity and adequacy lawsuits, and other dimensions of school-funding lawsuits have also been important, such as whether the case focuses on capital or operating spending or whether it addresses issues pertaining to all school districts or only a subset of needy school districts such as in the New Jersey *Abbott* rulings.[21] One of the most important distinctions among court rulings is their specificity. For example, Massachusetts's *McDuffy* decision found the state's school-funding system unconstitutional, but imposed no remedy.[22] On the other hand, New Jersey's *Abbot V* decision mandated a timetable of specific reforms that included particular curricular changes.[23]

Before turning to the effects of these lawsuits, three caveats are important. First, not all lawsuits were favorable to the plaintiffs. One reason that courts sometimes rejected school-funding lawsuits was that policy judgments about public education were the responsibility of the state legislature. For example, the highest court in Massachusetts argued, "Because decisions about where scarce public money will do the most good are laden with value judgments, those decisions are best left to our elected representatives."[24] Second, not all state legislatures restructured their school finance systems in response to a court mandate. In Ohio, where the school finance system was first ruled unconstitutional in 1997, as of 2007 the legislature had yet to restructure its school-funding system.[25] Finally, some states, such as Michigan, chose to restructure their school finance systems without being mandated to do so by a school-funding lawsuit.[26]

One question to ask regarding school-funding lawsuits is what impact they had on the level and distribution of school spending. Corcoran and Evans examined the period from 1972 to 2002 and found that spending per pupil rose by 9.2 percent more in states facing a court school-funding mandate than for states without such a mandate.[27] They also found that "within-state inequality fell as much as 15–19 percent between 1972 and 2002 in states with court mandated finance reform, relative to those without such orders."[28]

With respect to the more important question of whether school finance reform has raised student achievement, the evidence is mixed. Downes found that school finance reform tended to raise test scores and lower dropout rates, while Betts found the opposite.[29] Corcoran and Evans reviewed the literature and concluded that "assessments of the effects of finance reform on achievement have yielded quite varied results, quite likely due to the varied nature of these reforms."[30]

It is often claimed that school-funding lawsuits have led to reduced reliance on property taxes to fund education. Scrutiny of the empirical evidence leads to a more nuanced conclusion. Up until 1989, when equity lawsuits were the norm, states with independent school districts did reduce their reliance on property taxation to a modest degree, with the exception of California, which reduced its reliance on the property tax to a great degree. After 1989, when adequacy lawsuits were more typical, school-funding lawsuits had a negligible effect on the degree of a state's reliance on property taxes. McGuire and Papke argued that the turn to greater reliance on adequacy lawsuits may mean the pressure to reduce reliance on property-tax funding for education may abate somewhat.[31]

State Aid. State aid for schools takes different forms and falls under one of two categories: general and categorical aid. General aid typically constitutes the most important form of school aid while categorical aid provides funding for special programs (e.g., transportation) or particular pupils (e.g., special education students).

General aid, in turn, can take four basic forms: foundation grants, flat grants, district power-equalizing grants, and full state funding. [32] At present, foundation grants are the most commonly recommended form of general education grant used by forty states, so after briefly describing the other types of general aid, they will be the focus of this section.

Flat grants were the first types of school-funding grant employed, but today states rarely use flat grants, except as minor adjustments to other grants provided by a state. Flat grants can provide a certain number of dollars per school, per classroom, per teacher, or per pupil. District power-equalizing grants are a form of matching grant in which the per-pupil spending differences might remain, but spending differences result from varying tax rates reflecting local school preferences but not the unequal distribution of the local tax base.[33] The objective of this type of grant is to ensure that each school district can raise the same amount of revenue for a given increase in the district's tax rate. Hawaii is the best-known example, since there is a single school district and no school funding from the property tax.[34] There is no a priori reason why one requires a single district in order to have full funding, though. A state can have full funding with multiple districts, with the funding determined on the basis of fiscal capacity and fiscal need.[35]

Foundation grants are designed to ensure that per-pupil expenditures exceed a certain minimum or foundation amount in all school districts. In essence, foundation grants provide more aid to school districts with lesser ability to raise local revenues. Foundation grants accomplish this in the following way. First, a foundation level of spending is set. This may simply equal a certain number of dollars per pupil, or it may include adjustments for the varying costs of educating different pupils, or for variations in the cost of living across the state. Second, the state typically subtracts from the foundation level some common property-tax rate times the total value of the school district's tax base to determine the required local contribution. Sometimes the required local contribution is not based solely on property-tax revenues but depends on income-tax or sales-tax revenues or on household income even if the local government has no access to local option taxes. The state's foundation grant is set equal to the difference between the foundation level of spending and the required local contribution. John Yinger argued that:

> state supreme courts, policy makers, and scholars appear to have reached a consensus that a foundation plan with a foundation level based on a generous notion of educational adequacy, a required minimum tax rate, and some kind of educational cost adjustment forms the core of an acceptable reform of state education finance.[36]

The educational cost adjustments referenced by Yinger reflect the fact that not all students are equally costly to educate. English-language learners, low-income children, and children with disabilities require additional resources. State-aid formulas can take these cost differentials into account in different ways. Some states have supplemental aid programs or categorical aid programs distributed on the basis of economic disadvantage or special-education needs. Others weight students differently, so that an English-language learner might be given a weight in the basic school-aid formula of 1.25, indicating that such a student is estimated to require 25 percent more resources to educate than a student who is not an English-language learner.

The question of cost adjustments raises the question of whether state school aid is targeted to the neediest children. Education Trust, a nonprofit organization organized by the American Association for Higher Education, published a periodic report on state school-aid programs across the United States, which adjusts for the additional cost of educating low-income students or students with disabilities and also takes into account differences in the cost of living across each state. In 2006, Education Trust found that for most states *state* aid is not sufficiently targeted to high-poverty districts to compensate for the inequitable pattern of *local* government resources.[37] A more recent study of school finance looks at targeting of funds at an even more disaggregated level. Marguerite Roza examined allocation of funding by school instead of by school district, and she found that in most cases funding is not tracked in sufficient detail to enable the analyst to determine whether greater funding is allocated to impoverished schools than wealthy schools.[38]

Diversity among States. Any review of the role of state governments in financing education must note the wide degree of diversity among the states. Figure 20.3 shows how the role of state government in financing K–12 education differs

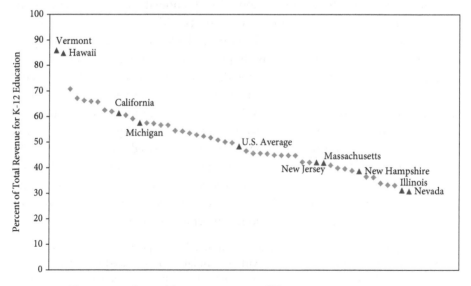

Figure 20.3 State aid as a percentage of K–12 revenue, 2007–2008
Source: National Center for Education Statistics, 2010.

among states. In states like Hawaii and Vermont, virtually all school funding comes from state sources (86.6 and 86.9 percent is funded by the state, respectively), but school finance is also very centralized in New Mexico (70.1 percent), Minnesota (69.5 percent), and North Carolina (63.0 percent) And it is not just the small to medium-sized states with high state-aid ratios: California is at 60.6 percent, which is well above the US average of 47.5 percent. At the other end of the spectrum, school finance is still mostly a local responsibility in states like Nevada (27.9 percent) and Illinois (27.1 percent).

Table 20.1 spotlights the great differences in education and education finance for seven selected states. States vary greatly in their demographic challenges, in their school district structures, in the degree to which they fund K-12 education, and in their outcomes. Students who are not native English speakers, who require special-education services, or who are from low-income families typically require greater resources than other children. Among the states featured in table 20.1, California stands out for having a high percentage of students with limited English proficiency (24 percent), especially compared to New Hampshire's 1.8 percent. The variation in the percentage of students requiring special education is not great, but the percentage of students from low-income families (measured as the percentage that is eligible for free or reduced price meals) ranges from over 50 percent in California to just over 20 percent in New Hampshire. States also vary in the amounts they spend per pupil (New Jersey spends nearly $16,000 per pupil while California spends less than $9,000), in the number of school districts, and in the number of students per district.

Educational Performance. One of the most important ways that states vary is in the educational performance of their schools. Although no standardized test is perfect, one of the most commonly cited measures of performance is the National Assessment of Educational Progress (NAEP), widely known as the "Nation's Report Card." In 2001, the reauthorization of the Elementary and Secondary Education Act known as No Child Left Behind (NCLB) mandated that every state participate in the NAEP in reading and mathematics for grades four and eight every two years, in part to serve as a way to gauge the level of each state's assessment and accountability system.[39] Using test scores for elementary and middle school students to gauge school performance is better than using scores on achievement tests that only college-bound students use, such as the Student Achievement Test (SAT).

High school graduation rates are the second widely used measure, though not all states have good data systems to track students through high school. Thus graduation rates can be defined in different ways. For example, some states report students who have passed the General Education Development (GED) test as having graduated from high school. By 2012, most states are expected to use a common definition of a high school graduation rate.[40]

Among the seven states in table 20.1, Massachusetts ranks highest with the highest NAEP scores, which reflect achievement for grades four and eight, and among the highest graduation rates, while California ranks the lowest on both measures. Massachusetts ranks first in the United States on fourth-grade math

Table 20.1 School finance in a nutshell, selected states

	California	Massachusetts	Michigan	New Hampshire	New Jersey	Hawaii	Illinois
Reliance on property tax, 2008 state and local property taxes as percentage of total state and local taxes; state rank (US average 21.1%)	19.5% (27th)	24.5% (11th)	24.3% (12th)	42.5% (1st)	45.1% (2nd)	13.4% (41st)	27.3% (6th)
State aid as percentage of elementary and secondary education revenues, 2007–2008	61.3%	41.9%	57.5%	38.6%	42.1%	84.8%	31.2%
Spending per pupil and rank, 2011, adjusted for regional cost differences; state rank	$8,852 (42nd)	$12,559 (11th)	$10,318 (31st)	$12,840 (10th)	$15,598 (3rd)	$12,457 (13th)	$10,030 (33rd)
Number of school districts, 2008–2009	960	352	552	178	616	1	869
Number of students, 2008–2009	6,322,528	958,910	1,659,921	197,934	1,381,420	179,478	2,119,707
Students/district, 2008–2009	6,586	2,724	3,007	1,112	2,243	179,478	2,439
Percentage of those with limited English proficiency, 2008–2009	24.0%	5.1%	3.7%	1.8%	0.9%	10.3%	9.7%
Percentage of special education, 2008–2009	10.5%	17.6%	14.0%	15.2%	16.6%	11.2%	15.0%

Percentage eligible for free and reduced price meals, 2005–2006	51.7%	30.7%	41.1%	20.5%	30.0%	41.7%	39.3%
Graduation rates, 2011	62.7% (41st)	77.3% (10th)	77.8% (6th)	76.2% (13th)	83.3% (1st)	65.1% (38th)	74.6% (18th)
2009 National Assessment of Educational Progress test, percentage scoring at or above basic, state rank							
Math, 4th grade	71.7% (47th)	92.4% (1st)	78.0% (40th)	92.1% (2nd)	87.5% (8th)	77.5% (42nd)	9.6% (36th)
Reading, 4th grade	53.9% (48th)	80.1% (1st)	64.1% (36th)	76.8% (2nd)	76.1% (3rd)	56.7% (45th)	64.7% (34th)
Math, 8th grade	59.1% (48th)	85.2% (2nd)	67.8% (37th)	81.6% (6th)	80.2% (8th)	65.0% (42nd)	72.6% (32nd)
Reading, 8th grade	63.6% (49th)	83.1% (6th)	72.0% (36th)	81.4% (10th)	83.4% (5th)	66.8% (44th)	76.5% (28th)

Sources: US Department of Education (2010a, 2010b, 2010c); US Census (2010); Editorial Projects in Education Research Center (2011).

and reading, second on eighth-grade math, and sixth on eighth-grade reading. In contrast, California ranks forty-seventh to forty-ninth on each. Furthermore, Massachusetts ranks tenth in the United States on its high school graduation rate and California ranks forty-first. An important caveat, however, is that these measures are not standardized for factors such as the composition of demographic groups by state.

Federal Finance and Regulation

The federal role in K-12 education has traditionally been much smaller than the state or local roles, but the importance of the federal government has increased over time, and it takes three forms: financial, regulatory, and agenda-setting.

As figure 20.1 revealed, the federal government played a negligible role in funding K-12 education before the 1940s. The federal share in financing increased gradually until 1965, when it jumped to nearly 10 percent with the passage of the Elementary and Secondary Education Act (ESEA). The largest component of ESEA, Title I, was intended to improve the academic achievement of disadvantaged, poor children. Through Title I, the federal government plays some role in redistributing resources both among and within states, sending funds to school districts based on the number of poor children in the district and the average school spending in the state, with a mandate to target funds to students whose performances fall short of adequate. However, studies have shown that state and local governments change their spending behaviors in response to this federal program with the result that Title I funding substitutes for, rather than supplements, state and local funding.[41]

Another milestone in the federal role in K-12 education was the creation of the Department of Education by President Jimmy Carter in 1979. During the Ronald Reagan administration, Secretary of Education Terrel Bell created the National Commission on Excellence in Education in order to investigate the state of US education. The commission produced an influential and often-cited report, *A Nation at Risk*, which painted a pessimistic picture of student achievement and called for a number of reforms, such as strengthening high school graduation course requirements and improving teacher preparation. The report is credited for helping spur nationwide interest in education reform.[42]

The federal role in K-12 education is not limited to funding and agenda-setting, but it includes regulation or mandates. One important example is the 1975 passage of the Education for All Handicapped Children Act, later renamed the Individuals with Disabilities Education Act (IDEA). This act provides funding for students with physical and cognitive disabilities, but it conditions the receipt of those funds on a complex set of regulations. In brief, each eligible student is guaranteed the right to a free and appropriate public education (FAPE) through the creation of an individualized education plan (IEP) as determined by a team of educators and service providers. Since 1975, the percentage of students in special education has grown and spending on special-education services constitutes a significant fraction—about 14 percent—of total K-12 spending.[43] Most of the funding for special education derives from state and local governments and there is continual pressure by some groups to increase the proportion of special-education services funded by the federal government.

The 2001 enactment of NCLB, which added a wide array of regulations on K-12 education, "has resulted in a stronger federal influence at the school and classroom level than ever before."[44] This is largely a result of new stringent regulations tied to an important federal-funding source. The stated goal of NCLB was to close the academic achievement gaps that currently exist between students of different races, special-education students, economically disadvantaged students, and other students. The central focus of NCLB is accountability, which includes a number of requirements.[45]

All states were required to adopt tests and to test students in grades three through eight and in high school on reading and mathematics. States could define proficiency as they choose but are required to report and disaggregate scores by race, ethnicity, family income, disability, or limited English-proficiency status. The mandated goal is for all students to achieve proficiency in reading and mathematics by 2013-2014. Although states are allowed to set their own timelines, federal rules triggered sanctions when a school did not make adequate yearly progress (AYP). These sanctions increased in severity, depending on how many years a school failed to make AYP and included such provisions as offering free tutoring, allowing school choice, or requiring school restructuring.

The law has been credited for shining a light on long-standing achievement gaps among students and encouraging educators to make the reduction of gaps a high priority. At the same time, the law has been soundly criticized for narrowing the curricula of many schools because testing is only mandated for reading and mathematics and for imposing sanctions that have no guarantee of improving student achievement.[46]

INTERNATIONAL EDUCATION COMPARISONS

Our economy is becoming increasingly global: international trade doubled as a percentage of world production over the last thirty years due to reduced trade barriers and because of lower costs of communication and transportation. For example, the cost of air travel fell from 87 cents per mile in 1930 to 9.5 cents per mile in 2000.[47] This puts American labor in competition with labor worldwide.

Many low-skilled jobs are likely to be filled overseas where labor costs are lower, providing fewer job opportunities for US youth who do not have a high school education. This means there is increasing pressure to make sure that all young people in the United States obtain a high-quality education with at least a high school diploma.

Recognizing that the United States is part of an increasingly global economy and that the country's K-12 system (e.g., high school) graduates must compete with others around the world, it is useful to compare elementary and secondary school structure, finance, and achievement in the United States to that of other countries. A wide range of useful comparative statistics is available for Organisation for Economic Co-operation and Development (OECD) countries.[48] It is best to be somewhat cautious in comparisons, however. Most OECD countries are not federal countries with substantial decentralization of finance and provision of education as in the United States. Moreover, many countries in the OECD are small countries (for example, the population of Hungary is about the same as Michigan; and Poland's population is about the same as that of California) with more homogeneous demographics than the United States, adding further cautions as to drawing strong conclusions between the United States and other countries. In addition, school systems are often different, with some countries tracking students by abilities at early ages, and others not using tracking until high school, as in the United States. For example, in some European countries, student achievement in primary grades determines the type of secondary school and course of study a student is allowed to choose. With those caveats in mind, test scores need to be compared first, then graduation rates, school structure, and school finance.

Since 2000, the Program for International Student Assessment (PISA) tests in math, reading, and science have been given every three years to fifteen-year-olds around the world. [49] Table 20.2 reports US scores and how they compare to the scores of other OECD countries. The US scores seventeenth out of sixty-five countries in reading, twenty-third in science, and thirty-first in mathematics.

Another international comparison is the *Trends in International Mathematics and Science* study, which reports test results for fourth- and eighth-grade students for thirty-six or forty-eight countries, including both many OECD countries and also non-OECD countries, such as Kazakhstan and Yemen.[50] In 2007, US scores ranked eighth out of thirty-six countries for fourth-grade science and eleventh out of forty-eight for eighth-grade science. A final measure of educational outcomes is the high school graduation rate. However, definitions for different countries may not be equivalent. Keeping that in mind, in 2007 the graduation rate in the United States ranked twentieth among twenty-eight OECD countries.

The last section of table 20.2 reports school finance comparisons. For public and private elementary school spending per pupil, the United States ranks second among OECD countries for per-pupil elementary school spending and fourth for secondary school spending. However, neither teacher pay nor pupils per teacher rank as highly.

Table 20.2 International comparisons of selected education indicators, 2007–2009

Indicator	Year	United States	OECD Average[1]	Best Ranked Country/Economy
Assessment Test Scores and Graduation Rates				
PISA math scores (15-yr-old students)	2009	487 (Rank 31 of 65)	496 (OECD and partner countries)[2,3]	600 (Shanghai-China)
PISA reading scores (15-yr-old students)	2009	500 (Rank 17 of 65)	493 (OECD and partner countries)	556 (Shanghai-China)
PISA science scores (15-yr-old students)	2009	502 (Rank 23 of 65)	501 (OECD and partner countries)	575 (Shanghai-China)
TIMSS: 4th-grade science	2007	539 (Rank 8 of 36)	474 (not OECD)	587 (Singapore)
TIMSS: 8th-grade science	2007	520 (Rank 11 of 48)	466 (not OECD)[4]	567 (Singapore)
Graduation rate	2008	76.7 (20 of 28)	80.0	97.2 (Germany)
Enrollment				
Percentage of students enrolled in public schools: Primary	2008	90.3 (23 of 31)	89.6	100 (Netherlands)
Percentage of students enrolled in public schools: Lower secondary	2008	91.1 (17 of 30)	83.2	100 (Netherlands and Ireland)
Percentage of students enrolled in public schools: Upper secondary	2008	91.4 (9 of 31)	82.0	100 (Netherlands)
School finance				
Per-student expenditures, public and private: Elementary	2007	$10,229 (Rank 2 of 28)	$6,741	$13,985 (Luxembourg)
Per student expenditures, public and private: Secondary	2007	$11,301 (Rank 4 of 29)	$8,267	$17,928 (Luxembourg)

(Continued)

Table 20.2 Continued

Indicator	Year	United States	OECD Average[1]	Best Ranked Country/Economy
Public expenditures on primary and secondary institutions as percentage of GDP	2007	3.7% (Rank 7 of 29)	3.3%	4.9% (Iceland)
Pupils per teacher, public and private: Primary	2008	14.3 (11 of 27)	16.4	10.5 (Poland)
Pupils per teacher, public and private: Secondary	2008	15.1 (23 of 29)	13.7	7.7 (Portugal)
Starting teacher salary/minimum training: Elementary (US dollars)	2008	$35,999 (6 of 29)	$28,949	$48,793 (Luxembourg)
Starting teacher salary/minimum training: Lower secondary (US dollars)	2008	$35,915 (7 out of 29)	$30,750	$71,508 (Luxembourg)
Starting teacher salary/minimum training: Upper secondary (US Dollars)	2008	$36,398 (7 of 28)	$32,563	$71,508 (Luxembourg)

Sources: OECD (2010a, 2010b); Snyder and Dillow (2010).

Notes: OECD member countries are Australia, Austria, Belgium, Canada, Chile, the Czech Republic, Denmark, Finland, France, Germany, Greece, Hungary, Iceland, Ireland, Israel, Italy, Japan, Korea, Luxembourg, Mexico, the Netherlands, New Zealand, Norway, Poland, Portugal, the Slovak Republic, Slovenia, Spain, Sweden, Switzerland, Turkey, the United Kingdom, and the United States.

[1] OECD partners may include countries and economies that have started the "accession process" to become members of the OECD, and nonmember countries that have developed "cooperative relations" with OECD. The partner countries that administered the 2009 PISA assessments are Albania, Argentina, Azerbaijan, Brazil, Bulgaria,

[2] Colombia, Costa Rica, Croatia, Georgia, Himachal Pradesh-India, Hong Kong, Indonesia, Jordan, Kazakhstan, Kyrgyzstan, Latvia, Liechtenstein, Lithuania, Macao, Malaysia, Malta, Mauritius, Miranda-Venezuela, Montenegro, Netherlands-Antilles, Panama, Peru, Thailand, Trinidad and Tobago, Tunisia, Uruguay, United Arab Emirates, and Vietnam.

[3] PISA: Programme for International Student Assessment.

[4] TIMSS: Trends in International Mathematics and Science.

The Changing Provision of Education

Structural changes in the economy, political forces, and technological change are all driving changes in the provision of education. Although many schools operate much as they did a century ago, the pressure for change is enormous, with a number of innovative schools providing glimpses into how education may evolve.

Reflecting the long-standing appreciation of the free market and the benefits of consumer choice there is a growing US trend toward choice-based education (see table 20.3). From 1999 to 2007, a greater proportion of K-12 students were home-schooled, had attended private schools, or had attended public charter schools relative to the traditional public school system in which students attend assigned schools.

The most frequent choice alternative to traditional public schools is the public charter school, which accounted for 15 percent of K-12 students in 2007, up from 14.3 percent in 1999. In 2010, forty states had charter schools and those schools educated over one million students nationwide. Charter schools are more likely to be located in a city, and they tend to have small enrollments and more racially diverse populations than traditional public schools. The choice option with the highest growth rate is homeschooling. In 1999, 1.7 percent of K-12 students were homeschooled; in 2007 that percentage was 2.9 percent.

Today's children grow up as digital natives, comfortable using computers from an early age to tap the resources of the Internet for entertainment, information gathering, or maintaining social connections. As one scholar described the experience of today's children and teens,

> They spend their days immersed in a "media diet," devouring entertainment, communication, and, well, any form of electronic media. They are master multitaskers, social networkers, electronic communicators and the first to rush to any new technology. They were born surrounded by technology, and with every

Table 20.3 K-12 students by school type, 1999–2007

	1999	2003	2007
Public School	88.4%	87.1%	85.6%
Assigned	*74.1%*	*72.1%*	*70.6%*
Chosen (including charter schools)	*14.3%*	*15.0%*	*15.0%*
Private	10.0%	10.8%	11.4%
Homeschool	1.7%	2.2%	2.9%
Charter School Enrollment	339,678	789,479	1,012,906
States with Charter Schools	32	35	42

Source: US Department of Education, National Center for Education Statistics (1999–2007).

passing year they add more tools to their electronic repertoire. They live in social networks such as *Facebook*, *MySpace*, and *Second Life* gathering friends; they text more than they talk on the phone; and they *Twitter* (or tweet) the night away, often sleeping with their cell phones vibrating by their sides.[51]

Traditional twentieth-century education, based on the agrarian calendar, with certain mandated days of annual seat time, within the physical boundaries of a school building, is increasingly out of sync with the experience of this generation. For these students, it is natural to use computers in their school work, including taking courses online, and for them to extend the school day beyond the traditional day to a nearly 24/7 endeavor.

Technological change has put much greater information at the fingertips of students and teachers. It also has the potential for improving education while lowering costs. The ease of using assessments to track individual student progress can help teachers individualize education, with the potential of raising achievement. Online courses are becoming increasingly popular and they have the potential for expanding curricular offerings, particularly for rural schools, while lowering costs.

CHALLENGES TO EDUCATION AND EDUCATION FINANCE

In the near term as the economy recovers from the Great Recession, fiscal pressures on schools are likely to be intense and growing. The federal government increased school aid through the American Recovery and Reinvestment Act,[52] but an extension of this federal stimulus targeted to education is unlikely given the huge federal budget deficits and increased public concern about the deficits. States face daunting budget pressures of their own, and many have cut school aid, and many more states are likely to do so. In the aftermath of the 2001 recession, states enrolling two-thirds of the nation's students cut real support for education and the last recession was even more severe.[53]

In the longer term, demographic challenges are likely to generate the greatest pressures on K-12 education. Between 1980 and 2025, the proportion of the population sixty-five and over is expected to increase from 11.3 percent to 18.2 percent while the proportion of the population that is school aged is expected to decline from 24.8 to 19.6 percent. This implies less support by taxpayers for property taxes to fund schools, although researchers disagree regarding the strength of that response. It also means that there will be increased demand for Medicaid funding for nursing-home care, which will tend to crowd out some school spending.[54]

At the same time the number of students with special needs, who require more resources and attention to educate, is growing and is expected to grow for the foreseeable future. This includes students with disabilities, with limited English proficiency, and with poorer family backgrounds. For example, today one in five children live in poverty and this fraction is expected to grow. One reflection of this changing student population is the prediction that, if current immigration trends in the United States continue, the majority of children will be from minority populations by 2050.[55]

With elementary and secondary education becoming more essential but fiscal pressures growing, it is difficult to be optimistic about the future of education. However, voters and politicians clearly value spending on education and both technology and education reformers promise a number of innovations. Hopefully, the high level of civic interest and potential for useful innovations will be up to the demographic and fiscal challenges. Both the well-being of our children and grandchildren and the health of our economy are at stake.

NOTES

Many thanks to Bethany Paquin for her research assistance and editing and to Adam Langley for his comments on previous drafts.

1 National Center for Education Statistics (2009).

2 US Department of Education, National Center for Education Statistics (2007).

3 Alaska, Hawaii, Maryland, and North Carolina are classified as dependent school districts because all school districts in these states are dependent. Other sources may classify Connecticut, Massachusetts, Rhode Island, Tennessee, and Virginia as dependent-district states because almost all districts in these states are dependent.

4 US Bureau of the Census (2008).

5 Table 2 in Keaton (2010).

6 New York City Department of Education, "About Us," http://schools.nyc.gov/AboutUs; and US Department of Education, National Center for Education Statistics, Common Core of Data, "Local Education Agency (School District) Universe Survey," 2008–2009, v.1.

7 McGuire and Papke (2008), 358. If a parent government, such as a municipal government, derives some of its revenue from the property tax, there is no definitive way to allocate revenues by source to a school department that is dependent on this parent government.

8 Ibid., 360.

9 *Serrano v. Priest*, 5 Cal.3d 584 (1971); Odden and Picus (2000), 12.

10 Pierce and Johnson (2006).

11 Yilmaz, Vaillancourt, and Dafflon (this volume) present the conceptual basis for this view.

12 Ladd and Hansen (1999), 232–233.

13 ACCESS (2011).

14 *McInnis v. Shapiro*, 293 F. Supp. 327 (ND Ill. 1968); *Burrus v. Wilkerson*, 310 F. Supp. 572 (W.D. Va.1969), aff'd per curiam, 397 US 44 (1970)

15 Murray, Nakib, and Rueben (2005), 96.

16 *Serrano v. Priest*, 5 Cal.3d 584, 487 P.2d 1241 (California 1971).

17 *San Antonio Independent School Dis. v. Rodriguez*, 411 US 1, 93 S. Ct. 1278, 36 L.Ed.2d 16 (1973).

18 *Serrano v. Priest*, 18 Cal.3d 728, 5557 P.2d 929 (California 1976), *Robinson v. Cahill*, 303 A.2d 273 (New Jersey 1973).

19 Koski and Hahnel (2008), 47.

20 *Rose v. Council for Better Education, Inc.* 790 S.W.2d 186 (Kentucky 1989).

21 There were ten such decisions, with the first being *Abbott v. Burke* 100 N.J. 269, 495 A.2d 376 (1985).

22 *McDuffy v. Secretary of the Executive Office of Education*, 415 Mass. 545, 615 N.E.2d 516 (1993).

23 *Abbott v. Burke* 153 N.J. 480, 710 A.2d 450 (1998).

24 *Hancock v. Driscoll*, 443 Mass. 428 (2005).

25 Kenyon (2007), 26–27.

26 Ibid., 28–29.

27 Corcoran and Evans (2008), 342.

28 Ibid., 340.

29 Downes (2002); Betts (2002).

30 Corcoran and Evans (2008), 346.

31 McGuire and Papke (2008).

32 For a general overview of state-to-local aid flows, see Fisher and Bristle (this volume)

33 Murray, Nakib, and Rueben (2005), 96; Evans, Murray, and Schwab (1997).

34 In 2008 in Hawaii, state revenues accounted for 84.8 percent of total K-12 revenues. Fees and charges for programs such as food services, activities, and summer school made up the 3 percent of public K-12 revenues from local sources. Hawaii receives no public education revenues from local property taxes. The remaining 12.21 percent of revenue came from federal sources. More recently, Vermont became a full funding state when its local property tax was mostly converted into a state tax. Thus, in Vermont, 85.9 percent of public K-12 revenues came from state sources. Another 7.9 percent of revenue came from federal sources and 6.3 percent came from local sources including local property taxes. (US Department of Education, National Center for Education Statistics, Common Core of Data [CCD], "National Public Education Financial Survey [NPEFS]," fiscal year 2008, Version 1a. US Department of Education, National Center for Education Statistics, 2010, Table 1, http://nces.ed.gov/pubs2010/expenditures/tables/table_01.asp.)

35 For a discussion of the differences between fiscal capacity and expenditure need, see Kenyon (2005); Yilmaz and Zahradnik (2008).

36 Yinger (2004), 46.

37 Education Trust (2006).

38 Roza (2010).

39 No Child Left Behind: Pub.L. 107–110, 115 Stat. 1425, enacted January 8, 2002.

40 In 2005, forty-five governors and twelve national organizations signed onto a compact on state high school graduation data. Eventually all fifty states agreed to voluntarily and gradually adopt a common formula for calculating their states' high school graduation rates.

41 Gordon (2008).

42 Vinovskis (2009), 17.

43 Harr, Parrish, and Chambers (2008), 574.

44 Gordon (2008), 305.

45 One readable, but critical, account of the major requirements of NCLB can be found in Ravitch (2010), 97–98.

46 Ravitch (2010).

47 Taylor and Weerapana (2009).

48 OECD member countries are Australia, Belgium, Canada, Chile, the Czech Republic, Denmark, Finland, France, Germany, Greece, Hungary, Iceland, Ireland, Israel, Italy, Japan, Korea, Luxembourg, Mexico, the Netherlands, New Zealand, Norway, Poland, Portugal, the Slovak Republic, Slovenia, Spain, Sweden, Switzerland, Turkey, the United Kingdom, and the United States. The only countries with a federal system of government other than the United States are Austria, Australia, Canada, Germany, and Switzerland. For a review of federal finance, see Griffiths (2005).

49 The Program for International Student Assessment (PISA) is sponsored by the OECD. The first survey was conducted in 2000 and more than seventy countries have participated so far.

50 Trends in International Mathematics and Science Study (TIMSS) began in 1995 and is organized by the International Association for the Evaluation of Educational Achievement.

51 Rosen (2010), 2.

52 American Recovery and Reinvestment Act (PL 111–5, February 17, 2009).

53 Donald J. Boyd, state and local financial update, annual meeting of the Government Investment Officers Association, May 18, 2011.

54 Wallace (this volume).

55 Frey (2011).

References

ACCESS (2011). National Access Network, Teachers College, Columbia University. State by State page. www.schoolfunding.info.

Betts, Julian R. (2002). "Discussion." In *Education in the 21st Century: Meeting the Challenges of a Changing World*, edited by Yolanda K. Kodryzycki. Boston: Federal Reserve Bank of Boston.

Corcoran, Sean P., and William N. Evans (2008). "Equity, Adequacy and the Evolving State Role in Education Finance." In *The Handbook of Research in Education Finance and Policy*, edited by Helen Ladd and Edward Fiske. New York: Routledge. 332–356.

Downes, Thomas (2002). "Do State Governments Matter?" In *Education in the 21st Century: Meeting the Challenges of a Changing World*, edited by Yolanda K. Kodryzycki. Boston: Federal Reserve Bank of Boston. 143–164.

Editorial Project in Education Research Center (2011). Education Counts Database. http://www.edcounts.org/createtable.

Education Trust (2006). *Funding Gaps.* http://www2.edtrust.org/EdTrust/Press+Room/Funding+Gap+2006.htm.

Evans, William N., Sheila E. Murray, and Robert M.. Schwab (1997). "Toward Increased Centralization in Public School Finance." In *Intergovernmental Fiscal Relations*, edited by Ronald Fisher. Boston: Kluwer Academic.

Frey, William H. (2011). "A Demographic Tipping Point among America's Three-Year-Olds." State of Metropolitan America, No. 26, Brookings Institution.

Gordon, Nora E. (2008). "The Changing Federal Role in Education Finance and Governance." In *The Handbook of Research in Education Finance and Policy*, edited by Helen Ladd and Edward Fiske. New York: Routledge. 295–313.

Griffiths, Ann L. (Ed.) (2005). *Handbook of Federal Countries.* Montreal: McGill-Queens University Press.

Harr, Jenifer J., Tom Parrish, and Jay Chambers (2008). "Special Education." In *The Handbook of Research in Education Finance and Policy*, edited by Helen Ladd and Edward Fiske. New York: Routledge. 573–590.

Keaton, P. (2010). "Numbers and Types of Public Elementary and Secondary Education Agencies from the Common Core of Data: School Year 2008–09." NCES 2010–346. National Center of Education Statistics, Institute of Education Sciences, US Department of Education, Washington, DC.

Kenyon, Daphne A. (2005). "Tax and Revenue Capacity and Effort, State and Local." In *The Encyclopedia of Taxation and Tax Policy*, edited by Joseph J. Cordes, Robert D. Ebel, and Jane G. Gravelle. Washington, DC: Urban Institute Press. 389–394.

Kenyon, Daphne A. (2007). *The Property Tax—School Funding Dilemma*. Cambridge, MA: Lincoln Institute of Land Policy.

Koski, William S., and Jesse Hahnel (2008). "The Past, Present, and Possible Future of Educational Finance Reform Litigation." In *The Handbook of Research in Education Finance and Policy*, edited by Helen Ladd and Edward Fiske. New York: Routledge. 42–60.

Ladd, Helen F., and Janet S. Hansen (Eds.) (1999). *Making Money Matter: Financing America's Schools*. Committee on Education Finance, Commission on Behavioral and Social Sciences and Education, National Research Council. Washington, DC: National Academy Press.

McGuire, Therese J., and Leslie E. Papke (2008). "Local Funding of Schools: The Property Tax and Its Alternatives." In *The Handbook of Research in Education Finance and Policy*, edited by Helen Ladd and Edward Fiske. New York: Routledge. 357–372.

Murray, Sheila, Yas Nakib, and Kim Rueben (2005). "Education Financing, State and Local." In *The Encyclopedia of Taxation and Tax Policy*, edited by Joseph J. Cordes, Robert D. Ebel, and Jane G. Gravelle. Washington, DC: Urban Institute Press. 95–100.

National Association of State Boards of Education (2010, October). *No Time to Wait: Creating Contemporary School Structures for All Students Today and Tomorrow*. Arlington, VA: National Association of State Boards of Education.

Odden, Allan R., and Lawrence O. Picus (2000). *School Finance: A Policy Perspective*. 2nd ed. Boston: McGraw-Hill.

Organisation for Economic Co-operation and Development (OECD) (2010a). *Education at a Glance 2010: OECD Indicators*. Paris: Organisation for Economic Cooperation and Development.

Organisation for Economic Co-operation and Development (OECD) (2010b). *PISA 2009 Results: What Students Know and Can Do: Student Performance in Reading, Mathematics and Science*. Vol. I. Paris: Organisation for Economic Cooperation and Development.

Pierce, Neal, and Curtis Johnson (2006, January 1). "Are New England Communities Too Small to be Governed Efficiently?" *The Sunday Telegraph*: E-4.

Ravitch, Diane (2010). *The Death and Life of the Great American School System: How Testing and Choice Are Undermining Education*. New York: Basic Books.

Rosen, Larry D. (2010). *Understanding the iGeneration and the Way They Learn*. New York: Palgrave Macmillan.

Roza, Marguerite (2010). *Educational Economics: Where Do School Funds Go?* Washington, DC: Urban Institute Press.

Siegel, Peggy M. (2010). *Learning, Technology, and the Future: Catalyzing a New Conversation*. Intel/Dell. www.dell.com.

Snyder, T. D., and Dillow, S. A. (2010). *Digest of Education Statistics 2009* (NCES 2010–013). National Center for Education Statistics, Institute of Education Sciences, US Department of Education. Washington, DC.

Taylor, John B., and Akila Weerapana (2009). *Principles of Macroeconomics.* Boston: Houghton Mifflin.

US Bureau of the Census (2008, February 25). *Census of Governments, Local Governments and Public School Systems by Type and State: 2007.* http://www.census.gov/govs/cog/GovOrgTab03ss.html.

US Census (2010, July 7). *State and Local Government Finances by Level of Government and by State: 2007–08.* http://www.census.gov/govs/estimate/

US Census. *Census of Governments,* various years.

US Department of Education (2010a). National Center for Education Statistics, Common Core of Data (CCD), National Public Education Financial Survey (NPEFS): Fiscal Year 2008, Version 1a. Washington, DC: Department of Education.

US Department of Education (2010b). National Center for Education Statistics, Common Core of Data (CCD), Local Education Agency Universe Survey: 2008–09, Version 1a. Washington, DC: US Department of Education.

US Department of Education (2010c). National Center for Education Statistics, National Assessment of Educational Progress (NAEP), 2007 and 2009 Mathematics Assessments, NAEP Data Explorer. Washington, DC: US Department of Education.

US Department of Education. National Center for Education Statistics, Parent Survey (Parent: 1999) and Parent and Family Involvement in Education Survey (PFI: 2003 and PFI: 2007) of the National Household Education Surveys. Washington, DC: US Department of Education.

Vinovskis, Maris A. (2009). *From a Nation at Risk to No Child Left Behind: National Education Goals and the Creation of Federal Education Policy.* New York: Teachers College Press.

Yinger, John. (2004). "State Aid and the Pursuit of Educational Equity: An Overview." In *Helping Children Left Behind: State Aid and the Pursuit of Educational Equity,* edited by John Yinger. Cambridge, MA: MIT Press. 3-57.

CHAPTER 21

....

THE SOCIAL SAFETY NET, HEALTH CARE, AND THE GREAT RECESSION

....

THOMAS GAIS, DONALD BOYD, AND LUCY DADAYAN

STATE governments play critical roles in implementing, financing, and making policy for the nation's social safety net. Their roles have changed in many ways in recent decades as a result of federal legislation, including the rapid expansion of Medicaid beginning in the 1980s, welfare reform in 1996, and the growth of federally financed yet state-administered nutrition assistance programs. The Great Recession of 2007–2009 and its aftermath at first appeared to provide the first real test of the post-welfare reform safety net's ability to respond to a large and persistent economic downturn. But the prerecession safety net did not stand alone. The 2009 federal stimulus package—the American Recovery and Reinvestment Act (ARRA)—provided an unprecedented amount of funding to reinforce the safety net, and it offered intriguing experiments in efforts by the national government to influence state policies, budgets, and institutions. There is little doubt that the federal stimulus helped the US safety net sustain more people than it would have had it not been enacted. As its provisions expire, however, questions arise about what safety net will emerge as states struggle to confront plummeting federal aid and to finance programs with volatile and eroding revenue systems.

WHAT IS THE SOCIAL SERVICES SAFETY NET?

We define the safety net as including programs designed primarily to assist people who have great difficulty in meeting basic needs such as food, clothing, shelter, and medical care, and people who have been unable to find and keep work. These difficulties may be the result of socioeconomic circumstances such as age, illness, or disability, or the result of external shocks such as economic recession or natural disaster. Depending on the program, assistance may be in the form of cash, services, or vouchers. We include in this definition programs financed by the federal or state general treasuries as well as programs that have a social insurance element such as unemployment insurance.

Under this broad definition, the federal behemoths Medicare and Social Security may be viewed as safety-net programs. But because the states have virtually no role in administering, financing, or making policy for these programs—and because they are available to all persons regardless of means or other economic circumstances—we exclude them from our analysis. Nonetheless, we include Medicare and Social Security in table 21.1 to show their size relative to other safety-net programs in the United States.[1]

In 2008, federal, state, and local spending on major safety-net programs other than Social Security and Medicare amounted to $697 billion (see table 21.1), or

Table 21.1 Federal and state-local spending on major safety-net programs ($ in billions, FY 2008 except as noted)

Function and program	Federal	State and local	Total
HEALTH CARE	206.5	154.1	360.7
Medicaid	199.6	151.1	350.7
State Children's Health Insurance Program (SCHIP)	6.9	3.0	10.0
CASH ASSISTANCE AND OTHER CASH PROGRAMS	137.1	55.9	193.1
Earned Income-Tax Credit (federal EITC and also state EITCs)	50.7	2.1	52.8
Unemployment Insurance (UI)	7.9	43.1	51.0
Supplemental Security Income (SSI)	38.7	4.4	43.0
Child tax credit	30.4	–	30.4
Temporary Assistance to Needy Families (TANF) cash assistance	5.8	4.2	10.0
Child support enforcement (administrative expenditures)	3.6	2.2	5.8

(Continued)

Table 21.1 Continued

Function and program	Federal	State and local	Total
FOOD AND NUTRITION	56.6	3.2	59.8
Food Stamps (Supplemental Nutrition Assistance Program - [SNAP])	37.5	3.2	40.7
Child nutrition programs	13.2	–	13.2
Women, Infants and Children (WIC) Nutrition Program	5.9	–	5.9
SOCIAL SERVICES/JOBS AND TRAINING	32.2	19.5	51.7
Foster Care, Adoption Assistance, and Social Services Block Grant (SSBG)	9.4	5.9	15.3
TANF noncash (child care, employment services, transportation assistance, diversion payments, etc.)	5.8	9.4	15.2
Child Care Development Fund (CCDF; including transfers from TANF)	8.5	2.4	10.9
Head Start	6.8	1.7	8.5
Homeless assistance	1.2	–	1.2
Community Services Block Grant (CSBG)	0.6	–	0
HOUSING	26.1	–	26.1
Section 8 rental assistance	18.5	–	18.5
Public housing	7.6	–	7.6
ENERGY	3.1	2.7	5.8
Low-Income Home Energy Assistance Program	3.1	2.7	5.8
Total, major safety-net programs (other than federal only)	461.7	235.4	697.1
SOCIAL SECURITY AND MEDICARE (FEDERAL ONLY)	1,086.8	–	1,086.8
Social Security	618.6	–	618.6
Medicare	468.2	–	4 68.2
Grand total, including federal-only programs	1,548.5	235.4	1,783.9

Sources: Data collected by the Rockefeller Institute from US Department of Health and Human Services; US Department of Labor; US Treasury Department; US Department of Agriculture; and US Department of Housing and Urban Development.

nearly 5 percent of the nation's gross domestic product (GDP). Two out of three dollars of this total are financed by the federal government; the remaining one-third ($235 billion) is supported by state and local government revenues. The vast majority of spending in the "State and Local" column is by state governments. Some local governments, however, particularly large cities and counties, help finance certain safety-net programs.

The programs in table 21.1 generally are federally established programs or state counterparts to those programs, such as state-matching expenditures under Medicaid. Spending data for these programs are available either from federal reporting systems or other central sources.[2] States have some standalone programs that are not included in the table because they are hard to track down and quantify, but we do not believe the amount of safety-net spending left out of the table is large.[3] Later in this chapter we analyze data from the Census Bureau's annual survey of state and local government finances, which gives a more complete picture of spending on social services, though with less program detail.

Table 21.2 provides a brief description of significant features of the most important of the programs listed in table 21.1. A few observations about table 21.1 are warranted:

- Health-care programs account for the largest share of safety-net programs, both for the federal government and for the states. Medicaid, the federal and state program that finances health care for the poor and medically needy, makes up half of all safety-net spending (excluding the federal-only programs of Social Security and Medicare) and is about three-quarters as large as Medicare, the federal health insurance program for the elderly.
- Cash assistance is the next largest category. Other than benefits for the elderly and the disabled, the bulk of these income supports go to people who have earned income or who had recently had jobs. Two of the largest cash assistance programs in the United States are administered through the federal tax system: the earned income-tax credit (EITC), a credit available to low-income working families; and the refundable child tax credit, which provides income-tax relief and refunds to low-income and middle-class working families with children, even to families who owe no federal tax. Supplemental Security Income (SSI), primarily funded and administered by the federal government, supports the economically needy, aged, blind, or disabled individuals. At the state level the largest cash assistance program is unemployment insurance (UI). Individuals who lose jobs involuntarily and have extensive work experience are generally eligible. The state share of UI is financed by experience-rated taxes imposed on employers. Temporary Assistance to Needy Families (TANF), the nation's traditional welfare program for low-income families with children, is jointly funded by federal and state governments but is much smaller than other major income-support programs. Another jointly funded program, Child Support Enforcement, provides legal assistance in establishing child support claims.
- Food and nutrition programs make up the next largest category, led by the Supplemental Nutrition Assistance Program (SNAP), formerly known as Food Stamps and still referred to by that name in many states. These

benefits are federally funded but states administer and pay half of the costs of administering SNAP.

- Social services are the next largest group of safety-net programs. This includes a variety of work supports such as job-seeking assistance, child care, and transportation assistance. They also include programs designed to help children who face poverty, abuse, and other crises.
- Housing and energy assistance programs round out the list of major supports for low-income Americans. Like the nutrition assistance programs, they provide important yet targeted income supports.

In general, table 21.1 shows that states contribute more of their own revenues to service programs, including health as well as social services. These are programs that typically require more administrative activities, and, by and large, state and local governments dominate the direct administration of public programs in the United States. By contrast, the national government puts more of its resources into income-support programs (if we include "vouchers" for food and housing as income supports), which typically demand relatively small bureaucracies to determine eligibility.

The Safety Net in the Context
of State and Local Budgets

The federal administrative data displayed in tables 21.1 and 21.2 are a useful way to understand the programs that make up the social safety net. But a complementary source of information that can trace trends and place the safety net in the context of overall state and local government spending is the US Census Bureau's Survey of State and Local Government Finances.[4] The Census survey has several strengths. It offers a long and nearly uninterrupted annual time series of state and local expenditures on important public functions. The categories it uses to classify public expenditures are stable, permitting comparisons over time even while federal and state programs come and go. The survey also collects data on programs wholly funded and operated by state and local governments, unlike the federal administrative data.

However, the survey also has limits. It does not show all US social welfare expenditures but only those that run through state or local government budgets. It does not, for instance, include the refundable portion of the federal EITC and most of the SSI program. It includes Food Stamp (now SNAP) administrative costs, because those are paid out of the states' own budgets. However, it does not encompass the costs of Food Stamp/SNAP benefits, which are paid by the federal government.

The Census survey expenditure data are organized into functional categories, one of which is "public welfare." Public welfare expenditures, which we call "safety-net expenditures" in this chapter, generally include spending on programs that support lower-income households, such as programs with means tests. To trace broad changes in safety-net spending, we organized the Census Bureau public welfare data into three types of expenditures:

- *Cash assistance*, including TANF cash assistance and its predecessor program, Aid to Families with Dependent Income (AFDC) as well as general assistance, home relief, refugee assistance, emergency relief, and state supplements SSI.
- *Medical assistance*, or payments to private health-care providers for medical assistance or health care on behalf of low-income or medically needy persons; these payments correspond roughly to expenditures under Medicaid and the State Child Health Insurance Program (SCHIP).
- *Social services*, which encompass a wide variety of services and benefits, including child-care subsidies, child welfare (programs to prevent abuse, neglect, and foster-care placement), foster-care and adoption assistance, social services for disabled persons, temporary shelters and other services for the homeless, welfare benefits other than cash assistance, administrative expenses to operate programs for low-income persons, and other payments to private vendors "for services and commodities other than medical, hospital, and health care." This category also includes cash or quasi-cash benefits for specific needs, such as low-income energy assistance and benefits provided through mechanisms outside traditional welfare payments. These mechanisms may include state refundable EITCs, individual development accounts, and "diversion" or one-time payments to help needy families avoid regular welfare.

These three types of expenditures totaled $405 billion across all US state and local governments in fiscal year 2008. The largest category was medical assistance, which made up 75 percent of safety-net expenditures. Social services constituted the second largest type, making up 21 percent. Cash assistance was only 5 percent of all Census-defined safety-net spending. The much smaller share of cash assistance programs in the Census data, when compared to the federal administrative data shown in table 21.1, reflects the fact that the Census spending data do not include unemployment benefits or tax credits (such as the EITC and the child tax credit), nor do they include benefits paid directly by the federal government, such as SNAP and most of SSI.

However, despite the differences between the Census data and the federal administrative data used in table 21.1, some of the same patterns appear. Most of the dollars spent by state and local governments on social welfare functions came from revenues raised by the federal government, which typically passed the money down to state and local public agencies through intergovernmental grants, such as Medicaid, TANF, and the Child Care and Development Block Grant (CCDBG).

Table 21.2 Important characteristics of selected safety-net programs

Program	Key features	Entitlement status	Origins
HEALTH CARE			
Medicaid and SCHIP	Federal-state program that pays for medical services for low-income persons and the medically needy. Disproportionate share of benefits are for elderly and disabled.	Open-ended entitlement, generally	Enacted 1965 as part of Great Society
CASH ASSISTANCE AND OTHER CASH PROGRAMS			
Earned income-tax credit	Entitlement—refundable tax credit for low-income workers with earnings and a qualifying child, and for some low-income workers without children	Open-ended entitlement, generally	Enacted 1975
Unemployment insurance (UI)	Provides time-limited benefits to individuals with sufficient work history, laid off through no fault of own.	Open-ended entitlement, generally, but time-limited	Enacted 1938
Supplemental Security Income (SSI)	Means-tested federally administered cash assistance program for aged, blind, and disabled persons with low incomes.	Yes, generally	Enacted 1972. Replaced predecessor federal programs.
Child tax credit	Federal income tax credit of up to $1,000 per child. Phases out at incomes above $100,000.	Yes, generally	Enacted 1997
TANF assistance	Temporary Assistance for Needy Families; time-limited cash assistance for low-income families with children	No. Block grant limits funds; lifetime limits for individuals; significant diversion efforts	Adopted as part of 1996 federal welfare reform. Successor to AFDC.
FOOD AND NUTRITION			
Supplemental Nutrition Assistance Program (SNAP); formerly, Food Stamps	Benefits available to most households that meet federal financial eligibility tests for limited monthly income and assets.	Open-ended entitlement	Enacted in 1961 as a pilot program. Expanded nationwide in 1975.

Sources: Program information collected by the Rockefeller Institute from US Department of Health and

Federal role	State role	Number of beneficiaries
HEALTH CARE		
Establish broad rules, allow waivers. Pay for approximately 55 percent of costs, depending on year. Federal share varies greatly across states.	Oversees states. Administer program. Select benefits to offer and eligibility criteria within federal parameters. Develop and evaluate waivers and other variations. Pay nonfederal share.	58.2 million beneficiaries in 2008, per CMS
CASH ASSISTANCE		
Federal EITC administered through federal income tax system.	No role in federal EITC. But twenty-four states have own EITC administered through state income taxes.	24.8 million families in 2008, per IRS
Establish general rules.	Administer program. Finance regular benefits and share in extended benefit costs.	9 million in 2010
Establish benefit levels and eligibility rules. Finance and administer SSI.	States can supplement federal SSI benefits.	8.6 million recipients in 2009
Entirely a federal program	None	35 million families in 2010 per TPC
Finance block grant. Establish broad rules. Grant waivers.	Administer program. Establish detailed rules within federal guidelines.	1.9 million families, 4.4 million recipients in 2010
FOOD AND NUTRITION		
Finance benefits. Define eligibility requirements, benefit levels, and administrative rules. Oversee state administration of program.	Within federal rules, states determine eligibility, calculate benefits, and issue monthly benefits.	40.3 million individuals in FY 2010 up from 26.3 million in FY 2007

Human Services; US Department of Labor; US Treasury Department; US Department of Agriculture.

Based on the Census data, of total safety-net spending in 2008, 62 percent ($246 billion) came from federal sources. State and local governments funded the remaining 38 percent ($149 billion) out of their own revenue sources.

Social welfare spending is a significant but not huge part of total state and local budgets: in 2008, it absorbed 17 percent of direct general expenditures. Spending on medical assistance constituted 12 percent of all direct general expenditures by state and local governments. Spending on social services made up 4 percent, while cash assistance expenditures were only 1 percent of total direct general expenditures.

Trends in the Social Safety Net before the Great Recession

An important fact about the safety net in the United States is its flux. New legislation, federal and state budget shifts, federal executive actions, gubernatorial initiatives, demographic changes, and economic crises all make their mark on the benefits and services that people receive as well as on their financing. Changes have been extensive throughout the past seventy-five years, but the most profound changes may be traced to the 1930s.

Policy Expansions through the 1970s

The modern social safety net in the United States began during the Great Depression with President Franklin Delano Roosevelt's "Second New Deal" and the Social Security Act of 1935. Among other things, the Social Security Act established grants to states to operate cash assistance programs for the blind, disabled, and the indigent elderly. It created AFDC, which provided cash assistance—with the benefits set and administered by states—to low-income children lacking at least one parent in the household. The Roosevelt administration also created the public housing program in 1937, which subsidized the building of public housing projects, owned and operated by local public housing authorities.[5]

These programs expanded moderately in participation, benefits, and expenditures through the early postwar years. But the greatest changes were introduced in the 1960s and early 1970s during President Lyndon B. Johnson's Great Society initiative. Most Great Society programs began small in terms of coverage and expenditures, but they widened the range of populations and social needs for political attention. By doing so, they established a programmatic base for much larger expansions in later decades.

The Great Society programs included Medicaid, a federal-state grant program that provided payments for medical assistance to populations eligible for welfare, including single-parent families, the blind and disabled, and the elderly poor; a pilot food stamp program (expanded to the nation as a whole in 1975), which offered monthly coupons to low-income households that they could use to purchase food; benefit increases under AFDC, particularly for families with earnings; expansions in public housing subsidies; establishment of the SSI program; and the creation or expansion of several social service programs, such as the Social Services Block Grant. These policy changes—combined with substantial growth in the US population, increases in low-income single-parent families, and other demographic and economic changes—pushed safety-net spending up rapidly through the mid-1970s.

NATIONAL SPENDING TRENDS

Safety-net spending ended its rapid growth in the late 1970s and early 1980s— especially when compared to changes in the number of low-income people in the United States. We can see this decline in the financial coverage of the safety net if we examine trends in inflation-adjusted expenditures per poor person by using the Census survey of state and local government finances.[6] Figure 21.1 shows annual changes in real safety-net spending per poor person from 1977 through 2008, bringing us to the first year of the Great Recession. From 1977 to 1978 and through 1982–1983, changes in safety-net expenditures per poor person (a rough indicator of need and potential eligibles) were negative.[7] This retrenchment was largely a consequence of cutbacks in AFDC benefits and other social programs in 1981 (the first year of the Reagan administration) and growth in the number of low-income families with children.

After this period of retrenchment, however, safety-net spending resumed growth through the early 2000s, even after adjusting for general inflation and the number of poor people. This growth slowed and reversed after 2001, and after 2005, adjusted safety-net spending began to decline. In 2008, for the first time since 1982–1983, real social welfare spending per poor person by state and local governments dropped for the third year in a row. The Great Recession thus began when the state and local safety nets were growing financially but when state and local safety nets had been losing resources for several years relative to the number of low-income households in the United States.

Because three out of four dollars spent on social welfare programs go to medical assistance, the drop in safety-net spending after 2005 was strongly affected by a recent decline in medical assistance spending. Figure 21.2 shows that medical

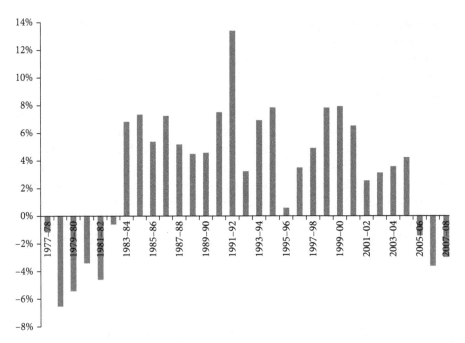

Figure 21.1 Percentage change in inflation-adjusted state and local spending on social welfare, per poor person, 1977–2008
Sources: Census Bureau and Bureau of Economic Analysis (GDP price index).

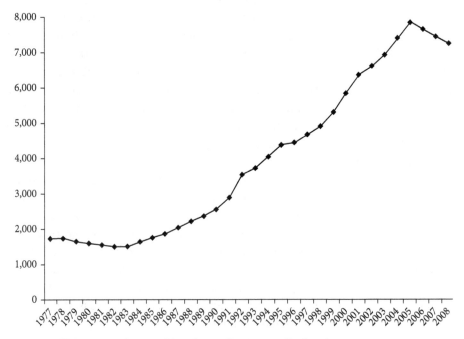

Figure 21.2 State and local spending on medical assistance per poor person, 2008 dollars, 1977–2008
Sources: Census Bureau and Bureau of Economic Analysis (GDP price index).

assistance spending fell each year after 2006 following a stretch of twenty-two years of uninterrupted growth. To the extent that the medical assistance category is a proxy for Medicaid, this long period of growth encompasses several distinct stages, with different forces driving costs in each period.[8] Yet the basic story over these two decades was the expansion of Medicaid from a program that primarily served families on welfare well into the 1980s, to one that served many poor elderly and disabled persons as well as a wider range of low-income families with children, including families not on welfare and often with incomes over the federal poverty level.[9] Spending growth was also driven by the general costs of health care; by expansions in the range of services covered under Medicaid; and by arrangements crafted by states with health-care providers to generate matching dollars to draw down federal dollars.[10]

The downturn after 2005 in medical assistance spending was attributable in large part to a shift in responsibility from the states to the federal government for the costs of prescription drugs used by "dual eligibles," that is, persons eligible for both Medicaid and Medicare. But although states got some long-run relief by shedding responsibility for the costs of pharmaceuticals for some Medicaid clients, this change is unlikely to slow Medicaid cost growth in the future.[11]

The slowdown and eventual downturn in social welfare spending after 2002, however, was not just an effect of Medicaid. Figure 21.3 shows the trends for cash assistance and social services in real spending per poor person. After moving more or less in tandem with each other from the late 1970s through the early 1990s, cash

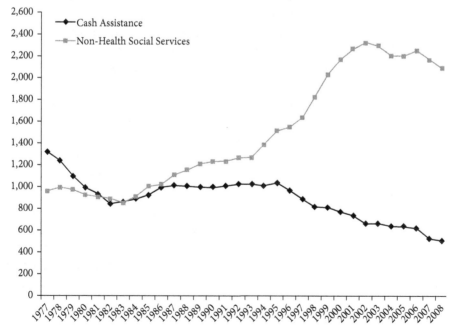

Figure 21.3 State and local spending on cash assistance and social services per poor person, 2008 dollars, 1977–2008
Sources: Census Bureau and Bureau of Economic Analysis (GDP price index).

assistance and social service expenditures began to move in different directions after 1994. Cash assistance expenditures declined persistently from 1995 to 2008, when it lost 60 percent of its real value per poor person. Social services spending, by contrast, grew between 1994 and 2002. But after 2002, following the end of the recession of the early 2000s, social services spending also began a consistent period of decline. It lost 22 percent of its real value per poor person between 2002 and 2008. Thus, the slowdown after 2002 in total social welfare spending was the result of a long-run decline in cash assistance, a more recent yet persistent drop in social services, and a recent and probably short-run decline in medical assistance.

The inflection point in social services spending in 2002 marked the end of a brief yet transformational period for social welfare spending, a period that began in the middle 1990s. Although real expenditures on cash assistance per poor person declined by $478 between 1993 and 2002 (a drop of 40 percent), that decline in spending was small compared to simultaneous increases in spending on social services (which grew by $1,043, an increase of 71 percent, between 1993 and 2002) and medical assistance (which swelled by $3,011, an increase of 73 percent, over the same period). These changes combined to expand total social welfare spending *and* shift the balance between different types of expenditures, away from cash assistance and toward health and social services.

What accounted for the decline in cash assistance and the expansion of social services in the 1990s? One factor was the economic growth of the 1990s. Cash assistance enrollments typically decline when unemployment falls.[12] Expanded access to the EITC and its increased value in the 1990s also dampened participation in welfare programs.[13] By contrast, social services tend to grow when unemployment is low, perhaps because most services are discretionary programs, and their funding may go up with the availability of greater revenues from state and federal governments.

Federal and state welfare reforms also contributed to the shift toward social services and away from cash assistance. In addition to substantial federal increases in child-care grants to the states, the 1996 Personal Responsibility and Work Opportunity Reconciliation Act (PRWORA) replaced AFDC, largely a cash assistance program, with the TANF block grant. The grant ended the entitlement to cash assistance and imposed restrictions on the receipt of cash assistance, including work requirements and time limits: these changes contributed to declines in cash assistance rolls.[14]

TANF also gave states the flexibility to apply their federal dollars and required state expenditures to services and other "nonassistance" programs for low-income families, largely to encourage and support work. "Nonassistance" are services or benefits for needy families that do not meet TANF's definition of "assistance," which encompasses "cash, payments, vouchers, and other forms of benefits designed to meet a family's ongoing basic needs," such as food, clothing, shelter, and utilities.[15] Nonassistance may include short-term diversion payments (nonrecurrent payments to needy families who agree not to apply for assistance), child-care subsidies for working families, refundable EITCs, case management and employment services, and transportation assistance.

Most of these services and benefits were "work supports," that is, benefits designed to help people get and keep jobs and augment earnings. Many states found it easy to invest more funds in services under TANF because of fiscal savings reaped from the large declines in welfare rolls. In 1997, the year after TANF was enacted, only 23 percent of state spending under TANF went to nonassistance services and benefits; by 2002, that percentage rose to 56 percent.[16] In fact, even this change underestimated the shift to services, because it did not include the block grant money that states transferred to their Social Service Block Grant programs or their Child Care Development Funds.

Beginning in 2002, however, circumstances changed. The economic downturn starting in late 2001 sharply cut state revenues at least through 2003 and made discretionary programs like most social services vulnerable to state cutbacks.[17] Also, after several years of rapid increases in services, TANF spending leveled off after 2001, as states spent down the surpluses they had built up in the 1990s from the block grant and as inflation eroded the value of federal assistance.[18] And even though welfare rolls fell during and after the 2001–2002 recession, the declines in enrollments were much smaller than in the 1990s—and thus fewer TANF dollars were available for work supports and services. In short, on the eve of the Great Recession, state and local spending was already losing ground relative to measures of need.

The safety net was not only shrinking, but its composition had also changed in the few years before the Great Recession. By 2008, cash assistance made up only 5 percent of state and local safety-net spending, down from 8 percent in 2001 (and 26 percent before the recession in 1982). By contrast, medical assistance spending was 74 percent of safety-net expenditures in 2008, up from 68 percent as recently as 2001 (and 46 percent in 1982). Social service spending was down to 21 percent of the safety-net total, compared to 24 percent in 2001. Before the effects of the Great Recession hit, the state and local safety net was thus dominated by medical assistance spending, while the share of spending going to cash assistance programs administered by the states was at a historic low.

Finally, another prerecession trend is worth noting: the growing role of the federal government in financing the overall safety net. We can see that in the state and local survey data described above: federal grants supported about 62 percent of all state and local safety-net expenditures in 2008, a slight decline from the early 2000s, but a substantial increase since the 1980s, when the federal share was between 54 and 57 percent.

But the shift to a greater reliance on federal financing is much greater when one considers several other developments. SNAP/FSP caseloads and expenditures began to climb in the early 2000s. SNAP/FSP benefits, which are fully funded by the federal government, increased from $22 billion to $37 billion between 2001 and 2008, a 70 percent increase, even after adjusting for inflation. SSI cases and benefits (which are largely paid for by the federal government) have grown, albeit more slowly, in recent years; real spending increased by 11 percent between 2001 and 2008.

Federal tax credits have also grown substantially, as the federal tax system became an increasingly important channel for augmenting the earnings of low-income workers. The federal EITC provided $47 billion to low-income earners, mostly families with children, in 2008; this was a 25 percent increase from 2001. The federal Child Tax Credit was established in 1997, and its refundable portion provides support to many low-income families with earnings.

How Safety-Net Programs
Respond to Recessions

Different safety-net programs may respond in different ways to the same economic shock. Some programs may be strongly affected by increases in eligible populations, such as the number of persons out of work or in poverty, or the number of individuals who have lost their health insurance. Other programs may be affected by declines in state revenues and increased competition for budget resources. Still, other programs may be little affected by either factor, if, for example, federal assistance is provided in the form of a fixed block grant. As we will find, these different responses did occur, and the differences contributed to important changes in the safety net.

Four factors might increase state programs' responsiveness to economic cycles:

1. whether the program is an open-ended entitlement, that is, one in which benefits go to individuals when they satisfy certain eligibility criteria, regardless of total expenditures;
2. whether the program's benefits are valuable, encouraged (or not discouraged due to administrative factors or cultural stigma), and quickly accessible;
3. whether the number of persons eligible for the program are strongly affected by short-term economic cycles; and
4. whether it is impracticable for policymakers or administrators to reduce benefits in response to short-run state fiscal conditions.

When these conditions are applied to unemployment insurance, the program would be expected to be very sensitive to changes in unemployment. Workers who lose their jobs involuntarily and have recent and consistent experience in the workforce are typically eligible, so the eligible population is usually composed of persons hurt by short-run economic changes. Unemployed workers are encouraged by the US Department of Labor to file for unemployment payments immediately after becoming unemployed. Benefit checks generally arrive two to three weeks after claims are filed. By putting income in the hands of families in difficult circumstances, most of the benefits are quickly spent by recipients. In fact, Moody's Economy.com estimates that raising or extending unemployment benefits in a recession has the second-highest "bang for the buck" among stimulus policies.[19]

The SNAP program has also been responsive, and in a countercyclical direction, to short-run economic changes. Its eligibility requirements are largely financial. For most clients, most of the time, eligibility does not depend on clients' behavior (such as their willingness to look for work), nor are benefits for most households time-limited (except for able-bodied persons without dependents). Benefits are indexed for inflation and are the same in all states. Moreover, eligibility processes have become easier for clients to handle in the last decade, and the federal government holds states accountable for timely processing of applications and benefits. Because eligibility is keyed to household income, "one would expect caseloads and outlays to have the strongest association with cyclical swings in business activity."[20] Ziliak, in fact, found that a one-percentage-point increase in the unemployment rate generates a 1.3 percent increase in "contemporaneous food stamp caseloads" and an even larger increase (2.3 percent) in caseloads after one year, perhaps due to persons taking time to apply for benefits after trying alternative sources of support.[21]

Spending and caseloads under AFDC—the program that TANF replaced in 1996—also responded in a countercyclical way to economic changes. Ziliak, for instance, found that the AFDC and Food Stamp caseloads moved together before federal welfare reform was enacted.[22] Powers analyzed safety-net cyclicality just as welfare reform was getting started and found that a one-percentage-point rise in unemployment would add 2.5 percentage points to AFDC and 4.5 percentage points to the Food Stamp program.[23]

However, there was little reason to expect that TANF would sustain this responsiveness. Powers recognized this possibility early, along with its implications. She warned that

> shifting funding responsibilities from Congress to the nation's statehouses will impose formidable cyclical burdens on the states. With entitlement status for benefits gone, state lawmakers could react to a recession-induced fiscal squeeze by tightening standards or reducing benefits, which would pass cyclical income risk down to households. Without compensating changes in other programs (most obviously, UI), reduced payments and decreased opportunities for participation will inevitably worsen the impact of a faltering economy on the well-being of the poorest Americans.[24]

Indeed, in 2001, the first recession after TANF was enacted, TANF caseloads did not rise as AFDC caseloads typically did. In some cases, states used their policy flexibility, as Powers predicted, to cut benefits or eligibility to reduce expenditures. States also used other means to keep welfare caseloads low. Many states maintained work requirements and procedural barriers, such as requiring an extensive work search before a family head could qualify for benefits. Also, by the early 2000s, many individuals who had been on welfare since welfare reforms went into effect began to hit the federal government's five-year lifetime limit and were ineligible for benefits regardless of their economic circumstances.

Other programs have also showed relatively little responsiveness to economic cycles, though for different reasons than TANF. Powers found that caseloads in the SSI—a federal entitlement—were not much affected by economic cycles (caseloads increased by 0.39 percent point to each percentage increase in unemployment), as one might expect given the fact that SSI eligibility not only depends on income levels but also on disability or age.[25]

Medicaid caseloads have shown moderate responsiveness to economic cycles. Powers found that each one percentage point increase in unemployment produced a 1.9 percent expansion in Medicaid cases.[26] However, the effects of such caseload increases on overall Medicaid spending are dampened by several factors. First, most Medicaid spending goes not to low-income households with children—whose income levels are sensitive to cyclical changes—but to disabled and elderly recipients, whose income levels are less affected by macroeconomic shifts. Second, even though eligibility for Medicaid benefits is an entitlement, states can alter benefit packages or services available to Medicaid recipients; change reimbursement rates to health-care providers; and even eliminate eligibility for some individuals if those persons are covered under an optional state category rather than a federally mandated category.

Finally, many nonhealth-service or benefit programs are discretionary and can be cut, in response to economic downturns and tight state budgets. States can reduce, for instance, their state matching dollars in many child welfare and child-care subsidy programs; cut back on administrative expenses for social programs (including those for federal programs like Food Stamps, Medicaid, and Child Support Enforcement); and slash or even eliminate programs fully funded by state own-source revenues. It should thus not be surprising that time-series analyses of state and local spending on nonhealth social services (using Census survey data) found that such spending was cyclical, not countercyclical. Increases in unemployment, that is, were associated with decreases in social services spending.[27]

In sum, we would expect that the Great Recession would have different effects on the expenditures and coverage of different programs. Some programs have been historically more responsive than others to growing economic needs. Other programs—notably cash assistance to low-income families with children—have undergone recent changes that might reduce their responsiveness to increases in unemployment or poverty. Still other programs, such as Food Stamps/SNAP, may have changed in the opposite direction.

THE 2007–2009 RECESSION
AND THE SOCIAL SAFETY NET

How has the Great Recession affected the social safety net? In many respects, the recession expanded and strengthened it. The combination of the sharp, severe economic downturn and a shift in political control over the national government led to a rapid, wide-ranging, and substantial infusion of federal funding in support of the national safety net in the form of the American Recovery and Reinvestment Act (ARRA) of 2009. No other post–World War II recession has generated such a large and timely expansion in the funding of safety-net programs. The 1982 recession, by contrast, was accompanied by a *contraction* in federal funding of social programs. The ARRA was short-lived—most of its supports for low-income families will end by 2012—and its full impact is still unclear. The post-ARRA safety net is likely to reveal not only many of the gaps that were evident before the Great Recession but also new challenges due to persistent fiscal pressures on states, high levels of long-term unemployment, added responsibilities caused by federal health-care reform, and the disproportionate location of vulnerable people in states with weak safety nets and state fiscal capacity.

Impact of the Great Recession on Demand for Safety-Net Services

The nation's most recent recession began in December 2007 and ended in June 2009 according to the National Bureau of Economic Research. It was severe. Real GDP fell 4.1 percent from peak to trough, much more than the 3.4 percent drop in the deep 1973 recession, and much deeper than the average of all recessions since World War II. The unemployment rate peaked at 10.1 percent in October 2009, far worse than all postwar recessions other than the 1981 recession when unemployment peaked at 10.8 percent. Between December 2007 and October 2009 the number of unemployed workers increased by 7.9 million, and as of September 2011 there were still 6.3 million more unemployed workers than at the start of the recession.

Unemployment spells associated with this recession have been much longer than in any prior recession. In 2009, 31.5 percent of unemployed workers had been out of work for six months or more, compared to 23.9 percent in 1983, the next-highest rate in the sixty-four years for which these measures are available.[28] Furthermore, for many workers the prospects of returning to their prior jobs were low. When employers have terminated workers in past recessions they have relied on temporary layoffs, increasing these layoffs as a share of total layoffs. But in 2009, for the first time in the forty-three-year span of these data, temporary layoffs actually decreased as a share of total layoffs.[29]

In addition to increased unemployment, this recession has produced a huge increase in the number of discouraged workers—people without jobs who, out of discouragement, have not looked for work in the previous four weeks and thus are not considered unemployed. From November 2007 (right before the recession started) through November 2010, the number of discouraged workers increased by 933,000, more than tripling.[30]

In part because of rising unemployment, the number of people in poverty has risen dramatically. Between 2007 and 2010 (the latest year of available data) the poverty rate rose from 12.5 percent to 15.1 percent, its highest level since 1993. Viewed differently, in a period in which the total US population grew by only 2.3 percent, the number of people in poverty increased by 23.9 percent, as shown in table 21.3. As the table also shows, the poverty increase was disproportionately concentrated among children and people of working age. By contrast, the number of elderly people living in poverty declined.[31]

Official poverty figures are imperfect measures of the stress created by recession. The estimates count cash income, including cash-based safety-net programs that can mitigate the effects of recession, such as unemployment compensation and cash assistance. Absent these programs, the stresses on individuals and families would have been greater still. However, the traditional poverty measure does not include the value of many other benefits, such as refundable tax credits and food stamps. As we will show, such benefits alleviated the effects of unemployment and reduced income on individuals and families in 2009, although some of this mitigation will soon vanish as many benefits enacted under the ARRA expire.

Table 21.3 Poverty increased substantially between 2007 and 2010 among children and people of working age

	2007	2010	Change	% change
	Number of people in poverty (thousands)			
Total number in poverty	37,276	46,180	8.904	23.9%
Children (under age 18)	13,324	16,401	3,077	23.1%
Working age (18–64)	20,396	26,258	5,889	28.9%
Elderly (65+)	3,556	3,520	−36	−1.0%
	Total population (thousands)			
Total population	298,699	305,688	6,989	2.3%
Children (under age 18)	73,996	74,494	498	0.7%
Working age (18–64)	187,913	192,015	4,102	2.2%
Elderly (65+)	36,790	39,179	2,389	6.5%
	Poverty rates (%)			
Total	12.5	15.1	2.6	
Children (under age 18)	18.0	22.0	4.0	
Working age (18–64)	10.9	13.7	2.8	
Elderly (65+)	9.7	9.0	−0.7	

Source: Income, Poverty and Health Insurance Coverage in the United States: 2010, US Census Bureau.

Impact of the Great Recession on State Capacity to Finance Services

Even before the Great Recession began to strain the safety net, it blew huge holes in states' capacities to pay for safety-net services. State-tax revenue fell far more sharply than in prior recessions, and far more sharply than the economy would suggest, as figure 21.4 shows. Between fiscal year 2008 and 2010, state-tax revenue fell by 10.8 percent, in nominal terms, with declines in forty-eight of fifty states.

Mainstream economic forecasters expect the economic recovery to be slow and many states expect it will take several years before tax revenue can return to its prerecession peak.[32] The outlook for states' abilities to finance safety-net services, or other services, is bleak.

ARRA and Federal Changes
for the Safety Net

The magnitude of the economic downturn encouraged the Obama administration and the 111th Congress to fashion the largest single economic stimulus package ever enacted by the US government. In February 2009, the ARRA was passed

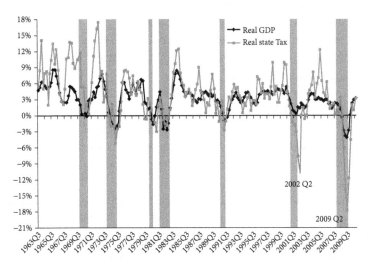

Figure 21.4 Percentage change in real state government taxes and real GDP vs. one year ago, quarterly data, 1963–2010

Notes: (1) Tax revevenue adjusted for inflation using GDP price index;
(2) Recession periods are shaded.

Sources: U.S. Census Bureau (taxes and Bureau of Economic Analysis
(real GDP and GDp price index).

and signed into law. The ARRA was designed to provide direct stimulus to the economy through tax cuts and capital spending programs, to provide fiscal relief to states and thereby forestall some state budget cuts (including cuts in safety-net programs), and to create direct expansions to the safety net. The main federal expansions of the safety net included the following:

- Federal Medicaid grants were increased by enhancing the FMAP, that is, by increasing the percentage of federal dollars supporting total state Medicaid expenditures. However, states that agreed to a higher FMAP also had to agree that they would not reduce eligibility for Medicaid or cut certain types of benefits.
- Unemployment Insurance was extended beyond the states' usual six months of benefits. The federal government typically authorizes temporary extensions, paid for by federal revenues, during recessions. (The federal government authorized another extension in December 2010, making UI benefits available through the end of calendar year 2011.)
- The federal government also gave states financial incentives to expand eligibility for their UI benefits, which typically cover only about one out of three workers. Part-time, low-income workers with interrupted work histories are usually not eligible for benefits.
- Federal refundable tax credits were created or expanded. The Child Tax Credit was increased, including the refundable credit for low-income families. A new Making Work Pay (MWP) credit was also included in the stimulus package, which was also available as a refundable credit to low-income workers. These expanded credits came on top of a separate increase in the value and coverage of the federal EITC.
- Food Stamp and SSI benefits were increased; in the case of Food Stamps or SNAP, the increase was large (13.6 percent). Each SSI recipient received a one-time payment of $250.
- A new funding source—the Emergency Fund—was made available to states through their TANF block grants. States could draw on the EF if they put up 20 percent of the costs in support of certain types of income supports: basic cash assistance, short-term "diversion" payments (e.g., one-time cash benefits to individuals or families in lieu of monthly cash payments), or subsidized work programs for welfare clients.
- Additional federal funds were provided for a variety of federal grants that supported services, including child care, Child Support Enforcement, homelessness protection, community services, workforce investment programs for youth, and foster-care and adoption assistance.

The size of the stimulus was breathtaking. Federal assistance to state and local governments jumped from 3.3 to an unprecedented 4.6 percent of GDP between federal fiscal years 2008 and 2010. Federal assistance in the social programs alone—including health, income security, and education/employment/social services—increased from 2.6 percent to 3.7 percent of GDP between 2008 and 2010 (see figure 21.5), with most of the increase due to the enhanced federal match for Medicaid.

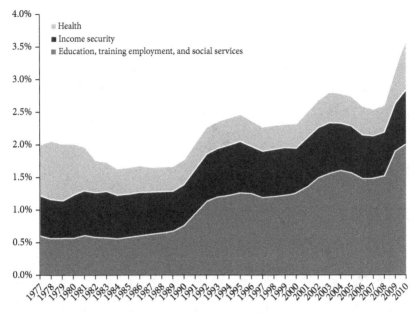

Figure 21.5 Federal assistance to state and local governments as a percentage
of GDP, 1977–2010
Sources: Budget of the United states Government and Bureau of Economic Analysis (GDP).

Yet the ARRA was more than just pump-priming. The federal government used the ARRA not only to stimulate the economy and sustain critical state and local programs, but it also used federal assistance to influence state budgets and policies and promote institutional reforms. As we will see, this effort to use the stimulus as leverage for policy change could also generate important differences across states in their safety nets, because some states responded to contingencies embedded in the ARRA and then can secure federal funding, while others did not.

How Did the Modified Safety Net Work?

As expected, different parts of the fragmented and mutable US safety net performed very differently during and after the Great Recession. With the help of the ARRA, this complex combination of programs met an enormous set of economic needs. But because some programs responded more strongly than others, some groups of people, and some needs, fared better than others.

To get some sense of the variation, figure 21.6 shows one measure of stress and several indicators of safety-net responses over the course of the recession. Each line represents the change in the number of individuals or households facing unemployment and enrolled in selected safety-net programs since the start of the recession. Two rough groupings of programs emerge from a comparison of the trends. UI claims, SNAP/Food Stamp households, and Medicaid enrollees all increased dramatically after the end of 2007, and in rough proportion to the number of unemployed people in the United States. By contrast, enrollments in TANF and related

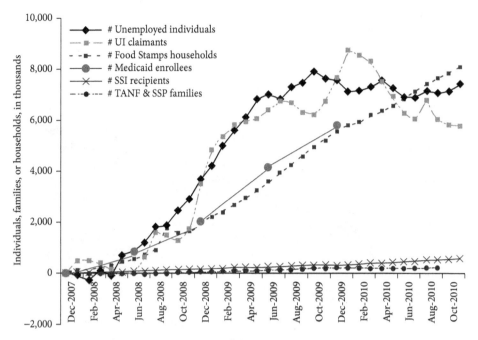

Figure 21.6 Changes since the start of the 2007 recession in the number of the
unemployed and in numbers receiving selected safety-net benefits
Sources: Bureau of Labor Statiscs (Unemployed individual), Department of Labor
(UI claimants), Department of Agriculture (Food stamps), Kaiser Family Foundation
(Medicaid enrollees), Social Security Administration (SSI recipients), Department of
Health &Human Services (TANF & SSp families).

state cash assistance programs—and, less surprisingly, participation in SSI—hardly
grew at all. These differences, along with the roles performed by the ARRA in each
of these programs, have had big implications for the future of the safety net.

Unemployment Insurance

The Federal-State Unemployment Insurance Program (UI) has expanded quickly
to meet economic needs, though with a lot of help from the federal government.
The regular UI program provides payments to people unemployed through no fault
of their own. States determine the size of the benefits, eligibility criteria, and the
maximum duration of payments. Most states provide benefits for up to twenty-six
weeks and the benefits are intended to replace 50 percent of unemployed workers'
wages, up to a maximum amount. In 2009, states replaced just under 47 percent of
workers' wages.[33] Benefits are financed from taxes that states levy on employers.

After these state-only benefits are exhausted, extended UI benefits may be
available if the state suffers from high unemployment. Extended benefits may run
for an additional thirteen weeks and their costs are shared equally by the federal
and state governments. The federal government may also extend UI benefits to
persons who have exhausted all other UI benefits by enacting temporary federal
benefits. The federal government pays the full costs of these benefits. Temporary

federal benefits were initially enacted in response to the Great Recession in July 2008 and were extended several times afterward; federal benefits were to be available through December 2011.

There is no doubt that the UI program was a key income support for unemployed people in the Great Recession. The rate of increase in the number of UI claimants after December 2007 was in fact greater than the rate of growth in the number of unemployed people. By November 2010 the number of people who were unemployed had increased by 7.4 million, an increase of 97 percent, while the number claiming UI had grown by 5.8 million, an increase of 196 percent.

Nonetheless, not all unemployed people were helped—not even most. The number of people receiving unemployment checks at any point in time was well below the number of people who are unemployed. In 2007, about 37 percent of unemployed workers received unemployment insurance.[34] Low-income families are particularly unlikely to receive UI benefits.[35] Such families are more likely to work part-time; their work experiences are often interrupted by child care, elder care, domestic violence, and other family-related problems; some workers are recent labor-market entrants with short wage histories. All of these conditions disqualified many unemployed people from UI benefits.

However, a provision in the ARRA offered states financial incentives to "modernize" their UI programs, such as qualifying people with only recent or part-time work experiences, or who left their jobs for personal reasons such as problems with daycare, caring for a sick family member, or relocating with a spouse.[36] Most states responded to the federal offer to subsidize UI eligibility expansions. As of January 2011, thirty-nine states agreed to adopt an "alternative base period," which would count workers' most recent earnings in qualifying for unemployment benefits; twenty-five states permitted benefits to people seeking part-time work; and eighteen states expanded eligibility to individuals who left jobs for "compelling family reasons."[37] Of these different options, past research suggests that the biggest payoff for low-income workers would be the adoption of the alternative base period, to include workers' most recent wages.[38]

This rapid shift in UI policies among most states may attest to the strength of the ARRA's financial incentives. Yet it is not yet clear how much real change has taken place in the reach of the UI program to low-income workers. The US Department of Labor's Office of Inspector General found that only $4 billion of the $7 billion that the ARRA offered for UI modernization had been applied for as of early 2011. Also, most of the states "were not able to provide data regarding claimants' payments under the new provisions."[39] Finally, many of the states that were hurt the most by the Great Recession—including Arizona, Florida, and California—did not choose to "modernize" their UI policies.

At the same time, state UI programs also experienced severe strains and limitations. The regular state UI program showed a drastic drop between 2009 and 2010 in the percentage of unemployed persons receiving benefits, from 40.1 percent to 30.1 percent.[40] The number of unemployed people exhausting their regular state benefits peaked as early as August 2009—at an unprecedented high of nearly 800,000. Since then, the extended and temporary federal benefits programs have had to absorb a growing share of the financial burden of assisting the unemployed. Even so, state UI programs face severe and growing financial problems. Net trust funds—total state funds available for UI benefits, minus what is owed to the federal government to pay back loans drawn when UI claims exceed state funds—plummeted to historic lows.[41] Because state UI benefits greatly exceeded state-funded accounts, states were forced to borrow from the federal government to pay benefits. By January 2011, thirty-one states owed the federal government an aggregate of $41.6 billion. These are debts that the states must pay back, which they often do by raising taxes on employers.

In sum, UI played an enormous role in helping unemployed individuals during the Great Recession. Yet it is still not clear whether it helped many low-income, young, or part-time workers. Also, the financing of the program increasingly relied on the federal government (see figure 21.7), either through federal loans to the states or temporary federal extensions of benefits. This federal absorption of costs may augur a weaker role for UI in the next few years, as the federal government may end its temporary extensions, and as some states may cut benefits or raise taxes to help pay back the federal government for its loans to state UI trust funds.

Supplemental Nutrition Assistance Program/Food Stamps

Figure 21.6 also shows that SNAP/FSP benefits—which are fully funded by the federal government—have also responded to growing economic needs as represented by the unemployment rate. The number of households receiving Food Stamps grew by 7.5 million between December 2007 and September 2010, an increase of 61 percent.

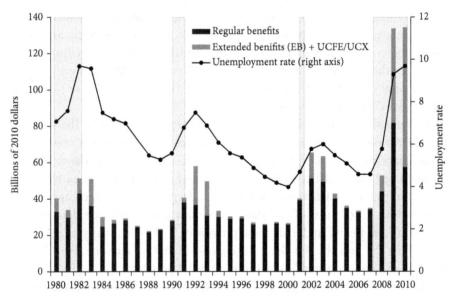

Figure 21.7 Unemployment rate and real unemployment benefits, by type, 1980–2010
Notes: (1) Adjusted for inflation; (2) Calender years; (3) Recession periods are shaded.
Sources: Bureau of Labor Statistics (unemployment rate), Department of Labor (unemployment benefits), Bureau of economic Analysis (GDP price index).

This rapid expansion was no surprise, because its origins preceded the Great Recession. Food Stamp caseloads have long shown strong countercyclical trends. SNAP benefits are available to most households with a net income under 133 percent of the federal poverty level, so as household income changes, it is only logical to expect changes in program participation. Caseloads rose sharply during, as well as one or two years after, the recessions of 1990 and 2001, while they fell during periods of economic growth and declining unemployment, like the middle and late 1990s.[42]

SNAP is much more accessible to low-income people than UI. In 2009, over 70 percent of recipient households reported no earnings.[43] And though UI reaches only about one out of three unemployed persons—and a much smaller proportion of low-income people who have lost jobs—SNAP reaches about two out of three eligible people, all of whom are in low-income households.[44] SNAP's accessibility has grown since 2002, when only a little more than half of eligible individuals participated in the Food Stamp Program. One event contributing to this growth was the federal Farm Bill of 2002, which gave states new policy options to make benefits easier to get and keep. Eligibility for certain immigrants was expanded; standard deductions used to determine eligibility were liberalized; performance measures were changed to give greater weight to accessibility; states were given options to simplify program rules; and electronic benefit systems were encouraged. Most states responded vigorously to these options, for instance, by reducing the need for face-to-face interviews and frequent recertifications.[45] With greater accessibility, SNAP benefits became increasingly delinked from welfare benefits; the percentage of households getting SNAP/FSP benefits *and* receiving welfare (AFDC/TANF) dropped from 37 percent in 1996 to 10 percent in 2009, while the number of SNAP households with earnings increased. Finally, FSP/SNAP benefits have grown in value. They are indexed to inflation, and the ARRA increased the maximum monthly benefits from $588 to $688 in the second half of 2009. Average monthly benefits to households grew in real terms by $202 to $272 between fiscal years 2001 and 2009.

In brief, SNAP benefits are now one of the most widely accessible income-support programs in the United States. Another important characteristic is its consistency across states. While TANF benefits vary enormously in value and accessibility across states—more on that below—the average monthly benefit per person under SNAP varies little from the national mean. In 2008, for instance, the average SNAP monthly benefit per person was $102, and only three states reported average benefits $10 more or less than that national average.[46]

Supplemental Security Income

SSI provides monthly income support to low-income families with disabled children, disabled working-age adults, and people sixty-five or older. The program is administered by the Social Security Administration, and its benefits are the same in all states. Its benefits are also comparatively large. Although benefits go to less than a third of those who get SNAP or EITC, the total benefits it pays out are larger than either of these programs.

SSI assistance caseloads have risen gradually in recent years, somewhat faster than the population. As figure 21.6 shows, this trend has continued since the Great Recession began in late 2007. We might expect some increase in SSI eligibility during economic downturns as more families who have disabled family members lose income. Also, states have financial incentives to move TANF recipients with disabilities that inhibit their employment to SSI, whose benefits are more generous than TANF's in most states. Perhaps more important, SSI benefits are fully paid for by the federal government, while TANF benefits are essentially paid for by both the federal and state governments (and local governments in a few states). There was indeed an increase in SSI caseloads of 0.6 million between December 2007 and November 2010, an increase of 8 percent—with most of the increase among children and nonelderly adults.[47] But given past research, it is unlikely that much of this growth was driven by macroeconomic changes.[48] SSI thus continues to be an important part of the safety net, but it still serves a small number of Americans, and it is not yet clear that the Great Recession has significantly changed the program's reach or role.

Tax Credits

In addition to UI and SNAP, federal tax credits were also expanded under the ARRA—in fact, they increased more than any other element of the safety net. The ARRA increased the Child Tax Credit (CTC) by $14.8 billion and the federal EITC by $4.6 billion. It also created Making Work Pay (MWP), which provided $116.2 billion to tax filers. All of these credits were refundable and offered low-income individuals and households support even if they did not owe federal income taxes, though the amounts going to low-income people under the CTC and MWP were much smaller than the total amounts listed above, because these credits went mostly to filers with moderate incomes.

In addition to these federal credits, twenty-three states have EITCs, and twenty of these are refundable. Most of these programs have not been cut back during the Great Recession.[49] In fact, the share of TANF spending (including state MOE expenditures) increased between 2007 and 2009, from 12.7 to 14.9 percent.[50] Refundable income-tax credits thus appear to be politically durable, even at the state level.

Data are not yet available to know with certainty the magnitude and effects of these tax-policy changes under the ARRA in helping low-income people in the United States. On the one hand, the credits (especially the refundable portions) make a lot of money available to a wide range of people, including low-income households. As people lose income, more and more may qualify for EITC. An estimate by the Center on Budget and Policy Priorities suggested that the tax provisions in the ARRA (MWP and CTC), along with the expansion of the EITC, kept 2.5 million people out of poverty in 2009, though these are estimates based on many assumptions and interpolations.[51] On the other hand, these credits are only available to people who have worked for some time during a calendar year. In a severe and prolonged recession, tax credits may decline in coverage and value. As figure 21.8 shows, it is difficult to draw any conclusions yet about the relative

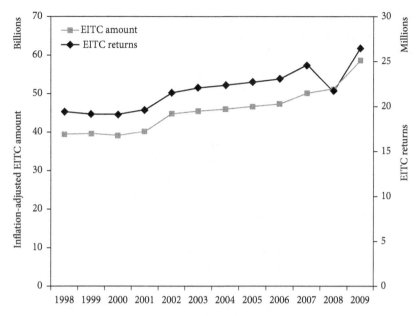

Figure 21.8 Federal EITC and returns, 1998–2009
Source: IRS, Statistics of Income Division, SOI Tax Stats, Table 2—Individual
Income and Tax Data.

strength of different dynamics in EITC usage in the Great Recession. The number
of tax returns claiming EITC credits fell sharply in 2008, the first year of the recession, but the number rebounded a year later in 2009.

One general weakness in using tax credits as part of the safety net is the infre-
quency of benefits; families may have to wait many months to receive federal-tax
refunds. The federal EITC until recently had an Advance Earned Income Tax
Credit program in which individuals who expected to qualify could receive estimated monthly payments from their employers. But so few tax filers used the program, it was terminated at the end of 2010.[52]

Temporary Assistance to Needy Families (Cash Assistance)

TANF cash assistance caseloads grew by 11 percent between December 2007 and
June 2010. Because TANF caseloads had shrunk to such low levels before the recession, the number of additional families on TANF assistance amounted to less than
0.2 million. Another way of looking at the small contribution of TANF assistance
to the safety net in the Great Recession is to consider its role in supporting poor
children. Even though the number of poor children grew by 2.1 million between
2007 and 2009, the number of children on TANF cash assistance increased only
by 0.4 million. In contrast, SNAP/FSP served 15.6 million children in 2009 (most
of which live in poor households), up from 12.7 million in 2007—an increase of 2.9
million, about seven times the increase in children supported by TANF.

Not only did SNAP/FSP serve many more low-income children than did TANF
cash assistance, it also provided more money. In 2009, TANF cash assistance

equaled $10.8 billion, including state as well as federally funded programs under TANF's authority.[53] In the same year, annualized SNAP benefits to low-income households with children—TANF's target population—equaled $35.7 billion, over three times the amount spent under TANF and related state programs.[54] Also unlike SNAP, TANF benefits vary enormously from state to state in terms of eligibility rules, work requirements, time limits, administrative practices, and the size of cash grants.[55] For instance, the maximum monthly benefits under TANF for a family of three and no income ranged, in 2009, from $170 in Mississippi and $185 in Tennessee, to $923 in Alaska, $721 in New York, and $694 (for families required to work) in California.[56]

What accounts for TANF's small role in supporting its target population: low-income children and their families? Unlike UI, SNAP, SSI, Medicaid, and the refundable tax credits, TANF is not an open-ended entitlement, available to everyone who meets certain eligibility requirements. States receive annual block grants, which have been largely unchanged even in nominal terms since they were first awarded in the late 1990s. As a result, inflation and the growing number of poor families with children since the 1990s have reduced federal TANF grants to states from a peak of $940 in 2000 to only $499 in 2009, a 47 percent decline.[57]

TANF programs can limit access to cash benefits in several ways. Cash assistance, in most states, is time-limited. Work or worklike activities (such as searching for work, participating in community service, or holding a job) are required of most families. But as TANF benefits have shrunk in real value over the years, and benefits in most states are reduced when a family earns income from a job, working even part-time while receiving benefits is often not worthwhile.[58] Also, complying with work requirements when few private-sector jobs are available may be difficult unless states offer other options.

States also have incentives to minimize cash assistance caseloads. Small caseloads save the states money they can then use to fund a wide variety of service programs: an especially important source of financial support during a recession, when state funding is scarce. States may also meet federal performance requirements more easily if they keep caseloads low. States are required to have 50 percent of their eligible heads of families participating in some combination of work-related activities or face possible reductions in their block grants from the federal government. However, to the extent that states reduce their caseloads from levels they reported in 2005, states' "work participation requirements" (the percentage of persons on assistance who must meet minimal work requirements) are reduced.

TANF caseloads actually fell during and soon after the 2001 recession. Perhaps in part to prevent that from happening again, the ARRA included a provision (the TANF Emergency Fund, or EF) that offered states additional TANF funds if a state commits to spending the grant money on cash assistance, one-time "diversion" cash grants, or subsidized jobs, and if the state pays 20 percent of the costs (while the federal government provides the remaining 80 percent). Even though states did not spend the entire Emergency Fund of $6.8 billion, they drew down $5 billion, or about 72 percent of total funds for which they were eligible (see table 21.4). Most of the funds were spent in fiscal year 2010 and represented a large boost in federal assistance under TANF, probably adding more than 20 percent to the total in that year.

As table 21.4 shows, states got approvals for short-term benefits and cash assistance more than for subsidized jobs. These programs were easier to roll out quickly, and states that committed the most to these functions were also more likely to draw down most of the emergency funds (EF) for which they were eligible.[59] However, federal funding for subsidized jobs under the EF was enormous in historical context. Under the EF, $1.3 billion was approved for subsidized job programs in thirty-nine states. This amount is about fifteen times greater than the $0.09 billion in federal funds spent by states on work subsidies under the regular TANF program in 2006, the highest level among prior years.

The subsidized jobs option also seemed to draw in states—like North Dakota, Kentucky, Florida, Mississippi, and Georgia—that had traditionally spent little on their TANF/AFDC programs. By contrast, states that have provided greater benefits to families under TANF and AFDC put more of their federal dollars into basic assistance (such as Washington, Oregon, or California) or short-term benefits (such as New York, New Jersey, Vermont, Wisconsin, and Minnesota). By providing multiple options for states, along with rewards for expansions, the TANF Emergency Fund thus appealed to a wide range of states. Nonetheless, these temporary extensions of the safety net were largely shut down after the EF expired in FY 2010.[60] In short, TANF showed some interesting responses to the ARRA. But even with the EF, its contribution to the safety net was, for the most part, marginal.

Medicaid

When a recession begins and unemployment rises, many people lose employer-based health insurance and some in turn become eligible for Medicaid, driving up enrollment and state and federal expenditures. In addition, costs for uncompensated care rise, much of which is financed through state budgets.

In a 2009 analysis, Holahan and Garrett estimated that an increase in unemployment from 4.6 percent to 10 percent (approximately what occurred in the 2007–2009 recession) would lead to a loss of employer-sponsored insurance by

Table 21.4 Approved federal funding under the ARRA's TANF Emergency Fund

Function	Amount approved (dollars)	Percentage of approved funds	Percentage of states approved for this function
Short-term benefits	2,046,898,770	41.3%	45%
Basic assistance	1,592,147,070	32.1%	42%
Subsidized jobs	1,314,363,330	26.5%	39%
Amount approved	**4,953,409,170**	**100.0%**	**49%**

Source: Office of Family Assistance, Administration for Children and Families; US Department of Health and Human Services.

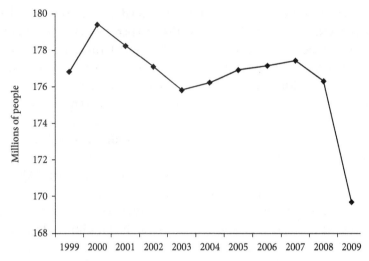

Figure 21.9 Number of people with reported employment-based health insurance, 1999–2009
Source: U.S. Census Bureau, Income, Poverty and Health Insurance Coverage
in the United States.

13.2 million people. They also estimated that 5.4 million more people enrolled in Medicaid and SCHIP; annual Medicaid expenditures would go up by $18.6 billion; and the costs of uncompensated care would rise by $7.2 billion.[61] Their expectations seem to be on track. Based on the Current Population Survey, the number of people reporting employer-based insurance coverage declined precipitously, as 7.8 million people lost coverage between 2008 and 2009 alone (figure 21.9), and declines probably continued in 2010.

While economic forces increased the demand for Medicaid, state budget gaps have in the past created incentives for states to cut funding, sometimes by restricting eligibility. However, the $87 billion in aid that state Medicaid programs were eligible to receive under the ARRA (plus later extensions through June 2011) was contingent on states meeting maintenance-of-eligibility requirements, including not having more restrictive standards, methodologies, and procedures in place than were in place on July 1, 2008.

In fact, the federal strategy appeared to work. Between December 2007 and December 2009 (the latest available data), total Medicaid enrollment increased by 5.8 million individuals, or 13.6 percent, reversing the previous trend of slowing enrollment growth, as figure 21.10 shows.[62] Nearly all states held steady or expanded their eligibility and enrollment rules in 2010, with about a third of the states expanding eligibility policies or easing enrollment and renewal procedures.[63] According to the GAO, children accounted for the greatest number of new enrollees, and the highest growth rate was among nondisabled nonelderly adults. States have estimated that enrollment growth averaged 8.5 percent in fiscal year 2010 and projected enrollment growth of 6.1 percent in fiscal year 2011.[64] Enrollment increases have contributed to a reported increase in Medicaid expenditures of 8.2 percent in fiscal year 2010 and will contribute to further increases in 2011. State funds decreased by 1 percent while federal funds increased by 14.4 percent over

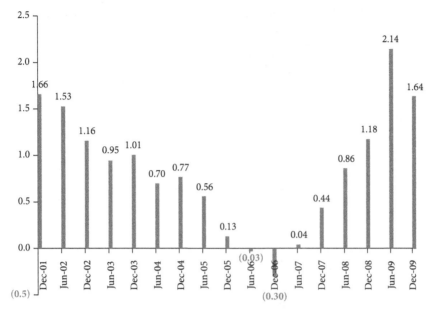

Figure 21.10 Semiannual changes in Medicaid enrollment,
December 2001–December 2009, millions of enrollees
Source: Compiled by the Health Management Associates from state
Medicaid enrollment reports, for the KCMU.

fiscal 2009 amounts. Both the Kaiser Commission on Medicaid and the Uninsured
and the Governmental Accountability Office report that states used the FMAP
increase primarily to cover increased enrollment.

Every state had an increase in Medicaid enrollment, although there was great
variation in the size of the increase (table 21.5). States in the west had higher-than-
average enrollment increases while northeastern states had lower-than-average
increases. According to an analysis by the GAO, western states also generally had
higher than average growth in unemployment and poverty rates during the recession, and higher rates of uninsurance before the recession. Many of the northeastern states had higher eligibility levels prior to the recession. The low growth in
Tennessee reflects a court decision that allowed it to re-determine eligibility for
certain individuals, resulting in an enrollment reduction of 100,000 individuals.

Although the ARRA prevented nearly all states from cutting eligibility for
Medicaid, it did not prohibit states from reducing optional services or benefits or
reducing provider payment rates. Nor did it prevent states from increasing reliance on provider taxes or other financing mechanisms. According to the GAO,
forty-six states reported taking action to help control Medicaid costs. By and large
those actions involved changing financing arrangements such as provider taxes
and intergovernmental transfers to generate additional revenue, or reduced provider payment rates.[65] Some states have also cut services. According to NASBO/
NGA's Fiscal Survey of the States, for fiscal year 2011, fourteen states planned
benefit restrictions, such as the elimination of covered benefits and application of
utilization controls or limits for existing benefits.[66]

Table 21.5 Medicaid enrollment during the Great Recession (thousands of enrollees), 2007–2009

	December 2007 enrollment	December 2009 enrollment	Change in enrollment	% change
United States	42,754	48,570	5,816	13.6%
Wisconsin	687	975	288	41.9%
Maryland	537	714	177	33.0%
Nevada	180	239	59	32.6%
Colorado	381	495	114	30.0%
Florida	2,083	2,677	594	28.5%
Arizona	944	1,204	260	27.5%
Oregon	338	427	89	26.3%
Utah	197	247	50	25.1%
Hawaii	184	226	42	23.0%
Alaska	78	94	17	21.4%
Iowa	324	392	68	21.0%
North Dakota	52	63	10	19.8%
Michigan	1,507	1,792	285	18.9%
Montana	81	96	15	18.3%
Indiana	796	941	145	18.3%
Delaware	149	174	25	17.1%
Washington	862	1,007	144	16.7%
Virginia	651	760	109	16.7%
Ohio	1,604	1,871	267	16.7%
Minnesota	590	687	96	16.3%
Idaho	170	196	27	15.7%
New Hampshire	111	128	17	15.7%
Georgia	1,253	1,447	195	15.6%
Wyoming	56	64	8	15.1%
New Mexico	388	446	58	14.9%
Nebraska	175	200	25	14.5%
Mississippi	521	596	75	14.4%
Illinois	1,992	2,270	277	13.9%

(Continued)

Table 21.5 Continued

	December 2007 enrollment	December 2009 enrollment	Change in enrollment	% change
New York	4,094	4,624	530	13.0%
Oklahoma	522	588	66	12.6%
Missouri	721	810	89	12.3%
District of Columbia	128	144	16	12.2%
Alabama	673	749	75	11.2%
North Carolina	1,206	1,335	130	10.7%
Vermont	121	134	13	10.5%
New Jersey	767	841	74	9.7%
Massachusetts	1,030	1,127	98	9.5%
Kansas	252	275	23	9.3%
South Dakota	90	98	8	9.2%
Louisiana	851	928	78	9.1%
West Virginia	303	330	27	9.0%
Kentucky	702	764	61	8.7%
Pennsylvania	1,894	2,053	159	8.4%
Texas	2,864	3,100	235	8.2%
Connecticut	421	455	34	8.0%
California	6,436	6,927	490	7.6%
South Carolina	619	652	33	5.3%
Arkansas	504	526	22	4.4%
Maine	259	269	9	3.6%
Rhode Island	163	166	3	2.1%
Tennessee	1,244	1,248	4	0.3%

Source: Kaiser Commission on Medicaid and the Uninsured (2010).

In sum, Medicaid's growing share of safety net expenditures in recent decades probably continued and even accelerated during and after the Great Recession. The program responded quickly to increased needs, and by choosing to accept federal ARRA funds, nearly all states were unable to cut eligibility, a tactic many states used in past recessions when they faced large budget deficits. States could and did find ways of reducing Medicaid costs in other ways: for instance, by trimming optional services or payments to health-care providers. Nonetheless, so long as the

ARRA was in effect, states had to look elsewhere for opportunities to cut benefits and services.

Social Services (Including TANF Nonassistance)

As already noted, social service expenditures at the state and local levels have been declining in real terms—and especially real dollars per poor person—since 2002. Unlike means-tested entitlements, social service programs are often discretionary, and their value has typically dropped during economic downturns, as states look for programs to cut. Other service programs are funded by fixed block grants from the federal government. Although these are not cut, their real value per poor person may decline in recessions. Also, states may use the block grants, if they can, to support programs not traditionally funded by such grants—and thus save some state funding.[67]

However, the ARRA may have countered some of these cyclical effects by increasing federal funding for many service programs, including the Workforce Investment Act ($4 billion), Head Start ($2.1 billion), the Child Care Development Block Grant ($2 billion), Emergency Shelter Grants ($1.5 billion), Community Development Block Grants ($1 billion), Child Support Enforcement ($1 billion), and the Community Services Block Grant ($1 billion).

It is difficult to get a clear picture of what happened to nonhealth social services after the start of the Great Recession. Although we do not have data from the Census Bureau's Survey of State and Local Governments for 2009—the data we used to describe historical patterns of safety-net spending—we do have data on *state* spending in that year, which includes two quarters for which ARRA money were available. Table 21.6 shows the nominal and inflation-adjusted expenditures on social services from 2007 to 2009. For comparison, it also shows state spending on medical and cash assistance. Since the recession began in December 2007, after the states enacted their fiscal year 2008 budgets, the 2009 expenditures reveal the first year in which most states budgeted after the recession began and the ARRA was enacted.

Table 21.6 shows that spending on social services increased over these years. Indeed, state spending increased in all three types of safety-net functions. Also, the increases were greater between 2008 and 2009, when the ARRA first came into play, than between 2007 and 2008. Social services spending grew substantially, by 10 percent (in real dollars), more than the rate of growth in medical assistance (5 percent) but less than the increase in cash assistance spending (15 percent).

Other evidence suggests that ARRA funding helped sustain these programs. The Census data break down the entire "public welfare" category into expenditures supported by federal transfers and those supported by state own-source revenues, and these amounts are shown at the bottom of table 21.6. Social welfare expenditures supported by states' own-source revenues dropped sharply between 2008 and 2009 (−16.3 percent), while federal transfers grew by 15.3 percent. Total funding of state safety-net programs increased by 5.9 percent.

Table 21.6 State expenditures on the safety net, 2007–2009 (local expenditures not included)

Function	Expenditures			Changes	
	2007	2008	2009	2007–2008	2008–2009
	Nominal dollars				
Medical assistance	273,530,418	288,518,175	305,251,109	5.5%	5.8%
Social services	45,171,535	47,447,930	52,759,701	5.0%	11.2%
Cash assistance	10,774,268	11,181,200	12,919,729	3.8%	15.5%
	Real dollars				
Medical assistance	282,065,618	291,228,064	305,251,109	3.2%	4.8%
Social services	46,581,061	47,893,582	52,759,701	2.8%	10.2%
Cash assistance	11,110,467	11,286,219	12,919,729	1.6%	14.5%
Source of funding					
	Nominal dollars				
State	95,997,525	103,634,401	87,611,447	8.0%	−15.5%
Federal	233,478,696	243,512,904	283,319,092	4.3%	16.3%
Real dollars					
State	98,993,017	104,607,781	87,611,447	5.7%	−16.3%
Federal	240,764,129	245,800,084	283,319,092	2.1%	15.3%
Total	339,757,146	350,407,865	370,930,539	3.1%	5.9%

Source: US Census Bureau.

Finally, states may have propped up social services through 2009 by drawing on their TANF block grants. As figure 21.11 shows, state spending on "nonassistance" has grown substantially since 2006; in 2009, two out of three dollars of state spending under TANF (including state maintenance of effort expenditures) went to nonassistance programs, such as child-care subsidies and employment services. However, the biggest growth in nonassistance spending between 2007 and 2009 occurred in the large catch-all category "Other." Although we do not have direct evidence, states may have used TANF to sustain a wide range of social services not previously subsidized by this funding stream.

Although national totals show growth in social services spending through 2009, some states did report cuts. Seven western and southern states (Arizona, Arkansas, Colorado, Delaware, Florida, Mississippi, and Virginia) reported nominal-dollar decreases in state spending on social services (based on the Census survey data) between 2008 and 2009. Cuts in discretionary programs may become particularly severe after 2010 as ARRA funds begin to expire. For instance, the

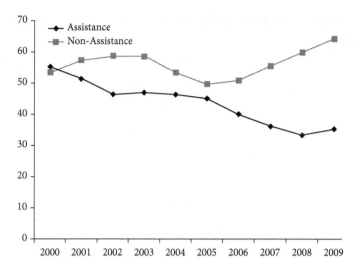

Figure 21.11 Real per capita TANF expenditures going to assistance
and Nonassistance, 2000–2009
Source: U.S. Department of Health and Human Services.

Center for Budget and Policy Priorities reported numerous reductions in discretionary items in state budgets for fiscal year 2011.[68] Child-care subsidies were cut in Texas, Massachusetts, and Ohio; California and Washington State eliminated such subsidies for families not on cash assistance.[69] Mental health services and services or income supports for the disabled (those not paid for by Medicaid) were reduced in many states, including Arizona, Georgia, Idaho, Illinois, Kansas, Michigan, Minnesota, Mississippi, New Hampshire, Ohio, and Washington. And some states reported to CBPP that they were closing human service offices or otherwise cutting back on staff for social programs. Idaho closed nine out of forty-five field offices, while Georgia cut staff handling eligibility for Food Stamps, Medicaid, and cash assistance.[70] Thus, although the ARRA staved off widespread and large cuts in social services through 2009, impressionistic evidence suggests that cuts may soon grow in number, range, and depth.

EFFECTS ON POVERTY

As of this writing, it is early to assess the effects of all these changes in the safety net on poverty; the most recent available measure of poverty rates is 2009. However, although the ARRA was not implemented until the last two quarters of 2009, poverty data from that year can provide clues about the effects of ARRA safety-net funding, the EITC increase, the continued expansion of SNAP, and other recent program changes on poverty.

To answer that question, we compare the percentage of persons living in households with incomes below the federal poverty level by using two measures of income: one measure that includes all significant sources of income except for safety-net programs, and one measure that also includes safety-net benefits. The difference between these two poverty-rate calculations is a rough estimate of the role of the safety net in keeping people out of poverty. In order to discern more subtle effects of the safety net, we also make these comparisons for different age groups: children (under eighteen), nonelderly adults (eighteen to sixty-four), and persons sixty-five years of age or older.

Figure 21.12 compares the percentages of people falling under the federal poverty level by using different definitions of income, from 2005 to 2009. Three graphs are shown. The top graph shows the percentages of people, by age, living in households that fall under the federal poverty level when we include *pre-safety net sources of income*, primarily after-tax market income and income from non-means-tested public programs. It includes earnings, interest income, rents, child support, employer contributions to health-care plans, and other nongovernment sources. It also includes benefits from non-means-tested public programs like Social Security, veterans' benefits, and the fungible value of Medicare. Unemployment assistance is not included in this measure of income, even though it is not strictly means-tested. We treat it as part of the safety net, as a critical source of income when many people lose their jobs. Finally, this measure of income is adjusted for taxes, except for the EITC, which is treated as a safety-net program.

The middle graph shows the percentage of persons (again, by age) in households whose incomes fall below the federal poverty line after adding income from means-tested programs (such as TANF cash assistance and SSI), EITC, UI, and major non-cash benefits (such as SNAP and Medicaid). The lowest graph in figure 21.12 shows the differences in poverty rates between estimates based on pre-safety-net income and those based on post-safety-net income.

The top graph reveals that poverty rates, before safety-net programs are counted, are quite different among the elderly, children, and nonelderly adults. Poverty is lowest among the elderly and highest among children. The trends are different too. The fastest growth was among children, whose poverty rates increased from 17.1 percent in 2006 to 20.8 percent in 2009. Poverty among adults between eighteen and sixty-four years of age began to increase a year later and grew from 11.3 percent in 2007 to 14.1 percent in 2009. In contrast, pre-safety-net income changed little among the elderly over this period, though it declined slightly after 2007. Poverty among the elderly would be much higher if we did not count Social Security and Medicare as income sources. But we do not treat these programs as part of the safety net, as people's eligibility for benefits is not based on demonstrated need.

The middle graph, which shows poverty rates after factoring in safety-net benefits, shows very different poverty levels and trends. Poverty rates are comparatively flat over this period when we include safety-net income. There is a slight increase in poverty among nonelderly adults after 2007, though much smaller than the increase when pre-safety-net income is considered. Children actually see a slight decline in poverty rates between 2008 and 2009, from 12.8 percent to 12.1 percent. Poverty levels and trends among the elderly, using post-safety-net income, are not much different from those estimated based on pre-safety-net income.

The bottom graph in figure 21.12 summarizes the effects of including safety-net programs in the poverty rate calculations; these are the differences between the pre- and post-safety-net poverty rates. All age groups see some reduction in poverty, but the biggest effects by far are found among children, followed by nonelderly adults. Also, the effects of the safety net on poverty rates among the nonelderly increased in 2009. The expansions in coverage and benefits discussed above—such as the ARRA safety-net provisions, the expanded EITC, and the accelerated growth in SNAP coverage—appear to have had an especially large impact on children, whose pre- and post-safety-net poverty rates differed by 8.7 percentage points (20.8 percent vs. 12.1 percent).[71]

In sum, safety-net programs have reduced poverty among all age groups, but the effects were larger among children and nonelderly adults in 2009. These effects may be even larger in 2010, when the ARRA's provisions were effective the entire year, not just the last two quarters. But the 2009 increase in the antipoverty effects of the safety net also implies that when the ARRA's funding of safety-net programs begins to vanish in 2011, and when federally subsidized UI payments expire at the end of the same year, poverty rates may increase substantially among children and nonelderly adults. (For more source information and definitions of income, see the endnote.)[72]

These large estimated effects of the ARRA do not, however, mean that the stimulus was efficient in affecting poverty throughout the nation. The ARRA often augmented but otherwise left existing allocation formulas in providing financial assistance to state governments. These formulas have generally not produced a redistribution of resources among states toward a more equal distribution of resources among states with large and small populations of low-income individuals. One reason is that, despite some special federal incentives to encourage fiscally weaker states to increase their funding of programs (like Medicaid and child welfare), state wealth and income have still traditionally been positively correlated with larger state safety-net programs funding thus went disproportionately to states that have been willing in the past to support safety-net programs, not necessarily to states with the greatest current economic needs. As figure 21.13 shows, federal funding under the ARRA on a poor-person basis was negatively related to the state's poverty rate in 2009. In other words, low-poverty states like Connecticut and New Hampshire received comparatively large federal infusions of safety-net assistance under the ARRA (in per-poor-person terms), while high-poverty states like Mississippi and Texas received less federal assistance. These differences among states are not new. But the fact that the ARRA reinforced these differences across states may have weakened the ARRA's impact on poverty reduction.

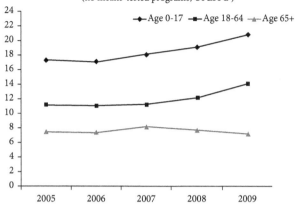

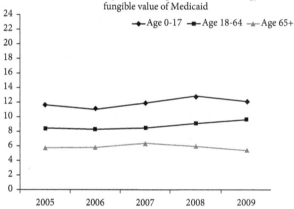

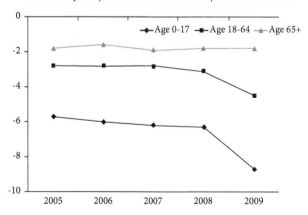

Figure 21.12 Percentages of persons in households under the federal poverty income threshold, before and after counting income from safety-net programs, 2004–2009
Source: U.S. Census Bureau. For More source information and definitions of income, see endnote 72.

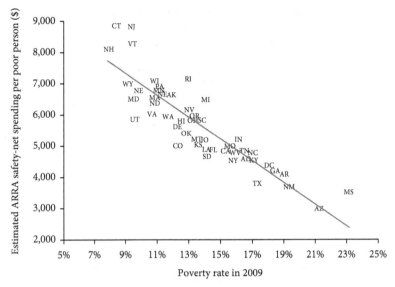

Figure 21.13 ARRA safety-net spending per poor person vs. poverty rate, by state
Sources: Census Bureau (poor people and poverty rate) and Center for
American Progress (ARRA safety net spending).

DID THE GREAT RECESSION CHANGE
THE SAFETY NET?

Before the Great Recession, there were good reasons to be concerned that the safety net would falter during a large economic shock. State cash assistance programs had been shrinking for a decade and a half, partly because of economic growth and reforms that promoted work rather than welfare. But the reforms also had the effect of making cash assistance less accessible (and less valuable) to family heads who were unable to find jobs. Social service expenditures and work supports, which had grown in the 1990s, began to shrink after 2002 and continued to do so through the first year of the Great Recession. UI, which had long failed to help most unemployed workers in the United States, covered even fewer workers just before the recession.

However, the safety net held up better than one might have expected. The value and accessibility of federal food assistance programs—particularly SNAP but also WIC and school or daycare meals programs—have grown rapidly since the early 2000s and established a broad-based set of supports available to many low-income households, especially those with children. The federal EITC program did not grow much in reach or value before the recession, but it continued to be an important income support for low-income families. SSI showed some expansion in coverage among disabled people and supported some families unable to manage the work requirements under TANF.

Yet the most important factor in bolstering the safety net during and after the Great Recession was the vast and rapid infusion of federal assistance—directly to individuals as well as through state and local governments—with the enactment and implementation of the American Recovery and Reinvestment Act and other federal actions in 2009. The stimulus added funding to a breathtakingly wide array of programs, including many income support and service programs targeted to people in economic distress. Within the safety net, the largest share of new funding went to Medicaid in the form of an enhanced federal match. But federal money also went to refundable tax credits, extended unemployment benefits, enhanced cash benefits under SNAP and SSI, and selected types of assistance under TANF. In addition, the ARRA offered funding for many other programs, including housing assistance, homelessness prevention, child-care subsidies, child welfare, and other services. In addition, the federal government, in separate actions, also increased benefits under the EITC as well as funding and eligibility for the Children's Health Insurance Program (CHIP).

The ARRA helped reverse the decline in resources that states devoted to cash assistance and social services, and it helped sustain Medicaid's coverage of low-income individuals despite the large budget deficits the states faced. It also demonstrated that the federal government can implement a large and timely stimulus that not only promotes economic recovery but also strengthens safety-net programs. That is no small feat. Prior stimulus packages have typically come late, often many months, sometimes years, after the end of the recession, and none provided the level of support for the social safety net that the ARRA did.

Nonetheless, the ARRA was a temporary measure. The enhanced Medicaid funding ended in mid-2011, while nearly all support ceased by 2012. Nor is anything like the ARRA likely to be re-enacted soon. It was produced in a crisis situation by a national government in which all branches other than the judiciary were controlled by a single party. It was pushed by a new administration with an interest not just in economic stimulus but also in supporting key programs and using fiscal incentives to reform and affect state policies and budgets. Each of these conditions was important in ARRA's enactment, yet there is no reason to expect that they will come together in future economic downturns.

Once the ARRA vanishes, financing the safety net will be difficult. Most state and local governments face severe budget shortfalls and may do so for many years.[73] Also, unemployment remains high and most professional forecasters expect rates to remain over 7 percent through 2014.[74] Questions then arise about the post-ARRA safety net: What is likely to happen to the safety net after the end of the ARRA? Where will there be strengths, and where will there be weaknesses or gaps?

When the ARRA expires, some elements of the safety net may remain strong. SNAP, other nutrition programs, and SSI have increased in value and take-up rates. The federal EITC and the refundable Child Tax Credit will continue to provide benefits to a wide range of low-income workers. CHIP funding and eligibility expansions will remain, and federal health-care reform increased eligibility for Medicaid to include all poor and near-poor individuals, up to 133 percent of the federal poverty level, beginning in 2014. All of these programs and expansions are highly reliant on continued federal funding. The federal government also pays more than 90 percent of the funds needed for Medicaid expansions under national health-care reform.

The federal government has also played an enormous role by extending UI benefits, but those extensions end after 2011. Most states now owe the federal government enormous sums due to loans they received automatically to support unemployment benefits after the states' own accounts were exhausted. To repay the federal government, some states may not only raise taxes on employers but also cut back on UI benefits. It is true that many states appeared to "modernize" their UI programs to cover a wider array of circumstances, including many that prevented low-income workers from receiving benefits. However, it is still not clear how much (if at all) these modernization initiatives will be fully implemented and lead to greater access to UI benefits, or whether the expansions will even survive after the federal incentives expire.

The biggest questions for the future involve programs, needs, and populations that rely in any significant extent on state or local funding and are not subject to a federal mandate. Such programs would include some child-care subsidies and child welfare programs (including foster care, adoption assistance, and protective services); general assistance programs; state-only service and benefit programs, such as at-risk youth services, after-school programs, pre-kindergarten programs, home visitation programs, and many services for the elderly and disabled; and many mental health, substance abuse, disability, dental, and other services not covered or mandatory under Medicaid.

Services and benefits offered under TANF are vulnerable too. During and soon after the previous recession, some states used their TANF and MOE dollars to sustain programs that had not traditionally relied on these sources in the past. This use of TANF may squeeze other service or benefit programs, particularly child-care subsidies, to which the block grant gave considerable support in prior years. The squeeze has been compounded by the fact that the block grant and associated MOE requirements have lost real value compared to the number of low-income families.

Implications for the Future

In sum, the nation's safety net may become more nationalized and concentrated among a few major programs. The nationalization and concentration are linked together. As discretionary service programs are squeezed or even eliminated by federal and state governments, entitlements like Medicaid, SNAP, SSI, UI, and EITC—which, except for regular UI and Medicaid, are almost fully funded by the federal government—may come to dominate the safety net even more than they do now. In particular, as states are required under federal health reform to change their eligibility standards toward a single threshold, this nationalization also means that state differences in the safety nets for low-income people may diminish.

The new safety net may also be administratively "light." While we saw a shift from benefits to social services and more intense supervisory methods in the

1990s—what Lawrence Mead called the "new paternalism"—recent trends suggest a shift toward less labor-intensive and more passive administrative approaches.[75] Rather than orientation meetings, service reviews, case management, and supervision of work search and participation—characteristics of the most developed TANF programs—the administrative face of the safety net may become website applications, tax forms, call centers, and other eligibility reviews. Instead of enforcing work through supervisory methods, the safety net offers access and rewards to low-income people who are working and/or able to seek assistance on their own. Indeed, as already noted, even TANF is moving in this direction, as a fast-growing share of TANF expenditures are going to refundable EITCs.

Although there may be merits in this move toward a more concentrated, nationalized, and administratively light safety net, there may also be gaping holes. Refundable tax credits may offer considerable support, but the support does not help families with short-term needs. Also, because tax benefits go only to people who have earnings, individuals with multiple barriers to employment will not benefit. For instance, the growing group of "disconnected single mothers" might be helped through intensive case management and outreach.[76] However, the shrinking of TANF, discretionary services, and state workforces may make such programs unfeasible in all but a few states.[77] More generally, cuts in discretionary programs may cause troubled families to lose access to services that might help them deal with substance abuse, domestic violence, illiteracy, or other fundamental barriers to the workforce. Another hole in the safety net may include young adults with little work experience, whose unemployment rates have been chronically high in recent years but who will get little help from UI even if the ARRA modernization efforts survive and are implemented.[78] Long-term unemployed people of many ages will run out of UI benefits and qualify for little outside of SNAP beginning in 2012.[79]

To sustain or recover a more balanced safety net—one that combines large national income-support programs with services that address more specific needs—will require the nation to reconcile the growing separation between the functions and capacities of the national and state governments. There are questions about the national government's fiscal capacity and political will to sustain its safety net. But those questions are not nearly as immediate and severe as the fiscal problems confronting state and local governments, and those fiscal problems may severely weaken states' administrative capacities. Yet the federal government cannot avoid using the states to implement critical parts of a balanced safety net. Only state and local governments have the administrative apparatus to put service programs into effect as well as more complex income-support programs like SNAP, and there is little near-term (or even long-term) political prospect of substantially increasing the size of the federal civilian bureaucracy. Nor would a federal takeover of financial *and* all policy and administrative functions necessarily perform as well as a smoothly working system of shared functions across governments.

There is value in permitting state variation and flexibility, not only to adjust general program objectives to the very different political cultures as well as the demographic, economic, and community characteristics found in different parts of the country, but also to give ample opportunities for innovation and experimentation, which may lead to national changes (such as we saw under Medicaid and AFDC waivers). Finally, a purely national safety net may limit what needs and populations may be served. In many cases, giving states a large role in devising policies and determining how to administer proposed programs has been critical in putting together national coalitions in the US Congress in support of controversial policies, as the growing role of states in the legislative history of the 2010 Affordable Care Act would attest.[80]

But it is not easy to see how the United States can continue to have a sharing of responsibilities over safety-net programs between the national and state governments if many of the states cannot sustain their financial roles. If the federal government continues to provide extensive and flexible financial support to states to help prop up their administrative and policy roles, it needs some sort of accountability. Efforts at intergovernmental accountability in the past have relied on state-matching formulas, data reporting, regulations, and performance measures and requirements. Yet many states will be challenged to deal with matching requirements, and the short history of TANF does not offer great hope for the effectiveness of performance measures. Too much "accountability" could restrict the reach of federal programs to the few states with greater financial resources and stronger bureaucracies. That is a troubling prospect now, as the greatest growth in the number of low-income children is found among a handful of states with lower fiscal capacities or traditionally small safety-net programs.[81] How to establish an effective partnership between the national and state governments in social welfare policy—a partnership that weds federal fiscal capacity with state and local administration in many states, not just the wealthiest or with the smallest needy populations—is surely one of the more difficult and important tasks for US social policies in the current decade.

NOTES

1 The table is based on the 2007–2008 federal fiscal year for programs where spending is readily available on that basis. Data for unemployment insurance and Supplemental Security Income were most readily available on a calendar-year basis and so 2008 calendar year data were used. Data for tax credits are based on the 2008 tax year.
2 For example, the table included data on state earned income-tax credits that have been compiled by the Center on Budget and Policy Priorities.
3 Lewin Group and the Rockefeller Institute of Government (2004). The article quantifies state-only programs for selected states.
4 The Census Bureau reported $404.6 billion of state and local government public welfare expenditures for 2008 and an additional $4.1 billion for administration of social insurance programs, for an expenditure total of $408.7 billion. This included the federal share of Medicaid and SCHIP expenditures but does not include either unemployment insurance expenditures or state tax credits. If we adjust the state and local expenditures in table 21.6 to add federal Medicaid and SCHIP and remove state tax credits and unemployment insurance, we arrive at a total of

$396.7 billion ($235.4 + 206.5 − 2.1—43.1). This is roughly comparable in concept to the Census numbers, and reasonably close in magnitude (about 3 percent less). The Census Bureau data are based on different collection methods and incorporate some differences in time periods and definitions. Undoubtedly some safety-net expenditures are recorded in categories other than the Census Bureau's "public welfare" category but nonetheless it is comforting that the numbers from two different sources are this close in magnitude.

5 Patterson (2010).

6 Gais, Dadayan, and Bae (2009). All expenditures are in 2006 dollars per person living under the federal poverty level. Inflation adjustments are based on the Bureau of Economic Analysis's State and Local Government Consumption Expenditures and Gross Investment Price Index for Gross Domestic Product. We divide by the three-year average of the number of poor persons in a particular year in order to reduce measurement error and volatility in calculations in each year.

7 Using the poverty population as a measure of need is not a perfect way of adjusting for the low-income populations targeted by these programs. For instance, many state Medicaid and SCHIP programs cover people with low incomes but who are not poor, while AFDC/TANF programs typically offer cash benefits only to families well below the federal poverty level. Also, most programs provide benefits or services to only some people living in poverty, such as families with children, homeless individuals, or those requiring child care. Nonetheless, the measure is a good approximation of differences in spending on needy persons across states and programs and over time.

8 Smith et al. (2008), 24; Gruber (2003).

9 US House of Representatives (2004), 15–48; Howard (2007), 95–98.

10 Coughlin et al. (2004).

11 Smith et al. (2008), 8.

12 Blank (2001).

13 Grogger (2004).

14 Blank (2001); Grogger (2004); Lurie (2006).

15 US House of Representatives (2004), 5–7.

16 US Department of Health and Human Services (2009).

17 Boyd (2008).

18 Lewin Group and the Rockefeller Institute of Government (2004).

19 Zandi (2009); Vroman (2010b).

20 Powers (1996).

21 Ziliak et al. (2003).

22 Ibid.

23 Powers (1996).

24 Ibid

25 Ibid.

26 Ibid.

27 Gais, Dadayan, and Bae (2009).

28 Vroman (2010a).

29 Ibid.

30 US Bureau of Labor Statistics, "Labor Statistics." We examine data for November to November because seasonally adjusted data on discouraged workers are not published by the US Bureau of Labor Statistics.

31 This decrease may not be statistically significant.

32 The National Conference of State Legislatures (2011) surveyed states about their projections regarding when they expect their tax revenues will return to peak levels. About half of the states made such projections, based on economic forecasts and existing tax laws. Three states expected revenue collections to reach previous peak levels during FY 2011, eight states during FY 2012, another eight in FY 2013, four in FY 2014, four in FY 2015, and one (CA) in FY 2016.

33 US Department of Labor, Employment & Training Administration, "Replacement Rates, US Average."

34 Stone, Greenstein, and Coven (2007).

35 Congressional Budget Office (2010).

36 Lancaster (2010).

37 US Department of Labor, Employment & Training Administration (2010).

38 Vroman (1995).

39 Office of Inspector General (2010).

40 US Department of Labor, Employment & Training Administration, "US Dept. of Labor Employment."

41 US Department of Labor, Employment & Training Administration, "Net Trust Fund in State Accounts."

42 Klerman and Danielson (2010).

43 US Department of Agriculture (2010a), 64.

44 Leftin (2010), 11.

45 Average certification periods of persons on SNAP/FSP increased from 9.6 months in 2002, to 12 months in 2009 (see table A-2 in US Department of Agriculture [2003, 2010a]).

46 US Department of Agriculture (2010b), 6.

47 Wiseman (2010).

48 Powers (1996); Mayer (2000).

49 Williams, Johnson, and Shure (2010).

50 Administration for Children and Families (2011).

51 Sherman (2011).

52 US Government Accountability Office (1992). See the report for a discussion of the Advance EITC and the reasons for its limited usage.

53 TANF expenditure data are available at US Department of Health and Human Services, Administration for Families and Children, "TANF Financial Data," at http://www.acf.hhs.gov/programs/ofs/data/.

54 US Department of Agriculture (2010a), 52.

55 Rowe, Murphy, and Mon (2010); Gais, Nathan, Lurie, and Kaplan (2001).

56 Rowe, Murphy, and Mon (2010), 92.

57 See note 49.

58 Schott and Finch (2010).

59 The sixteen states that spent more on basic assistance than on the other two functions spent an average of 80 percent of the total EF for which they were eligible. The thirteen states that spent the greatest proportion on subsidized jobs, by contrast, only spent 56 percent of their available funds. The remaining twenty states that put most of their EF funds into short-term benefits drew down an average of 69 percent of their available dollars.

60 Schott and Pavetti (2010).

61 Holahan and Garrett (2009).

62 Kaiser Commission (2010).

63 Heberlein et al. (2011).

64 Estimates and projections reported in the National Association of State Budget Officers and National Governors Association Fiscal Survey of the States, December 2010, and attributed to the Kaiser Commission on Medicaid and the Uninsured.

65 US Government Accountability Office (2010b), 17.

66 National Association of State Budget Officers and National Governors Association (2010).

67 Lewin Group and the Rockefeller Institute of Government (2004).

68 Johnson, Oliff, and Williams (2010).

69 Graman (2010); Lagos (2010). In California, Governor Schwarzenegger used the line-item veto on subsidies for families not on assistance, though the decision was temporarily stayed by a court.

70 Johnson, Oliff, and Williams (2010), 7–15.

71 Note that these comparisons are intended to estimate the effects of the safety net, not the ARRA. Elderly individuals, of course, benefited from several provisions of the ARRA, including increases in Social Security and veterans' benefits, but as already noted, we do not include these among safety-net programs.

72 Data were obtained from the US Census Bureau's Current Population Survey Table Creator II, available at http://www.census.gov/hhes/www/cpstc/apm/cpstc_altpov. html. Pre-safety-net income included the fifteen income components labeled as "market income," such as earnings, interested income, nongovernment benefits, and so on, except for source 40(a) "work-related expenses excluding child care (deducted from income)." It also included Social Security; federal and state income taxes (except EITC; note that all taxes are deducted from income); payroll taxes; property taxes; and educational assistance (government and nongovernment). Finally, pre-safety-net income included employer contributions to health-care plans and the fungible value of Medicare. Post-safety-net income included all the above sources plus unemployment compensation, public assistance (TANF and other cash welfare); SSI; federal EITC; SNAP; free and reduced-price school lunches; low-income energy assistance; public housing and rent subsidies (AHS-based estimates); and the fungible value of Medicaid.

73 Dadayan and Boyd (2011); National Conference of State Legislatures (2011); US Government Accountability Office (2010a).

74 Federal Reserve Bank of Philadelphia (2011).

75 Mead (1997).

76 Blank and Kovak (2008).

77 Boyd and Dadayan (2010).

78 Unemployment among eighteen- to nineteen-year-olds was 24.6 percent in January 2011. In the same month, unemployment was 15.2 percent among twenty- to twenty-four-year-olds. See table A-10 in US Department of Labor, Bureau of Labor Statistics (2011).

79 Long-term unemployment remained high in early 2011. The mean number of weeks in which unemployed persons in January 2011 were out of work was 36.9. About 44 percent of the unemployed have been so for twenty-seven weeks or more. See table A-12 in US Department of Labor, Bureau of Labor Statistics (2011).

80 For more on the role of states in permitting national policy coalitions to form, see Gais and Fossett (2005).

81 Between 1998 and 2008, the states with the largest growth in the number of poor children include Indiana, Kansas, Missouri, Colorado, Utah, Nevada, North Carolina, Georgia, Wisconsin, Texas, and Mississippi.

References

Administration for Children and Families, US Department of Health and Human Services (2011). "TANF Financial Data. http://www.acf.hhs.gov/programs/ofs/data/.

Blank, Rebecca (2001). "What Causes Public Assistance Cases to Grow?" *Journal of Human Resources* 36: 85–118.

Blank, Rebecca, and Brian Kovak (2008). "Helping Disconnected Single Mothers." Center on Children and Families, Brookings Institute, CCF Brief 38, http://www.brookings.edu/~/media/Files/rc/papers/2008/05_single_mothers_blank/05_single_mothers_blank.pdf.

Boyd, Donald, with the assistance of Lucy Dadayan (2008). "What Will Happen to State Government Finances in a Recession?" *Rockefeller Institute Fiscal Report*. The Nelson A. Rockefeller Institute of Government.

Boyd, Donald J., and Lucy Dadayan (2010). "State and Local Government Employment Are Down Since the Start of the Recession." *Data Alert* (Albany, NY: Rockefeller Institute). http://www.rockinst.org/newsroom/data_alerts/2010/08-10-govt_employment.aspx.

Congressional Budget Office (2010). "Cost Estimate for the Amendment in the Nature of a Substitute for H.R. 4872, Incorporating a Proposed Manager's Amendment." Made public on March 20, 2010.

Coughlin, Teresa A., Brian K. Bruen, and Jennifer King (2004). "States' Use of Medicaid UPL and DSH Financing Mechanisms." *Health Affairs* 23: 245–257.

Dadayan, Lucy, and Donald J. Boyd (2011). "State Tax Revenues Gained New Strength in Fourth Quarter." *State Revenue Report* No. 82. Albany, NY: Rockefeller Institute.

Elmendorf, Douglas (2009b, October 7). Letter to Honorable Max Baucus, Chairman of Committee on Finance United States Senate, Regarding Impact of Chairman's Mark, Congressional Budget Office.

Federal Reserve Bank of Philadelphia (2011). "First Quarter 2011 Survey of Professional Forecasters." http://www.phil.frb.org/research-and-data/real-time-center/survey-of-professional-forecasters/2011/survq111.cfm.

Gais, Thomas, and James Fossett (2005). "Federalism and the Executive Branch." In *The Executive Branch*, edited by Joel D. Aberbach and Mark A. Peterson. New York: Oxford University Press. 486–584.

Gais, Thomas, Richard Nathan, Irene Lurie, and Thomas Kaplan (2001). "Implementation of the Personal Responsibility Act of 1996." In *The New World of Welfare*, edited by Rebecca M. Blank and Ron Haskins. Washington, DC: Brookings Institution Press, 35–69.

Gais, Thomas, Lucy Dadayan, and Suho Bae (2009, November 19–20). "The Decline of States in Financing the U.S. Safety Net: Retrenchment in State and Local Social Welfare Spending, 1977–2007." Paper presented at "Reducing Poverty: Assessing Recent State Policy Innovations and Strategies," Emory University, Atlanta, Georgia.

Graman, Kevin (2010, November 13). "Cuts Hit Program Funding Childcare." *The Spokesman Review*.

Grogger, Jeffrey (2004). "Welfare Transitions in the 1990s: The Economy, Welfare Policy, and the EITC." *Journal of Policy Analysis and Management* 23: 671–695.

Gruber, Jonathan (2003). "Medicaid." In *Means Tested Transfer Programs in the United States*, edited by Robert A. Moffitt. Chicago: University of Chicago Press, 15–78.

Heberlein, Martha, Tricia Brooks, and Jocelyn Guyer (2011). "Holding Steady, Looking Ahead: Annual Findings of a 50-State Survey of Eligibility Rules, Enrollment and Renewal Procedures, and Cost Sharing Practices in Medicaid and CHIP, 2010–2011." Washington, DC: Kaiser Commission on Medicaid and the Uninsured.

Holahan, John, and Bowen Garrett (2009). "Rising Unemployment, Medicaid and the Uninsured." Washington, DC: The Urban Institute, For Henry J. Kaiser Family Foundation.

Howard, Christopher (2007). *The Welfare State Nobody Knows: Debunking Myths About U.S. Social Policy*. Princeton, NJ: Princeton University Press.

Johnson, Nicholas, Phil Oliff, and Erica Williams (2010). "An Update on State Budget Cuts." Washington, DC: Center on Budget and Policy Priorities. http://www.cbpp.org/files/3-13-08sfp.pdf.

Kaiser Commission on Medicaid and the Uninsured (2010). "Medicaid Enrollment: December 2009 Data Snapshot." http://www.kff.org/medicaid/upload/8050-02.pdf

Klerman, Jacob, and Caroline Danielson (2010). "The Changing Composition of the Supplemental Nutrition Assistance Program Caseload." Paper presented at the Annual Research Conference of the Association for Public Policy Analysis and Management, Boston, MA.

Lagos, Marisa (2010, December 6). "Democrats Try to Revive Childcare Subsidies." *San Francisco Chronicle*.

Lancaster, Loryn (2010, January). "Changes in Federal and State Unemployment Insurance Legislation in 2009." *Monthly Labor Review*:37–58.

Leftin, Joshua (2010). "Trends in Supplemental Nutrition Assistance Program Participation Rates: 2001 to 2008." Arlington, VA: US Department of Agriculture, Food and Nutrition Service.

Lewin Group and the Rockefeller Institute of Government (2004). "Spending on Social Welfare Programs in Rich and Poor States." Final Report. Washington, DC: US Department of Health and Human Services, Assistant Secretary for Planning and Evaluation. http://aspe.hhs.gov/hsp/social-welfare-spending04/index.htm.

Lurie, Irene (2006). *At the Front Lines of the Welfare System: A Perspective on the Decline in Welfare Caseloads*. Albany, NY: Rockefeller Institute Press.

Mayer, Susan E. (2000). "Why Welfare Caseloads Fluctuate: A Review of Research on AFDC, SSI, and Food Stamp Program." *Treasury Working Paper,* New Zealand Treasury. http://www.treasury.govt.nz/publications/research-policy/wp/2000/00-07/.

Mead, Lawrence M. (Ed.) (1997). *The New Paternalism: Supervisory Approaches to Poverty*. Washington, DC: The Brookings Institute.

National Association of State Budget Officers and National Governors Association (2010). "The Fiscal Survey of States." http://www.nasbo.org/LinkClick.aspx?fileticket=C6q1M3kxaEY%3d&tabid=38.

National Conference of State Legislatures (2011). "Projected State Revenue Growth in FY 2011 and Beyond." *NCSL Fiscal Brief*. Denver, CO: NCSL. http://www.ncsl.org/documents/fiscal/Projected_Revenue_Growth_in_FY_2011_and_Beyond.pdf.

Office of Inspector General, Employment and Training Administration, US Department of Labor (2010). "Recovery Act: More Than $1.3 Billion in Unemployment Insurance Modernization Incentive Payments Are Unlikely to Be Claimed by States." Report Number 18–10-012-03-315. Washington, D.C.: US Department of Labor.

Patterson, James T. (2010). *America's Struggle against Poverty in the Twentieth Century.* Cambridge, MA: Harvard University Press.

Powers, Elizabeth (1996). "Welfare Reform and the Cyclicality of Welfare Programs." Economic Commentary, Federal Reserve Bank of Cleveland. http://www. clevelandfed.org/research/commentary/1996/0696.htm.

Rowe, Gretchen, Mary Murphy, and Ei Yin Mon (2010). *Welfare Rules Databook.* Washington, DC: Urban Institute.

Schott, Liz, and Ife Finch (2010). "TANF Benefits Are Low and Have Not Kept Pace with Inflation." Report by the Center on Budget and Policy Priorities. http://www.cbpp. org/cms/index.cfm?fa=view&id=3306.

Schott, Liz, and LaDonna Pavetti (2010). "Walking Away from a Win-Win-Win: Subsidized Jobs Slated to End Soon Are Helping Families, Businesses, and Communities Weather the Recession." Center for Budget and Policy Priorities. http://www.cbpp.org/cms/index.cfm?fa=view&id=3274.

Sherman, Arloc (2011). "Despite Deep Recession and High Unemployment, Government Effort—Including the Recovery Act—Prevented Poverty from Rising in 2009, New Census Data Show." Report by the Center for Budget and Policy Priorities. Washington, DC.

Smith, Vernon, Kathleen Gifford, Eileen Ellis, Robin Rudowitz, Molly O'Malley, and Caryn Marks (2008). "Headed for a Crunch: An Update on Medicaid Spending, Coverage and Policy Heading into an Economic Downturn." Washington, DC: Kaiser Commission on Medicaid and the Uninsured. http://www. kff.org/medicaid/upload/7815.pdf.

Stone, Chad, Robert Greenstein, and Martha Coven (2007). "Addressing Longstanding Gaps in Unemployment Insurance Coverage." Center on Budget and Policy Priorities. http://www.cbpp.org/cms/?fa=view&id=517#_ftn1.

US Department of Agriculture. Food and Nutrition Service (2003). "Characteristics of Food Stamp Households: Fiscal Year 2002." *Nutrition Assistance Program Report Series.* Report No. FSP-03-CHAR02. Alexandria, VA: USDA.

US Department of Agriculture. Food and Nutrition Service (2010a). "Characteristics of Supplemental Nutrition Assistance Program Households: Fiscal Year 2009." *Nutrition Assistance Program Report Series.* Report No. SNAP-10-CHAR. Alexandria, VA: USDA.

US Department of Agriculture. Food and Nutrition Service (2010b). *Supplemental Nutrition Assistance Program State Activity Report: Federal Fiscal Year 2008.* Arlington, VA: USDA.

US Department of Health and Human Services, Administration for Children and Family (2009). "TANF Financial Data." http://www.acf.hhs.gov/programs/ofs/data/index. html.

US Department of Labor, Bureau of Labor Statistics (2011). "The Employment Situation— January 2011." News Release USDL-11-0129. Washington, DC: BLS.

US Department of Labor, Employment & Training Administration (2010). "UI Agreement: UI Modernization Incentive Payments: Information about Approved Applications." http://www.ows.doleta.gov/unemploy/laws.asp#modern.

US House of Representatives. Committee on Ways and Means (2004). *2004 Green Book, 108th Congress, 2nd Session.* Washington, DC: Government Printing Office.

US Government Accountability Office (2010a). "State and Local Governments Fiscal Outlook: March 2010 Update." *Report to the Congress.* GAO-10–358. Washington, DC: GAO.

US Government Accountability Office (2010b). "Recovery Act: Increased Medicaid Funds Aided Enrollment Growth, and Most States Reported Taking Steps to Sustain Their Programs." GAO-11–58. Washington, DC: GAO.

Vroman, Wayne (1995, January). "The Alternative Base Period in Unemployment Insurance: Final Report." *U.S. Department of Labor Occasional Paper.* Washington, DC: US Department of Labor.

Vroman, Wayne (2010a, January 15). "The Great Recession, Unemployment Insurance and Poverty." Paper prepared for the Georgetown University and Urban Institute Conference on Reducing Poverty and Economic Distress after ARRA.

Vroman, Wayne (2010b, July). "The Role of Unemployment Insurance as an Automatic Stabilizer during a Recession." The Urban Institute for IMPAQ International, LLC.

Williams, Erica, Nicholas Johnson, and Jon Shure (2010). "State Earned Income Tax Credit: 2010 Legislative Update." Center on Budget and Policy Priorities.

Wiseman, Michael (2010, January 15). "Supplemental Security Income for the Second Decade." Paper prepared for the conference "Reducing Poverty and Economic Distress after ARRA: The Most Promising Approaches." Washington, DC.

Zandi, Mark (2009, January 21). "The Economic Impact of the American Recovery and Reinvestment Act." *Moody's Economy.com.*

Ziliak, James P. Craig Gundersen, and David N. Figlio (2003). "Food Stamp Caseloads over the Business Cycle." *Southern Economic Journal* 69(4): 903–919.

CHAPTER 22

··

TRANSPORTATION
FINANCE

··

JONATHAN L. GIFFORD

FINANCING transportation in America presents a dizzying mosaic of funding sources and uses. Funding varies greatly across the individual transportation modes, both in the type of mechanisms used to raise revenues and the responsibility for spending for building and operating the nation's surface, air, and water transportation systems. These revenue-raising and spending chores are shared by local, state, and federal governments. An array of user fees levied at the various levels of government contribute a fraction of the support for each transportation mode. For example, motor fuel taxes raise a large share of funding for the nation's roadways, whereas in the public transit sector farebox revenues cover a much smaller portion of that mode's costs. Other revenues needed to support each of the transportation modes are raised from intergovernmental transfers, general funds, and a combination of dedicated property, sales, and other taxes. Transportation finance in the United States is a by-product of the nation's historical development and represents a legacy of political expediency and the dictates of economic necessity.

Today's reliance on the various forms of revenue depends heavily on the level of government responsible for the transportation facility or service. For example, local roads tend to fall under the control of local governments, which rely more heavily on property taxes than the fuel-tax-based state and national highway systems. One important lesson to draw from this financing structure is that as the levels of intergovernmental responsibility change—and by implication also the extent of intergovernmental transfers—so does the composition of the types of revenue-raising mechanisms that are used.

To understand transportation finance, this chapter will first survey on a mode-by-mode basis the funds that have been raised and expended for transportation purposes. At the finance level, each mode tells its own story, fundamentally because the infrastructure investment and day-to-day operations of each transportation system serve different types of traffic and reflect different roles and responsibilities for the public and private sectors. For example, in the United States the freight railroad system is operated primarily by private firms and thus recovers both operating and capital costs through transactions with shippers. As a result, there are relatively low levels of public subsidy payments and investment outlays. In contrast, public transit systems generally do not recover full operating costs from users and such charges rarely contribute to meeting capital costs. As a result, they generally receive public subsidies for both operating and capital expenses. A fundamental issue is the extent to which a transportation system supports itself by relying on user fees, and the extent to which it depends on government to raise and distribute the funding needed to sustain operations. In the following commentary, I first present individual discussions of the finances of highway, public transit, air, and water transportation, and then discuss the most salient trends and developments. I will conclude with a look forward into an uncertain future of how these transportation needs are to be financed in the years to come.

THE BIG PICTURE

Total governmental expenditures for transportation have more than tripled in the last half-century, from $83 billion in 1960 to $286 billion in 2010. (Throughout this chapter, dollar amounts are in 2006 dollars unless otherwise noted.) Across all modes of transportation, local governments have spent the most since about 1980, followed by states and then the federal government. In 2010, local governments spent $133 billion on transportation, the states spent $102 billion, and the federal government spent $98 billion. Ground transportation receives the greatest amount of federal support, for highways and transit, followed by air transport and water (figures 22.1 and 22.2).

A unifying theme that is observed in all modes is the intergovernmental nature of transportation spending. Federal and state governments transfer significant sums to local governments for transportation operating and capital expenses. In turn, states also receive substantial sums of federal funds. Sometimes localities make payments to states to perform transportation operations and investment (figure 22.3).

Many of these intergovernmental transfers are distributed by formula, such as the payout from the federal government's Highway Trust Fund to individual states. Other federal and state programs actively formulate specific transportation goals and award projects and programs that best achieve the desired goals. In these cases, local and state government transportation officials can understand what objectives

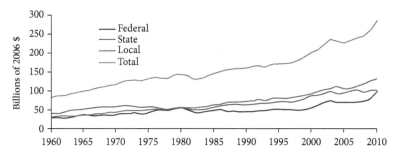

Figure 22.1 Transportation expenditures by government unit, FY 1960-2010
Note: Data prior to 2008 are actual; 2009–2010 data are estimated indexed
using CPI-U as reported by the Bureau of Labor Statistics.
Source: Federal expenditure data are from Budget of the US Government: Table 3.2 State
and Local government expenditure data are from US Census Bureau State and Local
Government Finances.

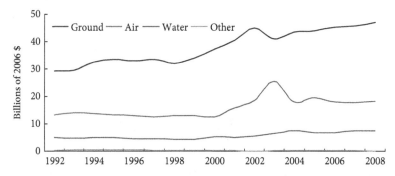

Figure 22.2 Federal government expenditures by mode: 1992–2008
Source: Federal expenditure data are from Budget of the US Government: Table 3.2,
indexed using CPI-U as reported by the Bureau of Labor Statistics.

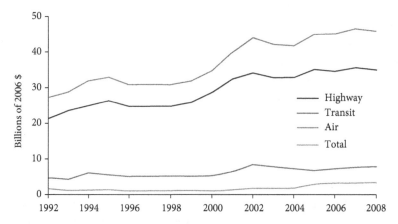

Figure 22.3 Federal intergovernmental transfers by mode: 1992–2008
Sources: US Census Bureau State and Local Government Finances, indexed using
CPI-U as reported by the Bureau of Labor Statistics; Christopher Chantrill. *Government
Spending Details: Federal State Local 1792-2016.* http://www.usgovernmentspending.com/
classic.html#usgs30260 (accessed March 11, 2011).

higher levels of government have in mind and then design projects accordingly. They also can substantially influence the funding they will receive. For example, under the "New Start" transit program, Federal Transit Administration (FTA) officials evaluate and select proposals for a new transit system according to very specific criteria.

In addition to formula and grant allocations, legislative "earmarks" have also been an important source of funding. Earmarks are funds allocated to a project in legislation or in the legislative history of a statute. Earmarks are particularly important—and controversial—in federal legislation. Congressional rules define an earmark in the following ways:

> [A] provision or report language included primarily at the request of a [member of Congress] providing, authorizing, or recommending a specific amount of discretionary budget authority, credit authority, or other spending authority for a contract, loan, loan guarantee, grant, loan authority, or other expenditure with or to an entity, or targeted to a specific State, locality or Congressional district, other than through a statutory or administrative formula-driven or competitive award process.[1]

Earmarks as a symbol of waste and political corruption became an issue in the 2010 congressional elections, and the newly elected Republican majority in the House of Representatives included a ban on earmark requests in the rules for Republican members as part of its reform agenda.[2] Reducing congressional influence on transportation-spending decisions will be an important change and may lessen the interest of legislators, who cannot promote individual transportation projects, for programs where they are not able to get "bringing home the bacon" credit.

HIGHWAYS, ROADS, AND STREETS

Highways, roads, and streets constitute the largest transportation investment in the United States, generating more than $166 billion in revenue and receiving $161 billion in government expenditures in 2006. In the past fifty years, the highway system has received $3.45 trillion in public investment (current dollars).[3] It would be difficult to imagine the United States, where the average person drives about 10,000 miles a year,[4] without its underlying infrastructure. The two most prominent systems are the Interstate Highway System and the National Highway System, which together total about 200,000 miles of roadway. State and local roads and streets make up another 2 million miles of roadway (figure 22.4).

Highway spending relative to aggregate travel has been steady at approximately $80 per billion vehicle miles of travel since about 1980. The much higher levels of spending in the years after 1956 reflect the high expenditures related to the deployment of the interstate highway system.

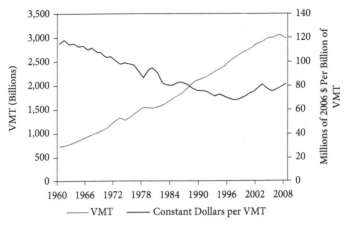

Figure 22.4 VMT-adjusted highway spending, 1960–2008
Source: Adopted from the model upon U.S., National Surface Transportation
Infrastructure Financing Commission. *Paying our way: a new framework for transportation finance*. Washington, D.C., February 26, 2009. Page 35. http://financecommission.
dot.gov/Documents/NSTIF_Commission_Final_Report_Advance%20Copy_Feb09.pdf

The nation's road network functions as an integrated whole, but the network at large is broken down into functional and administrative systems. Drivers may start a trip on a local subdivision street owned by a city, proceed onto a collector road owned by a county, then onto a state highway and an interstate highway, and possibly pay a toll to a private road operator along the way. Each system is separately managed by a different government authority, funded in various ways, and operated according to various standards.

To demonstrate this, consider the example given above. The city road may be funded by property taxes on local homes and businesses, and maintained by the city's department of public works. The county road may receive most of its funding from state transfers, and it may be maintained by a private firm contracted by the county. The state may fund its highway by using state gas-tax revenue, which pays for maintenance performed by the state department of transportation, with contributions received as transfers from the federal government. Finally, the interstate highway is partially paid for with the federal government's national gas-tax revenue, which it distributes to the states for spending on actual projects. It is likely all of the roads were built by private construction firms, contracted by various levels of government, and possibly funded by others.

This functional overlapping and intergovernmental intertwining provides the complicated basis for examining the actual financial structure. Given the complexity of highway finance, using year-specific data will most clearly demonstrate the distribution and magnitude of the various funding sources and the ultimate authorities responsible for road funding. The Federal Highway Administration provides the most comprehensive data on road finance in its biennial Conditions and Performance Report, which most recently was updated to 2008, using 2006 data.[5]

The first important observation is that more than half of highway expenditures are covered by user fees, or $93 billion in 2006. This funding includes motor fuel taxes, which in 2006 raised 36 percent of all revenue, and motor vehicle taxes and fees, which raised 15 percent. The data illustrate a high level of reliance on user fees at the federal level (figure 22.5). However, since 2008 the federal Highway Trust Fund has required $34.5 billion in "bailouts" from the general fund in order to remain solvent ($8 billion in 2008, $7 billion in 2009, and $19.5 billion in 2010, all figures in current dollars).

It is useful to note the differences between user fees and taxes in transportation. In the highway context, user fees refer to payments made by road users for building and maintaining roads. For example, the per-gallon gas "tax" paid by drivers purchasing motor fuel is roughly proportional to the extent to which they use road infrastructure. As such, it is part of the driver's total cost of travel, which is collected through gas taxes. A more direct form of user fee is the road toll. Due to a tolls' direct association with road use at a particular time and place, and the resulting assignment of a cost, toll payments are clearly economic transactions, as opposed to taxes. Vehicle registration and licensing fees are also user fees, but their lack of precise linkage between road use and resulting payments make the transactional nature less direct. However, when compared to nonuser tax-revenue sources, the difference becomes clear. Nonuser taxes are paid by all citizens in respective tax jurisdictions, regardless of their intensity of road usage. User fees, on the other hand, reflect to some degree a payment for actual road usage. When road systems can recover their costs by attracting enough drivers paying fees in one form or another, they are properly considered self-funded. As we consider

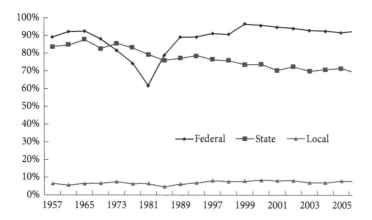

Figure 22.5 Percentage of highway revenue derived from user charges at each governmental level, 1957–2006
Source: U.S. Federal Highway Administration and U.S. Federal Transit Administration. *2008 status of the nation's highways, bridges, and transit: conditions and performance.* Report to Congress. Washington, D.C., n.d. Page 66, available at http://www.fhwa.dot. gov/policy/2008cpr/pdfs/cp2008.pdf

different highway systems, it is revealing to see which systems effectively "pay for themselves" and which rely on support from general funds.

One noteworthy exception to tolls as user charges occurs when toll revenues are used to support facilities other than those being used by the individuals paying the toll. Tolls are sometimes used to support other roadways and, in some cases, public transit services and facilities. For example, toll revenues on Virginia's Dulles Toll Road are being used to support the construction of a twenty-three-mile heavy rail transit line extending to Dulles International Airport and beyond. The most recent estimate of the cost to complete the transit line is up to $6.75 billion, depending on some station locations.[6] Arguably, some benefits accrue to road users when drivers shift from a congested highway to a transit system, thereby alleviating some congestion.

The second observation is that state governments play the largest role in highway finance. States have consistently contributed the greatest share of revenue to the highway systems, funding over half of all expenditures. In 2006 states funded $80.9 billion of road expenditures, compared to $36.3 billion by the federal government and $43.8 billion by local governments. When all intergovernmental transfers are included, using 2006 as a baseline, states are responsible for $100.1 billion in road spending, and they transferred another $15.8 billion to local governments (table 22.1).

This raises a third significant point. The sources of revenue that are used to fund highway expenditures are often intergovernmental, which means that the level of government that raises the revenue transfers it to another level of government to spend it. This pattern is most striking for the federal government, which transfers the large majority of its funding to the states, which do the spending. While the federal government raises a significant amount of revenue for highways, in 2006 it only directly spent $2.2 billion dollars on delivering transportation goods and services and transferred nearly all of its revenue to state governments. As a consequence, of the $100 billion that states spent in 2006 on highways, $32.8 billion came as transfers from the federal government, $65.1 billion was raised by the states themselves, and $2.2 billion came from local governments. Local governments display a similar pattern, spending $58.8 billion on highways in 2006, and receiving $15.8 billion of this amount from state governments.

A more detailed look at revenue shows a number of important differences among local, state, and federal funding sources. These include both differences in their reliance on user fees, transfers from other level of government, and the magnitude of their direct spending. For example, while the federal government raised nearly all of its highway revenue from user fees, $32.1 billion to be exact, local governments only raised $3.6 billion in user fees and $47.6 billion in nonuser fees (current dollars). Falling in between, state governments relied on user fees for about two-thirds of revenue raised. From this general picture, it is clear that road finance imposes the heaviest general taxing burdens on local governments, which do not have the same capacity to more directly charge highway users.[7]

Each level of government has a specific type of funding program. The federal government highway finance program is easiest to understand because it is uniform

Table 22.1 Direct expenditures for highways, by expending agencies and by type, 2006

| | (Billions of Dollars) | | | | |
	Federal	State	Local	Total	Percentage
CAPITAL OUTLAY	$0.5	$59.0	$19.2	$78.7	48.8%
Funded by Federal Government	*$0.5*	*$32.8*	*$1.4*	*$34.6*	*21.5%*
Funded by State or Local Governments	*$0.0*	*$26.2*	*$17.9*	*$44.1*	*27.4%*
NONCAPITAL EXPENDITURES					
Maintenance	0.2	12.6	18.6	31.3	19.4%
Highway and Traffic Services	0.0	4.7	4.4	9.1	5.7%
Administration	1.5	7.1	4.6	13.2	8.2%
Highway Patrol and Safety	0.0	7.7	6.8	14.5	9.0%
Interest on Debt	0.0	4.4	2.2	6.6	4.1%
Subtotal	$1.7	$36.5	$36.6	$74.7	46.4%
TOTAL, CURRENT EXPENDITURES	$2.2	$95.4	$55.8	$153.4	95.3%
BOND RETIREMENT	$0.0	$4.6	$3.0	$7.6	4.7%
TOTAL OF ALL EXPENDITURES	$2.2	$100.1	$58.8	$161.1	100.0%
Funded by Federal Government	*$2.2*	*$32.8*	*$1.4*	*$36.3*	*22.6%*
Funded by State Governments	*$0.0*	*$65.1*	*$15.8*	*$80.9*	*50.2%*
Funded by Local Governments	*$0.0*	*$2.2*	*$41.6*	*$43.8*	*27.2%*

Note: Amounts shown in italics are nonadditive to the rest of the table, which classifies spending by expending agency.
Source: US Federal Highway Administration and US Federal Transit Administration (2008), 6–7.

throughout the United States and has the single main source of fuel-tax revenue. Of the $34.8 billion of revenue raised by the federal government in 2006, nearly all came from user charges, mostly through the national fuel tax of 18.4 cents per gallon of gas and 24.4 cents per gallon of diesel. The federal government only directly spent $2.2 billion of its total revenue raised. The majority of federal funds are distributed among the states by a formula based on the lane-mileage of the interstate and national highways within each state, population, land area, fraction of land owned by the federal government, and other factors. This funding is largely restricted to capital spending on highways, and it covers over half of all state-level capital expenditures. In addition, states are responsible for funding highway operations, maintenance, administration, highway patrol, and other programs relating to highways.

To raise revenue, states also rely on user fees. In 2006, states raised $57.7 billion of their $83.7 billion total in revenue through user fees, with motor vehicle taxes contributing $19.1 billion and fuel taxes $31.9 billion. They also collected tolls totaling $6.7 billion. However, to raise the remaining $26 billion of their total contribution, states used a number of other revenue sources, including general funds, bonding, and other nontransportation funds. The states appropriated $4.9 billion of general funds to highways. They also use bonding more than any other level of government, raising $11.9 billion in 2006 for highways. Various investment income and other taxes and fees combined to raise another $9.2 billion for highways.

Highlighting the importance of intergovernmental transfers, the states actually spend a much higher amount of revenue than they raise, and at the same time they transfer significant amounts to local governments. The key to balancing this equation has been the inflow of federal funds. In 2006, states directly spent a total of $100.1 billion on highways, compared to the $83.7 billion in revenue they raised for that purpose from their own sources. Of this $83.7 billion, states transferred $15.8 billion to local governments. However, pushing funding up to the $100.1 billion level, the federal government transferred $32.8 billion to states, and local governments added another $2.2 billion to pay for state highway services in their respective localities. Reflecting the nation's federal system, the financing of highways is a complex, intertwined process.

State highway systems are broadly divided into rural and urban systems, which contain a variety of road types, including interstate highways, principal arterial roads, and smaller arterial and collector roads. Over half of state spending is concentrated on capital outlays, and the US Federal Highway Administration (FHWA) aggregates this spending by road type. The larger roads on the urban and rural systems receive the highest level of state spending. Overall, the rural systems received a total of $21.6 billion in state capital spending in 2006 and urban systems received $30.5 billion. More than three-quarters of this amount went into interstate highways and principal arterial roads, with less densely used minor arterial and collector roads falling more under the purview of local governments.[8]

The major theme of local government highway financing is their reliance on sources other than user fees. Instead, localities rely on property taxes, general fund revenues, and borrowing. One reason for this is that many states limit the authority of local governments to impose transportation fees and taxes. Also, gas taxes often do not work well in localities because residents have the option of accessing gas stations in adjacent localities that may have lower rates. In 2006, localities only collected $3.6 billion in fuel taxes, vehicle fees, and tolls, and they raised the remaining revenue of $47.6 billion by using nontransportation taxes and bonding. General-fund appropriations contributed the greatest share revenue of $19.6 billion in 2006.

Intergovernmental transfers to local governments play a significant role in the final direct expenditures of cities and counties. Substantial portions of state transportation budgets are often dedicated as formula payments to localities, or channeled into specific grant programs that seek to stimulate projects that satisfy statewide goals and criteria. States transferred a total of $15.8 billion to localities in 2006, and the federal government added another $1.4 billion.

In providing local road transportation, states and localities often work in partnerships that involve high levels of interaction and influence. The states typically have strong interests in promoting road standards, ensuring sufficient road capacity, and maintaining safe operations, while localities look to the state as ultimately responsible for providing the funding to achieve these goals. Most states operate under the "Dillon Rule," which deems local governments to be wholly an arm of a state government.[9] As a result, most local transportation programs rely on enabling legislation from the state government to function. State law generally allows some combination of local taxing authority and state transfer programs to satisfy funding needs. These authorities sometimes change frequently in response to shifting political pressures at both levels, and state legislators are likely to take a strong interest in promoting the transportation goals of the districts they represent.

PUBLIC TRANSIT

Public transit receives the second largest allocation of public funds for transportation after highways. In 2006, governments contributed a total of $30.9 billion to support the building and operation of public transit systems. Without this public investment, very few systems would be able to stay solvent. In total, public transit systems generated $12.5 billion in passenger fares and other revenue, or 14.6 percent of all transit-related revenue. In raising the remaining funds, local governments tend to have the greatest financial responsibilities. Local governments raise about half the public funding for public transportation, with federal and state governments paying roughly equal shares of the remaining half. In 2006 localities contributed $14.3 billion, the states contributed $8.6 billion, and the federal government contributed $8 billion (table 22.2).

The funds are divided between those spent on rail systems (which include commuter rail, heavy rail, and light rail) and on nonrail systems (which are primarily motor buses). For all these systems, separating capital funds from operating expenditures is a critical distinction in public transit finance. The rail systems received a total of $9 billion in capital funding in 2006, divided roughly evenly among heavy, light, and commuter rail systems. In addition, rail systems received $9.6 billion in operating subsidies. On the nonrail side, bus systems received around $3 billion in capital funding, but over $15 billion in operating subsidies.[10]

Surveying where these funds originate, which authorities spend them, and what types of expenditures they include provides an overview of public transit finance. Sales taxes and general funds are the largest funding sources for states and localities, but many other sources including property, fuel, and income taxes also are used. In 2006, sales taxes dedicated to public transit spending raised $2.4 billion for states and $4.8 billion for localities. States appropriated $2.4 billion from general funds and localities appropriated $3 billion for public transit purposes. A variety of other taxes, whether based on property, income, or

Table 22.2 Revenue sources for transit financing, 2006

	(Millions of Dollars)				
	Federal	State	Local	Total	Percentage
Public Funds	$8,075.5	$8,570.8	$14,261.8	$30,908.1	71.3%
General Fund	$1,615.1	$2,358.3	$3,014.6	$6,988.0	16.1%
Fuel Tax	$6,460.4	$549.5	$159.8	$7,169.7	16.5%
Income Tax		$195.1	$70.8	$265.9	0.6%
Sales Tax		$2,429.9	$4,797.6	$7,227.5	16.7%
Property Tax		$0.0	$547.3	$547.3	1.3%
Other Dedicated Taxes		$1,203.5	$1,163.6	$2,367.1	5.5%
Other Public Funds		$1,834.5	$4,508.1	$6,342.6	14.6%
System-Generated Revenue				$12,452.4	28.7%
Passenger Fares				$10,461.1	24.1%
Other Revenue				$1,991.3	4.6%
Total of All Sources				$43,360.5	100.0%

Source: US Federal Highway Administration and US Federal Transit Administration (2008), 6–35.

goods-specific purchases, and assorted other government receipts (mostly raised through borrowing and investment earnings) added another $8.6 billion to public transit funding.

In contrast to the assortment of state and local sources, almost all federal government revenue has come from a fixed formula transfer out of the Highway Trust Fund. In 1983, federal legislation established the Mass Transit Account within the Highway Trust Fund, which currently receives 2.86 cents per gallon of gas purchased. In 2006 this portion of the gas tax raised $8.1 billion in federal funds that were distributed to public transit systems. The FTA administers this funding, placing a focus on payments for capital investment. Although a decade ago the federal government funded over half of all public transit capital investment, as of 2006 transit systems received $5.5 billion in capital funding from the federal government, which amounted to 43.5 percent of total capital spending for that year.

Local governments make almost all the direct expenditures for public transit systems. The level of government where funding originates largely depends on whether the expenditures are for operating subsidies or capital outlays. The federal government has typically contributed less than 10 percent of all operating costs, but it funds more than 40 percent of all capital investments in public transit. Overall, capital expenditures are about one-third the size of operating expenditures. Capital expenditures, which totaled $12.7 billion in 2006, are generally not supported by fare box revenues and rely largely on government capital programs. While states contributed only $1.1 billion in 2006, federal and local governments both spent $5.5 billion on transit capital improvements. Operating expenditures totaled $30.6 billion in 2006, and system-generated fare box revenues covered approximately 40 percent of expenses. State and local governments provided the majority of the remaining operating funds. The federal government provided $2.5 billion on operating subsidies in 2006; states spent $6.6 billion and localities spent $8.9 billion.

AIRPORTS

The United States has an extensive system of public and private airports. The US Federal Aviation Administration (FAA) defines a "National Airport System" of 3,364 airports that are eligible for federal assistance.[11] Public airports are typically owned and operated by states, localities, or special authorities. The bulk of airline passenger traffic is concentrated in hub airports. The largest twenty-five hub airport areas, including seventy-one airports, carry 69 percent of the total passenger volume.[12]

Airport finance varies considerably by the size and type of airport. Commercial airports generate revenue through operations and most are able to recover operating expenses through various fees and charges, including gate and runway charges for airlines, parking fees for travelers, and concessions within the airport. Larger hub airports tend to receive more of their revenue from airlines. The reliance on airline revenue declines as hub size diminishes, with large hubs receiving 56 percent percent from airlines, and small hubs receiving 45 percent (figure 22.6).

When financing capital expansions, airports typically use anticipated cash flows from future operations to secure bonds. Between 2001 and 2005, airports spent an annual average of $13 billion in capital funding, which was projected in 2007 to rise to $14 billion per year through 2011. Funds raised through the sale of airport bonds covered half of this total, or $6.5 billion per year. These bonds were either issued by a local government authority or directly by the airport facility itself, which typically receives its charter from a local government. The second largest funding source is grants from the federal government, which come out of the Airport Improvement Program (AIP) of the Airport and Airway Trust Fund. Because this fund is generated through various aviation fees and taxes, federal grants can be viewed as a revolving fund returning portions of revenue back to airports. AIP grants to airports averaged $3.6 billion annually between 2001 and 2005.

The passenger facility charge (PFC) is the third major source of funding. Airports have the authority to charge a fee of up to $4.50 for each passenger that passes through the airport. PFCs raised an average of $2.2 billion each year between 2001 and 2005. Finally, states and localities contributed an annual average of $700 million to airport capital development between 2001 and 2005. Over half of

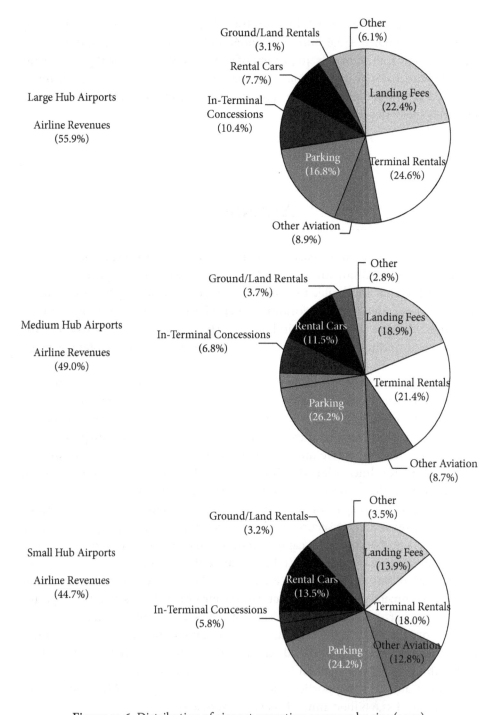

Figure 22.6 Distribution of airport operating revenues by size (2005)
Source: Nichol, Cindy. *Innovative Finance and Alternative Sources of Revenue for Airports*. Synthesis of Airport Practice. Washington, D.C.: Transportation Research Board, 2007, page 25, http://onlinepubs.trb.org/onlinepubs/acrp/acrp_syn_001.pdf

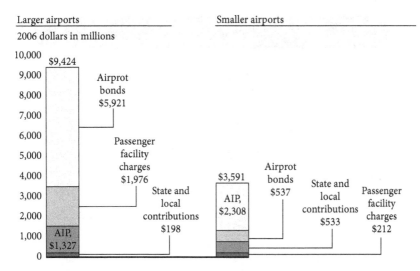

Figure 22.7 Airport capital funding sources by size of airport, 2001–2005 (annual average)
Note: Totals may not add up due to rounding
Source: U.S. Government Accountability Office. Airport Finance: Observations on
Planned *Airport Development Costs and Funding Levels and the Administration's
Proposed Changes in the Airport Improvement Program*. Washington D.C., June 2007.
Page 9. http://www.gao.gov/new.items/d07885.pdf

this funding went to small, general aviation airports, and larger airports serving
regular commercial traffic received less than one-quarter of the total (figure 22.7).[13]

PORTS

Like airports, most nonmilitary maritime ports are public utilities owned and
operated by states, localities, and special authorities. Container traffic is heavily
concentrated in a few large ports. The top three ports—Los Angeles, Long Beach,
and New York/New Jersey—receive 45 percent of the inbound container TEUs
(twenty-foot equivalent units). Bulk shipping is less concentrated; the top five ports
by shipment weight make up only 30 percent of the total (figure 22.8).

Ports generally receive relatively little public funding due to their ability to
generate revenue through operations with shipping companies. Port authorities
generally rely on local and state government charters, and they receive some public
investment in capital but are managed to fully recover expenses and make profit
that can be reinvested in capital outlays.

While port investment is highly localized and disaggregated, a US Maritime
Administration (MARAD) report in 2009 summarized total spending on ports

Port by shipment weight	Short tons (millions)	Port by container TEUs	Full TEUs (thousands)
South Louisiana, LA	229.0	Los Angeles, CA	5,497
Houston, TX	216.1	Long Beach, CA	5,131
New York, NY and NJ	157.2	New York/ New Jersey	4,047
Long Beach, CA	85.9	Savannah, GA	1,980
Beaumont, TX	81.4	Norfolk Harbor, VA	1,626
Corpus Christi, TX	81.1	Oakland, CA	1,579
Huntington-Tristate, WV-OH-PA	76.5	Seattle, WA	1,416
New Orleans, LA	76.0	Tacoma, WA	1,415
Los Angeles, CA	65.5	Houston, TX	1,400
Mobile, AL	64.5	Charleston, SC	1,369
Lake Charles, LA	64.2	Honolulu, HI	889
Plaquemines, LA	58.8	San Juan, PR	792
Texas City, TX	56.8	Port Everglades, FL	676
Baton Rouge, LA	54.6	Miami, FL	669
Tampa, FL	46.9	Jacksonville, FL	581
Duluth-Superior, MN and WI	46.5	Baltimore, MD	501
Baltimore, MD	41.3	Anchorage, AK	276
Norfolk Harbor, VA	39.7	New Orleans, LA	255
Pittsburgh, PA	38.1	Portland, OR	213
Paulsboro, NJ	38.0	Wilmington, DE	179
Total, top 20	1,618		30,493
Total, all ports	2,564		32,567

Figure 22.8 Top US ports by shipment weight and TEU volume, 2007
Note: Includes exports imports and domestic shipments.
Source: U.S. Bureau of Transportation Statistics. *Pocket Guide to Transportation 2010.*
Washington D.C. January 2010. Page 30. http://www.bts.gov/publications/
pocket_guide_to_transportation/2010/pdf/entire.pdf

up to 2006 and identified estimates of spending from 2007 and 2011. The report reflected expenditures for the thirty-five ports that had responded to MARAD's survey, out of a population of eighty-five ports that are members of the American Association of Port Authorities. Annual investment in port infrastructure totals around $1 to $2 billion dollars, with at least one-third of this funding coming from port revenues. Other sources include general obligation bonds issued by government authorities against their tax base, revenue bonds issued against future port revenues, loans from governments, and intergovernmental grants. However, the total amount of capital investment varies each year. For example, in 2004 and 2006 ports invested a total of about $1 billion in capital, but over $2 billion in 2005. Also, while less than one-third of funding came from port revenues for 2004 and 2006 investments, in 2005, nearly three-quarters of funding, or $1.4 billion, came from port revenues (current dollars). Looking forward, the study forecasted a total of $9.3 billion in port capital investment between 2007 and 2011 (current dollars).[14]

INNOVATIVE FINANCE

In recent years, government and transportation officials have sought to implement new types of financing for transportation infrastructure. The new programs include many tools for promoting transportation investment. Some programs authorize private developers to invest directly in infrastructure in return for rights to collect future revenues or sell the completed project. Other programs allow higher levels of government to secure debt incurred by lower levels of government that want to invest in transportation infrastructure immediately and pay it off over the coming years. In the past decade more than $20 billion of investment has been channeled through these new mechanisms.[15] (All references to dollars for the remainder of the chapter are current dollars unless otherwise noted.)

The innovative finance programs largely have come in response to strains on traditional methods of funding. With infrastructure costs and traffic demand growing faster than the transportation revenues available to fund investment, officials have had to search for new ways to provide and maintain critical infrastructure quickly rather than delay implementation indefinitely.

Two underlying features of transportation investment and usage are factored into the rise of these new financing programs. First, there are significant benefits to completing projects earlier. The sooner a project is completed, the sooner it begins to generate benefits of time savings and improved reliability. Second, some projects have the ability to self-finance through tolls, user fees, and other sources of revenue. Each of the programs outlined below combines the opportunity for accelerated completion and enhanced revenue-generating capacity.

PUBLIC-PRIVATE PARTNERSHIPS

Public-private partnerships (PPPs) are the most general type of innovative finance program, and these can refer to any situation whereby government authorities enter contractual agreements that give private firms more active roles in designing, building, operating, or owning transportation infrastructure. State and local governments take the initiative in facilitating PPPs, which first requires establishing a clear legal framework that establishes the terms of transportation infrastructure agreements. Once this step is completed, transportation authorities and private companies can identify projects eligible for private involvement and solicit or generate proposals from interested firms. The federal government has provided support for these programs by working to remove regulatory barriers that have impeded states in forming PPPs. For example, in 2004 the US Federal Highway Administration (FHWA) initiated a new procedure called "Special Experimental Project No. 15," which aimed to identify and remove regulatory requirements that were burdensome for PPPs.

Due to efforts at all levels of government and support from the private sector, PPPs have increased in popularity in recent years. As of 2008, the FHWA identified more than thirty PPPs that were either completed or in the planning stages. Most of these projects involved expansions of highway capacity, whether by adding lanes or constructing an entirely new right-of-way (tables 22.3 and 22.4).

Table 22.3 PPPs for the operation and maintenance of existing toll facilities in the United States, January 2005–May 2008

Project	Location	Cost of Concession	Type
Chicago Skyway	Illinois	$1.8 billion	Long-term concession to operate and maintain 7.8-mile toll road in Chicago
Indiana Toll Road	Indiana	$3.8 billion	Long-term concession to operate and maintain 157-mile toll road in northern Indiana
Pocahontas Parkway	Virginia	$150 million	Long-term concession to operate and maintain 14-mile toll road outside of Richmond and to build Richmond Airport Connector
Northwest Parkway	Colorado	$543 million	Long-term concession to operate and maintain 11-mile toll road outside of Denver and funding commitment for future expansions
Dulles Greenway	Virginia	$615 million	Refinancing long-term concession to operate and maintain 14-mile toll road between Leesburg and the Dulles International Airport
Pennsylvania Turnpike	Pennsylvania	$12.8 billion	Long-term concession to operate and maintain 531-mile turnpike (requires legislative approval)
Greenville Southern Connector	South Carolina	$219 million	Long-term concession to operate and maintain 16-mile toll road in Greenville, South Carolina
Alligator Alley	Florida	$350 million to $1 billion	Long-term concession to operate and maintain 78-mile toll road in South Florida

Source: US Department of Transportation (2008).

Table 22.4 PPPs for new-build highway and transit facilities in the United States, January 2005–May 2008

Project	Location	Type of PPP
TTC-35	Texas	Concessionaire responsible for preparation of master development plan and for some or all of the development, design, construction, financing, operation, and/or maintenance of an approximately 600-mile corridor from Mexico to Oklahoma
SH-130 Segments 5&6	Texas	Concession to design, build, finance, operate, and maintain an approximately $1.3 billion facility as the first segment of TTC-35 project
I-69/TTC	Texas	Concessionaire responsible for preparation of master development plan and for some or all of the development, design, construction, financing, operation, and/or maintenance of an approximately 650-mile corridor from Mexico to Texarkana/Shreveport
I-635	Texas	Concession to design, build, finance, operate, and maintain tolled managed lanes in Dallas/Fort Worth area
North Tarrant Express	Texas	Concession to design, build, finance, operate, and maintain tolled managed lanes and general lanes in North Tarrant County
DFW Connector	Texas	Concession to develop, design, and construct (and at TxDOT's sole option maintain) tolled managed lanes on the SH-114/SH-121 corridor in Dallas/Fort Worth area
Capital Beltway HOT Lanes	Virginia	Concession to design, build, finance, operate, and maintain HOT lanes on a fourteen-mile stretch of I-495 in northern Virginia
I-95/I-395 HOT Lanes	Virginia	Concession to design, build, finance, operate, and maintain HOT lanes on a fifty-six-mile stretch of I-95/I-395 in northern Virginia
US Route 460	Virginia	Concession to design, build, finance, operate, and maintain $1 billion to $2 billion improvements to Route 460 in southeastern Virginia

(Continued)

Table 22.4 Continued

Project	Location	Type of PPP
Midtown Corridor Tunnel	Virginia	Concession to modify the existing tunnel that links Portsmouth and Norfolk, construct a new parallel tunnel, and extend the freeway
Port of Miami Tunnel Project	Florida	Concession to design, build, finance, operate, and maintain a tunnel that provides access from the Port of Miami to the Florida mainland
I-595 Improvements	Florida	Concession to design, build, finance, operate, and maintain improvements on the I-595 corridor between I-75 and I-95
First Coast Outer Beltway	Florida	Concession to design, build, finance, operate, and maintain a limited access toll facility outside of Jacksonville
Northwest Corridor	Georgia	Concession to develop, design, and construct express toll lanes, BRT lanes, and possibly TOT lanes on I-75 and I-575 northwest of Atlanta
I-285 Northwest TOT Lanes	Georgia	Concession to design, build, finance, operate, and maintain TOT lanes on I-285 and I-20 northwest and west of Atlanta
GA-400 Crossroads Region	Georgia	Concession to design, construct, operate, and maintain HOT lanes on GA-400 north of Atlanta
I-20 Managed Lanes	Georgia	Concession to design, build, finance, operate, and maintain two managed lanes on the I-20 corridor east of Atlanta
Missouri Safe & Sound Bridge Program	Missouri	Concession to upgrade, finance, operate, and maintain more than 800 bridges in Missouri
Knik Arm Crossing Project	Alaska	Concession to design, build, finance, operate, and maintain a bridge that connects Anchorage to the Mat-Su borough
The Airport Parkway	Mississippi	Concession to develop, build, finance, operate, and maintain a parkway from downtown Jackson to the airport
Oakland Airport Connector	California	Concession to design, build, finance, operate, and maintain the Oakland Airport Connector

(Continued)

Table 22.4 Continued

Project	Location	Type of PPP
Denver RTD	Colorado	Concession to design, build, finance, operate, and maintain the East, Gold Line, and Commuter Line Maintenance Facility in the Denver area
Metro Solutions Phase II	Texas	Facility provider will be responsible for design and construction of civil works; furnishing and installation of equipment; initial operations and maintenance; and financing services for Light Rail projects in Houston
I-73	South Carolina	Concession to design, build, finance, operate, and maintain the eighty-mile portion of I-73, connecting Myrtle Beach with the North Carolina border
Mid-Currituck Bridge	North Carolina	Concession for new seven-mile bridge over Currituck Sound, connecting mainland and the Currituck County Outer Banks south of Corolla

Source: US Department of Transportation (2008).

Different models for accomplishing the involvement of private firms have been developed, which demonstrate that PPPs can have high degrees of flexibility and can be customized on a project-by-project basis. The list of models described below is not exhaustive, but it offers a good range of examples for how PPPs can be used:[16]

- "Private Contract-Fee Services"—Public agencies effectively "outsource" certain recurring functions, such as maintenance, operations, or finance, to private firms.
- "Design-Build"—Transportation authorities enter a contract with a firm to both design and build a project for a fixed fee.
- "Build-Operate-Transfer/Design-Build-Operate-Maintain"—A private firm enters a contract with a transportation authority to assume a full scope of responsibilities for a transportation project, including operations and maintenance after it completes construction.
- "Long-Term Lease Arrangements"—A private firm pays a transportation agency for the rights to operate and collect revenue from a toll road over the term of the lease.
- "Design-Build-Finance-Operate"—A transportation agency authorizes a private firm to have a large degree of financial and operational responsibility for a new infrastructure project it will build, but the agency retains some jurisdiction of control.

- "Build-Own-Operate"—A transportation agency authorizes a private firm to build a new infrastructure project, take complete ownership responsibilities, and pay for it by using the revenue it will collect in tolls.

In the United States, transportation-related PPPs have been used primarily for two purposes. The first purpose is to generate a large upfront payment for public authorities in consideration for a concession to operate a highway project for a long-term period. Highway projects that use PPP arrangements for this purpose are normally mature facilities with existing traffic, which provides comfort to the private sector that there is a stable customer stream to generate future toll revenue. In this case, public authorities make concessions of the operation and maintenance functions to private toll-road operators. The upfront payment for the concession then may be used for various purposes such as redeeming project indebtedness, funding a long-term reserve account, and funding various state and local programs. The Chicago Skyway and Indiana Toll Road projects belong to this type.

The second purpose may be to refinance existing projects and to help the owners bridge a gap in project financing. Some facilities may have been operated for only a few years and have not shown a strong performance in toll-revenue generation. Thus the project owners may explore PPPs as a remedy for restructuring debt and transferring risk. Two examples of this type of PPP are the Pocahontas Parkway project in Richmond, Virginia, and the Northwest Parkway in Denver, Colorado.

Transportation officials ultimately have the responsibility for determining what types of contracts are needed for private firms. In cases where the transportation agency has very weak financial capacity, it will be more likely to concede more operational and ownership rights to the contractor. In other cases, the agency can simply pay fees to contractors to perform those services that the agency cannot provide as efficiently. As is generally true in public procurement, when transportation authorities consider PPPs, it is important that they receive competitive bids that balance the project's costs to the public with the quality of infrastructure improvement and its operation.

The use of a PPP has had ideological and political dimensions. The administration of President George W. Bush was particularly disposed toward transportation PPPs, in part because a PPP provided a financing alternative to raising taxes, gas taxes in particular. The Obama administration so far has been less inclined to PPPs, although it has stated repeatedly its opposition to any tax increase during the recession. With the election of a Republican majority in the US House of Representatives in November 2010, the Obama administration has advanced a more "business-friendly" stance. It remains to be seen whether that will translate into the government's enthusiasm for PPPs as a mechanism for infrastructure finance.

With the emergence of PPPs and other transportation infrastructure projects eligible for debt financing, the federal government initiated a series of measures that were designed to streamline the PPP process and expand potential new finance arrangements. Each of the new regulatory changes, which are described below, provides incentives to transportation authorities that want to expand the use of private contracting and/or make greater use of debt financing.

PRIVATE ACTIVITY BONDS

Private activity bonds grant tax-exempt statuses to bonds issued on behalf of private firms that have contracted with public agencies to perform transportation work. The federal government's SAFETEA-LU Act amended the code of the Internal Revenue Service to provide tax exemption for up to $15 billion of transportation private-activity bonding, to be allocated by the Secretary of Transportation.[17] As of August 2010, the Department of Transportation had allocated funding for eight projects that used more than $4.7 billion of tax-exempt bonding. Of the $4.7 billion, bonds had been issued for $2 billion and the remainder has been allocated but not yet issued.[18]

THE GARVEE PROGRAM

The federal government also offers Grant Anticipation Revenue Vehicles (GARVEEs) to state transportation authorities. These allow the states to secure current borrowing by pledging future federal-aid funds as repayment sources. The 1995 National Highway System Act significantly enabled the GARVEE mechanism by expanding the amount of future aid that a state could dedicate to securing current borrowing. The federal government gives Grant Anticipation Notes (GANs) to states, which in turn use these to secure bonds from private financing sources. Since the program's inception, over $7 billion of GANs have been issued and used to obtain financing for transportation projects. The GARVEE program especially has been used to support PPPs, by granting a state the capacity to make upfront payments to private firms that can immediately begin designing and building infrastructure.[19]

As of early 2011, the federal surface transportation program had not been renewed and was operating under a short-term extension. That being the case, states have much less certainty about their future federal-aid allocations, and hence their ability to issue bonds against these funds may be curtailed. If and when the future funding levels are again enacted, the use of GARVEEs may rebound.

SECTION 129 LOANS

Starting in 1991, the federal government began allowing states to lend federal-aid highway funds to entities building eligible transportation projects rather than expending the funds directly. As funds are repaid, they can be used to fund other eligible projects. The use of Section 129 loans has been limited because of the creation of the TIFIA program in 1995.[20]

THE TIFIA PROGRAM

One of the most significant innovative finance programs is the Transportation Infrastructure Finance and Innovation Act (TIFIA), which sets up loan partnerships between the federal and state governments to provide financing for transportation projects. Congress passed the Federal Credit Reform Act (FCRA) of 1990 to establish the program, and under SAFETEA-LU it committed $122 million for each fiscal year between 2005 and 2009.

The TIFIA program uses direct loans, loan guarantees, and standby lines of credit to provide a projected $2.4 billion annually in credit assistance to infrastructure projects. The maximum maturity of TIFIA financing programs is thirty-five years, and the loans are subordinated to a project's other debts. TIFIA loans offer substantially lower interest rates than the market rate, and the borrowers do not need to start repayment for five years after substantial completion of the projects.[21]

There are a few thresholds for projects to be eligible for TIFIA financing assistance. First, only projects larger than $50 million, or above 33.3 percent of the state's federal-aid highway apportionment (whichever is lower), qualify. Also, the projects need to be included in the state's long-range transportation plan and the approved state transportation improvement program. Further, there must be dedicated revenue sources for repayment, such as tolls, user fees, and special taxes. Finally, privately sponsored projects are required to be supported by the public through being included in the state's transportation-planning documents.

As of July 2010, TIFIA had provided financial assistance to twenty-seven projects in thirteen states and territories, totaling $7.9 billion, and leveraging a total project investment of $29.4 billion. Examples of TIFIA-supported projects are a $150 million loan to the Route 895 Pocahontas Parkway (a ninety-nine-year lease by Transurban LLC) in 2006 and a $589 million direct loan for the I-495 Capital Beltway HOT lanes project.[22]

TIFIA's financing model has been so attractive that it has become oversubscribed, and the likelihood of any projects winning approval for TIFIA assistance is rapidly diminishing. For example, as of early 2010, there were thirty-nine applications totaling over $13 billion in assistance, of which only $1.5 billion could be assisted through TIFIA. As of early 2011, program authorization through SAFETEA-LU, which originally expired in 2009, had been extended until spring 2011.

STATE INFRASTRUCTURE BANKS

Another emerging tool of innovative finance is the use of state infrastructure banks (SIBs) to provide financing support to transportation projects.[23] The SIB vehicle acts as a "revolving fund," lending funds to support projects and receiving loan payments, which can then be used to lend for new projects. The "revolving fund" process is meant to demonstrate the self-sustaining benefits of a banking institution applied to transportation investment. First, public funding dedicated to banking purposes is designed to stay operational as opposed to leaving the state budget once distributed. Second, this funding can be turned into much larger-credit lines and accordingly multiply transportation investment capacity.

In its 2008 Conditions and Performance Report, the FHWA explained that "each SIB operates as a revolving fund and can finance a wide variety of surface transportation projects. As loans are repaid, additional funds become available to new loan applicants."[24] A survey of SIBs in the United States demonstrates how the process has worked. Federally chartered SIBs in thirty-two states, as of December 2008, had entered into 579 SIB loan agreements with a total dollar value of $5.56 billion. States have contributed additional funds and expanded total funding by credit leveraging, which means using existing funds to secure borrowing from private creditors. When faced with funding constraints, SIBs offer an opportunity to expand limited funds and encourage projects that self-collect revenue.

SIBs also develop ongoing relationships with the cities and counties that own and operate infrastructure in their states. This ongoing relationship adds value by helping such entities learn how to access the funding available from the SIBs, and hence to accelerate and expand the delivery of infrastructure in the state.

One variant type of SIB is a "state-only" SIB that receives initial capitalization and/or ongoing revenue only from the state, and not from the federal government. If the SIB lends for projects that receive no federal funding, then federal "strings"— such as labor, environmental, and "Buy America" requirements—do not attach. The absence of such strings can reduce project costs considerably as well as speed project completion.

SIB loans can play many roles in a project's financing. Most simply, an SIB loan might provide 100 percent of a project's costs. More typically, project financing is provided from a number of sources, including project-specific bonds, federal contributions, SIB loans, and contributions from state tax and trust funds. To the extent that a project is financed by loans and secured by tolls or other revenue, the loans may be structured in such a way that some loans are "superior" to others, so that they are paid off first. An SIB loan might be "subordinated" to other loans to reduce project costs, because bond markets demand lower interest rates from debts that are superior, other things being equal. An SIB loan might also allow deferred payment, so that interest accumulates and repayment commences only after a passage of up to five years or more.

DEVOLUTION

Local governments raise tens of billions of dollars for transportation. Nearly all cities have control over their internal road systems, as do counties in all states except Alaska, Virginia, West Virginia, and Delaware. As discussed earlier, states transfer billions of dollars of revenue each year to support these local operations. However, when revenue is not sufficient, either because of declines in state funding or unmet increases in transportation needs, local governments may look for alternatives by seeking to expand their own sources of revenue. In most states, local taxes require some form of state authorization, and then localities are permitted to implement taxes within the parameters set by the state. State officials may view additional tax authorizations as a "way out," effectively placing tax burdens on local governments. Conversely, local officials may resist these authorizations and lobby for sustained state financing. However, in many cases, local governments will respond to the tax allowances available in response to transportation needs. For example, the Self-Help Counties Coalition in California is a group of nineteen counties that advocates the use of voter-approved local tax measures to enable transportation projects that would otherwise not be funded.

While much of the funding interplay between state and local governments simply reflects transferring of revenue responsibility, the specific rise of local option transportation taxes signals a new trend of directly raising and channeling local revenue to transportation purposes. In 2001, researchers at the University of California, Berkeley, identified the use of local option transportation taxes in forty-six states, nearly all of which were adopted in the past thirty-five years. In the prior ten years at least twenty-one states had implemented new taxes of this type. Specifically, local option transportation taxes refer to local taxes that may vary within a state and are earmarked for transportation purposes. These can include fuel taxes, used in fifteen states; vehicle licensing or registration taxes, used in thirty-three states; sales taxes dedicated to transportation, used in thirty-three states; and property taxes dedicated to transportation, used in varying degrees by all states.[25]

FEDERAL ALLOCATIONS THROUGH
GRANTS AND FORMULAS

The federal government has traditionally relied heavily on fixed formulas to allocate funds to states for transportation purposes. As was noted, these formulas distribute funds among the states according to their respective populations, shares of highway mileage, and other demographic features. The chief example of this is the Highway Trust Fund, which apportions total revenue collected to states according to their respective shares of mileage of national highways, population, and gas-tax revenues, among other factors. While this technique provides an objective apportionment of funds, it does not recognize specific merits of certain projects over others. To better provide funding to the most deserving projects, the federal government has recently established competitive grant programs that evaluate different funding requests according to the merits of the projects. One example of this is the Transportation Investment Generating Economic Recovery (TIGER) program, a $1.5 billion grant program set up under the American Recovery and Reinvestment Act (ARRA) of 2009. The program required local and state governments seeking funding to complete applications, and projects were selected based on the Secretary of Transportation's evaluation of merit.

The call for a shift from a formula to a merit-based or performance-based selection mechanism for transportation investments arises out of a concern that formula programs tend to decentralize decision making and project selection to the government units receiving the formula allocations. The level of government providing the funds has often exercised relatively little control over the selection and prioritization of projects that contribute to broader social goals, not to mention meeting regional, state, or national transportation needs.[26]

Concluding Remarks

The major federal transportation programs are at a crossroads, with potentially profound implications for state and local governments. In the highway and transit areas, the federal Highway Trust Fund revenues are not sufficient to support projected program-spending levels, and the program has received "bailouts" from the federal general fund of approximately $40 billion as of January 2011. There is widespread agreement within the professional transportation and political communities that the federal surface transportation program is in dire need of restructuring. The problem is that there is little agreement on what shape such restructuring should take. On the one hand are proposals to simplify the federal program and concentrate its limited resources on clear national priorities such as freight and congestion. On the other are proposals to expand the program to support new goals such as "livability"—however defined—and metropolitan prosperity.[27]

As mentioned earlier, recent debates have focused on incorporating accountability and performance criteria in the allocation of funding, rather than relying on the traditional formula allocations. Indeed, President Obama himself, speaking on Labor Day in 2010, called for "reforming the haphazard and patchwork way we fund and maintain our infrastructure to focus less on wasteful earmarks and outdated formulas, and more on competition and innovation that gives us the best bang for the buck."[28] Formula programs have been the bedrock of federal highway policy since its modern inception in 1916, and for much of federal transit policy as well. A move from a formula-based allocation of programmatic funds toward some other structure, whether it is project-by-project cost-benefit analysis or evaluation according to some other criterion such as livability, portends substantial change to the surface transportation programs in future rounds of policy authorization.

On the aviation side of transportation issues, the federal aviation authorization as of this writing has also been stalled for more than three years. The FAA's NextGen program would upgrade the US air traffic control system from a mid-twentieth-century technology of ground-based radars to a modern system based on global positioning system (GPS) satellites. However, multiyear funding for the development and deployment of NextGen has not been forthcoming from Congress.

Prospects for additional federal transportation funding are all weaker in light of extraordinary pressures on the federal budget. Congress and the president appear to have no appetite for new taxes; liabilities for Medicare and Social Security entitlements are ballooning; and the national economy appears to be rebounding from the recession of 2008–2009 relatively slowly. Slow economic growth at present and the diminished prospects for such growth in the future are an impediment to undertaking new initiatives.

For states and localities, the erosion of federal support is both a challenge and an opportunity. The challenge resides in replacing declining federal funding in an economic and political climate that is not favorably disposed to any new taxes, while at the same time grappling with reduced state and local revenues for transportation resulting from the same recession.

The opportunity—perhaps difficult to discern in early 2011 as this is written— lies perhaps most squarely in the capacity of states and localities to make difficult choices and foster innovative approaches for the financing and development of transportation infrastructure and services. Possibilities include prospects for innovative finance and PPPs, reorganization and contracting out of transportation maintenance and operations, and an increasing reliance on user fees. Increasingly, the head-on collision in transportation finance will be between fiscal necessity and political acceptability.

Acknowledgments

Graduate students Nobuhiko Daito, Nathan Zebrowski, Zhenhua Chen, and Jing Li provided invaluable assistance in researching and writing this chapter. The chapter reflects the views of the author, and any remaining errors are fully the responsibility of the author.

Notes

1 Rules of the US Senate and US House of Representatives, quoted in Kirk, Mallett, and Peterman (2011), 3.
2 William Mallett, personal communication (January 14, 2011).
3 US Federal Highway Administration (2010b).
4 US Bureau of Transportation Statistics (2006).
5 US Federal Highway Administration and US Federal Transit Administration (2008).
6 Bolden (2010).
7 US Federal Highway Administration (2010a).
8 US Federal Highway Administration and US Federal Transit Administration (2008), 6–15.
9 "Local Government Authority—Home Rule & Dillon's Rule.".
10 US Federal Highway Administration and US Federal Transit Administration (2008), 6–35.
11 US Government Accountability Office (2007b) 5.
12 US Bureau of Transportation Statistics (2010), 2.
13 Ibid., 8–9.
14 US Maritime Administration (2009), 1–8.
15 US Printing Office (2001).
16 US Federal Highway Administration (2007); US Department of Transportation (2004).
17 *SAFETEA-LU*, sec. 11143.
18 US Federal Highway Administration (2011a).
19 US Printing Office (2001).
20 US Federal Highway Administration (2011b).
21 American Association of State Highway and Transportation Officials (2010).
22 US Federal Highway Administration (2010).
23 This section draws from Gifford (2010).
24 US Federal Highway Administration and US Federal Transit Administration (2008), 6–29.
25 Goldman, Corrett, and Wachs (2001); Goldman and Wachs (2003).
26 Critics have long complained that federal grant programs have long failed to provide appropriate incentives to promote national objectives in the use of funds. For example, see US Government Accountability Office (2007b).
27 Puentes (2008); Poole and Moore (2010); Transportation for America (2009); National Transportation Policy Project (2009); National Surface Transportation Infrastructure Financing Commission (2009); National Surface Transportation Policy and Revenue Study Commission (2008).
28 Stolberg and Walsh (2010).

References

American Association of State Highway and Transportation Officials (2010). "TIFIA: Transportation Infrastructure Finance and Innovation Act." *AASHTO Center for Excellence in Project Finance—Transportation Funding & Financing—Federal Credit Assistance.* http://www.transportation-finance.org/funding_financing/financing/credit_assistance/tifia.aspx.

Bolden, Michael D. (2010, December 7). "Lawmaker Seeks Auditor for Dulles Rail." *Washington Post*, http://voices.washingtonpost.com/dr-gridlock/2010/12/lawmaker_seeks_auditor_for_dul.html.

Gifford, Jonathan L. (2010, November 24). *State Infrastructure Banks: A Virginia Perspective*. George Mason University School of Public Policy Research Paper no. 2010-2032. ssrn.com/abstract=1714466.

Goldman, Todd, Sam Corrett, and Martin Wachs (2001). *Local Option Transportation Taxes: Part Two*. Berkeley: University of California, Berkeley, Institute of Transportation Studies.

Goldman, Todd, and Martin Wachs (2003, Winter). "A Quiet Revolution in Transportation Finance: The Rise of Local Option Transportation Taxes." *Transportation Quarterly* 57(1):19–32.

Kirk, Robert S., William J. Mallett, and David Randall Peterman (2011, January 3). *Transportation Spending Under an Earmark Ban*. Congressional Research Service, http://www.aashtojournal.org/Documents/January2011/earmarks.pdf.

"Local Government Authority—Home Rule & Dillon's Rule" (2010). National League of Cities official website, http://www.nlc.org/about_cities/cities_101/153.aspx.

National Surface Transportation Infrastructure Financing Commission (2009, February 26). *Paying Our Way: A New Framework for Transportation Finance*. Washington, DC. http://financecommission.dot.gov/Documents/NSTIF_Commission_Final_Report_Advance%20Copy_Feb09.pdf.

National Surface Transportation Policy and Revenue Study Commission (US) (2008). *Transportation for Tomorrow: Report of the National Surface Transportation Policy and Revenue Study Commission*. Washington, DC: National Surface Transportation Policy and Revenue Study Commission. http://digitalarchive.oclc.org/request?id%3Doclcnum%3A191092895.

National Transportation Policy Project (2009, June 9). *Performance Driven: A New Vision for U.S. Transportation Policy*. Washington, DC: Bipartisan Policy Center. http://www.bipartisanpolicy.org/sites/default/files/NTPP%20Report.pdf.

Poole, Robert W., and Adrian T. Moore (2010, August). *Restoring Trust in the Highway Trust Fund*. Reason Foundation.

Puentes, Robert (2008). *A Bridge to Somewhere: Rethinking American Transportation for the 21st Century*. Brookings Institution, Metropolitan Policy Program.

Safe, Accountable, Flexible, Efficient Transportation Equity Act: A Legacy for Users, P.L. 109–59 (2005, August 10).

Stolberg, Sheryl Gay, and Mary Williams Walsh (2010, September 6). "Obama Calls for $50 Billion Public Works Plan." *New York Times*, sec. US/Politics. http://www.nytimes.com/2010/09/07/us/politics/07obama.html?_r=1&scp=10&sq=obama%20labor%20day&st=cse.

Transportation for America (2009). *The Route to Reform: Blueprint for a 21st Century Federal Transportation Program*. Washington, DC. http://t4america.org/docs/blueprint_full.pdf.

US Bureau of Transportation Statistics (2010, January). *Pocket Guide to Transportation 2010*. Washington, DC. http://www.bts.gov/publications/pocket_guide_to_transportation/2010/pdf/entire.pdf.

US Bureau of Transportation Statistics (2006). "Table 5–3: Highway Vehicle-Miles Traveled (VMT)." http://www.bts.gov/publications/state_transportation_statistics/state_transportation_statistics_2006/html/table_05_03.html.

US Department of Transportation (2004). Report to Congress on Public-Private Partnerships. http://www.fhwa.dot.gov/reports/pppdec2004/index.htm.

US Department of Transportation (2008, July 18). *Innovation Wave: An Update on the Burgeoning Private Sector Role in U.S. Highway and Transit Infrastructure.* Washington, DC. http://www.fhwa.dot.gov/reports/pppwave/ppp_innovation_wave.pdf.

US Federal Highway Administration (2007). "User Guidebook on Implementing Public-Private Partnerships for Transportation Infrastructure Projects in the United States." http://www.fhwa.dot.gov/ipd/pdfs/ppp_user_guidebook_final_7–7-07.pdf.

US Federal Highway Administration (2010a). "Funding for Highways and Disposition of High-way-User Revenues, All Units of Government, 2008 1." *Highway Statistics 2008 Table HF-10.* http://www.fhwa.dot.gov/policyinformation/statistics/2008/hf10.cfm.

US Federal Highway Administration (2010b). "Total Receipts for Highways, by Function." *Highway Statistics 2008 Chart REC-C.* http://www.fhwa.dot.gov/policyinformation/statistics/2008/rec.cfm.

US Federal Highway Administration (2011a). "Private Activity Bonds (PABs)." *FHWA Office of Innovative Program Delivery: Innovative Finance.* http://www.fhwa.dot.gov/ipd/finance/tools_programs/federal_debt_financing/private_activity_bonds/index.htm.

US Federal Highway Administration (2011b). "Section 129 Loans." *FHWA Office of Innovative Program Delivery: Innovative Finance.* http://www.fhwa.dot.gov/ipd/finance/tools_programs/federal_credit_assistance/section_129/index.htm.

US Federal Highway Administration, and US Federal Transit Administration (2008). *2008 Status of the Nation's Highways, Bridges, and Transit: Conditions and Performance.* Report to Congress. Washington, DC. http://www.fhwa.dot.gov/policy/2008cpr/pdfs/cp2008.pdf.

US Government Accountability Office (2007a, June). *Airport Finance: Observations on Planned Airport Development Costs and Funding Levels and the Administration's Proposed Changes in the Airport Improvement Program.* Washington, DC, http://www.gao.gov/new.items/d07885.pdf.

US Government Accountability Office (2007b, July). "Surface Transportation Strategies to Make Existing Infrastructure Perform Better." Washington, DC. http://gpo.gov/cgi-bin/getdoc.cgi?dbname=gao&docid=f:d07920.pdf.

US Maritime Administration (2009, February). *U.S. Public Port Development Expenditure Report (FYs 2006 & 2007–2011).* Washington, DC. http://www.marad.dot.gov/documents/2006_port_expenditure_rpt_—_final.pdf.

US Printing Office (2001). *Budget of the United States Government.* http://www.gpo.gov/fdsys/pkg/BUDGET-2001-BUD/html/BUDGET-2001-BUD-8–9.htm.

CHAPTER 23

HOUSING POLICY: THE EVOLVING SUBNATIONAL ROLE

ROBERT M. BUCKLEY AND
ALEX F. SCHWARTZ

THIS chapter provides a general overview of US housing policy, with an emphasis on state and local programs and policies that subsidize housing for low-income households. The emphasis on the state and local dimension of housing policy is appropriate since beginning in the 1970s, when the federal government began to relinquish its role as the preeminent player in US housing policy. This was accomplished by the convergence of a variety of strategies, including the curtailment of highly centralized programs such as public housing, the growth of grants and tax policies that gave state and localities much more latitude to devise their own housing programs, and an increased emphasis on providing subsidies to people rather than to places. Moreover, as Penner notes, in an age of federal fiscal austerity the state and local roles in the allocation function are likely to increase in the coming years.[1]

But, that said, even as there is a shift toward an increased subnational role in housing policy for low-income families it is also true that the provision of affordable housing will nevertheless remain highly intergovernmental; thus, to have a understanding of the evolving subnational role in US housing policy one must have an understanding of the evolving nature of national housing policy

Accordingly, this chapter is divided into four sections.[2] The next section sets the context by summarizing key trends and patterns in the housing market and by tracing key features of the housing market, including data on tenure distributions, housing conditions, and costs. Particular emphasis is given to the role of increasing housing costs as these costs have become an increasingly important rationale for assisting lower-income families with their housing needs.

The next section focuses on national housing policy. It begins with a summary of federal housing assistance, including the different ways the tax code subsidizes homeowners and, to a much lesser degree, renters. It focuses on the extent to which tax subsidies for homeownership have benefited affluent homeowners far more than they have households of more modest means. From there, the chapter then examines a variety of subsidies for low-income housing, including, on the supply side, the Low-Income Housing Tax Credit (LITC), which is the largest active subsidy program for rental housing today as well as recent efforts to reform and rebuild public housing through the HOPE VI program for the revitalization of extremely distressed developments. We then discuss the main federal program to subsidize housing for lower-income families: demand-side subsidies—vouchers— which have been increasingly adopted in the United States and Europe.[3]

The third section focuses on programs designed and administered by state and local governments, often in close collaboration with nonprofit organizations. The section discusses how states and localities utilize federal block grants and tax-exempt bond financing for housing and how they are using the new tools of housing trust funds and inclusionary zoning to fund the development of affordable housing. It also summarizes the role of community development corporations and other nonprofit organizations as partners to state and local government in delivering housing assistance.

A final section offers concluding comments on the strengths and weaknesses of US housing policy and the evolving role of subnational governments.

HOUSING IN THE UNITED STATES: AN OVERVIEW

Few things influence as many aspects of life as housing. Housing provides far more than just shelter from the elements. As a home, housing is loaded with symbolic value. A house is valued for its location, its style, and its access to schools, parks, and other amenities.[4] It is also a major form of wealth for homeowners, the most widespread and largest single form of household wealth.[5] On the other hand, inadequate housing increases vulnerability to a wide range of troubles, such as health hazards. Residential location can influence the quality of education because of the access that housing provides to the best or worst schools. Moreover, vulnerability to crime is strongly influenced by residential location. People who live in distressed neighborhoods often face a far greater risk of being robbed or assaulted.[6]

Housing's Role in the Economy. From 1975 to 2008 the housing industry produced an average of 1.7 million new residential units each year. Although its production has been cyclical, housing output trended upward almost every year for the past twenty years, and when it did decline it did so only slightly. However, what was seen as an unbroken record of success came apart with the mortgage crisis and the collapse of the national housing market: housing starts plummeted in 2007, 2008, and 2009. The 554,000 total starts recorded in 2009 were a 73 percent decrease from 2005, the lowest level achieved since World War II.[7]

For the past quarter century, residential construction has been dominated by single-family homes, which accounted for 78 percent of the total in 2005, up from less than 56 percent in 1980. As will be discussed later, changes in the mortgage finance system and the federal income-tax code greatly reduced investment in rental housing and favored homeownership. In addition, as Glaeser has shown, local regulations in many areas have also placed severe constraints on multifamily housing development with the result that multifamily starts remain well below the volume of the early 1980s.[8]

Housing has also become larger and considerably more luxurious. The median size of owner-occupied homes increased steadily from 1,535 square feet in 1973 to 2,277 in 2007 so that the average American has almost 1,000 square feet of living space, more than double the average living space consumed in Great Britain, France, or Germany.[9] Multifamily units have also become larger, but not to nearly the same degree as single-family homes (indeed, by almost any standard). America is very well housed even if many people have to pay excessive amounts for it. To mention just a few dimensions of the scale of improvement: incomplete plumbing and other severe physical problems that were endemic at midcentury characterize only a tiny percentage of the housing stock today. Indeed, the 2000 Census stopped asking the question of whether a house lacked sewerage or a septic connection because in the previous Census only 1 percent of houses had this problem.[10] Similarly, the quality of the nation's housing stock has improved to the point that only a small portion is physically deficient.

This is a far cry from the time when the first building code and land use reforms were introduced in the late nineteenth and early twentieth centuries. President Franklin D. Roosevelt did not exaggerate when, in his second inaugural address, he spoke of "one third of a nation ill- housed." In 1940, fully 45 percent of households lived in homes without complete plumbing, especially in rural and southern areas. Unquestionably, housing conditions improved dramatically in the second half of the twentieth century, and by international or historical standards America is indeed very well housed.

Tenure.[11] The majority of people were renters until the 1940s. From 1940 to 1960 the national homeownership rate shot up from 44 to 62 percent, an increase driven by a variety of forces, not least the creation of the thirty-year, self-amortizing, fixed-rate mortgage under the auspices of the Federal Housing and Veterans Administrations. The homeownership rate peaked at over 69 percent in 2004 and has shifted downward since, reflecting both the run-up of housing prices of the housing bubble, and there was a surge in foreclosures after the housing bubble burst in 2007.

One fundamental difference across tenures is the relative affluence of homeowners and the increasing discrepancy between homeowner and renter incomes. The median household income of homeowners in 2007, at $61,700, was more than double that of renters, while it was only 75 percent greater in 1991. The differences are starker with regard to wealth. In 2007 the median net wealth of renters of $5,300 amounted to just 2 percent of the median for homeowners of $234,200.

Owners and renters also diverge in many other respects. Owners are far more likely to reside in detached single-family homes—85 percent of them do—and far less likely to live in multifamily housing, as 85 percent of dwellings with more than three units are rented. They are more likely to reside in the suburbs or outside metropolitan areas than in the central city. They are more likely to be white and less likely to be from a minority racial or ethnic group. Both tenure forms are equally likely to have children under eighteen, but owners are far more likely to be married couples and renters tend to be single females. Homeowners are more likely to be elderly, but less likely to live alone. They are far less likely than renters to live in poverty, and they spend a substantially smaller percentage of their income on housing-related expenses. Almost all homeowners have a car; nearly one-fifth of renters do not. Finally, even though the decline in the number living in "severely inadequate housing" fell from almost 11 percent of renter households in 1975 to less than 3 percent at present, renters are still more than twice as likely to reside in homes with moderate or severe physical deficiencies.

Affordability. Affordability of housing is of far greater concern than physical conditions or crowding. While fewer than 2 percent of all households now reside in severely deficient housing and fewer than 4 percent confront overcrowded conditions, more than 16 percent spend half or more of their income on housing expenses, including 24 percent of renters. Unlike the physical aspect of housing, affordability is not exclusively a housing problem. Rather, it encompasses income as well as cost. Housing, in other words, is more or less affordable because of changes in either housing expenses or income. To measure trends in affordability, the most common standard in the United States is 30 percent of income. Households spending 30 percent or more of their pretax income on housing are viewed as having a housing affordability problem. When housing-cost burdens exceed 50 percent of income, they are defined as being severe.

By these measures, more than 30 percent of all homeowners and more than 45 percent of all renters had a housing affordability problem in 2007. Moreover, for many of them the problem is severe and they do not receive any government assistance: half of all very low-income renters without any housing subsidy pay more than half of their income on rent or live in severely deficient housing, a problem not experienced by higher income families. For example, if we focus on the highest and lowest income levels we find that the bottom quartile of the income distribution accounts for 91 percent of all renters with severe cost burdens and 57 percent of all homeowners. The top two quartiles, in contrast, account for less than 1 percent of all renters and 16 percent of all homeowners with severe cost burdens. As would be expected from their lower incomes, renters confront severe cost burdens far more often than substandard housing.

Explaining the Affordability Problem. The pervasiveness of an affordability problem among poor renters is due to various reasons, the most important of which is the interplay between the functioning of the housing market and broader economic trends such as changes in income distribution.

As for the market's workings, perhaps the most important factor has been the apparent lack of policy responsiveness to the demands of low-income families, which in turn is fundamentally related to two factors: the way we have chosen to distribute subsidies—which Quigley, for example, describes as being closer to winning a sweepstakes than a process which induces better searches by households and more supply by landlords; and the way that housing market regulations constrain the functioning of the market so that supply is often slow to adjust.[12] Of course, one reason for the diminishing real incomes of renters is that many of the more affluent renters purchased homes over the past two decades, thus reducing the average income of renters by reducing the number of renters who have higher average incomes. Reducing the size of the pool of rental housing occupants by those at the high end of the income spectrum will necessarily reduce the average income of renters. But it is important to remember that these shifts within the housing market have taken place within the context of the nation's widening economic inequality.[13]

Regarding the broad trends, manifestations of the growing affordability problem are shown by DiPasquale and Murray, who show that across large metropolitan cities, real rents increased by 9 percent between 2000 and 2005 while at the same time that renter household income fell by about 5 percent, magnifying long-term trends that show that median renter income decreased while median gross rent increased.[14]

Moreover, while the lowest income renters have increased in number, they face what appears to be a shrinking supply of affordable housing. For example, while the number of extremely low-income renters (with incomes below 30 percent of area median family income) increased by nearly 1.6 million households from 1991 to 2005 (or 18 percent), the number of units that were affordable to these renters decreased by more than 400,000 (6 percent) due to higher income households "filtering" down into lower-priced housing, as well as to demolitions and the removal of 2 million units of lower-income housing from the stock.[15] As a result, there is relatively greater demand for lower-priced units and, not surprising, the rents of these units increased. At the same time, those with incomes above the median enjoyed a relative improvement in their circumstances. Again not surprisingly, only renters with incomes above 73 percent of area median have access to a supply of housing that is both affordable and available.

Similarly, Harvard's Joint Center for Housing Studies found striking decreases in the supply of older housing that was affordable to low-income families. From 1997 to 2007, about 30 percent of all housing renting for $400 or less (in 2007 prices) that was built before 1940 was torn down or otherwise removed from the stock, converted to owner occupancy or temporary usage, or shifted upward to a higher rental category.[16] These trends are especially alarming because older units account for most of the nation's affordable housing stock.

Also contributing to the shortage of affordable housing for low-income renters are reductions in the federally subsidized housing stock. The public housing
inventory decreased by nearly 250,000 units (18 percent), from 1991 to 2007, largely
reflecting the widespread demolition of distressed projects. Many of these projects
have been replaced with mixed-income developments, but the result is a net loss
of subsidized units. In addition, more than 150,000 units of privately owned but
federally subsidized housing have been lost since 1997 as owners decide against
renewing their subsidy contracts.[17]

Finally, at least part of the market's failure to provide housing affordable to
low-income renters stems from government regulations that govern the size, quality, and density of housing that can be built. Building code and zoning standards,
for example, impose minimum size requirements on all new housing—standards
that have questionable bearing on health and safety. Such size standards can simply price new housing out of reach for many low-income families; families may be
able to afford, say, 500-square-foot homes, but units of this size may fall below the
minimum requirement.

Land-use restrictions also inflate the cost of housing. Large-lot suburban zoning, for example, increases land costs per unit. Glaeser has shown that restrictions
on multifamily housing severely limit the supply of these forms of lower cost housing, increasing their costs and sharply reducing their availability.[18] Ultimately, while
the rapid growth in severe cost burdens among homeowners since the mid-1990s
is not well understood, it is, nevertheless, clear that neither policies nor trends in
income distribution have had a benevolent effect on the housing costs faced by
lower-income families.

Homelessness. No housing problem is as profound as is homelessness. Being
homeless puts one at the mercy of the elements, the kindness of family and friends,
and the workings of a variety of social welfare agencies. Without a home, it is
extremely difficult to find a job or to keep one. Homelessness makes it difficult
for children to attend school regularly and perhaps even more difficult to study
and learn. It places people at higher risk of illness, mental health problems, substance abuse, and crime. Unlike other housing problems, homelessness is by its
nature extremely difficult to quantify. Nevertheless, careful analysis of all the
available data implies that the central explanatory factors in explaining homelessness are the availability and cost of housing.[19] The study shows that when housing
is expensive and less available, homelessness increases. In short, despite the complexities involved at its core, homelessness—which the Department of Housing
and Urban Development estimates stands at over 640,000 in 2009—is yet another
manifestation of housing affordability problems.[20]

The US Department of Housing and Urban Development (HUD) has issued
annual reports since 2005 about the extent of homelessness in the nation. The
report for 2009 found that on a single night in January, more than 643,000 people
were homeless, including those in shelters and on the street. The report also
found that more than twice as many people, nearly 1.6 million, stayed in a homeless shelter or transitional housing during the twelve-month period ending on

September 30, 2009. This latter figure does not include people who were homeless but did not stay in shelters.[21]

FEDERAL HOUSING PROGRAMS

Given the complexity and pervasive effects that housing has on basic living conditions, it is perhaps not surprising that policy is seldom just about being sheltered. Nearly every housing program initiated since the nineteenth century has been motivated by concerns that go beyond the provision of decent and affordable housing. For example, the regulatory reforms of the late nineteenth and early twentieth centuries proscribing minimum standards for light, ventilation, fire safety, and sanitation derived at least as much from a desire to stem the spread of infectious disease and to curb antisocial behavior, as from a wish to improve living conditions for their own sake. Similarly, in passing the original public housing legislation in 1937, Congress was more interested in promoting employment in the construction trades than in providing low-income housing—a feature that, in many respects, carries through to the present set of supply-side subsidies. Policies also differ in the extent to which they rely on government agencies for program implementation. Some, such as public housing and rental vouchers, rely almost exclusively on government agencies, national and subnational alike; others involve partnerships with for-profit or nonprofit developers.

From the 1930s, when the government instituted the first national housing programs (FHA mortgage insurance, public housing), to the mid-1970s, the federal government devised, funded, and implemented virtually all housing programs. Programs were categorical, providing minimal latitude to states and localities. Cities and counties established public housing authorities (PHAs) to develop and manage public housing and subsequently administer the voucher program. But PHAs had very little autonomy. They were created in response to a court ruling that the federal government lacked constitutional authority to exercise powers of eminent domain to acquire sites for public housing.[22] In this delegation, local governments created PHAs to acquire land for public housing. They acquired sites for public housing and issued bonds to finance construction. The federal government paid the debt service on the bonds and issued rules and regulations regarding tenant eligibility standards, rent levels, construction and design standards, and virtually all other aspects of public housing. PHAs acted essentially as an arm of the federal government.

States and localities began to play a larger role in US housing policies in the mid-1970s when the government created the first block grant program, and in the years since, most of the government's new housing programs followed this approach. These include the Community Development Block Grant program, the HOME Investment Partnership program, and housing-related block grants for Native Americans, for homeless citizens and for persons with HIV/AIDS. In addition, the Low-Income Housing Tax Credit, the nation's largest active supply-side rental housing subsidy program, is analogous to a block grant, as will be discussed below.

Today, the federal government continues to fund the vast majority of the country's subsidy programs, but it does not dictate the terms of these programs to the same extent as before. States and localities now have considerably more say in deciding what kinds of housing should be subsidized, the kinds of households that should receive priority, where the housing should be built, the extent to which nonprofit or for-profit developers should be involved, and even over the type of subsidy provided.

One result of the shift to block grant-based funding is that with the exception of the voucher program and some much smaller programs, direct federal housing subsidy programs have not grown appreciably since the 1970s. Indeed, the total inventory of federal housing programs has diminished steadily since the 1990s, reflecting the demolition and redevelopment of public housing, and the loss of federally subsidized, privately owned housing due to prepayment of federally insured mortgages and the expiration of federal subsidy contracts.[23] From a budgetary standpoint, the government's "legacy" housing programs accounted for more than one-third of the HUD's total budget in fiscal year 2010. Vouchers account for another 42 percent. Block grants represented about 19 percent.[24]

The remainder of this section places particular emphasis on the four major types of national housing subsidies: tax and financial subsidies; the Low Income Housing Tax Credit; Public Housing, and housing vouchers. Again, this broad-brush approach to federal programs means that many of the smaller programs are not covered here.[25]

Tax and Financial Subsidies. Although many may associate housing policy in the United States with housing for low-income families (e.g., public housing), the federal government provides a much larger housing subsidy for the affluent in the form of tax benefits for homeownership. Whereas about 7 million low-income renters benefited from federal housing subsidies in 2008, more than 70 million homeowners received the benefits of tax-free income on the imputed rental income on their homes. Many of them also took mortgage interest deductions on their federal income taxes. Federal expenditures for direct housing assistance totaled less than $40.2 billion in 2008; at the same time, mortgage-interest deductions and other homeowner tax benefits approached $185 billion. Moreover, the lion's share of these benefits is regressively distributed to households with incomes above $100,000. Indeed, Poterba and Sinai show that households with incomes more than $250,000 per year receive more than ten times as much in such subsidies as do households with incomes between $40,000 and $75,000 (see table 23.1)[26].

In addition to the mortgage-interest deduction, other tax expenditures for homeownership include the deductibility of property-tax payments, reduced taxes

Table 23.1 Overview of federal housing expenditures (selected programs)

Budget Authority Fiscal 2011	$ Billions
Rental Vouchers	18.3
Project-Based Rental Assistance	9.3
Public Housing	6.7
Hope VI	0.1
Community Development Block Grants	3.3
Home Investment Partnership Program	1.6
Homeless Assistance Grants	1.9
Housing for the Elderly	0.4
Housing for Persons with Disabilities	0.15
Tax Expenditures, Fiscal 2007	
Homeowner Subsidies	152.2
Mortgage Interest Deduction	100.8
Property-Tax Deduction	16.6
Capital Gains Exemption	22.8
Investor Subsidies	29.5
Exclusion of Interest on State and Local Bonds	1890.0
Accelerated Depreciation	11.8
Low-Income Housing Tax Credit	5.8
Exemption from Passive-Loss Rules	8.8
Deferral of Income from Post-1997 Installment Sales	1.2

Source: National Low Income Housing Coalition (2011); Budget of the US Government.

on the sale of residential properties, the lack of tax on the imputed income from housing, and low-interest mortgages for first-time homebuyers financed by tax-exempt bonds.[27] The primary tax incentives for investing in rental housing consist of the low-income housing and historic rehabilitation tax credits and low-interest mortgages financed by tax-exempt bonds. In short, even without considering the assistance provided through the financial system, by Fannie Mae and Freddie Mac, two government-sponsored credit agencies, housing assistance is overwhelmingly targeted on homeowners and, to a considerable degree, on wealthier households.[28]

The Low-Income Housing Tax Credit. One of the largest subsidies for low-income rental housing is an item in the Internal Revenue Code. The Low-Income Housing Tax Credit, which was enacted as part of the Tax Reform Act of 1986, provides financial incentives to invest in low-income rental housing, and it now accommodates 1.9 million households, more households than the 1.2 million in public housing. In 2009 the cost to the US Treasury was $5.8 billion.[29] The LIHTC allows investors to reduce their federal income taxes by $1 for every dollar of tax credit received. Investors receive the credit for ten years; and the property must remain occupied by low-income households for at least fifteen years. The amount of the credit depends on the cost and location of the housing development and the proportion of units occupied by low-income households. Unlike other tax breaks associated with real estate, the LIHTC is not awarded automatically. Tax credits are usually assigned to individual housing developments by state housing finance agencies (HFAs). The total dollar amount of federal tax credits available is determined by state population. In 2010, states could allocate two dollars per capita per year in tax credits, with the amount adjusted for inflation thereafter. Developers apply to HFAs for tax credits. At least 10 percent of a state's tax-credit allocations must go to housing developed by nonprofit organizations. Tax law generally limits the market for LIHTC to corporate investors. In a sense, the tax-credit program is analogous to federal block grants, in that each state is allocated a fixed amount of tax credits and has considerable discretion over how the tax credits should be used.

Rental housing developments are eligible for the tax credit if at least 20 percent of their units are affordable to households earning up to 50 percent of the metropolitan area's median family income, or if at least 40 percent of the units are affordable to households earning 60 percent of the median. Most developers designate most (and often all) of the units in tax-credit projects for low-income occupancy to maximize the amount of credit they can receive and to have the option of marketing the units to households with somewhat higher incomes. The maximum allowable rent is set at 30 percent of 50 or 60 percent of median family income, depending on the proportion of tax-credit units within the development. It is important to note that, unlike other federal housing programs in which renters pay no more than 30 percent of their adjusted income on rent and the government makes up the difference, residents of tax-credit housing with incomes below the program's maximum limit can face a rent well above 30 percent.

The most recent assessment of housing financed through the LIHTC comes from a national Ernst and Young study of more than one million units.[30] The study tracks the financial performance of 14,000 developments from 2000 through 2005. It found that the properties performed relatively well. The median occupancy rate was 96 percent, and the properties generated a positive cash flow of $240 per unit. On the negative side, the study found that 18 percent of the properties reported an occupancy rate below 90 percent in 2005 and 34 percent reported a hard debt-coverage ratio of less than 1.0 and/or a negative cash flow. However, the study also noted that underperformance appears to often be a temporary condition, as relatively few properties repeat a subpar result from one year to the next. Only about 2 percent of the properties underperformed in each year of the study in terms of occupancy and 4 percent in terms of debt-coverage ratio and cash flow. The study also found that the properties in the sample showed a very low annualized foreclosure rate of 0.03 percent.

The LIHTC has avoided many of the problems that had afflicted its predecessors. It has been sufficiently flexible that states can tailor their programs to their individual needs and priorities, and it has been virtually devoid of scandal or impropriety. However, the financial crisis raises new questions about the program's sustainability and the wisdom of relying on tax credits and other incentives for private investment to produce low-income housing.

There are four issues that, together, raise questions regarding the efficiency of the LIHTC. The first focuses on its complexity. From the outset, the LIHTC has been criticized for its complexity. For example, Michael Stegman criticized the program for making the underwriting of low-income housing unduly complicated and cumbersome.[31] Besides being complicated, the program is inflexible, providing no incentive for developers to create mixed-income developments. As noted previously, the credit applies only to units slated for households with incomes less than 50 or 60 percent of the area median; units occupied by higher income renters receive no tax credit. Moreover, the tax credit's regulatory requirements make the management of mixed-income tax-credit developments especially burdensome.

The second concern focuses on continuing housing affordability. Rents in housing financed with tax credits are fixed at a set amount, so the percentage of income that tenants spend on housing may increase if their incomes decline and they may start out spending more than 30 percent of their income on rent. Consequently, while the increased effectiveness of the program enables developers to target more households with lower incomes than before, extremely low-income families can seldom afford tax-credit housing unless they also receive federal housing vouchers.

Third, the program does not always provide for the long-term sustainability of the housing it helped finance. Some tax-credit housing is at risk of converting to market-rate rents after the expiration of an initial fifteen-year affordability period. More important, such developments lack funding to replace major building systems. Federal and state governments have modified the tax-credit program to extend the minimum affordability period beyond fifteen years, and state and local governments have provided additional resources, including new tax credits, to help pay for capital improvements. However, such efforts would not have been necessary if the program had been designed differently.[32]

Finally, the issue of how efficient a tax shelter is relative to other forms of subsidy is a traditional problem of this means of finance. The costs to taxpayers of delivering a subsidy in this way are higher than are direct subsidies.[33]

Nevertheless, the LIHTC has evolved from an esoteric financial instrument to the most important source of equity for low-income rental housing in the country. It has replaced virtually all previous tax incentives for investing in rental housing. Not surprisingly, because this was a novel, untested tax incentive facing an uncertain future, investors initially purchased tax-credit properties at a steep discount. As a result, developers of tax-credit housing in the early years of the program were often forced to piece together multiple sources of debt and equity to supplement the tax-credit equity and the maximum attainable market-rate mortgage.

However, as the market grew accustomed to the LIHTC and Congress lifted the program's "sunset" provisions, investors have paid increasingly more for tax-credit properties. As a result, tax-credit equity has covered a growing share of total development costs, reducing the need for additional gap financing and allowing the housing to accommodate lower income households. The LIHTC, in short, became more efficient. Much more of the tax credit goes directly into bricks and mortar and much less is diverted to the investors' financial return or to syndication costs—although some of these gains have been reversed by the financial crisis of 2008–2009.

The financial crisis of 2008–2009 has highlighted other weaknesses in the program. It revealed that the program was highly dependent on the investments of a small number of large financial institutions. These institutions' demand for tax credits collapsed in 2008 as they racked up billions of dollars in mortgage-related losses, and some large institutions were closed down or taken over by the government. Looking ahead, the LIHTC, in the near term at least, will probably not produce as much equity for low-income housing as it had due to the lower profitability of the Great Recession. This subsidy is free from annual appropriation battles, but it is subject to the effects of business cycles on the demand for tax shelters, which will mean that developers will need additional sources of subsidy and may need to charge higher rents.

Public Housing. The Public Housing program originated in 1937 in one of the last major pieces of legislation passed during the New Deal. The legislation was revised many times and took several years to gain congressional approval. The program replaced a much smaller New Deal initiative that financed the development of low-income housing as part of a broader effort to support public works. The legislation authorized local public housing authorities (PHAs) to issue bonds to finance the development costs of public housing. The federal government was to pay the interest and principal on these bonds. The cost of operating public housing was to be covered by tenant rental payments.

In the past quarter century, however, far more resources have gone to the preservation and redevelopment of public housing than to the expansion of the program. The stock of public housing reached its peak of 1.4 million units in 1994; by 2008, it had declined by 19 percent for a loss of nearly 270,000 units. Only 5 percent of the public housing stock as of 2003 was built after 1985, and most of that replaced older public housing buildings that had been torn down. On the other hand, 57 percent of all public housing units were more than thirty years old in 2003.[34] Clearly this is a program that is not an active housing policy.

HOPE VI and the Transformation of Public Housing. Congress launched the HOPE VI program in 1993 to demolish and redevelop distressed public housing. Since its inception, hundreds of public housing projects across the nation have been transformed into housing developments that defy popular conceptions of public housing. Distressed public housing is being replaced by smaller scale, often mixed-income housing built to a design standard that would have been condemned as excessively lavish throughout the postwar period. The federal government has also sought to reduce the extreme concentration of poverty and crime within public housing through changes in tenant eligibility criteria and far more stringent eviction policies.

For the past twenty years, the HOPE VI program has been central to the transformation of public housing. It has funded the demolition of more than 150,000 units of distressed public housing and invested $6.1 billion in the redevelopment of 247 public housing projects. In so doing, it fundamentally changed the face of public housing.[35] Originally, HOPE VI focused on the physical reconstruction of public housing and resident empowerment, seeking to replace distressed public housing projects with lower density developments and a broader income mix than before by attracting working families whose low incomes made them eligible for public housing.

The program's goals soon became broader and more ambitious, encompassing "economic integration and poverty de-concentration, 'new urbanism,' and inner-city revitalization."[36] At the same time, the institutional look of traditional public housing was replaced by low-rise structures adorned with such features as front porches, bay windows, and gabled roofs. To help overcome the physical isolation of many public housing developments, HOPE VI projects are designed to blend in with the physical fabric of the surrounding community.

To improve safety, HOPE VI developments are often designed to give residents greater control over the areas just outside their homes. Traditional public housing featured common areas such as hallways, parking lots, and undifferentiated open space in which residents were often victimized by crime; HOPE VI designs give residents private and semiprivate spaces and can minimize public spaces over which residents are less likely to exert control. HOPE VI developments are also built with a higher level of amenity than the public housing they replaced. Apartments commonly include dishwashers, central air-conditioning, washers, and dryers. Such features, commonplace in market-rate housing, make it more feasible for HOPE VI developments to attract higher income households who, unlike typical public housing residents, have more options in the housing market.

To make improved design and construction possible, the HOPE VI program authorizes development costs per unit to be higher than has been allowed for public housing in the past. "In principle," wrote the authors of a major assessment of the HOPE VI program, "these higher development costs should pay off over time, not only in terms of better quality living environments, but also in lower maintenance costs. More specifically, well-designed and constructed housing is expected to reduce vandalism and hold up better in the face of normal wear and tear."[37]

In addition to innovations in development finance and design, the HOPE VI program has also engendered changes in the management of public housing. Participating PHAs frequently contract out the management of HOPE VI sites to private management firms. Instead of management organized on a highly centralized basis, as is the case for the vast majority of public housing, most HOPE VI developments are managed independently. Each site has its own operating budget, and operating costs and performance are tracked on a project-by-project basis. This approach, commonplace in the rest of the multifamily real estate sector, is demanded by private lenders who require accountability for their investments. HOPE VI has brought public housing and its residents into the mainstream. It has created a new market of private investors and lenders that now view mixed-income and mixed-finance public housing as a good investment. Housing authorities are able to draw on their HOPE VI partnerships and experiences to advance and inform all aspects of their management, operations, design, revitalization, and leveraging strategies.

Few would disagree that HOPE VI developments represent a dramatic improvement over the distressed public housing they replaced. However, the program does not necessarily improve the lives of all the residents of the original public housing. This is true for two reasons. First, by replacing large public housing developments with smaller scale, mixed-income projects, HOPE VI developments typically have fewer public housing units than the projects they supplant. For example, the program's redevelopment grants awarded from 1993 through 2007 involved the demolition of 96,226 public housing units and the rehabilitation of 11,961 other units. These will be replaced by 111,059 units. However, only 59,674 of these new units, 45 percent of what was redeveloped, can be considered equivalent to public housing in that they receive permanent operating subsidies of the magnitude necessary to support households with very low incomes. The other replacement units will receive shallower subsidies and serve families who are not necessarily eligible for public housing, or they will receive no subsidies and serve market-rate renters or homebuyers.[38]

A second and related criticism of HOPE VI concerns the fate of public housing residents who do not get to live in the new housing developed under the program. As of September 2008, only about 24 percent of the original public housing residents had relocated to completed HOPE VI developments (17,382 households) in contrast to expectations of housing authorities that participated that 38 percent of the original residents would move back to the completed developments. Not all residents of public housing projects redeveloped under HOPE VI are eligible to reside in the new housing that replaced the old. Local housing authorities and site managers have the latitude to devise and enforce stricter tenant eligibility criteria than are typical for public housing as a whole. HOPE VI developments may exclude families with poor credit histories, with criminal records, or who do not demonstrate acceptable housekeeping skills.[39]

Many of those displaced are re-housed under other assistance programs. For example, when residents of public housing slated for demolition under HOPE VI received rental vouchers, they moved from census tracts with an average poverty rate of 61 percent to tracts with an average rate of 27 percent. Moreover, about 40 percent of those who did not return to the original HOPE VI site now live in census tracts with poverty rates of less than 20 percent. Surveys of former residents reveal relatively high satisfaction with the quality of their new homes and neighborhoods. On the other hand, these former public housing residents continue to live in predominantly minority neighborhoods. One study reported that 40 percent of the relocated voucher holders had difficulty paying rent and/or utilities in the past year—largely because Section 8 recipients, unlike public housing residents, are responsible for their utility expenses; about half said they were having difficulty affording enough food.[40]

The future of HOPE VI is uncertain. Funding for the program had dwindled to $99.8 billion in fiscal 2011, down from $135 billion the previous year. At its peak, the program received more than $200 billion annually. The Obama administration has also sought to replace HOPE VI with a new program, the "Choice Neighborhoods Initiative." Initially funded at $250 million, it would "expand on the lessons of the HOPE VI program and help revitalize neighborhoods of high poverty through transformative investments in distressed public and assisted housing and closer linkages with school reform and early childhood interventions."[41]

Rental Housing Vouchers. The largest housing subsidy program that supports the largest number of low-income Americans, some 2.2 million families, is also the most inconspicuous in that it does not involve specific buildings or "projects." Whereas public housing and subsidy programs such as the LITHC for privately owned rental housing support the construction of specific buildings, vouchers enable low-income households to obtain housing that already exists in the private market. Compared to project-based subsidies, vouchers are less expensive to administer and cost less per unit of assistance and provide access to a wider range of neighborhoods and housing. However, having a voucher does not guarantee that a low-income household will be able to use the subsidy. To succeed, the household must find an apartment that does not exceed the program's maximum allowable rent, that complies with the programs standards for physical adequacy, and whose owner is willing to participate in the program.

Although rental vouchers were first proposed in legislative debates preceding the Public Housing Act of 1937 and were often promoted in subsequent policy discussions; vouchers did not become part of US housing policy until the 1970s. The Housing Act of 1974 established the first national voucher program, which subsequent legislation revised and refocused. As first designed, the Section 8 Existing Housing program provided rental certificates to households with incomes up to 80 percent of the area median. The certificates covered the difference between 25 percent of adjusted family income (later increased to 30 percent) and Fair Market Rent (FMR). FMRs are calculated annually for more than 2,600 housing markets. FMRs vary greatly from housing market to housing market. In fiscal year 2009, the FMR for a two-bedroom apartment in the metropolitan areas of the 50 states ranged from $512 to more than three times that level in Connecticut ($1,702). The mean FMR for the fifty largest metro areas in 2009 was $1,007 for a two-bedroom apartment.

In 1983 the government established the Freestanding Voucher program, a variant of the Existing Housing program. It gave households more choice by allowing them to spend more, or less, than 30 percent of their income on rent if they so choose. The program covered the difference between 30 percent of income and a "payment standard" (which housing authorities could set higher or lower than the FMR). The program allowed participants to reside in housing that cost more than the payment standard as long as they paid for the additional rent. Households who selected units costing less than the payment standard could retain a portion of the savings, thereby paying less than 30 percent of their income on rent.

The Quality Housing and Work Responsibility Act of 1998 merged the certificate and voucher programs into a single program, renamed the Housing Choice Voucher (HCV) program. The HCV retained several aspects of the voucher program. The legislation allowed housing authorities to establish multiple payment standards within the same metropolitan area to reflect internal differences in rent levels; more expensive sections could have higher payment standards and lower cost areas could have lower payment standards. It allowed each participant to spend more than 30 percent of income on housing if needed, but no more than 40 percent. It also permitted voucher holders to take their vouchers anywhere in the country. The legislation gave property owners more latitude in deciding whether to lease apartments to voucher holders. Finally, the legislation states that extremely low-income households (earning less than 30 percent of the area's median family income) must receive at least 75 percent of all vouchers issued annually.

By 2009, vouchers assisted more than 2.2 million households, more than any other federal housing program. As a percentage of all HUD-assisted households, vouchers increased from 34 percent in 1993 to 42 percent in 2008.[42] Whereas the number of households in public housing and other project-based subsidy programs has decreased since the early 1990s, the voucher program has continued to grow, if only in fits and starts.[43] About one-quarter of this growth derived from increases in the number of new, previously unserved households that provided federal housing assistance for the first time, and three-quarters reflected transfers of households from public housing and other project-based subsidy programs to the voucher program. The latter occurs when public housing projects are downsized and redeveloped under the HOPE VI program or when owners of subsidized housing choose to prepay their federally insured mortgage or otherwise opt out of the subsidy program.

Rental vouchers offer several advantages over project-based subsidy programs. They are far less expensive per unit, potentially allowing the government to assist more households with the same amount of funding. The General Accounting Office, for example, estimates that public housing redeveloped under the HOPE VI program will cost 27 percent more than vouchers over their thirty-year life cycle, and housing in metropolitan areas financed with low-income housing tax credits cost 15 percent more, after controlling for differences in location and unit size[44]

It is also clear that vouchers provide a greater degree of residential choice than project-based subsidy programs do, enabling recipients to live in a wider array of neighborhoods. Compared to public housing especially, but also to other project-based programs, a much smaller percentage of voucher holders live in economically distressed neighborhoods. However, the voucher program is no guarantee against racial segregation. Minority voucher holders usually reside in minority neighborhoods. Moreover, the geographic distribution of affordable rental units (i.e., renting for no more than a housing authority's voucher payment standard) constrains the potential for voucher holders to access middle-class neighborhoods of any racial composition. When affordable rental units are in short supply, vouchers are of limited value in promoting opportunity.

The nation's more than thirty years of experience with vouchers also underscores fundamental limitations with this approach. Some types of households fare better than others under the program, and it is decidedly less effective in tight housing markets. Large families, the elderly, and families and individuals with special needs tend to be less successful in finding housing with vouchers than other types of households and stand to benefit from project-based subsidies. Such subsidies also enable low-income people to reside in affluent neighborhoods with few affordable units. They can also promote racial integration. In areas with very tight rental markets, project-based programs increase the supply of low-cost housing.

Finally, the growth of the voucher program over time has become something of a political liability. The cumulative increase in low-income households issued housing vouchers, combined with the provision of vouchers to residents of public housing slated for demolition and to residents of privately owned housing whose owners are opting out of federal subsidy programs, has greatly increased the cost of the voucher program in the federal budget.

STATE AND LOCAL HOUSING POLICY AND THE NONPROFIT SECTOR

The federal government is no longer the preeminent player in US housing policy. Beginning in the late 1970s, state and local governments, along with a variety of nonprofit organizations, have become increasingly important to the development and implementation of housing policy and programs. The federal government encouraged this shift through the devolution of highly centralized programs, such as public housing, giving block grants that give states and localities much more latitude to devise their own housing programs. This shift reflects the scarcity of federal housing subsidies, as well as a change in the provision of much of the remaining subsidies from a centralized, categorical approach to one based on block grants. This section will explore the landscape of state and local housing policy, focusing on the uses for which block grants and other funds are invested. It will also discuss the role of community development corporations and other nonprofit organizations as a partner to state and local governments in delivering housing assistance.

Starting in the 1980s, when the Reagan administration sharply cut back growth in federal housing expenditures, states and localities had to find new ways of addressing their increasing housing needs. They needed to tap into new funding sources and develop their own programs. Between 1980 and the early 1990s the number of state-funded housing programs increased by 177 programs and by 2006, state expenditures in this area had more than doubled to $5.15 billion. Nevertheless, total state spending on housing and community development remained modest, never reaching 1 percent of total state expenditures.

The growth in housing and community development expenditures by local governments has been far larger than state spending, approaching $37 billion, which in real terms in 2006 was more than double the total in 1981. As with the states, this increase is much less impressive in the context of total local expenditures. Housing and community developments have accounted for about 2.5 percent of total expenditures since 1991, down from 2.9 percent in the 1980s.

Over the past quarter century, state and local governments have put in place an extremely broad array of housing programs, far too many to describe in a single chapter. Indeed, entire books are written on state and local housing programs alone.[45] The objective here is to sketch out some of the chief parameters of these programs—highlighting their funding sources, the type and duration of subsidies provided, the kinds of housing activities supported, the incomes and other characteristics of the households assisted, and their strengths and limitations.

We give special attention to four of the most widespread ways by which states and local governments fund or otherwise support low- and moderate-income housing: federal block grants, bond financing, housing trust funds, and inclusionary zoning. We also briefly discuss the role of different types of nonprofit organizations in implementing housing programs at the state and local levels.

Block Grants

Community Development Block Grants. The first step in the devolution of housing and other social programs occurred with the creation of the Community Development Block Grant (CDBG) program in 1974, which replaced eight federal programs. These categorical programs, including Urban Renewal and Model Cities, required states and local governments to compete to obtain funding for specific projects and gave recipients little leeway in how the funds could be spent. In contrast, the CDBG gave states and localities much more discretion in determining how the approximately $4 billion in federal funds may be used.

In order to receive block grant funds, states and localities must prepare a consolidated plan that identifies the housing needs of the state or municipality, lays out a strategy for meeting these needs, and specifies the resources for that strategy and how it will be implemented. They allow for a wide range of activities, including acquisition, disposition, or retention of real property; rehabilitation of residential and nonresidential buildings; social services; and economic development. The few functions CDBG is explicitly prohibited from funding include public works (government buildings, schools, airports, stadiums), general government facilities (e.g., park maintenance, street repairs), and political activities. At least 70 percent of CDBG expenditures must benefit low- and moderate-income persons, defined as up to 80 percent of area median income.

The CDBG allows for a wide range of housing-related expenditures, with one restriction that prohibits local governments from using CDBG funds to construct new residential buildings, except as a "last resort." Since its inception, about 28 percent of the program's funds have gone toward housing, mostly for housing rehabilitation. Nearly three-quarters of all CDBG housing expenditures in fiscal year 2008 went to housing rehabilitation.

In summary, the CDBG program has supported a wide range of community development projects and activities, many of which involve housing. It is easily the most flexible source of federal funding for housing and community development, and an evaluation of the program concluded that it has been very effective.[46] Similarly, a more recent study of the program's neighborhood impacts in seventeen cities found that neighborhood improvements are most pronounced when CDBG spending in a neighborhood exceeds a minimum threshold—that is, when CDBG is targeted to a limited number of neighborhoods.[47]

The main criticisms of the CDBG program have to do with its income targeting and the types of projects and activities that it sometimes supports. With the income eligibility standard set at 80 percent of the median income for the metropolitan area the program may be used to benefit a wide range of city residents, not necessarily the lowest-income households. Moreover, as previously noted, up to 30 percent of an area's CDBG allocation does not need to be targeted to any income group at all. In some cases, CDBG funds have been used in ways that harm low-income households, such as when CDBG-funded urban renewal projects displace local residents.[48]

The HOME Investment Partnership Program. In 1990, Congress created a second block grant program: the HOME Investment Partnership program. HOME is the nation's largest federal block grant program that focuses exclusively on affordable housing for low- and moderate-income households. The program gives state and local governments wide latitude in choosing how the almost $2 billion in funds may be spent; however, they must be spent on housing programs and projects, and the beneficiaries of these programs and projects must be low-income households. Cities and other local governments annually receive 60 percent of HOME funding and states receive 40 percent. As with the CDBG program, HUD uses a needs-based formula to allocate HOME funds to individual jurisdictions. Congress requires that all participating states and localities allocate no less than 15 percent of their annual HOME funding to community-based nonprofit organizations (Community Housing Development Organizations, or CHDOs). Congress also mandates that participating jurisdictions provide funds from other sources to partly match their HOME allocations.

Through March 2009, the HOME program has committed more than $27.7 billion to state and local governments, assisting 1.1 million renters and homeowners. Slightly more than half of total HOME funds have supported the development of low-income rental housing. About one-quarter has involved a variety of homebuyer activities and less than one-fifth has gone toward the rehabilitation of owner-occupied homes.

The broadest range of HOME-funded programs involves homebuyer assistance. These programs include home-purchase counseling, financial assistance for down payments and other closing costs, low-interest first or second mortgages to reduce monthly carrying costs, and subsidized development of housing for owner occupancy. The latter may involve subsidized new construction of homes targeted to low- and moderate-income families or the acquisition and rehabilitation of existing homes for sale to such households.

HOME-funded projects must assist households with incomes no higher than 80 percent of an area's median income and, in the case of rental housing, no more than 50 or 65 percent of the area median. In addition to its income-eligibility requirements, the HOME program also requires that the housing it assists remain affordable for a minimum number of years. Without additional subsidies, extremely low-income households (with incomes below 30 percent of the area median) are seldom able to afford housing developed with HOME funds. By itself, HOME rarely provides the "deep subsidies" associated with public housing and rental vouchers whereby the Public Housing Authority covers the difference between the rent and a fixed percentage of the tenant's income. Instead, HOME funds are usually used to subsidize the acquisition and/or development costs of a project, thereby reducing the amount of rental income needed to cover debt-service and other operating expenses. The HOME program is often used in conjunction with the LIHTC. For example, as of 2007, about 35 percent of all rental units with support from the HOME program also benefited from the LIHTC.[49]

In summary, the HOME and CDBG programs provide states and localities with broad latitude to customize housing programs to their individual needs and priorities. The chief limitation of these block grant programs is that they seldom provide subsidies large enough to house those with extremely low incomes and the greatest need for housing assistance.

Bond Financing

Tax-Exempt Private Activity Bonds. The first housing subsidy programs initiated by state governments usually involved tax-exempt bond financing of mortgages for first-time homebuyers and for multifamily rental housing developments. By exempting interest on these bonds from federal income tax, government agencies can pay lower interest rates to investors and use the proceeds of the bonds to finance low-interest mortgages. Tax-exempt housing bonds are generally issued by state housing finance agencies. Almost all of these agencies were founded from the 1960s through the 1980s. State housing finance agencies also issue housing-related bonds and administer the federal LIHTC program and state housing trust funds.

The federal government limits the amount of tax-exempt bonds—known as private activity bonds—that a state can issue in a given year. Private activity bonds can be used for several purposes besides housing (e.g., for economic development, water and sewer services, mass transit, and student loans). In fiscal year 2009, the maximum amount of private activity bonds a state could issue was $90 per state resident, translating into about $26 billion for the nation as a whole. In 2007, a statewide bonding authority ranged in size from $256.2 million for the smallest states to $3.1 billion for California.

The financial crisis that began in 2008 has severely impaired the market for tax-exempt bonds, making it extremely difficult for housing finance agencies to issue bonds at interest rates that are low enough to offer below-market-rate financing for housing. Even though the economic stimulus bill of 2008 gave states the capacity to issue $11 billion in additional housing bonds, the economic crisis rendered this resource nearly useless, and many "HFAs have been forced to curtail their lending significantly, while some have suspended lending altogether."[50]

Mortgage Revenue Bonds. Mortgage revenue bonds enable low- and moderate-income households to become homeowners for the first time by obtaining below-market-rate interest mortgages. Through 2007, state housing finance agencies had issued nearly $234 billion in these bonds, which have been used to finance more than 2.7 million mortgages. In 2007, these agencies issued $17.8 billion in bonds and closed more than 126,000 mortgage loans, and the median annual income of homebuyers using these mortgages was $36,806.[51]

Multifamily Housing Bonds. Although most multifamily bonds are tax-exempt, many states also issue taxable bonds, which are not subject to an annual volume cap. In 2007, for example, tax-exempt multifamily bond issues for new acquisition and/or development of new rental housing totaled $3.3 billion while taxable bond issues amounted to $555 million. Rental housing financed with multifamily bonds frequently receives additional subsidies as well. In 2007, 77 percent of all bond-financed rental housing also received the LIHTC and in fourteen states every bond-financed project also had tax credits.[52] Other common subsidy sources include HOME block grants, HOPE VI funds, and various forms of credit enhancement.

Federal regulations require that a minimum percentage of the units financed with tax-exempt bonds be occupied by low-income residents. As with housing funded with LIHTCs, households with incomes of up to 60 percent of the area median income must occupy at least 40 percent of the bond-financed property's units, or households with income of 50 percent or less of the median income must occupy 20 percent of the units. Of the 35,000 bond-financed units put in service in 2007, more than 82 percent went to families with incomes of 60 percent or less of the area median, including 28 percent to families earning less than 50 percent of median.

Housing Trust Funds

Housing trust funds are typically established with a dedicated funding source, and they are targeted to low- and moderate-income households. States, counties, and cities have established nearly 600 such trust funds, generating more than $1.6 billion annually for many types of housing assistance. Trust funds provide a flexible form of funding to help address local housing needs. Because they are based on revenue sources under the control of state and local governments, trust funds generally have far fewer restrictions on how they can be used than is the case for federal housing programs, even block grant programs. Trust funds are usually administered by governmental or quasi-governmental agencies operating under the guidance of a broad-based oversight board. With representation from banks, realtors, for-profit and nonprofit housing developers, advocacy organizations, labor unions, service providers, and low-income residents, these boards usually play an advisory role, though some have formal responsibilities in governing the funds, including the selection of the projects to receive funding from the trust funds. The first trust funds were created in the late 1970s, and the number of such trusts has been growing exponentially since.[53]

In total, housing trust funds generated about $1.6 billion annually as of 2006. State trust funds accounted for about 80 percent of this amount and city trust funds 17 percent. Housing trust funds support many different types of housing programs. They include new construction and the acquisition and rehabilitation of existing structures. Almost all trust funds are targeted to low- or moderate-income households. The most common designation is for households earning 80 percent of the area median income, although many trust funds target lower-income groups for at least some programs. About one in four trust funds focuses exclusively on the homeless or on other households with incomes below 50 percent of the median income.

While housing trust funds are an increasingly popular way of addressing local housing needs, it is important to recognize their limitations:

- Trust funds seldom provide the depth of subsidy associated with public housing and housing choice rental vouchers. Consequently, trust funds may not serve very low-income households.
- Although most trust funds require that the affordability of the housing they assist be preserved for a minimum period of time, these requirements often fall short of those imposed by federal housing programs.
- Trust funds are not ubiquitous; they are more prevalent in some states and regions than in others, thereby limiting their ability to meet the nation's housing needs.
- When they rely their basic funding on a highly volatile source of revenues such as deed recordation and transfer taxes, the ability of developers as well as city officials to systematically develop an affordable housing strategy is undermined. This is a particularly problematic matter if, when the volatile revenue flow is at a peak, the revenues are securitized and then committed to "projects in the pipeline" without regard for planning for the time when trust fund revenues will suddenly decline during an economic downturn.[54]

Inclusionary Zoning

Inclusionary zoning is used by a growing number of localities to increase the supply of "affordable" housing. It requires or encourages developers to designate a portion of the housing they produce for low- or moderate-income households.

For example, a developer building a 100-unit residential complex might be required to reserve twenty of these homes for families of modest means. Inclusionary zoning is appealing for two main reasons.

First, its ability to increase the supply of affordable housing as well as to promote economic diversity within affluent communities—enabling lower-income households to reside in areas with very little affordable housing; second, because it appears to have no public sector budgetary impact. Second, this type of zoning can take on many different forms, including mandatory requirements and voluntary inducements.

Localities differ widely in the amount of affordable housing they require private developers to build, the incomes of the targeted populations, and the length of time that units must remain affordable. As of 2004, about 600 mostly suburban communities had instituted some form of inclusionary zoning. The vast majority of these localities are in New Jersey, California, and Massachusetts, which require municipalities to address a portion of their region's housing needs. They commonly rely on inclusionary zoning to satisfy these requirements, in large part because it involves minimal direct public expenditures, even if the regulations place an implicit tax on developers.

Until the late 1990s, inclusionary zoning was overwhelmingly a suburban phenomenon, limited mostly to affluent suburbs with vibrant housing markets. In recent years, however, this zoning has been adopted by a growing number of cities, Inclusionary zoning ranks among the most popular means of producing affordable housing. It generates low- and moderate-income housing with little if any public expenditure and it increases the economic diversity within affluent communities. However, inclusionary zoning's accomplishments to date fall far short of such potential. Porter estimated that as of about 2003, inclusionary programs have produced 80,000 to 90,000 new housing units nationally, with about 65,000 located in states that mandate the provision of affordable housing (e.g., California, New Jersey).[55]

To sum up, local governments are increasingly turning to inclusionary zoning as one of several tools to help address their need for affordable housing. Although its ability to produce affordable housing with minimal explicit public subsidy makes it very appealing, inclusionary zoning as applied in most places is seldom able to meet more than a fraction of the need for low-cost housing. It also is not as free as it appears to be. It relies on implicit taxes and charging fees for services that in many ways concentrate the costs of subsidies on a limited tax base. Moreover, the amount of affordable housing produced through inclusionary zoning is directly tied to the volume of market-rate residential construction. Inclusionary zoning can be highly effective in communities with robust housing markets, but ineffective in areas with minimal amounts of new construction. Finally, for inclusionary zoning to provide housing affordable to very low-income households, additional sources of subsidy are almost always necessary.

Nonprofits and State and Local Programs. It is impossible to discuss the rise of state and local housing programs in isolation from the parallel growth of the nonprofit housing sector. Although state and local governments have devised numerous housing programs and established new sources of program funding, government agencies seldom build or renovate housing or provide other housing services directly. Instead, they partner with other groups to carry out these programs. In many places these organizations are often nonprofits. Frequently the relationship between government agencies and nonprofit housing groups is so close that, as Goetz puts it, "the distinction of the 'success' of the local public agency and the 'success' of the [nonprofit] becomes blurred."[56]

Nonprofit housing producers appeal to state and local governments for at least three reasons. First, most nonprofit housing groups are committed to keeping their housing affordable to low-income households indefinitely and, unlike many of their for-profit counterparts, have no desire to reap capital gains from the sale of the property or eventually to charge market-rate rents. Indeed, their nonprofit status derives from the fact that even though the developer must make "profits" to stay in business, those moneys must, by law, be plowed back into the business (e.g., there is no distribution of dividends to shareholders).

Second, nonprofits are often committed to serving the poorest, most needy families and provide an array of supportive services beyond housing—including employment counseling, child care, education, and more. Finally, nonprofits are sometimes the only groups willing or able to construct or rehabilitate housing in the toughest urban neighborhoods.[57]

The importance of the nonprofit sector is reflected in the requirement imposed by several major housing programs that state and local governments designate a minimum percentage of their funding to nonprofit housing groups—a percentage frequently exceeded by wide margins. Each state must assign at least 10 percent of its annual LIHTCs to housing developed by nonprofit organizations. The HOME program, as noted earlier, requires state and local governments to earmark at least 15 percent of their block grants to nonprofit CHDOs. Recognizing the importance of the nonprofit sector to the development of affordable housing, many state and local housing trust funds support the operations of these groups by providing funds for predevelopment costs, organizational capacity building, and administrative costs.

Although the present generation of nonprofit housing groups is quite diverse, varying widely in size and in the scope of services they provide, housing is integral to their work. In total, nonprofit organizations have produced nearly 1.5 million housing units for low- and moderate-income households, and they account for nearly one-third of all federally subsidized housing.

At risk of overgeneralization, it is useful to distinguish three types of nonprofit housing organizations. These categories include (1) community development corporations; (2) large citywide or regional nonprofit organizations; and (3) nonprofit providers of supportive housing for the homeless and others with special needs. Although the categories overlap to some extent, they cover most of the nonprofit housing landscape. We discuss only the first type, which probably accounts for the largest share of such housing provisions.[58]

Community Development Corporations (CDCs). These were first formed in the 1960s with support from the federal government and the Ford Foundation, but they were established in much larger numbers over the next thirty years. They focus largely on the housing and other needs of individual neighborhoods. Many also work in economic development, workforce development, and a variety of social services. According to one estimate, in 2005 there were 4,600 CDCs in operation. Collectively, by 2007 they had built or renovated 1.6 million units of low- and moderate-income housing since the 1960s. CDCs produced more than 96,000 units annually from 2005 to 2007, compared to about 62,000 from 1994 to 1998.[59]

CDCs perform many housing-related activities in addition to housing development. In the area of housing alone, many CDCs engage in homebuyer counseling, tenant counseling, homeless services, acquisition of existing housing, home repairs, and assistance with home-purchase financing. Outside the housing arena, some of the most common CDC activities include economic development, commercial real estate development, advocacy and community organizing, youth programs, job training and placement, homeless services, and emergency food assistance.

As of 2005, nearly 90 percent of all CDCs received at least $50,000 from federal programs—especially CDBG, HOME, and the LIHTC. From 1992 through 2008, state and local governments have designated an average of 21 percent of their HOME block grants for projects involving CDCs; this is well above the minimum allocation of 15 percent. Similarly, nonprofit organizations, including CDCs and others, account for more than 23 percent of all tax-credit developments put in service through 2006—far above the minimum requirement of 10 percent.

A number of studies have shown the challenges that CDCs confront:[60]

- **The need for multiple funding sources.** Most affordable housing projects require CDCs (and other developers) to assemble several sources of financing in order to underwrite a project. For example, a frequently cited study of CDC-sponsored housing developments found that the typical project received financing from an average of nearly eight separate sources.[61]
- **Undercapitalization.** Closely related to the need for multiple funding sources is the tendency for development projects to be undercapitalized— that is, underwritten with very narrow margins. Tight development budgets make it more difficult and costly to sustain the housing in the long term.
- **Financial Uncertainty.** Lack of long-term operating support causes CDCs to struggle to obtain funds to cover staff salaries and other operating expenses. In the absence of multiyear operating support, CDCs depend on short-term grants and development fees and other sources of revenue. Dependence on development fees is particularly risky because it requires a steady if not increasing flow of development projects from year to year. Relatedly, the long-term viability of CDC housing is of growing concern. The difficulties of providing affordable rental housing to low-income households do not stop with the completion of construction. Effective property and asset management are essential for sustaining the housing over the long haul.

In order to meet these challenges, CDCs solicit support from several sources in government, philanthropy, and elsewhere. Without this system, CDCs would be hard pressed to access the financial and technical resources essential for housing development and management. The single most important element of this support system is the national intermediaries: Enterprise Community Partners (until 2006, known as the Enterprise Foundation); the Local Initiatives Support Corporation (LISC); and Neighbor Works America (officially the Neighborhood Reinvestment Corporation). The Enterprise Foundation and the LISC provide a wide array of financial and technical assistance to hundreds of CDCs throughout the nation. They provide equity for rental housing development by syndicating LIHTCs and loans and grants to cover site acquisition and other predevelopment costs. They also provide training and professional development.

Since 1980, the LISC has helped 2,400 CDCs in more than 300 urban and rural communities construct or rehabilitate more than 244,000 low- and moderate-income housing units. In 2008, the LISC provided $49.5 million in grants to CDCs and raised $529 million in tax-credit equity for CDC development projects. From its founding in 1981 through 2007, Enterprise has raised on the order of $8 billion to help 2,500 nonprofit groups build over 200,000 units of affordable housing. In 2007, the organization provided $1 billion in grants, loans, and equity to nonprofit community developers and helped create or preserve more than 25,000 units of affordable housing.

CONCLUSION

To sum up, most of the innovation in housing policy since the 1980s has taken place subnationally, often in collaboration with the nonprofit sector. Most of the new housing built for low- and moderate-income families and individuals has been supported through state and local programs; direct federal funding has gone mostly to the preservation of subsidized housing built before the mid-1980s and for rental vouchers. However, much of the housing built and renovated by states and localities is funded with federal resources, including block grants (HOME and CDBG), LIHTCs, and tax-exempt bonds. With the notable exception of New York City, few places have drawn from their own resources (general revenue, capital budgets) to support the production or preservation of affordable housing. Additional funding for affordable housing often derives from housing trust funds, which are typically supported through fees generated from real estate transactions and from inclusionary zoning, which usually creates incentives or requirements for private developers to produce affordable housing.

State and local governments often have greater flexibility than federal agencies in designing programs more closely attuned to the needs of specific places and populations. However, state and local programs rarely offer the deep subsidies provided by federal programs that make it possible to house very low-income families.[62] Moreover, the resources that are available for state and local programs often depend on the strength of the local housing market, as in the case of housing trust funds and inclusionary zoning. Developments funded through state and local programs can seldom accommodate very low-income households unless they can pay much more than 30 percent of their income on rent. Moreover, few state and local programs will reduce rents when tenant income declines, as is routine with public housing and rental vouchers. Indeed, when very low-income families do reside in housing built through state and local programs—including the LIHTC— they usually receive federal rental vouchers or other additional subsidies. It does not appear, in other words, that state and local governments, working in concert with nonprofit housing groups, will ever be able to serve the neediest households without additional federal assistance.

The structure of US housing policy has changed considerably in the past quarter century and perhaps even more deeply in the past few years during the economic crisis. Subnational governments and nonprofits have grown from having low levels of activity to now providing more than $20 billion annually. At the same time, a large portion of the HUD's budget goes not to the expansion of affordable housing programs but to continuation of existing subsidies. In many ways, this sort of shift is appropriate. It recognizes the highly idiosyncratic nature of housing markets. In housing policy one size indeed does not fit all. Nor does the growth in subnational government involvement in housing assistance, for the most part, violate norms as to which level of government has a comparative advantage in providing subsidies. Most of these subnational expenditures are distributed from the federal government to lower tiers of government. In short, a great deal of innovation in addressing the housing problems of the poor has been developed.

However, the overall policy environment leaves much to be desired. Most fundamentally, housing assistance provided locally, whether it consists of federal block grants, tax credits, or locally funded programs, rarely provides a depth of subsidy sufficient for the poorest households—the population in greatest need of affordable housing. Most often, low-income households fortunate enough to receive federal rental vouchers are the only ones able to afford housing produced through state and local programs. But federal subsidy programs provide assistance for only 25 percent of the eligible population. As a result, the majority of low-income renters pay far more for housing than they can afford. Meanwhile, the federal government provides more than $150 billion annually in mortgage interest deductions and other tax benefits for homeowners, of whom at least half earn more than $100,000 annually. Moreover, local housing assistance increased, and locally imposed implicit taxes on the housing costs and availability for the poor also went up. Land-use controls, zoning ordinances, and a variety of impediments to developing multifamily housing make housing less affordable for the poor.

As a result of this badly structured overall policy environment, there is a nationwide surfeit of housing while housing costs are a severe and increasing burden, and housing availability for many of the poor is extremely limited. Much more can be done at the local level to lower these costs and increase housing availability for the poor, and, for many of the most important policy changes, state and local government action at the local level will be the key to improving conditions. Much more could also be done to make the distribution of housing subsidies less regressively distributed. In the end, it would indeed be surprising if the complicated, multilayered system of providing housing assistance does not undergo significant changes in the coming years, particularly in light of the enormous problems that arose in the sector in the recent financial crisis and economic downturn. However, without a clear understanding of the directions that will be taken on national tax, finance and housing policy, it is impossible to discern how subnational housing policy will evolve.

Notes

We would like to thank Skye Dobson for help in preparing the chapter.

1 Penner (this volume).
2 For more detail on programmatic detail and the quantification of what are often complicated programs and trends, see Schwartz (2010).
3 Housing programs for the homeless, elderly, and other populations with special needs are not discussed.
4 Van Vliet (1998).
5 See Flavin and Yamashia (2002) for recent evidence of this long-term and common condition in developed economies. See also Joint Center for Housing Studies (2009), 13–15.
6 Bratt (2000).
7 US Census Bureau (2010). For further detail on the dramatic decline of the national economy during the "Great Recession," see Francis (this volume).
8 Glaeser (2010)
9 Ibid.
10 Ibid.
11 The statistics on housing characteristics are from Schwartz (2010).
12 Quigley (2010).
13 Tilly (2006).
14 According to the Joint Center for Housing Studies (2009: 25), renter real income decreased by 28% while the median gross rent increased by 9 percent from 1998 to 2008.
15 US Department of Housing and Urban Development (2007), table A-13. See also Schwartz (2010), 35–38.
16 Joint Center for Housing Studies (2009), 26.
17 Schwartz (2010), 39.
18 Glaeser (2010).
19 Quigley (2001).
20 US Department of Housing and Urban Development (2010).
21 Ibid.
22 *United States v. Certain Lands in the City of Louisville.* See Hays (1995).
23 Schwartz (2010).
24 National Low Income Housing Coalition (2011).
25 See Schwartz (2010) for information on these programs and citations for many of the empirical findings presented here.

26 Poterba and Sinai (2008).

27 The mortgage interest deduction was over $79 billion, that of deductibility of state and local property taxes ($29 billion), the exclusion of imputed income ($27 billion), and capital gains exclusion (over $23 billion).

28 Until 2008 when Fannie Mae and Freddie Mac collapsed, the HUD also had regulatory authority over these institutions. The multibillion-dollar financial collapse of these institutions in 2009 provides a sense of the scale of federal support for homeownership.

29 Schwartz (2010), 90.

30 Ernst and Young (2007).

31 Stegman (1992), 363.

32 Schwartz and Melendez (2008).

33 See Burman and McFarland (2005) for further discussion of this issue.

34 Schwartz (2010).

35 Ibid.

36 Popkin et al. (2005) 14; Cisneros and Engdahl (2009).

37 Popkin et al (2005), 21.

38 Ibid.; Kingsley (2009).

39 Schwartz (2010).

40 Popkin et al. (2005), 30.

41 US Department of Housing and Urban Development (2009).

42 National Low Income Housing Coalition (2011).

43 Congress provided no funding for additional vouchers from fiscal years 1995 through 1998 and again from fiscal years 2003 through 2007. In total, the number of voucher holders has increased by 630,000 since fiscal year 1995.

44 US General Accounting Office (2002).

45 See, for example Goetz (1993); Stegman (1999); Keating & Krumholz (1999).

46 Walker et al. (1994).

47 Galster et al. (2004); see also Walker et al. (2002).

48 Gramlich (1998).

49 Schwartz (2010).

50 Thompson (2009).

51 National Council of State Housing Finance Agencies (2009).

52 Ibid.

53 Municipal and county trust funds are often established in response to state legislation designed to promote local trust funds. Thus, 250 of the 432 municipal trust funds identified in the Center for Community Change survey were established in New Jersey after the state passed legislation in 1992 that enabled localities to charge fees on private real estate development. Similarly, most of the eighty-two countywide housing trust funds were created in Pennsylvania after the state passed the 1992 Optional Affordable Housing Trust Fund Act. See Brooks (2007), 16.

54 Sexton (2010); Ebel (2010).

55 Porter (2004), 241.

56 Goetz (1993), 130.

57 Keyes et al. (1996).

58 See Schwartz (2010) for discussion of the other two approaches.

59 National Alliance of Community Economic Development Associations (2010).

60 Walker (1993); Goetz (1993); Stoutland (1999).

61 Hebert et al. (1993).

62 Mueller and Schwartz (2008); Pelletiere, Canzio et al. (2008).

References

Bostic, R. W., and B. L. Robinson (2003). "Do CRA Agreements Influence Lending Patterns?" *Real Estate Economics* 31(1): 23–51.

Bratt, R. G. (1992). "Federal Constraints and Retrenchment in Housing: The Opportunities and Limits of State and Local Governments." *The Journal of Law and Politics* 8(4): 651–699.

Bratt, R. G. (2000). "Housing and Family Well-Being." *Housing Studies* 17(1): 12–26.

Briggs, X. de S. (1998). "Brown Kids in White Suburbs: Housing Mobility and the Many Faces of Social Capital." *Housing Policy Debate* 9(1): 177–222.

Briggs, X. de S., S. J. Popkin, and J. Goering (2010). *Moving to Opportunity: The Story of an American Experiment to Fight Ghetto Poverty.* New York: Oxford University Press.

Brooks, M.E. (2007). Housing Trust Fund Progress Report 2007. Washington, DC: Center for Community Change. http://www.communitychange.org/our-projects/htf/our-projects/htf/other-media/HTF%2007%20final.pdf.

Burman, Leonard E., and Alastair McFarlane (2005). "Low-Income Housing Credit." In *The Encyclopedia of Taxation and Tax Policy*, edited by Joseph J. Cordes, Robert D. Ebel, and Jane G. Gravelle. 2nd ed. Washington, DC: The Urban Institute Press. 242–244.

Carliner, M. (1998). "Development of Federal Homeownership 'Policy.'" *Housing Policy Debate* 9(2): 299–321. http://www.mi.vt.edu/data/fi les/hpd%209(2)/hpd%209(2)_carliner.pdf.

Carr, J. H., and N. K. Kutty (Eds.) (2008). *Segregation: The Rising Costs for America.* New York: Routledge.

Case, K. E., and M. Marynchenko (2002). "Home Price Appreciation in Low- and Moderate-Income Markets." In *Low Income Homeownership: Examining the Unexamined Goal*, edited by N. E Retsinas and E. S. Belsky. Washington, DC: Brookings Institution Press. 239–256.

Cisneros, H. G., and L. Engdahl (Eds.) (2009). *From Despair to Hope: Hope VI and the New Promise of Public Housing in America's Cities.* Washington, DC: Brookings Institution.

Committee on Ways and Means, US House of Representatives (2008). *2008 Greenbook: Background Material and Data on the Programs within the Jurisdiction of the Committee on Ways and Means.* Washington, DC: US Government Printing Office.

Cummings, J. L., and D. DiPasquale (1999). The Low Income Housing Tax Credit: An Analysis of the First 10 Years. *Housing Policy Debate* 10(2): 251–307.

Davis, J. E. (2006). "Beyond Devolution and the Deep Blue Sea: What's a City or State to Do?" In *A Right to Housing: Foundation for a New Social Agenda*, edited by R. G. Bratt, M. E. Stone, and C. Hartman. Philadelphia: Temple University Press. 364–398.

DiPasquale, D., and J. L. Cummings (1992). "Financing Multifamily Rental Housing: The Changing Role of Lenders and Investors." *Housing Policy Debate* 3(1): 77–117.

DiPasquale, D., and M. Murray (2009). *The Evolution of Metropolitan Housing Affordability.* Bates College, Lewiston, Maine.

Ebel, Robert D. (2010). "Taxing Property Transactions: Commentary." In *Challenging the Conventional Wisdom on the Property Tax*, edited by Roy Bahl, Jorge Martinez-Vazquez, and Joan Youngman. Cambridge, MA: Lincoln Institute of Land Policy. 235–239.

Ernst and Young (2007). *Understanding the Dynamics IV: Housing Tax Credit Investment and Performance*. Washington, DC: Ernst and Young.

Flavin, M., and T. Yamashita (2002, March). "Owner-Occupied Housing and the Composition of the Household Portfolio." *American Economic Review* 92(1): 345–362.

Galster, G. C. (1997). "Comparing Demand-Side and Supply-Side Housing Policies: Submarket and Spatial Perspectives." *Housing Studies* 12(4): 561–577.

Galster, G., C., Walter, C. Hayes, E Boxall, and J. Johnson (2004). "Measuring the Impact of Community Development Block Grant Spending on Urban Neighborhoods." *Housing Policy Debate* 15 (4): 903–934.

GAO (US General Accounting Office) (1997). "Tax Credits: Opportunities to Improve the Low Income Housing Program." Washington, DC: GAO/GGD/RCED-97-55. http://www.gao.gov/archive/1997/g597055.pdf.

Glaeser, E. (2010). "Rethinking the Federal Bias towards Homeownership." Draft manuscript, Harvard University.

Glaeser, E., and J. Gyourko (2008). *Rethinking Federal Housing Policy: How to Make Housing Plentiful and Affordable*. Washington, DC: American Enterprise Institute.

Goetz, E. G. (1993). *Shelter Burden: Local Politics and Progressive Housing Policy*. Philadelphia: Temple University Press.

Goetz, E. G. (2003). *Clearing the Way: Deconcentrating the Poor in Urban America*. Washington, DC: Urban Institute Press.

Gramlich, E. (1998). "CDBG: An Action Guide to the Community Development Block Grant Program." Washington, DC: Center for Community Change. http://www.communitychange.org/shared/publications/downloads/CDBG.pdf.

Gramlich, E. (2007). *Subprime Mortgages: America's Latest Boom and Bust*. Washington, DC: Urban Institute.

Hays, A. (1995). *The Federal Government and Urban Housing*. 2nd ed. Albany: State University of New York Press.

Hebert, S., K. Heintz, C. Baron, N. Kay, & J.E. Wallace (1993). *Nonprofit Housing: Costs and Benefits. Final Report*. Washington, DC. Report prepared by Abt Associates, Inc., with Aspen Systems, Inc., for U.S. Department of Housing and Urban Development, Office of Policy Development and Research.

Joint Center for Housing Studies of Harvard University (2009). *State of the Nation's Housing 2009*. Cambridge, MA: Author. http://www.jchs.harvard.edu/publications/markets/son2009/son2009.pdf.

Keating, W. D., and N. Krumholz (1999). *Rebuilding Urban Neighborhoods: Achievements, Opportunities, and Limits*. Thousand Oaks, CA: Sage.

Keyes, L., A Schwartz, A. Vidal, and R Bratt (1996). "Networks and Nonprofits: Opportunities and Challenges in an Era of Federal Devolution." *Housing Policy Debate* 7(2): 201–229.

Khadduri, J., K. Burnett, and D. Rodda (2003). *Targeting Housing Production Subsidies: Literature Review*. Washington, DC: Abt Associates for US Department of Housing and Urban Development, Office of Policy Development and Research. http://www.huduser.org/Publications/pdf/TargetingLitReview.pdf.

Kingsley, G. T. (2009). "Appendix." In *From Despair to Hope: Hope VI and the New Promise of Public Housing in America's Cities*, edited by H. G. Cisneros & L. Engdahl. Washington, DC: Brookings Institution Press. 299-306.

Malpezzi, S. (1990). "Urban Housing and Financial Markets: Some International Comparisons." *Urban Studies* 27: 971–1022.

Mandelker, D. R., and H. A. Ellis (1998). "Exclusionary Zoning." In *The Encyclopedia of Housing*, edited by W. van Vliet. Thousand Oaks, CA: Sage. 160–161.

Marcuse, P. (1986). "Housing Policy and the Myth of the Benevolent State." In *Critical Perspectives on Housing*, edited by R. G. Bratt, C. Hartman, and A. Myerson. Philadelphia: Temple University Press. Chap. 14.

Melendez, E., and L. Servon (2008). "Reassessing the Role of Housing in Community-Based Urban Development." *Housing Policy Debate* 18(4): 751–783.

Mueller, E. J., and Schwartz, A. (2008) "Reversing the Tide: Will State and Local Governments House the Poor as Federal Direct Subsidies Decline?" *Journal of the American Planning Association* 74 (1): 122–135.

National Alliance of Community Economic Development Associations (2010). *Rising Above: Community Economic Development in a Changing Landscape*. Washington, DC: Author. http://naceda.org/pdfs/census-report-2010.pdf.

National Council of State Housing Finance Agencies (2009). *State HFA Factbook*. Washington, DC: Author.

National Low Income Housing Coalition (2011). "FY11 Budget Chart for Selected HUD Programs." Washington, DC: National Low Income Housing Coalition. http://www.nlihc.org/doc/FY11-Budget-Chart.pdf.

Nelson, K. P. (1992), "Housing Assistance Needs and the Housing Stock." *Journal of the American Planning Association* 58:85–102.

Nenno, M. K. (1998b). "State Governments." In *The Encyclopedia of Housing*, edited by W. van Vliet. Thousand Oaks, CA: Sage. 556–559.

Newman, S. J. (2008). "Does Housing Matter for Poor Families? A Critical Summary of Research and Issues Still to Be Resolved." *Journal of Policy Analysis and Management* 27(8): 895–925.

Newman, S. J., and A. B. Schnare (1997). "'...And a Suitable Living Environment': The Failure of Housing Programs to Deliver on Neighborhood Quality." *Housing Policy Debate* 8(4): 703–741. http://www.mi.vt.edu/data/files/hpd%208(4)/hpd%208(4)_newman.pdf.

Olsen, E. O. (1987). "The Demand and Supply of Housing Services: A Critical Review of the Empirical Literature." In *Handbook of Regional and Urban Economics*, vol. 2, edited by E. S. Mills. Amsterdam: Elsevier.

Olsen, E. O. (2001). *Housing Programs for Low-Income Households*. Working Paper 8208. Cambridge, MA: National Bureau of Economic Research.

Pelletiere, D. M. Canizio, M. Hargrave, and S. Crowley (2008). "Housing Assistance for Low Income Households: States Do Not Fill the Gap. Washington, D.C: National Low Income Housing Coalition.

Popkin, S. J., M. K. Cunningham, and M. Burt (2005). "Public Housing Transformation and the Hard to House." *Housing Policy Debate* 16(1): 1–24.

Porter, D. R. (2004). "The Promise and Practice of Inclusionary Zoning. In *Growth Management and Affordable Housing: Do They Conflict?* edited by A. Downs. Washington, DC: The Brookings Institution. Chap. 6.

Poterba, J., and T. Sinai (2008). "Tax Expenditures for Owner-Occupied Housing: Deductions for Property Taxes and Mortgage Interest and the Exclusion of Imputed Rental Income." *American Economic Review* 98 (2): 84–89.

Quigley, J. (2010, April). "Rental Assistance?" Paper prepared for the HUD Conference on Rental Housing. Washington DC.

Quigley, J. M., and S. Raphael (2004). "Is Housing Unaffordable? Why Isn't It More Affordable?" *Journal of Economic Perspectives* 18(1): 191–214.

Quigley, J., S. Raphael, and E. Smolensky (2001). "Homelessness in America, Homelessness in California." *Review of Economics and Statistics* 83(1): 37–51.

Retsinas, N. P., and E. S. Belsky (Eds.) (2002). *Low-Income Homeownership: Examining the Unexamined Goal.* Washington, DC: Brookings Institution Press.

Savage, H. A. (2009). *Who Could Afford to Buy a House in 2004?* Washington, DC: Census Housing Reports, H21/09–1. http://www.census.gov/prod/2009pubs/h121–09–01.pdf.

Schnare, A. B. (2001). "The Impact of Changes in Multifamily Housing Finance on Older Urban Areas." Discussion paper prepared for the Brookings Institution Center on Urban and Metropolitan Policy and the Harvard Joint Center for Housing Studies. http://www.brook.edu/es/urban/schnarefi nal.pdf.

Schuetz, J., R. Meltzer, and V. Been (2007, November 19). "The Effects of Inclusionary Zoning on Local Housing Markets: Lessons from the San Francisco, Washington DC and Suburban Boston Areas." Working paper. New York: New York University, Furman Center for Real Estate and Urban Policy. http://www.nhc.org/pdf/pub_chp_iz_08.pdf.

Schwartz, A. 1998. "Bank Lending to Minority and Low-Income Households and Neighborhoods: Do Community Reinvestment Act Agreements Make a Difference?" *Journal of Urban Affairs* 20: 269–301.

Schwartz, A. (2010). *Housing Policy in the United States: 2nd Edition.* New York: Routledge.

Schwartz, A., and E. Melendez (2008). "After Year 15: Challenges to the Preservation of Housing Financed with Low Income Housing Tax Credits." *Housing Policy Debate* 19(2): 261–294.

Sexton, Terry (2010). "Taxing Property Transactions Versus Taxing Property Ownership." In *Challenging the Conventional Wisdom on the Property Tax,* edited by Roy Bahl, Jorge Martinez-Vazquez, and Joan Youngman. Cambridge, MA: Lincoln Institute of Land Policy. 207–234.

Stegman, M. (1990). "The Role of Public Housing in a Revitalized National Housing Policy." In *Building Foundations: Housing and Federal Policy,* edited by D. DiPasquale and L.C. Keyes. Philadelphia: University of Pennsylvania Press. Chap. 13.

Stegman, M. A. (1992). "The Excessive Costs of Creative Finance: Growing Inefficiencies in the Production of Low-Income Housing." *Housing Policy Debate* 2(2): 357–373.

Stegman, M. A. (1999). *State and Local Housing Programs: A Rich Tapestry.* Washington, DC: Urban Land Institute.

Stoutland, S. (1999). Community Development Corporations: Mission, Strategy, and Accomplishments. In Urban Problems and Community Development, edited by R. F. Ferguson and W. T. Dickens. Washington, DC: Brookings Institution Press. Chap. 5.

Terner, I. D., and T. B. Cook (1990). "New Directions for Federal Housing Policy: The Role of the States." In *Building Foundations,* edited by D. DiPasquale and L. C. Keyes. Philadelphia: University of Pennsylvania Press. 13–35.

Thompson, B. (2009, February 3). Letter to U.S. Treasury Secretary Timothy Geithner. http://www.homemeanseverything.org/assets/NCSHALetterSecGeithner.pdf.

Tilly, Chris (2006). "The Economic Environment of Housing: Income Inequality and Insecurity." In *A Right to Housing,* edited by R. Bratt, M. Stone, and C. Hartman. Philadelphia: Temple University Press. 20–37.

Turner, M. A. (1998). "Moving Out of Poverty: Expanding Mobility and Choice through Tenant Based Housing Assistance." *Housing Policy Debate* 9(2): 373–394.

Turner, M. A., and G. T. Kingsley (2008). *Federal Programs for Addressing Low-Income Housing Needs: A Policy Primer*. Washington, DC: Urban Institute. http://www.urban.org/Uploaded-PDF/411798_low-income_housing.pdf.

US Census Bureau (2010). "New Privately Owned Housing Starts in the United States by Design and Purpose." http://www.census.gov/const/www/newresconstindex.html.

US Department of Housing and Urban Development (2007). *Affordable Housing Needs 2005: Report to Congress*. Washington, DC.

US Department of Housing and Urban Development (2009). FY2010 Budget: Road map for transformation. http://www.hud.gov/budgetsummary2010/fy10budget.pdf.

US Department of Housing and Urban Development, (2010). *First Annual Homelessness Assessment Report*. Washington, DC: Author.

US Department of Housing and Urban Development (2011). *Worst Case Housing Needs 2009: Report to Congress*. Washington, DC: Author.

US Department of Housing and Urban Development, Office of Community Planning and Development (2010). *The 2009 Annual Homeless Report to Congress*. Washington, DC: Author. http://www.hudhre.info/documents/5thHomelessAssessmentReport.pdf.

US General Accounting Office (2002a). "Federal Housing Assistance: Comparing the Characteristics and Costs of Housing Programs." Washington, DC: GAO-02-76. http://www.gao.gov/new.items/d0276.pdf.

Walker, C. (1993). "Nonprofit Housing Development: Status, Trends, and Prospects." *Housing Policy Debate* 4 (3): 369–414.

Walker, C., P. Dommel, A. Bogdon, H. Hatry, P Boxall, A. Abramson, R. Smith, and J. Silver (1994). "Federal Funds, Local Choices: An Evaluation of the Community Development Block Grant Program." Washington DC. Report prepared by The Urban Institute for the U.S. Department of Housing and Urban Development, Office of Policy Development and Research.

Walker, C., C. Hayes, G. Galster, P. Boxall, & J. Johnson (2002). "The Impact of CDBG Spending on Urban Neighborhoods." Washington, DC. Report prepared by The Urban Institute for the U.S. Department of Housing and Urban Development, Office of Policy Development and Research.

van Vliet, W. (1998). "Editor's Introduction." In *The Encyclopedia of Housing*, edited by W van Vliet. Thousand Oaks, CA: Sage.

Winnick, L. (1995). "The Triumph of Housing Allowance Programs: How a Fundamental Policy Conflict Was Resolved." *Cityscape: A Journal of Policy Development and Research* 1(3): 95–121.

CHAPTER 24

CAPITAL BUDGETING AND SPENDING

JUSTIN MARLOWE

CAPITAL spending by state and local governments, that is, investing in longer-lived physical assets, is of central concern in the provision of public services. Carrying out most every activity requires capital facilities. Education requires classrooms for teaching; transportation requires roads, waterways, tracks, runways, and terminal; and residents and businesses need water and sewer plants and solid-waste facilities to survive and to prosper. All these activities require planning for and investing in capital stock that lasts for years. The quantity and quality of such infrastucture investment combine to make up the "hardware" core for the economy. At each level, the stock of public capital is a key driver of its productivity. Ideally, governments at all levels should seek to maximize the benefits of such investment. But that seems particularly to be the case during periods of recession when the demand is high for targeted spending that has long-term benefits but that can also act as a timely economic stimulus.[1]

At the same time, overinvestment in public capital stocks that are nonessential and unproductive can crowd out private capital investment and create a drag on economic growth. Because of this implicit trade-off between too much and too little investment, a persistent conceptual issue in public capital investment is the identification of "optimal" spending levels, and the formulation of a spending plan that reflects those levels.[2]

Ideally, state and local capital-budgeting processes should be designed to address and attmept to solve these allocation problems. In practice, those processes tend to result in peculiar, inefficient allocations of capital resources. State and local governments tend to underinvest in public infrastructure.[3] They tend to manage capital spending pro-cyclically, cutting capital spending during recessions and then accelerating it during growth periods, even though capital spending is perhaps one of the best available tools to smooth income and consumption across the business cycle. Capital spending decisions often reflect near term politics more than they reflect a concern for long-term economic productivity. Many capital improvement projects are viewed in isolation and are disconnected from accomplishing broader strategic objectives. In light of these flaws, one of the field's central questions is how to reform capital budgeting and spending to promote greater efficiency and productivity. These calls for reform tend to grow louder during recessions, when capital budgeting's shortcomings are laid bare by fiscal stingencies and the opportunity costs of ineffective capital planning increase.

Criticisms of capital budgeting and the suggested reforms to the process are, of course, based on observations of past practice. If there was ever a time to reconfigure state and local capital-budgeting practices, that time is now. Public resources are more scarce than at any point in the past half century, and priority setting is the watchword for public resource allocation. For that reason, this chapter focuses on two questions. First, did capital spending decrease as a result of the Great Recession?[4] Past expereince suggests this often happens in periods of austerity, despite potential benefits to increasing capital spending during recessionary periods. Second, was the Great Recession a catalyst for reforms of capital-budgeting processes? The basis of comparison throughout is how capital-budgeting and spending practices had been changed in the wake of past recessions. A central feature in this discussion is deciphering the impact of the American Recovery and Reinvestment Act (the ARRA, or "stimulus bill") on state and local behavior.[5]

This chapter is organized in five parts. The next section provides a "lay of the land" regarding the nature of capital spending by state and local governments. Spending on stuctures, equipment, and land that make up the public capital stock and the associated costs that go with putting them in place are an integral part of providing public services. The following section then focuses on the practice of capital spending in state and local public finance and describes the perennial criticisms and reforms of capital-budgeting processes. Next, we turn to a description of how the Great Recession has affected capital spending levels, and that is followed by a discussion of the Recession's effect on capital planning and budgeting processes. The final section presents speculation on how the Great Recession may affect the intergovernmental relations surrounding capital budgeting. Emphasis throughout this chapter is on the contrasts between the past and present in order to speculate on what the future may hold.

State and Local Governmental
Capital Spending

State and local governments are major investors in the nation. Investments consist of the building of structures and the acquisition of plants, equipment, and land in the pursuit of government activities and purposes. For definitional purposes, investment encompasses those facilities that are owned (and usually operated) by governmental entities. The most comprehensive data on the government sector are collected by the US Bureau of the Census and we turn first to those figures for a comprehensive look at the level and nature of government capital spending.

Table 24.1 provides an overview of the capital outlays of governments at both the state and local levels for fiscal year 2008. As is indicated, the state and local sector had total expenditures of $2.8 trillion that year, of which $349 billion represented capital outlays. Of that amount, some $268 billion represented spending on construction, whereas the rest of the capital outlays was spent on buying machinery, equipment, and land. Total spending on capital outlays represented about 12 percent of all state and local government spending, and capital spending was relatively more important at the local government level (where the bulk of local utility spending takes place) than at the state level. The Bureau of the Census distinguishes between general government spending and that done for what it defined as utilities. The utilities, as a category, are generally much more capital-intensive than general government-direct expenditures. As may be seen in table 24.2, around 21 percent of total spending by government utilities was for capital outlays.

The importance of capital spending for governments differs among the various functional categories. As table 24.2 shows, capital spending in FY 2008 was highest in the education and highway categories when the state and local sector is viewed in the aggregate. On the other hand, states did their heaviest capital spending for highways and higher education, while localities invested mainly in elementary and secondary schools, general government structures, and local utilities. About two-thirds of all capital spending is done at the local government level and one-third at the state level. In many cases, however, the local governments will depend on state (or federal) aid transfers for the funds they spend on capital projects.

Table 24.1 Total expenditures and capital outlays: State and local governments in fiscal year 2008 (billions of dollars)

	State and local Governments	State Government	Local Government
Total expenditures	2,839	1,734	1,593
Capital outlay	349	113	236
Construction	268	92	176
Other capital outlay	81	21	60
Direct general expenditures	2,400	1,025	1,376
Capital outlay	307	107	200
Utility expenditures	193	26	167
Capital outlay	41	6	35

Source: US Bureau of the Census: Governmental Finances FY 2008.

Table 24.2 Capital outlays by functional category: State and local governments in fiscal year 2008 (billions of dollars)

Functional Category	State and local Total	State Government	Local Government
Higher education	27.0	22.5	4.5
Elementary and secondary	70.3	1.6	68.7
Hospitals	9.0	3.3	5.7
Highways	88.2	61.7	26.5
Correction	3.5	2.0	1.6
Natural resources	6.8	3.0	3.7
Parks and recreation	11.7	1.2	10.5
Sewerage	18.8	0.6	18.2
Solid waste management	2.4	0.3	2.1
Other general govt.	69.8	10.9	58.9
Utility cap. expenditure	41.3	5.9	35.4
Total capital outlay	348.8	113.0	235.8

Source: US Bureau of the Census: Governmental Finances FY (2008).

It is important to note that the individual projects that lie beneath these numbers come in a vast range of sizes. But each project's undertaking, when viewed in the context of the particular government making the outlays, is usually an important (and expensive) event that requires years of planning and preparation. The process of scheduling and financing capital projects is the main component of capital budgeting, which is discussed next.

CAPITAL BUDGETING: CONCEPT AND PRACTICE

Budgeting is a matter of aligning resources to needs for a given fiscal period. One common expression is that the budget must balance: that is, there is a "budget constraint" that requires that all resources used must equal those that are available during a period. In government, this means that the operating budget must balance revenues with current receipts. However, capital needs and the resources used to pay for them are treated differently. The reason for this is that most big "bricks and mortar" projects either require borrowing, which means going into debt with promises to repay in the future, or obtaining grant funds that usually carry various restrictions and requirements. A capital budget refers to the display of the sources and uses for capital items, which are usually defined as outlays for the construction of facilities, purchases of land and rights-of-way, and the acquisition of equipment that have economic lives that will extend beyond the current fiscal period. As a practical matter, most capital budgets also place a minimum dollar size on projects and have an expected life of at least two or three years. Another important distinction is the use of borrowed funds as a source of funds, something that the operating budget usually does not permit.

Another distinction in capital budgeting is between that part of the capital budget that is part of the current year budget (which otherwise focuses on current operations) and that part that represents a longer planning horizon. Thus, governments typically have a capital improvement plan (CIP) that schedules those capital outlays planned for the next five or six years, as well as a capital budget component embedded in the current year's budget. Each year, the current year "strip" of the capital budget is streamed into the current budget and a new out-year is added to the CIP. A typical sequence is to first fund the engineering and architectural costs ("soft costs") and land acquisition costs. After a year or so, these costs are followed by the actual costs of construction, which are often financed by debt issuance and bond funds. However, events and circumstances may hold up the actual construction and projects may stop and start depending on technical issues or competing needs for funds. A large project may stretch for several years, with the annual budgets showing the use of funds that were set aside and contracted out in earlier periods.

This fiscal planning cycle is important. As a technical matter, capital projects require engineering studies and plans and a lot of coordination among government departments and other affected parties, such as local utilities and property owners. They also require large amounts of money to be available when it is required to pay the bills. Last, operating budgets must be scheduled for changes as the projects come on line and need funds to operate. In short, capital projects are often a "big deal" that involves changes that reverberate throughout the physical plans of a jurisdiction and shape its future annual budgets for years to come.

Over time, critics have made two main criticisms of state and local capital budgeting. Both focus on the inefficiencies that often result from those processes. First is the propensity toward underinvestment. Many governments, not excluding the federal government, fail to spend enough on infrastructure maintenance, and they must then incur marginally higher costs to replace or rebuild that same infrastructure for no additional benefit. A related concern is that public infrastructure is not adequate to maximize potential economic growth and productivity. This is especially true for efficient energy transmission, telecommunications, and other infrastructure that are needed to support "new economy" initiatives.[6] Investment in these areas is far less than that made in traditional public infrastructure.

A second, more pointed criticism is that capital spending decisions are often driven by factors other than enhancing long-term economic productivity. The consequences of that bias are clear. Many entities favor spending on new infrastructure when proper maintenance of existing infrastructure will achieve the same objective at a lower cost. Much infrastructure spending happens away from population centers where it could have its greatest impact on private-sector economic output, and spending that could bolster rural economic output—telecommunications, public school infrastructure, small business incubators, and others—is a secondary concern behind highways and bridges.

There is considerable disagreement about the source of that "new facility fetish" in capital spending. On the one hand, many entities, particularly small local governments, lack the analytical capacity to consider the full consequences and trade-offs of capital-budgeting decisions. Previous empirical research shows that most capital-budgeting processes of local governments emphasize administrative expediency over analytical sophistication. The capital-budgeting process is often an end unto itself; a structured dialogue about capital project needs, regardless of the information that drives it, produces a more efficient allocation of resources than an ad hoc process or no process at all.[7] Nevertheless, the spending plans produced by these rudimentary processes rarely reflect any sort of cohesive set of strategic goals. The point is to have a budget, even if there is uncertainty about its core principles or objectives. This lack of connection to a broader set of objectives is usually a function of time and resource constraints, and not for want of political will or administrative acumen. Many administrators and elected officials in small jurisdictions simply do not have the time to develop themselves or to participate with others in an elaborate capital planning budgeting process.[8]

On the other hand, some believe capital-budgeting inefficiencies reflect voters' bias toward near-term, tangible benefits.[9] Many local leaders trade on this bias by prioritizing infrastructure spending with salient and immediately visible benefits, such as new streets and sidewalks, over less visible improvements to existing infrastructure that are essential for future economic development, like stormwater and sewer repairs. The basic desire to get re-elected also matters in this context. State and local officials often cannot resist the temptation to spend on visible, popular projects like community centers, public safety facilities, and rural highways. These "ribbon-cutting" projects are popular with voters, but they have dubious effects on private-sector productivity and, perhaps more important with respect to efficiency, place disproportionate demands on future capital maintenance budgets.

Regardless of its underlying cause, this tendency toward inefficiency is exacerbated in the peaks and troughs of the business cycle. Capital spending, especially for typical operations and maintenance, is considered "postponable" as a common target for cutbacks during recessions. This tendency was first documented in the literature on state and local responses to the recessions of the late 1970s and early 1980s.[10] On average, states and large cities reduced annual capital spending by an average of 30–50 percent during the worst years of those recessions. Those cuts shifted many jurisdictions' capital spending trajectories from being clearly upward to becoming clearly downward. For many, particularly large Rust Belt cities and small municipalities in the rural Midwest, spending was never restored to its pre-recession levels. The recessions of 1991–1992 and 2001–2002 had similar, though less severe, effects.[11]

Cutting capital spending is a pragmatic, if economically unwise, strategy to deal with recession. But if improperly managed, as cutbacks often are, they can further distort the relationship between capital spending and broader economic development goals. For instance, capital budget reductions during recessions often follow simple heuristics like across-the-board cuts and delays. These strategies are often employed without attention being paid to the complex cash flows of many capital projects, or to how subtle shifts in interest rates might affect financing and other costs. Moreover, project reprioritizations are often driven more by cash-flow considerations than by notions of longer-term productivity or efficiency concerns. Less expensive projects are often funded before larger, more expensive projects that could provide substantial local economic stimulus. Projects where debt has been issued and where borrowed money is available to spend, regardless of size or potential economic impact, are often kept on schedule. Ironically, the opposite is also often true. During economic growth periods, many entities use surplus current revenue resources to fund new capital projects on a pay-as-you-go basis, even though they also fund capital maintenance with those same surplus resources.[12] This can produce the proverbial vicious cycle: paying for new projects with surplus resources increases demand for maintenance funds that become even more scarce during the subsequent recession. These and other tendencies exacerbate capital budgeting's underlying inefficiencies.

That said, many jurisdictions have reformed their capital-budgeting processes to address these problems. How these reforms originate, how they are funded, and what determines their successful implementation are key topics in the contemporary state and local capital-budgeting literature. Some jurisdictions have enhanced technical capacity, mainly by investing in systems to forecast long-term relationships between capital spending and infrastructure performance. Some state transportation departments, for instance, have designed analytical tools that optimize the relationship between highway maintenance and pavement condition over time.[13] Some of these systems implicitly prioritize projects that bolster private economic productivity. For example, some public port authorities have developed benefit-cost frameworks to compare potential projects on the basis of improved trade and regional economic productivity.[14] But for the majority of states and municipalities, capital-budgeting processes could benefit from procedural reform, additional analytical capacity, and more transparency.

Unlike other areas of budgeting and financial management, where federal government practices have created top-down pressure to reform state and local practices—like procurement reform[15] or internal financial control[16]—the lack of a comprehensive capital budget for the federal government means state and local capital-budgeting reform will occur from the bottom up for the foreseeable future.

CAPITAL SPENDING LEVELS AND PRIORITIES

This section examines the Great Recession's impact to date on state and local capital spending levels and priority setting for capital projects. The analysis is based on three main data sources: (1) state and local government spending on fixed assets as reported in the National Income and Product Accounts; (2) figures from the audited financial statements of several hundred individual jurisdictions for fiscal years 2005–2009; and (3) a series of interviews and e-mail correspondence with capital-budgeting and finance staff from thirty state and local governments across the United States. These thirty jurisdictions were chosen because of convenience and availability, and, while diverse, they are not intended to form a statistically reliable sample.[17] But although the respondents do not compose a formal, random sample, the staff in these jurisdictions provided several valuable insights.

Aggregate Measures of Capital Spending

Most states and municipalities froze or reduced capital spending during fiscal years 2009 to 2011. Results from the National League of Cities' "City Fiscal Conditions" project (an ongoing survey of local government finance officers) report for 2010 indicated that 69 percent of cities delayed or canceled capital projects in 2010 in order to address budget shortfalls.[18] This was up from the 62 percent that employed this tactic in 2009, and up substantially from the 19 percent that enacted similar freezes in 2008. In fact, in 2008, 52 percent of cities had reported higher capital spending compared to 2007.[19] Survey data from the National Association of State Budget Officers (NASBO) suggest a similar pattern at the state level. According to those results, thirty-two states spent less on capital projects in FY 2008 than in FY 2007.[20] A similar, albeit smaller-scale survey revealed that 35 percent of California counties froze capital spending in FY 2009–2010. That figure was up from 29 percent in FY 2008–2009.[21] While the California suvey did not ask specifically about capital spending reductions (as opposed to freezes), the number of units that froze spending certainly implies that a majority of counties either froze or reduced capital spending. Taken together, this survey evidence suggests that reducing capital spending has been a "go-to" strategy for states and municipalities to address Recession-driven financial problems.

The National Income and Product Accounts (NIPA) maintained by the Bureau of Economic Analysis (BEA) provide more precise indicators of aggregate state and local capital spending. These data have two main advantages relative to the US Census and other sources. First, they cover the year 2009, whereas many other sources, including the Census and others, at the time of this writing, were only available through 2007 or 2008. Second, the BEA data make it possible to compare capital spending during the Great Recession to that occuring during the most recent recession in 2001–2002. The main disadvantage is divergent definitions.

Figures reported here are for spending on fixed assets, which the BEA defines as equipment, software, and structures, including owner-occupied housing built or acquired by state and local governments. Fixed assets are not synonymous with capital spending, but for most states and localities, the majority of capital spending is for fixed assets. So despite that drawback, these data provide a useful look at contemporary capital spending trends.

The NIPA data include both stock and flow variables. Stocks are the total value of state and local fixed assets in a given year, where the flow variables are the investment in fixed assets during the year. Stocks and flows are reported for several different functional categories of assets. Figure 24.1 presents these figures for the five largest categories: education, equipment and software, highways, water/sewer, and transportation. All figures are presented in constant 2009 dollars.

The comparisons shown in figure 24.1 indicate that capital spending reductions in the midst of the Great Recession were much greater than the reductions during the most recent recession in 2001–2002. Beginning in 2003—the first year after the 2001–2002 recession—the total value of state and local fixed assets increased across all program areas, with the most rapid increases occurring for highways and education. In 2008 that growth slowed, and total stocks in several areas then declined in 2009. By contrast, all stocks grew during the 2001–2002 recession. This pattern is also evident in the trends in fixed-asset investments. Annual investments were stable or increased following the 2001–2002 recession, then slowed in 2008, and then dropped substantially in 2009. Findings from both the above-cited surveys and the NIPA data suggest these reductions were proportional and uniform across different service areas, a pattern that is consistent with observations of past recessions.[22] According to the NASBO data, for instance, state spending cuts were proportional across higher education, transportation, corrections, environmental projects, housing, and other areas.

However, these data also suggest that investment levels remained comparatively high because of the federal stimulus, and they could drop precipitously once stimulus resources are exhausted. According to the NASBO data, thirty-four states estimated that capital spending would be greater in FY 2009 than in FY 2008, with much of that increase due to the arrival of ARRA resources.[23] Figure 24.1 illustrates how those resources affected fixed-asset stocks and flows in 2008 and 2009.

By contrast, consider the trends presented in figure 24.2. This figure shows "total gross investment" from the NIPA figures on government receipts and expenditures. Unlike capital asset levels, gross investment is not limited to capital assets and does not reflect depreciation or other consumption of fixed assets. It is simply the total investment expenditure for a particular time period. But given that most state and local investment is in fixed assets, it provides a reasonable indicator of current capital expenditure levels. This data series was available through the third quarter of 2010, which was the most current indicator on state and local capital spending. Figure 24.2 plots annual total gross investment for all states and local governments from the third quarter of 1996 through the third quarter of 2010. (Annual figures are third quarter to third quarter totals.)

State and Local Government Fixed Asset Stocks

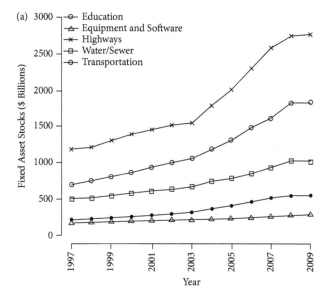

State and Local Government Fixed Asset Investments

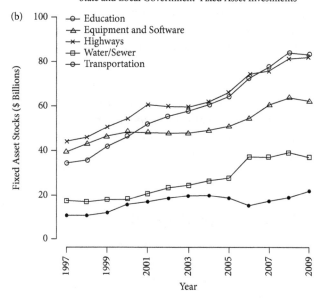

Figure 24.1 State and local government capital investment by functional area, 1997–2009
Source: Bureau of Economic Analysis, National Income and Product Accounts.

The BEA has also reported the ARRA's impact on several categories of government receipts and expenditures. Two of those categories—federal government "grants-in-aid" and federal government "capital grants"—provide a rough indication of the portion of state and local capital spending funded by the ARRA.[24] The solid line in figure 24.2 presents total gross investment from 1997 through the third

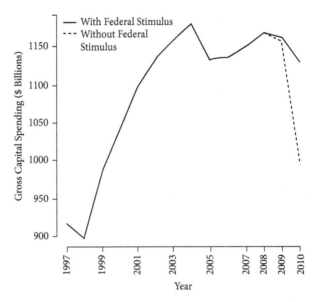

Figure 24.2 State and local government annual gross capital spending, 1997–2010
Source: Bureau of Economic Analysis, National Income and Product Accounts.

quarter of 2010, and the dashed line is total gross investment minus the ARRA-related grants-in-aid and capital grants from the first quarter of 2009 through the third quarter of 2010. These trends indicate that, from 2008 to 2010, gross investment decreased by $115 billion, or 3.5 percent. Without the ARRA, that decrease might have been closer to $177 billion, or a decrease of 15 percent. As ARRA resources are exhausted, and if a slow economic recovery brings slow growth in revenue collections, state and local capital spending levels in the years after 2010 might be closer to this hypothetical scenario, indicating a substantial reduction in capital spending by states and locailities.

Jurisdiction-Specific Capital Spending

The above aggregate figures suggest that the Great Recession led to decreases in state and local capital spending, with the potential for even larger decreases in the future. This naturally raises the question of how spending patterns in certain types of jurisdictions can contribute to or deviate from this overall trend. Different types of state and local governments have different capital needs. Capital upgrades for services that are both heavily regulated and essential, such as water and sewer utilities, are usually dictated by state and federal law and cannot be delayed in the event of a recession. By contrast, capital spending for traditional local government services that are not infrastructure intensive, such as public health and elections, are more elective in nature. They might be better candidates for project delays or cancelations. Thus, given the varying composition of capital spending, it's useful to examine the spending trends at the level of individual jurisdictions.

This level of detail raises several data quality and availability issues. First, relevant figures on capital spending for small and mid-sized cities are from the Census of Governments, the figures of which are only available through FY 2007. Second, there is substantial variation in the accounting and financial reporting of capital spending among state and local governments. For instance, some jurisdictions report capital maintenance as capital expenditures, whereas others report them as current expenditures in the general fund or some relevant capital projects fund. The Census and others who aggregate these types of data try to correct for these differences, but measurement error is inevitable.

Special districts and public authorities add an additional layer of complexity. Some of these entities report capital spending that overlaps capital spending by a general government(s), where others are independent jurisdictions with distinct capital-spending programs. To understand the Great Recession's impact on capital spending other than only at the aggregate state and local level, spending by districts and authorities must be separated from spending by other entities. This suggests that the better data sources for capital spending figures may be the annual financial statements prepared according to Generally Accepted Accounting Principles (GAAP), where the accounting treatment of capital spending will be more consistent across jurisdictions. Financial statements where public authorities are reported as standalone entities rather than as component units of a general government further illuminate these trends.

Fortunately, data drawn from annual financial reports are available on capital spending levels for individual states, cities, counties, and public authorities. Those data are available from Bloomberg and were collected for fiscal years 2005–2009.[25] Complete data were available for 1,752 cities, 720 counties, 43 states, and 558 public authorities.

These data include measures of capital "stock" and capital "flow." Capital "stock" is the accumulated value of a jurisdiction's capital assets at the end of the fiscal year. Stocks reflect the accumulated value of all the jurisdiction's previous capital spending.[26] "Flows" are changes in capital stocks over time. They indicate the entity's capital spending during a particular year. For example, if an entity's capital stock was $10 million at the end of year 1 and $11 million at the end of year 2, its capital asset inflow for year 2 would be $1 million or an increase of 10 percent. By contrast, if stock was $9 million at the end of year 2, it would have experienced an outflow of $1 million or a decrease of 10 percent. Stock and flow variables both include spending on new construction and on capital asset maintenance.

Here the focus is on a specific variable that measures capital stock: "net assets invested in capital assets, net of related debt." This is the jurisdiction's capital stock minus any unpaid debt—or "leverage"—used to finance its capital spending. Outstanding debt is often subtracted from capital asset values because it represents an external liability that reduces the "equity" value of the ownership on that asset. In this context it is especially important to consider oustanding debt because many entities financed some or most of their FY 2008 and FY 2009 capital spending with ARRA and other one-time, "pay-as-you-go" resources. This allowed these entities to increase their capital stocks and flows without taking on new debt burdens. In other words, the influx of federal aid was a substitute for increased borrowing.

In looking at various types of individual governments, it is also important to consider the size, scope, and scale of each jurisdiction's capital-spending needs. That is, a large individual capital project in a small jurisdiction with few existing capital assets will have a relatively large effect on capital flows, but that same project in a larger jurisdiction will have a smaller effect on flows. To control for those differences in size among the types of governments, the sample jurisdictions were grouped according to their total net assets (TNA), and the analysis that follows is organized according to those groups.[27]

Figure 24.3 presents the annual fixed-asset flows for the sampled jurisdictions. Results are presented separately for cities, counties, public authorities, and states. The lines indicate the average annual flow for each type of entity from FY 2005 to FY 2009. For example, in 2005 capital asset inflows for small counties were +9 percent. In other words, the value of the average small county's capital asset stock increased 9 percent from FY 2004 to FY 2005. From FY 2005 to FY 2006 the average capital flow for this same group of small counties was +12 percent. This suggests capital spending among these jurisdictions was higher overall in FY 2006

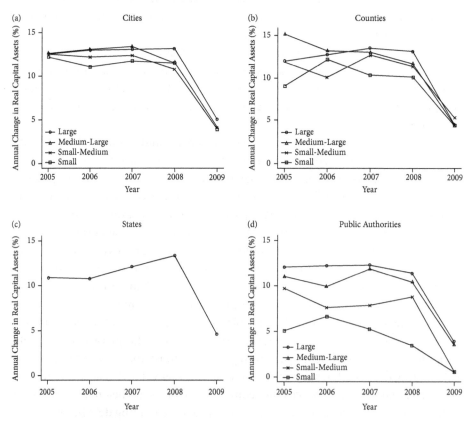

Figure 24.3 State and local government fixed asset "flows," 1997–2009
Source: Individual jurisdiction's comprehensive annual financial reports.

when compared to FY 2005.[28] All annual changes were based on constant 2009 dollars.

These data suggest three main conclusions. First, consistent with the foregoing discussion of NIPA data, spending trends were positive until 2008, then fell noticeably in 2009. For many jurisdictions—such as small and medium-large public authorities, and small counties—this shift began prior to 2008. Almost all jurisdictions experienced much smaller capital inflows beginning in 2009. Prior to FY 2009 capital asset values typically grew 8-12 percent annually, but in 2009 they grew by only 3-5 percent.

Second, capital asset stocks were well maintained through FY 2009, and it would take several years of shrinking capital asset values to "undo" the growth in values from 2005 to 2009. For some entities, like small public authorities, inflows were less than 1 percent in 2009, but nonetheless remianed positive. Considering the strong positive growth in values from 2005 through 2008, it would take several years of decline to shrink those values to their pre-2005 levels.

Such a decline, however, is quite possible given the nature and timing of the capital spending reductions that were reported as underway in many communities. Consider, for example, capital spending trends in the city of Overland Park, Kansas. Overland Park is a rapidly growing suburb of Kansas City, Missouri; its 2000 population was 149,080, and its 2008 population was an estimated 173,000. It maintains a five-year CIP that is among the most sophisticated in the country for cities of comparable size. The 2007–2011 version of that CIP included $228 million in projects. Following a series of reductions, the 2011–2015 version of that plan was valued at $121 million. Its reduced capital inflows for 2008 and 2009 reflected only a small portion of this initial reduction. Assuming the 2011–2015 budget is executed as planned, Overland Park's capital asset stock will lose 10 to 12 percent of its value every year from 2011 to 2015. This provides a good representation of how the lagged effects of the Great Recession might affect local capital asset stocks for the foreseeable future.

A third observation is that capital asset inflows have been quite similar for cities, regardless of size. Changes across different-sized counties were also quite uniform, especially in 2007–2009. Changes across public authorities, on the other hand, were noticeably different. Inflows for large authorities grew 5 to 7 percent faster than for small authorities, and rates for small-medium and medium-large authorities fell in between. But despite these differences, inflows for all authorities converged near 3 to 4 percent in FY 2009.

Capital Spending Priorities

In economic downturns, states and localities are put under pressure to reduce both their current operating and total capital spending levels. But the capital spending is usually more vulnerable. These outlays are often viewed as "postponable" and thus can be deferred with less immediate pain than reducing operating outlays.

Past practice during recessions has been to delay new capital projects, diverting resources from projects funded on a pay-as-you go basis, and restructuring existing borrowing and altering debt service schedules to free up money to meet current operating spending needs. These pro-cyclical actions can exacerbate the local effects of business-cycle fluctuations and can introduce new inefficiencies into the capital-budgeting process. Did this behavior occur during the Great Recession?

Interviews and and other correspondence with capital-budgeting staff suggest recent changes to capital spending priorities are both similar and different when compared to changes in past recessions. Like in past recessions, certain types of projects were often reduced as part of the initial response to the onset of the Great Recession. Roughly one-quarter of the jurisdictions from the survey analysis said they delayed or canceled projects that had been included in a previous capital budget. Almost all said cuts were concentrated in "noncore" service areas like parks, arts and culture, and animal control.

However, these responses also suggest behavior that was unique to the Great Recession: an emphasis on local economic stimulus. As mentioned, subnational capital spending is undoubtedly important to private-sector productivity. At the same time, traditional public finance theory says little about whether sub-national governments can or should attempt to stabilize local economic conditions during recessions.[29] That stabilization role may be unspecified in theory, but in practice many states and municipalities actively employ countercyclical stabilization tools like rainy-day funds. Empirical evidence so far on the effectiveness of those tools has been mixed.[30]

A natural extension of this countercyclical, Keynesian-style argument is that state and local capital spending can also stimulate local economic conditions. Many state and local officials apparently agree. More than one-third of the jurisdictions that replied said that they accelerated capital projects, and of almost all who did so, they said that the main motivation was to stimulate their local economy. More than half the accelerated projects were funded through bond proceeds or other resources that had been raised prior to the Great Recession. In many cases those projects were "too good to not accelerate" because estimated project costs dropped precipitously. Several local officials pointed out, for example, that bids for projects approved in 2008 and 2009 routinely came in at 50 to 60 percent of their original estimates. For that reason many jurisdictions accelerated, rather than reduced projects, moving them toward the front of their respective capital budget queues.

Some jurisdictions took this a step further and used capital projects as the centerpiece of a comprehensive "home-grown" local government stimulus effort. The city of Portland, Oregon, for instance, expedited $500 million of its $1.6 billion CIP. Projects with the greatest potential to immediately create local construction and other jobs created were most likely to be accelerated. The city of Tracy, California, made an even more aggressive effort. It compressed four years of planned capital projects into eighteen months. This compression, valued at $90 million, created an estimated 2,700 local construction jobs. Time will tell if these and similar efforts were successful. Evidence that they were successful could encourage others to think much differently about state and local governments' stabilization roles during future recessions.

REFORMING CAPITAL BUDGET-MAKING

Capital-spending levels have clearly shifted in the wake of the Great Recession. Some of that shift follows a pattern, observed during past recessions, of widespread cuts in maintenance spending and expensive capital items. But there is also evidence that, unlike in past recessions, efficiency has become a key consideration for many capital-planning decisions. Some jurisdictions for the first time are building efficiency concerns into capital programming models. For others, the Recession elevated that factor from just being one of many factors that drive capital budgeting, to the central factor. This emphasis on efficiency, even if only temporary, will likely affect how future capital budgets are made. The evidence so far suggests several changes and implications along those lines.

For many jurisdictions, establishing or reestablishing efficiency criteria has encouraged the development of a comprehensive approach to capital planning and resource allocation. Comprehensive in this context means that the capital budget includes a multiyear CIP that includes a needs assessment, financial condition analysis, and financial forecasting; the budget considers a range of options to finance and manage infrastructure, including public-private partnerships; the budget includes a clear statement of capital financing strategy; and the budget has a formal process to authorize and implement the capital budget.[31] For many entities, particularly small but growing municipalities, comprehensive capital planning has been unattractive because it tends to shift resources away from consumption-oriented "quality of life" infrastructure such as parks and community centers and toward investments in the basic infrastructure that a growing population demands. The administrator of a small city in Kansas explained this dynamic as follows: "My city has never had a well organized method or formal process for CIP. Initially I used goals and objective sessions until it produced 300% more work for administration and turned me into the bad guy in a public forum when I had to explain why sewer systems are more important than swing sets."[32]

But even in the absence of growth, maintaining their basic infrastructure has become the politically preferred alternative in some jurisdictions. A different small city official captured this alternative dynamic by saying, "When you're growing, taxpayers want to see that growth translate into better amenities and things that make their community special. When you're not growing they want you to take care of the basics so you can get back to making their community special once the recovery begins."[33]

In this slow-growth or no-growth scenario, comprehensive planning around basic infrastructure will become a useful tool. Until economic growth returns, many of these jurisdictions will remain reticent to spend on infrastructure to support contemplated population or business growth, especially if the prospects for growth are unlikely. Taken together, these findings suggest that the Great Recession and its aftermath may ultimately lead to widespread budget practices that encourage more prudence. Few resources, in other words, will engender greater care in how they are allocated.

Related to the shift toward comprehensiveness, a quarter of the respondents said the Recession caused their capital improvement planning to become "more rigorous" and/or "more quantitative." The public financial management literature generally suggests that impartial, analytical rigor is a substitute for political decision making on capital projects. That analytical rigor takes many forms. In one version, decisions about the CIP are guided by formal evaluation methods where projects are scored on dimensions like cost-effectiveness, benefits for public safety, implications for economic development, and other factors that implicitly discount near-term political desirability. Rigor can also imply allocating resources only in ways that are consistent with some predetermined principles, such as agreement with the strategic plan.[34] Five of the thirty entities said to that end that they had tried to incorporate core ideas and objectives from their local strategic plan into the CIP. In some cases those connections are abstract; "maintain high quality of life" is not an especially useful criterion for sorting though infrastructure demands. But other strategic goals, such as "promote targeted, sustainable economic development in new economy industries," provide useful guidance for capital-budgeting decisions.

The Stimulus and Intergovernmental Relations

Of all the ways the Great Recession has affected state and local capital budgeting, the most profound effects have been brought about, ironically, by the implementation of the ARRA stimulus progam. Empirical evidence to date on ARRA's effectiveness as a stimulus tool is mixed and has been surrounded by political controversy. Some feel it both spared the nation a much worse downturn and is responsible for the fragile recovery that commenced in late 2009.[35] Others believe the stimulus had zero net economic impact.[36] Yet others feel it is still too early to tell. But regardless of its impact on the macroeconomy, the ARRA did affect state and local capital-budgeting practices in several ways. Some of those effects were limited to intra-organizational processes. More important were the several changes to the intergovernmental relations surrounding capital budgeting.

In response to interviews done during the summer and fall of 2010, many capital-budgeting staff said that, to varying degrees, the ARRA's emphasis on "shovel-ready" projects meant temporarily uncoupling actual spending from existing capital-budgeting priorities.[37] For some jurisdictions the effect of that uncoupling was minor; high-priority, preplanned projects were quickly moved up in the queue, and the capital budget in effect progressed two years in the span of one year. For others, however, it meant a major departure from past practice. Perennially low-priority areas like sidewalk repair, highway signage, and rural road development became high-priority projects precisely because they could be quickly planned and executed. In the near term this might have induced some jurisdictions to shift future own-source capital resources and debt capacity away from higher priority projects, regardless of those projects' prior strategic importance. In that sense the stimulus, by displacing more valuable projects, may have exacerbated the bias toward suboptimal productivity outcomes. However, if low-priority projects had more potential to improve productivity, but were only low priority because of their lack of visibility or political salience, then the stimulus may have implicitly bolstered the overall emphasis on economic productivity. According to the finance director of a small community, "The stimulus really made us think about what kind of economic bang we would get for the federal government's buck, and what kind of bang we could get in the future from our own spending on capital projects."[38] In that sense, the stimulus may have brought "top-down" pressure to bear on reforming state and local capital budgets.

That said, the majority of survey participants said that the Great Recession's most profound impacts will be on the intergovernmental relations surrounding capital budgeting. This includes a variety of new potential problems for future capital-budgeting processes.

At one extreme, some feel the Great Recession in general and the ARRA in particular had been destructive forces. For instance, three different respondents noted that the sudden influx of ARRA resources exacerbated political conflict within multi-jurisdictional agencies—such as transportation planning boards, economic development agencies, homeland security coordinating agencies, and others—that were engaged in multilateral infrastructure planning. Stimulus resources allowed some jurisdictions to withdraw from these agencies and execute capital projects unilaterally, often with no plan for how to re-collaborate later. Others lamented that the ARRA program exacerbated horizontal inequities. Much of this is attributable to matching requirements attached to many ARRA-related programs. Respondents noted several instances where communities were allocated ARRA or other intergovernmental funding, only to see that funding retracted when they could not come up with the requisite own-source matching resources. To amplify the problem, many of those intergovernmental resources were redirected toward jurisdictions enjoying better financial positions, which were able to meet those matching requirements. Several capital-budgeting officials view this dynamic as shifting scarce capital resources from areas of the greatest need and greatest potential economic impact to areas of ostensibly less need.[39]

ARRA resources also introduced new substitution effects that will affect state and local capital budgets for some time. At the macro level, one line of thought suggests ARRA's overall effect was simply to substitute federal capital borrowing for that which otherwise would have been done by states and localities.[40] This behavior preserves some of states' and municipalities' scarce debt capacity for future projects. A key question going forward is how, if at all, that capacity might be allocated to future projects.

A more subtle but potentially more important substitution effect is the emergence of an odd new form of risk taking in capital budgeting, especially among small municipalities. In short, the potential for federal capital project resources has encouraged some jurisdictions to shift capital spending away from smaller projects and toward planning for much larger projects that have no demonstrable funding source. According to a small city administrator in the Midwest,

> My [city] Council is willing to forego street repaving this year and next year in order to have our [wastewater system upgrade project] "shovel ready" for the next round of stimulus money. I've tried to tell them this probably won't happen because the state and other federal agencies don't believe that project is necessary. But I can't persuade the Council otherwise.[41]

CONCLUSION

This chapter has considered how the Great Recession affected, and may continue to affect, capital budgeting and spending by state and local governments. The findings suggest three main conclusions. First, state and local capital spending slowed considerably with the Great Recession's onset. Overall, spending fell only slightly in fiscal year 2008, as the Recession was emerging, but then fell sharply in FY 2009 and FY 2010. Spending decreased at a faster rate in FY 2010 as many jurisdictions began to exhaust their ARRA resources and saw their one-source revenues in decline.[42] There was no clear pattern to these reductions. All types of jurisdictions—states, cities, counties, and public authorities—cut capital spending at similar rates. These combined effects suggest the Great Recession's effect on spending levels was consistent with, if slightly more intense, than the impacts of past recessions. Moreover, survey-based estimates indicated that declines in capital spending will continue through FY 2011 and FY 2012. If that happens, the Great Recession will have resulted in unprecedented declines in state and local capital spending.

Second, despite the declining spending levels, the Great Recession brought about some improvements to state and local capital-budgeting practices. Many jurisdictions redesigned their budgeting processes to produce tighter linkages between capital spending and broader community goals in areas like economic development and public safety. Many jurisdictions have responded to the new resource scarcity by formally realigning capital improvement planning with strategic plans and other statements of long-term objectives. Others have shifted resources away from new construction in order to increase future maintenance costs, and toward more efficient maintenance of existing infrastructure. Some have increased the level analytical sophistication in capital budgeting so as to better plan for costs and to better link resources with priorities.

A third and potentially deleterious effect is that the Great Recession strained intergovernmental relations regarding capital budgeting and spending. In short, federal-state and federal-local transfers designed to bolster local capital spending did sustain spending. But they also restructured capital budgeting in ways that will likely inhibit, rather than promote, intergovernmental cooperation in the future.

Capital spending slowed significantly during the Recession, but not as much as would have been the case had there not been the rapid influx of federal assistance. If, with the lapse of such aid, state and local capital spending levels continue to decline, then the values of infrastructure and fixed assets for many jurisdictions will fall. How rapid and widespread this decline will be remains to be seen. Correspondence and interviews with capital-budgeting staff around the country indicate that stringency will be accompanied by a strong desire for capital-budgeting reform. Pressed for resources, many jurisdictions for the first time are considering comprehensive approaches to capital budgeting, with thorough analysis that is driven by transparent criteria and quantifiable benefits.

NOTES

1 Aschauer (1989).; Munnell (1990); Garcia-Mila and McGuire (1992).
2 Holtz-Eakin (1996); Holtz-Eakin and Rosen (1989); Poterba (1996).
3 See Gramlich (1994), 1180–1189.
4 The Great Recession has been defined by authorities as the period from December 2007 until June 2009. The definition of recession is by convention defined by the National Bureau of Economic Research. As a practical matter, however, recessions are much more associated with those periods when unemployment levels exceed the "normal" levels. Were one to perceive that an unemployment rate in excess of 5 or 6 percent as being too high (which is commonly the case), then that nation was still experiencing recessionary conditions at the end of 2010, when the unemployment rate was nearly 10 percent. For the definition of recession, see the National Bureau of Economic Research website (www.nber.org/cycles/recessions.html).
5 See http://www.recovery.gov/About/Pages/The_Act.aspx.
6 Congressional Budget Office (2010b).
7 Marlowe et al. (2009).
8 Ibid., 41–43.
9 Gramlich (1994), 1182–1183.
10 Levine et al. (1981); Forrester (1993); Bland and Nunn (1992); MacManus (2004); Crain and Oakley (1995).
11 Pagano (2002).
12 Ibid.

13 Carroll et al. (2004).

14 Port of Seattle, WA (2010).

15 Kelman (1995).

16 Jakubowski (1995).

17 Those jurisdictions include the cities of Austin, TX; Brookings, OR; Burlingame, CA; Cedar Park, TX; East Pointe, GA; Keizer, OR; Klamath Falls, OR; Lexington, MA; Louisburg, KS; Ogallala, NE; Overland Park, KS; Palo Alto, CA; Pittsburgh, PA; Plano, TX; Portland, OR; Richland, WA; Steubenville, OH; Tracy, CA; Tulatin, OR; and (Village of) Waterford, WI. It also includes three counties: Arlington County, VA; Brevard County, FL; and Marquette County, MI. Public authorities included the Port of Seattle, WA; Houston, TX Unified School District; and (Chicago) Midway Airport. State entities included are the Office of Financial Management (Washington State); the Office of Budget and Policy Planning (Montana); and the Office of Administration, Division of Budget and Planning (Missouri). Where possible, interviewees also shared their observations of changes in public authorities' capital-budgeting practices. These jurisdictions are not meant to be a representative sample, but rather to provide a broadly representative body of qualitative insights into recent changes in capital-budgeting practices.

18 Hoene and Pagano (2010). See also Hoene and Pagano (2009) for earlier survey comparisons.

19 Ibid.

20 Ibid.

21 Sun (2010), 9–10.

22 National Association of State Budget Officers (2010).

23 National Association of State Budget Officers (2009).

24 Grants-in-aid to state and local governments include funding for "programs related to national defense, public safety, economic affairs, housing and community services, income security, and unemployment." Much, but not all, of this spending is for capital projects. Capital grants include grants for "highway and public transit infrastructure, construction, and restoration." Although most of this funding is for capital projects, a portion of it has bypassed states and municipalities. These data are available at http://www.bea.gov/recovery/pdf/arra_impact_table_01.pdf#page=1.

25 Municipalities include cities, counties, villages, towns, and townships. Public authorities include schools, hospitals, universities, utilities, airports, economic development districts, and community development districts. Bloomberg collects these data from these entities' annual audited financial reports. Bloomberg's main audience is investors, and in particular municipal bond investors, so the sample is admittedly skewed toward larger entities with higher levels of outstanding debt. While this excludes some smaller jurisdictions, it is also implicitly weighted toward those jurisdictions with more extensive capital budgeting and finance needs, which makes it appropriate for this analysis. Bloomberg distributes these data through its "Bloomberg Professional" terminals. For more information, see http://www.bloomberg.com/professional/fixed_income/.

26 Accumulated value is also known as "book value" or "accounting value." This value is most often determined at historical cost. Historical cost is determined by identifying the cost to build the asset at the time of its construction, adjusting that cost to present values (to account for the time value of money), and then depreciating the value over time. Capital investments in the asset, such as maintenance and upgrades, are also valued at cost and are depreciated. The nondepreciated costs are the assets' "book value." An alternative and lesser-used approach that is known as the modified method

determines asset values relative to the cost of maintaining the asset relative to some predetermined level of asset condition or performance.

27 The TNA is the difference between the jurisdiction's total governmentwide capital assets and its total governmentwide liabilities. It represents the government's "equity," or the portion of its assets that do not have an outside claim in the ownership. It increases as the entity's capital assets increase, which makes it a suitable basis for comparison across jurisdictions.

28 The size categories used were as follows: "small" governments had TNAs less than $32 million; "small-medium" had between $32 million and $86 million; "medium-large" governments had between $86 million and $281 million, and "large" governments had greater than $281 million. For public authorities those groups were also based on quartiles of TNA. "Small" authorities had TNAs less than $5 million (in constant 2009 dollars); "small-medium" authorities had greater than $5 million but less than $27 million; "medium-large" authorities had greater than $27 million but less than $114 million; "large" authorities had greater than $114 million. The states were not grouped by size. Standard deviations of the annual changes are not reported here, but they were uniform across all years and all types of jurisdictions.

29 Gramlich (1979); Gist (1988); Miller and Svara (2009).

30 Hou (2006); Wagner and Elder (2005); Marlowe (2005).

31 Marlowe et al. (2009), 19–24.

32 Marlowe (2010).

33 Ibid.

34 Marlowe et al. (2009), 62–85.

35 Congressional Budget Office (2010a). The CBO estimated that the ARRA's policies had accomplished the following in the second quarter of calendar year 2010:

- Raised the level of real (inflation-adjusted) gross domestic product (GDP) by between 1.7 percent and 4.5 percent
- Lowered the unemployment rate by between 0.7 percentage points and 1.8 percentage points
- Increased the number of people employed by between 1.4 million and 3.3 million
- Increased the number of full-time-equivalent (FTE) jobs by between 2 million to 4.8 million, compared with what those amounts would have been otherwise.

The effects of the ARRA on output and employment were expected to diminish during the second half of 2010 and beyond, as its funds run out.

36 Cogan and Taylor (2010).

37 Marlowe (2010). Also, see note 17 above.

38 Marlowe (2010).

39 Ibid.

40 Cogan and Taylor (2010).

41 Marlowe (2010).

42 See http://www.recovery.gov/About/Pages/The_Act.aspx.

References

Aschauer, David A. (1989, September/October). "Public Investment and Productivity Growth in the Group of Seven." *Federal Reserve Bank of Chicago Economic Perspectives* 13: 17–25.

Bland, Robert L., and Nunn, Samuel (1992). "The Impact of Capital Spending on Municipal Operating Budgets." *Public Budgeting & Finance* 12(2): 32–47.

Carroll, Deborah, Rita Cheng, Robert J. Eger, III, Lara Grusczynski, Justin Marlowe, Ali Roohanirad, and Hani Titi (2004). *Capital Preventative Maintenance.* Madison, WI: Midwest Regional University Transportation Consortium. http://www.mrutc.org/research/0301/index.htm. 27–30.

Cogan, John, and Taylor, John B. (2010). "What the Government Purchases Multiplier Actually Multiplied in the 2009 Stimulus Package." NBER Working Paper No. w16505.

Congressional Budget Office (2010a, July)." Estimated Impact of the American Recovery and Reinvestment Act on Employment and Economic Output from April 2010 through June 2010." Washington, DC: Congressional Budget Office.

Congressional Budget Office (2010b). *Public Spending on Water and Transportation Infrastructure.* Washington, DC: Congressional Budget Office. http://www.cbo.gov/doc.cfm?index=11940.

Crain, W. Mark, and Oakley, Lisa K. (1995). "The Politics of Infrastructure." *Journal of Law & Economics* 38(1): 1–17.

Forrester, John P. (1993). "Municipal Capital Budgeting: An Examination." *Public Budgeting & Finance* 13(2): 85–103.

Garcia-Mila, Teresa, and McGuire, Therese J. (1992). "The Contribution of Publicly Provided Inputs to States' Economies." *Regional Science & Urban Economics* 229.

Gist, John R. (1988). "Fiscal Austerity, Grant Structures, and Local Expenditure Response." *Policy Studies Journal* 16: 687–712.

Gramlich, Edward M. (1979). "Stimulating the Macro Economy through State and Local Governments." *American Economic Review Papers and Proceedings* 69(2): 180–185.

Gramlich, Edward M. (1994). "Infrastructure Investment: A Review Essay." *Journal of Economic Literature* 32(3): 1176–1196.

Hoene, Christopher W., and Pagano, Michael A. (2010). "City Fiscal Conditions in 2010." Washington, DC: National League of Cities. http://www.nlc.org/ASSETS/AE26793318A645C795C9CD11DAB3B39B/RB_CityFiscalConditions2010.pdf.

Hoene, Christopher W., and Pagano, Michael A. (2009). "City Fiscal Conditions in 2009." Washington, DC: National League of Cities. http://www.nlc.org/ASSETS/E0A769A03B464963A81410F40A0529BF/CityFiscalConditions_09%20(2).pdf.

Holtz-Eakin, Douglas (1996). "Bond Market Conditions and State-Local Capital Spending." *National Tax Journal* 44: 105–120.

Holtz-Eakin, Douglas, and Rosen, Harvey S. (1989). "The 'Rationality' of Municipal Capital Spending: Evidence from New Jersey." *Regional Science & Urban Economics* 19(3): 517–536.

Hou, Yilin (2006). "Budgeting for Fiscal Stability over the Business Cycle: A Countercyclical Fiscal Policy and the Multiyear Perspective on Budgeting." *Public Administration Review* 66(5): 730–741.

Jakubowski, Steven (1995). "Reporting on the Control Structures of Local Government under the Single Audit Act of 1984." *Public Budgeting & Finance* 15(1): 58–71.

Kelman, Steven (1995). *Unleashing Change: A Study of Organizational Renewal in Government.* Washington, DC: Brookings Institution.

Levine, Charles H., Irene S. Rubin, and George G. Wolohojian (1981). *The Politics of Retrenchment: How Local Governments Manage Fiscal Stress.* Beverly Hills, CA: Sage.

MacManus, Susan A. (2004). "'Bricks and Mortar' Politics: How Infrastructure Decisions Defeat Incumbents." *Public Budgeting & Finance* 24(1): 96–112.

Marlowe, Justin (2005). "Fiscal Slack and Countercyclical Expenditure Stabilization: A First Look at the Local Level." *Public Budgeting & Finance* 25(3): 48–72.

Marlowe, Justin (2010). "Municipal Capital Spending during the Bust." Working Paper, Evans School of Public Affairs, University of Washington.

Marlowe, Justin, William C. Rivenbark, and A. John Vogt (2009). *Capital Budgeting and Finance: A Guide for Local Governments.* Washington, DC: International City/County Management Association.

Miller, Gerald J., and Svara, James H. (Eds.) (2009). *Navigating the Fiscal Crisis: Tested Strategies for Local Leaders.* Phoenix: Arizona State University, Alliance for Innovation.

Munnell, Alicia H. (1990). "How Does Public Infrastructure Affect Regional Economic Performance?" In *Is There a Shortfall in Public Capital Investment?*, edited by Alicia H. Munnell. Boston: Federal Reserve Bank of Boston. 69–103.

National Association of State Budget Officers (2009). "The Fiscal Survey of the States, Fall 2009." Washington, DC: NASBO. http://www.nasbo.org/LinkClick.aspx?fileticket=dZSuPt3Slc8%3d&tabid=65.

National Association of State Budget Officers (2010). "The Fiscal Survey of the States, Spring 2010," Washington, DC: NASBO. http://www.nasbo.org/LinkClick.aspx?fileticket=gxz234BlUbo%3D&tabid=65.

Pagano, Michael (2002). "Municipal Capital Spending during the 'Boom.' " *Public Budgeting & Finance* 22(2): 1–20.

Port of Seattle, WA (2010). "Budget and Business Plan and Draft Plan of Finance. III-7." http://www.portseattle.org/downloads/about/2011_Budget_19_Whole_Budget.pdf.

Poterba, James M. (1996). "Capital Budgets, Borrowing Rules, and State Capital Spending." *Journal of Public Economics* 56(2): 165–187.

Sun, Jinping (2010). "Budget Strategy: A Survey of California County Governments." *California Journal of Politics and Policy* 2(1): 9–10. http://www.bepress.com/cjpp/vol2/iss1/3.

Wagner, Gary A., and Elder, Erick M. (2005). "The Role of Budget Stabilization Funds in Smoothing Government Expenditures over the Business Cycle." *Public Finance Review* 33(4): 439–465.

CHAPTER 25

FINANCIAL MARKETS AND STATE AND LOCAL GOVERNMENTS

JOHN E. PETERSEN AND RICHARD CICCARONE

THE first decade of the twenty-first century brought many changes to the financial markets in the United States and their most numerous and far-flung participants, the state and local governments. These governments, which have enjoyed ready and preferred access to the financial markets, have been important players, both as issuers of debt securities and as investors in the securities of others. Borrowing by these governments is in large part responsible for the accumulation of public infrastructure that provides the physical capital that supports the daily provision of basic utility services, the surface transportation network, and the various structures that house and the equipment used to support government services.[1] In addition to the sector's $2.8 trillion in financial liabilities, which it owed to others, the states and localities also had about $2.2 trillion in holdings of financial assets. These funds have been almost exclusively raised (or are invested) through the private financial markets.[2]

As robust as the numbers appear, they are products of past history. There is no question that the sector has been a major and successful component of the nation's financial system. The question is rather one of the continuing sustainability of the broad and successful performance of state and local borrowers in the face of current and future changes. That is, how has the market-oriented financial system by which these governments have financed themselves to the tune of trillions of dollars been altered by the events of the last few years? A key part of that question relates to the continuing creditworthiness of individual governments and their ability to contend with the increasingly sophisticated demands of the markets and their regulators.

In this chapter, we will dissect the various aspects of the changes in the financial markets themselves and how they affect state and local governments as participants. After a discussion of the aggregate balance sheet of state and local governments, there is a brief reprise of the financial market developments in the early 2000s and the meltdowns of 2007 and 2008, which affected state and local governments. As was true with the entire economy, the financial system debacle was followed by a widespread downturn in the nation's economy, which had a disproportionate impact on state and local government revenues. Meanwhile, the financial stresses led to major changes in the municipal bond market, largely centered on the demise of the bond insurers and the related disruptions in the credit-rating system. In addition, the decade-long onslaught of exotic financing structures, poorly understood by unsophisticated issuers led to a number of losses by governments.

Next, the chapter examines in greater detail the federal financial reform that was passed in 2010 and the impact on governmental borrowers (and their investment activities) of enhanced federal regulatory activity. As this is written, the financial reforms remain controversial and the content of the new regulatory scheme is uncertain. The chapter ends by outlining the major themes of a troubled and vexatious era regarding the financial condition of state and local governments and their access to the private financial markets.

The State and Local Government Sector: An Aggregate Balance Sheet

The state and local sector is large and sprawling. In the fifty sovereign states, there are approximately 90,000 local governments, ranging from 39,500 general units (such as cities, counties and townships) to 50,000 special districts, which perform a variety of limited governmental tasks, such as overseeing school districts and water-sewer districts.[3] Even those numbers understate the complexity of the sector, because these governments may issue debt and maintain funds that are restricted in purpose (the "special fund" doctrine). Thus, compiling the numbers (which is only done by a federal census every five years) is a substantial task. Nonetheless, the sector in the aggregate is a major component in the financial markets, both as a borrower and as an investor.

Table 25.1 provides an overview of the sector's balance sheet in a highly aggregated form. As of mid-2010, the state and local sector had $3 trillion in debt, the vast majority of which was in the form of credit market securities. While trade payables were substantial at $650 billion, the loans from the federal government were minuscule ($14 billion).[4] The second panel concerning state and local government debt makes a frequently missed distinction between "municipal securities outstanding" and state and local government debt. Both nonprofits and private corporations, under various state and local programs, may issue debt through (or on behalf of) state and local entities for public purposes. These obligations are referred to as "municipal securities," but the underlying obligors responsible

Table 25.1 State- and local-sector government assets and liabilities and municipal debt outstanding in 2000 and 2010 (second quarter) in billions of dollars

	2000	2010[1]	Percentage 2000 to 2010
State and Local Government Debt			
State and Local Government Securities	1,173	2,376	103%
Federal Government Loans	9	14	56%
Trade Payables	333	650	95%
Subtotal State and Local Debt	1,515	3,040	101%
"Municipal" Securities Debt Outstanding			
Nonprofit Entity Securities	132	267	102%
Private Corporate Securities	152	200	32%
State and Local Government Securities	1,173	2,376	103%
Subtotal Municipal Securities	1,457	2,843	95%
State and Local Government Assets			
Financial Assets of Governments	1,662	2,620	58%
Real Assets of Government (Depreciated)	4,286	8,152	90%
Subtotal State and Local Assets	5,948	10,772	81%
State and Local Retirement Fund			
Financial Assets	2,293	2,556	11%
Retirement Liabilities[2]	2,548	3,651	43%
Estimate of Unfunded Liability[3]	−255	−1,095	330%
Items: Gross US Domestic Product	*9,952*	*14,584*	*47%*
Total US Credit Market Debt	*27,138*	*52,120*	*92%*

[1] As of the end of the second quarter of 2010.
[2] Estimated by assuming a 90 percent funding ratio of assets to actuarial liabilities in 2000 and a 70 percent funding ratio in 2010.
[3] Subtraction of estimated liabilities from assets.
Sources: Federal Reserve Board, *Flow of Funds;* US Bureau of Economic Analysis; authors' estimates for retirement fund liabilities and unfunded liabilities.

for repayment are private-sector entities, such as business corporations, privately owned hospitals, and private colleges. That "nongovernmental" debt represents about 16.5 percent of the dollar volume of all municipal securities that were outstanding as of mid-2010. Following the custom of the financial markets, the term "municipal securities" and the specific marketplace they inhabit refer to both the governmental and nongovernmental debt instruments.

On the asset side of the balance sheet, state and local governments in the aggregate have both financial market and "real" assets (namely, land, structures, and equipment). While the value of the financial assets can be measured reasonably well by using public data sources, the value of the real assets (the depreciated value of structures, equipment, and land) can only be broadly estimated. Keeping that caveat in mind, the sector had an estimated $2.6 trillion in financial assets (not including those of the public retirement funds) and $8.2 trillion in real assets.[5] The financial asset holdings of state and local governments need to be assessed carefully. About half of that amount belongs to restricted (escrowed) accounts, which are dedicated to the payment of outstanding bonds that have been refinanced or the disbursement of bond proceeds. Most of the remaining half of assets is used to meet the liquidity needs in governments in their day-to-day operations, as well as various trust fund investments, excluding those of the retirement systems.

For state and local governments, a distinction is made between the assets of governments and those that are specifically restricted for retirement funds. The last panel of table 25.1 illustrates that as of mid-2010 state and local employee retirement funds had $2.6 trillion in assets. These assets are valued by the Federal Reserve on a market basis, reflecting their current evaluation in the financial markets. On the other hand, it is estimated that the present value of the retirement liabilities of these systems amounted to $3.6 trillion. As indicated in the footnote to the table, the dollar number regarding the total liability is only a rough estimate because of the variations in the actuarial assumptions that are used by the retirement plans. Nonetheless, a $1.1 trillion estimate of the underfunding of state and local pensions appears reasonable in view of the analysis of others.[6]

The last column of table 25.1 provides data on the growth of the various state and local government balance-sheet items for the period between 2000 and mid-2010. For purposes of comparison, the growth of national GDP and that of total credit-market debt outstanding are also shown in the final items of the table. For the period, state and local government debt grew much faster than GDP but at about the same rate as the total of credit-market debt outstanding. As may be seen, in table 25.1, the growth in state and local pension liabilities far outpaced the growth in assets and, as a result, the estimated unfunded grew greatly during the decade. While there is a galaxy of legal issues involved, much of this unfunded portion represents debt to the state and local governments. Unfortunately the unfunded pension liabilities are only part of the debt owed retirees: unfunded postretirement health benefits represent perhaps an equally large liability for governments.

THE GREAT MODERATION:
THE PRECRISIS YEARS

A look at the volume of borrowing in the early to mid-2000s by state and local governments provides a picture of relative calm and apparent prosperity. State and local governments had experienced a wrenching, but relatively brief, fiscal setback in the early 2000s. Tax receipts and spending slowed, but they recovered quickly and continued to grow. Municipal debt grew at a substantial and sustained rate after the stock market collapse and brief recession of 2001. Interest rates were falling on a sustained basis. As is illustrated in figure 25.1, there was a continuing down trend in municipal bond interest rates, as reflected in the Bond Buyer 20 Bond Index and the benchmark US Treasury twenty-year long-term bond interest rates. As imposing as the long-term municipal bond borrowing volume was during the great moderation of declining interest rates, seeds were being planted for more difficult times at the end of the decade.

Figure 25.2 presents the yearly long-term bond sales by state and local governments from 2000 to 2010. Bond sales are typically classified by the distinction between general obligation bonds (essentially tax-supported that involves the full-faith-and-credit or unlimited obligation of governments) versus "revenue" bonds (which represent a limited obligation, such as the pledging of specific project revenues). As may be seen, annual bond sales soared from around $200 billion in 2000 to $430 billion in 2007.

Two things are interesting about this period. For one, the states and localities used the bond markets extensively for refunding their outstanding debt. The other is that the tax-exempt market was busy in converting ostensibly long-term debt obligations into short-term securities. Over the decade, the volume of "new money" debt issued remained fairly static, while re-financings grew substantially

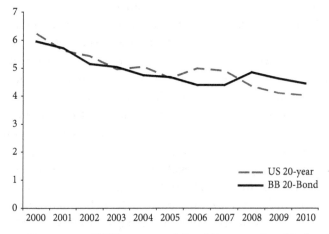

Figure 25.1 Twenty-year US Treasury and Bond Buyer 20 Bond Index: Interest rates in percentages, 2000–2010
Source: Federal Reserve.

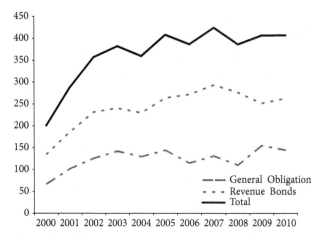

Figure 25.2 Municipal bond new issues by type of security (billions of dollars: 2000–2010)
Source: Securities Industry and Financial Markets Association (SIFMA).

in volume (see figure 25.3). There were several reasons for refinancing debt, but the important backdrop for this activity was the continuing decline in interest rates, including those on tax-exempt bonds. For example, governments could use the re-financings as a way to raise cash for other purposes by capitalizing on the increased value of their outstanding debt. As part of this decline in rates, especially those in the short-term end, governments were increasingly attracted to borrowing in the short-term money markets. Bankers and the bond insurers were inventive in making this possible.

Finding ready buyers for long-term tax-exempt bonds has always been a problem. The reason is that investors are uncertain about their own tax statuses beyond the immediate future and, just as important, that of future possible buyers if they wish to sell their holdings prior to maturity. Retail investors, individuals investing

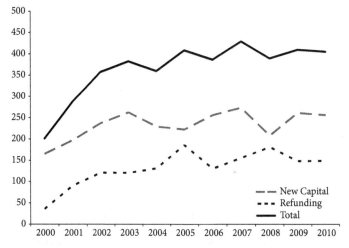

Figure 25.3 Municipal bonds: New capital and refunding (billions of dollars: 2000–2010)
Source: Securities Industry and Financial Markets Association (SIFMA).

directly or through funds, are the underlying core of the tax-exempt market. These investors have high incomes and lots of wealth. But these conservative investors shy away from owning bonds with maturities of more than ten or fifteen years and, as befits bond investors, are always worried about inflation.

The relatively weak demand by tax-exempt investors for the long maturity bonds has conflicted with the desire of governments to issue long-term debt. While income and wealth were growing among the better-off, the decline in the personal marginal income-tax rates, and the lowering of effective tax rates on alternative investments dampened investor enthusiasm for holding tax-exempt bonds in the 2000s. Thus, during the mid-decade (up to 2007), much of municipal bond finance was devoted to figuring out how to bridge the gap between long-term funding needed by governmental borrowers and the short-term desires of investors. Various types of structures were enlisted to accomplish this, ranging from tender-option bonds (TOBs), which were designed to arbitrage yield curves, to variable-rate-demand obligations (VRDOs) and auction-rate securities (ARSs), which effectively transformed long-term debt into short-term securities (see figure 25.4).

The TOB, VRDO, and ARS markets would become, in rapid succession, unhinged with the onset of the credit crisis in 2008. By the end of the decade, the Build America Bonds (BABs) were created as part of the stimulus program to enliven the market for municipal debt by selling federally subsidized taxable debt and luring a new set of investors. But the BABs program, too, would perish in December 2010 after an active, but brief and politically charged existence.

The tax-exempt yield curve had usually been steeper than the Treasury curve. Particularly in times of recession, the ratio of tax-exempt to taxable bond rates would climb. The tax-exempt yield curve was systematically steeper than the

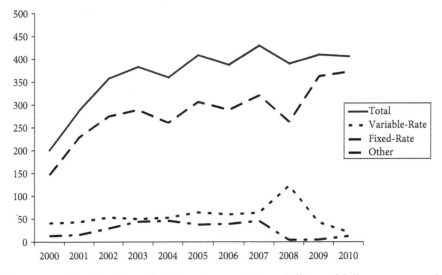

Figure 25.4 Municipal bond by interest payment type (billions of dollars: 2000–2010)
Source: Securities Industry and Financial Markets Association (SIFMA).

Treasury curve for most of the 1990s. But in the early 2000s, the relationship started to change. A group of investors, including the increasingly important hedge funds, noticed the systematic greater steepness of the tax-exempt yield curve and figured out ways to profit from it.

Taking advantage of the municipal market's "inefficiency," these investors bet one curve against the other. Using extensive leverage, they created the tender-option bond. The TOB device involved borrowing at a short term in the tax-exempt commercial paper market and using the proceeds to buy long-term tax-exempt bonds. Hedging was often used. Opposite positions were taken on taxable rates such as the London Interbank Offered Rate (LIBOR), with the idea of earning the additional income offered by the steeper municipal yield curve when compared to the taxable curve. It is estimated that at their peak in the mid-2000s, the TBO portfolios amounted to $300 billion to $500 billion and they were buying as much as a quarter of the annual long-term municipal bond offerings.[7]

The declining short-term rates had other attractions. States and localities, enticed by low short-term rates, also began selling auction-rate securities: these were nominally long-term bonds with an interest rate that were reset on a regular basis by auctions. The ARS market, using auctions run by dealers, transformed long-term debt into short-term paper. Again, the object was to tap the tax-exempt money-market funds. The municipal ARS market swelled to an estimated $200 billion in 2007. When bidders abruptly disappeared from the auctions in early 2008, many borrowers replaced their ARSs with VRDOs. Like ARS securities, variable-rate demand obligations are nominally long-term instruments with interest rates that reset regularly. A key difference between VRDOs and ARDs was that the former had a put option. The issuer, or a bank paid by it to provide liquidity facilities, was required to buy the securities back from the holder if they were put back. The advantage of the put feature is that the VRDO was thereby made attractive to the money market funds. With the demise of the ARDs and TBOs, the volume of VRDOs outstanding as of 2009 was estimated to total nearly $450 billion. Figure 25.4 illustrates the sudden surge of VRDO offerings in 2008, as the government issuers were forced to abandon their ARS fixed-rate securities, and the TBOs as a source of funds left the long-term municipal market.

Combining the impacts of the TOBs, the VRDOs, and the ARSs, hundreds of billions of long-term tax-exempt bonds were absorbed by leveraged hedge funds or converted into short-term paper. From 2002 to 2007, about 30 percent of all municipal borrowing was done either by VRDOs or ARSs. If one adds in the TBO effects, perhaps half of all tax-exempt borrowing was assisted by a conveyor belt that moved long-term obligations into de facto short-term securities. Without these long-to-short products, much more supply would have ended up in the long-term tax-exempt sector, pushing up long-term rates and steepening the yield curve. These devices made the tax-exempt yield curve about as flat as the Treasury curve, most of the time, from the early 2000s until the financial crisis struck.

Meltdown and Recession Hit the
Municipal Bond Market

Starting in 2007, a series of events, set off by the financial sector meltdown and the subsequent onset of the Great Recession rocked the municipal securities markets. In many ways, the municipal market was a bystander (but not always an innocent one) in the rapid sweep of financial devastation. However, even if it was only collateral damage, the market got its share of the misery. Moreover, the financial market meltdown soon delivered a tough second punch, the Great Recession, as the economy went into a steep decline and state and local government revenues fell off a cliff. This, in turn, fueled investor concerns that the municipal bond market would be wracked by defaults as overextended governments would be unable to pay the debt service on their bonds. The well-advertised fiscal difficulties on major states, such as California, New York, Arizona, Illinois, and Michigan, and a handful of hard-pressed local governments added fuel to the fire. Furthermore, the impact of the federal stimulus aid had dwindled rapidly and states and localities faced continuing budget shortfalls. Clearly, times had changed dramatically for both the issuers of bonds and their investors.

Collapse of the Bond Insurers

In 2007, the deflating housing bubble quickly capsized the municipal bond insurers, which until then had played a key role in the municipal market. In 2007, the last year that all the bond insurance firms were actively underwriting, the nine companies then active had provided new policies of about $200 billion in the new-issue tax-exempt market (insuring over 50 percent of the dollar volume of issuance). Insurance was seen as a way to improve the creditworthiness of bonds and ensure their liquidity. The credit ratings of the companies, virtually all of which were rated triple-A, were all-important in meeting various legal requirements and reassuring investors.

In a nutshell, the collapse happened as follows: the bond insurance companies, which historically had their origins in the municipal bond market, had undertaken large exposures to subprime mortgage debt. Starting in late 2007, their credit ratings plummeted. By 2010, only one bond insurance company (Assured Guaranty) was active underwriting policies, which by then represented only about 6 percent of the entire market.[8] Many banks, which also provided credit enhancements and liquidity facilities, were also drastically affected by market turmoil and rating downgrades. The plunging credit ratings of the various securities firms and credit enhancers led to widespread remarketing failures for insured auction rate and variable-rate securities.[9] Related to this, the subsequent collapse in late 2008 of the money market funds led to the demise of the tax-exempt commercial paper market. Investors were left with illiquid positions in low-yielding short-term debt, while issuers were left with high-cost loans when liquidity providers were forced to take back the unmarketable securities.

The pervasive and severe rating downgrading of the municipal bond insurers was a result of the drastic deterioration of the housing market and the downgrading of mortgage-backed securities, which the companies had insured. At the end of 2007, there were seven bond insurers with AAA ratings from all three credit-rating agencies; at the end of 2008, there were none. It is important to note that the rating downgrades were not caused by the insurers' holdings of municipal bonds. But the rating downgrades meant that investors in insured bonds found that they owned unrated debt, the market values of which plummeted.[10]

The explosive bankruptcy filing of Lehman Brothers in September 2008 and the accompanying market debacle led to a rapid sell-off in "risky" assets, including municipal securities, and a huge deleveraging of positions. The municipal market decline accelerated as falling net-asset values required the mutual funds to sell bonds so as to meet redemptions. Investors, who had used leverage to invest in municipal bond portfolios, were forced to liquidate their positions as collateral value dropped and financing costs for carrying positions spiked. Municipal interest rates jumped sharply and investors saw corresponding losses in the market value of their holdings.

For the month of December 2008, the key municipal market interest rate index, the Bond Buyer 20 soared to 5.56 percent, an interest rate fully 2.38 percentage points higher than the 3.18 percent rate on twenty-year US Treasuries.[11] Accompanying this pandemonium was the collapse of the short-term and variable-rate markets, as nervous investors withdrew funds from the tax-exempt money market funds.

INTEREST RATE SWAPS GO SOUR

During the pre-Recession salad days of the municipal market, investment firms were busy devising ways to make money from municipal issuers. In relationship to auction-rate bonds and the use of various special investment vehicles, novel approaches to managing debt and lowering interest costs gained purchase, as short-term rates were extremely attractive and there were manifold ways to leverage on the difference between short rates and longer-term rates. Thus, the use of interest-rate swaps grew rapidly. A typical swap deal was for the issuer to issue variable rate bonds and to pay the bank (or other counterparty) a fixed rate and to receive back a fluctuating short-term rate that lowered the borrower's net interest cost. It was a big business, with evidently $500 billion in municipal bond interest-rate swaps outstanding just before the financial crisis struck.[12] But when the markets collapsed in 2008 and short-term interest rates plunged, many issuers found themselves having to pay out a lot more to the banks than they received from them.

Unfortunately, the swap agreements were long-term in duration and the cost of getting out of ("unwinding") them became prohibitive. Meanwhile, issuers saw long-term rates plunge and were anxious to fix their debt service and lower their interest costs. Municipal issuers began to buy their way out of the interest-rate swaps, so they could borrow at lower long-term rates, but the decline in interest rates made these unwinding payments to their swap counterparties large. According to a recent article, failed swap deals by early 2010 had cost states, localities, and nonprofit issuers an estimated $4 billion in unwinding deals.[13] Among the largest swap-unwinding fees paid were those by Harvard University ($498 million), California Water Resources Department ($305 million), and the Bay Area Transit Authority of California ($105 million), but a myriad of much smaller issuers were thumped as well.[14]

A Market Respite Followed by Increasing Uncertainty

In early 2009 the market crisis in municipal bonds faded about as abruptly as it had erupted. The major factor was the broad-scale financial and economic intervention by the federal government and, most important for state and local governments, the rapid passage and implementation of the ARRA (stimulus program).[15] In addition, investors were drawn by unusually high rates of return on municipal securities that occurred the first few months, especially in comparison to the deeply sinking prices in the stock market and the low yields on US government bonds.

The year 2009 marked significant and remarkably positive changes for the municipal bond market. The surge of investor demand led to the market's best returns since 1995 and the best in any of the bond markets. An important factor was the new BABs program, an unexpected ingredient of the stimulus program, which opened up a new set of investors for municipal bonds. This federally subsidized taxable bond program, which is discussed below, led to a considerable substitution of taxable debt for tax-exempt debt, which substantially reduced the borrowing costs of state and local bond issuers.

But the restoration of calm in 2009 to the municipal market was to prove temporary. The year 2010, while notable for relatively low-interest costs for governmental issuers (in large part due to the BABs program), saw a series of follow-up punches landing on the municipal market. These had to do with the deteriorating financial prospects of several large governmental issuers. By spring it became increasingly evident that state and local finances were at an inflection point and that there were large changes afoot as regards the sector's fiscal resiliency and its capacity to support future debt. Local economies and, accordingly, their tax bases were not snapping back and were continuing to slide downhill. The Great Recession, felt nationwide and increasingly seen as being of long duration (and perhaps involving a double-dip relapse), clearly had sapped the vigor of state and local tax systems, pushing up welfare-related costs, and had curbed the governments' appetite for capital spending.

The financial markets' disastrous performance in the late 2000s had left a residue of concerns and complaints by investors and issuers alike. The wisdom of the bond market's increasingly complex transactions and the considerable and poorly understood risks attracted increasing attention. The severe interest-rate gyrations from late 2007 through early 2009 resulted in many instances of large losses incurred by municipal issuers that had engaged in what proved to be highly risky investment schemes, especially those involving swaps and investments in special investment vehicles.[16]

Perhaps most important in the long-term view of state and local finances was the overhang of unfunded public employee retirement benefit liabilities and the related health-care costs. The size of these obligations depended heavily on the credibility of actuarial assumptions used, and these were in many cases suspect. As the financial conditions of states and localities darkened, the public employee retirement obligations began to enter into debt calculations and their bulging magnitude sounded frightening alarms. Bond investors began to worry about how their claims would weigh against those of public employee retirees (whose pension funds were underfunded).[17]

The municipal market had glided along for many years by relying on the rating agencies to dissect the deals and set the general parameters of creditworthiness. The market disasters of 2007 and 2008, when the rating agencies sharply changed their minds about the claims-paying ability of the bond insurers, led to a wholesale lowering of ratings on insured transactions. Shorn of insurance-created creditworthiness, huge uncertainties arose that torpedoed the value of investors' portfolios. The downgrades also meant that, under the provisions of many loan contracts, issuers were forced to refinance (or fall back on expensive bank loans) in the face of difficult markets when their bonds could not be remarketed.

CREDIT RATINGS UNRAVEL

The credit-rating agencies came under attack in the wake of the subprime mortgage crisis, which subsequently has expanded into a major global financial (and economic) crisis. The crisis started to gather force in late 2006, initially triggered by a sharp rise in foreclosures in the subprime mortgage market in the United States. The infection spread rapidly into a global crisis and ignited a worldwide credit crunch and the subsequent Great Recession. While there are many players in the financial crisis, the three major credit-rating agencies played pivotal roles. By traditional practice, reinforced by federal and state laws and private contracts that required their use, the rating agencies had acted as the "gatekeepers" of the market. Their published ratings were used as the primary and authoritative gauge of credit quality and largely determined the relative interest rates on securities. The agencies were blamed most prominently in the wake of the financial crisis for giving investment-grade ratings to securitization transactions (often called "structured investments") that were backed by subprime mortgages and other (often similarly weak) underlying assets. It is a complicated story, but the impact of conferring overly optimistic credit ratings reverberated throughout the financial markets, demonstrating the systemic risk that the reliance on ratings entailed. The subsequent massive downgrading of the housing-related credits, as defaults began to threaten and occur, splashed into the municipal bond market.

Among the first casualties that directly affected municipal bonds were the bond insurance companies, which had not only insured a high percentage of the structured finance transactions but in the years just prior to 2007 had insured more than 50 percent of the new-issue municipal bonds in the market. The bond insurers had essentially built their business on the foundation of guaranteeing relatively low-risk municipal obligations. As the subprime-structured bond transactions imploded, bond insurers' ratings came under siege and were steadily downgraded. The first bond insurer casualty of the crisis was a niche company, ACA. The smallest of the guaranty companies, it specialized in lower-rated municipal bonds (mostly in the BBB and BB category) and nonmunicipal structured finance bonds. Standard & Poor's, which had confirmed its A rating with a stable outlook on the company's insured bonds on June 8, 2007, then downgraded it to CCC by December of that same year. In its June report, S&P downplayed the company's exposure to the subprime crisis and said this about ACA:

> The stable outlook reflects the company's refocused, lower risk business plan, its solid positions, its structured credit and CDO asset management business lines; and its sound capital position. The outlook also reflects Standard & Poor's expectations for improved market acceptance and penetration for ACA's public finance segment and significant loss development from the large, but high quality, exposure to subprime mortgage collateral.[18]

The insurer was a minor player in the municipal bond market and was only rated by one agency, but its fall took a major toll on banks and investment banks that had booked large portions of their portfolios with the ACA-protected bonds. As the unwinding of bond insurance ratings continued, the fallout cascaded to the general municipal market, which saw widespread downgrades occur on insured credit-enhanced municipal bonds. In turn, borrowing rates rose and illiquid markets developed for highly sophisticated municipal debt issues that were packaged with bond insurance, including ARSs. Moreover, the general municipal trading market became further strained as banks and dealer firms cut back their under-writing and trading activities in response to calls for additional internal capital needed to offset their subprime-related positions. Bear Stearns and Lehman, which were active players in the derivative and swap markets, made matters worse when they were forced to close their doors. Insured municipal bonds were put on a "ratings watch" in late 2007 and then were steadily downgraded in line with the decline in the ratings related to the insurers. [19] Investors as well as the rating agencies shifted their credit assessments from an overreliance on insurance to the underlying municipal bond security. Those credits that did not have an underlying rating from one of the three rating agencies were treated as nonrated and were left to be assessed by individual investors.

An early example of the rating agencies assigning what proved to be seriously overly optimistic ratings was found in the security known as Asset-Backed Commercial Paper.[20] The commercial paper was issued to finance pools of subprime mortgages, which were sold to investors. The market for subprime mortgages cooled in late 2006 as housing prices began to slump, foreclosures increased, and interest rates on the portfolios rose rapidly. The prices of commercial paper, which were exposed to the high-risk cash flows, declined sharply, causing large losses for investors. The initial rumblings of difficulty rapidly extended into short-term municipal markets, where credit enhancers scrambled for funds and dealers stopped supporting the market. The tax-exempt money market funds rapidly lost liquidity, and interest rates spiraled.

The subprime crisis and the massive collapse of the asset-back obligations was not the first time that the credit-rating agencies got it wrong, but never before had the implications been so globally sweeping in their severity. The attacks on the practices of the rating agencies, fueled by their mistakes that led to dramatic investor losses, had been fomenting for years. The Financial Reform Act (Dodd-Frank) passed in 2010 put the credit-rating agencies in the sights of regulators for further reform. That reform, whatever shape it eventually takes, promised to have substantial consequences for the municipal bond market.

How Credit-Rating Agencies Work

Credit-rating agencies are a homegrown American invention. They began in the United States in the 1860s when Henry Poor began to publish a manual comparing the creditworthiness of railroads. In 1910 John Moody started assigning credit ratings to railroads and state and local government debt obligations. By the 1930s, state and federal investment and banking laws were put in place that dictated credit ratings must be used to determine the suitability of debt for investment by public bodies and for determining the capital adequacy of regulated entities.

The diverse and far-flung nature of the municipal bond market, with its many thousands of small bond issues each year, underscored the usefulness of credit ratings.[21]

Credit-rating agencies are privately owned companies that assign credit ratings to debt obligations. Credit ratings are offered for all types of borrowers. The use of ratings was fostered by (1) financial institution regulation, (2) the use of various contractual "tests" in loan agreements, and (3) the "globalization" of the markets, whereby large numbers of borrowers can raise funds from a diverse set of investors. As a practical matter, credit ratings are used to classify the relative default risk of obligations issued by all entities: governments, corporations, banks, and nonprofit organizations. They are imperative for accessing the public capital markets. Credit ratings are the internationally recognized and observed measures of "basic" risk in the markets. They are the fundamental measure that most investors accept or, at least, provide a starting point for their estimation of "creditworthiness," which traditionally is seen as the likelihood that a loan will default.[22] Differences in interest rates are determined by relative risk, and the ratings are universally taken as proxies for risk: the lower a credit rating on a debt obligation, the higher the interest rate will have to be in order to attract lenders to compensate them for the greater risk.

In the day-to-day investment decision making, ratings are used by investors for deciding whether, given the level of interest rates, to invest in particular securities. While this concept of risk seems straightforward enough, life in the financial markets has become a lot more complicated. In practice, most investors look at a borrower's credit rating to determine a security's future trading value. But the agencies have maintained that this is not the purpose of credit ratings: it's wrong to assume "that ratings gauge the risk of trading losses, when, in fact, they look only at the probability of default."[23] Unfortunately, the pervasive use of ratings (and how they were interpreted) planted the seeds for systemic financial failures. When the ratings in the asset-backed market began to dive, it drove a complex process where, in knock-on fashion, ratings in other markets faltered. The municipal bond market, while not the source of the initial downgrades, was heavily hit by the concatenation of effects, and what had been a key player in municipal financing, the bond insurers, were essentially wiped out.

Credit ratings are published by using a simple alphabetic "grading" system. The symbols differ little among the major three rating agencies (see figure 25.5) and are easily understood. Ratings range from AAA for the most highly rated investment-grade products down to the C or D grades, which are used for those issues that are either near to or in default. The rating scale theoretically allows for a wide range of ratings to be assigned, but most ratings are clustered at the four "investment grades," which are BBB (or Baa) up to AAA. The AAA is the prime grade: the rating where there is asserted to be no measurable credit risk. For investors, the interpretation was that super-safe triple-A bond prices would always be dependably high in comparison to other obligations.

Bond Rating Symbols			Generic Definitions of Rating Categories	
Moody's	S&P	Fitch		
Aaa	AAA	AAA	Extremely Strong	
Aa	AA	AA	Very Strong	"Investment" Grades
A	A	A	Upper Medium	
Baa	BBB	BBB	Lower Medium	
Ba	BB	BB	Speculative	
B	B	B	Vulnerable	"Speculative" Grades
Caa - Ca	CCC - CC	CCC - CC	Very Vulnerable	
C	D	DDD	In Default	

Figure 25.5 Symbols and generic definitions of bond rating categories used by Moody's, Standard & Poors and Fitch

Notes: Moody's appends numeric suffixes of 1, 2 or 3 to ratings Aa through Caa to rank credits from the higher end (1) to the lower end (3) of that category. Hence, an A-1 rating symbol indicates a credit in the top tier of the A category. Similarly, S&P and Fitch may assign a "+" or "−" to a category symbol to refect a stronger or weaker position of the borrower within that particular category.

Sources: Moody's, Standard and Poors, and Fitch Investor Service.

PAST PERFORMANCE OF RATINGS

A basic question about credit ratings is how well they have performed in predicting financial failure, default, and bankruptcy. In general, until the egregious failure of the ratings given to the subprime and other asset-backed deals discussed above, the rating agencies in the post–Great Depression modern times had been spared systemic failures in seeing disaster coming. But, although much smaller in scale, there were previous crises. Previous modern-day (but isolated) disasters involved the Penn Central Railroad and Franklin Bank failures in the 1970s. In the municipal bond market, the plight of New York City (and other large cities) in the 1970s were worrisome but did not lead to any major defaults.[24]

The first major government to default since the Great Depression was Orange County, California. Its default and bankruptcy in 1994 were major events. The county had AA ratings from Moody's and S&P at the time it declared bankruptcy and then proceeded to sue the ratings firm, arguing that it gave the county too good a rating and failed to alert the agency to the County Treasurer's risky investment practices.[25] Although large amounts of Orange County debt were imperiled by the bankruptcy, a state-sponsored rescue package was quickly put together and the actual losses to investors were minimal. Investment-grade ratings were rapidly restored by the rating agencies. But, clearly, the county's precrisis high credit ratings were wrong.

Among other notable municipal bond market defaults, two of the largest government-related issues in modern times belonged to the Washington Public Power Supply System (WPPSS) and the Jefferson County, Alabama, Sewer Revenue Bonds.

The WPPSS bonds (Number 4 and 5) were rated A1/A+ prior to their default in June 1983 on $2.25 billion in bonds. This occurred when the Washington State Supreme Court invalidated the take-or-pay contracts with its municipal participants. Jefferson County, which was originally rated A3 by Moody's on its $3.2 billion of sewer revenue bonds, had technical defaults in 2008 on its failure to make collateral payments to banks involved with its derivative debt instruments. It is questionable whether the rating agencies could have anticipated the state court invalidation of the security used to back the WPPSS bonds; however, the huge nuclear power projects that were being financed with the WPPSS 4 and 5 project bonds were based on feasibility studies that called for optimistic electric load-growth projections. In the case of Jefferson County, Alabama, the cost feasibility for the project was linked to the use of variable-rate derivative structures that were highly dependent on the credit enhancement provided by bond insurers.

In the late 1990s, the financial markets were engulfed in the Asian financial crisis, which spread contagion throughout the world. Ratings were very much a part of the systemic failure. Corporate and sovereign ratings were massively downgraded as firms went bankrupt and countries' currencies depreciated, foreign reserves evaporated, and banking systems collapsed. The hard-pressed countries, short of exchange and frozen out of the private credit markets, trooped to the IMF for loans. Investment funds, restricted to holding investment-grade bonds, were forced to sell off assets as the ratings on their foreign holdings plummeted. While the agencies were roundly criticized for earlier overoptimism and acting too slowly in downgrading, they came through the crisis relatively unscathed regarding having to change their ways of doing business. In fact, the subsequent weakness of banks in many countries stifled bank lending and encouraged the use of the international bond markets and thus increased the importance of credit ratings.

Close behind the Asian crisis another credit shock followed in 2002, this time in the United States: the Enron bankruptcy. Overnight, a major US corporation collapsed from a market value of $62.3 billion to zero. Accounting fraud, which led to the demise of the major accounting firm Arthur Anderson and the loss of jobs of thousands, was at the heart of the failure. But the rating agencies were seen to be less than observant and acknowledged that they relied on deceptive financial statements from the corporation, which employed secretive, exotic financial structures.[26] The Enron scandal (and related crises at that time involving corporate finance) brought on a flurry of governmental investigation and, ultimately, the enactment of the Sarbanes-Oxley Act in 2002.[27] While most of the act's reform was aimed at auditing, governance, and corporate securities market-disclosure practices, it did bring renewed consideration of the structure of the rating agency business, the impact of ratings on the market, and the integrity and independence of the agencies' business practices.[28]

The major rating agencies have operated in an environment with high barriers to market entry. Aside from being in the business a long time and having accumulated thousands of clients and associated files, a major barrier to market entry by new firms was found in achieving the "NRSRO" designation that was bestowed upon rating agencies by the SEC. Investment and banking regulations over the years had in one fashion or another dictated the use of "nationally recognized statistical rating organizations" (or some phrase like that). But it was not until 1971 that the NRSRO concept was formalized. This was done by requiring a filing by such organizations with the SEC and the agency's issuance of a "no-action" letter that the firm could consider itself an NRSRO.[29] The process of getting the NRSRO designation from the SEC was somewhat mysterious, but the result was that only three firms achieved the NRSRO designation before 2007. Congress, slowly following up on the Sarbanes-Oxley Act, subsequently took steps to rectify this situation by passing the "Rating Reform Act of 2006."[30] Nonetheless, the Big Three firms continued to dominate the ratings business. Investors, while not happy about the lapses, obviously put a premium on having a few, easily understood ratings published by known entities. And issuers, faced with market demands, were willing to pay the rating fees.

Some incremental reforms of the rating agencies were in process at the time of the 2007–2008 blowup of the financial markets. The Rating Reform Act of 2006 made it easier for competing credit-rating agencies to obtain NRSRO recognition and it attempted to increase transparency of the industry by subjecting the NRSROs to limited oversight by the SEC. As subsequent events determined, the initiatives in the Rating Reform Act were quickly overwhelmed by the events of the 2007–2008 financial crisis.

CRITICISMS OF CREDIT-RATING AGENCIES

Over the years, there have been many criticisms of credit-rating agencies. Many have been somewhat esoteric, and until the Great Recession of 2007–2009, appeared to be far beyond the pale of most investors, not to mention being of any interest to the general public. But the unraveling of the ratings and the fate of the bond insurance companies brought the complaints into focus.

Monopolies of Opinion

There are many credit-rating firms located throughout the world, but only three firms now matter in the global markets: Moody's Investor Service, Standard & Poor's (S&P), and Fitch Ratings. Moody's and S&P between them represent roughly 80 percent of the international market in credit ratings. When these two are combined with Fitch Ratings, the "big three" rating agencies have control over 95 percent of the world's credit-rating market. Setting aside for the moment the issue of competition, which is a major issue of possible reforms, there are great advantages to the concentration of credit opinions. It means that investors (and regulators) need only keep track of a few (up to three) opinions and these opinions are easily understood in simple, comparable symbols. This system of letter-grade ratings and few providers made it easy to draw common comparative baselines in the markets. The drawback is that there is a lack of competition among the oligopoly of rating firms, the lack of which drives them to practice herding behavior with each making "acceptable" ratings, thus making it costly for one firm to take a tougher line.

A long-standing complaint has been a lack of competition in credit assessments due to the virtual monopoly that the "big three" rating agencies have in giving opinions. The agencies have been accused of monopoly pricing, and one investigation (on the verge of the 2007–2008 financial crisis striking) by the US Senate Banking Committee concluded that the credit-rating market is "an extremely concentrated and anti-competitive industry."[31] Moody's, the only one of the big three that is a publicly held corporation and had disclosed its undiluted financial results, reportedly had a profit margin of greater than 50 percent.[32]

There were many hurdles to overcome to increase competition and thus lessen the monopoly hold of the big three. At least until the "rating shopping" involved in the subprime mortgage fiasco, there had been little incentive for the big three to compete more directly. Most bond issuances in order to meet the legal requirements of institutional investors required at least two separate ratings. That meant that there was plenty of business for all and no real need to compete against each other in prices. Furthermore, credit rating had been a reputation-based industry, where newcomers face a daunting task in building up their name recognition and convincing issuers and investors to use their services (little attention is paid to ratings that aren't widely recognized). The *Economist* speculated that perhaps "credit ratings are a natural oligopoly, with new entrants offering a level of choice that investors simply don't want."[33] This "reputational" quality (reinforced by the huge number of regulatory requirements, not to mention the extensive references in bond contracts to the firms) makes the rating business very much like a public utility, where there are clearly economies of scale and networking.

Credit-Rating Models

For certain types of bond-security structures, especially those for structured finance, the assessment systems used to calculate ratings are now largely based on computer models, which are proprietary in nature. But such computer models, which rely on historical relationships, can present major problems with new markets and new instruments. Regarding the subprime crisis, the rating agencies used a set of projections that were "put together in one of the most benign markets for five years."[34] The projections assumed that the default rate on subprime mortgages (a financial instrument without a long history) would remain low, which proved devastatingly inaccurate.[35]

For example, the statistical models used to rate mortgage-backed investments, such as the controversial Goldman Sachs subprime deal (Abacus 2007-AC1), soon proved to be deeply flawed. The historical rates of foreclosure that the models used were based on early periods of stiffer lending standards (that subsequently were degraded in the subprime splurge), declining interest rates, and rapidly rising home prices. Like many, the rating agencies assumed that home prices would not decline. They also assumed that the complex investments linked to home loans were based on assets from around the nation and thus diversified. Both of those assumptions were wrong and the models were subject to manipulation, and investors around the world lost many billions of dollars. In the Abacus investment, for instance, 84 percent of the underlying bonds were downgraded within six months, many dropping from investment grade to default or near-default ratings.[36]

For Goldman Sachs and other banks, other conflicts arose, which seemed to give them undue influence over ratings. Expert analysts from the agencies were hired by the bankers to put together deals. Moreover, the models and procedures at the agencies became open to desired clients. The agencies received information about possible deals from banks and fed that data into their models, a process that allowed Wall Street firms to "massage" ratings by adjusting the data that were fed into the rating-agency models.[37]

Poor Surveillance and Stale Ratings

A persistent criticism of the credit-rating industry is that agencies did not carry out continuing surveillance on rated bonds and, as a result, did not downgrade an issuer's bond quickly enough, thus leaving investors hanging out to dry. This criticism arose in the corporate bond market following the failures of Enron (which was rated as investment grade four days before it went bankrupt), Global Crossing, Parmalat, and other corporations. It resurfaced in huge proportions with the subprime mortgage crisis. In that case, there were reports in 2006 that the subprime mortgage market was in deep trouble, but it was not until the summer of 2007 that the credit-rating agencies began to downgrade such investments. The credit-rating agencies responded to this criticism by pointing out that their ratings are only "opinions" and are thus a protected form of free speech. Furthermore, the agencies argued that their ratings "speak to one topic and one topic only—credit risk." They claimed that their ratings are not investment advice and that they shouldn't be held accountable for investors using them to make investment decisions.[38]

Inherent Conflict: The Issuer-Pays Business Model

Another criticism is that the credit-rating agencies have had too close of a relationship with those they rate and those who pay for the ratings. Critics charge that these economic relationships can lead to bankers and issuers exerting undue influence on the ratings process. Rating agencies meet with borrower representatives and their bankers and give advice as to what steps should be taken to maintain or improve credit ratings. Additionally, the agencies offered consultative advice to issuers and bankers on how to structure securities so as to achieve a desired rating, which proved to be a major problem in the subprime mortgage meltdown. At the heart of this criticism is how the credit-rating agencies are compensated: ratings must be high enough to meet (a paying) client's needs. If not, the clients have had two other agencies that can rate the bonds.

The rating agencies face conflicts of interest because the vast majority of their income comes from the borrowers that pay for ratings rather than from investors that subscribe to their services. That is to say, the agencies charge issuers to have their debt offerings rated rather than charging investors for access to ratings. Technology is a part of the problem: The rating agencies claim that charging the issuers is a necessity in this age of cheap photocopying, e-mail, and other communication technologies. But this predominant source of revenues, coupled with the agencies acting as consultants in advising how to structure new offerings so as to achieve a given rating (the agency will often then rate the product that it has consulted on), leaves the agencies vulnerable to a "pay-to-play" criticism.

Susceptibility to Corruption

A concern, especially in the aftermath of the subprime crisis, is with structured finance, products like the Abacus 2000-ACI deal mentioned above. In 2006, at the high point of structured financing, some 44 percent of Moody's revenues from rating Collateralized Debt Obligations (CDOs).[39] A congressional study found that investment banks and credit-rating agencies worked so closely on these financial products that the latter could be seen as helping to underwrite deals. This would expose the credit-rating agencies to lawsuits from unhappy investors. Also, with such a large percentage of revenues coming from structured finance, there was evidence of pressure on employees to keep the ratings on these products at high levels to keep revenue growing.[40]

The "sociology" of the financial markets had a role. The rating agencies, while viewed as gatekeepers to the financial markets, were not held in high esteem by the market participants that made more money. This became evident in the asset-backed securities crisis, where the rating agencies were influenced by their financial superiors: the more highly paid dealers and traders in the banks. Michael Lewis, in his book *The Big Short*, wrote about the pecking order of the rating-agency employees compared to the "high-roller" bankers they deal with:

> The price of the end product was driven by the rating assigned to it by the models used by Moody's and S&P. The inner workings of these models were, officially, secret: Moody's and S&P claimed they were impossible to game. But everyone knew that the people who ran the models were ripe for exploitation: "Guys who can't get a job on Wall Street work for Moody's [said one Wall Street trader]."[41]

The rating agencies, under pressure to analyze all the new "product," were too busy to look at individual mortgages in the pool but rather were relying on the general characteristics of the loan pools that were forming the credit. The aggregate data that were used could be manipulated to achieve the desired result: "Wall Street bond trading desks, staffed by people making seven figures a year, set out to coax from the brain-dead guys [asset-backed analysts] making high five figures the best possible ratings for the worst loans."[42]

Role of Ratings in Private Contracts

A further criticism is that the lowering of credit ratings can create a "death spiral" and "cliff effects" for issuers and investors. This happens because loans sometimes carry "rating triggers" that make them suddenly come due in full if a credit rating is lowered beyond a certain point. Because borrowers will rarely have the liquidity needed to pay their outstanding loans immediately, the credit-rating downgrade in essence sentences the company to death (bankruptcy). The rating triggers were a major factor in the use of credit derivatives or swaps. These contracts provided "insurance" so that, in case a bond is downgraded, the counterparty paid up. The large number of downgrades of the asset-backed and mortgage-backed bonds led to massive puts of the credit derivatives, causing huge drains on the "insurers" (the counterparties) in these transactions. Downgrading bond issues, especially to subinvestment-grade levels, also had serious implications for the breadth of investors that could participate in a new issue offering. The failure to maintain an investment-grade rating or sometimes the threat of a downgrading to junk status can spell the loss of market access to a borrower that needs additional capital or monies to refinance. This risk was even more evident in the municipal market, where credit enhancements had been so prevalent, and there were so many "nameless" small issuers.

THE MUNICIPAL RATING MODEL: RECALIBRATION

The credit-rating agencies have long played a major part in the operation of the municipal bond market, which is made up of a multitude of governmental issuers, many of whom are very small. In 2009, for example, $410 billion in long-term municipal bonds were issued, of which $397 billion were rated by one of the three major credit-rating agencies.[43] This pattern of the dominant role of credit ratings (and the three major rating firms) has occurred for many years, so it is likely that about 97 percent of all outstanding municipal debt (by par value) carries a credit rating. The ratings are important on determining investor demand for the bonds and thus have a large impact on the interest rates that governments pay. What happens to credit ratings and the firms that supply them is of intense interest to the thousands of state and local borrowers.

While rating agencies have been traditionally less reliant on a formula approach to assigning ratings to municipal bonds, the concept of a default history model has become more ingrained into the rating process, especially over the last ten years. Starting with the fact that the default rates on state and local obligations are far lower than for other types of fixed-income sectors, particularly corporate bonds, all three rating agencies implemented a form of "recalibration" that was meant to bring municipal bond ratings into line with those on other securities. The recalibrations were based on the individual rating agencies' historical default studies. As table 25.2 indicates, there have been substantial differences in default rates between corporate and municipal issues for years. Why that differential should exist was not clear and became contentious when state and local governments began to sell taxable bonds that competed directly with domestic corporate (and other taxable) securities.

In 2007, Moody's announced that it would begin using a Global Scale Rating approach to assessing taxable municipal bonds in order to provide parity of rating risk with other bond-rating scales used in the global markets. Moody's had examined municipal bond default history since 1970. Fitch called for a similar approach based on its own default studies, which looked at municipal bond defaults going back to 1980. Meanwhile, earlier in the decade S&P had stated that it would use its default studies to adjust ratings as they came up for periodic or new issue reviews. Once the credit crisis became full-blown in early 2008 and municipal issuers struggled with their liquidity needs and trading values, controversy over the parity of the

Table 25.2 Default rates of municipal versus corporate bonds

Rating	Issuer Type	Standard & Poor's	Moody's
AAA/Aaa	Municipal	.00%	.00%
	Corporate	50%	.69%
AA/Aa	Municipal	03%	.07%
	Corporate	54%	1.21%
A/A	Municipal	03%	.11%
	Corporate	2.05%	3.34%
BBB/Baa	Municipal	.16%	0.37%
	Corporate	4.85%	8.08%
"Invest. Grade"	Municipal	.06%	.16%
	Corporate	2.50%	4.21%

Sources: Moody's Investor Service (10-year average default record, 1970–2009); Standard & Poor's (15-year cumulative default records, 1986–2008 for municipal and 1981–2008 for corporate bonds).

ratings they received became intense. A number of state and local governments, led by the state of California, called for the rating agencies to elevate general obligation and essential service ratings based on their superior default performance relative to other fixed-income security classes.[44]

The movement to "recalibrate" municipal bond ratings was welcomed by governmental borrowers but it had its critics, primarily from the investment side. The primary objections from investors to the recalibration was that the very low default rate since the mid-1970s couldn't necessarily be counted on in the future just based on a historical model. The current day risks associated with state and local governments were fast changing and a growing base of liabilities for debt, pensions, and other retiree benefits would be an albatross for many weakened tax bases in the years ahead. The critics worried that the showdown in paying for essential services, retiree benefits, and infrastructure could be at odds with timely debt service despite the extremely strong bond-security pledges built into municipal bonds. Under the original Moody's Global Scale Rating proposal in 2007, most general obligation bonds were likely to be elevated to the Aa and Aaa grades. The last time that state and local general obligation bonds were this concentrated at the highest rating levels by Moody's was in 1929. In a seminal study on Depression defaults, George H. Hempel found that nearly 90 percent of the thirty-one cities with populations of more than 30,000 were rated Aaa (by Moody's) in 1929. Nearly 98 percent of the same group was rated Aa or better.[45] The study also noted that nearly 80 percent of the total dollar value for all defaulted issues were rated Aaa in 1929 and 94.4 percent were rated Aa or better. While the economic conditions and fiscal support efforts during the Great Depression were substantially worse and longer lasting than the Great Recession of 2008–2009, Hempel's work suggested that the rating firms had never anticipated the black swan severity of the Depression that not only rocked the stability of ratings but also the ability of hundreds of municipal bonds that defaulted in those years. Critics of the recalibration warned that modern historical default models in the post-Depression years, which occurred in a period of general growth and prosperity, might not be indicative of the risks moving forward.

Moody's and Fitch waited nearly two years after announcing their intentions in early 2008 to move toward overall recalibrations of municipal bonds. Both firms delayed implementation during the peak of the credit crisis in order to give the credit markets and the economy a chance to settle down. By the spring of 2010, both firms unveiled their recalibration programs. In its explanation of the changes, Moody's said that "the recalibration was intended to enhance the comparability of ratings across the Moody's rated universe." The firm added that "Moody's rated universe will result in an upward shift for most state and local government long-term municipal ratings by up to three notches. The degree of movement will be less for some sectors, most notably in the enterprises sectors which are largely already aligned with the ratings on the global scale." [46]

In its special report on "Recalibration of US Public Finance Ratings" issued on March 25, 2010, Fitch also said that "the intent of the recalibration is to ensure a greater degree of comparability across Fitch's global portfolio of credit ratings."

While the degree of recalibration depended on the municipal credit sector, it noted that the "state and local general obligation ratings and those dependent on them (e.g. appropriation based debt) will be adjusted upward two notches if the GO rating is currently rated 'A' to 'BBB-'and one notch upward if the GO is currently rated 'A+' or higher."[47]

THE REFORMS OF 2010

The Dodd-Frank Financial Reform Act was supposed to establish a new framework for directly regulating the NRSROs.[48] According to the act, the US Congress found that rating agencies are de facto "public utilities" and that there is "systemic importance of credit ratings and the reliance placed on credit ratings by individual and institutional investors and financial regulators." The activities and performance of NRSROs are "matters of national public interest, as credit-rating agencies are central to capital formation, investor confidence, and the efficient performance of the United States economy."[49]

The Financial Reform Act imposed new requirements on the NRSROs and a regulatory oversight framework to back it up. In summary, these requirements included increased authority to the SEC to regulate the ratings industry, with enhanced rule-making and enforcement powers and a new office in the SEC, the Office of Credit Ratings (the OCR), to coordinate activities. The legal liability of rating agencies was increased by lowering certain levels of pleading requirements regarding securities laws violations; removing former safe-harbor protections; and imposing filing requirements. In addition, many provisions of the act are aimed at the rating process and management supervision by the agencies in order to avoid conflicts of interest in the provision of credit ratings.

Under the new law, the rating agencies are required to publicly disclose more information, such as the performance record of their credit ratings and the procedures and methodologies used in the credit-rating process. A wide range of statutory references to NRSROs was rescinded and the SEC and other federal agencies were told to develop new standards of creditworthiness in their regulations. By mid-2010, the reforms were already under way. The Federal Deposit Insurance Corporation along with the Federal Reserve and other federal banking agencies, as required by the Financial Reform Act, were studying options to the use of externally procured credit ratings in bank capital evaluations. Among the options are using credit spreads more often, having the regulators develop their own risk metrics, and relying on the firm's existing internal models. The evaluation of alternatives is a huge task, as will be the adoption of any change. Regulators have relied on using credit ratings for decades. If external ratings are to be abandoned, the agencies will have to adopt an "extremely specific" alternative system.[50]

During consideration of the Financial Reform Act, a direct attack was made on the long-standing practice of banks and issuers in choosing the rating agencies to rate their offerings. Senator Al Franken of Minnesota, after citing the current model—where those being rated could choose the rating companies and pay them created a conflict of interest—then proposed creating a special board, overseen by the SEC, that would randomly assign rating agencies to transactions to do the ratings.[51] A major finding of the Senate investigative subcommittee, ascertaining the root causes of the financial meltdown, was the appearance of collusion between Wall Street banks and the rating agencies. Banks "shopped around" their deals, selecting the agency willing to confer the best rating. The individual deals earned an agency hundreds of thousands of dollars in fees. The results of the collaboration were startling, particularly in the case of subprime residential mortgage-backed securities: some 91 percent of the triple-A-rated bonds issued in 2007 had been downgraded to junk (that is, below investment grade) status by 2010.[52]

The Financial Reform Act and Municipal Securities

In July 2010, President Obama signed the Dodd-Frank Wall Street Reform and Consumer Protection Act (Financial Reform Act). The huge bill represented a massive restructuring of the nation's securities market and banking regulatory regimes, and it contained a host of new oversight powers for an array of regulatory bodies. As noted, the rating agencies were a major target for reform. The municipal securities market and other state and local government financial activities, while not being primary targets of financial reform, were swept up in the avalanche of legislative changes. The new regulations for implementing the act will take several years to be fully propagated, as will various studies to be conducted. But the impact promised to be substantial. The following commentary provides a brief summary of the act's major impacts on the municipal bond market.[53]

Expanded Roles for the MSRB and the SEC

The Financial Reform Act expanded the rule-making authority of the Municipal Securities Rulemaking Board (MSRB), the self-regulatory body of the municipal bond industry. The MSRB was established by Congress under the 1975 amendments to the Securities Exchange Act of 1934 to oversee broker-dealer transactions in municipal securities and related business activities. The purview of the MSRB was restricted to regulating dealer-brokers in municipal bonds; the government issuers themselves were exempted from the MSRB's oversight. Thus, the regulation of the municipal market is exerted through private-sector market professionals, an approach unique to that market, which has been controversial over the years.[54]

Prior to the act, the MSRB's regulatory reach extended only to dealer and broker transactions in municipal securities. However, many municipal financial transactions have involved financial products that did not meet the legal test of being "securities" per se. For example, transactions involving interest-rate swaps, credit derivatives, and investment contracts did not fall under the definitional umbrella of "securities." Falling between the regulatory cracks, many derivative transactions have been controversial and costly to governmental borrowers. The Financial Reform Act broadened the coverage of the MSRB to include such financial products when they involved governments or related entities.[55] The act created the Office of Municipal Securities within the SEC, which will serve as a liaison between the SEC and the MSRB. The director of the Office of Municipal Securities will report directly to the SEC chairman.

Municipal Financial Advisors

The new act brought into the MSRB's regulatory sphere municipal financial advisors, who had previously been unregulated. Financial advisors in the municipal bond market are those firms and individuals that assist in the design of transactions, the initial bond sale, and, often, the investment of bond proceeds, including the design and selection financial products that are often connected with bond sales. Advisors may provide other services such as feasibility or marketing studies.

The margins of what constitutes financial advisory activity can be elastic and shadowy. Advisors may be active players in the design and offering of bond issues or may simply be "helping" securities firms and banks drum up underwriting business (acting as deal finders). In other cases, accountants, lawyers, and engineers, in addition to offering the traditional advice of their profession, may be involved in the design and marketing of debt obligations of other financial transactions of a government. The Reform Act requires, for the first time, that municipal "advisors" be registered with the SEC, similar to the registration requirement for broker-dealers.[56] Perhaps most important, the act required the MSRB to develop fiduciary standards for advisors and authorized the MSRB to set professional standards for municipal advisors, such as prescribing testing of personnel and setting supervisory rules, as well as rules defining a municipal advisor's fiduciary duty to its clients.

Financial Products

The Reform Act gave the MSRB new powers to regulate transactions by municipal broker-dealers and advisors in municipal "financial products." Municipal financial products are defined as municipal derivatives, guaranteed investment contracts, and various investment strategies. Such investment products have been the source of considerable controversy (and litigation) over the past several years, as the municipal market has grown in complexity.[57] Among other things, the use of swaps is limited to governments that have minimum assets or that need to deal with a bank or broker. Moreover, the government must use a swap advisor. All swap transactions must be reported and listed in a repository.[58]

MSRB Board Composition

A complaint over the years has been that the MSRB was overweighted with industry representation and did not sufficiently reflect the broader public interests involved in oversight of the municipal market. Before the Reform Act, the board's membership was composed of five persons representing broker-dealers, five persons representing those commercial banks with municipal finance departments, and five persons representing the general public, including bond issuers. As a result of the act, the MSRB board was scheduled to have eight "public" members that are independent of any regulated entity and at least one of whom is to represent institutional investors and at least one of whom is to represent municipal entities. The other seven members will represent municipal dealers, bank municipal departments, and financial advisors.

Mandated Studies

The Reform Act mandated several studies should be done relating to, among other things, disclosure practices in the municipal securities market, the possible application of fiduciary standards to municipal broker and dealers, and the possible need to repeal or amend the Tower Amendment. That amendment, adopted when the securities laws were amended in the early 1970s to encompass the municipal market, limits the ability of the SEC or the MSRB to regulate municipal securities issuers directly by banning the SEC or the MSRB from requiring any filing prior to the issuance of securities. Any change in the Tower Amendment restrictions "would have significant ramifications for municipal securities issuers."[59] Closely related concerns are the mandated studies of the rating agencies and how they are to be regulated. The rating agencies, as we have discussed, play a huge role in the municipal securities markets on a wide variety of fronts.

The implications of the act for the municipal bond market appear to mean much more direct and detailed regulation of the municipal securities business. For years, the SEC has chafed from its inability to regulate directly the borrowing activities of state and local government borrowers.[60] A large part of the problem has been the extension over the years of tax exemption to debt that is not supported by general taxation but rather was self-supporting by the earnings from and assets invested in "private activities." For example, there have been long-standing provisions in the tax code that permit the use of tax-free bonds for commercial and industrial development purposes.[61] Not surprisingly, this commercially based "municipal" debt has proved to be much riskier than the traditional tax-supported debt or that of "garden variety" government-owned utilities, such as water and sewer bonds.

Changes in the Financial Markets

The role of subnational governments in the financial markets is unique to the United States. Unlike most countries, state and local governments are free to issue securities at their own behest and are responsible only for their own debts. Likewise, the federal government is constitutionally accountable only for its own debts as specifically approved by Congress. Neither the federal government nor the states assume debt under a joint and several legal liability, although the federal government, from time to time, has conferred federal guarantees on state and local obligations issued under specific programs. Nonetheless, the taxpayers of an individual state are responsible for their share of federal debt. State and local governments are not entitled legally to an automatic back-up or guarantee by the federal government; if a state and local government defaults on its debt, investors cannot count on the Treasury to step in and fix the problem.[62] This system of divided responsibilities has worked well during most of the history of the United States and has been a factor in letting state and local taxes adjust to local needs and willingness to take on different degrees of support for providing services to citizens.

The coexistence of the federal government and the states has been the basis for American public finance federalism, which calls for fiscal self-reliance between the central government and the local governments. Investors have understood that any state, local government, or its agency that fails to live within its means has meant that a bond could default without redress to the national government. With a few exceptions, that approach has been the tradition. During the nineteenth century, states, particularly in the South, defaulted on their bonds and, later, during the Great Depression of the 1930s when one state and hundreds of local governments missed their payments without an intervention by the federal government.[63] However, during the Great Depression, the federal government did get substantially involved in directly financing state and local governments through the Reconstruction Finance Corporation (RFC).[64]

The concept that governments must live within their means most likely checked the growth of subnational governments and their adoption of risky schemes. Likewise, credit analysis in the municipal bond market did not factor into bond pricing any expectation that the federal government would rescue a troubled state or local borrower in the event of a debt-service shortfall. The absence of a predetermined federal bailout expectation for troubled state and local governments avoided the moral hazard of dependency and intrinsically promoted market discipline among municipal bond borrowers. Over the years, the traditional idea of self-reliance within the federal system came to be balanced with the concept of a national framework of the public good. Depressed economic areas that could not provide certain basic services were deemed deserving of help from the national point of view. This balancing act required transfers of resources from richer areas to poorer ones. Wealth transfers have had both good and bad side effects, with the relative weights depending on one's political philosophy. On the positive side, transfers were used to support the overall growth of the nation and led to a stronger, more convergent, country. On the negative side, federal outlays funded "pork barrel" projects that were of dubious national benefit but appealed to special interests.

In recent decades, the federal government has become more active in matters that directly and indirectly affect state and local government financing. Federal aid to local governments and states through grants, revenue sharing, and stimulus packages to aid transportation, education, health care, and economic development all contribute to a lessened dogmatic approach to early fiscal federalism. While municipal debt has been an area in which the federal government has adhered to the original concept of letting the states stand on their creditworthiness, the concept of unstinting self-reliance does not appear as sacrosanct as it once did. In order to mitigate the serious repercussions of the credit crisis of 2007–2008 that spilled over into the Great Recession, the federal government took drastic steps to contain the impact by supporting the banking industry to keep it from failing and, subsequently, by enacting a $787 billion stimulus program. A substantial portion of the stimulus monies, around $140 billion, was channeled to the states and local governments. Spurred to greater action by the credit crisis, the federal government took on an active role in matters related to the municipal market—in terms of credit, tax exemption, and regulation.

Build America Bonds: The Taxable-Bond Option

One of the more innovative federal programs that grew out of the American Recovery and Reinvestment Act (the Recovery Act) in 2009 was the municipal bond program called Build America Bonds (BABs). This program was designed to lower the cost of borrowing for state and local governments to finance infrastructure and was unique in that federal subsidies were paid to help cover the debt service on municipal bonds that were sold on a taxable basis when issuers elected to offer them. Thus, the taxable bonds served as substitutes for tax-exempt securities.[65] The taxable BABs appealed to a broader investor class, including foreign investors and individual retirement accounts, which, because of their tax status, received little or no benefit from holding tax-free municipals.[66]

These investors looked at the municipal market with its historically extremely low default rate as an attractive alternative to corporate bonds. In addition, the fact that the federal government promised to pay 35 percent of the interest on BABs over their lifetimes moved the federal government a step closer in blurring the historic separation where the municipal market looked only to the means of state and local governments as a source of payment. To market traditionalists, the exchange of a federal subsidy for tax exemption on the bonds was another step eroding what was once thought as a constitutionally protected right of states under the Tenth Amendment.[67] By mid-2010, the issuing of BABs since the commencement of the program in April 2009 had amounted to over $90 billion. BABs sales were running about $10 billion a quarter, representing approximately 30 percent of all municipal bond issuances.[68] Figure 25.6 depicts in graphic fashion the impact of the BABs program in the two years of its existence.

While BABs clearly encouraged municipal bond sales, they were controversial, in large part because they were heavily utilized by major state borrowers that were under fiscal stress, namely California, Illinois, and New York. The BABs program, as enacted, had a sunset date at the end of 2010 but many market participants called for extending the program. Others argued that the expiration of the BABs program was needed because the federal subsidy to cover state and local debt encouraged issuance and unduly rewarded big-spending, high-debt states.[69]

As the BABs program's termination date approached, the tax-exempt municipal bond market began to suffer from increasing interest rates, as investors withdrew from tax-exempt bond funds. There were a variety of reasons for why

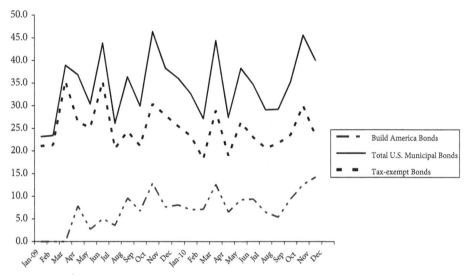

Figure 25.6 Total municipal bond sales, tax-exempt sales, Build America bond sales
(billions of dollars: monthly, 2009–2010)
Source: Securities Industry and Financial Markets Association (SIFMA).

investors became increasingly concerned about tax-exempt bonds, and it seems that a major factor was worry over what the loss of the BABs bonds would mean. If the BABs were terminated and no longer siphoning off the longer-maturity bonds, the tax-exempt rates would be expected to climb, perhaps substantially, in relation to other interest rates.[70] Unable to get reauthorization, the BABs taxable bond program expired December 31, 2010. During its short lifetime of eighteen months, however, the BABs program managed to move about $200 billion in state and local borrowing into the taxable-bond sector.

MARKET UNCERTAINTIES AT
THE END OF THE DECADE

At the end of 2010, the municipal bond market was in turmoil. Several factors caused the market difficulties, but a fundamental one was the widening concern that the enviable repayment record of debt service, with a default record many multiples better than that of private-sector debt, would come to an end. The alarms of possible state and local government defaults, which had been brewing since the well-advertised difficulties of Greece in the European Union in early 2010 and sub-sequent concerns boiled over to other European Union nations, such as Ireland. One of the major changes that had occurred was that US taxable state and local securities (primarily the BABs bonds) had entered (at least temporarily) into the international markets. This made them subject to comparison to the credits of the European Union countries, so that interest rates on the bonds could be compared.

The tax-exempt municipal bond market was rocked at the end of 2010 by the recommendations of the president's National Commission on Fiscal Responsibility and Reform.[71] Since the federal budget was last balanced in 2001, federal debt had grown dramatically, rising to 62 percent from 33 percent of GDP. The proposals in the commission's report were designed to reduce the federal deficit by nearly $4 trillion through 2020 to equal 2.3 percent of GDP, with a target of reducing it to 60 percent of GDP by 2023 and 40 percent by 2035. Under the commission's plan, federal revenue would be capped at 21 percent of GDP, and spending would be forced down to 22 percent and eventually 21 percent.[72] Also on the firing line were reductions in federal aid to state and local governments and the reductions or removal of a number of federal tax preferences favorable to state and local governments.

Structural Concerns

Given the chronically deteriorating nature of the federal government's fiscal situation and the seemingly deep-seated malaise of state and local finances, financial market participants had plenty of reasons to be concerned about the future structure of municipal bond market. Because the tax-exempt market is sensitive to marginal tax rates on income, the irony is that *higher* marginal federal-tax rates and the reduction of competing tax preferences would improve the demand for tax-exempt securities and lower their interest rates relative to other securities. But such changes as reducing in the deductibility of state and local taxes from the federal income tax and the loss of the mortgage interest deduction would make the burden of income taxes greater on state and local taxpayers and, perhaps, further reduce the value of housing, which is the major tax base for the local governments.

Another structural concern surrounded the future demand for long-term tax-exempt bonds. As noted, the BABs program had been exceedingly successful, particularly in the longer bond maturities (those exceeding ten years). Prior to the introduction of the BABs program, the longest maturities of tax-exempt securities had been supported by the extensive use of auction-rate and variable-rate securities, which effectively converted long-term bonds into short-term paper.[73] This restructuring of long-term debt into more easily sold short-term debt helped keep long-term interest rates lower. But it also masked a growing weakness in the market for long-term tax-exempt debt during the early to mid-2000s.[74] These devices imploded in 2007 and 2008 as the markets deteriorated and the interest rates on tax-exempt bonds rose rapidly in relationship to those on US Treasuries. However, in early 2008 the BABs had come to the rescue of the long-term municipal market, siphoning off the longer-term bonds with a generous 35 percent interest-rate subsidy. However, with the BABs on the brink of demise at the end of 2010, the prospects for long-term tax-exempt interest rates became menacing. Mirroring a sharp rise in long Treasury bond yields, intensified by the expiration of the BABs program as well as concerns about municipal credit quality, long-term municipal bond yields moved upward as well. In November 2010, tax-exempt mutual bond funds had a weekly withdrawal of nearly $5 billion dollars (the largest since October 2008). Investors, evidently spooked by the uncertain state of governmental fiscal affairs (at all levels), had anticipated that bond prices would fall and interest rates rise as the tax-exempt market lost the support of BABs. Moreover, investors were rattled by a bevy of market pessimists who were predicting that municipal bonds were on the verge of a wave of defaults.

WOULD STATE AND LOCAL DEBT BE PAID?

At the end of 2010, analysts asked if the many changes that the municipal market had undergone, coupled with the long-term dire fiscal straits of governments at all levels, were going to permanently change the relationship of these governments to the markets. The number one issue was that of looming defaults in the sector, a subject that had not been considered for eighty years. A major part of that issue was not just the bonded debt (market securities) that was outstanding, but, in addition, the other liabilities on the frequently incomplete and dated balance sheets of governments. As was noted at the outset of this chapter, the accumulation of underfunded pension benefits and various postretirement obligations are of great concern to investors. Not only were the amounts of these obligations in question, but also their legal standing was unknown: to what extent could pension benefits that were already promised to future government worker retirees be reduced?

In many states this restructuring of public employee benefits is evidently a constitutional question, as is their priority of claims versus bondholders.[75] Moreover, the estimation of the pension liabilities, the evaluation of the assets to support them, and the disclosure of such information in the case of the individual funds and for the sector as a whole were likewise subject to questioning.[76] This had already become an issue of action by the SEC, which had taken action against the state of New Jersey.[77] In the case of the state of Connecticut, for example, the bonded debt outstanding at the end of 2010 was $19.5 billion, but the state employee and teacher pension systems had an unfunded liability of $50 billion (if assets are valued at market values) and unfunded postretirement life insurance and health benefits were another $27.6 billion.[78] Thus, the repayment of the state's securities market debt amounted to only 20 percent of its total liabilities when retirement and postretirement benefits were included.[79]

By the end of 2010, comparisons were being made between the financial melt-down of the markets due to the subprime crisis and the perilous financial conditions that states and localities were experiencing. Some commentators argued that states and localities were overextended, especially given the substantial, if indefinite, overhang of pension and postretirement benefits, and their debts were shaky, akin to that which had been run up during the subprime mortgage crisis.[80] Of particular concern was the exhaustion of the federal stimulus funds, which had poured about $160 billion into the state and local sectors from 2009 through 2011.[81] Without the stimulus aid, states faced a $130 billion-dollar deficit in fiscal year 2012, according to the Center for Budget and Policy Priorities.[82] Reacting to increased credit concerns, at the end of 2010 and continuing into early 2011, the tax-exempt market suffered from a widespread retreat of the municipal bond money-market funds, which liquidated much of their positions, as tax-exempt rates rose sharply.

RECESSION, BUT NOT ANOTHER DEPRESSION

The ARRA stimulus, which brought considerable temporary relief, was not the only federal program that helped state and local governments get through the serious economic downturn that began in late 2007 with the collapse of the subprime housing market. Congressional enactment in late 2008 of the federal Troubled Asset Relief Program (TARP) bailout package bolstered financial institutions around the nation and played an important (if behind-the-scenes) role with respect to those municipal bonds that were secured by property taxes.[83] During the Great Depression of the 1930s, the absence of an early rescue package for the banks exacerbated losses to local governments from distressed real estate and unpaid property taxes, which contributed substantially to the hundreds of municipal borrowers that were unable to make timely payments on their bonds. Timely debt-service payments by municipal borrowers are heavily dependent on the timely receipt of tax and enterprise revenues and on the maintenance of sufficient cash balances.

Much like the Great Depression of the 1930s, the fall in housing prices was widespread in the Great Recession. Home values fell by as much as 44 percent in the hardest-hit states from 2007 to 2010.[84] Normally, the impact of falling real estate values on assessed valuation and property taxes lags within the trough of an economic downturn by one to three years because of the idiosyncratic mechanics of assessing properties and the setting of rates. The greatest risk to timely payment of those municipal bonds secured by ad valorem property taxes is the failure to collect property taxes in sufficient amounts to cover debt service. These deficiencies occurred in the 1930s because hundreds of banks either closed their doors without an appropriate successor or were unable to protect their collateral through advancing property-tax payments on delinquent loans.

According to George Hempel in his book *The Postwar Quality of State and Local Debt*, "Total state and local revenues remained at approximately the same level from 1927 through 1934, but the nature of these revenues shifted considerably. Cash revenues from property taxes declined from 60% to 48% of total revenues during the period, primarily because property values declined and the proportion of property taxes that were not collected rose."[85] Hempel further noted that "the proportion of property taxes that were uncollected in cities with over 50,000 residents rose from 4.7% in 1928 to 26.3% in 1933." Albeit they took a slight dip in the fourth quarter of 2010, running 3 percent below the fourth quarter of 2009, property-tax receipts during the Great Recession showed much greater stability than the dive they took in the 1930s.[86]

While the lagging reassessment process has helped to keep tax bills from falling fast, the big difference from the Great Depression period was that local governments maintained their high property-tax collection rates from 2007 to 2010. Collection rates showed only modest annual deterioration in the total percentage of the levy that they collected from prerecession levels. Evidence that property-tax collections remained relatively strong was found by examining the financial reporting documents provided by city borrowers. These showed that the median total collection rate had only fallen about 1 percent from 2007 through 2009 (99.5 percent to 98.7 percent).[87] Early reporters, which account for about one-half of the sample units, reported that FY 2010 showed the property-tax collection rate to be only a little weaker at 98.1 percent. In any event, the decline in the collections rate was nothing like the huge drop noted by Hempel as had happened during the early years of the Great Depression.

The demonstration of political will by the federal government at the time of a financial calamity to take steps to support the banking system was a major factor accounting for the much better tax-collection record following the credit crisis of 2008 than was the case during the Great Depression. The Troubled Asset Relief Program (TARP) enabled the vast majority of banks to stay healthy enough to pay property taxes in order to secure their collateral liens on the huge number of subprime delinquent loans. But, without those supports, many banks would have most likely not been in a position to pay those property taxes. This level of federal early intervention to protect the financial institutions did not happen during the Great Depression. By recapitalizing and consolidating many of the nation's large and small financial institutions, TARP and other liquidity-providing and various insuring measures helped to stabilize their balance sheets. That allowed most banks and mortgage servicers to protect their collateral on soured home and commercial mortgages by paying property taxes on delinquent mortgages until foreclosure. In those cases in which the loans were packaged into securitized mortgage pools, there were usually legal provisions that property taxes must be paid in accordance with requirements set by Fannie Mae and Freddie Mac. Thus, as long as these financial institutions or their successors remained strong enough to protect the collateral, the property taxes continued to be paid. The protection afforded by federal intervention to support the financial system cannot be taken for granted in the event of future financial and economic reversals. But the systemic dependency of governments on healthy financial institutions should be a consideration both in assessing credit quality in the state and local sectors and, one would hope, in designing future assistance programs.

CONCLUDING COMMENTS

State and local governments, as of early 2011, had enjoyed some recovery in their revenues as the nation's economy had slowly improved. But it was clear that long-term structural problems for states and localities would persist. According to the long-term forecasts performed by the GAO, the state and local sector in the coming years faced steadily growing operating deficits as the existing revenue system produced insufficient resources to meet the burgeoning spending needs embodied in existing spending programs.[88] Leading among these concerns about the state governments were the burdens of health-care spending and catching up on the unfunded liabilities for pensions and postretirement employee benefits. As states grappled with these issues, the knock-on effects would lead to reductions on capital spending, state employment, and employee wages, and the stream of transfers to individuals and their local governments. These adjustments will cause continuing stringency, not an instant collapse. The alternative of raising taxes appeared to have little public support and will collide with the need of the federal government itself to raise revenues. Discussions of comprehensive federal tax reform always contemplate removing the tax preferences that have favored state and local governments, with the present tax exemption of the interest income on state and local securities being a target.

Local governments are destined to suffer from the lingering hangover of the housing crisis in the form of slow-growing or even reduced property taxes and, more immediately, reductions in state aid (much of that stemming from reduced federal aid to the states). Faced with these challenges, the majority of them will need to implement a combination of increasing taxes and user charges, making spending cuts, and abandoning programs for which they no longer receive state or federal aid. A few municipalities will simply be unable or unwilling to take these actions. For a very few (mostly limited-purpose special districts), this may lead to a random default or a sporadic Chapter 9 bankruptcy. But, much more likely, the states will put together a rescue package, especially for general units of local government. In the last analysis, history should be a good guide, and final losses to investors will be less than the nominal default total. Debt may be restructured and amortization schedules will be extended in the process, but principal at the end of the day will get paid. But, even to the extent that there are losses, letter of credit banks and bond insurers will absorb much of them, insulating the individual bond investors.

Despite the current hardships and confusions, state and local governments, much like the nation's banking system, embody a sector that is just too big, and too essential, to be allowed to fail. Therefore, the traditions of payment of debts and continuing access to the financial markets will prevail.[89] Debt service is a fairly minor part of the annual spending by most governments and states and localities cannot afford to have the private markets close to them. Pension obligations present a long-term problem, but the solutions can also be undertaken over the long term and will be developed where the nation as a whole faces the issues of scaling back on past promises that assumed a trajectory of growth and prosperity that the future will not match. By the same token, the new sobriety will illuminate the reality that the nation as a whole cannot operate unless the day-to-day governmental functions are provided at the state and local level.

Notes

1 US Bureau of Economic Analysis (2010), table 11B. State and local government net physical capital stock at depreciated values was worth $8.2 trillion at the end of 2009, of which $2.7 trillion represents streets and highways; $1.9 trillion, education facilities; and $1 trillion, water and sewer facilities. See ibid., http://www.bea.gov/national/ FA2004, table 11B.

2 Unlike most countries, the subnational units in the United States access the markets at their own prerogative and without guarantees from the federal government.

3 US Census Bureau (2007 Census of Governments), http://www.census.gov/govs/cog/ GovOrgTab03ss.html.

4 Trade payables are the day-to-day short-term accounts payable of governments that owe money to vendors.

5 See US Census Bureau (2010), http://www.census.gov/govs/estimate/.

6 The Pew Center on the States (2010). State and local governments also faced fiscal pressure from other postemployment benefits (OPEB), the largest of which is typically retiree health benefits. The Governmental Accounting Standards Board (GASB) requires that governments account for the costs of OPEB as employees accrue the benefits, rather than when they are paid. But retiree health benefits have typically not been funded. Thus, OPEB liability is unfunded. Both the Pew Foundation and GAO have put the unfunded OPEB liabilities at around $550 billion as of 2010.

7 Seymour (2010).

8 Richard and Preston (2010), 41.

9 These are financial instruments that allow long-term instruments to be sold in short-term markets with ongoing resets of their rates. The provision of a liquidity facility to take up any unsold paper once rates were reset was a vital element.

10 Brad Gewehr, *UBS Risk Watch* (March 2, 2010), 3.

11 The interest rates on Aaa corporate bonds were at 5.05 percent in December 2008 and Baa corporate bonds were at 8.43 percent. (Moody's Investors Service monthly averages as reported in the Federal Reserve Board of Governors, *H-15 Release*). For an investor in municipal bonds (the average rating on the Bond Buyer 20 Index is around the Aa-AA bracket), the yield in December 2008 was equivalent to a before-tax yield of 8.55 percent for an investor in a 35 percent marginal tax bracket (5.58/(1-.35)).

12 IMF (as referenced in *Business Week*), November 21, 2010.

13 McDonald (2010), 83.

14 Ibid., 84.

15 The ARRA pumped roughly $140 billion of federal aid into state and local government budgets, with most of the additional spending occurring in 2009 and 2010.

16 See Robison, Wechsler, and Braun (2009).

17 Pew Center for the States (2010).

18 Standard & Poor's, Credit Report, *ACA* (April 2008).

19 A "ratings watch" is an announcement by a rating agency that it is examining a borrower's creditworthiness and may change its rating.

20 Kripalani (2007).

21 For an extensive history of the credit-rating industry and its impact on both financial markets and political policy, see Sinclair (2005).

22 Not all defaults are equal, because there may be differences in the speed and extent to which funds are recovered in the case of default.

23 "Measuring the Measurers" (2007).

24 New York City's debt restructuring was considered a default by some analysts because investors were forced to await principal payments on certain notes that were extended by the city.

25 See Sinclair (2005), 157–160. The county sued the bond underwriters as well as the rating agency and then collected $467 million from Merrill Lynch in a settlement. S&P settled for a partial refund ($140,000) of its rating fee. The agency successfully used its "First Amendment" defense against the county's accusation of reckless negligence. Under the First Amendment defense, the agency stated that it was exercising its right of free speech in giving its rating opinion.

26 Ibid.

27 Other corporate scandals leading up to investor losses and setting the stage for the act were those of Tyco, Worldcom, Global Crossing, and Adelphia.

28 Title 6 of the Sarbanes-Oxley Act mandated a study of the rating agencies and their regulation under the NRSRO status. The SEC was in the process of proposing regulations as the financial disaster of 2007–2008 struck and, subsequently, the SEC has been given new oversight responsibilities and enforcement powers under the Dodd-Frank Act of 2010.

29 Shorter and Seizinger (2009).

30 The 2006 Act streamlined the process for firms to receive an NRSRO designation and required that agencies receiving the designation submit their rating methodologies to the SEC. On September 24, 2007, the SEC issued a press release stating that it had granted seven credit-rating agencies the NRSRO status. Moody's, S&P, and Fitch were joined by A.M. Best Company, DBRS Ltd., Japan Credit Rating Agency Ltd., and Rating and Investment Information, Inc. US Securities and Exchange Commission (2007). But by that time, the financial crisis was overwhelming the markets.

31 USA Today (September 2007).

32 US Permanent Subcommittee on Investigation (2010), 5. Between 2000 and 2007, the average 53 percent operating margin of the rating agencies far outpaced that of other companies, such as Microsoft (36 percent) and Exxon (17 percent). See ibid.

33 "Measuring the Measurers" (2007).

34 *London Telegraph* (2007).

35 Examining in detail the subprime mortgage phenomenon, which precipitated the credit crunch of 2007, is beyond the scope of this chapter. The general contours can be found in several contemporary accounts. Edward Gramlich, a governor of the Federal Reserve Board, was an early alarm sounder, and he published in early 2007 a brief book that outlined the emergence of the subprime mortgage problem (Gramlich 2007). Fortunes were lost, but some were made. For an account of the rise and fall of the subprime market, see Lewis (2010).

36 The ABACUS deal was a "synthetic" CDO (collateral debt obligation), which was not backed by actual mortgages but rather where "referenced" to a set of such obligations. It was a way to speculate on the market by using a synthetic portfolio modeled after (but not containing) the underlying obligations.

37 Morgenson and Story (2010), B1.

38 Sinclair (2005) 152–53.

39 *London Telegraph* (2007).

40 Morgenson and Story (2010). As part of its inquiry, the Senate Subcommittee made public 581 pages of e-mail messages and other documents that suggested that executives and analysts at rating agencies took on new business from Wall Street, even though they recognized they couldn't properly analyze all of the banks' products. These documents also showed that in late 2006, workers at the agencies were worried that their assessments and the models they used were flawed. They were particularly concerned about models that were rating collateralized debt obligations like Abacus.

41 Lewis (2010), 98.

42 Ibid., 99.

43 Not all municipal bonds are rated by the agencies, but only very small, typically general-obligation securities are not rated. Of the total of 12,295 long-term municipal bonds issued in 2009, some 2,472 issues were not rated. But the unrated issues were only about $5.2 million in average size and were clearly aimed at local investors. SIFMA *Municipal Bond Credit Report Full Year* (2009) 7.

44 Noting the large variance in default rates between municipal and corporate bonds, California State Treasurer Bill Lockyer protested that the misaligned credit ratings were costing California jurisdictions about $4 billion in added debt service. CNBC News (2008).

45 Hempel (1971). *The Postwar Quality of Municipal Bonds* was republished later in 1971 as *The Postwar Quality of State and Local Debt* by the National Bureau of Economic Research.

46 Moody's Investor Service (2010).

47 Fitch Investor Service (2010).

48 Most provisions concerning the ratings agencies are found under Subtitle C of Title IX of the Dodd-Frank Act.

49 This analysis is based primarily on Moynihan, Nolan, Pagnano, and Williamson (2010).

50 Crittenden (2010).

51 Herszenhorn (2010). Senator Franken said this would allow smaller credit rating companies to compete against the Big Three. That idea did not make it into the final act and was replaced by a required study of the proposed random selection-rating scheme.

52 Blake (2010a).

53 According to common usage in the financial markets, the term "municipal" has an
   expansive meaning, and this terminology carries over to the act and its regulatory
   scope. A municipal entity is broadly defined to mean any state, political subdivision
   of a state, or municipal corporate instrumentality of a state, including (1) any agency,
   authority, or instrumentality of the state, political subdivision, or municipal corporate
   instrumentality; (2) any plan, program, or pool of assets sponsored or established by
   the state, political subdivision, or municipal corporate instrumentality or any agency,
   authority, or instrumentality thereof; and (3) any other issuer of municipal securities.
   See Fippinger, Herrington, and Sutcliff LLP (2010); Anderson and Woods (2010);
   Gaffney (2010).

54 The restriction on the MSRB's rule making regarding municipal issuers is found in the
   so-called Tower Amendment, which prohibited registration requirements on issuers
   and the direct application of MSRB rules to governments. The MSRB rules are subject
   to review and approval by the Securities and Exchange Commission (SEC).

55 There may be "obligated parties," which are not governmental issuers but on whose
   behalf a governmental unit may borrow. This is a very common "conduit" structure
   for not-for-profits and profit-making corporations that are used for various public and
   private purposes.

56 Defining a "financial advisor" is difficult. The act defines an advisor as one who
   provides advice to a municipal entity with respect to municipal financial products
   or the issuance of municipal securities. The definition specifically includes financial
   advisors, guaranteed investment-contract brokers, third-party marketers, placement
   agents, solicitors, deal finders, and swap providers. The definition excludes attorneys
   offering legal advice or providing services of a traditional legal nature, and engineers
   providing engineering advice. However, the status of various appointed (as opposed to
   elected) officials that serve on various governmental boards is unclear, as is their need
   to pay advisor registration fees.

57 The exact definition of these financial product forms and activities will be embodied
   in technical amendments to the bill. Regardless of the definitions, the new jurisdiction
   of the MSRB in respect to derivatives will overlap the new authority of the Commodity
   Futures Trading Commission (CFTC) and the SEC to regulate derivatives. These
   agencies will have to reach an accommodation with the MSRB on the issues to be
   covered by MSRB rules.

58 Several details on regulating swaps need to be worked out. However, it appears that
   state and local employee pension systems will be covered by the provisions. Swaps
   will be regulated by the CFTC, which will develop a "code of conduct" for dealers in
   dealing with state and local governments. See Gaffney (2010), 79.

59 See Anderson and Woods (2010), 2. The impact of the Tower Amendment, which
   was intended to restrict the powers of the federal government to regulate the state
   and local government bond issuers, is controversial. Some commentators think that
   while the amendment restricts the rule-making authority of the MRSB (an industry
   self-regulatory body), it has no real such constraints on the SEC, which is empowered
   under its general antifraud powers to place pre-issuance requirements for purposes
   of *preventing* fraud in the market. The definition of fraud is itself open to debate,
   depending under which sections of the securities laws the activity takes place. See
   Doty (2010), 670, note 920.

60 Under the Financial Reform Act, the SEC is to carry out a study to determine if its
   regulatory powers regarding the issuers of municipal securities should be increased.

61 According to the *Flow of Funds*, those municipal bond obligations that are liabilities of
   nonfinancial corporations amounted to $200 billion at the end of the second quarter

of 2010. Table l-211. Federal Reserve Board of Governors, *Flow of Funds* (September 17, 2010).

62 While the states do not have the power to print a national currency, they can issue securities (warrants) that can serve a similar function within a state and be used for paying state taxes and other money owed to the state. Warrants have been used on occasion by the states of Michigan and California.

63 Hempel (1971).

64 During the Depression years, the federal government was very active in state and local debt finance. The RFC, a federal corporation, financed $3 billion in relief payments to states and localities between 1932 and 1937. The loans, which were unpaid, were canceled in 1938. The RFC was active in the bond markets, bidding on bonds, and bought the $136 million refinancing bond issue of Arkansas (the one state that had defaulted during the Depression) in 1941. In addition, the RFC made loans on state and local self-liquidation projects, such as bridges, aqueducts, and toll roads. The Pennsylvania Turnpike was built with a $35 million RFC loan, as were the Oakland Bay Bridge ($70 million) and the Huey P. Long Bridge over the Mississippi at New Orleans ($17 million). The approximately $10 billion in RFC loans to state and local governments in the 1930s would be equal to $160 billion in current dollar (2010) terms. See Jones and Angly (1951).

65 Petersen (2010a).

66 Petersen (2010b).

67 A US Supreme Court ruling in 1983 (*South Carolina v. Baker*) decided that municipal bond tax exemption was a right subject to Congress statute and was not a constitutional issue.

68 SIFMA Municipal Credit Report (second quarter, 2010).

69 *Wall Street Journal*, Review and Outlook, Opinion (December 30, 2010); Malanga (2010).

70 According to one market observer, "If BABs did not exist, long-term yields on tax-exempts would be...about 50bp higher. [I]ssuers who qualify for BAB financing are saving close to 100bp by issuing long-term BABs relative to what their costs would be in a tax-exempt-only market, and issuers who do not qualify for BAB financing (hospitals, private activity bonds and refundings) are saving about 50bp." (Note: a basis point is 1/100th of a percentage point.) Friedlander (2010), 3.

71 The Commission was cochaired by Erskine Bowles and Alan Simpson. Eleven of the eighteen commission members voted in early December 2010 to accept the report. The report painted a bleak picture of the nation's fiscal situation, warning that the country faced staggering and unsustainable deficits without major reforms. In 2010, federal spending was nearly 24 percent of GDP. But with tax revenues at 15 percent of GDP, the budget deficit gap between spending and revenue was just under 9 percent of GDP.

72 Hume (2010).

73 Tender option bonds (TOBs) entailed borrowing at a short-term tax-exempt rate and using the proceeds to buy long-term tax-free bonds, hedging both with opposite positions on taxable rates such as the London Interbank Offered Rate. The strategy, used by hedge funds, was to earn an arbitrage profit by capturing the additional basis points offered by the municipal yield curve compared with the taxable curve. It has been estimated that there were $300 to $500 billion in TOBs in early 2007, which sopped up much of the supply of long-term tax-exempt bonds. See Seymour (2010).

74 One needs to be remembered that marginal income-tax rates were lowered during the 2000s, as well as the rates on capital gains and dividends, which are competing investments.

75 See Lav and McNichols (2011).

76 Sracke and Narens (2011).

77 Scannell and Neuman (2010).

78 Cooper and Walsh (2010), 1.

79 The state had about $97.1 billion in total liabilities, including an additional $2.3 billion in other obligations. Ibid.

80 This was the view of the analyst Meredith Whitney. Ibid.

81 That $159 billion in federal ARRA aid helped offset state deficits that totaled $360 billion for 2009 through 2011. By fiscal year 2012, only $6 billion in ARRA aid will be left unspent, but state deficits are estimated to be about $140 billion. Ibid.

82 Ibid.

83 Samuelson (2011),14. Of the $700 billion in aid approved under TARP, only $410 billion was used, of which $245 billion was distributed to banks. Virtually all of the bank assistance, which was distributed nationwide, had been repaid by early 2011 with interest and dividends. Nonetheless, the program was very unpopular with the public because it was perceived as being a bank bailout that did little for ordinary citizens.

84 The Federal Housing Finance Agency All-Transaction Index as cited in Boyd (2011).

85 Hempel (1971), 38–39.

86 US Census Bureau (2011).

87 Merritt Research Services (2011). The data derived from annual reports filed by cities for about 400 cities (total collections includes property-tax collections in the current year plus back payments, penalties, and foreclosure proceeds). Data are as of March 11, 2011.

88 GAO (2011). The analytical technique used is to measure the difference between the projected costs of services versus the revenues that would be produced under the existing revenue system. The gap is a measure of how much spending would need to be cut versus taxes raided so as to balance the aggregate budget.

89 See, for example, Sracke and Narens (2011). They argue, as do many other analysts, that the fiscal stresses, while great, are not going to lead to widespread defaults. As of this writing in mid-2011, that has been the case.

References

Anderson III, Arthur, and McGuire Woods (2010, August 3). "Dodd-Frank Financial Reform Act Will Impact Municipal Securities Market."

Blake, Rich (2010a, May 4). "Franken Targets Rating Agencies. ABC News.

Blake, Rich (2010b, July/August). "Down Graded." *Institutional Investor.*

Boyd, Donald (2011. March 18). "State and Local Financial Update." Rockefeller Institute of Government.

CNBC News (2008, April 29). "California Treasurer: Bond Raters Costing Us Big Bucks." http://www.cnbc.com/id/24372504.

Cooper, Michelle, and Mary Walsh (2010, December 5). "Mounting Debts by States Stoke Fears of Crisis." *New York Times*: 1.

Crittenden, Michael (2010, August 9). "Regulators Plan First Steps on Credit Ratings." *Wall Street Journal.* http://online.wsj.com/article/SB10001424052748704268004575417811362825370.

Courtois, Renee (2009, Spring). "Reforming the Raters." *Regional Focus.* Federal Reserve Bank of Richmond.

Dodd, Randall (2010, June). "Municipal Bombs." *Finance & Development*, Volume 47, Number 2. International Monetary Fund.

Doty, Robert (2010). *From Turmoil to Tomorrow*. American Governmental Financial Services, Sacramento, CA, http://turmoiltotomorrow.com.

Federal Reserve Board of Governors. *Flow of Funds*. Washington, DC (various numbers).

Federal Reserve Board of Governors. *H-15 Release*. Washington, DC (various numbers).

Fippinger, Robert, Orrick Herrington, and Sutcliff LLP (2010, July 16). "The Financial Reform Act of 2010."

Fitch Investor Service (2010, March 25). "Recalibration of US Public Finance Ratings."

Friedlander, George (2010, November 23). "U.S. Rates Special: The Build America Bond Program Is a Classic 'Win-Win' for Federal, State and Local Governments." *CITI Municipals*.

Gaffney, Susan (2010, August). "Financial Reform Act Affects State and Local Governments." *Government Finance Review*.

General Accountancy Office (2010, July). *State and Local Governments' Fiscal Outlook: March 2010 Update*, GAO-10-899. Washington, DC.

General Accountancy Office (2011, April). *State and Local Governments' Fiscal Outlook: March 2010 Update*, GAO-11-495. Washington, DC.

Gramlich, Edward (2007). *Subprime Mortgages: America's Latest Boom and Bust*. Washington DC: Urban Institute Press.

Hempel, George H. (1971). "The Postwar Quality of State and Local Debt." Cambridge, MA: National Bureau of Economic Research.

Hume, Lynn (2010, December 1). "Deficit Commission's Final Report Urges Ending Tax-Exempt Interest on New Munis." *Daily Bond Buyer*: 1.

Jones, Jesse, and Edward Angly (1951). *Fifty Billion Dollars*. New York: Macmillan.

Kripalani, Chandni (2007). "Credit Rating Agencies Raise Concerns Apropos Their Veracity." http://22dollars.com/2007/09/credit_rating_agencies_raise_concerns_apropos_their_veracity.php.

Herszenhorn, David (2010, June 15). "House-Senate Talks Drop New Credit-Rating Rules." *New York Times*. http://nytimes.com/2010/15.

Lav, Iris, and Elizabeth McNichol (2011, January 21). "Misunderstandings Regarding State Debt, Pensions, and Retirement Health Costs." Center for Budget and Policy Priorities.

Lewis, Michael (2010). *The Big Short*. New York: W.W. Norton.

London Telegraph (2007, August 20). "Fingers Pointed at Credit Rating Agency Monopoly." http://www.telegraph.co.uk/money/main.jhtml?xml=/money/2007/08/19/ccbull519.xml.

Lowenstein, Roger (2000). *When Genius Failed: The Rise and Fall of Long-Term Capital Management*. New York: Random House.

Malanga, Stephen (2010, July 31). "The Muni-Bond Debt Bomb...and How to Dismantle It." *Wall Street Journal*.

Malhotra, Heide, B. (2007, October 21). "Are Rating Agencies to Blame for the Credit Market Crunch?" *The Epoch Times*.

Mathis, H. Sean (2007). Congressional Testimony. US House Financial Services Committee. http://www.house.gov/apps/list/hearing/financialsvcs_dem/ht092707.shtml.

McDonald, Michael (2010, November 15). "A Wall Street Product That Soaks Taxpayers." *Bloomberg Newsweek*.

"Measuring the Measurers." (2007, May 31). *The Economist*. http://www.economist.com/finance/displaystory.cfm?story_id=9267952.

Merritt Research Services LLP (2011). Chicago. Illinois. Unpublished survey data provided to authors as of March 11, 2011.

Moody's Investor Service (2010, March). "Recalibration of Moody's U.S. Municipal Ratings to its Global Rating Scale."

Moynihan, Mary C., Anthony R. G. Nolan, Clair E. Pagnano, and Gwendolyn A. Williamson (2010, July 18). "Financial Reform Bill Strengthens Regulation, Expands Potential Liability of Credit Rating Agencies." *K-L Gates Newsstand*. http://www.klgates.com/newsstand/Detail.aspx?publication=6563.

Morgenson, Gretchen, and Louise Story (2010, April 23). "Rating Agency Data Helps Wall Street Firms." *New York Times*: B1.

Munnell, Alicia, Jean-Pierre Aubry, and Laura Quinby (2010, April). *The Funding of State and Local Pensions: 2009–2013*. Center for Retirement Research at Boston College.

Petersen, John (2010a, July). "Sacramento's Socratic Moment." *Governing*. http://www.governing.com/columns/public-finance/Similarities-Between-Sacramento-Athens.html.

Petersen, John (2010b, June). "Happy Birthday Babs." *Governing*. http://www.governing.com/topics/finance/Build-America-Bonds-Make-a-Mark.html.

Pew Center on the States (2010, February). *The Trillion Dollar Gap: Underfunded State Retirement Systems and the Roads to Reform*. Washington, DC.

Richard, Christine, and Darrell Preston (2010, September 8). "Ross Goes Where Buffet Fears to Tread." *Bloomberg Businessweek*: 41.

Robison Peter, Pat Wechsler, and Martin Braun (2009, October 28). "Back-Door Taxes Hit U.S. with Financing in the Dark." *Bloomberg*.

Samuelson, Robert (2011, April 4). TARP Success Halted Economic Collapse." *Washington Post*: A14.

Scannell, Kara, and Jeannette Neuman (2010, August 19). "SEC Sues New Jersey as States' Finances Stir Fears." *Wall Street Journal*.

Sloan, Allan (2007, October 16). "Junk Mortgages under the Microscope." *Fortune*.

Securities Industry and Financial Markets Association (SIFMA). *Municipal Credit Report* (various numbers).

Seymour, Dan (2010, November 29). "BABs: The Last Pillar Standing." *Daily Bond Buyer*: 1.

Sinclair, Timothy (2005). *The New Masters of Capital*. Ithaca: Cornell University Press.

Shorter, Gary, and Michael Seizinger (2009, September 3). "Credit Rating Agencies and Their Regulation." US Congressional Research Service, Washington, DC.

Sracke, Christian, and Joseph Narens (2011). *PIMCO Viewpoints: February, 2011*. Pacific Investments Management Company, Newport Beach, California.

US Bureau of Economic Analysis (2010, September). National Income Accounts. http://www.bea.gov/national/FA2004.

US Census Bureau (2011). State and Local Government Finance: Quarterly Summary of State and Local Tax Revenue. http://www2.census.gov/govs/qtax/information_sheet.pdf.

US Securities and Exchange Commission (2007). Division of Market Regulation. http://www.sec.gov/divisions/marketreg/ratingagency.htm.

US Senate, Permanent Subcommittee on Investigation (2010, April 23). "Memorandum: Wall Street and the Financial Crisis: The Role of the Credit Rating Agencies."

USA Today "Credit Rating Agencies Defend Track Record" September 26, 2007. http://www.usatoday.com/money/industries/banking/2007-09-26-congress-credit.

Wheeler, Brent (2007). "Would You Credit (Rate) It?" http://www.brentwheeler.com/finance.php?itemid=445.

CHAPTER 26

INFRASTRUCTURE PRIVATIZATION IN THE NEW MILLENNIUM

ELLEN DANNIN AND
LEE COKORINOS

THE framework for infrastructure privatization in the United States during the new millennium is a complex amalgam of finance; tax policy; federal, state, and local law; government subsidies; and ideology. It tends to be characterized by contracts of more than fifty years, which are not subject to the sort of oversight found, for example, in the United Kingdom. Explaining these features and their effects is the focus of this chapter. Privatization in the United States generally involves turning over to the private sector the control and operation of facilities and services formerly provided by the public sector. The legal and financial arrangements of privatization can vary greatly. However, those involving infrastructure privatization—often referred to as public-private partnerships, or PPPs or P3s—involve similar controlling principles and practices across the many types of infrastructure that have been privatized. For the sake of clarity and brevity, the focus here is on highway privatization and on important features and drivers of infrastructure privatization: (1) finance; (2) contract terms, (3) decision making; and (4) financial and nonfinancial costs.

PUBLIC AND PRIVATE
INFRASTRUCTURE FINANCE

For more than a century, state and local public infrastructure was primarily funded through the use of state and local taxes and by borrowing from the tax-exempt municipal bond market.[1] However, in the last half of the twentieth century, the federal government became a major participant in providing and facilitating financing. In 1956, the federal motor fuel tax was established specifically to finance construction and maintenance of America's interstate highway system and the state and local surface transportation infrastructure through a program of inter-governmental payments. That simple user-pay funding structure began to break down after 1993, the last year the gas tax was adjusted for inflation,[2] and since 2002, Highway Trust Fund spending has exceeded revenues.[3] The shortfall has been met in recent years with infusions from general revenues into the Highway Trust Fund, including $8 billion from the Treasury's General Fund in September 2008.[4] As a result, even though a significant amount of highway funding has been provided by taxpayers as a whole, the nation's transportation infrastructure has long suffered from severe underfunding. The instability and insufficiency of these funding sources has put surface transportation on the Government Accountability Office (GAO) High-Risk list.[5]

The decades' long failure to institute taxation policies to address public needs and the current economic crisis have left the nation with deteriorating infrastructure, including highways, water and waste systems, and education. When he introduced the Surface Transportation Authorization Act of 2009, Representative James Oberstar described a deep and widespread transportation crisis:

> Today, almost 61,000 miles (37 percent) of all lane miles on the NHS [National Highway System] are in poor or fair condition; more than 152,000 bridges—one of every four bridges in the United States—are structurally deficient or functionally obsolete; and more than 32,500 public transit buses and vans have exceeded their useful life. The nation's largest public transit agencies face an $80 billion maintenance backlog to bring their rail systems to a state of good repair and, within the next six years, almost every transit vehicle (55,000 vehicles) in rural America will need to be replaced.[6]

Infrastructure privatization has been used to fill the funding gap and is now part of a mix that includes congressional proposals to fund multimodal forms of transportation and President Obama's advocacy for a national infrastructure bank. Government budget shortfalls, large upfront payments by private contractors to states and cities, and shifting responsibility for upgrading and maintaining public assets now make privatization attractive. The roots of highway privatization, however, are many.

The ideological commitment to markets in the Clinton and Bush administrations is captured by Secretary of Transportation Mary Peters's praise for "market-based reforms of highway systems allowing for much greater reliance on tolling, particularly congestion pricing, private sector participation, and, thus, PPPs [while advocating] that the Federal role ought to be reduced and refocused in order to allow innovation at the state and local level."[7] That support included developing financial vehicles based on massive infusions of public money to attract private investment in public infrastructure. Today's PPP funding vehicles include the following:

> (1) Private Activity Bonds (PABs), created under the Safe, Accountable, Flexible, Efficient Transportation Equity Act: A Legacy for Users (SAFETEA-LU) of 2005 to subsidize private entities through preferences in the federal tax code that allow them to use tax-exempt bonds to provide low-cost financing for private projects that serve a public purpose, such as roads;[8] and
> (2) funding through the Transportation Infrastructure Finance and Innovation Act (TIFIA) of 1998, which provides loans, loan guarantees, and standby lines of credit.[9]

As part of the Obama administration's recovery and reinvestment program, which essentially saved the national infrastructure investment regime from collapse in the wake of the freezing up of credit markets, over $123 billion of Build America Bonds (BABs) were issued by state and local governments to shore up their capital spending, create jobs, and stimulate the economy. BABs, which are taxable municipal bonds, carry federal subsidies and special tax credits for bond issuers or bondholders.

Although it cannot be used to finance PPP deals, the BABs program rapidly became wildly popular with both public municipal bond issuers and an army of lobbyists from Wall Street firms and trade associations, who inundated Washington to press for its extension.[10] BABs, though issued by public entities, produce a cornucopia of fees and profits for the same Wall Street underwriters who are also involved in promoting infrastructure privatization.[11] But the BABs program was short-lived and was terminated at the end of 2010.

The prospects for state and local capital spending remain bleak, however, and the public asset privatization industry has plunged into these troubled waters. Beginning in the mid-1990s, a global industry has arisen to monetize public assets of all kinds and profit from the income streams thrown off by them under the rubric of the PPP model.

Originating in Australia, where Macquarie Bank pioneered the model for the long-term leasing of roads, airports, and other major public capital assets, this "alternative financing" industry was spurred forward in Europe by the efforts of major investment banks to purchase, lease, and build toll roads throughout the continent, and by the introduction in the United Kingdom of the Private Finance Initiative (PFI)[12] and similar programs throughout Canada.

With the onset of the US financial bubble and its accompanying bidding up of asset prices of all kinds, the privatization industry began aggressively targeting state and local governments in the United States, which it considers an underexploited market for PPPs, with offers of substantial upfront payments in return for long-term leases, extending from thirty to ninety-nine years, for toll roads.

Dozens of new private infrastructure funds were put together to cash in on what was expected to be a radical expansion of privatization.[13]

The bursting of the financial bubble late in the first decade of the twenty-first century left state and local governments in desperate straits with substandard public infrastructure that in some cases was an attractive privatization target. According to PricewaterhouseCooper, the "low pricing" for infrastructure "obtained in the first half of 2007" was driven by the massive explosion of complex forms of credit during the asset inflation bubble that reached its peak that year.[14] But the optimism was soon replaced by despair: the 2008 financial collapse created a crisis in the PPP model on a global scale.

In 2009, PPPs around the world experienced their lowest annual volume since 2006, with volume down 44 percent in Europe and 18 percent overall.[15] Unlisted infrastructure fund-raising declined to just $7.8 billion in the first half of 2009 from $44.8 billion in 2007—an 83 percent decline.[16] Citigroup estimated that nearly $8 trillion worth of assets were securitized by mid-2007, but this easy money had disappeared.[17] Desperate governments sent out global calls for financial support for infrastructure privatization, despite the substantial risks involved.[18] In the United States, the recession had three effects on public infrastructure privatization:

1. Greater federal support for highway privatization deals, mainly by providing low-interest loan financing (TIFIA) and increased limits on the $15 billion ceiling on tax-free private activity bonds (PABs). PABs allow the private developers and operators to tap into the tax-exempt bond market's lower interest rates, significantly bringing down their cost of borrowing.
2. Private-sector demands for governments to guarantee private returns on investment through regularly scheduled rentlike payments to the private contractor. As a result, there has been a shift in recent privatization deal proposals from the full concession model, in which the private contractor bears full financial responsibility, toward the "availability payment" model, in which the private contractor is paid for meeting specific milestones. Availability payment models for US transportation projects have been used for the upgrade of a 10.5-mile segment of I-595 in Fort Lauderdale, Florida; for construction of a Port of Miami tunnel; and for proposed projects in Texas and Denver.
3. Dramatically lower willingness by the private sector to take equity stakes in PPP projects and to provide large upfront payments in exchange for future revenues coupled with demands that the public sector invest directly and substantially in PPPs.

The privatization industry's efforts to shift financial responsibility from the private sector to the public sector will be an uphill battle politically, even though spending on infrastructure would create much-needed jobs at lower costs because of increased competition among construction contractors looking for projects. As Federal Reserve Chairman Ben Bernanke observed, "voters and policymakers may understandably be reluctant to approve new bond issues and take on additional costs for debt payments in a period of fiscal and economic stress."[19] Indeed, an initiative to curtail bond issuance was placed on the Colorado ballot for the 2010 election, and other states may take the same path.

There have also been countervailing forces. In April 6, 2010, Euromoney observed of the US market, "There are five main reasons why the US infrastructure market has not yet taken off: politics, public perception, the unions, the municipal bond market and the gap between buyers and sellers. Each of these problems is either being addressed or has simply stopped being an issue." Among the initiatives, Euromoney described a group of banks, infrastructure companies, and lawyers working in US infrastructure that, in early 2009, formed what they called the Working Group to revivify the market for private investment in infrastructure. Its members are Abertis, Allen & Overy LLP; Barclays Capital; Carlyle Infrastructure Partners; Chadbourne & Parke LLP; Citi Infrastructure Investors (CII); Credit Suisse; Debevoise & Plimpton; Freshfields Bruckhaus Deringer; Fulbright & Jaworski; Mayer Brown; McKenna Long & Aldridge LLP; Merrill Lynch; Morgan Stanley; RREEF; RBC Capital Markets; Scotia Capital; and UBS. As part of its campaign, the Working Group released a report called *Benefits of Private Investment in Infrastructure.*[20]

The result is public officials, who want to avoid the political risk of bond referenda, seeking private financing, even though its financial cost is likely to be much higher than that of traditional tax-exempt bonds.[21] Some officials may seek private funding through infrastructure privatization in order to provide government services, rather than increase tolls or water rates. Indeed, public officials see privatizing infrastructure as the solution to their financial and political problems, because it requires no public referendum or legislative votes on spending at a time in which issues of public debt and budgeting have become toxically politicized. Indeed, despite private investors' aim to shift as much financial risk as possible elsewhere, state and local governments in straitened circumstances still see privatization as attractive, including even the availability model, because it defers tough decisions on funding debt or operating payments to the future. This problem is only compounded over the long term. Private investors who now demand a premium for taking interest-rate or debt-cost risks are creating a future in which PPPs will funnel ever larger percentages of public budgets and user fees to private investors, rather than toward providing public services and infrastructure.

Securitization of PPP debt and the rise of a secondary market in public-asset equities and debt mean that schools and public buildings are traded like wheat futures. Keeping track of who owns public infrastructure and maintaining commitments to quality performance will become ever more difficult. As a result, state and local governments will find themselves confounded in planning their capital spending programs and assessing and monitoring their financing arrangements. Worse, government officials and the public have no one to turn to for advice except the cadre of underwriters, lawyers, and project advisors who regularly appear on every side of every deal.[22] As discussed in more details below, consultants on these deals are regularly paid a percentage rate based on the cost of the deal. These "success fees" that consultants demand entail the risk of biasing the advice that public officials must rely on—no matter how "competitive" the bidding is.[23]

The economic crisis has spurred the privatization industry's pursuit of public infrastructure, such as buildings, parking facilities, water and wastewater facilities, prisons, and public landfills. Just thirty-five deals in the pipeline in August 2010 were estimated to have "a market value of about $45 billion—more than ten times the $4 billion or so two years ago," with hundreds more deals being considered.[24] Public officials, desperate to raise funds for operating expenses and debt service, are increasingly tempted to "sell off" public assets at fire-sale prices. One banker recently said, "The moment the political pain from cutting services is more than the votes lost in selling assets, this market will take off."[25]

CONTRACT TERMS, REVENUES, AND STATE AND LOCAL GOVERNANCE

Most of the focus related to infrastructure privatization has been on financing. However, equally important, in terms of revenues for private contractors and investors and in terms of governance issues for state and local governments, are little-examined contract terms. These terms appear verbatim in contract after contract. It is too early to predict their full effects, but they have the power to freeze our transportation systems for the life of the contract, unless state and local governments buy their way out.

Terms Driven by the Tax Code

Infrastructure privatization contracts of fifty to ninety-nine years are common in the United States, despite the challenges of making accurate projections generations into the future as to the levels and patterns of use, interest rates, the performance of alternative investments, and technology. In the case of transportation infrastructure, predictions must take into account the effects of fuel prices, employment and housing patterns, and shifts to mass transit or telecommuting. Long contract terms also provoke intense public concern about losing control of vital public assets. Yet even though these problems could be eliminated or ameliorated with shorter contracts, investors show no interest in shortening the terms.

The explanation for this hesitancy can be found in the value to investors of highly accelerated amortization provided by the federal tax code when contract terms exceed the useful life of the infrastructure, giving investors "effective ownership" of the property, thus constituting a sale for tax purposes.[26] Effective ownership is demonstrated when the contract period exceeds the useful economic life of the property. "The Bureau of Economic Analysis estimates the service life of highways and streets to be 45 years, while the Chicago Skyway and Indiana Toll Road agreements were for terms of 99 and 75 years, respectively.... [W]hile the facts and circumstances of each transaction will control its tax treatment, these arrangements will most likely be viewed by the parties as a sale and purchase of a trade or business, and the concession agreement can be expected to include a provision describing the intended tax treatment in this manner."[27] Indeed, contracts state both the contract length and that the parties intend the transaction to be a sale for tax purposes in substantially similar language.[28] For example, § 2.8 of both the 2006 Indiana Toll Road agreement and the proposed 2008 Pennsylvania Turnpike agreement use similar language, saying that the parties intend the transactions to be sales for tax purposes.

New Mexico Senator Jeff Bingamon observed that "tax benefits are key to making these transactions economically attractive to the private companies."[29] He continued:

> I would like to say how troubled I am that a desire to derive generous federal tax benefits is driving exceedingly long lease lengths. [I]n order to take advantage of the tax code's 15-year cost recovery period, a lessor must have constructive ownership of the road. Constructive ownership is generally attained by having a lease that exceeds the 45-year period that the Bureau of Economic Analysis says is a road's "useful life." And so, parties will not enter these deals unless they are at least 45 years in length—and often longer, to follow tax advisors' guidance to be cautious. What we have, then, is the tax tail wagging the dog: Exceptionally long leases in order to recover capital outlays on an accelerated schedule. In essence, today's tax code provides a taxpayer subsidy for these companies that far exceeds what economic reality would dictate.
>
>   ... I, for one, think we ought to reconsider the perverse incentive that the tax code creates for such long leases—which now come at considerable expense to the nation's taxpayers.[30]

Who Bears the Risk?

Privatization proponents contend that, in addition to being a source of money, privatization shifts future financial risk to the private contractor,[31] as well as the financial rewards.[32] For example,

> In addition to revenue, the low amount of risk is also advantageous, says Dana Levenson, head of the North American infrastructure finance and advisory business at Royal Bank of Scotland. "Ultimately, if people don't want to park in downtown Chicago, the risk doesn't accrue to the city, it accrues to the investors," he says. "The investors accrue most of the risk and pay the lessor an upfront payment to assume that risk."[33]

However, common contract terms, such as "compensation events," noncompetition provisions, and "adverse actions" —found essentially verbatim across contracts—make the public the insurer of private contractors' anticipated financial return. Some contracts make the government's role as insurer explicit. For example, the Pocahontas Parkway agreement requires the government to protect the contractor's interests if competing transportation is contemplated,[34] and Virginia must reimburse the contractors on the Capital Beltway whenever carpools exceed 24 percent of the traffic on the carpool lanes for the next forty years "or until the builders make $100 million in profits." Since carpooling is encouraged by exempting carpools from tolls, those reimbursements must come from the Commonwealth's budget.[35] Other revenue guarantee terms are more indirect. For example, the Northwest Parkway contractors objected to improvements to nearby mass transit and roads "because they might hurt the parkway financially."[36] Contracts have required governments to take "traffic-calming" actions, such as narrowing roads, installing traffic lights, stop signs, speed bumps, and even blocking access to alternate routes—not for public needs—but in order to drive traffic volume to the privatized road.[37]

Other contract provisions treat government as a trespasser unless it has sought permission to enter the highway. For example, Section 3.7(a)(1) of the proposed Pennsylvania Turnpike contract says that the Commonwealth retains rights "to inspect the Turnpike or determine whether or not the Concessionaire is in compliance with its obligations under this Agreement or applicable Law" but only as long as it does so at reasonable times and upon reasonable prior notice. Failure to meet all requirements can require paying compensation to the contractor.

Indeed, even the government's ability to respond to emergencies is hedged with conditions. Proposed Pennsylvania contract § 3.7(a)(iii) allows access by emergency crews, but only if the Commonwealth *reasonably* believes that conditions are emergencies—as defined in the contract—and only if the method of entry complies with other parts of the contract, including giving notice "practicable under the circumstances." Indeed, permission to enter is required even if the private contractor has defaulted and the government needs to "make any necessary repairs to the Turnpike, perform any work therein and take any reasonable actions in connection therewith."[38]

Thus, actions to promote the public welfare are displaced by obligations to ensure the contractor's success[39] and impose the costs of risk onto the public. Two incidents involving the Indiana Toll Road illustrate two sorts of problems. First, in 2006, without consulting or notifying state and local governments, the Indiana Toll Road contractor placed sand-filled barrels in turn-arounds to prevent drivers from using them to avoid tolls and cause accidents. However, the barrels blocked emergency crews from getting to accidents as quickly as possible. The contractor refused to remove the barrels for several months while also failing to meet its obligation to prepare an emergency response plan for the toll road.[40] In September 2008, it was the State of Indiana that reimbursed the private Indiana Toll Road operator $447,000 for tolls waived for emergency evacuations during severe flooding,[41] rather than requiring that the contractor carry insurance for such events or build costs into the price of the infrastructure. Thus, privatizing the road left the public with less protection and power to protect itself and its interests when those needs conflicted with the contractor's rights to revenue.[42] Indeed, emergency evacuations may require parsing contract language and negotiating for access to roads by people with no transponders or money to pay tolls if lives are to be saved.

Private Contractors as a Fourth Branch of Government

"Adverse actions" give contractors the right to object to, and receive compensation for, legislative, administrative, judicial, and other decisions or actions that could affect a contractor's revenues, such as promoting carpooling or mass transit in order to lower urban congestion or air pollution. For example, Article 14 of the proposed Pennsylvania Turnpike contract requires compensating a private infrastructure contractor for new legislation, ordinances, rules, or regulations that principally affected it or private toll road operators or that was reasonably expected to cause a material adverse effect on the infrastructure's fair market value." San Diego's now bankrupt South Bay Expressway (SR 125) gave the private contractor rights to compensation if the state legislature, CalTrans, any administrative body, or voters created a law in any form, or court order, decree, or judgment would lead to acquiring part of the road, negatively affected the private contractor's rights, or that regulated or interfered with its right to collect tolls.[43]

The proposed Pennsylvania Turnpike Contract § 11.1(b) exempted the private contractor from complying with Federal Highway Administration rules and regulations—but not statutes—that induced compliance through financial incentives or disincentives. This, despite the normal hierarchy of laws means that federal laws trump state and local laws. Indeed, individual states have been allowed to cede control of parts of the Interstate Highway System to private investors even though traffic they carry is mostly interstate and their construction and maintenance are largely funded with federal money. Indeed, there is no mechanism to ensure that national interests are taken into account, nor has there been a federal definition of public interest or guidance on evaluating the public interest.[44] In the absence of such guidance, states have shown themselves willing to contract away public interests.[45]

To truly appreciate the implications of adverse action provisions it is helpful to know that they are a domestic form of "stabilization clause," contract terms originally created to protect corporate investors from risk of nationalization or expropriation.[46] Among other things, stabilization clauses protect international investments from changes in laws and other risks, such as the application of international and domestic human rights and environmental laws. A 2008 research project conducted for the International Finance Council and the United Nations Special Representative to the Secretary General on Business and Human Rights found, among other things, that "lenders often view stabilization clauses as an essential element of the bankability of an investment project, particularly in emerging markets.... They are particularly attractive in situations which involve 'long periods of time to recoup costs and become commercially viable.'"[47]

Entrepreneurs considering a multidecade contract with a government should be concerned about a state's power to harm anticipated profits. But is exempting firms from national and international law, treaties, and standards the best answer?[48] Critics of stabilization clauses have advocated full and meaningful disclosure of these terms before any contract is entered into[49] and the inclusion of language stating that the contractors "should refrain from asserting or advancing any claim against a host government or another party with respect to laws, regulations or measures relating to human rights, health, safety or the environment."[50]

The United Nations/IFC study of stabilization clauses found a split between OECD and non-OECD countries regarding the use of stabilization clauses. OECD countries either did not exempt companies from laws or had only limited exemptions, while exemptions tended to be included in contracts with non-OECD countries. OECD contracts generally took the view that laws of general applicability "are at the risk of the investor" with compensation only for new laws that have a discriminatory intent and impact against the investor.[51]

> Contracts and models from OECD countries appear to be based on principles of risk allocation that significantly limit the scope of stabilization clauses. Investors are expected to comply with all new laws, and to absorb the costs of compliance with all generally applicable laws. They must make efforts to minimize costs arising from complying with changes in law. The state compensates for discriminatory laws, and in some cases either shares the risk of laws aimed at the specific industry or project, or passes the costs on to users of the service.[52]

This controversial term, used in developing countries to exempt companies from laws, operates in the United States to elevate private contractors to a quasi-governmental status, giving them power over laws, judicial decisions, propositions voted on by the public, and other government actions that a contractor claims would affect its revenues.

In other words, infrastructure privatization contracts differ fundamentally from a simple bilateral contract in which money is exchanged for a product at one specific time. They concern the operation of and care for vital and expensive infrastructure over decades. That difference affects how to deal with claims of harm. Remedies for contract breaches are simplest when they can be measured by objective standards as to past losses. The standard remedy for future injuries and where it is difficult to measure the dollar value of harm is an injunction to stop the conduct. Opting for damages recognizes that an injunction is an inappropriate response to government actions and, perhaps, that the threat of money damages flowing into the distant future can have the same effect as an injunction: putting the brakes on government actions. These problems exist because of opting for the inflexibility of a contract that attempts to deal with uncertain future events that include revenues, expenses, quality of commitment to the relationship, overreaching, the economy, acts of nature, and costs of party compliance.

DECISION-MAKING PROCESSES

Infrastructure privatization affects government decision making in several ways. These effects have unfortunately been ignored. For example, the Government Accountability Office has issued many reports on highways, infrastructure, and their privatization without considering these contract provisions or their effects on state and local governments.[53] As discussed earlier, adverse actions impose contractual and financial limits on decisions and, in effect, give private contractors quasi-governmental status through their power over new laws, judicial decisions, and propositions voted on by the public, and other government actions. Indeed, such public-private hybrids may violate the nondelegation doctrine that bars private entities from exercising power that is inherently governmental. That is to say, the contracts give private contractors power over decisions that (1) affect the public interest, (2) are normally made by public officials, and (3) are subject to public oversight, disclosure, and accountability—oversight that does not apply to private contractors.[54] Thus, they give contractors perquisites of government but without the oversight and accountability obligations imposed by state and federal constitutions and law on government.[55]

Narrow Decision-Making Processes

Second, the process for deciding whether to privatize infrastructure has generally not involved any—let alone a rigorous—cost-benefit analysis. Contract terms, their significance, their effects, or even a summary of the terms are rarely made public before the contract is consummated, nor are opportunities for effective public comment provided while the decision is pending. Even government officials responsible for voting on the contracts have been denied access to the full contracts and the time to read and assess the terms before making a decision. For example, the Chicago City Council was forced to approve a complex, one-hundred-plus-page agreement to lease its 36,000 parking meters to a private company for seventy-five years only two days after being given access to its details. The public at large was given no opportunity for review or comment.[56]

Important information, revealed only after the contract was signed, showed that the city received far less than the infrastructure was worth. The Chicago Inspector General found that Chicago had relinquished future parking-meter revenue with a present value of approximately $2.13 billion in exchange for $1.15 billion, 46 percent less than its value.[57] Documents released by the contractors for investors a year later forecast that Chicago drivers would pay the Morgan Stanley, Abu Dhabi Investment Authority, and Allianz Capital Partners partnership at least $11.6 billion over the seventy-five-year contract term, roughly ten times the amount paid for the lease in 2008, for an expected profit of $9.58 billion before interest, taxes, and depreciation.[58]

The Chicago Inspector General found that justifications for privatizing the parking meters were false: (1) Chicago had not needed to shift the decision to a private contractor in order to raise rates, (2) the city had demonstrated in other situations that it had the political will to do so, and (3) Chicago could have extracted the same amount of revenue from its parking meters as a private operator by making the same capital improvements.[59] In retrospect, it is clear that this hasty decision, made without public involvement or full consideration, has ceded more than parking-meter fees to the private contractor.

Decisions to privatize infrastructure have been made because government officials have low-balled the infrastructure's estimated value in order to make agreement more likely when a much higher bid is received.

> When determining whether to sell the Indiana Toll Road to a private firm, Indiana justified the sale as being in the public interest because the highest bid of $3.8 billion far exceeded the $2 billion that the state initially thought it would earn from the sale. The City of Chicago similarly justified its sale of the Chicago Skyway to a private entity by comparing its estimate of the Skyway's worth of $800–900 million to the winning bid of $1.8 billion. In addition to using price to justify the sale as in the public interest, both governments used a bidding process that ensured the winner would be picked on price alone, ignoring other intangible factors when making their determinations.[60]

Even when more information is provided, decision-making processes have not been commensurate with the serious consequences of the decision.

> While a few states have used factors other than asset valuation as the conclusive factor in their public interest determination, even these multifaceted decisions rely almost solely on financial factors. When evaluating the benefits of using a PPP to construct the Newberg-Dundee bypass, Oregon compared the costs of using a PPP to the estimated costs of using traditional procurement methods....
>
> Texas similarly required that the state Department of Transportation create a "shadow bid" for two PPP projects to allow the state to compare the bids received from project bidders with the long-term costs and benefits of undertaking the project as a public endeavor. In determining whether undertaking these projects was in the public interest, Texas considered criteria other than pure asset valuation.[61]

Unfortunately, a narrow focus on dollars has been the norm.

The obligations that legislative, executive, and judicial bodies owe the public must be altered by privatization agreements that require state and local bodies to act with an eye to effects their decisions will or could have on private contractors' revenues.

Decisions Based on Faulty Information

As bad as no information is, having access to what seems to be full information but is not accurate is worse. Public officials charged with deciding whether to privatize public infrastructure may be able to evaluate technical information, but they have no ability to evaluate the quality of that technical information. For example, traffic projections, which are an important component of pricing infrastructure privatization, have been highly inaccurate. A study of fourteen urban toll roads by J. P. Morgan Securities found that only two projects had revenues that exceeded projections during the first four years of operation, and ten projects' "revenues fell short by 20 percent to 75 percent."[62] A 2006 *Denver Post* investigation found that more than 75 percent of toll roads in eight states failed to meet traffic projections in their first three years, and, when there were incentives to inflate factors underlying projections, the figures were off by "34.5 percent to 67.5 percent of their estimated traffic in their first year of operation" and were still dramatically off in their third year. That result may be explained by knowing that the three companies that do most of the revenue projections have an interest in seeing the roads get built. According to Robert Bain, a London-based analyst for bond-rating agency Standard & Poor's who has conducted international studies of toll roads, "Quite often, people shop around until they find the people who provide the numbers."[63] In some cases, consultants on traffic studies were promised lucrative jobs or contracts if a road were built.[64]

Governments that lack expertise will, quite reasonably, retain advisors with the experience acquired while working for infrastructure contractors, investors, and governments. These revolving-door relationships create actual or potential conflicts of interest,[65] while also providing windows into the mechanics and incentives related to infrastructure privatization deals. For example, the law firm Mayer Brown was a consultant for the Commonwealth of Pennsylvania on the Pennsylvania Turnpike deal.[66] It has experience, as well, on the Chicago Midway Airport, Chicago Skyway, Colorado Northwest Parkway, Indiana Toll Road, Chicago Public Parking System, Corredor Sur Toll Road, IIRSA Sur Toll Road, and Jorge Chávez International Airport.[67] It has also served as an advisor to governments and on infrastructure investment-fund formation projects for Macquarie, UBS Global Asset Management, and LS Power.[68] Investigative reporters revealed that, in the case of the Chicago parking meters, the city's financial advisors "were working on other multibillion-dollar deals with the company that emerged as the winning bidder, Morgan Stanley." This was the case even though such overlapping relationships violated the city's contracting rules.[69]

Morgan Stanley,[70] an unsuccessful bidder on the Pennsylvania Turnpike, became an advisor to Governor Rendell on the deal.[71] At the time that Morgan Stanley was advising Pennsylvania, the Morgan Stanley Infrastructure Partners investment fund had amassed over $4 billion to invest in other deals.[72] In October 2006, Morgan Stanley Infrastructure and the French contractor LAZ were given the ninety-nine-year lease for Chicago's downtown underground parking garages. Two years later, in 2008, Morgan Stanley was part of a consortium called Chicago Parking Meters, LLC, that leased Chicago's parking meters for seventy-five years.[73]

These close-knit, revolving-door relationships help explain the striking similarity of wording found in infrastructure privatization contracts. Many provisions in the proposed Pennsylvania Turnpike contract are found, verbatim, in other privatization contracts. According to Mayer Brown, the lease agreement it worked on in its role as co-counsel for the State of Indiana on the Indiana Toll Road "followed in many respects the form we developed for the Chicago Skyway transaction."[74] While advising Governor Rendell, Morgan Stanley had an incentive to create and preserve contract terms, such as adverse action provisions, that would favor investors, rather than the Commonwealth. The existence of such incentives, not whether they were acted on, creates ethical issues. The only benefit to Pennsylvanians from including these terms seems to be that no private contractor would agree to a contract without them.

Another problematic incentive that can affect independent judgment and the ability to represent the public interest is paying advisors based on their reaching a deal and on the dollar amount of the deal. The "success fee," which compensates advisors only if a deal is consummated, is standard procedure in infrastructure privatization transactions.[75] While tying fees to reaching a deal and the dollar value of a deal creates incentives to negotiate the highest amount possible, it creates even stronger incentives to focus only on deals and dollars while overlooking how other contract terms affect the public interest. In other words, success payment structures are also an inducement to recommend a contract, even if a deal is not the best option for the public.[76]

The consultants on the Pennsylvania Turnpike deal were paid a success fee based on a percentage of either a privatization or bond deal.[77] Thus, Morgan Stanley had an incentive to "recommend the largest transaction possible rather than a course of action which may be more balanced and more prudently serve the needs of the Commonwealth and its residents."[78]

Unfortunately, even experienced government officials seem unaware of the perverse incentives created by such a pay structure. For example, Roy Kienitz, Pennsylvania Governor Rendell's deputy chief of staff, said of Morgan Stanley's role in the privatization of the Pennsylvania Turnpike: "Morgan Stanley was not going to make any decisions. 'They don't have the power. People in this building, the general assembly and the governor, they will set the terms.' " He said that Morgan Stanley was strictly prohibited under the terms of its employment by the state from working for any bidder and from bidding. He said its compensation is proportional to the value of any deal consummated to give the company an incentive to work to maximize benefits to the state. If Morgan Stanley were paid a fixed fee it wouldn't have that incentive.[79]

Other countries concluded that the government must develop its own expertise, rather than rely on industry consultants, and, thus, they have developed special governmental bodies charged with overseeing privatization. For example, Spain's Ministry of Public Works oversees the performance of PPP projects during construction and operation, including monitoring the reliability of the infrastructure and conformance with the concession terms.[80] The United Kingdom's many permanent governmental and quasi-governmental bodies handle issues related to infrastructure privatization, thus treating infrastructure privatization as a regulated monopoly. Those bodies include the private finance initiative (PFI) created in 1992 and, more recently, Partnerships UK, the National Audit Office (NAO), the Public Accounts Committee, the Audit Commission, Infrastructure UK (IUK), the Centre for the Protection of National Infrastructure (CPNI), and the Infrastructure Planning Commission.[81] In addition, the UK's Treasury issues standardized contract terms accompanied by explanations, whose three main objectives are to promote a common understanding of the main risks of these projects, allow consistency of approach and pricing, and reduce the time and costs of negotiation by using "a standard approach without extended negotiations."[82] In addition to providing these structures and guidance, infrastructure privatization contracts, particularly in Europe, tend to be far shorter than those in the United States. The result is a process within the UK that protects the public interest beyond simply raising cash and providing transportation. However, those entities that are quasi-public or subject to regulation within the UK and Europe are allowed to operate with no regulations to protect the public interest when they operate in the United States.

The Costs of Infrastructure Privatization Contracts

Focusing on dollars has caused many states and cities to lose sight of those things we value but cannot price. It has also made us oblivious to important financial and nonfinancial costs of infrastructure privatization, in particular (1) costs of government subsidies; (2) costs of requiring the public to reimburse the contractor for anticipated lost revenues; and (3) contractual limits on actions that public entities can take.

Costs of Government Subsidies

Of the dollars invested in infrastructure privatization, public money makes up the largest percentage. Sources of just federal money include Private Activity Bonds (PABs); [83] the Transportation Infrastructure Finance and Innovation Act (TIFIA) of 1998; foregone taxes provided through highly accelerated amortization of infrastructure investments; and reimbursements to private contractors for claims that government actions have decreased anticipated revenues. An analysis of the Capitol Beltway's funding finds that less than 20 percent of the upfront funds came from the private investors. The rest was provided from government funds or government subsidies, including low-interest loans, direct subsidies, tax deductions, and other public sources:

> Of the total $1.9 billion (and rising), Fluor-Transurban is contributing only $349 million in private equity. Meanwhile, the state is paying $409 million and the Federal Highway Administration is lending Fluor $585 million in low-interest loans and $586 million in subsidized bonds. Taxpayers are also on the hook every year for the next 40 years for the carpool fees charged to the state account.[84]

So great is public investment that it suggests that there would be no private-sector interest in infrastructure privatization but for the array of public subsidies and public risk taking.

Contractor reimbursement provisions in infrastructure privatization contracts, such as adverse action and compensation events, and tax subsidies to induce private investment in infrastructure may, perversely, severely limit state and local governments' ability to provide for the public welfare for decades. First, they risk violating the contract if a competing facility is built. Second, their budgets are strained by the loss of taxes on investor revenues, which, but for tax incentives might have been invested in taxable activities. Third, providing highly accelerated depreciation of infrastructure investments further impoverishes the federal government by foregoing tax revenues and, accordingly, its ability to assist states. By depressing future government revenues, these tax breaks also risk exacerbating the financial problems that privatization is supposed to address.

The Congressional Budget Office and Joint Committee on Taxation warn:

> Concerns about economic efficiency are particularly acute for the federal tax preferences that help finance private-sector investment in infrastructure, because those preferences risk transferring resources from taxpayers to private investors without obtaining a commensurate payoff in terms of the value of the infrastructure services that would not have been provided without that subsidy. For example, the fact that those infrastructure facilities are in private hands indicates that owners can capture—through user fees and other charges—a sizable portion of the value of the services they provide. Hence, public benefits from those investments may be small relative to those of infrastructure owned and operated by government, and determining the appropriate degree of subsidy—or whether any is warranted—may be difficult. If the private-sector investment would have taken place even without a subsidy, then the tax preference simply shifts resources from taxpayers to private investors. Because tax preferences for private-sector borrowers lower the cost of financing and hence the return needed to make an investment attractive, they can also reallocate capital from profitable projects to projects that otherwise would not have been undertaken, thereby potentially reducing economic growth.[85]

Consider, then, the costs of these public and private investments and the potential revenue government at all levels has lost in facilitating them. In the case of Chicago's parking meters, it is estimated that Chicago drivers will pay the private contractor more than $11.6 billion in parking fees over the next seventy-five years. Indeed, the Morgan Stanley-led partnership has used aggressive parking-fee hikes to make a return of more than 80 cents per dollar of projected revenue, twenty times the 4.84 cents on a dollar earned by the concession owner at O'Hare and Midway airports in 2009.[86] Chicago would probably not have raised parking fees to these levels, but between what it was charging and the level of the partnership's fee hikes, it could have had access to a regular stream of income, not been subject to compensation demands by the contractors, could have retained control, and been able to focus on the public interest.

Costs of Requiring the Public to Reimburse the Contractor for Anticipated Lost Revenues

Choice among competitors in the free market is supposed to spur better performance and lower costs. However, standard infrastructure privatization agreements forbid competition.[87] Those contract provisions undermine the basic argument for private operation. Of course, private contractors are concerned that a government's power to legislate can decrease revenues.[88] That business concern is not unique to infrastructure privatization. Government decisions affect people and institutions in many ways, and corporations regularly lobby for favorable treatment. It is interesting here that, even though there is no evidence of a taking, the contracts require that contractors be reimbursed for the effects of legal changes as if a taking had occurred.

Briefly, the Fifth Amendment to the US Constitution requires paying just compensation when private property is taken for public use. Government regulation may affect the value of land to its owner, but the Supreme Court has permitted governments to issue regulations or take actions that affect private property but which are reasonably related to the government's power to protect the public health, safety, and the general welfare without being obligated to pay compensation. The Court has also held that a valid government action or regulation that significantly affects the value or use of private property may be a regulatory taking. In that case, the property's owner has a right to compensation. To be a taking requiring compensation, the effect of the government action must be the functional equivalent of an actual taking of title through an eminent domain proceeding. Infrastructure privatization contracts, however, require compensation for a wide range of government actions that fall far short of a taking. They include no equivalent provisions reimbursing government for actions that protect and enhance a private contractor's revenues. This issue cries out for attention. Perhaps, rather than providing compensation as a matter of contract, we should consider whether the effect of a new law is actually a taking or just part of the fallout of changes that occur over time, requiring no compensation.

The Federal Highway Administration in 2008 promoted revenue reimbursements in lieu of (or with) noncompetition agreements,[89] without considering other alternatives available to private investors. Governments actions may lower or raise private revenues, but governments do not take those actions in order to harm private contractors' revenues but, rather, to promote the public interest. Revenue subsidies for private contractors make it harder for governments to protect the public interest, including making "it difficult for public transportation agencies to address safety and congestion problems on highways and adjacent streets."[90]

Reimbursement terms create incentives to make claims in order to build revenues. Alan Lowenthal, the chair of the California Senate Transportation and Housing Committee, testified before the US Congressional Committee on Transportation and Infrastructure: "Working with a private entity may be a contentious, potentially litigious endeavor for public agencies because private companies may work to protect their investment over the public interest."[91] In the first quarter of 2009, the City of Chicago was liable to the parking-meter contractor for more than $106,000 in claimed lost income for street repair and street closings, and these amounts will rise over time. CBS reported, "According to a document attached to the city contract, the most valuable spaces in the city are along Madison Street—68 of them. If they were out for a year, the company could expect to be reimbursed a small fortune. Krislov estimates it could cost $559,057 a year, or about $8,000 a space."[92]

Contractual Limits on Actions That Public Entities Can Take

A 2008 GAO review of surface transportation recognized the government's struggle to accommodate many competing goals.[93] Recent infrastructure privatization contractors have added to those goals by making the government their own attorney general, agent, or lobbyist; or have the government pay for not making sufficient efforts to protect the contractor from competition. Such competition can stem from governmental efforts to provide other modes of transportation. For example, the Pocahontas Parkway contract required that the government exercise "all discretionary authority available to it under Laws, Regulations and Ordinances to prevent any other governmental or private entity from developing Competitive Transportation Facilities, including but not limited to connections to State Highways."[94] The Chicago Parking Meter Contract required the city to "use its reasonable efforts to oppose and challenge Such action by any such other Governmental Authority."[95]

The proposed Surface Transportation Authorization Act of 2009 recognized that we must address transportation needs as an "intermodal" system, rather than as a collection of discrete and separate modes of transportation.[96] However, an important barrier to intermodalism is to be found in infrastructure privatization contract terms that freeze the status quo for generations and could leave the public with obsolete transportation systems or an expensive featherbedding system. This was the case with Hungary's M-5, which imposed private and localized impediments to regional planning and integrated systems.[97]

Requiring the government to insure the contractor's income complicates—and may even eliminate—options for addressing important public issues for the life of the contract, such as reducing air pollution, environmental degradation, and urban and suburban congestion; promoting public health; and tackling other problems related to car-focused transportation. Revenues from privatized infrastructure, including highways, parking meters, and parking garages, will certainly be affected by the promotion of mass transit or other alternatives to driving, closing or narrowing streets to provide more urban green space, and other actions, such as those set out in PlaNYC's ambitious program.[98] The contracts also directly affect "national uniformity in highway operation, interstate commerce, the mobility of low-income households, and traffic diversion,"[99] for the life of the contract, with effects continuing long after it expires.

Noncompetition and adverse action terms hamper governance, first, by creating divided loyalties. Public officials who privatize infrastructure in order to serve the public's needs find themselves compelled to prevent or impede public access to protect the private investors. The public may feel betrayed by their public servants, as when the existence of noncompete agreements came to light in Colorado and California.[100]

Contracting with the government means making a deal with a party with the power to alter conditions that directly affect the value of the contract to the other party and with a party that has an obligation to act in the public's interest. Infrastructure privatization contracts that force the government to choose between being perpetually in breach of a contract or not meeting its obligations to the citizenry is certainly not good practice. Yet this is what the contract for the Chicago parking meters seems to contemplate in its provisions on Reserved Powers Adverse Actions.[101] It is worth considering whether, rather than being a solution to the problem, the necessity of including these provisions may be an important signal as to the merits of using privatization as a way to provide infrastructure. Contract terms that hold back progress, impose extra costs on the public, and even force suboptimal decisions are a high price to pay for financing infrastructure, especially when there are other options for raising money.

A much better solution may already exist. For decades, the federal gas tax funded our transportation infrastructure and could continue doing so on as a pay-as-you-go system.[102] That tax no longer meets funding needs because (1) the increased use of fuel-efficient vehicles has driven down fuel tax revenues per mile driven,[103] (2) the federal gas tax is not indexed for inflation, and (3) the tax has been stuck at 18.4 cents per gallon since 1993.[104] The problem is that there is no political will to set the tax at a level that will provide the funds needed for maintaining and building our country's infrastructure. State fuel taxes have also not kept pace with inflation. The combined federal and state rates vary widely among the states, from California at 67.4 and Hawaii at 63.4 cents to Wyoming at 32.4 and Alaska at 26.4 cents. The unsurprising result is insufficient money generated by fuel taxes, with the federal government meeting the revenue shortfall by taking money from other pressing needs. Because of funding problems and other challenges, surface transportation programs remain on the GAO's High-Risk list.[105] The nation cannot build and maintain roads when the Highway Trust Fund account is depleted, and continued borrowing from the General Fund of the Treasury to replenish the account is not a real solution.[106]

Looking Toward the Future

The United States' experience of leasing public infrastructure has been brief and limited to a time of radical change and deep economic dislocation that shows no sign of abating. As a result, there are many open questions about the current operation and future of infrastructure. Three examples show the breadth of issues we face.

First, infrastructure privatization has been seen as a novel innovation in financing, building, operating, and maintaining infrastructure. However, it seems likely we will come to see that there are extant useful analogies and experiences we can use to understand this phenomenon. As discussed earlier, the revenue-guarantee terms—the adverse action or stabilization clauses—may be better understood as fitting within the takings context. That perspective and experience may find a fairer and superior way to address investor concerns that led to their creation while better protecting the public interest. We would also benefit from putting adverse actions into context by recalling that government actions and laws are meant to effect change. We do not pay compensation just because a new law is passed and someone claims it has a negative effect on them. Changes to law have always had negative and positive effects that legislators must weigh when deciding how to vote. In short, we have the means to better understand these contracts and make decisions about them that promote the public's interests.

Second, we can benefit from domestic and international experiences. For example, we may want to emulate the United Kingdom's decision to provide infrastructure through a network of agencies that give oversight and guidance related to public infrastructure. We might also want to consider the merits of legislation, such as the proposed Surface Transportation Amendment Act of 2009. That law has a number of very good features that would address pressing transportation needs while also protecting the public interest. We should also improve and update the funding mechanisms used for most of the last fifty years. Put simply, the least expensive way to provide high-quality infrastructure may be through our taxes, rather than relying on private investors and complex decades-long contracts.

Finally, we need to prepare for the current lawsuits and those that are germinating within current and future deals, as well as their effects. Two lawsuits filed in late 2010 are the South Bay Expressway (SR 125) bankruptcy and the Professional Engineers in California Government lawsuit over the decision to lease the Presidio

Parkway. The South Bay Expressway bankruptcy led to numerous claims and counterclaims by developers, operators, and other stakeholders. The Presidio Parkway lawsuit followed on the heels of a campaign against the lease.

These and other infrastructure privatization lawsuits will clog our courts for years. They present a mixture of complex law and politics. As to the law, at a minimum, the ownership/leasehold/contractual arrangements and the involvement of international parties mean that we can expect courts to have to deal with issues such as asserting jurisdiction over international parties. The complexity of the substantive and procedural legal issues will grow over time, as decades-long contracts are subcontracted and changes of all sorts affect the terms and value of the contracts. Among the issues the courts will have to sort out are the following: Who can be liable? Who is injured and has standing to sue? How will damages be calculated? Was there adequate disclosure? How will the public interest be protected? The politics will take place in a time when, for many vocal people, taxes and government are toxic, while others feel betrayed that their governments would place in private hands any infrastructure that was paid for by public dollars.

These and other looming issues related to infrastructure privatization will provide interesting times for those involved in state and local finance and governance.

Notes

1 For a background on infrastructure and infrastructure funding in the United States, see Orszag (2008); US Government Accountability Office (2006).
2 US PIRG Education Fund (2010), 6; Enright (2007).
3 Mallett (2008), 3–4.
4 Government Accountability Office (2009), 1, 10.
5 Government Accountability Office (2010), summary page.
6 House Committee on Transportation and Infrastructure (2009b), 3.
7 Mallett (2008), 5.
8 Perez and March (2006), 14; Joint Committee on Taxation (2008), 15–18. Private activity bonds make it possible to secure loans for these projects at a lower interest rate because the bond purchasers do not have to pay federal taxes on the incomes they receive. Furst (2005).
9 Federal Highway Administration (n.d.-b); California Department of Transportation (n.d).
10 Dutton (2010).
11 Creswell (2010).
12 HM Treasury (n.d.).
13 Ryan Orr of the Stanford Collaboratory for Research on Global Projects identified seventy-two new funds created in 2006–2007 alone that raised more than $160 billion for infrastructure investments. Orr (2007). See also Orr and Kennedy (2008).
14 PricewaterhouseCooper (2008).
15 Dealogic (2010), 5.
16 Preqin (2010), 2.

17 Tett (2010).

18 Burger, Tyson, Karpowicz, and Coelho (2009).

19 Bernanke (2010).

20 Lord (2010); The Working Group (2009).

21 Enright (2007), 6.

22 Dannin (2011).

23 Chancellor and Silva (2007).

24 Dugan (2010).

25 Lord (2010).

26 Perez and March (2006), 14; Joint Committee on Taxation (2008), 15–18; Furst (2005).

27 Kleinbard (2008); see also Hecker (2008); Joint Committee on Taxation (2008).

28 Bingaman (2008).

29 Ibid.

30 Ibid.

31 Slone (n.d.), 24–25.

32 Kansas T-Link (2008), 3–32 to 3–33.("By moving to private participation in toll roads, the public benefits from private assumption of risk as well as from the availability of private capital, and it is appropriate that investors be paid to produce those public benefits.")

33 Hamerman (2008), 3.

34 Federal Highway Administration (2005a).

35 Weiss (2008), C06; Kattula (2009a, 2009b).

36 Leib (2008); [City of] Golden, Colorado (2009), 1, 7, 11. For examples, see US PIRG Education Fund (2009), Appendix A; Pagano (2009), 373–74 (2009); Leib (2006).

37 THENEWSPAPER.COM (2006, 2007); Sclar (2009).

38 Pennsylvania Turnpike Contract (Proposed) (2008) § 3.7(a) (ii) 42.

39 MacInnes (2008).

40 Stowe (2006), B-3; *Chicago Tribune* (2006), 3.

41 US PIRG Education Fund (2009) 18–19; Associated Press (2008).

42 Kim (2006).

43 Pennsylvania Turnpike Contract (Proposed) (2008) § 14.1, 89–90; Federal Highway Administration (2005b); [Chicago Parking Meter Contract] (2008), § 14.3 Reserved Powers Adverse Actions.

44 Hecker (2008), 10–11.

45 *Washington Times* (2009).

46 Ayine, Blanco, Cotula, Djiré, Gonzalez, Kotey, Khan, Reyes, Ward, and Yusuf (2005), 5. For an overview of international infrastructure privatization, see Likosky (2006).

47 Shemberg and Aizawa (2008), vii, 5.

48 International Bar Association Working Group (2009), 11.

49 Ibid., 19.

50 Ibid., 33.

51 Shemberg and Aizawa (2008), 10, 25.

52 Ibid., xi.

53 See, e.g., Government Accountability Office (2009). The GAO discussed noncompete agreements in Government Accountability Office (2008b), 35–36.

54 Dannin (2006).

55 Slone (n.d), 25–27.

56 Office of the Chicago Inspector General (2009), 1–2.

57 Ibid., 23–24.

58 Preston (2010).

59 Office of the Chicago Inspector General (2009), 26–27.

60 Gaffey (2010), 356 n.28, 359–361.

61 Ibid., 360.

62 Congressional Budget Office (1997), 18–19.

63 Plunkett (2006a, 2006b); Wilson (2010).

64 Plunkett (2006a, 2006b); Wilson (2010); Dannin (2011).

65 For examples, see American Bar Association (2010), Rules 1.7–1.9.

66 Crimmins (2009), 10001.

67 Mayer Brown (n.d.-a); Mayer Brown (n.d.-b).

68 Mayer Brown (n.d.-c).

69 Joravsky and Dumke (2009).

70 Morgan Stanley (n.d.).

71 Nussbaum (2007a).

72 Hamerman (2008), 3; Morgan Stanley (2008); Holman (2008).

73 Hamerman (2008); Crimmins (2009).

74 Mayer Brown (n.d.-b).

75 Rendell Press Release (2007); Crimmins (2009).

76 Barnes (2007); Joravsky and Dumke (2009).

77 Erdley (2007).

78 Nussbaum (2007b).

79 Keinitz is now Undersecretary of Transportation for Policy in the Obama administration. *TollRoad News* (2007).

80 Gaffey (2010), 363.

81 Gaffey (2010), 361–62; UK Centre for the Protection of National Infrastructure (n.d.); UK Infrastructure Planning Commission (n.d.).

82 UK Treasury (2007).

83 Perez and March (2006), 14; see also Joint Committee on Taxation (2008), 15–18; Furst (2005).

84 Kattula (2009a); Kattula (2009b).

85 Congressional Budget Office and Joint Committee on Taxation (2009).

86 Preston (2010).

87 US PIRG Education Fund (2009).

88 Orr (2007), 11; Orr and Kennedy (2008), 123.

89 Federal Highway Administration (2008), 31, 61.

90 Bingaman (2008).

91 Lowenthal (2007), 2.

92 CBS Broadcasting (2010).

93 Government Accountability Office (2008b), 26–28.

94 Federal Highway Administration (2005a).

95 Authorization for Execution of Concession and Lease Agreement and Amendment of Titles 2, 3, 9, and 10 of Municipal Code of Chicago in Connection with Chicago Metered Parking System, Passed by the City Council of the City of Chicago in Special Meeting Dec. 4, 2008; [Chicago Parking Meter Contract], § 14.5.

96 House Committee on Transportation and Infrastructure (2009a), 10.

97 Siposs (2005).

98 http://www.nyc.gov/html/planyc2030/html/home/home.shtml.

99 Mallett (2008).

100 Sorid (2005).

101 [Chicago Parking Meter Contract] (2008), §14.3.

102 Kansas Turnpike Authority and Kansas Department of Transportation (2008), 2–11.

103 Pagano (2009), 358.

104 Energy Information Administration (2010), 152; Mallett (2008), 3, 4.

105 Government Accountability Office (2010).

106 Ibid.; Government Accountability Office (2009), 1, 10; Federal Highway Administration (n.d.-b).

References

American Bar Association (2010). *Model Rules of Professional Conduct Concerning the Client-Lawyer Relationship.* http://www.abanet.org/cpr/mrpc/mrpc_toc.html.

Associated Press (2008, September 20). "State to Pay Spanish-Australian Consortium for Waived Fees on Toll Road."

Ayine, Dominic, Hernán Blanco, Lorenzo Cotula, Moussa Djiré, Candy Gonzalez, Nii Ashie Kotey, Shaheen Rafi Khan, Bernardo Reyes, Halina Ward, and Moeed Yusuf (2005, October). *Lifting the Lid on Foreign Investment Contracts: The Real Deal for Sustainable Development,* International Institute for Environment and Development, Sustainable Markets Briefing Paper No.1. http://www.iied.org/pubs/display.php?o=16007IIED.

Barnes, Tom (2007, May 22). "Turnpike Lease Looks Good on Paper: Rendell Advisers Present a Study Seeing Potential for Big Profits." *Pittsburgh Post-Gazette.* http://www.post-gazette.com/pg/07142/788007-147.stm.

Bernanke, Ben S. (2010, August 2). "Challenges for the Economy and State Governments." Speech at the Annual Meeting of the Southern Legislative Conference of the Council of State Governments, Charleston, South Carolina.

Bingaman, Jeff (2008, July 28). "Statement." *Hearing on Tax and Financing Aspects of Highway Public-Private Partnerships.*

Burger, Philippe, Justin Tyson, Izabela Karpowicz, and Maria Delgado Coelho (2009, July). "The Effects of the Financial Crisis on Public-Private Partnerships." IMF Working Paper WP/09/144. http://www.imf.org/external/pubs/ft/wp/2009/wp09144.pdf.

California Department of Transportation (n.d.). "Transportation Infrastructure Finance and Innovation Act (TIFIA) of 1998." http://www.dot.ca.gov/hq/innovfinance/tifia.htm.

Carlisle, Linda E. (2008, July 24). "Tax and Financing Aspects of Highway Public-Private Partnerships." Testimony before the Subcommittee on Energy, Natural Resources and Infrastructure of the Committee on Finance.

CBS Broadcasting (2010, February 5). "Report: Parking Meter Firm Gets Paid Even When Streets Closed." http://www.wbbm780.com/pages/6296597.php?contentType=4&contentId=5535568.

Chancellor, Edward, and Lauren Silva (2007, June 4). "Macquarie's Secret Recipe: 'Black Box' Valuation Model That Yields Profits for Funds Presents Credibility Problem." *Wall Street Journal.*

[Chicago Parking Meter Contract] (2008, December 4). "Authorization for Execution of Concession and Lease Agreement and Amendment of Titles 2, 3, 9 and 10 of Municipal Code of Chicago in Connection with Chicago Metered Parking System, Passed by the City Council of the City of Chicago in Special Meeting."

Chicago Tribune (2006, September 3). "Transportation—Quick Trips." *Chicago Tribune.*

[City of] Golden, Colorado (2009, July 22). "Letter to Chairman and Transportation Commissioners, Transportation Commission of Colorado."

Congressional Budget Office (1997, February). "Toll Roads: A Review of Recent Experience." http://www.cbo.gov/ftpdocs/40xx/doc4014/1997doc03-Entire.pdf.

Congressional Budget Office and Joint Committee on Taxation (2009, October). "Subsidizing Infrastructure Investment with Tax-Preferred Bonds." http://www.cbo. gov/ftpdocs/106xx/doc10667/10-26-TaxPreferredBonds.pdf.

Creswell, Julie (2010, June 15). "Stimulus Bond Program Has Unforeseen Costs." *The New York Times.*

Crimmins, Jerry (2009, April 21). "Privatization Deals May Be Tougher Now; But Are Not Dead; Lawyer Says." *Chicago Daily Law Bulletin*: 10001.

Dannin, Ellen (2006). "Red Tape or Accountability: Privatization, Public-ization, and Public Values." *Cornell Journal of Law and Public Policy* 15: 1111.

Dannin, Ellen (2011). "Crumbling Infrastructure—Crumbling Democracy Infrastructure Privatization Contracts and Their Effects on State and Local Governance." *Northwestern Journal Law and Social Policy* 5.

Dealogic (2010, January 11). Press Release: Project Finance Review. 5.

Deloitte Research (2007). *Closing America's Infrastructure Gap: The Role of Public-Private Partnerships.* http://www.deloitte.com/assets/Dcom-UnitedStates/Local%20Assets/ Documents/us_ps_PPPUS_final%281%29.pdf.

Dugan, Ianthe Jeanne (2010, August 23). "Facing Budget Gaps, Cities Sell Parking, Airports, Zoo." *Wall Street Journal.*

Dutton, Audrey (2010, August 11). "Build America Bonds: Lobbyists Line Up to Push BAB Extension." *The Bond Buyer.*

Energy Information Administration (2010, May). *Petroleum Marketing Monthly.* 152. http://www.eia.doe.gov/pub/oil_gas/petroleum/data_publications/petroleum_ marketing_monthly/current/pdf/enote.pdf.

Enright, Dennis J. (2007, June 1). "The Public versus Private Toll Road Choice in the United States." Address to the Council of State Governments (CSG) Eastern Regional Conference. http://www.csgeast.org/Annual_Meeting/2007/present/budget2.enright.pdf.

Erdley, Debra (2007, April 5). "Wall Street Mobilizes to Cash in on Privatizing Public Assets." *Pittsburgh Tribune-Review.* http://www.pittsburghlive.com/x/pittsburghtrib/ s_501218.html.

Federal Highway Administration (2005a, September). "Public Private Partnerships: PPP Agreements (Pocahontas Parkway)." http://www.fhwa.dot.gov/PPP/agreements_ pocahontas.htm.

Federal Highway Administration (2005b, September). "Public Private Partnerships: PPP Agreements (South Bay Expressway (SR 125)." Agreement. http://www.fhwa.dot.gov/ PPP/agreements_sr125.htm.

Federal Highway Administration (2008, July 18). "Innovation Wave: An Update on the Burgeoning Private Sector Role in U.S. Highway and Transit Infrastructure." http:// www.fhwa.dot.gov/reports/pppwave/ppp_innovation_wave.pdf.

Federal Highway Administration (n.d.-a). "Financing Federal-Aid Highways." http:// www.fhwa.dot.gov/reports/fifahiwy/fifahi05.htm.

Federal Highway Administration (n.d.-b). "Innovative Program Delivery: TIFIA." http:// www.fhwa.dot.gov/ipd/tifia/.

Furst, Tony (2005, September). "Freight Provisions in SAFETEA-LU." *Federal Highway Administration, U.S. Department of Transportation.* http://www.fhwa.dot.gov/ freightplanning/safetea_lu.htm.

Gaffey, David W. (2010). "Outsourcing Infrastructure: Expanding the Use of Public-Private Partnerships in the United States." *Public Contracting Law Journal* 39:351.

Government Accountability Office (2008a, February). "Highway Public-Private Partnerships: More Rigorous Up-front Analysis Could Better Secure Potential Benefits and Protect the Public Interest, GAO-08–44."

Government Accountability Office (2008b, March). "Surface Transportation: Restructured Federal Approach Needed for More Focused, Performance-Based, and Sustainable Programs GAO-08–400."

Government Accountability Office (2009, June 25). "Highway Trust Fund: Options for Improving Sustainability and Mechanisms to Manage Solvency, GAO-09–845T."

Government Accountability Office (2010, June 30). "Highway Trust Fund: Nearly All States Received More Funding Than They Contributed in Highway Taxes Since 2005, GAO-10–780."

Hamerman, Joshua (2008, December 8). "More Infrastructure Privatization Coming; Latest Chicago Deal Highlights the Growth of a Developed Market for Infrastructure Privatization in the US." *Investment Dealers' Digest* 74.

Hecker, JayEtta Z. (2008, July 24). "Highway Public-Private Partnerships, Securing Potential Benefits, and Protecting the Public Interest Could Result from More Rigorous Up-front Analysis GAO-08–1052T." Testimony Before the Senate Subcommittee on Energy, Natural Resources, and Infrastructure, Committee on Finance.

Hepworth, Annabel, and Jared Owens (2010, September 1). "Clem7 Tunnel Losses Endanger Public-Private Infrastructure." *The Australian*. http://www.theaustralian. com.au/news/nation/clem7-tunnel-losses-endanger-public-private-infrastructure/ story-e6frg6nf-1225912550578.

HM Treasury (n.d.). "Public Private Partnerships." http://www.hm-treasury.gov.uk/ ppp_index.htm.

Holman, Kelly (2008, May 12). "Infrastructure Investment Speeds Up—Morgan Stanley and Global Infrastructure Partners Are Latest to Raise Investment Vehicles for the Space." *Investment Dealers Digest*. http://www.iddmagazine.com/news/181743–1.html.

House Committee on Transportation and Infrastructure (2009a, June 18). "The Surface Transportation Authorization Act of 2009: A Blueprint for Investment and Reform."

House Committee on Transportation and Infrastructure (2009b, June 18). "The Surface Transportation Authorization Act of 2009: A Blueprint for Investment and Reform, Executive Summary."

International Bar Association Working Group on the OECD Guidelines for Multinational Enterprises (2009, November 30). "Response to the UK Consultation on the Terms of Reference for an Update of the OECD Guidelines for Multinational Enterprises UK Department for Business, Innovation and Skills." http://oecdwatch. org/publications-en/Publication_3290/at_download/fullfile.

Joint Committee on Taxation (2008, July 8). "Overview of Selected Tax Provisions Relating to the Financing of Surface Transportation Infrastructure (JCX-56–08)."

Joravsky, Ben, and Mick Dumke (2009, June 18). "The Parking Meter Fiasco: Part III The Insiders." *Chicago Reader*. http://www.chicagoreader.com/ chicago_parking_meters_3/.

Kansas T-Link (2008, November). "Using Tolls to Support Needed Transportation Projects: A Resource for Kansas Policymakers." http://www.kansastlink. com/downloads/VI%20Using%20Tolls%20to%20Support%20Needed%20 Transportation%20Projects.pdf.

Kansas Turnpike Authority and Kansas Department of Transportation (2008, January). "Using Tolls to Support Needed Transportation Projects: A Resource for Kansas Policymakers." http://www.kansastlink.com/downloads/VI%20Using%20Tolls%20to%20Support%20Needed%20Transportation%20Projects.pdf.

Kattula, Steve (2009a, November 11). "Corporate Welfare and the Beltway HOT Lanes, Part 2: You Better Not Carpool (Too Much)." *Greater Greater Washington.* http://greatergreaterwashington.org/post.cgi?id=4041.

Kattula, Steve (2009b, November 18). "Corporate Welfare and the Beltway Hot Lanes, Part 3: Don't Worry Until It's Too Late." *Greater Greater Washington.* http://greatergreaterwashington.org/post.cgi?id=4102.

Kim, Theodore (2006, October 17). "States Considering Privatizing Highways Can Study Indiana Toll Road Experience." *USA Today*: 10A.

Kleinbard, Edward D. (2008, July 24). "Tax and Financing Aspects of Highway Public-Private Partnerships." Testimony before the Subcommittee on Energy, Natural Resources, and Infrastructure of the Committee on Finance.

Leib, Jeffrey (2006, May 30). "A Fork in C-470: May Sway How State Adds Lanes." *Denver Post.* http://www.denverpost.com/news/ci_3878766.

Leib, Jeffrey (2008, July 24). "Toll Firm Objects to Work on W. 160th: The 'Non-Compete' Clause for the Northwest Parkway Raises Legislative Concerns." *Denver Post.* http://www.denverpost.com/news/ci_9976830.

Likosky, Michael B. (2006). *Law, Infrastructure, and Human Rights.* New York: Cambridge University Press.

Lord, Nick (2010, April 6). "Privatization: The Road to Wiping Out the US Deficit." *Euromoney.* http://www.euromoney.com/Print.aspx?ArticleID=2459161.

Lowenthal, Allen (2007, January). "Tolls, User Fees, and Public-Private Partnerships: The Future of Transportation Finance in California?" Information Hearing of the US Senate Transportation and Housing Committee.

MacInnes, Judy (2008, September 11). "Cintra's August Traffic Falls on Main Concessions." *Reuters.* http://uk.reuters.com/article/rbssIndustryMaterialsUtilitiesNews/idUKLB70560420080911.

Mallett, William J. (2008, July 9). "Public-Private Partnerships in Highway and Transit Infrastructure Provision(RL34567)." *Congressional Research Service.*

Mayer Brown (n.d.-a) "Infrastructure Privatization Experience." http://www.mayerbrown.com/infrastructure/index.asp?nid=11539.

Mayer Brown (n.d.-b) "Infrastructure Practice." http://www.mayerbrown.com/infrastructure/.

Mayer Brown (n.d.-c) "Infrastructure Investment Funds." http://www.mayerbrown.com/infrastructure/index.asp?nid=11440.

Morgan Stanley (2008, May 12). "Press Release: Morgan Stanley Closes $4.0 Billion Global Infrastructure Fund." http://www.morganstanley.com/about/press/articles/193468f4–555c-11dd-adaf-ab43576ea42b.html.

Morgan Stanley (n.d.) http://www.morganstanley.com/index.html.

Nussbaum, Paul (2007a, March 20). "Pa. Turnpike Lease Plans 'Proprietary;' Penndot Is Keeping 48 Firms' Plans for Running the Toll Road Secret from Legislators Even as the Governor Makes His Pitch." *Philadelphia Inquirer.*

Nussbaum, Paul (2007b, May 22). "Turnpike Lease Plan Sent to Pa. Legislature: Gov. Rendell's Proposal to Raise Money for State Transportation Projects Faces Major Opposition." *Philadelphia Inquirer.*

Office of the Chicago Inspector General (2009, June 2). *Report of Inspector General's Findings and Recommendations: An Analysis of the Lease of the City's Parking Meters.*

Orr, Ryan J. (2007). *The Rise of Infrastructure Funds, Global Infrastructure Report 2007.* London: Project Finance International.

Orr, Ryan J., and Jeremy R. Kennedy (2008, April 1). "Highlights of Recent Trends in Global Infrastructure: New Players and Revised Game Rules." *Transnational Corporations.* http://www.allbusiness.com/trade-development/economic-development/11699033–1.html investments.

Orszag, Peter R. (2008, July 10). Statement of Peter R. Orszag, Director of the Congressional Budget Office, Before the United States Senate Committee on Finance, Investing in Infrastructure.

Pagano, Celeste (2009). "Proceed with Caution: Avoiding Hazards in Toll Road Privatizations." *St. John's Law Review* 83: 351.

Pennsylvania Turnpike Contract (Proposed) (2008).

Perez, Benjamin G., and James W. March (2006, August 2–3). "Public-Private Partnerships and the Development of Transport Infrastructure: Trends on Both Sides of the Atlantic." First International Conference on Funding Transportation Infrastructure, Institute of Public Economics at the University of Alberta, Banff Centre, Alberta, Canada. http://financecommission.dot.gov/Documents/Background%20Documents/perez_banff_ppp_final.pdf.

PlaNYC (n.d.). http://www.nyc.gov/html/planyc2030/html/home/home.shtml.

Plunkett, Chuck (2006a, May 28). "Roads to Riches: Paved with Bad Projections." *Denver Post.* http://www.denverpost.com/news/ci_3871773.

Plunkett, Chuck (2006b, May 29). "No 2-Way Street: When Landowners Help Pay the Toll." *Denver Post.* http://www.denverpost.com/news/ci_3876477.

Preqin (2010, July). *Infrastructure Spotlight* 3:7.

Preston, Darrell (2010, August 12). "A Windfall for Investors, a Loss for Chicago: Critics Say the Windy City Will Lose Billions over the Life of a $1.15 Billion Contract to Run the City's Parking Meters." *BusinessWeek.* http://www.businessweek.com/magazine/content/10_34/b4192044579970.htm.

PricewaterhouseCooper (2008, December). "Infrastructure Finance—Surviving the Credit Crunch."

Rendell Press Release (2007, March 29). "Governor Rendell Announces Selection of Financial Adviser for Transportation Funding Options, Morgan Stanley & Co. To Analyze All Options, Including Turnpike's Proposal." http://www.state.pa.us/papower/cwp/view.asp?A=11&Q=461198.

Sclar, Elliott D. (2009, October 1). "The Political-Economics of Private Infrastructure Finance: The New Sub Prime." Address to the Association of Collegiate Schools of Planning, Crystal City, VA.

Shemberg, Andrea and Motoko Aizawa (2008, March 11). *Stabilization Clauses and Human Rights: A Research Project Conducted for IFC and the United Nations Special Representative to the Secretary General on Business and Human Rights.* http://www.ifc.org/ifcext/enviro.nsf/AttachmentsByTitle/p_StabilizationClausesandHumanRights/$FILE/Stabilization+Paper.pdf.

Siposs, Árpád G. (2005, April 11–13). *Tolling on the Hungarian Motorway Network.* Piarc Seminar on Road Pricing with Emphasis on Financing, Regulation and Equity.

Slone, Sean (n.d.). *Transportation and Infrastructure Finance: A CSG National Report.* http://www.csg.org/pubs/Documents/TransportationInfrastructureFinance.pdf.

Sorid, Daniel (2005, August 11). "Colorado Highway 'Slowdown' Sparks Debate on Toll Roads." *Reuters.* http://corridornews.blogspot.com/2005_08_01_archive.html.

Staff of the Joint Committee on Taxation (2008, July 10). "Overview of Selected Tax Provisions Relating to the Financing of Surface Transportation Infrastructure." Before the Senate Committee on Finance. http://www.jct.gov/x-56-08.pdf.

Stowe, Joshua (2006, November 11). "U-Turn Safety Barriers on Toll Road Finished; Emergency Crews Still Training on Median Bypass." *South Bend Tribune (Indiana)*: B-3.

Tett, Gillian (2010, June 23). "Collapsed Debt Market Poses Dilemma For G20." *Financial Times*. http://www.ft.com/cms/s/0/7200fb68-7eec-11df-8398-00144feabdc0.html.

The Working Group (2009). *The Benefits of Private Investment in Infrastructure 2009*. http://www2.vlaanderen.be/pps/documenten/benefits_of_private_investment_in_infrastructure.pdf.

THENEWSPAPER.COM (2006, February 3). "Australia: Traffic Lights Modified to Funnel Traffic into Toll Tunnel." *THENEWSPAPER.COM*. http://www.thenewspaper.com/news/09/936.asp.

THENEWSPAPER.COM (2007, October 19). "Texas: Speed Limit May Be Lowered to Boost Toll Revenue." *THENEWSPAPER.COM*. http://thenewspaper.com/news/20/2025.asp.

TollRoad News (2007, May 21). "Longterm Lease of Turnpike Likely Best Value for Pennsylvania—Gov Rendell Seeking Law for a Concession." *TollRoad News*. http://www.tollroadsnews.com/node/145.

UK Centre for the Protection of National Infrastructure (n.d.). http://www.cpni.gov.uk/.

UK Infrastructure Planning Commission (n.d.) http://infrastructure.independent.gov.uk/.

UK Treasury (2007, March). "Standardisation of PFI Contracts, Version 4." http://www.hm-treasury.gov.uk/d/pfi_sopc4pu101_210307.pdf.

US Government Accountability Office (2006). "Highway Finance: States' Expanding Use of Tolling Illustrates Diverse Challenges and Strategies, GAO-06-554."

US PIRG Education Fund (2009). *Private Roads, Public Costs: The Facts about Toll Road Privatization and How to Protect the Public*. http://www.uspirg.org/uploads/H5/Ql/H5QloNcoPVeVJwymwlURRw/Private-Roads-Public-Costs.pdf.

US PIRG Education Fund (2010). *Road Work Ahead: Holding Government Accountable for Fixing America's Crumbling Roads and Bridges*.

Washington Post (n.d.). "Head Count: Tracking Obama's Appointments: Roy Kienitz." http://projects.washingtonpost.com/2009/federal-appointments/person/roy-kienitz/.

Washington Times (2009, July 13). "Editorial: Not So HOT Lanes." http://www.washingtontimes.com/news/2009/jul/13/not-so-hot-lanes/.

Weiss, Eric M. (2008, July 20). "Toll-Lanes Contract Could Cost State-Deal to Allow Free Carpooling on Beltway Project Might Leave Va. Owing Millions." *Washington Post*.

Wilson, Stuart (2010, September 7). "Clem7 Motorway Investors Did Not Get the Whole Picture." *The Australian*. http://www.theaustralian.com.au/business/opinion/clem7-motorway-investors-did-not-get-the-whole-picture/story-e6frg9q6-1225915021261.

CHAPTER 27

....

FINANCIAL EMERGENCIES: DEFAULT AND BANKRUPTCY

....

JAMES E. SPIOTTO

EVERY economic downturn has the potential to threaten existing state and local government debt financing and the provision of essential services. Aging infrastructure, exploding unfunded pension obligations and an ever-increasing demand for social programs—all are occurring in an era of downward adjustment of US home values, widespread foreclosures, financial products of "mass destruction" and declining predictability of property, sale, and income-tax revenues—have elevated the possibility of municipal and state default and insolvency to the forefront of US concerns. When placed in the context of the greater risks of financial market meltdowns and national government debt crises, both domestic and foreign, the ability of existing mechanisms to deal with municipal and state defaults and insolvencies in the United States must be carefully considered.

In this chapter I explore the historical underpinnings of efforts to restructure municipal debt in times of financial crisis, and I provide selected examples of successes and failures of such efforts in the United States and the advantages and disadvantages of the existing statutory framework for municipal bankruptcy in the United States. The issue of a sovereign debt resolution mechanism for states also will be discussed. I conclude with recommendations for alternative municipal and state debt resolution mechanisms.

Background: The State and Local Government Debt Bubble in the United States

The outstanding debt of state and local governments in the United States has almost doubled from \$1.5 trillion in 2000 to \$2.8 trillion at the end of 2009.[1] This latter figure does not include over \$1 trillion of unfunded public employee pension liabilities and estimated unfunded postretirement health liabilities of \$700 billion.[2] Nor does it include the required debt financing over the next five years to bring infrastructure up to acceptable standards, which may amount to \$2.5 trillion.[3] While the exact magnitude of the overall liability is sketchy, the reality of this debt bubble mandates an effective means of dealing with the financial stresses for states and localities that are bound to follow.[4]

The Causes and Examples of Subsovereign Debt Default in the United States

In the United States, causes of default by municipalities have included weakened economic conditions, financing developed to pay for nonessential services, problems with the feasibility of projects and industries, fraud, municipal mismanagement, unwillingness to repay debt, and the impacts from natural and man-made disasters.

In particular, economic depression led to major municipal bond defaults in the past, including in 1837 with Mobile, Alabama; 1843 for Bridgeport, Connecticut; 1857 for Chicago and Philadelphia; the 1860s, in which thirteen states repudiated reconstruction and war debt; 1873 for Mobile once again; and 1877 for Pittsburgh.[5] The defaults of the 1800s led to a movement away from the "moral obligation" bond and to the institution of many of the protective measures that are now taken for granted, such as statutory authority, debt limitations, use of bond counsel, and rating agencies.[6] Examples of nonessential services that have resulted in municipal defaults include failed health-care projects; a railroad station without a working railroad; real estate speculation; refuse-burning facilities such as in Harrisburg, Pennsylvania; and a large housing development on Guam. Historically, the largest number of municipal defaults have occurred with respect to projects involving real estate development (particularly in nonessential service districts) and health-care transactions. Defaults involving municipal projects relating to the provision of essential services, infrastructure, or public safety are rare. Ill-conceived financing has also caused defaults. Examples of projects and industries lacking adequate feasibility studies have included a Harrisburg, Pennsylvania, incinerator and the Washington Public Power Supply System (WPPSS). The irrational investment strategies of Orange County, California, in the early 1990s approached the fraud level. In addition, unwillingness to pay was the basis for the repudiations in the 1860s, the WPPSS default, and the Chapter 9 filing by Orange County, California, one of the wealthiest local governments in the United States. Natural and man-made disasters leading to defaults have included the tort liability for an employee in South Tucson and a hurricane leading to massive default in Galveston, Texas, in the early 1900s.

To put the recent history of municipal defaults in perspective, according to Moody's Investor Services, between 1970 and 2009, there were fifty-four rated municipal bond defaults compared to 1,707 rated corporate defaults, and 78 percent of the rated municipal defaults were in the health-care and housing-project finance sectors.[7] Similarly, according to Standard and Poor's, between 1986 and 2008, there were thirty-nine rated municipal defaults compared to 1,604 rated corporate defaults.[8] According to Municipal Market Advisors, the overall number of municipal issues, rated and nonrated, that had payment defaults to bondholders in 2009 was 187, and 495 issuers filed notices of some type of impairment such as payment default or reserve draw.[9] Currently, there are approximately 90,000 governmental units involved in the $2.8 trillion municipal market of today. Nevertheless, economic conditions from time to time have and will lead to municipal defaults and financially troubled municipalities.

THE SEARCH FOR A
DEBT-RESTRUCTURING MECHANISM

The history of government debt defaults makes it clear that the city or state with an unsustainable debt burden needs to find a fresh start. The question, of course, is "how should that be done"? The answer to this dilemma has perplexed units of local government from antiquity to the present. Indeed, the Greeks and Romans regarded the discharge of debt and equitable liquidation of assets as a necessary ingredient of a civilized society.[10]

Because of the very purpose of local government—the most basic way that people organize themselves to live together and enjoy public safety and basic services—the traditional receivership approach of rapid repayment of defaulted indebtedness with a concomitant reduction in services is an unpopular mechanism. On the other hand, in the past, repudiation of government debt, refusal to pay valid obligations, has been all too common, not only in Europe, Latin America, and Asia during times of war or economic crisis, but even in the United States in the nineteenth century following overexpansion and improvident issuance of public debt, especially after the Civil War in the South. While repudiation in some form or another, as opposed to receivership, has been a popular means of avoiding debt payment, it is obviously short-sighted. Repudiation of validly issued public debt destroys the credit rating for the issuer and makes any subsequent return to the public-debt markets problematic at best. A real fix requires a fresh start, which does not impair necessary credit perception going forward, and which does not destroy the debtor municipality in the name of fiscal discipline. The popular use of Band-Aids applied to mask the problem only leads to an increasingly deteriorating situation. All too often, governmental bodies have been content to simply demonstrate some activity rather than fully address systemic problems. Tough decisions are left to the next administration while officeholders support insufficient budget reductions, deferral of current liabilities such as unfunded pension obligations, borrowing to fund current excessive operating costs, and promised increased salaries and pension benefits that are neither sustainable nor affordable. A mechanism needs to be devised to address the need of the municipality or state and its citizens for liquidity and to provide a path to a viable financial future while, at the same time, to deal with the need for prompt repayment of legitimate debt in whole or in part.

Grappling with Municipal Default

Since 1839, less than 10,000 municipal defaults have occurred among all municipal and state entities. Almost half of these defaults occurred between 1929 and 1937, a direct result of the Great Depression of 1929. Since 1937[11] in the United States, 249 subsovereign entities have filed for municipal debt adjustment (legislated by federal law, currently commonly known as Chapter 9). As will be discussed, the Tenth Amendment to the Constitution has prevented Congress from legislating mandatory action with respect to insolvency of the individual sovereign states.

In the early years of the republic, defaults occurred in various transportation projects, such as canal and railroad building, where the governments frequently lent assistance to private developers. As noted, many municipal defaults more recently have arisen in connection with health-care projects, conduit issues in which the municipal debt suffers because of failed private businesses or in conjunction with special service districts that are similarly tied to the fortunes of private business, particularly real estate development.[12] A brief review of major US municipal defaults is instructive in highlighting the issues that any statutory scheme to provide a mechanism for municipal debt adjustment must anticipate.

The New York and Cleveland Experiences

In the late 1970s, both New York and Cleveland faced major financial crises stemming from the lack of reliable accounting and financing controls and the market's response thereto and the basic fact that general-fund expenditures exceeded revenues. Both cities averted financial disaster by borrowing from their states in order to pay overdue debts, in the case of New York City, the State Municipal Assistance Corporation. Cleveland coupled a loan from the State of Ohio with the sale of bonds to Cleveland banks. Municipal bankruptcy was not seriously considered by either city.[13]

The San Jose School District and Medley, Florida

Labor problems coupled with the California Proposition 13 restrictions on real estate taxes were the primary causes for the San Jose School District's filing for bankruptcy in 1983. Medley, Florida, was the subject of numerous judgments and writs of mandamus issued in favor of creditors. The San Jose School District and Medley, Florida, both used the mechanism of instituting Chapter 9 bankruptcy proceedings but, nevertheless, each insisted on paying public-bond obligations that had been incurred before the filing.[14] Despite the general prohibition against paying interest and principal during a bankruptcy where the debtor is insolvent, municipal bondholders continued to be paid in both of these cases. The San Jose School District case ultimately was dismissed, and the plan of adjustment in the Medley, Florida, case did not alter or impair bonded indebtedness.

The Washington Public Power Supply System

In 1976, the Washington Public Power Supply System (WPPSS), a multistate electric utility system in the Northwest, entered into agreements with eighty-eight public utilities under which each participant utility purchased a percentage of the capability of two nuclear power projects to be built, commonly known as WPPSS 4&5. The participant agreements contained a "hell or high water" proviso that meant the obligations must be paid even if the plants were never built or operated. The legal opinion rendered in connection with the financing noted that seventy-seven participants were authorized to join in a joint action agency but was silent as to the others. Prior to the completion of construction, it was determined that there was a lack of demand for the power, and the projects were terminated. A subsequent Washington Supreme Court decision determined that the certain participant utilities had lacked the authority to enter into the participant agreements, which were to fund principal and interest on the bonds that were issued to pay for the projects, and hence the utilities did not have to pay.[15] This resulted in the then-largest municipal bond default in US history. Nevertheless, municipal bankruptcy was not pursued by WPPSS. Rather, extensive and expensive litigation ensued, and bond-holders received far less than the full payment of principal and interest on the securities that had been issued to pay the terminated projects.

Colorado Special Districts

In the real estate boom of the 1980s, special districts were created in Colorado, which then issued special assessment bonds to finance the infrastructure for residential real estate development. These special districts are municipalities under the language of the United States Bankruptcy Code. In light of the unique nature and limited purpose of these special districts, a liquidation or bankruptcy was the only logical mechanism for dealing with the bond defaults once the Colorado real estate market faced a significant downturn. Ironically, the municipal bankruptcies of these tiny districts have produced much of the legal precedent interpreting the federal municipal bankruptcy law.[16]

Bridgeport, Connecticut

In 1991, Bridgeport, Connecticut, suffering under the impact of urban flight, shocked the municipal finance community by filing a petition under Chapter 9 of the Federal Bankruptcy Code. Bridgeport was the first real "city" of over 100,000 in population in recent history to default on an issue of municipal debt and to file for bankruptcy. It employed some 4,000 people pursuant to union contracts to deliver services to approximately 150,000 citizens. The State of Connecticut moved to dismiss the bankruptcy petition, and the court granted the dismissal, finding that financial difficulties short of insolvency were not a sufficient basis for Chapter 9 relief.[17] In that case, Bridgeport was unable to establish insolvency at the time of filing although it made a showing of prospective problems. Thus, municipal bankruptcy was not a vehicle to permit Bridgeport to restructure predictable future problems.

Philadelphia

Also in 1991, Philadelphia encountered a financial crisis. Through the cooperation of the State of Pennsylvania, default was avoided. Special legislation, the Pennsylvania Intergovernmental Cooperation Authority Act for Cities of the First Class, was enacted that permitted an authority to issue securities to refund the obligations of the city. Certain taxes were dedicated to the repayment of those bonds, and an authority monitored collective bargaining and other budget issues that had contributed to the financial crisis.

Orange County, California

In 1994, Orange County, California, suffered a devastating liquidity crisis stemming from an unwise leveraged investment policy in derivatives and rising interest rates. Additionally, the county experienced a severe tax-revenue shortfall. Unlike New York, Philadelphia, and Cleveland, however, Orange County resorted to municipal bankruptcy rather than turning to other measures to avoid default, such as increasing its sales tax 1 percent to equal the rate in Los Angeles County. In order to borrow to pay off existing debt obligations, Orange County incurred a ten to twenty-three basis point penalty because of its status as a bankrupt issuer, costing Orange County over $60 million.[18]

Vallejo, California

In 2008, Vallejo, California, filed for Chapter 9, claiming insolvency and the failure of city workers to address necessary adjustments for collective bargaining agreements for salaries and benefits.[19] Reportedly, salaries and benefits for public safety workers accounted for at least 80 percent of Vallejo's general-fund budget. After a lengthy legal skirmish over the eligibility of Vallejo to file for municipal bankruptcy, the district court affirmed the bankruptcy court's rejection of a collective bargaining agreement with the electrical workers, including the bankruptcy court's finding that the agreement was burdensome and that the city had made reasonable efforts to reach an agreement with the union. An appeal to the Court of Appeals followed. Whatever the outcome, the Chapter 9 procedure has been expensive, time-consuming, and not an obvious solution to a municipality facing labor problems.

These varied experiences reveal a resort to Chapter 9 by relatively smaller municipalities, with the exception of Orange County. Most major municipalities have been assisted by their states in dealing with financial crises that could cripple state and other local governments in the process. The default by Harrisburg, Pennsylvania, on loan payments in connection with the bonds to finance its incinerator expansion has negatively affected the city's creditworthiness.[20] In October 2010, the State of Pennsylvania provided state aid to avert a default on the city's general obligation bonds while the insurer for the incinerator bonds has sought the appointment of a receiver. The state is also working with the city to secure financing for operating funds. While the mayor has discussed the possibility of selling municipal assets or raising taxes to address the crisis, others have advocated a Chapter 9 filing. Similarly the initial response of Central Falls, Rhode Island, was to seek the appointment of a state court receiver to take charge of the city's finances, rather than turn to the bankruptcy court.

CHAPTER 9 OF THE BANKRUPTCY CODE

Chapter 9 originated with the Great Depression and citizens' disgust with the cost of the unproductive but distracting litigation over a city's inability to pay current obligations due to the drastic decline in revenues. After various attempts between 1934 and 1937 to craft legislation that would pass constitutional scrutiny and demonstrate appropriate respect for state sovereignty, Chapter 9 was born. Not every governmental unit can maintain a case under Chapter 9. The Bankruptcy Code prescribes in detail the qualifications for an entity to be a debtor under Chapter 9, which pertains to the adjustment of debts of a municipality. The entity must be a municipality, specifically authorized under state law to be a debtor, insolvent, willing to effectuate a plan, and either have obtained the agreement of creditors holding the majority amount of the claim of each class that the municipality intends to impair or have attempted to negotiate in good faith, but was unable to do so or it was impractical to negotiate with creditors or a creditor is attempting to obtain a preference.[21]

Only a "municipality" may be a debtor under Chapter 9 of the Bankruptcy Code. Furthermore, only a municipality can initiate a Chapter 9 proceeding. Under the provisions of the Bankruptcy Code, a municipality is defined as a "political subdivision or public agency or instrumentality of the state."[22] A municipality is not eligible to be a debtor under any other chapter of the US Bankruptcy Code.

Initiation of a Chapter 9 Proceeding

There can be no involuntary Chapter 9 proceeding (in which the filing is made by one other than the debtor) so no one other than the municipality can initiate a Chapter 9 filing. Not only are involuntary proceedings constitutionally prohibited, but there is no statutory basis for an involuntary action. On the other hand, a state is a sovereign and, as a sovereign, it is not subject to federal bankruptcy legislation and hence not eligible to file a Chapter 9 petition. In addition to the requirement that a municipality be a subdivision of an agency or a subdivision or instrumentality of the state, it must be specifically authorized to file a Chapter 9 proceeding by the state.[23] The states have adopted different approaches to this requirement. Fifteen states have statutory provisions in which the state specifically authorizes filing. Another nine states authorize a filing conditioned on a further act of the state, an elected official or a state entity. Three states grant limited authorization and two states prohibit filing, but one of them has an exception to the prohibition. The remaining twenty-one states are either unclear or do not have specific authorization with respect to filing.[24] The issue of the ability to be a Chapter 9 debtor has been a frequent threshold question in municipal bankruptcy cases.[25] While the characterization of certain public and private partnerships may be open to question, most special service districts formed under a state's statute to perform certain public services or provide public utilities should qualify as municipalities. However, this initial question of authority to file can absorb precious court time while the municipality is in extreme financial difficulty. Regardless of the constitutional requirement that such analysis be performed, the requirement obviously impairs the utility of Chapter 9 as a restructuring mechanism when time is of the essence.

Only an Insolvent Municipality Can Use Chapter 9

Chapter 9 requires that a municipality be insolvent under the statutory definition to proceed as a Chapter 9 debtor. Under the Bankruptcy Code, a municipality is insolvent when its financial condition is such that the municipality is generally not paying its debts as they become due, unless such debts are the subject of a bona fide dispute, or the municipality is unable to pay its debts as they become due. The insolvency analysis focuses on the filing date and the financial capability of the municipality at that moment in time. Accordingly, a number of troubled cities and towns have been unable to proceed under Chapter 9 as they have not been deemed insolvent under the statutory definition.

For example, the Bridgeport, Connecticut, Chapter 9 case was dismissed because the evidence only supported a finding that Bridgeport might be unable to meet its debt obligations in the future.[26] In other words, there must be a determination of insolvency without substantial regard to either future potential revenues or shortfalls. The issue of insolvency occupied the early months of the Vallejo bankruptcy. In that case, the United States Bankruptcy Appellate Panel of the Ninth Circuit ultimately rejected the challenge to the insolvency of Vallejo brought by numerous unions.[27] The Appellate Panel affirmed the ruling of the Bankruptcy Court that insolvency is determined on a cash-flow basis, which required Vallejo to demonstrate an inability to pay debts due within the next year. Part of the controversy involved various city special funds, which Vallejo contended were restricted, and the union opposing the filing asserted that money from such funds could be used to support general-fund obligations. The court was willing to accept expert testimony regarding the restricted nature of various funds. The Appellate Panel also affirmed the Bankruptcy Court's ruling that a further reduction of municipal services would threaten Vallejo's ability to provide for the basic health and safety of its citizens and was not mandated. While the ruling of insolvency permitted the Chapter 9 proceeding to go forward, the ruling on insolvency came over a year after the filing of the bankruptcy petition. Although the litigants were certainly entitled to raise legitimate legal issues, the Vallejo dispute as to insolvency highlights the challenges a municipality faces in attempting to utilize Chapter 9 to provide relief in an emergency situation.

Required Maintenance of Municipal Services

Depending upon the statutory mission of the municipality, there are certain necessary and basic municipal services that must be provided that the Chapter 9 court cannot frustrate. Section 903 of the Bankruptcy Code specifically provides that Chapter 9 should not interfere with the power of a state, by legislation or otherwise, to control its municipalities. As a corollary, § 904 of the Bankruptcy Code limits the ability of the court to interfere with the governmental powers of the debtor, any of the property or the revenues of the debtor, or the debtor's use or enjoyment of income-producing property. This is consistent with the Tenth Amendment prohibition against the federal government's interference with the sovereign power of the states. Accordingly, certain revenues and activities of the municipal body that may be the cause of the insolvency may not be able to be restrained, curtailed, or modified without the consent of the municipality.

Compensation of Professionals for the Debtor Municipality

The fees of professionals employed by the municipality during the case are not subject to court review or approval. While this permits greater leeway for a debtor municipality to compensate its professionals, there also is no requirement in Chapter 9 compelling the compensation of such professionals by a cash-strapped municipality. Particularly in special-purpose district bankruptcies, where funds are scarce, the source of payment of fees for counsel to the debtor is the issue that must be resolved if the debtor is to receive adequate representation.

Postpetition Security Interest, Statutory Liens, and Special Revenues

While outside of a Chapter 9 proceeding, general obligation bonds of a municipality are widely regarded as superior investments with the full faith and credit of the municipality backing them, in a Chapter 9 proceeding revenue bonds secured by a pledge of special revenue may receive better treatment. In a corporate bankruptcy context, § 552 of the Bankruptcy Code provides that property acquired by the estate or the debtor after commencement of a case is not subject to any lien resulting from a security agreement entered into by the debtor before the commencement of the case. There had been concern, before the adoption of the Municipal Bankruptcy

Amendments in 1988 that, consistent with § 552(a) of the Bankruptcy Code, the pledge of revenues by a municipality would terminate upon a Chapter 9 filing, and general creditors of the municipality could seek payment from the pledged revenues.

This concern was addressed by § 928 of the Bankruptcy Code, which renders § 552(a) inapplicable in a Chapter 9 to revenue bonds secured by special revenues.[28] Thus, in the case of special revenues, the security interest remains valid and unenforceable even though such revenues are received after a Chapter 9 filing. On the other hand, to the extent that a general obligation bond does not have any pledged revenues that qualify as special revenues, there are no revenues necessarily earmarked or paid to the general obligation bondholder during the bankruptcy proceeding, and such bonds would be treated as general unsecured claims. Conversely, the revenue bondholder only receives payment of special revenues postpetition and the bondholders have no claim against nonpledged assets. The addition of the special revenues concept into Chapter 9, as part of the 1988 Amendments, was to ensure a means of financing that could not have the source of payment voided by a subsequent Chapter 9 filing, a feature desired by financially distressed municipalities who require a means of financing with an unquestionable source of payment.

Another method of avoiding the effect of § 552(a) is through the prepetition enactment of a statutory lien creating the pledge rather than a security interest. This approach was recognized by the District Court on appeal in the Orange County bankruptcy. There, the court found that the lien securing tax and revenue anticipation notes pursuant to a California statute authorizing the county to pledge assets to secure notes was a statutory lien. Because the statute imposed the pledge, not a security agreement, it survived the filing of a Chapter 9 petition.[29]

The significance of special revenues and statutory liens was illustrated by the case of the Sierra Kings Health Care District,[30] in which a court order reaffirmed the fact that a Chapter 9 proceeding does not interfere with notes, bonds, or municipal obligations that are paid from the pledge of taxes or revenues, which are special revenues or subject to a statutory lien. Of special significance is the fact that the court confirmed, for the first time, the postpetition effectiveness of a municipality's pledge of *ad valorem* taxes, which qualified as both a special revenue pledge and a statutory lien. The Chapter 9 proceeding did not affect the timely payment on these bonds according to their terms.

Treatment of Municipal Bond Debt

Prepetition claims, including those of general obligation bonds, are not required to receive payment after filing until there are a plan of arrangement and the effective date. A different result is accorded to holders of special revenue bonds and bonds that enjoy a statutory pledge of revenues that can only be used to pay principal and interest on the bonds. Generally, securities that are subject to annual appropriation and have no statutory or contractual pledge of revenues are treated as unsecured

TYPE OF BONDS/NOTES	BANKRUPTCY EFFECTS
General Obligation Bonds	Post-petition, a court may treat general obligation bonds without a statutory lien as unsecured debt and order a restructuring of the bonds. Payment on the bonds during the bankruptcy proceeding likely will cease. Pre-petition, general obligation bonds are backed by the unlimited taxing power of the municipality (its "full faith and credit") and are historically subject to conditions such as voter authorization, limitations on particular purposes, or debt limitation to a percentage of assessed valuation on the power of municipal entities to incur such debts.
General Obligation Bonds plus Pledged Revenues	Assuming that the general obligation pledge is an actual pledge of revenue and to the extent that it may be classified as a Statutory Lien or Special Revenues, this secured issuance will be respected to the degree it is consistent and authorized under state law. A Pledge of Revenues that is not a Statutory Lien or Special Revenues may be attacked as not being a valid continuing Post-Petition Lien under Section 552 of the Bankruptcy Code. This position may be questioned under Section 904 of the Bankruptcy Code given the prohibition that the Court not interfere with the Government Affairs or Revenues of the Municipality.
Special Revenue Bonds	A pledge on special revenue bonds will survive a bankruptcy filing. Pre-petition, a special revenue bond is an obligation to repay solely and only from revenues of a municipal enterprise (net of operations and maintenance costs) that are pledged to bondholders. The contemplated remedy for default often focuses on a covenant to charge rates sufficient to amortize the debt. Defaulted bondholders are expected to seek mandamus in court to require the municipal borrower to raise its rates.
Revenues subject to Statutory Lien	Assuming the pledge is authorized under state law through a statutory lien, the Bankruptcy Court should respect that statutory lien. Thus, as long as the revenues are subject to a statutory lien, payments to the bondholders should be protected post-petition.

Figure 27.1 How municipal bond debt is treated in a Chapter 9 proceeding
Source: Spiotto 2010a: 77.

obligations in accordance with their terms. Thus, a general obligation bond without any pledge of special revenues or special statutory priority can be treated like any other unsecured claim of a vendor, worker, or trade. Figure 27.1 is a chart summarizing the priority of payment of municipal debt in a Chapter 9 proceeding. Figure 27.2 is a chart illustrating the overall priorities in Chapter 9.

Status of Payments to Bondholders

Chapter 9 of the Bankruptcy Code provides that a transfer of property of the debtor to or for the benefit of any holder of a bond or note on account of such a bond or note may not be avoided under § 547 of the Bankruptcy Code. Section 547 outside of Chapter 9 permits the avoidance of any transfers to or for the benefit of a creditor made on account of an antecedent debt while the debtor was insolvent within ninety days of the date of the filing of a petition. While this section refers to bonds

TYPE OF CLAIM	EXPLANATION
1. Obligations secured by a statutory lien to the extent of the value of the collateral.[ab]	Debt (Bonds, Trans, Rans) issued pursuant to statute that itself imposes a pledge. (There may be delay in payments due to automatic stay - unless stay is lifted - but ultimately will be paid.)
2. Obligations secured by Special Revenues (subject to necessary operating expenses of such project or System) to the extent of the value of the collateral.[ab] These obligations are often non-recourse and, in the event of default, the bondholders have no claim against non-pledged assets.	Special Revenue Bonds secured by any of the following: (A) receipts derived from the ownership, operation, or disposition of projects or systems of the debtor that are primarily used or intended to be used primarily to provide transportation, utility, or other services, including the proceeds of borrowings to finance the projects or systems; (B) special excise taxes imposed on particular activities or transactions; (C) incremental tax receipts from the benefited area in the case of tax-increment financing; (D) other revenues or receipts derived from particular functions of the debtor, whether or not the debtor has other functions; or (E) taxes specially levied to finance one or more projects or systems, excluding receipts from general property, sales, or income taxes (other than tax-increment financing) levied to finance the general purposes of the debtor.[c] There should be no delay in payment since automatic stay is lifted under Section 922(d).
3. Secured Lien based on Bond Resolution or contractual provisions that does not meet test of Statutory Lien or Special Revenues to the extent perfected prepetition, subject to the value of prepetition property or proceeds thereof.[c]	Under language of Sections 522 and 958, liens on such collateral would not continue postpetition. After giving value to the prepetition lien on property or proceeds, there is an unsecured claim to the extent there is recourse to the municipality or Debtor. You may expect the creditor to argue that pursuant to Section 904, the Court cannot interfere with the property or revenues of the Debtor, and that includes the grant of security to such secured creditor.
4. Obligations secured by a municipal facility lease financing.	Under Section 929 of the Bankruptcy Code, even if the transaction is styled as a municipal lease, a financing lease will be treated as long-term debt and secured to the extent of the value of the facility.
5. Administrative Expenses (which would include expenses incurred in connection with the Chapter 9 case itself).[d] Chapter 9 incorporates Section 507(a)(2) which, by its terms, provides a priority for administrative expenses allowed under Section 503(b). These would include the expenses of a committee or indenture trustee making a substantial contribution in a Chapter 9 case.	Pursuant to Section 943, all amounts must be disclosed and be reasonable for a Plan of Adjustment to be confirmed.

Figure 27.2 How municipal bond debt is treated in a Chapter 9 proceeding (priority of payment)

Source: Spiotto 2010b: 55.

6. Unsecured Debt includes:

A. Senior Unsecured Claims with benefit of subordination paid to the extent of available funds (without any obligation to raise taxes) which include any of B, C, D, or E below.

B. General Obligation Bonds.

Secured by the "full faith and credit" of the issuing municipality. Postpetition, a court may treat general obligation bonds without a statutory lien or Special Revenues pledge as unsecured debt and order a restructuring of the bonds. Payment on the bonds during the bankruptcy proceeding likely will cease.

C. Trade.

Vendors, suppliers, contracting parties for goods or services.

Payment will likely cease for prepetition goods or services.[e]

These do not enjoy any priority, unlike in a Chapter 11.[f]

D. Obligations for Accrued but Unpaid Prepetition Wages and Pensions and other Employee Benefits.

E. Unsecured portion of secured indebtedness.

F. Subordinated Unsecured Claims.

Any debt subordinated by statue or by contract to other debt would be appropriately subordinated and paid only to the extent senior claims are paid in full. Senior debt would receive *pro rata* distribution (taking unsecured claim and subordinated claim in aggregate) attributable to subordinated debt until paid.

---

[a] Chapter 9 incorporates Section 506(c) of the Bankruptcy Code which imposes a surcharge for preserving or disposing of collateral. Since the municipality cannot mortgage city hall or the police headquarters, municipal securities tend to be secured by a pledge of a revenue stream. Hence, it is seldom a surcharge will be imposed. (But see Nos. 3 and 4) incorporates Section 364(d) of the Bankruptcy Code which permits a debtor to obtain post-petition credit secured by a senior or equal lien on property of the estate that is subject to a lien if the prior lien holder is adequately protected.

[b] Chapter 9 that is not a Statutory Lien or Special Revenues may be attacked as not being a valid continuing Post-Petition Lien under Section 552 of the Bankruptcy Code.

[c] A Pledge of Revenues.

[d] These expenses strictly relate to the costs of the Bankruptcy. Because the Bankruptcy Court cannot interfere with the government and affairs of the municipality, general operating expenses of the municipality are not within the control of the Court, are not discharged and will remain liabilities of the municipality after the confirmation of a plan or dismissal of the case.

[e] Section 503(b)(9) provides for a priority claim to be paid on Confirmation of a Plan for the value of goods provided prepetition within 20 days of the Petition Date.

[f] Chapter 9 does not incorporate Section 1113 of the Bankruptcy Code, which imposes special provisions for the rejection of collative bargaining agreements (making the standard less restrictive, *i.e.*, "impairs ability to rehabilitate"), or Sections 507(a)(4) and (5), which give a priority (before payment of unsecured claims) to wages, salaries, commissions, vacation, severance, sick leave or contribution to pension plans of currently $11,725 per employee.

Figure 27.2 Continued

or notes, there is nothing in the legislative history to support the view that this provision is limited only to instruments bearing such titles. The legislative intent appears to be that § 926(b) of the Bankruptcy Code should be applicable to and protect all forms of municipal debt.[31]

Contracts, Leases, and Collective Bargaining Agreements

On February 22, 1984, in *National Labor of Relations Board v. Bildisco & Bildisco*,[32] the US Supreme Court held § 365(a) of the Bankruptcy Code provides that, with certain limitations, the debtor may unilaterally assume or reject any executory contract of the debtor including a collective bargaining agreement. The test set forth in *Bildisco* was whether the debtor could show both that the agreement burdens the estate and that the equities balance in favor of rejection. Unions were outraged with this result. Congress responded to that decision by adding to the Chapter 11 provisions (corporate bankruptcy) § 1113 of the Bankruptcy Code, which set a much more difficult test to reject collective bargaining agreements in a Chapter 11 case. In addition, § 1113 sets a detailed procedure that must be followed for the rejection of a collective bargaining agreement. Under § 1113(c), the court will approve an application for rejection of a collective bargaining agreement only if the court finds that (a) the debtor has, prior to the hearing, made a proposal to modify the collective bargaining agreement that is necessary to permit the debtor to reorganize, (b) the authorized representative of the employees has refused to accept such proposal without cause and (c) the balance of the equities clearly favors rejection of such agreement. This more difficult test has *not* been incorporated into Chapter 9 even though there was an effort to do so in the 1980s and 1990s. Although such efforts by labor unions continue, the *Bildisco* standard appears to be applicable to Chapter 9 debtors. However, as evidenced by the Vallejo case, despite the more lenient test to reject a municipal collective bargaining agreement, the nature of the litigation process and the time and expense involved in obtaining a final order with respect to such an emotional and political issue is likely to absorb the attention of the municipality and take many months to reach a conclusion.

MECHANISMS OTHER THAN CHAPTER 9
TO RESOLVE THE PENSION CRISIS

Chapter 9 as it currently exists, although containing many sought-after protections for municipal bond investors, is not the optimal mechanism for dealing with the debt bubble and public pension crisis. This is especially so from the perspective of the municipal securities market. There are three impediments when it comes to resolving the excess burden of public employee pension liabilities. First, as previously explained, Chapter 9 can only be invoked by the municipality itself. There is no such thing as an involuntary Chapter 9 petition. Therefore, Chapter 9 provides a means of restructuring only if the municipality is receptive to embrace it. Second, for constitutional reasons, the bankruptcy court has no control over the government and affairs of a municipality. This is a far cry from a Chapter 11 proceeding in which the court virtually controls the expenditures postpetition and out of the ordinary operation of the Chapter 11 debtor. Even in a Chapter 9 proceeding, the debtor does not need the court's permission to expend substantial funds. Thus, if the goal of a restructuring is to impose strict controls on the receipts and expenditures of a municipality, Chapter 9 does not provide this. Third, Chapter 9 permits the rejection of executory contracts (i.e., collective bargaining agreements) based on a far more relaxed standard than Chapter 11. This should be attractive to the municipality and contrary to the interests of organized labor. However, both political reality and procedural delays limit the effectiveness of using Chapter 9 to significantly rewrite collective bargaining agreements quickly enough to provide timely relief to a municipality. The Vallejo, California, case illustrates the limited effectiveness of Chapter 9 to provide speedy assistance to a municipality burdened with labor agreements it can no longer afford. Moreover, Chapter 9 does not enhance the revenues or sources of funds necessary for a municipality to orchestrate a turnaround of its fortunes.

Accordingly, given the municipal debt bubble and unfunded pension crisis, an alternative vehicle to assist troubled municipalities should be explored. As the Harrisburg situation illustrates, local governmental bodies experiencing financial distress often benefit by the resort to state assistance. Currently, a number of states have adopted legislation providing for such an authority, each with its own unique features. The municipal bond market would benefit by a uniform approach to a state financing and oversight authority that could provide the teeth and sources of revenues that Chapter 9 does not. The oversight authority can provide review and input on budgets and expenditures. The oversight authority could determine in a quasi-judicial manner whether mediation or arbitration would be helpful and what pension or wage benefits are sustainable and affordable. Unlike a Chapter 9 in which all debtor-credit relationships must be dealt with, the authority can be focused on the particular problems affecting the municipality. Further, the authority could be given the power to require a referendum of local taxpayers on the question of levying additional taxes or the power to provide increased taxing sources. Additionally, a quasi-judicial determination of targeted issues and authorization if necessary that a prepackaged agreement be filed could be made. The authority could adjust pension and wage benefits to current sustainable and affordable levels to preserve the ability to provide essential services and prevent a government meltdown.[33] Because the state itself would enact the legislation, and it is not imposed by the federal government, no federal constitutional issues should be presented.

An Oversight Authority for
Municipalities in Financial Crisis

Chapter 9 of the Bankruptcy Code was not intended as the exclusive remedy for municipal bodies unable to meet their current debt obligations to work out their problems. Local governmental bodies experiencing financial distress are often assisted by the resort to a state-created financing and oversight authority with various degrees of control. Since 1930, numerous states have adopted legislation providing for a state agency or other party to act as a receiver when a local governmental unit defaults on its financial obligations.

For example, in Pennsylvania, state law provides a procedure for declaring a municipality as distressed and subsequently authorizing the appointment of a distressed municipality coordinator. Known as Act 47,[34] the Pennsylvania statute requires the formulation of a fiscal plan unique to the distressed municipality that will enable the municipality to remedy its distressed status and gives such municipality the option of formulating its own fiscal plan. Act 47 requires the State of Pennsylvania to withhold all state funds from the municipality except those considered absolutely essential when a municipality refuses to adopt a fiscal solvency plan. Finally, if needed, Act 47 authorizes a distressed municipality to file a municipal debt readjustment under federal law. In 2003, Pittsburgh was found to be financially distressed under Act 47 because it had maintained a deficit for all governmental and proprietary funds for the years 1998 through 2002. Subsequently, Harrisburg sought enrollment in Pennsylvania's Act 47 program, rather than immediately pursuing a Chapter 9. As previously noted, Philadelphia has the benefit of separate legislation and is the only municipality in Pennsylvania that is not subject to Act 47. As of 2010, of the twenty-six municipalities that entered Act 47 supervision, only six have sought to have the distress determined rescinded and the rest have not formally sought to change this status.[35]

As evidenced by the Pennsylvania experience, given the stigma of bankruptcy and the delay inherent in the Chapter 9 process, consideration should first be given by municipalities to the use of state agencies and finance or refinance authorities. In many cases, these approaches will be preferable to municipal bankruptcy. Historically, state-refinancing authorities and commissions for municipalities have not dealt with the adjustment of debt but rather with providing funds for continued provision of municipal services (grants or loans), refocusing municipal services to other governmental bodies and requiring a balanced budget going forward. Debt adjustment by agreement of the parties may need to be a part of the agency's powers given the current burden on municipalities. The state may, by state statute (intergovernmental cooperation act or refinancing authority), step in to provide the bridge financing or refinancing of troubled debt for its municipalities, transfer certain services to other governmental agencies to reduce their expenditures, grant funds to municipalities to bridge the financial crisis, loan funds to the municipality on terms that are realistic or payable out of state-tax sources that can be offset, and provide for the use of state taxes payable to the municipality to ensure essential municipal services.

Rather than the somewhat cumbersome Chapter 9 process, the state authority can be tailored to a specific situation and common ground can be sought on which the municipality and creditors can agree without the necessity of having bankruptcy court supervision. There is some precedent for this approach. State-created agencies such as a state agency for emergency municipal finance have prevented a number of municipalities from being forced to seek relief under Chapter 9 and have allowed a number of troubled municipalities to work out their problems under state supervision while providing bondholders the insurance that the amounts still owed them will be paid. This was done in New York City in 1975 and 1976 with the creation of the Municipal Assistance Corporation and also in Chicago in 1980 with the creation of the Chicago School Finance Authority. The existence and operation of both of these entities have been upheld in court proceedings. Similarly, Ohio has a local fiscal emergency act that bondholders may invoke in the event of default that introduces a commission to intervene in the municipality's affairs.[36]

While state legislation differs widely, past experience suggests a structure for a successful municipal financial oversight authority. The creation of a state commission, which can function as a refinancing authority, provides basic advantages. The new authority has financial credibility and access to the capital markets if it has an assured source of revenue to pay debt service isolated from bankruptcy

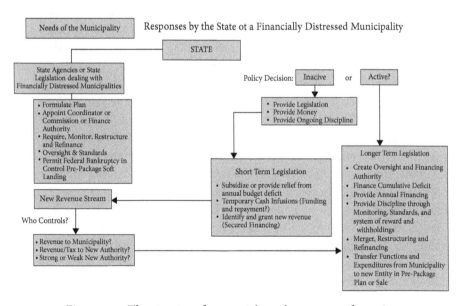

Figure 27.3 The structure for oversight and emergency financing
Source: Spiotto 2010a: 100.

and other credit risks. Further, an independent authority can use various fiscal tools to enforce fiscal discipline on a local government because it is removed from political pressure. The authority can provide liquidity financing, require balanced budgets, provide economic discipline and reporting, issue debt in the state name or the name of a separate entity to obtain market credibility and access for the benefit of the municipality, gather information as to the true financial situation, possess the power to negotiate debt restructuring, review services or costs that could be transferred to other governmental bodies, have the right to intercept tax revenues and focus use on essential services and costs, negotiate with creditors, formulate a plan, and ultimately adopt a plan for the restructuring of the debt of the municipality. The authority would monitor compliance with any restructuring plan. If the plan does not result in a return to financial health, then a possible federal bankruptcy filing could be pursued, more likely than not, in the form of a prepackaged plan. Figure 27.3 illustrates the possible structure of a refinance authority.

The Dilemma Facing Financially Troubled States

The Tenth Amendment to the US Constitution, which is part of the Bill of Rights, reflects the sovereign nature of the states and the Constitution's principle of federalism by providing that powers not granted to the federal government or prohibited to the states by the Constitution are reserved to the states or to the people. Accordingly, Congress cannot legislate to impose an involuntary debt-restructuring procedure on the states. A state is not a municipality within the statutory definition, and hence it cannot be a debtor under Chapter 9 of the Bankruptcy Code, except by voluntarily adopting such procedures as its own. However, the states, like other sovereigns, can become overburdened with debt and suffer from shrinking revenues. In particular, the aging infrastructure of the states, growing pension obligations, flight of industry and shrinking tax base are driving many states to the brink of financial disaster with no uniform legislation being in place to govern workout efforts. The lack of uniform state law can result in confusion within the securities markets and can make analysis of the soundness of state indebtedness difficult. Uniform mechanisms for states, like other sovereigns, to utilize in the event of financial distress should be considered.[37] On the global stage, for example, both Greece and Ireland have received emergency funds from the European Financial Stability Facility established by the European Union applying similar principles.[38]

ALTERNATIVES TO CHAPTER 9 FOR STATES

A sovereign debt resolution mechanism (SDRM) needs to be explored that could apply to the US states and could be utilized by nation-states as well. While a number of structures can be utilized, there are several leading approaches to an SDRM. On the most basic level, provision can be made for an entity to house the composition of creditors. In other words, a legal forum would be provided for creditors to meet to reach consensus, on a voluntary basis, as to what can be paid, to whom, and what should be forgiven.

Future debt financing also can include a "collective action clause," which is meeting with increased approval in European debt financings. The collective action clause would be included in the governing documents of a financing, whereby a majority or supermajority of parties (debtholders) to that contract have the power to bind all holders to a debt restructuring and, if need be, forgiveness of debt. This type of provision is not currently acceptable in the US capital markets where the requirement traditionally has been that all holders must consent to the modification of principal or interest on debt outside of the bankruptcy procedure.[39]

Another SDRM approach can be the mandatory inclusion of arbitration clauses in state contracts. One shortcoming is that arbitration does not have the transparency and creditor participation that sophisticated institutions may require. Arbitration in commercial agreements is often avoided by major institutions, and the same could be true of sovereign debt agreements.

In international finance, informal groups of creditors have gathered together to study ways of assisting troubled sovereigns dealing with unsustainable debt. These groups could serve as models for an SDRM. The Paris Club meets periodically in France and is attended by representatives of the world's wealthiest nations, including the United States. The Paris Club considers, on a confidential basis, requests from beleaguered countries, especially those whose debt stems from military conflict or dictatorship. The Paris Club structures a suggested debt rescheduling or debt cancellation as an alternative to default. The decisions are not legally binding but frequently honored. The London Club, composed primarily of major commercial banks, meets on an ad hoc basis on request. But it shares the goal of the Paris Club of reduced payments rather than defaults. Thus, the London Club is an informal group of private creditors as compared to the Paris Club of public lenders.

Should the informal approach of the club procedure be unworkable, then a bankruptcy court for sovereigns could be developed that, as applied to the sovereign states in the United States, could be structured on a voluntary basis in order to avoid the Tenth Amendment issues raised by the Bankruptcy Code.

Finally, a dispute resolution forum could be created as an SDRM to verify and reconcile claims and possibly act as a sovereign debt-restructuring court or sovereign debt tribunal, characterized by independence, expertise, neutrality, and predictability. Dispute resolution procedures would include an attempt to reach agreement among the parties. Any restructuring plan would have the vote of the majority of creditors and the ultimate hammer of a sovereign debt tribunal deciding what the path would be if a restructuring plan cannot be approved.

Conclusion

State and local government debt financing in the United States has a proud and successful history. With the exception of the default by Arkansas on highway bonds in 1933, which were quickly refinanced, states have not defaulted on their general obligations since the 1800s. In that era, thirteen states repudiated indebtedness that represented, for the most part, the unacceptable overspending of the carpetbagger era after the Civil War. With few exceptions, municipalities generally have paid their essential service-debt obligations. This historical fact is no accident. State and local governments have relied heavily on cheap financing for funding to bridge uneven tax revenues and to provide needed infrastructure and essential governmental services. Having that financing available and inexpensive has allowed state and local governments to chart their own destinies and to develop infrastructure and essential services to suit their tastes and circumstances. However, individuals and market participants now question whether this historic pattern will continue. The reaffirmation of the historical precedent of paying their obligations is essential for state and local governments if they are to weather the current storms as well as those that are on the horizon. Similar question and debate as to the dependability of municipal debt existed in the 1930s during the Great Depression and the annihilating lawsuits that municipalities faced for delayed or failed payments due to insufficient tax revenues.[40] That situation brought about Chapter 9, not as a universal remedy, but as a last resort when all else failed.

In recent history, Chapter 9 has been rarely used but it is always there as the ultimate safety valve. State and municipalities have done almost anything to meet their payment obligations and to avoid default and repudiation of their obligations. Certainly part of the reason has been the need for access to the bond market and inexpensive financing. But another motivation has been that, in meeting these obligations, the municipality should be assured that its citizens will continue to receive essential services and there will be steady progress. Anything less leads to eventual disaster.

The current crises of unfunded pension liabilities, aging infrastructure, increased costs of health, education, and safety needs must lead to new, creative ways for states and municipalities to meet their obligations of providing essential and improving services for a better tomorrow. A less creative and somewhat simplistic approach would be the increased use of Chapter 9 by municipalities and the creation of a bankruptcy court for the states to alleviate the current financial distress. Bankruptcy courts and tribunals do not provide bridge financing or the interim provision of essential services. Bankruptcy affects virtually all constituents, taxpayers, government workers, suppliers, and essential services, and it is an expensive, time-consuming, disruptive process that only can be used when there is no feasible alternative. As I have indicated, better options need to be considered and put in place before disaster strikes.

Our future in part depends on our capacity not to take the easy path but to address real problems directly while not destroying that which has worked and is working. Perhaps the next generation of sovereign debt-resolution mechanisms will be tied to increased legislative use of oversight, assistance, and refinancing authorities that can transfer certain burdensome services to other entities, provide bridge financing, and, if needed, identify appropriate new tax sources and coordinate on a regional or state level to ensure that the problem is solved and not transferred to another. The new mechanism should not be an approach that affects all constituents, including those who are not part of the problem. Rather, the mechanism should be a scalpel to deal surgically with the problem in a discreet method that does not adversely affect that which works. This will lead to a new, effective mechanism that is less expensive, less intrusive, and more focused on precisely what is broken. We have seen in New York City, Cleveland, Philadelphia, and other distressed situations a glimpse of these future resolution mechanisms. The purpose of this chapter is not only to describe what has happened, what has worked, and how it has been done, but also to point to new and creative mechanisms that can help ease the pain of financial distress and lead to financial health and a brighter future for all.

NOTES

1 For 2000 numbers, see US Census Bureau, Federal, State and Local Governments, State and Local Government Finances (published July 2008), available at http://www.census.gov/compendia/statab/2010/tables/10s0423.pdf.

2 See, generally, the Pew Center on the States (2010); Wilshire Consulting (2010); Spiotto (2010b).

3 James Spiotto, The Government Debt Tsunami (April 2010), available at http://chapman.com/publications.php.

4 Ibid.

5 Hillhouse (1936).

6 In the nineteenth century, during the period of repudiation of state and local government securities (thirteen states repudiated indebtedness in connection with the Civil War and carpetbagger era) and the municipal experience with railroad bonds (which led to the prohibition of the granting of creditor aid by the state to

any private corporations), the role of bond counsel was instituted. State statutes and legislation transformed the then perceived moral obligation into a legal obligation. There was clarification that there was no sovereign immunity defense to the payment of state and local government debt offerings. In 1876, Judge John Forest Dillon published his important article "The Law of Municipal Bonds," 2 *Southern Law Review* 437 (1876), in which he discussed the power of municipalities to issue securities in the light of existing court decisions. Earlier, as the Chief Justice of the Iowa Supreme Court, Judge Dillon also authored two seminal opinions establishing a modern rule of law by which the powers of local government are evaluated. He had also authored a treatise on municipal corporations, which was an essential book on the topic. Before long, purchasers of municipal bonds (and underwriters) began to seek the opinion of Judge Dillon regarding the legality and enforceability of the bonds they were considering purchasing. Soon, other firms of attorneys also began to specialize in this work, eventually leading to the role of bond counsel as we understand it today.

7 Moody's Investor Service, *U.S. Municipal Bond Defaults and Recoveries, 1970–2009*; Moody's Investor Service, *Corporate Default and Recovery Rates, 1920–2009*, for a contrast of the 1970–2009 period. See also Citigroup Global Markets Inc., *Municipal Credit Quality in Recessions and Depressions*, January 2009.

8 Standard and Poor's, *2009 Global Corporate Default Study and Ratings Transition* (March 17, 2010); Standard and Poor's, *U.S. Municipal Ratings Transition and Defaults, 1986–2009* (March 11, 2009).

9 Dunstan McNichol, "Budget Cuts May Avert Any 'Blip' in Muni Bankruptcies," Bloomberg.com (April 29, 2010), available at http://www.bloomberg.com/apps/news?pid=20670001dsid=aysoinVpqDq4.

10 In Greece, in 500 B.C., the towns of Atarneus and Assos defaulted on debt owed to a banker, Eubulus. A receivership was established and the banker acted as the receiver for the towns for many years until the debt was repaid. Eubulus controlled the taxes that were required to be paid and the services the citizens would receive. In the fourth century B.C., ten of the thirteen Greek municipalities of the Attic Maritime Association had defaulted on loans from the Delos Temple. These Greek municipalities suffered the same fate of receivership. George Calhoun, *The Business Life of Ancient Athens* (Chicago: University of Chicago Press, 1926).

11 Federal municipal bankruptcy legislation first passed constitutional scrutiny in 1937. Prior versions of municipal bankruptcy legislation had been found unconstitutional as violating the Tenth Amendment.

12 In other words, municipal defaults are more likely where the debt is a private activity or conduit obligation (securities issued by a governmental entity on behalf of a private nonprofit organization or in order to incentivize economic development) as opposed to financing the direct workings of government.

13 The Municipal Bankruptcy Amendments, Pub. L. No. 100-597 (1988), enacted after the New York and Cleveland experiences, allowed municipalities to be able to borrow funds without fear of avoidance of the obligations due to insolvency, including the introduction of the concept of "special revenues."

14 The California Education Code § 15251 provided that taxes levied to pay principal, interest, and serve as the security for the bonds could only be used for such bonds.

15 Perhaps as a result of the WPPSS debacle, the Securities and Exchange Commission adopted continuing disclosure obligations through amendments to Rule 15c2–12 in 1994 to include secondary market disclosure.

16 Case law arising from an early Colorado special-service district filing held that express statutory authorization under state law was not required to be a Chapter 9 debtor. *In re Villages at Castle Rock Dist. No. 4*, 145 B.R. 76 (Bankr. D. Colo. 1990). Subsequently, the 1994 amendments to the Bankruptcy Code required that municipalities be *specifically* authorized to be debtors under Chapter 9, perhaps as a result of the ruling that general powers were sufficient to support a municipal bankruptcy filing. 140 Cong. Rec. H. 10771 (October 4, 1994).

17 *In re City of Bridgeport*, 132 B.R. 85 (Bankr. D. Conn. 1991).

18 Baldassare (1998); 11 USC § 109(c).

19 Andrew Ward, "Is Vallejo Really Broke? Its Unions Want to Know," *The Bond Buyer*, July 25, 2008, p. 1.

20 Michael Cooper, "An Incinerator Becomes Harrisburg's Money Pit," *New York Times*, May 20, 2010, sec.1, p. A14.

21 11 USC § 109(c).

22 11 USC § 101.

23 The following are statutory provisions in which states have authorized Chapter 9 filings for certain governmental entities.

  Fifteen states that specifically authorize municipal bankruptcies:
  Ala. Code 1975 § 11–81–3
  Ariz. Rev. Stat. Ann. § 35–603
  Ark. Code Ann. § 14–74–103
  Cal. Gov't Code § 53760
  Idaho Code Ann. § 67–3903
  Ky. Rev. Stat Ann. § 66.400
  Minn. Stat. Ann. § 471.831
  Mo. Ann. Stat. § 427.100
  Mont. Code Ann. § 7–7–132
  Neb. Rev. St. § 13–402
  N.Y. Local Finance Law § 85.80
  Okla. Stat. Ann. tit. 62 §§ 281, 283
  S.C. Code Ann. § 6–1–10
  Tex. Loc. Gov't Code § 140.001
  Wash. Rev. Code § 39.64.040

  Nine states that *conditionally* authorize municipal bankruptcies:
  Conn. Gen. Stat. Ann. § 7–566
  Fla. Stat. Ann. § 218.01
  La. Rev. Stat. Ann. § 39–619
  Mich. Comp. Laws § 141.1222
  N.J. Stat. Ann. § 52:27–40
  N.C. Gen. Stat. Ann. § 23–48
  Ohio Rev. Code Ann. § 133.36
  53 Pa. Stat. Ann. § 11701.261
  Rhode Island S. 2997 Substitute A, Jan. Sess. 2010 (RI 2010) (approved by Senate on June 9, 2010 and by House on June 10, 2010)

  Three states with limited authorization for municipal bankruptcies:
  Colorado has enacted legislation specifically authorizing its beleaguered special taxing districts to file a petition under Chapter 9. Section 32–1–1403 of the Colorado revised statutes states that "any insolvent taxing district is hereby authorized to file a petition authorized by federal bankruptcy law and to take any and all action

necessary or proper to carry out the plan filed with said petition" (CRS § 37–32–102
(Drainage & Irrigation District))
Oregon permits Irrigation and Drainage Districts to file (Or. Rev. Stat. § 548.705)
Illinois—specific authorization solely for the Illinois Power Agency (20 Ill Comp.
Stat. Ann. 3855/1–20(b)(15)). The Local Government Financing and Supervision
Act permits that commission to recommend that the Legislature authorize a
filing but it is not specific authorization (20 Ill. Comp. Stat. Ann. 320/9(b)(4))
Two states prohibit filing but one has an exception
Iowa generally prohibits filing Chapter 9 (Ia. Code Ann. § 76.16) but allows filing
for insolvency caused by debt involuntarily incurred and not covered by insurance
proceeds (Ia. Code Ann. § 76.16A)
Georgia prohibits the filing of Chapter 9 bankruptcy (Ga. Code Ann. § 36–80-5)
These distinctions grow out of the Bridgeport, Connecticut, case in 1991 where the
state of Connecticut objected to the city's filing and the change in the Bankruptcy
Code in 1994 to require specific authorization to file by the municipality. Prior to that,
any municipality not specifically prohibited that had the ability to sue or be sued could
file for Chapter 9.

24 Spiotto (2010a).

25 In the matter of *In re County of Orange*, the court held that the Orange County
Investment Pool, as an instrumentality and creation of the County of Orange, was not
an instrumentality of the state and, hence, not a municipality. *In re County of Orange*,
183 B.R. 594 (Bankr. C.D. Cal. 1995).

26 *In re City of Bridgeport*, 132 B.R. 85 (Bankr. Conn. 1991).

27 *In re City of Vallejo*, 408 B.R. 280 (B.A.P. 9th Cir. 2009).

28 Section 902 of the Bankruptcy Code defines "special revenues" as

(A) receipts derived from the ownership, operation or disposition of projects or
systems of the debtor that are primarily used or intended to be used primarily
to provide transportation, utility or other services, including the proceeds of
borrowings to finance the project or systems;

(B) special excise taxes imposed on particular activities or transactions;

(C) incremental tax receipts from the benefited area in the case of tax-increment
financing;

(D) other revenues or receipts derived from particular functions of the debtor,
whether or not the debtor has other functions; or

(E) taxes specifically levied to finance one or more projects or systems, excluding
receipts from general property, sales, or income taxes (other than tax-increment
financing) levied to finance the general purposes of the debtor.

This concept was added to Chapter 9 as part of the Municipal Bankruptcy
Amendments of 1988 as Congress sought to provide a form of financing that was
immune from avoidance or other adverse effect of bankruptcy.

29 *In re County of Orange*, 189 B.R. 499 (C.D. Ca. 1995).

30 *In re Sierra Kings Health Care District*, Case No. 09–19728 (Bankr. E.D. Ca. Sept. 13, 2010).

31 See S. Rep. No. 506, 100th Cong.; 2nd Sess. 7 (1988).

32 465 US 513 (1984).

33 In the case of *Faitoute Iron & Steel Co. v. City of Asbury Park*, 316 US 502 (1942), the
New Jersey Municipal Finance Act provided that a state agency could place a bankrupt
local government into receivership. Under the law, similar to a plan of adjustment for
a Chapter 9 municipal bankruptcy action, the interested parties could devise a plan

that would be binding on nonconsenting creditors if a state court decided that the municipality could not otherwise pay its creditors and the plan was in the best interest of all creditors. Id. at 504. After certain bondholders dissented, the court determined that the plan helped the city meet its obligations more effectively. "The necessity compelled by unexpected financial conditions to modify an original arrangement for discharging a city's debt is implied in every such obligation for the very reason that thereby the obligation is discharged, not impaired." Id. at 511. The court then found that the plan protected creditors and was not in violation of the Contract Clause. Id. at 513. See also *U.S. Trust v. New Jersey*, 431 US 1, 25–28 (1997).

34 Pennsylvania enacted the Municipalities Financial Recovery Act in 1987, 53 PS § 11701.101 et seq. Due to financial difficulties, in 1991, the General Assembly suspended the provisions of Act 47 as they applied to the City of Philadelphia by the enactment of the Pennsylvania Intergovernmental Cooperation Authority Act for Cities of the First Class, Act 6 of 1991. 53 Pa.C.S. § 731 et seq.

35 Elizabeth Stelle, "Harrisburg Considers Bankruptcy, Act 47," *Commonwealth Foundation*, October 27, 2010, available at www.commonwealthfoundation.org/policyblog.

36 Ohio Rev. Code §§ 118.01–118.99; North Carolina, through its Local Government Finance Act, N.S. Stat. §§ 159–1 also provides for the appointment of a commission that could ultimately assume control of financial affairs in the event of a bond default.

37 The restructuring models utilized by sovereigns is instructive. See Patrick Bolton, "Toward a Statutory Approach to Sovereign Debt Restructuring: Lessons from Corporate Bankruptcy Practice Around the World," *IMF Staff Papers* 50 (2003); Randall Dodd, "Sovereign Debt Restructuring," *The Financier*, 9 (2002); John Murray Brown, "Europe Signs up to Irish Rescue," *Financial Times* (November 21, 2010), available at http://www.FT.com/cms/s/0/9338047c-f5a0-11df-99d6-00144feab49ahtml.

38 Jan Strupczewski and Padraic Halpin, "Ireland in Aid Talks with EU, Rescue Likely," Reuters, November 12, 2010.

39 See Trust Indenture Act of 1939, Section 316(b).

40 See, generally, Advisory Committee on Intergovernmental Relations (1973), 11–16.

References

Advisory Commission on Intergovernmental Relations (1985). "Bankruptcies, Defaults and Other Local Government Financial Emergencies." Washington: ACIR.

Advisory Commission on Intergovernmental Relations (1973). "City Financial Emergencies: The Intergovernmental Dimension." Washington: ACIR.

Baldassare, Mark (1998). *When Government Fails: The Orange County Bankruptcy.* Berkeley: University of California Press.

Gewehr, Brad (2010, March). "Municipal Bonds: The Road Ahead." *UBS Risk Watch*.

Hempel, George H (1971). *The Postwar Quality of State and Local Debt.* Cambridge, MA: National Bureau of Economic Research.

Hillhouse, A. M. (1936). *Municipal Bonds: A Century of Experience.* New York: Prentice Hall.

Leigland, James, and Lamb, Robert (1986). *Who Is to Blame for the WPPSS Disaster.* Cambridge, MA: Ballinger.

Pew Center on the States (2010). "The Trillion Dollar Gap: Underfunded State Retirement Systems and the Roads to Reform." Washington, DC.

Spiotto, James (2010a). "Historical and Legal Strength of State and Local Government Debt Financing." Chapman and Cutler LLP, http://chapman.com/publications.php.

Spiotto, James (2010b). "Unfunded Pension Obligations: Is Chapter 9 the Ultimate Remedy? Is There a Better Resolution Mechanism?" Chapman and Cutler LLP, http://www.chapman.com/media/news/media.907.pdf.

Wilshire Consulting (2010, March). *Wilshire Report on State Retirement Systems: Funding Levels and Asset Allocation.* Santa Monica, CA.

GOVERNMENT FINANCIAL-REPORTING STANDARDS: REVIEWING THE PAST AND PRESENT, ANTICIPATING THE FUTURE

CRAIG D. SHOULDERS AND
ROBERT J. FREEMAN

THIS chapter explores recent changes in the financial-reporting standards for state and local governments. The area may appear arcane to many. but the impact of the rules that underlie the accurate and timely reporting of the financial condition and operations of governments are widespread. Establishing the accountability of governments depends on reporting of their myriad of financial activities in a systematic, clear, and timely way. While there is not perfect conformity in following the reporting requirements established by the Governmental Accounting Standards Board (GASB), the degree to which governments report their finances in accordance with those standards has increased over the past three decades and is expected to continue to do so. In considering financial reporting, one should note that during the course of a year governments will account for their transactions in a manner consistent with their budgets, the accounts of which often differ from Generally Accepted Accounting Principles (GAAP). Governments then convert the accounting information captured during the year from their budgetary basis to the basis of accounting required by the GASB for financial-reporting purposes at the end of the year. The typical cycle is that the GAAP-based accounts are compiled and tallied and then reviewed by an auditor, who opines that the resulting reports are in conformance with the GAAP standards (or notes where they are not).

The GASB has no authority over budgeting practices or over internal budgetary reporting practices. However, until recently budgetary reporting—that is, comparing budgeted with actual results on the budgetary basis and in enough detail to demonstrate budgetary compliance—was a central part of GAAP financial-reporting requirements. Budgetary reports on the general fund and major special-revenue funds are still required, at least as required supplementary information, by current standards. Issues unique to budgetary control and budgetary reporting for management purposes are not within the scope of this chapter but are covered in several governmental accounting textbooks.[1]

The predominant focus of state and local government accounting and financial reporting during the past decade has been implementation of the financial-reporting model adopted in 1999 when the Governmental Accounting Standards Board (GASB) issued *Statement No. 34*, "Basic Financial Statements—and Management's Discussion and Analysis—for State and Local Governments."[2] Adoption of this model—particularly with its requirement that governmentwide financial statements must be presented as part of the basic financial statements required to comply with GAAP—was heralded as a landmark event in the evolution of government financial reporting. Most of the GASB's recent standards-setting efforts have been directed toward issues related to the implementation and improvement of those governmentwide financial statements, including such "headline" issues as reporting postemployment employee benefits. Other efforts have focused on reporting information outside the traditional purview of financial statements and financial reporting.[3] The only standard per se to affect governmental fund financial statements significantly since GASB *Statement No. 34* is a recently issued standard that changed the fund-balance classifications and modified the governmental fund definitions.

Other key developments over the past decade have included the GASB's progress on its conceptual framework projects, the extensive publication of implementation guides, interpretations, and technical bulletins. Also, of significance are the establishment of a federal funding source for the GASB to stabilize its finances and an array of other developments outside the direct purview of standards setting— such as concerted efforts by the US Securities and Exchange Commission (SEC) to expand its influence in this area.

We briefly review some aspects of the new reporting model in identifying the trends that suggest where financial reporting for state and local governments may be heading. But we do not cover that model in depth. The basic model is widely understood. Nonetheless, its impacts on the financial-reporting and standards-setting initiatives over the past decade have been pervasive.

We begin this chapter by considering the expanding roles of the accounting standards-setting bodies and the significant changes in the government financial-reporting model: the nature and content of the required financial statements, the growing body of optional or advisory financial-reporting guidance, and the changing emphases of the GASB. After a review of the GASB's current focus and the impact of sundry issues now affecting government accounting and reporting, we conclude with a discussion of where emerging developments may lead the GASB and the discipline of accounting and reporting over the next ten to fifteen years.

EXPANDING ROLES OF STANDARDS SETTERS FOR ACCOUNTING

Traditionally, standards setting for accounting was focused almost exclusively on establishing guidance for reporting in financial statements required to comply with GAAP. However, a recent private-sector concepts statement on the objectives of general-purpose financial *reporting* (developed by the Financial Accounting Standards Board (FASB) in conjunction with the International Accounting Standards Board (IASB)—expanded the scope of the FASB's standards-setting role. The FASB states in the basis for conclusions of that statement:

> Consistent with the Board's responsibilities, the Conceptual Framework establishes an objective of financial *reporting* and not just of financial statements. Financial statements are a central part of financial reporting, and most of the issues that the Board addresses involve financial statements. Although the scope of FASB Concepts Statement No. 1, *Objectives of Financial Reporting by Business Enterprises,* was financial reporting, the other FASB Concepts Statements focused on financial statements. The scope of the IASB's *Framework for the Preparation and Presentation of Financial Statements,* which was published by the IASB's predecessor body in 1989...dealt with financial statements only. Therefore, for both Boards the scope of the Conceptual Framework is broader.[4]

Financial-Reporting Objectives Broader Than Financial-Statement Objectives

Government accounting-standards setters, particularly the GASB, have been at the forefront of this expansion of the conceptual scope of financial reporting. GASB *Concepts Statement No. 1,* "Objectives of Financial Reporting," stated that the board takes a "broad view of public accountability and anticipates that not all financial-reporting objectives of state and local governmental entities can be accomplished through [presenting basic financial statements, notes to the financial statements, and required supplementary information]."[5] Indeed, according to that Statement No. 1 another objective of financial reporting is that "financial reporting should provide information to assist users in assessing the service efforts, costs, and accomplishments of the governmental entity."[6] The GASB launched a major project on service efforts and accomplishments early in its existence and currently is considering economic-condition reporting and the presentation of forward-looking information. The GASB chairman recently stated that popular reporting—such as citizen-oriented summary reports—and service efforts and accomplishments reporting warrant additional research and consideration from the GASB as well.[7]

GASB Financial-Statement Guidance Includes Nonmandatory Financial Statements

Government financial-reporting guidance has long included requirements for an introductory section and a statistical section when a government issues a comprehensive annual financial report (CAFR). However, prior to the National Council on Governmental Accounting (NCGA), which was the immediate forerunner of the GASB, issuance of NCGA Statement 1, the presentation of *all* fund financial statements was required by GAAP. A unique aspect of government reporting began with the issuance of that NCGA Statement 1. It set forth that there are different levels of financial statements, not all of which are required to be presented by GAAP. Clearly then, the GASB's financial-reporting standards are meant to go beyond the traditional understanding of the scope of GAAP.

Government financial reporting has changed dramatically over the past forty or so years and more changes appear likely in the coming years. The nature and direction of past changes, the current GASB projects, and the current difficult environment for government finances provide indications of the potential nature and direction of future changes.

CHANGES IN THE GOVERNMENT FINANCIAL-REPORTING MODEL

Financial reporting for governmental activities such as public safety, education, and human services has evolved. Formerly, it was focused almost exclusively on providing accountability for the use of budgetary and financial resources. Now, it is taking on a closer relationship to the decision-making process in government, and it has taken on a dual focus on both operational accountability and accountability for financial resources (with budgetary accountability being given something of a secondary status).[8] Traditionally, only reporting for business-type activities focused on operational accountability—defined by the GASB as "governments' responsibility to report the extent to which they have met their operating objectives efficiently and effectively, using all resources available for that purpose, and whether they can continue to meet their objectives for the foreseeable future." In addition to an increasing emphasis on operational accountability for governmental activities, the GASB appears to be on the verge of an additional, broader focus as well. While the GASB has been the instrument of much of this change during its first twenty-five years, the groundwork was laid in part before the GASB was formed.

Pre-NCGA Statement 1

Governmental accounting standards established by several National Committees on Governmental Accounting (committees of the Government Finance Officers Association, or GFOA, which was previously known as the Municipal Finance Officers Association) were in effect from 1968 until 1979. These early standards had three primary characteristics:

- an emphasis on legal and budgetary accountability and budgetary reporting,
- a focus of reporting upon the individual funds, and
- use of the modified accrual basis for reporting general government activities using both governmental funds and nonfund account groups.

Independent audits of government financial statements for conformity with GAAP were not yet commonplace. However, the municipal bond market was growing and maturing, creating an increasing need for comparable and believable financial statements. Also, the spread of federal assistance programs entailed increasing requirements for accounting for and reporting on the use of grant funds. Hence, the demand for GAAP financial statements and audits of those statements was expanding.

The fiscal crisis in New York City and several other cities in the mid-1970s brought renewed attention to government financial reporting—both regarding the financial statements required by the reporting standards of that day and the lack of compliance with those standards.[9] Many of the issues that the GASB has addressed over its existence gained popular attention during that time period. These concerns include lack of cost of services information, the reporting model, interperiod equity, pensions and other postemployment benefits, the government reporting entity, and service efforts and accomplishments reporting.[10]

NCGA Statement No. 1, issued in 1979, added a new feature to government financial reporting. One criticism of the previous standards was that there were no financial statements covering the reporting government as a whole. In an attempt to address this issue, the NCGA required, for the first time, a set of government financial statements covering more than a single fund. These *combined* financial statements were intended to provide a "larger picture" view of a government's over-all financial position and activities—and focused on fund types and account groups rather than on individual funds. The exception to this comprehensive view was that a combined budgetary comparison statement was required to be presented cover-ing the general fund and each special-revenue fund with a legally adopted annual budget. Fund-type financial statements reported aggregated amounts for all funds in a fund type. For instance, the combined statement of revenues, expenditures, and changes in fund balances for governmental funds and expendable trust funds could have the following reporting columns under NCGA Statement 1:

Governmental Fund Types				Fiduciary Fund Type	Totals
General	Special Revenue	Debt Service	Capital Projects	Expendable Trust	Memorandum Only

The general-fund column, of course, was always a report for that individual fund. However, each of the other columns could, and typically did, report the aggregated data of all funds of a particular fund type. Thus, the amounts reported in the special-revenue funds column might be the total for two or three special-revenue funds or even for ten or eleven of them, depending solely on how many funds of that type a government had.

The NCGA intended that the above-described combined statements should be provided *in addition* to the individual-fund financial statements, and Statement 1 communicated this intent. The combined financial statements were to be the reporting pinnacle: that is, the most aggregated statements in a financial-reporting pyramid. In that pyramid, individual-fund detail was to be provided in combin-ing financial statements for each fund type, and in some cases, by individual-fund financial statements. Neither consolidating nor consolidated financial statements were permitted.

Although the NCGA's preference for both combined and combining and individual-fund financial statements to be presented was clearly stated in NCGA Statement 1, it did identify that the *combined* financial statements, known as *gen-eral-purpose financial statements and the notes to those financial statements*, would make up the minimum acceptable scope of annual audits. Therefore, while the expectation was that individual-fund financial reporting would continue to be the norm—and indeed was and still is required by law or regulation in many states—GAAP no longer required it. Thus, governments could receive an unqualified opinion for reporting in accordance with GAAP without issuing either combin-ing or individual-fund financial statements. The combined financial statements and notes alone sufficed. This provision created an early example of what might be referred to as "optional GAAP financial statements." Thus, under the NCGA

Statement 1 reporting model, most of the financial statements in a CAFR's financial section were not required by GAAP.

While technically they were optional under GAAP, most governments that presented GAAP financial statements at the time either were required by law or regulation to present a comprehensive annual financial report (or at least the financial section of a CAFR) or opted to do so. Likewise, most governments that issued a CAFR obtained audits of both their general-purpose financial statements and their combining and individual-fund financial statements. Too, the fund structure used for reporting purposes in the combining and individual-fund financial statements tended to mirror the fund structure used for internal management purposes, though this was not required directly in the standards. As time passed, more governments—even though presenting the entire CAFR—began the practice of having audits covering only the general-purpose financial statements and notes. In such audits, the remainder of the information in the CAFR, including the combining and individual-fund financial statements, was considered supplementary information.

The NCGA Model Comes under Fire

These new financial statements did not adequately address all of the issues raised in the mid- to late 1970s. In particular, government financial statements came under fire because critics said they did not adequately reflect intergenerational equity, which came to be known as interperiod equity. The concern was with the time dimension reflected in the financial reports. Current-year citizens potentially could enjoy a high level of services and defer payment of much of the bill for those services to future generations of taxpayers without this deferral of those costs being reflected clearly in the financial statements. In effect, by not paying the full costs of services consumed, the current generation of users was in effect borrowing from future generations with no recognition of the growing debt on the books. The resulting "unfunded liabilities" for items such as employee-compensated absences, pensions, and other postemployment benefits (primarily retiree health benefits) associated for services already rendered were not reported adequately under existing standards. Even after attempts to address this issue, the NCGA Statement 1 prescribed financial statements were considered by critics as ineffective (or even useless) from an interperiod equity perspective. Indeed, the fund-type financial statements of NCGA Statement 1 were widely viewed as ineffective for any purpose.

GASB Statement No. 34: The Dual-Perspective Reporting Model Is Established

When established in 1984, one of the GASB's most prominent charges was to develop a better financial-reporting model. One expectation was that the new reporting model would better reflect interperiod (intergenerational) equity. GASB *Statement No. 34*, issued in 1999, was the culmination of fifteen years of GASB efforts to fulfill this charge. GASB *Statement No. 34* is the basis for the current financial-reporting model. It stated that the basic financial statements consist of the following components:

- Two *governmentwide* financial statements that (1) report the primary government in two parts—governmental (general government) activities and business-type activities—and (2) also report most component units (legally those separate entities that are included in the government financial reporting entity) of a government separate from the primary government. The flow of economic resources (revenue and expense) measurement focus is required for the governmentwide financial statements, which include a statement of net assets and a statement of activities.
- Three sets of *fund* financial statements—governmental funds, proprietary funds, and fiduciary funds. The individual-fund financial statements included in these fund financial statements are for the general fund, any other *major* governmental fund, and any *major* enterprise fund.[11] Internal service funds and fiduciary funds are reported only by fund type. The flow of economic resources measurement focus is required for all fund financial statements except the governmental funds, which use modified accrual accounting (flow of current financial resources measurement focus).

Budgetary statements or schedules for the general fund and for any annually budgeted major special-revenue fund are permitted to be included in the basic financial statements or may be presented as required supplemental information (RSI). Budgetary statements or schedules of any other governmental fund, including any other major governmental funds, are not permitted to be included in the basic financial statements or in the required supplementary information.

Financial statements reporting on individual *nonmajor* funds are not required. If a government opts to publish a comprehensive annual financial report (CAFR), the GASB requires combining and individual-fund financial statements in addition to the basic financial statements. These additional statements, if presented, must comply with additional guidance provided by the GASB covering the structure and content of a government's comprehensive report (the CAFR). While a government may have these additional statements audited, many treat them as supplemental information that is not subject to audit. The absence of these statements does not affect the auditor's opinion on a government's basic financial statements. GAAP do not require presentation of a comprehensive annual financial report, essentially making all current-fund financial reporting except for the three sets of fund financial statements' "optional GAAP." It should be noted that governments with outstanding bonds commonly present an entire CAFR even though most of its contents exceed the minimum required by GAAP.

The basis for conclusions in GASB Concepts Statement No. 3, Communications in General Purpose External Financial Reports That Contain Basic Financial Statements, expresses one way of thinking of "optional GAAP" stating:

> Some respondents were concerned that the definition of supplementary information (SI) [noting] that presentations in SI often are required by regulatory bodies and, therefore, although considered voluntary from a standards-setting perspective, are not truly voluntary. The Board decided to remove the reference to "voluntary" in the Concepts Statement and to clarify that SI may be required by law or regulation although the GASB does not require its presentation. The Board also clarified that preparers of governmental financial reports should follow applicable GASB-issued or GASB-cleared guidance for any information that they present in SI.[12]

Changing Emphases in Reporting

Three underlying developments that occurred concurrently with these changes in reporting standards—whether viewed as resulting from them or causing them— are essential to understand. Clearly, they reflect that the focus of accountability has changed and is continuing to change government financial reporting. These developments are (1) the elimination of budgetary accountability as a central focus of government basic financial statements, (2) the erosion of fund reporting, and (3) the emergence of demonstrating interperiod equity as a central reporting objective, along with the evolution of that concept from one understood as a budgetary and funds flow concept to a revenue- and expense-based capital maintenance concept. A fourth development, alluded to earlier, has been the GASB's extension of its reporting requirements beyond those normally achieved primarily through financial statements and notes.

Decline of Budgetary Reporting in the Basic Financial Statements

Budgetary statements initially were the *only* required financial statements in government financial reports in the early semiformal and formal guidance that served as GAAP for governments.[13] Indeed, given the importance of the legally adopted annual budget in government decision making, control, and accountability— and the fact that budgets were adopted for funds used to account for and control resources restricted for various purposes—fund financial reporting was a logical part of this budgetary reporting requirement.

The need for proper budgetary reporting and accountability—including demonstrating that restricted resources were used only for the restricted purpose(s)—has been almost a given throughout most of the modern history of government financial-reporting standards prior to GASB *Statement No. 34*. Indeed, GASB's *Concepts Statement 1*, "Objectives of Financial Reporting," recognizes the importance of fiscal accountability. The financial-reporting objectives concept statement clearly reflects the importance of budgetary accountability and accountability for restricted resources in government.

"Accountability" is the *paramount* financial-reporting objective according to the GASB concepts statement, and one primary use of financial statements is to assess accountability by "comparing actual financial results with the legally adopted budget."[14] Further, one of the financial-reporting objectives set forth in the concepts statement is "financial reporting should demonstrate whether resources were obtained and used in accordance with the entity's legally adopted budget; it should also demonstrate compliance with other finance-related legal or contractual requirements."[15]

While the "objectives" concepts statement indicates that the financial-reporting objectives will not all be met through financial statements, clearly financial statements were the norm at the time that the concepts statement was issued and likely was the means that the board expected to be used to achieve its budgetary reporting objectives. Following the issuance of GASB *Statement No. 34*, however, budgetary comparisons for most governmental funds are not *permitted* to be presented as part of the basic financial statements, and none are *required* to be presented in that manner. Consequently, budgetary comparison statements have gone from (a) being required for every governmental fund with a legally adopted annual budget (prior to NCGA Statement 1) to (b) being required for the general fund and each special-revenue fund with a legally adopted annual budget (NCGA Statement 1) to (c) budgetary comparison statements for only the general fund and any major special-revenue fund being an *optional* part of the *basic* financial statements under current GAAP. Budgetary comparisons for other special-revenue funds or for any funds of the other fund types are not even part of required supplementary information. Budgetary comparison statements for other governmental funds with legally adopted annual budgets still are included in the comprehensive annual financial report and typically are treated as other supplementary information.[16]

Funds as an Internal Accountability and Control Mechanism Only

Another occurrence over the past twenty years that may eventually impact government financial-reporting requirements is that fund accounting has increasingly been viewed as useful solely for internal purposes. Of the numerous types of entities for which some version of fund reporting was once required for external reporting purposes, only state and local governments still are required to report funds externally. Even in state and local government reporting, the required fund reporting already is much less extensive than in the past.

Major fund reporting has been praised as an improvement over the fund-type reporting that satisfied GAAP requirements under NCGA Statement 1. But it often means that only one or two funds besides the general fund are reported individually in the basic financial statements. Too, there is no significant GAAP guidance as to when individual funds of a fund type are required as opposed to establishing one broader purpose fund for reporting purposes. Consequently, many governments do not adhere to traditional assumptions about fund structure. For instance, the traditional presumption that each capital project financed by a separate major bond issue will be reported in a separate capital projects fund is applied by some governments whereas others aggregate all capital projects funds used for internal purposes into a single capital projects fund for external financial-reporting purposes—even when financed by different major bond issues or major grants. These and other circumstances led some to argue that only the governmentwide statements are comparable.

Government colleges and universities that grant bachelor's degrees traditionally have issued fund financial reports and theoretically could still do so. However, under GASB *Statement No. 35,* "Basic Financial Statements—and Management's Discussion and Analysis—for Public Colleges and Universities," these universities typically are reported externally as enterprise activities. Many, if not most, of these colleges and universities still operate during the year using the traditional college and university fund accounting structure. This demonstrates as clearly as any example the difference between internal and external fund structures that exist already in governments.

The Rise and Evolution of Interperiod Equity

As discussed earlier, a common criticism of governmental fund financial reporting under the NGCA *Statement 1* model was that the governmental fund financial statements did not alert users if a government was incurring significant liabilities to cover current costs incurred for items such as claims and judgments, compensated absences, and postemployment benefits (specifically pensions at the time). This criticism resulted in part from the scrutiny resulting from the fiscal crisis in New York City and several other large governments during the 1970s. The largest portion of these liabilities—referred to as "operating debt"—and changes in them, often was long term in nature and was reflected primarily in the combined balance sheet and the notes to the financial statements. This treatment, adopted in *NCGA Statement 4,* "Accounting and Financial Reporting Principles for Claims and Judgments and Compensated Absences," has been applied to governmental fund reporting of many other items, including pensions and other postemployment benefits.[17] Critics at that time asserted that this approach failed to reflect *interperiod equity* appropriately.

Demonstrating interperiod equity began to be viewed as an important goal for government financial statements, however, and after failed attempts by the NCGA to address these and other criticisms of its reporting model, the GASB was formed in 1984. A review of the GASB's early literature and projects shows that the interperiod equity as understood by the GASB went through an evolution in the board's early years. Its initial concepts statement—"Objectives of Financial Reporting"—specifically states one financial-reporting objective as "financial reporting should provide information to determine whether current-year revenues were sufficient to pay for current-year services [interperiod equity]."[18]

When *Concepts Statement No. 1* was adopted in the initial stages of the GASB's development of a new financial-reporting model, interperiod equity was understood as an objective that could be met using the flow of financial resources information. Indeed, the GASB's initial attempt to establish a new reporting model was based on a measurement focus and basis of accounting standard for governmental-fund operating statements that was expected to form the foundation of financial reporting going forward. That standard, which the GASB never permitted to be implemented, would have required governments to report governmental-fund operations using a flow of total financial resources measurement focus. The summary of that standard—GASB *Statement No. 11*, "Measurement Focus and Basis of Accounting—Governmental Fund Operating Statements," states [with emphases added]:

> The measurement focus for governmental fund operating statements should be the *flow of financial resources* measurement focus. The operating results expressed using this measurement focus *show the extent to which financial resources obtained during a period are sufficient to cover claims incurred during that period against financial resources.* This measurement focus considers financial resources only and uses an accrual basis of accounting referred to as the *modified accrual* basis.
>
> The flow of financial resources measurement focus for governmental fund operating statements is responsive to the government environment and the needs of users of government financial reports. This measurement focus *is based on the concept of accountability, which includes measuring* **interperiod equity**—*whether current-year revenues were sufficient to pay for current-year services.* It also considers the performance goals and measures of governmental-type activities, the intent and effect of budgets and other financial controls, and the use of fund accounting to achieve and demonstrate legal compliance and to enhance financial administration.[19]

After issuing *Statement No. 11*, the GASB struggled with how to implement the flow of a total financial resources measurement focus in the context of governmental fund balance sheets. In the midst of the failing effort to develop comprehensive implementation guidance for the flow of total financial resources approach in *Statement No. 11*, the GASB began to debate and develop a dual-perspective model. This model cast aside the flow of the total financial resources model altogether and called for fund financial statements not unlike those of the past except that they would include individual-fund reporting only for individual funds.

Combined financial statements also would be eliminated. Governmentwide financial statements presenting flows and balances of economic resources (revenue- and expense-based) information would be presented. The latter financial statements were intended to achieve the objective of demonstrating interperiod equity among others. This step morphed the GASB's interperiod equity concept from a flow of financial resources concept to a capital maintenance concept not unlike that applied in business accounting. This dual-perspective concept was developed into the government financial-reporting model established in GASB *Statement No. 34.*

The GASB never seemed to conceive that certain objectives of financial reporting—such as cost of services information and service efforts and accomplishments information—could be met with budgetary or flow of financial resources information. However, the meaning and intent of the interperiod equity information seemed to alter dramatically during the twelve years between the issuance of GASB *Concepts Statement 1* in 1987 and GASB *Statement No. 34* in 1999. The discussion in the appendices of *Concepts Statement 1* described a notion of interperiod equity that can be closely associated with budgetary reporting and/or modified accrual accounting. *Concepts Statement 1* stated:

> The concept of intergenerational equity, or interperiod equity as the Board refers to it, is reflected in the balanced budget requirements and debt issuance limitations of many state statutes and local ordinances. Virtually all states currently have balanced budget requirements of some type. Some states, for example, are bound by law to "raise revenue sufficient to defray the expenses of the state for each fiscal year." Some may even require a deficit in one year to be made up in the following year, a concept of budgetary balance over a multiyear period.[20]

At the same time the statement indicated that other states' budget laws are not consistent with this notion of interperiod equity:

> The budgetary requirements of certain other states, and such practices as "off-budget" financing, however, may not result in true balanced budgets, in the sense that current-period revenues are sufficient to pay for current-period services. One state statute, for example, views debt proceeds as a revenue source and authorizes the governor to recommend ways to "balance" the budget "whether by an increase in the indebtedness of the state, by the imposition of new taxes, by increased rates on existing taxes or otherwise."[21]

However, *Concepts Statement 1* asserted:

> The notions of accountability and interperiod equity developed in this section are readily adaptable to governmental budgetary and fiscal planning processes. For example, some suggest that one method of meeting objectives of accountability and interperiod equity would be to make budgetary estimates of the effects of new expenditure commitments resulting from such factors as new laws, program decisions, and major capital projects. They note that these commitments add significantly to taxpayer burdens in future years. This information could be disclosed through five-year revenue and expenditure projections issued after each legislative session and would be a logical extension of single-year budgeting requirements.[22]

By the time the GASB issued *Statement No. 34* in 1999, the GASB's concept of interperiod equity apparently was very different. Indeed, the basis for conclusions discussed interperiod equity in the context of operational accountability, as opposed to fiscal accountability, and asserted that flow of economic resource information on an aggregated basis was needed to demonstrate the extent to which current period revenues are sufficient to pay for current period services. The preface to the statement said that one of the advantages of the governmentwide reporting requirement is that it will help users "evaluate whether the government's current-year revenues were sufficient to pay for current-year services."

Interperiod equity as it is conceived today is as a flow of economic resources (revenue- and expense-based) concept. Whether discussing financial statement issues or economic condition reporting, it is a goal that the GASB seeks to achieve. But, with respect to activities that are not financed by direct charges for services, it is a concept that can only be addressed at a highly aggregated level, not at a governmental fund level. Interperiod equity addresses whether the *overall* costs of the basket of services provided by a government in a particular year is provided for by the *overall* revenues raised from the constituency (primarily taxes) and other revenue sources (primarily intergovernmental revenues) during the year. The concept suggests that, if interperiod equity is achieved, a government's net assets (i.e., assets minus liabilities) will not change during the year.

GASB *Statement No. 34* was heralded as a landmark standard primarily because it required state and local governments to present governmentwide, revenue- and expense-based financial statements for the first time in the history of government financial-reporting standards. GASB *Statement No. 34* ushered in other more subtle changes. Since the standard's adoption, its efforts have been oriented largely toward projects that impact primarily the governmentwide financial statements and proprietary-fund financial statements (which use the same measurement focus and basis of accounting). This is true of key GASB projects like pensions and other postemployment benefits (OPEB), derivatives, pollution remediation, intangibles, and so on.

GASB's Current Focus

Understanding the GASB's current focus and direction is important to anticipating where government financial reporting might be in ten to fifteen years. Since the new reporting model was established—with a change to major fund reporting—the GASB's agenda has been driven largely by issues affecting the governmentwide financial statements (and proprietary-fund financial statements) and cost of services information. Since adopting its new reporting model the GASB has issued major standards on OPEB, intangible assets, impairment of capital assets, derivative instruments, pollution remediation obligations, and termination benefits. None affected accounting and reporting for governmental funds in a noteworthy way, and most had no effect at all. Areas in which the GASB currently spends time and energy include postemployment benefits, economic condition/fiscal sustainability, electronic reporting, and service efforts and accomplishments. Improving timeliness of reporting, forward-looking information, and popular reporting are other areas of interest voiced by the GASB chairman.

Postemployment Benefits

Postemployment benefits (current work is on pension benefits but later will be on other postretirement benefits) is the project on the GASB's current agenda, and this effort has the potential to have one of the most dramatic effects on the reported financial condition of governments since GASB *Statement No. 34* established the new reporting model. The GASB's preliminary views indicate that the board is leaning toward requiring governments' unfunded actuarial accrued pension liabilities to be reported in the statement of net assets. Many expect that this requirement for pensions ultimately will be implemented, followed by a similar requirement for the unfunded liability for other postemployment benefits. The high level of interest in this area and the probability that the GASB will require the unfunded actuarial accrued pension liability and the unfunded actuarial accrued OPEB liability to be reported in the governmentwide (and proprietary fund) financial statements are heightened by the attention that postemployment benefits have received in the media during the current fiscal crisis. Both professional publications and public media contain many assertions that the current level of benefits is not sustainable. Moreover, the reduction in benefits in the private sector has created a more stark contrast with the level and types of public employee benefits. Finally, a brief review of state governments' statements of net assets and required supplementary information suggests that many states will have negative balances in their governmental activities' total net assets and some in primary government total net assets if the proposed guidance is adopted.

The potential impact of such a requirement is indisputable. Consider, for instance, that the State of New York's March 31, 2010, governmentwide Statement of Net Assets reported total primary government net assets of $28.1 billion and its required supplementary information disclosed an unfunded actuarial liability for OPEB (based on a 2008 actuarial valuation) of $56.8 billion. While some of this liability is included in its financial statements already, reporting all of it in the governmentwide financial statements would result in a total primary government net assets deficit of as much as $20 billion. In 2009, one study reported that the unfunded actuarial accrued liabilities for OPEB were over $250 billion total for the ten most populous states. As always, governmental fund accounting and reporting are not expected to be affected.[23]

Economic Condition/Fiscal Sustainability and Forward-Looking Information

The October 2010 board meeting minutes posted on the GASB website focus attention on the discussion of economic condition and fiscal sustainability—and on forward-looking information and projections. The minutes indicate [emphases added]:

> The Board began deliberations on: (1) whether or not *forward-looking information* is necessary for users to make an assessment of a governmental entity's fiscal sustainability, (2) whether or not the qualitative characteristics identified and described in Concepts Statement No. 1, Objectives of Financial Reporting, apply to forward-looking information, and (3) what specific measures are necessary for users to assess the types of forward-looking information generally associated with the first three broad categories (*ability* to generate inflows of resources, *ability* to honor current service commitments, and *ability* to meet financial obligations and commitments) of information tentatively agreed upon by the Board at a previous meeting. The specific measures were identified by research participants and confirmed by task force member feedback. The Board reached a tentative agreement that *forward-looking information is necessary* for users to make an assessment of a governmental entity's *fiscal sustainability.*[24]

The board also reached tentative agreement in October 2010 on specific measures that it considered conceptually essential to assist users to assess a government's fiscal accountability. Included were individual measures that can be used to measure a government's ability to:

- Generate inflows of resources;
- Honor current service commitments; and
- Meet financial obligations and commitments.[25]

The board also has indicated that it does not intend to consider service efforts and accomplishments information further as part of this project on fiscal sustainability. The GASB chairman offered arguments for forward-looking information in the financial reports in a separate article presented on the website. He suggested that Concepts Statement 1 contemplated such information being presented. It seems doubtful, however, that the board members at that time or those involved in the due process leading to the Concepts Statement actually conceived of such information as that being proposed.[26]

Service Efforts and Accomplishments

The GASB has researched service efforts and accomplishments measures and reporting almost from its inception. The second concepts statement addressed this area, and the GASB recently began to issue practice guidance in this area. With respect to service efforts and accomplishments (SEA), it is important to note several facts. The GASB Board:

- Currently issues only voluntary reporting guidance on service efforts and accomplishments;
- Continues to work to establish service efforts and accomplishments reporting guidance;
- Has the prerogative to make this voluntary guidance mandatory in the future if there is a change in its perceived role;
- Might need to change the voluntary status of this guidance if it requires or endorses specific SEA measures in the future—either in the statistical ection of the CAFR or in other reports; and
- Is a recognized authority among governments, which makes even voluntary guidance from the GASB apt to carry weight. Failure to follow that voluntary guidance might create a "burden of proof" issue for a government if it provides service efforts and accomplishments reports that do not follow such voluntary guidance and is deemed to be misleading.

Most SEA data are apt to rely on cost of services data not provided in governmental fund financial statements, thereby requiring a focus on revenue and expense data but likely at a more detailed level than generally presented in the governmentwide financial statements.

Service efforts and accomplishments reporting by governments has been a controversial area for the GASB. The GFOA along with several other national organizations involved in the government accounting and finance area has taken a strong stand against the GASB's involvement in this area. In essence, they consider it beyond the scope of the GASB's authority. Further, the argument has been made that SEA should be limited to the budget process. The GASB at least temporarily addressed the controversy by making its guidance in this area voluntary rather than mandatory.[27]

Electronic Reporting

The GASB is monitoring electronic reporting (that which takes place on government websites) and has been involved in efforts to develop a prototype model for government reporting in electronic format. Higher priority projects have prevented recent progress in this area but the GASB chairman has indicated that he considers this an effort worth the GASB's time and effort in the future—particularly given the need to provide information on a timelier basis.[28]

Popular Reporting

Popular reporting is another area that the GASB chairman has said the GASB should pay more attention to in the future. Popular reporting has been encouraged on an experimental basis for many years. One of the most concerted recent efforts related to reporting that falls in this category is the Association of Government Accountants' (AGA's) "citizen-centric" reporting initiative. This program has an objective of encouraging "snapshot reports of government finances to supplement traditional financial information." The AGA began an awards program in 2009 to encourage and recognize excellence in citizen-centric reporting. The judging guidelines for that program include a requirement for timely presentation of the reports, after receipt of a clean audit opinion:

> [The] Report is issued in a timely manner following the close of the entity's fiscal year:
> a. First-year report submitted to AGA: must be within 6 months with a clean audit
> b. Second-year report submitted to AGA: must be within 5 months with a clean audit
> c. Third-year report submitted to AGA: must be within 4 months with a clean audit
> d. Fourth-year and beyond report submitted to AGA: must be within 3 months with a clean audit.[29]

Besides the content components of the judging, which include performance data as well as financial data, it should be noted that a submission for the reports requires increasingly shorter time frames during which the audited financial statements also must have been prepared and published. This program is one of several sources calling for increasingly shorter time frames for governments to publish their audited annual financial statements.

Report Timeliness

The timeliness of government financial reports has been a concern for many ever since GAAP reporting for governments began to be more common. For many years, it was considered at least minimally acceptable for a government's financial report to be issued not more than six months after the end of its fiscal year.[30] However, the timing of the reports is gaining growing attention. There is pressure that the electronic lag in publishing reports be shortened dramatically. The chairman of the GASB and the president and CEO of the American Institute of Certified Public Accountants (AICPA) have urged that governments report on a timely basis—within three to six months after the fiscal year end. They note that the GASB's user research indicates that lack of timely reporting is a major problem, particularly for bond analysts.[31] The Government Finance Officers Association has issued a "best practice" communication on improving the timeliness of government reports with suggestions on how to accomplish this.[32] The AGA citizen-centric reporting excellence program noted above ultimately would require audited financial statements to be available within three months. And the SEC clearly does not consider issuance of financial statements six months after the end of the year to be appropriate. One SEC commissioner stated in a speech, "With the appropriate authority, the Commission could mandate that municipal disclosures be issued in a time period that makes critical information available when investment decisions are made. I think we greatly underestimate the timeliness of information problem in the muni market today."[33]

While improved timeliness of financial reports clearly is desirable, at some point it will come only by devoting additional time and resources to speed up the reporting and auditing process or by affecting the content required in government financial reports. In one early call for more timely reporting, the proponents specifically pointed out that they believe this will require issuance of only governmentwide financial statements. [34]

The Conceptual Framework—Measurement and Recognition

The GASB's concepts statements do not constitute GAAP. However, once a concepts statement is adopted, its influence on future standards is significant. As the GASB chairman has explained, "The primary goal of GASB's conceptual framework...is to set the underlying philosophy and the boundaries for judgment that will guide GASB in resolving accounting and financial reporting issues."[35]

The GASB's current conceptual framework project is on measurement and recognition of information—that is, when information should be reported and how the information should be measured. The most daunting aspect of this for the board appears to relate to the flow of current financial resources model. However, early indications are that the board is dismissing the current manifestation of that model—which *Statement No. 34* project described as an ad hoc collection of practices over time that is not conceptually coherent. This implies that the GASB is not likely to develop a concepts statement that current modified accrual accounting for governmental funds fits well. If this is the case, future standards are apt to change governmental fund reporting significantly.

OTHER FACTORS

Additional developments are likely to affect the future of government financial reporting. These include the growing influence of the federal government in the municipal bond market and in the realm of standards setting and the continuing push for the convergence of accounting standards.

Growing Federal Interest

Another phenomenon taking place currently is a growing potential for federal influence on government financial reporting. It arises from at least four sources:

- The federal interest in repealing the Tower Amendment, which limits the ability of the Municipal Securities Rulemaking Board to regulate the disclosure requirements for state and local government bond issuers
- The increasing federal role and power in the municipal bond market
- Changes in the bond market resulting from the fiscal crisis and the related increase in involvement of retail investors in this market
- The federal funding of the GASB as provided for in the Dodd-Frank Act

The federal government, especially the SEC, believes that it needs additional control and influence over the municipal bond market and municipal bond issuers in order to protect investors. The SEC's motivation to achieve this additional control and influence likely was increased by the fiscal strains felt by governments as a result of the 2007–2009 recession, including the bankruptcy of Vallejo, California, and rumors of potential additional municipal bankruptcy filings. Several possible avenues to increase the SEC's influence are being explored and may be pursued by the federal government.[36]

The Tower Amendment: Should It Be Repealed?

A key impediment to greater SEC influence over state and local government financial reporting is the Tower Amendment to the SEC Act of 1934. That amendment prevents the SEC and the Municipal Securities Rulemaking Board from requiring:

> any issuer of municipal securities, directly or indirectly through a purchaser or prospective purchaser of securities from the issuer, to file with the Commission or the Board prior to the sale of such securities by the issuer any application, report, or document in connection with the issuance, sale, or distribution of such securities.[37]

The Wall Street Reform and Consumer Protection Act requires that the US Government Accountability Office conduct a study of disclosures required of municipal bond issuers compared to those of corporate issuers and make recommendations regarding those disclosures, including whether the Tower Amendment should be repealed. The act also creates an Office of Municipal Securities within the SEC, which will coordinate with the Municipal Securities Rulemaking Board for rulemaking and enforcement actions.

The SEC commissioner in charge of a nationwide inquiry in 2010–2011 on the municipal bond market indicated in an interview that establishing more timely and uniform disclosure standards was very important: "What we're going to do is try to be broad, concentrating on some of the hot topics, particularly the concerns we've heard from both institutional and individual investors."[38] One of the disclosure issues [the SEC commissioner] planned to explore was the timeliness and quality of issuers' secondary market filings, including annual financial statements. The fact that some government issuers do not provide their annual reports until more than six months after the close of their fiscal years is considered a real problem because of the pressure that the recession has created on state and local finances.[39]

The Municipal Bond Market

The effect of the fiscal crisis on the municipal bond market has provided additional impetus for the SEC to push for more authority over that market. First, the strategy of acquiring municipal bond insurance from AAA-rated bond insurance companies, once a common means used by many governments to gain access to the market at a reasonable cost, is no longer available. From among several AAA-rated bond insurance companies prior to the fiscal crisis, only one remains a major active insurer and none are AAA-rated. The potential for municipal bankruptcies is a growing concern for many. Large numbers of individual investors, either directly or through their wealth managers, directly invest in municipal bonds—often intending to hold them to maturity. The SEC has expressed concern about the fact that municipal issuers do not provide as timely disclosures as do corporate issuers, and it has argued that it needs more regulatory authority related to municipal issuers to protect the investing public.[40]

Federal Funding for GASB

Yet another indirect effect of the 2007–2009 recession and the ensuing fiscal crisis was that the federal government now provides a funding source for the GASB, which addressed the board's long-standing financial struggles. The Dodd-Frank Act provided for a fee to be assessed on new municipal bond issuances to supply a stable financing source for the GASB. The act also stated that the SEC cannot be involved, directly or indirectly, with the GASB's agenda or with setting GAAP. Although the provisions are intended to protect state and local government standards setting from federal influence, history suggests skepticism about the long-term effectiveness of this restraint.

Convergence of Accounting Standards

Another significant recent trend in accounting and auditing has been the move to harmonize standards internationally. Moreover, this has been achieved effectively. The focus of most efforts and attention on internationalization of financial-reporting standards has related to private-sector business standards. In part, this emphasis results from the globalization of the world economies and the trading of international companies on the exchanges of different countries. The SEC allows companies headquartered in other countries but traded on US stock exchanges to report using International Financial Reporting Standards (IFRS) without reconciling their statements to US GAAP.

Currently, the FASB and the International Accounting Standards Board have multiple joint projects designed to develop common standards and by which they hope to increase the probability of achieving convergence of US and international financial-reporting standards. At the same time, the SEC is studying whether to require US public companies to report using international accounting standards beginning in 2015. Even if this goal is not achieved, it no doubt will be revisited in the future.

Many have believed that internationalization of business-reporting standards was a certainty and the AICPA has already begun limited testing regarding IFRS on the Uniform Certified Public Accountants Examination. However, recent news reflects that a global standard is *not* a certainty. The chairman of the IASB trustee group, Tommaso Padoa-Schioppa, stated recently, "The aspiration of having global standards depends very much on the adoption of global standards by the United States and this is highly uncertain."[41]

Further, despite significant efforts, the FASB and the IASB have not found common ground on some key concepts. Certain European governments have exercised influence, causing the IASB to overhaul one of its standards and the European Union (EU) adoption of individual standards is not a given. The likelihood of the US accepting standards that are subject to political or financial pressure from various governments in the EU presumably is low. Similarly, other governments are not likely to accept it if the United States subsequently attempts to use political or financial pressure to influence international standards setting.

It is doubtful that convergence of US government accounting standards and international public-sector accounting standards will occur before there is substantial additional progress on the international convergence of business accounting standards. However, once such convergence is achieved, pressure for the convergence of government accounting standards—first for national governments, then for subnational governments—is apt to increase. Foremost among advocates for convergence will be the SEC and the Forum of Firms. The GASB and the International Public Standards Accounting Standards Board (IPSASB) have coordinated research efforts on projects of mutual interest because of the project on capital assets impairment, which led to issuance of the GASB's standard on accounting and financial reporting for impairment of capital assets and insurance recoveries. Too, the GASB commits significant time and effort to monitoring and participating in the standards-setting efforts of the IPSASB—particularly through the membership of its Director of Research on the IPSASB. Finally, one should recognize that convergence of GASB financial-reporting standards with those of either the FASB or the IPSASB can only occur in the context of governmentwide revenue- and expense-based financial statements. Anything else would require major, inconceivable changes in the standards of those other bodies.

The Future of Government Financial Reporting

Envisioning what the status of state and local government financial reporting will be ten to fifteen years from now is a daunting task. Virtually no one foresaw in 1984 that just fifteen years later the GASB would have adopted a reporting model like that required by *Statement No. 34*. In today's standards-setting environment—where a far larger portion of a report that contains basic financial statements is apt to be devoted to supplemental information beyond that which is required—it is important to distinguish between what one expects will be required in the future to warrant an unqualified opinion that financial statements comply with GAAP and what will be required for that supplemental information a government chooses to present in the same financial report. Nonetheless, it is interesting and potentially fruitful to consider where the tide of the forces at play today seem likely to lead.

The Tide

With that in mind, we offer the following observations about where we think things stand as of early 2011.

- GAAP for governments has moved from an individual-fund focus to an increasingly aggregated entity focus.
- Demonstrating interperiod equity is and will continue to be considered an essential objective of financial reporting and will necessarily require revenue and expense (cost of service) data reported at a highly aggregated level.
- Continuing and intensifying pressure for more timely reporting will be met more realistically with highly aggregated financial statements like governmentwide financial statements rather than with disaggregated statements presented with fund reporting. This factor may affect what, if any, fund and component unit financial statements are included in the basic financial statements versus supplemental information in the future.
- Gathering audited information for the basic financial statements of multiple discretely presented component units is an added challenge if the goal is for financial reports containing that audited information to be available in a significantly shorter time period than is currently achieved.

- Governments are the only entities for which fund financial reporting is still required for external reporting in accordance with GAAP.
- With its concepts statements providing justification, the GASB is likely to propose significant changes in governmental fund financial statements and, perhaps, in the modified accrual basis of accounting.
- For the GASB to make fundamental changes in the level of fund financial statements that are included in the basic financial statement requirements, the GASB would need to adopt a governmentwide cash-flow statement to create a complete set of governmentwide financial statements.
- General-fund financial statements are the only individual-fund financial statements that have been required for compliance with GAAP under every set of reporting standards that has been adopted to date. It might be difficult to establish a consensus supporting basic financial statements that do not include at least general-fund financial statements.
- The federal government, especially the SEC, is likely to gain more authority in the municipal bond market in coming years. If a rash of municipal bankruptcies should occur, as some expect, this authority could expand quickly and broadly—especially if significant numbers of "retail" individual investors are harmed. If governments make it through this period without significant increases in defaults and bankruptcies, the arguments for more SEC authority and criticisms of the current timing and types of information provided should be minimized. More SEC authority suggests more pressure for more timely reports and a likely preference for aggregated revenue and expense financial statements over fund financial statements. Of course, for revenue debt that is not a general obligation of the government, the SEC requirements might be met with reports covering only the component of a government subject to the obligation.
- Unfunded actuarial liabilities for both pensions and OPEB are virtually certain to be required in governmentwide financial statements. Doing so will dramatically reduce many primary governments' net assets as reported in the governmentwide statement of net assets.
- To the extent that governmentwide revenue and expense financial statements are the only or virtually only financial statements required in the basic financial statements, convergence with FASB standards and with international public-sector accounting standards could be achieved to a far greater extent than is commonly considered possible.
- The status of budgetary reporting was diminished by *Statement No. 34.* Technically, a government can get an unqualified opinion on its financial statements without presenting any budgetary statements or schedules, though it is doubtful that this happens.
- For most funds under current GAAP (i.e., nonmajor funds), no individual fund information is required in the basic financial statements.
- Electronic reporting, particularly with the ability to drill down to different levels of information, can be a valuable tool for users and can increase timeliness of user access to financial reports. However, it cannot solve

many of the problems that result in reports currently becoming available four to six months after the end of a fiscal year.

- Convergence of standards—either with the FASB or the IPSASB—is virtually impossible if the basic financial statements continue to require fund financial statements.
- As popular reporting becomes more widespread, the likelihood of the GASB providing guidance for these reports to standardize at least some elements of them will increase. Popular reporting on a timely basis using audited financial information is more compatible with aggregated data use. Service efforts and accomplishments data presented in such reports could create pressure for the GASB to make its voluntary guidance mandatory.
- The expansion of the scope of financial-reporting standards is apt to continue. The GASB is likely to require additional economic condition/fiscal sustainability information, including forward-looking information in the statistical section of a CAFR.

Where Does the Tide Take Us?

Given the above observations on current trends, it would not be surprising to find fundamentally different basic financial statements in place in the future. The most controversial of these changes might include:

- Requiring that basic financial statements include a governmentwide statement of cash flows
- Changing the substance of modified accrual accounting
- Removing most, if not all, fund financial statements from the basic financial statements
- Removing discretely presented component-unit data from the basic financial statements
- Expanding the statistical section to provide additional economic condition/ fiscal sustainability information, including forward-looking information
- Having new GASB requirements related to SEA and to popular reporting

Leverage for these changes will come from pressures to present the basic financial statements on a more timely basis, a creeping increase in the SEC's influence and authority in the municipal bond market, and the predisposition of the SEC and of many practitioners—particularly the regular stream entering the government accounting and auditing arena from the foundation of a business accounting and auditing career—to prefer aggregated revenue- and expense-based reporting. The preference or need for expense-based information to meet several of the GASB's ongoing financial-reporting goals, including reflecting interperiod equity and cost of services information, economic condition/sustainability information, and SEA, will add to the argument for a focus on aggregated revenue- and expense-based financial statements. The continuing desire for popular reporting of some type will be another factor.

Governmentwide Statement of Cash Flows

Requiring a governmentwide statement of cash flows would be a prerequisite to making significant changes in the fund financial statements required to be included in the basic financial statements. A governmentwide cash-flow statement is not a new idea and would be necessary for the governmentwide statements alone to constitute a complete set of basic financial statements. The GASB was thinking in terms of a statement like this at the time it issued GASB *Statement No. 9*, "Reporting Cash Flows of Proprietary and Nonexpendable Trust Funds and Governmental Entities That Use Proprietary Fund Accounting." Part of the reasoning for some of the classifications required by this statement was their potential for use in reporting general government cash flows, according to its basis for conclusions. Of course, the reporting model developed along a different path than was expected at that time, but the requirements of *Statement No. 9* would make developing a governmentwide cash-flow statement requirement readily achievable.

Changes to Modified Accrual Accounting

Given the expectation that the concepts statement on measurement and recognition will be based on a definition of the flow of current financial resources measurement focus that varies meaningfully from current practice, the measurement focus used for governmental funds likely will change over the next decade. Whether these changes will affect both the balance sheet and the operating statement versus just one or the other is difficult to predict. Likewise, it is difficult at this point to predict how dramatic those changes will be given the early stage of this critical concepts statement project. Hopefully, the outcome of the project and any future impacts on standards will result in positive improvements to current GAAP.

Removing Fund Financial Statements from Basic Financial Statements

Instituting a government cash-flow statement requirement would permit the GASB to shift most fund financial statements, if desired, from the basic financial statements to supplemental information in a CAFR. It may be difficult to get consensus on such a shift—particularly if it means a total removal of all fund financial statements from basic financial statements. The one set of fund financial statements most likely to continue to be reported as part of the basic financial statements is the general-fund financial statements. These statements have always been required under every variation of GAAP financial-reporting requirements, and the general fund is the most important governmental fund as well as the one most known to the citizenry. However, even the general-fund financial statements may be relegated to required supplementary information by that point in the future. The current option of reporting general and major special-revenue fund budgetary comparisons as required supplementary information has set the precedent for such a possibility.

DISCRETELY PRESENTED COMPONENT-UNITS PRESENTATION

In addition to most (or all) fund financial statements being removed from basic financial statements, pressure to increase the timeliness of audited basic financial statements may provide an impetus for other changes. Many governments have multiple discretely presented component units—these averaged approximately sixteen per state government in 2005. Incorporating the financial statements of those units is one of the practical impediments to improving the timing of issuance of the basic financial statements. It is conceivable that discretely presented component-unit financial statement information might be removed from the face of the basic financial statements. Besides the practical challenges that reporting these units in the basic statements presents, the GASB's long-standing position is that the focal purpose of these financial statements is to report the primary government. If this is the case, it is possible to build an argument for relegating much, if not all, of this information to supplemental or required supplemental information status. One key factor against this happening is the fact that some discretely presented component units are so closely aligned with the related primary government that exclusion from the basic financial statements might not be acceptable. For instance, state colleges and universities are discretely presented component units in some states.

OTHER LIKELY DEVELOPMENTS

In addition to the possible changes to basic financial statements, a number of other developments are likely to occur in the future.

Electronic Reporting

Given the current state of electronic access to financial reports, it is not much of a risk to suggest that some form of electronic access to financial reports will be the norm, and this may be required for large governments. A government version of XBRL or some other taxonomy will be used. The GASB may attempt to standardize this taxonomy for financial-reporting purposes.

Popular Reporting

Popular reporting in some form will continue to be encouraged. It is a reporting form that accommodates a presentation of broad financial information along with selected service efforts and economic condition information. The GASB may attempt to establish guidance with respect to such reports when they are issued. However, it is more likely that other priorities will take precedence and prevent this step from occurring in the next fifteen years.

Forward-Looking Information

Forward-looking information is likely to become a GASB requirement as the GASB continues to focus on interperiod equity, economic conditions, and fiscal sustainability in addition to more traditional uses of government financial reporting. It is very likely that most, if not all, of this information will be part of supplementary information that will not be encompassed directly by auditors' opinions.

THE COUNTERVAILING FORCES

As is usually the case, there are factors that may prevent some of these developments. In particular, this is true with regard to whether only the governmentwide financial statements are required in the future. Laws without enforcement mechanisms would in substance be recommendations that people choose whether to comply with. This is true as well with accounting standards. Standards not backed by a meaningful enforcement mechanism essentially are advisory. Governments' history of compliance with financial-reporting standards that are advisory (i.e., optional GAAP) is sketchy at best.

By far, the most significant and pervasive enforcement mechanism supporting the GASB standards is the need for a government to comply with those standards in order to receive an unqualified opinion on its financial statements. As discussed earlier, this enforcement mechanism essentially now supports only the basic financial statements, the notes to those statements, and required supplementary information. Indeed, it could be argued that it supports requirements for required supplementary information only in a secondary fashion.

Of course, in some cases additional financial statements are required by law or regulation, are needed to satisfy the bond market, or may be required by the Government Finance Officers Association or Association of School Business Officers financial-reporting excellence award programs. Even in these cases, audit coverage may not be required for the financial statements and other information that are not part of the basic financial statements and related notes.

It is possible that if the only part of a financial section that were required by the GASB to comply with GAAP is the governmentwide financial statements (or the governmentwide financial statements and the general-fund financial statements), some states that now require local governments to present the full financial section of a CAFR would reduce that requirement to the basic financial statements. Indeed, if they do not do so, because of a perceived need for the information either by the bond market or their constituencies, it would call into question the results of the GASB's own due process conclusion.

When the GASB excludes certain financial statements from basic financial statements and notes (and particularly if they are also excluded from required supplementary information), the apparent conclusion—after due process—is that those statements or other information are not essential for users of financial reports. If numerous states continue to require additional fund financial statements to be presented and the bond-market participants demand them or reward their supply via reduced interest-cost and increased market accessibility, it suggests that one key subset of the users (bond investors) and representatives of a second set of users (citizens) disagree with the GASB's conclusions about user information needs. For these and other users to rely heavily on unaudited financial statements would put these users at risks. Thus, the more that the GASB places information in this unaudited supplemental information section rather than in the audited basic financial statements, the greater is the ultimate risk of user decisions being based on misleading information. There may be a tendency for citizens, some of the growing numbers of bond-market participants, and other users to presume that all financial statements presented within a report containing audited financial statements can be relied upon with much the same confidence as the audited financial statements that they accompany—even though the audit report clearly states otherwise. Indeed, to the extent that these users need this information, they will have few, if any, alternative places to turn for most of it.

In the end, the most influential determinant on how far the GASB moves toward the governmentwide financial statements becoming sufficient to satisfy minimum financial-reporting requirements under GAAP likely will be municipal bond-market participants. The most extreme possibilities we have outlined above seem difficult to fathom at times. That is because our anecdotal evidence from discussions with bond analysts and others indicate that they find the more detailed information in the fund financial statements and in the broader comprehensive annual financial reports more useful than the governmentwide financial statements. In part, this derives from the fact that many bond issues are not general obligation bond issues. In part, it may result from the fact that for governmental activities the magnitude of the general capital assets and general long-term liabilities tend to overwhelm the remaining assets and liabilities. There are other factors as well. If bond-market participants continue to rely on fund financial information and demand that there be audited information (as opposed to information that has not been subject to audit), this alone could prevent fund financial statements from being removed from basic financial statements.

NOTES

1 See Freeman et al. (2011); See also Wilson et al. (2010); Granof and Khumawala (2011).
2 GASB (1999).
3 See Patton and Freeman (2009), 20–26; Bean (2009), 26–32. See also Gauthier (2001), 9–11.
4 Financial Accounting Standards Board (2010), chapter 1, and chapter 3, para. BC1.4.
5 GASB (1987), para. 8.
6 Ibid., para. 77c.
7 Attmore (2009), 20–24.
8 Freeman and Shoulders (2010), 22–28.
9 Cockrill et al. (1976), 5.
10 Hogan and Mottola (1978), 6–7.
11 Major funds are those identified as the individual governmental funds and individual enterprise funds most important to financial statement users. Any of these funds that fit this description may be reported as major funds (i.e.., reported individually). However, the general fund is always a major fund and any other governmental fund or any enterprise fund that meets specified size criteria must be reported as major funds. Nonmajor governmental funds are aggregated in a single column in the governmental funds financial statements, and nonmajor enterprise funds are aggregated in a single column in the proprietary funds financial statements.
12 GASB (2007), para. 59.
13 National Committee on Municipal Accounting (1936).
14 GASB (1987), para. 32.
15 Ibid., para. 77b.
16 See Freeman and Shoulders (2010), 22–28, for detailed coverage of the evolution of the budgetary reporting related to GAAP guidance over time.
17 See, for example, GASB (2000) for an interpretation of NCGA Statements 1, 4, and 5; NCGA Interpretation 8; and GASB Statements 10, 16, and 18; GASB (1994); GASB (2004); GASB (2006).
18 GASB (1987), para. 77.
19 GASB (1990), summary.
20 GASB (1987), para. 84.
21 Ibid.
22 Ibid., para. 87.
23 Ives (2010), 46.
24 GASB (2010).
25 These individual measures included the following: (1) To measure a governmental entity's ability to generate inflows of resources: (i) *projections* of the bases for major

own-source inflows of resources, (ii) *projections* of individual major inflows of resources and total inflows of resources along with explanations of the known causes of resource fluctuations (including nonrecurring resources), and (iii) *projections* of the percentage of total inflows of resources represented by each major individual inflow of resources; (2) To measure a governmental entity's ability to honor current service commitments: (i) *projections* of current types and levels of major programs and functions, (ii) *projections* of individual major outflows of resources and total outflows of resources along with explanations of the known causes of resource fluctuations, and (iii) *projections* of the percentage of total outflows of resources represented by each major individual outflow of resources; (3) To measure a governmental entity's ability to meet financial obligations and commitments: (i) *projections* of future major individual financial obligations and total financial obligations including pensions, OPEB, and long-term contracts, (ii) *projections* of annual debt service payments (principle [*sic*] and interest), and (iii) *projections* of key debt measures and overlapping debt.

26 Attmore (2010), 8–9.

27 See Government Finance Officers Association (1993, 2002). For a contrary view, see McCall and Klay (2009), 52–57.

28 Attmore (2009a), 23.

29 Association of Government Accountants (2010). The remaining judging guidelines are (1) How the entity is organized/operates (items such as vision statement and strategic goals), (2) Key accomplishments surrounding key missions and service and/or along with selected performance measures, (3) Bar and/or pie charts to display revenues and expenses, (4) Similar statements are listed: An independent audit was conducted, resulting in a clean audit opinion. Complete financial information can be found at www.xyz.gov, (5) Future challenges affecting the entity, (6) Similar statements are listed: We want to hear from you. Do you like this report? Do you believe it should include any other information? Please let us know by contacting xxx, (7) Report is "free" of technical accounting language, (8) Report incorporates pictures and other graphics to make it visually appealing, (9) Report has been distributed (hardcopy, posted to website, and/or posted in newspaper).

30 For many years Standard & Poor's had a policy statement on municipal accounting and financial reporting that indicated that reports should be issued within six months after the end of the fiscal year. Its current criteria indicate that receipt of a Certificate of Achievement for Excellence in Financial Reporting from the Government Finance Officers Association has a favorable ratings impact. That program requires governments to submit reports to the program within not more than six months after the government's fiscal year end. The criteria for the program are available at gfoa.org.

31 Attmore and Melancon (2010).

32 Government Finance Officers Association (2008).

33 Walter (2009), 21.

34 Cockrill et al. (1976), 14.

35 Attmore (2009b), 8.

36 See particularly the speech by Commissioner Elisse B. Walter cited above and the requirements of the Wall Street Reform and Consumer Protection Act (known as the Dodd-Frank Act) for studies of the Tower Amendment and of the effectiveness of the GASB's financial-reporting standards.

37 Section 15B(d) Securities Exchange Act of 1934.

38 Ackerman (2010).

39 Ibid.

40 Rosenstiel (2010), 10–15.

41 Christodoulou (2010).

REFERENCES

Ackerman, Andrew (2010, July 21). "SEC Eyes Regulatory Road Show." *The Bond Buyer.*
  http://www.bondbuyer.com/issues/119_387/sec_regulatory_road_show-
  1015011–1.html.

Association of Government Accountants (2010, December 31). "AGA's Certificate of
  Excellence in Citizen-Centric Reporting." http://agacgfm.org/citizen/award.aspx.

Attmore, Robert H. (2009a, Fall). "A Look Forward from the GASB Chairman." *Journal
  of Government Financial Management*: 20–24.

Attmore, Robert H. (2009b, Winter). "What Is the Significance of GASB's Conceptual
  Framework?" *Journal of Government Financial Management*: 8–10.

Attmore, Robert H. (2010, Winter) "Forward-Looking Information: What It Is and Why
  It Matters." *Journal of Government Financial Management*: 8–9.

Attmore, Robert H., and Barry C. Melancon (2010, July 15). "Trust in Timing: Timely
  Financial Reporting Can Reap A Government Many Rewards." *Governing.* http://
  www.governing.com/topics/finance/timely-financial-reporting.html.

Bean, David R. (2009, Fall). "A Look Back at 25 Years of High-Quality Standards-Setting."
  Journal of Government Financial Management: 26–32.

Christodoulou, Mario (2010, July 14). "U.S. Adoption of IFRS Remains Highly
  Uncertain." *Accountancy Age.* http://www.accountancyage.com/aa/news/1808566/
  us-adoption-ifrs-remains-highly-uncertain-trustee-warns.

Cockrill, Robert M, Morton Meyerson, James L. Savage, Earl C. Keller, and Michael W.
  Maher (1976). *Financial Disclosure Practices of the American Cities: A Public Report.*
  New York: Coopers & Lybrand.

Financial Accounting Standards Board (2010). *Concepts Statement No. 8.* "Conceptual
  Framework for Financial Reporting, Chapter 1: The Objective of General Purpose
  Financial Reporting, and Chapter 3: Qualitative Characteristics of Useful Financial
  Information." Norwalk, CT: FASB. para. BC1.4.

Freeman, Robert J., and Craig D. Shoulders (2010, August 20). "Modified Accrual
  Accounting: Accountability Centered and Decision Useful." *Government Finance
  Review*: 22–28.

Freeman, Robert J., Craig D. Shoulders, Gregory S. Allison, Terry K. Patton, and G.
  Robert Smith (2011). *Governmental and Nonprofit Accounting: Theory and Practice.*
  Revised 9th ed. Upper Saddle River, NJ: Prentice-Hall.

Gauthier, Stephen J. (2001, June). "Then and Now: 65 Years of the Blue Book."
  Government Finance Review: 9–11.

Government Finance Officers Association (GFOA) (1993). Public Policy Statements.
  "Service Efforts and Accomplishments Reporting."

Government Finance Officers Association (GFOA) (2002). "Performance Measurement
  and the Governmental Accounting Standards Board."

Government Finance Officers Association (GFOA) (2008). "Best Practices: Improving the
  Timeliness of Financial Reports." www.gfoa.org.

Governmental Accounting Standards Board (GASB) (1987). *Concepts Statement No. 1.*
  "Objectives of Financial Reporting." Norwalk, CT: GASB.

Governmental Accounting Standards Board (GASB) (1990). *Statement No. 11.*
  "Measurement Focus and Basis of Accounting—Governmental Fund Operating
  Statements." Norwalk, CT: GASB.

Governmental Accounting Standards Board (GASB) (1994). *Statement No. 27.* "Accounting for Pensions by State and Local Governmental Employers." Norwalk, CT: GASB.

Governmental Accounting Standards Board (GASB) (1999). *Statement No. 34.* "Basic Financial Statements—and Management's Discussion and Analysis—for State and Local Governments." Norwalk, CT: GASB.

Governmental Accounting Standards Board (GASB) (2000). *Interpretation No. 6.* "Recognition and Measurement of Certain Liabilities and Expenditures in Governmental Fund Financial Statements."

Governmental Accounting Standards Board (GASB) (2004). *Statement No. 45.* "Accounting and Financial Reporting by Employers for Postemployment Benefits Other Than Pensions." Norwalk, CT: GASB.

Governmental Accounting Standards Board (GASB) (2006). *Statement No. 49.* "Accounting and Financial Reporting for Pollution Remediation Obligations." Norwalk, CT: GASB.

Governmental Accounting Standards Board (GASB) (2007). *Concepts Statement No. 3.* "Communications in General Purpose External Financial Reports That Contain Basic Financial Statements." Norwalk, CT: GASB.

Governmental Accounting Standards Board (GASB) (2010). Minutes of Meeting, October 25, 26, and 28, 2010. http://www.gasb.org.

Granof, Michael H., and Saleha B. Khumawala (2011). *Government and Not-for-Profit Accounting: Concepts and Practices.* 5th ed. Hoboken, NJ: John Wiley & Sons.

Hogan, James A., and Anthony J. Mottola (1978). *Financial Disclosure Practices of the American Cities II: Closing the Communications Gap.* New York: Coopers & Lybrand.

Ives, Martin (2010, Summer). "Financial Reporting of Retiree Health Care Benefits: An Assessment." *Journal of Government Financial Management.* 42–48.

McCall, Sam M., and William E. Klay (2009, Fall). "Accountability Has Always Been the Cornerstone of Accountability." *Journal of Government Financial Management*: 52–57.

National Committee on Municipal Accounting (1936). *Bulletin No. 6.* "Municipal Accounting Statements." Chicago: Municipal Finance Officers Association.

Patton, Terry K., and Robert J. Freeman (2009, April). "The GASB Turns 25: A Retrospective." *Government Finance Review*: 20–26.

Rosenstiel, Paul (2010, February). "The New World of Selling Bonds." *Government Finance Review*: 10–15.

Wall Street Reform and Consumer Protection Act (Dodd-Frank Act). July 21, 2010.

Walter, Elisse B. (2009, October 28). "Speech by SEC Commissioner: Regulation of the Municipal Securities Market: Investors Are Not Second-Class Citizens." Speech delivered at the 10th Annual A. A. Sommer Jr. Corporate, Securities and Financial Law Lecture. New York.

Wilson, Earl, Jacqueline Reck, and Susan Kattelus (2010). *Accounting for Governmental and Nonprofit Entities.* 15th ed. New York: McGraw-Hill.

CHAPTER 29

PULLBACK MANAGEMENT: STATE BUDGETING UNDER FISCAL STRESS

CAROLYN BOURDEAUX AND
W. BARTLEY HILDRETH

MOST public budgeting and finance textbooks describe US state budgetary processes as an orderly cycle of preparation, approval, execution, and evaluation. In the middle to late twentieth century, when state governments were accustomed to steady growth or only marginal declines, state budgeters experienced exactly this type of regular rhythm to the budget process. Over the past two decades (1989–2009), for example, states averaged year-over-year increases in revenues on the order of 5 to 5.5 percent[1] and a roughly equivalent growth in expenditures.[2] Yet, natural disasters, economic shocks, overoptimistic revenue forecasts, and even elections and changing policy agendas can disrupt this process and create the need for significant midyear adjustments.

The financial crisis of 2008 through 2010 provides an important window onto state systems for managing midyear budget adjustments. In fiscal year (FY) 2009, twenty-four states had budget gaps of greater than 10 percent of the originally enacted budget, while forty-five states had shortfalls greater than 5 percent. For many, the vast majority of the gap had to be closed during the fiscal year as state financial officers realized they had significantly overshot their FY 2009 revenue estimate.[3] In Georgia, for example, FY 2009 state general-fund revenues fell by

17 percent from the original revenue estimate. The state closed a $245 million budget gap prior to the beginning of the fiscal year but then closed a $3.3 billion state general-funds gap during the course of the fiscal year. By FY 2010 the economic outlook was grim; however, many states still had to manage significant midyear shortfalls as forecasters were unable to predict the bottom of the recession.[4] Georgia closed a $1.7 billion gap over the course of FY 2010, a reduction equivalent to 10 percent of its state general-funds budget.

To manage through these declines, state processes of budget execution became one of continuous budget revision. States leaned heavily on provisions in their constitutions or in state statute that provided mechanisms for midyear budget adjustments. This chapter examines the state responses as well as the states' abilities to respond to these midyear shortfalls. The current literature on midyear "pullback" management is limited, and so the following analysis adopts an exploratory approach to understanding the dilemmas faced by states. As such, this analysis draws on five case studies that represent different approaches to managing midyear shortfalls, ranging from states that cede significant authority to the governor to those that require significant legislative involvement in midyear decision making.

What all the cases reveal is that states faced a balancing act. On the one hand, governors needed to be able to respond quickly to rapidly declining revenues in order to keep the budget balanced at the end of the fiscal year and to avoid cash-flow problems. On the other hand, the executive authority to act with dispatch conflicted with legislative authority to establish policy priorities through the budget, a founding tenet of American constitutional democracy. The cases show that an aggressive executive can advance his or her policy priorities through the special powers available during a period of pullback management, while, at the same time, legislative involvement did not necessarily undermine the state's ability to respond quickly to the crisis. The analysis concludes with some criteria that states should consider when designing systems for response to significant and unexpected declines in revenues.

Literature on Revisions
to the Adopted Budget

The dilemmas around revisions to the adopted budget are colored by executive and legislative tensions. Generally, scholars have observed that budget gamesmanship does not end with the passage of the budget,[5] and one early study highlighted the strategic actions that could be used to revise the adopted budget during the year, through accounting tricks, interfund transfers, shifting between programs, and intentionally underestimating revenues.[6] However, generally, the empirical work on midyear budget revisions is limited.

Changes to the adopted budget can occur in either or both of two ways. The legislature can make a legal change in the appropriation amount in either a mid-year session or by an interim board or committee it empowers, or the executive can utilize selected powers to withhold funds or transfer funds from reserves or across budget accounts to address the deficit.

The literature observing legislative midyear activities is particularly thin. Thomas P. Lauth described the Georgia General Assembly's process of making special midyear appropriation adjustment and concluded that this process has become an established system for adapting to midyear changes in the state's adopted budget.[7] He also observed that this midyear process could be problematic in years of surplus insofar as the legislature takes up items (most notably special projects) that do not compete with priorities in the rest of the budget during this process.[8] Meagan M. Jordan described the Arkansas legislature's budget strategy, which anticipates potential midyear changes by dividing the budget into three major categories with the first category funded (or cut) before the next category is funded, depending on the revenues available.[9]

Analysis of executive activities is somewhat broader. Over the course of the twentieth century, scholars have observed that the executive branch, both state and federal, has become more aggressive in using its authority over budget execution to withhold and transfer funds.[10] One of the significant executive tools is the process known in the states as allotments and for the federal government as apportionment (as provided for by the Antideficiency Act of 1906).[11] While the literature treats allotments as a mechanism to divide a spending unit's total yearly appropriations into monthly or quarterly spending allocations to control against ending the fiscal year with spending in excess of the legally appropriated amount,[12] there is a void in the actual study of allotments or in the use of allotments to deal with rapidly declining revenues.

Making midyear adjustments to the adopted budget is also referred to as "rebudgeting."[13] Revenue flows below (above) budget estimates and unexpected expenditure needs can undermine the fixed annual budget, thereby necessitating one or more mid-course corrections. The public finance literature examining state budgeting tends to downplay the implications of executive midyear adjustments, finding that they are primarily a response to technical or economic conditions. John P. Forrester and Daniel R. Mullins found that, among cities, the difficulty in correctly estimating revenues and spending was more likely to lead to rebudgeting than unanticipated changes in the legal or economic environment or even political concerns.[14] Forrester (1993) drew the same conclusion for the state of Missouri.[15] A survey of state budget directors in 2000–2001 found that executive budget officers viewed the ability to withhold funds as a key tool to keep the budget balanced during periods of revenue shortfall, but not as a particularly effective means of advancing gubernatorial policy priorities.[16]

By way of contrast, reviews of the presidential use of impoundment authority showed an evolution that suggests that gubernatorial withholding authorities could be used more aggressively to advance executive priorities. Impoundment authority, which allows the president to withhold or reduce appropriations, in many cases resembles the gubernatorial authority to withhold allotments. Prior to the 1970s, the legal framework around impoundments was relatively vague, and presidents could and did impound funds with few restrictions—but they used this authority sparingly. In the early 1970s, President Richard M. Nixon began to use impoundment authority aggressively to target domestic programs that he believed should be eliminated. This action provoked a congressional backlash and resulted in the Congressional Budget and Impoundment Control Act of 1974, which not only curtailed executive withholding of funds but also strengthened congressional institutional capacity to craft and evaluate the budget. After some modifications, the act eventually required the president to submit any rescissions to Congress for approval and sharply limited the conditions under which the president could even defer spending funds. Congress further tasked the Comptroller General with monitoring executive spending and reporting any deferrals or rescissions that were not reported to Congress by the president.[17] Since then, executive use of rescissions and withholdings has declined to the extent that President George W. Bush did not use this authority at all in the 2000s, and Congress itself became more likely to make rescissions than the president would.[18]

The Legal Dilemma

Recent reviews in law journals of gubernatorial withholding authorities are also less sanguine about gubernatorial "rebudgeting" powers, expressing concern that such authority can be used aggressively as a tool to advance executive power relative to the legislative branch and that this tool could encroach on the legislative "power of the purse."[19] The basic legal dilemma is a tension between legislative prerogatives over budgetary decision making relative to executive authority to execute the budget within a balanced-budget framework.

Legislative control over the budget has deep roots in Anglo-Saxon democracy, extending back to the Magna Carta. The US Constitution is explicit that "no money shall be drawn from Treasury, but in consequence of appropriations made by law." This explicit authority is mirrored in state constitutional arrangements.[20] Constitutional scholars have argued that this power may not be delegated away by Congress,[21] and many state constitutions often have even stronger nondelegation standards.[22]

On the other hand, unlike at the federal level, state governors are charged with executing the state budget in such a way as to avoid a year-end deficit—a rule enforced by the external de facto requirements of capital markets aided by the credit-rating agencies.[23] The withholding or rescission sections of state codes often refer to balanced-budget requirements when establishing an executive authority to withhold or move funds without legislative involvement. In situations where such executive authority is vague or is not established in law, a governor may use this requirement to legally ground his or her authority to withhold funds through the allotment process or to move funds from reserves or nongeneral-fund accounts in order to respond to a revenue shortfall.[24]

The recent downturn has prompted extensive discussion within some states about executive impoundments and appropriate processes for making midyear budgetary changes. In New York, the Lieutenant Governor called for increasing executive authority to withhold funds. A study analyzing executive authority to address budget gaps during the fiscal year concluded that "legislation and/or constitutional amendment could usefully clarify the status of this existing gubernatorial power."[25] In New Mexico, the legislature delegated some of its authority to authorize the governor to take action to adjust midyear shortfalls.[26] On the other hand, the aggressive use of gubernatorial powers to withhold funds has caused a host of lawsuits, including ones in Arizona, New Jersey, New York, Minnesota, Connecticut, Mississippi, New Hampshire, and Kansas.[27]

Current Institutional Arrangements

Most states do allow governors to withhold funds in the event of a deficit, but the institutional arrangements vary. The National Association of State Budget Officers (NASBO) and the National Conference of State Legislators (NCSL) provide an initial framework. NASBO's survey of executive budget authority captures two dimensions of the state arrangements: (1) whether the governor can reduce the enacted budget without legislative approval, and (2) whether there are restrictions on this authority. NASBO's 2008 survey recorded that the governors of thirty-eight states had the ability to reduce the enacted budget and in eleven states this authority is "unrestricted," although it may be bounded by a percentage amount or limited to certain parts of the budget. The remaining states required some sort of legislative approval or otherwise restricted the circumstances under which governors can reduce funds.[28]

The NCSL arranged executive midyear adjustment authority roughly as follows:

- The governor has complete authority to withhold funds as needed, typically with some notification to the legislature (ten states)
- The governor can withhold funds but only up to a certain percentage or dollar amount (six states)
- The governor can withhold but only equally across the board, sometimes with selected exceptions (ten states)
- The governor can withhold allotments but not change appropriations (the legal authority to spend), typically indicating some sort of temporary withholding arrangement until the legislature can come into session and formally adopt reductions (ten states)
- Legislative approval is required for some or all reductions (twenty states)
- Other arrangements (thirteen states)[29]

These different institutional arrangements suggest that states may have different mechanisms of mediating the executive-legislative tension and that some may be more successful than others in allowing a state to both respond rapidly to a fiscal crisis without giving the executive extraordinary authority to re-organize budgetary priorities. This analysis leverages the opportunity of the past two years to examine a cross-section of state experiences with re-budgeting. Examining a series of case studies, we explore the following questions: (1) What were the challenges that states faced in managing through the downturn? (2) How did the institutional arrangements influence the state's response? (3) Do these institutional arrangements raise policy questions about too little executive authority or too much? And, if so, what might be policy solutions to these dilemmas?

CONTEXT AND CASE STUDIES

The case studies were selected to review a range of gubernatorial authorities and the subsequent impact on the state's ability to stay balanced. Using the NASBO and NCSL criteria as well as personal knowledge of state circumstances, the states range from North Carolina, where the governor has almost unlimited authority to withhold funds and move funds from reserves into the general fund of the budget, to Nevada, where the governor has almost no authority to withhold or move funds without legislative approval. In the middle of the range are Minnesota, New York, and Georgia. In Minnesota, the governor has extensive authority to withhold funds, much like in North Carolina, but the case illustrates the complications that arise when the governor has an aggressive agenda to reduce funds. In Georgia, the governor's authority is technically more limited, but again, an aggressive governor can use the authorities available and exploit vague legal language and a passive legislature to advance a policy agenda. Finally, the governor in New York is relatively constrained to consult with the legislature, although not as much as in Nevada. This case illustrates some of the dangers associated with the inability to take early and effective action to address a fiscal crisis.

Two conditions set the context for continuous budget revision. First, in most states, revenue forecasters were unable to predict when the state would reach the bottom of the fiscal crisis, requiring the executive branch to respond quickly to changing circumstances as revenues declined. Second, most states had to end the year with balanced budgets (or some approximation thereof), which meant that the states *had* to respond to declining revenues by raising revenues or curtailing spending as the new revenue estimates were produced. Combined, these factors forced states to re-budget continually throughout the fiscal year to try to bring their budgets into balance. The five cases touch on each state's institutional context and go through the timeline of the decline in the budget with a brief review of major executive and legislative actions taken to address the shortfalls. Each case ends with an analysis of the issues raised by that experience.

North Carolina

Institutional Context: North Carolina has a biennial budget with annual legislative sessions. During even-numbered years when the state is in the middle of the biennium, the General Assembly will meet for a brief session and make adjustments to the budget for the upcoming year, but generally the legislature does not make changes, or only makes minor changes, to the current fiscal year budget.[30] The revenue estimate has evolved in North Carolina into a consensus estimation process developed jointly by the executive and legislative fiscal economists. During the downturn, they produced monthly updates for the governor and General Assembly. The executive and legislative branches are constitutionally required to enact a balanced budget, and importantly, the state is *statutorily* required to end the fiscal year with a balanced budget, one of only eight states to have such a year-end mandate.[31]

Although generally considered a "weak governor" state,[32] North Carolina gives the governor significant authority to manage through fiscal downturn. In the North Carolina statute on "methods to avoid a deficit," appropriations are clearly defined as being conditional on "necessity" and "availability of funds": "Each appropriation is maximum and conditional. The expenditures authorized by an appropriation from a fund shall be made only if necessary and only if the aggregate revenues to the fund during each fiscal year of the biennium, when added to any unreserved fund balance from the previous fiscal year, are sufficient to support the expenditures."[33]

Once the governor's Budget Director determines that the revenues are insufficient to fund the state budget, he or she must notify the General Assembly of the downturn and provide them with a general outline of a plan to bring it into balance. This was done through an Executive Order in FY 2009 and FY 2010. After this action, the governor (or by extension the Budget Director) has wide latitude to take action to keep the budget in balance. She may withhold funds across the budget differentially as necessary. There are a few exceptions. The governor may make reductions only after "making adequate provision for the prompt payment of principal and interest on bonds and notes."[34] Also, the governor may not unilaterally reduce the judicial budget or expropriate tax revenues that the state collects on behalf of localities.[35]

North Carolina's governors have also interpreted their authority as allowing them to transfer funds out of segregated accounts such as their highway trust fund and lottery and tobacco reserves into the general fund. These funds have a "special object" or purpose defined in statute, which in normal circumstances would limit their use. This authority was challenged in 2002 when the governor moved funds out of the highway trust fund to the general fund to cover shortfalls, and in 2010 the court ruled in a split decision that the governor had exceeded his authority by moving these funds, although the legislature could move the funds.[36] However, the current governor has argued that the case does not set a precedent as this ruling was limited to the particular 2002 action.[37] The governor used this authority broadly in 2009, drawing funds from a host of reserves and trust funds, including the capital improvement funds, repair and renovation reserves, Disaster Relief Reserve, Lottery Reserve, Tobacco Trust Fund, and Health and Wellness Trust Fund.[38]

FY 2009 Events: Across FY 2009, the governor's office changed hands. The previous governor, Mike Easley, had made some preparation for the downturn by issuing an executive order and initiating withholding of allotments at 2 percent. However, by the time the new governor, Bev Perdue, took office in January 2009, the state economists reported that a 2.5 percent shortfall had become a 10 percent shortfall from the original $20,489 billion budget. The new governor issued a revised executive order and initiated allotment withholding at 7 percent, prohibited purchase orders, travel and training, all capital improvements, and all hiring. The General Assembly was informed of the plans but their advice was not solicited. In February, the Office of State Budget Management (OSBM) began to transfer funds from reserves and trust funds into the state general fund to keep state operations running.

By April, it became apparent that the state would miss the original revenue estimate by as much as 15 percent. Executive budget staff described this period as one of near "martial law." The OSBM directed agencies to stop all purchases, informing them that allotments would only be released for payroll, utilities, financial aid, state aid as required by law, and debt service. All purchase orders for goods not received by April 16 had to be canceled. This policy did have a disproportionate impact on agencies that had higher expenditures at the end of the fiscal year, most notably the state university system, which was able to maintain operations by relying on internal reserves. The state instituted a flexible furlough program equivalent to a pay reduction of 0.5 percent.

By May, the legislative and executive state economists had revised their joint estimate again to $17.682 billion. The OSBM withdrew funds from the budget stabilization reserve, other reserves across the budget, and ultimately backfilled the remaining shortfall with the recently passed federal stimulus funds,[39] including budget stabilization funds and Medicaid funds. The state also slowed the issuance of tax refunds, although no late penalties were incurred in FY 2009 for the delays. By the end of the fiscal year, the state had managed through a $3.22 billion shortfall from the original budget or a 15.4 percent decline in state-fund revenues across the course of the fiscal year.

FY 2010 Events: Managing the FY 2010 budget was more straightforward than the FY 2009 scenario because the state only had around a $681 million midyear shortfall. Even as the governor was managing through the 2009 decline, the state legislature was struggling to craft the FY 2010–2011 biennial budget. During budget consideration, the revenue estimate for FY 2010 changed from $18.862 billion to $17.516. After two continuing resolutions, the legislature reached agreement in early August. The plan included $1.4 billion in tax increases and $1.7 billion in cuts.

In August, immediately after the budget had passed, the OSBM began withholding 5 percent allotments (with some adjustments for education, Medicaid, and debt service), in preparation for a potential year-end shortfall. At the end of the year, recognizing that there was still around a $200 million shortfall, the OSBM covered part of the shortfall with some unanticipated savings from corporate income-tax refunds and slowed the release of individual income-tax refunds to keep the state balanced through the end of the year. In 2010, the state did end up paying interest to taxpayers who experienced delayed tax refunds.

Other Actions of Interest: In 2010, making adjustments to the FY 2011 budget, the General Assembly, in consultation with the governor's office, took an additional step of building into the budget a list of options to cover a potential shortfall if Congress failed to approve additional stimulus assistance to states. These optional cuts were listed in priority order.

Analysis: North Carolina's process illustrates strong gubernatorial power and was relatively free of conflict. The governor was able to respond quickly to the precipitous decline between January and April, both withholding expenditures and pulling available reserves into the general fund. Even with the refunds, the state did not end either year with substantial liabilities pushed into future fiscal years, where, as will be seen, other states pushed billions into future fiscal years.

There was no effort by the General Assembly to reverse significant gubernatorial actions even though the legislature was in session during the withholding process and could have taken action. The North Carolina legislature can also call itself into session, and this latent power to challenge executive authority may act as some constraint on executive choices. This cross-branch comity was also likely driven by the executive and legislative branches being controlled by the same political party, and the governor did not advance an aggressive policy agenda through withholding. However, the governor's authority in North Carolina resembles the federal executive authority prior to 1974, where the president had significant impoundment power but did not use it aggressively. The national example suggests the potential for a governor in North Carolina to use this authority more aggressively to advance a policy agenda.

Minnesota

Like North Carolina, Minnesota provides significant discretion to the governor to impound or "unallot" funds; however, the Minnesota case illustrates the conflict that can occur when the executive chooses to aggressively leverage this authority to advance a policy agenda. This case also shows why scholars might be concerned about separation of powers.

Institutional Context: Minnesota adopts biennium budget appropriations in odd-numbered years. The legislature can make midyear budget adjustments in a session usually held in the even-numbered year, but the legislature is limited to meeting a maximum of 120 days during the two-year period. Revenue forecasts are issued in February and November by the executive branch.[40] The revenue estimates bind the budget, and the executive and legislative branches are required by statute to pass a balanced budget. Although the state does not have to end the year in balance, the governor's Commissioner of Management and Budget is charged with maintaining the balance throughout the fiscal year. The state law on unallotment states:

> If the commissioner determines that probable receipts for the general fund will be less than anticipated, and that the amount available for the remainder of the biennium will be less than needed, the commissioner shall, with the approval of the governor, and after consulting with the Legislative Advisory Commission, reduce the amount in the budget reserve account as needed to balance expenditures with revenue. An additional deficit shall...be made up by reducing unexpended allotments of any prior appropriation or transfer. Notwithstanding any other law to the contrary, the commissioner is empowered to defer or suspend prior statutorily created obligations, which would prevent effecting such reductions.[41]

The governor also has the authority to utilize the state rainy-day fund to cover any shortfalls. Although the governor (and by extension the Commissioner of Management of Budget) cannot raid other trust funds and reserves to put into the general fund, the Commissioner does have the authority to borrow from selected trust funds and reserves to manage cash flow in the general fund as long as the funds are repaid within the biennium. The executive branch is statutorily prohibited from using funds such as bond proceeds, highway funds, and federal funds.[42]

FY 2009 Events: In FY 2009, the state managed through an $890 million shortfall—or 2.51 percent of the $35.5 billion biennium general-funds budget—with modest unallotments of around $271 million, the use of the entire budget stabilization fund, and the use of federal stimulus funds. Forty-one percent of the unallotments came from reducing city and county aid and reducing local reimbursements for a homestead credit.[43]

FY 2010 Events: In FY 2010, however, the situation was more serious. In January 2009, Governor Tim Pawlenty presented a FY 2010–2011 biennium budget that closed a $4.8 billion shortfall created by an anticipated $36.7 billion in current services expenditures relative to $31.9 billion in anticipated revenues. Embedded in the governor's proposal were new spending initiatives, tax cuts, and an effort to replenish the state reserves, which increased the shortfall by $860 million.[44] Overall, to fill the shortfall, the governor proposed spending reductions of around $2.5 billion; however, importantly, he also proposed a $1.77 billion shift of payments to school districts from the FY 2010–2011 biennium to the FY 2012–2013 biennium plus a plan for "increasing revenues" by moving $1.9 billion out of a health-care access reserve fund and terminating the program for low-income residents who did not qualify for Medicaid.[45] In February 2009, the economists revised their forecast to a $4.6 billion shortfall based in part on use of a projected year-end surplus from 2009. However, this forecast also included a $1.2 billion additional decline in revenues, which was offset by $1.4 billion in federal stimulus funds.[46] The governor proposed a revised budget plan, making some modest restorations of funding.[47]

Although the legislature adopted a substantial amount of the plan, including delaying payments to school districts, the legislature also passed a tax increase of $979.6 million for the biennium, rejecting a number of the proposed cuts in local aid, property-tax relief, and health care. On May 9, 2009, the governor vetoed the revenue bill containing the tax increases, and the legislature subsequently failed to override the veto. In the middle of the month, the legislature passed appropriations bills reducing the deficit to $2.8 billion, which the governor signed with a few line-item vetoes. On May 18, the legislature passed another revenue bill that would cover the remaining $2.8 billion deficit with the tax increases and authorization to shift the education funding to the FY 2012–2013 biennium. The governor vetoed the legislation and then on July 1 he directed the Commissioner of Management and Budget to inform the General Assembly that the state faced a budgetary shortfall. The Commissioner then proceeded to make unallotments that implemented much of the original budget proposed by the governor in January.[48] This action drew a lawsuit from organizations affected by the unallotment actions, charging that the executive had usurped legislative-appropriating authorities.

As the courts considered the matter, an additional $994 million hole opened in the FY 2010 budget. In February 2010, the governor proposed a revised supplemental budget plan that leaned heavily on cuts to local aid and federal stimulus, but also included tax cuts. The General Assembly was still deliberating on this proposal when the state Supreme Court ruled in May 2010 that the governor's use of unallotment power in July of the prior year was against the law.[49] Although the court upheld the constitutionality of the executive authority for unallotments, it ruled that the use of unallotments in this situation was invalid because the forecasted budget deficit "was neither unknown nor unanticipated when the appropriation bills became law."[50] Moreover, "the authority of the Governor to unallot is an authority intended to save the state in times of a previously unforeseen budget crisis, it is not meant to be used as a weapon by the executive branch to break a stalemate in budget negotiations with the Legislature or to rewrite the appropriations bill."[51]

This court decision rendered $2.43 billion in unallotments invalid in the last month of the fiscal year. Additionally, the General Assembly had not fully resolved the $994 million additional shortfall. Although the General Assembly had won the legal battle over unallotments and established a future precedent, they lost the more immediate battle over the cuts. By this point in the fiscal year, the cuts had already been in place for eleven months, and the legislature was forced to agree to almost all of the governor's original unallotment plan.[52]

During FY 2010, the state also experienced significant cash-flow problems, leading the Department of Management and Budget to borrow $1 billion from other reserve funds, including those held for the state colleges and universities, special-revenue funds, and the health-care access fund. Meanwhile, for FY 2011, the governor's staff developed a plan that included delaying payments to local governments and school districts, as well as corporate refund payments. The state also established a line of credit for $600 million.

Analysis: The Minnesota case illustrates the separation of powers issues raised by executive authority. This conflict may be more visible in Minnesota because the governor's office and the legislature were controlled by different political parties. Although the power of unallotment had not previously been used aggressively by governors,[53] action by Governor Pawlenty to advance his agenda shows the latent power in these legal provisions. The courts established some constraint by creating a temporal boundary, namely that a balanced budget must be passed prior to the governor taking action to balance the budget. However, the governor still retains significant authority to subvert legislative priorities early in the fiscal year if the revenues appear to be lagging, and importantly, the executive branch determines the revenue estimate required to trigger such action.

This case also illustrates another important issue, which is that if the members of the legislature meet late in the fiscal year, they may have difficulty unwinding executive choices made early in the fiscal year. In the FY 2010 instance, this dilemma was pushed to the extreme when the unallotment lawsuit was not resolved until May, too late in the fiscal year to reverse spending reductions initiated in July of the prior year.

Additionally, Minnesota experienced extensive cash-flow problems, delayed payments to local governments, and pushed substantial liabilities into future fiscal years—a poor budget practice that mirrors the problems in New York, which prompted a call for increased gubernatorial authority. Strong gubernatorial authority does not in and of itself lead to better fiscal practices. On the other hand, the Minnesota budget office does have clear statutory authority to use these mechanisms when needed.

Georgia

Although the Georgia governor is generally considered to have strong executive authority over the budget,[54] technically, the governor's legal ability to adjust the budget midyear is more constrained than in either Minnesota or North Carolina.[55] However, despite limitations, the authority available can be quite strong if used aggressively by the governor.

Institutional Context: Georgia has an annual budget with annual legislative sessions. Each year the General Assembly meets for forty legislative days (around three months) and takes up a budget amending the current year budget and the budget for the upcoming fiscal year. The governor sets the revenue estimate for both the amended midyear budget and the upcoming continuation budget, and this revenue estimate binds the legislatively adopted budget. If the governor determines that the state faces a midyear revenue shortfall, the governor may withhold funds until the General Assembly convenes in January, but he cannot change appropriations. The law is unclear as to whether the governor must notify the legislature of the proposed shortfall or of any changes in allotment withholding. In practice, the governor has usually notified legislative leadership in advance. The drafters of the law clearly envisioned that the General Assembly would be able to address any shortfalls during the legislative session in January and that this would provide sufficient oversight of the gubernatorial authority to withhold funds. After the session has adjourned, if there is an additional shortfall, the governor can call a special session or can withhold, but only across the board. Generally, the governor can call a special session at any time on a selected topic. The General Assembly can also call itself into special session but only with a three-fifths vote of all the members, certifying that an emergency exists in the affairs of the state.

Georgia has several other institutional features that are important. Georgia's budget is not particularly fragmented across fund sources. Although highway funds and lottery funds are restricted-fund sources, Georgia's state operations are primarily funded out of the state general fund, and as a result, the governor has control of almost the entire state-funds budget when he or she needs to reduce or transfer funds due to a budgetary shortfall. Finally, a governor can access the revenue shortfall reserve by pegging a revenue estimate too high, which builds in a presumption of use of the reserve, or the governor can formally authorize the release of funds from the reserve and build this into his or her revenue estimate.

FY 2009: In FY 2009, Georgia's state general-fund revenues declined by $3.3 billion, 17 percent from the original revenue forecast. Much like North Carolina, during the year, the Governor's Office of Planning and Budget (OPB) began progressively withholding allotments. However, unlike North Carolina, early on these withholdings reflected gubernatorial priorities. In particular, Governor Sonny Perdue eliminated a Homeowners Tax Relief Grant (HTRG), a program that his predecessor had instituted. This program was administered by reimbursing local governments for a reduction in the assessed value of homestead properties; however, the governor charged that local governments had just increased the millage rate in response. The state had budgeted $428 million for local reimbursements in FY 2009.

As the local governments began to realize what was happening, they protested that they had already sent out their tax bills, and they now would either have to absorb the loss of state revenues or re-send the tax bills (where they would prominently display the fact that this tax increase was courtesy of the state General Assembly). Not surprisingly, both the House and the Senate membership sided with the local governments.

In January, the governor introduced his proposed FY 2009 budget, which included $2.2 billion in reductions, 11 percent below the original budget as passed. In March, he lowered his revenue estimate by an additional $500 million. Most state agencies were now absorbing 8 percent cuts. At the same time, the legislature was concerned with how to replace the HTRG funding, but it had few options at this point in the year. The state was projected to spend around $4.5 billion in the final quarter, which meant that the General Assembly would have had to make the equivalent of 10 percent in additional cuts across all agencies to cover the HTRG. The arrival of federal stimulus funds finally broke the executive-legislative stalemate and allowed the HTRG to be funded for one additional year.

The FY 2009 drama was not over yet though. On June 19, after the General Assembly had adjourned, the governor issued a memorandum reducing the revenue estimate by an additional $274 million, or 1.5 percent below the budget as passed. Presumably, the governor could have called the General Assembly back into session, but instead, he chose to formally lower the revenue estimate again and invoke his authority to withhold allotments across the board: 25 percent of the final month's allotment. This authority had never before been invoked and it precipitated a series of problems.

First, the budget was out of balance, or at least it was unclear whether a "balanced budget" meant that expenditures were in alignment with *available revenues* or expenditures needed to be in alignment with *appropriations*, which in turn needed to be in alignment with available revenues. Only the General Assembly could adjust appropriations. Some agency financial officers argued that they were only legally bound to keep their budgets balanced to their appropriations, not "available revenues." The state Attorney General's office finally issued special instructions that agencies could only spend to revenue availability as defined through the allotment process and should not look at the appropriations as "revenues."

Second, in an unofficial opinion that provoked some dissent, the Attorney General declared that across-the-board withholding applied to the legislative and judicial branches as well. Neither branch had been notified in advance of this year-end withholding strategy. The judicial branch had payroll obligations that it had to meet and it simply ran over budget, creating a series of audit exceptions that in an executive branch agency would have exposed the budget officers to personal liability for overspending their budgets. Both the legislative and judicial branches sent letters to the governor stating that although they were going to honor the exigencies of the fiscal crisis, they did not agree with the legal basis for the withholding.

Although the law required "across-the-board cuts," the availability of stimulus funds allowed the governor to avoid this stricture by adding federal funds as needed across different agencies. The governor used the funds to mitigate the cut to the Department of Revenue, the Department of Corrections, and other selected agencies. At the year's end, the state also slowed the processing of income-tax refunds, incurring a small interest penalty.

FY 2010: In FY 2010, the situation was repeated, though on a smaller scale, with a year-end shortfall of $1.7 billion rather than $3.3 billion. The most interesting variation was that at the year's end, the OPB again anticipated a shortfall after the General Assembly left. However, instead of reducing the revenue estimate, the OPB pulled back more informally, essentially "inviting" agencies to reduce their final budget by 0.5 percent. This approach avoided both the showdown with the General Assembly and allowed the OPB to reduce revenues differently for different agencies. The governor also again made use of the flexibility of stimulus funds. The state ended the year in balance but during the course of the year had suffered substantial cash-flow problems, such that major payments to vendors had to be delayed and income-tax refund processing was initially slowed. However, the year ended with the state substantially in balance with no payments pushed into future fiscal years and all tax refunds delivered on time.

Analysis: As Georgia's case shows, governors can use even limited re-budgeting authorities aggressively, and to the extent that the governor's agenda coincides with eliminating programs or reducing government spending can use this tool effectively to scale back government. Even in states where the General Assembly considers midyear budget revisions, the governor can leverage the ability to withhold funds early in the fiscal year to make funding restoration for a program more difficult. The Georgia case also underscores the vague nature of legislative versus executive authorities. In Georgia, appropriations are a maximum (as they are in many states), thus opening the door to informal agreements between the executive and agencies to withhold funds.

New York

If Minnesota and Georgia raise red flags because of executive encroachment on legislative power of the purse, the New York state case illustrates the possible problems of too little executive control.

Institutional Context: The New York State legislature is considered to be a fully "professionalized" legislative body that meets annually with no limit to the session length. New York's budget is annual, and the legislature can and does amend the current year budget repeatedly during the year, as well as take other actions, such as tax cuts or increases, that affect the budget. Significantly, although the General Assembly must pass a balanced budget, the state does not have to end the year with a balanced budget.

The governor's budget authority is considered strong;[56] however, the governor's ability to withhold funds is limited and poorly defined in statute or the constitution. By tradition, his or her authority to withhold allotments is limited to "state agency operations" that make up around 26 percent of the total state-funds budget. Within this modest sphere, the governor has substantial authority to withhold differentially and across-the-board.[57] The remainder of the budget includes payments of state aid to local governments and school districts and a host of special-revenue funds that have statutorily dedicated purposes and cannot be touched without legislative authority.

FY 2009: New York's FY 2009 was not quite as bad as other states in part because its fiscal year ended earlier (in March) and so the precipitous and unanticipated declines that affected other states in April through June were entirely absorbed in New York's FY 2010 budget. The state initiated withholding like many other states, but perhaps the most notable event in FY 2008 and then into FY 2009, was the authority granted by the General Assembly to authorize "blanket" sweeps of special-revenue accounts of an amount up to $100 million in 2008, and in increasing amounts in the following years.[58]

One other FY 2009 issue that foreshadows some of the problems in FY 2010 was the failure of the General Assembly, and to some degree the governor, to make decisions early in the fiscal year. In October 2008, the Department of Budget (DOB) projected a $1.5 billion gap out of a $56 billion adopted general-fund budget, partly caused by declining revenues, but also partly caused by problems in one-time funds failing to materialize.[59] This prompted Governor David Patterson to call a November special session for the General Assembly to approve cuts, revenue increases, and the use of one-time funds from public authorities and fund sweeps. The General Assembly met but failed to act on the governor's proposals. In December 2008, the governor proposed a $2 billion deficit reduction plan, but this time it was heavily reliant on fund sweeps and other sources of one-time funds because there was no longer time to take action on many of the original November proposals. In February 2009, the General Assembly approved a deficit reduction plan to cover what had become a $2.2 billion shortfall.[60]

FY 2010: The state began FY 2010 anticipating an $18 billion gap between revenues and their projected "current services budget" (the budget required to keep services at their current levels). On April 3, 2009, the governor and legislature reached agreement to close this gap. The plan included an additional $6 billion in cuts (from the FY 2009 plan), $5.2 billion in revenue increases, $1 billion in one-time funds, and $5 billion in stimulus.[61]

By the time of the first quarterly update in July 2009, the DOB estimated that there would be an additional $2.1 billion shortfall and again imposed across-the-board reductions for state operations.[62] By October, this gap had grown to $3.2 billion and the governor called the General Assembly into a special session in November to make cuts to balance the budget. At this point the Department of Budget started to warn of serious cash-flow problems and indicated that they were going to start borrowing from the short-term investment pool and delay making payments to the state's retirement plan in order to manage cash. The budget office issued a warning that the state might be out of cash by December.[63]

On December 2, 2009, the legislature approved a reduction plan that included $2.7 billion in savings but left a $414 million shortfall. Further, apparently the legislature agreed that any additional shortfall that emerged would simply be carried into FY 2011. Despite these actions, the state posted a negative balance in the state general fund, and the governor had to order the Department of Budget to delay payments to school districts due to an insufficient cash balance. This action drew a lawsuit from the statewide associations of school boards, teachers, school superintendents, and school administrators. Although the governor reported an escalating shortfall through the remainder of the fiscal year, neither the governor nor the General Assembly acted on this problem, and by the year's end, the state shifted a $3 billion deficit into FY 2011, primarily through delaying payments to school districts and local governments.[64]

Analysis: In general, New York's management of the fiscal crisis in 2009 and 2010 was primarily a joint executive-legislative exercise, with the governor calling on the General Assembly to manage the downturn. By most accounts, the General Assembly repeatedly failed to adequately address the shortfalls and this caused serious cash-flow problems for the executive branch and year-end overruns. This prompted a call by the lieutenant governor and the State Comptroller for the General Assembly to give the governor increased authority to manage the crisis, and the Speaker of the House introduced legislation to make this change.[65] The New York case also illustrates the importance of being able to withhold funds early in the process. As the General Assembly delayed action, the crisis escalated, and the state was forced to rely increasingly on one-time measures or pushing payments into future fiscal years in order to reach a balance.

Nevada

Nevada provides an illustration of limited executive authority, but, unlike New York, the state was relatively successful in reaching a resolution to the budget crisis.

Institutional Context: Nevada has a biennial budget and a biennial legislative session. The legislature is in session for five to six months on odd-numbered years. During the interim, the legislative Interim Finance Committee (IFC) is authorized to approve certain fiscal transfers and other changes to agency "work plans." The IFC is not able to change the law or make transfers from certain reserves and trust funds. Additionally, the state's revenue estimate is set by a nonpartisan panel of economists (the Economic Forum), which convenes in November and May. The governor can request that the panel produce a revenue estimate at other times of the year as well. Additionally, the governor has the sole authority to call a special session and is the only one who can set the agenda for the special session.

Overall, both the Nevada legislature and the governor must deal with inherently weak institutional powers. For example, the Nevada legislature is in session only once every other year, while the governor does not have line-item veto authority.[66] Furthermore, the governor's authority to withhold funds is also weak, although prior to 2008, the executive branch had interpreted its authority as quite broad as long as any withholding was couched as setting aside a "reserve." In 2008, this authority was challenged by the legislature's IFC, and the Attorney General issued an opinion supporting the IFC's position that the IFC had to approve any changes to agency work plans that involved a reduction greater than 10 percent, or $50,000 (whichever was less).

FY 2008–2009: Nevada's fiscal problems began earlier than some of the other states. In the fall of 2007, the Budget Division asked agencies to set aside "reserves" of 4.5 percent. By early 2008, the IFC challenged the ability of Governor Jim Gibbons to alter the agency work plans in this way. One legislator complained that the Department of Corrections was proposing to close a prison in his district, while another worried about the impact on schools and public health. All complained that they had not been consulted in the governor's plans to reduce the budget.[67] One legislator pointed out that the governor did not possess line-item veto authority, but his ability to create reserves in effect created a kind of "back-door" line-item veto.[68] The state controller then asked the Attorney General to issue an opinion on this conflict, and in May 2008 the Attorney General ruled that despite the long-standing practice of allowing the governor to order "reserves," changes in the agency work plans required IFC approval. The governor could ask for expedited approval when the situation required and the IFC would have to approve within fifteen days or the proposals would be deemed approved. In emergency situations, the executive could act unilaterally.[69]

The governor had initiated the 4.5 percent withholding in the fall, but he submitted the plans to the IFC for approval immediately thereafter. His proposals were approved in large part. At a prior meeting the IFC had approved work plans that included a delay of almost all construction projects.

In May, the state was anticipating around a $274 million shortfall in FY 2008, but an $898 million shortfall for the biennium, or a 13 percent shortfall from the original biennial budget of $6.8 billion. By June, the shortfall for the biennium had grown to $1 billion, and the governor called a special session in part to repeal legal provisions such as pay increases that were going into effect in FY 2009 and in part to move a number of special funds and reserves into the state general fund. On June 27, the legislature convened for a one-day special session and ratified most of the governor's changes, but not all. The governor issued a statement expressing general satisfaction with the session, but he had some reservations about the legislative decision to cut funds for textbooks for K–12 students and to not allow him to securitize the state's tobacco revenues.[70]

In the fall of 2008, as the state's situation worsened, agencies were asked to prepare for a 4 percent cut, followed quickly by another call for 4 to 11 percent reductions. By December it became apparent that the state's shortfall had grown by $309 million for a total biennial shortfall of $1.5 billion, or 22 percent of the original budget. The Division of Budget asked the agencies to identify 10 and 20 percent reductions for the governor's proposal for the upcoming FY 2010–2011 biennial budget. Meanwhile in December the governor convened another special session to address the FY 2009 problems. The General Assembly covered the remaining shortfall by endorsing the governor's proposed reductions, transferring additional reserves to the general fund, as well as making administrative changes to the administration of taxes and fees and allowing the state treasurer to borrow for state cash-flow purposes up to $160 million from the state-run local government investment pool, with repayment and interest due in full in four years. By the year's end, the state's revenues had declined an additional $208.5 million, but the shortfalls were resolved by accessing federal stimulus funds.

FY 2010: Consideration of the budget for FY 2010–2011 began only a few months after the December 2008 special session, but at this point the legislature had shifted from Republican control to Democratic control while the governor was Republican. The new legislature made a number of cuts, including suspending pay increases, a temporary pay cut of 4.6 percent through a one-day-a-month furlough, and a generic 1.4 percent across-the-board cut, asking agencies to determine how it would be administered. The legislature also passed legislation increasing taxes by $1.332 billion, including an increase in the sales tax and payroll tax. The governor vetoed this proposal, offering up an alternative plan of securitization of tobacco revenues and additional cuts to K-12 education, but the legislature overrode the veto and the tax increases went into effect in July.

By December it was apparent that the state would not make budget in FY 2010. The Economic Forum projected a $384 million shortfall in FY 2010 and an $888 million shortfall for the biennium. In response, the governor ordered agencies to plan for 6, 8, and 10 percent reductions, with a proposed implementation date of March 1, and he convened a special session in mid-February. For their part, the General Assembly passed a revised budget with a range of budgetary cuts, including 10 percent cuts to many agencies and 6.9 percent cuts to K-12 education and higher education. In addition, the legislature agreed to transfer funds into the general fund and move $164 million in stimulus funds out of FY 2011 and into FY 2010. The state ended the year within budget, despite having filled an effective $2.3 billion or 35 percent shortfall from the original FY 2008–2009 budget.

Analysis: The Nevada case raises some interesting questions. Even though the state dealt with a shortfall as devastating as the other states, ultimately the situation was resolved with substantial legislative input. Nevada did have to absorb the cost of multiple special sessions, but unlike New York, the legislature resolved the problems put before it. The midyear delegation of authority from the General Assembly to the IFC does raise some concerns similar to the delegation of midyear authority to the governor since the state constitution could be interpreted as placing appropriations authority with the General Assembly as a whole rather than with a committee.[71]

Gubernatorial Withholding and Impoundment Authorities

These five cases reveal that strong gubernatorial authority does not in and of itself lead to better fiscal practices any more than strong legislative authority lends itself to poor fiscal practices. North Carolina and Nevada operated on opposite ends of the executive authority continuum, but both states appear to have had similar outcomes, maintaining a fiscal balance under extreme duress. The principal difference seems to be that Nevada required several special sessions to reach a balanced budget, and the legislature modified some of the governor's agenda. Meanwhile, Minnesota and New York, with a strong and weak governor, respectively, both ended up pushing significant liabilities into future budgets. Yet in Minnesota the governor used his withholding authority to actively promote his budgetary priorities and subvert legislative ones. Although there is little evidence from the case studies that a particular level of gubernatorial authority is more conducive to good fiscal practices, there is clear evidence that certain institutional arrangements are more conducive to executive encroachment on the traditional legislative authority over the budget.

The fundamental concerns that states face with the midyear adjustment process are the following:

1. Allowing the state to respond quickly and effectively to dramatically changing fiscal circumstances across the fiscal year, and
2. Respecting the constitutional principle that authority for budgeting resides with the legislature.

Based on the five cases reviewed, there is no evidence that these two criteria are mutually exclusive. States face certain practical concerns during a fiscal crisis. Spending needs to be restrained quickly when the depth of the fiscal crisis becomes apparent, and in this particular crisis, states often needed to respond multiple times when forecasters were unable to predict the bottom of the downturn. The reason for speed is that with every day that goes by more money is spent and there is less that can be saved within the fiscal year. A related issue is that budget directors also need the ability to manage cash flow effectively as reserves are spent down, and the state begins to operate on a much thinner margin.

The primary arguments against broader involvement of the legislatures is that (1) legislatures, such as the one in New York, may simply fail to respond to the crisis forcing the state into a deficit; and (2) legislatures may take longer to respond by virtue of the deliberative processes that they require and thus hinder the ability of the state to respond quickly to the crisis. In response to the problem of legislative inaction, ultimately, no institutional arrangement can force state legislatures or governors to make wise decisions. A governor can fail to address a fiscal crisis as well. New York's specific fiscal problems predated the 2008–2010 crisis. Among the issues identified in New York's budget process are (1) relatively weak balanced-budget requirements[72] and (2) a fragmented budget structure that lacks transparency.[73] Additionally, the New York problem was partly created by failing to withhold funds sufficiently earlier in the year. A simple solution might be to allow the governor to withhold broadly, subject to legislative review and approval within a certain time period.

In response to the second concern, it is not hard to envision institutional arrangements that balance legislative authority over the budget with the need to act with dispatch. Most states manage special sessions over the course of a few days, and most fiscal crises, unlike a natural disaster, require an expeditious but not necessarily immediate response. As shown, both Nevada and New York were able to convene special sessions relatively rapidly. Again, such a concern could be easily addressed by allowing the governor to withhold broadly early in the fiscal year (or when needed), but limiting the time period to one within which the legislature can reasonably be convened and complete business, such as within sixty days.

At present, states such as Georgia allow the governor to withhold funds until the legislature convenes in January, but in many cases, January is too late for the legislature to actually change the governor's plan for a fiscal year that ends on June 30.

In the case of the HTRG in Georgia, there was simply too much money that would have had to be found at the year's end. In other cases, the implementation of a cut was complete: the employees laid off, the contracts canceled, the prison closed, the program defunct. At this point, restoring the cut may be more expensive than just replacing the original dollar amount. This same problem was evident in Minnesota and Nevada, although driven by slow court responses to the governors' efforts to withhold funds early in the year.

Another problem might be that at the end of the year, an unexpected shortfall might not allow the legislature enough time to convene. On the one hand, few states statutorily require the state to *end* the year in balance (most simply require executive introduction and legislative adoption of a balanced budget).[74] On the other hand, there are serious cash-flow issues associated with pushing obligations into future fiscal years, and given the positive effects of strong norms of fiscal balance, states should consider a year-end remedy. If there truly is not time to convene a special session (perhaps there are only sixty days left in the fiscal year), one option would be to allow the governor to make an emergency declaration, such as one an executive might issue for a natural disaster and to act accordingly. Legislative priorities are protected to some degree at this point in the fiscal year because agency spending plans have been implemented for most of the year.

It is worth noting that in Georgia and North Carolina, conversations with fiscal staff indicated that the legislature did not particularly *want* to act to address the midyear fiscal shortfall. Of course in Georgia by failing to act, the legislature found itself boxed in on the issue of the HTRG. However, one of the central legal principles surrounding separation of powers and the legislative power to establish appropriations is that the power of the purse is delegated by the people to the legislature, and thus, the legislature cannot subsequently delegate this authority to the executive or to a legislative board or committee. Recognizing that at times delegation may be required, should a legislature choose to delegate, most state judiciaries require some sort of "clear standard" outlining the conditions under which delegation might occur or setting out procedures for triggering such authority. Further, the more authority that is delegated, the clearer the standard should be.[75]

Referencing exactly this sort of standard, the court in the Minnesota case noted that the current statute did not establish a temporal boundary for the exercise of gubernatorial authority nor was the definition of "deficit" clear, even though a declaration of a deficit triggered the exercise of extraordinary executive authority. This problem of vagueness surrounding the triggering of executive authority occurs in other states as well. In Georgia, the governor is authorized to take action to withhold funds to prevent a shortfall, but there is no required "event" that can formally recognize a shortfall. As a result, the governor may just start withholding funds, with the general public or General Assembly none the wiser. Similar issues were raised in Nevada[76] and New York,[77] and some research suggests this issue is present in a host of other states as well.[78] The remedy does not seem impossible; presumably in states where the revenue forecast is completed by consensus, a finding by the panel or set of economists that determines the revenue estimate could trigger executive withholding. In states where the governor unilaterally sets the revenue estimate, the situation may be more difficult, but at least the governor can clearly define and publicly announce the revenue shortfall that is triggering the withholding. In the context of a limited period for withholding, this might be sufficient because the legislature would rapidly reconvene to address any particular abuse of this authority.

A further issue with addressing midyear shortfalls occurs in states where legislatures have tried to preserve their authority and the original scope of their budget agreement by limiting the governor's discretion to "across-the-board withholding" or limitations on what can be withheld. Both strategies have limited efficacy. For states that set a percentage or dollar value, the actual impact of this restriction varies based on the amount. Nevada restricts the governor to a withholding limit of 10 percent, or $50,000 (whichever is less), a constraint so restrictive that it effectively requires the governor to solicit legislative approval in almost any deficit situation. At the other end of the continuum, some limits are so generous and allow the governor so much discretion that they appear to place almost no serious constraint at all on the governor. For instance, Maryland's maximum reduction is 25 percent of any appropriation, while Virginia sets the limit at 15 percent of any agency's appropriation.[79]

The "across-the-board" withholding criteria are also limited in their usefulness particularly in a serious deficit situation, because all agencies may not be able to sustain the same magnitude of reduction. According to the NCSL survey, only ten states require this type of strategy, and the experience of Georgia suggests that it either causes significant problems, or the governor will find ways around it. Other states with similar criteria, such as Oregon, simply ended up calling multiple special sessions. Fundamentally, it is hard to understand why these stop-gap measures should substitute for simply calling a special session. They are either of such limited usefulness that the executive branch finds ways to subvert the intent of the provision, they prompt a special session, or if actually used, they create such distortions that a special session would have been more desirable in their place.

Other Models: One other model is for the legislature to establish a plan for reductions in advance that the executive must use when facing an unexpected fiscal shortfall. In Arkansas the General Assembly sets broad priorities every two years, but detailed programs are left up to the governor. These priorities are expressed in the budget by categorizing line items as "A," "A1," and "B," with the expectation that "A" will be funded completely before "A1," and so on. State-revenue estimates determine the funding level. If, for example, the governor's official forecast of revenue collections adjusts expected revenues below the amount sufficient to fund the "A" category completely, then an equal share is cut from each agency allocation within that priority category. For the fiscal year ending June 30, 2010, the official estimate of May 4, 2010, revised the funding to 94.73 percent of the "A" allocation.

CONCLUSION

The experience of the states between FY 2008 and FY 2010 provided a unique opportunity to see a variety of state responses to a commonly experienced fiscal crisis. During the Great Recession, many state revenue forecasters were unable to detect the bottom of the recession creating a situation where state officials were forced to severely pull back on spending or to lean heavily on reserves in order to keep their budgets in balance during the fiscal year. Fundamental to this experience was a tension created by the need to act quickly to changing circumstances, typically an executive responsibility, while respecting legislative prerogatives for setting fiscal priorities.

Although more research in this area is warranted, the case studies reviewed in this chapter suggest that different state institutional arrangements may mediate this tension better than others. Many states delegate substantial authority to the executive branch to make midyear fiscal adjustments and while many governors use this delegated authority with discretion, the case studies also showed several circumstances where these authorities could be used quite aggressively to advance an agenda and undermine legislative priorities. On the other hand, state officials need to be able to act quickly to withhold funds in the face of rapidly declining revenues; however, these cases show that legislatures can develop mechanisms through special sessions or committees authorized to act in their stead that can allow the state to respond in a timely manner to a downturn while still providing some check on executive authority.

NOTES

1 Boyd and Dadayan (2010), 1–2.
2 National Governors Association and National Association of State Budget Officers (2009), 8.
3 McNichol and Lav (2009).
4 Francis (this volume); McNichol, Oliff, and Johnson (2010).
5 Rubin (1985).
6 Hale and Douglass (1977).
7 Lauth (1988).
8 Lauth (2002).
9 Jordan (2006).
10 Schick (1964).
11 Antideficiency Act, 31 USC sect. 1341 (a)(1)(A).
12 Mikesell (2011).
13 Forrester and Mullins (1992).
14 Douglas and Hoffman (2002).
15 Forrester (1993)
16 Douglas and Hoffman (2002).
17 Keith (2008); McMurtry (1997).

18 Wlezien (1994); Gibson (2010); Poling (2009).

19 Siewert (2011); Myers (2010).

20 Ibid.

21 Stith (1988). See also Justice Kennedy's discussion of the president's line-item veto authority in *Clinton v. City of New York*, 524 US 417.

22 Kincaid (this volume); Rossi (1999).

23 Hou and Smith (2006); Hildreth and Zorn (2005).

24 Siewert (2011). For an example from North Carolina, see *County of Cabarrus et al. v. Norris L. Tolson*, Secretary of Revenue of the State of North Carolina, 2005. No. COA04-594. For a complete list of state code sections where gubernatorial authority is established see National Conference of State Legislatures (n.d.).

25 Ward (2010).

26 Jennings (2010).

27 Siewert (2011), footnote 99.

28 National Association of State Budget Officers (2008).

29 National Conference of State Legislatures (n.d.).

30 Based on interviews with executive and legislative fiscal staff (August 2010).

31 Hou and Smith (2006).

32 Beyle (2008).

33 North Carolina Code Section 143C-6-2(a).

34 North Carolina State Code Section G.S. 143C-4-1.

35 Based on North Carolina State Code Section G.S. 143C-6-2; interview with executive budget staff (October 2010).

36 Staff (2010).

37 Owens (2009).

38 Based on materials provided by legislative and executive fiscal staff on strategies used to balance the FY 2009 budget.

39 The American Recovery and Reinvestment Act (ARRA) of 2009, Public Law 111-5.

40 Minnesota Statute 16A.103.

41 Minnesota Statute 16A.152 (subd.4).

42 Marx (2010).

43 Massman (2009).

44 Office of Governor Tim Pawlenty (2009b); Fiscal Analysis Department (2009).

45 Fiscal Analysis Department (2009).

46 Minnesota Department of Management & Budget (2009).

47 Office of Governor Tim Pawlenty (2009a).

48 Massman (2010).

49 Ibid.

50 *Deanna Brayton, et al. v. Tim Pawlenty, et al.*, 781 N.W. 2d 357, 9 (2010).

51 Ibid.

52 Massman (2010).

53 Siewert (2011); Minnesota Legislative Reference Library (2010).

54 Lauth (2006).

55 The Georgia case is based on the senior author's extensive personal experience with the Georgia budget. Carolyn Bourdeaux was Director of the Georgia Senate Budget and Evaluation Office at the time.

56 Beyle (2008).

57 Ward (2010).

58 DiNapoli (2010).

59 New York Department of the Budget (2008).
60 New York Department of the Budget (2009a).
61 Ibid.
62 New York Department of the Budget (2009b).
63 New York Department of the Budget (2009c).
64 DiNapoli (2010).
65 Ward (2010).
66 Beyle (2008).
67 Fiscal Analysis Division (2008).
68 Myers (2010).
69 Masto (2008).
70 Press Office (2008).
71 Myers (2010).
72 Bifulco and Duncombe (2010).
73 DiNapoli (2010).
74 Hou and Smith (2006).
75 Siewert (2011); Rossi (1999).
76 Myers (2010).
77 Ward (2010).
78 Siewert (2011).
79 For an overview of types of executive authorities, see National Association of State Budget Officers (2008); National Conference of State Legislatures (n.d.).

References

American Recovery and Reinvestment Act of 2009, Public Law 111–5.
Antideficiency Act, 31 USC Sect. 1341 (a)(1)(A).
Beyle, Thad (2008). "Gubernatorial Power." http://www.unc.edu/~beyle/gubnewpwr.html.
Bifulco, Robert, and William Duncombe (2010). "Budget Deficits in the States: New York." *Public Budgeting & Finance* 30(1): 58–79.
Boyd, Donald, and Lucy Dadayan (2010). "Revenue Declines Less Severe, but State's Fiscal Crisis Is Far from Over." Albany, NY: Nelson A. Rockefeller Institute of Government.
Clinton v. City of New York, 424 US 417.
Congressional Budget and Impoundment Control Act of 1974, 31 USC Sect. 601–688.
County of Cabarrus et al v. Norris L Tolson, Secretary of Revenue of the State of North Carolina 2005, No. COA04–594.
Deanna Brayton, et al. v. Tim Pawlenty, et al., 781 N.W. 2d 357 (2010).
DiNapoli, Thomas P. (2010). "New York's Deficit Shuffle." http://www.osc.state.ny.us.
Douglas, James, and Kim Hoffman (2002). "Impoundment at the State Level: Executive Power and Budget Impact." *American Review of Public Administration* 34(3): 252–258.
Fiscal Analysis Department (2009). "An Overview of Governor Tim Pawlenty's Fy2010–11 Biennial Budget Recommendations." St. Paul: Minnesota House of Representatives.
Fiscal Analysis Division (2008). "Minutes of the January 24, 2008 Meeting of the Interim Finance Committee." Carson City, NV: Legislative Council Bureau.
Forrester, John P. (1993). "The Rebudgeting Process in State Government: The Case of Missouri." *American Review of Public Administration* 23(2): 155–178.
Forrester, John P., and Daniel R. Mullins (1992). "Rebudgeting: The Serial Nature of Municipal Budgetary Processes." *Public Administration Review* 52(5): 467–473.

Gibson, Lynn (2010). "Updated Rescission Statistics, Fiscal Years 1974–2009." Washington, DC: US Government Accountability Office.

Hale, George E., and Scott R. Douglass (1977). "The Politics of Budget Execution: Financial Manipulation in State and Local Government." *Administration & Society* 9(3): 367–378.

Hildreth, W. Bartley, and Kurt Zorn (2005). "The Evolution of the State and Local Government Debt Market Over the Past Quarter Century." *Public Budgeting & Finance* Special Issue: 127–153.

Hou, Yilin, and Daniel L. Smith (2006). "A Framework for Understanding State Balanced Budget Requirement Systems: Reexamining Distinctive Features and an Operational Definition." *Public Budgeting & Finance* 26(3): 22–45.

Jennings, Trip (2010, March 1). "Budget Proposal Gives Governor More Power to Cut Spending." *The New Mexico Independent.*

Jordan, Meagan M. (2006). "Arkansas Revenue Stabilization Act: Stabilizing Programmatic Impact through Prioritized Revenue Distribution." *State & Local Government Review* 38(2): 104–111.

Keith, Robert (2008). *Introduction to the Federal Budget Process.* Washington, DC: Congressional Research Service.

Lauth, Thomas P. (1988). "Mid-Year Appropriations in Georgia: Allocating the 'Surplus.' " *International Journal of Public Administration* 11(5): 531–550.

Lauth, Thomas P. (2002). "The Midyear Appropriation in Georgia: A Threat to Comprehensiveness." *State & Local Government Review* 34(3): 198–204.

Lauth, Thomas P. (2006). "Georgia: Shared Power and Fiscal Conservatism." In *Budgeting in the States: Institutions, Processes, and Policies,* edited by Edward Clynch and Thomas Lauth. Westport, CT: Praeger. 33–54.

Marx, Bill (2010). "State General Fund Cash Flow." St. Paul: Fiscal Analysis Department, Minnesota House of Representative.

Massman, Matt (2009). "Governor's Unallotments Fy2008–2009 General Fund Budget." St. Paul: Office of Counsel, Research and Fiscal Analysis, Minnesota Senate.

Massman, Matt (2010). "General Fund Budget Summary 2010 End-of-Session." St. Paul: Office of Counsel, Research and Fiscal Analysis, Minnesota Senate.

Masto, Catherine Cortez (2008). Opinion No. 2008-04. Carson City: State of Nevada, Office of the Attorney General.

McMurtry, Virginia A. (1997). "The Impoundment Control Act of 1974: Restraining or Reviving Presidential Power?" *Public Budgeting & Finance* 17(3): 39–61.

McNichol, Elizabeth, and Iris Lav (2009). "New Fiscal Year Brings No Relief from Unprecedented State Budget Problems." Washington, DC: Center on Budget and Policy Priorities.

McNichol, Elizabeth, Phil Oliff, and Nicholas Johnson (2010). "States Continue to Feel Recession's Impact." Washington, DC: Center on Budget and Policy Priorities.

Mikesell, John (2011). *Fiscal Administration: Analysis and Applications for the Public Sector.* 8th ed. Boston: Wadsworth.

Minnesota Department of Management & Budget (2009). "Highlights: February Forecast." St. Paul: Minnesota Department of Management & Budget.

Minnesota Legislative Reference Library (2010). "Resources on Minnesota Issues: Unallotment." St. Paul: Minnesota Legislative Reference Library.

Myers, Joanna (2010). "Note: When the Governor Legislates: Post-Enactment Budget Changes and the Separation of Powers in Nevada." *Nevada Law Journal* 10(229).

National Association of State Budget Officers (2008). "Budget Processes in the States." Washington, DC: National Association of State Budget Officers.

National Conference of State Legislatures (n.d.). "Executive Authority to Cut the Enacted Budget." http://www.ncsl.org/default.aspx?tabid=12589.

National Governors Association and National Association of State Budget Officers (2009). "The Fiscal Survey of States." Washington, DC: National Association of State Budget Officers.

New York Department of the Budget (2008). "2008–09 Financial Plan Mid-Year Update Report." Albany: New York Department of the Budget

New York Department of the Budget (2009a). "2009–10 Enacted Budget Financial Plan." Albany: New York Department of the Budget.

New York Department of the Budget (2009b). "2009–10 Financial Plan First Quarter Update Report." Albany: New York Department of the Budget.

New York Department of the Budget (2009c). "2009–10 Financial Plan Mid-Year Update Report." Albany: New York Department of the Budget.

Office of Governor Tim Pawlenty (2009a). "Press Release: Governor Pawlenty's Budget Recommendations Maintain Priorities, Position State for Recovery." St. Paul, MN: Office of the Governor.

Office of Governor Tim Pawlenty (2009b). "Press Release: Governor Pawlenty Presents Balanced Budget That Sets Priorities and Positions Minnesota for Success." St. Paul, MN: Office of the Governor.

Owens, Adam (2009, April 9). "Perdue Again Taps Trust Funds for Spending." WRAL.com. http://www.wral.com/news/local/politics/story/4924381/.

Poling, Susan (2009). "Impoundment Control Act: Use and Impact of Rescission Procedures." Washington, DC: Goverment Accountability Office, GAO-10-320T.

Press Office (2008). "The Governor Issued the Following Statement Today after Signing the Bills from the Special Session Balancing the Budget for the Remainder of the Biennium." Carson City, NV: Office of the Governor.

Rossi, Jim (1999). "Institutional Design and the Lingering Legacy of Antifederalist Separation of Powers Ideals in the States." *Vanderbilt Law Review* 52(1167).

Rubin, Irene (1985). *Shrinking the Government: The Effects of Cutbacks on Five Federal Agencies.* New York: Longman.

Schick, Allen (1964). "Control Patterns in State Budget Execution." *Public Administration Review* 24(2): 97–106.

Siewert, Tyler J. (2011). "The Cloying Use of Unallotment: Curbing Executive Branch Appropriations Reductions During Fiscal Emergencies." *Minnesota Law Review* 95.

Staff (2010). "Split Supreme Court Means Easley Loses in Highway Trust Fund Dispute." *Carolina Journal Online.*

Stith, Kate (1988). "Congress' Power of the Purse." *Yale Law Journal* 97(7): 1343–1396.

Ward, Robert (2010). "Gubernatorial Powers to Address Budget Gaps During the Fiscal Year: New York Governors Lack Broad Authority Commonly Found in Other States." Albany: Nelson A. Rockefeller Institute of Government.

Wlezien, Christopher (1994). "The Politics of Impoundments." *Political Research Quarterly* 47(1): 59–84.

CHAPTER 30

....

PUBLIC EMPLOYEE PENSIONS AND INVESTMENTS

....

SIONA LISTOKIN-SMITH

NINETEEN million public employees are covered by state and local retirement systems. Public pension funds exist at most jurisdiction levels, and they are tailored for teachers, safety workers, sanitation workers, judges, legislators, school janitors, and civil servants, among other occupations.[1] These funds control a total of $3.2 trillion in assets, and they face up to $3 trillion in unfunded liabilities.[2] Large public employee retirement systems are influential in corporate governance and management at many of the most important corporations in the country; at the same time, many funds are dealing with catastrophic financial losses after complex investment products went sour in the 2008 financial crisis. Many state and local governments are currently faced with rapidly increasing annual contributions to pension and health-care funds to pay for benefits promised years earlier.

In short, there are many reasons why the health of state and local public pension systems is a pressing financial, political, and policy issue. While the fall in asset values since 2007 has made pension finances a prominent public concern, the underlying forces affecting public pension funds at the turn of the decade have been fairly stable for two decades: changing demographics and fewer active employees compared to retirees along with stretched state and local budgets. In addition to these constants, recent changes in the accounting rules they observe have highlighted liabilities that are tied to retirement health-care benefits. As fiscal tensions and an aging population come to a head, plan beneficiaries, taxpayers, and credit markets will continue to assess the ability of the pension plans to efficiently fulfill their role. At the forefront are concerns that public pension funds will not be adequate to pay for promised benefits, and past administration of state and local retirement policies and funds have set up a potential budget time bomb.

While there is wide variation in the financial health of the 2,000 plans in the United States, there is no question that many jurisdictions face serious funding problems in their retirement systems. Even if investment returns jump to the previous decade's highs, many systems are underfunded; essentially, the funds are borrowing against the future, affecting taxpayers, public servants, and future public service. Strategies to address these gaps—which could include raising employee and employer contribution rates, adjusting benefits for future employees (and possibly current employees), shifting financial management, and changing the very structure of the systems—must be implemented soon.

This chapter provides an overview of US state and local public employee retirement systems. The data presented come from multiple sources, including the US 2008 Census, the Bureau of Labor Statistics, the Public Fund Survey, the Government Accountability Office, the National Center on State Legislatures, and the Pew Center on the States. The first section of the chapter describes the structure, finances, and history of state and local pension plans. This section introduces the fundamentals of state and local retirement systems, and it presents the current state of affairs in these systems following the financial market collapse of 2007–2008. The next section summarizes major areas of recent research concerning public pension plans, including health benefits and liabilities, actuarial methodology and assumptions, shifts into defined contribution plans, and governance and investment management. The final section outlines the effects of the recent financial and fiscal crises and examines steps taken to address the unfunded liabilities. It argues that reforms to date have been too incremental, and serious structural shifts must be undertaken to pay for the retirement and health benefits already promised to active employees while remaining competitive employers in the future.

PUBLIC PENSION PLAN STRUCTURE

Public employee retirement systems provide retirement income and other benefits to former state and local employees. While there is variation as to how employees in different occupations are clustered and the ways public pension systems are structured, the vast majority of the funds are set up as defined benefit (DB) plans: 84 percent of state and local government employees have access to DB plans.[3] Defined benefit systems promise a specified retirement benefit to be collected in the future, generally with minimal years of service and age requirements. The specified benefits frequently include cost-of-living adjustments (COLAs). In contrast, defined contribution (DC) plans accumulate funds for an employee throughout his or her tenure; upon retirement, the employee draws on the invested assets and bears the risk as what their level will be. Only three states—Alaska, Michigan, and Nebraska—have mandatory DC plans for some or all employees (Nebraska's plan is cash-balance).[4] In addition, most states have established voluntary supplemental DC plans that permit employees to take advantage of tax deferment of savings.[5]

Perhaps more than any other aspect of compensation, the structure of state and local pension funds has diverged greatly from private-sector retirement arrangements. Over the past two decades, the percentage of private-sector employees with DB retirement access declined from 32 percent to 21 percent. Many more employees are not offered retirement packages at all by their employers. In addition, state and local government employees receive a greater share of their compensation from benefits than private-sector workers. A 2010 employee compensation study from the Bureau of Labor Statistics showed that 8 percent of public employee annual compensation comes in the form of employer contributions to retirement benefits, with 0.8 percent of total compensation tied to defined contribution plans. For private industry employees, 3.5 percent of compensation is from retirement and savings, with 2 percent of total compensation tied to defined contribution plans.[6]

Public employee retirement systems frequently offer more than retirement income benefits. Retirement benefits generally consist of both pension payments and retiree health benefits.[7] According to a 2006 Workforce Economics Inc. survey, all states but Nebraska offer supplemental health coverage to Medicare, and many states pay the employee premiums. All states provide health coverage to retirees that are not eligible for Medicare. While there is greater variability in access to other types of benefits, retirees are frequently offered prescription drug coverage, dental and vision insurance, and life and disability insurance.[8]

Table 30.1 offers an overview of state and local pension plans since 1995 by using data from the 2008 Census Bureau. There are 2,550 different plans covering nineteen million active and inactive members. In 2008, almost eight million beneficiaries received pension benefits from the plans. The major demographic and financial issues now facing the funds become clear when looking at rudimentary data about the systems. The ratio of active to inactive members (aggregated in the table) has declined from about 5:1 in 1995 to 3.3:1 in 2008. In addition, the annual expenditures of the funds on benefits have increased greatly, from $58 billion to $175 billion.

Public Pension Plan History

Pension benefits have been offered to selected groups of public employees since the mid-1800s. In fact, officers of the Continental Army threatened desertion in 1783 over the failure to honor salary and pension promises.[9] Civilian pensions lagged behind military benefits, though cities and municipalities were leaders in

Table 30.1 Overview of state and local pension plans

	1995	2000	2005	2008
Number of Plans	2,284	2,209	2,656	2,550
State	*200*	*218*	*222*	*218*
Local	*2,084*	*1,991*	*2,434*	*2,332*
Membership (in Millions)	14.7	16.8	18.1	19.1
State	*13.1*	*15.1*	*16.2*	*17.2*
Local	*1.7*	*1.8*	*1.8*	*1.9*
Beneficiaries Receiving Payments (in Millions)	5.0	6.3	7.0	7.7
State	*4.0*	*4.8*	*5.8*	*6.6*
Local	*1.0*	*1.5*	*1.1*	*1.1*
Assets (in $ Billions)	1,118.3	2,168.6	2,675.1	3,190.1
State	*913.9*	*1,798.0*	*2,226.4*	*2,663.8*
Local	*204.4*	*370.7*	*448.8*	*526.3*
Expenditures (in $ Billions)	63.6	100.5	156.1	193.8
State	*49.5*	*79.5*	*126.8*	*157.4*
Local	*14.1*	*21.0*	*29.3*	*36.4*

Source: US Census Bureau (2008).

offering benefits to police and fire workers (though many of the plans were self-funded).[10] Massachusetts created the first state fund for general employees in 1911, and eventually state-sponsored teachers' funds became the norm due to the states' control over school spending in the local school districts. Public-sector coverage became more widespread after the passage of the Federal Employees Retirement Act in 1920.

After 1920, the structure of public pension funds began to form into its modern shape. Employees and employers contributed, sometimes evenly, to a retirement fund. When Social Security was first created in 1935, the federal government was constitutionally blocked from taxing state and local governments, thus state and local employees were excluded from Social Security coverage. This was changed in 1950 when special coverage provisions for public employees were added to the Social Security Act (SSA) for those public employee systems that chose to join.[11] Not all plan sponsors voluntarily joined Social Security, resulting in divergent benefit and contribution schedules for the plans paying taxes to and covered by the SSA. About three quarters of state and local employees were covered by Social Security as of 1998, according to the House Ways and Means Committee.

Federal legislation continued to play a major role in state and local pension fund development following the Employee Retirement Income Security Act of 1974 (ERISA). ERISA applied only to private employee pension plans, and it outlined eligibility requirements and fiduciary responsibilities. Many public systems adopted ERISA's "prudent man" standard for management of the fund, and they then expanded their investment horizons outside of the state and Treasury debt instruments to include a broader range of investment securities. As greater portions of the funds' assets were invested in equities, the pension systems' financial health fluctuated with the stock market. This move to equities was beneficial through much of the 1980s to 2000s, though market downturns during these decades were increasingly problematic for fund finances. Nonetheless, as table 30.1 illustrates, public pension fund assets grew exponentially between 1995 and 2008 from $1.1 trillion to $3.2 trillion; assets in nongovernment securities, in particular, grew from $744 billion to $2.4 trillion.

Pension Plan Funding

Retirement benefits, particularly defined benefit systems, require managed funding to set aside sufficient assets to pay future promises for services provided today. Plan sponsors and (often) employees together contribute a portion of the employee compensation to a pension fund, ensuring proper funding of current and future obligations. The contributions are determined by actuarial calculations of the benefit liability, a discounted sum of future benefits given assumptions about retirement age, final salary levels, and longevity. The accumulated fund is invested, with the investment returns adding to the assets. Pension systems are considered fully funded if the fund assets on hand, given the multitude of assumptions regarding future performance, can cover the liability. There is no federal requirement for full funding by state and local government funds and these funds frequently fall below 100 percent funding ratios. In this case, some combination of higher future contributions and increased investment returns will be needed to cover the shortfall.

Pension systems provide audited reports with funding information. The Government Accounting Standards Board (GASB) established the financial accounting standards for pension funds, and over the past three decades they have issued statements updating the accepted reporting principles. Public employee retirement systems have standardized rules for reporting benefit liabilities. However, other critical aspects of the actuarial valuations are open to pension assumptions. In 1994, the GASB issued Statements 25 and 27, establishing more complete standards for reporting pension liabilities.[12] The rate at which future liabilities are discounted, along with expected increases in salary and price levels vary between funds, can have a large influence on the actuarially determined contribution rates.[13]

The variation in the actuarial assumptions can make it difficult to evaluate the financial health of the different systems. Nonetheless, the funding ratio is typically used as a marker of plan finances and is frequently compared across funds.

According to the Pew Center on the States, the states' systems were 84 percent funded in 2010, corresponding to $2.3 trillion in assets compared with $2.8 trillion in long-term liabilities. The Public Fund survey, which covers state and local plans, reported an average 80.9 percent actuarial funding ratio for fiscal year (FY) 2009. Other estimates place the funding ratio lower, at 78 percent.[14] Table 30.2 includes data on funding ratios and displays other key elements of plan funding.

It is worth noting that public pension plans should not necessarily aim for full funding (100 percent) all of the time. Considering the risk profiles of plan sponsors and the amortization period that is available to fund benefits, there could be financial benefits to a lower funding ratio.[15] Indeed, a 2008 GAO report found that many officials knowledgeable in and dealing with state and local government funds believed that 80 percent funding ratios are adequate.[16]

Eligibility and Rules

Public pension systems are frequently divided by occupation. This differentiation allows the pension funds to address the needs of different workers. For example, safety workers frequently retire early and are particularly interested in disability and survivor benefits. In addition, public employees make different contributions. Data from the Public Fund Survey, which includes 126 state

Table 30.2 Public pension plan funding, investments, and structure

	General	Teacher	Safety	Local	Total
Total Assets ($ Billions)	1118.5	536.1	132.3	324.3	2111.2
Equities	51.8%	54.2%	50.5%	49.1%	51.70%
Domestic Fixed Income	27.9%	24.8%	28.2%	32.7%	28.10%
International Fixed Income	1.1%	1.1%	1.1%	0.2%	0.90%
Real Estate	6.2%	7.1%	8.9%	5.5%	6.40%
Alternatives	9.0%	9.2%	8.6%	7.1%	8.70%
Cash	2.4%	2.1%	2.7%	3.2%	2.50%
Other	1.7%	1.8%	0.0%	2.2%	1.70%
Funding Ratio	78.9	76.5	91.3	85.4	80.6
Benefit Multiplier	1.98%	2.05%	2.19%	1.94%	2.03%
Contributions					
Employee	5.34%	7.34%	5.94%	6.14%	6.43%
Employer	12.15%	11.14%	6.24%	12.29%	11.31%

Source: Public Fund Survey; data generally dated from June 30, 2009, actuarial valuations.

and local plans with combined assets totaling $2.1 trillion covering 13.3 million members, show that public safety workers frequently have different eligibility requirements than other government employees. While it is difficult to average the rules for normal retirement ages and years of service across plans, police and fire employee retirement plans frequently have normal retirement ages of fifty after twenty years of service, significantly lower than other employees. In general employee plans, where public safety, general, and/or teacher employees are covered by the same systems, the retirement rules and benefit provisions may vary by occupation.

In contrast to most private-sector DB plans, most public employees make contributions to the pension fund, often calculated as a percentage of current salary.[17] It is notable that many state and local employee DB contributions are made to qualified funds and are not counted as taxable income.[18] When the benefits are eventually paid to the retirees, these amounts plus interest are subject to federal taxes. According to the Public Fund Survey, employees contribute an average of 6.4 percent of salary. Safety workers typically contribute more, to compensate for their shorter service requirement. Plan sponsors are meant to contribute the amount necessary to cover new benefit obligations accrued over the period and a portion of any unfunded liability. In 2009, the public employer contribution to DB plans averaged 11.3 percent (see table 30.2).

Generally, benefits are calculated using DB benefit formulas, which could include the number of years worked, a final average salary, and a multiplier. Again, it is difficult to compare multipliers across plans, but the Public Fund Survey shows that flat plans typically average between 1.6 percent to 2.5 percent of salary (many systems used a tiered multiplier). Final average salaries used as a basis of benefits are calculated considering the last one to five years of service. According to 2006 Census reports, a total of $151.7 billion in pension benefits were given to about seven million state and local government retirees and/or beneficiaries, or an average of $1,700 in monthly retirement benefits.[19] As a rough comparison, the average monthly Social Security benefit is $1,070.[20]

In addition to monthly retirement benefits specified by formulas, most plans offer COLAs. These benefit augmentations can be automatic, based on a percentage of the Consumer Price Index or another inflation measure. COLAs can also be ad hoc, generally as approved by the sponsor's legislature. Less frequently, adjustments are flat, as in the case of the Arkansas Public Employee Retirement System, which has an automatic 3 percent compounded postretirement benefit increase provision.[21]

Given the difficulty in general labor markets and government budgeting following the financial crisis, there has been a fair amount of focus on comparing public and private compensation, with a particular examination of benefits.[22] The Bureau of Labor Statistics (BLS) estimates average hourly total compensation in 2009 for state and local employees as $39.66, and retirement benefits contribute about $3.16 per hour to that figure. For private-sector employees, average hourly compensation is $27.42, with $0.94 per hour coming from retirement benefits.

Other studies show that public-sector retirement benefits are nearly twice as high as private-sector DB retirement benefits.[23]

However, figures like this can be misleading, and good comparisons are, in fact, not straightforward. For one thing, state and local employees are typically older and better educated than the general pool of private-sector workers, which naturally skews public-sector employee compensation higher.[24] In addition, the Internal Revenue Code or other federal legislation does not treat plans comparably. Private plans are regulated by ERISA and their defined benefits are partly insured by the federal Pension Benefit Guaranty Corporation. Many public-sector systems, on the other hand, qualify under the 414(h) (2) section of the tax code, which allow the annual contributions to be pretax, before federal and municipal taxes are deducted. Because private pension plans do not qualify, private employees typically do not contribute comparable percentages of salary (as these contributions would come after tax).[25] Benefits often make up a larger portion of total employee compensation among state and local workers, which may inflate the differences between public and private employees.[26] Finally, some public-sector retirement benefits are higher in order to compensate for the lack of Social Security.

Another difference between public and private employees concerns the benefit protections afforded to public-sector retirees. Legal protections for promised public employee DB retirement income have ranged from constitutional provisions to legislated rules as to status of the pension trust fund and the benefit guarantee.[27] Employees generally have legal rights to accrued benefits, and they have successfully defended these rights in court.[28] In fact, it can be difficult to change benefit structures for current employees, even if they are not yet vested. For this reason, benefit changes are frequently applicable only to new hires. As will be discussed later in the chapter, a number of states are testing these legal protections by changing retirement benefits, COLAs, and service requirements for current employees, as a response to the financial and budget crises.

Pension Investments

With $3.2 trillion in assets, the state and local pension systems in the United States are among the largest institutional investors in the world. Asset growth has been pronounced in recent decades. In 1985, public pension system assets totaled about $400 billion. By 1993, pension system assets totaled about $1 trillion, and this amount has tripled over the following seventeen years. Much of this increase is due in part to a reallocation of asset investments into equities. As shown in table 30.2, about half of system assets were invested in equities in FY 2009, up from 22 percent in 1980. In addition to equities, investments in alternative investments, private equity, and hedge funds have also grown. Historically, the shift out of fixed-income securities into equities and various alternatives is associated with higher risks and returns. The best illustrations of this change are the effects of the 2008 financial crisis on pension fund assets, where a total of $1 trillion in equity asset value was lost between October 2007 and October 2008.[29]

The shift in asset allocation over the past two decades followed the effective end of "legal lists," where states restricted the asset classes and geographic diversification of assets to limit risk and control investment strategies. Up through the 1990s, a number of states (Indiana, South Carolina, and West Virginia) had prohibited investment in equities, particularly international securities. Many states still limit the allocation of assets into equities to mitigate risk.[30] As investment policy shifted and the assumed rate of return increased, the investment objectives grew more ambitious. Target portfolios now reflect high presumed investment returns with large equity asset allocation; the resulting rate assumptions have implications for pension accounting that are discussed in the next section.

Recent Research

There are a number of issues that have demanded particular attention from practitioners and academics regarding state and local government employee retirement systems. Having introduced the basic structure and current state of public pension funds, this section will expand key areas of research on issues affecting systems in the last decade. These include other postemployment benefits, variability of actuarial methods, pension governance, and defined contribution plans.

Other Postemployment Benefits

Many pension systems offer retirees benefits in addition to retirement income. The most substantial nonpension benefit in terms of cost is health-care benefits, but it can also include dental, life, disability, and long-term care insurance.[31] Health-care benefits include pre-Medicare health insurance and Medicare-eligible health benefits. In 2004, the GASB approved GASB Statements 43 and 45, which established standards for measuring and reporting postemployment benefits other than pensions. The rules in the statements were phased in over two years from 2006 to 2008 for different-sized pension systems and were meant to augment the 1994 GASB statements that excluded health benefits. Public-sector employers are required to provide actuarial statements for other postemployment benefits (OPEB) that conform to Generally Accepted Accounting Principles (GAAP), reporting the unfunded liability and the required contribution necessary to achieve full funding with amortization.[32] Importantly, the GASB standards do not require funding the liability; plans can (continue to) use pay-as-you-go financing, although governments that set up a trust fund to prefund obligations can use a higher discount rate for OPEB actuarial calculations.[33]

The actuarial statements conforming to the new standards reveal a total of $530 billion in unfunded OPEB liabilities for states and up to another $500 billion for local systems.[34] Other studies estimate the total unfunded OPEB liability as substantially higher, up to $1.6 trillion.[35] There are wide disparities in the relative sizes of the states' OPEB liabilities. For example, New Jersey, Hawaii, and Connecticut have OPEB-unfunded liabilities larger than their state budgets, while a number of states' liabilities are less than 2 percent of their annual state budgets. Typically, states that pay a greater portion of health-care insurance premiums have larger unfunded liabilities.[36] In 2008, fourteen states required retirees to pay the full cost of their insurance premiums, while fourteen states paid the entire premium amounts.[37] The rest required retirees to pay a portion of the premiums. At the same time, current annual OPEB payments are smaller than retirement benefits, even for states with large per capita obligations.

Future payments, however, may not be as manageable. According to the GAO, public-sector employers have not prefunded OPEBs because health-care costs were less expensive when the benefits were first offered and the health-care inflation rate is less predictable.[38] In addition to fundamental budgeting concerns, this liability can affect credit ratings. To date, the governments' plan of action to deal with the OPEB obligations appears more important than the actual size of the liability for ratings. The three major rating agencies issued public statements in 2007 indicating that they will consider a "government's approach to addressing its OPEB liability, as well as the magnitude of the liability itself, into its analysis of the main credit factors."[39]

Pay-as-you-go financing will eventually become a significant annual expense for many jurisdictions. As the actuarially determined unfunded liability is now required on accounting statements, governments may consider prefunding their OPEB obligations. There are a number of options for prefunding the liability and reducing the future obligations. First, it is important to note that most OPEB benefits do not have the same legal protections as retirement pension benefits; employers can change the level of health-care benefits and the premiums required by beneficiaries. Changing the nature of the OPEBs is not mutually exclusive to considering ways to prefund the obligations. Much like retirement benefits, paying for unfunded liabilities would entail establishing a fund and contributing payments to cover current annual payments and the amortized future costs. Eleven states already had OPEB trust funds in 2001; many more states were planning to or had already created funds following the new GASB rules.[40] The trust funds can be separate from a pension fund, or pooled together for administration. Like pension funds, OPEB funds will enable employers to issue OPEB bonds, which offer the same benefits and costs as pension obligation bonds. There are a number of types of OPEB trusts that qualify under different sections of the Internal Revenue Code.

Actuarial Assumptions

As the preceding sections make clear, much of the discussion about public pension funds regards their funding status. The method of calculating a system's liability and the value of its assets is therefore a critical dimension of pension funds. Plans generally project future service and calculate contribution rates as a percentage of salary. Plan assets are smoothed for investment gains and losses over a period of time to avoid sharp changes in funding levels. In addition, state and local plans specify their discount rates for liabilities in the actuarial reports, and most state plans use a rate between 7 percent and 8.5 percent. This practice has generated a lot of criticism, and federal legislation prevents private DB pension plans from using such high discount rates.[41] In practice, however, GASB Statement 25 proposes that the discount rate "should be based on an estimated long-term investment yield for the plan, with consideration given to the nature and mix of current and expected plan investment."[42] According to a study by Callan Associates, public pension plans had a median annual return of 9.3 percent over the past twenty-five years, but over the past ten years the return has dropped to 3.9 percent.[43] The long-term return on investment corresponds to the plans' high discount rates, and, based on historical performance, the return on investment follows the GASB guidelines.

However, there appears to be a divide between academics and practitioners regarding the appropriate standards for discount rates.[44] Generally, economists consider the riskiness of the liabilities when determining the rate, rather than the expected growth of the dedicated asset funds.[45] Considering the protections that many promised retirement benefits enjoy and the relative safety of future earned benefits, the pension fund liabilities themselves will not likely experience significant variation. The appropriate discount rate is akin to the risk-free interest rate. Because this rate is considerably lower than the investment rate returns of 8 percent or so, the newly calculated liability is significantly higher than financial statements would suggest. Recent studies estimate the unfunded liabilities of state-sponsored plans at $3.23 trillion when using Treasury bills and bond yields.[46] Furthermore, linking liability discount rates with investment yields encourages risky investment strategies that have a higher average return but greater risk.

There are practical reasons why the actuarial discount rate tends to be considerably higher than the risk-free interest rate. As outlined by Peskin, a higher discount rate can reduce costs and risks for plan sponsors and taxpayers.[47] Because lower rates would raise the actuarially required contribution (ARC), the plan's assets would rise; surplus assets (over 100 percent of funding) tend to be used to increase benefits. Given the "stickiness" of budgets, the relative bargaining positions of plan members and the temporal disconnect between those officials promising higher benefits and those in office when the expense is due, it may be in sponsors' best interests to underfund liabilities. Of course, there are also the immediate benefits to employers: using a higher discount rate, or increasing the riskiness of investment assets, decreases the required contribution as a percentage of salary.

Using the projected investment return as the discount rate has other, more legitimate benefits. A study comparing conventional actuarial methods to "market-value liability" methods suggests that using risk-free bond yields would result in erratic contribution levels.[48] Given the reality of the budgeting process, these fluctuations are less practical than the smoothed contribution rates as a percentage of payroll.

There have been recent efforts to standardize the discount rates that different public pension funds have used to calculate their liabilities. In the fall and winter of 2010, the GASB solicited comments to a proposal that has been considered for about four years. The GASB had thought about standardizing rules for the discount rate assumptions. One possibility for the discount rate included a blend of the presumed investment returns and the risk-free rate, where only the unfunded liability would need to be discounted at the lower rate. In February 2011, Republican congressmen introduced legislation that would require state and local pension funds to use only the risk-free rate when discounting liabilities.

There are a number of other important economic assumptions required for valuation, including the future rate of inflation (especially important for plans that have automatic COLAs) and the health-care inflation rate. In addition, demographic assumptions are not all standardized across programs; these include retirement ages, mortality and disability rates, and terminations. There are also different actuarial cost methods that are approved by the GASB; these include normal entry age, projected unit credit, aggregate cost, and frozen entry age.[49] According to the Public Fund Survey, in FY 2008 the vast majority of plans were using the normal entry age cost method (65 percent of plans), followed by the projected unit credit method (13 percent). The normal entry age method uses an individual participant's age when he or she becomes a member, then calculates pension benefits based on future expected salary. The benefit costs are calculated as a dollar amount or percentage of the individual's salary from entry through retirement. In contrast, the projected unit cost uses the individual's projected final salary to estimate benefits and adjusts for the number of service years credited. The major difference between the two methods is the rate at which liabilities accrue; normal costs are considerably higher in early years when using the normal entry age cost method.

Contribution Rate Volatility

Given the range of actuarial methods and assumptions, combined with the volatility in market forces and rates of inflation, it is perhaps not surprising that plan sponsors have experienced a fair amount of instability in their annual contributions (employee contributions are generally more steady). This volatility can be difficult for state and local governments' budget planning. The problem is exacerbated when plan sponsors do not contribute the full actuarially required contribution or when they take a "pension holiday" by not making any contributions; this not only increases the unfunded liability, but also ensures that contribution rates will vary even more in future years.

Figure 30.1 shows the average contribution rates that state and local governments paid between 1997 and 2008, with data compiled from the Pew Center on the States and the Public Fund Survey. Contributions decreased between 1997 and 2002, despite declining investment returns and the 2001 recession, which resulted in negative returns. Contribution rates then increased through FY 2004, at one point going up by almost 30 percent in one year. Since then, employer contribution rates have cycled up and down. In many cases, the changes in rates have reflected the (lagged) movements of the equity markets. Pension holidays, however, have taken place in both fiscally flush and tight years. For example, New Jersey reduced state and local contributions to the state system by $1.5 billion in the mid-1990s while the fund earned high returns from its increasingly equity-based investments. Following the financial collapse in 2008, the state legislated a "pension holiday," allowing sponsors to skip contributions in 2009 to ease other budget pressures.[50] While New Jersey is a prominent case, it is estimated that only half of the state pension plans contributed the full ARC in 2006.[51] The average percentage of ARC actually paid by state plans since 1997 is shown in figure 30.1.

There are a number of strategies available to smooth contribution rates. First, plans can control the growth of fundamental aspects of retirement liabilities,

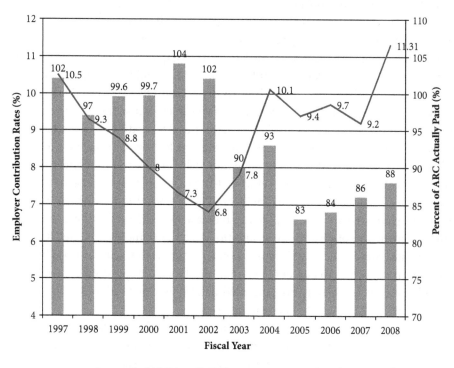

Figure 30.1 Average contribution rates and average percentage of ARC paid
Source: 1997–2000 Pew Center on the States; 2001-2008 Public Fund Survey.

notably benefit increases. This would address an underlying source of growth that contributes to volatility in employer contribution rates. On the actuarial side, plans can examine methods to smooth the ARC. Investment returns can be smoothed over a five-year period to absorb both losses and rapid gains to the fund assets. Indeed, some systems had contribution rates equal to zero during the high-return years of the 1990s.[52] The smoothing period can be extended, though this will likewise understate funding problems during bear markets. More substantially, systems can shift the distribution of fund assets to less volatile asset classes, and away from equities and alternative investments. While this would result in lower average returns, thereby increasing the overall employer contribution rate, it would make the ARC more regular and create less budgeting havoc. Funds can set contribution rate floors or mandate a fixed rate, thereby trading off flexibility for continuity—and possibly creating other funding issues.[53] Of course, these strategies are less meaningful if plan sponsors do not regularly pay the ARC and, instead, budget what is fiscally available.

Defined Contribution

As mentioned earlier in the chapter, the DB structure of most public-sector retirement plans is markedly different than in the private sector, which increasingly offers DC plans if a retirement benefit is available at all. While the implications of shifting more state and local government retirement plans to a DC structure will be discussed along with other reforms later in the chapter, this section focuses primarily on the structural elements and current status of public-sector DC plans.

DC plans eliminate much funding risk. Because DB plans promise specific benefits to retirees, plan sponsors must appropriately value their future benefit obligations and assets used to fund those liabilities. Depending on the strength of the retirement promise—and typically in state and local governments, the promised benefits are on par with general obligation debt, or risk-free for beneficiaries—state and local governments must set aside funds for beneficiary benefits through contributions, investment returns, or debt. The temporal issues inherent in any retirement plan predisposes DB plans to increase benefits that will accrue in the future, frequently in place of more straightforward salary increases. The DC structure alleviates these issues for the plan sponsor by shifting the focus from benefits to be paid in the future to current contributions. Once the specified contributions are made every year, there is no unfunded liability and the risk of future performance of the fund is borne by the beneficiaries.

While plan sponsors obviate their funding risk with DC plans, beneficiaries bear greater risk in their retirement income. DC plan members do not have specified retirement benefits, but rather they must live off of the assets accumulated during employment. Because assets can grow at variable rates, and there is uncertainty as to how long retirees will require income, beneficiaries in DC plans carry much of the risks that are pooled up to the plan sponsor in comparable DB plans. In addition, the smaller asset pools belonging to plan members do not benefit from some economies of scale in investment opportunities and administration costs. One of the few benefits of DC plans to plan members is the portability of benefits to other state programs or beyond the systems altogether.[54]

It is not surprising, therefore, that public-sector employees have largely resisted shifting from DB to DC plans. While a number of states offer DC plans as supplements to DB plans, only Alaska, Nebraska, and Michigan have mandatory DC plans for general state employees hired after a certain date; Utah will offer a choice between a DC and hybrid plan for new employees beginning in 2011.[55] Six other states offer optional DC plans for general employees and teachers, and many states offer DC plans to higher education faculty. In 2002, the governor of California proposed shifting new California public employees into a DC plan. The resulting protests and considerable political backlash ended this possibility. Five other states have hybrid plans, which combine elements of DC and DB plans; generally, employee contributions go to DC accounts while employer contributions go to a DB fund.

Pension Fund Governance and Activism

In many respects, public pension fund administration is a subset of normal human resource management that occurs in every jurisdiction. The unique nature of the retirement system fund, however, creates political and economic elements unlike any other program involving public employee compensation and taxpayer funds. Legislatures and public employee retirement system administrators, typically led by a governing board, have a responsibility to plan beneficiaries expecting to receive retirement benefits while mitigating risk to the general taxpaying population through prudent management of benefit promises, contributions, and asset investment. While these populations are not necessarily at odds, governing boards frequently correspond to a mix of constituents in order to ensure competing interests are represented. Trustees on the governing board are elected by plan members (active and retired), appointed by the employer, or serve ex officio; the latter members are frequently elected to their positions in a general election. According to a 2006 National Education Association survey, the median governing board has nine trustees, and plan members elect half of the trustees.[56]

How much governance influences key aspects of the retirement plans is a matter for debate. In a series of papers, Hsin and Mitchell found that the number of trustees elected by plan members is correlated with high employer contribution rates and lower funding levels.[57] Other papers have shown mixed effects.[58] The expected correlation is unclear. On one hand, elected trustees may be interested in expanding benefits and COLAs, which increases liabilities, and may not be particularly knowledgeable about investment strategies. On the other hand, beneficiary representatives have a vested stake in the financial health of the funds, have a strong incumbency rate, and are less interested in special interest-group politics involved in a general election.

From a practical standpoint, more important than the quantitative analysis of pension fund governance influence is the recent attention paid to the economic and political connections of legislators, ex officio trustees, unions, and funding policies. The *New York Times* has run over three dozen articles—many placed on the front page—that deal specifically with retirement benefits and/or pension funds and political relationships over the past five years (this count does not include articles dealing primarily with pension fund finances). A 2009 study similarly indicated that "prior to the 1980s, state and local pensions were not on the radar screen of interest groups," but the visibility of special interest group activity has grown since then.[59] While the governance structure has remained constant in a number of the pension plans in recent decades, the political economy surrounding the plans is shifting, with public employee unions gaining strength relative to private unions and the discrepancy between public and private compensation growing.

A related issue involves public pension fund activism. As investors, public pension plans are among the most active institutional investors in terms of proxy proposals, long-term ownership, and public attempts to influence corporate strategy.[60] The increase in ownership activism could be in part a consequence of the political factors in pension governance mentioned above; it is also a natural effect of the rising pension assets invested in corporate equities. As large, long-term shareholders, public pension plans can monitor corporate management to maximize investment return. Retirement systems may also be interested in social causes that are not necessarily related to maximizing long-term return, though these desires can be concurrent.[61]

Public pension plan activism has occurred in the form of shareholder proposals, director nominations, and informal communications with management.[62] A particularly prominent example is the California Public Employee Retirement System's (CALPERS) "Double Bottom Line" initiative that began in 2000. The initiative made investment decisions based on social, rather than financial, decisions by excluding firms in certain industries and those with poor labor rights records. In September 2010, the SEC passed a proposal granting proxy access to institutional investors with ownership profiles similar to public pension plans. The National Association of State Retirement Administrators (NASRA) and the major public pension plans supported wider proxy access in order to increase the shareholders' ability to nominate directors to corporate boards.

Pension fund activism can improve investment returns by restraining corporate management rent extraction from shareholders. However, limiting the investment portfolio or focusing on nonfinancial elements of securities can reduce the overall returns, in contrast to the prudent man standards governing most public pension fund boards. While it is hard to estimate whether public pension fund activism improves the fund value, there have been a few studies that investigate the effect of activism on equity values, which indirectly measures financial impact for the funds. The evidence is mixed. A study on the CALPERS "Double Bottom Line" program found that activism had a positive effect on share prices for targeted firms.[63] Other studies considering a broader sample of public pension fund ownership found an insignificant or negative effect of public pension fund activism on equity value.[64]

State and local government pension plans' interactions with corporations and the equity market go far beyond their influence on equity values. As substantial investors, public pension plans are very much affected by the markets. Given the financial downturns of the 2000s, there is additional scrutiny as to the degree of investment risk taken by funds run by trustees without substantial investment experience. Investment risk should vary with retirement horizons, the ratio of active to retired employees, and return assumptions. A look at the data, however, reveals that there is relatively little variation in the share of assets invested in risky securities (that is, in assets other than US government debt), and it is not correlated as expected to the variables mentioned.[65] Almost all state funds have 50–70 percent of their assets in equity; an average of 7.4 percent is invested in private placement equity. Wilshire Associates reported allocations into private placement equity as high as 21 percent. The financial crisis also highlighted fund investments in over-the-counter derivatives, exemplified by a local multidistrict Wisconsin teacher's fund that lost $200 million in collateralized debt obligations.[66] The cumulative impact of the financial crisis on pension fund assets is discussed in more detail in the next section.

THE IMPACT OF THE FINANCIAL CRISIS AND PATHS TO REFORM

As this chapter has made clear, a number of policy issues are facing state and local pension funds. There is no greater issue than the financial outlook of the DB plans; this matter is even more urgent following the financial crisis in 2007–2008 and the subsequent declines in equity values and in state and local governments' fiscal outlooks. The full extent of the crisis will be felt over the next few years as funds that smooth investment returns realize the decline in their assets. In addition, tight state and local budgets are squeezing annual contributions to the funds, exasperating the funding problems and threatening the ability to bridge the funding gap in the future. The sharp declines in assets and funding status have sparked reactions from plan sponsors, spurring some to attempt changes to promised benefits, shifts in investment allocation, and other reforms. It is worth noting, however, that many plans had structural underfunding issues before the crisis.

According to Census data, the largest one hundred public funds lost $835 billion of value in the recent recession, and as a result FY 2010 benefit payouts amounted to almost 8 percent of total fund assets. Through 2009, 58 percent of funds had funding ratios below 80 percent, a distribution not seen for fifteen years.[67] Optimistic economic scenarios estimate that the 2013 funding ratio to average 76 percent, assuming contribution rates remain steady.

Plan sponsors are responding to the financial crisis in a number of ways. States have enacted and proposed legislation to deal with their funding issues in 2010 and 2011.[68] According to the National Conference on State Legislatures, the proposals offered by state legislatures and governors in 2011 regarding state pension and health-care benefits are extensive. They include increasing employee contributions (fifteen states), reducing benefits or raising the retirement age for new employees (eleven states), and limiting pension "spiking" or artificial increases to final years' salary (six states). More radically, five states (Illinois, Kansas, Massachusetts, New Hampshire, and New Jersey) have proposals that would reduce benefits or increase the retirement age for existing employees. Proposals, of course, are not equivalent to legislation, but the activity in 2010 suggests that more legislatures are taking real steps toward reform. According to the National Conference on State Legislatures, nineteen states have enacted major changes to their plans since January 2010. Table 30.3 details some of the changes proposed in response to the financial crisis as well as general funding problems between 2009 and 2010. The actions can be grouped in three categories: changes to lower the future funding requirement, changes to increase the funding ratio, and changes to relieve current

Table 30.3 Public pension responses to the financial crisis, FY 2009–2010

Reform/Legislation	States
Benefits Reduction	AZ, CO, IA, IL, LA, MI, MN, MO, MS, NJ, NV, RI, SD, TX, UT, VA, VT
Employee Contribution Increase	CO, IA, LA, MI, MN, MO, MS, UT, VA, VT, WY
Employee Contribution Increase for Active Employees	CO, IA, MN, MS, VT, WY
Increasing Service/Retirement Age Requirement	AZ, CO, IL, MI, MO, MS, NV, NM, RI, TX, UT, VA, VT
Increase in Final Average Salary Period	AZ, IA, IL, LA, MI, NJ, VA
Reduced COLAs	CO, GA, IL, LA, MI, MN, NV, RI, SD, UT, VA
Reduced COLAs for Current Retirees	CO, MN, SD
Changes Away from DB Plans	MI, UT

Source: 2009 and 2010 NCSL Annual Report on State Pension Legislation.

funding requirements. A number of states have made benefits less generous, by either increasing service requirements or extending the final pay average period. Nine states (Vermont, Michigan, Colorado, Utah, Virginia, Illinois, Missouri, Mississippi, and Arizona) increased the retirement age and service requirements in 2010, and four states (New Jersey, Minnesota, Iowa, and Missouri) increased vesting requirements for 2011. Louisiana was the only state to lower requirements by decreasing the vesting period. Nine states have reduced benefits for early retirement outright; in Colorado, this change extends to active employees.

In the second category of legislative changes, ten states increased employee contributions in 2010—four of these states (Missouri, Utah, Virginia, and Wyoming) introduced employee contributions for the first time for current employees and future hires. Perhaps the most radical changes include reducing postretirement benefit increases (generally through COLAs). Eight states changed COLAs; in Minnesota, South Dakota, and Colorado these changes apply to current employees and retirees. Given the protections afforded to benefits, many of these decisions are being challenged in court.

States have also taken action to provide themselves with funding relief, through new pension obligation bonds (POBs), temporarily reducing employer contributions, and extending the amortization period in order to lower the ARC. Other states are changing demographic and economic assumptions. Washington delayed the adoption of new mortality tables and reduced the projected salary growth. New York State is lowering its discount rate from 8 percent to 7.5 percent; Utah and Pennsylvania made similar moves in 2008 and 2009, respectively. The use of POBs was attractive for states that legally could not put off contributions or borrow from the fund, or POBs were considered a prudent financial strategy to arbitrage future equity performance and provide spending relief. As with all arbitrage opportunities, timing and specifics of the issuers will have significant effects on the overall performance of POBs.[69]

Less formally, some states and local plan sponsors have deferred or reduced contribution payments for a temporary period. For example, Virginia delayed paying $620 million to its state retirement system for FY 2010. Governor Rell in Connecticut had also deferred payments to the pension plan and had proposed eliminating the pension benefit guarantee for future employees. California had seriously considered borrowing $2 billion from CALPERS, while the New York legislature agreed to allow the state and municipalities to borrow $6 billion from the pension fund in order to pay the required annual contributions.[70]

These latter moves represent short-term fixes. The legislative changes that reduce the growth of future funding needs and increase contributions from both plan sponsors and employees are more sustainable and address the structural funding problems. It is perhaps surprising that the recession and subsequent unfunded liability has not led to more proposals for fundamental changes to public pension structure. Only two states have enacted major changes to parts of their retirement systems. Utah will begin requiring employees to choose between a DC and a hybrid plan, and Michigan created a new hybrid plan for newly hired state teachers.

Substantially more states have committees looking into switching to DC plans, but to date there is no reform wave in pension structure. In part, this may be due to political realities. Many legislatures are cutting pay, jobs, and services; state representatives may not have the political appetite to tackle major changes in the public employee retirement structure. Surely, many elected officials observed the political fallout from the failed DC proposal in California in the early 2000s. Less radical structural changes, such as opening eligibility for Social Security in the 23 percent of systems that currently do not qualify for SSA, have similarly been absent in the recent two years.

In addition to dealing with retirement benefit liabilities, state and local governments are going to have to deal with the OPEB liabilities revealed since the passage of GASB Statements 43 and 45. Many states have shifted from pay-as-you-go plans to more strategic planning to pay for the estimated costs. Plan sponsors have issued OPEB bonds, borrowing to prefund the obligation. While this entails exchanging flexible liabilities for rigid interest debt, the new GASB standards include accounting rules that makes this option favorable. In addition, a number of states are proposing changes to their retiree health insurance plans over the next five years.[71] More than half of the states have increased cost sharing, in some cases requiring employee contributions for the first time. Five states have diminished health benefits for future retirees since 2004, and more retirees will probably face higher deductibles and co-pays. Because OPEB liabilities are so dependent on the rate of health-care inflation, sponsors will need to prefund growing costs; unfortunately, it appears that most state actuarial reports use a long-term medical inflation rate of about 5 percent, down from the 10–14 percent levels that have been the norm recently.[72] Even a 1 percent difference in the inflation assumptions can change the amount of the unfunded liability by 20 percent.

Looking Ahead

Surveying the landscape of issues facing state and local government employee retirement systems illuminates a number of policy ideas and concerns. On average, public pension funds are in trouble, and the unfunded liability will strain already tight public budgets as benefit obligations become due. Not all systems, however, are having difficulty. Any description of public pension fund reform must distinguish between those state and local government funds facing severe funding problems and those that have been responsibly managing their retirement systems. At the same time, it is wrong to claim that there is not a funding crisis in public pension funds or that there wasn't a crisis before the recent market declines.

For the plan sponsors with actuarial funding ratios over 90 percent following the decline in equity values in 2008, the current obligations require modest, but not inconsequential, adjustments to contributions, investments, and assumptions. Reforms could include a mix of the legislative moves taken in 2010 to improve the funding picture described above: using more realistic actuarial assumptions, setting contribution floors, reducing the generosity of benefit structures, and sharing costs with employees. Even these steps may not be sufficient in states that appear well funded at first glance. Utah offers a good example of a state that had responsibly funded its state plan, yet it faced looming increases in required contributions following the financial crisis. In 2008, Utah had a funding ratio of 96.5 percent but projected a 70.5 percent funding ratio by 2013. This was partly due to the 22 percent decline in the plan's asset value in 2008. When the state considered what the ARC would need to be, when given a discount rate of 7 percent, it found that contributions would have to rise by 75 percent. Eventually, Utah made the radical decision to close its DB plan to new employees and it offered a DC or hybrid plan choice.[73]

In those states facing severe underfunding—the list of such states varies over time, but it typically includes Connecticut, Illinois, Kansas, Kentucky, Massachusetts, New Jersey, Oklahoma, Rhode Island, and West Virginia—more dramatic reforms are necessary. Increasing employee contributions or extending the service requirement will not be sufficient to fill the unfunded gap, which reaches over 30 percent. State and local governments have relied heavily on investment returns to fund liabilities, and they did not pay the ARC in full; in New Jersey, strong equity performance in the late 1990s left the state system 106 percent funded, and in the following eight years, state contributions averaged less than half of the ARC.[74] States that are now in trouble have generally also offered more generous benefit terms in the 1990s through the early 2000s. Though there is less aggregate data available on increases in unconventional benefit costs, many states are concerned about the rate of retirees returning to work (double-dipping) and artificially high final salaries that increase the benefit base.[75]

What should reforms look like in states that have severe pension funding problems? First, governments must commit to assessing their pension obligations realistically, regardless of the GASB actuarial requirements that may result from new accounting rules or federal legislation. This means using a lower rate of return on investments to realistic levels to discount future benefits and realistic salary growth expectations. Plan sponsors do not have to choose between rates of 3 or 8 percent. Rather, there is a middle ground that reflects the expected return on a portfolio conservatively—and passively—invested in equities and alternative investments. For example, corporations use a discount rate of about 6 percent, reflecting the risk that corporations may go out of business. Governments will need to find an enforcement mechanism for paying the required pension contributions every year, in all market conditions. Laws or constitutional requirements can enforce this practice. In states with the legal room to increase employee contribution rates, employee rates must rise. Employee contribution rates can be set at a fraction of the sponsor's rate, raising employees' stakes in any change in benefits or asset management. Finally, governments should contain future benefit increases by tying them to higher employee contributions and/or requiring taxpayer approval, as has been implemented in San Francisco, for example.

All of the above reforms only concern the benefits promised to current employees and retirees. Future employees have no guarantees, and they are not an effective special-interest group. If the above reforms cannot be implemented in full, governments must admit that they cannot commit to acting as responsible stewards of employees' retirement security; these states should shift to hybrid or DC plans for new employees. While this change could affect future recruitment and retention, and is not necessary in all state and local governments, it is the fiscally responsible action. In addition, the 23 percent of plans that are currently not eligible for Social Security should apply for qualification.

In its recent 2010 report, the Pew Center on the States contended that part of the $1 trillion funding gap counts as "good news": the size of the unfunded liability has spurred calls for reform from policymakers across the country. Certainly, high-profile legislation in Wisconsin and Michigan regarding employee contributions to retirement pension and health funds in 2011 has increased public awareness about the issue and spurred new energy from both ends of the political spectrum to close the funding gaps. However, looking across the state and local pension plans in this country that are in the most serious financial trouble, there does not appear to be gathering momentum for the package of fundamental reforms highlighted above, and the most frequently invoked fix involves cutting benefits for future employees. In the midst of tight state and local budgets, legislatures must fund the steep losses in pension assets following the recession. At the same time, they must consider that their true natures, for better and worse, have in many cases led to generous and unfunded benefit increases, risky investments, and sloppy accounting. While raising funding ratios in the near-term, policymakers need to commit themselves in the long term to state and local governments' financial well-being.

NOTES

1 US Census Bureau (2008).
2 Novy-Marx and Rauh (2009), 3: 2; US Census Bureau (2008).
3 Wiatrowski (2009), 1.
4 Snell (2010), 1–3. Cash balance plans are similar to DB plans, in that employers bear the investment risk, but balances are expressed as a lump sum rather than a periodic payment.
5 GAO (2008), 5.
6 Bureau of Labor Statistics (2010).
7 GAO (2008), 5.
8 Ibid.
9 Stewart (2005), 85.
10 Clark, Craig, and Wilson (2003), 167. Self-funded plans are based on employee, not employer, contributions.
11 Clark, Craig, and Ahmed (2009), 239–271.
12 GAO (2007), 62.
13 Munnell, Haverstick, and Aubry (2008), 1–12.
14 Munnell, Aubry, and Quinby (2010), 4.
15 Ibid.
16 GAO (2008), 2.

17 Munnell and Soto (2007), 1.
18 GAO (2008), 10.
19 Ibid., 1.
20 Social Security Administration (2010), 1.
21 Peng (2008), 40.
22 Edwards (2010); Bender and Heywood (2010). Following a delayed budget vote in Wisconsin pertaining to public employee benefits in early 2011, there were numerous articles written about this issue.
23 The Pew Center on the States (2007), 12–14.
24 Bender and Heywood (2010).
25 GAO (2007), 8.
26 Bender and Heywood (2010).
27 GAO (2007), 19.
28 Brown and Wilcox (2009), 538–542.
29 Munnell, Aubry, and Muldoon (2008), 1.
30 Peng (2008).
31 Ibid.
32 Clark (2009), 5.
33 Peng (2008).
34 Clark (2009), 1.
35 Edwards and Gokhale (2006); Zion and Varshney (2007).
36 Clark (2009), 3.
37 Robinson et al. (2008), 3–11.
38 GAO (2008), 21.
39 Moran (2007), 13.
40 Wisniewski (2005).
41 Waring (2009), 32.
42 Brown and Wilcox (2009), 540.
43 Reilly (2010).
44 Brown and Wilcox (2009), 538.
45 Novy-Marx and Rauh (2009), 1.
46 Ibid.
47 Peskin (2001).
48 Jones, Murphy, and Zorn (2009), 1.
49 Peng (2008).
50 Benner (2009).
51 Barrett and Greene (2007), 1.
52 Young (2009), 75–85.
53 Ibid.
54 Fore (2001).
55 Snell (2010a).
56 Peng (2008).
57 Hsin and Mitchell (2010).
58 Munnell, Haverstick, and Aubry (2008).
59 Almeida, Kenneally, and Madland (2009).
60 Johnson and Greening (1999); Qui (2003); Romano (1993).
61 Barber (2009), 271–294.
62 David, Bloom, and Hillman (2007), 1.
63 Barber (2009).

64 Woidtke (2002).

65 Lucas and Zeldes (2009), 16.

66 Duhigg and Dougherty (2008).

67 Munnell, Aubry, and Quinby (2010).

68 Snell (2010b, 2011).

69 Munnell et al. (2010), 3.

70 Hakim (2010).

71 Kearney et al. (2009).

72 Clark (2009), 8.

73 Liljenquist (2010).

74 It is worth noting that New Jersey is also involved in what could be a harbinger of future pension issues with the Securities and Exchange Commission (SEC). In August, New Jersey reached a settlement with the SEC over a charge that the state had fraudulently marketed municipal bonds by misrepresenting their pension liability. The fraud charge was filed following the creation of an SEC unit dedicated to investigating pension funds and municipal securities.

75 A number of pension systems allow retirees earning pension income to return to work, thus earning a salary and retirement income at the same time ("double-dipping"). Because retirement benefits are based on the employee's salary during the final years of employment, it is possible to increase the pension benefit by "spiking" salaries during the final years of work.

References

Almeida, B., Kenneally, K., and Madland, D. (2009). "The New Intersection on the Road to Retirement: Public Pensions, Economics, Perceptions, Politics, and Interest Groups." In *The Future of Public Employee Retirement Systems*, edited by Olivia Mitchell and Gary Anderson. New York: Oxford University Press. 294.

Barber, B. M. (2009). "Pension Fund Activism: The Double-Edged Sword." In *The Future of Public Employee Retirement Systems*, edited by Olivia Mitchell and Gary Anderson. New York: Oxford University Press. 271.

Barrett, K., and Greene, R. (2007). "The $3 Trillion Challenge." *Governing* 21(1): 26–32.

Bender, K., and Heywood, J. (2010, April). "Out of Balance? Comparing Public and Private Sector Compensation over 20 Years." Center for State and Local Government Excellence.

Benner, K. (2009, May 12). "The Public Pension Bomb." *CNNMoney.com*. Retrieved September 25, 2010, from http://money.cnn.com/2009/05/12/news/economy/benner_pension.fortune/index.htm.

Brown, J. R., and Wilcox, D. W. (2009). "Discounting State and Local Pension Liabilities." *American Economic Review* 99(2): 538–542.

Bureau of Labor Statistics. (2010, June). "Employer Costs for Employee Compensation— June 2010." US Department of Labor.

Clark, R. L. (2009). "Will Public Sector Retiree Health Benefit Plans Survive? Economic and Policy Implications of Unfunded Liabilities." *American Economic Review* 99(2): 533–537.

Clark, R. L., Craig, L. A., and Ahmed, N. (2009). "The Evolution of Public Sector Pension Plans in the United States." In *The Future of Public Employee Retirement Systems*, edited by Olivia Mitchell and Gary Anderson. New York: Oxford University Press. 239–271.

Clark, R. L., Craig, L. A., and Wilson, J. W. (2003). *A History of Public Sector Pensions in the United States.* Philadelphia: University of Pennsylvania Press.

David, P., Bloom, M., and Hillman, A. J. (2007). "Investor Activism, Managerial Responsiveness, and Corporate Social Performance." *Strategic Management Journal* 28(1): 91–100.

Duhigg, Charles, and Carter Dougherty (2008, November 1). "From Midwest to M.T.A., Pain from Global Gamble," *New York Times.* http://www.nytimes.com/2008/11/02/business/02global.html

Edwards, C. (2010, January). "Employee Compensation in State and Local Governments." Cato Institute.

Edwards, C., and Gokhale, J. (2006). "Unfunded State and Local Health Costs: $1.4 Trillion." *Cato Institute Tax and Budget Bulletin* 40.

Fore, D. (2001). "Going Private in the Public Sector: The Transition from Defined Benefit to Defined Contribution Pension Plans." In *Pensions in the Public Sector,* edited by Olivia S. Mitchell and Edwin C. Hustead. Philadelphia: University of Pennsylvania Press.

GAO (2007, September). "State and Local Government Retiree Benefits: Current Status of Benefit Structures, Protections and Fiscal Outlook for Funding Future Costs." Government Accountability Office.

GAO (2008, January). "State and Local Government Retiree Benefits: Current Funded Status of Pension and Health Benefits." Government Accountability Office.

Hakim, D. (2010, June 11). "State Plan Makes Fund Both Borrower and Lender." *New York Times:* A1.

Hsin, P. L., and Mitchell, O. (2010). "The Political Economy of Public Pensions: Pension Funding, Governance, and Fiscal Stress." *Revista de Analisis Economico–Economic Analysis Review* 9(1): 151.

Johnson, R. A., and Greening, D. W. (1999). "The Effects of Corporate Governance and Institutional Ownership Types on Corporate Social Performance." *Academy of Management Journal* 42(5): 564–576.

Jones, N. L., Murphy, B. B., and Zorn, P. (2009, May). "Actuarial Methods and Public Pension Funding Objectives: An Empirical Examination." *Public Pension Finance Symposium* Vol. 2.

Kearney, R. C., Clark, R. L., Coggburn, J. D., Daley, D., and Robinson, C. (2009, July). "At a Crossroads: The Financing and Future of Health Benefits for State and Local Government Retirees." Center for State and Local Government Excellence.

Liljenquist, D. (2010, July 27). "Pension Crisis: The 2010 Utah Response." PowerPoint presentation at the NCSL 2010 Legislative Summit, Louisville, Kentucky. Retrieved from http://www.ncsl.org/?tabid=21105.

Lucas, D. J., and Zeldes, S. P. (2009). "How Should Public Pension Plans Invest?" *American Economic Review* 99(2): 527–532.

Moran, M. (2007, Summer). "The Trillion Dollar Question: What Is Your GASB Number?" Goldman Sachs Global Markets Institute.

Munnell, A., Aubry, J. P., and Muldoon, D. (2008). "The Financial Crisis and State/Local Defined Benefit Plans." *Issues in Brief:* 8–19.

Munnell, A. H., Aubry, J. P., and Quinby, L. (2010). "The Funding of State and Local Pensions: 2009–2013." *Issues in Brief.*

Munnell, A. H., Calabrese, T., Monk, A., and Aubry, J. P. (2010). "Pension Obligation Bonds: Financial Crisis Exposes Risks." Center for Retirement Research at Boston College.

Munnell, A. H., Haverstick, K., and Aubry, J. P. (2008). "Why Does Funding Status Vary among State and Local Plans?" *Boston College Center for Retirement Research Brief.*

Munnell, A. H., and Soto, M. (2007). "State and Local Pensions Are Different from Private Plans." Center for Retirement Research at Boston College.

Novy-Marx, Robert, and Joshua D. Rauh (2009). "The Liabilities and Risks of State-Sponsored Pension Plans." *Journal of Economic Perspectives* 23(4): 191–210.

Peng, J. (2008). *State and Local Pension Fund Management.* CRC Press.

Peskin, Michael. (2001). "Asset/Liability Management in the Public Sector." In *Pensions in the Public Sector,* edited by Olivia S. Mitchell and Edwin C. Hustead. Philadelphia: University of Pennsylvania Press. 195-217.

Pew Center on the States. (2007). "Promise with a Price: Public Sector Retirement Benefits." Pew Center on the States.

Qui, L. (2003). "Public Pension Fund Activism and M&A Activity." Yale School of Management, International Center of Finance.

Reilly, D. (2010, September 18). "Pension Gaps Loom Larger." *Wall Street Journal.*

Robinson, C., Kearney, R., Clark, R., Daley, D., and Coggburn, J. (2008, September). "Retiree Health Plans: A National Assessment." Center for State and Local Government Excellence.

Romano, R. (1993). "Public Pension Fund Activism in Corporate Governance Reconsidered." *Columbia Law Review* 93(795): 801–804.

Snell, R. (2010a, June). "State Defined Contribution and Hybrid Pension Plans." National Conference of State Legislatures.

Snell, R. (2010b, September 1). "Pensions and Retirement Plan Enactments in 2010 State Legislatures." National Conference of State Legislatures.

Snell, R. (2011, March 10). "Selected 2011 State Pension Reform Proposals." National Conference of State Legislatures.

Social Security Administration. (2010, August). "Monthly Statistical Snapshot, August 2010." SSA Research, Statistics and Policy Analysis. Retrieved from http://www.ssa.gov/policy/docs/quickfacts/stat_snapshot/.

Stewart, R. E. (2005). *American Military History: The United States Army and the Forging of a Nation, 1775–1917.* American Military History Vol. 1. Washington, DC: United States Army Center of Military History.

US Census Bureau. (2008). "Finances of Selected State and Local Government Employee Retirement Systems." Retrieved from http://www.census.gov/govs/retire/.

Waring, M. B. (2009, May). "A Pension Rosetta Stone: Reconciling Actuarial Science and Pension Accounting with Economic Values." *Public Pension Finance Symposium, Society of Actuaries,* Vol. 4.

Wiatrowski, W. (2009). "The Structure of State and Local Government Retirement Benefits, 2008." Bureau of Labor Statistics. Retrieved from http://www.bls.gov/opub/cwc/cm20090218aro1p1.htm.

Wisniewski, S. C. (2005). "Potential State Government Practices Impact of the New GASB Accounting Standard for Retiree Health Benefits." *Public Budgeting & Finance* 25(1): 104–118.

Woidtke, T. (2002). "Agents Watching Agents? Evidence from Pension Fund Ownership and Firm Value." *Journal of Financial Economics* 63(1): 99–131.

Young, P. (2009). "Public Pensions and State and Local Budgets: Can Contribution Rate Cyclicality Be Better Managed?" In *The Future of Public Employee Retirement Systems,* edited by Olivia Mitchell and Gary Anderson. New York: Oxford University Press. 75-85.

Zion, D., and Varshney, A. (2007). "You Dropped a Bomb on Me, GASB." Credit Suisse.

PART IV

LOOKING AHEAD

Reforming and Restructuring

CHAPTER 31

ACCOMPLISHING STATE BUDGET POLICY AND PROCESS REFORMS

IRIS J. LAV

STATES and localities pursue a myriad of less-than-optimal tax and budget policies, most of which have been discussed thoroughly over the past two or three decades. Many of these dysfunctions are rooted in policies adopted in the middle of the last century and were never updated as the world around them had changed. They are not the policies one would choose if one were starting a totally new state—from scratch—in the twenty-first century. But starting over is a mere fantasy. And so, unfortunately, is the idea that state budget problems will be solved by radically restructuring state policies.

Despite the hackneyed label for states of being called "laboratories of democracy," state budget policy—particularly state-tax policy—has been profoundly conservative, in the sense of being resistant to change, for a very long time.[1] With a couple of exceptions, such as Connecticut's adoption of an income tax two decades ago, changes enacted by states over the past twenty-five years have largely been quite modest and incremental. Given this history, it is unlikely that current dysfunctions will be remedied by sweeping reform. I would argue that, to be politically viable, solutions to state problems in the foreseeable future have to build on and reform existing policies. Large disruptions to those policies or radical changes in direction have to be kept to a minimum as policies are adjusted, or voters will not accept the changes.

Reform is necessary to allow the maintenance of at least the current level of programs and services states and localities provide, which cannot be supported over time under current revenue policies. There is strong evidence, despite a lot of rhetoric to the contrary, that people want their services and will vote to maintain them when given choices and adequate information to understand the choices. Colorado-like TABOR tax and expenditure limitations have been rejected in every state in which they were proposed between 2006 and 2009, both by more than twenty legislatures in which it was seriously considered and on the ballots of Maine, Nebraska, Oregon, and Washington. Oregon voters approved a large tax increase on the ballot in 2009 rather than experience major service cuts. And polling frequently shows that vague desires to cut government services overall quickly crumble when specific service cuts in education, health, public safety, or other areas are mentioned. People need and value the services that states and localities provide. And while the election season of 2010 suggests that people value their services but don't want to pay for them – the "free lunch" syndrome – it remains to be seen if this is a passing phenomenon or a fundamental change. Because a "free lunch" is not possible, it is likely that people will return to being willing to pay for the services they value.

State and local fiscal problems that urgently need to be addressed to achieve the goal of maintaining services fall into two broad categories: cyclical and structural. Cyclical problems result in a major part from forces outside of the jurisdiction; a recession or natural disaster will cause revenue to decline and service needs to rise, creating deficits that have to be closed under the balanced-budget requirements of most jurisdictions. Structural problems result from the internal policies and practices of the jurisdiction. In particular, most states have revenue systems that grow more slowly than is necessary to maintain their existing level of services—a situation known as a "structural deficit." Obviously, states have more control over fixing the structural problems to address long-term adequacy, and these problems will be the primary focus of this chapter.[2] Both policy changes and budget process changes that could alleviate structural deficits, and to some degree cyclical problems, will be considered.

The policy changes necessary to fix state structural problems are well known in the public finance community. They include extending sales taxes to include services and remote sales, enacting or improving progressive income taxes, and maintaining flexible property taxes. Some of these changes are supported by experts and policymakers over a wide spectrum of political persuasions; others are more controversial. Nevertheless, there is less need to develop new policy approaches than there is to find new ways of achieving the known solutions to the problems. All too often, changes in the tax structure such as an expansion of the sales tax to include more services or changes in income-tax brackets or rates are introduced in the heat of a legislative session focused on closing a deficit. When these proposals are defeated, as they most often are, the defeat is used as evidence that the change cannot be accomplished. Even when the reforms are proposed in a governor's budget released before a legislative session, the opposition often has a chance to get out its negative message before the proponents can muster support for the proposal. It is relatively easy to villainize a proposed change when adequate public preparation has not been conducted.

A better approach is needed if change is to occur. Key elements of a better approach would include designing simple reforms that the public can understand, preparing the ground with affected constituencies before making a public proposal, using modern opinion research and a range of communications techniques to help design proposed reforms and educate the public, and investigating the possibility of coordinated reforms across states in a region.

In addition, the role of the budget process in permitting or preventing the development of structural deficits is often overlooked. There are, of course, those who use the existence of structural deficits or other budget problems as a springboard to propose extreme budget-process changes such as limits on the growth of revenues or expenditures (tax and expenditure limitations, or TELs) such as Colorado's TABOR. Rigid, formulaic restrictions do not solve the problem, however; they just codify existing problems, prevent reforms, and limit a state's flexibility to meet residents' needs. Reforms such as multiyear budgeting based on current services (baselines) could facilitate public understanding and scrutiny of the implications of policymakers' proposals. Light would be shed on phased-in, multiyear tax cuts or program expansions, which can create structural problems. Moreover, the adoption at the state level of a mechanism similar to the federal pay-as-you-go policy known as PAYGO—in which tax reductions or program increases over the baseline would have to be offset by other tax or program changes to create budget neutrality—could help ensure that new structural deficits are not created by policy changes.

PART I: STRUCTURAL PROBLEMS AND POTENTIAL SOLUTIONS

Most states have one overarching structural problem, sometimes with many manifestations. The basic structural problem is that state revenues do not grow sufficiently from year to year to finance the growth of expenditures, assuming no statutory changes in either revenues or expenditures. Theoretically, this basic problem could be solved either by lowering the rate of growth of expenditures or by increasing the rate of growth of revenues.

Expenditures

In practice, however, states and localities do not have as much control over the rate of growth of their expenditures as they seem to have. The two biggest areas of state expenditures are education and health care. Nearly two-thirds of state general-fund spending (excluding spending from federal funds, restricted funds, or bond proceeds) is for elementary and secondary education (34.5 percent), higher education (11.3 percent) and Medicaid (16.3 percent). States also have other health expenditures for public employee and retiree health insurance, and for prisoners.[3] Local governments spend about 35 percent of their own source funds on K–12 education.[4]

Educating children is by labor-intensive. Most parents don't want their children taught by computers in the classroom; they demand well-qualified teachers and classrooms that allow the teachers to teach effectively. While in a former era highly qualified women and members of minorities became teachers because they had few other career opportunities, attracting qualified teachers now requires paying competitive compensation. For this and a variety of other reasons, the cost of K–12 education for states and localities has grown faster than the economy over the past twenty years, rising from 3.58 percent of GDP in 1988 to 4.02 percent of GDP in 2008.[5] As the population ages and the ratio of potential teachers to school-aged children declines, these costs may have to rise still more rather than less rapidly.[6] In addition, there is evidence that as half the teachers become eligible for retirement in the next decade, the quality of teachers will decline unless salaries are increased substantially. A McKinsey report estimates that it would cost $30 billion to increase the percentage of new teachers drawn from the top third of their college classes from the current very low 14 percent to 68 percent.[7] (The report also projects large economic gains if this were to be done.) Thus, in most states, there is limited potential for lowering the growth rate in education costs (absent declining enrollments) without sacrificing quality.[8]

Health-care costs are even more problematic. The rate of growth of health-care costs is a national phenomenon, not something that can be controlled to any significant degree by any one state. Health-care cost growth affects the cost of Medicaid, the cost of health insurance for current public-sector workers and retirees, and a variety of other health-related programs that states and localities operate. Current projections by the Government Accountability Office (GAO) show that state and local health-care costs are growing more rapidly than GDP over the foreseeable future.[9] While this rate of growth is unsustainable for both federal and state budgets, it is a larger problem for state budgets because annual state revenue growth generally is lower than federal revenue growth. The GAO has projected that state and local revenue growth will lag behind GDP growth, as it characteristically has, while health-care cost growth will exceed GDP growth, meaning that health-related costs will absorb ever larger portions of state and local budgets under current projections. Controlling health-care costs—preventing this scenario from being played out—will require national solutions, but it is highly unlikely that the rate of health-care cost growth will drop below the rate of state revenue growth in the near future.

There may be the potential for states to enact some efficiency measures in education and health, but the effect of such changes on long-term growth trends generally is modest. For example, there is a current focus on ways to reduce the compensation of teachers and other employees through changes in pensions and retiree health insurance coverage. Changes in pensions would primarily affect costs twenty to thirty years from now, given the protections for the pensions of current employees that are embedded in state constitutions and case law. Moreover, many states have underfunded pension plans, and any reductions in benefits is likely to be offset by the need for increased contributions to reach full funding over the next thirty years.[10] By contrast, some changes in retiree health benefits, which generally do not have such legal protections, could affect nearer-term costs and cost growth as the baby boomers retire.

There are also other, smaller areas of the budget such as corrections and economic development for which there is the potential to reduce costs and perhaps cost growth. While important to do so, these areas are not a large enough percentage of state budgets to make more than a quite small difference in long-term growth trends.

While it is difficult for states to control the underlying, ongoing growth in costs in some of the largest areas of the budget, states do have control over the way the path of budget growth is changed by legislation. Governors and legislatures have to agree on proposed statutory policy changes that increase expenditures or the rate of growth of expenditures—the expansion of programs or the enactment of new programs. As will be discussed below in the section on the budget process, an important part of preventing structural deficits from developing or worsening is ensuring that sufficient revenue will be available to fund the long-term cost of any newly created expenditure. Or to put it another way, (a) additional revenues need to be available to fund the additional expenditures through the foreseeable future, and (b) the inherent growth rate of the revenues expected to support the additional expenditures should be equal to the inherent growth rate of the expenditures. A classic example of legislation that violates this principle is the expansion of eligibility for a health-care program that is "paid for" by an increase in the cigarette tax. (Cigarette taxes have a slow growth rate or even decline over time because they are levied on a per-pack basis and the rate of smoking is declining. Health-care costs are growing substantially, creating a mismatch of expenditure and revenue growth.) The PAYGO proposal described below is an attempt to suggest a mechanism that could require close consideration of how new programs will be financed over the long term.

Revenues

Because of the difficulty of controlling some of the major cost drivers of expenditures, it is important to consider ways to raise the rate of growth of state and local revenues and the potential paths to achieving that goal. In any given state and for any particular base level of services that legislators or voters in that state may have chosen, the growth rate of revenue is the key issue.

Sales Taxes

Some of the best-known problems of state and local revenues are in sales taxes. Two sets of problems are particularly important. First, most states have excessively narrow sales-tax bases. Sales taxes were designed in an era in which the sales of services played little role in the economy, and most states exclude most sales of services from taxation. According to the Federation of Tax Administrators, a majority of states apply their sales taxes to less than one-third of the 168 potentially taxable services that the FTA includes in its survey of state practices.[11] Five of the forty-five states with sales taxes impose them on fewer than twenty services. Second, all states with sales taxes are losing large amounts of revenue on purchases their residents make through the Internet and catalogs because of the Supreme Court decisions of 1967 and 1992[12] that bar states from requiring sellers without "nexus"—traditionally defined as a physical presence in the state—to collect and remit the taxes. These two problems require very different types of solutions.

Expanding the Sales Tax to Services

The problems caused by omitting services from the sales-tax base became widely recognized in the 1980s; ever since that time, various states have tried to address the problem. Two unsuccessful attempts early on in Florida and Massachusetts to expand their sales-tax bases to include most or all services—where legislation was enacted and subsequently repealed before taking effect—arguably poisoned the well and made states shy away from trying to solve the problem in one comprehensive reform effort.

In theory, other states could have learned from the political "mistakes" of Florida and Massachusetts and then moved forward. The Florida legislation, passed in 1986 to take effect in 1987, eliminated (sunset) exemptions for all services including professional, insurance, and personal services. A variety of factors led to the repeal of the expansion, most notably the decision to use a formula to determine what portion of services purchased by multistate companies would be taxed by Florida. This resulted in the taxation of advertising revenue based on the amount of advertising that appeared in Florida media, and this arrangement motivated advertisers to use their resources to encourage popular opposition to the tax. The tax became caught up in demagoguery as well as a political campaign before accurate information about the tax was widely disseminated. James Francis, the director of research in the Florida Department of Revenue at the time, identified three lessons for other states wanting to go down this road:

1. The piecemeal approach to service taxation is not the appropriate method because [if it is done piecemeal] the politically toughest but most important measure will likely never be taken;
2. A method must be found to make the self-serving, antitax posture of the media obvious for what it is. One approach would be to tax advertising sales in a separate bill, after a general-service tax has been implemented

and accepted by the public; another would be to tax advertising in a different—yet constitutional—manner, such as by denying the deductibility of advertising and promotional expenses for income-tax purposes; and

3. It must be recognized from the outset that the pro-tax coalition must proceed on a consensus basis both before and after enactment.

In other words, Francis stressed the importance of a full expansion, but he also warned proponents to expect opposition and look for ways to neutralize it. He also stressed the importance of building an effective and cohesive coalition that advocates for the change.[13]

The Massachusetts experience yields related lessons. In July 1990 Massachusetts enacted an expansion to many different enumerated services, including some but not all categories of professional services. The decision to move ahead with the expansion was made in the late spring, so only a quick set of hearings was held before enactment. Like Florida, Massachusetts sought to apportion services consumed by multistate businesses using formulas that attempted to reflect the share consumed in Massachusetts. Both the definitions of the professional services to be taxed and the apportionment effort came immediately under attack. As in Florida, the expansion became an issue in a political campaign, with the end result that the sales tax on services was repealed two days after it went into effect.[14]

Despite the potential for following Francis's advice and the lessons of Massachusetts to overcome the obstacles to a full expansion to services, no state enacted such a broad expansion after the Florida and Massachusetts attempts. States did not follow Francis's first point, which most felt was not good advice, but instead they have attempted piecemeal or incremental expansions to services—with mixed results. A few were modestly successful. In 2006, New Jersey added roughly a dozen services to its sales-tax base. At the time the state said this would yield more than $400 million in new revenue each year, a 5 percent increase in sales-tax receipts. Arkansas added about fifteen services in 2004 that boosted sales-tax revenue by about 1 percent. By contrast, a revenue-neutral expansion enacted in 2009 in Maine that would have boosted sales-tax revenue about 4.4 percent in exchange for lower income-tax rates was repealed the subsequent year through a "people's veto" ballot measure. (See the discussion below.) Recent expansions in Maryland and Michigan ran into similar opposition and had to be rolled back. And other efforts have been stopped in their tracks by organized opposition to taxing specific services included in expansion packages, such as bowling alleys and yoga instruction.

The popular opposition to expanding sales taxes to encompass services—especially those services primarily purchased by households—is somewhat surprising. The sales tax is routinely found to be the best-liked of all state and local taxes and sales tax-rate increases typically engender far less opposition than other forms of tax increases. The opposition to taxation of services seems to be a bit outside of rational considerations. Why would, for example, relatively well-off residents of the District of Columbia who for many years have paid sales tax on dry cleaning services vehemently object to paying sales taxes on the cost of their yoga lessons?

The obstacles to expanding the sales-tax base are political rather than substantive, and it is critical to find ways to overcome these obstacles. The sales tax must be modernized to reflect today's economy if it is to survive as one of the two major sources of revenue for states and as an important revenue source for localities in many states. It also has to be modernized to prevent the decline of sales-tax revenue from substantially lagging economic growth. But it has become obvious that an expansion to cover services will not sell itself to the public or businesses. It is not enough to write an expansion into a governor's budget or into a piece of legislation. There are a number of ways that an incremental, yet broad expansion of the sales tax to services—as well as other reforms—could be given a greater chance for success. Using more modern and intense efforts to bring about reform will be discussed below in the section "Modern Methods for Modernization."

If a straight expansion to encompass more services is not possible, there are some "back-door" methods that in some states could be more appealing, albeit less desirable, than an expansion of the retail sales tax. Services could be taxed at the business level instead of the consumer level through a gross receipts tax or a value-added tax (VAT) that operates as a primary business tax or an alternative corporate income tax. And if the federal government adopts a VAT that ultimately is collected at the retail level, as a variety of experts have suggested will be necessary to sustain federal obligations for the long term (although politically difficult to enact), states would likely have an opportunity to piggyback on the broad base of a federal VAT either in place of or in addition to their own sales taxes.[15]

Taxing Remote Sales

The other major sales-tax problem is the inability of states to tax most remote sales, that is, sales that are made to state residents through the Internet or from a catalog from sellers that do not have nexus (a physical presence) in the state. The tax on such purchases that legally is due is known as the "use tax"—a tax on purchases from out of state that are brought into the state for use. While use taxes are legally due from state residents who purchase goods in this way, they are extremely hard to collect effectively from individuals. Estimates suggest that states and localities will lose about $23 billion in 2012 from the inability to collect these taxes.[16]

There are two streams of effort moving to remedy this problem that costs states billions of dollars in lost revenue each year. One is the Simplified Sales Tax Project (SSTP). It was started in 1999 to encourage states to simplify and harmonize their sales taxes, because the two Supreme Court decisions that excused remote sellers from the duty to collect the taxes (made in 1967 and 1992, before the Internet age) cited the complexity of the many rates and bases around the country as the major reason that states could not require remote retailers to collect and remit the tax. By early 2010, twenty states were full members of the project: they have enacted sales-tax revisions that meet the project's criteria, and the committee of states is working through a number of thorny issues that have deterred other states, including large states like California, Florida, New York, and Texas, from joining.[17] The premise of the project is that simplification will either encourage remote retailers to voluntarily collect and remit taxes, or it will result in Congress enacting a law that overrides the Supreme Court decision. Legislation to that effect was introduced in Congress in 2010, but prospects for enactment are uncertain.

Another thread is also moving forward on taxing remote sales. A number of states are taking individual action to compel payment of the taxes. In 2008, New York State enacted a law that expands the interpretation of "nexus" to include companies that use in-state businesses—affiliates—to promote sales and thus increase the number of companies required to collect and remit sales taxes.[18] Rhode Island and North Carolina enacted similar laws in 2009. In 2010, Colorado enacted a law that requires all remote sellers that do not collect and remit sales taxes to notify their Colorado customers that they may owe sales tax on their purchases, and also to tell the state each year the total dollar value of items purchased by each purchaser—which should result in far greater payment of use taxes owed by residents. The lists provided to Colorado by the online retailers would theoretically allow the state to send bills to their residents for the taxes due.

With efforts moving forward on so many fronts, it is likely that this problem ultimately will be solved. Because the volume of remote sales is likely to continue growing each year for the foreseeable future, the states' ability to collect these taxes is important to maintaining a revenue growth rate that can sustain necessary expenditures.

Personal Income Tax

The personal income tax is important because maintaining a strong income tax is the best way a state can improve the overall growth of its revenues to match the necessary growth of its expenditures. State personal income taxes, no matter what their design, generally grow more rapidly relative to economic growth in good economic times than sales and excise taxes or other types of state revenues. Progressive income taxes, with graduated rates, grow more strongly than flat-rate or nearly flat-rate taxes.

Some theorists and policymakers are concerned because a progressive income tax both grows more rapidly in good economic times and declines more rapidly during recessions (although the rate of decline arguably depends on what types of income are hardest hit in a recession: wages or investment income). While a decline during a recession is an issue, it can be handled outside of the income tax itself by maintaining more adequate rainy-day funds and other measures. Without a strong income tax, most states will continue to experience total revenues that grow more slowly than the economy, be susceptible to developing structural deficits, and will not be able to meet obligations in health care, education, and other areas in the future.

The prospects for incremental reform of the personal income tax are mixed. While there is pressure to improve income taxes in states that have them and adopt them in states that do not, there also is pressure from the political right to eliminate state income taxes and rely entirely on consumption taxes to support what inevitably would have to be a much lower level of services.[19] Nevertheless, reform seems likely in some areas.

One potential area for reform of the income tax is curbing tax expenditures. In most states, personal income tax revenue, and potentially revenue growth, is eroded by tax expenditures of varying kinds that rarely are reexamined. Although most states produce tax-expenditure reports or budgets, most also are far from comprehensive and have lacked the information needed by policymakers to make informed judgments about whether tax expenditures are worthwhile. During the Great Recession, states showed renewed interest in examining the value of their tax expenditures. The large federal deficits are also provoking interest in this issue at the federal level; because most states key their personal income-tax provisions to the federal code, reductions of federal tax expenditures could also improve state revenues. One area of state personal income-tax expenditures that merits particular scrutiny is the tendency of states to provide large nonmeans-tested tax breaks to retirees and senior citizens; as the population ages, these will become increasingly unaffordable. Another is the myriad of tax breaks of unexamined and doubtful efficacy that states provide to businesses, some of which are structured as entities that pay personal rather than corporate income tax. Other tax expenditures are peculiar to a small number of states, such as allowing a deduction for federal taxes paid.

States lacking income taxes may or may not consider enacting them within the next decade. There are nine states that lack a broad personal income tax, including the very large states of Florida and Texas as well as Alaska, New Hampshire, Nevada, South Dakota, Tennessee (which has a tax on dividend and interest income only), Washington, and Wyoming. While some of these states are likely never to adopt an income tax, the odds are reasonable that at least New Hampshire and Washington will do so sometime in the next decade. These states are having significant difficulty managing their responsibilities absent an income tax and some important forces within these states are discussing the possibility of adopting an income tax of some sort. In November 2010, citizens in Washington State voted down an initiative that would have created an income tax solely levied on high earners, with rates ranging from 5 percent on residents with incomes exceeding $200,000 for individuals and $400,000 for joint filers to 9 percent on individuals with incomes above $500,000 and joint filers with incomes above $1 million.[20] Nevertheless, it is possible, and perhaps likely, that a proposal with more modest rates and the ability to deduct certain items could gain acceptance in the not-too-distant future.

Another potential area is rate reform. There are seven other states that levy their income tax at a flat rate, and several additional states in which the value of the brackets has eroded over so many years that the impact of their tax resembles a flat-rate tax. Improving the rate structure would seem to be an easy way to increase the growth of revenues, but like expanding the sales tax to services it has been difficult to achieve. Such a change would require a constitutional amendment in some flat-rate states such as Illinois and Pennsylvania. The long-standing fiscal problems in Illinois that were exacerbated and became all too obvious during the Great Recession suggest that Illinois may ultimately change its tax structure in this way, despite the difficulty of amending its constitution. Connecticut changed its nearly flat-rate structure to a graduated tax in 2009, suggesting that such a change may be possible in some states—but again this would require the lead time and intense preparation and education activities described below.

Property Tax

Property-tax revenue is less tied to the rate of economic growth than is the sales tax or the personal income tax. In normal economic times, the growth rate of property-tax revenue depends on the rate of growth of the value of existing homes, the rate of growth of new home construction and purchases, and a property-tax rate that is set either locally or statewide. The assessed value of property and/or the tax rate is subject to various constraints in different states, as discussed below. Where flexible, rates applied to assessed values may be set at levels that offset either significant increases or decreases in property valuation, depending on the amounts needed to balance the jurisdiction's budget, thereby controlling the rate of growth in property-tax revenues. In addition, housing values may or may not decline during economic downturns. In the 2001 recession, housing values remained stable or were growing. But housing values dropped precipitously in the 2008–2010 recession, especially in states such as Arizona, Nevada, and Florida, in which a particularly large real estate bubble burst. In other words, the property tax reacts to a different set of variables than economically sensitive taxes such as the sales tax or the income tax.

In theory, property-tax revenues could always grow in tandem with economic growth, assuming that property values are growing with the economy, *if* tax rates could always be adjusted to allow that to occur. A significant number of states, however, have constitutional or statutory limits on assessment growth, on tax rates, or on annual growth of property-tax revenues. Many if not most of these limits were adopted following periods in which there was rapid growth in property values and rates were not adjusted downward; therefore, property-tax revenues—as well as homeowners' property-tax bills—grew rapidly. Now, however, many limits hold the growth in property-tax revenues below the rate of growth of the economy in normal years, making it very difficult to maintain schools and other local government services that rely on property taxes for support. For example, limits in at least seven states allow for only 3 percent nominal annual growth or less in property-tax revenue, and other states have related limits on assessments or rates that may produce the same result.[21]

In states that do not already have limits, and in states in which limits allow for property-tax revenue to grow reasonably along with economic growth, it is important to avoid adoption of limits or tightening of existing limits. Arguably, the best way to do that is to provide a property-tax relief regime that prevents homeowners' and renters' property-tax bills from becoming unaffordable; it is particularly important to protect groups that are highly sensitive to property taxes, such as low-income residents and elderly residents on fixed incomes.

States have experimented over time with a lot of different types of property-tax relief schemes. There are homestead exemptions that exempt the first specified amount of a property's value from taxation for owner-occupied homes; since these are first dollar exemptions, they do not address the growth in property taxes. There are also a variety of state-financed property-tax credits. Some of these require homeowners (and sometimes renters) to apply for the credit on a standalone form, while others may be claimed on the state income-tax forms. Each of these methods has a drawback. The participation rate is relatively low if residents are required to submit a special form to claim their credit. For example, a 2006 analysis found that only 41 percent of eligible Maine residents applied for the state's circuit breaker when the state required a special form. Participation tends to be higher for credits claimed as part of the income tax, but residents often do not associate the income-tax credit with their property-tax bills but rather view it as a reduction in their income taxes.[22]

Vermont is one state that has moved toward solving this conundrum. As a number of states do, Vermont provides "circuit-breaker" property-tax relief, that is, property-tax relief that is related to the income of the homeowner or renter. In its purest form, a circuit breaker prevents property tax from exceeding a specified percentage of a homeowner's or a renter's income; this arguably is the most effective form of property-tax relief.[23] In Vermont, homeowners may be eligible for property-tax relief if their income is below $97,000 a year, depending on a home's value. (Renters with incomes below $47,000 may claim rebates.) A special form must be filed to claim the credit, which may be filed either with state income-tax forms or separate from them. What is unique about Vermont's program, however, is that the credit is paid to the town in which the homeowner lives, rather than to the homeowner. The town then directly reduces the homeowner's property-tax bill by the amount of the credit. The intention is to ensure that residents connect the property-tax relief with their property-tax bill, then reliably reap the benefit. Although there has been no formal evaluation, the general sense is that the connection has been strengthened in residents' perceptions. This is a promising direction other states may want to consider.

EXPERIENCE WITH REFORM: KEEP IT SIMPLE AND BE PREPARED

There have been very few successful state-tax reforms in recent years that have addressed the issues of modernization of tax systems and improving revenue growth rates to alleviate structural deficits. Some that have been enacted, such as in Louisiana and Maine, have subsequently been partially or fully repealed. And a number of efforts in other states have failed. Some important lessons may be drawn from these experiences.

Louisiana. In November 2002 Louisiana voters approved the "Stelly Plan" that eliminated sales taxes on necessities (groceries, prescription drugs, utilities) and raised the individual income-tax rates. The plan was designed to be "revenue neutral," but it was understood that the income tax in Louisiana grows more rapidly than other taxes relative to economic growth, and so long-term improvement in revenue growth was expected. Despite the voter adoption of the Stelly Plan (by a narrow margin) and estimates that it would leave unchanged or reduce the taxes of 87 percent of single filers, 92 percent of heads of households, and 74 percent of joint filers, it remained something of an unpopular "whipping boy" in the state's political process. Because it is difficult for individuals to perceive how much less sales tax they pay in a year but they can see the increase in their income-tax liability, many middle-class taxpayers were convinced (probably erroneously) that their taxes had increased under Stelly. In 2008, the Stelly income-tax increases were repealed.

Maine. In June 2009 the Maine Legislature passed a bill, which the governor signed, that would change the state's income-tax, sales-tax, and property-tax relief program. As in Louisiana, this reform was designed to be revenue neutral. But in something of a mirror image of Louisiana's Stelly, the Maine plan lowered income taxes for what was claimed to be 95.6 percent of Maine households, and the state made up the funds by extending the sales tax to more services such as installation, repair, and maintenance services; transportation and courier services; personal property services; and amusement, entertainment, and recreation services. It also increased the sales tax on prepared food, lodging, and car rentals—an effort to "export" a portion of the increased taxes to tourists. Estimates suggest that the combined result would have been a tax reduction for 87 percent of the state's households.[24] Nevertheless, sufficient petition signatures were submitted to put a "People's Veto" of this reform on the June 2010 ballot. The reform was repealed by an approximately 60 percent to 40 percent vote without ever having taken effect. Those who urged repeal argued that it was a tax increase on average-income Mainers and a tax cut for the wealthy—a position not supported by the analysis but which evidently sounded plausible for a tax-reform plan that had several moving pieces.

Other States. The efforts of Florida, Massachusetts, Michigan, and Maryland to expand the sales-tax base to services were mentioned above. In addition, it should be noted that there was a small trend between 2006 and 2008 to "swap" property taxes for sales taxes; Idaho, South Carolina, and Texas increased their state sales taxes in order to eliminate some property taxes that supported schools. Michigan did a similar, more complicated swap in 1993. Far from helping to solve structural deficit problems, however, the state revenues in each case fell short of the amount of property taxes foregone—in part because of the slower growth of sales-tax revenues (and in Michigan's case also cigarette-tax revenues) than the property tax it replaced. Nevertheless, the swaps were acceptable to the voters (who were told future revenues would be adequate). The ability to make such swaps may just reflect the preference of voters for sales taxes over property taxes and not have much bearing on the ability to reform taxes in ways that reduce or eliminate structural deficits.

Modern Methods for Modernization

Just as revenue systems around the country need to be modernized to be viable in the twenty-first century, perhaps so do the methods by which reforms are proposed and supported. The following are five principles that could improve the prospects for reforms to succeed.

First, it is important to keep the reform simple. As much as policy analysts or state officials might understand that it is good policy to trade-off certain types of taxes for others, the electorate is very skeptical of that approach (with the exception of swapping sales taxes for property taxes, of which the public should be more suspicious than they are). As in the examples above, the evidence suggests that people tend to believe that a complicated reform cannot be good for them—no matter what the facts of the situation are.

Second, reform efforts should be better prepared and less ad hoc. It has been all too common for a legislature to slip in a modest expansion of the sales-tax base in the final effort to fill a revenue gap and balance a budget. This usually triggers an immediate attack by the affected industries and thus allows negative publicity to get ahead of clear public explanations of the need for the policy, discussion of alternatives, or negotiations about what is or is not included. This occurred in the District of Columbia in 2010, when a huge outcry by yoga studio patrons—arguably people who could afford an extra dollar per lesson—derailed an end-of-budget negotiations proposal.[25] Policymakers should attempt to get buy-in from affected industries, if possible, before introducing related legislation.

Third, reform efforts should be treated more like a campaign. Reform efforts could begin with focus groups and polling to determine, for example, how people perceive expansions to services, what bothers them, what services are "out of bounds" in the minds of the electorate, and how best to discuss such issues. For example, the equity arguments of taxing lawn services as well as lawn mowers seem obvious to policymakers; it is important to know why it often is rejected by a public that generally approves of sales taxes. Similarly, modern, sophisticated opinion research could help policymakers understand why people who often claim on polls to be in favor of more heavily taxing higher-income households balk when it comes to actually changing the state income tax—and what combination of provisions could make a change acceptable. It has not been successful for policy wonks or politicians to sit in a room and design a reform. Care also needs to be taken to ensure that catering to constituencies doesn't undermine the purpose of the reform.

Fourth, once a plan is tested and decided on, the campaign mode needs to continue through the public education and messaging phase. A reform needs to be more than just incorporated into a proposed executive budget or piece of legislation. A prior step would be to communicate the proposal and its justification through all the modern ways people receive information, give feedback, and participate in discussions—including social media.

Campaign tactics are much more likely to be used in states in which the reform is being proposed as a ballot measure. The recent failure of the TABOR proposals in the four states in which they reached the ballot (twice in Maine, and once each in Nebraska, Oregon, and Washington) and the successful tax increase on the ballot in Oregon suggest that using solid campaign tactics can make the difference. But using the campaign mode should not be limited just to ballot measures. It is also important to use these methods if the legislature is going to be considering a reform—something that almost never is done.

It is particularly important to use a campaign to connect the revenues under consideration to the services that people value. Often this is a connection that is difficult for the electorate to grasp, and public education can play an important role in highlighting it. Interestingly, in the successful "people's veto" of Maine's enacted reform (described above), the forces attempting to preserve the reform framed it as a tax cut rather than as a way to maintain or improve public services in the long run.

Fifth, and finally, it may be necessary to have some level of regional coordination. A proposed expansion of the sales tax to services or other reforms often engender fears of revenue leakage over borders or even fears (usually unjustified) of out-migration. A reform effort should be cognizant of what is happening in neighboring states. Ideally, similar or parallel campaigns should be run in several states at once. Nonprofits, advocates, or other organizations outside of the government in neighboring states may be possible partners for encouraging and facilitating this type of coordination.

Preventing Structural Deficits

Structural deficits can develop or deepen when recurring expenditures are increased without adequate revenues that grow in tandem with the expenditures they support. Deficits also can develop or deepen when taxes or other revenues are cut below the level needed to support expenditures, or when the design or mix of taxes is changed in a way that reduces the growth rate of total revenues without also reducing the level or growth rate of expenditures. Improved budget practices could provide a warning to policymakers and the public when proposed actions are likely to create or deepen budget problems over the long term and, thereby, allow independent watchdogs and the media to make that information widely known.

Most of the potential improvements briefly discussed below are used by some states but are by no means universally adopted. Reforming these processes may be a fruitful way for states to begin reforming their budgets and taxes, because the process changes do not necessarily upset specific constituencies to an extent that would engender concerted or organized opposition—as some of the policy changes inevitably do. In addition, a new idea for budget control that is not yet used by any state is suggested.

Multiyear Budgeting

A change in a spending program, or in the tax code, is sometimes designed in such a way that it has a modest budget impact in the initial year or biennium, but then has a much larger one in subsequent years. Policymakers routinely engage in this type of backloading in order to squeeze their initiatives into annual or biennial balanced-budget requirements, leaving to subsequent governors and legislatures the problem of how to balance future budgets.

If states provide budget data only for the immediate budget period, and/or limit their fiscal-impact estimates to that period, it is difficult to detect these tactics or to gauge whether those future impacts are affordable. Thus, little consideration typically is given to longer-term implications of the policy changes.

According to the National Association of State Budget Officers, about fourteen states provide budget data that extend four years beyond the current budget cycle.[26] As described below, however, many of these states fail to base those budgets on meaningful out-year forecasts. At the other extreme, about eighteen states consider only the current budget cycle or one additional year beyond. Ideally, states should include a review of a five-year period in their budgets.

Current Services

Multiyear budgeting will not accomplish its purpose if projections are not done properly. Expenditures should be projected based on "current services" or a "baseline" analysis.

A current services analysis tells us how much it will cost to continue existing policies and programs—the current level of state services and benefits—in future years. In such an analysis, current-year spending is projected forward, based on expected changes in the number of people requiring those services and benefits, and on expected changes in the per-person cost. Costs typically are adjusted by some measure of price inflation, often with special indices used to project increases in costs, such as in the case of health-care costs. The federal Congressional Budget Office projects future costs in this way.

A current services analysis creates a baseline of what it would cost to continue the government as it is, given existing programs and revenue policies. It does not commit the state to continue all programs and benefits; it just provides an accurate base on which to consider whatever changes are desired.

Only thirteen states and DC use current services budgeting. [27] To the extent that the other states do multiyear projections, they tend to assume nominal expenditures will stay constant. Thus their multiyear projections are not realistic pictures of the future health of the state. Less than a handful of states, including Connecticut and Pennsylvania, prepare detailed multiyear budgets on a current services basis as a regular part of their budgets, although a few others such as Louisiana and Kansas do so at a summary level.

Revenue Projections

Most states project the revenue side of their budgets based on economic forecasts. States generally have some type of in-house forecasting model—in some cases it is a complex micro-simulation model—either under control of the governor's budget office or the legislative fiscal office. In some states, both the legislative and the executive branches have the capacity to do revenue forecasts, and the dueling forecasts sometimes become a debating point in the political process. This has been fairly common in New York, for example.

Other states have sought to insulate the revenue-forecasting process and have created a council made up of economists and other outsiders that create the revenue forecasts. In states such as Florida that follow this approach, the forecast generally is accepted by all parties to the budget debate. Slightly fewer than half the states use a consensus-forecasting process, in which representatives from the executive and legislative branches—usually aided by testimony and advice from outside economists and advisors—are required to agree on an economic and revenue forecast. Some other states rely on a board of economists to prepare the forecasts.[28] Arguably, these are the preferable process by which revenue forecasts should be done, because it reduces the incentive among all parties to "pick-and-choose" to select the most favorable forecast.

Fiscal Notes and Legislative Fiscal Offices

Policymakers and the public need good tools to evaluate proposed changes in budgets and taxation. An important tool is a fiscal note, which is a document that accompanies a piece of legislation and explains how much the legislation will cost or save.

States vary in the degree to which they require fiscal notes, the agency that is responsible for preparing them, and the thoroughness of the information presented. Some states require fiscal notes only for the initial introduction of a bill, while others require revised notes as bills are amended and move through the legislative process. States also differ in the number of years for which the fiscal note estimates budgetary impact; as is the case for proposed budgets, fiscal notes should include projections over the next five years. The best fiscal notes also provide other data, such as who will benefit (or lose) from a proposal and its impacts on local governments.

Fiscal notes may be prepared by the governor's budget office, by a partisan legislative entity (that is, staff employed by the majority part in the legislature), or by a nonpartisan legislative fiscal office. Obviously, only the latter source can generally be depended on to be fully free of political slant. Legislative fiscal offices (either partisan or nonpartisan) also are more accessible to legislators wanting to have an analysis done before proposing legislation.

Legislative fiscal offices also perform other important analytic functions, often looking at the effectiveness and cost of policies in a broader context than at individual pieces of legislation, and typically providing an independent analysis of the executive's proposed budget. Nevertheless, a good legislative fiscal office is only one more voice in the policy process, and by itself it is no guarantee of improved policies. For example, California and Illinois both have good nonpartisan legislative fiscal offices. But California's and Illinois's budget practices are far from exemplary; both states have large, ongoing structural deficits—as does the federal government despite high-quality forecasts by the Congressional Budget Office.

Tax Expenditure Scrutiny

"Tax expenditure" is the term for tax breaks that function more or less similarly to on-budget spending. For example, a state can provide grants or vouchers to low-income working parents to help them afford child care, or it can provide child-care tax credits through its income tax. Many states do both. The goals are roughly similar, but the beneficiaries of the vouchers tend to be low-income residents while the beneficiaries of the tax credit tend to be middle- or upper-income residents. Similarly, many states provide income-tax or sales-tax breaks to businesses that engage in certain types of activities, make investments, or hire workers, as an alternative to on-budget grant programs for which businesses meeting certain criteria can apply.

When these and similar types of subsidies are part of the annual or biennial budget, they tend to receive some level of scrutiny. Especially in periods of fiscal stress when states are searching for ways to cut spending, there is likely to be discussion over whether subsidies in the form of cash outlays are efficient and effective. When the subsidies are provided through the tax code, however, that type of scrutiny rarely takes place; even when deficits develop and budgets are cut "across the board," tax expenditures are exempted from the cuts. Moreover, unlike direct spending, tax expenditures typically are uncapped; if the cost of a tax expenditure exceeds expectations, there is no automatic mechanism to stop the revenue loss. Structural deficits may deepen if tax expenditures continue to grow rapidly when revenues are growing only slowly or declining in an economic downturn.

Some states do not even know how much they "spend" in terms of foregone revenues through preferences in the tax code. Eight states do not prepare tax-expenditure budgets or reports, and the reports of a number of others contain minimal information.[29] Very few states make a serious effort at evaluating the effectiveness of their tax expenditures. And no state, not even one that may produce a tax-expenditure budget at the same time as its regular budget, treats tax expenditures in a manner comparable to on-budget spending. That is, no state decides at budget time whether to "re-appropriate" its tax-expenditure line items as it does for its on-budget spending line items, nor has any state included tax expenditures when it has cut expenditures "across the board."

States could improve their tax-expenditure reporting by including information about the cost of the tax expenditure, the type of recipients, and evidence about outputs and outcomes similar to those that should be available for on-budget expenditures. States should also have formal mechanisms to review all tax expenditures periodically and to determine whether or not each of them makes sense to continue.

PAYGO Budgeting

Finally, avoiding structural deficits may require a way to utilize these substantive budget process reforms within the political budget process.

For the last several decades, activists and analysts have sought a budget control mechanism that will prevent irresponsible state budget policies from prevailing—and creating structural deficits—and encourage responsible budget choices. This concern has resulted in the adoption over the years of tax and expenditure limitations (TELs) of varying kinds in some states, the most stringent of which is TABOR in Colorado. Even though many recent attempts in this area have failed, there still is lots of discussion and continuing efforts toward adopting such limits. This desire for tighter budget control also has led a number of states to adopt supermajority requirements, term limits, and similar policies. The tightest constitutional TELs have ratcheted down expenditures and service provision. But they have not resulted in a desirable form of responsible budget policies that prioritize budgetary expenditures, tax expenditures, and revenue policy in a way that best provides for the needs of state residents. And supermajority requirements in California have famously brought the state to a complete and dysfunctional budget impasse.[30]

A better alternative may be a PAYGO (or pay-as-you-go) system for individual pieces of legislation, similar to that which the federal government successfully used in the 1990s and which has recently been reenacted.[31] Under PAYGO, any proposal or legislation that would increase spending or reduce taxes above the current services baseline would have to be offset by a cut in another program or an increase in a revenue source.

- When PAYGO was being seriously adhered to by the federal government in the 1990s, it was very effective in holding down deficits. One important advantage of the federal PAYGO was that it made Congress more likely to scrutinize tax expenditures (the special breaks in the tax code) to come up with "offsets" to help pay for tax cuts or spending increases. So a desired spending increase may be paired with a reduction or elimination of a special-interest tax break. In the absence of PAYGO, such tax-expenditure programs delivered through the tax code rarely receive attention or scrutiny, as discussed above.
- The bigger advantage is that applying PAYGO to each appropriation or tax change does not usurp the authority of the legislature in the way that a formula in a TEL or a supermajority requirement does, and so it does not rob policymakers of the flexibility needed to properly run a state. It also makes the legislative proponent of each expenditure increase or tax cut responsible for the consequences of its actions.
- PAYGO does not prevent program expansions or tax reductions—or the needed restructuring of revenue sources. It just ensures that they are enacted and implemented in a fiscally responsible manner.

No state has tried such a PAYGO-style budget-control mechanism to date. Obviously, this could only be implemented in states that do baseline or current services budgeting, quality revenue forecasts, and multiyear budgets. It is an idea worth trying.

CONCLUSION

The structural revenue problems of states, exacerbated by cyclical downturns, are likely to lead over time to reduced levels of public services—unless reforms are enacted. But there is no need to say that the future has to be one in which public services cannot be afforded. And the idea that there will be some radical change in the way states finance services is also improbable. Instead, the problems behind structural deficits can be specifically identified and remedied.

While there is strong evidence that the public does not desire fewer or lower-quality public services, it also is becoming common wisdom that the necessary reforms to pay for them are so unpopular as to be impossible to achieve. The common wisdom, however, appears to be based on an incorrect interpretation of the history of fiscal reform efforts. Arguably, it is not a reform per se that is the problem but rather the way it has been undertaken. Just as tax systems are in urgent need of modernization, so too are the methods through which reforms are sought in need of modernization. Keeping reforms simple, conducting adequate preparation and consultations before reforms are introduced, and using modern methods of opinion research and updated modes of communication can all enhance the probability of a proposal's success.

Finally, state budget processes also need to be modernized to prevent structural deficits from developing or deepening. Attempts to simply limit overall spending or revenues through rigid formulas and severe caps can distort the budget-making process and cause a damaging loss of flexibility. Multiyear budgeting techniques that carefully and clearly cost-out programs, and display the effects of changes in tax policy as well as direct spending totals, can help avoid long-term mismatches of revenues and expenditures that deepen structural problems. States should also consider the more novel PAYGO approach of balancing changes in expenditures with changes in revenues within the rubric of an overall balanced operating budget.

Notes

1 States have been more willing to experiment with social policy, such as welfare reform or health-care reform, than with tax policy.
2 The concentration of this chapter on structural problems of long-term adequacy is not intended to minimize the importance of other structural issues, such as the equity of revenue systems, that are outside of its scope.
3 National Association of State Budget Officers (2009).
4 US Census Bureau (2008).
5 Ibid.
6 The Census projects that the ratio of adults aged twenty-five to sixty-and to children aged six to seventeen will decline from 1.5 in 2010 to 1.4 in 2030. US Census Bureau, Population Division (2008).
7 Auguste et al. (2010).
8 There is a growing debate over whether pensions and retiree health benefits for teachers are too high and could be reduced. Most changes in those areas, particularly in pensions, would have little impact over the next decade or two because pensions for current workers are largely protected by state constitutions and case law. Some savings could be made by changing retiree health benefits, which are not so protected in most states. There is a question, however, about whether states and localities would have to increase current compensation if they decreased deferred compensation in order to attract good teachers.
9 US Government Accountability Office (2010), 11.
10 Munnell et al. (2010).
11 Federation of Tax Administrators (2008).
12 *National Bellas Hess v. Department of Revenue,* 386 US (1967): *Quill Corp. v. North Dakota,* 504 US 298 (1992).
13 Francis (1988), 145.
14 Bruskin and Parker (1991).
15 A federal VAT potentially could, however, have some negative effects on state and local revenues. In particular, a federal consumption tax could compete with state and local retail sales taxes, making it difficult to raise sales taxes when necessary. In addition, should a state desire to piggy-back on a federal VAT rather than levy its own retail

sales tax, there would be significant complexity involved in coordinating the federal and state VAT, particularly with respect to local government sales taxes.

16 Recent estimates of the revenue loss were presented at a July 13, 2010, meeting of the Streamlined Sales Tax Governing Board. William Fox, University of Tennessee Professor of Business and one of the leading experts on this issue, found that in 2012 states will lose $11.4 billion in sales tax on purchases made on the Internet. Lorrie Brown, an economist with the Washington State Department of Revenue, estimated that the revenue loss from uncollected taxes on catalog and other non-Internet remote sales to be an additional 11.8 billion in the same year—for a total loss from all remote sales at $23 billion.

17 Streamlined Sales Tax Governing Board, Inc., http://www.streamlinedsalestax.org/index.php?page=faqs and https://www.sstregister.org/sellers/SellerFAQs.Aspx

18 Mazerov (2009).

19 McNichol and Johnson (2010).

20 Ballotpedia (2010).

21 Lyons and Lav (2007), 18–19.

22 Lyons, Farkas, and Johnson (2007).

23 Ibid.

24 Dan Coyne, "Tax Reform Delivers Benefits to Maine Households," Maine Center for Economic Policy, April 19, 2010.

25 Kerstetter (2010).

26 National Association of State Budget Officers (2009).

27 McNichol and Okwuje (2006)

28 National Conference of State Legislatures (2009).

29 Levitis et al. (2009).

30 In November 2010 California voters approved Proposition 25, a ballot initiative that eliminates the supermajority requirement for enacting a budget. At the same time, it approved Proposition 26, which extended the supermajority requirement for raising taxes to include increases in certain fees. It also changed the definition of revenue measures for which a supermajority is required. Previously, a supermajority was required for any legislation that resulted in a net increase in taxes. Under the new law, a supermajority is required to approve any measure that would increase taxes on any single taxpayer in California, even if the tax package as a whole is revenue neutral. The retention and tightening of the supermajority requirement to raise taxes and fees will continue to hamper the ability of the legislature to reach budget solutions and is likely to result in continuing gridlock. See California Budget Project, *Proposition 26: Should State and Local Governments Be Required to Meet Higher Voting Thresholds to Raise Revenues?* September 2010, http://www.cbp.org/pdfs/2010/100922_Proposition_%2026.pdf.

31 Center on Budget and Policy Priorities (2009).

References
....

Auguste, Byron, Paul Kihn, and Matt Miller (2010, September). "Closing the Talent Gap: Attracting and Retaining Top-Third Graduates to Careers in Teaching." McKinsey & Company.

Ballotpedia (2010). "Washington Income Tax, Initiative 1098." http://www.ballotpedia.org/wiki/index.php/Washington_Income_Tax,_Initiative_1098_(2010).

Bruskin, Samuel B., and Kathleen King Parker (1991). "State Sales Taxes on Services: Massachusetts as a Case Study." *The Tax Lawyer* 45. Tax Law, 49.

Center on Budget and Policy Priorities (2009, March 5). "Policy Basics: Congress's "Pay-as-You-Go" Budget Rule." http://www.cbpp.org/files/policybasics-paygo.pdf.

Federation of Tax Administrators (2008). "Sales Taxation of Services—2007 Update." http://www.taxadmin.org/fta/pub/services/btn/0708.html.

Francis, James (1988). "The Florida Sales Tax on Services: What Really Went Wrong." In *The Unfinished Agenda for State Tax Reform*, edited by Steven Gold. Washington, DC: National Conference of State Legislatures.

Kerstetter, Katie (2010, May 6). "Why It Makes Sense to Modernize the Sales Tax—Yes, Even to Include Yoga Studios." Washington, DC: Fiscal Policy Institute. http://www.dcfpi.org/why-it-makes-sense-to-expand-the-sales-tax-%e2%80%93-yes-even-to-yoga-studios.

Levitis, Jason, Nicholas Johnson, and Jeremy Koulish (2009, April). "Promoting State Budget Accountability through Tax Expenditure Reporting." Washington, DC: Center on Budget and Policy Priorities.

Lyons, Karen, and Iris J. Lav (2007, June). *The Problems with Property Tax Revenue Caps.* Washington, DC: Center on Budget and Policy Priorities.

Lyons, Karen, Sarah Farkas, and Nicholas Johnson (2007, March). "The Property Tax Circuit Breaker: An Introductions and Survey of Current Programs." Washington, DC: Center on Budget and Policy Priorities.

Mazerov, Michael (2009, July). "New York's 'Amazon Law': An Important Tool for Collecting Taxes Owed on Internet Purchases." Washington, DC: Center on Budget and Policy Priorities.

McNichol, Elizabeth, and Ifie Okwuje (2006, December). "The Current Services Baseline: A Tool for Making Sensible Budget Choices." Washington, DC: Center on Budget and Policy Priorities.

McNichol, Elizabeth, and Nicholas Johnson (2010, September). "Fair Tax Proposals to Replace State Income and Business Taxes with Expanded Sales Tax Would Create Serious Problems." Washington, DC: Center on Budget and Policy Priorities.

Munnell, Alicia H., Jean-Pierre Aubry, and Laura Quinby (2010, October). "The Impact of Public Pensions on State and Local Budgets." Boston: Center for Retirement Research at Boston College.

National Association of State Budget Officers (2008). "Budget Processes in the States." Washington, DC: NASBO.

National Association of State Budget Officers (2009). "State Expenditure Report, Fiscal Year 2008." Washington, DC: NASBO.

National Bellas Hess v. Department of Revenue, 386 US (1967).

National Conference of State Legislatures (2009, October). "Revenue Forecast." http://www.ncsl.org/default.aspx?tabid=18793.

Quill Corp. v. North Dakota, 504 US 298 (1992).

US Census Bureau, Population Division (2008, August 14). "Projections of the Population by Selected Age Groups and Sex for the United States: 2010 to 2050 (NP2008-T2)."

US Census Bureau (2008). "Annual Survey of State and Local Government Finance."

US Government Accountability Office (2010, March). "State and Local Governments' Fiscal Outlook: March 2010 Update." GAO-10-358.

CHAPTER 32

···

FISCAL AUSTERITY AND THE FUTURE OF FEDERALISM

···

RUDOLPH G. PENNER

ALMOST certainly, fiscal relationships among federal, state, and local governments will change significantly in the future. The federal government is saddled with an unsustainable set of tax and spending policies and the policy changes necessary to restore fiscal stability are far larger and more painful than anything that the American public has experienced since World War II. State and local governments will be forced to adjust to a new world of federal fiscal austerity.

On the domestic spending side of the federal budget, the deepest problems lie in just two areas: Social Security and health care. In 2007, before the surge in spending related to the Great Recession, the Social Security, Medicare, and Medicaid programs accounted for almost 50 percent of noninterest spending. Those three entitlement programs are growing faster than the economy and tax revenues. Meanwhile, the overall federal tax impact has been remarkably constant, varying between 17 and 19 percent of the GDP for all but eleven of the past fifty years. Partly because of the Great Recession, the total federal tax burden fell below 15 percent of GDP in fiscal 2010, the lowest level since 1950.

The single most important reason for fiscal unsustainability is the rapid rise in health costs. It is caused by two factors. First, the population is aging, with a surge in the second and third decades of the twenty-first century as large cohorts of baby boomers reach retirement age and become eligible for Medicare.[1] As they age and live longer, they are also more likely to require Medicaid to pay for long-term care. Second, age-sex adjusted health costs per capita are projected to rise annually by about 2 percentage points more than income per capita in the decades ahead, as they have over the past four decades. Federal health-reform legislation, enacted in 2010, is unlikely to dampen this trend. The new law adds to Medicaid spending, creates a new subsidy for the purchase of health insurance, but also reduces the growth of Medicare spending. Although there are elements of the health reform that may dampen cost growth somewhat, the growth of health spending will almost certainly continue to constitute the number one long-run federal budget problem. That is true even if the law is implemented as it was written, but it is very likely that some of the cost-saving measures, especially those cutting Medicare reimbursements, will have to be moderated. Health costs are likely to remain a major budget problem for the states as well, as Medicaid continues its inexorable growth and health reform adds even more responsibilities to that highly troubled program. Medicaid spending financed by state governments has far outstripped total state spending as it has risen from about 7½ percent of state budgets in 1985 to almost 13 percent in 2008. Total Medicaid spending was $338 billion in 2008 with $192 billion coming from the federal government and $146 billion from the states. The interests of federal and state governments are bound to clash as the federal government tries to unload a greater share of health costs onto the states and the states would like to do the opposite.[2] Although Social Security outlays do not present as large a long-run problem as health costs do, Social Security will create very significant upward pressures on spending, especially over the next twenty years, as baby boomers retire in large numbers, drawing benefits for decades.

If Social Security and our health programs are not significantly reformed, if other programs grow at the same rate as GDP, and if the tax burden impact is at its average level of the past fifty years, the national debt will soar. The long-run budget projections of the Congressional Budget Office[3] have the federal debt reaching 100 percent of GDP in 2023 and 200 percent in 2037 under their "alternative fiscal scenario," which assumes a more realistic combination of tax and spending policies than if current law remains unchanged.

It is very unlikely that we shall ever see federal debt climbing as high as 200 percent of GDP. Long before that happens, domestic and foreign investors will become nervous about lending money to the US government, and interest rates will soar and the foreign exchange value of the dollar may plummet. At that point, we shall have no choice but to radically reform spending and tax policy. Hopefully, it will be done as the result of a timely deliberative process and not as a panicked reaction to a financial crisis. In the worst of all possible worlds, countries try to inflate their way out of budget crises. That works for a time,[4] but the hyperinflation that follows wreaks havoc on the economy[5] and on individuals holding assets denominated in money terms. Eventually, almost everyone stops using money and governments gain little by continuing to print it.

The long-run budget problem has been apparent for decades, but the need to confront it was intensified by the Great Recession of 2007–2009. The economic downturn slashed revenues and raised spending on unemployment insurance and other safety-net programs. It also provoked the passage of a huge stimulus package, now estimated to cost $814 billion, and required a bailout of the financial and auto sectors, which was designed to prevent a collapse from becoming a calamity.[6] As a result, the national debt in the hands of the public soared from 40 percent of GDP at the end of fiscal year 2008 to 62 percent at the end of 2010.

By some measures, the Great Recession was the most severe economic downturn since World War II and it is not surprising that it caused the budget deficit to explode.[7] Normally, after a severe recession, revenues revive, safety-net spending declines, any stimulus package expires, and the budget deficit shrinks rapidly. It has been, in fact, expected that under the Obama administration's budget policies, as stated in February 2010, the budget deficit will decline from 10 percent of GDP in 2010—a post-World War II record—to a bit under 4 percent in 2014.[8] That decline is not enough, however, to prevent the national debt from rising faster than our incomes and by the end of 2014, debt will be over 70 percent of GDP.

Ominously, the deficit is expected to rise after 2014, even though the economic recovery is expected to continue. The increase accelerates after 2018 and by the end of 2020 the debt is expected to be 77 percent of GDP under the economic and technical assumptions in the administration's budget and about 90 percent using Congressional Budget Office (CBO) assumptions.[9] Not surprisingly, the main culprits in the increase in the deficit are health, interest, and Social Security in that order of importance. Interest costs are expected to rise by 4½times between 2010 and 2020 because of the large increase in the debt and an assumed relatively small increase in interest rates.[10]

Although Social Security and health spending present the most serious problems on the spending side of the federal budget, it is unlikely that fiscal consolidation will reform only those programs. It is popular among politicians and quite legitimate to say that everything on the tax and spending side of the budget must be "on the table." That implies that there will be intense downward pressures on grants-in-aid; there will be efforts to have the states and localities take on more of the responsibility for public services; and there may be federally mandated increases in state and local spending. Because it is essentially impossible to solve the entire budget problem on the spending side of the budget, federal tax increases become very likely, and these are bound to encroach on the ability of the state and local sectors to raise revenues. The President's Commission on Fiscal Responsibility and Reform released a set of recommendations in December 2010 that addressed the long-run budget problem.[11] Through 2020 it imposes almost $3 of spending cuts, including associated reductions in the interest bill, for every $1 dollar of revenue increases. It so happens that the British austerity program also released in 2010 claimed the same ratio of spending cuts to revenue increases.[12] It is clearly a popular approach to deficit reduction.

FEDERAL GRANTS

Grants to state and local governments are of considerable significance to both the federal budget and the budgets of state and local governments.[13] In 2008, before the federal budget was distorted by stimulus programs, outlays for grants amounted to $461.3 billion, or 15.5 percent of total federal outlays. This was equivalent to 20.1 percent of total state and local receipts.[14] Figures 32.1, 32.2, and 32.3 depict the history of total grants as a percentage of GDP, of the federal budget, and of state and local spending.

Classified by budget function, the largest grant expenditure, by far, is for health, constituting almost one-half of grant outlays. Medicaid grants constituted more than 90 percent of total health grants. Grants for income security made up the second most important budget category, accounting for about 20 percent of total grant spending.

Medicaid—Federal grants for Medicaid finance somewhat more than one-half of Medicaid costs with the states responsible for the remainder. As noted previously, the program has severely pressured state budgets because it has far outgrown tax revenues and other forms of spending. Its costs are driven mainly by health-cost growth per recipient and by the aging of the population. Unlike Medicare, Medicaid covers expenses for long-term care.

In the past, the Medicaid program has grown so rapidly that it has squeezed out other types of state spending. Peter Orszag,[15] the former OMB director for President Obama, has emphasized its negative impact on state spending for higher

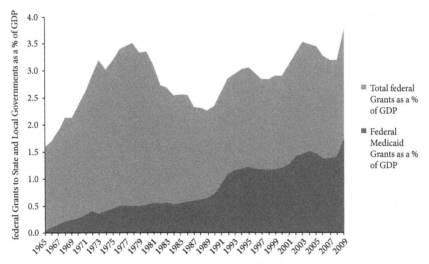

Figure 32.1 Federal grants for medical and total federal grants to state and local governments as a percentage of GDP, 1965–2009
Source: Historical Tables, Budget of the U.S. Government, Office of Management and Budget, 2011.

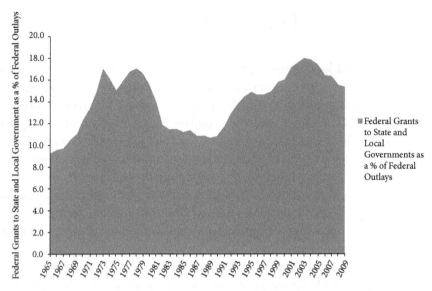

Figure 32.2 Federal grants to state and local governments as a percentage
of federal outlays, 1965–2009
Source: Historical Tables, Budget of the U.S. Government, Office of
Management and Budget, 2011.

education. If one examines only the effect on federal grants, it can be argued that
Medicaid grants have had a negative effect on almost all other types of grant spending. As shown in figure 32.1, total federal grants remained almost constant relative
to GDP for the past three decades, falling from a peak of 3.5 in 1978 to 3.2 percent
in 2008. However, non-Medicaid grants fell from 3.0 to 1.8 percent of GDP over

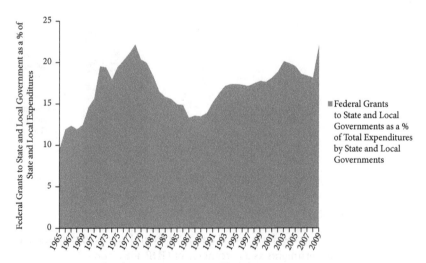

Figure 32.3 Federal grants to state and local governments as a percentage
of total state and local government expenditures, 1965–2009
Source: Table 3.2 and table 3.3, National Income and Product Accounts, Bureau of
Ecconomic **Analysis.**

the period while Medicaid grants almost tripled in importance, rising from 0.5 to 1.4 percent of GDP.

The program is expanded significantly by the new federal health plan. States will pay a much smaller share of the costs of this expansion than they do of the costs of the older program, but nevertheless, the health-care expansion will somewhat intensify the budget pain associated with Medicaid.[16]

It is difficult to imagine getting the federal budget under control without curbing the growth of health costs. It is harder to speculate on how health-care cost constraints might affect the Medicaid program. The CBO did not assume that much saving would come from the cost restraints contained in the new health reform, but if such measures could be effectively strengthened, it could take some of the budget pressure off Medicaid and so redound to the benefit of states.

It is possible to envision more radical changes. Today, Medicare and Medicaid have essentially open-ended budgets. The programs describe who is eligible and the treatments that they can receive while excluding very few medical procedures. Then the programs pay for treatments for whoever walks in the door. States have some control over defining eligibility and determining reimbursement rates under Medicaid, but these are crude instruments for controlling costs. The federal government attempts to control Medicare budgets by controlling reimbursements with a price control system whose complexity rivals the price controls of the old Soviet Union.[17] Again, this represents a very crude approach to cost control. In some countries with nationalized health systems, such as Canada and the United Kingdom, the systems have to operate under a fixed budget. They then ration services to fit under the budget, admittedly in a somewhat nontransparent manner. There are intense political pressures to raise the budgets faster than GDP every year, but at least they have a tool that directly controls costs and is not available in the United States.

Medicare and Medicaid could be put on fixed budgets by using some sort of voucher system for Medicare and block grants for Medicaid. The value of the voucher could be income- and age-related. In a block-grant regime, there would be intense political pressure on states to supplement federal assistance with their own money. There would also be restraints on the states' ability to game the system in ways that now artificially increase the federal government's cost share. The president's fiscal commission suggests the possibility of putting Medicare and other health programs on a fixed budget as one possible option in achieving their goal of limiting health-cost growth to GDP growth plus 1 percent after 2020.[18]

Many other arrangements are possible. States could be given full responsibility for financing Medicaid for the nonelderly while the federal government took over Medicaid for the elderly population. That might not be a bad deal for the states in the longer run given the continual aging of the population and the prospect of very large increases in the cost of long-term care.

The future financial impact of Medicaid on states will depend to some degree on how the federal budget reform evolves. If it comes about as the result of a rational process that leads to a mega-budget deal similar to those occurring in 1990 and 1993, there will be more time to work on improving the efficiency of the system.

This might be accomplished by modifying the health plan passed in 2010, so as to strengthen those features that create some hope for cost control. Federal fiscal austerity could, of course, take a less desirable form. A mega-budget deal could shift costs from the federal to state and local governments and to the private sector regardless of what happens to the efficiency of the health system.

If policymakers must reform the budget in response to a budget-induced crisis in financial markets, the pressures to shift costs quickly "downward" from the federal government to state and local governments and to the private sector will intensify and there will be less time for efficiency-enhancing reforms. To the extent that private individuals and companies bear more of a burden, they will be resistant to any state or local tax increases or benefit cuts.

Constraints on Medicaid seem inevitable even if a large part of the federal budget problem is solved using tax increases. On its current path, health spending is heading for 100 percent of GDP and tax increases cannot keep up with such a path without raising tax rates almost every year until the economy is driven into the ground. Eventually health-cost growth must be slowed to the growth of GDP or below and we cannot afford to wait very long before starting a process that will achieve this goal.

Grants Other Than Medicaid—It seems inevitable that nonhealth grants will experience unrelenting downward pressure as federal budget problems intensify. Figures 32.4 and 32.5 reflect the ups and downs of non-Medicaid grants as a proportion of GDP and of total federal spending.

Non-Medicaid grants rose rapidly relative to GDP between 1965 and the late 1970s as Great Society programs grew and permeated the budget. Non-Medicaid

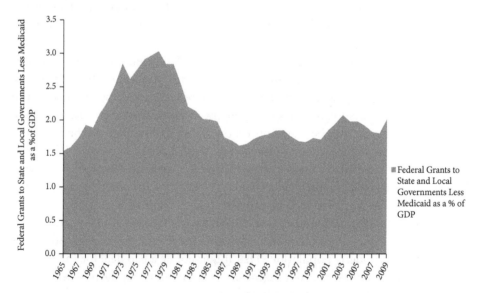

Figure 32.4 Federal grants to state and local governments less Medicaid
as a percentage of GDP, 1965–2009
Source: Historical Tables, Budget of the U.S. Government, Office of
Management and Budget, 2011.

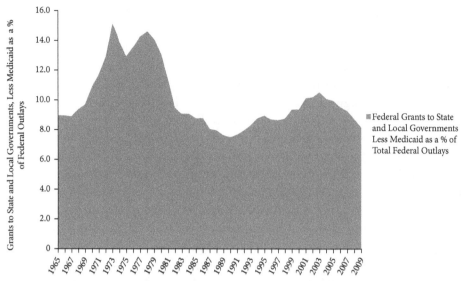

Figure 32.5 Federal grants to state and local governments less Medicaid
as a percentage of total federal outlays, 1965–2009
Source: Historical Tables, Budget of the U.S. Government, Office of
Management and Budget, 2011.

grants peaked in 1978 at slightly above 3 percent of GDP. But as inflation roared
and budget deficits became a major concern, the Carter administration began cutting back. That began a long decline under President Reagan and the first President
Bush, perhaps abetted by the Gramm-Rudman-Hollings budget law that set deficit
targets after 1985.

It is a bit puzzling that grants rose a bit relative to GDP in the early 1990s.
That was an era of austerity invoked by the major budget deals of 1990 and 1993.
Discretionary appropriations, which fund most non-Medicaid grants, were capped
after 1990 by the Budget Enforcement Act. However, the recession of 1990 probably
played a role by depressing GDP and increasing income security spending at a very
rapid pace between 1990 and 1994.

After Republicans took over the House of Representatives in 1994, there was
again a period of restraint and the grant-to-GDP ratio fell slightly. But restraint went
out the window when a budget surplus emerged by complete surprise in 1998. After
that the Republicans "went native" in the eyes of conservatives and President Bush,
and Congress did little to clamp down on spending during his first term. Of course,
they were confronted by the recession of 2001, which resulted in a very large increase
in income-security spending in that year. In addition, security and defense spending soared because of the 9/11 attacks and the subsequent wars in Afghanistan and
Iraq. Grants fell relative to GDP in the second Bush term and then blipped upward
in Obama's first year because of the Great Recession and the stimulus program.

Figure 32.5 examines non-Medicaid grants as a percentage of total federal outlays. It reveals that grants were treated more harshly than other federal

expenditures during the long period of restraint during the Reagan and elder Bush's administrations. They then rose relative to other spending through the younger Bush's first term but then fell through 2009, because nongrant spending was inflated by the stimulus program.

Is there anything in the historical record that gives us a clue as to how non-Medicaid grants might respond to the long period of fiscal austerity that will be necessary to get federal deficits under control? That will depend to some degree on whether pro- or antigovernment forces are in control of Congress when we as a nation finally decide to act on our long-run budget problem. But rising public concern over deficits and the intense hostility toward tax increases manifested in the election of 2010 would seem to favor antigovernment forces politically and suggests that the response to rising deficits is likely to resemble the record of the 1980s.

Grants are more likely to suffer relatively if fiscal austerity is the response to a financial crisis. It will be necessary to act quickly to show investors that we are serious about fiscal discipline. It is difficult to reign in Social Security and Medicare quickly because that so disrupts retirement planning. Phased-in reforms of Social Security and Medicare might be enacted, but participants in financial and dollar markets may lack confidence that we will carry out such reforms. That puts the pressure on discretionary spending that can be controlled almost immediately. Non-Medicaid grants will not fare well under these circumstances.

Are some grants more vulnerable than others during a long period of fiscal austerity? That is a difficult question to answer. There was some fiscal restraint in the 2001 federal budget, which recommended freezing nonsecurity, discretionary spending for three years. Subsequently, the Obama administration further recommended freezing civil service pay for two years. Freezes or across-the-board cuts are popular when spending growth must be slowed. It avoids the need to favor one program over another. That is to say, you do not have to be very specific about your priorities. A similar strategy appears in the report of the president's fiscal commission. It recommends a pay freeze for three years, a reduction in the size of the federal civil service, and the need for civil servants to pay more for their fringe benefits. It is difficult to say how such measures will affect programs for state and local governments. The programs may remain intact, but there may be fewer civil servants to administer them.

However, it is also true that some types of spending are easier to cut than others. If cutting is necessary, there is a strong temptation to cut investment. Postponing a project is not as disruptive as curtailing an ongoing program. That would indicate that infrastructure spending and research and development could suffer disproportionately. There may also be a tendency to cut programs that aid constituencies that are not very powerful politically. That may not bode well for the poor.

In the end, the choice of what to cut will depend on the relative political popularity of programs and the degree of support from special-interest groups when budget reform finally occurs. It is striking how different types of grants have been popular at different times since World War II. In the late 1950s and early 1960s, the focus was on the interstate highway system. For almost all the program's history, it was entirely financed by a dedicated revenue source: the gas tax. By the late 1960s and through most of the 1970s, programs related to the Great Society grew very rapidly. Between 1966 and 1978, grants for income security grew 13 percent per year. Grants for community development exploded over the same time period from far less than $1 billion to $4.5 billion—a rate well over 20 percent per year. In recent years, much of the focus has been on education with President Bush's No Child Left Behind initiative and President Obama's follow-on called Race to the Top. It is probably difficult to cut any type of grant significantly when it is at the height of its popularity. But popularity can be fleeting. Many of the fiscal conservatives elected in 2010 would like to eliminate the Department of Education and greatly reduce the federal government's role in education. On the other hand, public opinion polls suggest that federal spending on education remains very popular.[19]

DEVOLUTION AND THE FEDERAL BUDGET

Will a long period of fiscal austerity cause the federal government to push more public responsibilities "down"? The previous section argued that federal financial support for many activities is likely to be curtailed, but that is different from totally abandoning the federal government's role in helping to provide significant public goods and services through state and local governments.

There are factors that favor greater devolution, but there are also strong forces that make it unlikely. First, devolution is certainly a way of constraining federal spending and could be carried out more quickly than reforming Social Security and Medicare. Second, the federal government has taken more and more responsibility over the decades for financing activities that traditionally were predominantly financed by state and local governments. There are good intellectual arguments for reversing this trend.[20] Third, federal politicians have traditionally enjoyed the power over the allocation of resources that they get from an expanded federal role and they have been reluctant to give it up, even when faced with severe budget pressures. The 111th Congress, elected in 2010, still contains a large number of traditionalists. But there will be about one hundred new members of the House—a very large turnover by historical standards. Many of the new Republicans—and there are about 85 of them—are extreme fiscal conservatives. The fate of devolution will, to some degree, be determined by the outcome of clashes between the old and new guard.

The outcome will also depend crucially on how much of the long-run budget problem is solved by raising taxes and how much by cutting the growth of spending. It will also depend on how successful we are at curbing the growth of health costs.

The prospects for and contours of increased devolution will depend largely on the particulars of how the long-term federal deficit problem is solved. In 2010, the

National Academies of Science and Public Administration published the report of a committee on "Choosing the Nation's Fiscal Future."[21] The report compiled four packages of options that would put the federal budget on a sustainable path. In one, all the adjustment came on the spending side of the budget while the total tax burden remained at its long-run historical level. Although this package dramatically slowed health spending to the rate necessitated only by the aging of the population and solved Social Security's financial problem by slowing the growth of benefits rather than by raising payroll taxes, it proved necessary to also take a draconian approach to discretionary spending in order to get the budget under control.

Both defense and nondefense spending had to be severely limited. On the nondefense side, almost everything had to be cut to avoid a tax increase and that could not be done without moving fiscal responsibilities to the states and localities. At first, it was assumed that a part of the added financial burden imposed on the states would be covered by block grants, but those grants would be allowed to erode over time. An appendix to the report provides a long list of federally financed activities that would ultimately be turned over to states and localities.[22]

When one examines the nature of the spending reforms necessary to avoid all tax increases, they appear to be highly implausible politically. The other three packages compiled in the report involved some increase in taxes[23] and one solved the entire problem on the tax side of the budget. It will be discussed later. Where some portion of the federal budget problem was cured by using tax increases, devolution became less necessary. But that was only possible if Social Security was reformed to some degree and health-cost spending growth was slowed.

There will certainly be arguments, mostly made by traditional conservatives, in favor of moving responsibilities "downward." Two interesting cases involve surface transportation and education.

Surface Transportation Grants

Historically, the federal government had a relatively minor role in road transportation until President Eisenhower promoted the interstate highway system in the 1950s. At the time, it could be argued that there was a strong national interest in developing an efficient, nationally integrated highway system. But over the decades the system has evolved in ways that weaken the argument for a strong federal role.

The federal grant system that supports highways is hopelessly complicated, but the largest amount of money is provided in the form of a formula block grant. Minimum effort requirements are imposed on states, but they are rarely binding. Consequently, states tend to get the same amount of money regardless of how much of their own money they spend on roads. Theoretically, the highway block grant does not encourage road building and maintenance any more than would a general revenue-sharing grant. Contrary to this theory, empirical evidence suggests that the grant does in fact encourage spending on roads.[24] But given the grant's peculiar structure, there is no guarantee that it will continue to have a strong impact on road building.

In the past, the grant had a strong redistributive element in that it tried to serve a national purpose by equalizing the ability of states to finance road building. However, states that paid more in federal fuel taxes than they got in highway grants constantly complained and the redistributive elements of the formula have been weakened over time.

Another major change involves the way in which federal highway spending is financed. Originally, there was a very close connection between the revenues generated by the federal fuel tax and federal spending on roads. There are many arguments against dedicated financing of this type. The most important is that it is unlikely that a dedicated tax will finance exactly the right amount of construction as might be determined by benefit-cost analysis. But a dedicated tax also has desirable features. It appears to be fair to have highway users finance the bulk of highway spending. And it promotes budget discipline by forcing a tax increase if there is a desire for more spending.

All the desirable features of the federal surface transportation financing system have eroded over time. The link between fuel-tax revenues and highway construction was weakened by devoting part of the proceeds to mass transit and, for a time, to ethanol subsidies. Antitax fervor has prevented any increase in the fuel tax since 1993 when in earlier years the tax was at least raised periodically to reflect inflation. Because of a lack of dedicated tax revenues, Congress has recently resorted to general-revenue (deficit) financing to fund the system, thus greatly reducing the budget discipline inherent in the old system. The president's fiscal commission advocates a 15 cent per-gallon increase in the gasoline tax in order to eliminate the program's deficit. By implication, it supports the current federal highway program despite the stringency that it imposes on other types of domestic spending.

There is also a question as to whether the federal government should be supporting mass transit. Certainly, mass transit serves social purposes such as reducing pollution and road congestion, but those benefits redound overwhelmingly to local communities. Should federal taxpayers in areas of the country that see little benefit be expected to share the financial load?

Because surface transportation grants are no longer as effective in serving a national purpose and because the program is now less disciplined fiscally, there is an argument for conveying the responsibility for such spending and control over the federal fuel tax to state and local governments. Because the fuel tax no longer entirely finances the expenditures of the program, this is equivalent to a "shifting the deficit down" strategy. However, although the generosity of federal highway grant funding may be reduced, complete devolution of the responsibility for highways and mass transit is unlikely to follow, even in the face of severe federal fiscal austerity. Surface transportation has been an area in which politicians can be very visible in providing projects for their districts. They have used earmarks to direct funds to specific projects; they can be present at groundbreaking ceremonies; and they can cut the ribbon when the project opens. Earmarks have such a bad name among fiscal conservatives that there has been a vigorous debate, largely between newly elected and more senior Republican elected members, as to whether they should be banned for the 112th Congress. But an earmark ban will not stop members of Congress from cutting ribbons at the initiation of highway projects financed by ordinary appropriations. Again, it should be emphasized that federal highway financing could still be cut severely, even though the federal government retains strict control over what remains.

Public Education Grants

Grants for primary and secondary education provoke the same types of arguments that surround programs for surface transportation. There is a national interest in having a well-educated work force, because it is conducive to economic growth, just as there is a national interest in having an efficient, integrated highway system. But education is an area that has traditionally been mainly the purview of local government. It is argued that local voters know best what is needed for the schools in their communities.

A federal Department of Education was not created until 1979. In 1965, grants for education were less than $1 billion. But they doubled in 1966 and they then grew at an annual rate of over 11 percent per year for the next fourteen years. They leveled off during President Reagan's first term, but then grew over 7 percent per year through 2000.

President George W. Bush made education one of his highest priorities with his No Child Left Behind program, and education grants grew at 12.5 percent per year during his first term. Growth slowed in Bush's second term, but President Obama chose to increase resources on education as part of his stimulus program. Education grants rose an astounding 34.5 percent between 2008 and 2009. A portion of this assistance was extended in 2010, allegedly to avoid teacher layoffs but more accurately as a tool for providing generalized fiscal assistance to states.

The vast increase in the federal education budget since 1965 indicates the extent to which education has become an important national priority. However, this increase has been accompanied by federal regulations and requirements. Although localities and states are still responsible for most funding for primary and secondary education, the increase in the federal financial role and its increased power over educational policy represents a sea change that provides testimony for the political popularity of education spending. Nevertheless, it is an area that is more controversial than highways. As noted previously, many fiscal conservatives want to do away with the federal Department of Education and return responsibility to the state and local sectors. Surface transportation and education were discussed merely as examples in which a large federal role did not emerge until well after World War II, but in which a federal role is now so heavily entrenched that federal politicians are very unlikely to devolve much responsibility. Similar arguments can be applied to welfare (much of which was not federalized until the early 1970s), worker training, and a host of other activities where good arguments can be made for devolution, but where they are unlikely to prevail.

Although wholesale devolution can probably be ruled out in the face of federal fiscal austerity, it must be re-emphasized that it is quite different from saying that the federal government will continue to support activities, such as highways and education, at the levels of the recent past. Financial support is very likely to be curtailed. It is just unlikely to be ended entirely for important functions in which all types of governments play an important role.

Unfunded Mandates That Increase State and Local Expenditures

It is very tempting for federal politicians to mandate that state and local governments satisfy certain social objectives without the federal government paying any of the cost. That way the federal government seems to be getting something for nothing. In fact, the practice was tempting enough and occurred frequently enough that the state and local sectors demanded and received procedural protections against the activity. Under the Unfunded Mandates Reform Act of 1995, protection was also afforded to the private sector.

Legislation requires that the CBO prepare an estimate of any costs imposed on state and local governments by bills that are reported out of committees. The threshold for reporting estimates was $50 million in 1996. It rose with inflation and reached $69 million in 2009.[25] In practice, the CBO must estimate the cost of almost every mandate to see if it breaches the threshold.

If a bill containing a mandate reaches the House or Senate floor and does not provide sufficient financing to cover the mandated expenditure or loss of revenues, points of order can be raised against it. From 1996 to 2009, only eleven bills imposing mandates were enacted that exceeded the cost of the threshold. That amounted to about 1 percent of all the public laws enacted during that period. Of the eleven bills, only one provided sufficient funds to pay for the cost of the mandate.

It could be said that in ten cases the law failed in that the threat of a point of order was not sufficient to prevent the enactment of the unfunded mandate. However, proponents of the unfunded mandates law would counter that many more mandates would have been enacted without it. In other words, they believe that it acts as an effective deterrent. That is very difficult to prove or disprove conclusively. It is true that many more laws imposing mandates are reported out of committee than are ever enacted, but that is also true of laws not imposing mandates.

It is certainly true that federal fiscal austerity will greatly increase the pressure to achieve social ends by passing unfunded mandates. Would Congress go so far as to eliminate procedural protections that make the practice difficult? I very much doubt it. There would be a firestorm of protests from state and local governments; the law has long been embedded in congressional procedures; and most federal legislators know that it is not right to force state and local governments to do something without compensating them. Presuming that current procedural protections are retained, federal fiscal pressures might still result in some increase in unfunded mandates, but such activity has imposed such low costs on state and local governments in recent years so that even a doubling or tripling of such costs would not have a major impact on state and local budgets.

It must be emphasized that I am talking about mandates that receive absolutely no funding. When the federal government provides grants, it is not at all shy about mandating how they are used. For example, Medicaid is controlled very strictly. Very often, grants-receiving governments could use grants more productively if they were controlled less rigidly. It is quite possible that if the federal government decides to devolve some functions, it would first provide some support with block grants that provide considerable freedom in how the money is used. However, one would expect the support for the grants to erode over time.

TAX POLICY

As noted previously, it is essentially certain that tax burdens will have to be raised in order to control the federal budget deficit. The spending cuts that are necessary to keep the tax burden constant are too draconian to be politically plausible. However, it is also certain that there will be a bitter battle over exactly how much of the solution will come from slowing spending growth and how much from raising taxes.

There are four broad options for raising tax burdens:

1. Personal income, payroll, corporate, and other tax rates can simply be raised without doing anything else.
2. Various deductions and exclusions (sometimes known as loopholes) can be eliminated selectively.
3. A new tax can be created, such as a value-added tax (VAT) or a carbon tax.
4. There can be a very radical income-tax reform that would eliminate essentially all deductions and exclusions from the personal and corporate systems. Additional revenues could then be raised with tax rates that are considerably lower than in existing law.

Obviously, the four options could be combined, but a very radical tax reform would eliminate the need to do anything else. Of course, anything that increases the federal tax burden makes state and local taxes more painful.

In the previously cited Academies' report, one package of options showed the tax increases that would be necessary to stabilize the national debt if spending programs remained on their current path. (Some health-policy reform is necessary to slow spending growth eventually or else health costs will consume the entire gross national product.) This increasing-the-taxes package is just as implausible as is a package that would avoid any tax increase. It would imply that by the 2040s, the federal tax burden would have to be raised about 50 percent above the average level of the past fifty years. Even though it is implausible, it is interesting to examine the types of tax changes that might be necessary to finance this large a government.

Two strategies were devised in the Academies' report. In one, all personal tax rates were initially raised proportionally to finance the increased spending. However, the top tax rate reached 50 percent by 2020 and given the inefficiencies and inequities inherent in our current tax structure, it was decided that that was a practical upper limit. After 2020, a VAT was imposed. Its rate had to be raised constantly until it reached 14.6 percent in 2080.

In the other strategy, the personal tax system was radically reformed. All deductions, exclusions, and credits were eliminated except for those benefiting low-income earners and those encouraging saving. Also, the exclusion for employer- provided health insurance was retained, but limited absolutely to the average cost of health plans in 2009. The tax rate on capital gains and dividends was limited to 15 percent. This reform allowed sufficient revenues to be raised to initially finance the high spending path with two bracket rates of 10 and 25 percent. The rates had to be raised a bit by 2020, but the top rate remained below 30 percent. After that, rates could be lowered, because the reformed tax structure causes revenues to rise very rapidly. That is partly because of the limit on the health insurance exclusion. If it is unrestrained, the cost of the exclusion will rise very rapidly because of growing health costs.[26]

In the report's packages of options that limit spending growth, the tax rates in the reformed system can be constantly lowered while still providing enough revenue to solve the budget problem. This outcome makes radical tax reform look very appealing. But radical tax reform is also very difficult politically, because it creates so many winners and losers, the losers being those who currently make heavy use of deductions, credits, and exclusions. The losers tend to oppose reform much more intensely than the winners support it. Although radical tax reform is extremely difficult, it cannot be ruled out when the nation finally faces up to its budget problem. Reform has some appeal to conservatives because it keeps marginal tax rates very low, and it should have some appeal to liberals because otherwise the current complexity of the tax code allows much manipulation and enables rich people to get away with paying very low tax rates.

A radical federal-tax reform would put considerable pressure on states and localities with income taxes to make their systems conform with the federal rules.[27] This need not lose revenues for state and local governments and may even raise such revenues as it did in 1986, but it can be a disruption and impose extra administrative costs on the state and local systems.

Most proposals for radical tax reform eliminate the deduction for state and local taxes. This deduction survived the last radical reform in 1986, but there is no guarantee that it will survive the next one. It is interesting that all of the radical tax-reform proposals described by the president's fiscal commission would eliminate the state and local tax deduction as would the radical tax reforms described in the Academies' report and in a report by the Bipartisan Policy Center (*Restoring America's Future*).[28]

The state and local tax deduction significantly eases the pain imposed by state and local income and real estate taxes. At the top federal rate of 35 percent that prevailed in 2010, an extra state or local income or property tax of one dollar costs the taxpayer only 65 cents. The president's fiscal commission also proposed eliminating the tax exemption for the interest on newly issued municipal bonds, a policy that could greatly increase state and local borrowing costs.

Even if the nation chooses to eschew radical tax reform, there are many proposals to raise revenues by either eliminating certain tax deductions selectively or paring them back by converting them to tax credits or using either phase-outs or proportionate reductions.[29] To the extent that such partial reforms diminish the value of state and local deductions, they make the current levels of state and local taxes more burdensome and strengthen the opposition to increasing them.

State and local governments rely heavily on sales taxes. In 2008, they constituted 23 percent of current receipts as defined by the national income accounts. If the federal government decides to raise revenues with a new tax, it is very likely to be a consumption tax, such as a VAT[30] or an energy tax. A VAT, although collected differently, applies to a base that is similar, but it has some important differences from the base used by retail sales taxes. (See below.) If the federal government decides to raise revenues by imposing a new VAT, there will be direct competition over this base and it will be very much more difficult for states and localities to raise their sales-tax rates. An energy tax would affect only part of the sales-tax base but would very directly affect the states' ability to raise fuel taxes and to a lesser extent would affect taxes on other sales as well.

The intensity of the competition arising from a federal VAT will depend on the level of its rate. The rate could be quite low for the first decade or so, if it is designed simply to supplement the revenues provided by the existing tax system. However, some proposals hope to diminish political opposition to a VAT by imposing a relatively high rate and using some of the revenue to reduce the burden of the personal and perhaps the corporate income-tax rate. For example, Graetz[31] would impose a 15 percent rate and eliminate personal income taxes on individuals with less than $100,000 of income. Such a high rate would very much inhibit state and local governments' ability to squeeze more revenues out of the same tax base.

Quite a different proposal would create a VAT that is earmarked to finance health expenditures.[32] Because the VAT rate would have to be raised if health-cost growth exceeded the growth of the VAT tax base, the proposal would presumably create a political incentive to dampen the rate of health-cost growth. A VAT that was large enough to finance Medicare, Medicaid, and the new subsidies provided by health reform would be substantial enough that it would compete with state and local sales taxes.

It is theoretically possible to envision a fairly large federal VAT, a part of whose proceeds are distributed back to the states and localities to compensate them for competing with their sales taxes. Australia levies a national VAT and distributes all of its proceeds in a redistributive manner.[33] However, there are no US grants today that attempt to explicitly compensate for differences in the tax capacity of subnational governments, though the data are available to do so.[34] (Medicaid has a redistributive effect, but only because Medicaid largely serves poor people.) A revenue-sharing VAT would not seem to be consistent with American traditions.

Would the creation of a federal VAT encourage states to create their own VATs and substitute them for their retail sales taxes? There are strong arguments for such a reform. States could simply piggyback their own VAT rates on top of the federal rate and so reduce administrative costs. Moreover, most retail sales taxes exempt a large portion of the service sector of the economy. Because services are growing faster than the production of physical goods, sales-tax revenue tends not to keep up with the growth of state economies. A VAT can be easily designed to cover almost all the service sector. (Financial services create special, but not insurmountable, problems.) The retail sales taxes of state and local governments very often tax business-to-business transactions in addition to taxing final consumption. This can create different, unfair, and inefficient tax burdens on different types of consumption, because in some cases, inputs to the production of goods and services will be taxed and then the good or service will be taxed yet again when it is sold at retail. A VAT eliminates any burden on business-to-business transactions. Despite the advantages of moving to a VAT, particularly if the federal government adopts one, the states have shown little inclination to move in this direction.[35]

There would be many complex interactions in administering a new federal VAT and the existing retail tax system. In some cases, the existence of a federal VAT might improve the administration of retail sales taxes. For example, the federal government might be able to assist in reducing tax evasion.[36]

Thus far, I have not discussed the most direct approach to raising federal revenues and that is simply to increase the rates in the existing system. It may be the most direct approach, but it is also the least desirable. Our personal and corporate income-tax systems are highly inefficient because of the combination of high marginal rates and numerous deductions, exclusions, and credits that reduce revenues. This combination of high rates and a multitude of tax preferences can induce people to make economic choices based on tax law rather than on what is best for the economy. The corporate income tax is particularly inefficient. Most OECD countries have been reducing their corporate income rates. The United States is left with the second highest marginal rate of taxation among the thirty OECD countries, but it also has a relatively low average rate because of numerous deductions and exclusions. The extreme inefficiency of the US corporate tax makes it very unlikely that there will be any attempt to raise extra revenue by raising corporate rates. Consequently, there will not be increased competition with state business taxes unless the United States embarks on a fundamental corporate-tax reform.

The top marginal rate in the personal tax is lower than it has been during some periods of the past, but it is still high enough to create significant inequities and inefficiencies. In 2010 the top rate was 35 percent. The president and Congress agreed in December 2010 to maintain this rate for another two years. But if the Bush tax cuts for the more affluent are allowed to expire eventually, the top rate will rise to 39.6 percent. The health reform will add a 3.8 percent tax on investment income, including capital gains.[37] There are certain instances in which the top rate can be pushed higher by the phase-out of deductions. Add state income taxes and the top marginal rate often begins to get uncomfortably close to 50 percent and may exceed this level where there are also local income taxes. As rates go up, the pursuit of tax avoidance schemes intensifies and there is likely to be more illegal tax evasion. That should discourage federal legislators from using income-tax rate increases in the current system to raise revenues and should reduce the possibility of increased competition with state and local personal income taxes.

CONCLUSIONS

Federal budget policies will have to change. That is a forecast that can be made with certainty. Otherwise, the federal deficit and debt will explode. Although it can be said that the entire problem rests on the spending side of the budget and that it is only Social Security and health benefits that are growing faster than tax revenues, it is very likely that budget reforms will affect almost all spending areas and that overall tax burdens will have to rise. It is a popular political refrain that "everything must be on the table."

However, once everything is on the table there will be bitter fights as to how much of the problem must be solved with spending restraint and how much with tax increases. On the spending side, there will be intense competition among programs as to how a limited amount of resources should be divided. On the tax side, the argument will be over whether we need a new tax, a radical tax reform, or whether we can make do with raising rates in the existing system and by closing a few "loopholes."

There are so many options for closing the federal deficit that it is difficult to say with certainty exactly how state and local governments will fare in the budget battles of the future. It is, however, virtually certain that they will experience considerable pain. If a large portion of the federal problem is solved with tax increases, it will be very much harder for a state or local government to raise its own taxes. A federal VAT will particularly limit the ability of the state and local governments to tax retail sales and the elimination of the federal income-tax deduction for state and local taxes will make state and local sales, income, and real estate taxes more painful.[38]

Significant federal tax increases will take some pressure off the spending side of the federal budget, but it is still probable that grants will be constrained.

That includes the grant for Medicaid, but here there is a dim ray of hope. Federal budget pressures may induce the federal government to pursue health-cost control measures more vigorously. To the extent that they improve the efficiency of the Medicaid program, the states could reap a benefit. Unfortunately, the possible impact of the many cost controls embodied in health reform is so uncertain that the CBO was reluctant to assume that there would be significant savings.[39]

Although the federal government will be tempted to pass the responsibility for some activities "down," the temptation will be muted by the fact that federal politicians really like the power conveyed by controlling those activities. Federal politicians will also be tempted to mandate that lower state and local governments supply certain social goods and services without any compensation, but procedural controls limit this activity and those controls are unlikely to be eliminated.

The amount of fiscal pain imposed on governments will also depend to some degree on how federal budget reform comes about. If there is a mega-budget deal that results from a careful deliberative process, there will be more time to design and to phase in long-run health and Social Security reforms. That will take some of the pressure off discretionary spending, which finances the bulk of non-Medicaid grants. If it takes a financial crisis to provoke reforms, it will be necessary to act quickly and that probably means that discretionary cuts and tax increases will be more dramatic.

Although it is highly uncertain exactly how and when the intergovernmental financial system will change, change is inevitable. State and local governments should be strong advocates for federal budget reform. It will be easier to protect their interests if reform results from a deliberative process rather than from an economic or political crisis.

NOTES

1 See the essay by Sally Wallace in this volume.
2 Hood (2010), 127–141.
3 Congressional Budget Office (2010a).
4 It would work less well in the United States than in most developed countries, because US debt has an unusually short maturity. About 30 percent of the total has to be refinanced every year and that means that interest costs would rise quickly as inflation rises, thus countering the erosion of the real value of the debt.
5 For example, it becomes impossible to fulfill contracts written in money terms; civil service salaries become worth very little; and more generally, public benefits and wages are eroded. This happens even if benefits and wages are indexed to inflation. No indexing process can operate rapidly enough to keep up with a hyperinflation.
6 For a rationale from the man who initiated the bailouts, see Bush (2010).
7 Francis in this volume discusses empirically the depth of the Great Recession.
8 Office of Management and Budget (2010).
9 Congressional Budget Office (2010a).
10 Portions of the above have been drawn from Palmer and Penner (2010).

11 Not counting interest saving, the split is about 70 percent spending reduction and 30 revenue increases. National Commission on Fiscal Responsibility and Reform (2010).

12 The British plan can be found at www.hm-treasury.gov.uk/spend_sr2010_documents. htm.

13 For a full discussion, see Scheppach, this volume.

14 The receipts total is from the national income accounts. As measured by the Census, grants are a slightly lower percentage of receipts. The Census measure includes receipts related to state and local pensions. The NIA includes only the net surplus or deficit of state and locally owned businesses whereas the Census reports the sales and expenditures on a gross basis.

15 Orszag (2010).

16 Congressional Budget Office. (2010c); Angeles (2010).

17 Gabrielli et al. (2009). For a description of diagnosis-related groups (DRG), see Mayes (2007).

18 National Commission on Fiscal Responsibility and Reform. (2010).

19 Public opinion polls conducted by Fox News in 2006 and the National Opinion Research Center (NORC) between 1985 and 2006. The results have been compiled by the American Enterprise Institute: Bowman et al. (2010).

20 Nivola (2007).

21 National Research Council and National Academy of Public Administration (2010). The commission was jointly chaired by Rudolph Penner and John Palmer.

22 The appendices to the report were not printed. They can be found at www. ourfiscalfuture.org.

23 The two packages that involved both tax increases and reductions in the rate of growth of spending differed little in the implied size of government. They mainly differed in the choice of priorities. One protected benefits going to the elderly. That meant that there was less money left over for investing in things like infrastructure and education.

24 Dye and McGuire (1992).

25 Congressional Budget Office (2010b).

26 The new health-reform law does not limit the health-care exclusion, but it will impose a "luxury tax" on very expensive policies starting in 2018.

27 A few states simply add a surtax or "piggyback" tax to the taxpayer's federal tax liability.

28 Bipartisan Policy Center, the Debt Reduction Task Force (2010).

29 The effect of a phase-out on the after-tax cost of an extra dollar of state and local taxes depends on how the phase-out is constructed. Current law reduces itemized deductions by 3 percent income above a threshold for most people subjected to the phase-out. Because the reduction depends on income and not the amount of deductions, the cost of an extra dollar of tax equals the tax minus the person's marginal tax rate. However, the reduction is limited to 80 percent of total deductions. For those affected by the limit, the cost of an extra dollar of state and local tax is increased.

30 A VAT has been recommended by the Bipartisan Policy Center, the Debt Reduction Task Force (2010).

31 Graetz (2008).

32 Burman (2008).

33 Perry (2010).

34 There once was a general revenue-sharing grant in the 1970s, but it did not last very long. See Nathan et al. (1977). For the most recent methodology and estimates of the fifty states and the District of Columbia, see Yilmaz and Zahradnik (2008).

35 For a review of state practice, see Hines (2003) and Ebel and Kalambokidis (2005).
36 McLure (2010).
37 National Research Council and National Academy of Public Administration (2010).
38 In states with no income taxes, individuals are allowed to deduct sales taxes.
39 For a discussion, see Palmer and Penner (2010).

References

Angeles, January (2010, October 21). "Some Recent Reports Overstate the Effect on State Budgets of the Medicaid Expansions in the Health Reform Law." Center on Budget Policy and Priorities.

Bipartisan Policy Center, the Debt Reduction Task Force (2010). "Restoring America's Future." http://bipartisanpolicy.org/sites/default/files/FINAL%20DRTF%20 REPORT%2011.16.10.pdf.

Bowman, Karlyn, Rugg, Andrew, and Marsico, Jennifer (2010). "Are Attitudes Changing about the Proper Role of the Federal Government?" AEI Public Opinion Studies, American Enterprise Institute for Public Policy Research. Accessed December 21, 2010, at http://www.aei.org/docLib/RoleOfGovernment.pdf.

Burman, Leonard E. (2008). "Testimony on a Blueprint for Tax Reform and Health Reform before the Senate Committee on Finance." Text from the Tax Policy Center, Urban Institute. http://www.taxpolicycenter.org/UploadedPDF/901167_Burman_reform.pdf.

Bush, George W. (2010). *Decision Points*. New York: Crown.

Committee on Ways and Means (2004). "2004 Green Book." US House of Representatives (108th Congress), Committee on Ways and Means.

Congressional Budget Office (2010a). "A Preliminary Analysis of the President's Budget and an Update of CBO's Budget and Economic Outlook." Congress of the United States, Congressional Budget Office.

Congressional Budget Office (2010b). "A Review of the CBO Activities in 2009 under the Unfunded Mandates Reform Act." Congress of the United States, Congressional Budget Office.

Congressional Budget Office (2010c). "H.R. 4872, Reconciliation Act of 2010 (Final Health Care Legislation): Cost Estimate for the Amendment in the Nature of a Substitute for H.R. 4872, Incorporating a Proposed Manager's Amendment Made Public on March 20, 2010." Congress of the United States, Congressional Budget Office.

Dye, Richard F., and Therese J. McGuire (1992, October). "The Effect of Earmarked Revenues on the Level and Composition of Expenditures." *Public Finance Quarterly* 20(4): 543–556.

Ebel, Robert, and Laura Kalambokidis (2005). "Value-added Tax, State." In *The Encyclopedia of Taxation and Tax Policy*, edited by Joseph Cordes, Robert Ebel, and Jane Gravelle. Washington, DC: Urban Institute Press. 464–467.

Gabrielli, Andrea, Layon, A. Joseph, and Yu, Mihae (2009). *Civetta, Taylor & Kirby's Critical Care*. Philadelphia: Lippincott Williams & Wilkins.

Graetz, Michael (2008). *100 Million Unnecessary Returns: A Simple, Fair, and Competitive Tax Plan for the United States*. New Haven: Yale University Press.

Hines, James R., Jr. (2003) "Michigan's Flirtation with the Single Business Tax". *In Michigan at the Millennium*, edited by Charles L. Ballard, Douglas C. Crake, Paul N. Courant, Ronald Fisher and Elizabeth R. Gerber. East Lansing: Michigan State University Press. 60–28.

Hood, John (2010, Summer). "How to Fix Medicaid." *National Affairs* 4: 127–141.

Mayes, Rick (2007, January). "The Origins, Development, and Passage of Medicare's Revolutionary Prospective Payment System." *Journal of the History of Medicine and Allied Sciences* 62(1): 21–55.

McLure, Charles E. (2010). "How to Coordinate State and Local Sales Taxes with a Federal Value-Added Tax." *Tax Law Review* 63(3): 639–704.

National Commission on Fiscal Responsibility and Reform (2010). "The Moment of Truth." Washington, DC.

National Research Council and National Academy of Public Administration (2010). *Choosing the Nation's Fiscal Future.* Committee on the Fiscal Future of the United States. Washington, DC: National Academics Press.

National State Association of Budget Officers (2009). "State Expenditure Report 2008." National State Association of Budget Officers.

Nathan, Richard P. Adams, Charles F. Jr., and associates with the assistance of Junean, Andre, and Fossett, James W. (1977). *Revenue Sharing: The Second Round.* Washington, DC: Brookings Institution.

Nivola, Pietro S. (2007, July). "Rediscovering Federalism." Issues in Governance Studies, no.10, Brookings Institution. Accessed December 21, 2010, at http://www.brookings. edu/papers/2007/07governance_nivola.aspx.

Office of Management and Budget (2010). "Mid-Session Review: Budget of the US Government, Fiscal Year 2011." Office of Management and Budget.

Orszag, Peter (2010, September 18). "A Health Care Plan for Colleges." *New York Times.* http://www.nytimes.com/2010/09/19/opinion/19orszag.html?_r=1&ref=peter_orszag.

Palmer, John L., and Rudolph G. Penner (2010). *Have Recent Budget Policies Contributed to Long-Run Fiscal Stability?* Washington, DC: Urban Institute.

Perry, Victoria J. (2010). "International Experiences in Implementing VATs in Federal Jurisdictions: A Summary." *Tax Law Review* 63(3): 623–638.

Yilmaz, Yesim, and Robert Zahradnik (2008). "Measuring the Fiscal Capacity of the District of Columbia: A Comparison of Revenue Capacity and Expenditure Need, FY 2005." *Annual Proceedings of the National Tax Association.* Washington, DC: National Tax Association.

CHAPTER 33

....

ACHIEVING FISCAL SUSTAINABILITY FOR STATE AND LOCAL GOVERNMENTS

....

ROBERT B. WARD

PERHAPS the most fundamental rule of economics holds that resources are always limited. In the context of governmental budgets, this concept of scarcity means we inevitably have fewer dollars than policymakers or voters might like. Since the founding of the nation, states have struggled to balance limited revenues with expenditure demands that can seem nearly limitless.[1]

Such concerns have typically related to the immediate year's budget, the coming year (or biennium in states with two-year cycles), and—less commonly—another year or two in the future. In the first decade of the twenty-first century, however, observers of state and local finances expressed increasing alarm over an emerging picture of long-term, structural imbalances. The question of whether expenditure commitments can be met within available revenue streams, over the course of coming decades, is captured in the concept of fiscal sustainability.

That concept can be analyzed in varied ways, so I first summarize varying ways of thinking about fiscal sustainability. I briefly review recent trends in state and local finances, with particular attention to expenditure commitments that are difficult to change—taking on the character of entitlements—and thus create risks to fiscal sustainability. I then touch on the importance of budgetary culture and finally examine potential paths to significant changes in state and local budget practices that might be brought about by new financial reporting rules as well as actions by state and local policymakers and/or the federal government.

LOOKING AHEAD

WHAT IS FISCAL SUSTAINABILITY?

The concept of a long-term budgetary balance is not new. Fiscal monitors and public-policy practitioners have long talked and written about "structural" balance, meaning that revenues and expenditures are not only aligned in a current year but are projected to remain so in years to come.[2] Broad concern about fiscal sustainability arose after the turn of the twenty-first century as a brief national recession in 2001 reduced state-tax revenues by unexpectedly sharp levels and observers increasingly perceived a confluence of long-term trends such as higher health-care costs, unfunded commitments for pensions and other expenditures, and the failure of certain tax revenues to keep pace with growth in their economic bases. In simple terms, the concept extends the "structural balance" concept into a longer time frame—over several decades, rather than years. Markers of the growth in concern include a 2008 conference held by the National Tax Association (NTA) and partner organizations, creation of an NTA "Fiscal Sustainability Working Group" the same year, and reports from various sources in recent years on topics such as unfunded pension and health-care commitments.

While general understanding of the issue is clear, "fiscal sustainability" may mean different things to different people. This chapter will not attempt to define the term beyond the broad concept. However, readers should be aware of such differences, which may direct analysis and research—perhaps even solutions—in varied directions. A summary of several approaches to the definition of fiscal sustainability follows.

The Federal Accounting Standards Advisory Board (FASAB), which promulgates such standards for the US government, adopted Standard No. 36, "Reporting Comprehensive Long-Term Fiscal Projections for the U.S. Government," in 2009. In a summary, the FASAB said the new standard would help readers of the comprehensive financial report assess "whether future budgetary resources will likely be sufficient to sustain public services and to meet obligations as they come due." For a basic financial statement in the US government's consolidated financial report, the new standard requires the present value of projected receipts and noninterest spending under current policy without change; the relationship of such amounts to projected gross domestic product (GDP); and changes in the present value of such receipts and spending from the prior year. Required supplementary information includes the likely impact of delaying corrective action in case a fiscal gap exists and alternative scenarios of trends including projected deficits or surpluses. Underlying assumptions and factors influencing such trends must be included as well. The rules were to be implemented following a three-year transition period starting in fiscal year 2010.[3]

The Governmental Accounting Standards Board (GASB), which sets accounting and financial-reporting standards for most state and local governments, began in 2005 to study the possibility of including fiscal sustainability among the issues that governments must address in certain public financial reports. If the board ultimately establishes standards in this area, its definition will settle the field for state and local financial reports, and for many related purposes. As of late 2010, the board had not adopted a definition of the term. A draft circulated early in the board's research provided this language: "Fiscal sustainability is a government's ability and willingness to generate inflows of resources necessary to honor current service commitments and to meet financial obligations as they come due, without transferring financial obligations to future periods that do not result in commensurate benefits."[4] The GASB and its staff have since explored key concepts and potentially detailed definitions for the elements of fiscal sustainability.

The Government Accountability Office, which has constructed long-range projections of aggregate state and local fiscal balance, defines "fiscal sustainability" as "the ability of the sector to cover its current expenditures out of current receipts."[5] Other standards-setting entities have taken up the sustainability issue as well. The staff of the International Public Sector Accounting Standards Board has used this terminology:

> At a very high level, long-term fiscal sustainability reporting involves an assessment of the extent to which service delivery can be maintained at existing levels, and the extent to which governmental obligations to citizens under existing legal frameworks can be met from predicted inflows over a predetermined future period.[6]

Academic researchers have offered several attempts at definition. One admirably simple formulation held that fiscal sustainability "relates to the government's ability to maintain its current policies while remaining solvent."[7] Another suggested the following: "At the state and local level, fiscal sustainability is the long-run capability of a government to consistently meet its financial responsibilities. It reflects the adequacy of available revenue to ensure the continued provision of the service and capital levels that the public demands."[8]

One issue in attempting to define fiscal sustainability relates to the variability of relevant terms. Examination of balance or imbalance among physical units—grams, meters, and so on—is based on fixed, measurable values of those terms. A gram is always one-thousandth of a kilogram, which in turn is the mass of a liter of water—and, under normal conditions, that mass is always the same. A meter is defined in relation to the speed of light in a vacuum, which is similarly constant. Defining the nature of a budget balance, in the short or long term, inherently requires a juxtaposition of elements that have no fixed value. It's hard to conceive, for example, how elected or appointed officials—or academic researchers, for that matter—might determine "the service and capital levels that the public demands," especially with regard to each of the many subsets of governmental budgets. Similarly elusive, for purposes of measurement, is any government's "willingness to generate inflows of resources." Such a concept certainly relates to one of the most important elements of fiscal practices and sustainability—the budgetary culture in a given jurisdiction (a topic addressed later in this chapter). But how could the cultural attribute be assessed—with surveys of voters, or of future elected officials? If such elements of fiscal sustainability cannot be measured, neither can sustainability itself.

Another issue relates to whether expenditures or revenues—or both—are considered susceptible to changes in policy. The early-draft GASB language cited above treats "current service commitments" and "financial obligations" as factors that might be balanced with changes in a third factor ("inflows of resources") but does not seem to contemplate the possibility of changes in service commitments. "Obligations" might inherently be unchangeable, but state and local governments increase and reduce services every year.

Financial Reporting on Fiscal Sustainability

After five years of research and deliberation, in late 2010 the GASB was well into a project that might result in new rules for state and local government reporting on fiscal sustainability. With additional work scheduled through most of the following year, any new rules in this area from the GASB were unlikely to emerge before 2012, and possibly later.

GASB staff and board members had reached a consensus, however, that "forward-looking information is necessary for users to make an assessment of a governmental entity's fiscal sustainability." Discussions centered around the concept that "the ability to meet financial obligations and commitments, the effects of interdependencies between governmental entities, the potential effects of the underlying environment within which a governmental entity operates, and the ability and willingness of a governmental entity to make decisions that will keep it sound are categories of information necessary for users to make an assessment of a governmental entity's fiscal sustainability." Each of those elements includes several subsets. For example, regarding the "ability to meet financial obligations and commitments," specific issues include debt and debt service information, postemployment benefit information including pensions and other postemployment benefits, capital asset and infrastructure information, and information on contractual obligations.[9]

Looking Back: The Rise of "Entitlement" Spending

State and local government expenditures have risen over time as population growth increased demand for services; economic growth generated more resources to support new and expanded programs; evolving social mores produced expectations of a higher quality in life that in part would be met by government; and increasingly influential interest groups such as public-employee unions enhanced political rewards for increases in government spending. Revenue systems are larger and more broad-based than they were decades ago, so sharp declines in overall revenues are rare. For many modern elected leaders, heightened expectations on the part of voters and politically active interest groups make today's policy calculus significantly different from that of several decades ago.

The classic illustration is public education, the largest single area of state and local expenditures both a century ago (23 percent of the total in 1902) and recently (29 percent as of 2008).[10] As early as the mid-1800s, states reflected changing social attitudes by beginning to enact laws and constitutional requirements establishing free public education as a universal right. Over many decades, the flow of dollars into public schools expanded almost continuously both because the population was expanding and because the resource base was growing—especially for taxes on incomes and property values. But spending considerations were aligned closely with revenue realities, and increases occasionally were reversed when economic disruptions reduced tax collections. From the 1929–1930 school year to that of 1933–1934, for example, state and local expenditures on public elementary and secondary schools fell by 25 percent. The cause was not that voters had turned against education, or that enrollments had plummeted. Rather, the economy and tax revenues (particularly property taxes for local school districts) had taken sharp declines. Education spending did not regain its pre-Depression levels until 1940.[11]

That was then. Over the last three to four decades, education and certain other expenditures have become less responsive to the business cycle. Annual budget increases continue to reflect the strength of the economy, in broad form. But, reminiscent of entitlement programs at the federal level, expenditures in some categories are increasingly shaped by political, demographic, and institutional forces that make adjustments more difficult when revenues do not keep pace with spending patterns. In addition to education, the most important examples of these—though specifics vary from state to state—are publicly funded health-care and public-employee compensation (including pension and health benefits).

Take education. In contrast to the early 1930s, a 25 percent reduction in school spending is inconceivable today. State-tax revenues in 2009 and early 2010 took their sharpest drop since the Depression—yet it seems unlikely that overall K-12 expenditures fell by even 5 percent, or one-fifth as much as during the first years of the collapse in the early 1930s. (Limitations of publicly available data make such conclusions uncertain until at least 2011.) To be sure, the extraordinary injection of federal funds helped cushion state and local budgets during the worst of the fiscal impact from the Great Recession. And most states' tax bases now are much larger and more resilient than those of eighty years ago, so greater resiliency for expenditures should be expected. But more robust tax bases and the approval of special federal funding are also, in significant measure, reflections of voters' heightened expectations for public services.

A second example of entitlement-like expenditures is Medicaid, which represents the bulk of state costs for public health care. While many states greeted the creation of Medicaid in 1965 as an opportunity to draw new assistance from Washington, the unexpected growth in costs generated second thoughts within just a few years. (For example, in New York, Governor Nelson A. Rockefeller signed legislation in 1968—two years after bringing Medicaid to New York—cutting the program by some $300 million.) By the 1990s, continual growth in costs for what had already become a large part of state budgets produced widespread, repeated efforts to limit expenditures through adoption of managed care and other steps. Such cost-saving initiatives have had some success. Still, Medicaid expenditures have continued to increase not only in absolute terms but in relation to overall state revenues and budgets, as shown in table 33.1. As represented by Census data on vendor payments, Medicaid represented the equivalent of more than 22 percent of state-tax revenues in 2008—up sharply from 8.4 percent some three decades earlier. Relative to states' general expenditures, the program has grown from roughly one in twenty dollars, to one in eight more recently.

As of 2008, state and local governments spent a total of $868 billion on K-12 education or Medicaid vendor payments, according to Census data. Adding $129 billion in expenditures on hospitals, some 41 percent of combined state and local budgets were committed to health care and education. These are the programmatic categories for which voter surveys tend to show especially strong support, and in which the political influence of employees and providers has become most powerful.

One element of the dramatic growth in state and local expenditures during the second half of the twentieth century—reflected in education statistics and elsewhere—was a significant increase in both employment and employee compensation. States and localities (including school districts) employed 4.7 million Americans in 1955, or 9.3 percent of total nonagricultural jobs. The proportion rose almost continuously until 1975, when it reached 15.5 percent. It then declined by one to two percentage points for most of the ensuing decades (with absolute numbers of employees rising in most years, but not as much as overall employment). During the broad economic slowdown starting in 2008, the state and local government share of all jobs rose above 15 percent once again. However, state and local employment, reacting to fiscal pressures, began to decline thereafter.[12]

As of 2010, benefit costs for state and local government employees averaged some $13.60 an hour nationwide, nearly two-thirds more than the average in the

Table 33.1 Growing Medicaid commitments for states

	1977	1992	2008
Vendor payments as percentage of tax revenue, all states	8.4%	16.7%	22.3%
Vendor payments as percentage of direct general expenditures	5.4%	9.6%	12.3%

Source: Author calculations from US Census Bureau data.

private sector. Benefits represented more than 34 percent of compensation in the state and local sector compared to a little over 29 percent for private industry. Benefit costs for these government workers were rising more rapidly than those for private-sector workers, both in dollar terms and as a share of total compensation.[13]

Two major types of employee benefits—pension and health insurance—are among the central topics of concern when government officials and outside observers analyze fiscal sustainability.

Most state and local governments in the United States provide defined-benefit pension plans. This contrasts with most private-sector employers, who have generally changed to defined-contribution programs such as 401K plans if they provide retirement benefits at all. In addition, states and localities tend to offer more generous health coverage to their employees than typical private-sector businesses and nonprofit entities—and many public-sector retirees continue to enjoy employer-sponsored health coverage, while such benefits are rare in the private sector. Rising awareness of the cost of such benefits has taken place along with—and been a central part of—increasing concern about fiscal sustainability generally.

By one 2010 estimate, states faced a $1 trillion gap between the amount they had set aside for employee retirement benefits (pensions and health coverage), and the likely actual cost of such commitments.[14] Another study put the estimate of underfunding, for states' pensions alone, at $3.2 trillion.[15] Differences in such estimates reflect, among other things, varying assessments of the proper actuarial procedures to be used in the calculation of pension liabilities. Either figure would at least double the formally recognized liabilities for states, relative to traditional reporting of such liabilities as bonds and other obligations.

Such figures are useful for understanding that states (and local governments, whose employee benefit structures are generally similar) will be confronting sizable new financial challenges. They illustrate the environment in which governments will enact and manage annual budgets over the course of many years, but do not provide specific insights into the impact on those budgets—for example, the extent to which increased annual costs for employee and retiree health benefits might require higher taxes or crowd out other spending.

A number of states have taken steps in recent years to change their pension systems—reducing benefits or requiring higher employee contributions for defined-benefit plans, or moving from defined-benefit to defined-contribution systems. Still, many jurisdictions have no firm grasp on how pensions and health-care benefits may affect annual budgets in the medium-term to long-term future. These compensation costs remain a large, growing, and largely undefined challenge for year-to-year fiscal sustainability.

As noted earlier, the recent requirement that states and most local-government employers estimate and report their long-term liabilities for retirees' health-care and other benefits has dramatically increased public attention to such costs. Unlike public pensions in many states, these benefits typically do not have constitutional or statutory protection. Thus, they may be susceptible to somewhat more rapid change than pensions, as governments are forced to confront trade-offs between employee compensation and other expenditures.

LOOKING FORWARD: MORE OF THE SAME?

The factors that have contributed most to rising expenditures by states and localities are likely—along with political, economic, and institutional conditions that limit growth in tax revenues—to create ongoing hurdles to fiscal sustainability.

The GAO, in a series of reports starting in 2008, noted the impact of health-care expenditures for both the general public and for state and local government employees: "The primary driver of the fiscal pressure confronting the state and local sector is the continued growth in health-related costs."[16] Like numerous other observers, the GAO has forecasted that demand for health-care expenditures will become more intense as the nation's population ages and health-care costs generally continue to outpace overall inflation or growth in the economy.

To be sure, various uncertainties make precise estimates regarding future Medicaid expenditures inherently risky. However, several major factors suggest that pressures for spending on publicly funded health care are likely to increase. The proportion of private-sector workers covered by employer-sponsored health insurance has decreased, and it will likely further decline. Federal health-care legislation signed by President Obama in 2010 requires states to cover millions of individuals who were previously ineligible for Medicaid (although additional federal aid will offset at least some new costs). As members of the baby-boom generation progress through older age, more Americans will seek help paying for nursing homes and other long-term care. In some states and in Washington, unions representing health-care workers have become powerful political actors. Expenditure trends in Medicaid inherently reflect costs in the broader health-care marketplace, which have proven hard to change—as evidenced by the outcome of the national legislation mentioned above.

States continually, and especially during periods of revenue declines, seek ways to restrain Medicaid spending. But doing so is complicated because Medicaid includes a variety of major programs including general health coverage for those with lower incomes; long-term care for the elderly; and lifetime care for many individuals with developmental disabilities. Because states receive federal funding for half or more of every Medicaid dollar they spend, reducing their own expenditures by a given amount may mean significantly larger reductions in overall support for health care and other programs. Finally, Medicaid is increasingly viewed more like Medicare as a support to which middle-class and even wealthier Americans are entitled when they need it. That makes any restrictions on expenditures significantly more politically difficult than if the program were viewed as assistance for the poor.

In the second half of the twentieth century, education became the largest element of state and local budgets because of a near-universal belief in its central importance to the realization of individual and societal potential. Americans increasingly came to regard education as a competitive necessity for the nation, in an ever more integrated global economy. Such concerns are likely to remain, and perhaps grow further in importance, over coming decades. Some economists suggest that education and other public-sector jobs are especially susceptible to "cost disease"—in which wages and salaries rise despite a lack of gains in employee productivity—and thus resistant to restructuring for cost-effectiveness.

As other chapters describe in greater detail, revenue constraints represent a key element in concerns over fiscal sustainability. Contrary to occasional suggestions that outdated tax systems have produced diminishing revenues, combined tax revenues for states and localities have grown faster than population and inflation, and they have remained essentially constant as a share of the nation's economic output since the mid-1970s.

As shown in figure 33.1, state taxes and local taxes each equated to slightly less than 4 percent of GDP in the early 1960s. Increased expenditures on Medicaid, education, and other programs drove state-tax collections up to roughly 5.5 percent of GDP from the mid-1970s through the early 1990s. With that increase, combined state and local levies rose by one-third, as a proportion of GDP—from 7.3 percent to 9.8 percent—from 1961 to 1973. Since the mid-1970s, tax revenues from both levels of government have remained relatively constant, varying within a range of 8.8 to 9.8 percent of the economy. These figures capture the entirety of thousands of

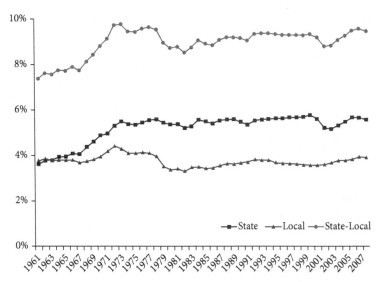

Figure 33.1 State-local government tax revenue as percentage of GDP, FY 1961–2008
Source: US Census Bureau (tax revenue); Bureau of Economic Analysis (GDP).

policy choices by state and local officials over an extended period. If the net results of such decisions can be considered to represent the wishes of voters, as expressed through their elected representatives, American taxpayers may have reached an equilibrium point regarding demand for public services and acceptability of state and local taxes. Such equilibrium points may change over time, however—as was the case in the 1960s and early 1970s when voter preferences for an expanded social safety net brought new costs.

What Might Bring Sustainable Budgeting?

Increased concern over fiscal sustainability for states and localities flows from the perception that elected officials in these jurisdictions have generally not dealt adequately with the issue. Indeed, while gaps between the pace of expenditures and revenues constitute the essentials of unsustainable budgets, those elements do not arise of their own volition. Rather, they reflect the actions and inactions of individuals in thousands of government offices. If elected leaders are to address fiscal sustainability more seriously, what might be the impetus? What might the mechanics look like?

At least two types of external forces seem possible: fiscal pressure from the federal government, and regulatory direction from the GASB. A third possibility is an evolution in budgetary cultures—which vary from one jurisdiction to another and may change in response to voter attitudes as well as institutional reforms shaped by political elites.

Federal aid increased as a share of state and local government revenues over the past half-century—from less than 12 percent in 1960 to around 20 percent in 2008. (The great majority of such revenue has flowed to states, with some of that passing through to municipalities and school districts.) In programmatic areas such as health care, social welfare, special education, transportation, and environmental quality, federal funding is often the most important driving force in program design. Even relatively small increments of aid from Washington can generate significant policy changes. The Obama administration's Race to the Top program, for example, drove major new developments in state policies regarding charter schools and teacher evaluation—even though state officials knew that such changes would not guarantee additional aid and that any new funding from the program would be relatively small in the context of overall education spending. Governors and legislatures generally perceive their budgetary resources as tightly limited and make a high priority of any opportunity to obtain any new, "free" assistance.

Many observers—no doubt including a majority of those who run state and local governments—argue that equity and other considerations require a larger overall federal role in funding domestic services. An increase in Washington's responsibility for costs that are currently borne by subnational jurisdictions could answer at least a major part of the sustainability question for states and localities. To be sure, such a development appears highly unlikely in the near term. Yet elections in 2012 and thereafter may bring policymakers who are more sympathetic to the troubles of the states. Even in that case, however, a significant shifting of costs to Washington seems unlikely unless the federal government also adds significantly to its own revenue base, either with new forms of taxation or increases in existing income-tax rates. In recent years, as the issue of fiscal sustainability has gained increasing attention, the national Republican Party has become dominated by an ideology of smaller government and limited spending. Given the philosophy dominating one of the two major national parties, the expansion of federal taxes will not be accomplished easily. Similarly, using any new federal resources to aid states, rather than to address the growth of national budget deficits, would be opposed by many members of Congress. Still, such changes cannot be ruled out. Even Ronald Reagan, the hero of small-government Republicans, agreed to some tax increases both when he was governor of California and later when he was president.

If the idea of significant increases in federal assistance for states does gain traction, it seems likely that it would be accompanied by a discussion of new requirements to promote fiscal sustainability. Critics of increased government spending could be expected to push for stricter balanced-budget rules—and perhaps for extending such rules to promote long-term sustainability—rather than the one-year requirements that are now in place. Some would likely argue for new, or stricter, limits on state or local expenditures or taxes. Perhaps a higher level of assistance would be accompanied by specific policy requirements related to more cost-efficient staffing levels, or restrictions on the assignment of students to special education (an especially costly area of K-12 instruction where the federal government already plays a major role).

Consideration of major new federal involvement in states' fiscal affairs is complicated by long-standing debates over limits on the national government's authority in such matters. States retain sovereignty, even after more than a century of rising influence from Washington. Any attempt by Congress to impose budgetary rules on states would face broad skepticism on constitutional grounds. Conceivably, a grand bargain could emerge, in which the federal government's broader resource base assumes a greater share of state and local costs, on the condition that state policymakers take defined steps to ensure that increased assistance would not simply produce larger and still unbalanced budgets. Even such a voluntary relinquishment of state authority might be subject to challenge by interests opposed to either the limits on states or to the expansion of federal responsibilities. Such questions are premature, however, until (and unless) the political will to place such options on the agenda has emerged.

In addition to issues of federal expenditures, national tax policy may have dramatic implications for state and local governments. Serious discussion of federal tax reform re-emerged in 2010, and it seemed likely to continue due to rising concerns over the nation's large budget deficits and the complexity of the tax code.

Potential changes at the national level include reductions in rates and broadening of the tax based for federal personal and corporate income taxes, as occurred in 1986. (A series of incremental changes over the ensuing quarter-century raised rates, and these changes introduced significant numbers of new credits and deductions along with greater complexity.) Other options include enactment of a national value-added tax (VAT), a form of consumption tax in which businesses pay tax on the difference between their total sales and their purchases of inputs.[17] Any such changes would have substantial impacts—some likely positive, some negative, and all hard to predict with certainty—on state and local government fiscal sustainability.

Absent any one-size-fits-all change in Washington's relationships with the states, elected leaders in fifty capitals (and those in thousands of local government entities) will find their own paths to budgetary balance. Such approaches can be expected to vary dramatically, just as budget practices and problems differ already. For example, can California reduce the voter-imposed gridlock that combines mandated proportions of education spending with high hurdles to the enactment of tax increases? Will Tennessee, Washington, and six other states join the rest of the nation in making income taxes a central plank in their revenue structures? How will elected officials, especially in those states whose political cultures encourage high spending, provide quality educational services without continual, above-inflation increases in costs?

While Congress can exert a broad influence on state budgetary choices, the accounting and financial-reporting functions of states and localities are the GASB's realm. As discussed earlier in this chapter, the board has considered setting standards that might come into play in governments' comprehensive annual financial reports or other public documents. New rules from the GASB could have major ramifications for states and localities, ultimately providing important new information for policymakers, researchers, and the public. A related step by the organization in 2004, the promulgation of a rule regarding public reporting of estimated long-range costs for retiree health coverage and other postemployment benefits, significantly increased attention to that particular area of state and local finance and fiscal sustainability in general.

Any action by the GASB would cause policymakers and voters to pay more attention to fiscal sustainability. However, greater transparency for long-term budget challenges alone will not produce any policy change. The GASB does not have enforcement authority. Compliance with its standards is enforced through the laws of some individual states and through the audit process, when auditors render opinions on the fairness of financial statement presentations in conformity with the GASB's rules. If there were a GASB standard on fiscal sustainability, many states and localities would report long-term projections for spending exceeding those for revenues. Such transparency alone would not directly force any change in fiscal practices—as evidenced, for example, by experience in New York, where continual projections of out-year gaps have not produced structurally balanced budgets. All else equal, however, increased attention to long-term budget challenges would at a minimum lead to more long-term thinking about policy choices.

THE ROLE OF BUDGETARY CULTURE

Ultimate responsibility for state and local budgets lies not with US Congress, nor with those who make the rules for accounting and financial reporting, but with elected leaders and voters in every jurisdiction that raises and spends public dollars. The choices made by these men and women define budgetary cultures that vary just as natural environments, social habits, and economic activities differ from state to state and from city to city.

Like the political cultures of which they are a significant element, budgetary cultures are difficult to measure. Clearly, states and localities vary in their fiscal policy choices, such as the overall level of resources they raise from taxpayers and the way they distribute those dollars among competing programs and services. They also differ in the extent to which they value budgetary balance and sustainability.

One way to think about variation in this area is through use of the representative expenditure system (RES). As applied over the years by Tannenwald, Yilmaz, and others, RES measurements include the level of expenditure need—"the amount that a state would have to spend on its residents to provide services on a par with the national average.... For example, all other things being equal, a state with a large percentage of its population between the ages of 5 and 18 has a higher need for spending on education than one with fewer school age children."[18] States that spend more than their apparent expenditure need are said to have high levels of expenditure effort. Thus, for example, Mississippi is perceived to have the highest expenditure need of any state—but an expenditure effort that is among the lowest. Hawaii's need for public expenditures is the lowest in the nation, but its expenditure effort is among the highest when using this measure.

Such assessments may or may not accurately capture the reality of need and effort in specific states. The concept such assessments attempt to illustrate—that states' policy choices differ in ways that are not fully explained by variations in economic assets and fiscal capacity—is undeniable.

So, too, there are differences in the importance that state officials (and, presumably, voters) attach to issues of budget process—including short-term balance and long-term sustainability. Some states, but not all, have adopted constitutional limits on debt, taxes, and/or expenditures, and such limits vary in strictness. States differ in institutional rules such as the authority they grant governors to impound legislative appropriations when budget gaps arise during the fiscal year.[19] Such arrangements represent one aspect of budgetary cultures. Also important—sometimes more so—are unwritten expectations, as well as the willingness on the part of some elected leaders to take steps that others will not. Examples of such actions in recent years include steps that Governors Chris Christie of New Jersey and Mitch Daniels of Indiana took in 2009 to trim education and other expenditures beyond the level of reductions in many other states. On the revenue side of the equation, policymakers in Connecticut and New York chose to increase income taxes in 2009. Their actions contrasted with Illinois, which considered but did not take such a step (nor limit its spending sharply); instead Illinois borrowed billions of dollars to pay current expenditures, giving the state perhaps the most critical short-term budget crisis in the nation.

Elected leaders make choices—or refuse to make them—based partly on what they perceive the will of the electorate to be. But voters, many of whom pay little attention to public affairs at any level, often care more about national and local issues than state policies. Budgetary balance is seldom the most salient of concerns; most citizens care more about levels of taxes or services (and many focus their attention on issues such as war and the health of the economy). Periodically, national budget deficits produce high levels of voter concern—in the presidential election of 1992, for example, and in the congressional elections of 2010. But even such sporadic attention is harder to find at the state level. Broader trends in citizens' views may also come into play—such as opinions about the level of personal indebtedness that individuals find acceptable. Given the generally low importance that voters apparently assign to balanced budgets, there is little wonder that elected leaders have often ignored the issue of fiscal sustainability.

Daniel Patrick Moynihan considered his most important conclusion, after forty years of working in and studying government, to be this: "The central conservative truth is that it is culture, not politics, that determines the success of a society. The central liberal truth is that politics can change a culture and save it from itself. Thanks to this interaction, we're a better society in nearly all respects than we were."[20] Changes to budgetary rules that promote more long-term planning could, then, help lead to new budgetary cultures. Examples might include shifting more budget-making authority from legislatures to governors, who tend to have a greater political stake in avoiding fiscal crises and thus more interest in a multiyear balance.

While state officials are in near unanimity as to the long-term nature of the fiscal problems confronting them, existing budget practices do not promote multiyear thinking, let alone planning. Half the states do not forecast tax revenues beyond the current year and the year immediately following. Twenty states do make some forecasts of revenues at least three years into the future.[21] Only a handful of states, however, issue multiyear projections of overall balance or imbalance.

Is Broad Change Coming?

In the 1960s, state governments entered a period of major growth and change. Legislatures created or expanded programs, including Medicaid, special education for children with disabilities, and environmental protection; they imposed new taxes and charges to pay for these services. The expansion of state govern-ments was accompanied—and in part driven—by significant changes in the pro-cesses that determine representation and policymaking. Legislatures became more "professional," with larger staffs to provide expertise and political balance to the governors whose offices had taken an increasing share of influence during the preceding half-century. They also became more representative, due to court decisions on reapportionment and an increasing political participation by minor-ity groups.

It is possible that such a period of consensus for greater activism will return. In the context of fiscal sustainability, such an evolution in voter attitudes could mean support for higher taxes. As state and local governments seek to eliminate signifi-cant, structural budget gaps, elected leaders will look to make changes on both the expenditure and revenue sides of the budget. Other chapters in this volume exam-ine barriers to the expansion of state and local tax systems. Here, it may suffice to note that the last period of major change in state fiscal systems—during the 1960s and 1970s—included major revenue increases:

> During this era of renewed recognition, state governments perpetuated the long-standing trend toward professionalism and centralization. Legislative reforms realized the goals set by the Council of State Governments in 1946. Judicial changes followed the course charted by Arthur Vanderbilt in the 1940s, and the states did not invent any major new taxes but simply continued the shift to income and sales taxes begun in the early decades of the twentieth century. The 1960s and 1970s were not so much an era of innovation as one of realization. Laggard states realized reforms pioneered in earlier decades and worked to fulfill goals that had guided state-level reformers throughout much of the twentieth century.[22]

If a new era of voter support for more activist state governments emerges, some states may create or increase income taxes, while others may expand sales taxes. Property taxes remain subject to especially high levels of voter anger and opposi-tion. If anything, developments in the political environment may lead to dimin-ished growth in that source of revenues—an especially critical element of local government and school budgets.

Whether significant new revenues are available or not, state and local leaders will almost certainly continue to look for reductions in the growth of expendi-tures. There, the challenge of finding political will for change is compounded by the absence of knowledge on *how to change*. States and localities have clear options for increasing taxes and other revenues: raising rates for income and sales taxes, broadening the bases of these taxes, increasing charges for university tuition and hospital services, and instituting local fees on property owners and consumers of municipal services. In the realm of expenditures, cutting services is the most obvious means to control costs. But there may be a limit to the level of service reductions that voters will accept—especially given that services such as health care are increasingly considered entitlements for the middle-class as well as the poor. At some point within the next decade or so, Medicaid and other health-care expenditures are likely to supplant education as the largest cost center that governors and legislatures must address when balancing budgets. Such an evolution in the nature of public finance may have implications that are difficult to predict.

The alternative to saving money by cutting services is to make publicly funded programs more cost-effective on a unit basis. In education, this may mean changing the way in which K-12 classroom services are provided. Options may include using fewer highly qualified, higher-paid teachers and more lower-paid teaching assistants; placing more emphasis on technology-based and distance learning; and reducing the growth of employee compensation (including benefit costs) over time. In health care, economists and others have identified approaches including reducing the volume of high-cost services provided near the end of life; shifting routine care out of hospitals and into lower-cost community care centers; and improving health outcomes through changes in diet and exercise.

For state and local policymakers, and for active citizens, the challenge of identifying and successfully implementing these kinds of changes may be at least as great as the problem of developing political will. Powerful interest groups could oppose many of these changes. For example, teacher unions would likely object to a reduced number of classroom teachers. Also, hospital owners, board members, and unions have worked to block transfers of resources from their institutions to other services.

Meanwhile, citizens and policymakers can assume that currently unforeseen challenges will arise. New demands for services and expenditures can be expected as social needs shift over time. To cite one possibility, changes in the national and global economy have made employment less predictable and reliable for many workers. Such a development raises questions as to whether the nation's social safety net should be augmented to account for a potential increase in the proportion of workers who are unemployed or underemployed at any given time. If so, any expansion of public support services might occur within social welfare programs that require significant state (or state and local) funding. Also, such changes might fall within programs (such as unemployment insurance) that fall outside state and local government budgets but that draw on the same taxable resources as those budgets do. Either development would pose some level of additional challenge for fiscal sustainability.

It has always been the case that states get through—often, "muddle through" may be more accurate—extended periods of budgetary problems. In ways that are difficult or impossible to predict, elected and appointed officials with varying backgrounds, ideologies, and expertise will be challenged to enact budgets that provide essential services and raise adequate revenue to pay the cost. In 2011, a number of states took steps to improve their structural financial stability. Illinois enacted large increases in its taxes on personal income (which rose from 3 to 5 percent) and corporate income (from 4.8 to 7 percent). A number of states took significant actions on the expenditure side of the budget. New York eliminated long-standing statutory provisions that had the effect of driving above-inflation increases in education and health-care spending. Wisconsin and Ohio enacted changes in collective-bargaining laws that are likely to limit future growth in employee compensation costs. All of these decisions were controversial and can be debated on their merits. Whatever other impacts may result, each action moved a given jurisdiction in the direction of fiscal sustainability—and is likely to be considered elsewhere as budget pressures force further changes.

WHAT'S AT STAKE?

Citizens, policymakers, advocates, and researchers may debate the appropriate size and nature of governmental budgets. Such issues are separate from the question of whether a given set of revenue and expenditure policies is sustainable. Often, the most popular spending and tax policies will not be sustainable. Indeed, the problem of fiscal sustainability arises precisely because elected leaders have increasingly responded affirmatively to voters' desires for more spending without creating more taxes.

The longer that states and localities structure their budgets in unsustainable ways, the more likely it will be that undesirable results will emerge. Failure to solve the problem of fiscal sustainability will not result in state governments going out of business. The majority of local entities will continue, as well (although some will likely be eliminated through consolidation or other action). Failure will, however, almost certainly bring some mixture of the following:

- Damage to human services resulting from sudden, unplanned reductions in expenditures—and thus exacerbation of inequities between the neediest and those in middle- and upper-income levels;
- Loss of physical infrastructure, leading to degradation of transportation and other services that have long been considered among the most fundamental of governmental purposes;
- Higher costs for taxpayers and users of services, beyond what might be needed otherwise;
- More borrowing, meaning additional resources going to debt service rather than services, and current costs being shifted to future generations.

One troubling manifestation of state and local governments' refusal or inability to deal adequately with budget challenges is increased monetization of capital and financial assets to pay for current expenditures. A number of jurisdictions have resorted to selling or mortgaging assets that previously were assumed to be off-limits for budget-balancing purposes. Such steps allow governments to maintain expenditures at higher levels than ongoing revenues allow. Once such extraordinary revenue measures are exhausted, elected and appointed officials will still

:ed to find ways to balance budgets. Meanwhile, such steps will have left higher
ebts, new costs for purchasing or renting office space, new expenditures for
replacement capital assets, and other costly legacies.

If the late economist Mancur Olson was correct, the deep problems facing
American state and local governments may stem in part from the nation's history
of success. Olson argued that the longer a society enjoys political stability, the more
likely it will develop powerful special-interest constituencies that retard efficiency
in the overall economy and in government.[23] This theory may help explain the
difficulty that states and localities have in changing large, costly public programs
such as education and health care. On its face, Olson's idea may be less helpful
in understanding the attitudes of most voters, including their stated preference
for balanced budgets but with a reluctance to support either limited spending or
higher taxes. Yet Olson also suggested that "information about collective goods is
itself a collective good and accordingly there is normally little of it. When igno-
rance is often a rational strategy for constituents, there is a substantial possibility
that an interest group or political leader will not act in accord with the interest of
constituents."[24]

State and local elected leaders will be forced to deal with increasing fiscal
challenges in one way or another. They will choose particular paths based partly
on whether voters become involved and better informed about major decisions
relating to state and local government budgets. Sharp declines in the number of
state capitol reporters and in newspaper circulation likely mean that typical voters are less informed about state policy issues today than they were a decade or
two ago. To be sure, online news and information sources provide increasingly
rich data and policy discussions for those readers who are interested and able to
access them.[25] Such websites and blogs, however, are representative of a media
environment that has become more atomized over the past decade or two—such
that those with a particular interest may become very knowledgeable, and those
with lesser interest receive little information because they do not seek it out.
The majority of voters may remain relatively uninterested in state and local fiscal problems at least until the impact on services, taxes, and public employees
becomes severe enough to demand attention—a development that has already
begun to occur in some jurisdictions and will likely occur elsewhere relatively
soon. Whether through their anger or their apathy, voters will shape the environment in which elected leaders choose varied responses to the challenges of
fiscal sustainability.

NOTES

Selected observations in this chapter have been influenced by the previous writings of
Don Boyd, Senior Fellow at the Rockefeller Institute; and Richard P. Nathan, former
Director of the Rockefeller Institute. The author is also grateful to Lucy Dadayan,
Senior Policy Analyst at the Institute, for important research and data assistance.

1 In *Federalist No. 12*, Alexander Hamilton wrote, "Tax laws have in vain been multiplied; new methods to enforce the collection have in vain been tried; the public expectation has been uniformly disappointed, and the treasuries of the states have remained empty."

2 See, for example, Gold (1995).

3 Federal Accounting Standards Advisory Board (2009).

4 Governmental Accounting Standards Board (2005).

5 Government Accountability Office (2008).

6 International Public Sector Accounting Standards Board (2008).

7 Burnside (2004).

8 Chapman (2008).

9 The GASB's work in this area is ongoing. Readers may wish to consult www.gasb.org for updates.

10 Author's calculations from US Census Bureau data.

11 Snyder (1993).

12 Author's calculations from US Bureau of Labor Statistics data. However, from the peak of 2008 to March 2011, state and local employment went into decline, with a reduction of about 450,000 jobs. See BLS News Release (April 1, 2011), www.bls.gov.news.release/pdf.

13 Ibid.

14 Pew Center on the States (2010).

15 Novy-Marx and Rauh (2009).

16 The quote is from Government Accountability Office (2010). Similar comments appear in other GAO reports on the topic.

17 See, for example, Gale and Harris (2010).

18 See, for example, Yilmaz et al. (2006), vi.

19 Ward (2010).

20 Weisman (2009).

21 http://www.ncsl.org/documents/fiscal/Projected_Revenue_Growth_in_FY_2011_and_Beyond.pdf.

22 Teaford (2002), 196.

23 Olson (1982).

24 Ibid., 52.

25 See, for example, www.stateline.org for information on state policy developments generally and www.statehealthfacts.org for data on health indicators, health-care finance, and related topics.

References

Burnside, Craig (2004). "Assessing New Approaches to Fiscal Sustainability Analysis." In *Debt Sustainability Analysis*. Washington, DC: World Bank.

Chapman, Jeffrey I. (2008, December). "State and Local Fiscal Sustainability: The Challenges." *Public Administration Review* Vol. 68, Issue Supplement.

Federal Accounting Standards Advisory Board (2009, September 28). "Reporting Comprehensive Long-Term Fiscal Projections for the U.S. Government: Statement of Federal Financial Accounting Standards 36." Washington, DC.

Gale, William G., and Benjamin H. Harris (2010, July). "A Value-Added Tax for the United States: Part of the Solution." Urban-Brookings Tax Policy Center.

Gold, Stephen D. (Ed.) (1995). *The Fiscal Crisis of the States: Lessons for the Future.* Washington, DC: Georgetown University Press.

Government Accountability Office (2008). "State and Local Fiscal Challenges: Rising Health Care Costs Drive Long-Term and Immediate Pressures."

Government Accountability Office (2010, July). "Fiscal Pressures Could Have Implications for Future Delivery of Intergovernmental Programs." Report GAO-10-899.

Governmental Accounting Standards Board (2005). "Minutes of Meetings, August 9–11." www.gasb.org.

Governmental Accounting Standards Board. Project Pages for "Economic Condition Reporting: Fiscal Sustainability." Updates available at www.gasb.org.

International Public Sector Accounting Standards Board (2008, March). *Long-Term Fiscal Sustainability Reporting.* New York: International Federation of Accountants.

Novy-Marx, Robert, and Joshua D. Rauh (2009). "The Liabilities and Risks of State-Sponsored Pension Plans." *Journal of Economic Perspectives* 23(4): 191–210.

Olson, Mancur (1982). *The Rise and Decline of Nations: Economic Growth, Stagflation and Social Rigidities.* New Haven, CT: Yale University Press.

Pew Center on the States (2010, February). "The Trillion-Dollar Gap: Underfunded State Retirement Systems and the Roads to Reform." Washington, DC.

Snyder, Thomas D. (Ed.) (1993, January). *120 Years of American Education: A Statistical Portrait.* National Center on Education Statistics.

Teaford, John C. (2002). *The Rise of the States: Evolution of American State Government.* Baltimore: Johns Hopkins University Press.

US Government Accountability Office. Various reports on state and local government fiscal challenges. Available via www.gao.gov.

Ward, Robert B. (2010, June 17). "Gubernatorial Powers to Address Budget Gaps during the Fiscal Year." Albany NY: Nelson A. Rockefeller Institute of Government.

Ward, Robert B. and Lucy Dadayan (2009). "State and Local Finance: Increasing Focus on Fiscal Sustainability." *Publius: The Journal of Federalism* 39(3).

Weisman, Steven R. (Ed.) (2009). *Daniel Patrick Moynihan: A Portrait in Letters of an American Visionary.* New York: Public Affairs.

Yilmaz, Yesim, Sonya Hoo, Matthew Nagowski, Kim Rueben, and Robert Tannenwald (2006). *Measuring Fiscal Disparities across the U.S. States: A Representative Revenue System/Representative Expenditure System Approach Fiscal Year 2002.* Washington, DC: Urban-Brookings Tax Policy Center and Fiscal Reserve Bank of Boston.

CHAPTER 34

··

THE
INTERGOVERNMENTAL
GRANT SYSTEM

··

RAYMOND C. SCHEPPACH

FEDERAL grants have long been a major component of state and local government revenues. After World War II, these grants grew, with fits and starts, from under 10 percent of the sector's total revenues in the late 1940s to well over 20 percent of revenues by the early 1970s. Total grants from the federal government to state and local governments reached $399 billion in 2008, which was about 20 percent of state and local governments' total current revenues for that year and down only slightly from the 23 percent figure for 1978.[1] The most significant change over that thirty-year period was that health-care grants, driven by the growth of Medicaid, rose from 12 percent to 20 percent of the federal total. That overall stability in the federal aid share of state funding came to an abrupt halt in 2009 with the Great Recession and the enactment of the American Recovery and Reinvestment Act (ARRA) and its subsequent extensions. The future intergovernmental relationship will be dramatically different as a result not only of ARRA but also as a result of the enactment of health-care reform, the Patient Protection and Affordability Care Act (ACA), in 2010.

History will write the two-year period of 2009 to 2010 as a watershed moment in the fiscal relationships among federal, state, and local governments. To stabilize the US economy after the financial meltdown, the ARRA and its extensions provided $103 billion of federal aid in flexible Medicaid and $48 billion in education funds to the states, enabling states to limit budget cuts and tax increases. There was also another $100 billion in funds that came to states in transportation, weatherization, and other grants that were not flexible but in fact were spent in existing programs. Federal grants dramatically increased as a percentage of total state revenues, from 26.3 percent to 34.7 percent, between 2009 and 2010.[2] These federal actions were the second fiscal bailout for states in six years; the federal government had also provided $20 billion—$10 billion in Medicaid and $10 billion in general-revenue sharing—in 2003. These two fiscal relief packages are clear harbingers for the future.

Paradoxically, right in the middle of bailing out the states with $103 billion in Medicaid funds in 2009, Congress also mandated a significantly larger Medicaid burden on the states as part of the ACA health-care reform. Even before the Great Recession, it was questionable whether state revenues would grow sufficiently to fund this additional fiscal burden; afterward, it became almost impossible. If the health-care legislation is not substantially modified, it will require both additional fiscal relief by the federal government every couple of years and significant cuts in education and infrastructure investments, thereby lowering long-run productivity and economic growth.

When one looks at the intergovernmental fiscal system as it was in 2008, especially Medicaid, given its growing importance, and then traces the recurring policy debates over the last thirty years, it is vividly clear that the events of 2009 and 2010 are "game changers" that will completely transform the future fiscal relationship between the federal government and state and local governments.

THE EXISTING INTERGOVERNMENTAL FISCAL FRAMEWORK

State and local revenues grew from about $786 billion in 1978 to a little over $2 trillion in 2008, the peak year for spending, just before the financial meltdown.[3] About 68 percent of 2008 revenues were general tax receipts from the three major tax sources—income, property, and sales taxes—and another $251 billion came from other fees and taxes, which may be dedicated to specific types of spending (that is, the funds are restricted in some way). Finally, federal grants to state and local governments were about $399 billion, or 20 percent of total state and local revenues, in 2008. It is interesting that the share was down only slightly from 23 percent in 1978 (see figure 34.1).

State and local government expenditures on health care (depicted in figure 34.2) grew from 12 percent to 20 percent of spending from 1978 to 2008, while most other types of spending were down as proportions of the total. Even education fell from 40 percent to 36 percent during this time frame. Essentially, it was the growth of Medicaid that was driving health-care spending.

Total state and local revenues 1978

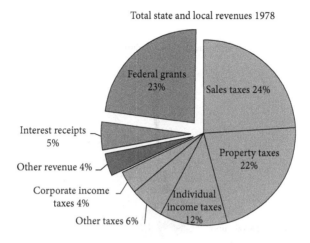

Total state and local revenues 2008

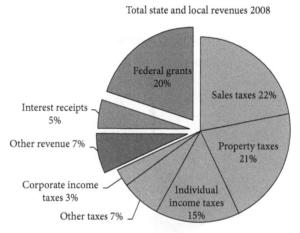

Figure 34.1 State and local revenues, by type, 1978 and 2008
Note: Federal grants as a percentage of state and local revenues declined from 23 percent in 1978 to 14 percent in 1988 and then gradually increased to 20 percent in 2008.
Source: GAO analysis of historical data from the Bureau of Economic Analysis's National Income and Product Accounts.

This can be seen vividly in figure 34.3, which shows that health care, as a percentage of federal grants, increased from 21 percent in 1978 to 57 percent in 2008. Education grew to 11 percent in 2008. Thus, close to 70 percent of federal grants were for health and education. The Medicaid program continues as an individual entitlement. It is the only major program that remains a state-administered individual entitlement, because Aid to Families with Dependent Children (AFDC) was converted to the Temporary Assistance for Needy Families (TANF) block grant in 1996.[4]

Of the 2008 total, there was $399 billion[5] in federal grants to state and local governments, of which $200 billion was for Medicaid. Federal Medicaid and other health programs grew from 21 percent to 57 percent from 1978 to 2008 as seen in

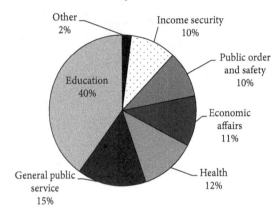

State and Local expenditures 1978

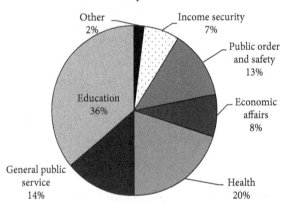

State and Local expenditures 2008

Figure 34.2 State and local expenditures, by category, 1978 and 2008
Note: The other category includes Housing and Community Services and Recreation
and Culture. Economic affairs include transportation, space, agriculture, and natural
resources. Health includes Medicaid. General public service includes interest payments
and tax collection and financial management services. Income security includes
disability, welfare, and social services. State and local government pension contributions
are considered part of employee compensation and accounted for within the categories.
Source: GAO analysis of historical data from the Bureau of Economic
Analysis's National Income and Product Accounts.

figure 34.3; all other functions shrank with the exception of education. Another
$50 billion was for fourteen small entitlement or mandatory programs, from
TANF to the social services block grant to vaccines for children. There was thus
an additional $150 billion in several hundred discretionary grants.[6] Some of those
are categorical grants that have very narrowly defined objectives and uses. Others
are block grants, such as the Community Development Block Grant, that have a

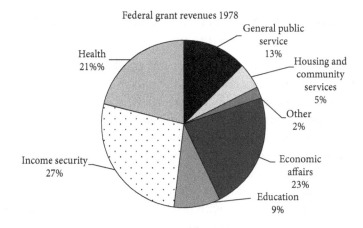

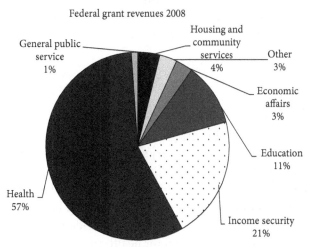

Figure 34.3 Federal grants to state and local governments
Note: Medicaid grants comprised 90 percent of health grants in 2008. 'Other' includes
national defense, public order and safety, and recreation and culture.
Source: GAO analysis of historical data from the Bureau of Economic
Analysis's National Income and Product Accounts.

broader range of eligible activities; these were usually created by combining several
categorical grants. There are also project grants that have a narrower purpose than
the categorical grants and that may be time-limited. Both the categorical and block
grants may have requirements for matching by state and local governments, as well
as maintenance-of-effort requirements, which prohibit states from withdrawing
state funding. Finally, there also exist formula grants, in which funds are distributed through a formula, for example, based on the number of people in a state or
on a measure of personal income. The larger formula grants include highway and
transit at $50 billion; Section 8 housing at $16 billion; and special education and
Title I education for the disadvantaged, at $14 billion and $11 billion, respectively,
in 2008.[7]

THE EFFICIENCY OF THE GRANTS SYSTEM

With oversight of hundreds of small categorical grants, the entire system has been rather inefficient. Many states accept grant funds even though they do not need additional funding in the area of focus and will be short in other, higher-priority areas. Administrative costs to both the federal government and state and local governments are significant because of the various regulations, alternative matching requirements, and audit procedures. Few performance requirements exist beyond the normal auditing. It would be far more efficient to move to eight or ten broad block grants (for example, for infrastructure, social services, education and training, economic development, etc.), with negotiated performance standards, and to allow state and local governments to combine funds across block grants via waiver processes. Such an approach would allow significant cuts in funding levels because administrative costs would go down dramatically.

The Early Programs

The first federal-state health grant program of importance was the Sheppard-Towner Act of 1921. The grants were very small, with the first $5,000 granted directly to the state and an additional $5,000 that was matched by the state. A major expansion occurred during the New Deal in two of the eleven titles of the Social Security Act of 1935: Title V grants were for maternal and child health and Title VI was for public health. By 1936 the federal government provided more than $500 million in intergovernmental grants, much of it for health care for low-income individuals.[8]

In 1950 Congress created medical vendor payments through an amendment to the Social Security Act. The amendment authorized federal grants to states to make direct payments to health-care providers, mostly for nursing homes for low-income individuals. The next major expansion of the federal role was the Kerr-Mills Act, passed in 1960, which established a low-income health-care program with a comprehensive benefit package, with eligibility based on a means test.

Medicaid

Medicaid represented over 50 percent of total federal grants to states and localities in 2008. Moreover, it is growing rapidly and is now about 22 percent of an average state budget. It is therefore critical to understand both how it evolved and the factors that contribute to its rapid growth.

The major push for expanded health care in the United States came in the late 1950s and early 1960s. After several attempts to create a universal care program, Medicare for the elderly was passed as part of the Social Security Act in 1965.

Medicaid was created at the same time, essentially as an afterthought. It incorporated vendor payments as well as the Kerr-Mills approach, that is, direct payments to providers and benefits eligibility based on a means test.

The original cost estimate for the Medicaid program was $238 million per year. However, by 1967, even though only thirty-seven states had programs, spending was already 57 percent above the estimate, largely because states established generous eligibility standards.

At the time, many US citizens believed that the biggest health-care problems had been fixed, because the needs of both the elderly and the poor had been met. Other citizens continued to push for universal health care. Without a national consensus on universal care, however, Medicaid became the program of default to fill needs for health care. Over time, long-term care, comprehensive benefits for the disabled, and comprehensive benefits for some nonpoor uninsured were covered by Medicaid. Although the original designers of the Medicaid program did not envision that it would become a major funder of long-term care, long-term care has nevertheless become a huge component of the program. In 2006, long-term care spending was $178 billion, and 40 percent was paid by Medicaid.[9] Long-term care is also now the fastest-growing component, and with the demographic changes that are coming, it will continue to be the fastest growing.

It would be better public policy to incorporate the long-term care portion of Medicaid into Medicare. That would not only allow a continuum of care for the elderly but also substantially reduce the number of individuals who are eligible for both Medicare and Medicaid benefits, because in those cases both state and federal governments are providing uncoordinated benefits for the same individual, with the accompanying inefficiency and confusion. Substantial inefficiency results because the incentives for Medicaid and Medicare are not aligned to enable both levels of government to work together to reduce costs. An alternative for long-term care would be to enact a separate program, with a separate income stream, to eliminate dual eligibility.

The designers of the Medicaid program also did not foresee that it would be expanded to include any nonpoor uninsured. Eligibility was originally tied to cash assistance programs for poor families and children. That tie eroded over time, as the federal government during the late 1980s allowed states to expand eligibility for children, pregnant women, and infants. Federal policy shifted in 1988, from options to a combination of options and mandates, to increase coverage for pregnant women and children above the poverty level. States usually pushed for options but often opposed mandated coverage. The program grew very rapidly during the 1980s and 1990s through expansions of eligibility and benefits and because of the increasing cost of health care.

Today Medicaid covers about fifty-eight million people (over 19 percent of the nation's population) primarily in three distinct populations: low-income women and children, the disabled, and low-income seniors. The coverage for women and children is relatively inexpensive, but coverage for the disabled and long-term care is relatively expensive.

Medicaid is the most expensive entitlement, with total federal and state spending for it at about $350 billion in 2008. Of that, an average 57 percent is paid by the federal government and 43 percent is paid by states.[10] The share that states pay depends on their per capita personal income. Thus very-low-income states such as Mississippi may pay only 23 percent of their Medicaid costs, while many wealthier states, such as Connecticut and New York, pay 50 percent, which is the cap. The shares are adjusted annually. It is interesting that Medicaid is the only major federal-state program that redistributes funding from wealthier states (based on higher federal tax revenues) to low-income states. The formula was one of the great policy compromises regarding equity among the states.

From 1965 to the middle 1990s, Medicaid was expanded partly by the states, by exercising options, and then by the federal government through mandates. The program has both core and optional benefits and core and optional eligible populations, but the political reality is that few real options exist. For example, home- and community-based long-term care is an option on paper but not in reality.

Reimbursement rates for physicians also differ substantially by state, with the average being about 72 percent of Medicare rates.[11] Some states, such as California, pay physicians as little as 56 percent of Medicare rates. This is a problem particularly for primary care physicians. It is a real obstacle to health-care access in many states, as physicians are unwilling to accept such low payments. In addition, each state has been able to set its own poverty level for eligibility for the various populations.

Medicaid has become a double-edged sword. States supported it in the early 1980s, when they had options to modify eligibility, because it was helpful to have the federal government share the cost of expansions. When the program matured in the late 1980s and early 1990s, however, it became the "Pac-Man" of state government, often eating up a state's entire yearly increase in revenues, particularly from 2000 to 2008. In 2008, it cost states $146 billion and the federal government $192 billion. At about 22 percent of the average state budget, expenditures for Medicaid are now slightly greater than those made by states for all elementary and secondary education. Although states have implemented many cost-control strategies, affecting the cost dramatically is difficult. Most states now would argue that state Medicaid spending is out of line relative to elementary, secondary, and higher education and infrastructure spending.

THE POLICY DEBATES ALONG THE WAY

Over the last thirty years the appropriate structure of federal aid to state and local governments has been the subject of much debate. Many of the issues, such as changing Medicaid to a block grant or consolidating a number of categorical grants into a block grant, have been raised numerous times.

Medicaid

From the standpoint of federalism, it is appropriate that the federal government should have responsibility for the elderly, that is, the retired and nonworking population, and should administer and fund programs, such as Social Security and Medicare, for them. It can also be logically argued that states should be responsible for health care for low-income individuals, so that it can be coordinated with other programs such as welfare, job training, and food stamps. The level of government that administers a program need not be the same level of government that funds it. Once long-term care became a major part of Medicaid, however, there was no longer a clear division of responsibility because a high percentage of recipients of long-term care were elderly, and many others were not in the workforce. The responsibility for individuals in long-term care facilities and in home- and community-based care should be integrated with other programs for the elderly that the federal government administers.

Another point of debate has been whether, instead of an entitlement, Medicaid should be converted to a block grant to states. Overall, it is very difficult to create a block grant for a rapidly growing program, such as one that has appropriate incentives for efficiency and can apportion risk fairly between the federal government and individual states. This is particularly true when the growth rates of eligible populations are different and the cost of health care also differs substantially from state to state.

Categorical versus Block Grants

Also debated has been the efficiency of converting a number of categorical grants into a single block grant. There is substantial merit in this approach, because states are often willing to accept reduced funding in exchange for greater flexibility. The greatest success of this approach was in 1981, under President Ronald Reagan's "new federalism," when Congress converted seventy-seven categorical grants worth $8 billion into nine block grants.[12] Over time, however, Congress added set-asides, which limit flexibility, and funding levels were further eroded as former advocates no longer supported the broad purpose of the grants.

General Revenue Sharing

On October 20, 1972, President Richard Nixon signed the bill that created general revenue sharing, which provided one-third of its funding to the 38,000 local governments and Indian tribes and two-thirds to the fifty state governments. Between 1972 and 1986, $87 billion flowed to state and local governments without restrictions as to how the funds would be spent. The goal was both to relieve state and local governments of fiscal stress and also to allow units of government close to the people determine spending priorities.[13] Support for this general funding concept gradually eroded in Congress, primarily because of the lack of a defined purpose. The concept was brought back in 2003, when Congress passed a $20 billion fiscal relief package, with $10 billion in general revenue sharing and $10 billion in Medicaid assistance.

The Big Swap and Welfare Reform

In his 1982 State of the Union address, President Reagan stunned both Republican legislators and state governors with his "big swap." He was interested not only in streamlining the intergovernmental system but also in decentralizing government decisions and cutting the federal budget. Reagan was willing to have the federal government take over Medicaid in exchange for the states' taking over of AFDC and the food stamps program, both of which were entitlements. An interesting note is that he also wanted to convert AFDC into a block grant (as eventually happened in 1996). The presidential initiative also included reversions of forty-three major categorical grants, with $28 billion in federal excise taxes, to the states.[14]

Looking back, the swap would have increased the efficiency of health-care programs because one level of government would have been administering the two largest government health-care programs. That would have eliminated many of the problems created by dual eligibility and would have eased the path toward universal health care. It would also have increased the efficiency of the welfare program, as it would have integrated it better with work programs in the states. Perhaps most important, it would have freed states of the fiscal burden of Medicaid and allowed them to concentrate on the education and training of a productive workforce and on infrastructure investment. During the fiscal crisis of today, it is likely that many governors look back at the swap and ask why governors walked away from the plan in 1982.

In 1935, as part of the Social Security Act, the AFDC program was created to provide cash assistance to poor women with children. The individual states set the level of the cash payments. For years the program drew the criticism of conservatives who argued that entitlement created cycles of dependency among the children of the recipient families. In 1986, Governor Tommy Thompson of Wisconsin created a program that funded education and training along with child care, in order to help AFDC recipients find jobs, and the program also applied time limits for the funding. Over the next decade, states experimented with attaching time limits and work requirements to AFDC, eventually leading to the enactment of TANF.[15] This was a fundamental change in policy because it converted the program from an entitlement for cash assistance into a work program with time limits and work requirements. It included education and training and child-care assistance, to help support work, and it also provided Medicaid for a transition work period. Democratic support for the entitlement had gradually eroded as Republicans became more willing to accept education, training, and child-care support provisions to support welfare recipients' transitions to work.

THE GREAT RECESSION

The so-called Great Recession, which began in December 2007 and was declared officially over in June 2009, had an unprecedented, immediate impact on state governments. More important, it will continue to have an impact for years to come. Furthermore, because the ARRA, enacted in February 2009, and its extension provided $151 billion of flexible money to the states, the Great Recession had a huge impact on the federal-state fiscal relationship. It was the second state fiscal bailout by the federal government in six years.

From the time that the National Association of State Budget Officers (NASBO) began collecting state budget data in 1978, it had found an actual decline in state spending and revenues only once, in 1983, and that decline was less than 1 percent. In the Great Recession, however, state revenues were down for five continuous quarters—from the last calendar quarter of 2008 through the last quarter of 2009—by 4 percent, 12.2 percent, 16.8 percent, 11.5 percent, and 4 percent, respectively. Not until the first quarter of 2010 did revenues go up, and then by just 2.5 percent, mostly as a result of large tax increases in New York and California. At the time of this writing, at the end of 2010, revenues had been up for two additional quarters in a row, by 2.3 percent and 3.9 percent.[16]

The Three Stages

Analysis of previous recessions shows clearly that their biggest impact on state governments occurred one, two, and at times three years after the recession was declared to be over. The first stage of impact, caused by the trough in state-tax revenues, mostly income taxes, coincides with the peak in unemployment, which occurs very late in the cycle. The budget impact of the revenue decline is exacerbated by the explosion in Medicaid costs, which also generally occurs late in the cycle, after people lose their jobs, look unsuccessfully for other employment, and only then come on the Medicaid rolls, often with children.

Unfortunately, given the depth and breadth of the Great Recession, two additional stages are to be expected that will continue the fiscal problems of state governments. The second stage will occur because states will likely not attain their 2008 revenue levels again until 2013 or 2014, in view of what has become a jobless recovery. This would mean virtually no state revenue growth for five years, compared to 6.5 percent average yearly growth from 1978 to 2008. The final stage of the impact will be the period, perhaps from 2015 to 2018, when states will have to meet the spending needs they have deferred. Those makeup needs run the spectrum, from upgrading management information systems, to performing maintenance on structures, to rebuilding rainy-day funds, to enhancing contributions to state pension funds. The latter is a huge cost, because some states have not made contributions over the last few years, and some have even borrowed from pension trust funds.

According to the Pew Center on the States, the unfunded liability of those pension funds and retiree health benefits programs now amounts to about $1 trillion.

To meet their balanced-budget requirements, states cut about $75 billion of spending and raised taxes and fees by another $31.4 billion in 2008–2010. The cuts and tax increases would have been significantly more severe if the federal government had not enacted the American Recovery and Reimbursement Act (ARRA) and its extensions.

American Recovery and Reimbursement Act

About $246 billion from the ARRA economic recovery package went to states, or through states, in existing state programs from highways to weatherization.[17] Of that total, however, $135 billion in designated Medicaid and education funds was, in fact, flexible because the infusion of federal Medicaid money allowed the states to withdraw their own matching share and reallocate it as needed to other programs. Similarly, the education money could be allocated across elementary, secondary, and higher education. This represented about 30 percent of most state budgets, so these funds were also quite flexible. However, the ARRA included maintenance-of-effort (MOE) provisions for both Medicaid and education. A state could not cut Medicaid eligibility or cut education funding below the level of preceding years. Overall, the ARRA was quite effective. Unlike most previous fiscal policy initiatives, it was not too late; in fact it was timely and helped to stabilize both the aggregate economy and state spending. Because of requirements that they balance their budgets, states would have had both to cut spending and to increase taxes substantially more without the ARRA. Both steps would be pro-cyclical and thus would make the recession deeper and longer. The federal funding allowed states to limit such actions.

Medicaid and Education Extensions

Before its August 2010 recess, Congress passed and the president signed a $16 billion, two-quarter extension of Medicaid funding covering the period from January 1 to June 30, 2011, or through the end of state fiscal year 2011. This action was seen as a bridge to state fiscal year 2012, when state revenues were hoped to rebound.

The extension for education was vastly different from the original ARRA education funding. This act required that 98 percent of the money must pass through states to local school districts, many of which would roll the funds over to state fiscal year 2012. It also subjected states to strict new MOE requirements for elementary and secondary education, as well as higher education, so that some states were required to increase education funding at the same time that localities were receiving the additional federal funds. Local property-tax revenues did not fall as sharply as state revenues did because of the lagging impact of the decline in property values, and local governments also increased tax rates to maintain their revenues during the downturn. In sum, the combination of state MOE and the additional federal education funds provided many local school districts with adequate funds, when other state or local spending priorities were not being met. The two ARRA extensions in 2010 provided additional funding through state fiscal year 2011 but set up a major "cliff" in funding in fiscal year 2012, if the economy is slow to recover.

All the ARRA flexible funds and the extensions meant that $151 billion came to the states, and an additional $10 billion went through states to local governments. Although the latter did not assist states directly, it relieved them of some pressure by stabilizing local governments and school districts.

The goal of ARRA funds and the extensions was twofold: first, to help stabilize the overall economy (many economists recommended offsetting potential state budget cuts and tax increases as the most effective macroeconomic policy), and second, to bail out the states to save state jobs, particularly in education (educators often represent a voting bloc for Democrats), and enable states to continue to provide health care for low-income women and children.

Despite numerous recommendations to change the Medicaid formula to automatically adjust the federal share to be countercyclical, that is, to provide a bigger federal share when unemployment increases during a downturn, this has never been done. In the ARRA, however, every state received an increase of 6.2 percentage points in the federal share of Medicaid funding, and states with higher-than-average unemployment rates received significant bonuses. It will be interesting to see if researchers find that this experiment was effective and whether it leads to countercyclical changes to the Medicaid program.

As noted, the ARRA came on the heels of an earlier federal bailout effort. In May 2003 the federal government enacted $20 billion in fiscal relief for the states. Increasing the federal Medicaid match rate for all states by 2.95 percentage points brought $10 billion, and an additional $10 billion came from general revenue sharing. That was the first time that Medicaid was given additional funding during a downturn, and it clearly set the stage for Medicaid assistance in 2009.

The "New Normal"

As previously stated, before the Great Recession, state revenue growth averaged 6.5 percent yearly from 1978 to 2008. Revenue growth also jumped 8.9 percent in both 2005 and in 2006 when many homeowners, enticed by low interest rates and rising home prices, took equity out of their houses and spent it. That not only accelerated the growth of the gross domestic product (GDP) but also increased state revenues from sales and income taxes.[18]

But even when state revenues recover from the financial meltdown later in this decade, the long-run trend of state and local government revenues will likely be flatter than the 6.5 percent growth of the last three decades. The reason is that the

US economy will likely be growing more slowly because much higher federal debt will require higher long-term interest rates. Additional regulation, higher tax rates at all three levels of government, and a more competitive global economy will also slow growth. A volatile international trading environment due to currency fluctuations, as each country attempts to gain an economic advantage by devaluing currency, is also to be expected.

From 2008 to 2010, states have (1) reorganized and combined agencies; (2) sold state assets; and (3) consolidated real estate management and purchases and made significant cuts across most agencies and budget functions. Even so, given the expected "new normal" revenue path, states will need to continue to downsize. They will have to do that by reexamining core services such as corrections, elementary and secondary education, and higher education and by significantly redesigning delivery systems so that they are sustainable over the long term. For K–12 education, for example, districts will need to streamline services and explore ways to reduce costs without jeopardizing student achievement. They may need to close underutilized schools and consolidate districts with small numbers of pupils. Similar strategies need to be adopted for other core services. State pensions must be part of the downsizing, in the face of their huge unfunded liability for retiree pension and health-care benefits and because most of the state pension systems are defined-benefit plans, as opposed to defined-contribution plans, and employee contributions are limited.[17] Only through such redesign efforts will states be able to meet their balanced-budget requirements and maintain appropriate services in the changed environment.

As recently as fiscal year 2009, federal funds accounted for 26.3 percent of total state spending. By 2010, however, federal funds were 34.7 percent of total state spending, as a result of the enactment of the ARRA and its extension and the states' dramatic spending cuts.[19]

Health-Care Reform

After several attempts at universal health-care reform, from the administration of President Truman to those of Nixon and Clinton, the ACA law was finally enacted on March 23, 2010. On one hand, the timing—during the Great Recession—was poor. On the other hand, Democrats had a political opportunity in their large majority in the House of Representatives and almost filibuster-proof majority in the Senate, in addition to the presidency. President Barack Obama had campaigned on the issue. But it was the Democratic leadership on Capitol Hill (Senate Majority Leader Harry Reid and particularly House Speaker Nancy Pelosi) who pushed the reform over the finish line. They had waited a long time for such a political opportunity. The act, however, passed with no Republican votes in either the House of

Representatives or the Senate. Although some early negotiations took place with several Republicans in the Senate, they did not last long, and the Democrats decided to push for enactment.

The new health-care law was modeled after the plan that the Commonwealth of Massachusetts had enacted four years earlier in 2006. Both the federal and Massachusetts plans include (1) limits on medical underwriting, (2) a requirement that individuals purchase health insurance, (3) a mandate on most businesses to provide health-care coverage, (4) an expansion of Medicaid, (5) additional subsidies for low-income individuals not eligible for Medicaid to purchase insurance, and (6) a "connector" in Massachusetts, which is similar to the "exchange" at the federal level, in which small businesses, individuals, and all of the federally subsidized, non-Medicaid populations can purchase health insurance from among several plans. Neither the Massachusetts plan nor the one Congress enacted, however, built in any serious cost-control strategies. The plan that was enacted was essentially the one originally produced by the Senate, which was relatively state friendly and placed a premium on state implementation, whereas the House plan had a much stronger federal role. From a state perspective, there are essentially three main areas for implementation: (1) Medicaid expansion, (2) the decisions concerning the exchange, and (3) the phasing out of medical underwriting. From the standpoint of federalism, or the federal-state fiscal relationship, it is the first two areas that are critically important.

Medicaid Expansion

The ACA law essentially makes everyone in a state whose income is 138 percent or less of the determined poverty level as eligible for Medicaid. For this newly eligible population—all those above the current, state-determined poverty level but at or less than 138 percent of the level—each state will receive a 100 percent federal subsidy for the first several years, which is then phased down to about 90 percent on a permanent basis. A few states, such as Massachusetts and Vermont, which had already expanded coverage to most low-income individuals, would receive a windfall under the ACA, but most states would have to pay a share of the cost of the expansion. The Congressional Budget Office (CBO) estimated that states will have to pay an additional $20 billion over the next ten years.[20]

Debate continues among Medicaid experts about the actual cost to states. Some think that it will be lower than the CBO estimates, but others hold that it will be higher. One problem is that about 12 million individuals who are currently eligible for Medicaid are not enrolled. The CBO and others assume that few of them will enroll under the act. But if even 20 percent of these individuals do enroll, the cost to states will be huge because they will come on the rolls at the current state-federal matching rate, not the enhanced match for the newly eligible population. Second, all cost estimates assume that the states' reimbursement rates to physicians will not increase above the current average of 72 percent. Again, if a state makes even marginal upward adjustments in this reimbursement rate to maintain access, it will be extremely expensive, as it would affect the entire Medicaid population, not just the newly eligible population.

Raising the Medicaid eligibility cut-off point to 138 percent of the poverty level and eliminating the existing program will make about 15 million additional people eligible for Medicaid. That is about one-half of the increase in coverage for the entire act.

While it is possible to argue that individuals up to 100 percent of the determined poverty level should be eligible for Medicaid, because they are the most vulnerable, those individuals with salaries between 100 percent and 138 percent of the poverty level were brought into Medicaid primarily to save the federal government money. Essentially, there are three sources of savings. First, on average, the federal government reduces its costs because the state pays about 10 percent for the cost of the newly eligible populations. Second, the state reimbursement rate for physicians is only 72 percent of the Medicare rate for physicians. Third, if this population received health care through the exchanges, the federal subsidy would be based on the market rates for health care, that is, not only on average above the Medicaid rate but above the Medicare rate.

In sum, the federal government under the provisions of the ACA has substantially increased the cost of health care to the states at a time when the states were in the worst fiscal situation in at least thirty years. This burden over the long run will force the states to make significant cuts in education and infrastructure funding.

While the federal government had bailed out states with more than $100 billion for Medicaid during the Great Recession, it also prepared both the next short-run and the next long-run Medicaid crises for the states. The only way that states will avoid huge cuts in education will be if the federal government continues to bail them out every couple of years.

The Exchange

An exchange, as envisioned by the ACA health-care law, is simply a place where individuals who do not receive health insurance from their place of work or the government (through Medicare or Medicaid) can purchase insurance, choosing among a number of plans. Essentially it establishes an orderly marketplace for buyers and sellers. As provided in the act, a state has to decide, and be determined ready by the US Department of Health and Human Services, by January 1, 2013, to take responsibility to create a health insurance exchange. If the state decides not to develop the exchange, then the federal government will do it. From the state perspective, a number of important political and policy issues are part of this decision.

On one hand, a significant number of Republican governors and state attorneys general are suing the federal government over the individual mandate and the Medicaid mandate and thus do not want to implement the act. On the other hand, the business community and most of the health-care plans and providers prefer that the states operate the exchanges. One of the critical issues is that the eligibility system of the exchange must be integrated with Medicaid eligibility, which means that individual states will still be accountable for establishing comprehensive eligibility systems even if the federal government is running the exchange in the state. If a state decides to create the exchange, then it must make a number of other decisions, such as whether the exchange will be part of the state government or will be a nonprofit organization. Individuals who would likely purchase through the exchange would be those previously in the individual market, the newly subsidized population (that is, those who had salaries between 138 percent and 400 percent of poverty) and small businesses.

From the standpoint of federalism, over the long run, state decisions regarding exchanges are critical. Today, all low-income federal programs are administered by states—food stamps, Medicaid, TANF, and others. The programs may be 100 percent federally funded or a shared fiscal responsibility, as Medicaid and TANF, but they are all administered by the states.

If a number of states default to the federal government on operating exchanges, it will be the first time that the federal government runs a program for low-income individuals in a state. Among domestic programs now, the federal government administers programs only for the elderly, that is, Medicare and Social Security. This could be a game changer, as it could lead to significant federal intrusion into the administration of domestic programs.

A New Accountability

For those states that choose to create health insurance exchanges, there will be a new accountability for health-care costs. After the ACA reform is fully implemented there will be 75 million individuals on Medicaid; 50 million to 60 million, and possibly more, in exchanges; and 3 million state employees in programs that the states either run directly or oversee. This means that about 130 million individuals across the country will be looking to states to control health-care costs. In fact, the argument can be made that the people who will be purchasing health plans through the exchange will be the most price-sensitive, as they include the non-Medicaid subsidized population, young single individuals who do not want to purchase health care at all, and small businesses. This will be the group that advocates the loudest for states to act to control costs.

If cost increases in the future are similar to GDP growth, then governors and state legislators will not become involved. But if health-care costs continue to rise at rates of 8 percent, 9 percent, or 10 percent a year, then the political leadership in states will be called on to act. The pressure for action will be strengthened because Medicaid will most likely jump from 22 percent of the average state budget to 28 percent, not only as a result of the health-care reform act but also because of the $75 billion that was cut out of other state programs during the Great Recession.

This new accountability will likely require states to create all-payer databases from claims data that are already collected by the health-care plans. Such information can help determine what is driving health-care costs in the states. For example, is it the number of MRIs or the cost per MRI that is increasing, and who are the high-cost providers? Based on this information, states will likely begin to convene stakeholders, from providers to health plans to small businesses, to discuss the cost problem. Over time, this could lead to additional price and quality transparency, payment reforms, and possibly more price regulation, all of which may help to bring down the costs of health care. It is becoming increasingly obvious that cost control must be done state by state for all payers. Federal cuts in Medicaid or Medicare would merely be shifted to the other payers, whereas an all-payer approach could limit the shifting.

Three main conclusions are to be drawn regarding passage of the ACA. First, the federal government shifted a significant funding responsibility onto the states at a time when they can least afford it. It will create a need for additional federal bailouts in the future and for significant cuts in state education and infrastructure funding that the nation can ill afford. Second, to the extent that states default to the federal government on health insurance exchanges, it opens the door to federal administration of other low-income programs. That would be a significant change in one of the basic tenets of federalism. Third, it shifts accountability from the federal government to the states for health-care cost containment: only in the states can this be done on a multipayer basis, because all health care is local. This could be positive in the long run.

A LOOK FORWARD

State and local governments have had structural deficits for decades because of the explosion of health-care spending and because their tax systems were built for a manufacturing economy of the 1950s and not for a high-technology, international, service-oriented economy of the twenty-first century. The primary culprit is sales taxes, which generally do not apply to services, to many goods sold over the Internet, or to Internet downloads. Alternatively stated, states tax old-economy goods that are stagnant, not new-economy services that are growing. Although state and local governments have adjusted taxes and spending over time, they also have shifted to more debt financing for operations and run up huge unfunded liabilities in their pension and retiree health-benefit systems. Managing these increased liabilities would have been very difficult even if revenues returned to the 6.5 percent growth that states witnessed from 1978 to 2008, but with the "new normal" of slower growth in revenues, more likely in the 4 percent to 5 percent range, continued budget cutting will be necessary.

A Government Accountability Office report published just before the ACA was enacted calculated that the state and local sector would have to cut spending by 12.3 percent every year between now and 2058 to eliminate the sector's structural deficit. Although that percentage seems high, it supports the point of a large and growing structural deficit.[21]

It will be a challenge for state revenues to cover the increased interest costs on municipal bonds and other debt, the current Medicaid program, and huge unfunded pension liabilities. There is little capacity to accommodate the additional Medicaid burden from passage of the ACA. There are thus essentially only two possibilities for the future of health-care reform: first, it is possible the law will be substantially modified to limit the financial burden on the states. Second, if it is implemented as currently written, then the federal government will have to continue to provide Medicaid bailouts to the states every couple of years, as it did in 2003 and 2009. Even then, the states will have to continue to reduce spending on education and infrastructure.

Stated another way, the states will be increasingly dependent on the federal government, as Medicaid increases substantially as a share of state spending. This is clearly an acceleration of the change whereby health-care costs are absorbing a significantly greater portion of state revenues. It will also mean substantially more volatility and uncertainty in all forms of state spending.

Given the size of the federal deficit, there will also have to be significant cuts in grants to state and local governments over the next decade. This will likely be done through consolidation of categorical grants, the elimination of many small grants, and cuts in the broader block grants. Although such steps will be politically difficult, because these programs are in the domestic discretionary funding category they will be far easier to cut than national defense spending or the other major entitlements of Social Security, Medicaid, and Medicare.

In summary, four major trends will transform the future federal-state relationship:

- Because of both the growth in the base Medicaid program and the expansion in the ACA, federal grants will become a significantly larger part of total revenues for state and local governments. State and local governments will depend more on the federal government.
- The mix in federal grants will change dramatically, as health care becomes a significantly larger share, and as education, training, social services, and transportation become a smaller share.
- Because of the growth in Medicaid, the federal government will have to continue short-run bailouts every couple of years, as in 2003 and 2009, and that federal support will be more volatile and less certain.
- Health-care spending will grow for all three levels of government, forcing reductions in public investment in education and training and public infrastructure. That, in turn, will reduce the nation's long-run competitiveness, productivity, and economic growth as well as the real wages and real incomes of citizens.

None of these trends are positive for the nation. The growth of federal health-care entitlements erodes public investment in human and infrastructure capital. It makes health-care cost containment a top national priority. However, it may take another financial crisis for the nation to face this growing problem.

Notes

1 US Government Accountability Office (2010). Estimates in the report are based on the Bureau of Economic Analysis's national income and product accounts definition, which differs slightly from the budget estimates.

2 National Association of State Budget Officers (2010). When one uses the national income definitions and data for the sector, the federal share of all state and local government current revenues was running about 25 percent by the middle of 2009. Most federal aid is provided directly to the states, although much is passed on to localities through programs operated by the states. See Bureau of Economic Analysis, National Income Accounts, Table 3.3: State and Local Government Current Receipts and Expenditures.

3 US Government Accountability Office (2010).

4 Although states administer the Food Stamp program, only the administrative costs, not the actual benefit payments, are considered grants to states.

5 The Medicaid total includes benefits and the state administrative costs paid by the federal government.

6 The exact budget treatment of these individual programs differs considerably across programs, but the programs all differ from discretionary grants that are appropriated on a year-by-year basis.

7 Unpublished estimates of major discretionary and mandatory program funding (2008 Federal Funds Information for State).

8 Grogan and Smith (2008).

9 Kaiser Commission on Medicaid and the Uninsured (2010).

10 Ibid.

11 Zuckerman, Williams, and Stockley (2009).

12 Benton (1986).

13 Canada (2003).

14 Maguire (2009).

15 Haskins (2008).

16 Dadayan and Boyd (2010).

17 From unpublished estimates by the staff of the National Governors Association, Washington, DC.

18 Pew Center on the States (2010).

19 National Association of State Budget Officers (2010).

20 Cost estimates from the Congressional Budget Office.

21 US Government Accountability Office (July 2010).

References

Benton, J. Edwin (1986). "Economic Considerations and Reagan's New Federalism Swap Proposals." *Publius* 16(2): 17–32.

Canada, Ben (2003). *Federal Grants to State and Local Governments: A Brief History.* Washington, DC: Congressional Research Service.

Dadayan, Lucy, and Donald Boyd (2010, November). *State Tax Revenues Rebound Further, Growing for the Third Straight Quarter.* Nelson A. Rockefeller Institute of Government. Albany: University of Albany, State University of New York.

Grogan, Colleen M., and Vernon K. Smith (2008). "From Charity Care to Medicaid: Governors, States and the Transformation of America's Health Care." In *A Legacy of Innovation: Governors and Public Policy*, edited by Ethan G. Sribnick. Philadelphia: University of Pennsylvania Press.

Haskins, Ron (2008). "Governors and the Development of American Social Policy." In *A Legacy of Innovation, Governors and Public Policy*, edited by Ethan G. Sribnick. Philadelphia: University of Pennsylvania Press.

Kaiser Commission on Medicaid and the Uninsured (2010, October). *Medicaid and Long-Term Care Services and Supports*. Fact sheet. Washington, DC: Kaiser Family Foundation.

Maguire, Stephen (2009). *General Revenue Sharing: Background and Analysis*. Washington, DC: Congressional Research Service.

National Association of State Budget Officers (NASBO) (2010). *The Fiscal Survey of the States*. Washington, DC: National Association of State Budget Officers.

Pew Center on the States (2010). *State Pensions and Retiree Health Benefits: The Trillion Dollar Gap*. Washington, DC: Pew Center on the States.

US Government Accountability Office (2010, July 30). *State and Local Governments: Fiscal Pressures Could Have Implications for Future Delivery of Intergovernmental Programs*. GAO Report no. 10–899. Washington, DC: US Government Accountability Office.

Zuckerman, Stephen, Aimee F. Williams, and Karen E. Stockley (2009). *Trends in Medicaid Physician Fees, 2003–2008*. Health Tracking Project Hope. Washington, DC. Available at www. healthaffairs.org.

CHAPTER 35

....

COMMUNITY ASSOCIATIONS AT MIDDLE AGE: CONSIDERING THE OPTIONS

....

ROBERT H. NELSON

THE first condominium development in the United States, Greystoke in Salt Lake City, Utah, was built only about fifty years ago, in 1962. Homeowner associations and cooperatives have been around much longer but these three forms of American collective housing ownership as recently as 1970 represented only about 1 percent of US housing. By 2010, however, there were more than 300,000 community associations housing more than 60 million Americans, or 20 percent of the US population.[1] Between 1980 and 2000, half the new housing in the United States was built and organized under the private governance of a community association. The rise of community associations has been perhaps the leading development for American housing and local governance of the past half century.[2]

As a more recent institution in American life, much of the public policy concern up to now has related to the manner of forming and then operating and maintaining community associations. The structure of community association governance is set in place by the land developer before there are any residents ("unit owners" in the language of the field). New buyers must then agree to the terms of this governance as a condition of purchase. Once they become owners, they are financially responsible for paying unit assessments and then gradually assume a growing role in association governance. When the development is completed and the housing units have been sold, the developer leaves and the unit owners take over the full control and management of the association. There can be, however, a lengthy period of transition in which the developer is still holding and selling units, while other units have already been sold and occupied. Managing this transition fairly for both developers and unit owners can be complicated.[3] Laws have had to be written and association rules devised to oversee the process of transferring final control from the developer to the unit owners.

As community associations move into middle age, however, new issues are demanding attention. Developers (in the writing of the founding documents) and policymakers now need to address more fully the question of the appropriate lifetime of a community association and how the middle and, potentially ending, stage might be handled. Should some failing community associations now go out of business altogether? How might this be accomplished? Should other community associations with major operating problems be reorganized? And, again, what is the best mechanism for accomplishing this?

Termination or Reorganization as an Option

One option that may become attractive for some community associations is outright termination. The association might be facing increasing difficulties in meeting its financial obligations; the revenues from unit owner assessments might not be enough to cover basic maintenance and other costs. If the infrastructure is deteriorating, there might be large capital costs that unit owners are not able to, or are not willing, to cover. The properties of the community association might deteriorate until they are no longer functional, depressing unit values and possibly posing safety hazards and other problems. When they have large mortgages, some unit owners might walk away from their properties entirely rather than pay a large special assessment.

In other cases the unit owners of a community association may simply have decided that it does not work for them.[4] The internal politics may be dysfunctional, perhaps due to a lack of volunteer leadership, a large number of transient renters (instead of permanent homeowners), or deeper structural reasons (the association may have diverse unit owners with widely varying and conflicting common-service interests and demands and who are never likely to agree).[5] One option is for the unit owners to move out one by one. If enough owners are dissatisfied, however, it might make more sense to terminate the association altogether. A new association with new rules might be reconstituted, or, in the case of a homeowners' association, the units might simply be transferred to individual ownership alone. Another possibility would be to sell everything in the association—all the individually and collectively owned properties alike—in one package to a developer. If the developer is willing to pay enough, this could even be a financially lucrative option for the association unit owners.

In the long run, community association terminations are most likely to reflect the simple reality of changing economic circumstances. As time passes, the original use of community association properties may become outmoded. When it was first built, for example, a community association of townhouses might have been well suited to its location. But a new subway stop could have opened nearby, radically altering the economic calculus. A large new apartment complex might now be a much more profitable land use—creating land values multiple times higher per unit than the current townhouse values. Unit owners might be able to realize a large windfall gain by selling and moving out collectively. This would pose a new kind of transitional problem for community associations, including the termination of an existing association. As time goes by, and existing community associations age, more and more will become uneconomic for the sites they occupy. To date, there has been little planning and analysis of how an association might end its lifetime.

The Uniform Planned Community Act (UPCA) and the Uniform Common Interest Ownership Act (UCIOA), drafted in 1980 and 1982 by the National Conference of Commissioners on Uniform State Laws, contemplate the possibility of the outright termination of a community association. These model state laws require a favorable vote of 80 percent or more of the unit owners, with further provisions specifying the fair treatment of unit owners during such a process. The UPCA and the UCIOA models were adopted in part by several states but most states have chosen to tailor their own community association legal regimes. In any case, there have been few terminations of community associations in the United States based on a voluntary 80 percent vote of the unit owners.

The UPCA and UCIOA, moreover, contemplated the complete sale of the community association assets (including both individually and collectively owned properties) only in the case of a single building organized as a condominium. As land values change over time, however, there will also be homeowners' associations with many individual homes (and "vertical" condominiums with multiple structures) that would find it profitable to sell out everything for a brand-new form of land use at the site. In such cases, a whole new set of issues would have to be addressed, including the appropriate decision-making procedure to terminate the association, the speed and process of unit owner exits, and the allocation formula for distributing the total association sale proceeds among the unit owners.

Bankruptcy of Community Associations

In the near term, issues of reorganizing or terminating a community association are most likely to arise in the context of a bankruptcy filing. Association bankruptcies have been rare in the past. However, the number of filings has been increasing in recent years with the sharp housing-market downturn and the general deterioration in economic conditions. Bank foreclosures on unit owners in some parts of the country have been common, leaving individual properties unoccupied for significant periods. Many associations have had trouble collecting assessments from economically distressed residents. Overall, the financial health of many community associations has deteriorated sharply since 2007, posing real risks of bankruptcy in some cases.

Community associations have been particularly prominent in the fastest growing states such as Florida, Arizona, Nevada, and California. In 1990, for example, 19 percent of all condominium associations in the United States were in Florida, and 18 percent were in California. It is in these same fast-growing states where the housing-market downturn has also been most severe. According to one 2010 estimate, two-thirds of all Arizona mortgage holders were "under water" (the amount of the mortgage was greater than the value of the property), creating an incentive for owners to simply walk away from properties. Also as of 2010, an estimated 10 percent of unit owners in Arizona community associations had either abandoned their units or been forced out by foreclosures. Overall, as one observer found, there were a growing number of Arizona homeowners' associations where "delinquencies have reached alarming proportions, placing some [homeowners' associations] under serious threat of bankruptcy."[6]

There is no good data source on the total numbers of community associations that have filed for bankruptcy. In Florida, however, media reports of bankruptcy filings have been appearing with growing frequency.[7] In 2009 the Legacy Park community association filed for bankruptcy, owing partly to an unpaid debt of $105,000 for cable television services provided by Comcast.[8] In another Florida case, the Maison Grande condominium in Miami Beach, facing $1 million in debts, and with 100 unit owners delinquent on their assessments, filed in 2009 for bankruptcy.[9] This is just the tip of the iceberg in terms of potential community association bankruptcies in Florida, especially if the law of bankruptcy for community associations were to be clarified and otherwise improved. At one Florida law firm there were so many "association clients [who] have inquired about filing for bankruptcy" that the firm had launched a comprehensive study of the benefits and costs of bankruptcy.[10]

Although only a few community associations have so far filed for bankruptcy in Florida, many more developers of new community associations have been going bankrupt. They have been hit by the severe housing-market downturn in which a new Florida condominium unit that was expected to sell for perhaps $200,000 in 2006 now might well bring in only $75,000 (and in some cases as little as $25,000). In such cases the developer of a new community association may have sold some of the association units but will still have been left with many others unsold before running out of money. Bankruptcy court trustees may combine the remaining unsold units for sale as a single package, using the proceeds to satisfy the demands of the creditors. For example, with the developer still owing more than $22 million, a bankruptcy court in 2010 sold off more than 60,000 square feet of condominium unit space, fifty-six parking-space reservations, and fifteen storage areas in the twenty-eight-story Onyx on the Bay tower in downtown Miami. New firms have emerged—one goes by the name "Condo Vultures"—that specialize in the purchase of vacant units in severely distressed community associations in Florida.[11]

If bankruptcies of community associations themselves (rather than of the developers) become more widespread, it will be desirable to revisit and rewrite the bankruptcy laws to take account of the special circumstances of associations. Community associations at present are legally established as nonprofit corporations. As a result, they now file for bankruptcy under either the general provisions of Chapter 7 or Chapter 11 of the federal Bankruptcy Code, the former providing for complete liquidation of the corporation and the latter for its reorganization (and subsequent emergence from bankruptcy).[12] The provisions of corporate bankruptcy law, however, are—reasonably enough—designed primarily for the circumstances of a private business corporation.[13] This can prove an awkward fit for a community association. The unit owners of a homeowners' association, for example, are legally analogous to the shareholders of a business corporation. But the application of limited liability to homeowner association unit owners can be inappropriate; the homeowners' association is not an entrepreneurial and profit-seeking body but in fact functions more in the manner of a government that serves the unit owners.

Kristin Davidson, a bankruptcy analyst, commented in a 2004 article that "the Bankruptcy Code is not equipped to address the unique characteristics and functions of community associations with excessive debt." Under current bankruptcy proceedings as applied to community associations, in many cases "either residents are tremendously burdened by the associations debt, or creditors suffer from little to no recovery of the debt."[14] Given the few previous cases and the complexity of the issues raised, there are few court precedents and widespread uncertainty exists as to the actual application of bankruptcy law to community associations. Some reorganization or liquidation options that would make the most sense for a bankrupt community association are not legally available to the bankruptcy court at present.[15]

Before taking up such matters in greater detail, it will be helpful to provide some background by reviewing briefly the rise of community associations since the 1970s and their unusual combination of private and public features. A community association is appropriately regarded as both a quasi-private and a quasi-public institution.

A MAJOR SOCIAL DEVELOPMENT

The rise of community associations since the 1960s has resulted in major changes in the character of American housing, property rights, and local governments.[16] Instead of public zoning, community associations shift much of the burden of

regulation of neighborhood land use to a new private body, thus significantly altering the manner of designing, building, and regulating neighborhood development
across the United States. In terms of property rights, community associations follow in the path of the spread of corporate ownership in the late nineteenth century,
which saw the transformation of American businesses from being predominantly
owned by individuals to predominantly collective ownership. We are now seeing
a similar transition in the ownership of American housing from predominantly
individual to—as it now seems will be the case in the future—predominantly collective ownership.

With the rise of community associations, many US local governments are for
practical purposes being decentralized to the neighborhood scale. Private management firms now often substitute for the past role of local public employees in
overseeing neighborhood land-use regulation and the provision of common services. It is also a large new experiment in grass-roots governance and local democracy. Around 2 million Americans now serve—the terms are typically two to three
years—on the boards of directors of community associations. For some of them,
this experience serves as a springboard into involvement with the wider American
political process.

In the 1960s and 1970s, a neighborhood movement in the United States advocated the transfer of many government responsibilities from counties and municipalities to individual neighborhoods. The leading advocates at the time were
proposing a reorganization of local government within the public sector. But this
never happened. There was too much institutional resistance to such a basic change
that would have affected so many existing local governments and their residents.
Instead, to many people's surprise, there was a successful private neighborhood
movement. The shift of governing responsibilities to private community associations has been rapidly transforming the organization and the workings of local
government in the United States, decentralizing it to the neighborhood scale and
privatizing it.[17]

The Functioning of Community Associations

There are three kinds of community associations—homeowners' associations,
condominiums, and cooperatives—and each has a different legal form. In a homeowners' association, the unit owners individually own their homes and then also
belong to the homeowners' association, which is a separate nonprofit corporation
that owns and manages the common areas. With condominiums, the common
areas are owned by the unit owners as "tenants in common," while each owner also
holds a legal entitlement to occupy his individual unit. Some commentators believe
that this legal difference may become important for bankruptcy purposes because
in a condominium there is less legal separation of the unit owners from the association itself, and thus potentially less protection against liabilities for the financial
and other obligations of the whole condominium association.[18]

As legally nonprofit corporations, much of the law of community associations derives from business corporation precedents. This extends to the significant role played by state governments (Delaware, in the case of many business corporations) in setting the terms of corporate governance, extending to governing structure, voting procedures, and many other matters. In states such as California and Florida, given the large numbers of community associations, the state legislature has routinely modified the state legal framework—at times seeming to make important changes almost every year. The overall trend has been toward increasing state oversight. In Nevada, for example, state laws in 1997, 1999, and 2003 made homeowners' associations subject to the following new controls:[19]

- Fines that associations can levy are capped at $100.
- Association boards must receive approval from their residents before starting litigation.
- Board elections must be held every two years and proxy votes during board elections are prohibited.
- Foreclosure based on nonpayment of fines is banned.
- Education for property managers is required.
- Annual meetings with announced agendas are required.
- A mechanism for recalling association board members must be in place.

Despite its private status, a community association functions in many ways like a form of government. The association has the power to levy "assessments"— amounting to a form of private taxation. If a unit owner fails to pay the assessments, the community association has the right to foreclose on the unit; this practice has spawned widespread tensions between associations and unit owners who are behind on their payments. Community associations can control the finest details of exterior property use, such as the house-paint color, where a bush can be planted, whether a fence is allowable, the manner of lawn care, the locations for car parking, and so on and so forth. This authority is all laid out in the "covenants, conditions and restrictions" (the CC&Rs) that are the governing documents—in effect, the neighborhood "constitution"—to which the unit owners have agreed in advance. A community association can be as small as a single building or as large as a city of 50,000. But more typically it is of neighborhood size and is around 200 to 400 housing units with a total population of perhaps 500 to 1,000 residents.

A community association will also provide certain common services. These may include typical municipal services such as garbage collection, street repair and lighting, and snow removal. Many associations also provide private security patrols. An estimated 10 to 20 percent of associations maintain a gate—the so-called gated communities.[20] The associations mow the lawns, trim the trees, and otherwise maintain the common areas belonging to the unit owners collectively. Many Americans may today want less government at the national level; but at the neighborhood level, they seemingly want more.

Associations frequently provide and oversee the use of recreational facilities such as swimming pools, tennis courts, and golf courses. Many of them now provide park areas and other open spaces for people to go for a walk, jog on a trail, or do some bird watching. Associations commonly sponsor public events such as community dinners, singles gatherings, or speeches by prominent individuals. Basically, if a collective service mainly affects a single neighborhood, and there are no major economies of scale, it is increasingly likely that it is now being provided in the United States by a community association. The actual delivery, to be sure, may be by an outside private contractor who performs this service for a number of different associations.

Community Associations: Transforming Local Governance

The rapid spread of community associations does not mean that there is no longer a need for local government in the public sector. But in areas where community associations have proliferated, local public governments now mainly focus on matters with a wider territorial scope—such as sewer systems, water supplies, air pollution controls, arterial highways, and provision of criminal justice. Such local public governments are also typically larger, often a center-city municipality or a large and powerful county government in the suburbs. Schools are also generally public at present but the few economies of scale—especially at the elementary school level—would make it possible in many cases for an individual school to serve a single community association. As charter schools become more common, it is easy to imagine charter schools being organized in the future—sometimes as part of the development process—and serving mainly elementary school students from a particular association.

For people living in the Northeast and Midwest, they are often surprised to learn of the large impact that community associations are having elsewhere in the United States on the American system of local governance. The Northeast and Midwest were mostly developed prior to the 1960s, and thus many areas do not have community associations (except for individual condominiums). In the newer and more rapidly developing parts of the South and West, however, community associations have proliferated and have become omnipresent. In these places, including large parts of states such as Florida, Texas, Arizona, Nevada, and California, almost all new large residential development now comes with a community association. In California as of 2004, about 60 percent of all new housing in the state was being built with a community association.[21]

The large differences between the systems of local government in the older and newer parts of the United States are illustrated in table 35.1. According to the 2007 Census of Governments, the Chicago metropolitan area has 570 general-purpose local governments (excluding schools and other special districts) in the public sector. The Detroit area has 215 local governments; St. Louis has 397; and Cleveland has 167. Of course, this is not true everywhere. The Buffalo metropolitan area has only 65 general-purpose local governments. That is partly because the Buffalo area

Table 35.1 Total general-purpose local governments (county, municipality, or township) by metropolitan area, 2007

Older Metropolitan Areas	Number of Local Governments
Buffalo (1.2 million population)	65
Chicago (9.2 million)	570
Cincinnati (2.0 million)	253
Cleveland (2.9 million)	167
Detroit (5.5 million)	215
Milwaukee (1.7 million)	94
Minneapolis (3.0 million)	339
Philadelphia (5.1 million)	386
Pittsburgh (2.4 million)	464
St. Louis (2.6 million)	397
Newer Metropolitan Areas	
Austin (1.2 million)	52
Las Vegas (1.6 million)	6
Miami (3.9 million)	106
Orlando (1.6 million)	40
Phoenix (3.3 million)	35
Raleigh-Durham (1.2 million)	30
San Diego (2.8 million)	19
Tampa (2.4 million)	39

Source: 2007 Census of Governments.

has only 1.1 million people, and it never had any booming suburban development in the twentieth century. So Buffalo's population is mostly fitted into a local governing structure inherited from the nineteenth and early twentieth centuries with a dominant central city.

With some such exceptions, the older parts of the United States fit a common pattern. In the suburbs, there are hundreds of public-sector municipalities—including townships in some states—that provide the more localized services. Many of these small suburban municipal governments have only one or a few neighborhoods. In the central city, there are large consolidated municipal governments encompassing at least a few hundred thousand people, typically formed one hundred or more years ago.

The pattern is much different in the South and West, however. Since the 1960s, Nevada has been the fastest-growing state (and it also has suffered disproportionately in the economic downturn of the Great Recession). The Las Vegas metropolitan area with its 1.6 million people has a grand total of six local governments in the public sector. There are only nineteen municipalities in the entire state of Nevada, along with its sixteen counties. Does this mean that Nevada residents have a special taste for large government at the local level or that they dislike small government? The answer, of course, is the opposite. Nevadans have a strong liking for government at the neighborhood scale but are obtaining such decentralized governance privately through community associations. Indeed, Nevada is filled with many hundreds of community associations. There, the associations are playing the role that small municipal governments in the public sector play in the Boston, New York, and Chicago suburbs—and in most of the rest of the suburban Northeast and Midwest. In the South and West, Nevada is an extreme case but similar patterns are found in many parts of these regions.

In Florida, the Orlando metropolitan area, for example, has 2.1 million people and only forty general-purpose local governments. The Tampa metropolitan area has 2.7 million people and thirty-nine local governments. Compare these figures to Cincinnati, whose metropolitan area has 2.2 million people and 253 local governments. Arizona is more like Nevada, with only ninety municipal governments in the entire state. Shifting back to the Midwest, Minnesota has a population similar to Arizona and has 854 municipalities. It also has 1,788 towns and townships, which are the functional equivalents of municipalities. There are 35 general-purpose local governments in the Phoenix metropolitan area (including two county governments), while the Minneapolis metropolitan area has 339 such governments.

Practical Implications

The increasingly private status has many practical implications for the conduct of local governments. Voting rights are allocated in community associations on the basis of property ownership. Owning a unit in a community association in this respect is like owning stock in a business corporation. A common arrangement is one vote for each unit. If four adults share one unit, they still get only one vote to share. One person who owns four units gets four votes. If I own a unit in Massachusetts where I spend the summer, and another unit in Florida where I spend the winter, I can vote in both places. A Norwegian can also vote if he owns a unit in Florida, whether or not he is a US citizen, and independent of the actual amount of time he resides there.

Overall, unless constrained by state laws, the private status of community associations gives them wider freedom to innovate in many areas of internal operations and governance. This reflects the fact that in general there are fewer legal and constitutional constraints on a private organization, as compared with a local government in the public sector. One area of difference is the application of rights such as freedom of speech and assembly. A community association can ban political signs on lawns, for example. It could deny the right for residents to have a protest march. In general, constitutional rights that would apply in a public context may not apply within a community association.

I once learned about the greater flexibility of community associations from personal experience. My father belonged to a community association in the Shenandoah Valley of Virginia. The association was having trouble passing an amendment to its founding documents, even though this was not controversial. It was simply that not enough unit owners were voting to meet the minimum vote requirement for passage. The association came up with a clever solution: convert the referendum into a lottery or raffle as well.[22] With this added incentive, more unit owners voted, and the amendment passed. It was a practical device to stimulate greater turnout; this was legal for a private community association but probably illegal for a local government in the public sector. (In the United States, a municipality is not supposed to pay people to vote in public elections.)

Consider another example where paying would probably be illegal publicly, but would be legal privately. Let us say a new convenience store wants to move into a neighborhood. A private community association in concept could sell rights to use a suitable location within the common areas. It would simply be another transaction such as occurs routinely in the buying and selling of rights in the private sector. If some unit owners were adversely affected, the sale proceeds might be used in part to compensate them. In this way the whole neighborhood might benefit from easy access to a conveniently located store. While few (if any) such transactions have occurred to date, Robert Ellickson, a Yale law professor, has long proposed the use of such methods as a way of resolving not-in-my-backyard (NIMBY) conflicts that are internal to neighborhoods.[23] In the public sector, however, this would probably be impossible even in concept. Changes in regulations to allow new uses are not supposed to be for sale, even in win-win situations where all parties benefit from and are agreeable to the transfer of rights.[24]

Proposed Institutional Reforms at Middle Age

With the rise of community associations in American life now dating back at least forty years, it is appropriate to consider needed institutional changes that address problems identified by this experience. As suggested above, the prospect of more association bankruptcies and the major deficiencies of bankruptcy law as applied to community associations show the need for new attention to this area of the law. It would be part of a wider consideration of the possible means by which a community association might be reorganized or terminated.

Termination by Bankruptcy

As noted above, a community association can now file for bankruptcy under either Chapter 7 or Chapter 11 of the Federal Bankruptcy Code. Under Chapter 7 as traditionally applied in the business sector, the liquidation of an entire corporation is contemplated. The properties of the corporation are assembled and then sold for as much as they can bring in. With the oversight of the bankruptcy court, the sale revenues are divided up among the various creditors of the corporation to reflect the relative seniority of debt obligations. In a typical case, many creditors receive only partial compensation for the debts owed to them. Having a junior status, the stock holders of the corporation frequently receive nothing.

Legally, a homeowners' association fits this corporate model. The homeowners' association corresponds to the business corporation and the unit owners are the corporate shareholders. If a Chapter 7 bankruptcy were to occur, the association would then presumably be liquidated, the common areas and other common properties sold, and the unit owners would lose any rights in these common areas. Under provisions for limited corporate liability, the unit owners would presumably still be left with the possession of their individual homes.

This model, however, poses a number of difficulties in the case of homeowners' associations. Many of the collective assets of the association itself may be difficult or impossible to separate from the individual units. What happens to an association street that is within the common areas and serves the unit owners living along this particular street? Would it have any sale value, other than to the owners, and who might otherwise buy it? Similarly, what about an association clubhouse, swimming pool, or tennis court that is surrounded by individually owned units? Some parts of the common areas might be suitable for development and have a significant value in a new use. But the highest value development of such areas might be incompatible with the existing homes. Even if the unit owners could be compelled to agree to a sale by their bankruptcy circumstances, would such incompatible development be allowed under public zoning laws? Such complications partly reflect the fact that a homeowners' association serves in the role of a private government, as well as having similarities to a business corporation.

As compared with a public municipality, the private status of a community association makes for one large difference. If the functions and boundaries of a municipality become outmoded, it would be difficult (if not impossible) to sell the municipally and individually owned properties collectively. A community association could, however, opt for termination and the sale of all the association assets, including both collectively and individually owned properties. While this is a rare event to date, at least one such sale did occur recently in Seattle. The Laurelton Terrace condominium occupied six acres adjacent to the Children's Hospital and Regional Medical Center. Wanting to expand, the hospital agreed to pay $93 million for the full set of Laurelton condominium properties, amounting to $614,000 per unit owner—fully 2.5 times the recent average of $241,000 in the individual sale of units. In a 2008 vote, 120 unit owners favored the package sale of all the condominium properties: three opposed it, and twelve did not vote. Until 1990, Washington State law required unanimity for such a transaction; but the state in that year enacted a law providing for such a termination of an association with a favorable vote of greater than 80 percent. This law, however, applied only prospectively to new associations. The state legislature, however, solved the problem by amending the law in 2008 to allow transactions such as the Laurelton sale to proceed.[25]

In another case, the unit owners of the Parker Place condominium in Wallingford, Connecticut, opted for the termination of the association and the sale of all the units, as also authorized by state law with an 80 percent favorable vote. In this case, however, seeking to gain control over all the properties, a private developer had already bought up 80 percent of the association units in individual purchases. Then, exercising his rights under state law, in August 2008 he informed the remaining twenty-two unit owners, many of whom did not want to terminate the association, of his intentions. As his lawyer wrote, "as an owner of 80 percent of the units, my client can accomplish this without your cooperation or that of any other unit owners."[26]

A Chapter 7 bankruptcy—with suitably revised bankruptcy laws—might be another vehicle for accomplishing a complete termination, and without such a high supermajority required. Not only the common areas but also the individual units would be vacated and transferred to a new buyer who would redevelop the site in a brand-new use. Admittedly, this is a severe remedy that bankruptcy courts might be reluctant to impose unilaterally. Yet there will be many circumstances such as the Seattle example, where such "complete" termination might be workable or even economically desirable for everyone concerned. There might even be enough development value in a brand-new use to satisfy the creditors and to create a financial windfall for the unit owners. Society might benefit as well from the more efficient use of the land. Even when this is not the case, complete termination of a bankrupt association may be the only fair way to resolve the claims of the creditors while leaving some substantial amounts for the unit owners.

If all the properties of a community association are sold as a single package as part of a bankruptcy proceeding, a suitable rule will be required for determining the distribution of the proceeds among the creditors and the unit owners. This will be a matter presumably for a bankruptcy court to address. A fair distribution among unit owners will itself raise some difficult issues. The formula used to allocate voting shares in the association may not be appropriate for the purpose of allocating total sale revenues from all the association properties. Voting rights may be allocated as one per unit, for example, even though these units may now have significantly different sale values. Some unit owners may have made major improvements in their properties. Others may have let their properties run down. How would such matters be factored into the unit owner distribution formula?

Given the current absence of answers to such questions, and the uncertain legal prospects for a complete termination, very few (if any) community associations have pursued liquidation under Chapter 7 of the bankruptcy law. With legal clarification and a newly written bankruptcy chapter for community associations, many more might do so.

Reorganization of Community Associations

The limited number of community associations filing for bankruptcy to date have almost all done so under Chapter 11, which provides for the reorganization of a corporation and its eventual emergence from bankruptcy as a viable organization. Even in these cases, major uncertainties remain in the application of Chapter 11 to community associations. A key question is the extent to which unit owners are sheltered in a bankruptcy proceeding. Can, or should, a bankruptcy court require the unit owners to contribute to the final settlement with creditors by means of an assessment? If that is allowed, many unit owners might incur large and unexpected financial burdens, some of whom may not have the necessary financial resources themselves. If the unit owners are instead legally protected from such unit owner assessments (as their limited liability might be interpreted to require in the case of a homeowners' association), the creditors may be denied significant recovery on the debts owed to them. The common areas of the community association may by themselves have limited sale value. Whether a bankruptcy court could order the sale of the common areas alone, and whether this would make any sense as a matter of sound land-use planning, are more unresolved questions.

A better solution might be to allow the creditors to take charge of the association, temporarily replacing some (or all) of the current board of directors with at least a majority of new members selected by the creditors (thus putting the association in a form of "receivership"). The new creditor-dominated board might be authorized to operate the swimming pool, golf course, and other recreational facilities, potentially increasing charges for their use. It might do the same for the clubhouse, parking lots, and other possible sources of new revenue. Subject to the oversight of the bankruptcy trustee, unit owner assessments might also be increased, using some of the funds for community association maintenance and operation, and some to pay off the association debts. When the creditors were paid off as required by the bankruptcy court, the full control of the board of directors would be returned to the unit owners.

It might be desirable, however, to revisit the operating rules and other elements of the CC&Rs. If the bankruptcy of the association was attributable in part to a poorly functioning set of association operating rules and procedures, the bankruptcy court might be authorized to reorganize the association, requiring the development of new rules and procedures. If, for example, past association limits on major new assessments (perhaps a requirement for a high supermajority vote of the unit owners) had resulted in the chronic underfunding and undermaintenance of the association infrastructure, the bankruptcy court might vacate these limits.

Or the bankruptcy court might order that an outside management firm be hired (for some limited time period) to handle some of the routine affairs of the association. Even the internal association rules for selecting and running the board of directors might be fair game in the bankruptcy proceeding. The goal would be to set in place a new set of association governing rules that would prevent the association from returning to bankruptcy in the future.

Other New Means of Termination and Reorganization

The advantage of bankruptcy is that, having reached the edge of disaster, bankruptcy law allows for—and even compels—radical solutions that might otherwise be prevented by various existing institutional obstacles to change. It would be preferable in many cases, however, to take action before reaching such dire straits. One might suggest that community associations already have the authority to revisit their decision-making and other governing rules and procedures. Most CC&Rs do allow for amendments to the founding documents of the association. As noted above, however, high supermajorities and other hurdles normally make such amendments difficult. Some community associations have sought to change specific restrictions relating to allowable uses of properties (parking rules, for example). But few community associations have ever undertaken a basic internal reorganization of their own systems of governance, following their existing rules for amending their "constitutions."

Even when basic changes might be available and desirable, it would typically require a heroic entrepreneurial effort to bring them about within an association. The disincentives for individuals to participate in collective actions (the strong incentive to be a "free rider") limit the likelihood that any one unit owner would be willing to take on such a large responsibility.[27] Thus, in practice, even when they have significant operating problems that may be widely recognized within a community association, the great majority of associations simply make do with the status quo.

A few associations, it might be noted, do have provisions in their founding documents to renew the terms of governance periodically. University Park, the oldest private community in Irvine, California, includes provisions in the CC&Rs that require that the architectural review committee be reauthorized every forty years. Absent a majority vote at that point by the unit owners, the association land-use restrictions automatically expire—as happened in 2008, partly because the association had barely been aware of this provision of its founding documents.[28] In Florida, a 1963 law requires that certain community associations must renew their restrictions every thirty years, although there seems to have been little awareness of and enforcement of this legal requirement to date.[29]

These procedures, however, are limited in their application and have arbitrary time frames. Recognizing that community association circumstances can change

significantly, new state laws might be written to make it easier for community associations, acting on their own, to change their rules and procedures relating to termination and reorganization. The state might also oversee such changes to ensure
that individual unit owners are treated fairly. Rather than a court proceeding, however, this would probably better be regarded as an administrative responsibility of
a state agency charged with overseeing community associating affairs (many if not
all states already have such agencies).

States might thus enact new laws to oversee the termination of a community
association. The state rules would clarify that termination options could include
the package sale of the entire set of association properties, both those individually
and collectively owned. Economic motives—the possibility of large gains in total
unit owner values—would normally be the driving force. But strong dissatisfaction with the past internal workings of the association might also come into play.
It might take a vote of 70 percent of the unit owners to commence an association
process of "complete" termination. State laws might specify certain criteria for an
acceptable termination process, including fair treatment of all the unit owners in
the distribution of the total revenues received in the sale process. The state would
then either approve or disapprove the termination plan. Provision would be made
for a high final vote of approval—perhaps requiring 80 percent of the unit owners
in favor—before any actual complete collective sale of the association properties
could occur.

New state laws might also be rewritten to facilitate the internal reorganization
of a community association as a more normal procedure before a crisis and potentially before the extreme of bankruptcy is reached. A favorable vote of perhaps
60 percent of the unit owners might be sufficient to initiate such a process and
a 70 percent vote would be needed to give final approval. The full set of existing
CC&Rs, often written long ago by the developer, might come under review. Many
associations have tight restrictions that may no longer have the support of most
unit owners. There are wide complaints about the "dictatorial" behavior of some
community association boards. The basic operating rules of the association could
thus be revisited. The types of association decisions that are subject to a full vote
of all the unit owners might be reconsidered. Procedures for collecting delinquent
assessments and fines might be revised. Election procedures (use of proxy voting,
for example) might come under review.

State laws for community associations assume that the association should be
organized along the lines of a business corporation. The reality is, however, that a
community association also performs many functions that are more like a local
government. The scope for reorganization of community associations thus might
also be extended to making more fundamental changes in the governing structure
of the association.[30] Perhaps some associations would like a greater separation of
powers internally—they might want the private equivalent of an elected "mayor"
to manage the association's "executive branch." There could be wide freedom to
innovate, borrowing as appropriate from both the business corporation and the
local public governance models. Association board members are now volunteers

but in some larger associations they might be paid in the future, including some outside board members who could bring valuable forms of expertise (for now, only unit owners can be board members).

Retrofitting Community Associations

The popularity of community associations in newly developing parts of the United States suggests that the association model might be extended more broadly to older areas of the country. It might be desirable to establish new legal authority to allow the "retrofitting" of a community association in an existing neighborhood.[31] An older neighborhood, for example, that is now governed within a larger political jurisdiction might decide that it wants its own neighborhood government. At present, it could obtain its own government only through municipal incorporation at the neighborhood level, thus creating a neighborhood public government. With a change in state law, the range of choice might be expanded to also allow another option, incorporation as a private government—a community association—for this neighborhood. As discussed above, community associations have various advantages relative to public governments—even as they also have some disadvantages that could also be factored into the neighborhood's analysis of its needs and its final choice of a new governing form.[32]

As a new state law might provide, retrofitting a community association to an existing neighborhood might work as follows.[33] If a group of neighborhood property owners wanted to create their own new private community association, they would gather signatures on a petition. If enough neighborhood owners signed, neighborhood representatives and the existing local public government (normally of considerably wider geographic scope than the neighborhood) would work out a transfer agreement. It would cover streets (some of which might be turned over to the private association), local service-provision responsibilities, divisions of regulatory authority, parkland and other recreational areas, and other such matters. After that, and following the circulation of information to the public, the property owners in the neighborhood would vote. It might take, say, a vote of 80 percent of the property owners to form a new community association to govern the neighborhood.

Such retroactive establishment of new community associations might be particularly helpful in stimulating the redevelopment of poor inner city and other distressed older urban neighborhoods. A community association in such an area could provide a whole new degree of security of persons and of investment. Given the new legal flexibility afforded by its private status, it might even put up gates and control entry, thereby becoming an inner-city gated community. If a distressed urban neighborhood could keep out potentially threatening elements, many of these neighborhoods might become much more attractive for redevelopment. If anyone now needs gates, it is not in the suburbs but in the inner cities. Investment might flood in.[34] Business improvement districts (BIDs) have some of the features of a community association and have already shown such benefits.[35] But their powers are limited in comparison to a full-fledged community association.

A New Response to *Kelo*

The 2005 *Kelo* decision of the Supreme Court, involving the city of New London, Connecticut, highlighted some of the problems of urban land assembly. The use of eminent domain—approved by the court—is troublesome for a number of reasons. But it is still true that there is a need to assemble large urban parcels, potentially involving many ownerships, if coordinated private land development is to occur in older parts of many cities. Such land assembly, however, is difficult under the current land-use system. Individual properties normally have to be assembled one by one in an assembly process that can be long and cumbersome. There are also likely to be significant inequities among existing land owners. Speculators and the last holdouts often gain a disproportionate share of the ultimate total value of the land as an assembled package ready for redevelopment.

A possible solution would be to retrofit a community association for the express purpose of selling a whole neighborhood.[36] The association would in effect be created to be the new bargaining agent for the neighborhood property owners collectively. If they received a high-enough offer from a land developer, and a sufficient supermajority of unit owners voted in favor of a sale, the association might then be sold off as a complete package of properties according to wider rules for such a complete termination of an association. The problems of the current role of land speculators in purchasing individual neighborhood properties early in the process and the possible disproportionate gains from being a late holdout would be much reduced. The financial rewards to the average property owner in the neighborhood would be correspondingly increased. By facilitating the assembly of large parcels of urban land, newly comprehensive—as opposed to the current piecemeal process of—private redevelopment would be significantly increased.[37] By such a process of "internalizing the externalities" in urban land development, the overall efficiency and aesthetic attractiveness of land use in America's cities might be significantly enhanced.

As compared with the use of eminent domain for land assembly, moreover, this proposal would have two major advantages. First, the sale price for the fully assembled package of land would be set by direct negotiations between the unit owners acting collectively and a potential developer. Second, the decision to accept or reject a developer offer would be made by the unit owners themselves. Under eminent domain, by contrast, a wider city or other public government acts unilaterally to make such decisions. It is understandable that neighborhood residents may be angry and upset, if they feel they have not been adequately compensated or simply do not want to move and are forced to do so by state coercion. A retrofitted community association would put such decisions on a collective voluntary private basis (although a limited minority of outvoted unit owners in the association could admittedly be forced to move out against their wishes).

At present, however, lacking such a procedure for the collective sale of whole neighborhoods, any such efforts would require unanimous consent of the property owners. Indeed, a few neighborhoods around the United States have attempted to organize themselves on a unanimous basis to sell their properties collectively. A handful has even succeeded. In 1988 in Arlington, Virginia, all twenty-four property owners in the Courtland neighborhood—located near a new subway stop—banded together to sell all their properties collectively to the Moyarta Corporation. By working together, they were able to double the existing values of their homes. But most such efforts have failed to win the necessary unanimous consent to create a collective bargaining body. Given the very high transaction costs, the great majority of neighborhoods that might have benefited significantly from collective bargaining have never tried to organize themselves in the first place.

LOCAL GOVERNANCE AS AN ECONOMIC PROBLEM IN "INDUSTRIAL ORGANIZATION"

A main advantage derived from the private status of a community association is the greater flexibility it introduces into the metropolitan land-use system and its governance. It is easier to contemplate the complete termination or the major reorganization of a private local government, as compared with that of a public local government. When the government is private, market incentives can be brought into play in motivating and guiding such a process of governmental change. If some of the proposals made in this chapter—which are dependent on a private status—are adopted, it would become easier to end the life of a community association and to commit the land to a brand-new set of uses with suitable new structures of private governance.

Many commentators have observed that local governments in the United States, even when they are nominally public, actually function more like private units.[38] Zoning for many purposes is better regarded as a de facto collective property right than as a form of public regulation for the public good.[39] Community associations make the private status official, thus giving private forces a greater ability to shape the system of local governance. Indeed, if local governance is reconceived to be a private activity, the economics of local governance might be newly understood as economic problems of "industrial organization," employing analytical tools long applied by economists to the study of the steel, automobile, computer, and many other private industries.

Transaction Costs and Other Issues

In the ordinary business world, large corporations have typically won out over small firms in the market. These large business corporations are in effect small, private "planned economies" based internally on central planning and management (although perhaps making use of marketlike incentives). Since the pioneering work of Oliver Williamson in the 1970s, a "new institutional economics" has shed greater light on the transaction costs and other economic forces that can yield more or less vertical and horizontal integration within an industry.[40]

In a metropolitan system of local governance, there are similar economic issues of transaction costs and economies of scale that will influence the desirability of various governmental outcomes. A larger unit of local government might be able to deliver services such as water and sewer systems at lower costs. A big city may have access to various forms of specialized professional knowledge. A large city, however, might be at a significant disadvantage in other respects. It might be difficult to create a system of positive incentives that will serve to motivate a large city bureaucracy. Large city size will involve a greater diversity of citizens and thus require greater divergences between service demands and the common levels of citywide services that are typically provided. As a mayor of Chicago once declared in resisting a further expansion of city boundaries, "The ideal city is compact. With its area fully occupied, the care of all branches of administration can be applied to all sections expeditiously and well." In response to any proposals "to increase this territory" of Chicago, the appropriate response should be "instant and emphatic discouragement."[41]

Government at the scale of a small neighborhood also may not be ideal. The time burdens required for full democratic participation and other transaction costs of neighborhood governance may be large for each housing unit owner. Economies of scale in service delivery may be impossible to achieve. A neighborhood should be large enough to offer a self-contained physical environment of high quality. In general, there will be trade-offs between various benefits and costs associated with larger and smaller sizes of neighborhoods and their governments.[42]

In New York State, the village of Macedon addressed such issues in a study of the benefits and costs of dissolving its small public government. Some responsibilities might have been transferred to the wider town government in which the village was located. Other responsibilities might have been assumed by newly created special districts. Overall, the study estimated that property owners in Macedon could each save $204 per year (for a representative home worth $100,000) by terminating the village government and abolishing or redistributing its functions.[43] Following this study, however, the residents of the village voted 257 to 228 in a referendum against the termination proposal. In this case, the benefits of keeping a small village government closer to home apparently outweighed the potential financial gains of governmental consolidation in the minds of the voters.

A More Flexible Process of Local Adjustment

In an ordinary business corporation, each investor joins by purchasing shares. Later changes in the "citizenship" of a business organization are accomplished by buying and selling the stock. One corporation thus can take over the physical assets of another corporation by buying out most of its stockholders. Mergers and acquisitions, along with divestitures, are a routine part of life in the American business world. All these ownership changes entail moderate transaction costs. Stockholders who disapprove of the way a corporation is being run can "exit" from the organization simply by selling their shares on Wall Street.

In principle, the "industrial organization" of the "business" of a local government in the United States, like other "industrial" sectors, could also be determined by a process of competition in the marketplace. Ronald Oakerson, who in the mid-1980s directed a study of the structures of local governance across the United States for the US Advisory Commission on Intergovernmental Relations (ACIR), took this view. As Oakerson wrote, "Of central importance is the authority to create, modify, and dissolve [local service] provision units. The structure of the provision side—including the variety of provision units—depends on who can exercise this authority and under what conditions."[44] In this way, a competitive process of selection of the fittest among many local governments of many possible sizes and types could drive the local governance system.

Oakerson argued that the ability to create new neighborhood-level institutions of local governance was a large missing element in the American system. As he explained, "What is essential is that small-scale communities have the capability to organize themselves to act collectively with respect to common problems. This requires that locally defined communities be able to self-govern, exercising the powers of government within a limited sphere—limited in terms of both territory and the scope of authority." Many goods and services could best be "provided on a 'neighborhood' scale."[45] At present, however, the governance structures of metropolitan areas in the United States "tend to preclude or inhibit the development of smaller, nested provision units—neighborhood governments—within [wider city] boundaries."[46] As a result, neighborhood forms of governance are often simply left out of the competition to determine the future metropolitan structure of local governance.

Oakerson said little about the major legal changes that are necessary to make the formation of new local governments much easier and to simplify the processes of boundary adjustment. Moreover, although Oakerson clearly recognized the growing importance of private community associations, he did not necessarily advocate them as the main preferred instrument of a newly flexible and competitive system of neighborhood governance. Yet, a large advantage of the community association with its private status is its greater ease of integration into a more marketlike system of local governance. If the private constitution of a community association is properly written, it can allow for the routine expansion, contraction, termination, or other modification of the community association and its boundaries, as a private business act and as economic circumstances change.

It would be helpful, for example, if more community association founding documents provided for private "divestitures" of appropriate subunits of the association, assuming a contiguous subgroup within a neighborhood wanted to leave. Legally, this should be easier to accomplish than the current rules that control the secession of a subunit from an existing municipal government in the public sector. There could be a well-defined process in community association documents for appropriate private "acquisitions" of new areas as well. If few community associations have thus far considered such matters, it is partly because the governance institution of the community association in the United States is still fairly new. As more and more community associations have reached middle-age status, attention should now shift to the processes by which needed changes in the boundaries and organization of local private governance can be made.[47]

In this manner, it would be possible to come closer to Oakerson's vision of a trial-and-error process to resolve the many trade-offs among local governing forms.

> There is no fully objective way of determining an appropriate set of provision units apart from the expressed preferences of local citizens for public goods and services. The ease with which a single provision unit can satisfy individual preferences decreases with the preference heterogeneity of the community. By the same token, the ability to satisfy diverse preferences increases with an increase in the number of provision units in a local public economy—at least up to some point. The creation of provision units is constrained by the expected transaction costs of organizing and operating an additional unit. Transaction costs include the costs of citizen participation. The choice is between greater preference satisfaction, obtained by creating an additional provision unit, and lower transaction costs. Citizens face a trade-off that only they can decide.[48]

CONCLUSION

Community associations represent a major American shift toward collective private ownership of housing, following in the path of the rise of the private business corporation one hundred years ago. In many ways, these community-based organizations constitute either an alternative to, or augmentation of, many of the services that traditionally have been provided by local governments. But, as the economy and demographics change, the associated "aging" process of this type of governance can bring problems. The laws controlling the chartering, organizing, governing, and other aspects of these corporations have been significantly revised many times. These changes have come about from experience gained with various corporate forms of business ownership and from the responses to problems and opportunities that have been discovered by businessmen, researchers, and other observers. As more and more community associations age, this area of collective property ownership will increasingly need a full retrospective assessment. New state laws and other initiatives will be needed to correct problems and achieve opportunities as both are identified over time.

Notes

1 By comparison, there were 89,476 local public governments of all kinds as found in the 2007 Census of Governments, including 19,491 municipalities, 16,519 townships (similar to municipalities), and 3,033 counties, all of these in the category of "general purpose governments." In addition, there were 50,432 "special purpose governments," including 13,051 school districts and 37,381 other types of special districts.
2 Nelson (2005a).
3 Hyatt (1998).
4 Low (2003).
5 Alexander (1989).
6 Anderson (2010).
7 Association bankruptcies were being reflected in the financial markets with the widespread defaults on special-district bonds that have been sold to finance infrastructure in the new communities. Of the approximately $10 billion special-district bonds outstanding in Florida, about $2 to $3 billion were approaching default in early 2010. See Sigo (2010).
8 McClatchy-Tribune Information Services (2010).
9 Sheridan (2009).
10 Ibid.
11 Holsman and Vanderhoof (2010).
12 Pinkerton (2009).
13 USCourts.gov (2010).
14 Davidson (2004), 583, 631.
15 Davidson (2004) proposes that community associations should instead file for bankruptcy under Chapter 9, which applies to municipalities and other public governments. While it would help with some problems, however, this would create other new difficulties. I propose that a brand-new chapter of the bankruptcy law instead be written that is specifically designed for the circumstances of community associations. I also propose other institutional changes outside bankruptcy that would facilitate the termination and reorganization of community associations as they face new economic and other challenges in middle age.
16 McKenzie (1994); Dilger (1992); Barton and Silverman (1994); Hyatt (1998); Stabile (2000).
17 Nelson (2005a).
18 Davidson (2004).
19 This is based on an informal tabulation by the author from local newspapers.
20 Blakely and Snyder (1997).
21 Lyon (2004), iii.
22 Each ballot submitted became in effect a lottery ticket. The first prize was $300, second was $200, and third was $100. (The author heard about this technique because his father won the $100 prize.)
23 Ellickson (1973).

24 Fennell (2000).

25 Pryne (2008).

26 Prevost (2008).

27 A "free rider" is one who benefits from a publicly provided good or service, but it does not contribute anything or at least not a fair share to the paying for that benefit.

28 Bird (2008).

29 Berger (2010).

30 For various proposals, see Nelson (2005a), Part V.

31 Ibid., Part IV; Nelson (2005b). See also Nelson (1999).

32 Nelson (2008).

33 Nelson (2006).

34 See Norcross, McKenzie, and Nelson (2008).

35 Nelson, McKenzie, and Norcross (2008).

36 Nelson and Norcross (2009).

37 Michael Heller and David Hills make a similar proposal as a means of facilitating urban land assembly (although not framed as the retrofitting of a community association). Heller and Hills (2008).

38 Popenoe (1985).

39 See Nelson (1977); also Fischel (1985). Zoning thus facilitates the decentralization of local government and competition among government units, creating a rough approximation of a market process and market efficiencies. See Tiebout (1956); Oates (1972, 2006).

40 See Williamson (1975); also Furubotn and Richter (1997).

41 Comment in 1902 of Chicago mayor Carter H. Harrison, quoted in Jackson (1985), 150.

42 Breton (1996).

43 Curry (2008).

44 Oakerson (1999), 81. This is a revised edition of Oakerson's original 1987 report done for the Advisory Commission on Intergovernmental Relations.

45 Ibid., 127, 85.

46 Ibid., 86.

47 See Liebmann (2000).

48 Oakerson (1999), 115.

References

Advisory Commission on Intergovernmental Relations. (1978). *Metropolitan America: Challenge to Federalism*. New York: Arno Press.

Alexander, Gregory S. (1989, November). "Dilemmas of Group Autonomy: Residential Associations and Community," *Cornell Law Review* 75: 1–61.

Anderson, J. Craig (2010, August 29). "Homeowners Associations Facing Own Crisis Amid Foreclosures." *The Arizona Republic*.

Barton, Stephen E., and Carol J. Silverman (Eds.) (1994). *Common Interest Communities: Private Governments and the Public Interest*. Berkeley: Institute of Governmental Studies Press, University of California.

Berger, Donna DiMaggio (2010, July 18). "Are Your HOA Governing Documents Set to Expire Soon?" *Sun Sentinel*.

Bird, Cameron. (2008, July 1). "Irvine Village Loses Architectural Control." *Orange County Register*.

Blakely, Edward J., and Mary Gail Snyder. (1997). *Fortress America: Gated Communities in the United States*. Washington, DC: Brookings Institution Press.

Breton, Albert. (1996). *Competitive Governments: An Economic Theory of Politics and Public Finance*. New York: Cambridge University Press.

Briffault, Richard. (1996, May). "The Local Government Boundary Problem in Metropolitan Areas." *Stanford Law Review* 48: 1115–1171.

Curry, Tracey (2008, March 16). "Finally, It's Decision Time in Macedon." *Courier Journal*.

Davidson, Kristin L. (2004, Spring). "Bankruptcy Protection for Community Associations as Debtors." *Emory Bankruptcy Developments Journal* 20: 583–632.

Dilger, Robert Jay. (1992). *Neighborhood Politics: Residential Community Associations in American Governance*. New York: New York University Press.

Ellickson, Robert C. (1973, Summer). "Alternatives to Zoning: Covenants, Nuisance Rules, and Fines as Land Use Controls." *University of Chicago Law Review* 40: 681–781.

Fennell, Lee Anne (2000, October). "Hard Bargains and Real Steals: Land Use Exactions Revisited." *Iowa Law Review* 86: 1–85.

Fischel, William A. (1985). *The Economics of Zoning Laws: A Property Rights Approach to American Land Use Controls*. Baltimore: Johns Hopkins University Press.

Furubotn, Eirik G., and Rudolf Richter. (1997). *Institutions and Economic Theory: The Contribution of the New Institutional Economics*. Ann Arbor: University of Michigan Press.

Heller, Michael, and Rick Hills (2008, April). "Land Assembly Districts." *Harvard Law Review* 121(6): 1467–1527.

Holsman, Melissa E., and Nadia Vanderhoof (2010, October 8). "Owners of Apartment-to-Condo Conversions Feel Burn of Mangled Economy." *PCPalm*.

Hyatt, Amanda G. (1966). *Transition from Developer Control*. 2nd ed., GAP Report 3. Alexandria, VA: Community Associations Institute.

Hyatt, Wayne S. (1998, Winter). "Common Interest Communities: Evolution and Reinvention." *John Marshall Law Review* 31: 303–395.

Jackson, Kenneth T. (1985). *Crabgrass Frontier: The Suburbanization of the United States*. New York: Oxford University Press.

Liebmann, George W. (2000, Winter). "Land Readjustment for America: A Proposal for a Statute." *The Urban Lawyer* 32(1): 1–20.

Low, Setha. (2003). *Behind the Gates: Life, Security and the Pursuit of Happiness in Fortress America*. New York: Routledge.

Lyon, David W. (2004). "Foreword." In *Planned Developments in California: Private Communities and Public Life*, edited by Tracy W. Gordon. San Francisco: Public Policy Institute of California. iii–v.

McClatchy-Tribune Information Services (2010). http://www.mcclatchydc.com/2010/commentary.Legacy html.

McKenzie, Evan. (1994). *Privatopia: Homeowner Associations and the Rise of Residential Private Government*. New Haven: Yale University Press.

Nelson, Robert H. (1977). *Zoning and Property Rights: An Analysis of the American System of Land Use Regulation*. Cambridge, MA: MIT Press.

Nelson, Robert H. (1999, Summer). "Privatizing the Neighborhood: A Proposal to Replace Zoning with Collective Private Property Rights to Existing Neighborhoods." *George Mason Law Review* 7: 827–880.

Nelson, Robert H. (2005a). *Private Neighborhoods and the Transformation of Local Government*. Washington, DC: Urban Institute Press.

Nelson, Robert H. (2005b, September/October). "Retro Metro." *Common Ground*.

Nelson, Robert H. (2006, November). "New Community Associations for Established Neighborhoods." *Review of Policy Research* 23.

Nelson, Robert H. (2008). "Community Associations: Decentralizing Local Government Privately." In *Fiscal Decentralization and Land Policies*, edited by Gregory K. Ingram and Yu-Hung Hong. Cambridge, MA: Lincoln Institute of Land Policy. 332–355.

Nelson, Robert H., Kyle McKenzie, and Eileen Norcross (2008). *Lessons from Business Improvement Districts: Building on Past Successes*. Arlington, VA: Mercatus Center, Policy Primer No. 5.

Nelson, Robert H., and Eileen Norcross (2009). *Moving Past Kelo: A New Institution for Land Assembly: Collective Neighborhood Bargaining Associations (CNBAs)*. Arlington, VA: Mercatus Center. Policy Comment No. 23.

Norcross, Eileen, Kyle McKenzie and Robert H. Nelson (2008). *From BIDs to RIDs: Creating Residential Improvement Districts*. Arlington, VA: Mercatus Center. Policy Comment No. 20.

Oakerson, Ronald J. (1999). *Governing Local Public Economies: Creating the Civic Metropolis*. Oakland, CA: Institute for Contemporary Studies Press.

Oates, Wallace E. (1972). *Fiscal Federalism*. New York: Harcourt Brace Jovanovich.

Oates, Wallace E. (2006). "The Many Faces of the Tiebout Model." In *The Tiebout Model at Fifty: Essays in Public Economics in Honor of Wallace Oates,* edited by William A. Fischel. Cambridge, MA: Lincoln Institute of Land Policy. 21–45.

Pinkerton, Trevor G. (2009). "Escaping the Death Spiral of Dues and Debt: Bankruptcy and Condominium Debtors." *Emory Bankruptcy Developments Journal* 26: 125–166.

Popenoe, David. (1985). *Private Pleasure, Public Plight: American Metropolitan Community Life in Comparative Perspective* New Brunswick, NJ: Transaction.

Prevost, Lisa (2008, September 28). "Condo Owners Forced to Sell." *New York Times*.

Pryne, Eric (2008, February 22). "Children's Hospital Agrees to Buy Condos." *Seattle Times*.

Shanklin, Mary (2010, August 19). "Homeowners Associations Buck Cable Bills." *Orlando Sentinel*.

Sheridan, Terry (2009, July 8). "Bankruptcy: $1 Million Debt Sends Condo Association into Chapter 11." *Daily Business Review*. http://www.dailybusinessreview.com/Web_Blog_Stories/2009/July/Maison_bankruptcy.html.

Sigo, Shelly (2010, February 10). "Dirt Bonds Drying Up in Florida." *The Bond Buyer*. http://www.bondbuyer.com/issues/119_276/Florida-CCD-defaults-report.

Stabile, Donald R. (2000). *Community Associations: The Emergence and Acceptance of a Quiet Innovation in Housing*. Westport, CT: Greenwood Press.

Stansel, Dean. (2002). *Interjurisdictional Competition and Local Economic Performance: A Cross-Sectional Examination of US Metropolitan Areas*. Fairfax, VA: Working Paper, Department of Economics, George Mason University.

Tiebout, Charles M. (1956). "A Pure Theory of Local Expenditures." *Journal of Political Economy* 64(4): 416–424.

US Courts.gov (2010). "Bankruptcy Basics: Process." Federal Courts website. http://www.uscourts.gov/FederalCourts/Bankruptcy/BankruptcyBasics/Process.aspx.

Williamson, Oliver E. (1975). *Markets and Hierarchies: Analysis and Antitrust Implications*. New York: Free Press.

INDEX

....